Lecture Notes in Computer Science

Lecture Notes in Artificial Intelligence   16075
Founding Editor

Jörg Siekmann

Series Editors

Randy Goebel, *University of Alberta, Edmonton, Canada*
Wolfgang Wahlster, *DFKI, Berlin, Germany*
Zhi-Hua Zhou, *Nanjing University, Nanjing, China*

The series Lecture Notes in Artificial Intelligence (LNAI) was established in 1988 as a topical subseries of LNCS devoted to artificial intelligence.

The series publishes state-of-the-art research results at a high level. As with the LNCS mother series, the mission of the series is to serve the international R & D community by providing an invaluable service, mainly focused on the publication of conference and workshop proceedings and postproceedings.

Takayuki Matsuno · Honghai Liu · Lianqing Liu ·
Zhouping Yin · Xiangyang Zhu · Weihong Ren ·
Zhiyong Wang · Yixuan Sheng
Editors

Intelligent Robotics and Applications

18th International Conference, ICIRA 2025
Okayama, Japan, August 6–9, 2025
Proceedings, Part II

Springer

Editors
Takayuki Matsuno
Okayama University
Okayama, Japan

Honghai Liu
Harbin Institute of Technology
Shenzhen, China

Lianqing Liu
Shenyang Institute of Automation
Shenyang, China

Zhouping Yin
Huazhong University of Science
and Technology
Wuhan, China

Xiangyang Zhu
Shanghai Jiao Tong University
Shanghai, China

Weihong Ren
Harbin Institute of Technology
Shenzhen, China

Zhiyong Wang
Harbin Institute of Technology
Shenzhen, China

Yixuan Sheng
Harbin Institute of Technology
Shenzhen, China

ISSN 0302-9743 ISSN 1611-3349 (electronic)
Lecture Notes in Artificial Intelligence
ISBN 978-981-95-2097-8 ISBN 978-981-95-2098-5 (eBook)
https://doi.org/10.1007/978-981-95-2098-5

LNCS Sublibrary: SL7 – Artificial Intelligence

© The Editor(s) (if applicable) and The Author(s), under exclusive license
to Springer Nature Singapore Pte Ltd. 2026

This work is subject to copyright. All rights are solely and exclusively licensed by the Publisher, whether the whole or part of the material is concerned, specifically the rights of translation, reprinting, reuse of illustrations, recitation, broadcasting, reproduction on microfilms or in any other physical way, and transmission or information storage and retrieval, electronic adaptation, computer software, or by similar or dissimilar methodology now known or hereafter developed.
The use of general descriptive names, registered names, trademarks, service marks, etc. in this publication does not imply, even in the absence of a specific statement, that such names are exempt from the relevant protective laws and regulations and therefore free for general use.
The publisher, the authors and the editors are safe to assume that the advice and information in this book are believed to be true and accurate at the date of publication. Neither the publisher nor the authors or the editors give a warranty, expressed or implied, with respect to the material contained herein or for any errors or omissions that may have been made. The publisher remains neutral with regard to jurisdictional claims in published maps and institutional affiliations.

This Springer imprint is published by the registered company Springer Nature Singapore Pte Ltd.
The registered company address is: 152 Beach Road, #21-01/04 Gateway East, Singapore 189721, Singapore

If disposing of this product, please recycle the paper.

Preface

With the theme "AI & Robotics for Smart Society", the 18th International Conference on Intelligent Robotics and Applications (ICIRA 2025) was held in Okayama, Japan, from August 6 to 9, 2025. The conference aimed to promote high-level academic exchange and innovation in robotics and artificial intelligence, providing a global platform for researchers, engineers, and practitioners to present their latest achievements and explore emerging trends in intelligent robotics and its applications to society.

ICIRA 2025 was organized by Okayama University, and co-organized by Harbin Institute of Technology. It was technically co-sponsored by Springer. The conference received a total of 329 paper submissions from around the world. Each submitted paper underwent a rigorous peer-review process, with at least three independent reviewers per paper. Based on the reviewers' evaluations and the discussions by the Program Committee, 165 high-quality papers were accepted for publication in *Springer's Lecture Notes in Artificial Intelligence (LNAI)* series. Among these, 107 papers were presented orally and 58 papers were presented as posters.

ICIRA 2025 featured 2 plenary speeches and 8 keynote speeches, delivered by internationally renowned scholars in the field. The technical sessions covered a wide range of topics, including intelligent perception and control, human–robot interaction, robotic manipulation, biomedical and rehabilitation robotics, soft robotics, and machine learning for robotics. The conference provided a vibrant and inspiring environment for academic exchange and collaboration.

We would like to extend our heartfelt appreciation to all the authors for their valuable contributions, and to the plenary and keynote speakers for sharing their insights. We also thank the reviewers for their professional and constructive evaluations. Special thanks are due to all members of the Organizing Committee, the Technical Program Committee, and the local volunteers for their dedication and efforts that ensured the success of ICIRA 2025.

August 2025

Takayuki Matsuno
Honghai Liu
Lianqing Liu
Zhouping Yin
Xiangyang Zhu
Weihong Ren
Zhiyong Wang
Yixuan Sheng

Organization

Honorary Chair

Youlun Xiong — Huazhong University of Science and Technology, China

General Chairs

Takayuki Matsuno — Okayama University, Japan
Honghai Liu — Harbin Institute of Technology, Shenzhen, China
Lianqing Liu — Shenyang Institute of Automation, Chinese Academy of Sciences, China
Zhouping Yin — Huazhong University of Science and Technology, China
Xiangyang Zhu — Shanghai Jiao Tong University, China

Program Chairs

Guoying Gu — Shanghai Jiao Tong University, China
Duanling Li — Beijing University of Posts and Telecommunications, China
Yuichiro Toda — Okayama University, Japan
Xinyu Wu — Shenzhen Institutes of Advanced Technology, Chinese Academy of Sciences, China
Hui Zhang — Hunan University, China

Publication Chairs

Weihong Ren — Harbin Institute of Technology, Shenzhen, China
Zhiyong Wang — Harbin Institute of Technology, Shenzhen, China
Yixuan Sheng — Harbin Institute of Technology, Shenzhen, China

Award Committee Chair

Limin Zhu — Shanghai Jiao Tong University, China

International Chairs

Zhiyong Chen	University of Newcastle, Australia
Naoyuki Kubota	Tokyo Metropolitan University, Japan
Zhaojie Ju	University of Portsmouth, UK
Eric Perreault	Northwestern University, USA
Hesheng Wang	Shanghai Jiao Tong University, China
Peter Xu	University of Auckland, New Zealand
Simon Yang	University of Guelph, Canada
Xingchen Yang	Imperial College London, UK
Houxiang Zhang	Norwegian University of Science and Technology, Norway

Advisory Committee

Jorge Angeles	McGill University, Canada
Tamio Arai	University of Tokyo, Japan
Hegao Cai	Harbin Institute of Technology, China
Tianyou Chai	Northeastern University, China
Jie Chen	Tongji University, China
Jiansheng Dai	King's College London, UK
Zongquan Deng	Harbin Institute of Technology, China
Han Ding	Huazhong University of Science and Technology, China
Xilun Ding	Beihang University, China
Baoyan Duan	Xidian University, China
Xisheng Feng	Shenyang Institute of Automation, Chinese Academy of Sciences, China
Toshio Fukuda	Nagoya University, Japan
Jianda Han	Shenyang Institute of Automation, Chinese Academy of Sciences, China
Qiang Huang	Beijing Institute of Technology, China
Oussama Khatib	Stanford University, USA
Yinan Lai	National Natural Science Foundation of China, China
Jangmyung Lee	Pusan National University, South Korea

Zhongqin Lin	Shanghai Jiao Tong University, China
Hong Liu	Harbin Institute of Technology, China
Honghai Liu	University of Portsmouth, UK
Shugen Ma	Ritsumeikan University, Japan
Daokui Qu	SIASUN, China
Min Tan	Institute of Automation, Chinese Academy of Sciences, China
Kevin Warwick	Coventry University, UK
Guobiao Wang	National Natural Science Foundation of China, China
Tianmiao Wang	Beihang University, China
Tianran Wang	Shenyang Institute of Automation, Chinese Academy of Sciences, China
Yuechao Wang	Shenyang Institute of Automation, Chinese Academy of Sciences, China
Bogdan M. Wilamowski	Auburn University, USA
Ming Xie	Nanyang Technological University, Singapore
Yangsheng Xu	Chinese University of Hong Kong, China
Huayong Yang	Zhejiang University, China
Jie Zhaoc	Harbin Institute of Technology, China
Nanning Zheng	Xi'an Jiaotong University, China
Xiangyang Zhu	Shanghai Jiao Tong University, China

Contents – Part II

Hand-Centric Human-Robot Collaboration Advances in Perception, Control, and Interaction

Electrotactile Artifact Denoising via Function Interpolation for Integrated sEMG-Based Prosthetic Control 3
  Lina Guo, Yalong Tong, Yazhou Li, Peiyao Wang, Yi Wang, and Kairu Li

Admittance-Controlled Compliant Remote Center-of-Motion for Tele-Operated Transurethral Resection 16
  Chunheng Lu, Siqin Yang, Zhihong Song, Yu Shen, and Junchen Wang

Bioinspired Prosthetic Hand System with Multimodal Sensory Fusion for Naturalistic Grasping Behaviors 27
  Yue Zheng, Xiangxin Li, Lin Wang, Lan Tian, Xugang Jiang, Haoshi Zhang, and Guanglin Li

RoboImagine: A Robotic Video Generation Model, for Autoregressive Long-Term Task Video Generation with Geometric and Dynamic Consistency Augmentation 37
  Conglin Wang, Hongkun Yang, Chuanjiang Li, Siqi Wen, Yiming Gan, and Shuai Liang

A Soft-Skin Facial Robot Capable of Real-Time Emotion-Driven Actuation Through Visual Perception 54
  Xuanhe Fan, Huijuan Zhao, Shuangjiang He, Li Li, and Li Yu

Enhancing Robustness of Hand Gesture Recognition Against Sensor Data Loss by Fusing High-Density sEMG and Kinematics 67
  Yushuai Yan, Chengyu Lin, Chenglong Fu, and Yuquan Leng

Simulation-Driven Learning for Vision-Based Tactile Force Reconstruction in Surgical Master Manipulators Using Random Marker Particles 79
  Hui Chu, Xizhe Zang, Peng Wang, and Xu Wang

A Low-Cost Multisensor IMU-VIO Framework for Real-Time Full-Body Human Pose Estimation 91
  Lele Li, Zedong Liu, Dawei Liang, Chuanyu Si, Haotian Ju, Shouyi Zhang, Haoxiang Zhang, Hongwei Jing, Jian Qi, Tianjiao Zheng, and Yanhe Zhu

Shape Matching Method Based on Growing Neural Gas 103
    Jiaqi Zhang, Yuichiro Toda, and Takayuki Matsuno

Enhancing 4D ViT-Driven Gesture Recognition with Decomposed
HD-sEMG 114
    Yaolun Jin and Yinfeng Fang

Intelligent Technology in Healthcare

Mamdani Fuzzy Assessment System for Oral Motor Exercise Tasks 129
    Chyan Zheng Siow, Qingwei Song, Yuqi Zhang, Zongying Liu,
    Adnan Rachmat Anom Besari, and Naoyuki Kubota

Motion Planning of Self-balancing Exoskeleton Robot Based
on Spring-Loaded Inverted Pendulum 143
    Chenhao Wu, Jinke Li, Zengle Ren, Shisheng Zhang, Xueyan Shen,
    and Xinyu Wu

Doctor-Centered Mixed Reality Tele-Guidance Training System Design 155
    Yanzhuo Wang, Keyi Wang, Lan Wang, Haochu Chen, and Jinghang Li

A Novel Deep Learning Enhanced Particle Swarm Optimization
for Puncture Path Planning 166
    Jianfeng Yao, Zhuang Fu, Canhui Wu, Zi Fang, Bang Liu, and Fei Jing

Driving Logic Optimization and Fine Control of a Peripheral Electrical
Stimulator Based on FPGA 175
    Kening Gong, Li Jiang, Xiaoran Tang, and Hong Liu

Design and Implementation of a 4-DOF Wearable Assisted Puncture Robot 184
    Canhui Wu, Zhuang Fu, Jianfeng Yao, Zi Fang, Bang Liu, and Fei Jing

Towards Early Intervention of Knee Osteoarthritis: A Wearable System
for Gait Analysis and Functional Evaluation 197
    Haolan Xian, Changjiang Lei, Jinglin Zhou, Changquan Liu, Wei Sun,
    Zhiyong Wang, Chenglong Fu, and Yuquan Leng

A Flexible Fruit Wearable System for Real-Time and Long-Term Tomato
Growth Monitoring 210
    Xin Zhao, Qin Jiang, Yihui Fan, Han Ding, and Zhigang Wu

LLM-Based Structured Information Extraction for Urinary Incontinence
from Multi-modal Clinical Data 222
    Tianyu Wu, Mingxiang Luo, Xueyan Shen, Shengxiang Liang,
    Xinyu Wu, and Wujing Cao

A Tactile-Driven Multiple Instance Learning Framework for Automated
Industrial Detection 234
   *Jingnan Wang, Pengjie Qin, Chuwen Huang, Yaling Wang, Yue Ma,
Meng Yin, Wujing Cao, and Xinyu Wu*

Hip Joint Angle Prediction for Lower Limb Continuous Movement
in Multitasking Scenarios 244
   Zixiang Yang, Hao Lu, Xin Shi, Pengjie Qin, Yujie Chen, and Wujing Cao

Design of a Soft Pneumatic Exosuit for Stroke-Induced Knee Rehabilitation ... 255
   *Jinglin Zhou, Changjiang Lei, Haolan Xian, Yuanwen Zhang,
Chenglong Fu, and Yuquan Leng*

Dynamic Collision Avoidance for Slave Instruments in Robotic Cardiac
Surgery 266
   Xizhe Zang, Peng Wang, Xu Wang, and Hui Chu

Benchmarking State-of-the-Art Lower Limb Joint Moment Estimator
Against Advanced Time Series Models 275
   *Hamza Azam, Wenzhu Xu, Haoyu Wang, Luying Feng, Ahmad Irshad,
Canjun Yang, Mitja Gerževič, and Wei Yang*

A Mixed Reality-Based SSMVEP Brain-Computer Interface
for Exoskeletons 285
   *Xiuyuan Wu, Yichen Lin, Xinyang Du, Zengle Ren, Wujing Cao,
Meng Yin, and Yue Ma*

Outward Electrical Impedance Tomography for Atherosclerotic Arterial
Wall Detection 297
   Yanbo Hu, Zhenyu Cheng, Yichen Lin, and Xiaojing Long

A CNN–LSTM-Based Prediction Method of Lower-Limb Parameters
Across Multiple Locomotion Modes 309
   *Wenke Lu, Yue Ma, Haoran Zhang, Yichen Lin, Xinyu Wu, Wujing Cao,
Meng Yin, and Jianquan Sun*

Binocular Vision-Based Spatiotemporal Feature Fusion Model for Elderly
Fall Risk Prediction 322
   *Guangyu Liang, Chen Wang, Rui Zou, Jiatong Cui, Ziyun Ge,
and Zeng-Guang Hou*

Advanced Localization, Navigation and Control Technologies in Intelligent Robotic Systems

Lie Group Variational Integrators For Hybrid Flexible-Rigid Multibody System Dynamics Based on Projective Geometric Algebra 337
   Guangzhen Sun and Ye Ding

High-Order Adaptive Integration of Contact Dynamics in MuJoCo 349
   Hongchen Li and Ye Ding

Path Planning in the Anode Block Area for Underwater Cleaning Robots 361
   Ang Gao, Bocong Li, Hang Su, and Canjun Yang

Experimental Optimization of Clap-and-Fling Wing Stroke Kinematics and Geometry Configuration 373
   Wenjie Dai, Yuhan Liu, and Xuan Wang

Agile and Versatile Bipedal Robot Tracking Control Through Reinforcement Learning 385
   Han Zheng, Jiayi Li, Linqi Ye, Houde Liu, and Bin Liang

Multi-robot Path Planning Based on IPPO Reinforcement Learning and Imitation Learning 397
   Wen Ma, Gedong Jiang, Liming Wang, Zhipeng Li, Guo Li, and Feng Li

Design and Control of a Multi-UAV Cabin System 409
   Weilun Guo, Xinxing Mu, Weimin Li, Runze Liu, and Ningning Song

M2PT Dataset: A Multi-motion Pattern Dataset for SLAM Evaluation on Diverse Terrains 421
   Yan Dong, Junru Chen, Enci Xu, and Bin Han

Design and Evaluation of a Generic Safe Control Transition System for Human-Machine Cooperative Driving 433
   Yaowei Sun and Dachuan Li

Research on Robotic Visual Inspection Path and Pose Planning for Automotive Paint Defects Considering Curvature Weights 446
   Minghui Yang, Yun Cheng, Chaoqun Wu, Huayi Cai, and Ruoyuan Jiang

Multi-agent Active Exploration Framework Based on Topological Map Fusion for Indoor Environments 459
   Chenyu Bao, Junjie Hu, Shaobin Ling, Guoquan Ye, and Tin Lun Lam

An Attention-Based Diffusion Policy with Hybrid Farthest Point Sampling
for Robotic Intelligent Manipulation 471
   Yifei Dong, Yi An, Tiantian Xu, and Sheng Xu

Relative Pose Estimation of Substation Equipment for UAV Inspection
via Deep Point Cloud Registration 483
   *Jianming Liu, Duanjiao Li, Ying Zhang, Yun Chen, Shengbo Liu,
Chao Yang, Ning Ding, Xufang Pang, and Jianguo Zhang*

Wearable Robotics for Gait Analysis, Training, and Rehabilitation

Humanoid Locomotion with Roller Screw-Driven Knee Joints: Design,
Control, and Deployment 497
   *Yuchen Lin, Tian Xia, Mengdi Wang, Zhenwei Zhang, Honglei Lu,
Tao Ding, Yuhao Zhang, Xingwei Zhao, and Bo Tao*

Design and Implementation of a Multifunctional Desktop Pet Robot Dog
Based on Arduino Nano and ESP32-S3 509
   Di Li, Junkai Lin, Siqi Hou, and Yanyan Ji

From Sim-to-Real to Learn-in-Real: Real-World Online Learning
for Humanoid Robots 521
   Rankun Li, Yuhang Xie, Linqing Zhu, Linqi Ye, Qingdu Li, and Yan Peng

Smart Shoe System for Accurate Gait Phase Recognition 534
   Jiachen Wang, Jiakang Wang, Tian Liang, and Huanghe Zhang

Wearable AI-Driven Smart Insole for Long-Term Monitoring
of Lower-Limb Joint Mobility: A Pilot Study 545
   *Dinghuang Zhang, Yuxiang Huang, Ying Liu, Zhe Ding, Liucheng Guo,
and Dalin Zhou*

Tri-Plane Rhythmic Signal Generation and Adaptive Oscillator Tracking:
A Novel Framework for Motion Analysis 557
   *Haoran Zhang, Yichen Lin, Xiuyuan Wu, Yu Zhu, Xinyang Du,
Xiangyang Wang, Jianquan Sun, and Yue Ma*

A Marker-Free Motion Capture System Built on Unsynchronized Cameras 567
   *Haofei Hou, Shunyi Zhao, Zuxin Fan, Wei Jin, Jintao Zhu,
Lecheng Ruan, and Qining Wang*

Embodied Intelligence in Biomimetic Robotics, Humanoid Robotics

Fluid Dynamics Around a Whisker 581
   Md.Mahbub Alam and Xiaoyu Shi

Interaction-Friendly Trajectories via Torque-and-Jerk-Constrained
Optimization 589
   *Shize Zhao, Tianjiao Zheng, Chengzhi Wang, Sikai Zhao, Yanhe Zhu,
and Jie Zhao*

Tactile Servo Control Based on Reinforcement Learning Applied
to Flexible Wires Manipulation 601
   *Yihan Shan, Changle Li, Zhe Gao, Gangfeng Liu, Xuehe Zhang,
Chong Yao, Zhantao Xu, and Jie Zhao*

An In-Situ Excitation Trajectory Optimizer for Industrial Robots
in Constrained Space with Human Collaboration 613
   *Chengzhi Wang, Haotian Ju, Zhiyuan Yang, Tianjiao Zheng,
Shize Zhao, Sikai Zhao, Dawei Liang, Hegao Cai, Jie Zhao,
and Yanhe Zhu*

Terrain-Adaptive Bipedal Locomotion via Reinforcement Learning
with Human-Inspired Stepping Strategy 624
   Yunpeng Liang, Yanzheng Zhao, and Weixin Yan

Research on Autonomously Exterior Wall Spraying Technology
for Tethered Unmanned Aerial Vehicles 637
   *Liang Gao, Xu'an Zhao, Xu'ning Zhao, Tianjiao Zheng, Liyi Li,
and Jie Zhao*

A Study of the Effectiveness of Various Combined Control Schemes
Based on MPC and WBC in Humanoid Control 650
   Yinhui Chen, Dachuan Liu, Shilong Sun, Wenfu Xu, and Qingbin Gao

Development and Autonomous Tracking of Miniature Continuum
Endscope for Intraocular Microsurgery 662
   *Chunbo Wang, Taixian Jin, Yunfei Wang, Zhuowen Zhang,
Haoyan Zhang, Jiaqi Zhang, Jian Liang, Lei Zhong, He Zhang,
and Jie Zhao*

Air-Ground-Wall Robot with Multimodal Morphological Adaptation 675
   Juanxia Zhou, Jiajun Xu, Mengcheng Zhao, Peixin Wang, and Youfu Li

Design and Human-Robot Collaborative Control of Reconfigurable
Supernumerary Robotic Limb for Overhead Work 686
 *Peixin Wang, Jiajun Xu, Mengcheng Zhao, Juanxia Zhou, Xingyu Liu,
 and Youfu Li*

Learning Whole-Body Motion Control Through Instruction Learning
and Human Motion Data 698
 Zhipeng Xu, Kaixuan Chen, Linqi Ye, and Boyang Xing

Author Index 711

Hand-Centric Human-Robot Collaboration Advances in Perception, Control, and Interaction

Electrotactile Artifact Denoising via Function Interpolation for Integrated sEMG-Based Prosthetic Control

Lina Guo[1], Yalong Tong[1], Yazhou Li[1], Peiyao Wang[1], Yi Wang[2(✉)], and Kairu Li[1(✉)]

[1] Shenyang University of Technology, Shenyang 110870, China
Kairu.li@sut.edu.cn
[2] Luxun Academy of Fine Arts, Dalian, China
wangyi_Icoh@lumei.edu.cn

Abstract. Electrotactile stimulation may cause severe interference with the acquisition and analysis of surface electromyography (sEMG) signals, adversely affecting the control performance of sEMG-based prosthetic hands. Therefore, it is necessary to remove the interference from the electrical stimulation signal to enhance the accuracy of sEMG-based gesture recognition under electrotactile feedback. This paper proposes an electrical stimulation artifact removal method based on function interpolation. An sEMG gesture database was established, including three types of signals—original raw-tata, filtered-data and comblined-data. Experiment results show that the proposed method outperforms wavelet thresholding and adaptive filtering in terms of signal-to-noise ratio (15.52) and root mean square error (5.01). Vision Transformer (ViT) classification model was introduced for gesture recognition. The offline recognition accuracy of sEMG signals influenced by electrotactile feedback was increased from about 60% to about 90%. Online experiments were further conducted to validate its artifact de-noising performance.

Keywords: sEMG · Wavelet Decomposition · Function Interpolation · Gesture Recognition

1 Introduction

Surface electromyography (sEMG) signals refer to the electrical signals that trigger muscle movements and reflect the degree of muscle contraction [1]. Electromyographic signals can analyze the motion intentions of the human body and drive the motion control systems of intelligent bionic prostheses. In order to further improve the control of intelligent prosthetic hands by sEMG signals for people with disabilities, Researchers have proposed a theory that integrates intelligent bionic hands with electro-tactile feedback into one. In practical research, the output of electrical stimulation signals will generate artifact interference in the acquisition of sEMG signals, which instead affects the forward control of the bionic hand. Therefore, in the field of intelligent prosthetic hand control with electro-tactile feedback, how to eliminate the interference of electrical stimulation artifacts remains a challenging task.

Based on the differences between electrical stimulation signals and sEMG signals, that is, electrical stimulation signals are concentrated in the high-frequency range (several hundred hertz to several thousand hertz) with higher amplitudes, while sEMG signals are concentrated in the low-frequency range (20–500 Hz) with lower amplitudes (in the microvolt to millivolt range) [2–6], in the face of low-level stimulation currents under electrotactile feedback, traditional EMG signal denoising methods, such as Butterworth bandpass filtering [7]. Wavelet packet decomposition [8] and other single methods can filter out high-frequency information, however, these methods do not take into account the overlapping effective features between the original EMG signals and the electrical stimulation artifacts, and are thus unable to filter out this information. Therefore, it is necessary to propose targeted and effective methods based on the particularity of this electrical stimulation artifact. Manickan C et al. [9] employed the designed cascaded least mean squares adaptive filter to obtain clean signals by filtering the EMG signals containing electrical stimulation artifacts. The team headed by Dosen S [10] utilized the Time-division multiplexing (TDM) method. They avoided the interference of stimulation artifacts by conducting the acquisition of EMG signals and electrical stimulation separately in non-overlapping time windows. Wang Jinwei et al. used continuous wavelet transform to decompose the signal containing artifacts by frequency and then removed the artifacts using a threshold-based localization method, followed by signal reconstruction [11]. Hu Wei et al. proposed a denoising method combining Empirical Mode Decomposition (EMD) and wavelet thresholding for EMG signals containing electrical stimulation artifacts, achieving better SNR values than the single EMD algorithm [12]. However, these studies only compared the time-domain waveforms before and after denoising or used a single SNR value, lacking multi-faceted experimental validation. On the basis of the above - mentioned studies, this paper first conducts a comparative analysis using two evaluation metrics, SNR and RMSE. Secondly, from the perspectives of offline accuracy and online practical applications of different signals, it comprehensively validates the effectiveness of the denoising method proposed in this paper. The specific content is divided into two parts. First, in terms of frequency, wavelet decomposition is performed on the signal containing electrical stimulation artifacts to obtain decomposition signals in different frequency ranges. Secondly, functional interpolation was applied to the high-frequency components during amplitude processing to effectively suppress the interference caused by electrical stimulation artifacts.

This paper proposes a function interpolation-based method for removing electrical stimulation artifacts. First, the original signal is decomposed using wavelet transform to separate high-frequency and low-frequency components. Then, an adaptive thresholding method is applied to the high-frequency part to identify artifacts, which are subsequently processed using function interpolation. Finally, the signal is reconstructed to obtain the artifact-free result. Figure 1 shows the flowchart of the denoising method proposed in this paper, and the principles of the algorithms are described as follows.

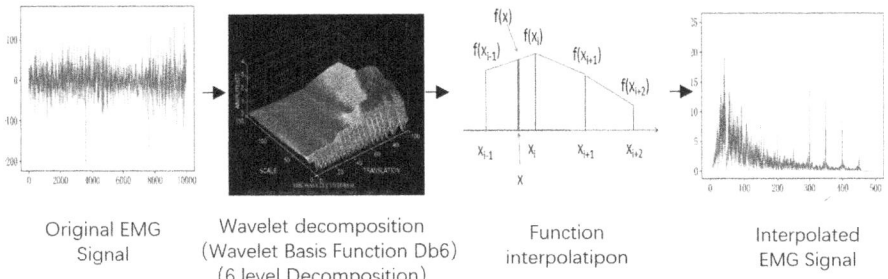

Fig. 1. Function Interpolation Framework Based on Wavelet Transform

2 Method

2.1 Wavelet Transform

The wavelet transform is a multi-scale signal analysis method [13], and its excellent denoising performance is widely appreciated. The basic principle of wavelet threshold denoising is to perform a wavelet transform on the original signal $s(t)$ by selecting an appropriate wavelet basis and decomposition level, resulting in a set of wavelet decomposition coefficients C_j.

$$C_j = W(s(t)) \tag{1}$$

In the equation, denotes the wavelet transform, and j represents the number of wavelet decomposition levels.

2.2 Function Interpolation

Function interpolation is an important mathematical tool widely used in signal processing, numerical computation, and data analysis [14]. When dealing with artifacts in signals (such as electrical stimulation artifacts in sEMG signals), function interpolation provides an effective solution. By using known signal data points, function interpolation can reconstruct the signal in regions affected by artifacts, thereby removing the artifacts and restoring the authenticity of the signal. Common interpolation methods include linear interpolation, polynomial interpolation, spline interpolation, and Lagrange interpolation [15, 16], among others. The expressions for different interpolation functions are shown as follows.

Linear interpolation: Given two points (x_0, y_0) (x_1, y_1), the calculation formula is:

$$\frac{y - y_0}{x - x_0} = \frac{y_1 - y_0}{x_1 - x_0} \tag{4}$$

Polynomial interpolation:

$$f = a_n x^n + a_{n-1} x^{n-1} + \ldots + a_1 x + a_0 \tag{5}$$

Spline interpolation:

$$S_i(x) = a_i(x - x_i)^3 + b_i(x - x_i)^2 + c_i(x - x_i) + d_i \tag{6}$$

In this case, a_i, b_i, c_i and d_i are the quantities that need to be determined.

Since electrical stimulation artifacts are primarily concentrated in the high-frequency components of sEMG signals, this paper first applies wavelet decomposition to the acquired signal to extract components from different frequency domains. Then, for each decomposition level, multiple interpolation functions are employed, and the most suitable interpolation method and wavelet level are selected for artifact removal.

2.3 ViT Gesture Recognition Model

ViT (Vision Transformer) is a vision processing model based on the Transformer architecture [18]. The ViT model consists of three main components: patch embedding, Transformer encoder, and classification head. ViT divides the input image into a sequence of small image patches, which are then represented and fed into the Transformer architecture to process the entire image. One of the key advantages of ViT is its ability to handle the entire image directly without relying on convolutional neural networks (CNNs), capturing global relationships through local patch interactions. Since both the images processed by the Vision Transformer (ViT) and electromyographic (EMG) signals are two-dimensional data, this paper applies the ViT model to EMG signal processing despite differences in the dimensions of their input shapes. Specifically, the original image input size of the ViT model is 224×224, while in this paper, the input size is adjusted to 36×36 to meet the input requirements of EMG signals.

3 Experiment

3.1 sEMG Dataset Establishment

This work involved human subjects in its research. Approval of all ethical and experimental procedures and protocols was granted by Ethic Committee of Harbin Institute of Technology.

In this study, five healthy subjects were selected as the objects for collecting sEMG signals. A total of six common hand gestures were chosen, namely hand opening, fist clenching, OK gesture, wrist pronation, wrist supination, and thumb abduction. The offline data acquisition platform and the selected gestures are shown in Fig. 2 and Fig. 3.

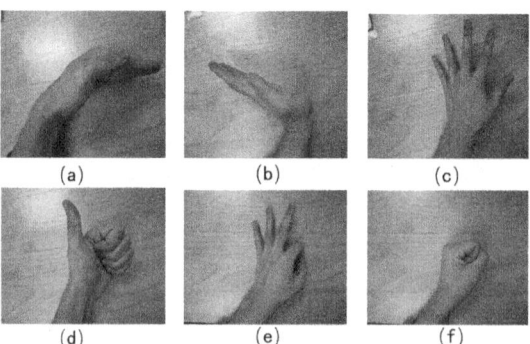

Fig. 2. Gesture action selection

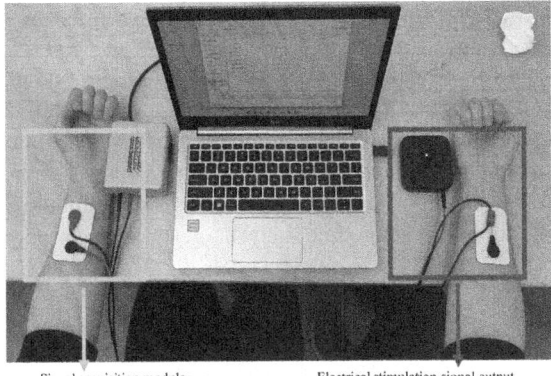

Fig. 3. Offline data collection platform

In the sEMG signal acquisition experiment, channels 1 to 4 correspond to the flexor carpi radialis, flexor carpi ulnaris, palmaris longus, and brachioradialis muscles, respectively. The sampling frequency is 1000 Hz. Before the experiment, the subject's forearm skin was cleaned with an alcohol swab to reduce impedance and enhance electrode adhesion. The subject first relaxes for 3 to 5 minutes, then each type of movement is recorded for 10 seconds. After each movement, there is a rest of 1 to 2 minutes. Each type of movement is repeated 10 times to form one session, and a 20-minute rest is taken between sessions to reduce muscle fatigue.

In the sEMG combined with electrotactile stimulation experiment, sEMG acquisition was conducted while the electrotactile stimulation was applied. Considering the strong electrical influence of electrical stimulation on sEMG signals, the electrotactile stimulation was instead applied to the other arm rather than the same arm where the sEMG electrodes were placed. The stimulation parameters were set at an amplitude of 3 mA and a pulse width of 100 μs, with a pattern of 2 seconds of stimulation followed by 2 seconds of rest. The subjects perceived the stimulation mildly and experienced no discomfort.

During the experimental process, the collected sEMG signal data were mainly divided into three categories: Raw-data, Combined-data, and Filtered-data, respectively. The specific meanings they represent are shown in Table 1.

Table 1. Database classification

	Representative Meaning
Raw-data	Raw surface electromyography (sEMG) signals without contamination
Combined-data	sEMG signals containing electrical stimulation artifacts
Filtered-data	sEMG signals after removal of electrical stimulation artifacts

3.2 Online Experimental Platform

In this paper, the BainRobotics intelligent bionic hand is used to conduct real-time gesture recognition experiments. While collecting sEMG data from one arm and outputting the corresponding movements, an electrical stimulation experiment is carried out on the other arm. The real-time gesture recognition platform is set up as shown in Fig. 4 below, which consists of three parts: the armband signal acquisition module of the bionic hand, the electrical stimulation output module, and the gesture action output module of the bionic hand.

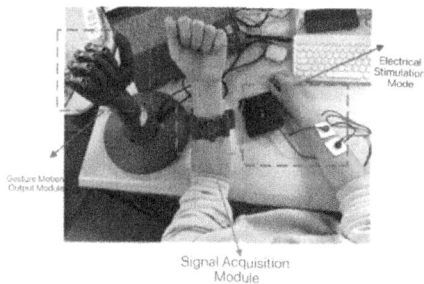

Fig. 4. Real time gesture recognition experimental platform

4 Results

4.1 Results of the Offline Experiment

Evaluation indexes after removing the electrical stimulation artifacts. In this paper, two calculation parameters, namely the Signal to Noise Ratio (SNR) and the Root Mean Square Error (RMSE), are used to evaluate the denoising performance [17]. The following are the calculation formulas of the two parameters:

$$SNR = 10 \lg \left[\frac{\sum_{i=1}^{n}(X_i)^2}{\sum_{i=1}^{n}(Y_i - X_i)^2} \right] \quad (7)$$

$$RMSE = \sqrt{\frac{\sum_{i=1}^{n}(Y_i - X_i)^2}{n}} \quad (8)$$

Among them, X_i is the collected original sEMG signal, Y_i is the signal after removing the electrical stimulation artifacts from the sEMG signal containing such artifacts, and n is the sample data of sEMG. The larger the SNR value is, the more effective information there is after denoising the signal, and the better the denoising effect is. RMSE is used to evaluate the deviation between the reconstructed signal and the original signal. The smaller its value is, the better the denoising effect of this method is.

To select the interpolation function most suitable for artifact removal, this paper first applies different interpolation methods to denoise the Combined-data dataset. The results are shown in Table 2.

Table 2. SNR and RMSE values under different interpolation functions

	Linear interpolation	Quadratic polynomial interpolation	Cubic polynomial interpolation	Quartic polynomial interpolation	Spline interpolation
SNR	8.70	15.52	15.52	15.51	8.70
RMSE	10.4508	5.0139	5.0141	5.0215	10.4516

Based on Table 2, quadratic polynomial interpolation demonstrates higher SNR and lower RMSE after denoising, indicating superior overall performance compared to other interpolation methods. Therefore, this paper adopts the quadratic polynomial interpolation function for denoising surface EMG signals contaminated with electrical stimulation artifacts in subsequent experiments.

After selecting the interpolation function, in order to further verify whether the electrical stimulation signal is in the high-frequency part of the signal and whether it is applicable to different populations, this paper uses the wavelet decomposition method for the sEMG signals in the Combined-data database, after selecting the db6 wavelet basis function and decomposing the signal into six layers to capture the signal characteristics in different frequency bands, the interpolation process is carried out layer by layer for each decomposed layer of the signal. As a result, the reconstructed signals, spectrograms under different layers, and the values of two evaluation indexes are obtained, as shown in Table 3.

It can be seen from the above table that after the interpolation processing of the first layer of the decomposed signal, the values of SNR and RMSE are superior to those of the reconstructed signals of other layers, and it is applicable to the signal characteristics of different subjects.

Table 3. SNR/RMSE values interpolated by different subjects at different decomposition levels

	1	2	3	4	5	6
Subject1	20.54/9.03	11.52/25.48	5.43/51.38	1.63/79.56	0.21/93.71	0.03/95.73
Subject2	18.04/11.54	11.53/24.41	5.63/48.15	1.52/77.32	0.32/88.73	0.12/90.80
Subject3	18.76/8.36	10.01/22.90	4.82/41.62	1.41/61.66	0.32/69.92	0.04/72.16
Subject4	17.43/8.31	10.61/18.22	4.93/35.04	1.04/54.84	0.13/60.92	0.02/61.70
Subject5	16.86/4.72	8.69/12.09	3.16/22.88	0.72/30.28	0.12/32.44	0.06/32.68

It can be seen from the above table that after the interpolation processing of the first layer of the decomposed signal, the values of SNR and RMSE are superior to those of the reconstructed signals of other layers, and it is applicable to the signal characteristics of different subjects.

Through the above experiments, this paper finally chooses to use the quadratic polynomial function to perform the denoising process with the interpolation method on the first layer of the decomposed signal.

At the same time, a comparative experiment is carried out between the method in this paper and the wavelet threshold denoising method as well as the adaptive filtering method. The results of the evaluation indexes finally obtained are shown in Table 4.

Table 4. Comparison of evaluation indexes of different denoising methods

Subjects	Evaluation Indexes	Wavelet Thresh-olding	Adaptive Filtering	Function Interpolation
Subject1	SNR/RMSE	9.26/10.45	7.82/31.14	15.52/5.01
Subject2		12.08/10.45	9.25/41.78	17.51/5.54
Subject3		7.04/10.46	7.16/22.93	16.10/3.64
Subject4		12.24/10.45	10.46/41.25	18.51/4.90
Subject5		4.68/10.54	10.38/14.52	20.17/1.41

It can be known from the above results that the two evaluation indexes of the method in this paper are both superior to the other two processing methods in terms of denoising. Figure 5, 6, 7 and 8 are respectively the results of the signal containing electrical stimulation artifacts, wavelet threshold denoising, adaptive filtering and function interpolation denoising. In the time-domain signals and spectrograms, the wavelet threshold denoising still retains the characteristic parts of the electrical stimulation artifacts, and there is no obvious removal of interference; the adaptive filtering method filters out a large number of signal features, including the features of the original signal, so it is not suitable for subsequent data analysis. However, when the method in this paper removes the electrical stimulation artifacts, it filters out the high-frequency features of the artifacts while retaining most of the information of the electromyogram signals.

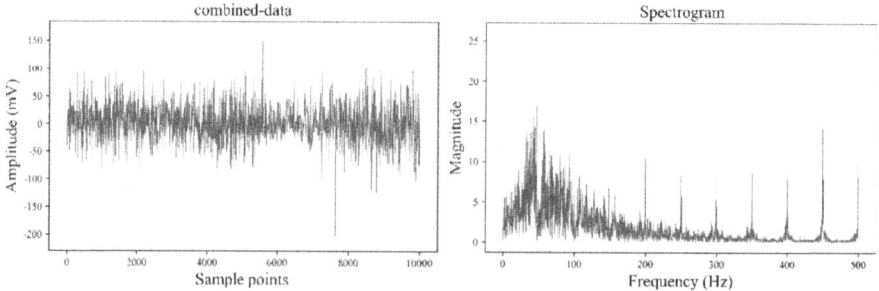

Fig. 5. Electrically stimulated artifact signals

Electrotactile Artifact Denoising via Function Interpolation 11

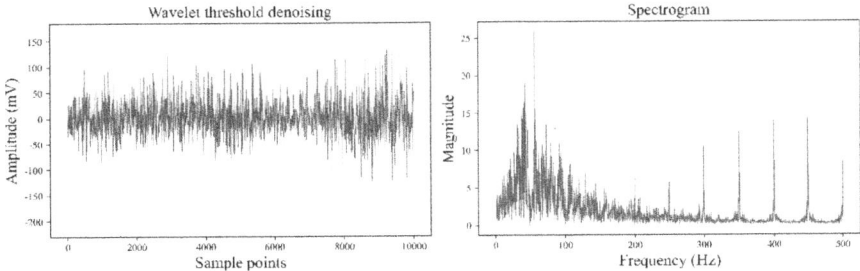

Fig. 6. Wavelet threshold denoising

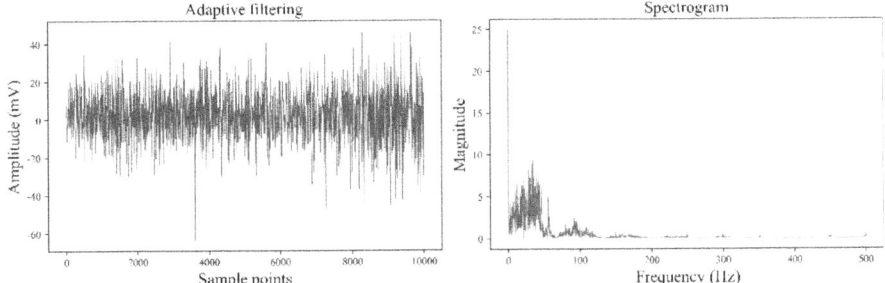

Fig. 7. Adaptive filtering

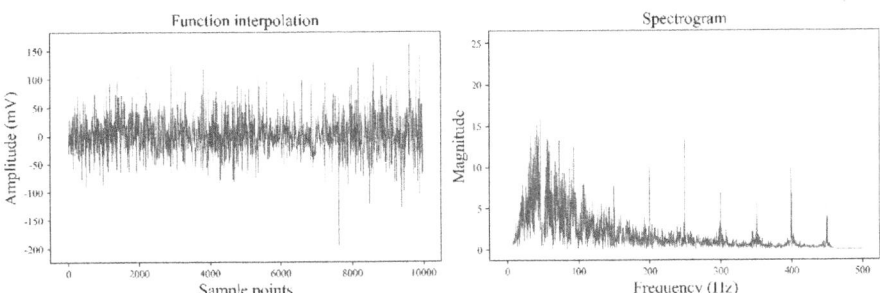

Fig. 8. Function interpolation

In order to further verify the feasibility of the denoising method based on function interpolation, this paper will illustrate it from the perspective of offline recognition accuracy on the basis of two evaluation indexes, namely SNR and RMSE.

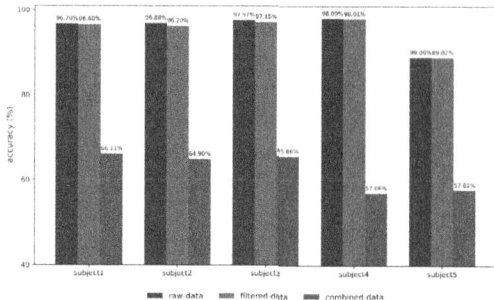

Fig. 9. Offline gesture recognition accuracy based on three types of datasets

Figure 9 shows the recognition accuracies of five subjects across three types of datasets. The original data achieved the highest accuracy (approximately 98%), while the artifact-contaminated data had the lowest (around 60%). After artifact removal, the accuracy lay between the two and closely approached that of the original data, confirming the effectiveness of the denoising method. Taking Subject 4 as an example, the confusion matrices for the three datasets are illustrated.

From the confusion matrix in Fig. 10, it can be concluded that (a) represents the original electromyogram signal, and there are not many misidentifications of movements. However, (b), under the interference of electrical stimulation artifacts, has a large number of recognition errors, from this, it can be seen that the electrical stimulation signal has a huge impact on data collection and recognition, which in turn affects the forward control of the bionic hand. The recognition effect after removing these artifacts is shown in Figure (c). There were 28 misclassification errors between Gesture 3 (inversion) and Gesture 4 (eversion). This may be attributed to the fact that both actions engage the same muscles, resulting in low feature separability after artifact removal. Consequently, this affects the accuracy of threshold-based classification.

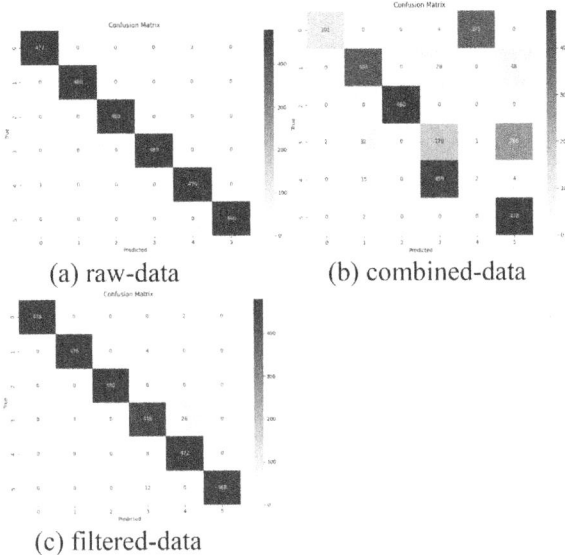

Fig. 10. Confusion matrices for gesture recognition based on three types of datasets

4.2 Results of the Online Experiment

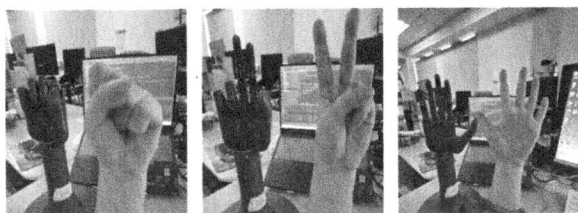

Fig. 11. Real time gesture action output results

The output results of the real-time gesture recognition experiment are reflected through the real-time movements of the bionic hand. Since the bionic hand is incapable of performing wrist movements, three gestures, namely fist clenching, the "V" sign gesture (scissors hand gesture), and hand opening, are chosen for the real-time experiment. This experiment captures the user's hand movements by collecting sEMG signals and utilizes a recognition algorithm to convert them in real time into corresponding actions of the bionic hand. The specific results are shown in Fig. 11.

5 Conclusion

To remove the interference of electrical stimulation artifacts generated by electro-tactile feedback, this paper proposes a denoising method based on wavelet decomposition and function interpolation. First, wavelet decomposition is used to locate the high-frequency components where the artifacts are located. Then, quadratic polynomial interpolation processing is performed on the target components. Finally, the components are reconstructed to achieve denoising. In offline experiments, this method achieved 18.51 and 4.90 in two key indicators of signal-to-noise ratio and root mean square error, respectively, significantly outperforming traditional wavelet threshold denoising and adaptive filtering methods. At the same time, the offline accuracy experiment shows that the accuracy of the original signal is 98.72%, and the denoised signal still remains at 98.02%, fully demonstrating the effectiveness of the method. In real-time experiments, the bionic hand can accurately recognize three different hand gestures even under the interference of electrical stimulation.

Although the proposed method demonstrates denoising performance, it still faces several challenges. In the current experiments, signal acquisition and electrical stimulation are applied to separate upper limbs, which is unfavorable for the integration of an electro-tactile feedback system in bionic hands. Additionally, the electrical stimulation parameters used are fixed, making it difficult to meet the demands of dynamic tactile feedback in real-world applications. Future research will focus on removing artifacts caused by real-time varying electrical stimulation, aiming to enhance the practicality and interactive experience of bionic hand systems with electro-tactile feedback capabilities.

Acknowledgement. This work is partly supported by the LiaoNing Revitalization Talents Program (Grant No. XLYC2203104) and the Research Fund of Liaoning Provincial Department of Education (Grant No. LJ222410142058).

References

1. Tian, J., Zhu, H., Lu, C., et al.: A novel passive occupational shoulder exoskeleton with adjustable peak assistive torque angle for overhead tasks. IEEE Trans. Biomed. Eng. **72**(2), 734–746 (2024)
2. Inoue, Y., Yamanoi, Y., Kuroda, Y., et al.: Development of a waterproof emg sensor for improved signal quality by using load balancing. IEEE Sens. J. **25**(9), 14617–14628 (2025)
3. Wang, F., Chen, X., Roelfsema, P.R.: Comparison of electrical microstimulation artifact removal methods for high-channel-count prostheses. J. Neurosci. Methods **408**, 110169 (2024)
4. Kang, P., Jiang, S., He, B.: Diffusion-driven deep decoding: advancing EMG-based hand skill learning for environment-free human–robot interaction. IEEE/ASME Trans. Mechatron. 1–11 (2025)
5. Kaliyaperumal, G., Karthick, P.A.: MODWT based analysis of facial EMG For assessing muscle fatigue: implications for rehabilitation and HCI systems. In: 2024 International Conference On Brain Computer Interface & Healthcare Technologies (iCon-BCIHT), pp. 243–248 (2024)
6. Amberg, M.L., Suppelt, S., Altmann, A.A., et al.: Integration of EMG electrodes by disruptive 3D printing into a mandibular brace. In: 2024 IEEE Sensors, pp. 1–4 (2024)
7. Kang, X., Handayani, D.O.D., Yaacob, H.: Comparison between butterworth bandpass and stationary wavelet transform filter for electroencephalography signal. IOP Conf. Ser. Mater. Sci. Eng. **1077**(1), 012024 (2021)
8. Zhang, G., Morin, E., Zhang, Y., et al.: Non-invasive detection of low-level muscle fatigue using surface EMG with wavelet decomposition. In: 2018 40th Annual International Conference of the IEEE Engineering in Medicine and Biology Society (EMBC), pp. 5648–5651 (2018)

9. Manickam, C., Govindasamy, M., Muthusamy, S., Paramasivam, M.: A novel method for design and implementation of systolic associative cascaded variable leaky least mean square adaptive filter for denoising of ECG signals. Wirel. Pers. Commun. **137**(2), 1029–1043 (2024)
10. Dosen, S., Schaeffer, M.C., Farina, D.: Time-division multiplexing for myoelectric closed-loop control using electrotactile feedback. J. Neuroeng. Rehabil. **11**, 1–10 (2014)
11. Wang, J., Le, C., Xiu, K., et al.: LDA-BPNN bimanual gesture recognition algorithm based on surface EMG signals. Sens. Microsyst. **42**(06), 158–160, 168 (2023)
12. Hu, W.: Design and implementation of a functional electrical stimulation system driven by EEMD-denoised surface EMG signals. Hefei University of Technology (2021)
13. To, A.C., Moore, J.R., Glaser, S.D.: Wavelet denoising techniques with applications to experimental geophysical data. Signal Process. **89**(2), 144–160 (2009)
14. Tan, W., Fang, M., Duan, F., et al.: Research on 3D laser image denoising algorithm based on cubic spline interpolation function. J. Central South Univ. (Sci. Technol.) **51**(09), 2496–2503 (2020)
15. Ruikar, S.D., Doye, D.D.: Image denoising using tri nonlinear and nearest neighbor interpolation with wavelet transform. Int. J. Inf. Technol. Comput. Sci. **4**(9), 36 (2012)
16. Zhang, D., Zhang, D.: Wavelet transform. In: Fundamentals of Image Data Mining: Analysis, Features, Classification and Retrieval, pp. 35–44 (2019)
17. Frančič, A., Holobar, A.: On the reuse of motor unit filters in high density surface electromyograms recorded at different contraction levels. IEEE Access **9**, 115227–115236 (2021)
18. Tian, Y., Wang, Y., Wang, J.: Key issues in vision transformer research: current status and prospects. Acta Automatica Sinica **48**(04), 957–979 (2022)

Admittance-Controlled Compliant Remote Center-of-Motion for Tele-Operated Transurethral Resection

Chunheng Lu[1], Siqin Yang[1], Zhihong Song[2], Yu Shen[3], and Junchen Wang[1(✉)]

[1] School of Mechanical Engineering and Automation, Beihang University, Beijing, China
wangjunchen@buaa.edu.cn
[2] Research Institute of Aero-Engine, Beihang University, Beijing, China
[3] School of Biomedical Engineering, Tsinghua University, Beijing, China

Abstract. Transurethral resection of the prostate (TURP) is a crucial procedure that significantly improves the quality of life for aging males with benign prostatic hyperplasia (BPH). During TURP, a long surgical instrument is inserted into the patient's body through the urethra and operated under a remote center-of-motion (RCM) constraint. Robot-assisted TURP with tele-operation combines operator expertise with robotic precision. However, unexpected disturbances such as patient movement or unintentional squeeze leads to large force at the RCM constraint, potentially causing damage to delicate tissues. In this paper, we propose an intuitive task space motion controller with a compliant RCM constraint for tele-operated robot-assisted TURP. The key finding is the combination of a programmable online RCM motion planner and a 6 degree-of-freedom task space admittance controller. The controller achieves high RCM accuracy in the absence of external disturbances, while maintaining compliant behavior to reduce contact forces when disturbances occur. Experiments were performed on a collaborative surgical manipulator to simulate robotic TURP. The results demonstrate that the average RCM precision and the tool tip accuracy were 0.35 mm and 0.30 mm, respectively, under undisturbed conditions. Under applied external disturbances, the proposed compliant RCM controller could significantly reduce the contact force at the RCM by at least 80% compared to the rigid RCM constraint, verifying the effectiveness of our method.

Keywords: Minimally invasive surgical robots · admittance control · compliant remote center of motion

1 Introduction

Lower urinary tract symptoms (LUTS) associated with benign prostatic hyperplasia (BPH) are common complaint among the aging male [1]. Transurethral resection of the prostate (TURP) has been the gold standard for treating BPH in patients with the prostate volume of ≤ 80 ml [2]. In TURP, a straight and rigid instrument called resectoscope is inserted into the prostate through the urethra to excise enlarged tissue using electrocautery, and the motion should be controlled to meet remote center-of-motion (RCM) constraint to prevent damage to the healthy tissue [3]. During the electrosurgical resection process, the resectoscope cuts tissue with high-frequency electrical current, keeping the contact force at the tip minimal enough to be neglected [4]. The surgeon faces challenges such as hand tremors, prolonged operational fatigue, and contamination risks. Robot-assisted TURP with tele-operation can help to provide better ergonomics as well as increase precision and dexterity [5].

Many researches on robot-assisted urology surgery have been developed. The Da Vinci® and Hugo™ RAS robots have been widely used in robot-assisted radical prostatectomy to overcome the limitations of resectoscope surgery [6]. Both robots can only perform position control without compliance. In addition to the commercial robot systems, there are also some research systems under development. Vanderbilt University has developed a robotic system for transurethral bladder surgery and surveillance [7]. Kuang *et al.* proposed a teleoperation-based continuum robot system to handle the challenges with rigid surgical tools in transurethral surgery [8]. The method proposed in our research will be integrated with existing medical devices such as endoscopes, to enhance the versatility and usability, while maintaining high precision in robot-assisted surgery.

For TURP robot system, the RCM constraint must be satisfied. Active programmable RCM motion control with a robotic manipulator is more flexible and suitable for general purpose application. The RCM constraint can be formulated based on the kinematics of manipulators [9,10]. Aghakhani *et al.* proposed a kinematics control method in task space based on Jacobian matrix [11]. This kind of RCM constraint generation method requires the desired trajectory of the tool tip as control inputs, which is more suitable for image-based visual servoing [12]. However, these methods are not intuitive for tele-operated robots, since for tele-operation, the desired trajectory is from the interaction device at the master side in real-time.

In TURP, unexpected disturbance (like patient's movement caused by obturator nerve reflex [13]) can cause squeeze at the incision and may damage healthy tissues. To avoid this issue, the RCM constraint needs to be compliant. Su *et al.* proposed an impedance control based robot assist minimally invasive surgery (RA-MIS) method [14–16], in which a manipulator with joint torque controller is required. Although there are some researches achieving impedance control without torque sensors [17,18], the impedance control is still subject to dynamics uncertainties, which may result in poor RCM accuracy. Different from impedance control, admittance control has the advantages of high motion accuracy and adaptability to low-cost manipulators with only position control interface [19]. In TURP, the instrument primarily interacts with soft tissue, which makes admittance control appropriate. Kastritsi *et al.* decoupled the motion space from the RCM constraint space. By mapping user forces to the motion space and applying joint admittance control, human-robot interaction with RCM constraint was achieved [10]. But the surgical task and RCM constraint are in Cartesian space, it is not intuitive to use joint admittance to ensure compliance.

In our previous work, a screw theory-based programmable RCM motion planner for TURP was proposed [20], but the compliance of RCM constraint had not been concerned. In this paper, we combined the online RCM motion planner with a 6-DoF task space admittance controller [21] to propose a control method with compliant RCM constraint for tele-operated transurethral resection. The proposed controller has good RCM accuracy as well as compliant behavior in response to external disturbance.

2 Method

2.1 6-DoF Admittance Control

The aim of admittance control is to establish a mass-damping-spring relationship between the robot end-effector's pose displacement and the external wrench as follows [22]

$$\mathcal{M}(\ddot{X} - \ddot{X}_d) + \mathcal{B}(\dot{X} - \dot{X}_d) + \mathcal{K}(X - X_d) = \mathcal{F} \tag{1}$$

where $\mathcal{M}$, $\mathcal{B}$, $\mathcal{K}$ are positive definite matrices representing virtual inertia, damping and stiffness coefficients of the system respectively, $\mathcal{F}$ is the robot-environment interaction wrench. X_d and X represent the desired and real pose in task space. $X_e = X - X_d$ denote the pose displacements. Rewrite $X_e = (r_e^T, p_e^T)^T$, and decouple Eq. (1) into the rotational and positional dynamics as follows

$$\mathcal{M}_r \ddot{r}_e + \mathcal{B}_r \dot{r}_e + \mathcal{K}_r r_e = \mathcal{F}^m \tag{2}$$

$$\mathcal{M}_p \ddot{p}_e + \mathcal{B}_p \dot{p}_e + \mathcal{K}_p p_e = \mathcal{F}^f \tag{3}$$

where $r_e \in \mathbb{R}^3$ and $p_e \in \mathbb{R}^3$ are the rotational and positional displacements, and $\mathcal{F}^m \in \mathbb{R}^3$ and $\mathcal{F}^f \in \mathbb{R}^3$ represent moment and force respectively.

As illustrated in Fig. 1, $T_d = (R_d, t_d)$ is the desired trajectory with ω_d and v_d the angular and linear velocity expressed in spatial frame {s}. The actual trajectory of the robot is denoted by $T = (R, t)$ with ω and v the actual angular and linear velocity expressed also in frame {s}.

Using the exponential coordinate expression described in our previous work [21], the rotational and positional displacements r_e^k and p_e^k expressed in body frame {b} are given by

$$e^{r_e^k} = (R^k)^T R_d^k \tag{4}$$

$$p_e^k = (R^k)^T (t_d^k - t^k) \tag{5}$$

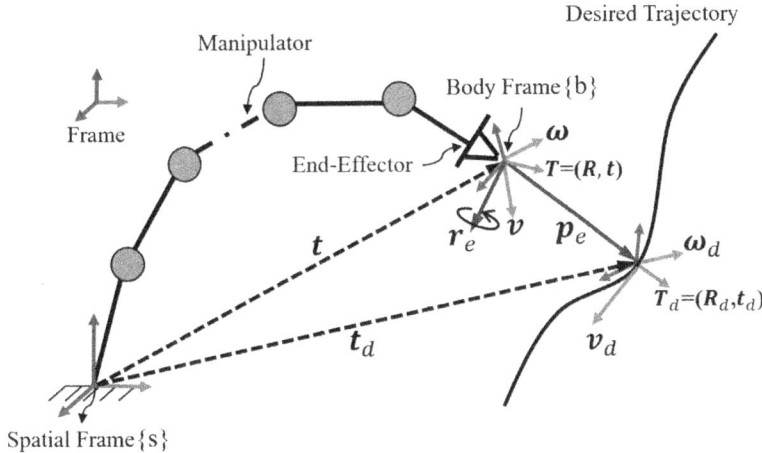

Fig. 1. Frames and notations.

where the right superscript k represents the data within k control period. The first derivatives $\dot{r}_e^k$ and $\dot{p}_e^k$ are

$$\dot{r}_e^k = A^{-1}(r_e^k)(R_d^k)^{\mathrm{T}}\left(\omega_d^k - R^k J_{b\omega}(\theta^k)\dot{\theta}^k\right) \tag{6}$$

$$\dot{p}_e^k = -[J_{b\omega}(\theta^k)\dot{\theta}^k]p_e^k + (R^k)^{\mathrm{T}}v_d^k - J_{bv}(\theta^k)\dot{\theta}^k \tag{7}$$

where $J_b(\theta) = (J_{b\omega}^{\mathrm{T}}, J_{bv}^{\mathrm{T}})^{\mathrm{T}}$ represents body Jacobian matrix and $[\bullet]$ represents the skew-symmetric matrix of the vector. The expression of $A(r_e)$ is

$$A(r_e) = I_3 - \frac{1 - \cos\|r_e\|}{\|r_e\|^2}[r_e] + \frac{\|r_e\| - \sin\|r_e\|}{\|r_e\|^3}[r_e]^2 \tag{8}$$

where $\|r_e\|$ represents the norm of r_e and $I_3 \in \mathbb{R}^{3\times 3}$ denote the 3-dimensional identity matrix.

After getting the displacements and their first derivatives in current control cycle $r_e^k, p_e^k, \dot{r}_e^k, \dot{p}_e^k$, the second-order differential admittance control equation (2) and (3) can be solved to get the displacements at next step r_e^{k+1}, p_e^{k+1}, which are used to adjust the desired motion for compliance. The proof is shown in [21].

2.2 Compliant RCM Constraint

As illustrated in Fig. 2, $^b p_{rcm}$ is the RCM point expressed in body frame $\{b\}$ at the initial pose T_0. T_0 is the homogeneous transformation matrix of $\{b\}$ relativeÂăto $\{s\}$. An RCM Coordinate system $^b\hat{x}_{rcm}$-$^b\hat{y}_{rcm}$-$^b\hat{z}_{rcm}$ is established with $^b p_{rcm}$ as the original point. $^b\hat{z}_{rcm}$ is defined along the tool feed direction, and x-y axes of RCM frame is freely defined as long as satisfying the Cartesian right-hand coordinate system. $^b\hat{x}_{rcm}$, $^b\hat{y}_{rcm}$ and $^b\hat{z}_{rcm}$ are the representation of three axes of RCM frame expressed in body frame $\{b\}$.

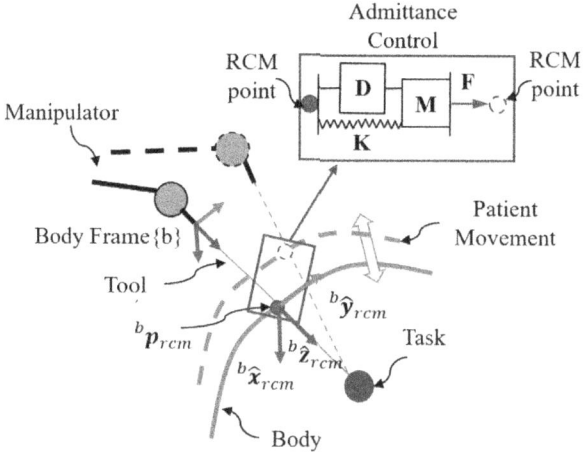

Fig. 2. Admittance controlled compliant RCM constraint.

The 4-DoF RCM motion can be expressed as the body frame {b} rotating about the spatial axis $(^b\boldsymbol{p}_{rcm}, ^b\hat{\boldsymbol{x}}_{rcm})$, $(^b\boldsymbol{p}_{rcm}, ^b\hat{\boldsymbol{y}}_{rcm})$, $(^b\boldsymbol{p}_{rcm}, ^b\hat{\boldsymbol{z}}_{rcm})$ in sequence and translating along $^b\hat{\boldsymbol{z}}_{rcm}$ direction. Represent it as screw motions, that is, rotating α, β, γ, d sequentially around 4 unit screw axes $\mathcal{S}_1$, $\mathcal{S}_2$, $\mathcal{S}_3$, $\mathcal{S}_4$, whose specific expression can be found in [20]. The final RCM constraint expressed in the form of product of exponential is

$$\delta\boldsymbol{T}^k(\alpha^k, \beta^k, \gamma^k, d^k) = e^{[\mathcal{S}_1]\alpha^k} e^{[\mathcal{S}_2]\beta^k} e^{[\mathcal{S}_3]\gamma^k} e^{[\mathcal{S}_4]d^k} \qquad (9)$$

The rotations α^k, β^k, γ^k, d^k are obtained by the master device controlled by human operator in control cycle k. With the initial pose of the tool $\boldsymbol{T}_0$, the desired pose satisfying RCM constraint is

$$\boldsymbol{T}_d^k(\alpha^k, \beta^k, \gamma^k, d^k) = \boldsymbol{T}_0 \delta\boldsymbol{T}(\alpha^k, \beta^k, \gamma^k, d^k) \qquad (10)$$

The desired pose at next cycle $\boldsymbol{T}_d^{k+1}$ can be estimated by $\boldsymbol{T}_d^k$ and $\boldsymbol{\mathcal{V}}_d^k = \left((\boldsymbol{\omega}_d^k)^{\mathrm{T}}, (\boldsymbol{v}_d^k)^{\mathrm{T}}\right)^{\mathrm{T}} \in \mathbb{R}^6$

$$\boldsymbol{T}_d^{k+1} = \boldsymbol{T}_d^k e^{\left[\mathrm{Ad}_{\boldsymbol{T}_{bs}^k} \boldsymbol{\mathcal{V}}_d^k \delta t\right]} \qquad (11)$$

where δt is the control cycle and $\mathrm{Ad}_{\boldsymbol{T}_{bs}^k} \in \mathbb{R}^{6\times 6}$ is the adjoint matrix of $\boldsymbol{T}_{bs}^k$. $\boldsymbol{T}_{bs}^k$ is a homogeneous transformation matrix of frame {s} with respect to frame {b}

$$\boldsymbol{T}_{bs}^k = \begin{pmatrix} (\boldsymbol{R}_d^k)^{-1} & 0 \\ 0 & 1 \end{pmatrix} \qquad (12)$$

To achieve the compliant RCM, $\boldsymbol{T}_d^{k+1}$, obtained through master-slave control and satisfied RCM constraints, will be adjusted by displacements $\boldsymbol{r}_e^{k+1}$ and $\boldsymbol{p}_e^{k+1}$ calculated in 2.1 to obtain the final target pose for the next cycle $\boldsymbol{T}^{k+1}$

$$R^{k+1} = R_d^{k+1} e^{[-r_e^{k+1}]} \tag{13}$$
$$t^{k+1} = t_d^{k+1} - R^{k+1} p_e^{k+1} \tag{14}$$

By controlling the robot to move body frame {b} to the target pose $T^{k+1} = (R^{k+1}, t^{k+1})$, the compliant RCM control can be achieved.

3 Experiments and Results

3.1 Experimental setup

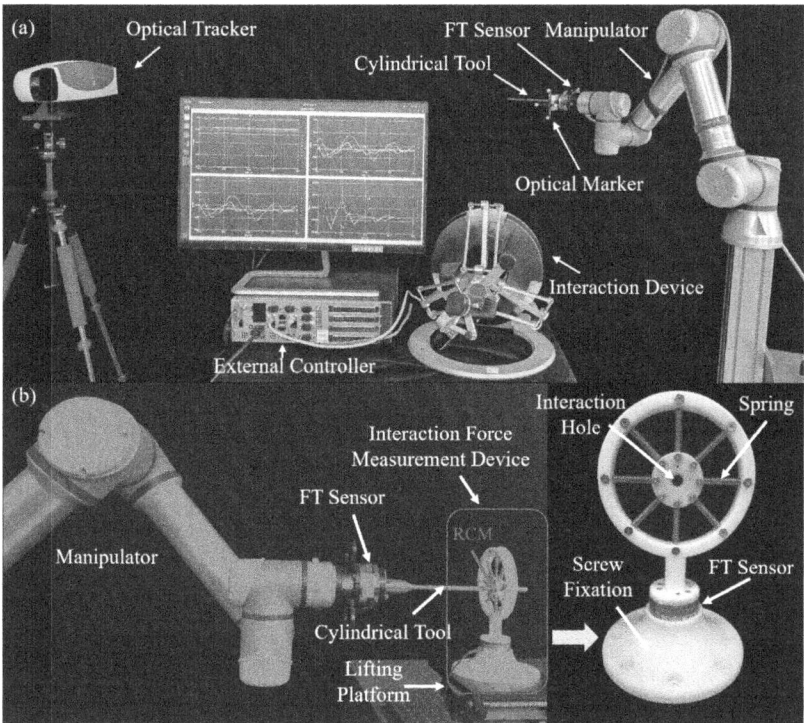

Fig. 3. Experimental setup. (a) Experimental scene. (b) Interaction force evaluation at the RCM.

The proposed compliant RCM control was evaluated on our previously developed transurethral surgical robot [20]. The experimental scene is shown in Fig. 3(a). Since the control can be performed on a low-cost position controlled manipulator, in our experiments a UR5e robot (Universal Robot) was used to replace the Kuka iiwa robot in [20]. A six dimensional FT sensor (Gamma, ATI) was installed on the flange of the manipulator and a long rigid cylindrical tool was attached

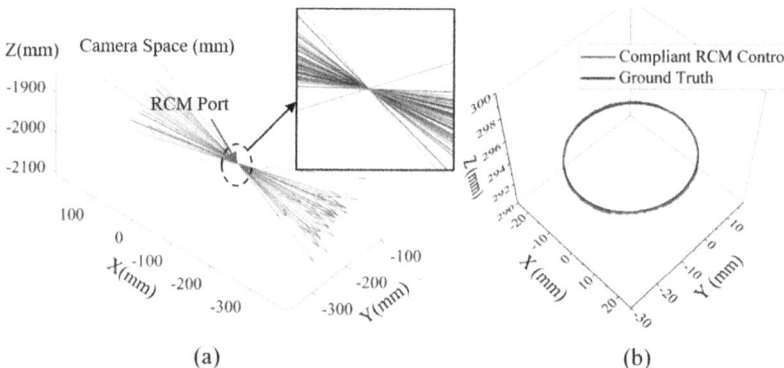

Fig. 4. Captured trajectories of the tool shafts (a) and the tool tip (b) during the motion with compliant RCM constraint in free space.

to the overload side of the FT sensor to simulate a laparoscope. An industrial computer (MIC-770 V2, ADVANTECH Co., Ltd.) was employed as the external controller of the UR robot with an operating system of Ubuntu 20.04 with RT-Preempt patch installed for real-time control. The control algorithms were implemented in C++ and ran on the external controller with the control cycle $\delta t = 2$ ms. The controller sent target pose commands in every control cycle to the UR robot with the real-time data exchange (RTDE) protocol. An optical tracker (Polaris Vega, NDI) was employed to capture the motion of the surgical tool by tracking an optical marker attached on the tool. An interaction device (Omega 7, Force Dimension) was used as the mater device to remotely send desired motion to the manipulator. In all experiments, admittance control parameters were $\mathcal{M}_r = \text{diag}(0.05, 0.05, 0.05)$, $\mathcal{B}_r = \text{diag}(7,7,7)$, $\mathcal{K}_r = \text{diag}(10, 10, 10)$, $\mathcal{M}_p = \text{diag}(0.5, 0.5, 0.5)$, $\mathcal{B}_p = \text{diag}(70, 70, 70)$, $\mathcal{K}_p = \text{diag}(100, 100, 100)$.

3.2 RCM Constraint Accuracy

Table 1. RCM Metric Results (Unit: mm)

No.	1	2	3	4	5	Mean
Rigid RCM Control	0.31	0.37	0.32	0.36	0.38	0.35
Compliant RCM Control	0.31	0.38	0.34	0.35	0.35	0.35

Experiments were performed to evaluate the tracking accuracy of RCM constraint under proposed compliant method in free space. The manipulator was controlled in a tele-operated mode to pivot with RCM constraint. The desired RCM trajectory was generated from the interaction device shown in Fig. 3(a) by the operator at the master side. The RCM was set to be on the shaft of the cylindrical tool at a distance of 150 mm to the flange. The optical tracker shown in Fig. 3(a) was used to capture the motion of the tool. The RCM metric proposed in [20] was used to evaluate the accuracy of the compliant RCM trajectory following.

Five tele-operated RCM control experiments were performed and Table 1 summarizes the RCM metric evaluation results by calculating the root-mean-square (RMS) distance of the RCM to the captured tool shafts by the tracker. For comparison, the RCM control method in our previous work [20] (referred to as "rigid RCM control") was also performed. As is expected, the compliant RCM controllers had similar RCM accuracy (mean RCM metric of 0.35 mm) to the rigid RCM controller. Welch's t-test was performed on the results of the two groups, yielding p=0.914 (p>0.05), indicating no statistically significant difference in RCM accuracy between the two methods in free space. Fig. 4 (a) visualizes the captured trajectories of the tool shafts by the optical tracker during the motion.

3.3 Tool Tip Following Accuracy

Table 2. Tip Following Accuracy (Unit: mm)

No.	1	2	3	4	5	Mean
Rigid RCM Control	0.29	0.30	0.30	0.30	0.30	0.30
Compliant RCM Control	0.30	0.31	0.30	0.30	0.30	0.30

The control accuracy of the surgical tool tip is also important for robotic surgery. A circle with a radius of 19 mm was planned as the desired trajectory of the tool tip. The robot was controlled automatically by program so that the tool tip followed the circle with the RCM constraint at an angular velocity of 40°/s. The real trajectory of the tip was recorded by the optical tracker. This was achieved by tracking the optical marker attached to the tool with the known tip offset in the marker frame. The captured tool tip was finally transformed to the flange frame at the motion beginning using the hand-eye calibration matrix. Since the planned circular path was also based on the flange frame at the motion beginning, the two paths were compared directly to calculate the RMS error.

For both rigid and compliant RCM controller, five experiments were performed and Table 2 summarizes the RMS errors between the ideal paths and the actual paths. Fig. 4 (b) visualizes the captured trajectories of the tool tip compared with the ground truth. As is expected, the compliant RCM controllers had similar tool tip following accuracy (mean RMS error of 0.30 mm) to rigid RCM controller in free space. The result ($p = 0.195$, $p > 0.05$) indicates no statistically significant difference in tool tip accuracy between the two methods under the condition.

3.4 Interaction Force Evaluation at RCM

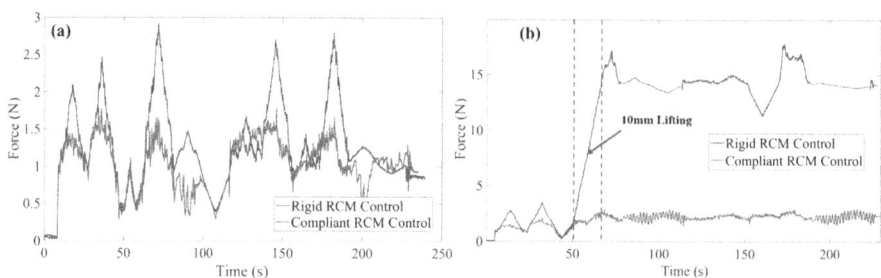

Fig. 5. Interaction force at the RCM. (a) Without lifting. (b) With lifting of 10 mm during the motion.

Table 3. Mean Interaction Force at RCM (Unit: N)

Without Lifting	1	2	3	4	5
Rigid RCM Control	1.30	1.26	1.76	1.23	1.36
Compliant RCM Control	0.88	0.97	0.97	1.01	1.00
Reduction Rate	32%	23%	45%	18%	27%
10 mm Lifting	1	2	3	4	5
Rigid RCM Control	12.08	10.95	10.94	10.43	10.68
Compliant RCM Control	2.09	1.96	1.95	1.94	1.96
Reduction Rate	83%	82%	82%	81%	81%

The experimental setup is shown in Fig. 3(b). An interaction force measurement device was designed to evaluate the interaction force at the RCM. The device mainly consists of inner and outer frames which are connected by six springs, and a six dimensional FT sensor (Mini45, ATI) was fixed on a lifting platform which would be used to lift the device to simulate patient move. The robot was programmed to perform pivoting motion with RCM constraint. The RCM of the cylindrical tool was originally aligned with the insertion hole of the inner frame. The interaction force was measured during the motion with the rigid and compliant RCM controller, respectively. Then the lifting platform was raised by 10 mm at 50 s to squeeze the cylindrical tool. The interaction force was measured again during the motion with two controllers, respectively. For each controller, five experiments were performed.

The results are summarized in Table 3. As we can see, the compliant RCM control yielded minimal interaction force. The maximum interaction force was only 1.01 N without "patient move" and it was only 2.09N in the case that the "patient" squeezed the "surgical tool". The proposed compliant RCM control could significantly reduce the contact force compared with the rigid control in both two cases (maximum reduction rate of 83%). The results (p = 0.011 for no lifting and p = 0.001 for 10 mm lifting, both p < 0.05) indicate a statistically significant difference in interaction force between the two methods at the 95% confidence level. Figure 5 shows the interaction force with and without lifting under different control strategies. The rigid RCM control yielded large interaction force because the controller tried to minimize the position error, while the admittance controller endowed the robot with compliant behavior to reduce the interaction force, which could enhance the safety of robot assisted TURP surgery. The RCM deviated from the original position when suffering from interaction force and returned to its original position when the force decreased.

4 Conclusion

We have proposed a compliant RCM control method for transurethral resection by combining a screw theory-based RCM motion planner and a 6-DoF task space admittance controller.

Comprehensive experiments have been performed, and the results show that the proposed compliant RCM control method not only has the same RCM precision and the tool tip accuracy as the rigid RCM control, but also can effectively reduce the interaction force at the RCM, enhancing the safety of the tele-operated TURP surgery.

Acknowledgement. This work was supported in part by the Natural Science Foundation of China under Grant 62173014, Grant U22A2051; and in part by the Natural Science Foundation of Beijing Municipality under Grant L232037; and in part by the Beijing Municipal Science and Technology Project under Grant Z231100004823011, Grant Z221100007422013.

References

1. Gravas, S., et al.: Summary paper on the 2023 European association of urology guidelines on the management of non-neurogenic male lower urinary tract symptoms. Eur. Urol. **84**(2), 207–222 (2023)
2. Miernik, A., Gratzke, C.: Current treatment for benign prostatic hyperplasia. Dtsch. Arztebl. Int. **117**(49), 843–854 (2020)
3. Bian, G.B., et al.: Learning surgical skills under the RCM constraint from demonstrations in robot-assisted minimally invasive surgery. Expert Syst. Appl. **225**, 120134 (2023)
4. Geavlete, P., Niţă, G., Geavlete, B.: Chapter 2 - endoscopic electroresection of benign prostatic adenoma (turp). In: Geavlete, P.A. (ed.) Endoscopic Diagnosis and Treatment in Prostate Pathology, pp. 9–66. Academic Press, San Diego (2016)
5. Hislop, J., Tirosh, O., Isaksson, M., Mccormick, J., Hensman, C.: Perceived comfort and tool usability during robot-assisted and traditional laparoscopic surgery: a survey study. J. Robot. Surg. 18(1), 15 (2024). https://doi.org/10.1007/s11701-023-01785-7

6. Brime Menendez, R., et al.: Da Vinci vs. Hugo Ras for robot-assisted radical prostatectomy: a prospective comparative single-center study. World J. Urol. **42**(1), 336 (2024)
7. Herrell, S.D., Webster, R., Simaan, N.: Future robotic platforms in urologic surgery: recent developments. Curr. Opin. Urol. **24**(1), 118–126 (2014)
8. Kuang, H., Wang, X., Zhao, C., Zhu, C., Xu, K.: Proof-of-concept development of the distal module of a cystoscope transurethral continuum surgical robotic system. IEEE Robot. Autom. Lett. **9**(11), 10002–10009 (2024)
9. Colan, J., Davila, A., Fozilov, K., Hasegawa, Y.: A concurrent framework for constrained inverse kinematics of minimally invasive surgical robots. Sensors **23**(6), 3328 (2023)
10. Kastritsi, T., Doulgeri, Z.: A controller to impose a RCM for hands-on robotic-assisted minimally invasive surgery. IEEE Trans. Med. Robot. Bionics **3**(2), 392–401 (2021)
11. Aghakhani, N., Geravand, M., Shahriari, N., Vendittelli, M., Oriolo, G.: Task control with remote center of motion constraint for minimally invasive robotic surgery. In: 2013 Proceedings of the IEEE International Conference on Robotics and Automation (ICRA), pp. 5807–5812. IEEE (2013)
12. Wang, X., Tan, N.: Cerebellum-inspired model-free tracking control and visual servoing of a rigid-flexible hybrid robotic endoscope with RCM constraints. IEEE Trans. Ind. Electron. **70**(12), 12626–12635 (2023)
13. Wu, J., et al.: Comparison of different methods of obturator nerve block in transurethral resection of bladder tumors: a systematic review and network meta-analysis. Cancer Med. **12**(5), 5420–5435 (2023)
14. Su, H., Yang, C., Ferrigno, G., De Momi, E.: Improved human–robot collaborative control of redundant robot for teleoperated minimally invasive surgery. IEEE Robot. Autom. Lett. **4**(2), 1447–1453 (2019)
15. Su, H., Mariani, A., Ovur, S.E., Menciassi, A., Ferrigno, G., De Momi, E.: Toward teaching by demonstration for robot-assisted minimally invasive surgery. IEEE Trans. Autom. Sci. Eng. **18**(2), 484–494 (2021)
16. Su, H., Qi, W., Chen, J., Zhang, D.: Fuzzy approximation-based task-space control of robot manipulators with remote center of motion constraint. IEEE Trans. Fuzzy Syst. **30**(6), 1564–1573 (2022)
17. Liu, D., Wang, J., Wang, S.: Force-sensorless active compliance control for environment interactive robotic systems. IEEE/ASME Trans. Mechatron. **30**, 1–11 (2024)
18. Li, Y., Bian, H., Wang, L.: Parameters identification and contact interaction control of redundant robot based on dynamic model. Physica Scripta **99**(8), 085270 (2024). https://dx.doi.org/10.1088/1402-4896/ad6512
19. Ott, C., Mukherjee, R., Nakamura, Y.: A hybrid system framework for unified impedance and admittance control. J. Intell. Robot. Syst. **78**, 359–375 (2015)
20. Sun, Z., Wang, T., Lu, C., Shen, Y., Wang, J.: Robotic system with programmable motion constraint for transurethral resection. Int. J. Comput. Assist. Radiol. Surgery **17**(5), 895–902 (2022)
21. Wang, J., Lu, C., Lv, Y., Yang, S., Zhang, M., Shen, Y.: Task space compliant control and six-dimensional force regulation toward automated robotic ultrasound imaging. IEEE Trans. Autom. Sci. Eng. **21**, 1–12 (2023)
22. Albu-Schäffer, A., Hirzinger, G.: Cartesian compliant control strategies for light-weight, flexible joint robots. In: Bicchi, A., Prattichizzo, D., Christensen, H.I. (eds.), pp. 135–151. Springer, Heidelberg (2003). https://doi.org/10.1007/3-540-36224-X_9

Bioinspired Prosthetic Hand System with Multimodal Sensory Fusion for Naturalistic Grasping Behaviors

Yue Zheng[1,2], Xiangxin Li[1,2], Lin Wang[1,2], Lan Tian[1,2], Xugang Jiang[1,2], Haoshi Zhang[1,2(✉)], and Guanglin Li[1,2(✉)]

[1] Shenzhen Institute of Advanced Technology, Chinese Academy of Sciences (CAS), Shenzhen 518055, China
{Zhanghaoshi,gl.li}@siat.ac.cn

[2] Shenzhen Institutes of Advanced Technology, Guangdong-Hong Kong-Macao Joint Laboratory of Human-Machine Intelligence-Synergy Systems, Chinese Academy of Sciences, Shenzhen 518055, China

Abstract. This paper presents an innovative bionic prosthetic hand control system and a hybrid control method, which aims to improve the functionality and trajectory bionicity of traditional myoelectric prostheses. The grasping process is divided into two phases: pre-grasping and grasping. Visual perception is incorporated during the pre-grasping phase to identify the target object and autonomously plan a human-like grasping trajectory. In the grasping phase, myoelectric signals initiate the corresponding actions. A two-step correction method (TSCM) for improving grasping trajectories is proposed, which maps the motion of a human hand onto a prosthetic hand. The method reduces the mean average absolute error (MAPE) of the trajectories between the human and prosthetic hands by 3.24%. The actual tripod grasping experiments of the prosthetic hand indicate that the hybrid control method proposed in this paper significantly enhances the bionicity of movement. The mean correlation coefficients of the movement trajectories of the human and prosthetic hands in the x and y directions reached 0.989 and 0.872, respectively. And the mean MAPE value in the x and y directions is 4.28% and 4.80% respectively. The method described in this paper will contribute to achieving more natural and efficient human-machine collaborative control of prosthetic hands.

Keywords: Prosthetic Hand · Hybrid Control · Grasping

1 Introduction

Due to the high dexterity of human hands, they play a significant role in the activities of daily life (ADLs). The two main functions of human hands are grasping and manipulation, which account for about 80% of ADLs [1]. The loss of hand function exerts a substantial hindrance on the capacity of amputees to carry out ADLs and participate in social interactions [2, 3]. Therefore, using a prosthetic hand is crucial for individuals who have undergone upper arm amputations. According to statistics, the number of people with physical disabilities in China is up to 24.72 million. Wearing intelligent prostheses is important for amputees to restore lost limb function. However, the fact that existing commercial prostheses still generally have defects such as single and rigid movement patterns, limited functions, and less environmental adaptability leads to the poor acceptance and high abandonment rate of the prostheses [4].

In rehabilitation engineering, endowing the prosthetic hand with functions similar to human hands has become a research hotspot and a significant challenge [2]. With the improvement of biomechatronic systems and neural engineering technologies, people's expectations for prosthetic hands are no longer limited to simple limb replacement but aim for higher functionality and naturalness, enabling them to assist amputees more effectively in completing various complex tasks in ADLs. Myoelectric prosthetic hands are currently the most widely used, which collect electromyography (EMG) signals from the residual limb muscles to decode the user's movement intentions in real time and control the prosthetic hand to perform corresponding actions accordingly [5, 6]. This control method, which is based on EMG signals, has attracted much attention due to its intuitiveness. However, despite the introduction of advanced signal processing techniques such as pattern recognition, synchronous proportional control, machine learning, and neural networks in the control of prosthetic hand systems, research and improvement on the grasping function mainly focus on increasing the number of grasping patterns, rarely consider the grasping process. This results in significant differences between the grasping trajectory planning and the movement patterns of a natural human hand.

Artificial vision has recently been introduced as a new means of prosthetic hand control [7]. It enables environment perception and assists in interpreting the user intention. The hybrid control method integrates vision and EMG to improve the control performance of the prosthetic hand [8]. The Harbin Institute of Technology has developed a hybrid myoelectric control system designated as i-MYO. This system first selects the grasping type through eye tracking of the interface within the AR helmet and subsequently uses EMG signals to regulate the prosthetic hand proportionally [9]. The University of Science and Technology of China manipulates the prosthesis by integrating EMG and vision signals obtained from a depth camera attached to the elbow of the prosthesis [10]. North Carolina State University also utilizes an EMG and vision-based control method. However, in their case, the camera is attached to the wrist of a gripper [11]. However, these studies focus on selecting the grasping pattern, which ignores the naturalness when the prosthetic hand proceeds with the grasping object. For instance, the vision signals are supplied by devices attached externally to the prosthetic hand, which fails to achieve a humanoid prosthetic hand appearance [11–13]. In some research, a gripper is used instead of a prosthetic hand [8]. Moreover, the system cannot provide a natural grasping trajectory similar to that of natural hands.

In this paper, we center on the natural and bionic features of the prosthetic hand during the grasping process. A novel hybrid control method is proposed to allow the prosthetic hand to execute continuous, coordinated, and human-like grasping motions. The proposed method fused the vision and EMG single to select the suitable grasping gesture. Then, a two-stage trajectory planning method provides the prosthetic hand with a human-like grasping trajectory. The contributions of this paper are as follows: build an eye-in-hand prosthetic hand system, the trajectory of the prosthetic hand is rectified via the two-step correction method (TSCM). By adopting the hybrid control strategy that integrates EMG and visual information, the anthropomorphic characteristics of the prosthetic hand while grasping the target object are enhanced. The rest of this article is structured as follows. Section 2 introduces the experimental apparatus and the hybrid control method. Section 3 evaluates the method. Section 4 concludes the paper.

2 Method

2.1 Experimental Apparatus and Procedure

A healthy subject was recruited instead of an amputee because this paper aims to estimate the feasibility of the proposed control method. The healthy participant could accelerate the experiment and decrease the uncertainty brought by the residual limb of amputees. This experiment was approved by the Shenzhen Institutes of Advanced Technology, Chinese Academy of Sciences. The subject gave consent for the publication of his photographs for scientific purposes. A socket was specially designed for the healthy subject to utilize the prosthetic hand, establishing a connection between the subjects and the prosthesis.

The experiment utilized a self-designed prosthetic hand with six active degrees of freedom (DOFs). The five prosthetic fingers were modularized, and the flexion and extension of each finger are actuated independently. Simultaneously, an additional motor governs the adduction and abduction of the thumb. Six Maxon Epos4 control drivers were utilized to control the prosthetic hand. In order to augment the perceptual capabilities of the system, a diverse range of sensors have been incorporated into the prosthetic hand. These encompass contact force sensors at each fingertip, which furnish contact information when contacting the grasping object. Position sensors are situated at each rotational joint, offering real-time finger gestures. A RGB-D camera is integrated into the palm of the prosthetic hand, providing immediate and interpretable information about the target object and its surroundings during the grasping process. The force and RGB-D signals are transferred to the laptop via USB. Position signals are gathered by the MAXON driver in the form of multi-analog signals and then transmitted to the laptop through CAN communication. In order to recognize the user's motion intention from the decoded EMG signal, eight surface EMG electrodes were placed on the participant's forearm. A self-developed portable EMG signal processing device with an 8-channel EMG acquisition and a real-time processing function powered by a battery was used to collect the EMG signals [14]. The EMG classification results are gathered by the MAXON driver in the form of multi-digital signals and then transmitted to the laptop through CAN communication. The structure of the experimental apparatus is displayed in Fig. 1.

The procedure of the experiment is simple. The target object for grasping is placed on the desk. The participant was asked to grasp the target object with the prosthetic hand as naturally as using a natural hand. Prior to the commencement of the formal experiment, the subjects were asked to acquaint themselves with the control process. They were also instructed to don the designed prosthetic system and utilize the hybrid control method proposed in the following section to grasp the target object. The sensing data were recorded and processed during the experiment, as detailed in Sect. 3.

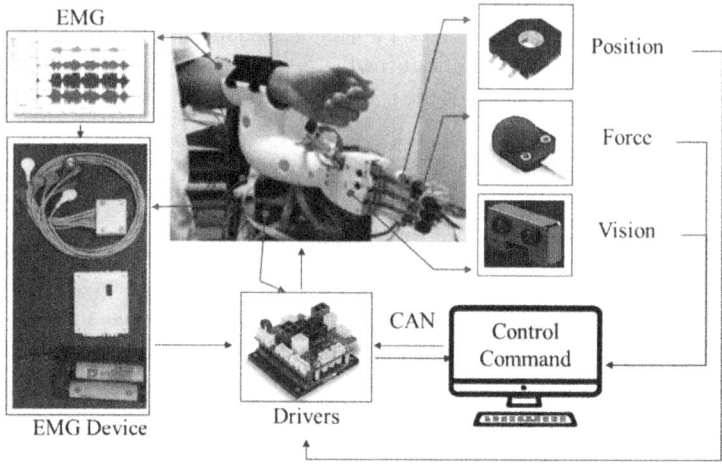

Fig. 1. The structure of the experimental apparatus.

2.2 The Hybrid Control Method

In the traditional method of controlling the grasping of prosthetic hands using EMG signals, the movement trajectory of the prosthetic hand during the approach toward the target object is usually disregarded. The relative position between the prosthetic hand and the target object relies only upon the human eyes, and the grasping action is executed when the position is considered appropriate by the user. This approach results in discontinuity and naturalness within the grasping process. Furthermore, long-term prosthesis control with myoelectric signals induces muscle fatigue and elevates the user's cognitive burden. Therefore, to improve the effectiveness and efficiency of prosthetic hand control, this study presents a human-centered, human-machine collaborative hybrid control approach. This method divides the grasping process into two distinct stages: the approach stage and the grasp stage. During the approach stage, the system automatically selects and maps the most suitable grasping gesture according to the target object type, enabling the prosthetic hand to pre-adjust to the corresponding grasping configuration during the approach. When the user ascertains that the prosthetic hand has reached the ideal position, the grasping action can be accomplished via EMG signals. Significantly, suppose the user detects any deviation in the grasping gesture during the process. In that case, they can interrupt and readjust the grasping process at any time by utilizing the rest gesture command of the EMG signal.

2.3 Trajectory Planning Method

This study employed a two-step correction method to rectify the human hand movement trajectory. This was done to maximize the reachability of the prosthetic hand movement, thus mimicking the natural grasping behavior of humans. During the approach toward the target object, the system intelligently identifies the object to determine the grasping gesture. Then, it completes the pre-shaping of the gesture in accordance with anthropomorphic trajectory planning. The DB9 part of the Ninapro dataset was utilized to offer the trajectory of the human hand. This DB9 dataset records the kinematic information of healthy individuals grasping different objects via the Cyberglove-II data glove. The kinematic data of grasping a tennis ball was chosen as a representative sample, encompassing the 22 joint angles of the human hand and the sampling time. Based on human grasping habits discussed in the reference literature [16], we completed mapping the relative distance between the human hand trajectory and the target object, generating the human hand grasping trajectory.

The key to achieving human-like grasping trajectories lies in establishing an accurate mapping relationship between the joint angles of the human hand and those of the prosthetic hand. To this end, we developed the kinematic DH models for both the human and prosthetic hands. We transformed the joint angles of the human hand into fingertip trajectories and then corrected these trajectories according to the reachability of the prosthetic hand. Subsequently, these trajectories were converted into the joint angles of the prosthetic hand using inverse kinematics methods. Given the absence of abduction and adduction DOFs in the metacarpophalangeal (MCP) joints of the self-developed prosthetic hand and the movement limitations of the wrist joint, we simplified the human hand DH model to 16 DOFs. To ensure that the prosthetic hand's trajectory can closely approximate that of the human hand, we designed a two-step correction approach to complete the reachability transformation of the trajectory.

In the first step, the trajectory was corrected based on geometric dimensions. Specifically, the human hand trajectory was proportionally scaled according to the size ratio of the prosthetic hand to the human hand. In the second step, the trajectory was adjusted based on geometric configuration. This was accomplished by computing the minimum Euclidean distance between each point of the human hand trajectory and that of the prosthetic hand trajectory. Consequently, the prosthetic hand's joint angles closest to the human hand trajectory were determined. The process is shown in Fig. 2.

2.4 Data Analysis

The recorded EMG signals were first analyzed offline with Matlab software. To efficiently mitigate the interference of power-line noise, a 50 Hz notch filter was utilized. Subsequently, the continuous EMG recordings were segmented and concatenated into a series of analysis windows, each window being 150 ms in duration with a 50-ms overlap, facilitating the extraction of time-domain features. We selected four representative time-domain features, namely the absolute mean value, waveform length, zero crossing and slope sign changes. By implementing the Linear Discriminant Analysis (LDA) method, we successfully classified and identified three commonly used actions: hand open, hand close and rest.

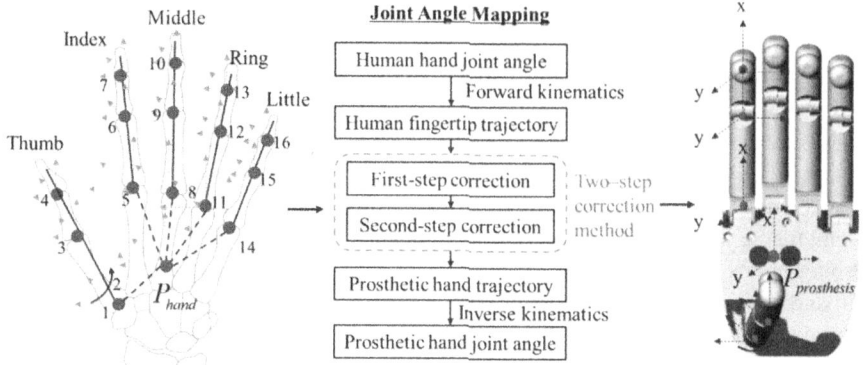

Fig. 2. The two-step correction method for joint angle mapping between the human and prosthetic hands in trajectory planning.

Typical grasping gestures employed by humans encompass the cylinder grasp, tripod grasp, sphere grasp, and so on [15]. According to the existing grasping dataset YCB (Yale-CMU-Berkeley) and the types and shapes of commonly used objects in ADLs, a tennis ball, which exhibits a spherical shape, was chosen as the experimental target object in this research. The corresponding grasping gesture for the tennis ball is the tripod grasp. By integrating the existing YCB database with the images acquired by an RGB-D camera, a training dataset for visual recognition was established. The depth RGB camera can simultaneously capture color and depth images at 30 frames per second. The Yolov8-based model was employed for training and target recognition to determine the object name, confidence level, and relative distance between the target objects and the prosthetic hand.

3 Results and Analysis

After the trajectory was rectified using the two-step correction method, the comparison results of the positions of the fingertips of the human hand and the prosthetic hand in the tripod gesture (comprising the thumb, index finger, and middle finger) in the x and y directions were presented. in Fig. 3(a). Due to the fact that the thumb in the tripod gesture remains opposite to that of the other four fingers, the adduction and abduction movements are disregarded. The horizontal axis represents the joint angle, and the shaded area indicates the position difference between the positions of the human and prosthetic hands. From Fig. 3(a), it can be seen that when the flexion angle is small, the position difference in the y-direction between the human hand and the prosthetic hand is minimal. However, this difference gradually becomes more pronounced as the flexion angle increases. This is mainly due to the structure limitation of the prosthetic hand, which result in some unreachable positions. In the x-direction, the position difference between the human and prosthetic hands remains relatively small. Figure 3(b) further depicts the mean absolute percentage error (MAPE) between the human and prosthetic hands at different joint angles, which is calculated by Eq. (1). The MAPE between the human and prosthetic hands within the joints' angle range of 0–90° before and after the application of TSCM is summarized in Table 1. After optimization by the TSCM, the MAPE was reduced by 3.24%, from 9.74% before correction to 6.20% after correction, demonstrating the effectiveness of this approach in enhancing accuracy.

$$MAPE = \frac{1}{n}\sum_{i=1}^{n}\left|\frac{p_{pi} - p_{hi}}{p_{pi}}\right| \times 100\% \tag{1}$$

where p_{pi} presents the prosthetic hand trajectory, while p_{hi} resents the human hand trajectory, n denotes the number of sampling points.

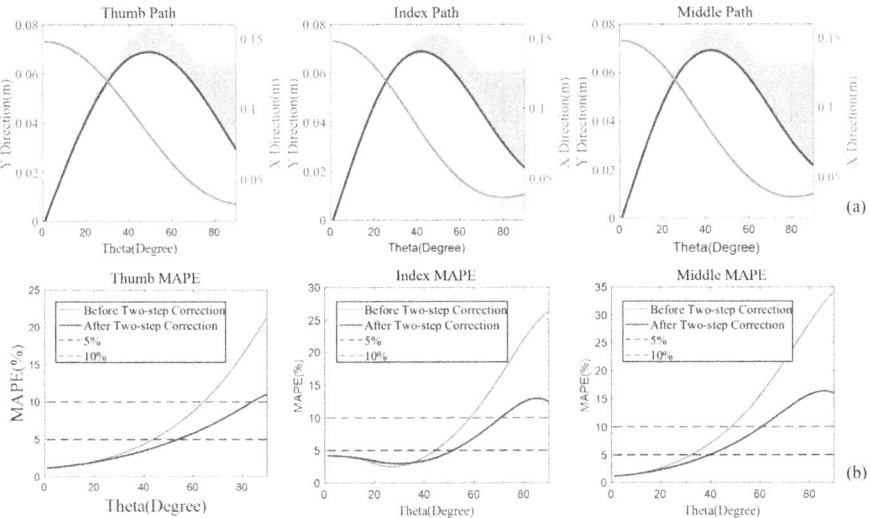

Fig. 3. (a) The comparison of the trajectories of the human and prosthetic hands (b) The MAPE of the human hand and prosthetic hand trajectories before and after the application of the TSCM.

Table 1. The MAPE between the human and prosthetic hands after two-step correction method.

Direction	Thumb	Index	Middle	Mean
Before TSCM	7.35%	9.48%	12.4%	9.74%
After TSCM	4.79%	6.30%	7.51%	6.2%

The rectified motion trajectory was designated as the target trajectory of the prosthetic hand. The proposed hybrid control approach was employed to direct the prosthetic hand to mimic the object-grasping action of the human hand. Subsequently, a detailed comparison was carried out between the grasping trajectories of the prosthetic and human hands, with the results presented in Fig. 4. The Fig. 4(a) represents the fingertip trajectories of the human and the prosthetic hands in the x and y directions during the tripod grasp. The horizontal axis represents the relative distance between the hands and the target object. The shaded areas represent the positional discrepancies between the prosthetic and human hands at corresponding distances. In contrast to the scenario without visual guidance, the grasping action of the prosthetic hand with visual guidance significantly enhanced its similarity to the grasping action of the human hand. Through visual guidance, the mean correlation coefficient between trajectories of the human and prosthetic hands is 0.989 in the x direction and 0.877 in the y direction, as computed by Eq. (2).

$$r_p = \frac{\sum_{i=1}^{n}(p_{hi} - \hat{p}_h)(p_{pi} - \hat{p}_p)}{\sqrt{\sum_{i=1}^{n}(p_{hi} - \hat{p}_h)^2}\sqrt{\sum_{i=1}^{n}(p_{pi} - \hat{p}_p)^2}} \quad (2)$$

p_h and p_p represent the fingertip positions of the human hand and the prosthetic hand at the same relative distance from the target object, respectively. Symbol $\wedge$ represents the means of p_h and p_p. Figure 4(b) presents the MAPE between the trajectories of the human and prosthetic hands at different relative distances after three experiments, which is also summarized in Table 2. During the tripod grasp, the mean MAPE value in the x direction is 4.28% and in the y direction is 4.80%. During the prosthetic hand's toward to the target object, the MAPE between the trajectories of the human and prosthetic hands predominantly remained below 10% in both the x and y directions. In certain positions, the difference is comparatively large. This is primarily attributable to the fact that the structural constraints of the prosthetic hand challenges in reach specific positions of the human hand.

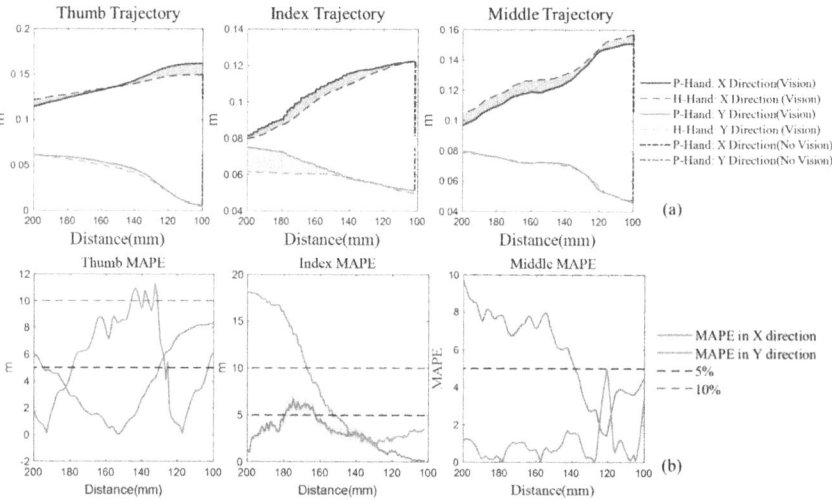

Fig. 4. (a) The trajectories of human and prosthetic hands in x and y directions during the tripod grasp (b) The MAPE between the trajectories of the human and prosthetic hands at different relative distances.

Table 2. The MAPE between the trajectories of the human and prosthetic hands in real experiments.

Direction	Thumb	Index	Middle	Mean
x	4.11%	2.94%	5.8%	4.28%
y	5.55%	7.89%	0.98%	4.80%

4 Conclusion and Future Work

The experiment in this paper indicates that the proposed visual-EMG hybrid control strategy significantly enhances the bionicity of the grasping trajectory of the prosthetic hand. After the application of TSCM, the MAPE between the trajectories of the prosthetic and human hands is decreased by 3.24%. Through visual guidance, the mean correlation coefficients of the trajectories of the human and prosthetic hands in the x and y directions during the real tripod grasp experiments reached 0.989 and 0.872, respectively. And the mean MAPE value in the x and y directions is 4.28% and 4.80%, respectively. Despite the fact that the MAPE is comparatively large at certain positions due to the mechanical structure constraints of the prosthetic hand, the multimodal perception and kinematic mapping endow the prosthetic hand with autonomous decision-making capabilities and improve its grasping biomicity, facilitating the transition of the prosthetic from the functional substitution paradigm to the natural interaction paradigm. This is beneficial for achieving more natural and efficient human-machine collaborative control of the prosthetic hand.

Future research efforts will be centered on further optimizing the multimodal perception system, refining the mechanical structure design, enhancing the precision of kinematic mapping, strengthening the autonomous decision-making capabilities, enabling user interaction and personalized adjustment, and exploring long-term stability and reliability. These endeavors aim to achieve more natural and efficient human-machine collaborative control of prosthetic hands.

Acknowledgement. This work was supported in part by Guangdong Basic and Applied Basic Research Foundation (2022A1515110142), the grants from Shenzhen Science and Technology Program (#JCYJ20240813154800002), Guangdong Basic and Applied Basic Research Foundation (2024A1515011973).

References

1. Zheng, Y., Li, X., Tian, L., Li, G.: Function-oriented optimization design method for underactuated tendon-driven humanoid prosthetic hand. Front. Mech. Eng. **17**(3), 40 (2022)
2. Yue, Z., et al.: A prosthetic hand system with human-like grasping by combining EMG and visual information. In: 30th International Conference on Mechatronics and Machine Vision in Practice (M2VIP) (2024)

3. Yuan, B., Hu, D., Gu, S., Xiao, S., Song, F.: The global burden of traumatic amputation in 204 countries and territories. Front. Public Health **11**, 1258853 (2023)
4. Salminger, S., et al.: Current rates of prosthetic usage in upper-limb amputees - have innovations had an impact on device acceptance? Disabil. Rehabil. **44**(14), 3708–3713 (2022)
5. Li, X., Tian, L., Zheng, Y., Samuel, O.W., Fang, P., Wang, L., Li, G.: A new strategy based on feature filtering technique for improving the real-time control performance of myoelectric prostheses. Biomed. Signal Process. Control **70**, 10296 (2021)
6. Chen, Z., Min, H., Wang, D., Xia, Z., Sun, F., Fang, B.: A review of myoelectric control for prosthetic hand manipulation. Biomimetics (Basel) **8**(3), 328 (2023)
7. Gionfrida, L., Kim, D., Scaramuzza, D., Farina, D., Howe, R.D.: Wearable robots for the real world need vision. Sci. Rob. **9**(90), eadj8812 (2024)
8. Zhong, B., Huang, H., Lobaton, E.: Reliable vision-based grasping target recognition for upper limb prostheses. IEEE Trans Cybern **52**(3), 1750–1762 (2022)
9. Shi, C., Yang, D., Zhao, J., Jiang, L.: i-MYO: A hybrid prosthetic hand control system based on eye-tracking, augmented reality and myoelectric signal (2022)
10. Huang, J., Li, Z., Xia, H., Chen, G., Meng, Q.: Cross-modal integration and transfer learning using fuzzy logic techniques for intelligent upper limb prosthesis. IEEE Trans. Fuzzy Syst. **31**(4), 1267–1280 (2022)
11. Castro, M.N., Dosen, S.: Continuous semi-autonomous prosthesis control using a depth sensor on the hand. Front. Neurorobot. **16**, 814973 (2022)
12. Vasile, F., Maiettini, E., Pasquale, G., Florio, A., Boccardo, N., Natale, L.: Grasp Pre-shape selection by synthetic training: eye-in-hand shared control on the hannes prosthesis. CoRR abs/2203.09812 (2022)
13. Cirelli, G., Tamantini, C., Cordella, L.P., Cordella, F.: A semiautonomous control strategy based on computer vision for a hand-wrist prosthesis. Robotics **12**(6), 152 (2023)
14. Tian, L., et al.: An intelligent prosthetic system for EMG pattern recognition based prosthesis control. In: 2022 IEEE International Conference on Cyborg and Bionic Systems, pp. 70–77 (2022)
15. Cutkosky, M.R.: On grasp choice, grasp models, and the design of hands for manufacturing tasks. IEEE Trans. Robot. Autom. **5**(3), 269–279 (1989)
16. Zandigohar, M., et al.: Multimodal fusion of EMG and vision for human grasp intent inference in prosthetic hand control, vol. 11 (2024)

RoboImagine: A Robotic Video Generation Model, for Autoregressive Long-Term Task Video Generation with Geometric and Dynamic Consistency Augmentation

Conglin Wang[1], Hongkun Yang[2], Chuanjiang Li[1], Siqi Wen[3], Yiming Gan[1], and Shuai Liang[1(✉)]

[1] Institute of Computing Technology, Chinese Academy of Sciences, Beijing 100190, China
{wangconglin,lichuanjiang1013,ganyiming,liangshuai}@ict.ac.cn
[2] New York University, New York, USA
hy2363@nyu.edu
[3] Beijing Jiaotong University, Beijing 100044, China
22722030@bjtu.edu.cn

Abstract. Robot learning aims to complete diverse tasks. End-to-end VLA models, achieving significant performance, but struggling on data dependency. Recently, video generation models (VGMs) as a world model provides a new perspective, enabling robots to generalize across tasks by 'imagining' future states. However, computing bottleneck leading to limited-length video output, not applicable for long-term tasks. In this paper, we train a image-text conditioned robotic video generation model, named **RoboImagine**, aiming to generate long-term robotic manipulation videos, with visual-semantic-dynamic conformity. We build an autoregressive long-term video generation pipeline based on a VLM as task-complete-verifier, in which RoboImagine is designed with dynamic and geometric consistency augmentation to get continuous and smooth motions between generated clips. Systematic experiments are implemented, showing that we are able to generate longe-term robotic manipulation videos with continuous motion, achieveing average success rate increment of 150% than that of w/o augmentation method. Our method effectively generalize on unseen simulation and real world cases. The generated video is mapped into end-effector actions, through a visual inverse dynamic model. We open source our work with link: https://github.com/Egbert-Lannister/Robo-Imagine.

Keywords: Robotic manipulation · Video generation · World model

1 Introduction

With rapid evolvement of robotics and artificial intelligence, robot learning has emerged as a pivotal technology, increasingly becoming a focal point of research.

The primary objective is to learn a strategy that enable robots to perform a diversity of tasks successfully and robustly across environments. Effectiveness and safety are two key factors on robotic manipulation, especially in human involved environment or collision sensitive industrial productions.

To achieve task generalization, existing methodologies have proposed different solutions. Hierarchical structures [8,13,33] combining LLM as high-level task planner and individual algorithm modules as low-level executors, enabling long-term task but restricted by predefined skills, with limited flexibility.

Recent years, VLA models [2,4,5,11,20,24,34], as a promising solution, have achieved significant results on robotic manipulations. However, VLA models illustrate heavy data dependency, restricting the generalization across tasks and environments. Latent visual action model [6,9,32,37] propose to train an unified form of latent action tokens, which utilizes VQ-VAE [30] to learn latent motion between consecutive frames across a wide range of video dataset, including internet scope and robotic scope. The learned latent action followed with action head is further finetuned with target task data for exact applications. Latent action is able to learn the potential key feature between frames, but requires multi-stage for training and lack of consideration on long-term task.

Video generation models (VGMs) [3,17,19,36], as a world model provides a new perspective, enabling robots to generalize across tasks and environments by 'imagining' future states. VGMs provide a 'think before action' mechanism, which is crucial when task is unfamiliar or collision sensitive. However, due to the computing limitation, diffusion based VGMs often output short-length clips which is not suitable for long-term tasks [1,15,21,28,31]. Even there are solutions such as autoregressive video generation method VLP [14], its recursive tree search consumes large computing resources. Besides, the geometric and dynamic consistency between clips should be further considered. SkillDiffuser [23] is another work utilizing robotic video generation for complicated tasks, but only trained on pre-defined skill sets leading to less flexibility.

To address this, we train a diffusion-based robotic video generation model, named **RoboImagine** to 'imagine' robot videos across tasks and environments. In addition, We introduce a Visual Language Model (VLM) as task-completeness evaluator to regressively generating long-term videos until task fulfilled. In order to generate continuous and smooth robot videos, when connecting sequential generated clips together, we use three consecutive frames as image condition, within which, the pixel difference provides key implicit representations, namely the objects motion velocity and acceleration at last clip end. This leading to a reasonable following generated video with motion continuity and smoothness, avoiding abrupt actions. Besides the static and dynamic pixel between conditional consecutive frames providing shape and location constrains on generated video, guaranteeing the geometric consistency between clips. In contrast, single frame conditioned video generation may expose problems on ambiguous motion direction and shows less geometric consistency. The generated video is further mapped into 7-DoF robotic end-effector action through a trained visual inverse dynamic model (VID).

In this paper, we mainly make three contributions:

(1) We finetune a diffusion-based robotic video generation model, RoboImagine, conditioned with text and consecutive images (providing visual-spatial-dynamic information including motion velocity and acceleration, leading to smooth trajectory when generated video, conditioned with former video ending frames), guaranteeing the geometric and dynamic consistency between clips.
(2) We design an autoregressive long-term video generation paradigm, using VLM as contextual task-complete verifier to iteratively generating video clips until task done, which can also be used to identify anomalies in generated video before real world execution, forming a 'think before action' mechanism.
(3) We trained a ViT-based visual inverse dynamic model (VID) to map video into end-effector action. And systematic experiments are implemented to verify the effectiveness of video generation and VID model between baselines.

The following of this paper is organized that, Sect. 2 introduces RoboImagine video generation model with geometric and dynamic augmentation, which is integrated in an autoregressive long-term video generation framework through VLM task-evaluator. The generated video is further mapped in to end-effector action by visual inverse dynamic model. In Sect. 3, systematic baseline tests are implemented, including video generation quality, long video generation continuity evaluation and VID action prediction.

2 Method

2.1 Overview and Setup

RoboImagine pipeline consists of three parts: a text-image conditioned, diffusion video generator, an autoregressive long-term video generation paradigm enabled by a VLM task-complete evaluator and a visual inverse dynamics model (VID) mapping video into end-effector actions.

At timestep t, given inputs comprise of consecutive observation images O_{t-2}, O_{t-1}, O_t as visual condition and an goal text instruction I_t, the robotic system ψ executes a sequence of actions $a_{t:t+m}$ to accomplish the task in an end-to-end manner:

$$a_{t:t+m} = \psi_{t-2}((O_{t-2}, O_{t-1}, O_t), I_t), \tag{1}$$

where m denotes the predicted action horizon. We divide this process into video generation phrase followed with action mapping phrase.

2.2 Robotic Video Generation

In RoboImagine, we employ a Denoising Diffusion Probabilistic Model (DDPM) [18,27] as the core module to generate video frames aligned with image-text conditions. A DDPM consists of two Markov chains: a forward diffusion

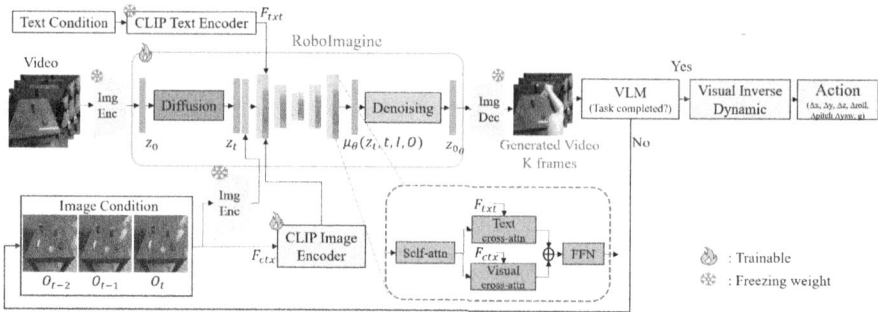

The last 3 frames of the previous video, implicitly representing **(1) dynamic information of velocity and acceleration,** **(2) geometric information of shape and location restriction,** relace as new input images condition for regressive video generation

Fig. 1. Framework of our RoboImagine model. RoboImagine is a U-Net-based diffusion video generation model. At timestep t, inputs: text instruction I, 3 consecutive condition images (O_{t-2}, O_{t-1}, O_t). (O_{t-2}, O_{t-1}, O_t) represent implicit geometrics (shapes and locations) and dynamic (motion velocity and acceleration) conditions of task, in order to achieve coherent and smooth motion between generated clips, under autoregressive long-term video generation framework. We employ a VLM as task-completion evaluator to generate long-term video. If VLM feedbacks task incomplete, RoboImagine continues to generate videos until task fulfilled. Output: generated robotic manipulation video, which is mapped into end-effector 7-DoF actions by visual inverse dynamic model.

process and a reverse generative process. The forward process gradually perturbs the data into noise. Given a data distribution $x_0 \sim q(x_0)$, the forward Markov process generates a sequence of random variables $x_1, x_2, \ldots, x_T$ via a transition kernel $q(x_t|x_{t-1})$. The joint distribution of $x_1, \ldots, x_T$ conditioned on x_0, denoted $q(x_1, \ldots, x_T|x_0)$, can be factorized as:

$$q(x_1, \ldots, x_T|x_0) = \prod_{t=1}^{T} q(x_t|x_{t-1}), \quad (2)$$

Typically, the forward transition kernel is designed as:

$$q(x_t|x_{t-1}) = \mathcal{N}(x_t; \sqrt{1-\beta_t}x_{t-1}, \beta_t I) \quad (3)$$

where $\beta_t \in (0,1)$ is a hyperparameter chosen prior to model training, controlling the level of noise injection to progressively approximate a simple prior distribution, such as a standard Gaussian distribution.

The reverse process learns to reverse the noise injection perturbation, generating images or video frames consistent with the input conditions. We utilize a Gaussian prior distribution $p(x_T) = \mathcal{N}(x_T; 0, I)$ and a learnable denoising model $p_\theta(x_{t-1}|x_t)$ to iteratively predict the injected noise from forward process:

$$p_\theta(x_{t-1}|x_t) = \mathcal{N}(x_{t-1}; \mu_\theta(x_t, t), \Sigma_\theta(x_t, t)) \quad (4)$$

where θ denotes the model parameters.

Based on this, we make modifications on a DDPM-based model, DynamiCrafter, to effectively guide video generation align with input conditions (images, text), as shown in Fig. 1. The natural language task description I_t is processed by the pre-trained CLIP text encoder [26], generating semantic embeddings. Simultaneously, RoboImagine receives 3 consecutive images O_{t-2}, O_{t-1}, O_t, where t is timestep. On the one hand, O_{t-2}, O_{t-1}, O_t represent the global task scene evolvement and implicit dynamic information including objects moving velocity and acceleration. On the other hand, the three continuous frames also implicitly describe the dynamic and static parts in the scene, which is a visual prompt for the model to distinguish effective motion in the video and retain shapes and location in the view. During training, the 3 consecutive images condition is chosen randomly, enabling to guide our model to generate video geometrically and dynamically align with any task stage. Furthermore, this is also a special design for autoregressive video generation through VLM task-completeverification, as we need to generate video referring the last generated video ending frames, guaranteeing the geometric, semantic and dynamic conformity, in order to obtain long-term coherent and smooth trajectories. Images are encoded by the VAE encoder and CLIP image encoder to extract global and local visual feature, then concatenated and aligned with text encoding in a shared latent space, to guide the de denoising process through cross attention respectively, ensuring alignment with task description, visual spatial feature, visual dynamics then generated frames.

The core of RoboImagine is a diffusion model based on denoising U-Net, which iteratively refines noise-initialized latent variables to produce video frames. Initially, VAE encodes video frames, representing the task scene and objects, into latent variable z_0, which undergoes gradual noise addition diffusion process and resulting a noisy latent variable z_t. z_t, combined with conditional information (text and images embeddings), processed by denoising U-Net to iteratively remove noise. The denoised results form the conditioned robotic video, Fig. 1.

2.3 VLM-Based AutoRegressive Long-Term Video Generation

One limitation of diffusion-based VGMs is that they can only generate short video clips due to the limited computing source, unsuitable for long-term task. To address this, we adopts an autoregressive approach to enable RoboImagine to iteratively generate latter video according to its former generated video frames, Fig. 1. Specifically, the generated video frames are fed into a task-completeness evaluator, a Visual Language Model (VLM) (ChatGPT-4o [25]), which feedbacks whether the generated frames semantically represent 'task-is-done'. If task is uncompleted, RoboImagine takes the last 3 generated frames as new initial condition images (with geometric and dynamic information), combining with text instruction, re-inputs and re-proceeds to generate the next segment video. If VLM feedbacks task is done, video generation stops. This autoregressive approach allows RoboImagine to generate longer, visual coherent, motion smooth videos while ensuring alignment with the specified task instruction.

Video task-complete determination is a challenging problem. Evaluation is multidimensional, including temporal consistency, dynamic degree, text2video alignment, factual consistency and so on. Facing this issue, VideoAgent [28] evaluated by humans, UniPi [15] trained a success classifier that takes the last frame of a generated video and predicts whether the task is successful or not, which achieves 72.6%(scratch) and 77.1%(pretrained) success rate.

Since task is composed of a series of actions, it is not sufficient to judge whether the task is completed solely based on a single tail frame, which may be not even the key frame. Therefore, We consider the key frames span the task. We first extract 5 key frames from the video by computing the biggest image histograms. Then, the key images are horizontally stitched together to form one image that can represent the task evolvement. Lastly, we input the combined image to GPT4o with multimodal analysis capabilities to determine whether the task has been completed, which achieves 82.1% success rate. In the experiment, we found that the model can perform object detection, frame to frame motion analysis, and temporal sequence checking on images like humans. This VLM task-evaluator is used to determine the video generation success rate of different baseline in Sect. 3, Table 1. Besides, it can also be used to identify collisions, accidents or abnormal kinematics in generated video, before real world execution, avoiding risks.

2.4 Visual Inverse Dynamic Model

We trained a visual inverse dynamic model (VID) as the action head, which takes two generated video consecutive frames (O_t, O_{t+1}) as inputs and outputs 7-DoF robot end-effector incremental position, rotation, and gripper state action $(\Delta x, \Delta y, \Delta z, \Delta roll, \Delta pitch, \Delta yaw, g)$. When applied with RoboImagine, VID takes generated video target frame $I_t + 1$ and real-time observation frame O_t as inputs, and outputs incremental action a_t, leading current robot state O_t converge to target state $I_t + 1$, Fig. 2. Different from conventional inverse dynamic directly using two generated frames in an open-loop control, our method use real-time observation frame as feedback compared with generative leading frame, outputs action correction in close-loop, eliminating accumulation errors. This method could both guarantee the control accuracy and maintain high computational efficiency compared with MPC methods. Our VID is backboned with pretrained ViT-base model(ViT-B) [12]. We apply a customized loss function, which includes a MSE action loss and an extra action direction penalty, guiding correct motion direction and amplitude.

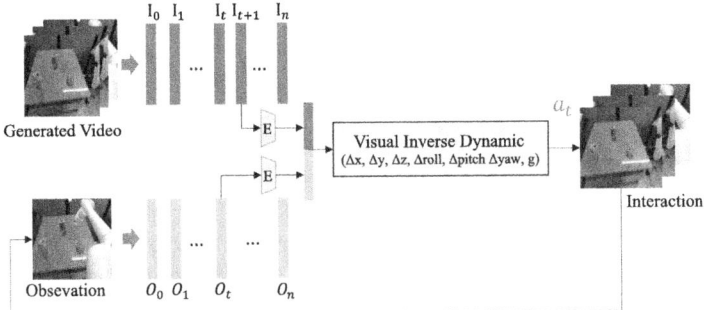

Fig. 2. Visual inverse dynamic model, guided by RoboImagine generated video, outputs 7-DoF robot end-effector action by comparing guiding video frames and real-time observation frame.

3 Experiment

3.1 Experimental Setup

RoboImagine builds on a fine-tuned DynamiCrafter [35], outputting 16-frame shot clips. We fine-tuned this framework on RT-X [10], including RT-1 [5], Berkeley Bridge [16] and Berkeley Autolab UR5 [7], utilizing only 2,552 samples (RT-1: 40.1%, Bridge: 40.1%, UR5: 19.8%), across three robot arms (RT-1 Google-robot, WidowX, and UR5). The dataset consists of 12 categories, 302 objects, and 1092 tasks, among them top 30 objects with the highest frequencies (>55 times), while other 272 objects appeared less than 55 times. We utilize six NVIDIA A100 GPUs with 40G memory each for training, with 934 epochs, 100000 steps, and learning rate of 1.0e−05. The model was trained for three days. We referred to Octo [29] and Simpler [22], and built simulations for RT-1 to verify the performance.

3.2 Video Generation Generalization

Our video generation experiments include three parts, (1) Performance on thousands of tasks from three datasets (seen-familiar samples, unseen-familiar samples), (2) Generalization in simulation and real-world environments (unseen-unfamiliar-simulation samples, unseen-unfamiliar-real-world samples), (3) Enhancement of Long Video Generation Capability by VLM Strategy.

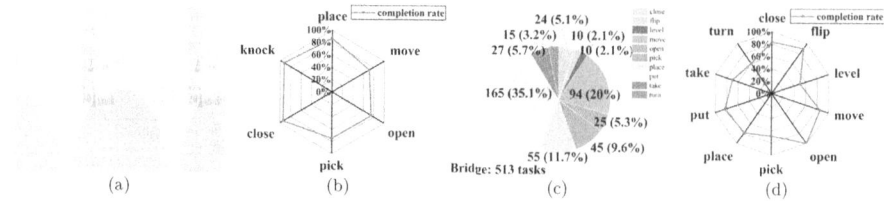

Fig. 3. RoboImagine generalization experimental results. (a) 599 tasks distribution across 6 major categories of RT-1 test dataset. (b) corresponding success rates of RT-1 test dataset. (c) 513 tasks distribution across 10 major categories of Bridge test dataset. (d) corresponding success rates of Bridge test dataset.

Generalization on Test Datasets. We performed video generation on the RT-1 and Bridge test datasets. The statistical results of these two experiments are shown in Fig. 3, Fig. 3 (a)(c) shows the tasks distribution, namely 599 tasks (6 categories: place/move/open/pick/close/knock) on RT-1 and 513 tasks (10 categories: close/flip/level/move/open/pick/place/put/take/turn) on Bridge. Figure 3 (b)(d) were success rate on RT-1 (78.5%) and Bridge (80.4%) test datasets respectively.

Figure 4 and Fig. 5 show that in the test dataset, the RT-1 Google-robot and Bridge WidowX robot can successfully complete the tasks they have seen before such as pick/put/close (same tasks, different environments). Experiment results prove that our model is able to identify target object distinguish from background, understand the instruction intention, spatial relationships, light-shadow and occlusion rendering.

Fig. 4. Video generation qualitative results for RT-1, seen task but different configurations in test dataset. (a) Pick coke can. (b) Pick apple. (c) Pick chocolate. (d) Open top drawer. (e) Close top drawer.

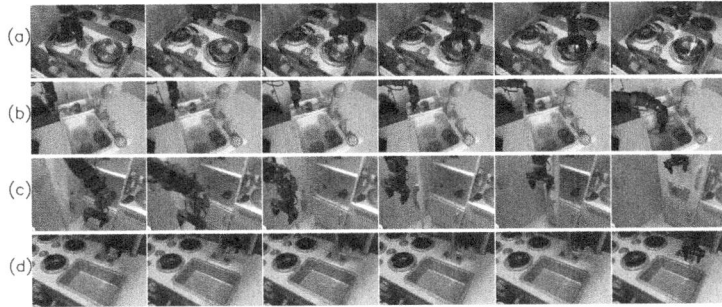

Fig. 5. Video generation qualitative results for Bridge, seen task but different configurations in test dataset. (a) Take broccoli out of pan. (b) Put carrot on plate. (c) Close fridge. (d) Open tap.

Our model also demonstrates strong generalization in environments and tasks never seen before (different tasks, different environments). We selected 10 tasks on RT-1 and Bridge each, which have never appeared on the training dataset before, for one-shot video generation, including tasks of move/place/put/pick, as shown in Fig. 6. In Fig. 6 (Left) RT-1(a)(b)(d)(e), RT-1 Google-robot can accurately grab the target object white bowl, blue chip bag, blue plastic bottle, and apple nearby the reference object. Figure 6 RT-1(e) has proven that tasks can also even be completed inside drawers. In Fig. 6 (Right) Bridge, WidowX can understand relative positional relationships, such as "left of the pot" in Fig. 6 Bridge(b) and "top left of the table" in Fig. 6 Bridge(c). In Fig. 6 Bridge(a)(d)(e), WidowX can place objects at specified locations.

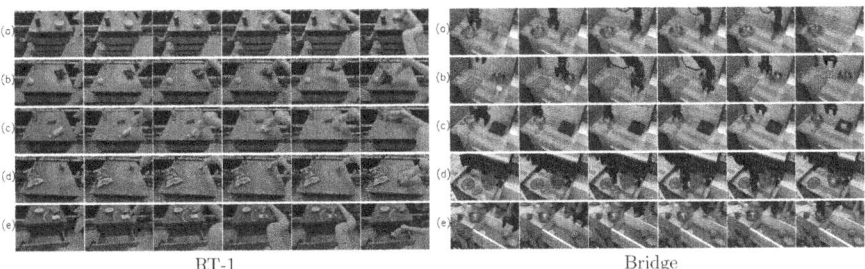

RT-1　　　　　　　　　　　　　Bridge

Fig. 6. Video generation quantitative results of unseen scenes in RT-1 and Bridge, unseen tasks. RT-1 (Left): (a) Move white bowl near water bottle. (b) Move blue chip bag near orange. (c) Move blue plastic bottle near coke can. (d) Move apple near brown chip bag (e) Place sponge into top drawer. **Bridge (Right):** (a) Move the blue spoon to the left of the pot. (b) pick blue brush and place it on the top left of the table. (c) Put the cheese onto the cloth. (d) Put sushi in pot cardboard fence. (e) put can in pot. (Color figure online)

Generalization in Unseen Simulation and Real Environments. To further assess our model's generalization, we first evaluate our model with RT-1 tasks in simulation environment, where items were randomly placed on drawers. Our model demonstrated robust Sim-to-Real generalization, generating accurate picking up manipulation videos. We created four distinct simulation environments, with varied in backgrounds, desktop categories, desktop texture, random coke can poses and spatial configurations. As shown in Fig. 7 left side, the robot successfully completed the assigned tasks, pick up coke can stably, further affirming the model's adaptability and robustness.

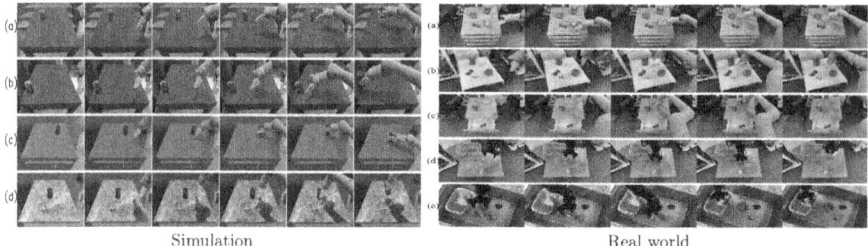

Fig. 7. Video generation in unseen scenes in simulation and real world for generalization test. **Simulation (Left):** Pick coke can with different backgrounds (a)(b) and different texture (c)(d). **Real world (Right):** (a) Move orange near apple. (b) Pick up banana. (c) Pick up green chips. (d) Pick up carrot. (e) Move banana to drying rack.

Eventually, We set up three scenarios from real-world environment, which the model never seen before, including two different drawers (one wooden, one white plastics), and one kitchen sink environment, to test the model's generalization. As shown in Fig. 7 right side, Real world video generation results (a)(b)(c) are drawers from different camera view, with objects randomly placed. We can see that RT-1 Google-robot successfully completed the task of 'move orange near apple', 'pick up banana', and 'pick up green chips'. Figure 7 right side, Real world (d)(e) shows that Bridge WidowX robot successfully completed the task of 'pick up carrot', and 'move banana to drying rack' in both drawers and kitchen environment. Figure 7 demonstrates our model's strong generalization capability across simulation and real-world scenarios.

3.3 Comparison Baselines

Video Quality Evaluation. Here, we choose AVDC [21], VideoAgent [28] and This&That [31] as baseline to make comparison experiments. Compared to single image and text conditions in AVDC [21], we use multiple consecutive images and text as conditions to achieve better graphic consistency, geometrically and semantically guiding diffusion (with global and local visual spatial and dynamic conditions) to generate clearer video (AVDC with only global visual condition), as shown in Fig. 8.

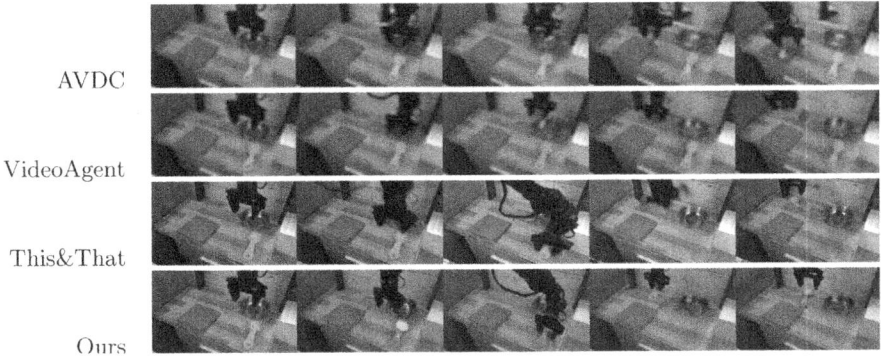

Fig. 8. Qualitative result comparison between AVDC, VideoAgent, This&That and our model. RoboImagine generates higher-resolution video, and under randomly selected tasks, our model shows a higher success rate.

We further make an comparison with This&That, a diffusion model with additional pixel instruction control. This&That requires complicated multi stage training, namely, a hand-annotated-label pretrained end-effector detection model for end-effector relabel in datasets before video generation training. Besides, AVDC, VideoAgent, This&That need to be separately trained for different embodiments and without consideration for long-term video generation.

Different from the above three baselines, RoboImagine is only one model trained on different datasets with geometric and dynamic augmentation. The Bridge dataset video generation success rate comparison with baselines are shown in Table 1. RoboImagine achieved overall success rate of 80%, while AVDC was 65%, VideoAgent was 59%, This&That was 75%. The success rate judgment is based on the VLM GPT4o, as we proposed in Sect. 2.3.

Table 1. Video generation success rate baseline comparison on different tasks (AVDC, VideoAgent, This&That, RoboImagine).

	AVDC	VideoAgent	This&That	RoboImagine(ours)
Move	63% (59/94)	63% (59/94)	74% (70/94)	**85% (80/94)**
Open	96% (24/25)	**100% (25/25)**	**100% (25/25)**	**100% (25/25)**
Place	62% (34/55)	55% (30/55)	76% (42/55)	**78% (43/55)**
Flip	80% (8/10)	60% (6/10)	70% (7/10)	**90% (9/10)**
Pick	53% (24/45)	40% (18/45)	**78% (35/45)**	69% (31/45)
Level	**90% (9/10)**	80% (8/10)	50% (5/10)	50% (5/10)
Close	71% (17/24)	50% (12/24)	**83% (20/24)**	**83% (20/24)**
Take	67% (18/27)	41% (11/27)	**81% (22/27)**	70% (19/27)
Put	65% (108/165)	64% (106/165)	70% (115/165)	**83% (137/165)**
Turn	33% (5/15)	27% (4/15)	**80% (12/15)**	60% (9/15)
Overall	65% (306/470)	59% (279/470)	75% (353/470)	**80% (378/470)**

We also conducted video quality quantitative baseline comparison experiments on Bridge dataset with AVDC, VideoAgent, This&That, as shown in Table 2. The results show that RoboImagine is able to generate more qualified videos, which approximate ground-truth videos. MSE, FID and FVD indicate the difference between generated videos and ground-truth videos, the values lower, the better. As a result, MSE of Robo-Imagine decreased by 33%–52% compared to baselines, while FID decreased by 7%–43%, and FVD decreased by 9%–65%. CLIP score and SSIM represent the similarity between the generated videos and ground-truth videos, the values higher, the better. Eventually, CLIP score of Robo-Imagine increased by 15%–16% compared to baselines, while SSIM value increased by 28%–34%. This illustrates that RoboImagine has the potential to generate more reasonable videos to guide robotic manipulations. We also provide a qualitative result comparison as shown in Fig. 8, the result shows that our model is able to generate higher resolution and semantically correct video which is important in robotic tasks.

Table 2. Generated video baseline quantitative comparison (AVDC, VideoAgent, This&That, RoboImagine).

Method	MSE ↓	FID ↓	FVD ↓	CLIPScore ↑	SSIM ↑
AVDC	1696	40	1615	0.75	0.49
VideoAgent	2187	38.38	1519	0.74	0.48
This&That	2345	24.84	622	0.83	0.45
RoboImagine-Bridge(Ours)	**1019**	**22**	**523**	**0.88**	**0.70**
RoboImagine(Ours)	1133	23	569	**0.88**	0.68

3.4 Autoregressive Long-Term Video Generation

Long-Term Video Generation Success Rate. For long-term video generation, adapting VLM as task-complete-verifier, we generate video frames autogressively in a close-loop until task done, on RT-1, Bridge and UR5 datasets (20 videos on each dataset), illustrated in Fig. 1. As results shown in Fig. 9, the clips within red bounding box represent former generated clip, whose last frames condition the following generated clips within blue bounding box. We make a comparison between generated long videos, w/ and w/o geometric and dynamic augmentation methods namely. We can find that method w/ geometric and dynamic augmentation shows spatial fidelity and smooth motion between the adjacent videos, enabling task being planned reasonably and smoothly, showing higher task success rate, which is totally opposite in w/o augmentation case. The relative long video generation success rate results are summarized in Table 3. With geometric and dynamic augmentation, our model achieve a success rate of 55%, 80%, 75% on RT-1, Bridge and UR5, while the method without augmentation achive success rate of 20%, 15%, 30%. Our model get a sucess rate increment of 175%, 433%, 150%, as summarized in Table 3.

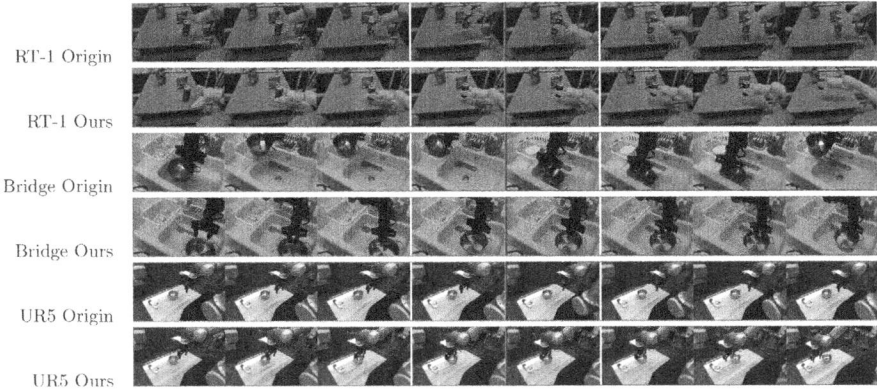

Fig. 9. Long-term video generation qualitative results, w/ and w/o geometric and dynamic augmentation. Each sub-figure is composed of two consecutive generated clips, of which the right side one (blue bounding box) is conditioned by the left side one (red bounding box). Experiments implemented on RT-1, Bridge and UR5 datasets. Rt-1: Pick pepsi can. Bridge: Put pot or pan from sink into drying rack. UR5: Put the ranch bottle into the pot. Sub-figures with 'Origin' subtitles indicate results that latter video is generated conditioned with only last one frame from former video, showing poor geometric and dynamic consistency, with position distribution offsets and abrupt unreasonable actions. Sub-figures with 'Ours' subtitles indicate results that latter video is generated conditioned with last consecutive frames from former video, showing consistent geometric distribution and continuous actions between video phrases. (Color figure online)

Table 3. Long-Term vodeo generation success rate on RT-1, Bridge and UR5, w/ and w/o geometric and dynamic augmentation. SR is short for Success Rate.

Dataset	Method	SR	Dataset	Method	SR	Dataset	Method	SR
RT-1	w/o augmentation	20%	Bridge	w/o augmentation	15%	UR5	w/o augmentation	30%
RT-1	**Ours**	**55%**	Bridge	**Ours**	**80%**	UR5	**Ours**	**75%**

Geometric and Dynamic Consistency of Stitched Long-Term Video. To further estimate the long-term video generation quality, we make a comparison between models w/ and w/o geometric and dynamic augmentation, generating long video under autoregressive framework. We generate long 20 videos each on RT-1, Bridge and UR5 datasets. The long-term video is composed of various generated clips, among which each clip is conditioned from its previous clip, stopping generation until VLM verify task-complete, Fig. 9. As a result, we estimate the video geometric consistency and dynamic consistency respectively, which represent the video's spatial fidelity and motion smoothness. First, we estimate the geometric consistency between the previous video's last frame and the following video's first frame, w/ (RoboImagine) and w/o geometric and dynamic augmentation. In experiments, we find that the generated video without geometric augmentation, exposing the spatial consistency issue leading to distorted shapes, deviant locations and abrupt actions, which are intolerable for real world robotic application. Hence, we make quantitative estimation on the geometric fidelity between the previous video's last frame and the following video's first frame, focusing on the MSE (the lower the better), SSIM (the higher the better), CLIPScore(the higher the better) and FID (the lower the better). The relative results are summarized in Table 4. We can find that on the three datasets, our model consistently outperforms than method without geometric augmentation. Second, we estimate the dynamic consistency between the previous video's last frame and the following video's second frame, w/ (RoboImagine) and w/o geometric and dynamic augmentation. Dynamics in videos play a key role to achieve motion direction, speed and even acceleration information, avoiding abrupt or misleading actions, which does not conform physics laws. Hence, we make quantitative estimation on the dynamic consistency between the previous video's last frame and the following video's second frame, focusing on the MSE (the lower the better), SSIM (the higher the better), CLIPScore(the higher the better), Optical Flow Magnitude (the lower the better) and Optical Flow direction standard deviation (the lower the better). The relative results are summarized in Table 5. We can find that on the three datasets, our model consistently outperforms than method without dynamic augmentation leading to smooth motions, Fig. 9.

Table 4. Geometric consistency evaluation between the last frame of previous video and the first frame of following video, under autoregressive generation frame work, w/ (RoboImagine) and w/o geometric and dynamic augmentation

Dataset	Method	MSE ↓	SSIM ↑	CLIPScore ↑	FID ↓
RT1	w/o augmentation	1238.34	0.73	0.85	180.68
RT1	**Ours**	**11.73**	**0.96**	**0.97**	**13.86**
Bridge	w/o augmentation	1585.16	0.75	0.91	140.12
Bridge	**Ours**	**30.58**	**0.94**	**0.97**	**14.41**
UR5	w/o augmentation	2022.78	0.66	0.92	159.26
UR5	**Ours**	**21.34**	**0.94**	**0.97**	**13.79**

Table 5. Dynamic consistency evaluation between the last frame of previous video and the second frame of following video, under autoregressive generation frame work, w/ (RoboImagine) and w/o geometric and dynamic augmentation

Dataset	Method	MSE ↓	SSIM ↑	CLIPScore ↑	OpticalFlow Magnitude ↓	OpticalFlow Dir-STD ↓
RT1	w/o augmentation	1205.04	0.74	0.86	3.41	**1.86**
RT1	**Ours**	**12.16**	**0.96**	**0.97**	**0.18**	1.89
Bridge	w/o augmentation	1590.86	0.75	0.91	2.84	1.82
Bridge	**Ours**	**31.65**	**0.94**	**0.98**	**0.22**	**1.78**
UR5	w/o augmentation	1999.14	0.66	0.92	5.53	1.84
UR5	**Ours**	**20.82**	**0.94**	**0.98**	**0.17**	1.84

3.5 Visual Inverse Dynamic Model

Experimental Setup. We trained one visual inverse dynamic model span various datasets including Bridge, Berkeley Autolab UR5, RT-1. For each dataset, we choose at least 2000 samples with video observations and their corresponding robotic action. We trained the inverse dynamic model for 20 epochs with AdamW optimizer with batchsize of 64, learning rate of 1e−4, 1000 linear warm up steps and 0.15 dropout rate for better robustness. One Nvidia A100 GPU is used for model training.

Baseline Comparison. We use *HiP* and *RoboDreamer* inverse dynamic as the baseline, with 1200 RT-1 tasks, 1000 Bridge tasks, and 1000 RT-1 + Bridge tasks, results shown in Table 6. The loss calculation includes two terms: the mean squared error (MSE) between the predicted action $\hat{a}$ and ground-truth action a, and a directional penalty that enforces alignment in motion direction. The total loss is formulated as:

$$\mathcal{L}_{\text{VID}} = MSE(\hat{a}, a) + \lambda \cdot MSE(sign(\hat{a}), sign(a)),$$

where $sign(.)$ denotes the action direction ($[-1, 0, 1]$) on each degree, and λ is a weighting coefficient. The directional penalty encourages the predicted action to additionally align with the correct motion direction. RoboImagine VID demonstrates high training and test accuracy under this loss design.

Table 6. VID baseline comparison, with *HiP* and *RoboDreamer* inverse dynamic, on RT-1, Bridge and UR5 datasets.

Model	RT-1		Bridge		RT-1 + Bridge	
	Train Loss	Test Loss	Train Loss	Test Loss	Train Loss	Test Loss
Hip(VC-1)	0.0173	0.0468	0.0422	**0.0784**	0.0995	0.1085
RoboDreamer(ResNet18)	**0.01294**	**0.0396**	0.03264	0.0867	0.0248	**0.0624**
RoboImagine(Ours)	0.0135	0.0459	**0.008**	0.0995	**0.0078**	0.0695

4 Conclusion

In this paper, we proposed RoboImagine, a generalized robotic video generation model with geometric and dynamic augmentation across tasks and environments. RoboImagine illustrates strong generalization capability even in unseen real-world and simulation scenes. This work provides a new perspective enabling robot to 'think before action' guaranteeing accuracy and safty simultaneously. By using a VLM as task-completion evaluator, we enable RoboImagine to autoregressively generate long-term videos, with coherent and smooth motion thanks to the design of using consecutive images condition containing geometric and dynamic restrictions. We also trained a visual inverse dynamic model, mapping video-action cross tasks and environments. For the future work, we will further combine video generation and action head together in order to eliminate accumulated error from hierarchical structure. Besides, generating image with diffusion model is time consuming, and video and action generation separation will accelerate inference speed.

References

1. Ajay, A., et al.: Compositional foundation models for hierarchical planning. Adv. Neural Inf. Process. Syst. **36** (2024)
2. Black, K., et al.: $\pi 0$: a vision-language-action flow model for general robot control (2024). https://arxiv.org/abs/2410.24164
3. Blattmann, A., et al.: Stable video diffusion: scaling latent video diffusion models to large datasets. arXiv preprint arXiv:2311.15127 (2023)
4. Brohan, A., et al.: RT-2: vision-language-action models transfer web knowledge to robotic control. arXiv preprint arXiv:2307.15818 (2023)
5. Brohan, A., et al.: Rt-1: Robotics transformer for real-world control at scale. arXiv preprint arXiv:2212.06817 (2022)
6. Bu, Q., et al.: UniVLA: learning to act anywhere with task-centric latent actions. arXiv preprint arXiv:2505.06111 (2025)
7. Chen, L.Y., Adebola, S., Goldberg, K.: Berkeley UR5 demonstration dataset. https://sites.google.com/view/berkeley-ur5/home
8. Chen, X., et al.: Pali-x: on scaling up a multilingual vision and language model. arXiv preprint arXiv:2305.18565 (2023)
9. Chen, Y., et al.: MOTO: latent motion token as the bridging language for robot manipulation. arXiv preprint arXiv:2412.04445 (2024)
10. Collaboration, O.X.E., et al.: Open X-embodiment: robotic learning datasets and RT-X models. https://arxiv.org/abs/2310.08864 (2023)
11. Deng, S., et al.: GraspVLA: a grasping foundation model pre-trained on billion-scale synthetic action data. arXiv preprint arXiv:2505.03233 (2025)
12. Dosovitskiy, A., et al.: An image is worth 16x16 words: transformers for image recognition at scale. In: International Conference on Learning Representations (2021). https://openreview.net/forum?id=YicbFdNTTy
13. Driess, D., et al.: Palm-e: an embodied multimodal language model. arXiv preprint arXiv:2303.03378 (2023)
14. Du, Y., et al.: Video language planning. arXiv preprint arXiv:2310.10625 (2023)
15. Du, Y., et al.: Learning universal policies via text-guided video generation. Adv. Neural Inf. Process. Syst. **36** (2024)
16. Ebert, F., et al.: Bridge data: boosting generalization of robotic skills with cross-domain datasets. CoRR arxiv:2109.13396 (2021)
17. He, Y., Yang, T., Zhang, Y., Shan, Y., Chen, Q.: Latent video diffusion models for high-fidelity long video generation. arXiv preprint arXiv:2211.13221 (2022)
18. Ho, J., Jain, A., Abbeel, P.: Denoising diffusion probabilistic models. Adv. Neural. Inf. Process. Syst. **33**, 6840–6851 (2020)
19. Ho, J., Salimans, T., Gritsenko, A., Chan, W., Norouzi, M., Fleet, D.J.: Video diffusion models. Adv. Neural. Inf. Process. Syst. **35**, 8633–8646 (2022)
20. Kim, M.J., et al.: OpenVLA: an open-source vision-language-action model. arXiv preprint arXiv:2406.09246 (2024)

21. Ko, P.C., Mao, J., Du, Y., Sun, S.H., Tenenbaum, J.B.: Learning to act from actionless videos through dense correspondences. arXiv:2310.08576 (2023)
22. Li, X., et al.: Evaluating real-world robot manipulation policies in simulation (2024). https://arxiv.org/abs/2405.05941
23. Liang, Z., Mu, Y., Ma, H., Tomizuka, M., Ding, M., Luo, P.: SkillDiffuser: interpretable hierarchical planning via skill abstractions in diffusion-based task execution. In: Proceedings of the IEEE/CVF Conference on Computer Vision and Pattern Recognition, pp. 16467–16476 (2024)
24. Liu, S., et al.: RDT-1B: a diffusion foundation model for bimanual manipulation. arXiv preprint arXiv:2410.07864 (2024)
25. OpenAI, Achiam, J., et al.: GPT-4 technical report (2024). https://arxiv.org/abs/2303.08774
26. Radford, A., et al.: Learning transferable visual models from natural language supervision. In: International Conference on Machine Learning, pp. 8748–8763. PMLR (2021)
27. Sohl-Dickstein, J., Weiss, E., Maheswaranathan, N., Ganguli, S.: Deep unsupervised learning using nonequilibrium thermodynamics. In: International Conference on Machine Learning, pp. 2256–2265. PMLR (2015)
28. Soni, A., et al.: VideoAgent: self-improving video generation (2024). https://arxiv.org/abs/2410.10076
29. Team, O.M., et al.: Octo: an open-source generalist robot policy (2024). https://arxiv.org/abs/2405.12213
30. Van Den Oord, A., Vinyals, O., et al.: Neural discrete representation learning. Adv. Neural Inf. Process. Syst. **30** (2017)
31. Wang, B., et al.: This&that: language-gesture controlled video generation for robot planning. arXiv preprint arXiv:2407.05530 (2024)
32. Wang, L., Chen, X., Zhao, J., He, K.: Scaling proprioceptive-visual learning with heterogeneous pre-trained transformers. Adv. Neural. Inf. Process. Syst. **37**, 124420–124450 (2024)
33. Wang, Z., et al.: Karma: augmenting embodied AI agents with long-and-short term memory systems. arXiv preprint arXiv:2409.14908 (2024)
34. Wen, J., et al.: Diffusion-vla: scaling robot foundation models via unified diffusion and autoregression. arXiv preprint arXiv:2412.03293 (2024)
35. Xing, J., et al.: DynamiCrafter: animating open-domain images with video diffusion priors. In: Leonardis, A., Ricci, E., Roth, S., Russakovsky, O., Sattler, T., Varol, G. (eds.) European Conference on Computer Vision, pp. 399–417. Springer, Heidelberg (2025). https://doi.org/10.1007/978-3-031-72952-2_23
36. Xing, Z., et al.: A survey on video diffusion models. ACM Comput. Surv. **57**, 1–42 (2023)
37. Ye, S., et al.: Latent action pretraining from videos. arXiv preprint arXiv:2410.11758 (2024)

A Soft-Skin Facial Robot Capable of Real-Time Emotion-Driven Actuation Through Visual Perception

Xuanhe Fan[1], Huijuan Zhao[1,3], Shuangjiang He[1,3], Li Li[2], and Li Yu[1,3]([✉])

[1] School of Electronic Information and Communications, Huazhong University of Science and Technology, Wuhan 430074, Hubei, China
[2] School of Future Technology, Huazhong University of Science and Technology, Wuhan 430074, Hubei, China
[3] Research Institute of Huazhong University of Science and Technology in Shenzhen, Shenzhen 518057, Guangdong, China
hustlyu@hust.edu.cn

Abstract. Existing facial robotic systems often suffer from high costs, limited flexibility in expression imitation, and a lack of adaptability to diverse facial identities, resulting in suboptimal replication of human-like expressions. This work designs YU-F01, a low-cost soft-skin facial robot capable of real-time emotion-driven actuation through visual perception. The system integrates computer vision and a multi-actuator facial mechanism to enable dynamic expression imitation. The main innovations include: (1) a landmark-based hierarchical mapping framework that converts facial keypoints into coordinated servo movements, allowing for adaptive expression replication across different facial structures; (2) a Polling-based Multi-actuator Synchronous Control Framework (PMSCF) that enables pseudo-parallel control of 16 servos on a microcontroller, reducing flash and memory usage by 21% and 44%, respectively, compared to RTOS solutions; (3) a Bio-inspired mechanical design featuring E600# silicone skin (Shore 0 ± 2 hardness) and an optimized linkage system, capable of simulating 12 key Facial Action Coding System (FACS) action units, all of which cost less than 70 dollars for the robot. Experimental results show that the robot can accurately capture expressions across multiple models, and its expression imitation achieves a PCC of 89.7%, demonstrating strong expression replication capability.

Keywords: Humanoid robot · facial expression imitation · real-time control · action unit mapping · Bio-inspired control

1 Introduction

Humanoid robots have emerged as a prominent research focus in robotics, with one key objective being to improve human-robot interaction (HRI) to improve user acceptance [1]. However, current studies are predominantly focused on control of body motion, while facial expressions are often reduced to displays on screens [2], lacking biomimetic and dynamic expressiveness. In fact, facial expressions are a critical medium for emotional HRI [3]. Therefore, it is important to create biomimetic facial robots that can imitate humans expressions [4,5].

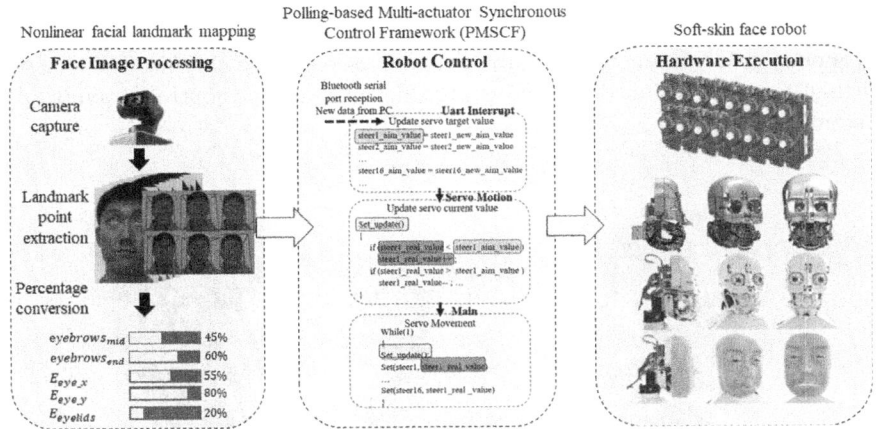

Fig. 1. The overall pipeline of our work.

Previous studies mainly used pre-programmed movements to make robot faces show expressions. These methods could create basic emotions, like happy or angry looks. However, the robot's expressions often looked stiff and unnatural [6]. They couldn't copy the small, subtle changes in real human facial movements. Subsequently, some researchers have obtained dynamic parameters by comparing the current face to a static face [7], but have limited the flexibility of dynamic interactions between different people. These examples show that facial robots need better adaptability and real-time responsiveness.

Among other approaches, creating dynamic, realistic, and resource-efficient facial systems that can adapt to human emotions remains a significant challenge. Issues such as expressiveness fidelity, identity adaptability, and computational efficiency severely limit scalability and practical deployment [8,9]. For instance, EVA employed servo-driven mechanisms for facial control but were constrained by thermal throttling due to reliance on Raspberry Pi hardware [10], while their fixed facial parameters hindered individual adaptability. Similarly, Liu et al. [11]. Improved cross-identity compatibility by modeling facial key-point motion percentages, yet their system was designed for sign-language collaboration. These cases underscore the limitations of rigid, predefined expression mappings in traditional approaches.

To overcome the above challenges, we designed the YU-F01 facial soft skin robot by introducing the following three innovations, and the overall pipeline of our work is shown in the Fig. 1.

1. Hardware Optimization: Replacing the Raspberry Pi with the STM32F103-C8T6 microcontroller and PCA9685 servo controller eliminates

thermal issues, reduces power consumption, and supports scalable actuator control with 16 PWM channels.

2. Adaptive Perception: A nonlinear facial landmark mapping algorithm using 476 keypoints enables region-specific, adaptive facial expression control, improving robustness across individuals.

3. Lightweight Control Framework: The Polling-based Multi-actuator Synchronous Control Framework (PMSCF) achieves s-level synchronization of servos without the need for an RTOS, ensuring efficient real-time control for embedded systems.

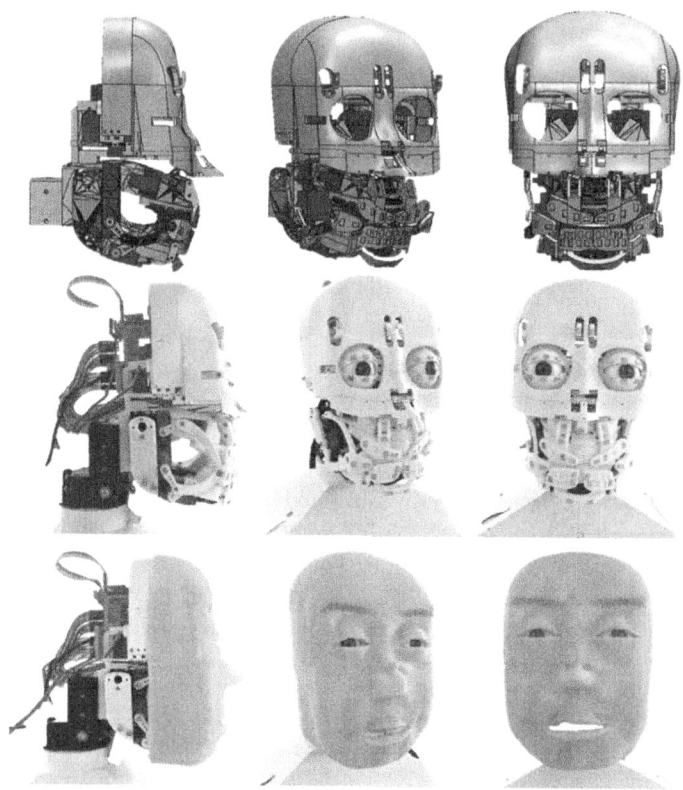

Fig. 2. The Overall view of the facial robot.

2 Overview of Hardware Components

The YU-F01 is mainly composed of the following components: eye-driving mechanism, jaw-driving mechanism, mouth-driving mechanism, face mask structure, and silicone skin. Key components used include an STM32F103C8T6 minimum system board, a 16-channel PWM output module PCA9685, 15 SG90 micro servos, one MG996R metal gear servo, a 12V, 1.3A DC switching power supply, several magnetic adhesive patches, and various 3D-printed structures made of PLA material. The overall structure of the flexible-skinned facial robot is shown in the Fig. 2.

The servo configuration and kinematic function mapping of YU-F01 is shown in Table 1. The eye-driving mechanism consist of eight SG90 servos, four-bar linkages, and two servo-driven eyebrow brackets that drive the movement of the left and right eyes in terms of up, down, left, and right rotations, eyelid closure, and eyebrow movements. The jaw-driving mechanism consists of one MG996R metal gear motor and a servo-driven jaw joint. The mouth-driving mechanism consists of six SG90 servos, two five-bar linkages, and two four-bar linkages. The face mask structure is mainly used to support the silicone skin on the face, preventing skin indentation caused by servo stretching, while one SG90 servo and a direct-drive rod are used to control the vertical movement of the nose muscles. The silicone skin is made of E600# AB silicone, with a Shore hardness of $0\pm2°$ and tear strength and elongation close to that of human skin.

Table 1. Servo Configuration and Kinematic Function Mapping

Servo No.	Controlled Area	AU	Movement Type	Mechanical Implementation
M1, M2	Left/Right Eye Horizontal Rotation	61/62	±30° H R	Four-bar linkage + Universal joint
M3, M4	Left/Right Eye Vertical Rotation	63/64	±30° V R	Four-bar linkage + Universal joint
M5	Inner Eyebrow Lift/Lower	1/4	0–8 mm V D	Servo-driven eyebrow bracket
M6	Outer Eyebrow Lift/Lower	2/4	0–8 mm V D	Servo-driven eyebrow bracket
M7	Nose Movement	9	0–10 mm V S	Servo-driven nose muscle bracket
M8, M9	Left/Right Mouth Corner Lift	12	0–20 mm V D	Five-bar linkage
M10, M11	Left/Right Mouth Corner Lateral Movement	10/12	0–6 mm H D	Five-bar linkage
M12	Upper Lip Lift	10	0–10 mm V D	Four-bar linkage combination
M13	Lower Lip Drop	16	0–8 mm V D	Four-bar linkage combination
M14	Jaw Opening/Closing	26/27	0-60° V R	Servo-driven jaw bracket
M15	Upper Eyelid Open/Close	5/43	0-60° V R	Four-bar linkage
M16	Lower Eyelid Micro Movement	7	0-60° R	Four-bar linkage

V: Vertical, H: Horizontal, R: Rotation, D: Displacement, S: Stretch.

In our facial robot design, servos simulate the stretching of facial muscles. However, the human face is composed of approximately 43 muscles. Fitting 43 servos in the limited space of the robot's head is challenging. Therefore, to improve the robot's facial expressions, we refer to the Facial Action Coding System (FACS), which uses servos to mimic the most commonly used muscles in basic expressions. An updated definition of 64 Action Units (AUs), corresponding to different facial muscles, has been developed.

3 Robot Drive Method

3.1 Nonlinear Mapping of Facial Action Units

Many expression imitation methods require a neutral face during initialization, limiting performance when initial frames are non-neutral [7]. For that, we propose a hierarchical keypoint mapping framework, assigning multiple facial landmarks to each servo and defining region-specific mappings. This improves both cross-subject adaptability and real-time response.

To reduce sensitivity to individual keypoint errors, we employ nonlinear mapping of multiple landmarks. A total of 476 facial keypoints are extracted using Mediapipe [14], with their mapping to servo control illustrated in Fig. 3.

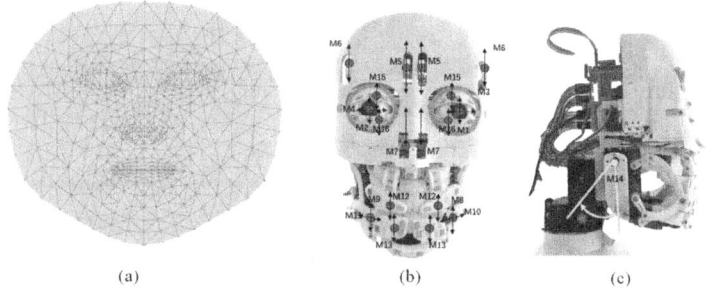

Fig. 3. Figure (a): 476 facial keypoints from Mediapipe. Figure (b)(c): 16 servo-controlled robot nodes corresponding to the control.

Although the detected facial landmarks perfectly align with the servo control points, a one-to-one mapping may introduce errors due to lighting or movement. Therefore, in the facial landmark mapping, we treat the key points corresponding to the facial Action Units (AUs) as a group of mapped points.

Additionally, we are inspired by other work [12], to make the computed values adaptable to each face, this work uses relative values rather than absolute values to represent joint movement, i.e., using percentages instead of absolute pixel coordinates.

This work uses Mediapipe to detect iris landmarks in both eyes to determine iris position. The calculations for the right and left irises are similar, so only the specific formula for the percentage movement of the right iris is listed in the Eq. 1:

$$Percent_{RHiris} = \frac{ED[33, CoM(468,469,470,471,472)]}{ED[33,133]}$$

$$Percent_{RViris} = \frac{ED[CoM(144,145,153), CoM(468,469,470,471,472)]}{ED[CoM(144,145,153), CoM(158,159,160)]}$$
(1)

Where $Percent$ represents the percentage of movement at the key position, R stands for "$Right$," H for "$Horizontal$," V for "$Vertical$," ED is the Euclidean distance between the two points, and CoM is the Center of Mass. The numbers refer to the landmark indices.

The Eyelid closure has an absolute zero (fully closed state). However, unlike the iris, eyelid opening lacks reference points. We calculate opening percentage as the ratio of eyelid separation to eye-corner width, modeling movement as spherical rotation (like the eyeball). Accounting for mechanical limits, we set maximum rotation at 60°, giving $Max_{open} = EyeWidth \times sin60°$. Since the calculation methods for the left and right eyelids are similar, the specific formula for the right eyelid movement percentage is presented in Eq. 2:

$$Percent_{Reyelid} = \frac{ED[CoM(144,145,153), CoM(158,159,160)]}{ED[33,133]}$$
(2)

Jaw movement affects facial length, but individual differences prevent absolute measurements. We instead track relative chin displacement along the head's vertical axis between frames to control rotation. The calculation method is detailed in Eq. 3:

$$Jaw = \frac{ED[CoM(109,10,338), CoM(148,152,377)]}{Height}$$

$$Percent_{jaw} = Jaw_{now} - Jaw_{last}$$
(3)

Mouth control focuses on four regions: upper/lower lips and mouth corners. Since lip muscles move collectively, we analyze curvature between lip landmarks to determine mouth shape and lip positions, as shown in Eq. 4:

$$k_c = \frac{4 \cdot Area(\triangle ABC)}{\|AB\| \cdot \|BC\| \cdot \|CA\|}$$

$$Percent_{Ulip} = k_c \cdot CoM[78, 308]$$
(4)

Where kc is the calculated curvature, U represents the upper lip, and L represents the lower lip. Using landmarks 78/13/308 (U) and 78/14/308 (L), we compute curvature as radius reciprocal, scaled by distance between landmarks 78-308 for percentage.

For mouth corners, we calculate movement percentage as the ratio between mouth-corner midpoint to upper lip distance and total lip height, as shown in Eq. 5:

$$Percent_{Clip} = \frac{ED[Mid(78, 308), CoM(82, 13, 312)]}{ED[CoM(87, 14, 317), CoM(82, 13, 312)]} \tag{5}$$

Where Mid represents the midpoint between two points, and $Clip$ represents the mouth corner.

For the eyebrow mapping, similar to the mouth, each person's eyebrow height and size are different, so background templates cannot be used to calculate relative values. This work calculates the eyebrow movement percentage based on the slope of the eyebrow. The specific formula is shown in Eq. 6:

$$k_c = \frac{n \cdot \sum_{i=landmark}^{n} x_i y_i - \sum_{i=landmark}^{n} x_i \sum_{i=landmark}^{n} y_i}{n \cdot \sum_{i=landmark}^{n} x_i^2 - (\sum_{i=landmark}^{n} x_i)^2}$$

$$Percent_{eyebrow} = \frac{k_c + 1}{2} \tag{6}$$

Where n is the number of points used to calculate the slope. In this work, n is set to 3, with the left eyebrow landmarks being Landmarks 285, 282, 276 and the right eyebrow landmarks being Landmarks 55, 52, 46. At the same time, we limit the slope value within the range of $[-1, 1]$ due to mechanical dead zones and the actual range of eyebrow movement. The final percentage is calculated using Eq. (6).

3.2 Robot Control Methods

The robot consoles receive the corresponding percentage signals from the image processing console, and then convert them into actual servo motion commands. To ensure the correctness of the data transmission, we used data packets and sequence numbers. In addition, to prevent the mechanical structures from obstructing each other, we limit the range of motion of the mechanical structures. In this way, the range of motion can be mapped to the received percentage signals and the servo assignment equation is shown Eq. 7:

$$Servo_{aim} = Servo_{base} + Percent \cdot Servo_{range} \tag{7}$$

Where $Servo_{aim}$ is the target servo value, $Servo_{base}$ denotes the baseline position, $Percent$ is the movement percentage from the upper-level system, and $Servo_{range}$ defines the servo's motion span based on mechanical limits.

We propose a Polling-based Multi-actuator Synchronous Control Framework (PMSCF) for coordinated multi-servo control. Without relying on an RTOS, this polling-based design enables pseudo-parallelism with minimal resource overhead, making it suitable for low-cost MCUs like STM32F103C8T6.

Dynamic speed control is achieved via linear interpolation, adjusting step size in real time based on current-to-target ratios. A unified timestamp and sequential scanning ensure synchronous updates of all 16 servos within each control cycle, effectively avoiding desynchronization typically seen in RTOS-based systems.

4 Experiments

In this work, we design a soft-skin facial expression robot YU-F01. We propose an expression control framework based on hierarchical mapping of keypoints (PMSCF), which accurately maps face keypoints to the corresponding parts of the robot's face. Then we propose a synchronized multi-actuator control framework based on a polling mechanism, which can control the motion of 16 motors by simulating parallel operation in a microcontroller. Therefore, we evaluate our face robot by testing both expression generation and expression following.

4.1 Emoji Generation

This study evaluates the effectiveness of six basic facial expressions (Happiness, Sadness, Anger, Fear, Surprise, Disgust) generated by a humanoid robot. We compare facial keypoint detection results from three methods—OpenCV Haar, Dlib, and OpenFace—to assess expression recognizability and feature accuracy.

As shown in Fig. 4, each expression displays distinct features (e.g., upturned mouth for Happiness, downturned for Sadness, furrowed brows for Anger), serving as evaluation references.

All three detection methods successfully identified key facial areas, confirming the clarity of features like mouth corners, eyebrows, and eyes. OpenCV Haar marked keypoints with red dots and blue boxes using Haar features. Dlib, based on HOG and regression trees, offered denser points, especially around the mouth and eyes. OpenFace, using deep learning, provided the most precise keypoints, particularly around the eyes and nose.

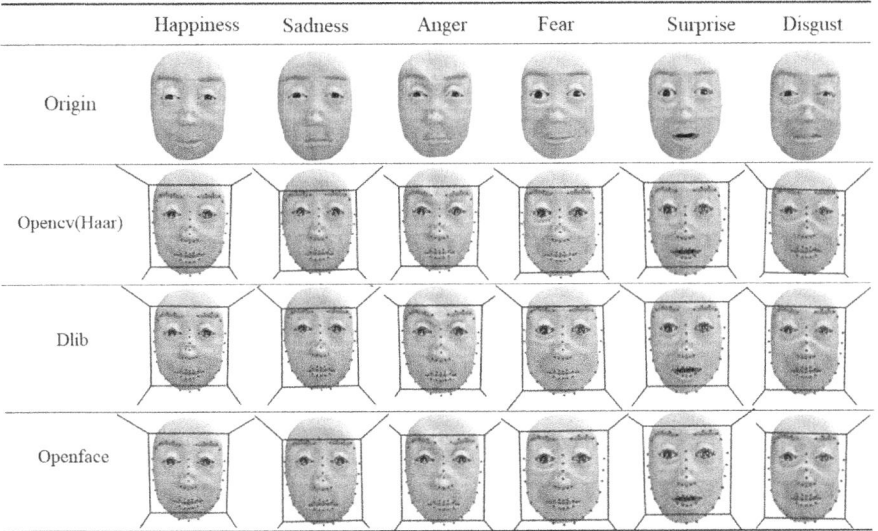

Fig. 4. Recognizing Different Emotions Using Different Face Recognition Methods.

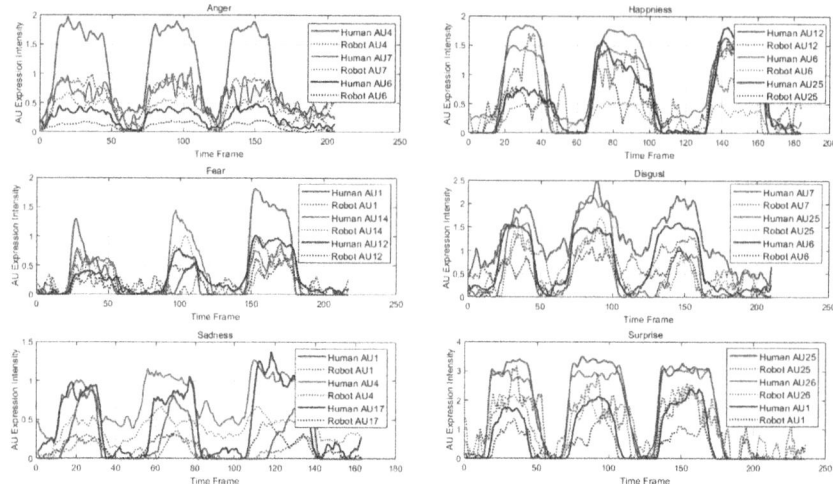

Fig. 5. Six Emotional Human and Robot Faces AU Motion Amplitude Comparison.

The methods consistently captured specific expressions: Happiness and Sadness through mouth corner movements; Anger via furrowed brows; Fear by wide-open eyes; Surprise by an open mouth, with Dlib detecting finer mouth details; and Disgust mainly through nose wrinkling, where OpenFace provided the most accurate keypoints. These results confirm the robot's expressions are distinctive and reliably recognized by common detection methods.

4.2 Expression Imitation

In this experiment, we use OpenFace for keypoint tracking, and to evaluate how accurately the robot follows human facial movements, we compared the facial expressions of the humanoid robot with those of human subjects. We used a camera to simultaneously photograph the human face and the robot face, and then the human face made the same expression three times in a row. In order to make the display clearer, we chose the three AU with the largest amplitude of movement in each expression for comparison. The results are shown in Fig. 5 (Table 2).

Table 2. Six emotions human face and robot face corresponding to AU of PCC

Emotion	1st	2nd	3rd
Anger	(AU4) 0.958	(AU7) 0.894	(AU6) 0.924
Happiness	(AU12) 0.861	(AU6) 0.890	(AU25) 0.907
Fear	(AU1) 0.870	(AU14) 0.915	(AU12) 0.828
Disgust	(AU7) 0.888	(AU25) 0.920	(AU6) 0.902
Sadness	(AU1) 0.908	(AU4) 0.880	(AU17) 0.916
Surprise	(AU25) 0.887	(AU26) 0.918	(AU1) 0.882

1st, 2nd, 3rd represent the three AUs with the largest motion respectively

The Pearson Correlation Coefficient (PCC) is a statistical measure used to assess the strength of the linear relationship between two variables. In this context, it is used to evaluate how accurately our facial recognition robot follows the face. The results are in the Table 3 show that although the robot's facial movements are smaller than human's due to the limitations of the actuator, the average PCC value is 89.7% in all six expressions. This demonstrates the high accuracy of the robot's ability to replicate the dynamics of human facial expressions. For example, in the "angry" expression, the robot accurately replicated the movements of the furrowed brow (AU04) and the clenched eyes (AU07) despite the small amplitude.

The robot showed strong consistency in replicating the relative movements of key facial features such as eyebrows, lips, and cheeks. For example, in "Happiness," the robot highly realistically mimicked the movements of the corners of the mouth pulling up (AU12) and the cheeks rising (AU06). Thus despite actuator limitations, the robot's expressions are dynamic and recognizable.

It is worth to mention that our proposed approach reduces flash memory usage by 21% (from 30.5 KB to 24.1 KB) and RAM consumption by 44% (from 9.3 KB to 5.2 KB) compared to a conventional FreeRTOS on the STM32F103C8T6 platform. Because such optimizations can be directly translated into extended functionality within existing hardware constraints or reduced production costs by deploying on lower-cost microcontrollers.

4.3 Landmark Map

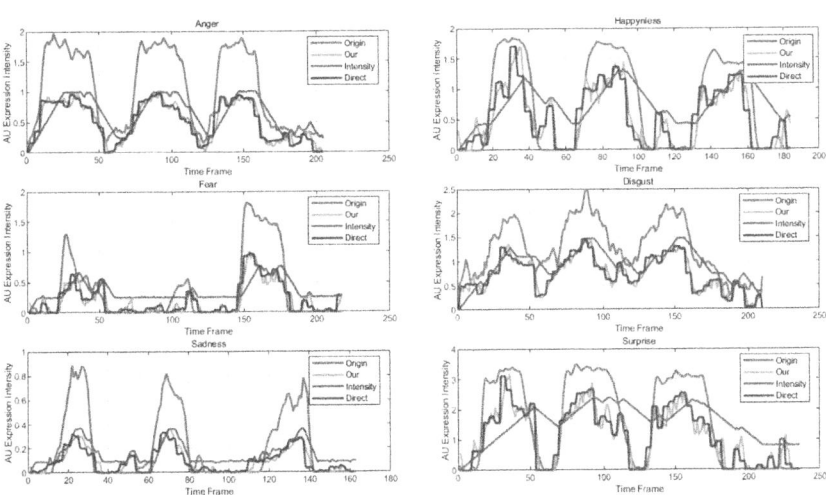

Fig. 6. Comparison of different mapping methods in six expressions.

Table 3. Six emotions human face and robot face corresponding to AU of PCC

Emotion	Our	Intensity	Direct
Anger(AU4)	**0.958**	0.801	0.949
Happiness(AU12)	**0.861**	0.626	0.823
Fear(AU1)	**0.902**	0.734	0.897
Disgust(AU7)	**0.888**	0.805	0.870
Sadness(AU1)	**0.908**	0.811	0.857
Surprise(AU25)	0.887	0.510	**0.897**

To evaluate the effectiveness of the proposed method, we compare it with two commonly used approaches. The first approach maps facial expressions by categorizing them into different intensity levels [15]. The second directly detects facial keypoints and maps them to servo movements [7]. In our experiments, all three methods, including ours, use OpenFace for facial keypoint detection to ensure consistency. We selected the Action Unit (AU) with the largest amplitude variation for comparison, in order to minimize the influence of minor movements from other AUs. The experimental results are shown in Fig. 6, and the corresponding Pearson Correlation Coefficients (PCC) are listed in Table 3. The average PCCs for our method, the intensity-based method, and the direct mapping method are 0.901, 0.715, and 0.882, respectively. These results show that our method has a higher correlation with the other two methods.

5 Conclusions

This work presents YU-F01, a soft-skin facial robot system designed to enable real-time, emotion-driven actuation through visual perception. The system translates 476 MediaPipe keypoints into coordinated servo movements, effectively replicating facial expressions across various structures with a pearson correlation coefficient (PCC) ranging from 90.1%. A Polling-based Multi-actuator Synchronous Control Framework (PMSCF) is proposed, which synchronizes 16 servos on an STM32F103C8T6 microcontroller with microsecond-level precision. This approach reduces flash and RAM usage by 21% and 44%, respectively, compared to traditional RTOS-based solutions, while maintaining real-time performance. The system uses E600# silicone skin and optimized linkages to emulate 12 key Facial Action Coding System (FACS) action units, achieving a PCC of 89.7% in OpenFace AU detection for the six basic facial expressions. The experimental results demonstrate the effectiveness of the proposed system, validating its capability to accurately replicate facial expressions and perform emotion-driven actuation.

Compared to previous work, the total cost of our hardware is no more than $70, which provides a solution for low-cost facial robot fabrication, solving the problem that robots always have expensive price for fabrication. Based on this,

this work is able to adapt to imitate the expressions of people with different identities with good expressiveness, which solves the problem that facial imitation is only good in single identity face. In future work, we will continue to explore methods for facial robots to improve on the intensity of their expressions, such that they are able to show more bionic expressions.

Acknowledgement. This work was supported in part by the Interdisciplinary Research Program of HUST (2024JCYJ034), Shenzhen Sci.&Tech. Program (GJHZ-20240218114706012), and the Future Technology Taihu Innovation Fund of HUST (2024-A-4). The computation was completed in the HPC Platform of Huazhong University of Science and Technology.

References

1. Chevalier, P., Kompatsiari, K., Ciardo, F., Wykowska, A.: Examining joint attention with the use of humanoid robots-a new approach to study fundamental mechanisms of social cognition. Psychon. Bull. Rev. **27**(2), 217–236 (2019). https://doi.org/10.3758/s13423-019-01689-4
2. Jo, S., Hong, S.: The development of human-robot interaction design for optimal emotional expression in social robots used by older people: design of robot facial expressions and gestures. IEEE Access **13**, 21367–21381 (2025). https://doi.org/10.1109/ACCESS.2025.3534845
3. Bermano, A.H., et al.: Facial performance enhancement using dynamic shape space analysis. ACM Trans. Graph. (TOG) **33**(2), 1–12 (2014). https://doi.org/10.1145/2546276
4. Field, M., Stirling, D., Pan, Z., Naghdy, F.: Learning trajectories for robot programing by demonstration using a coordinated mixture of factor analyzers. IEEE Trans. Cybern. **46**(3), 706–717 (2016). https://doi.org/10.1109/TCYB.2015.2414277
5. Liu, X., Chen, Y., Li, J., Cangelosi, A.: Real-time robotic mirrored behavior of facial expressions and head motions based on lightweight networks. IEEE Internet Things J. **10**(2), 1401–1413 (2023). https://doi.org/10.1109/JIOT.2022.3205123
6. Hashimoto, T., Hiramatsu, S., Kobayashi, H.: Development of face robot for emotional communication between human and robot. In: 2006 International Conference on Mechatronics and Automation, pp. 25–30. IEEE, Luoyang, China (2006). https://doi.org/10.1109/ICMA.2006.257429
7. Hu, Y., et al.: Human-robot facial coexpression. Sci. Robot. **9**, eadi4724 (2024). https://doi.org/10.1126/scirobotics.adi4724
8. Lin, C.Y., Huang, C.C., Cheng, L.C.: An expressional simplified mechanism in anthropomorphic face robot design. Robotica **34**(3), 652–670 (2016). https://doi.org/10.1017/S0263574714001787
9. Asheber, W.T., Lin, C.Y., Yen, S.H.: Humanoid head face mechanism with expandable facial expressions. Int. J. Adv. Rob. Syst. **13**(1), 29 (2016). https://doi.org/10.5772/62181
10. Randhavane, T., Bera, A., Kapsaskis, K., Sheth, R., Gray, K., Manocha, D.: EVA: generating emotional behavior of virtual agents using expressive features of gait and gaze. In: ACM Symposium on Applied Perception 2019 (SAP 2019), pp. 1–10. New York, USA (2019). https://doi.org/10.1145/3343036.3343129

11. Liu, N., et al.: A lightweight network-based sign language robot with facial mirroring and speech system. Expert Syst. Appl. **262**, 125492 (2025). https://doi.org/10.1016/j.eswa.2024.125492
12. Chen, B., Hu, Y., Li, L., Cummings, S., Lipson, H.: Smile like you mean it: driving animatronic robotic face with learned models. In: 2021 IEEE International Conference on Robotics and Automation (ICRA), pp. 2739–2746. IEEE, Xi'an, China (2021). https://doi.org/10.1109/ICRA48506.2021.9560797
13. Ekman, P., Rosenberg, E.L.: What the face reveals: basic and applied studies of spontaneous expression using the facial action coding system (FACS). Oxford University Press, New York (2005). https://doi.org/10.1093/acprof:oso/9780195179644.001.0001
14. Lugaresi, C., et al.: MediaPipe: a framework for building perception pipelines. arXiv preprint arXiv:1906.08172 (2019). https://doi.org/10.48550/arXiv.1906.08172
15. Park, J.W., Lee, H.S., Chung, M.J.: Generation of realistic robot facial expressions for human robot interaction. J. Intell. Robot. Syst. **2**, 443–462 (2014). https://doi.org/10.1007/s10846-014-0066-1

Enhancing Robustness of Hand Gesture Recognition Against Sensor Data Loss by Fusing High-Density sEMG and Kinematics

Yushuai Yan[1], Chengyu Lin[1], Chenglong Fu[1], and Yuquan Leng[2(✉)]

[1] Department of Mechanical and Energy Engineering, Southern University of Science and Technology, Shenzhen, China
[2] School of Biomedical Engineering and the State Key Laboratory of Robotics and Systems, Harbin Institute of Technology at Shenzhen, Shenzhen, China
lengyuquan@hit.edu.cn

Abstract. The seamless integration of humans with digital environments hinges on robust and intuitive control interfaces, making accurate hand gesture recognition crucial for effective human-computer interaction (HCI). However, systems relying solely on kinematic sensors, such as data gloves, often exhibit a sharp performance decline when faced with partial data loss–a common occurrence in real-world scenarios that undermines their practical reliability. To address this robustness challenge, this study proposes and evaluates a multi-modal fusion framework leveraging Convolutional Neural Networks (CNNs). The framework integrates 64-channel High-Density surface Electromyography (HD-sEMG), which captures underlying motor intent, with kinematic information (finger joint angles and wrist posture) from a data glove. We classify a challenging set of 12 fine-grained gestures, composed of 4 distinct finger pinch types combined with 3 wrist postures. Experimental results demonstrate that under ideal, complete data conditions, the proposed multi-modal model achieves a high average classification accuracy of 98.4%, modestly outperforming single-modality counterparts. More importantly, a robustness evaluation simulating a 30% random loss of finger angle sensor channels revealed that while the accuracy of the kinematics-only model plummeted to 52.62%, our multi-modal fusion model maintained a significantly higher accuracy of 83.83%. These findings quantitatively confirm that the fusion of HD-sEMG with kinematic data provides a critical layer of redundancy, substantially enhancing the robustness of gesture recognition systems against incomplete or degraded sensor information. This work provides valuable insights for the development of highly reliable and practical HCI systems prepared for real-world operational uncertainties.

Keywords: Hand Gesture Recognition · HD-sEMG · Multimodal Fusion · Robustness · Convolutional Neural Network

1 Introduction

Precise hand gesture recognition is fundamental to achieving a new generation of efficient human-computer interaction (HCI) [14], immersive virtual/augmented reality (VR/AR) experiences [8], and advanced assistive rehabilitation technologies [12,17]. Among various sensing technologies, data gloves have gained prominence as a common motion capture device. They offer high-fidelity kinematic information about finger joint articulations and wrist postures, making them highly effective for gesture classification tasks under laboratory conditions [6]. However, this reliance on a single kinematic modality introduces a critical vulnerability. In practical applications, these systems are susceptible to significant performance degradation due to sensor malfunctions, improper device wear, or signal loss, which severely limits their reliability and usability in complex and dynamic real-world environments [10].

To overcome the limitations of single-modality systems, researchers have turned to complementary data sources [15]. Surface electromyography (sEMG) signals, which non-invasively capture the electrical potentials generated by muscle contractions, offer a unique window into the user's underlying motor intent, often before the motion is fully executed [13]. In particular, High-Density sEMG (HD-sEMG) technology, which utilizes multi-channel electrode arrays to acquire detailed spatial maps of muscle activity, offers new technical avenues for robustly recognizing complex and subtle gestures [4]. The fusion of EMG with kinematic data, therefore, holds the potential for synergistic enhancement, combining the direct motion measurement of data gloves with the intent-driven information from sEMG to improve both accuracy and robustness [7]. Although existing research has explored the accuracy improvements of multi-modal fusion under ideal conditions [11], the robustness of such fused systems in the face of partial loss of key sensor information still requires deeper, quantitative investigation.

This study directly addresses this gap by investigating the resilience of a multi-modal gesture recognition system. We focus on a challenging set of 12 gesture classes, formed by combining 4 fine finger pinch motions with 3 distinct wrist postures. We propose a multi-modal fusion method based on Convolutional Neural Networks (CNNs), designed to integrate 64-channel HD-sEMG signals with kinematic data from a data glove. The central hypothesis of this work is that the redundant and complementary information provided by HD-sEMG can compensate for failures in the kinematic data stream. To test this, we first establish baseline classification performance for models using only EMG, only kinematics, and the fused data under ideal conditions. Subsequently, the core contribution of this work is a systematic evaluation of the robustness of the multi-modal fusion model against the kinematics-only model under simulated sensor degradation. This is achieved through a degradation test involving random dropout of finger angle sensor channels. Our experimental results demonstrate that while the accuracy gain from fusion is modest with complete data, the introduction of HD-sEMG dramatically enhances the system's ability to maintain performance when finger angle information is partially missing, thus highlighting its immense value in building truly reliable HCI systems.

2 Method

2.1 Data Acquisition

This study collected right-hand gesture data from four healthy, right-handed subjects (all adult males, with no known neuromuscular disorders). As shown in Fig. 1, the experimental gesture set was designed to be challenging, comprising 12 composite gestures [9]. These gestures were formed by combining four fine finger pinch actions (thumb tip to the index, middle, ring, and little finger tips, respectively) with three distinct wrist postures (neutral, flexion, and extension). This set was chosen to evaluate the system's ability to distinguish between subtle finger movements while simultaneously accounting for gross limb posture changes, a common requirement in practical applications.

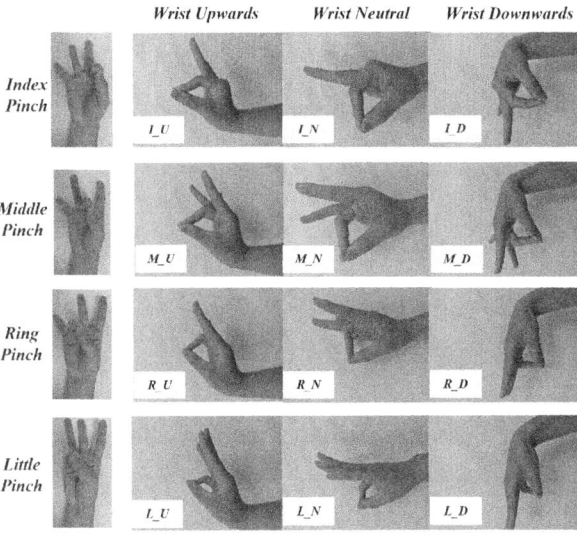

Fig. 1. The 12 gesture categories used in this study, illustrating the combination of four pinch types with three wrist postures. The labels assigned to each gesture in the dataset (e.g., I_U for Index-Upwards) are also displayed.

We synchronously collected 64-channel HD-sEMG signals and hand kinematic data. As depicted in Fig. 2, the HD-sEMG electrode array was strategically placed to cover the primary flexor and extensor muscle groups of the forearm and the extensor groups on the dorsum of the hand, which are critically involved in producing the target gestures [3]. The signals were sampled at 2000 Hz. A data glove was used to record 19 finger joint angles and to obtain wrist posture quaternions via Inertial Measurement Units (IMUs) attached to the back of the hand and the forearm. The kinematic data was upsampled to match the EMG sampling rate to ensure precise temporal alignment. During the experiment, each subject repeated each gesture class five times. The protocol for each trial consisted of a 5-second static gesture execution following a visual cue, a 2-second transition period for the hand to return to a neutral state, and a subsequent 5-second rest period before the next trial began. A representative sample of the synchronized data is shown in Fig. 3. State markers were used to log the gesture execution segments for subsequent data analysis.

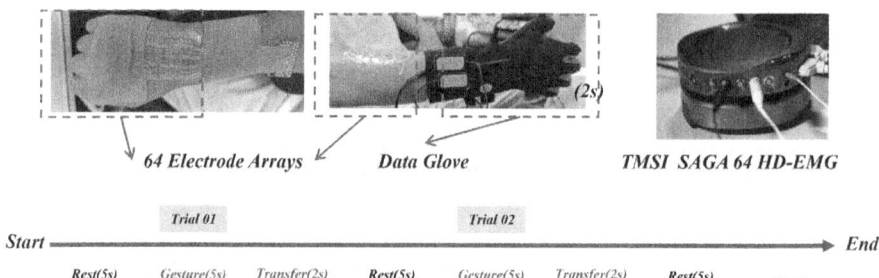

Fig. 2. Data acquisition setup and experimental protocol. HD-sEMG signals were collected using a TMSI SAGA system (64 channels), and kinematic data were recorded with a data glove. The full protocol for each trial consisted of a 5 s rest period, a 5 s static gesture hold, and a 2 s transition period for the hand to return to a neutral state.

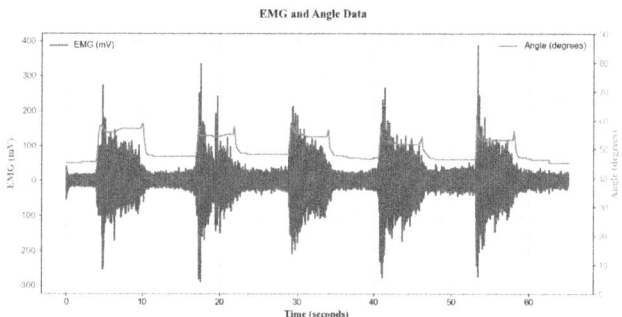

Fig. 3. The experimental protocol for a single trial. Each cycle involved a 5 s rest, a 5 s static gesture hold, and a 2 s transition period before the next trial began.

2.2 Data Preprocessing

To ensure data quality and extract features suitable for subsequent model training, we performed the following key preprocessing steps on the raw multi-modal data:

HD-sEMG Signal Processing. The raw 64-channel HD-sEMG signals were first clipped to an amplitude range of $[-600\mu V, 600\mu V]$. Subsequently, to remove the pervasive 50 Hz power-line interference, a common artifact in biopotential recordings (sampling rate $F_s = 2000$ Hz), a second-order IIR digital notch filter with a quality factor of $Q = 30$ was applied [5]. The transfer function $H_{notch}(z)$ of this type of filter can be expressed as[1]:

$$H_{notch}(z) = G \frac{1 - 2\cos(\omega_0)z^{-1} + z^{-2}}{1 - 2r\cos(\omega_0)z^{-1} + r^2 z^{-2}} \tag{1}$$

where $\omega_0 = 2\pi f_0 / F_s$ is the normalized notch frequency, r is the pole radius related to the quality factor Q ($0 < r < 1$) controlling the notch bandwidth, and G is a gain factor to ensure unit gain at other frequencies. Next, to isolate the frequency band containing the most relevant neuromuscular information and suppress low-frequency motion artifacts and high-frequency noise, the signals were passed through a fourth-order Butterworth band-pass filter from 20 Hz to 450 Hz. All filtering operations were implemented using the zero-phase `filtfilt` function to prevent the introduction of phase distortion, which is critical for preserving the temporal relationship between muscle activation patterns.

Kinematic Data Processing. The 19-dimensional finger joint angle data provided by the data glove, representing the direct skeletal configuration, were used directly as kinematic features. For wrist posture, the data glove provided two quaternions: the hand posture quaternion $q_{hand} = [w_h, x_h, y_h, z_h]$ and the forearm posture quaternion $q_{forearm} = [w_f, x_f, y_f, z_f]$. These two quaternions were independently converted into 3D Euler angle sequences using the following standard conversion formulas:

$$\phi = \mathrm{atan2}(2(wx + yz), 1 - 2(x^2 + y^2)) \tag{2}$$
$$\theta = \mathrm{asin}(2(wy - zx)) \tag{3}$$
$$\psi = \mathrm{atan2}(2(wz + xy), 1 - 2(y^2 + z^2)) \tag{4}$$

While quaternions avoid the issue of gimbal lock, converting them to Euler angles provides a more interpretable feature space and allows the model to process wrist orientation through distinct, decoupled channels (roll, pitch, yaw). This resulted in two sets of 3D Euler angle sequences, representing the absolute postures of the hand and forearm, respectively. These two sequences were time-aligned and concatenated to form a 6-dimensional feature vector for wrist-related posture.

Data Segmentation and Dataset Construction. To transform the continuous time-series data into discrete samples suitable for training a supervised classifier, a sliding window approach was employed. From the five independent gesture execution segments labeled "Gesture" within each CSV file, data segments were extracted using a sliding window of length $W = 500$ samples (250 ms) with a stride of $S = 200$ samples (100 ms) [2]. A window size of 250 ms was chosen as it

---

[1] The specific coefficients are computed by the `scipy.signal.iirnotch` function based on the center frequency f_0, sampling rate F_s, and quality factor Q.

is long enough to capture a stable and representative pattern of muscle activation and hand posture, yet short enough for potential real-time applications. The 60% overlap (150 ms) resulting from the 100 ms stride serves both to augment the size of the training dataset and to ensure a smooth, dense sampling of the gesture execution period. This process yielded 48 samples from each 5-second trial. Finally, data segments from all subjects were aggregated to form a multimodal dataset containing preprocessed EMG segments ($X_{emg} \in \mathbb{R}^{N \times 64 \times 500}$), finger angle segments ($X_{finger} \in \mathbb{R}^{N \times 19 \times 500}$), 6-dimensional wrist-related Euler angle segments ($X_{wrist} \in \mathbb{R}^{N \times 6 \times 500}$), along with their corresponding class labels ($Y \in \{0, \ldots, 11\}^N$), subject IDs, and intra-subject trial IDs (1–5). Here, N represents the total number of samples.

2.3 Model Architectures

This study compared three models based on 1D Convolutional Neural Networks (CNNs): (1) **EMG CNN**: This model used only the 64-channel HD-sEMG signals and consisted of three convolutional blocks (filter counts 128-256-128, kernel sizes 7-5-3) followed by an adaptive average pooling layer and a fully connected classification layer. (2) **Kinematics CNN**: This model used the 19-dimensional finger angles and 6-dimensional wrist Euler angles, processed through two parallel CNN branches (each with two convolutional blocks) to extract features separately [1]. The features were then concatenated and fed into a fully connected layer for classification. (3) **MultiModal CNN**: This model integrates the inputs of the previous two models using a late fusion strategy, as shown in Fig. 4 [16]. It comprises three parallel CNN branches to independently extract high-level features from the HD-sEMG, finger angle, and wrist posture data streams. The features extracted from each branch are transformed by an adaptive average pooling layer and then concatenated into a single, unified feature vector. This vector is finally passed to a fully connected network for classification into the 12 gesture classes. This architecture allows the model to learn modality-specific representations before combining them for a final decision. All models employed Batch Normalization, ReLU activation, and Dropout after key layers to improve training stability and prevent overfitting.

2.4 Model Training and Evaluation

The models were trained by optimizing the multi-class cross-entropy loss function. For a classification problem with M classes, the cross-entropy loss L_{CE} for a single sample is defined as:

$$L_{CE} = -\sum_{i=1}^{M} y_i \log(\hat{y}_i) \tag{5}$$

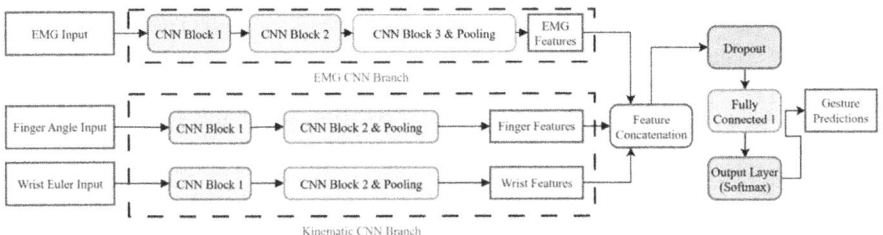

Fig. 4. Architecture of the MultiModal CNN. The model contains three parallel branches to process HD-sEMG, finger angle, and wrist posture data, which are fused via feature concatenation (a late fusion strategy).

where y_i is the true label of the sample (one-hot encoded, with $y_i = 1$ if the class is i, and 0 otherwise), and $\hat{y}_i$ is the model's predicted probability that the sample belongs to class i.

The model was optimized using the Adam optimizer (learning rate $\eta = 1 \times 10^{-3}$, weight decay $\lambda = 1 \times 10^{-4}$) with a batch size of 128. To prevent overfitting, an early stopping strategy was employed (patience = 7, monitoring validation loss, min_delta = 10^{-3}). To rigorously evaluate generalization performance, we conducted a Leave-One-Group-Out Cross-Validation (LOGO-CV) based on the five intra-subject repetition trials, partitioning the data into 5 folds. In each fold, data from four trial IDs were used for training, and the remaining one was used for testing. The primary evaluation metric was the average classification accuracy across the folds.

2.5 Robustness Degradation Test

To evaluate the models' robustness to partial sensor information loss, we conducted a degradation test on the MultiModal CNN and Kinematics CNN. During the testing phase of the cross-validation, we simulated random loss of finger angle sensor channels by randomly selecting a certain percentage (10%, 20%, and 30%) of the input finger angle data channels (X_{finger}) and setting their values to zero for the entire test set. This process simulates catastrophic failure of a subset of sensors. The EMG and wrist posture data remained unchanged. By comparing the degradation in model accuracy at different channel loss ratios, we assessed the quantitative contribution of HD-sEMG to system robustness.

3 Experimental Results

3.1 Model Performance Comparison

To establish a performance baseline, we first evaluated the classification performance of the three designed CNN models on the original, undisturbed dataset. Using a Leave-One-Group-Out Cross-Validation (LOGO-CV) strategy based on the five intra-subject repetition trials, the average accuracies of the models on the 12-class gesture recognition task are presented in Table 1. The results reveal several key insights.

The EMG CNN model, relying solely on HD-sEMG, achieved a respectable average accuracy of 93.73% ± 1.32%, demonstrating that muscle activation patterns alone contain sufficient information to distinguish these fine gestures. The Kinematics CNN model, using only data glove information, performed slightly better, reaching an accuracy of 94.4% ± 0.62%. This suggests that for these static, well-defined postures, the final skeletal configuration is a highly discriminative feature. As hypothesized, by fusing both modalities, the MultiModal CNN achieved the best performance. Its average accuracy increased to a near-perfect 98.4% ± 0.3%, which is a statistically significant improvement over both single-modality models. This confirms the benefit of multi-modal fusion even under ideal conditions, likely because the model learns to leverage the complementary nature of motor intent (EMG) and executed action (kinematics). These results provide a strong baseline for the subsequent robustness analysis (Fig. 5).

Table 1. Average classification performance of different models on the full dataset (5-fold LOGO-CV). Values are reported as mean ± standard deviation.

Model	EMG	Kinematics	MultiModal
Average Acc (%)	93.73 ± 1.32	94.4 ± 0.62	98.4 ± 0.3

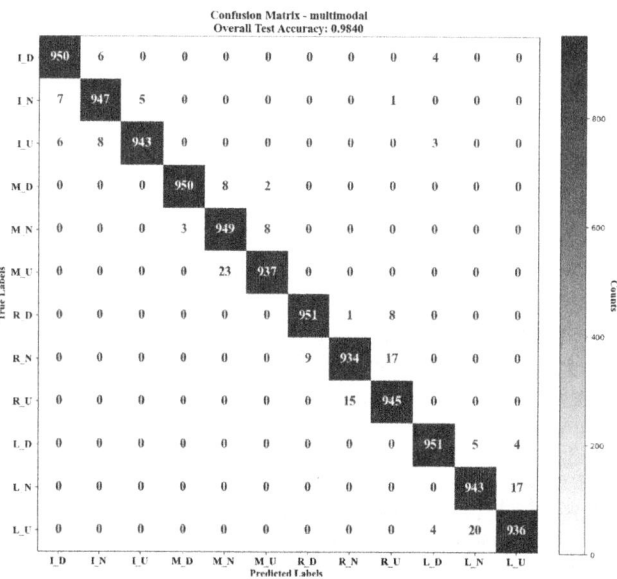

Fig. 5. Confusion matrix of the MultiModal CNN on the full dataset. The average accuracy reaches 98.4%.

3.2 Robustness Evaluation Under Finger Angle Channel Loss

To evaluate the models' robustness against the loss of key kinematic information, we conducted a degradation test on the MultiModal CNN and Kinematics CNN by randomly dropping finger angle channels. During the testing phase of the 5-fold LOGO-CV, we randomly selected 10%, 20%, and 30% of the input finger angle channels (X_{finger}) and set their values to zero. The HD-sEMG and wrist posture data remained intact.

As shown in the performance degradation curves in Fig. 6, a clear and dramatic difference in resilience emerges between the two models. With no channel loss (0%), both models perform well, consistent with our baseline results. However, as the proportion of dropped finger angle channels increases, the performance of the Kinematics CNN, which is entirely dependent on this information, deteriorates rapidly and catastrophically. Its accuracy plummets to just 52.62% at a 30% channel loss, a level of performance that is unacceptable for any practical application.

In stark contrast, the MultiModal CNN demonstrates remarkable resilience. While its accuracy does decrease, the degradation is far more graceful. Even with 30% of its finger kinematic sensor information completely lost, the model maintained an average accuracy of 83.83% (Fig. 7). This result strongly suggests that when the kinematic data stream becomes unreliable, the model effectively learns to shift its reliance onto the intact HD-sEMG data stream to make a correct prediction. This behavior clearly demonstrates that the introduction of HD-sEMG information acts as a powerful stabilizing factor, significantly enhancing the system's overall robustness and fault tolerance.

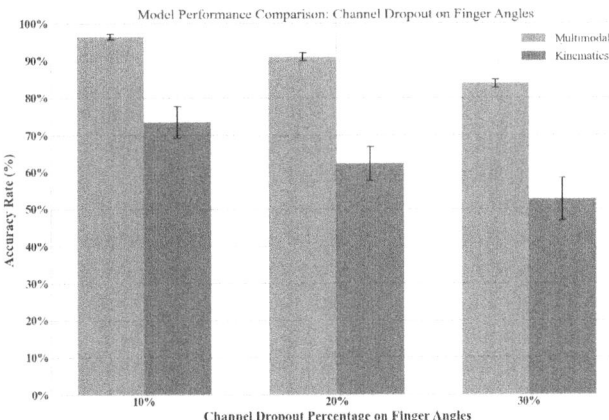

Fig. 6. Comparison of average test accuracy between the MultiModal CNN and the Kinematics-Only CNN under different finger angle channel dropout ratios.

These results provide strong evidence that the inclusion of HD-sEMG can significantly enhance the robustness and reliability of gesture recognition systems when facing partial failure of key kinematic sensors.

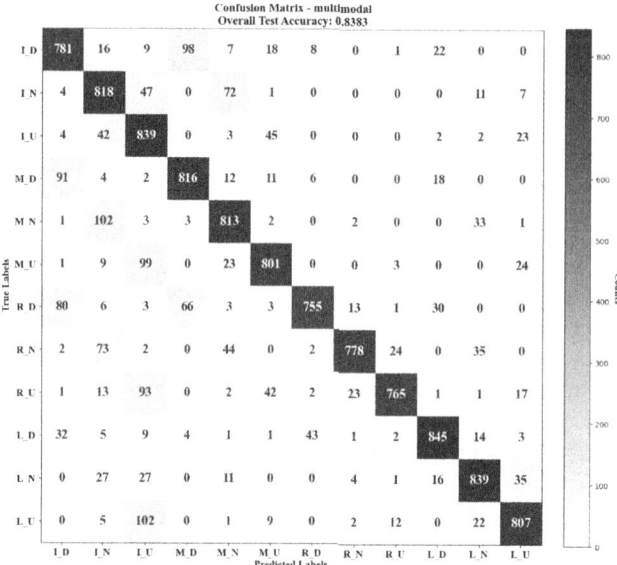

Fig. 7. Confusion matrix and average accuracy of the MultiModal CNN with 30% finger angle channel dropout.

4 Conclusions

This study designed and evaluated a multi-modal CNN recognition system for 12 fine-grained hand gestures, with a primary focus on assessing robustness against sensor data loss. The experimental results show that the multi-modal model, fusing HD-sEMG and kinematic data, achieved a superior average accuracy of 98.4% under ideal conditions. More critically, the study demonstrates that this fusion provides substantial resilience in non-ideal scenarios. When simulating a 30% loss of finger angle sensor channels, the fusion model's accuracy was maintained at a robust 83.83%, significantly outperforming the kinematics-only model, whose performance collapsed to 52.62%. This key finding confirms that the introduction of HD-sEMG, which captures motor intent, can effectively compensate for the partial loss of key kinematic sensor information, thereby providing a vital safety net for system reliability.

The implications of this work extend beyond a simple accuracy benchmark, shifting the evaluation paradigm towards reliability and robustness, which are paramount for real-world HCI. Our findings provide strong evidence and a valuable architectural reference for developing human-computer interaction applications that are not just accurate in the lab, but dependable in the wild. Future work will proceed along three main avenues: (1) exploring more advanced fusion mechanisms, such as attention-based models, to enable the network to dynamically weight the importance of each modality based on data quality; (2) extending the evaluation framework to include dynamic gestures, which are more representative of natural human motion; and (3) validating the proposed framework's performance across a larger and more diverse subject population to ensure its generalizability.

Acknowledgments. This work was supported by National Key R&D Program of China [Grant: 2024YFC3082800], the National Natural Science Foundation of China [Grant: 52175272], Guangdong Basic and Applied Basic Research Foundation [Grant: 2024B1515020008 and 2023B1515130007], Shenzhen Science and Technology Program [Grant: RCYX20231211090345058, JCYJ20220530114809021].

Disclosure of Funding. The authors have no competing interests to declare that are relevant to the content of this article.

References

1. Multi-stream CNN: learning representations based on human-related regions for action recognition. Pattern Recognit.**79**, 32–43 (2018)
2. Bo, L., Banghua, Y., Shouwei, G., Yan, L., Zhuang, H., Wang, W.: Hand gesture recognition using SEMG signals based on CNN. In: 2021 40th Chinese Control Conference (CCC), pp. 7180–7184 (2021)
3. Chamberland, F., et al.: Novel wearable HD-EMG sensor with shift-robust gesture recognition using deep learning. IEEE Trans. Biomed. Circ. Syst. **17**(5), 968–984 (2023)
4. Chen, J., Bi, S., Zhang, G., Cao, G.: High-density surface EMG-based gesture recognition using a 3D convolutional neural network. Sensors **20**(4) (2020)
5. Cunanan, D.V., et al.: Mitigation of noise on surface electromyography (SEMG) signals through signal filtering algorithms. In: TENCON 2024 - 2024 IEEE Region 10 Conference (TENCON), pp. 715–718 (2024)
6. Fu, Q., Fu, J., Guo, J., Guo, S., Li, X.: Gesture recognition based on BP neural network and data glove. In: 2020 IEEE International Conference on Mechatronics and Automation (ICMA), pp. 1918–1922 (2020)
7. Gong, L., Cheng, Y., Zhang, H., Wang, Y., Zhao, P.: A multi-model fusion framework to enhance SEMG-based gesture recognition assisted by visual features. In: 2024 IEEE International Conference on Robotics and Biomimetics (ROBIO), pp. 2300–2305 (2024)
8. Guo, L., Lu, Z., Yao, L.: Human-machine interaction sensing technology based on hand gesture recognition: a review. IEEE Trans. Hum. Mach. Syst. **51**(4), 300–309 (2021)
9. Jiang, X., et al.: Open access dataset, toolbox and benchmark processing results of high-density surface electromyogram recordings. IEEE Trans. Neural Syst. Rehabil. Eng. **29**, 1035–1046 (2021)
10. Leng, Y., Zhang, Y., Zhang, W., He, X., Zhou, W.: Attitude analysis of reachable space for spatial manipulator. In: The 27th Chinese Control and Decision Conference (2015 CCDC), pp. 4927–4931 (2015)
11. Li, G., Wan, B., Su, K., Huo, J., Jiang, C., Wang, F.: SEMG and IMU data-based hand gesture recognition method using multistream CNN with a fine-tuning transfer framework. IEEE Sens. J. **23**(24), 31414–31424 (2023)
12. Lin, C., Zhang, C., Xu, J., Liu, R., Leng, Y., Fu, C.: Neural correlation of EEG and eye movement in natural grasping intention estimation. IEEE Trans. Neural Syst. Rehabil. Eng. **31**, 4329–4337 (2023)

13. Qiu, H., Liao, Y., Chen, Y., Xie, L.: A comfortable wrist-worn gesture recognition system via HD-SEMG. In: 2023 IEEE 18th Conference on Industrial Electronics and Applications (ICIEA), pp. 1369–1372 (2023)
14. Saini, R., Maan, V.: Human activity and gesture recognition: a review. In: 2020 International Conference on Emerging Trends in Communication, Control and Computing (ICONC3), pp. 1–2 (2020)
15. Xu, Y., et al.: A powered prosthetic hand with vision system for enhancing the anthropopathic grasp. IEEE Trans. Neural Syst. Rehabil. Eng. **33**, 1827–1840 (2025)
16. Yang, R., Deng, H., Xu, W., Wang, X., Li, C.: Multi-stream CNN-SVM hybrid model for gesture recognition based on SEMG signals. In: 2023 6th International Conference on Electronics Technology (ICET), pp. 1435–1440 (2023)
17. Zhong, X.C., et al.: Plug-and-play SEMG-driven hand gesture recognition with subdomain adaptation for exoskeleton rehabilitation gloves. IEEE Trans. Instrum. Meas. **74**, 1–10 (2025)

Simulation-Driven Learning for Vision-Based Tactile Force Reconstruction in Surgical Master Manipulators Using Random Marker Particles

Hui Chu, Xizhe Zang[✉], Peng Wang, and Xu Wang

State Key Laboratory of Robotics and System, Harbin Institute of Technology, Harbin 150001, China
zangxizhe@hit.edu.cn

Abstract. This paper proposes a vision-based tactile perception unit tailored for force sensing in the master manipulator of surgical robotic systems. The unit is capable of perceiving three-dimensional force distributions during object interaction, providing critical tactile feedback for precise and safe surgical manipulation. Based on the principle of marker-particle tactile sensing, the system features high spatial resolution, a large sensing area, and low fabrication cost. Tactile images are obtained by capturing the displacement of embedded marker particles during contact using a camera, and are subsequently used as input to a neural network to reconstruct the surface force distribution in real time.

To enable large-scale data acquisition, a simulation platform was developed to automatically generate various contact scenarios. Parametric control and scripting in ANSYS were employed to simulate different contact conditions and obtain the corresponding 3D force distribution data. The fidelity of the simulated data was validated by comparing the ANSYS results with measurements from physical force sensors. The neural network adopts an encoder-decoder architecture composed of convolutional and deconvolutional layers and is trained in TensorFlow to perform force distribution estimation and contact pattern recognition.

Finally, the accuracy of contact force estimation was quantitatively evaluated. A robotic end-effector integrated with the tactile perception unit was constructed, and object grasping experiments were conducted to validate the effectiveness of the proposed system.

Keywords: master manipulator · tactile image perception · 3D tactile force distribution · ANSYS simulation · convolutional neural network · marker particles

1 Introduction

As robots are increasingly deployed in complex and dynamic environments—including medical procedures such as minimally invasive surgery—there is a growing demand for tactile sensing systems with high spatial resolution, large sensing areas, and compliant interfaces. In particular, in surgical robotic systems, accurate perception of contact forces at the master manipulator is critical for achieving intuitive, stable, and safe teleoperation. As show in Fig. 1.

Vision-based tactile sensing systems have gained significant attention in recent years due to their simple mechanical structure, rich information output, and low fabrication cost, making them promising candidates for integration into high-performance surgical force feedback systems.

These systems can be generally classified into three categories[1]: The first type utilizes deformable light-guiding plates, where contact alters the refractive index and thereby changes light reflection, enabling a camera to detect contact areas [2, 3]. The second type relies on the surface reflection changes of a deform-able membrane to infer contact shape and texture. Such approaches are used in [4] to detect object textures and in [5, 6] to estimate object poses. The third type tracks the displacement of embedded marker particles in a soft transparent medium to reconstruct internal deformation and estimate contact force distributions. This approach has been applied to contact localization in [7, 8], force estimation in [9], and slip detection in [10].

However, a major challenge remains: the difficulty in acquiring high-quality training data. Collecting labeled tactile images requires precise mechanical setups and accurate force measurements, where each sample must undergo a physical contact process—making it costly, time-consuming, and prone to labeling errors. Furthermore, the relationship between observed particle displacements and actual force distributions is highly nonlinear, posing significant challenges for model generalization to real-world scenarios. Therefore, improving data efficiency and sim-to-real generalization capability is essential for advancing vision-based tactile sensing.

To address these issues, we propose a marker-particle-based vision tactile sensing unit and develop an automated simulation platform using ANSYS finite element modeling. This platform parametrically generates large-scale datasets of contact images and corresponding 3D force distributions. We combine these simulated samples with real tactile images to train an encoder-decoder convolutional neural network for force reconstruction, and introduce a network to assist with contact condition recognition. Finally, the sensing unit is integrated into a robotic gripper and validated through diverse grasping experiments to evaluate its effectiveness in real-world manipulation.

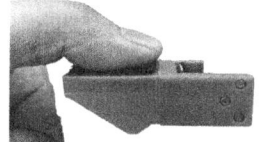

Fig. 1. Human–robot manual interaction

2 Design of the Tactile Sensing Unit

The tactile sensing unit aims to convert contact forces into recognizable image features for subsequent processing and intelligent perception. It should meet the following criteria: High sensitivity to subtle force variations; Stable, high-quality imaging with clear, recognizable features; Simple structure and manufacturability using accessible materials and mature processes; Stable packaging with good sealing and interference resistance; Good system compatibility for integration into control and perception frameworks.

The key dimensional specifications of the tactile perception unit are as follows: a working surface area of 32 × 32 mm, a spatial resolution of 1 × 1 mm, an overall thickness of less than 34 mm, and a maximum detectable contact depth of 2.5 mm.

2.1 Marker Particle Distribution Design

Marker particles are the primary source of visual features. Black microspheres (~0.4 mm diameter) are adhered to the inner surface of the flexible layer in a pseudo-random uniform pattern to avoid clustering or gaps. This distribution ensures stable, non-redundant visual features under various deformation states, facilitating robust image-based force reconstruction.

This section focuses on the optimization of marker particle distribution. During contact, the compliant medium inside the tactile sensor deforms, causing embedded particles to shift. The camera captures these displacements, which are used to reconstruct contact force information. The distinctiveness of particle displacement is a key factor in the fidelity of tactile data, and it is strongly influenced by the spatial distribution of particles. Therefore, optimizing their placement is essential for improving sensing performance. To systematically evaluate how particle position affects displacement characteristics, this study employs ANSYS finite element simulations to model the deformation of the medium under various contact conditions. The results provide a theoretical foundation for optimizing particle distribution.

The state of a marker particle within the compliant medium is characterized by its three-dimensional position and the resulting three-dimensional displacement caused by the deformation of the tactile sensing unit, denoted as vectors p and x, respectively. Since the particles reside in 3D space while the camera observes a 2D image plane, the observed position and displacement are represented as 2D vectors, denoted p' and x'. The projection from 3D space to the 2D image plane, governed by the camera imaging model, is defined as: $f_p : p \to p'$

$$p' = \left[p_x \cdot \frac{vs}{(p_z+u)} \quad p_y \cdot \frac{vs}{(p_z+u)} \right] \tag{1}$$

After deriving the projection transformation formula that maps the 3D positions of marker particles to the camera's 2D image plane, ANSYS finite element simulations are used to model the contact deformation behavior of the compliant medium in the tactile sensing unit. Displacement data from nodes at different spatial locations are extracted to evaluate how the distribution of marker particles affects the saliency of tactile information in the resulting image.

First, a finite element model of the tactile sensing unit is constructed and simulated under standard contact conditions (as shown in Fig. 2). The displacement data of the contact-region nodes are then exported as structured text files. The compliant medium is divided into five layers based on depth, and displacement data from each layer are analyzed separately.

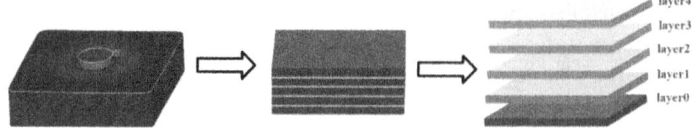

Fig. 2. Contact simulation of the tactile sensing unit and layer-wise slicing analysis of the conversion medium

Finally, using the projection function defined in (Eq. 1), the 3D displacement vectors are projected onto the image plane, producing the 2D displacement distribution map shown in Fig. 3.

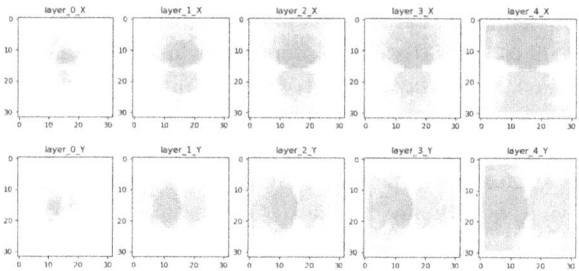

Fig. 3. Projection of layer-wise displacement distributions in the image coordinate system

The projected displacement of marker particles increases with depth in the compliant medium, offering insight into their optimal spatial distribution. In deeper layers, contact-induced deformation is limited, resulting in negligible particle displacement. In contrast, particles near the surface undergo more substantial deformation and thus greater displacement. To improve the responsiveness of the tactile sensing unit, particles should be primarily concentrated within the top 1 mm of the medium. Moreover, deeper particles can obscure the camera's view of upper-layer particles, hindering accurate force reconstruction. A surface-near distribution not only avoids visual occlusion but also ensures that both normal and tangential contact forces produce distinct displacement patterns, thereby enhancing the sensor's capability for multi-dimensional contact perception.

2.2 Design and Fabrication of the Tactile Sensing Unit

The structure of the tactile sensing unit is shown in Fig. 4 From top to bottom, it consists of a light-shielding layer, marker medium, transparent medium, support body, LED light board, transparent acrylic plate, camera, reflective mirror, and housing.

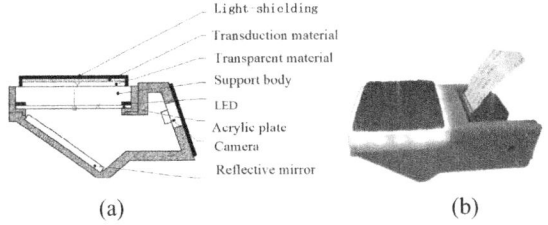

Fig. 4. Tactile sensing unit. (a) Structural diagram. (b) Physical prototype

The light-shielding layer, made of black silicone, effectively blocks ambient light interference, enhancing imaging stability. The transduction material, composed of transparent silicone embedded with marker particles, is the core component for tactile signal encoding. Its softness determines sensitivity and measurement range. Marker particles are distributed only in the upper layer to minimize occlusion and improve image clarity. The support body, made of stiffer transparent silicone, provides structural support with negligible deformation and facilitates uniform light diffusion. The LED board includes 16 evenly distributed LEDs along the periphery, ensuring uniform illumination and improving particle visibility. The transparent acrylic plate enhances structural stiffness, smooths the optical interface, and allows easy maintenance. A reflective mirror redirects the optical path, enabling a more compact mechanical layout. The entire structure consists of a transduction sub-housing, main housing, and auxiliary housing, assembled in a nested configuration.

3 Auto Data Collection and Training Sample Construction

To enable neural networks to interpret tactile images and obtain the three-dimensional force distribution and contact state of the tactile sensing unit, a large number of high-quality data samples must be collected. The input data for neural network training should consist of images showing the displacement of randomly distributed marker particles under contact conditions, while the output data should include the corresponding 3D force distribution and contact state. The data collection process includes two parts: first, a contact simulation platform is used to replicate the tactile unit's interaction with objects and capture both marker particle images and contact position information in real time; second, ANSYS simulations are employed to model the deformation response of the tactile unit under different contact conditions, providing surface 3D force distribution data to label the training samples.

3.1 Data Collection Method

To train a neural network with high accuracy and generalization capability, it is essential to construct a large-scale, high-dimensional, and well-labeled dataset. To this end, an automated data acquisition framework was developed, integrating several key components. As show in Fig. 5, An automated contact simulation platform was designed to execute predefined contact motions and collect batches of tactile images efficiently. In parallel, a variety of contact probes with different geometries. Furthermore, ANSYS was employed for synchronized parametric simulations of each contact event, generating high-fidelity 3D force distributions that serve as accurate ground-truth labels for supervised neural network training.

The data acquisition process involves four main stages. First, randomized contact parameters—including the initial pose and motion increments—are generated and saved to a parameter file. Then, the simulation platform parses these parameters, drives the actuator accordingly, and simultaneously collects tactile images and force measurements. In parallel, ANSYS executes synchronized simulations using the same parameter set to compute the corresponding 3D force distributions. Finally, all tactile images, contact positions, and simulation results are saved in standardized formats to support supervised neural network training.

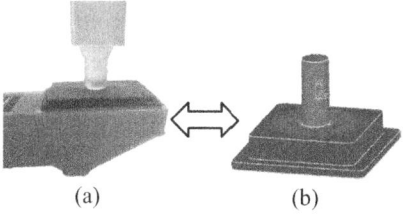

Fig. 5. (a) Real-world data acquisition. (b) ANSYS simulation data collection

To ensure the fidelity of simulated force distributions, we first characterized the key mechanical properties (including Young's modulus and Poisson's ratio) of the compliant medium through standardized material tests, and precisely assigned these parameters to the ANSYS simulation model. During physical data acquisition, a high-precision single-axis force sensor integrated into the simulation platform provided ground-truth measurements of contact forces. After completing, comparative analysis between ANSYS simulations and physical sensor measurements demonstrated consistency.

Through this process, approximately 7,000 samples were collected. The use of simplified geometries ensured modeling efficiency and simulation accuracy, while more complex shapes were reserved for testing. This framework provides a robust dataset for training models capable of handling diverse and realistic contact scenarios.

As shown in Fig. 6, various contact probes with different geometries were designed and fabricated. These probes help generate high-dimensional and varied training samples, enabling the network to adapt more effectively to complex contact scenarios.

Fig. 6. Various types of probes used for sample acquisition

3.2 Training Dataset Preparation

The collected data samples should undergo preprocessing. First, cropping and resizing are applied to ensure accurate spatial correspondence between the tactile images and the 3D force distribution. Second, brightness equalization is performed to address uneven illumination in the raw images, thereby improving image quality and reducing training complexity. Third, the 3D force data obtained from ANSYS simulations are smoothed and normalized to better reflect realistic force distribution patterns. Finally, data augmentation techniques are used to expand the dataset and enhance the network's generalization ability.

After the above preprocessing steps, standardized sample instances were obtained, as shown in Fig. 7 These standardized samples provide high-quality data for subsequent neural network training and analysis.

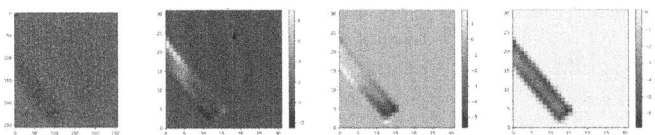

Fig. 7. The preprocessed image is used as the input X to the neural network, and the corresponding 3D force distribution is taken as the output Y for training and prediction.

4 Tactile Image-Driven Neural Network for 3D Force Distribution

This study employs a fully convolutional neural network composed of convolutional and deconvolutional layers, with a depth of 45 layers and incorporating residual connections. Use residual networks address this issue by adding the input directly to the output before activation. Leveraging the local inductive bias of convolutional and deconvolutional neural networks significantly improves the accuracy of 3D force distribution prediction.

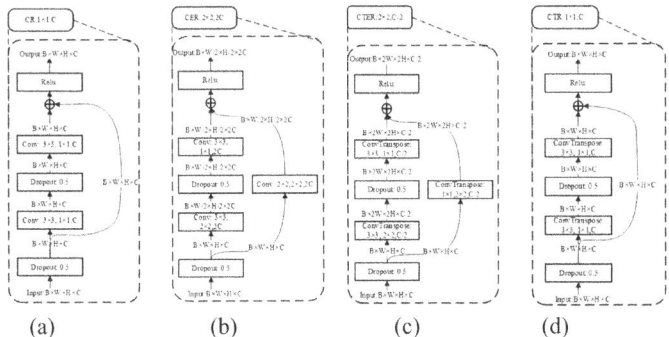

Fig. 8. Sub-layer structures (a) CR layer. (b) CER layer. (c) CTR layer. (d) CTER layer

As shown in Fig. 8(a), the CR layer has two 3 × 3 convolutional layers with stride 1, keeping input size and channels unchanged. Input passes Dropout, first convolution uses ReLU, second does not. Their outputs are added and activated by ReLU (Eq. 2).

$$x = Dropout(Input)$$
$$Output = Relu(Conv1(Conv0(x) + x)) \quad (2)$$

Figure 8(b) shows the CER layer with three convolutions: conv0 (2×2 kernel, stride 2, channels doubled, no activation), conv1 (3×3, stride 2, channels doubled, ReLU), conv2 (3×3, stride 1, channels unchanged, no activation). CER halves spatial size and doubles channels (Eq. 3), enhancing global feature abstraction.

$$x = Dropout(Input)$$
$$Output = Relu(Conv2(Conv1(x)) + Conv0(x)) \quad (3)$$

Decoder in Fig. 8(c) mirrors encoder but uses transposed convolutions. CTR has two transposed convolutions preserving size (Eq. 4). CTER has three: convT0 (1×1, stride 2, channels halved, no activation), convT1 (3×3, stride 2, channels halved, ReLU), convT2 (3×3, stride 1, channels unchanged, no activation). CTER doubles spatial size and halves channels (Eq. 5), decoding global features to local details.

$$x = Dropout(Input)$$
$$Output = Relu(ConvT1(ConvT0(x)) + x) \quad (4)$$

$$x = Dropout(Input)$$
$$Output = Relu(ConvT2(ConvT1(x)) + ConvT0(x)) \quad (5)$$

Encoder stacks CR and CER (Fig. 9(a)) encoding inputs to abstract features; decoder stacks CTR and CTER (Fig. 9(b)) decoding back to local features.

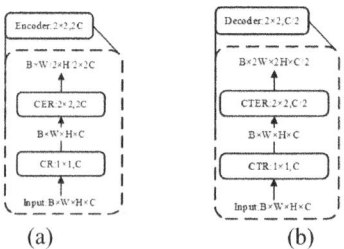

Fig. 9. Encoder and Decoder Architecture. (a) Encoder Structure. (b) Decoder Structure

The full network (Fig. 10) contains 6 encoders and 10 decoders. Input is $256 \times 256 \times 2$ grayscale images of original and contact states; output is multi-head $32 \times 32 \times 1$ force maps for X, Y, Z axes. Skip connections fuse local and global features from different layers, improving prediction.

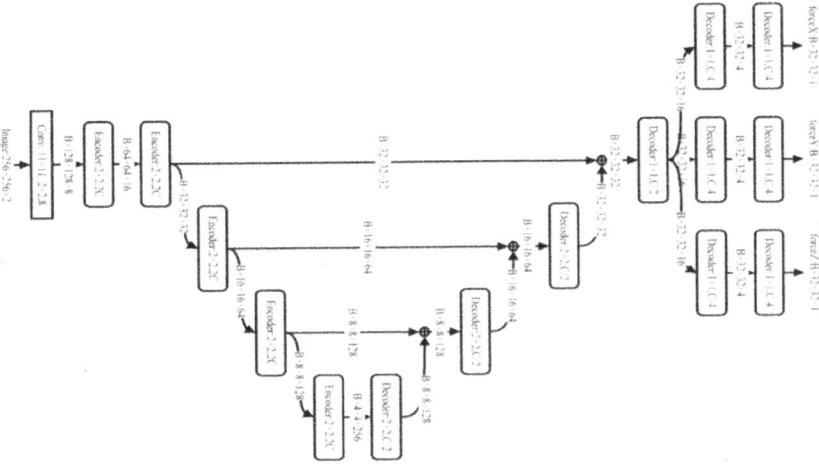

Fig. 10. Architecture of the neural network for 3d force distribution prediction

5 Evaluation and Practical Testing of the Tactile Sensing Unit

This chapter evaluates the performance of the tactile sensing unit, focusing on its accuracy in force perception and contact position localization. Experiments involving contact with various objects are conducted to assess its ability to recognize surface shapes. Additionally, the sensing unit is integrated into the end-effector of an xArm 6-DOF robotic arm to further validate its contact localization capability in practical applications. It is important to emphasize that the sensor captures a distributed 3D force field rather than a single resultant force.

5.1 Force Accuracy Evaluation

To evaluate the tactile sensing unit, a 4 mm radius circular probe was used to apply indentation over a 17 × 17 grid with 2 mm spacing. At each grid point, 36 indentations were made in 0.2 mm increments along the Z-axis, resulting in 10,404 data samples. Ground truth Z-axis forces were recorded using a uniaxial force sensor, and the corresponding 3D force distributions were predicted by the tactile unit.

In Fig. 11, Results show that the sensor has a dead zone: for indentations under 0.6 mm, the output remains near zero, even when the contact force reaches 0.35 N. As indentation increases, the error gradually grows, with a sharp rise beyond 2.5 mm (approximately 6.1 N). Since the sensor outputs a distributed force field, both the dead zone and effective range depend on probe geometry and contact conditions. For this probe, the dead-zone error is around 0.35 N.

At one test point, the maximum deviation between predicted and reference force within the valid range was 0.378 N, corresponding to a linearity error of 6.3%.

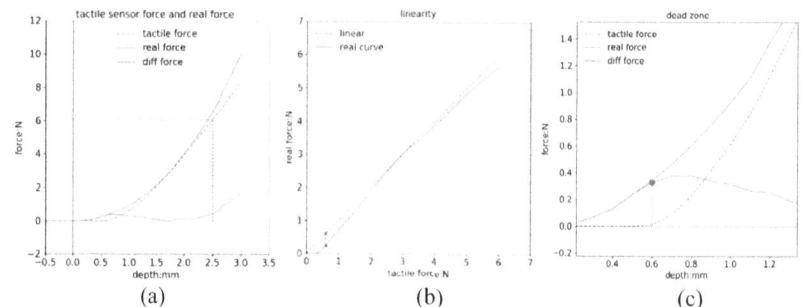

Fig. 11. (a) Comparison of actual and predicted pressure at position 24 mm × 20 mm. (b) Dead zone error evaluation. (c) Linearity error evaluation

5.2 Surface Contact Recognition Test

The tactile sensor designed in this study features a large working area, allowing approximate recognition of the partial shape of small objects through a single effective contact. As shown in Fig. 12, various objects were randomly contacted with the tactile sensing unit to evaluate its shape recognition performance.

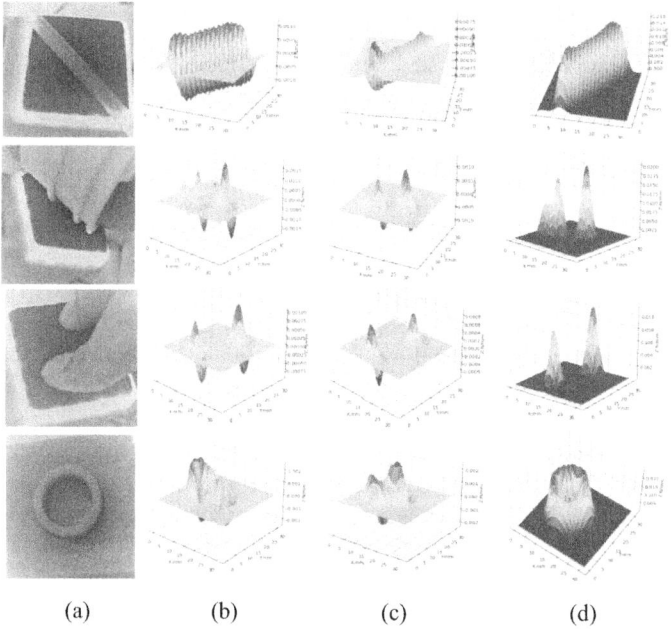

Fig. 12. Contact testing between the tactile sensing unit and objects of various shapes. (a) State of contact. (b) Force distribution of X. (c) Force distribution of Y.(d). Force distribution of Z.

The 3D force visualization results demonstrate that the tactile sensor can not only detect the distribution of contact forces, but also infer the local shape features of the contacted object based on the force distribution information.

5.3 Grasp Pose Detection and Contact Position Correction

This experiment assumes that only the approximate position of the target object is known, without precise pose information. Under this condition, a parallel gripper attempts to grasp the object, but the exact contact location remains uncertain. After the grasp, the tactile sensing unit captures the 3D force distribution and analyzes it to estimate the actual contact position. This enables accurate adjustment of the robot arm to achieve precise object placement. As shown in Fig. 13, four grasps at different positions were conducted to validate this capability.

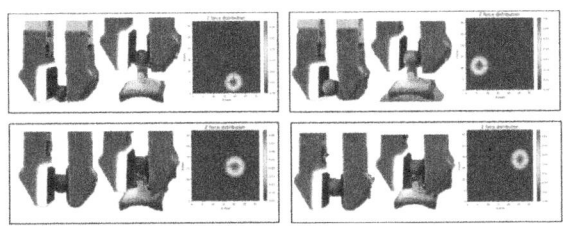

Fig. 13. Tactile sensing unit for contact position detection and precise placement

Furthermore, the tactile sensing unit can detect grasp pose errors caused by misalignment, such as off-center or incomplete grasps that may lead to failure. By analyzing the measured 3D force distribution, the system calculates the resultant force and its point of application to identify deviations from the ideal grasp. Based on this information, the robot can adaptively adjust its grasp position and reattempt the operation, improving both success rate and stability. These results highlight the unit's capability in contact pose estimation and enhancing manipulation robustness, particularly in precision tasks such as surgical tool handling.

6 Conclusion

This study presents the design and implementation of a marker-particle-based tactile sensing unit, along with an automated simulation-driven data collection platform for efficiently constructing and labeling training datasets. This significantly enriches the data diversity used for neural network training. Evaluation results demonstrate that simulation-based data acquisition not only ensures the realism and reliability of the samples but also greatly improves data collection efficiency, thus enhancing overall model performance.

The proposed neural network adopts a deep encoder–decoder architecture, integrating residual and transposed convolution modules to extract both local and global spatial features. This enables accurate prediction of high-resolution, multidimensional force distributions from 2D marker displacement maps. The tactile sensing unit exhibits favorable mechanical characteristics, including good linearity, a practical sensing range, and acceptable dead-zone behavior.

In practical evaluations, the system achieves precise estimation of contact position and orientation and is capable of automatically compensating for misalignments during grasping. When integrated into the master manipulator of a surgical robotic system, the proposed solution provides intuitive and high-fidelity force feedback, significantly enhancing the operator's perception and control accuracy during delicate procedures such as minimally invasive surgery.

In conclusion, this work offers a reliable and scalable approach to vision-enhanced tactile force perception, with strong potential for application in surgical teleoperation, robotic-assisted procedures, and other high-precision human–robot interaction scenarios.

Acknowledgments. This work is funded by National Key Research and Development Program of China under grant no. 2022YFB4700802.

References

1. Shimonomura, K.: Tactile image sensors employing camera: a review. Sensors **19**(18), 3933 (2019)
2. Ohka, M., Kobayashi, H., Tanaka, J., Mitsuya, Y.: An experimental optical three-axis tactile sensor featured with hemispherical surface. J. Adv. Mech. Des. Syst. Manuf. **2**, 860–873 (2008)
3. Shimonomura, K., Nakashima, H., Nozu, K.: Robotic grasp control with high-resolution combined tactile and proximity sensing. In: Proceedings of the IEEE International Conference on Robotics and Automation, Stockholm, Sweden, 16–21 May 2016. pp. 138–143 (2016)
4. James, J., Pestell, N., Lepora, N.: Slip detection with a biomimetic tactile sensor. IEEE Robot. Autom. Lett. **3**, 3340–3346 (2018)
5. Nozu, K., Shimonomura, K.: Robotic bolt insertion and tightening based on in-hand object localization and force sensing. In: Proceedings of the IEEE/ASME International Conference on Advanced Intelligent Mechatronics, Auckland, New Zealand, 9–12 July 2018 (2018)
6. Li, R., et al.: Localization and manipulation of small parts using GelSight tactile sensing. In: Proceedings of the IEEE/RSJ International Conference on Intelligent Robots and Systems, Chicago, IL, USA, 14–18 September 2014, pp. 3988–3993 (2014)
7. Sferrazza, C., D'Andrea, R.: Design, motivation and evaluation of a full-resolution optical tactile sensor. Sensors **19**, 928 (2019)
8. Cramphorn, L., Lloyd, J., Lepora, N.F.: Voronoi features for tactile sensing: direct inference of pressure, shear, and contact locations. In: Proceedings of the IEEE International Conference on Robotics and Automation, Brisbane, QLD, Australia, 21–25 May 2018, pp. 2752–2757 (2018)
9. Kamiyama, K., Kajimoto, H., Kawakami, N., Tachi, S.: Evaluation of a vision-based tactile sensor. In: Proceedings of the IEEE International Conference on Robotics and Automation, New Orleans, LA, USA, 26 April–1 May 2004, pp. 1542–1547 (2024)
10. Yuan, W., Li, R., Srinivasan, M., Adelson, E.: Measurement of shear and slip with a GelSight tactile sensor. In: Proceedings of the IEEE International Conference on Robotics and Automation, Seattle, WA, USA, 26–30 May 2015, pp. 304–311 (2015)

A Low-Cost Multisensor IMU-VIO Framework for Real-Time Full-Body Human Pose Estimation

Lele Li, Zedong Liu, Dawei Liang, Chuanyu Si, Haotian Ju, Shouyi Zhang, Haoxiang Zhang, Hongwei Jing, Jian Qi, Tianjiao Zheng[✉], and Yanhe Zhu[✉]

State Key Laboratory of Robotics and System, Harbin Institute of Technology, Harbin 150001, China
{zhengtj,yhzhu}@hit.edu.cn

Abstract. This paper presents a low-cost and robust human pose estimation framework that fuses Inertial Measurement Units (IMUs) with Visual-inertial Odometry (VIO). A custom-designed wireless IMU module and distributed hardware architecture enable real-time estimation of 3D orientations using a quaternion-based Extended Kalman Filter (EKF). A hybrid static-dynamic alignment method is introduced to precisely map IMU frames to anatomical body frames. Based on this alignment, joint angles between adjacent body segments are computed, and the global body position is tracked via a pelvis-mounted VIO sensor. The proposed system is validated through visualization in the MuJoCo simulation platform, where full-body motion is accurately reproduced. Experimental results demonstrate the method's high real-time performance and accuracy in reconstructing natural human motion, highlighting its applicability to wearable sensing and human-robot interaction.

Keywords: Human-robot Interaction · Human Pose Estimation · Wearable Sensing

1 Introduction

Human Pose Estimation (HPE) has long been a core and challenging topic in the field of Human-Robot Interaction (HRI) [1–3]. Its fundamental objective is to accurately infer the three-dimensional spatial configuration of key human body joints from sensor or image data. With the rapid advancements in deep learning and multimodal sensing technologies, HPE has become increasingly essential across a wide range of practical applications, including medical rehabilitation, sports performance analysis, and human-robot interaction, among others.

The most widely adopted category of human pose estimation techniques is vision-based methods [4–6]. These approaches typically utilize monocular or multi-camera systems to capture image sequences of the human body and employ deep learning architectures to infer 2D or 3D joint positions. Vision-based methods offer a non-intrusive, low-cost, and easily deployable solution. However, the accuracy of these systems is highly sensitive to visual conditions [7,8]. The second major class comprises inertial sensor-based methods, which utilize wearable Inertial Measurement Units (IMUs) to continuously record tri-axial accelerometer and gyroscope data from different body segments [9–12]. IMU-based systems are advantageous in environments where visual sensing is unreliable, such as low-light, occluded, or outdoor conditions. However, a significant limitation of IMU-based systems lies in cumulative drift and sensor noise, which lead to increasing pose estimation errors over time. The third category includes high-precision optical motion capture systems, such as Vicon or OptiTrack, which are widely recognized as the gold standard in human motion analysis [13–15]. However, their practical deployment is hindered by high costs, complex setup procedures, and strong dependency on controlled environments, making them unsuitable for large-scale or mobile real-world applications.

This work proposes a multimodal human pose estimation framework that fuses Inertial Measurement Units (IMUs) with Visual-inertial Odometry (VIO). The proposed method leverages the high responsiveness of IMUs in capturing rapid local body movements, while simultaneously exploiting the global spatial awareness and mapping capabilities of vision-based odometry. This fusion yields a low-cost, low-latency, and highly robust pose estimation architecture suitable for real-world deployment.

2 System Design

2.1 Hardware Architecture

The system adopts a hardware design philosophy centered on modularity, low power consumption, and wearable integration. A compact and highly integrated wireless IMU module was custom-developed to support multi-node human pose estimation. With physical dimensions of only 22mm × 25mm × 13mm, the module is optimized for flexible attachment to key body segments such as the forearms, thighs, or back. Unlike traditional wired motion capture systems, this solution eliminates cable constraints, significantly enhancing user mobility and system deployability. The module supports quick replacement, spatial decoupling, and stable operation in dynamic scenarios. As shown in Fig. 1, the module demonstrates excellent wearability and a high degree of system integration.

The system employs the ESP32-C6 as its central microcontroller, offering robust edge computing capabilities and extensive wireless communication protocols. The chip natively supports Wi-Fi 6, Bluetooth 5.2, and IEEE 802.15.4 (enabling Zigbee and Thread), allowing flexible communication topologies including peer-to-peer, star, or mesh networks. With a maximum clock speed of 160 MHz and 512 KB of internal SRAM, the ESP32-C6 efficiently handles intermediate processing tasks such as sensor data acquisition, filtering, and fusion. It also features multiple low-power operation modes and interrupt-based wakeup mechanisms, which are critical for extending battery life in wearable applications. The chip supports diverse peripheral interfaces (e.g., I^2C, SPI,

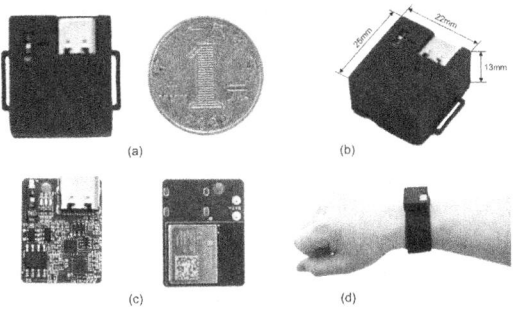

Fig. 1. Overview and structural illustration of the wireless IMU module. (a) Front view of the module compared with a 1-Yuan coin, highlighting its small form factor; (b) 3D dimensions of the module (22mm × 25mm × 13mm), demonstrating its compact structure; (c) Internal PCB layout showing the top and bottom sides, including the main controller, power management circuit, IMU, and Type-C interface; (d) Wearability demonstration of the module worn on the forearm using a wristband.

UART), enabling easy integration with sensors, displays, or memory modules, and laying the foundation for scalable multi-node architectures.

The core sensing unit of the module is the ICM-20948, a 9-axis Inertial Measurement Unit (IMU) that integrates a 3-axis accelerometer, 3-axis gyroscope, and 3-axis magnetometer. It supports data output rates up to 1.125 kHz, making it suitable for capturing fast, dynamic body movements. The sensor features an internal Digital Motion Processor, which enables onboard sensor fusion and preliminary attitude estimation, thereby offloading computational demand from the main processor and improving system responsiveness. In terms of performance, the sensor exhibits high measurement accuracy and low noise: gyroscope sensitivity error is ±1.5%, nonlinearity ±0.1%; accelerometer sensitivity error is ±0.5%, nonlinearity ±0.5%; magnetometer sensitivity scale factor error is ±0.15 μT/LSB. These characteristics ensure high-fidelity motion tracking in complex, real-world environments.

To ensure safe and reliable power supply, the module integrates a comprehensive power management system, including a 3.7V lithium battery and an intelligent charge-discharge controller. The power management circuitry supports overcharge, over-discharge, and overcurrent protection, enhancing system safety and prolonging battery lifespan. Real-time battery status monitoring is implemented, enabling dynamic power management and timely alerts. A Type-C port is incorporated into the module design, providing a unified interface for firmware flashing, serial communication, and battery charging, thereby streamlining system maintenance and debugging.

2.2 Communication Architecture and Network Topology

Within each IMU module, high-speed and reliable data exchange between the inertial measurement unit (ICM-20948) and the microcontroller (ESP32-C6) is achieved via an I^{2}C bus interface. The I^{2}C protocol offers a lightweight and stable communication structure, with clearly defined master-slave roles, making it well-suited for low-power embedded systems. In the present design, the IMU sampling rate is configured at 100 Hz, which is sufficient for capturing continuous pose transitions in typical human motion. This frequency provides a practical trade-off between accuracy and energy efficiency, ensuring consistent data availability for downstream processing while supporting long-duration wearable applications.

For multi-node deployment, the system adopts a star network topology, in which a central master node (e.g., edge server, mobile device, or upper computer) coordinates multiple distributed IMU modules functioning as peripheral nodes. Each module communicates wirelessly with the master node using protocols supported by the ESP32-C6 chip, namely Wi-Fi (via UDP) or Zigbee (via IEEE 802.15.4). Wi-Fi-based communication is ideal for high-throughput and long-range applications in open environments, offering flexible network scalability. In contrast, Zigbee is optimized for low-power, interference-resilient communication and is more suitable for indoor scenarios with a high density of sensor nodes (Fig. 2).

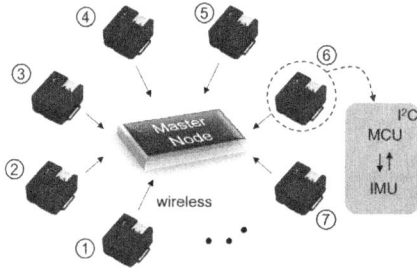

Fig. 2. Schematic of the system communication architecture. Multiple wireless IMU modules form a star topology with the master node via Wi-Fi (UDP) or Zigbee, while each module internally connects its microcontroller unit (MCU) and IMU through an I^{2}C interface for sensor data acquisition.

To ensure communication stability and orderly data transmission, each IMU module undergoes identity binding and network registration during the system initialization phase. A unique identifier (ID) is assigned to each node, and the central controller dynamically allocates communication ports to prevent channel collisions and data loss. This distributed binding scheme supports hot-plugging and dynamic scalability, enabling flexible configuration in complex interactive environments. Sensor data are transmitted at regular intervals, and basic retransmission mechanisms are implemented to improve robustness under unreliable wireless conditions.

At the protocol level, a custom lightweight data encapsulation format is employed to balance communication efficiency with ease of parsing. Each transmitted data packet includes raw sensor measurements (acceleration, angular velocity, magnetometer), timestamps and module ID, enabling unified parsing and synchronization at the master node. This compact format minimizes transmission overhead, improves real-time responsiveness, and provides a scalable foundation for future extensions such as on-node data fusion, compression, or edge inference. The overall communication framework supports high scalability, robust deployment, and consistent performance, making it well-suited for dense, distributed human pose estimation systems.

3 Human Pose Estimation Algorithm

3.1 Quaternion-Based Extended Kalman Filter for IMU Orientation Estimation

For each standalone IMU module, raw sensor outputs, including triaxial acceleration, angular velocity, and magnetic field strength, are preprocessed to suppress noise prior to entering the filter. A first-order low-pass filter is applied to smooth the signal and eliminate high-frequency artifacts, described by:

$$x_t = \alpha x_{t_0} + (1-\alpha)x_{t-1} \tag{1}$$

where x_{t_0} is the current sample, x_t is the filtered output, and α is a tunable smoothing factor. This filtering process improves the stability of subsequent pose estimation without compromising temporal responsiveness.

To achieve reliable sensor fusion, the system implements an Extended Kalman Filter (EKF) based on quaternion representation. The state vector is defined as a unit quaternion $q = [q_0, q_1, q_2, q_3]^\top$, which models the 3D orientation of the module.

The continuous-time formulation of the state equation is as follows:

$$\dot{q} = \frac{1}{2}\Omega(\boldsymbol{\omega})q \tag{2}$$

$$\Omega(\boldsymbol{\omega}) = \begin{bmatrix} 0 & -\omega_x & -\omega_y & -\omega_z \\ \omega_x & 0 & \omega_z & -\omega_y \\ \omega_y & -\omega_z & 0 & \omega_x \\ \omega_z & \omega_y & -\omega_x & 0 \end{bmatrix} \tag{3}$$

where $\Omega(\boldsymbol{\omega})$ is a skew-symmetric matrix constructed from angular velocity. The state prediction is driven by gyroscope data:

$$q_{k|k-1} = q_{k-1} + \frac{1}{2}\Delta t \cdot \Omega(\boldsymbol{\omega}_{k-1})q_{k-1} \tag{4}$$

In the observation update stage, the accelerometer and magnetometer are used to provide gravity and geomagnetic direction references, respectively. These are incorporated through a nonlinear observation function $h(\mathbf{x}_k)$ to correct the predicted state. Specifically, the accelerometer offers a reliable estimate of the gravity vector, while the magnetometer provides heading information to stabilize orientation. Together, they counteract the drift that arises from pure gyroscope integration.

The measurement vector is defined as:

$$\mathbf{z}_k = \begin{bmatrix} \mathbf{a}_k \\ \mathbf{m}_k \end{bmatrix} \quad (5)$$

representing the normalized accelerometer (gravity) and magnetometer (magnetic north) readings. The function $h(\mathbf{x}_k)$ computes the expected sensor readings based on the current quaternion state.

The observation residual is computed as:

$$\mathbf{y}_k = \mathbf{z}_k - h(\hat{\mathbf{x}}_{k|k-1}) \quad (6)$$

The Jacobian matrix of the observation model is then calculated:

$$\mathbf{H}_k = \left. \frac{\partial h(\mathbf{x})}{\partial \mathbf{x}} \right|_{\hat{\mathbf{x}}_{k|k-1}} \quad (7)$$

Next, the Kalman gain is derived:

$$\mathbf{K}_k = \mathbf{P}_{k|k-1} \mathbf{H}_k^\top (\mathbf{H}_k \mathbf{P}_{k|k-1} \mathbf{H}_k^\top + \mathbf{R}_k)^{-1} \quad (8)$$

The state is updated using the residual and gain:

$$\hat{\mathbf{x}}_{k|k} = \hat{\mathbf{x}}_{k|k-1} + \mathbf{K}_k \mathbf{y}_k \quad (9)$$

And the error covariance matrix is updated as:

$$\mathbf{P}_{k|k} = (\mathbf{I} - \mathbf{K}_k \mathbf{H}_k) \mathbf{P}_{k|k-1} \quad (10)$$

This EKF update cycle allows sensor fusion to occur at each time step, combining fast but drift-prone gyroscope data with stable but noisy accelerometer and magnetometer readings. As a result, the system achieves a balance between responsiveness and robustness, making it well-suited for motion capture and real-time pose estimation in unconstrained environments.

3.2 Hybrid Sensor-to-Body Frame Alignment and Human Pose Estimation

In biomechanical modeling, the human body is often abstracted as a multi-link system composed of rigid segments connected by joints, such as the shoulders, elbows, hips, and knees. Each limb is treated as a rigid link, and joint motion is represented by relative rotations between adjacent segments. To estimate joint angles and body posture during motion, we adopt a simplified kinematic model based on this rigid-body assumption. The local coordinate systems and sensor placement are illustrated in Fig. 3.

Specifically, nine IMU modules are attached to the body at the following locations: upper arms (left and right), forearms (left and right), thighs (left and right), shanks (left and right), and the upper back (thoracic region). Additionally, an Intel RealSense T265 visual-inertial odometry (VIO) sensor is mounted at the front of the pelvis, serving as the reference for global body motion tracking. For modeling purposes, we assume all sensors are rigidly affixed to their corresponding body segments, meaning there is no relative movement or positional drift between the hardware and the human body during motion.

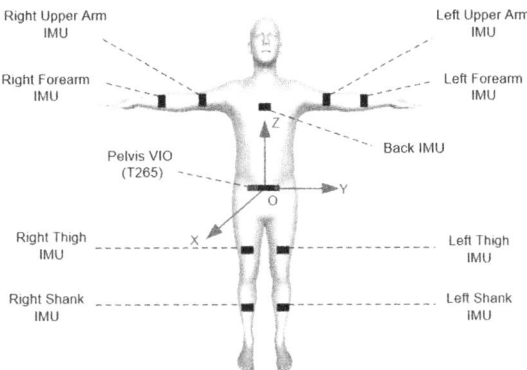

Fig. 3. Overview of sensor (IMU and VIO) placement and body coordinate definition.

In the context of human pose estimation, it is essential to first identify the dominant axis of rotation for different body movements. For example, torso flexion and extension are typically modeled as rotations around the Y-axis of the anatomical body frame. However, in practical scenarios, the axes of the wearable IMU sensors rarely align perfectly with those of the human anatomical coordinate system. This misalignment makes it difficult to directly infer the orientation of the body frame in the global (world) coordinate system using raw IMU measurements.

To address this issue, we propose a sensor-to-body coordinate alignment method that combines both static postural calibration and guided dynamic movement. In this approach, users are instructed to adopt specific static postures to capture baseline orientation vectors, followed by performing isolated rotational motions to characterize the orientation of the anatomical axes within the local sensor frame. This hybrid alignment procedure enables efficient mapping between the IMU and body coordinate frames without requiring any external reference system, thus providing a unified reference basis for subsequent pose estimation tasks.

As shown in Fig. 4(a), the first step involves Pelvis VIO Alignment, which establishes a rigid-body mapping between the coordinate system of the VIO sen-

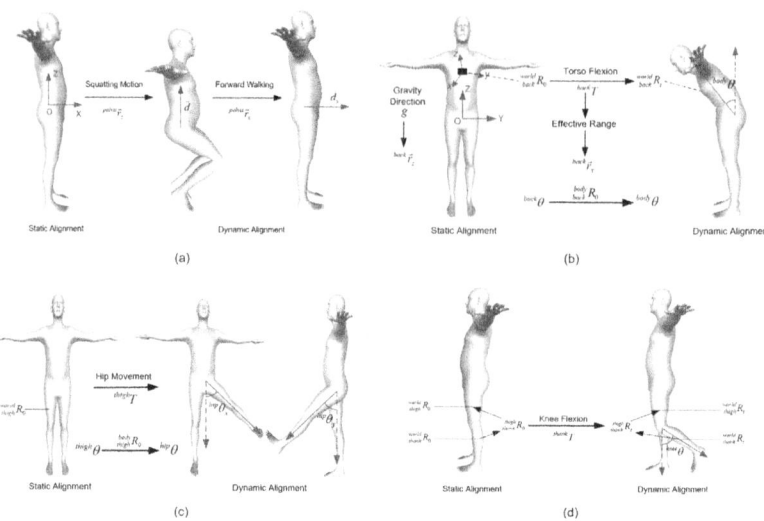

Fig. 4. Hybrid Sensor-to-Body Frame Alignment and Human Pose Estimation Process. (a) Pelvis VIO Alignment. (b) Back Frame Alignment and Pose Estimation. (c) Hip (or Shoulder) Frame Alignment and Pose Estimation. (d) Knee (or Elbow) Frame Alignment and Pose Estimation.

sor and the anatomical coordinate system of the human body. The procedure begins with the subject performing repeated squat movements while standing in place. This motion induces dominant displacement along the body's vertical direction, corresponding to the Z-axis of the body frame. Approximately 1000 translation vectors are recorded from the VIO sensor. Each vector is normalized to unit length, then its absolute values are averaged and normalized, denoted as $^{pelvis}\vec{r}_z$. The resulting vector represents the Z-axis of the body frame expressed in the VIO coordinate system. Next, the subject performs a short, straight forward walking motion. This induces dominant translation along the body's X-axis (forward direction). The same process is applied to the VIO translation vectors, yielding the X-axis of the body frame in the VIO coordinate system, denoted as $^{pelvis}\vec{r}_x$. Finally, the Y-axis is computed via the right-hand rule using the cross product of the obtained X and Z vectors, denoted as $^{pelvis}\vec{r}_y$. This completes the construction of the body coordinate frame in the VIO coordinate system, enabling accurate frame alignment for subsequent pose estimation.

Based on this procedure, the rotation matrix from the VIO coordinate system to the body coordinate system is constructed as:

$$^{body}_{pelvis}\mathbf{R} = \begin{bmatrix} ^{pelvis}\vec{r}_x \\ ^{pelvis}\vec{r}_y \\ ^{pelvis}\vec{r}_z \end{bmatrix} \quad (11)$$

Figure 4(b), (c), and (d) illustrate the alignment of IMU sensor axes with the anatomical coordinate system and the subsequent pose estimation process.

As shown in Fig. 4 (b), when the subject is in a static upright position, the linear acceleration measured by the back-mounted IMU corresponds primarily to gravity. This vector points along the negative Z-axis of the body frame and is normalized to obtain $^{back}\vec{r}_z$. Next, the subject performs multiple torso flexion movements, which are predominantly rotations about the body's Y-axis. By analyzing the sequence of IMU orientation changes during these motions, the principal rotation axis $^{back}\vec{r}_y = (n_x, n_y, n_z)$ can be extracted. Let $^{back}\mathbf{T}$ denote the IMU's orientation matrix, then:

$$^{back}\mathbf{T} = \begin{bmatrix} a_{11} & a_{12} & a_{13} \\ a_{21} & a_{22} & a_{33} \\ a_{31} & a_{32} & a_{33} \end{bmatrix} \quad (12)$$

$$\begin{cases} \theta = \arccos(\dfrac{a_{11} + a_{22} + a_{33} - 1}{2}) \\ n_x = (a_{32} - a_{23})/(2\sin\theta) \\ n_y = (a_{13} - a_{31})/(2\sin\theta) \\ n_z = (a_{21} - a_{12})/(2\sin\theta) \end{cases} \quad (13)$$

With both $\vec{r}_z$ and $\vec{r}_y$ determined, the right-hand rule is applied to compute the X-axis direction as: $^{back}\vec{r}_x = ^{back}\vec{r}_y \times ^{back}\vec{r}_z$. The rotation matrix from the back IMU to the body coordinate system is constructed as:

$$^{body}_{back}\mathbf{R} = \begin{bmatrix} ^{back}\vec{r}_x \\ ^{back}\vec{r}_y \\ ^{back}\vec{r}_z \end{bmatrix} \quad (14)$$

Let $\mathbf{R}_t$ denote the rotation matrix of the back-mounted IMU at time t. The anatomical orientation of the back is then given by:

$$^{body}\mathbf{R}_t = ^{body}_{back}\mathbf{R} \cdot \mathbf{R}_t \cdot ^{body}_{back}\mathbf{R}^{-1} \quad (15)$$

From the resulting rotation matrix $^{body}\mathbf{R}_t$, the three-axis orientation angles, namely θ_x, θ_y, and θ_z, can be extracted as follows:

$$^{body}\mathbf{R}_t = \begin{bmatrix} r_{11} & r_{12} & r_{13} \\ r_{21} & r_{22} & r_{33} \\ r_{31} & r_{32} & r_{33} \end{bmatrix} \quad (16)$$

$$\begin{cases} \theta_x = \arctan 2(r_{32}, r_{33}) \\ \theta_y = \arctan 2(-r_{31}, \sqrt{r_{11}^2 + r_{21}^2}) \\ \theta_z = \arctan 2(r_{21}, r_{11}) \end{cases} \quad (17)$$

The same approach can be extended to other body-mounted IMU modules by applying the hybrid sensor-to-body frame alignment method to each anatomical segment. Once the local body-aligned coordinate frame is established for each IMU, the orientation data from each sensor can be transformed accordingly to yield the posture of the corresponding body part. In parallel, the global spatial motion, including position and heading, is obtained from the T265 visual-inertial odometry sensor mounted at the pelvis. This framework enables a multi-level motion representation, where global locomotion and local joint movements are captured simultaneously. It provides a high-fidelity and flexible foundation for full-body human pose reconstruction in dynamic, real-world environments.

4 Experiments and Results

To evaluate the real-time performance and accuracy of the proposed pose estimation algorithm, we employed the MuJoCo [16] physics engine to visualize the reconstructed human motion in a virtual environment. During the experiment, the subject continuously performed natural body movements, while the system computed human body pose from IMU orientation data in real time. The computed postures were used to drive a human model in MuJoCo, enabling visual feedback of the motion, as illustrated in Fig. 5.

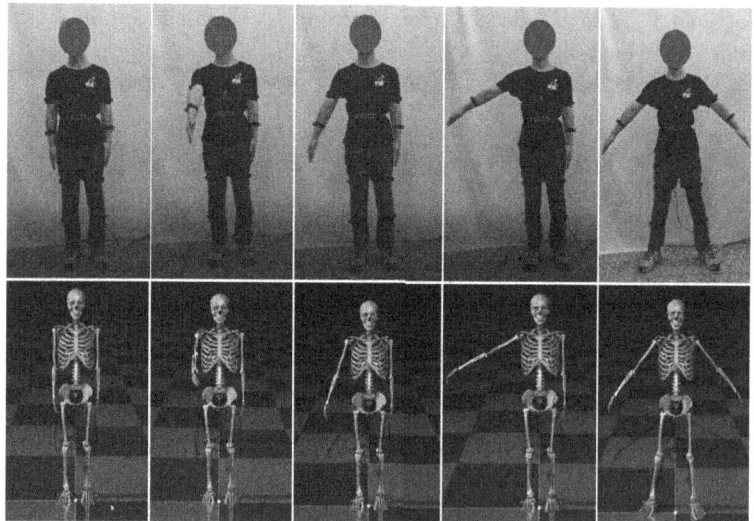

Fig. 5. The experimenter, equipped with IMUs and a T265 VIO, performed a series of movements and the Mujoco simulation visualized the human pose estimation results.

In the walking trial, joint angles and angular velocities of all tracked joints were recorded. From the full dataset, three consecutive gait cycles were extracted, each normalized to a gait percentage scale from 0% to 100%. We differentiate the angle over time intervals as joint's angular velocity. The results are shown in Fig. 6. The results show clear periodic patterns and bilateral symmetry across gait cycles, indicating consistent and accurate joint reconstruction.

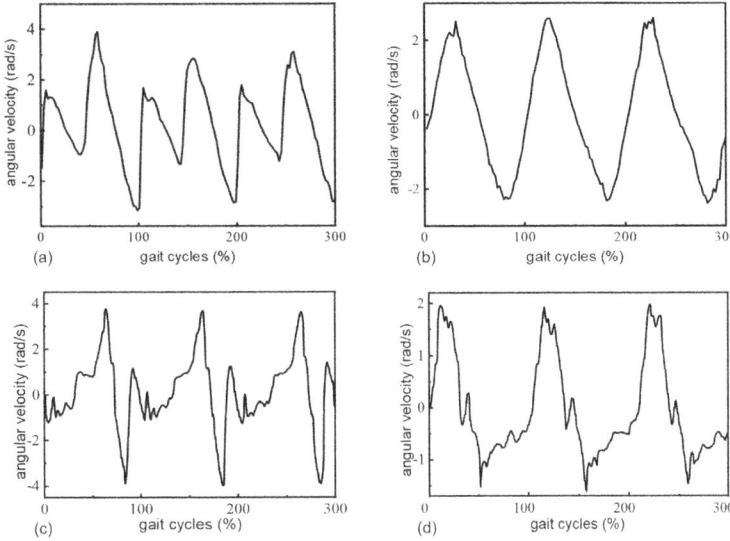

Fig. 6. Angular velocity (dq/dt) of different joints. (a) elbow joint. (b) shoulder joint. (c) knee joint. (d) hip joint.

Overall, the experimental results demonstrate that the proposed system achieves high real-time performance and accuracy. It can compute joint kinematics quickly and reliably, and replicate diverse human motions in the visualization platform with high fidelity, thereby accomplishing the core objective of full-body pose estimation and motion reconstruction.

5 Conclusion

The proposed human pose estimation system, which fuses IMU data with visual-inertial odometry, demonstrates an effective integration of modular hardware, hybrid coordinate alignment, and real-time quaternion-based filtering. Without relying on external infrastructure, the system successfully reconstructs full-body motion, including both global trajectories and joint-level angular kinematics. Experimental results validate its responsiveness, accuracy, and scalability, making it well-suited for applications such as motion tracking, rehabilitation, and human-robot interaction. Future work will focus on integrating the system into human-robot interaction pipelines, enabling motion imitation, collaborative control, and training data generation for robotics.

Acknowledgments. This work was supported by the National Natural Science Foundation of China (NSFC) (No. 52435001 & No. 52025054) and the fellowship of China Postdoctoral Science Foundation (No. 2022M710957).

References

1. Munea, T.L., Jembre, Y.Z., Weldegebriel, H.T., Chen, L., Huang, C., Yang, C.: The progress of human pose estimation: a survey and taxonomy of models applied in 2D human pose estimation. IEEE Access **8**, 133330–133348 (2020)
2. Sigal, L.: Human pose estimation. In: Computer Vision: A Reference Guide, pp. 1–20 (2021)
3. Zheng, C., et al.: Deep learning-based human pose estimation: a survey. ACM Comput. Surv. **56**(1), 1–37 (2023)
4. Lan, G., Wu, Y., Hu, F., Hao, Q.: Vision-based human pose estimation via deep learning: a survey. IEEE Trans. Hum.-Mach. Syst. **53**(1), 253–268 (2022)
5. Gong, W., et al.: Human pose estimation from monocular images: a comprehensive survey. Sensor **16**(12), 1966 (2016)
6. Sun, K., Xiao, B., Liu, D., Wang, J.: Deep high-resolution representation learning for human pose estimation. In: Proceedings of the IEEE/CVF Conference on Computer Vision and Pattern Recognition, pp. 5693–5703 (2019)
7. Dubey, S., Dixit, M.: A comprehensive survey on human pose estimation approaches. Multimedia Syst. **29**(1), 167–195 (2023)
8. Xiaohan Nie, B., Xiong, C., Zhu, S.C.: Joint action recognition and pose estimation from video. In: Proceedings of the IEEE Conference on Computer Vision and Pattern Recognition, pp. 1293–1301 (2015)
9. Zhao, J.: A review of wearable IMU (inertial-measurement-unit)-based pose estimation and drift reduction technologies. J. Phys. Conf. Ser. **1087**, 042003. IOP Publishing (2018)
10. Zhang, Z., Wang, C., Qin, W., Zeng, W.: Fusing wearable IMUs with multi-view images for human pose estimation: a geometric approach. In: Proceedings of the IEEE/CVF Conference on Computer Vision and Pattern Recognition, pp. 2200–2209 (2020)
11. McGrath, T., Stirling, L.: Body-worn IMU-based human hip and knee kinematics estimation during treadmill walking. Sensors **22**(7), 2544 (2022)
12. Pathirana, P.N., Karunarathne, M.S., Williams, G.L., Nam, P.T., Durrant-Whyte, H.: Robust and accurate capture of human joint pose using an inertial sensor. IEEE J. Transl. Eng. Health Med. **6**, 1–11 (2018)
13. Zeng, J., He, X., Hu, Y., Zhang, Y., Yang, H., Zhou, S.: Research status of data application based on optical motion capture technology. In: 2021 2nd International Conference on Artificial Intelligence and Information Systems, pp. 1–8 (2021)
14. Schlagenhauf, F., Sreeram, S., Singhose, W.: Comparison of kinect and vicon motion capture of upper-body joint angle tracking. In: 2018 IEEE 14th International Conference on Control and Automation (ICCA), pp. 674–679. IEEE (2018)
15. Ota, M., et al.: Verification of reliability and validity of motion analysis systems during bilateral squat using human pose tracking algorithm. Gait Posture **80**, 62–67 (2020)
16. Todorov, E., Erez, T., Tassa, Y.: MuJoCo: a physics engine for model-based control. In: 2012 IEEE/RSJ International Conference on Intelligent Robots and Systems, pp. 5026–5033. IEEE (2012)

Shape Matching Method Based on Growing Neural Gas

Jiaqi Zhang, Yuichiro Toda[✉], and Takayuki Matsuno

Okayama University, Okayama, Japan
ytoda@okayama-u.ac.jp

Abstract. Shape recognition is a major challenge in computer vision. Different approaches and tools have been used to solve this problem. To capture the invariant features of both local shape details and visual parts, we construct a graph that contains the topological and geometrical properties of the object, then based on the coordinate and relation of its vertices, we propose a multi-scale descriptor which is robust to rotation and noise. In this work, we define three types of invariants to capture the shape features from different aspects. Since a semi-global scale-space information is contained in the descriptor, matching can be conducted between different scales, making it possible to handle shearing and scale variation simultaneously. To validate the invariance and robustness of our proposed method, we perform an experiment and discuss the effectiveness of the proposed method.

Keywords: Shape matching · Growing Neural Gas · Image processing

1 Introduction

Shape matching amounts to developing computational methods for comparing shapes that agree as much as possible with the human notion of shape similarity. The problem has significant theoretical interest and a wide range of applications, including, but not limited to object detection and recognition, content-based retrieval of images, and image registration. To perform shape matching, most of the existing methods [1–8] define shape representations and descriptors which are then compared through appropriately selected methods and metrics. The quality of the shape-matching process depends on whether its final outcome agrees with human judgment. Shape matching is a very challenging problem. Shapes to be matched are typically the result of some kind of segmentation process which, being imperfect, may introduce a considerable amount of noise that needs to be tolerated. In most cases, arbitrary differences in scale and orientation should not affect the matching process. Due to viewpoint dependencies and shape articulations and deformations, different 2D image projections of the shape of the same 3D object may differ considerably. Further complications are caused by occlusions which force shape matching to be based on partial evidence. In this particular case, the best matching of an open contour with part of a closed contour needs to be established [9,10]. Last but not least, in realistic settings, all of the above complicating factors do not appear in isolation but contribute collectively to increasing the complexity of the matching problem.

In this paper, we use the growing neural gas (GNG) [11] algorithm to construct a GNG graph model of input data incrementally. The number of vertices of the graph does not depend on the size of the image and it is not sensitive to articulation and noise on the boundary. In this graph, every vertex has a coordinate, so that we can use the geometrical properties of the graph as well. We use both topological and geometrical properties of this graph to extract meaningful features from the image. Both theoretic discussions and experimental results show that our method is invariant to articulation, noise, occlusion, rotation, and scale.

2 Method

2.1 Descriptor Generation

For a shape-matching and retrieval engine, a good performance is significantly relevant to three properties of shape representation: invariance, discrimination, and robustness. In the shape matching, both small intra-class distances and large inter-class distances are expected, which rely on the invariance and the discrimination of the descriptor, respectively. The robustness is also necessary for both large-scale disturbance, e.g., partial occlusion, and small-scale disturbance, e.g., high-frequency noise, which are two critical roadblocks for a good retrieval result. However, it is very hard to well satisfy these properties simultaneously, especially for complex shapes. In this section, we will introduce how and why we use the GNG method to generate a robust descriptor. We use a graph to approximate the object. The vertices are scattered almost uniformly inside the object. The main steps are:

1. Constructing a graph that models the object using the growing neural gas (GNG) algorithm. The constructed graph is called the GNG graph.
2. Extracting the outer boundary of the GNG graph, using computational geometry approaches and extracting geometrical and topological features from this graph.
3. Measuring the similarity between objects using a dynamic programming algorithm.

The system consists of three main parts, the first part is floor guide map recognition and intelligence extraction, the second part is the matching of robot's local map (generated by slam) and guide map information, and the third part is the path planning based on area distribution.

Advantages of GNG Graph Our method is based on a GNG graph. This graph must have the following properties:

- The vertices are placed almost uniformly inside the object and the edges have almost equal lengths.
- The topology generated by GNG eliminates the need for distances between vertices to be computed in Euclidean space and only requires finding point-to-point connectivity relationships, which drastically reduces the computational effort required to generate the descriptor.
- The number of vertices is fixed and does not depend on the size of the object.
- The graph is robust to noises. It ignores holes and cracks inside and on the boundary of the object.

Different approaches can be chosen to construct this graph. We used the GNG algorithm because it satisfies the mentioned properties, the running time is acceptable, and can be extended to 3D object representation and object tracking. Also, since the structure is not fixed but adaptable, GNG can learn new evolving patterns in an online learning process and is able to adapt to dynamic changing operating conditions.

Boundary Extraction In this phase, we extract the outer boundary of the GNG graph. If the graph is 2-connected, then the outer boundary is a cycle, otherwise, it is a closed walk. So, we can store its vertices in a cyclic array, C, in a clockwise order of appearance. The idea is similar to the idea of a convex hull algorithm. The full steps are like:

1. Find the rightmost vertex v and its neighbor u with the smallest clockwise angle with the vertical upward ray starting at v. Insert v and u in C.
2. Consider the two last vertices i and $i-1$ in C, and for all vertices j, adjacent to i, compute the size of the clockwise angle between the edges $i, i-1$ and i, j. Select a vertex with a minimum angle as the next vertex on the boundary and insert it in C.
3. If the last two vertices in C are equal to initial vertices (u and v), exit otherwise go to step 3. (This helps pass the cut vertex if it exists.)

Fig. 1 shows an example of a GNG graph and its outer boundary.

Feature Extraction Although the vertices on the outer boundary of a GNG graph capture special information about the object, the relation between the boundary and internal vertices can provide new topological features that lead to better recognition. We introduce features for each vertex on the outer boundary, then compute and combine these features to describe the global and local properties of the shape. The features are perimeter(P), boundary-in-disc (B) and convex hull-area (CH) for outer boundary vertices of GNG. Given the GNG graph of an object, let $U = u_1, u_2, ..., u_n$ define the sequence of outer boundary vertices in clockwise order. A feature vector $F_i = (P_i, B_i, CH_i)$ is computed for every outer boundary vertex $u_i, i \in 1, ..., n$. F_i consists of three features P_i, B_i, CH_i with lengths $|Pi| = m1, |Bi| = m2, |CHi| = m3$ and $\sum_{j=1}^{3} m_j = m$. So F_i can

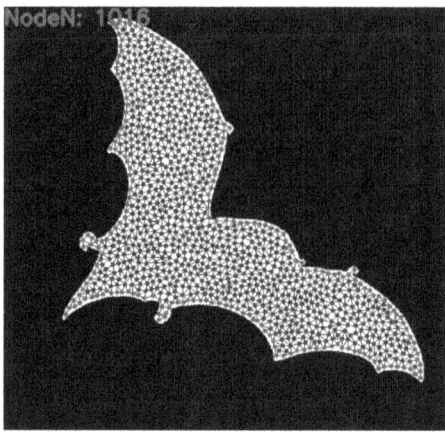

Fig. 1. GNG structure and contour detection on a binary image.

be considered as a m-dimensional vector. We compute F_i for every outer boundary vertex $u_i, i \in 1, ..., n$ and define $\boldsymbol{F} = \boldsymbol{F}(U) = (\boldsymbol{F_1}, \boldsymbol{F_2}, \boldsymbol{F_3}, ..., \boldsymbol{F_n})$ which is a $m \times n$ matrix. Let G be the GNG graph of an object and $V(G)$ be the set of vertices in G. For every two vertices $v, u \in V(G)$, $d(u, v)$ shows their distance in G. For every outer boundary vertex u_i and for every integer j, let $\boldsymbol{D_j}(u_i) = v \in V(G) : d(v, u_i) \leq j$ be the discrete disc of radius j around u_i and $D_j(u_i) = v \in V(G) : d(v, u_i) = j$ be the boundary of the discrete disc. Figure 2 shows the discrete discs around a vertex in a sample image. We define three features P, B, and CH for a given GNG graph with outer boundary vertices $U = u_1, u_2, ..., u_n$ as follows (shown as Fig. 2)

- Perimeter (P): For each outer boundary vertex u_i, perimeter counts the number of vertices that are in $D_j(u_i)$ for $j \in 1, ..., m_1$. Small values of j describe local properties, while larger values represent global properties of the shape. (See Fig. 4a).
- Boundary-in-disc (B): The number of outer boundary vertices inside $D_j(u_i)$ for each outer boundary vertex u_i where $j \in 1, ..., m_2$ is called boundary-in-disc. If the boundary has peaks and troughs inside the disc, this number is bigger, so this feature can keep the shape of the boundary if it is computed for different radii.
- Convex hull-area (CH): For each outer boundary vertex u_i and integer $j \in 1, 2, ..., m3$, let S be the convex hull of vertices in $D_j(u_i)$ that are on the outer boundary of G(the green line). Let the number of vertices of $D_j(u_i)$ that are inside S be d, the value of $3\sqrt{d}$ is called convex hull-area.

Since the descriptor does not contain any orientation factors, the descriptor is robust to rotation. An example of a pattern and its three descriptors is shown in Fig. 3, where it can be seen that the descriptor is almost unchanged after rotation.

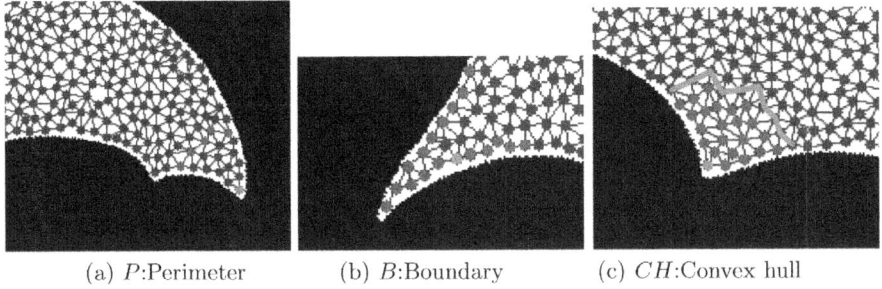

(a) P:Perimeter (b) B:Boundary (c) CH:Convex hull

Fig. 2. Definition of the three elements of descriptor, where the green node is the current node and the number of the red nodes refer to the value of the descriptor. (Color figure online)

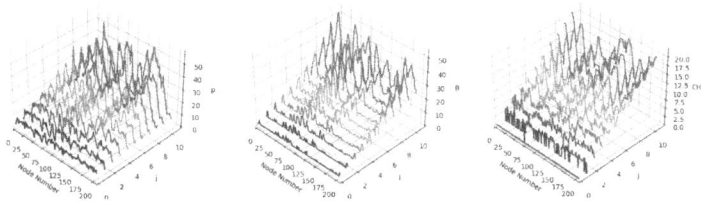

Fig. 3. Descriptor of the bat shape.

2.2 Matching

Scale-Space Scale-space theory is a framework for multi-scale signal representation developed by the computer vision, image processing and signal processing communities with complementary motivations from physics and biological vision. It is a formal theory for handling image structures at different scales, by representing an image as a one-parameter family of smoothed images, the scale-space representation, parametrized by the size of the smoothing kernel used for suppressing fine-scale structures. The parameter t in this family is referred to as the scale parameter, with the interpretation that image structures of spatial size smaller than about $\sqrt{t}$ have largely been smoothed away in the scale-space level at scale t. The main type of scale space is the linear (Gaussian) scale space, which has wide applicability as well as the attractive property of being possible to derive from a small set of scale-space axioms and this framework allows visual operations to be made scale invariant. Some of the major existing image feature matching algorithms such as SIFT, SURF, and ORB have used this idea to make the algorithm scale invariant.

However, unlike image matching, in shape matching we do not have information about brightness, color and the number of pixels available tends to be much smaller, which means that matching feature descriptors as separate entities would be next to impossible. However, since shape information tends to be in binary form, this makes the extraction of its contours much more stable compared to images. Thanks to our contour-based descriptor construction above, we can eliminate the effects of scale inhomogeneity by comparing them in scale space. It is worth mentioning that we do not do this for the purpose of comparing similar graphs, since that kind of problem can be solved more simply by homogenizing the number of points in the topology. What we need to do is to perform partial matching between graphs with scale differences. This means that we need to deal with both the numerical differences due to scaling and the sampling interval differences due to shearing. We will introduce our matching method in the rest of this chapter.

Scale Estimation To solve the map-matching problem we mentioned above, we first divide the graph into template and to-be-matched parts, and the graph as a template tends to have higher resolution and sharper edges. The graph as template tends to have higher resolution and sharper edges, but is only a part of the to-be-matched graph. We use higher density parameters in it to generate GNG structures for more accurate information. In order to match between different scales, we first need to determine the maximum local feature range. This is in consideration of the fact that a larger feature range will distort the local features as the clipped region will have a larger effect on the descriptor, while a smaller feature range will probably not describe the graph correctly. We use the following discriminant to determine the maximum local feature range j_{max}.

$$j_{max} = max \ j, \quad s.t. \frac{|P_j| + |B_j| + |CH_j|}{|P_{j-1}| + |B_{j-1}| + |CH_{j-1}|} > \beta \quad (1)$$

where β is a threshold set empirically, the following figures show the value of j_{max} in some shapes.

Shape Matching To conduct a matching between two shapes I and I', we simply calculate the dissimilarity between their descriptors. An intuitive idea is to compare their invariant functions directly. However, as discussed above, the density of the topology, i.e. the scale of the image, is not normalized. To solve this problem, we will try to match over a range of scales and find the scale that minimizes the matching difference.

Let the scale factor be α, implying that the dissimilarity of the match is minimized when A is scaled by α^{-1}. For each shape, we take three layers of its descriptor for matching. In the template, the first layer $l_{I1} = j_{Imax}$, the second layer $l_{I2} = j_{Imax}^{-\frac{1}{2}}$, and the third layer $l_I = j_{Imax}^{-\frac{1}{4}}$. Accordingly, the first layer to be matched in shape B $l_{I'1}$ should be $\alpha^{-1} l_{I'1}$, and $l_{I'2} = \alpha^{-1} l_{I2}$, $l_{I'3} = \alpha^{-1} l_{I3}$.

Since in the vast majority of cases, the values of these strata are not integers, this is due to the fact that we treat the values of the descriptors as scale-continuous, but in practice, it is impossible to sample an infinite number of values, and therefore we need to estimate it by the values of the neighboring layers. For a non-integer layer value l, we use the following formula to compute the value in its descriptor.

$$P_l(i) = (l - \lfloor l \rfloor)P_{\lfloor l \rfloor}(i) + (\lceil l \rceil - l)P_{\lceil l \rceil}(i) \qquad (2)$$

$$B_l(i) = (l - \lfloor l \rfloor)B_{\lfloor l \rfloor}(i) + (\lceil l \rceil - l)B_{\lceil l \rceil}(i) \qquad (3)$$

$$CH_l(i) = (l - \lfloor l \rfloor)CH_{\lfloor l \rfloor}(i) + (\lceil l \rceil - l)CH_{\lceil l \rceil}(i) \qquad (4)$$

Another problem is that the contour points of the two shapes should be aligned beforehand. In this work, dynamic programming (DP) is employed to find the best correspondence between two shapes. When describing the two shapes with point sequences on their extracted contours: $I = p_1, p_2, ..., p_{nI}$ and $I' = q_1, q_2, ..., q_{nI'}$. The matching cost of two points p_i and $q_{i'}$ is defined as the Euclidean distance of their descriptor:

$$d(p_i, q_{i'}) =$$

$$\sum_{k=1}^{3} \frac{l_{I1}}{l_{Ik}} \sqrt{dP_k(i,i') + dB_k(i,i') + dCH_k(i,i')} \qquad (5)$$

where

$$dP_k(i,i') = \left(\frac{P^I_{l_{Ik}}(i) - \alpha P^{I'}_{l_{I'k}}(i')}{P^I_{l_{Ik}}(i)}\right)^2$$

$$dB_k(i,i') = \left(\frac{B^I_{l_{Ik}}(i) - \alpha B^{I'}_{l_{I'k}}(i')}{B^I_{l_{Ik}}(i)}\right)^2$$

$$dCH_k(i,i') = \left(\frac{CH^I_{l_{Ik}}(i) - \alpha CH^{I'}_{l_{I'k}}(i')}{CH^I_{l_{Ik}}(i)}\right)^2$$

and the cost matrix $\mathbf{D}$ represents the set of costs between all pairs of points

$$D(I,I') = \begin{bmatrix} d(p_1,q_1) & d(p_1,q_2) & d(p_1,q_3) & \cdots \\ d(p_2,q_1) & d(p_2,q_2) & d(p_2,q_3) & \cdots \\ d(p_3,q_1) & d(p_3,q_2) & d(p_3,q_3) & \cdots \\ \cdots & \cdots & \cdots & \cdots \end{bmatrix} \qquad (6)$$

A matching π from I to I' is defined as a mapping from $p1, p2, ..., pn$ to $q_1, q_2, ..., q_m$ where p_i is mapped to $q_{\pi(i)}$ if $\pi(i) = 0$ and otherwise p_i remains unmapped. The mapping π should minimize the matching cost function $f_{I,I'}(\pi)$:

$$f_{I,I'}(\pi) = \sum_{i=1}^{n'} d(p_i, q_{\pi(i')}) \tag{7}$$

where

$$n' = min(\lfloor \alpha^{-1} n_A \rfloor, n_B) \tag{8}$$

3 Results

In this section, we will evaluate the capability of the proposed method in three aspects: (1) demonstrate the invariant properties of the proposed IMD descriptor for articulated deformation, partial occlusion and intra-class variation including rotation and scale variation; (2) evaluate the representative and discriminative power by shape matching and retrieval experiments on benchmark datasets, including the MPEG-7 [19] dataset.

3.1 MPEG-7 Dataset

The MPEG-7 is a standard dataset that is widely used to test the capability of shape-matching and retrieval methods. It consists of 1400 binary images divided into 70 shape classes and each class contains 20 shapes.

3.2 Descriptor Similarity

Since the matching is performed in scale-space, the matching is scale-invariant. It is worth noting that since the patterns in the mpeg7 dataset are complete, they can be homogenized simply by using the pattern area size. However, our algorithm is not exactly designed for this purpose; we were originally designed so that the algorithm would still be able to match when one of the patterns is incomplete, which would lead to reduced accuracy in the retrieval test. Figure 4 shows the element P in the descriptor of a bat pattern.

Figure 5 shows a slice of the interpreter ($j = 5$), and we can see that the interpreters for the first through third patterns show a high degree of consistency, despite the varying size and orientation of the patterns. However, the interpreter for the fourth pattern is different from the other three due to the fact that our interpreter does not have mirror symmetry and the direction of the contour is always clockwise. In our intended usage scenario, mirror symmetry invariance is not needed because architectural guide maps and SLAM local maps are never mirror-flipped, which will also give us some disadvantages in our tests.

Figure 6 illustrates the matching results of pattern 1 with the other three patterns, and it can be seen that the second and third patterns match relatively well, while the fourth match is less effective due to mirror symmetry matching.

Shape Matching Method Based on Growing Neural Gas 111

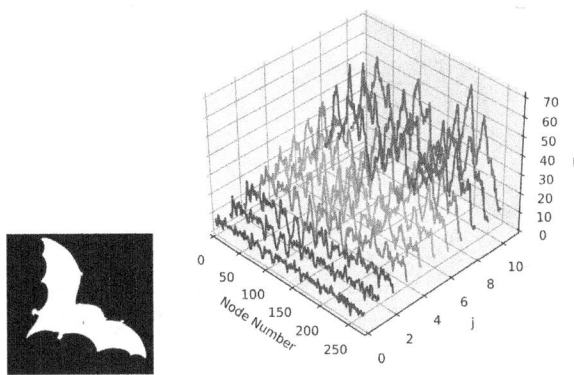

Fig. 4. Parameter P of four bat patterns.

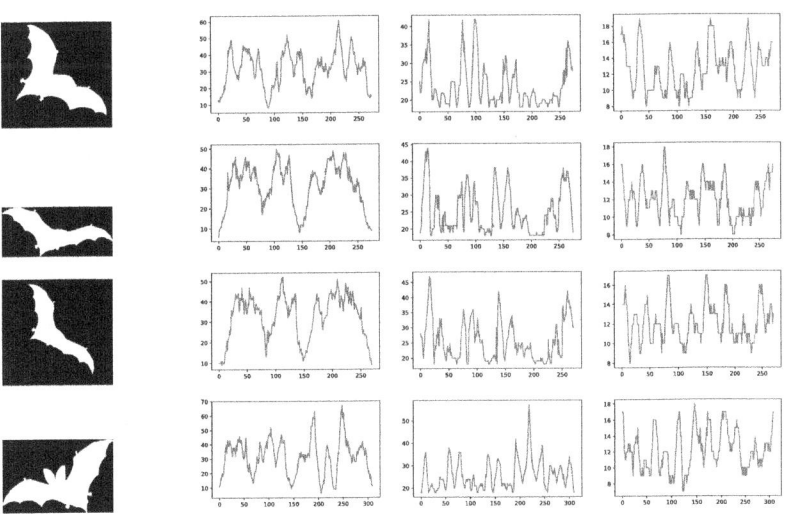

Fig. 5. A slice of the descriptor where $j = 5$ of four bat patterns.

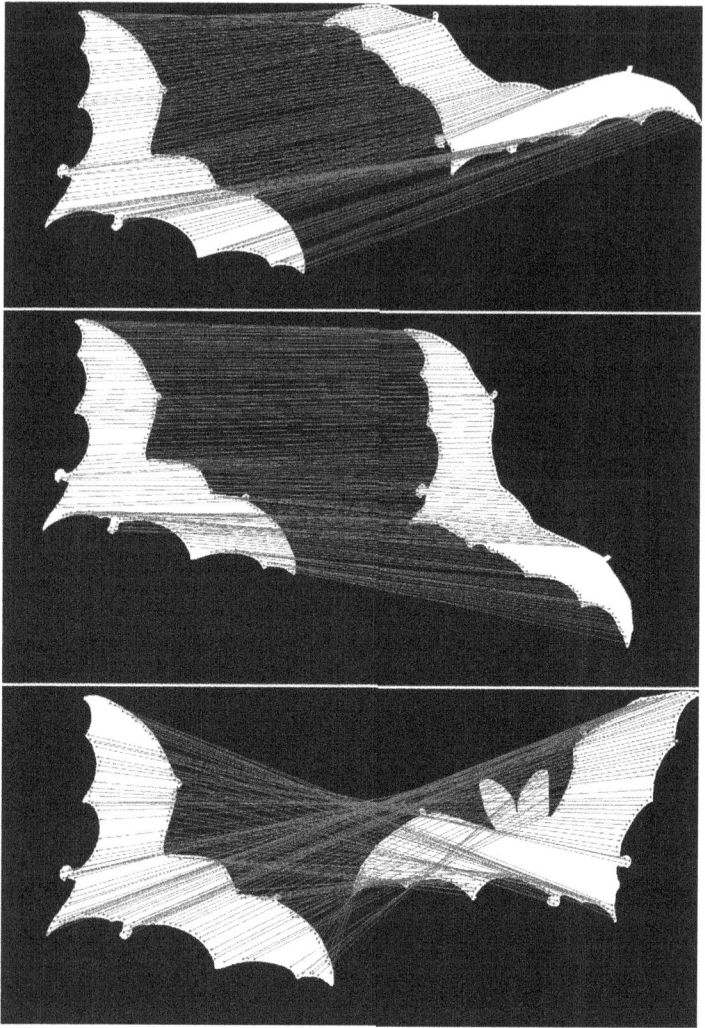

Fig. 6. Matching results between bat patterns.

4 Conclusion

With shape descriptors computed from GNG-generated topologies with different scale information, we successfully matched patterns that were simultaneously scaled and cropped. However, to meet the requirements of real-world use, some problems remain to be solved:

1. The density of the nodes is controlled manually, an algorithm that could automatically control the density is needed.

2. The results of the retrieval test prove that the current retrieval rate of this method for shapes is not satisfactory, and the calculation method of the matching error needs to be improved to improve the retrieval accuracy.
3. The nodes are matched one by one, we need to consider the situation in which the contour is somehow slightly deformed.
4. The transformation matrix between the two figures, i.e., the relationship between the sample image and the image remaining to be matched has to be calculated.

Acknowledgments. This work is supported by JSPS KAKENHI Grant Number JP24K20870 and JP25K03187.

References

1. Arica, N., Vural, F.T.Y.: A perceptual shape descriptor. In: Proceedings of the 16th International Conference on Pattern Recognition (ICPR'02), vol. 2, pp. 375–378. IEEE Computer Society (2002)
2. Backes, A.R., Casanova, D., Bruno, O.M.: A complex network-based approach for boundary shape analysis. Pattern Recogn. **42**(1), 54–67 (2009)
3. Belongie, S., Mori, G., Malik, J.: Matching with shape contexts. In: IEEE Workshop on Content-based access of Image and Video-Libraries, p. 20 (2000)
4. Torres, R.S., Falcão, A.X.: Contour salience descriptors for effective image retrieval and analysis. Image Vis. Comput. J. **25**(1), 3–13 (2007)
5. Ebrahim, Y., Ahmed, M., Abdelsalam, W., Chau, S.C.: Shape representation and description using the Hilbert curve. Pattern Recogn. Lett. **30**(4), 348–358 (2009)
6. Felzenszwalb, P.F., Schwartz, J.D.: Hierarchical matching of deformable shapes. In: IEEE Conference on Computer Vision and Pattern Recognition, pp. 1–8 (2007)
7. Ling, H., Jacobs, W.W.: Shape classification using the inner-distance. IEEE Trans. Pattern Anal. Mach. Intell. **29**(2), 286–299 (2007)
8. Wu, A., Tsang, P.W.M., Yuen, T.Y.F., Yeung, L.F.: Affine invariant object shape matching using genetic algorithm with multi-parent orthogonal recombination and migrant principle. Appl. Soft Comput. **9**(1), 282–289 (2009)
9. Cui, M., Femiani, J., Hu, J., Wonka, P., Razdan, A.: Curve matching for open 2D curves. Pattern Recogn. Lett. **30**(1), 1–10 (2009)
10. Latecki, L.J., Megalooikonomou, V., Wang, Q.A., Yu, D.: An elastic partial shape matching technique. Pattern Recogn. **40**(11), 3069–3080 (2007)
11. Fritzke, B.: A growing neural gas network learns topologies. In: Advances in Neural Information Processing Systems 7: Proceedings of the 1994 Conference, pp. 625–632. MIT Press (1995)

Enhancing 4D ViT-Driven Gesture Recognition with Decomposed HD-sEMG

Yaolun Jin[1] and Yinfeng Fang[2(✉)]

[1] School of Communication Engineering, Hangzhou Dianzi University, Hangzhou 310018, China
yaolun.jin@hdu.edu.cn
[2] Hangzhou Dianzi University, Hangzhou 310018, China
yinfeng.fang@hdu.edu.cn

Abstract. High-density surface electromyography (HD-sEMG) provides rich spatial and temporal muscle activity data, enabling accurate gesture classification. However, there are limited studies applying HD-sEMG decomposition techniques within deep learning frameworks. Despite their physiological relevance, the potential of these methods to enhance model performance through informative feature representation remains underexplored.

A novel dual-branch 4D Vision Transformer (d4D-ViT) is introduced, leveraging a publicly available 128-channel HD-sEMG dataset. This architecture fuses raw sEMG signals with MUAP peak-to-peak image features, capturing both temporal dynamics and spatial patterns. The design adapts vision-based modeling to the HD-sEMG domain while preserving biosignal characteristics. The model was evaluated on data from 19 subjects using five-fold cross-validation, achieving an average accuracy of $90.33 \pm 6.80\%$ and outperforming existing methods.

Ablation studies confirm the effectiveness of the dual-branch approach, demonstrating consistent improvements over single-branch models. This work highlights the benefits of integrating decomposition-derived features with deep learning for HD-sEMG signal processing and offers insights into future multimodal biosignal analysis.

Keywords: HD-sEMG Decomposition · Hand Gesture Recognition · 4D ViT

1 Introduction

With the rapid development of human-computer interaction technologies [2], sEMG-based gesture recognition has become a key technology in applications such as prosthetics, virtual reality, and smart environments. HD-sEMG provides rich spatial and temporal information about muscle activity through non-invasive acquisition, making it a promising signal source for intuitive and accurate gesture classification. Compared to conventional sEMG systems with limited channel counts, HD-sEMG enables more detailed mapping of neuromuscular activation patterns, offering greater potential for decoding complex hand movements.

Recent studies on the publicly available 128-channel HD-sEMG dataset [8] have explored various feature extraction and modeling strategies [1,5,11]. Traditional approaches such as Deep Wavelet Scattering [1] and Riemannian manifold analysis [5] have laid a solid theoretical foundation for understanding sEMG signal characteristics by leveraging time-frequency and geometric representations. These methods often rely on domain-specific preprocessing and feature engineering, which can improve interpretability but may limit adaptability across different tasks or subjects.

More recently, image-inspired modeling approaches [11,12] have demonstrated the feasibility of cross-domain model transfer by treating sEMG data as spatially structured signals. These methods leverage the representational flexibility of vision-based architectures and have shown improved performance over traditional CNNs and RNNs. However, most existing works focus solely on raw signal inputs or engineered features in isolation, and rarely explore how multiple complementary representations can be jointly modeled to better capture the complexity of biosignals.

In this work, we propose d4D-ViT that effectively fuses raw sEMG signals and MUAP peak-to-peak image features. Our experiments demonstrate that this architecture not only outperforms existing methods but also better captures the spatiotemporal characteristics of HD-sEMG data. By integrating both direct sensor measurements and physiologically informed decomposition features, our approach bridges the gap between signal interpretation and deep learning modeling, opening new possibilities for multimodal biosignal analysis.

2 Methodology

2.1 Original HD-sEMG Dataset

The study is based on the HD-sEMG dataset constructed by Malevsevic et al. [8], which includes 128-channel EMG signals collected from the forearms of 20 healthy volunteers. Each participant performed 65 different hand gestures, ranging from simple finger flexions and extensions to complex movements simulating daily activities or specific hand signs. The signals were acquired using the Quattrocento biomedical amplifier system at a sampling rate of 2048 Hz, with hardware high-pass and low-pass filters set at 10 Hz and 900 Hz, respectively, to enhance signal quality and reduce noise. Each electrode consists of an 8×8 matrix with a 10 mm inter-contact distance, ensuring effective coverage of the forearm's major muscle groups. Signals were recorded in differential mode to suppress common-mode noise, significantly improving the signal-to-noise ratio. Post-acquisition offline processing included a third-order zero-phase bandpass Butterworth filter to eliminate power-line interference, and synchronization pulses were used to align the time axes across all acquisition devices. This dataset provides high-quality raw signals and serves as a solid foundation for further analysis.

2.2 Raw Feature Training Set Generation

This section outlines the extraction of continuous HD-sEMG signals and their segmentation into five non-overlapping subsets for end-to-end learning (referred to as raw feature sets). It also presents a novel 4D image-based representation of HD-sEMG signals.

In end-to-end learning, no manual feature extraction is performed. Since the dataset had already been hardware-filtered, only signal segmentation was applied. Each of the 20 participants contributed one raw feature set. For each participant, two recordings–extensor and flexor muscle signals–are available, with spatial dimensions corresponding to 8×8 electrode arrays. Gesture labels (1–65) and repetition counts (1-5) were used to guide segmentation. Based on repetitions, each subject's data were divided into five folds, and each fold was segmented into 65 gesture classes using a sliding window approach [1,7,10,16].

An HD-sEMG signal can be represented as $\boldsymbol{S}_{\text{Ext}}, \boldsymbol{S}_{\text{Flex}} \in \mathbb{R}^{1 \times L \times 8 \times 8}$, where L is the temporal length. With window size W and stride S, $N = \lfloor \frac{L-W}{S} + 1 \rfloor$ samples are generated. The i-th sample is:

$$\boldsymbol{S}i = \text{concat}(\boldsymbol{S}_{\text{Ext}}[:, Wi : W(i+1)-1, :, :], \boldsymbol{S}_{\text{Flex}}[:, Wi : W(i+1)-1, :, :], \dim = 0), \quad (1)$$

where $\boldsymbol{S}_i \in \mathbb{R}^{2 \times W \times 8 \times 8}$, $i \in [0, N)$.

Instead of treating HD-sEMG as conventional 2D multi-channel signals, we propose viewing it as a 4D structure that is analogous to color images. This allows the use of computer vision models for EMG signal analysis.

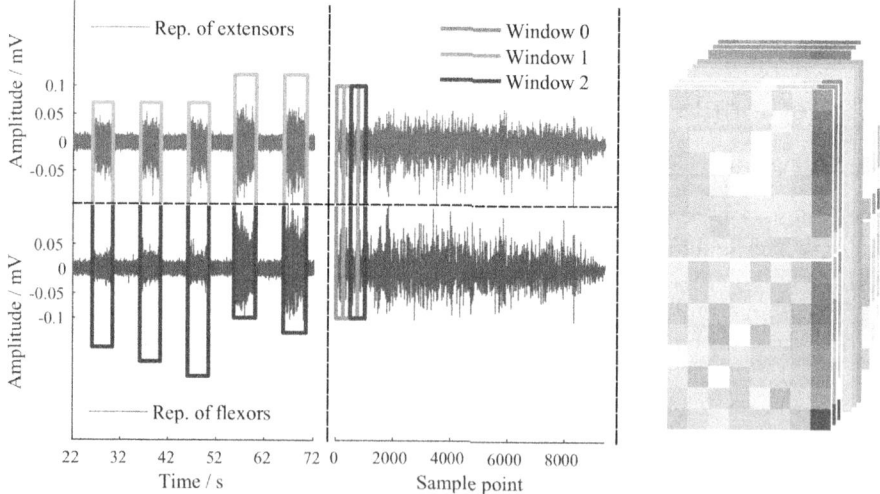

Fig. 1. Schematic Diagram of Dataset Preprocessing. The red signals represent sEMG signals from the extensors, while the blue signals represent sEMG signals from the flexors. (a) Illustrates the method for dividing the original dataset into 5 folds with 65 gesture classes. (b) Demonstrates the approach for extracting samples using a sliding window. (c) Shows a specific example of an HD-sEMG 3D Color Image sample. (Color figure online)

2.3 MUAPs Peak-to-Peak Image Feature Training Set Generation

Feature engineering for HD-sEMG signals was performed on windowed samples rather than full-length signals, ensuring that no information from the training set leaked into the validation process. In particular, the generation of MUAP peak-to-peak features was based solely on the raw feature training set, not the entire original dataset, due to the sensitivity of the blind source separation method to signal length.

The HD-sEMG decomposition algorithm used in this study was proposed by Negro et al. [13] and combines Independent Component Analysis (ICA) with Convolution Kernel Compensation (CKC) [6]. This method first applies an ICA-like fixed-point algorithm to extract initial Motor Unit Spike Trains (MUSTs). These results are then refined using CKC; the Coefficient of Variation (CoV) measures consistency, and the Silhouette Coefficient (SIL) evaluates separation quality. Decomposition outcomes are accepted or rejected based on SIL thresholds, ensuring high-quality MUSTs.

Next, spike-triggered averaging (STA) [3] was applied to estimate Motor Unit Action Potentials (MUAPs) from the extracted MUSTs. For each MUST j, with spike times $T_j = \{t_1, t_2, \ldots\}$, and a given sample $S \in \mathbb{R}^{2 \times W \times 8 \times 8}$, MUAPs were computed using pre- and post-spike windows defined by parameters L and R, respectively:

$$A[i, k, m, n] = \frac{1}{\text{card}(T_j)} \sum_{t \in T_j} S[i, (t-L+k), m, n], \quad \text{for } k = 0, 1, \ldots, L+R, \quad (2)$$

resulting in $P \in \mathbb{R}^{2 \times N_{\text{MUST}} \times 8 \times 8}$, where the second dimension reflects the number of decomposed MUSTs.

Finally, peak-to-peak images were constructed by computing the difference between the maximum and minimum values across the temporal dimension:

$$P[i, j, m, n] = \max(A[i, :, m, n]) - \min(A[i, :, m, n]), \quad (3)$$

resulting in $P \in \mathbb{R}^{2 \times N_{\text{MUST}} \times 8 \times 8}$.

2.4 The Proposed 4D ViT

This section provides a detailed explanation of the 4D Input Vision Transformer with single backbone (s4D-ViT) adopted in this paper, with particular emphasis on core components such as patch embedding, position embedding, multi-head self-attention mechanism (MHSA), and feed-forward neural network (FFN). We also explore the implementation details, laying the theoretical foundation for a variant based on the s4D-ViT: the d4D-ViT. This variant enhances the capability to handle more input features by parallelizing two s4D-ViT models. When discussing these variants, our focus is on their structural frameworks and how to effectively utilize these structures to process the increased input feature dimensionality.

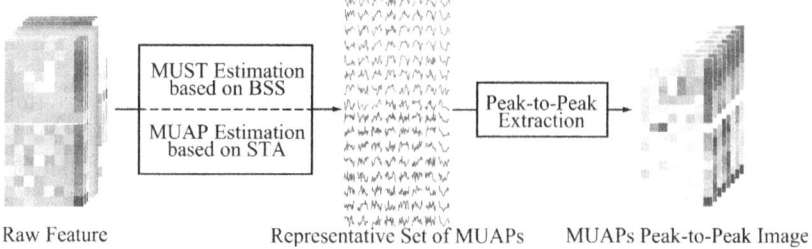

Fig. 2. MUAPs Peak-to-Peak Image Feature Extraction: the figure illustrates the extraction process. Initially, raw features are processed through Blind Source Separation (BSS) methods to estimate 8 MUSTs. Subsequently, these MUSTs are combined with the raw features and processed through STA technique to estimate the corresponding 8 sets of MUAPs. Finally, the peak-to-peak values of each set are extracted and concatenated to construct the MUAP Peak-to-Peak Image Feature.

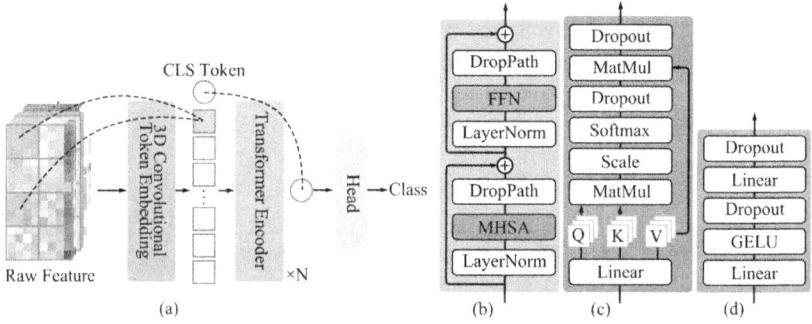

Fig. 3. The Pipeline of s4D-ViT. (a) Overall architecture, showing the schematic process of converting 4D input into tokens through the 3D Convolutional Token Embedding layer. (b) Details of the Transformer Encoder. (c) Details of the MHSA module. (d) Details of the FFN module.

3D Convolutional Token Embedding To process 4D HD-sEMG signals, this work adapts the Vision Transformer (ViT) [4] by introducing a 3D convolutional token embedding module. Given an input sample $S \in \mathbb{R}^{c_s \times d_s \times h_s \times w_s}$, where $c_s = 2$ denotes the two electrode plates and d_s is the temporal (window) dimension, each plate has an 8×8 spatial layout ($h_s = w_s = 8$).

The input is divided into non-overlapping 3D patches $P \in \mathbb{R}^{c_p \times d_p \times h_p \times w_p}$, with $c_p = c_s = 2$, and patch dimensions chosen to evenly divide the input. This results in $n_p = n_d \times n_h \times n_w$ patches per sample. These patches are flattened and linearly projected into tokens using 3D convolution, inspired by the CvT architecture [18].

For a batch of inputs $X_{\text{PAin}} \in \mathbb{R}^{b \times c_s \times d_s \times h_s \times w_s}$, a 3D convolution with kernel size and stride matching the patch dimensions maps each patch to a d_{embed}-dimensional token. The output is reshaped to $X'_{\text{PA}} \in \mathbb{R}^{b \times n_p \times d_{\text{embed}}}$. A learnable

CLS token T_cls is then prepended to the token sequence:

$$X_\text{PAout} = \text{concat}(\text{repeat}(T_\text{cls}, b), X'_\text{PA}), \tag{4}$$

resulting in $X_\text{PAout} \in \mathbb{R}^{b \times n_\text{t} \times d_\text{embed}}$, where $n_\text{t} = 1 + n_\text{p}$.

Since the transformer encoder processes tokens independently, positional information must be explicitly encoded. A trainable positional embedding $P \in \mathbb{R}^{1 \times n_\text{t} \times d_\text{embed}}$ is added to preserve temporal and spatial structure:

$$X_\text{POout} = X_\text{PAout} + \text{repeat}(P, b). \tag{5}$$

Transformer Encoder This study employs a classic transformer encoder for feature extraction from HD-sEMG signals. For simplicity, we omit the batch size dimension b. The input tensor to the encoder is $X_\text{EN} \in \mathbb{R}^{n_\text{t} \times d_\text{embed}}$, derived from position embedding. The encoder operations can be summarized as:

$$Y_\text{En} = X_\text{En} + \text{DropPath}(\text{MHSA}(\text{LayerNorm}(X_\text{En}))), \tag{6}$$

$$Z_\text{En} = Y_\text{En} + \text{DropPath}(\text{FFN}(\text{LayerNorm}(Y_\text{En}))), \tag{7}$$

where $Y_\text{En}, Z_\text{En} \in \mathbb{R}^{n_\text{t} \times d_\text{embed}}$.

The Multi-Head Self-Attention (MHSA) module takes an input tensor $X_\text{AttnIn} \in \mathbb{R}^{n_\text{t} \times d_\text{embed}}$ and expands it via a linear transformation:

$$X_\text{Attn} = X_\text{AttnIn} W_\text{AttnIn}, \tag{8}$$

where $X_\text{Attn} \in \mathbb{R}^{n_\text{t} \times 3d_\text{embed}}$. This step generates query (Q), key (K), and value (V) vectors:

$$X'_\text{Attn} = \text{reshape}(X_\text{Attn}, [n_\text{t}, 3, n_\text{h}, d_\text{h}]), \tag{9}$$

$$[Q \ K \ V] = X_\text{QKV} = \text{permute}(X'_\text{Attn}, [1, 2, 0, 3]). \tag{10}$$

Here, n_h is the number of heads and d_h is the dimension per head. Scaled dot-product attention is applied:

$$X''_\text{Attn} = \text{Attention}(Q, K, V) = \text{softmax}(\frac{QK^\text{T}}{\sqrt{d_\text{h}}})V. \tag{11}$$

The output is reshaped and passed through a linear layer:

$$X_\text{AttnOut} = X'''_\text{Attn} W_\text{AttnOut}. \tag{12}$$

The Feed-Forward Neural Network (FFN) module processes the output with a sequence of layers: a linear layer, GELU activation, Dropout, another linear layer, and Dropout. This introduces non-linearity to complement the linear nature of attention mechanisms, enhancing the model's ability to capture complex patterns.

By integrating non-linear transformations, FFN improves the learning capacity and expressiveness of the model, making it more effective in handling intricate data relationships. The use of two linear layers with activations and Dropout facilitates complex transformations in high-dimensional space, crucial for robust feature extraction and representation learning.

2.5 The Proposed D4D-ViT

As illustrated in Fig. 4, d4D-ViT represents parallel extensions of the s4D-ViT architecture. Since both backbones process feature maps from the same perspective, they can conveniently share the same interface. However, since the two types of features used in this study have distinct interpretations along the second dimension, different patch embedding strategies are designed accordingly.

Let the two types of features be denoted as $F_{\text{Raw}}, F_{\text{Mptop}} \in \mathbb{R}^{c_s \times d_s \times h_s \times w_s}$, where $c_s = 2, h_s = w_s = 8$. For F_{Raw}, $d_s = W = 512$, representing the window size, allowing flexible selection of the patch size to balance signal resolution in both temporal and spatial domains. For F_{Mptop}, $d_s = 8$ indicates the number of MUs in the decomposition result. The MUAPs Peak-to-Peak Image Feature fixes the depth of the patches as $d_p = 1$, while the height and width are set according to the required spatial resolution.

The head consists of a linear layer, a LayerNorm, and another linear layer to fuse the CLS tokens from the two backbones and generate the final prediction.

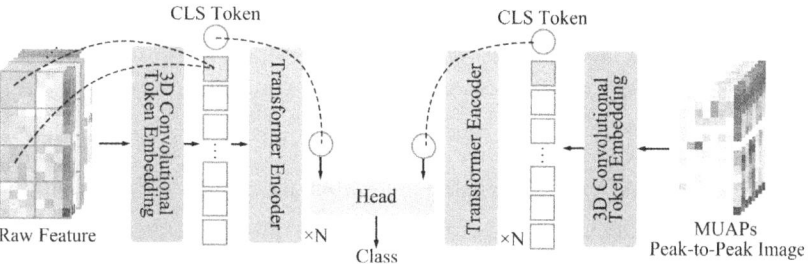

Fig. 4. The Pipeline of d4D-ViT.

3 Experiments

3.1 Environment and Parameter Settings

In this study, the model construction and training validation programs were developed using LibTorch, the C++ API of PyTorch. The experimental platform was configured with a 13th Gen Intel® Core™ i7-13700KF CPU, two 16 GB DDR5 memory modules, and an NVIDIA GeForce RTX 4080 SUPER GPU. All experiments employed a within-subject five-fold cross-validation method, where each subject's repeated gestures served sequentially as the validation set to ensure comprehensive and reliable evaluation.

For the backbone network taking Raw Features as input, we set the patch size to $d_p = h_p = w_p = 8$. For the backbone utilizing the MUAPs Peak-to-Peak Features as inputs, we set the patch size to $d_p = 1, h_p = w_p = 8$. For simplicity and efficiency, all other hyperparameters were kept consistent between the two backbones: an embedding dimension $d_{\text{embed}} = 288$, a single encoder layer, 12 heads in the Multi-Head Self-Attention (MHSA) module, a feed-forward network (FFN) intermediate dimension four times the embedding dimension (i.e., 1152), and a dropout rate of 0.3 for all dropout layers. Given the single encoder layer, the drop path rate was set to 0.0. The head comprised a linear layer with output dimension equal to its input dimension, a LayerNorm layer, and a linear layer mapping the features to classifications among 65 gesture classes. The model was trained for 41 epochs (from 0 to 40) with a batch size of 256, utilizing the Adam optimizer configured with $\beta_1 = 0.9$, $\beta_2 = 0.999$, and a weight decay of 0.001. The first two epochs were used for warm-up, during which the learning rate followed: $(0.9 \times \text{epoch}/2 + 0.1) \times 1 \times 10^{-4}$. Subsequently, the learning rate followed a cosine annealing schedule with warm-up, where the initial learning rate was set to $\alpha = 0.001$ and the warm-up period was $W = 2$ epochs. The specific formula for the learning rate adjustment is as follows:

$$\eta = \begin{cases} (0.9 \times \frac{t}{W} + 0.1) \times \alpha, & t \leq W \\ \max(0.5 \times (1 + \cos(\pi \times \frac{t-W}{T-W})) \times \alpha, \frac{\alpha}{10}), & t > W \end{cases}. \tag{13}$$

3.2 Benchmarking Against Existing Models

To evaluate the effectiveness of the proposed 4D ViT model, we extensively reviewed various related works that employed the same dataset [8] for gesture recognition, including but not limited to Graph Neural Networks and Long Short-Term Memory Networks. However, because all relevant studies are either closed-source or semi-open-source, it was not possible to conduct a direct comparison under identical experimental conditions. Therefore, differences in computational platforms and configurations may affect the performance results. Nevertheless, this study aims to demonstrate the potential and advantages of the d4D-ViT model within our experimental setup.

Specifically, the works cited in [1,7] lack detailed descriptions of how the training and validation sets were divided, which could introduce bias in performance estimation due to improper sample allocation. Additionally, reference [5] does not specify the settings for window size and stride, which can have significant implications on the distribution of sample data and subsequent analysis results. Consequently, these studies and their corresponding models were excluded from our comparative analysis.

For the remaining relevant studies that meet the criteria, this paper provides detailed information on their window sizes and strides, training-validation set divisions, feature engineering methods, and final classification accuracies in subsequent sections. This approach facilitates a more systematic and scientific comparative analysis.

3.3 Ablation Study on Single-Branch Architectures

To assess the effective utilization of both the Raw Feature and the MUAP Peak-to-Peak Image Feature, as well as the contribution of dual-branch feature fusion in d4D-ViT, we designed a set of ablation experiments based on single-branch variants.

We constructed two single-branch models: s4D-ViT (Raw Feature, R) and s4D-ViT (MUAP Peak-to-Peak Image Feature, Mptop), which were derived from the full dual-branch d4D-ViT model. Specifically, we modified the architecture by removing the linear layer in the head that was originally responsible for fusing the dual-branch features. The input dimensions of the LayerNorm and the final linear layer were also adjusted accordingly. The rest of the architecture remained identical to that of d4D-ViT.

All models were trained and evaluated under the same hyperparameter settings and training/validation data splits. We performed five-fold cross-validation across 19 subjects and compared the average accuracy of the three models to evaluate the effectiveness of each modality and the contribution of dual-branch feature fusion.

4 Results and Discussion

4.1 Benchmarking Against Existing Models

Table 1 summarizes the five-fold cross-validation results of the proposed d4D-ViT model across 19 subjects, including per-fold accuracy, per-subject averages, and the overall average validation accuracy. The model achieves an average accuracy of $90.33 \pm 6.80\%$, demonstrating stable performance across different folds and subjects.

As shown in Table 2, the d4D-ViT model outperforms previous approaches under a consistent evaluation protocol across the same dataset, most of which are based on handcrafted features or conventional CNN-based architectures.

Among the compared models, the work cited in [11] achieves the highest previously reported accuracy of $89.34 \pm 2.61\%$. Our model extends previous designs by incorporating similar feature inputs (e.g., MUAP peak-to-peak images) into a dual-branch ViT architecture that enables more effective feature fusion and representation learning. This structural enhancement may therefore contribute to the observed performance improvement.

It should be noted that differences in training protocols and reporting practices across studies may hinder direct comparisons of variance or stability metrics. Nevertheless, our results demonstrate the effectiveness of the proposed method within the current experimental setup.

Table 1. Five-fold Cross-validation Accuracy of the d4D-ViT Model on 19 Subjects. It includes the average accuracy per subject, the average accuracy per fold, and the final average accuracy, with data deviation measured using the sample standard deviation.

subject	Fold 1 (%)	Fold 2 (%)	Fold 3 (%)	Fold 4 (%)	Fold 5 (%)	Average (%)
s1	83.60	92.89	97.60	97.36	93.79	93.05 ± 5.08
s2	89.16	96.34	97.16	94.15	93.98	94.16 ± 2.78
s3	68.88	92.16	96.53	94.11	88.84	88.10 ± 9.94
s4	83.14	96.23	95.40	95.91	92.27	92.59 ± 4.93
s6	75.46	87.66	92.93	93.43	86.16	87.13 ± 6.49
s7	84.14	91.37	93.85	92.98	86.65	89.80 ± 3.77
s8	87.97	95.69	96.71	98.34	92.00	94.14 ± 3.72
s9	80.56	92.17	96.51	95.03	89.96	90.84 ± 5.62
s10	79.91	94.43	92.08	93.21	87.04	89.33 ± 5.34
s11	80.47	95.65	92.69	93.65	90.57	90.61 ± 5.32
s12	85.21	97.98	94.97	94.89	92.62	93.14 ± 4.31
s13	73.82	84.90	84.41	82.33	81.57	81.41 ± 3.99
s14	84.84	90.04	94.68	96.08	92.25	91.58 ± 3.95
s15	75.14	92.57	95.42	91.12	86.19	88.09 ± 7.13
s16	71.43	83.33	86.60	85.49	81.25	81.62 ± 5.42
s17	87.94	98.22	98.50	97.41	96.39	95.69 ± 3.94
s18	85.36	94.84	91.68	95.45	94.92	92.45 ± 3.79
s19	71.52	87.62	92.08	87.35	86.08	84.93 ± 7.00
s20	96.14	97.46	98.70	98.85	96.52	97.53 ± 1.10
Average (%)	81.30 ± 7.11	92.71 ± 4.35	94.13 ± 3.75	93.53 ± 4.32	89.95 ± 4.55	**90.33 ± 6.80**

4.2 Ablation Study on Single-Branch Architectures

Table 3 presents the average validation accuracy and sample standard deviation across 19 subjects, comparing the dual-branch d4D-ViT model with its two single-branch variants: s4D-ViT (R), which uses only raw features, and s4D-ViT (Mptop), which uses only MUAP peak-to-peak image features.

Both single-branch models achieve comparable performance, with average accuracies of 87.07 ± 7.22% and 87.21 ± 7.89%, respectively. These results indicate that both input modalities provide informative features for the classification task and that each branch alone is capable of achieving reasonable performance. However, the dual-branch d4D-ViT model outperforms both single-branch variants with an average improvement of approximately 3.13.2% points, achieving an overall accuracy of 90.33 ± 6.80%.

Table 2. Comparison of classification accuracy and STD obtained by the other works on our utilized dataset.

Reference	Window Size, Stride (ms)	Feature Engineering	Train / Test Split	Accuracy (%)
Ref. [15]	200, 10	Min-Max Norm, μ-Law Norm	5-Fold Cross Validation	83.33
Ref. [16]	200, 10	Min-Max Norm, μ-Law Norm	5-Fold Cross Validation	84.60
Ref. [12]	32, 16	LPF, μ-Law Norm	5-Fold Cross Validation	84.62 ± 3.07
Ref. [11]	250, 125	MUAP Peak-to-Peak Image	5-Fold Cross Validation	86.64 ± 3.10
Ref. [17]	200, 10	BPF, Z-Score Norm	Fold 1, 3, 4 / Fold 2, 5	87.60
Ref. [11]	250, 125	LPF, μ-Law Norm	5-Fold Cross Validation	89.34 ± 2.61
d4D-ViT	250, 125	Raw Signals, MUAP Peak-to-Peak Image	5-Fold Cross Validation	**90.33 ± 6.80**

This performance gain indicates that the proposed dual-branch architecture effectively captures complementary information from both feature modalities. The consistent improvement observed across all five folds suggests that the feature fusion mechanism enhances the model's generalization and robustness.

Table 3. The table provides the average validation accuracy and sample standard deviation across 19 subjects for each fold, for the three models.

Model	Fold 1 (%)	Fold 2 (%)	Fold 3 (%)	Fold 4 (%)	Fold 5 (%)	Average (%)
s4D-ViT (R)	76.53 ± 5.90	89.52 ± 4.52	91.67 ± 3.84	90.88 ± 4.29	86.73 ± 4.76	87.07 ± 7.22
s4D-ViT (Mptop)	78.01 ± 8.07	89.93 ± 5.65	90.87 ± 5.52	90.59 ± 6.09	86.66 ± 6.05	87.21 ± 7.89
d4D-ViT	81.30 ± 7.11	92.71 ± 4.35	94.13 ± 3.75	93.53 ± 4.32	89.95 ± 4.55	**90.33 ± 6.80**

4.3 Discussion

The rationale for not conducting within-subject experiments is evident from the data in Table 1. Physiological signals such as sEMG exhibit considerable inter-subject variability. Even within the same subject, factors like electrode displacement or changes in physiological state can cause significant signal fluctuations. Specifically, as shown in Table 1, when Fold 1 is used as the validation set and Folds 25 as the training sets, the recognition accuracy is significantly lower than in other configurations.

We hypothesize that during a subject's first execution of a gesture, the motor unit physiology must be re-established, leading to notable changes in the generated sEMG signals. In subsequent repetitions, where the physiological logic remains stable, the underlying features of the signals are largely preserved from the initial action. In other words, evidence suggests the presence of a Muscle Memory phenomenon in sEMG signals, akin to observations reported in studies on Muscle Fatigue [9,14].

Given the uncertainties inherent in real-world gesture execution, we recommend that researchers adopt randomized gesture sequences during dataset collection, rather than repeating each gesture multiple times consecutively. Although this approach increases data collection complexity and cost, mitigating the sEMG Memory phenomenon is crucial for constructing a more generalized and robust dataset.

5 Conclusion

In this work, we propose a dual-branch 4D Vision Transformer (d4D-ViT) for sEMG-based gesture recognition, designed to effectively fuse raw signals with MUAP peak-to-peak image features. Evaluated on 19 subjects through five-fold cross-validation, the model achieved an average accuracy of $90.33 \pm 6.80\%$, outperforming existing approaches under comparable experimental settings.

Ablation studies demonstrated that each single-branch variant (raw-only or MUAP-only) achieved approximately 87% accuracy, whereas the dual-branch architecture improved performance by approximately 3% points, highlighting the benefits of feature fusion.

The observed performance variations across folds suggest potential "Muscle Memory" effects in repeated gestures, indicating the importance of adopting randomized data collection protocols to enhance model generalization.

Overall, d4D-ViT represents a promising framework for multimodal sEMG modeling and provides meaningful insights into the nature of surface electromyographic signals.

References

1. Al Taee, A.A., Khushaba, R.N., Zia, T., Al-Jumaily, A.: The effectiveness of narrowing the window size for LD & HD EMG channels based on novel deep learning wavelet scattering transform feature extraction approach. In: 2022 44th Annual International Conference of the IEEE Engineering in Medicine & Biology Society (EMBC), pp. 3698–3701. IEEE (2022)
2. Chen, C., et al.: Hand gesture recognition based on motor unit spike trains decoded from high-density electromyography. Biomed. Signal Process. Control **55**, 101637 (2020)
3. Dayan, P., Abbott, L.F.: Theoretical neuroscience: computational and mathematical modeling of neural systems. MIT press (2005)
4. Dosovitskiy, A., et al.: An image is worth 16×16 words: transformers for image recognition at scale. arXiv preprint arXiv:2010.11929 (2020)
5. Gowda, H.T., Miller, L.M.: Topology of surface electromyogram signals: hand gesture decoding on Riemannian manifolds. J. Neural Eng. **21**(3), 036047 (2024)
6. Holobar, A., Zazula, D.: Multichannel blind source separation using convolution kernel compensation. IEEE Trans. Signal Process. **55**(9), 4487–4496 (2007)
7. Khushaba, R.N., Nazarpour, K.: Decoding HD-EMG signals for myoelectric control-how small can the analysis window size be? IEEE Robot. Autom. Lett. **6**(4), 8569–8574 (2021)
8. Malešević, N., et al.: A database of high-density surface electromyogram signals comprising 65 isometric hand gestures. Sci. Data **8**(1), 63 (2021)

9. Marco, G., Alberto, B., Taian, V.: Surface EMG and muscle fatigue: multi-channel approaches to the study of myoelectric manifestations of muscle fatigue. Physiol. Meas. **38**(5), R27 (2017)
10. Massa, S.M., Riboni, D., Nazarpour, K.: Graph neural networks for HD EMG-based movement intention recognition: an initial investigation. In: 2022 IEEE International Conference on Recent Advances in Systems Science and Engineering (RASSE), pp. 1–4. IEEE (2022)
11. Montazerin, M., Rahimian, E., Naderkhani, F., Atashzar, S.F., Alinejad-Rokny, H., Mohammadi, A.: Hydra-HGR: a hybrid transformer-based architecture for fusion of macroscopic and microscopic neural drive information. In: ICASSP 2023-2023 IEEE International Conference on Acoustics, Speech and Signal Processing (ICASSP), pp. 1–5. IEEE (2023)
12. Montazerin, M., Zabihi, S., Rahimian, E., Mohammadi, A., Naderkhani, F.: ViT-HGR: vision transformer-based hand gesture recognition from high density surface EMG signals. In: 2022 44th Annual International Conference of the IEEE Engineering in Medicine & Biology Society (EMBC), pp. 5115–5119. IEEE (2022)
13. Negro, F., Muceli, S., Castronovo, A.M., Holobar, A., Farina, D.: Multi-channel intramuscular and surface EMG decomposition by convolutive blind source separation. J. Neural Eng. **13**(2), 026027 (2016)
14. PA, K., et al.: Automated detection of muscle fatigue conditions from cyclostationary based geometric features of surface electromyography signals. Comput. Methods Biomech. Biomed. Eng. **25**(3) (2022)
15. Sun, T., Hu, Q., Libby, J., Atashzar, S.F.: Deep heterogeneous dilation of LSTM for transient-phase gesture prediction through high-density electromyography: Towards application in neurorobotics. IEEE Robot. Autom. Lett. **7**(2), 2851–2858 (2022)
16. Sun, T., Libby, J., Rizzo, J., Atashzar, S.F.: Deep augmentation for electrode shift compensation in transient high-density SEMG: towards application in neurorobotics. In: 2022 IEEE/RSJ International Conference on Intelligent Robots and Systems (IROS), pp. 6148–6153. IEEE (2022)
17. Tyacke, E., Gupta, K., Patel, J., Katoch, R., Atashzar, S.F.: From unstable electrode contacts to reliable control: a deep learning approach for HD-SEMG in neurorobotics. In: 2024 IEEE International Conference on Robotics and Automation (ICRA), pp. 7874–7879. IEEE (2024)
18. Wu, H., et al.: CVT: introducing convolutions to vision transformers. In: Proceedings of the IEEE/CVF International Conference on Computer Vision, pp. 22–31 (2021)

Intelligent Technology in Healthcare

Mamdani Fuzzy Assessment System for Oral Motor Exercise Tasks

Chyan Zheng Siow[1], Qingwei Song[1(✉)], Yuqi Zhang[1], Zongying Liu[3], Adnan Rachmat Anom Besari[1,2], and Naoyuki Kubota[1]

[1] Tokyo Metropolitan University, Tokyo 191-0065, Japan
qingwei-song@ed.tmu.ac.jp
[2] Politeknik Elektronika Negeri Surabaya, Surabaya 60111, Indonesia
[3] Dalian Maritime University, Dalian 116026, LiaoNing, China

Abstract. Oral motor exercises are important for people of all ages, especially the elderly, as they help maintain optimal oral health, including activities such as eating, swallowing, and speaking. Visually recognizing oral movements can be challenging due to subtle variations in individual facial expressions. Furthermore, even when accurately recognized, judging the effectiveness of these exercises can be difficult. To address these challenges, this paper proposes to utilize machine learning models for recognition and then evaluate oral motor exercises using a Mamdani fuzzy inference system. The Wang-Mendel method has been shown to be effective in generating interpretable fuzzy systems by generating fuzzy rules directly from numerical data. However, it must be acknowledged that the main application of rules generated by this method is for recognition purposes rather than for exercise evaluation. In response to this limitation, this paper proposes a new method to filter out effective variables from Wang-Mendel method rules and use these variables to generate inference rules for the Mamdani fuzzy inference system for the assessment task. In order to evaluate the effectiveness of the proposed method, 13 different oral motor exercise datasets of 9 college students were collected. Experimental results demonstrate the effectiveness of the proposed method in rejecting unlearned exercises and recalibrate predictions, achieving an accuracy of 73% under leave-one-subject-out cross validation.

Keywords: oral motor exercises · Mamdani fuzzy inference system · assessment system · facial blendshape coefficients · reject options · recalibrate predictions

1 Introduction

The use of technology in the field of rehabilitation has been the focus of extensive research in recent years. Technologies such as robotic exoskeletons [1], virtual reality (VR) [2] and wearable devices have opened up new avenues for rehabilitation and assessment by integrating artificial intelligence (AI). The scope of rehabilitation covers a wide range, including physical aspects such as fingers, arms, hands and legs, as well as cognitive aspects such as memory, attention and understanding. Injured, ill or disabled individuals require rehabilitation to restore and enhance their physical and cognitive abilities. In addition to this, an important aspect that deserves great attention is the decline in physical and functional reserves of normal people, a phenomenon often referred to as "frailty".

Oral frailty has always been overlooked. Oral frailty refers to the decline in oral function that is common among older adults [3]. It includes difficulty chewing and swallowing, which may be due to age-related changes in oral structure and function. This condition may lead to malnutrition, reduced quality of life, and an increased risk of general frailty. To resolve this, we can perform oral motor exercises daily to maintain such oral function. To motivate the elderly or people to perform such exercises every day, we can develop a monitoring AI at the washbasin to guide and evaluate such exercises.

Several techniques have been developed to recognize such exercises, including k-nearest neighbors (KNN), decision trees, support vector machine (SVM), multi-layer perceptrons (MLP), and convolutional neural network (CNN). This system has shown high accuracy; however, it is flawed in two aspects: The first is the reject option [4]. The reject option is to discard unlearned exercises or unsuccessful exercises because deep learning may incorrectly classify unlearned exercises as learned [5], which may lead to incorrect conclusions about the lifelog of a person. The second missing feature is the evaluation score, which determines how well the exercise was performed. To address these deficiencies, a new approach is proposed in this paper. The approach involves implementing the Mamdani inference fuzzy system integrated with a machine learning model to remedy the above shortcomings.

The Mamdani fuzzy inference system, developed by Professor Ebrahim Mamdani in 1975 [6], is a prominent example of a fuzzy logic system. It has gained great popularity in the field of control systems and decision-making processes due to its intuitive and rule-based approach. These rule-based approaches allow for easy modification of rules to evaluate the effectiveness of an exercise and to recognize and reject falsely recognized categories. The integration of facial blendshape coefficient extraction functions as inputs to fuzzy models has been facilitated [7]. For example, a rule is established stating that if "jaw opening" then is "yawing". However, this coefficient varies greatly between individuals, with some people having a smiling default expression while others having a serious expression, resulting in different values for these coefficients. To address this challenge, we propose to use delta coefficients as inputs to the fuzzy model. First, the default coefficients of the subjects are recorded, and then the delta coefficients are calculated as the difference between these default coefficients. However, determining the evaluation score from the input features remains a significant challenge. Fortunately, the advent of the Wang-Mendel method [8] has made it possible to generate rules from raw data. However, this process often generates a large number of redundant rules, which affects the evaluation of exercise performance. Therefore, this paper proposes a new method to screen out effective variables from these rules and use the effective variables to generate assessment rules, thereby forming a Mamdani fuzzy assessment system.

To verify the effectiveness of the proposed method, we collected 13 different sets of oral motor exercises from 9 college students. The experimental results show that the normalized coefficient in the prediction of the machine learning model is stable. In addition, the proposed Mamdani fuzzy assessment system successfully eliminates the unlearned categories and recalibrate predictions.

This paper is organized as follows. Section 2 reviews related work. Section 3 discusses the overall oral motor exercise assessment model. Section 4 describes the setup and data collection in detail. Section 5 presents and discuss the effectiveness of the proposed approach. In the last two section, we discuss and conclude the paper, highlighting the core aspects of the proposed approach and suggesting future research directions.

2 Related Work

Rejecting options is not a novel idea, as neural networks can easily recognize input data based on the data they have learned, but it is not good at rejecting those non-learned categories. In order to distinguish these unlearned categories, additional unknown data needs to be collected as unlearned categories. This in turn increases the cost of data collection. In previous methods, the k-means algorithm is used to generate key nodes (i.e., key information) from the data of each category [5]. Subsequently, the activation score of each key feature is calculated in the inference phase. If the key node is not activated, it can be inferred that the incoming data has not been learned. Another similar study implemented a two-stage rejection option where a machine learning model was employed after the threshold-based decision of the fuzzy classifier. In cases where the class labels predicted by the machine learning model and the fuzzy classifier were the same, the fuzzy classifier would output the predicted class label without rejection [4]. In this paper, we propose a method that emulates the two-stage rejection option technique described in a previous paper. In the initial stage, a machine learning model is employed, and in the subsequent stage, a Mamdani fuzzy inference system is employed. A notable feature of our method is the introduction of a new technique that can efficiently generate rules from data and use these rules to reject categories that the machine learning model has not yet learned. This approach eliminates the necessity for the machine learning model to absorb additional unknown data, a task that can place a heavy burden on complex models.

Exercise assessment is essential to determine the current condition of the user, especially in rehabilitation tasks. In this type of assessment, fuzzy inference systems emerge as the best approach, primarily because they are able to provide the user with an inference score and an error tolerance, allowing errors during movement to be ignored. This error tolerance is important because it can improve an individual's self-efficacy, thereby facilitating their adherence to an exercise program. In earlier studies, a topological approach was initially employed to recognize essential exercise postures [9]. These postures were subsequently converted into fuzzy membership functions. Afterwards, the similarity scores with the essential postures were calculated and then incorporated into the fuzzy inference system to accomplish the assessment task. From their experiments, it was demonstrated that a fuzzy system could be used to calculate the score of a user performing simple exercises and reject those erroneous exercises by setting a threshold. While the effectiveness of this approach in recognizing similarities with basic exercise postures has been demonstrated, its limitations become apparent when oral motor exercises are considered. There are two reasons for this limitation: first, there are a large number of facial action units; second, there is little difference between facial coefficients.

3 Proposed Method

Mamdani fuzzy inference system can be a viable rejection and evaluation tool, depending on the specification of rules during the inference process. Manually constructing rules is a challenging task; therefore, this paper adopts the Wang-Mendel method to generate potential rules from data. However, the rules output by Wang-Mendel are redundant and some rules are unnecessary. To address this challenge, a new method is proposed to filter out effective variables from the generated rules and use these effective variables to generate assessment rules for the fuzzy inference system. The proposed method is shown in Fig. 1, which illustrates the overall system architecture.

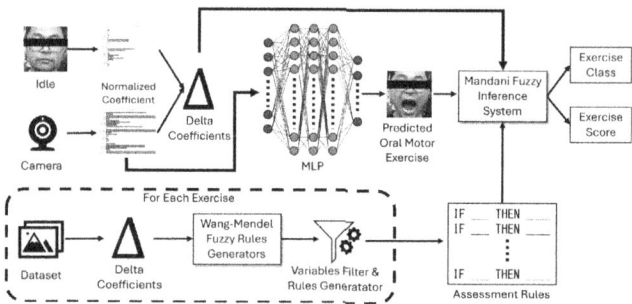

Fig. 1. The overall system of the proposed method to oral motor exercise recognition and assessment task.

3.1 Facial Blendshape Coefficient

This paper utilizes facial blendshape coefficients provided by MediaPipe [7], which contain 52 facial features. However, not all features are equally applicable to oral motor training. Therefore, this paper only uses features related to the mouth, namely "jaw forward", "jaw left", "jaw open", "jaw right", "mouth close", "mouth dimple left", "mouth dimple right", "mouth frown left", "mouth frown right", "mouth funnel", "mouth left", "mouth lower down left", "mouth lower down right", "mouth press left", "mouth press right", "mouth pucker", "mouth right", "mouth roll lower", "mouth roll upper", "mouth shrug lower", "mouth shrug upper", "mouth smile left", "mouth smile right", "mouth stretch left", "mouth stretch right", "mouth upper up left", and "mouth upper up right".

It is well known that the idle facial features vary from person to person, with some people showing a smile while others display a serious expression. This paper exploits the delta feature between any facial feature and idle facial features. This approach enables a fuzzy assessment system to discern the difference and then provide an evaluation score. To illustrate this concept, consider a subject with a downward curvature of the mouth. Although the subject's smile may not be obvious, it can be discerned and evaluated through discernible differences.

Before calculating the delta coefficient, the data is normalized according to the interquartile range (IQR). IQR is a measure of the statistical dispersion or distribution of a data set. It is often used to measure outlier data. In this article, the IQR of each feature is calculated using the entire data set, and then the data is normalized using the upper bound as follows:

$$Q_k^R \leftarrow Q_k^3 - Q_k^1, \forall k \in x_i \qquad (1)$$

$$\dot{x}_{i,k} \leftarrow \max\left(\frac{x_{i,k}}{Q_k^3 + 1.5 \times Q_k^R}, 1\right), \forall i \in X \qquad (2)$$

where Q_k^R is IQR of k-th feature, Q_k^3 represents the 75th percentile of k-th feature, Q_k^1 represents the 25th percentile of k-th feature, x_i is the i-th datum of the dataset X, and $\dot{x}$ is the normalized coefficients.

After obtaining the normalized coefficient, we subtract it from the recorded idle coefficient, the formula is as follows:

$$\ddot{x}_i^p \leftarrow |\dot{x}_i^p - \dot{x}^{p,idle}| \qquad (3)$$

where $\dot{x}^{p,idle}$ is the normalized idle coefficient of p-th person, and $\ddot{x}$ is the delta coefficients.

3.2 Machine Learning Model

Machine learning models can be divided into the following categories: supervised learning models, including KNN, decision trees, MLP, echo state networks (ESNs) [10], and deep learning. This article uses standard MLP because they can learn directly from data and can effectively handle uncertain data, which is far superior to KNNs and decision trees. In addition, MLPs require fewer parameter settings than ESNs. But for deep learning models such as Transformers, this method is more advantageous. However, it has a premise: it requires a lot of data.

The MLP model uses 4 hidden layers, each with 64 neurons, and each hidden layer has a ReLU activation function. The network structure is: 27 inputs > Linear[27 × 64] > ReLU > Linear[64 × 64] > ReLU > Linear[64 × 64] > ReLU > Linear[64 × 13] > 13 outputs. The Adam optimization function is used for training, the learning rate is 0.0001, and the cross entropy loss is calculated.

3.3 Assessment Rules Generator

Mamdani fuzzy inference system is a rule structure that simulates human reasoning and can help experts and non-experts understand and explain the logic behind decisions. However, generating rules from data and feature lists is very time-consuming. Therefore, this paper first generates fuzzy rules through the Wang-Mendel method, which can directly extract fuzzy rules from data without any prior knowledge [11]. However, the noise in the data can greatly reduce the effectiveness of the Wang-Mendel method and lead to the generation of redundant rules [12]. It should also be noted that some rules and their variables may be illogical in terms of model evaluation. Therefore, after obtaining the fuzzy rules through the Wang-Mendel method, the variables considered meaningful in each rule are screened out and used to create new rules for the assessment task.

Initially, the Wang-Mendel antecedents are divided into nine different membership regions for each feature, and the consequents terms are either accepted or rejected. Therefore, rules are generated for each class. During the training phase, each class (accepted consequent term) is compared with the remaining classes (rejected consequent term). After this, only the remaining rules contain accepted term in the consequent, as shown below:

$$R^c \leftarrow \{r_j | q_j = \text{accepted}\}, \forall j \in R^c \quad (4)$$

where R^c are the all the rules r of c-th class obtained from Wang-Mendel method, and q_j is the consequent term of j-th rule.

After filtering these rules, the next step is to filter the effective variables. In this context, effective variables are those that are considered effective in the oral exercise assessment measurement. For illustration, the "Yawning" oral exercise is only validated by the "Open Jaw" variable. Therefore, to filter out the effective variables for each category, the data for the specific class c is input into the Mamdani fuzzy inference system using R^c rules. Subsequently, only the variables whose last 4 antecedent membership regions had at least 0.1 membership result were filtered out as follows:

$$V^c \leftarrow \{k | q > 5 \wedge f(r^c_{j,q}, x^c_{i,k}) > 0.1\}, \forall j \in R^c, \forall i \in x^c \quad (5)$$

where $r^c_{j,q}$ is the j-th rule, q-th antecedent membership region, $f(r^c_{j,q}, x^c_{i,k})$ return the membership result based on the antecedent membership regions using the k-th variable value of x, and V^c is those filtered variables which are effective in measuring c-th oral exercise assessment.

After the effective variables are determined, the next step is to formulate assessment rules based on these effective variables. In this paper, the consequent

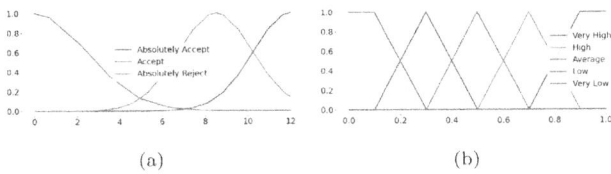

Fig. 2. (a) The consequent membership of the Mamdani fuzzy inference system for the assessment task. (b) The antecedent membership of the Mamdani fuzzy inference system for the assessment task.

for the assessment task is divided into three terms: "absolutely reject", "accept" and "absolutely accept". The range is set to 0 to 12, as shown in Fig. 2a. The consequent membership can be extended with additional terms to enhance the comprehensibility of the interpretation; however, for the purpose of this study, using three terms in the consequent membership function is sufficient.

After determining the membership of the consequent, the next step is to determine the membership of the antecedent. The antecedent membership is used as the input to the Mamdani fuzzy inference system to fuzzify the crisp value (delta coefficient). This paper suggests categorizing the antecedent into five terms: "very low", "low", "average", "high", and "very high", which is sufficient to cover the fuzzification process. Figure 2b provides an illustration of the antecedent membership.

At this point, assessment rules will generated. These rules come from antecedent, consequent, and effective variables. The structure of these assessment rules is as follows:

$$\text{if } V_k^c \text{ is } A_q \text{ then } c \text{ is } Q_l \qquad (6)$$

where V_k^c is the k-th effective variables of the class c, A_q is the q-th terms of antecedent membership, and Q_l is l-th terms of consequent membership.

The antecedents range from "very low" to "very high", and the consequents range from "absolutely reject" to "absolutely accept". As shown in the fuzzy rule example, each variable will have three consequents, and therefore three rules. This is because the antecedent is a continuous term, and the rules can be constructed as if-else statements, starting with the highest term and then going down to the lower terms. Therefore, the most appropriate highest term must be determined as the starting point for each variable. The data of the class is then input into the antecedent membership to determine the membership value of each term. The term with the minimum membership value of 0.5 is selected and the highest antecedent term is used to develop the highest consequent term rule. Subsequent antecedent terms are then used to develop subsequent consequent term rules, and this process is only repeated for positive consequents. The following assessment rules were generated for each effective variable in each class:

$$\hat{q}_k \leftarrow \arg\max_{\forall q \in A} \left(f(A_q, x_{i,k}^c) > 0.5 \right) \qquad (7)$$

$$\text{if } V_k^c \text{ is } A_{\hat{q}_k} \quad \text{then} \quad c \text{ is } Q_3 \tag{8}$$

$$\text{if } V_k^c \text{ is } A_{\hat{q}_k-1} \quad \text{then} \quad c \text{ is } Q_2 \tag{9}$$

$$\text{if } V_k^c \text{ is } A_1 \quad \text{then} \quad c \text{ is } Q_1 \tag{10}$$

where $\hat{q}$ is the highest antecedent term, Q_3, Q_2, and Q_1 are "absolutely accept", "accept", and "absolutely reject", respectively, $f(A_{q_k}, x_{i,k}^c)$ returns the membership value of the q-th antecedent membership region using the kth variable value of datum x, and A_1 is the "very low" antecedent membership region. All these assessment rules are stored as $\dot{R}$.

3.4 Mamdani Fuzzy Assessment System

The final stage of the proposed method requires using the assessment rules to perform the reject option task using the Mamdani fuzzy inference system. The Mamdani fuzzy inference system consists of four main steps, which are summarized as follows:

Step 1: Fuzzification. The delta coefficients are converted into fuzzy values using the antecedent membership function.

Step 2: Rule Evaluation. Apply the assessment rules $\dot{R}$ to determine the consequent membership for each class.

Step 3: Aggregation. The outputs of all rules for each class must be combined. First, minimum implication is performed, and then the resulting membership of each class are combined by selecting the maximum value from them.

Step 4: Defuzzification. Convert the aggregated fuzzy output into a exercise score using center of gravity (cog).

After completing the above four steps, each oral motor exercise will receive a score, which will be used for rejection and assessment tasks. For the learning machine model, the implementation of the Softmax function facilitates the calculation of the predicted probability of each learned class, and then selects the class with the highest probability as the prediction result of the learning machine model. However, when the probabilities of two classes are very close, misclassification may occur. To address this potential problem, we use the exercise score to calibrate and reject those misclassified categories. Specifically, if the exercise score of the predicted class is less than 2, it is judged to be very low and the exercise is rejected. On the contrary, if the exercise score of the next highest probability class is higher than 2, it is considered accurate and is selected as the final prediction output. This if-else process can be described by the following formula:

$$y \leftarrow \begin{cases} \arg\max(\hat{y}) & \text{if } S[\arg\max(\hat{y})] > 2 \\ \arg\max_{\hat{y} \neq \max(\hat{y})}(\hat{y}) & \text{if } S[\arg\max_{\hat{y} \neq \max(\hat{y})}(\hat{y})] > 2 \\ 0 & \text{otherwise} \end{cases} \tag{11}$$

where $\hat{y}$ is the predicted probability of each learned class, S is the score of each oral exercise, and y is the final prediction output.

4 Implementation

This section delineates the setup and data collection procedures. The experiments detailed in this paper were conducted on Ubuntu 22.04 (Intel Xeon E-2286M), and the Python programming language was utilized for the execution of the experiments.

4.1 Oral Motor Exercise Dataset

A total of 13 oral motor exercises were included in this study, 3 of which involved directional movements, specifically left and right. These exercises were carefully designed to mimic the exercises previously outlined in the RehabMyPatient[1] YouTube channel, with the goal of ensuring that the elderly could easily master them. These exercises included "Smile", "Kiss", "Yawning", "Puffer", "Fish", "Ghost", "Smirking Left", "Smirking Right", "Teeth", "Jaw Left", "Jaw Right", "Mouth Left", and "Mouth Right". To collect the dataset, a webcam was mounted on top of a monitor and the user was instructed to perform the exercises in front of it. The webcam used in this study was a high-definition eMeet C960 with a field of view (diagonal) of 90°, recorded at a resolution of 640 × 480, and a frame rate of 30 FPS. Nine university students were invited to perform each exercise in front of the camera, and the images were then captured and saved. In addition, their idle faces were captured. The captured image set is shown in Fig. 3.

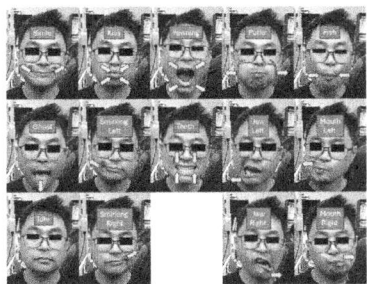

Fig. 3. The 13 oral motor exercises used in this study, including idle facial for subtraction to form delta coefficients.

The collected dataset contains a total of 126 images from 9 different subjects. To determine the effectiveness of the model, leave-one-subject-out cross-validation was used. Furthermore, in all subsequent experiments, to verify the performance of the rejection option, idle faces were used in the testing phase instead of the training phase.

---

[1] https://www.youtube.com/@RehabMyPatient.

5 Experiments

Two experiments are conducted in this section. The first experiment aims to evaluate the effectiveness of the blendshape coefficients. The last experiment aims to evaluate the effectiveness of the proposed Mamdani fuzzy assessment system.

5.1 Facial Blendshape Coefficient

A series of experiments were conducted to validate the blendshape coefficients. These experiments were conducted on various machine learning models using four different types of inputs: original face images, blendshape coefficients, normalized coefficients, and delta coefficients. Each learning model was trained for 1,000 epochs. The results of these comparisons are shown in Table 1.

Table 1. The accuracy results of different learning models on different input types.

Model	Facial Images	Blendshape Coefficients	Normalized Coefficients	Delta Coefficients
CNN	56.35±16.30	n/a	n/a	n/a
KNN	n/a	60.32±13.93	61.11±12.65	57.14±17.50
Decision Tree	n/a	60.32±11.22	58.73±10.53	50.00±15.79
SVM	n/a	**66.67±14.68**	63.49±13.65	61.90±20.20
Proposed MLP	n/a	65.87±17.10	65.08±12.35	60.32±17.85

Bold text indicates the best performance of these combinations.

The tabular results show that using the blendshape coefficients results in superior performance compared to using the original image. Analysis of the coefficients shows that the normalized coefficients show higher stability compared to the unnormalized ones, as evidenced by the results of the standard deviation analysis. Among the range of methods studied, SVM without normalized coefficients shows superior performance compared to the other methods. However, SVM does not generate probabilistic outputs for each class, while MLP has this capability.

5.2 Mamdani Fuzzy Assessment System

This paper proposes a scheme to implement Mamdani fuzzy system in order to perform rejection task and generate exercise scores for assessment task. In order to reject uncertain and unlearned predictions, the model is tested using idle face data, and the overall accuracy results are shown in Table 2. It should be noted that the experiments use normalized data on machine learning models.

Table 2. The accuracy results of different learning models using Mamdani fuzzy system for rejection task.

Model	No Rejection	Reject Only	Reject & Adjust
KNN	61.11±12.65	68.25±12.65	n/a
Decision Tree	58.73±10.53	65.08±11.88	n/a
SVM	63.49±13.65	70.63±13.65	n/a
Proposed MLP	65.08±12.35	72.22±12.35	**73.81±12.60**

Bold text indicates the best performance of these combinations.

The tabular results show that implementing the proposed assessment system can improve recognition accuracy by rejecting unlearned classes (idle faces) or uncertain predictions. In addition, it can also facilitate prediction recalibration of the results. To illustrate this point, Fig. 4 shows three confusion matrices illustrating the states before rejection, after rejection, and after prediction recalibration. The confusion matrices show that ID 0 acts as an idle face, preventing the MLP model from recognizing it. However, after implementing the proposed assessment system, it is rejected as an idle face. Notably, three other data points are also rejected as idle faces. However, after recalibrating the predictions, two of them are successfully re-identified as the correct class.

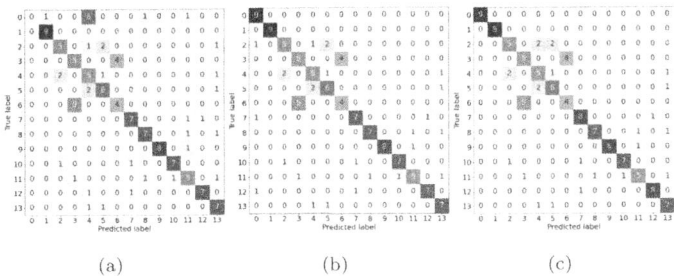

Fig. 4. The confusion matrix of the proposed method. (a) Before rejection. (b) After rejection. (c) After prediction recalibration.

6 Discussion

This paper proposes an assessment model that combines a machine learning model with a Mamdani fuzzy inference system. The assessment task consists of rejecting unlearned categories and unsuccessful exerises while providing scores for these recognized exercises. Three different "yawning" exercises of the same individual were captured and the scored exercises were calculated, as shown in

Fig. 5. The results obtained from these exercises showed a correlation with the physical strength level of the individual performing the "yawning" action, thus achieving the main goal of this study.

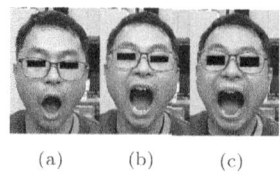

(a) (b) (c)

Fig. 5. The exercise score generated from the proposed Mamdani fuzzy assessment system. (a) Score: 5.48. (b) Score: 8.96. (c) Score: 10.33.

Nevertheless, the proposed method is not without limitations in real-time applications. Performance evaluation of the proposed method showed an FPS of 20 when executed in real time. The proposed method handles the assessment task for each image separately; therefore, the input image depends on the illumination of the ambient light. This can cause fluctuations in the blendshape coefficients and thus lead to unstable exercise scores, even in cases where a person is constantly performing the same action. To ensure stability, future research should be conducted on temporal recognition and temporal fuzzy assessment systems.

A notable limitation of this study is the limited size of the dataset used during the experimental phase. In addition, the range of input features is also limited. In the original configuration, the facial blendshape coefficients totaled 52, which were subsequently reduced to 27. However, these 27 coefficients are insufficient to resolve all action units of the face. Therefore, as the amount of data and coefficients increase, the number of assessment rules will increase, resulting in a decrease in FPS when executed in real time. This computational overhead represents a significant limitation of classical fuzzy inference systems. Therefore, there are compelling reasons to explore quantum computing in fuzzy systems [13]. By exploiting the inherent parallelism and efficiency of quantum computing, quantum fuzzy systems can perform complex computations and process large datasets with greater efficiency than conventional systems [14]. Furthermore, the application of quantum computing in the generation of fuzzy rules from large amount data represents an area that necessitates further exploration.

7 Conclusion

This paper proposes a fuzzy assessment system to evaluate oral motor exercise. First, the Wang-Mendal method is used to generate rules from the data. Then, effective variables are screened from the generated rules and subsequently used to generate assessment rules for the Mamdani fuzzy inference system. The proposed assessment system generates exercise scores that can be used to reject option tasks and recalibrate predictions. This approach addresses the limitations of machine learning models, which are often unable to reject non-learned categories and provide exercise scores after recognition.

Experimental results demonstrate the effectiveness of the Mamdani fuzzy assessment system in rejecting unlearned classes and recalibrating predictions, thereby achieving 73% accuracy on an recorded oral motor exercise dataset. Furthermore, the system's ability to evaluate exercises by assigning scores to users in real time (FPS: 20) is noteworthy. However, given the image-based recognition nature of the proposed approach, the input features exhibit variability, resulting in unstable exercise score generation. To address the above limitations, this study proposes future approaches that combine temporal recognition and temporal fuzzy assessment systems with quantum computing. These future approaches are expected to facilitate the generation of fuzzy rules from large datasets and the real-time execution of complex fuzzy assessment system.

Acknowledgment. This work was partially supported by Japan Science and Technology Agency (JST), Moonshot R&D, under grant number JPMJMS2034, and Tokyo Metropolitan University (TMU) Local 5G research support. The authors greatly appreciate the scholarship support from the Japan Ministry of Education, Culture, Sports, Science, and Technology (MEXT).

References

1. Shi, D., Zhang, W., Zhang, W., Ding, X.: A review on lower limb rehabilitation exoskeleton robots. Chin. J. Mech. Eng. **32**(1), 1–11 (2019)
2. Sekiguchi, T., Obo, T., Matsuda, T., Kubota, N.: Structural coupling system for cognitive modeling in immersive VR assessment tasks. J. Adv. Comput. Intell. Intell. Inf. **28**(6), 1240–1250 (2024)
3. Morley, J.E.: Oral frailty, pp. 683–684 (2020)
4. Nojima, Y., Kawano, K., Shimahara, H., Vernon, E., Masuyama, N., Ishibuchi, H.: Fuzzy classifiers with a two-stage reject option. In: 2023 IEEE International Conference on Fuzzy Systems (FUZZ), pp. 1–6. IEEE (2023)
5. Siow, C.Z., Dou, W., Song, Q., Chuquirachi, F., Obo, T., Kubota, N.: Use k-means-generated nodes to distinguish learned from non-learned exercises. In: IECON 2023-49th Annual Conference of the IEEE Industrial Electronics Society, pp. 1–6. IEEE (2023)
6. Mamdani, E.H., Assilian, S.: An experiment in linguistic synthesis with a fuzzy logic controller. Int. J. Man Mach. Stud. **7**(1), 1–13 (1975)
7. Lugaresi, C., et al.: Mediapipe: a framework for building perception pipelines. arXiv preprint arXiv:1906.08172 (2019)
8. Wang, L.-X., Mendel, J.M.: Generating fuzzy rules by learning from examples. IEEE Trans. Syst. Man Cybern. **22**(6), 1414–1427 (1992)
9. Siow, C.Z., Chin, W.H., Kubota, N.: Evaluating simple exercises with a fuzzy system based on human skeleton poses. In: IEEE International Conference on Fuzzy Systems (FUZZ) 2023, pp. 1–6 (2023)
10. Liu, Z., Zhang, W., Pan, M., Loo, C.K., Pasupa, K.: Weighted error-output recurrent Xavier echo state network for concept drift handling in water level prediction. Appl. Soft Comput. **165**, 112055 (2024)

11. Wang, L.-X.: The WM method completed: a flexible fuzzy system approach to data mining. IEEE Trans. Fuzzy Syst. **11**(6), 768–782 (2003)
12. Zhai, Y., Lv, Z., Zhao, J., Wang, W., Leung, H.: Data-driven inference modeling based on an on-line wang-mendel fuzzy approach. Inf. Sci. **551**, 113–127 (2021)
13. Acampora, G., Schiattarella, R., Vitiello, A.: On the implementation of fuzzy inference engines on quantum computers. IEEE Trans. Fuzzy Syst. **31**(5), 1419–1433 (2023)
14. Pourabdollah, A., Acampora, G., Schiattarella, R.: Fuzzy logic on quantum annealers. IEEE Trans. Fuzzy Syst. **30**(8), 3389–3394 (2022)

Motion Planning of Self-balancing Exoskeleton Robot Based on Spring-Loaded Inverted Pendulum

Chenhao Wu[1], Jinke Li[1(✉)], Zengle Ren[1], Shisheng Zhang[1], Xueyan Shen[2], and Xinyu Wu[1,3]

[1] Guangdong Provincial Key Lab of Robotics and Intelligent System, Shenzhen Institute of Advanced Technology, Chinese Academy of Sciences, Shenzhen 518055, China
jk.li@siat.ac.cn
[2] Department of Rehabilitation Medicine, Huashan Hospital, Fudan University, Shanghai, China
[3] State Key Laboratory of Biomedical Imaging Science and System, Shenzhen 518055, China

Abstract. Self-balancing lower-limb exoskeletons (SBLLE) have huge potential in rehabilitation applications. In this paper, we propose an effective control framework to let SBLLE walk human-like. By modeling the exoskeleton as a spring-loaded inverted pendulum (SLIP), we designed a motion trajectory generator based on zero-moment point (ZMP), which enables the center of mass (CoM) fluctuate during the walking process. Then, we design a controller to indirectly control the actual ZMP by controlling the trajectory of CoM, which can reduce the influence caused by wearers of different weight. The results demonstrate notable advances in the achievement of autonomous and balanced walking movements, highlighting the effectiveness of the proposed framework.

Keywords: Self-balancing exoskeleton · Walking control · Spring-loaded inverted pendulum

1 Introduction

In the field of clinical practice, existing research has shown that lower-limb exoskeleton robots can provide assistance in walking and rehabilitation for paralyzed individuals [1]. Actually, a large number of patients suffer from spinal cord injury in China and more in the world [2]. Spinal cord injury will cause paralysis and so on. These patients need lower-limb exoskeleton robots to help them in daily life.

Normal lower-limb exoskeletons cannot maintain their own balance while providing assistance, and thus require the intervention of auxiliary devices such as crutches during use to keep the system stable. There are several such exoskeletons, for example: Rewalk [3], Ekso [4], HAL [5], Indego [6]. However, the prolonged use of devices such as crutches can cause certain damage to the upper limbs of the patient. In fact, there are a large number of patients with spinal cord injury in the world, among whom a considerable number of patients do not have sufficient upper limb strength to use assistive devices [7]. As a result, self-balancing lower-limb exoskeleton is needed by these patients to provide assistance.

Self-balancing lower-limb exoskeletons (SBLLE) can ensure the balance of human-machine hybrid system without any assistance while walking. As a result, they can meet the rehabilitation and walking assistance needs of paraplegic and tetraplegia patients. Existing researches usually use linear inverted pendulum to simplify the system, which consider the height of center of mass (CoM) remains unchanged [8]. It's inconsistent with the fact that the CoM fluctuates during the walking process of ordinary people and may cause discomfort while wearing. It's important for the SBLLE to have a human-like gait to improve wearing comfort.

Another simplified model commonly used in the motion planning of biped robots is the spring-loaded Inverted Pendulum (SLIP) model [9]. The existing of the spring enables it to simulate the running and jumping states more realistically. A lot of variant SLIP have also been proposed for the study of robot motion gait. J.G. Keetelaar put forward the SLIP model with variable stiffness, making the moving state of the legs more similar to that of humans [10]. Garofalo G proposed the fully actuated SLIP model to enable biped robots to walk stably [11].

Due to the particularity of the SBLLE system, its control strategy needs to consider two aspects. First is to guarantee the stability during walking. Second is to handle the random disturbance caused by the wearer. As a consequence, its motion planning needs to construct a two-layer decision-making framework, the upper layer determines the target trajectory through global path planning, and the lower layer generates specific gait parameters based on stability constraints, thereby achieving the autonomous walking ability without auxiliary support.

The main purpose of this paper is to achieve the human-like CoM fluctuation of SBLLE during stable walking. The ZMP(Zero-moment point) transfer trajectory is planned according to the walking law of the human body. The CoM trajectory during the walking process is planned offline through the motion trajectory generator based on ZMP. Then the CoM trajectory is controlled online through a PD controller to reduce disturbance caused by the wearer. The whole control framework is shown in Fig. 1. The main contribution of the paper can be summarized as follows:

- Planning the trajectory of the CoM in the vertical direction so that the motion of the CoM in the vertical direction is more similar to a normal human being.
- By solving the ZMP equation for the SLIP, the preview controller calculates the horizontal CoM trajectory, which minimizes the error between the actual ZMP and the planned ZMP of SBLLE.
- To enhance walking stability and safety during walking, a controller was introduced in this paper.

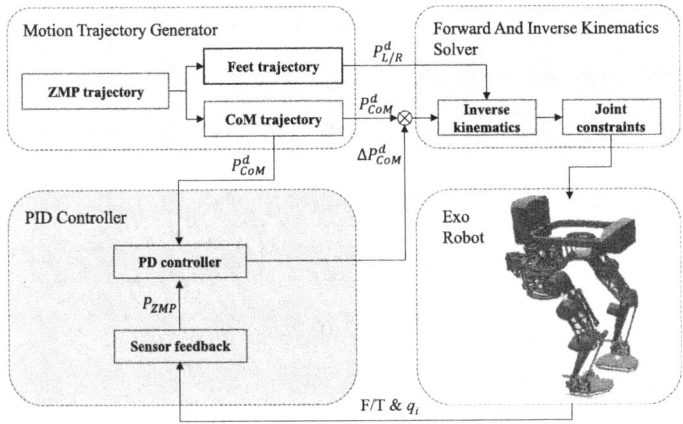

Fig. 1. Proposed control framework for stable and safe exoskeleton walking.

2 Modeling

2.1 Dynamic Model of The SLIP

The SLIP model [12] has been widely used in the research of biped robots. The SLIP model can simulate the change of the CoM in the vertical direction accurately during the motion process, and has achieved excellent results in various kinds of jumping and running robots [13,14], and the bipedal SLIP model has been proved to simulate the walking process of human beings well [15].

The model used for walking, shown in Fig. 2, is simply given by two massless linear springs connected to the CoM. Although the model have two springs, it has the same dynamic equation with SLIP during single support phase, because of its massless springs. By switching between single support phase and double support phase, shown in Fig. 3, SLIP can realize walking smoothly.

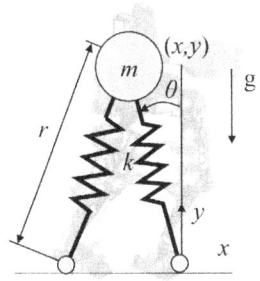

Fig. 2. Bipedal SLIP model.

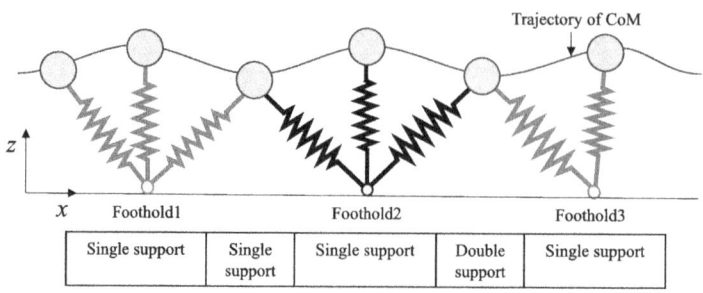

Fig. 3. Bipedal SLIP walking state.

Using the following notation: m for the total mass, k and r for the stiffness and length of the spring, r_0 for the rest length of the spring, x for the CoM position, and g for the Earth's gravitational acceleration, the dynamic equation of the single support phase can be written as:

$$\begin{cases} m\ddot{r} - mr\dot{\theta}^2 + k(r - r_0) + mg\cos\theta = 0 \\ mr^2\ddot{\theta} + 2mr\dot{r}\dot{\theta} - mgr\sin\theta = 0 \end{cases} \quad (1)$$

There exists a second-order non-integrable term $r\dot{\theta}^2$, so the dynamical equations under the single support phase of the SLIP model cannot be solved to an exact analytical solution, which makes the subsequent control difficult. The solution will be presented in next chapter.

2.2 ZMP Equation of the SLIP and Its Transfer Trajectory

To ensure the stability of SBLLE while walking, ZMP need to be kept in the convex hull of the contact points between the robot's feet and the ground [16]. So we need the ZMP equation of the SLIP first. Consider the center of the two feet in the initial state as the origin of the world coordinate system, and the forward direction as the x-direction. The CoM position x and the planned foot placement position P_x must satisfy the equation below:

$$P_x = x - \frac{(z - P_z)\ddot{x}}{\ddot{z} + g} . \quad (2)$$

where z is the height of the CoM, and g is the Earth's gravitational acceleration.

In this paper, the robot walks on flat surface, so considers P_z to be 0. Thus, the ZMP equation turns into:

$$P_x = x - \frac{z\ddot{x}}{\ddot{z} + g} . \quad (3)$$

The ZMP transfer trajectory of the exoskeleton when walking straight is shown in Fig. 4. The trajectory takes the transfer of the ZMP within the foot during walking into account, which is more similar to the walking habit of normal human.

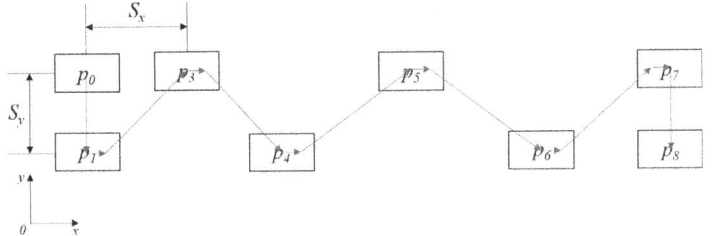

Fig. 4. ZMP transfer trajectory planned.

3 Motion Trajectory Generator

3.1 Vertical Motion Trajectory of CoM

Since the dynamical equations of SLIP can't be solved accurately, we can plan the vertical motion trajectory of CoM by the walking law of human [17].

In order to reduce the impact force when switching legs and to increase the stability during walking, we consider the height of the CoM keep constant during the double support phase, which means that the velocity and acceleration of the SLIP model in the vertical direction are both 0. A complete stepping cycle contains two single support phases and two double support phases, and two complete stepping cycles are carried out in the walking process. In this paper, the gait parameters are 2 s for a double support phase and 4 s for a single support phase, the change in height of the CoM is 4 cm. Finally, based on the gait parameters, we can get the desired CoM trajectory in the vertical direction by using quintic polynomial curve.

3.2 Horizontal Motion Trajectory of CoM

After planning the vertical trajectory of CoM, the horizontal trajectory of CoM is needed. Notice that the actual ZMP moves when the robot is moving. In order to make the trajectory of the actual ZMP have less error with the planned ZMP trajectory, we use preview controller to control the horizontal trajectory of the CoM to reduce the error. The framework of preview control is shown in Fig. 5.

Regarding $u_x = \dddot{x}$ as the input of SLIP, rewrite Eq. (3) into the state as:

$$\begin{cases} \dfrac{d}{dt} \begin{bmatrix} x \\ \dot{x} \\ \ddot{x} \end{bmatrix} = \begin{bmatrix} 0 & 1 & 0 \\ 0 & 0 & 1 \\ 0 & 0 & 0 \end{bmatrix} \begin{bmatrix} x \\ \dot{x} \\ \ddot{x} \end{bmatrix} + \begin{bmatrix} 0 \\ 0 \\ 1 \end{bmatrix} u_x \\ P_x = \begin{bmatrix} 1 & 0 & -\dfrac{z}{\ddot{z}+g} \end{bmatrix} \begin{bmatrix} x \\ \dot{x} \\ \ddot{x} \end{bmatrix} \end{cases} \quad (4)$$

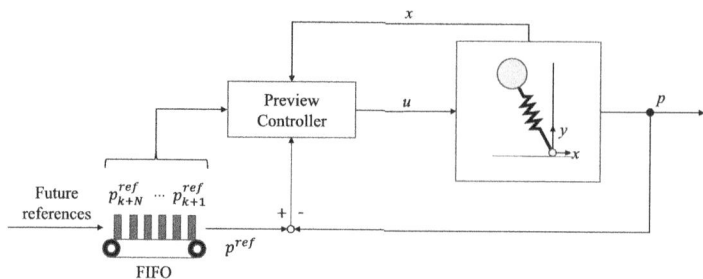

Fig. 5. Framework Of Preview Control.

Then discretize Eq. (4) with a control cycle time of T, we have the state-space equation expressed as:

$$\begin{cases} x(k+1) = Ax(k) + Bu(k) \\ P_x = Cx(k) \end{cases} \quad (5)$$

where

$$\begin{cases} A = \begin{bmatrix} 1 & \Delta t & \frac{\Delta t^2}{2} \\ 0 & 1 & \Delta t \\ 0 & 0 & 1 \end{bmatrix} \\ B = \begin{bmatrix} \frac{\Delta t^3}{6} & \frac{\Delta t^2}{2} & \Delta t \end{bmatrix}^T \\ C = \begin{bmatrix} 1 & 0 & -\frac{z}{\ddot{z}+g} \end{bmatrix} \end{cases} \quad (6)$$

By using the ZMP trajectory planned, we can express the problem as an optimal problem by minimizing [18].

$$J = \sum_{j=k}^{\infty} [Q_e e^2(j) + \Delta x^T Q_x \Delta x(j) + R\Delta u^2(j)] \quad (7)$$

where $e(j) = P(j) - P^{ref}(j)$, $\Delta x = x_k - x_{k-1}$ and $\Delta u = u_k - u_{k-1}$, Q_e, Q_x and R are symmetric nonnegative definite matrices.

By taking the reference values of the next N steps as input, the input function is obtained as:

$$u(k) = -G_i \sum_{i=0}^{k} e(k) - G_x x(k) - \sum_{j=1}^{N} G_p(j) P^{ref}(k+j) \quad (8)$$

In Eq. (8), G_i, G_x, $G_p(j)$ can be obtained by the following equations:

$$\begin{cases} \begin{bmatrix} G_i \\ G_x \end{bmatrix} = (R + \hat{B}^T P \hat{B})^{-1} \hat{B}^T P \hat{A} \\ G_p(j) = (R + \hat{B}^T P \hat{B})^{-1} \hat{B}^T ((\hat{A} - \hat{B}K)^T)^{j-1} \hat{C}^T Q \end{cases} \quad (9)$$

By solving the Riccati equation, we can obtain P [19]:

$$P = \hat{A}^T P \hat{A} + \hat{C}^T Q \hat{C} - \hat{A}^T P \hat{B}(R + \hat{B}^T P \hat{B})^{-1} \hat{B} P \hat{A} . \tag{10}$$

where $Q = diag(Q_e, Q_x)$, $\hat{A}$ and $\hat{B}$ are the expansion form of A and B.

3.3 Final Motion Trajectory

After obtaining the trajectory of the CoM, we need to obtain the swinging trajectory of the feet. In order to maintain the stability of the robot during walking process, it's generally required that the speed and acceleration of the swing leg at the beginning and end of the swing are both 0. Therefore, the swing trajectory can be obtained by a quintic polynomial curve, which can be expressed as:

$$h(t) = a_0 + a_1 t + a_2 t^2 + a_3 t^3 + a_4 t^4 + a_5 t^5 . \tag{11}$$

where h is the position of feet.

Lastly, the motion trajectory of the robot in Cartesian space is generated, which is shown in Fig. 6. By using preview controller, the actual ZMP can track the desired ZMP well, which keeps the robot in stable. Then, we can obtain the reference motion trajectory of the robot in joint space by inverse kinematics solution.

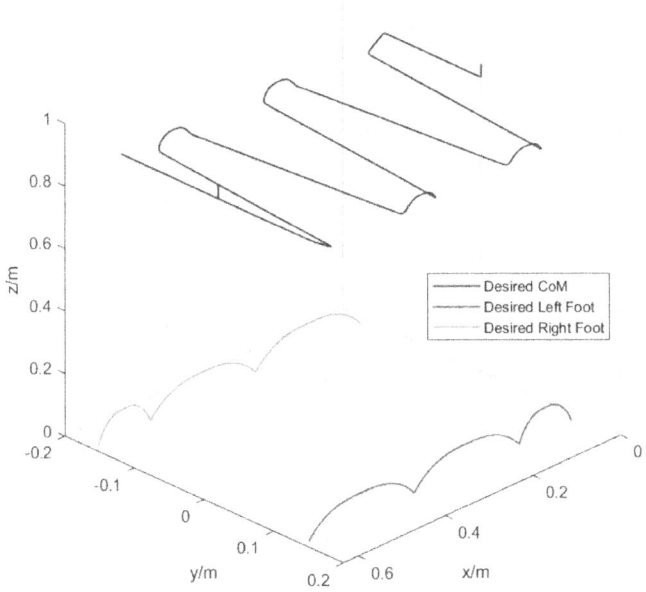

Fig. 6. Stereo image of the planned trajectory.

4 Design of Controller

In generating walking gaits based on the ZMP, the process can be viewed as a offline ZMP tracking problem. However, different wearers may cause different CoM deviations and lead to instability if only ZMP references is tracked. In order to increase the stability of SBLLE during walking, we need to design a controller to avoid falling while walking. So we design a PD controller to indirectly control the ZMP trajectory by controlling the acceleration of the CoM, which makes sure wearers of different weight can be carried safely.

According to Eq. (3), ZMP is determined by its CoM. By controlling the CoM, we can control the ZMP indirectly, which can be expressed as:

$$\Delta \ddot{x}(k) = K_p \Delta P_x(k) + K_D[\Delta P_x(k) - \Delta P_x(k-1)] \ . \tag{12}$$

where $\Delta P_x = P_x^d - P_x$, P_x^d is the desired ZMP in X-axis.

We can obtain the compensation of CoM by numerical iteration, expressed as:

$$\begin{cases} \Delta \dot{x} = \Delta \dot{x} + \Delta \ddot{x} \cdot T \\ \Delta x = \Delta x + \Delta \dot{x} \cdot T \ . \end{cases} \tag{13}$$

where sample time $T = 0.001$ s.

By adding the compensation to the desired trajectory of CoM, it enables the actual ZMP to track the desired ZMP trajectory, expressed as:

$$x = x^d + \Delta x \ . \tag{14}$$

where x^d is the desired CoM trajectory.

Since the CoM equations in the X-axis and Y-axis have the same formulation, the same process can be done to the CoM in Y-axis, which can be expressed as:

$$y = y^d + \Delta y \ . \tag{15}$$

where y^d is the desired CoM trajectory.

In summary, by using the feedback ZMP position, the PD controller can calculate compensation. Then, the ZMP trajectory can be controlled by adding the compensation to the desired CoM trajectory, which can control the ZMP trajectory, to reduce the influence caused by wearers of different weight.

5 Experiment and Discussion

The final control framework obtained in this paper is shown in Fig. 1. To test the effectiveness of the control framework, we conducted a series of contrastive experiments to test the tracking results of ZMP trajectories by simulating the situation of wearers of different weights. The experiments was conducted on Matlab and CoppeliaSim. The exoskeleton used is the AutoLEE-II lower-limb exoskeleton [20], features 12 DOFs (3 hip, 1 knee and 2 ankle per limb) for natural joint articulation. Dual 6-axis F/T sensors in footplates monitor ground reactions to calculate the actual ZMP. The motion trajectory is first generated by Matlab and subsequently the dynamics are simulated by CoppeliaSim.

Figure 7 shows AutoLEE-II can walk forward stably on a flat ground in CoppeliaSim. Then, we simulated the situation of three body weights for 60 kg, 70 kg and 80 kg, and compared them with the reference trajectory, shown in Fig. 8 and Fig. 9.

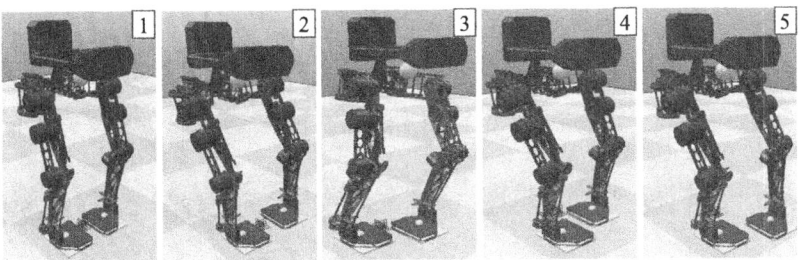

Fig. 7. The illustration for AutoLEE-II walking forward in simulation.

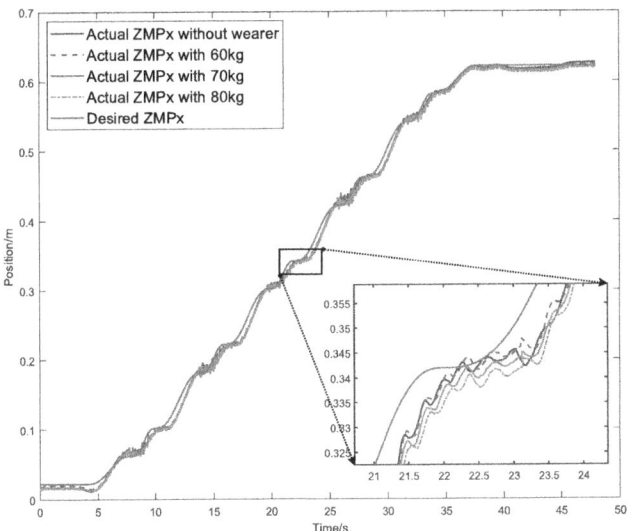

Fig. 8. ZMP result with different wearers in X-axis.

Figure 8 shows the result of ZMP tracking in X-axis in the comparative experiment. Due to the fact that the weight of the human body is mainly concentrated in the upper body and its position located back from the center of the robot,

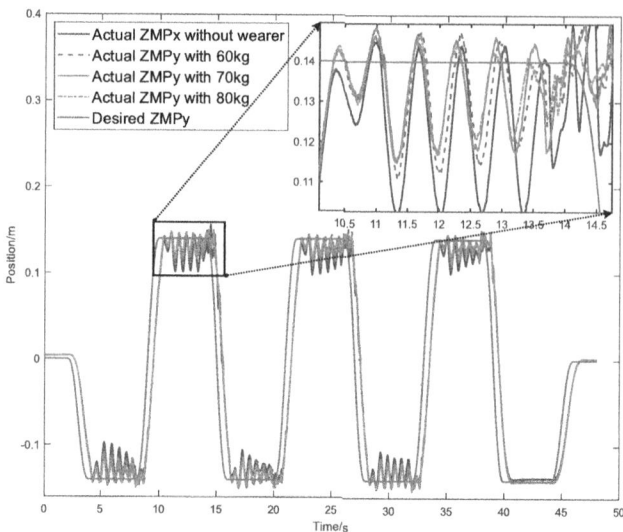

Fig. 9. ZMP result with different wearers in Y-axis.

it leads to a smaller ZMP in X-axis compared to unloading. As a result, when the wearer's weight varies, it leads to a steady-state error in the ZMP on the x-axis, which increases when the weight becomes heavier. By calculation, when the wearer weighs 80 kg, the maximum absolute error of ZMP in X-axis is 0.0203 m, which means the ZMP in X-axis stays within the support polygon and the foot is stable while walking.

Figure 9 shows the result of ZMP tracking in Y-axis in the comparative experiment. When the human body wears an exoskeleton and walks, the upper body deflects less, the lower body deflects with the exoskeleton. Since the body weight is more concentrated in the upper body, so the CoM of the human-machine hybrid system will have a smaller deviation during the walking process when there is a wearer compared to the unloaded state. The heavier wearer's weight, the smaller the relative deflection. By calculation, when unloaded, the maximum absolute error of ZMP in Y-axis is 0.0428 m, which means the ZMP in Y-axis stays within the support polygon and the foot is stable while walking.

6 Conclusion

This paper presents a walking trajectory generation method for the self-balancing exoskeleton.

First, the motion trajectories are determined offline using the preview controller based on ZMP. Then, we use PD controller, which uses force sensor feedback, to control the CoM trajectory online in order to keep the actual ZMP trajectory stay in position. To evaluate the effectiveness of the control framework, comparative experiments were conducted with unloaded state and wearers of 60 kg, 70 kg, 80 kg. The experiments show that the exoskeleton can achieve stable walking under the control framework.

In the future, we will conduct more experiments on AutoLEE-II with different feedback control strategies to further reduce the error of ZMP during walking process.

Acknowledgement. This work was supported in part by the Science, Technology, and Innovation Commission of Shenzhen Municipality (Grant No. KCXFZ20230731093401004), in part by the National Natural Science Foundation of China (Grant No. 62403452), in part by Shenzhen Science and Technology Program (Grant No. RCBS20231211090523046), and in part by Guangdong Basic and Applied Basic Research Foundation (Grant No. 2023A1515110891).

References

1. Plaza, A., Hernandez, M., Puyuelo, G., Garces, E., Garcia, E.: Lower-limb medical and rehabilitation exoskeletons: a review of the current designs. IEEE Rev. Biomed. Eng. **16**, 278–291 (2023)
2. Qiu, J.: China spinal cord injury network: changes from within. Lancet Neurol. **8**(7), 606–607 (2009)
3. Esquenazi, A., Talaty, M., Packel, A., Saulino, M.: The rewalk powered exoskeleton to restore ambulatory function to individuals with thoracic-level motor-complete spinal cord injury. Am. J. Phys. Med. Rehabil. **91**(11), 911 (2012)
4. Milia, P., et al.: Neurorehabilitation in paraplegic patients with an active powered exoskeleton (EKSO). Dig. Med. **2**(4), 163 (2016)
5. Sankai, Y.: Leading edge of cybernics: robot suit hal. In: 2006 SICE-ICASE International Joint Conference, pp. P-1–P-2 (2006)
6. Tefertiller, C., et al.: Initial outcomes from a multicenter study utilizing the indego powered exoskeleton in spinal cord injury. Topics Spinal Cord Injury Rehabil. **24**(1), 78–85 (2017)
7. Center, N.S.C.I.S.: Traumatic spinal cord injury facts and figures at a glance. birmingham, al: University of alabama at birmingham (2025)
8. Kajita, S., Kanehiro, F., Kaneko, K., Yokoi, K., Hirukawa, H.: The 3d linear inverted pendulum mode: a simple modeling for a biped walking pattern generation. In: Proceedings 2001 IEEE/RSJ International Conference on Intelligent Robots and Systems. (Cat. No.01CH37180), vol. 1, pp. 239–246 (2001)
9. Ghigliazza, R.M., Altendorfer, R., Holmes, P., Koditschek, D.: A simply stabilized running model. SIAM Rev. **47**(3), 519–549 (2005)
10. Ketelaar, J., Visser, L., Stramigioli, S., Carloni, R.: Controller design for a bipedal walking robot using variable stiffness actuators. In: 2013 IEEE International Conference on Robotics and Automation, pp. 5650–5655 (2013)
11. Garofalo, G., Ott, C., Albu-Schäffer, A.: Walking control of fully actuated robots based on the bipedal slip model. In: 2012 IEEE International Conference on Robotics and Automation, pp. 1456–1463 (2012)
12. Blickhan, R.: The spring-mass model for running and hopping. J. Biomech. **22**(11), 1217–1227 (1989)
13. Wieber, P.B.: Trajectory free linear model predictive control for stable walking in the presence of strong perturbations. In: 2006 6th IEEE-RAS International Conference on Humanoid Robots, pp. 137–142 (2006)

14. Li, Y., Jiang, Y., Hosoda, K.: Design and sequential jumping experimental validation of a musculoskeletal bipedal robot based on the spring-loaded inverted pendulum model. Front. Rob. AI **11** (2024)
15. Whittington, B.R., Thelen, D.G.: A simple mass-spring model with roller feet can induce the ground reactions observed in human walking. J. Biomech. Eng. **131**, 011013 (2008)
16. Kajita, S., et al.: Biped walking pattern generation by using preview control of zero-moment point. In: 2003 IEEE International Conference on Robotics and Automation (Cat. No.03CH37422), vol. 2, pp. 1620–1626 (2003)
17. Liu, Y., Wensing, P.M., Orin, D.E., Zheng, Y.F.: Dynamic walking in a humanoid robot based on a 3d actuated dual-slip model. In: 2015 IEEE International Conference on Robotics and Automation (ICRA), pp. 5710–5717 (2015)
18. Park, J., Youm, Y.: General zmp preview control for bipedal walking. In: Proceedings 2007 IEEE International Conference on Robotics and Automation, pp. 2682–2687 (2007)
19. Arnold, W., Laub, A.: Generalized eigenproblem algorithms and software for algebraic Riccati equations. Proc. IEEE **72**(12), 1746–1754 (1984)
20. Tian, D., et al.: Bionic design and control of a 12-dof self-balancing walking exoskeleton. IEEE Trans. Autom. Sci. Eng. **22**, 8292–8302 (2025)

Doctor-Centered Mixed Reality Tele-Guidance Training System Design

Yanzhuo Wang, Keyi Wang(✉), Lan Wang, Haochu Chen, and Jinghang Li

Harbin Engineering University, Harbin, Heilongjiang, China
wangkeyi@hrbeu.edu.cn

Abstract. Aiming at the problems of weak human-machine interaction on the doctor-side and insufficient visualization of patient movement information in the tele-rehabilitation system, the paper proposes a doctor-centered mixed reality tele-guidance training system, based on a self-developed doctor-patient interactive cable-driven lower limb rehabilitation robot platform. The solution constructs a high-precision virtual simulation mapping system and a mixed reality collaboration module to achieve real-time synchronization of patient movement states and multi-dimensional visual assessment. Static virtualization employs parameterized engineering models to ensure mapping accuracy, while dynamic virtualization utilizes inverse kinematics control strategies for joint motion trajectory mapping. The mixed reality collaboration module integrates Unity3D with HoloLens2 platforms to form a bidirectional closed-loop system for bioinformation acquisition, command transmission, and safety monitoring. Experimental results demonstrate that the root mean square error of trajectory tracking at the patient-side end is 20.28 mm, with rapid doctor-side interaction response. This confirms that the proposed method significantly enhances doctors' real-time perception and dynamic adjustment capabilities during tele-rehabilitation processes, offering novel design insights for doctor-side interaction in remote rehabilitation systems.

Keywords: Mixed Reality · Cable Driven lower limb Rehabilitation Robot · Tele-Guidance Training System · Human-Machine Interaction Interface

1 Introduction

With the intensification of population aging and the rising incidence of diseases such as stroke, brain/spinal cord injuries, the number of patients with lower limb motor dysfunction continues to increase [1]. Traditional rehabilitation models face severe challenges, including uneven distribution of medical resources [2], shortages of professional rehabilitation therapists [3], and poor regional accessibility [4]. In this context, tele-rehabilitation technology has emerged as a critical breakthrough for improving rehabilitation accessibility due to its unique advantage of transcending spatiotemporal constraints.

Cable-driven rehabilitation robots (CDRR) demonstrate distinctive strengths in lower limb rehabilitation with high compliance, load capacity, and expansive workspace [5].

However, existing research focuses on patient-side development, with limited attention to doctor-side human-machine interaction (HMI) mechanisms. Current approaches fall into two categories: One approach relies on establishing doctor-patient interaction channels through haptic feedback, such as the teleoperation control strategy for CDRR proposed by Saracino et al. [6], and the home-based tele-rehabilitation system developed by Liu Yi et al. [7, 8]. The other approach utilizes video monitoring and parameter adjustment to enable tele-guidance, such as Miao et al.'s video communication-based rehabilitation system for guiding patients in remote training [9], and Garzo et al.'s Arm-Assist platform for upper limb tele-rehabilitation [10]. However, it is difficult to convey intuitively patient motion data and rehabilitation effects in the above systems, hindering doctors from obtaining clear, actionable feedback for assessing progress.

In the tele-rehabilitation system, real-time monitoring of patients 'training status is paramount, while doctor-guided rehabilitation systems serve as the prerequisite for effective training. The current research trench is to improving patient engagement and data visualization through virtual reality (VR) and augmented reality (AR) technologies. Wang et al. developed a VR-based lower limb rehabilitation system to enhance patient participation [11]. The other team developed an AR-based brain-computer interface for HMI [12]. Pinto et al. designed an audio-visual feedback system to apply AR technology to walking assistance [13]. Pasquale et al. combined AR-BCI integration to achieve visual monitoring of children's rehabilitation trajectory [14]. On the other hand, digital twin technology has been gradually adopted in tele-rehabilitation, such as: Wang et al. proposed the automatic gait control system for motion data synchronization [15]. Sosa-Méndez et al. built an upper limb multi-domain coupling model with virtual-physical mapping [16]. However, the above researches mostly focus on the patient-side experiences, and the development of HMI for the doctor is obviously insufficient. Specifically, the combination of doctor tele-guidance and MR is adequately insufficient, and it is impossible to better present patient motion data and evaluation effects to doctors.

To address these limitations, this paper proposes an innovative doctor-centered mixed reality tele-guidance training system (MRTGTS) through self-developed cable-driven lower limb rehabilitation robot (CDLLRR) platform. The solution achieves three code functionalities through the construction of high-precision virtual simulation mapping system (HPVSMS) and a MR collaboration module: 1. HPVSMS enables real-time synchronization of the patient's movement information. 2. MR collaborative interface provides multi-dimensional visualization dashboards for doctors. 3. Remote collaboration mechanism enables doctors to conduct remote demonstrations and adjust movements via MR technology.

2 Mixed Reality Tele-Guidance Training System Design

2.1 Doctor-Patient Interactive Cable-Driven Lower Limb Rehabilitation Robot

The system employs a self-developed CDLLRR [4, 17, 18], which establishes a closed-loop control system through the doctor-side part (left side of Fig. 1) and the patient-side part (right side of Fig. 1). Among them, the doctor-side part is equipped with a simulated lower extremity and a force feedback device; and the patient-side part adopts a rigid-flexible hybrid drive module, integrating servo motors, parallel mechanism and multi-degree of freedom traction module; Bidirectional data synchronization between the two parts is achieved through TCP/IP protocol.

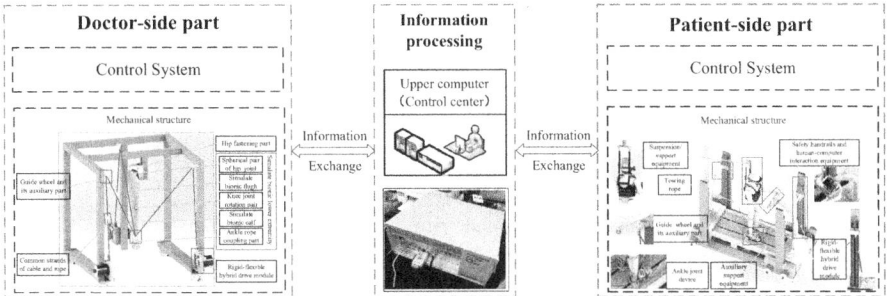

Fig. 1. The overall design of the CDLLRR and the detailed structural diagrams of each part.

2.2 Robots and Patient Physical Entities Virtualization Analysis

The core of MRTGTS lies in establishing HPVSMS. In this paper, multi-dimensional virtualization processing of CDLLRR and patients is carried out through a hierarchical modeling approach: the topological structure and biomechanical characteristics of the mechanism are analyzed at the static level, while the dynamic level reconstruction captures cable tension transmission dynamics and limb trajectory patterns, and finally building a real-time interactive simulation environment for human-machine collaboration.

Static Virtualization

The static modeling adopts a differentiated modeling approach: For the patient-side part, a parametric engineering model is built through SolidWorks, optimized by 3D rendering in 3dsMax, and then imported into the Unity3D to establish an interactive virtual prototype with millimeter-level accuracy (see Fig. 2a); The patient's biological model is based on an open-source 3D biomechanics model library, and a 3D human model with significant joint anatomical features is selected (see Fig. 2b). The joint structure is obvious, enabling accurately mapping of the real-time state of the lower limb kinematic chain.

 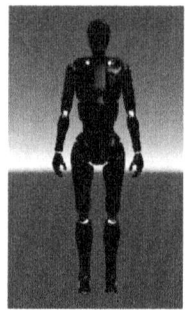

(a) Geometric modeling of patient-side part (b) Human body model

Fig. 2. Static geometric modeling of both patient-side part and patient

Robot Dynamic Virtualization

Kinematics Analysis

Dynamic virtualization modeling focuses on accurate simulation of the motion characteristics of physical entities. For the patient-side part in the gait flexion and extension training mode (see Fig. 3b), three cable co-drive models are designed: the cable1/2 is connected to the torque motor 1/2 through guide wheels respectively to form a sagittal traction unit; The cable 3 is linked with the torque motor 3 through a dynamic adjustment module integrating a screw slider to form a reconfigurable sagittal drive unit. This topology uses a space vector synthesis algorithm to achieve precision control of the ankle joint motion trajectory. At the same time, it uses the displacement compensation mechanism of the slider mechanism to effectively balance the cable tension distribution during the training process and improve the dynamic stability and safety.

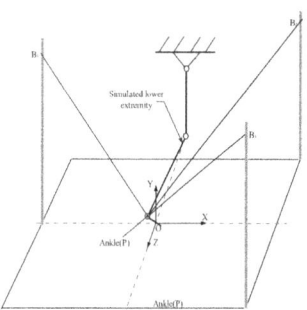 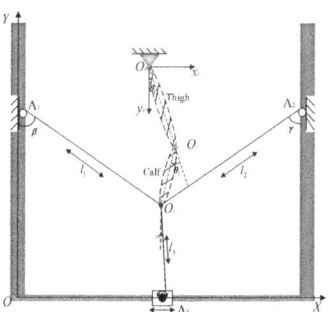

(a) Doctor-side simplified structural diagram (b) Patient-side simplified structural diagram

Fig. 3. Mechanism diagram of doctor-patient interactive CDLLRR

From the simplified model of the patient-side part, the length of the cable is defined as:

$$l_i = (\boldsymbol{L}_i^T \boldsymbol{L}_i)^{1/2} = \sqrt{(x_i - x_{o2})^2 + (y_i - y_{o2})^2} \tag{1}$$

Based on the geometric analysis of the simplified model, the spatial coordinates of the ankle joint in the global coordinate system $O\text{-}XY$ can be determined as:

$$\begin{bmatrix} x_{o2} \\ y_{o2} \end{bmatrix} = \begin{bmatrix} x_P + l_1 \sin\theta_1 + l_2 \sin(\theta_1+\theta_2) \\ y_P - l_1 \cos\theta_1 - l_2 \cos(\theta_1+\theta_2) \end{bmatrix} = \begin{bmatrix} \frac{l_1^2 + x_{A2}^2 - l_2^2}{2x_{A2}} \\ y_{A2} - \frac{\sqrt{4x_{A2}^2 l_1^2 - (l_1^2 + x_{A2}^2 - l_2^2)^2}}{2x_{A2}^2} \end{bmatrix} \quad (2)$$

In the equation, (x_p, y_p) and (x_{Ai}, y_{Ai}) represent O_p and A_i respectively, which are the coordinate points in the global coordinate system $O\text{-}XY$.

Aiming at the motion planning problem of rigid linkages, an angle bisector motion planning strategy is adopted. This strategy can control the cable tension within a small fluctuation range by optimizing the direction of traction [19]. Such characteristic makes the constraint of the lower limb traction point more stable, thereby providing better stability and safety protection for patients during training. Based on the above analysis, the motion planning function of A_3 is:

$$\begin{bmatrix} x_{A3} \\ y_{A3} \end{bmatrix} = \begin{bmatrix} \frac{(l_2-l_1)(x_{o2}^2+y_{o2}^2-l_1l_2-y_B^2)+l_1x_B^2}{2(l_1x_B+l_2x_{o2}-l_1x_{o2})} \\ 0 \end{bmatrix} \quad (3)$$

Dynamics and Control Strategy Analysis
Considering the requirements of human-robot collaborative control in remote rehabilitation scenarios, the paper adopts the improved PD control strategy based on Anderson's method (IPDAM) that we previously developed [4]. This approach makes the rehabilitation robot have excellent position tracking performance while maintaining force transparency and system stability, the schematic diagram is shown in Fig. 4.

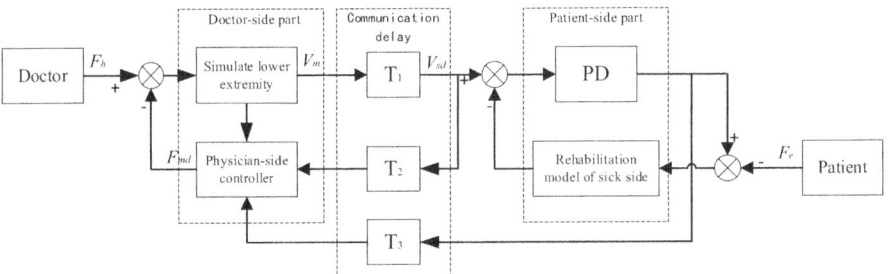

Fig. 4. Schematic diagram of IPDAM

From the schematic diagram of IPDAM, the dynamic model of the doctor-side part is:

$$F_h(t) - F_{md}(t) = M_m \dot{V}_m(t) + B_m V_m(t) \quad (4)$$

The dynamic model of the patient-side part is:

$$F_s(t) - F_e(t) = M_s \dot{V}_s(t) + B_s V_s(t) \quad (5)$$

The mathematical model of the IPDAM can be obtained as follows:

$$\begin{cases} F_{md}(t) = F_s(t - t_2(t)) + n^2(V_m(t) - V_{sd}(t - t_2(t))) \\ F_s(t) = K_{Ps} \int (V_{sd}(t) - V_s(t))dt + K_{Ds}(V_{sd}(t) - V_s(t)) \end{cases} \quad (6)$$

where M, V, B is mass, velocity, velocity damping coefficients and respectively; s denotes the complex variables of function after *Laplace* transformation; F_{md} is the force which fed back from patient-side to doctor-side after correction; F_s is the force of patient-side's position tracking control; V_{sd} is the corrected doctor-side speed received by the patient-side; K_P, K_D is the proportional and differential coefficients of the patient-side controller respectively; t_1, t_2 is communication time-delay from doctor-side to patient-side and patient-side to doctor-side respectively; n^2 is the characteristic impedance of Anderson method.

In order to ensure the stability of the aforementioned control system, *Liewellyn* criterion [20] is used for verification. The detailed validation procedures have been verified in the previous paper [4]. Since the primary purpose of this paper is not to innovate control strategy, further elaboration on this aspect will not be provided herein.

Patient Dynamic Virtualization

The control logic of CDLLRR is that a parallel cable-driven mechanism drives the ankle joint to move, thereby inducing gait movement in the lower limbs. In order to accurately realize dynamic simulation of lower limb motions in virtual environments, accurate inverse kinematic (IK) control of human lower limbs is needed. In this paper, the lower limb is simplified into a two-link mechanism for control, and the lower limb motion control model is built based on the Unity 3D's IK system. Therefore, the Two-Bone IK Constraint component is selected to realize human IK functionality.

2.3 Mixed Reality Collaboration Module Design

The MR collaboration module establishes a virtual-physical interactive mechanism through the Unity3D's 3D motion data fusion engine and the HoloLens2 MR platform. The system integrates the three core modules: biometric parameter collection, training command transmission and security monitoring, establishing a bidirectional closed-loop system between virtual part and physical part. Doctors can control the patient-side equipment via the doctor-side actuator, while the MR interface synchronously displays the patient's motion information, forming a closed-loop rehabilitation framework. This can allow doctors to dynamically optimize training plans based on quantitative indicators.

Based on Unity 3D Human-Machine Interaction System

The core function of the HMI system is the visual display of the expected input and actual output of CDLLRR, among which the output visualization depends on the virtual-real synchronization of CDLLRR. In order to realize these core functions, the user interface (UI) and virtual model driver of the HMI system need to be designed.

The UI of the HMI system consists of a 3D visualization scene and a HMI control panel. The 3D scene module includes a patient-side model, a virtual human body model and an environmental scene model, achieving dynamic synchronization between physical entities and virtual space through virtual-real mapping technology. The HMI control panel integrates multi-modal operation interfaces, covering real-time control, virtual-real synchronization interfaces and graphical displays. The 3D scene and the HMI panel achieve visual collaboration through a unified rendering engine, enabling doctors to maintain environmental awareness while ensuring intuitive operational interaction and status monitoring within the MR environment. The UI display effect is shown in Fig. 5.

The modular control architecture (see Fig. 6) is implemented using C# scripting to apply dynamic behavioral constraints to the virtual models. The system core functions include: 1. IK-based joint angles resolution to drive model motion; 2. Feedforward control algorithms to generate motor drive commands; 3. Coordinating multi-module operation with a global state machine. Static classes are used to centrally manage key parameters such as hip/knee joint angle, ankle joint position and motor rotation angle to ensure global uniqueness of the data.

Fig. 5. The UI of HMI system

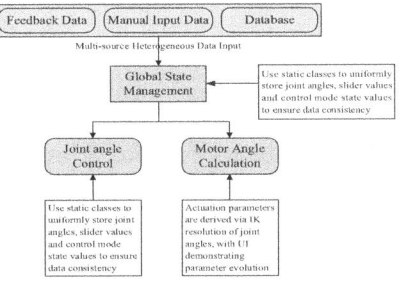

Fig. 6. C# scripting program

Based on HoloLens2 Platform Deployment

In response to the hardware performance limitations of HoloLens2, a remote streaming architecture based on PC and head-side display is adopted: high-load scene rendering and logical operations are completed on the PC, and video streams are transmitted in real-time to HoloLens2 through the local area network, thereby reducing device memory consumption. The deployment process is illustrated in Fig. 7.

As shown in Fig. 8, the system uses virtual-reality hybrid display technology to construct the MR interface: interactive robot models, UI interaction panels and dynamic gesture recognition frameworks are superimposed in the virtual scene, and the black background area is a perspective window. Doctors can use the client to observe the real-time movement status of the robot and the patient, enabling rehabilitation assessment and dynamic parameter adjustments.

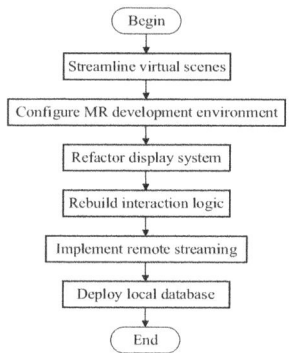
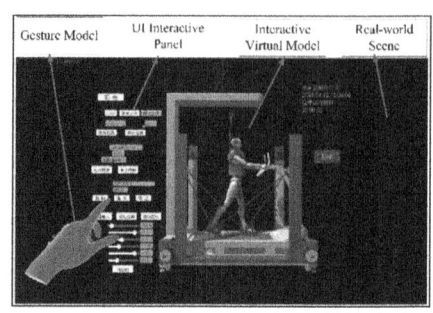

Fig. 8. HoloLens2 runtime effect diagram

Fig. 7. HoloLens2 Deployment

3 Experimental Study

In this paper, the FAB motion capture system is used to collect ankle joint motion trajectory and kinematic data during lower limb flexion-extension gait movements. The experimental subjects, a healthy young male (25 years old, 168 cm in height, 57 kg in weight), was selected according to international adult anthropometric standards. The human simulation model and biomechanical analysis system were constructed through the OpenSim platform, and the simulation data was used to compensate and correct the raw FAB measured data. Finally, this process enabled the construction of reference angle curve of the hip and knee joint (see Fig. 9a, b). Meanwhile, the theoretical ankle joint motion trajectory (see Fig. 9c) was obtained by substituting these data into Eq. (2).

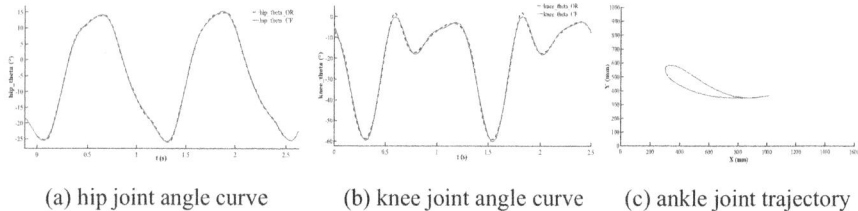

(a) hip joint angle curve   (b) knee joint angle curve   (c) ankle joint trajectory

Fig. 9. Limb kinematic data during gait flexion-extension training

The results show that the generated ankle joint motion trajectory is highly consistent with normal human gait characteristics, and the kinematic parameters conform to the physiological gait cycle patterns. The high-precision fitting of hip and knee joint angle data ($R^2 > 0.9996$) and the physiological consistency of the ankle joint trajectory collectively validate the effectiveness of the planned trajectory.

Experimental rehabilitation training researches were carried out based on the desired trajectory obtained from aforementioned motion plan. The doctor reproduced this trajectory using the simulated lower extremity, which was transmitted to the patient-side through the control system and information feedback loop, and patient-side part drove end effector to track the trajectory through the cable. During experiments, the UI of

HMI system provided real-time synchronized display of quantitative indicators including patient motion information and motor rotation angles data (see Fig. 10). The experiment evaluated tracking performance using root mean square error (RMSE), and incorporated visual feedback obtained by doctors through an interactive interface to verify the system's applicability.

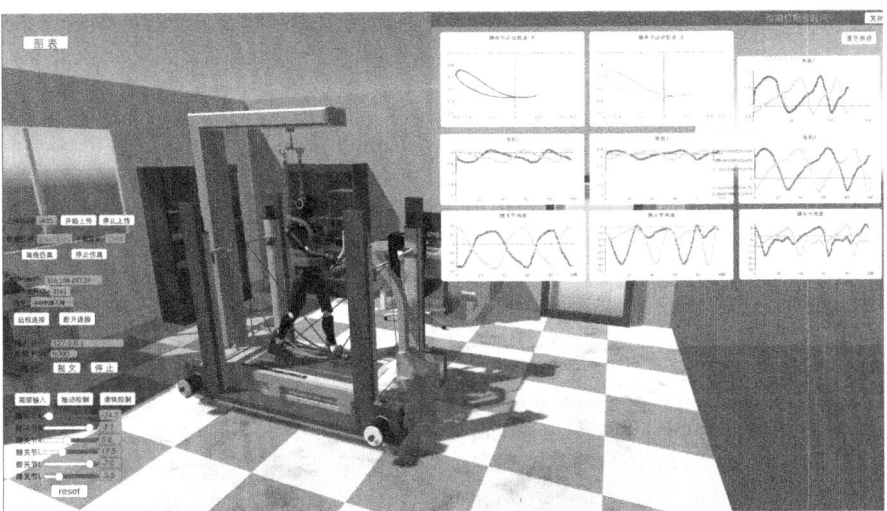

Fig. 10. Visualization of Virtual-Real Synchronization in UI of HMI system

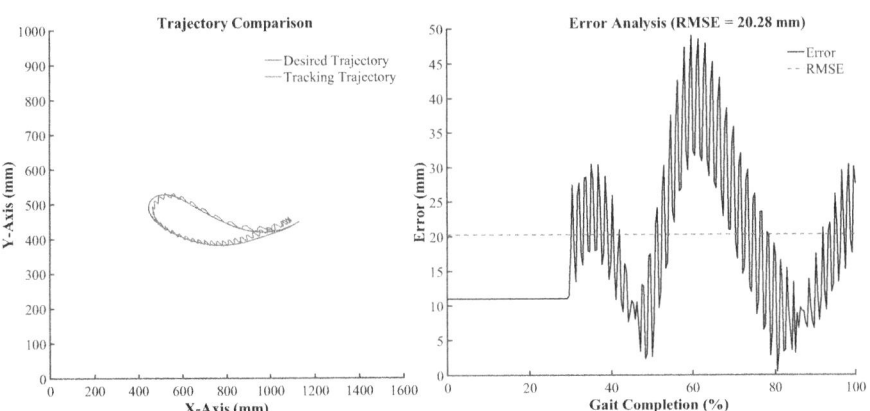

Fig. 11. Trajectory tracking experimental results

Experimental results show that the motion trend between the tracking trajectory of the end effector of patient-side part and the desired trajectory of the doctor-side part is consistent. And as illustrated in Fig. 11, the error fluctuations remained below 50 mm, with an RMSE of 20.28 mm between the two trajectories, the result indicate that the tele-rehabilitation system has excellent tracking accuracy. Additionally, the UI of HMI system synchronously displays statistical panels such as the time-position trajectory plots of the ankle joint, the angle analysis diagram of the hip joint and knee joint, and the motor rotation angle diagram. The multi-modal visual data enables doctors to accurately identify relevant parameters such as motion trajectories, providing quantitative foundations for establishing a data-driven rehabilitation evaluation framework.

4 Conclusion

This paper proposes a MRTGTS, aiming to solve the problems of low interaction efficiency and non-intuitive information feedback during remote rehabilitation. First, multi-dimensional virtualization processing is carried out on the patient-side part and patient through a hierarchical modeling approach, aiming to establish the HPVSMS. Secondly, the MR collaboration module has been developed based on Unity3D and HoloLens2, integrating 3D visualization scenes and remote streaming technology. This enables doctors to monitor the patient's motion status in real time through the HMI interface, allowing for real-time rehabilitation assessment and training adjustment. Finally, experiments verify the effectiveness of the proposed approach and motion planning method, and the feasibility of the HMI interface in practical applications was confirmed.

The introduction of MRTGTS for doctors has significantly improved doctors' ability to quantitatively analyze rehabilitation status, and provided new insights for the doctor-side interactive design of remote rehabilitation systems. Future research will extend to multi-patient collaborative training scenarios and develop intelligent rehabilitation assessment algorithms to enhance system versatility; concurrently, we will implement phased validation with real clinical data and quantifiable performance metrics to ensure methodological rigor.

Acknowledgments. This work is funded by the National Science Foundation of China (Grant Number: 52175006), the Heilongjiang Province Natural Science Foundation (Grant Number: LH2023E064) and the Ningbo Province 'Yongjiang Innovation and Science Initiative 2035' (Grant Number: 2024Z200).

References

1. Lu, Z., Jie, Z., Yao, L., et al.: The human-machine interaction methods and strategies for upper and lower extremity rehabilitation robots: a review. IEEE Sens. J. **24**(9), 13773–137872024 (2024)
2. Babaiasl, M., Mahdioun, S.H., et al.: A review of technological and clinical aspects of robot-aided rehabilitation of upper-extremity after stroke. Disabil. Rehabil. Assist. Technol. **11**(4), 263–280 (2016)
3. Sheng, B., Xie, S., Tang, L., et al.: An industrial robot-based rehabilitation system for bilateral exercises. IEEE Access **7**, 151282–151294 (2019)
4. Wang, Y.Z., Wang, L., Wang, K.Y., et al.: Research on a new cable-driven lower limb rehabilitation robot with bilateral coordination control. Proc. Inst. Mech. Engineers Part C-J. Mech. Eng. Sci. **238**(14), 7143–7154 (2024)

5. Alapati, S., Seth, D., Nakka, S., et al.: Validation of cable-driven experimental setup to assess movements made with elbow joint assistance. Appl. Sci.-Basel **15**(4), 1892 (2025)
6. Saracino, A., Oude-Vrielink, T.J.C., Menciassi, A., et al.: Haptic intracorporeal palpation using a cable-driven parallel robot: a user study. IEEE Trans. Biomed. Eng. **67**(12), 3452–3463 (2020)
7. Zareinia, K., Maddahi, Y., Ng, C., et al.: Performance evaluation of haptic hand-controllers in a robot-assisted surgical system. Int. J. Med. Rob. Comput. Assist. Surg. **11**(4), 486–501 (2015)
8. Liu, Y., Guo, S., Yang, Z., et al.: A home-based tele-rehabilitation system with enhanced therapist-patient remote interaction: a feasibility study. IEEE J. Biomed. Health Inform. **26**(8), 4176–4186 (2022)
9. Miao, M., Gao, X., Zhu, W.: A construction method of lower limb rehabilitation robot with remote control system. Appl. Sci. **11**(2), 867 (2021)
10. Garzo, A., Jung, J.H., Arcas-Ruiz-Ruano, J., et al.: Armassist: a telerehabilitation solution for upper-limb rehabilitation at home. IEEE Robot. Autom. Mag. **30**(1), 62–71 (2022)
11. Guo, X.H., Wang, J., Yang, Y., et al.: Active and passive training system of lower limb rehabilitation based on virtual reality. J. Xi'an Jiaotong Univ. **50**(2), 124–131 (2016)
12. Wang, F., Wen, Y., Bi, J., et al.: A portable SSVEP-BCI system for rehabilitation exoskeleton in augmented reality environment. Biomed. Signal Process. Control **83**, 104664 (2023)
13. Pinto-Fernández, D., Gómez, M., Rodrigues, C., et al.: Augmented reality feedback for exoskeleton-assisted walking. a feasibility study. In: 2023 International Conference on Rehabilitation Robotics (ICORR), pp. 1–6. IEEE, Singapore (2023)
14. Arpaia, P., Duraccio, L., Moccaldi, N., et al.: Wearable brain–computer interface instrumentation for robot-based rehabilitation by augmented reality. IEEE Trans. Instrum. Meas. **69**(9), 6362–6371 (2020)
15. Wang, W., He, Y., Li, F., et al.: Digital twin rehabilitation system based on self-balancing lower limb exoskeleton. Technol. Health Care **31**(1), 103–115 (2023)
16. Sosa-Méndez, D., García-Cena, C.E.: Robotic digital twin as a training platform for rehabilitation health personnel. Enfoque UTE. **14**(3), 19–26 (2023)
17. Li, J.H., Wang, K.Y., Wang, Y.Z., et al.: Motion planning for a cable-driven lower limb rehabilitation robot with movable distal anchor points. J. Bionic Eng. **20**(4), 1585–1596 (2023)
18. Wang, K.Y., Wang, Y.L., Yin, P.C.: Design and remote collaboration control of asymmetric rigid flexible hybrid-driven lower limb rehabilitation robot. Proc. Inst. Mech. Engineers Part C-J. Mech. Eng. Sci. **236**(3), 1796–1814 (2021)
19. Wang, Y.L., Wang, K.Y., Zhang, Z.X., et al.: Mechanical characteristics analysis of a bionic muscle cable-driven lower limb rehabilitation robot. J. Mech. Med. Biol. **20**(10), 2040037 (2020)
20. Jazayeri, A., Tavakoli, M.: Revisiting Llewellyn's absolute stability criterion for bilateral teleoperation systems under non-passive operator or environment. In: 2012 IEEE/RSJ International Conference on Intelligent Robots and Systems. vol. 106, pp.70–75. IEEE, Algarve (2012)

A Novel Deep Learning Enhanced Particle Swarm Optimization for Puncture Path Planning

Jianfeng Yao, Zhuang Fu[✉], Canhui Wu, Zi Fang, Bang Liu, and Fei Jing

School of Mechanical Engineering, Shanghai Jiao Tong University, Shanghai, China
zhfu@sjtu.edu.cn

Abstract. Flexible needle insertion has emerged as a promising technique for minimally invasive procedures, yet their curved trajectories make feasible path planning challenging. In this study, we propose a novel deep learning enhanced particle swarm optimization (EPSO) algorithm for puncture path planning. A dense network-based model is first trained to generate a spatial probability distribution of optimal paths. This guidance is then integrated into the key components of PSO—initialization, and velocity update—to enhance sampling efficiency and trajectory quality. The proposed method generates smoother, shorter, and safer needle trajectories while maintaining rapid convergence performance. Experiments demonstrate the effectiveness and generalizability of the approach across diverse scenarios, suggesting its potential for clinical application in image guided interventions.

Keywords: Path Planning · Particle Swarm Optimization · Deep Learning Method · Surgical Robotics

1 Introduction

Lung malignant tumors remain one of the most morbid and lethal cancers worldwide [1]. Minimally invasive procedures such as percutaneous needle biopsy and ablation have become critical clinical options for early diagnosis and local control of tumors [2]. However, traditional rigid puncture needles often struggle to simultaneously balance path shortening, safety and targeting accuracy when traversing critical structures such as blood vessels or bronchi. This can therefore increase the risk of complications such as pneumothorax, bleeding and targeting errors. Flexible beveled-tip needles with controllable bending curvature offer new possibilities for obstacle avoidance and precise localization, but also present more complex path planning challenges.

To overcome the limitations of rigid needle in obstacle avoidance and targeting accuracy, researchers have proposed various curved path planning approaches. Sampling-based methods, such as RRT*/IRRT*, are widely used for steerable needle path planning due to their strong global exploration capabilities [11]. Patil et al. proposed an interactive RRT-based planner that integrates reachable region sampling and duty-cycling control strategy, which can generate multiple curvature feasible insertion paths in obstacle-rich environments [3]. Based on IRRT*, Xiong et al. incorporated the flexible needle kinematic constraints into the sampling extension and introduced a comprehensive length-safety-circularity evaluation metric [4]. They realized the generation of continuous optimal curve paths which is more suitable for the clinical needs than the traditional RRT. Huang et al. proposed a target directed TRBi-RRT algorithm that utilizes variable arc planning to enable obstacle-avoiding insertion of flexible needles [5]. Experimental results demonstrated a targeting error of no more than 4 mm, with shorter paths and fewer nodes, thereby improving the efficiency and accuracy of robot-assisted minimally interventions. Ensuring safety, smooth trajectories, and real-time adaptability is essential for clinical feasibility, similar to the design principles seen in wearable medical devices for tremor suppression, which emphasize precise control and patient comfort [8].

Deep learning has demonstrated powerful feature abstraction and representation capabilities in tasks such as medical image segmentation and surgical navigation. In recent years, researchers have begun exploring the integration of neural networks with traditional algorithms to enhance the intelligence and generalizability of path planning systems. Wang et al. proposed NRRT*, which utilizes CNN-predicted optimal path probability distributions to guide RRT* sampling, significantly reducing the optimization time and memory overhead while maintaining probabilistic completeness and asymptotic optimality [6]. Huang et al. proposed NIRRT* which utilize PointNet++ to guide ellipsoidal internal sampling and ensure the connectivity through the Neural Connect Network. They significantly improved the initial solving speed and optimal convergence rate [7]. More recently, Yao et al. proposed NG-RRT*, which fuses a 3D U-Net based entry point selector and an optimal path predictor to accelerate convergence and produce smoother, kinematically feasible needle paths in complex 3D anatomies [12].

Although the aforementioned studies have demonstrated the effectiveness of learning-based heuristics in path planning, no prior work has yet achieved a deep integration of neural network with particle swarm optimization (PSO) for flexible lung needle path planning. Existing PSO-based methods remain limited to heuristic parameter tuning and lack prior guidance driven by medical imaging and anatomical data, which constrains their applicability in complex clinical scenarios.

In summary, sampling-based and numerical algorithms have made progress in flexible needle puncture, but there is still room for improvement in terms of convergence speed and curve continuity. PSO provides a natural framework for continuous curve optimization, but is limited by the inefficiency of early search due to stochasticity. To solve the above problems, we propose a novel deep learning enhanced particle swarm optimization for puncture path planning. Firstly, we design and train a neural network to predict the possible distribution of sampling paths. Then, we enhanced the particle swarm optimization (EPSO) algorithm through two injection channels: initialization, and velocity/position update modulation. The proposed method achieves shorter, smoother, and safer puncture trajectories while maintaining real-time computational performance, thereby improving its clinical feasibility.

2 Method

2.1 Unicycle Kinematic Model

The flexible needle can avoid critical anatomical structures, due to its bevel tip and elastic body. During puncture, the tip of the needle is bent to one side by the asymmetric reaction force of the tissue, resulting in a circular trajectory. Researchers have proposed a variety of kinematic models based on this characteristic, the most widely used of which is the unicycle model [9]. As shown in Fig. 1, the motion of the bevel-tip needle can be controlled by two degrees of freedom: the feed velocity v along the axis and the rotational velocity ω around the axis. The pose of the needle tip can be represented as $q = [x, y, \theta]$, where x and y are the coordinates in the needle tip's reference frame, and θ is the rotation angle around the needle's axis. The motion of the needle tip can be expressed by the following equation, where λ is $+1$ or -1, depending on the direction of the bevel angle.

$$\begin{bmatrix} \dot{y} \\ \dot{x} \\ \dot{\theta} \end{bmatrix} = \begin{bmatrix} \cos\theta & -\sin\theta & 0 \\ \sin\theta & \cos\theta & 0 \\ 0 & 0 & \lambda \end{bmatrix} \times \begin{bmatrix} v \\ 0 \\ \omega \end{bmatrix} \quad (1)$$

The radius of the arc can be controlled by adjusting the duty cycle of the feed and rotation. This relationship can be expressed as: $r = r_1/(1 - \alpha)$, where $\alpha = T_{spin}/(T_{spin} + T_{ins})$ is the duty cycle factor of the rotation period within the entire puncture cycle, and r_1 is the natural radius of the circular trajectory of the flexible needle without rotation. As a result, any arc trajectory with a radius larger than the natural radius can be achieved (such as r_2 or r_3 in Fig. 1).

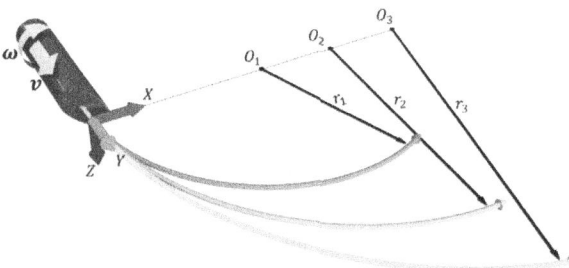

Fig. 1. Variable curvature trajectory for the bevel-tip needle with inputs ω and v.

2.2 Sampling Guidance Network

In this section, we describe the structure and implementation details of our network. We use gridded 2D maps to represent CT images. Based on the typical anatomical dimensions of the thoracic cavity, our map size is 384×256 with a resolution of $1\ mm^2$. We represent the properties of each pixel by assigning a value to it. 0 means empty space, 1 indicates obstacles, 2 and 3 representing the start and target, respectively. We use A* to label the optimal paths in the map for training the model to predict the sampling routes.

Our proposed model is shown in Fig. 2. We designed our model based on DenseNet. DenseNet replaces the traditional single convolutional layer with a "dense block + transition layer" in the encoding-decoding framework. The output of any layer is cascaded with the feature maps of all subsequent layers, thus enabling feature reuse and significantly reducing parameter redundancy.

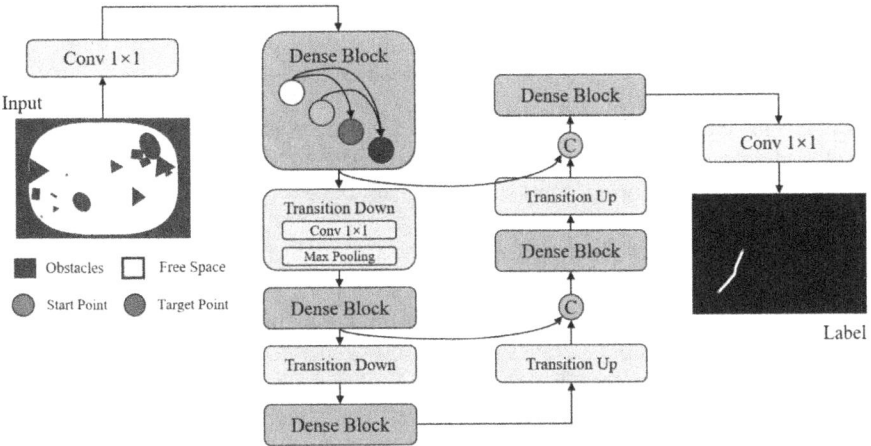

Fig. 2. Schematic diagram of the structure of the sampling guidance network

The input to the model is a map with four channels (empty space, obstacles, start and target points). And the model will output a sampling guidance probability heat map with the same size. The encoder of the network consists of three dense blocks which progressively achieve downsampling. Each dense block contains four 3×3 convolutional layers, with a growth rate of $k = 8$. Since each dense block brings an increase in the number of channels, excessive use may over-complicate the model. To address this, each dense block is followed by a transition layer composed of a convolutional layer and an max pooling layer, which halves the spatial resolution while controlling channel growth. The decoder mirrors the encoder architecture and incorporates skip connections by directly concatenating dense features from the corresponding encoder layers. Finally, a 1×1 convolutional layer is used to generate a single channel probability heatmap, indicating the likelihood of each location being part of the optimal path. We use the cross-entropy between the probability heat map and the binary labels as the loss function.

2.3 Enhanced Particle Swarm Optimization

After obtaining the probability heat map P from the neural network, we propose a novel enhanced particle swarm optimization (EPSO) as a global searcher for puncture paths. To ensure that the searching process balances both global optimality and safety requirements of clinical applications, we tightly integrated the neural network output with the two core components of particle swarm optimization: particle initialization, and velocity update.

First, to ensure that the path can actually be executed in the 2D plane by the flexible needle, the path x is parameterized as a sequence of up to M arc segments:

$$x = [\kappa_1, l_1, \ldots, \kappa_M, l_M] \in \mathbb{R}^{2M} \tag{2}$$

where the curvature κ_i and the arc length l_i together define the circular arc trajectory. Synthesizing the feasibility of operator operation, this study takes $M \leq 6$. In this parameter space, we design the following multi-objective cost function:

$$J(x) = w_1 L(x) + w_2 C(x) + w_3 R(x) + w_4 S(x) \tag{3}$$

where L is the total path length, C is the mean curvature, R is the exponential penalty for the closest distance from the trajectory to the risk structure, and S restricts mutations in the curvature of neighboring segments. In the subsequent experiments, the parameters we take are $w = [0.6, 0.2, 0.1, 0.1]$.

In standard PSO, the initial distribution of particle clusters is often highly randomized, leading to inefficient early exploration. In out method, we first select the top 1% of high-confidence clusters from the P and use them as particle initialization control points, while the rest of the particles are randomly generated in space. This step allows the initial solution set to focus directly on regions of high feasibility, while the remaining random particles maintain the search diversity.

Subsequently, on the basis of the traditional velocity update formulae:

$$\mathbf{v}_i^{t+1} = \omega \mathbf{v}_i^t + c_1 r_1 \left(\mathbf{p}_i^{best} - \mathbf{x}_i^t \right) + c_2 r_2 \left(\mathbf{g}^{best} - \mathbf{x}_i^t \right) \tag{4}$$

We introduce a third neural network injection $c_3 r_3 \left(m_i^t - x_i^t \right)$, where m_i^t is the pointing of the particle's current position on the probability gradient field ∇P. This guidance mechanism is equivalent to superimposing a gravitational force in velocity space that aligns with the local "reachable upward direction", which can effectively shorten the number of steps for particles to reach the high-confidence region.

3 Experiments and Discussion

All the computation is conducted on a laptop equipped with i7-13650HX@4.9 GHz CPU, NVIDA RTX 4060 laptop GPU, and 32G RAM.

3.1 Experimental Setup

We constructed 5000 2D maps as our dataset, and the training and validation sets were divided in the ratio of 8:2. Our maps were set to approximate the size of a common CT image, while the thoracic region requiring path planning only occupies a portion of the map. To prevent the algorithm from planning paths into irrelevant areas, we first label regions outside the thoracic cavity as obstacles. To model the geometry of the thoracic, we approximate its shape using a super ellipse $\left(\left|\frac{x}{a}\right|^3 + \left|\frac{y}{b}\right|^3 = 1 \right)$. This representation captures the general contour of the thorax while facilitating efficient computation and obstacle labeling within the voxel space.

To simulate critical anatomical structures that must be avoided during needle insertion, we randomly place multiple obstacles—such as circles, ellipses, rectangles, and triangles—on each synthetic map. The number and positions of these obstacles are randomized to increase the diversity and complexity of the simulated planning scenarios. We set the puncture entry point on the super ellipse (randomized by angle), and the target point inside the ellipse. In order to make the trained model adaptable to common clinical puncture depths, the Eulerian distance between the start and the target in each map is limited to between 30–120 [10]. We use A* to obtain the optimal path for each map. In order to reduce the difficulty of learning and improve the quality of subsequent sampling, we expand the optimal paths by one pixel and use them as labels.

3.2 Path Planning Under Different Puncture Depth

To evaluate the performance of EPSO at different surgical depths, we synthesized 150 maps of the test set according to the Euclidean distance between the starting point and the target point: shallow (30–60 mm), medium (60–90 mm) and deep (90–120 mm). The definitions of thorax and obstruction are the same as previously described. The planning results of EPSO in three maps are shown in Fig. 3. EPSO successfully plans feasible puncture paths in all the maps through multiple rounds of iterative optimization. Combined with the circular trajectory characteristics, EPSO can directly obtain smooth and continuous trajectories without post-processing. At the same time, this method can directly control the number of arc segments in the trajectory by adjusting particle parameters, which avoids the problem of too many turns in traditional methods such as RRT*.

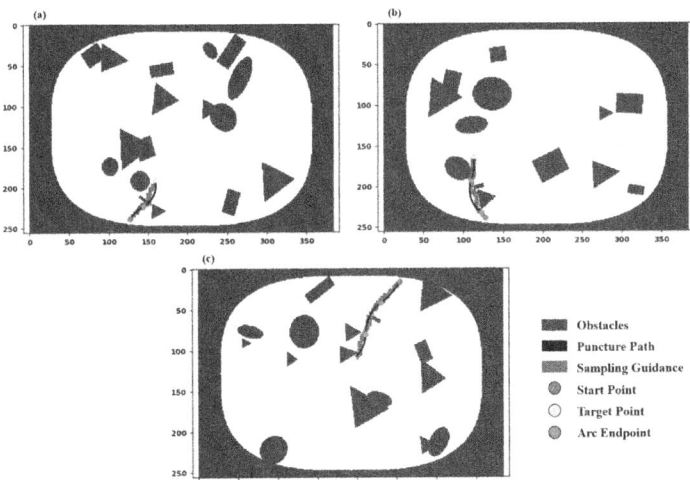

Fig. 3. Puncture paths of EPSO in three types of maps. a) shallow (30–60 mm); b) medium (60–90 mm); c) deep (90–120 mm).

We further compared the proposed algorithm with Genetic Algorithm (GA) and Particle Swarm Optimization (PSO), as illustrated in Fig. 4. In general, the integrated cost curve shifts upward and shows more fluctuations as the puncture depth increases. However, EPSO, which introduces the neural guidance, always maintains the fastest descending speed and the smallest variance. In shallow scenarios, EPSO reduced the path cost to approximately 49 within the first 20 iterations, outperforming PSO and GA by 2.2% and 3.2%, respectively. As the insertion depth increased to medium levels, its advantage became more pronounced, stabilizing around 80 by iteration 30, while PSO and GA plateaued at 82 and 85, respectively. When the puncture depth exceeded 90mm, the global search capabilities of traditional evolutionary algorithms significantly deteriorated. GA exhibited increasing variance and the slowest convergence, while PSO showed a secondary cost drop around iteration 120 but was still outperformed by EPSO with a 1.7 margin.

Across the three insertion depth levels, EPSO required only 37 ± 9 iterations to reach 95% of its final performance, outperforming PSO (86 ± 15) and GA (112 ± 24). It consistently achieved the lowest convergence costs: 49.1 ± 0.4, 80.2 ± 0.6, and 109.3 ± 0.9 for shallow, medium, and deep scenarios, respectively. These results demonstrate that neural guidance not only improves global search efficiency but also suppresses early-stage drift and oscillation in the particle swarm, enabling rapid convergence and stable generation of high-quality puncture paths across all depth scenarios.

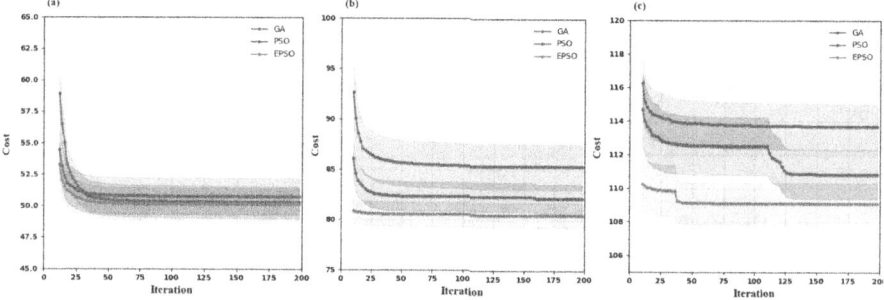

Fig. 4. Convergence curves of GA, PSO and EPSO in three scenarios. a) shallow (30–60 mm); b) medium (60–90 mm); c) deep (90–120 mm).

3.3 Path Planning Under Different Initialization Ratios

Finally, to investigate the contribution of neural guidance during the initialization phase of the particle swarm, we conducted experiments on medium-depth scenarios from the validation set. Specifically, we configured 0%, 25%, 50%, and 75% of the particles to be initialized using neural network guidance, with the remaining particles sampled uniformly at random. These configurations are denoted as EPSO_0, EPSO_25, EPSO_50, and EPSO_75, respectively. Figure 5 presents the average convergence curves and a magnified view of the critical convergence region to analyze the effect of guidance proportion on performance.

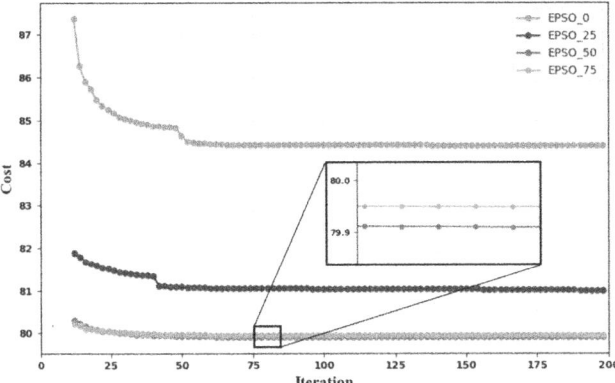

Fig. 5. Convergence curves for different initialized mixing ratios.

As the heuristic percentage increases, the algorithm shows consistent improvements in two areas. The first is the speed of convergence: While EPSO_0 with complete randomization takes about 50 iterations to reach 95% termination cost, EPSO_25 reduces this number to 32. When the proportion increases above 50%, the curve plateaus within 20 iterations. Next is the final cost: EPSO_0 stabilizes at around 84.4. After adding a quarter of the heuristic particles, the cost drops to 81.1. The marginal gain decreases efficiently as the proportion continues to increase up to 50% and 75%, with termination values of 79.91 and 79.95, respectively. Statistical tests show that the difference between 50% and 75% is indistinguishable within the 95% confidence interval, but both are significantly better than 25% and 0%.

The experimental results indicate that incorporating even a small proportion of neural prior can effectively reduce the search space and improve convergence efficiency. When the proportion of guided particles exceeds 50%, the algorithm has already leveraged sufficient information about the feasible region, and further increasing the ratio yields diminishing returns. Therefore, we recommend using 50% heuristic initialization as the default configuration, striking a favorable balance between local optimization and global exploration.

4 Conclusion

In this work, we introduce an end-to-end puncture path planning framework that unifies convolutional neural inference with particle based global optimization. A Dense Network predictor learns from A*-labelled maps and output the possibility heatmap of feasible trajectories. While the enhanced PSO (EPSO) exploits this information to steer the swarm toward promising regions, accelerate convergence and refine continuous arc–line sequences that respect flexible needle kinematics. Simulations across varying insertion depths confirm that the proposed EPSO consistently outperforms traditional PSO and Genetic Algorithm in terms of convergence speed, and path synthesis quality. Further experiments on initial population configurations demonstrate that even a small proportion of neural guided particles can effectively enhance the planner's performance, highlighting the practicality of the hybrid initialization strategy that combines heuristic and random sampling.

In summary, by marrying neural network with evolutionary optimization, the proposed method provides a practical and efficient solution for trajectory planning in minimally invasive procedures, and lays the groundwork for future integration with real-time surgical navigation systems.

References

1. James, S.L., Abate, D., Abate, K.H., et al.: Global, regional, and national incidence, prevalence, and years lived with disability for 354 diseases and injuries for 195 countries and territories, 1990–2017: a systematic analysis for the Global Burden of Disease Study 2017. Lancet **392**(10159), 1789–1858 (2018)
2. Zhang, S., Chen, J., Sun, H., et al.: A scientometric review of medical flexible needle systems in surgery: signal processing, navigation and control. SIViP **18**(Suppl 1), 627–642 (2024)
3. Patil, S., Alterovitz, R.: Interactive motion planning for steerable needles in 3D environments with obstacles. In: 2010 3rd IEEE RAS & EMBS International Conference on Biomedical Robotics and Biomechatronics, pp. 893–899. IEEE (2010)
4. Xiong, J., Li, X., Gan, Y., et al.: Path planning for flexible needle insertion system based on improved rapidly-exploring random tree algorithm. In: 2015 IEEE International Conference on Information and Automation, pp. 1545–1550. IEEE (2015)
5. Huang, Y., Zhang, F.: Variable curvature path planning for robot-assisted flexible needle insertion based on improved Bi-RRT algorithm. IEEE Trans. Instrument. Meas. **73**, 11–14 (2024)
6. Wang, J., Chi, W., Li, C., et al.: Neural RRT*: learning-based optimal path planning. IEEE Trans. Autom. Sci. Eng. **17**(4), 1748–1758 (2020)
7. Huang, Z., Chen, H., Pohovey, J., et al. Neural informed rrt*: learning-based path planning with point cloud state representations under admissible ellipsoidal constraints. In: 2024 IEEE International Conference on Robotics and Automation (ICRA), pp. 8742–8748. IEEE (2024)
8. Gong, K., Guo, C., Guo, W., et al.: Research on tremor suppression strategies under a constant current peripheral electrical stimulation device for Parkinson's disease. IEEE Trans. Neural Syst. Rehabil. Eng. **32**, 3071–3083 (2024)
9. Aghdam, A.N., Liu, P.X.: A novel path planner for steerable bevel-tip needles to reach multiple targets with obstacles. IEEE Trans. Instrum. Meas. **69**(10), 7636–7645 (2020)
10. Guimarães, M.D., Marchiori, E., Hochhegger, B., et al.: CT-guided biopsy of lung lesions: defining the best needle option for a specific diagnosis. Clinics **69**, 335–340 (2014)
11. Huang, Y., Yu, L., Zhang, F.: A survey on puncture models and path planning algorithms of bevel-tipped flexible needles. Heliyon **10**(3), e25002 (2024)
12. Jianfeng, Y., et al.: Neural-guided RRT*: learning-based planning of entry point and puncture path for steerable bevel-tip needle insertion. IEEE Robot. Autom. Let. **10**(9), 9016–9023 (2025)

Driving Logic Optimization and Fine Control of a Peripheral Electrical Stimulator Based on FPGA

Kening Gong, Li Jiang(✉), Xiaoran Tang, and Hong Liu

Harbin Institute of Technology, Harbin 150006, Heilongjiang, China
jiangli01@hit.edu.cn

Abstract. Peripheral electrical stimulation is a key robotic-assisted rehabilitation technology widely used for intelligent functional recovery and nervous system reconstruction. Currently, peripheral electrical stimulators are predominantly applied in clinical settings such as hospitals, but they often face challenges including large device size, limited portability, and inflexible parameter tuning. Traditional stimulators for functional electrical stimulation and transcutaneous nerve stimulation cannot fully meet the increasing demands for personalized, multi-channel, and real-time adaptive control. To overcome these limitations, this paper presents a lightweight, low-frequency peripheral electrical stimulator driven by FPGA. The device features high current control accuracy at the 0.1 mA level and pulse width precision at the microsecond level, combined with wearability, programmability, and wireless communication capabilities. It delivers stable output current with fast response times, supports multiple stimulation waveforms, and offers flexible parameter adjustments, effectively accommodating individualized patient needs. This advancement significantly improves stimulation safety, precision, and user comfort. The proposed design offers a promising technical solution for the miniaturization, intelligent control, and personalized application of peripheral electrical stimulation devices, with potential to enhance clinical rehabilitation outcomes.

Keywords: Peripheral Electrical Stimulation · FPGA-driven Stimulator · Wearable Rehabilitation Device

1 Introduction

Neurological disorders and musculoskeletal impairments are leading causes of long-term disability worldwide, significantly reducing patients' quality of life and increasing healthcare burdens [1, 2]. Rehabilitation strategies aimed at restoring motor function and enhancing neural plasticity have become essential components in clinical treatment protocols [3]. Among these, robotic-assisted rehabilitation technologies have attracted considerable attention due to their potential to provide precise, repetitive, and adaptive interventions that promote functional recovery [4–7].

Peripheral electrical stimulation (PES) represents a crucial modality within robotic rehabilitation systems, offering non-invasive means to activate muscles and nerves to restore motor control and facilitate neural reorganization [8]. PES has been widely applied in intelligent functional recovery and nervous system reconstruction, showing promising clinical outcomes for patients with stroke, spinal cord injury, and neurodegenerative diseases [9, 10]. Traditional PES devices are typically utilized in hospital or specialized clinical settings, characterized by bulky hardware, limited portability, and often lack flexible programmability [11]. These limitations constrain their practical application in daily life and long-term home-based rehabilitation.

Moreover, conventional PES systems commonly suffer from inadequate current control precision and limited capability for multi-channel stimulation [12], which restricts the adaptability and effectiveness of therapy tailored to individual patient needs. High precision in current amplitude and pulse timing is essential to ensure safe, effective stimulation while minimizing discomfort and adverse effects [13]. Meanwhile, the growing demand for wearable and user-friendly devices necessitates the development of compact, lightweight stimulators capable of real-time, multi-channel programmable control [14].

Addressing these challenges, recent research efforts have focused on integrating advanced hardware platforms, such as field-programmable gate arrays (FPGA), to achieve high-performance stimulation with flexible programmability and miniaturization. FPGA-driven stimulators provide rapid signal processing, precise timing control, and customizable waveform generation, making them well-suited for next-generation wearable rehabilitation devices [15]. However, the development of lightweight, low-frequency, multi-channel PES systems that balance portability, precision, and programmability remains an open technical challenge.

In this context, this paper proposes a novel FPGA-based lightweight peripheral electrical stimulator designed to overcome the limitations of existing devices. The proposed system achieves current control accuracy at the sub-milliampere level and pulse width precision at the microsecond scale, combined with wearable form factor and wireless communication capabilities. This innovation aims to facilitate personalized, adaptive rehabilitation interventions beyond clinical environments, ultimately improving patient autonomy and rehabilitation outcomes.

2 Method

2.1 Hardware Architecture and Implementation

The system employs the Xilinx ZYNQ 7020 as the control core, integrated with a high-precision constant current output module, to design and implement a lightweight, low-frequency peripheral electrical stimulator. The overall hardware architecture is depicted in Fig. 1 and primarily comprises the FPGA control unit, a boost converter module, a bridge-type current output module, an expandable multi-channel electrode interface, and a wireless communication module. In response to clinical demands for low-frequency stimulation parameters, the system is capable of generating current pulses with microsecond-level temporal resolution. The boost converter is employed to elevate the current to the required amplitude, ensuring effective transmission and application of stimulation waveforms.

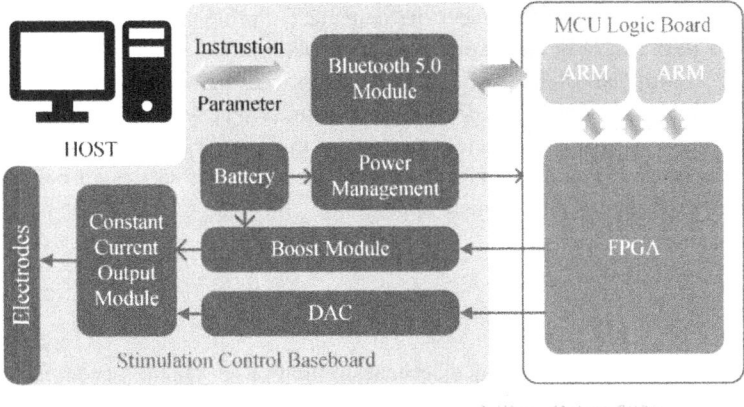

Fig. 1. System architecture of the wearable FPGA-based low-frequency electrical stimulator. The system comprises five main functional modules: an FPGA control unit, a boost converter, a constant current output module, a multi-channel electrode interface, and a Bluetooth communication module. Signal generation and modulation are coordinated via the FPGA, with wireless control enabled by Bluetooth 5.0.

The Xilinx ZYNQ 7020 integrates a dual-core ARM Cortex-A9 processor with an FPGA programmable logic unit. Leveraging its superior computational and real-time processing capabilities, the FPGA is responsible for precise generation and timing control of low-level pulse waveforms. The FPGA drives the constant current source circuit via a digital-to-analog converter (DAC), achieving high-precision current control. The constant current output module utilizes a closed-loop feedback control strategy to dynamically regulate the current output, ensuring stability and safety, effectively mitigating risks of discomfort or tissue damage caused by current fluctuations during stimulation.

The device adopts a modular design supporting flexible expansion and switching of multi-channel electrode interfaces, accommodating the diverse stimulation requirements of complex muscle groups. To meet the demands of prolonged wear, the mechanical structure is designed to be lightweight and compact, with flexible circuit board layouts enhancing comfort and adaptability. The wireless communication module, based on embedded Bluetooth technology, facilitates real-time data exchange and remote parameter adjustment between the device and host computers or mobile terminals, significantly improving portability and user experience. The overall design balances high performance, portability, and clinical applicability, fulfilling rehabilitation needs across multiple scenarios.

2.2 Stimulation Parameters and Signal Generation

To meet the demands of functional electrical stimulation (FES), the system incorporates a finely tuned driving logic architecture that supports flexible configuration of core parameters, including current amplitude, pulse frequency, and pulse width. The output current ranges from 0 to 65.28 mA and is modulated via an 8-bit digital-to-analog converter (DAC) with a resolution of 0.256 mA, allowing precise control of stimulation intensity. Pulse frequency is continuously adjustable from 1 to 256 Hz, and pulse width is configurable between 2 and 510 μs, covering the parameter space commonly used in clinical low-frequency neuromuscular applications.

The system supports both monophasic rectangular and symmetric biphasic waveforms, which are dynamically synthesized within the FPGA through parameter-driven control schemes. These waveform modes can be rapidly reconfigured in real time, enabling flexible stimulation strategies for varied therapeutic contexts. To ensure stimulation safety and minimize charge buildup, symmetric biphasic pulses are adopted as the default waveform.

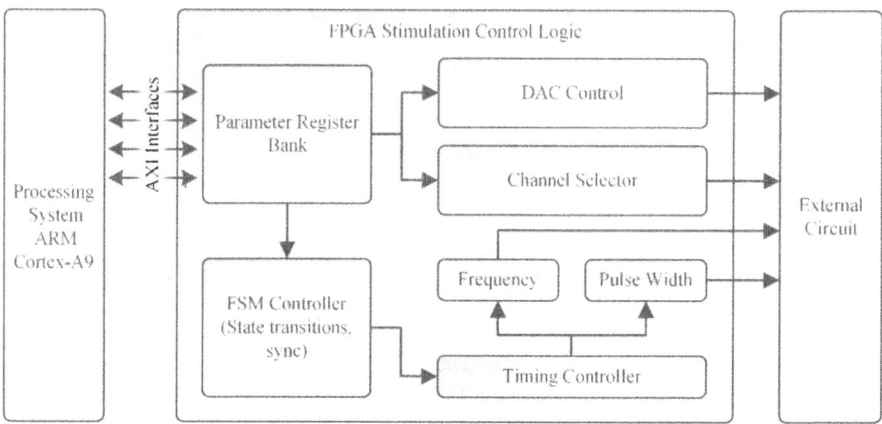

Fig. 2. Functional block diagram of the FPGA-based stimulation control architecture. The system comprises parameter configuration, precise timing and waveform control, FSM-guided logic coordination, DAC-based current modulation, and multi-channel output selection. All modules are dynamically configurable and optimized for high-resolution, safe, and synchronized stimulation delivery.

As illustrated in Fig. 2, the FPGA-based control architecture is built upon modular driving logic units, including a parameter register bank, pulse generator, timing controller, finite state machine (FSM), and channel selector. The FSM coordinates the entire stimulation cycle with microsecond-level temporal precision, orchestrating waveform generation, DAC output, timing synchronization, channel switching, and post-pulse charge balancing. Pulse frequency and width are modulated via dedicated counters and comparators, while the pulse timing and amplitude are handled by a tightly integrated timing-pulse-DAC pathway, ensuring highly deterministic control.

Fine control is further enhanced by the system's ability to support dynamic reconfiguration during runtime. All stimulation parameters are remotely adjustable via the host interface and are directly mapped to internal FPGA registers. Multi-channel coordination is achieved through the channel selector, which enables precise and synchronized output across multiple stimulation sites. These design choices—tight timing control, real-time reconfigurability, and scalable channel management—jointly realize an optimized stimulation driving logic, establishing a robust foundation for advanced features such as closed-loop feedback, spatiotemporal modulation, and intelligent control policies.

2.3 System Performance Evaluation and Application Validation

To comprehensively evaluate the performance of the proposed electrical stimulator, we conducted a series of hardware-level tests focusing on current output accuracy, pulse timing precision, system latency, and signal stability.

For current output verification, the stimulator output was connected in series with a 1 kΩ resistive load to emulate the impedance of human skin. A high-precision clamp-type current probe (HIOKI) was used to capture the stimulation waveform, and an Agilent digital oscilloscope was used for real-time signal visualization. As the DAC control word varied, the actual output current was measured and compared with theoretical values.

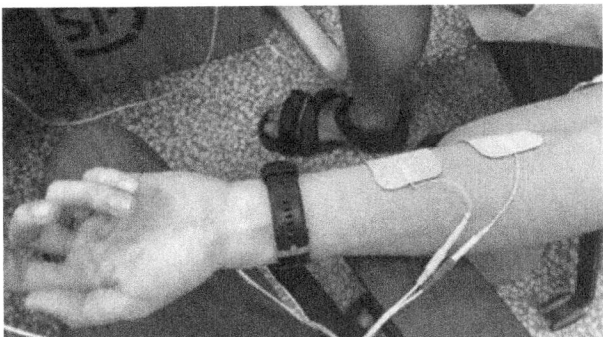

Fig. 3. Electrode placement on the forearm for human subject testing. Biphasic pulses (20 Hz, 200 μs, 5–20 mA) were applied to flexor and extensor muscles to evaluate stimulation-induced contraction.

Pulse width accuracy was assessed by configuring the system to output rectangular pulses with programmable durations ranging from 2 to 510 μs. These pulses were captured directly via a high-speed oscilloscope. The measured pulse widths closely matched the programmed values, validating the system's microsecond-level temporal precision, which is critical for consistent neuromuscular recruitment.

To verify the system's practical applicability, a human subject experiment was conducted. As shown in Fig. 3, surface electrodes were placed over the motor points of the forearm flexor and extensor muscles. The stimulation waveform was configured as symmetric biphasic rectangular pulses at 20 Hz with a pulse width of 200 µs and a current amplitude ranging from 5 to 20 mA. The subject was seated in a relaxed position, and visible muscle contractions were observed and recorded in response to stimulation. No adverse effects such as discomfort or delayed response were noted during the session.

3 Result and Discussion

3.1 Stimulation Output Performance

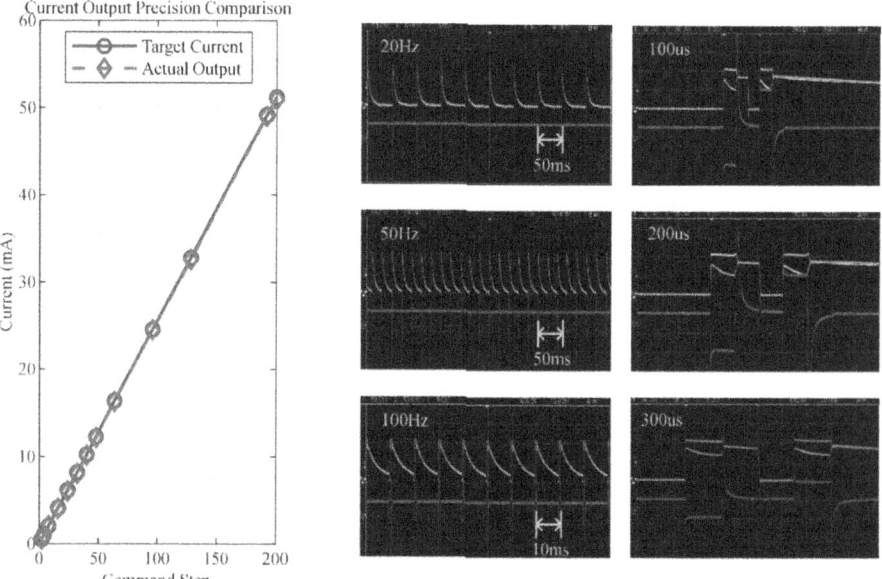

Fig. 4. Evaluation of current output and pulse timing. (Left) Output current shows high linearity and 0.256 mA resolution across DAC steps. (Right) Oscilloscope waveforms at different frequencies and pulse widths confirm accurate microsecond-level timing control.

The stimulator demonstrated excellent consistency and precision in both current amplitude control and temporal waveform shaping. As shown in Fig. 4 (left), the actual output current tracked the target current with high fidelity across the entire DAC range. The linear relationship between the command steps and measured output confirmed that the system supports fine-grained control with a resolution of 0.256 mA. The maximum deviation was within ± 2%, indicating reliable amplitude modulation for clinical stimulation demands.

In terms of temporal control, the system exhibited accurate and stable waveform output under various frequencies (20 Hz, 50 Hz, and 100 Hz) and pulse widths (100 μs, 200 μs, and 300 μs), as illustrated in Fig. 4 (right). All observed inter-pulse intervals and pulse durations matched the programmed parameters with minimal distortion or jitter. This microsecond-level timing precision is critical for neuromuscular recruitment efficiency, phase-controlled stimulation, and closed-loop timing schemes.

The observed performance confirms that the stimulator offers not only programmable flexibility but also hardware-level consistency, making it suitable for high-fidelity applications such as graded muscle activation, multi-site coordination, and protocol-dependent waveform optimization.

3.2 Stimulation Output Performance

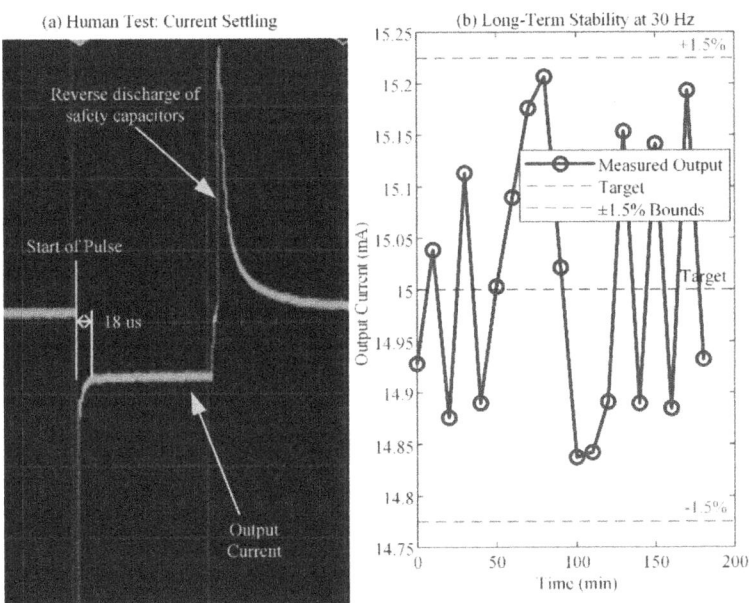

Fig. 5. Current stability performance evaluation. (a) Current settling during human stimulation, with 18 μs rise time and a reverse discharge due to safety capacitors. (b) Current stability over 3 h stimulation into a 1 kΩ load at 30 Hz, within ± 1.5% deviation.

The dynamic performance of the stimulator was evaluated in terms of its response speed and long-term output stability. These properties are essential for reliable use in real-time neuromodulation and closed-loop control systems.

Figure 5(a) shows the output current waveform measured during biphasic stimulation on a human subject. The output current reached a stable value within approximately 18 μs after pulse initiation, indicating rapid current settling. Notably, a reverse discharge was observed at the trailing edge of the pulse due to safety capacitors across the electrode-tissue interface, which is expected and physiologically safe in surface stimulation applications.

To assess long-term stability, the system was configured to deliver continuous stimulation at 30 Hz with a fixed amplitude of 15 mA into a 1 kΩ resistive load. As illustrated in Fig. 5(b), the output current was sampled every 10 min over a 3-h period. The measured current fluctuated within ±1.5% of the target value, and no waveform distortion or drift was observed. This demonstrates the system's ability to maintain consistent output over extended operation.

Overall, the stimulator achieves both fast transient response and high long-term stability, confirming its applicability for precise and sustained neuromuscular stimulation in both experimental and clinical environments.

4 Conclusion

In this study, we developed a compact, high-precision, FPGA-based wearable electrical stimulation system that integrates low-latency signal control, multi-parameter programmability, and wireless communication on a unified PCB. The system supports fine-grained control of current amplitude (0–65.28 mA, 0.256 mA resolution), pulse width (2–510 μs), and stimulation frequency (1–256 Hz), with waveform generation and output coordination managed entirely through on-chip driving logic.

Performance evaluation demonstrated that the system achieves excellent linearity in current output, microsecond-level pulse timing accuracy, and consistent multi-channel synchronization. Real-time responsiveness (≤ 20 μs) and long-term stability (±1.5% current deviation over 3 h) further validate its robustness for clinical and experimental use.

Preliminary human subject experiments confirmed the system's capability to evoke controlled muscle activation using biphasic stimulation waveforms. The results support its application in functional rehabilitation, neuromuscular research, and closed-loop motor control systems.

Future work will focus on integrating sensory feedback, implementing adaptive stimulation strategies, and expanding multi-site coordination for more complex movement restoration scenarios.

References

1. Foltynie, T., Bruno, V., Fox, S., Kühn, A.A., Lindop, F., Lees, A.J.: Medical, surgical, and physical treatments for Parkinson's disease. The Lancet. **403**, 305–324 (2024)
2. Postuma, R.B., et al.: MDS clinical diagnostic criteria for Parkinson's disease: MDS-PD Clinical Diagnostic Criteria. Mov. Disord. **30**, 1591–1601 (2015)
3. Schrag, A., Horsfall, L., Walters, K., Noyce, A., Petersen, I.: Prediagnostic presentations of Parkinson's disease in primary care: a case-control study. Lancet Neurol. **14**, 57–64 (2015)
4. Rocon, E., Belda-Lois, J.M., Ruiz, A.F., Manto, M., Moreno, J.C., Pons, J.L.: Design and validation of a rehabilitation robotic exoskeleton for tremor assessment and suppression. IEEE Trans. Neural Syst. Rehabil. Eng. **15**, 367–378 (2007)

5. Zhang, Z., Chu, B., Liu, Y., Li, Z., Owens, D.H.: Multimuscle functional-electrical-stimulation-based wrist tremor suppression using repetitive control. IEEE/ASME Trans. Mechatron. **27**, 3988–3998 (2022)
6. Habibollahi, Z., Zhou, Y., Jenkins, M.E., Garland, S.J., Naish, M.D., Trejos, A.L.: Multimodal tremor suppression of the wrist using FES and electric motors–a simulation study. IEEE Robot. Autom. Lett. **8**, 7543–7550 (2023)
7. Zhou, Y., Ibrahim, A., Hardy, K.G., Jenkins, M.E., Naish, M.D., Trejos, A.L.: Design and preliminary performance assessment of a wearable tremor suppression glove. IEEE Trans. Biomed. Eng. **68**, 2846–2857 (2021)
8. Dideriksen, J.L., et al.: Electrical stimulation of afferent pathways for the suppression of pathological Tremor. Front. Neurosci. **11** (2017)
9. Hao, M.-Z., et al.: Inhibition of Parkinsonian tremor with cutaneous afferent evoked by transcutaneous electrical nerve stimulation. J NeuroEngineering Rehabil. **14**, 75 (2017)
10. Meng, L., Jin, M., Zhu, X., Ming, D.: Peripherical electrical stimulation for parkinsonian tremor: a systematic review. Front. Aging Neurosci. **14**, 795454 (2022)
11. Widjaja, F., Shee, C.Y., Au, W.L., Poignet, P., Ang, W.T.: Using electromechanical delay for real-time anti-phase tremor attenuation system using Functional Electrical Stimulation. In: 2011 IEEE International Conference on Robotics and Automation, pp. 3694–3699. IEEE, Shanghai (2011)
12. Pascual-Valdunciel, A., et al.: Peripheral electrical stimulation to reduce pathological tremor: a review. J. NeuroEng. Rehabil. **18**, 33 (2021)
13. Pahwa, R., et al.: An acute randomized controlled trial of noninvasive peripheral nerve stimulation in essential tremor. Neuromodulation: Technol, Neural Interface **22**, 537–545 (2019)
14. Gong, K., Guo, C., Guo, W., Jiang, L., Liu, H.: Research on tremor suppression strategies under a constant current peripheral electrical stimulation device for parkinson's disease. IEEE Trans. Neural Syst. Rehabil. Eng. **32**, 3071–3083 (2024)
15. Khan, M.I., Da Silva, B.: Harnessing FPGA technology for energy-efficient wearable medical devices. Electronics **13**, 4094 (2024)

Design and Implementation of a 4-DOF Wearable Assisted Puncture Robot

Canhui Wu, Zhuang Fu[✉], Jianfeng Yao, Zi Fang, Bang Liu, and Fei Jing

School of Mechanical Engineering, Shanghai Jiao Tong University, Shanghai, China
zhfu@sjtu.edu.cn

Abstract. Puncture is a widely used surgical technique in medicine that plays a crucial role in cancer treatment. Traditional puncture surgeries require the collaboration of multiple surgeons, and the success rate relies heavily on their experience and skills. Robot technology can overcome the limitations of manual puncture effectively by improving operational accuracy and stability. This has made puncture robots a key area of focus in the field of medical robotics. In this paper, the design of a 4-Degree-of-Freedom (DOF) wearable assisted puncture robot is proposed. The robot consists of two distinct mechanisms: a position adjustment mechanism and an angle adjustment mechanism. These two mechanisms enable the planar movement of two center blocks, and translate it into the translation and pitch of the puncture needle. Kinematic analysis of the designed robot mechanism is conducted and establishes the relationship between the inputs and the outputs. Based on this proposed robot design, a prototype was manufactured that achieves the original design goals of being lightweight (0.44 kg) and compact (170 mm × 170 mm × 72 mm). The prototype can adjust the position, yaw angle and pitch angle of the puncture needle cannula. The puncture operation can then be performed by passing the needle through the cannula.

Keywords: Puncture Robot · Wearable Robot · Kinematic Analysis

1 Introduction

Cancer has become a major public health problem that is commonly faced worldwide, posing a serious threat to human health and life safety. Puncture, a surgical operation of significant prevalence, plays a crucial role in the treatment of cancer. Percutaneous puncture is usually performed with the assistance of medical imaging technology, by inserting a puncture needle into the patient's body until the target is reached, for sample extraction or drug injection. During the process of cancer treatment, puncture is an essential part of both the preoperative biopsy and the ablation therapy. Conventional puncture requires the collaborative efforts of multiple surgeons. The chief surgeon will select the appropriate position and angle based on ultrasound imaging or computed tomography (CT) findings, and manually insert the puncture needle into the patient's body. The success rate heavily depends on the experience and skills. In the event of the puncture needle failing to reach the target precisely, it is necessary to withdraw the needle and re-punctured the target. This process can cause discomfort and anxiety in the patient, and there is even a risk of damaging other healthy tissues. Furthermore, repeated punctures will result in an increase in operation time, an escalation in physical exertion of the surgeon, and a decline in the precision of the procedure.

In recent years, the concept of puncture robots has emerged, with the invention of numerous prototypes in this field. The utilization of puncture robots helps overcome several limitations inherent to conventional manual puncture. The employment of robotic mechanism ensures the secure fastening of the puncture needle, thereby preventing vibration. The combination of different sensors enables surgeons to obtain data during the puncture process in real time and respond to potential emergencies. Diverse mechanical structures and control algorithms enable the robot to adaptively and reliably cope with different puncture scenarios, reducing the reliance on the surgeon's expertise. Therefore, puncture robots have demonstrated potential advantages over conventional manual puncture, including high accuracy, strong perception and high stability. This can effectively increase the success rate of puncture and reduce medical costs and surgeons' working intensity.

In the early iterations of the puncture robot, the mechanism mainly comprised mechanical arms and was typically fixed to the beds. In 2003, Stoianovici et al. from Johns Hopkins University designed and developed the Acubot, which possesses 6 DOFs and is capable of performing positioning, orientation and needle insertion respectively. This technology is specifically designed for operating needles or other slender surgical instruments within the limited space of imaging equipment, and has been demonstrated to be suitable for X-ray guided puncture, with an average error of 1.44 mm in clinical trials [1]. In 2005, Innomedic designed and developed the INNOMOTION system, which uses a 5-DOF pneumatic drive arm and a 180° track to complete the positioning and guidance of surgical instruments. The device is composed entirely of non-metallic materials, which allows it to achieve percutaneous intervention guided by CT or MRI, with positioning accuracy that met requirements in tests under different field strength. At a target distance of 100 mm, the average deviation is less than 0.5 mm [2]. Fischer et al. from Johns Hopkins University designed and developed a puncture robot for prostate cancer, which is compatible with the MRI environment and uses real-time imaging for precise positioning. The robot has been engineered to execute two primary translational motions (vertical and horizontal) and two rotational motions to adjust the posture of the needle. Specific application movements such as needle insertion, cannula retraction, and needle rotation can also be performed manually or automatically [3]. Song et al. from Nankai University designed and developed a spinal surgery robot. The robot employs a 5-DOF operating mechanism that can drive the joints to the designated positions according to the instructions of the control system. A locking device is used to ensure the stability of each joint. In addition, a surgical navigation system was developed, which can generate virtual 3D images based on the patient's CT scans. It is advantageous for surgeons to observe the trajectory of the puncture needle [4]. In 2013, Inoue et al. from Okayama University designed and developed a triangular link robot, adopting a control method combining PID control and gravity compensation. Experimental findings have demonstrated that the accuracy error range of the end effector was between 1 mm and 1.5 mm [5].

To enable mobility between different consulting rooms, some puncture robots are also installed on platforms equipped with wheels. In 2011, Duan et al. from Beijing Institute of Technology designed and developed a microwave ablation robot that was guided by ultrasound. The robot can guide a 5-DOF puncture needle to the designated position and posture. The surgeon then inserts the puncture needle actively to complete the surgical procedure. In experiments conducted on animals, the systematic error has been shown to be less than 2.5 mm, meeting the requirements for ultrasound-guided ablation surgery [6]. In 2016, Liu et al. from Beijing University of Technology designed and developed a joint puncture robot, which has a large working space and good flexibility. The workstation can receive the patient's CT images, map them into three-dimensional images, obtain the joint angle according to the puncture path set by the doctor, and direct the robot to the target puncture position [7].

The popularization of lightweight design has led to the emergence of the Light Puncture Robot (LPR). This kind of robot can be placed directly on the patient for puncture, thus avoiding the deviation of the puncture point caused by the patient's respiratory movement. In 2008, Bricault et al. from the University of Grenoble adopted this concept and developed a percutaneous surgical robot that is compatible with CT and MRI. The LPR possesses 5 DOFs and is divided into two components. The primary component is a needle holder directly placed on the patient, which is used to achieve the rotation, feed and pitch of the needle. The other part includes a support frame and four translating actuators, which are used to achieve translational movements over the patient's body. The device weighs only 1 kg. The translation accuracy at small distances is less than 1°, and the deviation for a puncture with a depth of 6 cm is less than 2 mm [8]. Maurin et al. from the University of Strasbourg has designed and developed the CT-Bot. CT-Bot adopts a 5-DOF parallel structure, has a hemispherical working space, and can be directly worn on patients. The robot is capable of performing interventional surgeries with the guidance of CT scanning imaging. In the experimental test, the position error was found to be 0.76 mm and the angle error was 0.45° [9]. In 2016, Hata et al. from Harvard Medical School in the United States designed and developed a cryoablation robot for renal cancer. In the body model experiment, when the depth was 80 mm, the puncture accuracy could reach 0.3 mm [10]. In 2017, XACT Robotics designed and developed the ACE system, which can adjust the moving probe to reach the precise target in the patient's body in real time based on CT images and in coordination with the patient's respiratory movements. The accuracy error of the probe is less than 1.7 mm, and the average puncture time is less than 8.5 min [11]. In 2018, NDR Medical Technology designed and developed the ANT-X system, which uses spherical joints to assist in clamping the puncture needle. The system has been developed to adjust the posture of the puncture needle based on CT images. The puncture needle is then inserted into the patient's body by the surgeon to complete the procedure [12]. This focus on lightweight, wearable, and patient-friendly design is also seen in the development of peripheral stimulation devices for tremor management [13]. In parallel with wearable platform design, learning-guided planning has advanced entry point selection and puncture path optimization, demonstrating great application potential [14].

This paper introduces a new type of 4-DOF wearable assisted puncture robot with a novel mechanical structure, as shown in Fig. 1. The robot can adjust the posture of the puncture needle in order to align with the specific requirements of the surgical procedure. Furthermore, the robot is characterized by its compact size and light weight, which makes it portable for surgeons and wearable for patients.

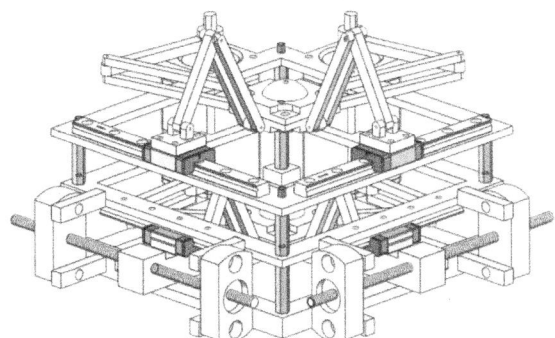

Fig. 1. 4-DOF Wearable Assisted Puncture Robot

2 Mechanical Design

The puncture robot has 4 DOFs and is divided into two parts: the position adjustment mechanism and the angle adjustment mechanism.

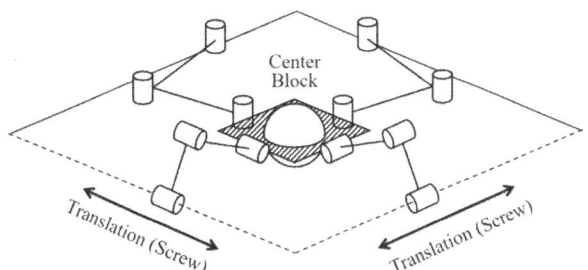

Fig. 2. Position Adjustment Mechanism

As shown in Fig. 2, the position adjustment mechanism is located at the lower layer of the robot. This part adopts a dual-screw mechanism, whose function is to adjust the insertion position of the puncture needle. The two screws respectively drive a slider along the guide rail. The slider is connected to two adjacent sides of the center block through two connecting rods, thereby achieving the linear movement of the center block in two mutually perpendicular directions. The remaining two adjacent sides of the center block are fixed on the base through another two connecting rods to ensure that the center block moves within the same horizontal plane.

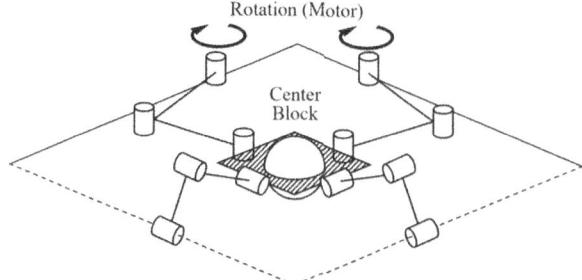

Fig. 3. Angle Adjustment Mechanism

As shown in Fig. 3, the angle adjustment mechanism is located at the upper layer of the robot. This part adopts a parallel SCARA mechanism, whose function is to adjust the entry angle of the puncture needle. The movement of the centre block is achieved by the synchronized operation of two motors, each powering two connecting rods. The remaining two adjacent sides of the center block are fixed on the slider through connecting rods. The slider can slide freely on the guide rail, providing support for the center block and ensuring the stiffness of the angle adjustment mechanism.

Both mechanisms are possessed of 2 DOFs. While they are similar in mechanism principle, they differ in driving method. When the surgeon attached the robot to the patient, a preliminary positioning of the puncture position had already been made. During the implementation of the puncture, the position adjustment mechanism only required minor adjustments, thus necessitating a relatively small working space. However, given the position adjustment mechanism's lower location within the robot, the movable height is constrained. Therefore, the utilization of screw in this mechanism is based on its capacity to facilitate a compact design and uncomplicated control. In order to achieve different needle insertion angles and thereby meet different surgical requirements, it is necessary for the angle adjustment mechanism to achieve as large a working space as possible. However, given the necessity to minimize overall size of the robot, its range of motion is constrained. Therefore, the parallel SCARA, driven by motors, can achieve large-scale planar movement within a confined space.

The position adjustment mechanism and the angle adjustment mechanism both involve a center block, and each center block comprises a ball that can rotate in all directions. A through hole is incorporated into each ball. A cannula is inserted through the hole to fit with two balls. In the ball of the position adjustment mechanism, there is a baffle that serves to restrict the radial movement of the cannula. Therefore, through these two spherical joints, the translational motions of the two center blocks in their respective planes are transformed into the translational and pitch motions of the cannula. When the mechanism moves to the designated position and angle, the surgeon manually inserts the puncture needle through the cannula in order to complete the puncture procedure.

3 Kinematic Analysis

3.1 Forward Kinematics

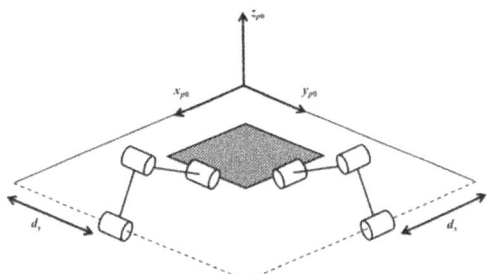

Fig. 4. Forward Kinematics Schematic of the Position Adjustment Mechanism

The forward kinematics schematic of the position adjustment mechanism is shown in Fig. 4. The inputs are the displacements of the two screws, represented by d_x and d_y respectively. The position of the center block (x_p, y_p, z_p) can be obtained through Eqs. (1) and (2):

$$x_p = d_x \tag{1}$$

$$y_p = d_y \tag{2}$$

z_p is a constant value that depends on the height of the position adjustment mechanism and remains unchanged during its movement.

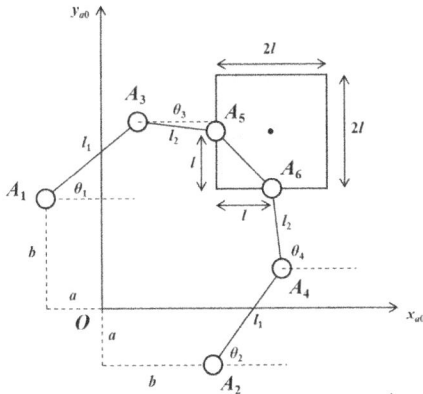

Fig. 5. Forward Kinematics Schematic of the Angle Adjustment Mechanism

The forward kinematics schematic of the angle adjustment mechanism is shown in Fig. 5. The inputs are the rotation angles of the two motors, represented by θ_1 and θ_2

respectively. The coordinates of each joint are:

$$A_1(a, b) \tag{3}$$

$$A_2(b, a) \tag{4}$$

$$A_3(a + l_1\cos\theta_1, b + l_1\sin\theta_1) \tag{5}$$

$$A_4(b + l_1\cos\theta_2, a + l_1\sin\theta_2) \tag{6}$$

$$A_5(a + l_1\cos\theta_1 + l_2\cos\theta_3, b + l_1\sin\theta_1 + l_2\sin\theta_3) \tag{7}$$

$$A_6(b + l_1\cos\theta_2 + l_2\cos\theta_4, a + l_1\sin\theta_2 + l_2\sin\theta_4) \tag{8}$$

As the distance and slope between A_5 and A_6 are fixed, their coordinates must satisfy the following equations:

$$\begin{cases} a + l_1\cos\theta_1 + l_2\cos\theta_3 + l = b + l_1\cos\theta_2 + l_2\cos\theta_4 \\ b + l_1\sin\theta_1 + l_2\sin\theta_3 - l = a + l_1\sin\theta_2 + l_2\sin\theta_4 \end{cases} \tag{9}$$

d, l, l_1 and l_2 are known constants. Therefore, the expressions for θ_3 and θ_4 are:

$$\begin{cases} \cos\theta_3 - \cos\theta_4 = \frac{l_1(\cos\theta_2 - \cos\theta_1) - a + b - l}{l_2} \stackrel{\text{def}}{=} M \\ \sin\theta_3 - \sin\theta_4 = \frac{l_1(\sin\theta_2 - \sin\theta_1) + a - b + l}{l_2} \stackrel{\text{def}}{=} N \end{cases} \tag{10}$$

According to the motion characteristics of the mechanism, the values of θ_3 and θ_4 are not arbitrary, but are constrained within a specific range. By solving Eq. (10), we can obtain θ_3 and θ_4:

$$\begin{cases} \theta_3 = \cot^{-1}\left(-\frac{N}{M}\right) - \sin^{-1}\left(\frac{\sqrt{M^2+N^2}}{2}\right) \\ \theta_4 = \cot^{-1}\left(-\frac{N}{M}\right) + \sin^{-1}\left(\frac{\sqrt{M^2+N^2}}{2}\right) \end{cases} \tag{11}$$

The position of the center block (x_a, y_a, z_a) can be obtained through Eqs. (12) and (13):

$$x_a = a + l_1\cos\theta_1 + l_2\cos\theta_3 + l = b + l_1\cos\theta_2 + l_2\cos\theta_4 \tag{12}$$

$$y_a = b + l_1\sin\theta_1 + l_2\sin\theta_3 = a + l_1\sin\theta_2 + l_2\sin\theta_4 + l \tag{13}$$

Similarly, z_a is a constant value that depends on the height of the angle adjustment mechanism and remains unchanged during its movement.

As is shown in Fig. 6, based on the coordinates of the two center blocks, the insertion position $(x_d, y_d, 0)$, yaw angle φ and pitch angle θ of the puncture needle can be obtained through Eqs. (14) to (17):

$$x_d = \frac{z_a x_p - z_p x_a}{z_a - z_p} \tag{14}$$

$$y_d = \frac{z_a y_p - z_p y_a}{z_a - z_p} \quad (15)$$

$$\varphi = \tan^{-1}\left(\frac{y_a - y_p}{x_a - x_p}\right) \quad (16)$$

$$\theta = \tan^{-1}\left(\frac{z_a - z_p}{\sqrt{(x_a - x_p)^2 + (y_a - y_p)^2}}\right) \quad (17)$$

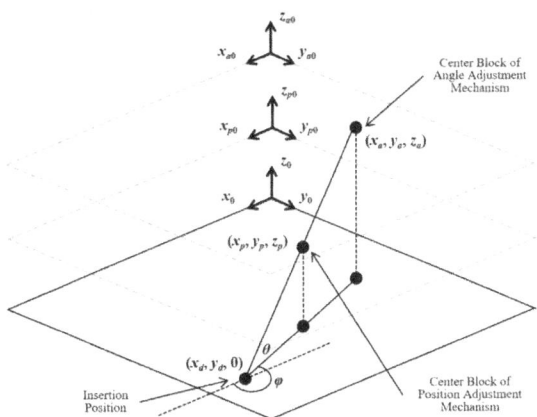

Fig. 6. Posture of the Puncture Needle

3.2 Inverse Kinematics

When the insertion position $(x_d, y_d, 0)$, yaw angle φ and pitch angle θ of the puncture needle are given, since the heights of the two center blocks z_p, z_a have been determined by the mechanism, the positions of the two center blocks can be obtained according to Eqs. (18) and (19):

$$\begin{bmatrix} z_a & -z_p \\ -1 & 1 \end{bmatrix}\begin{bmatrix} x_p \\ x_a \end{bmatrix} = \begin{bmatrix} x_d(z_a - z_p) \\ \frac{(z_a - z_p)\cos\varphi}{\tan\theta} \end{bmatrix}, \quad \begin{bmatrix} x_p \\ x_a \end{bmatrix} = \begin{bmatrix} z_a & -z_p \\ -1 & 1 \end{bmatrix}^{-1}\begin{bmatrix} x_d(z_a - z_p) \\ \frac{(z_a - z_p)\cos\varphi}{\tan\theta} \end{bmatrix} \quad (18)$$

$$\begin{bmatrix} z_a & -z_p \\ -1 & 1 \end{bmatrix}\begin{bmatrix} y_p \\ y_a \end{bmatrix} = \begin{bmatrix} y_d(z_a - z_p) \\ \frac{(z_a - z_p)\sin\varphi}{\tan\theta} \end{bmatrix}, \quad \begin{bmatrix} y_p \\ y_a \end{bmatrix} = \begin{bmatrix} z_a & -z_p \\ -1 & 1 \end{bmatrix}^{-1}\begin{bmatrix} y_d(z_a - z_p) \\ \frac{(z_a - z_p)\sin\varphi}{\tan\theta} \end{bmatrix} \quad (19)$$

In the position adjustment mechanism, the inputs of the two screws can be directly obtained from the position of the center block through Eqs. (20) and (21):

$$d_x = x_p \quad (20)$$

$$d_y = y_p \quad (21)$$

In the angle adjustment mechanism, $\theta_1, \theta_2, \theta_3$ and θ_4 satisfy:

$$\begin{cases} l_1 \cos\theta_1 + l_2 \cos\theta_3 = x_a - a - l \\ l_1 \sin\theta_1 + l_2 \sin\theta_3 = y_a - b \end{cases} \tag{22}$$

$$\begin{cases} l_1 \cos\theta_2 + l_2 \cos\theta_4 = x_a - b \\ l_1 \sin\theta_2 + l_2 \sin\theta_4 = y_a - a - l \end{cases} \tag{23}$$

From Eqs. (22) and (23) we may deduce that:

$$\cos(\theta_1 - \theta_3) = \frac{(x_a - a - l)^2 + (y_a - b)^2 - l_1^2 - l_2^2}{2 l_1 l_2} \stackrel{\text{def}}{=} P_1 \tag{24}$$

$$\cos(\theta_2 - \theta_4) = \frac{(x_a - b)^2 + (y_a - a - l)^2 - l_1^2 - l_2^2}{2 l_1 l_2} \stackrel{\text{def}}{=} P_2 \tag{25}$$

According to the motion characteristics of the mechanism, the arm $A_1 A_3 A_5$ is positioned with the elbow in an upward direction, and the arm $A_2 A_4 A_6$ is positioned with the elbow in an downward direction. Therefore:

$$\sin(\theta_1 - \theta_3) = \sqrt{1 - P_1^2} > 0 \tag{26}$$

$$\sin(\theta_2 - \theta_4) = -\sqrt{1 - P_2^2} < 0 \tag{27}$$

The inputs of the two motors can be obtained through:

$$\theta_1 = \cos^{-1} \frac{(l_1 + l_2 P_1)(x_a - a - l) - l_2 \sqrt{1 - P_1^2}(y_a - b)}{l_1^2 + l_1^2 + 2 l_1 l_2 P_1} \tag{28}$$

$$\theta_2 = \sin^{-1} \frac{(l_1 + l_2 P_2)(y_a - a - l) - l_2 \sqrt{1 - P_2^2}(x_a - b)}{l_1^2 + l_1^2 + 2 l_1 l_2 P_2} \tag{29}$$

4 Experiment

4.1 Prototype Manufacture

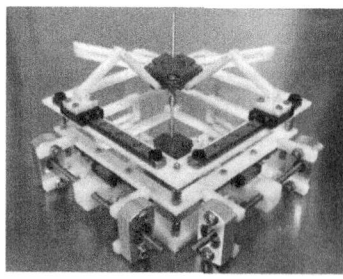

Fig. 7. Prototype of the Wearable Assisted Puncture Robot

As shown in Fig. 7, the structural components of the prototype are manufactured through 3D printing, selecting resin as the material. The mass of the prototype, without the installation of the motors, is 0.44 kg, and its dimensions are 170 mm × 170 mm × 72 mm.

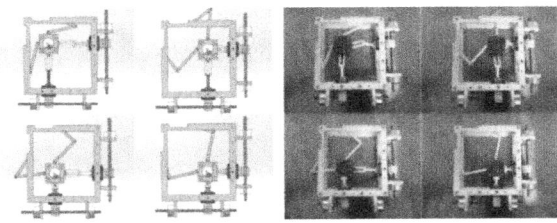

Fig. 8. Motion Range of the Position Adjustment Mechanism

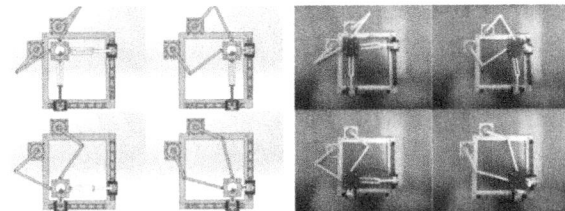

Fig. 9. Motion Range of the Angle Adjustment Mechanism

As shown in Fig. 8, the range of motion for the position adjustment mechanism is 30 mm × 30 mm, with a height of 13.5 mm for its center block. As shown in Fig. 9, the range of motion for the angle adjustment mechanism is 60 mm × 60 mm, with a height of 63 mm for its center block.

The base of the prototype is installed on an elastic band. By winding the elastic band around the patient's body, the robot can be worn. For different puncture targets, the length of the elastic band can be adjusted and different winding positions can be chosen for fixation.

4.2 Kinematics Simulation

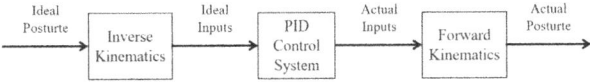

Fig. 10. Motion Control Simulation System

As shown in Fig. 10, a motion control simulation system was constructed with MATLAB. Given the expected posture of the puncture needle, the expected joint variables of the robot are obtained through inverse kinematics. The drivers are then provided with the corresponding step inputs. Finally, the actual posture of the puncture needle is obtained through forward kinematics in order to determine whether it meets the expectation.

The posture parameters and steady time are shown in Table 1. In the simulation, the steady time is selected when the deviation is 0.1 mm or 0.5°. The changing process of the puncture needle's posture parameters in Experiment No.1 ($x_d = 40$ mm, $y_d = 40$ mm, $\varphi = 10°$, $\theta = 80°$) is shown in Fig. 11. The simulation results demonstrate that, based on the results of the kinematic analysis and the constructed control system, the robot can achieve the adjustment of the posture.

Table 1. Steady Time under Different Posture Parameters

	X-Coordinate of the Insertion Position x_d (mm)	Y-Coordinate of the Insertion Position y_d (mm)	Yaw Angle φ (°)	Pitch Angle θ(°)	Steady Time (s)
1	40	40	10	85	4.088
2	30	30	100	75	6.580
3	60	60	35	75	4.196
4	40	60	50	80	4.920

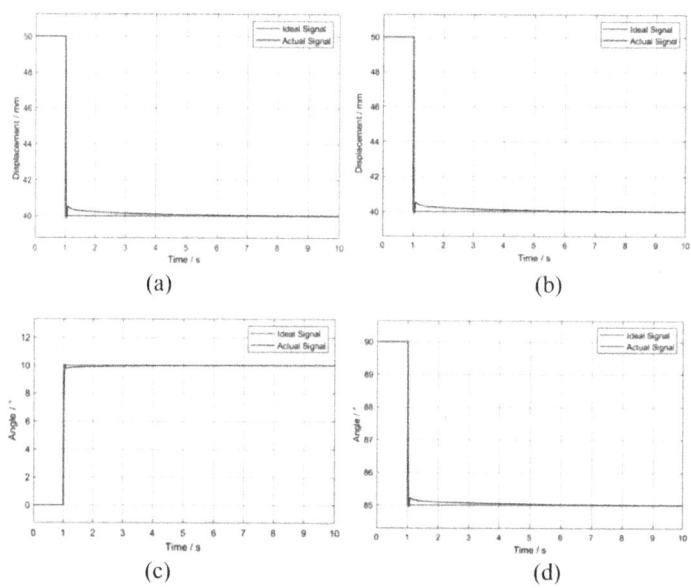

Fig. 11. Posture Change of the Puncture Needle. (a) X-Coordinate of the Insertion Position x_d. (b) Y-Coordinate of the Insertion Position y_d. (c) Yaw Angle φ. (d) Pitch Angle θ.

5 Conclusion

This paper proposes the design of a 4-DOF wearable assisted puncture robot. The robot is composed of two distinct mechanisms: a position adjustment mechanism and an angle adjustment mechanism. Both two parts realize the planar movement of a center block and convert this movement into the translation and pitch of the puncture needle through a spherical pair. The kinematic analysis of the designed robot mechanism is conducted and establishes the relationship between the input and the output. A prototype was manufactured based on the proposed robot design, with a mass of 0.44 kg and dimensions of 170 mm × 170 mm × 72 mm, which meets the original design intention of being lightweight and compact.

In the future, the structural optimization and motion control of the puncture robot will continue. Furthermore, in order to ensure compatibility with CT or MRI, all metal materials will be replaced with magnetically compatible materials. In order to make the robot more automated, the cannula design will be improved to achieve the feed and rotation of the puncture needle.

References

1. Stoianovici, D., Cleary, K., Patriciu, A., et al.: AcuBot: a robot for radiological interventions. IEEE Trans. Robot. Autom. **19**(5), 927–930 (2003)
2. Melzer, A., Gutmann, B., Remmele, T., et al.: INNOMOTION for percutaneous image-guided interventions. IEEE Eng. Med. Biol. Mag. **27**(3), 66–73 (2008)
3. Fischer, G.S., Iordachita, I., Csoma, C., et al.: MRI-compatible pneumatic robot for transperineal prostate needle placement. IEEE/ASME Trans. Mechatron. **13**(3), 295–305 (2008)
4. Song, Y., An, G., Zhang, J., et al.: Medical robotic system for minimally invasive spine surgery. In: 2008 2nd International Conference on Bioinformatics and Biomedical Engineering, pp. 1703–1706. IEEE (2008)
5. Inoue, T., Matsuno, T., Yanou, A., et al.: Development of a minimally invasive Robotic Interventional Radiology for treatment of lung cancer -Manufacture of a basic mechanism and verification experiment-. In: The SICE Annual Conference 2013, Nagoya, Japan, pp. 2646–2651 (2013)
6. Duan, X., Guo, Q., Liu, T., et al.: Experimental research on the ultrasound-guided positioning system of microwave ablation surgical robot. In: 2012 IEEE International Conference on Automation and Logistics, pp. 545–549. IEEE (2012)
7. Liu, R., Guo, J., Kang, C.: Joint type puncture robot research. In: 2016 3rd International Conference on Information Science and Control Engineering (ICISCE), pp. 1006–1010. IEEE (2016)
8. Bricault, I., Zemiti, N., Jouniaux, E., et al.: Light puncture robot for CT and MRI interventions. IEEE Eng. Med. Biol. Mag. **27**(3), 42–50 (2008)
9. Maurin, B., Bayle, B., Piccin, O., et al.: A patient-mounted robotic platform for CT-scan guided procedures. IEEE Trans. Biomed. Eng. **55**(10), 2417–2425 (2008)
10. Hata, N., Song, S.E., Olubiyi, O., et al.: Body-mounted robotic instrument guide for image-guided cryotherapy of renal cancer. Med. Phys. **43**(2), 843–853 (2016)
11. Arnold, O., Borodets, E.: Automated insertion device. US201716303536 (2021)

12. Mon, M.O., Ramesh, H.G., KianTai, C., et al.: Automated Needle Targeting with X-ray (ANT-X) - robot-assisted device for percutaneous nephrolithotomy (PCNL) with its first successful use in human. J. Endourol. **35**(6), e919–e919 (2018)
13. Gong, K., Guo, C., Guo, W., et al.: Research on tremor suppression strategies under a constant current peripheral electrical stimulation device for Parkinson's disease. IEEE Trans. Neural Syst. Rehabil. Eng. **32**, 3071–3083 (2024)
14. Jianfeng, Y., et al.: Neural-guided RRT*: Learning-based planning of entry point and puncture path for steerable bevel-tip needle insertion. IEEE Robot. Autom. Let. **10**(9), 9016–9023 (2025)

Towards Early Intervention of Knee Osteoarthritis: A Wearable System for Gait Analysis and Functional Evaluation

Haolan Xian[1], Changjiang Lei[1], Jinglin Zhou[1], Changquan Liu[2], Wei Sun[2], Zhiyong Wang[3], Chenglong Fu[1], and Yuquan Leng[1,3(✉)]

[1] Department of Mechanical and Energy Engineering, Southern University of Science and Technology, Shenzhen 518055, Guangdong, China
[2] Department of Orthopedics, Shenzhen Second People's Hospital/First Affiliated Hospital of Shenzhen University Health Science Center, Shenzhen 518035, Guangdong, China
[3] School of Biomedical Engineering and State Key Lab of Robotics and Systems, Harbin Institute of Technology (Shenzhen), Shenzhen 518067, Guangdong, China
lengyuquan@hit.edu.cn

Abstract. Degenerative osteoarthritis (DOA) impairs joint function and quality of life. Early detection and intervention can prevent further deterioration, yet identifying the disease at an early stage remains challenging. This work presents a wearable system for gait-based DOA screening, integrating seven IMUs and two pressure insoles to estimate kinematics and kinetics of lower limb during walking. The system was validated with optical motion capture and force plates system, with high correlation in joint angle and moment ($R^2 \geq 0.97$). It was then deployed in clinical settings to collect gait data from knee osteoarthritis (KOA) patients. We introduce three functional metrics: stance-phase knee range of motion (SKRoM), full-phase knee range of motion (FKRoM), and maximum knee moment (MKM) to quantify joint deficits and compensatory patterns. Additionally, these metrics are associated with KOA and may serve as potential targets for early intervention.

Keywords: Wearable device · Osteoarthritis screening · Gait analysis · Early intervention

1 Introduction

Osteoarthritis is becoming a global disease burden [15] with the rapid aging of the global population [6]. A study suggested that there will be approximately 642 million arthritis patients in the whole world by 2050, accounting for about 8 % of global population [17]. Among them, degenerative osteoarthritis (DOA)

H. Xian and C. Lei—Contributed equally to this paper and share first authorship.

is the most prevalent subtype, characterized by the progressive degeneration of articular cartilage and bone remodeling. DOA often leads to joint pain, swelling, and deformity, significantly impairing patients' mobility and quality of life.

Currently, there is no definitive cure for DOA, largely due to its multifactorial etiology involving genetics, biomechanics, metabolism, and inflammation [16]. Existing treatment strategies mainly focus on symptom management through pharmacological intervention and, in severe cases, joint replacement surgery. Increasing evidence suggests that early intervention, prior to the onset of chronic pain or irreversible joint damage, may substantially improve clinical outcomes [7,10]. However, diagnosing DOA at an early stage remains a major challenge. Conventional imaging modalities such as X-ray and magnetic resonance imaging often fail to detect early pathological changes. Recent research has shown that neuromuscular abnormalities, which manifest as subtle alterations in gait and postural control, may appear in the early phases of DOA [5,18,19]. D'Souza et al. [4] show that there is an association between sagittal plane biomechanics with patellofemoral OA progression. Therefore, gait analysis presents a promising method for early detection and monitoring of disease progression.

There are currently two primary approaches for human gait analysis: lab-based systems [1,13] and wearable systems [9,11]. Lab-based methods, such as optical motion capture systems combined with force plates, provide high-precision measurements of kinematic and kinetic parameters. However, these systems are expensive, require specialized facilities and are not suitable for routine clinical or community use. Costello et al. [3] predicted the deterioration of cartilage by means of data from human walking on a walkway embedded with a force plate and identified some indicators for early intervention for cartilage worsening, including peak ground reaction force (GRF) and so on. In contrast, wearable systems, based on inertial measurement units (IMUs), pressure sensors, surface electromyography (sEMG) and so on, offer a portable and cost-effective choice, enabling biomechanical assessment in natural environments. Scherpereel et al. collected lower-limb biomechanics data during cyclic and non-cyclic activities with a wearable collection system consisting of IMU and sEMG [14]. Manupibul et al. designed a portable gait measurement system in lower extremities with integration of insole snesor and IMU and it is validated by motion capture system [11]. Therefore, wearable approach is a promising way to gait analysis for large-scale screening and early intervening of DOA.

In this study, we proposed a wearable system designed for large-scale collection of lower-limb biomechanical data. The system comprises six IMUs placed on the thighs, shanks and feet, one IMU on the waist, and two pressure insoles. To validate the system's performance, we first compared its output with data obtained from a gold-standard laboratory setup, including motion capture and force plates. We then deployed the system in a clinical setting to monitor patients diagnosed with knee osteoarthritis (KOA), collecting gait data to assess joint function and biomechanical patterns. The key contributions of this work are as follows:

1. We developed a compact and deployable wearable system capable of capturing human gait kinematics and dynamics in real-world settings, offering a practical tool for the assessment of degenerative joint conditions.
2. The system's accuracy was validated against laboratory-grade equipment, demonstrating its feasibility for clinical use.
3. With its low cost and ease of use, the system has the potential for large-scale biomechanical screening, providing valuable data to support early diagnosis and intervention for DOA (Fig. 1).

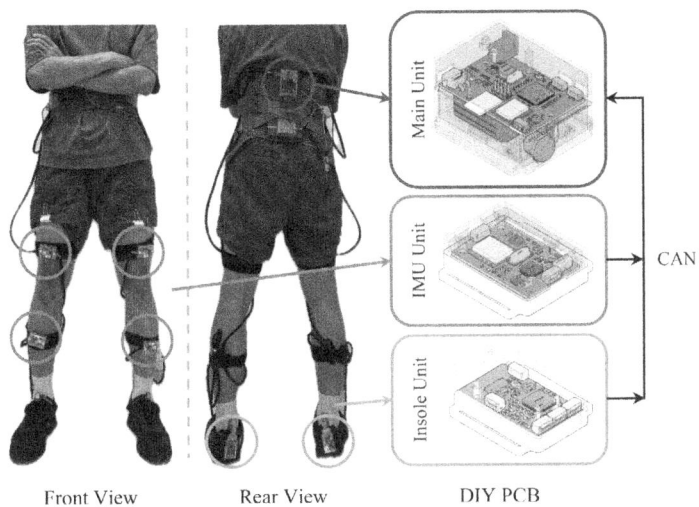

Fig. 1. Data collection system.

2 Data Collection System

2.1 Sensor Selection

To capture lower-limb biomechanical data for early diagnosis of DOA, we designed a wearable system that emphasizes practicality, scalability and clinical applicability. Currently, the mainstream methods for acquiring lower-limb biomechanical data can be mainly categorized into two approaches.

One approach simplifies the lower-limb into a kinematic model, such as a four-link model to represent trunk, thigh, shank and foot [2]. In this model, IMUs are attached to each segment to track the relative orientations of the body parts. When combined with external measurements like GRF, inverse dynamics can be appled to estimate joint moments and powers [11]. The other approach involves directly measuring neuromuscular activity using sEMG or ultrasound imaging to monitor muscle activation [8,12]. However, these techniques require precise electrode or probe placement over specific muscles, which may require professional setup. Such limitations could hinder their applicability in larger-scale screening or long-term monitoring. Therefore, the system proposed in the work adopts a hybrid solution based on wearable IMUs and pressure insoles. Specifically, we use:

1. Six 9-DOF IMUs mounted on the lower limbs: one on each foot, shank and thigh.
2. One IMU on the waist to serve as a global reference.
3. Two pressure insoles, each embedded with 18 force-sensitive resistor sensors, to estimate vertical GRF and center of pressure (CoP).

2.2 Hardware Design

The data collection system consists of slave modules and master modules shown as Fig. Slave modules are responsible for acquiring and providing data to master modules. And master module is responsible to process the original data and transmit to computer.

The slave modules, motion measured units (MMUs) and GRF measured units (GMUs), are placed on lower limb and under foot of wearer respectively. A MMU is equipped with an ARM micro-controller (STM32F103) and an IMU (JY901B, WitMotion, Shenzhen, China). The pose of MMU is estimated by a Kalman filter with the data from accelerometers and gyroscopes. A GMU is implemented on an ARM micro-controller (STM32F405) and one insole sensor (Crownto, Anhui, China). The insole sensors have been calibrated by force plate (see associated details in *Insole sensor calibraion*). Pressure signal of the insole sensor is collected by an analog-to-digital converter on the GMU. All of the data from slave modules is transmitted to a controller area network (CAN) bus.

The main electronic module is placed inside the electronic house. The data collection and procession unit (DCPU), an ARM micro-controller (STM32H723), collects and analyses the data from CAN bus and transmit the data to computer through Bluetooth, including joint angle, moment and so on.

The system is fully self-contained and does not need any external connection during operation. All data is transmitted to computer through a wireless module at 100 Hz for data logging. A 24V lithium battery is selected as power supply and provides power to all electronic modules.

2.3 Sensor Calibration and Data Procession

IMU Sensor Calibration. Due to variability in IMU placement, calibration is required to ensure accurate joint angle estimation. We model the thigh-knee-shank as a two-link hinge and assume rigid attachment between the IMUs and the limbs.

Let $\mathbf{j}_{world}$ be the knee rotation axis in the world frame. Its representations in the thigh and shank IMU frames are $\mathbf{j}_{thigh}$ and $\mathbf{j}_{shank}$, with corresponding rotation matrices $\mathbf{R}_{thigh}^{world}$ and $\mathbf{R}_{shank}^{world}$. We estimate $\mathbf{j}_{thigh}$ and $\mathbf{j}_{shank}$ by solving:

$$\min_{\mathbf{j}_{\text{thigh}}, \mathbf{j}_{\text{shank}}} \left\| \mathbf{R}_{\text{thigh}}^{\text{world}} \cdot \mathbf{j}_{\text{thigh}} - \mathbf{R}_{\text{shank}}^{\text{world}} \cdot \mathbf{j}_{\text{shank}} \right\|^2 \quad (1)$$

After identifying the joint axis, reference vectors $\mathbf{v}_{\text{thigh}}$ and $\mathbf{v}_{\text{shank}}$ are constructed in the joint plane orthogonal to the axis. The knee angle θ is computed from their transformed world vectors $\mathbf{V}_1$ and $\mathbf{V}_2$ as:

$$\theta = \arccos(\mathbf{V}_1 \cdot \mathbf{V}_2) \quad (2)$$

To determine the sign of the angle, we compute:

$$\mathbf{d} = (\mathbf{V}_1 \times \mathbf{V}_2) \cdot (\mathbf{R}_{\text{thigh}}^{\text{world}} \cdot \mathbf{j}_{\text{thigh}}) \quad (3)$$

If $\mathbf{d} < 0$, then θ is negative. This procedure ensures accurate knee flexion-extension angle estimation despite mounting differences.

Insole Sensor Calibration. To estimate vertical GRF, each insole is embedded with 18 piezoresistive sensors grouped into six rows. Due to sensor variability, calibration is necessary to relate sensor outputs to true GRF values.

The raw signals from each row i are summed as:

$$P_i(t) = \sum_{j \in \mathcal{R}_i} s_j(t), \quad i = 1, 2, ..., 6 \quad (4)$$

These row-wise sums form the pressure vector:

$$\mathbf{P}(t) = [P_1(t), P_2(t), ..., P_6(t)]^T \quad (5)$$

Using force plate measurements as ground-truth $F_{true}(t)$, a linear regression model is fitted:

$$\hat{F}(t) = \mathbf{w}^T \mathbf{P}(t) + b \quad (6)$$

The weights $\mathbf{w}$ and bias b are optimized by minimizing the squared error:

$$\min_{\mathbf{w}, b} \sum_t (F_{true}(t) - \mathbf{w}^T \mathbf{P}(t) - b)^2 \quad (7)$$

Data Processing. Nine-axis IMUs are mounted on the waist, thighs, shanks, and feet. Each provides orientation data via sensor fusion. The orientation of each segment i is represented by rotation matrix $\mathbf{R}_i(t)$. The relative rotation between adjacent segments is:

$$\mathbf{R}_{ij}(t) = \mathbf{R}_j^{-1}(t)\mathbf{R}_i(t) \quad (8)$$

Angular velocity $\boldsymbol{\omega}_i(t)$ is directly measured, while angular acceleration is estimated via:

$$\boldsymbol{\alpha}_i(t) = \frac{d\boldsymbol{\omega}_i(t)}{dt} \quad (9)$$

The vertical GRF is estimated by Eq. 6. The center of pressure (CoP) along the anterior-posterior axis is:

$$x_{\text{CoP}}(t) = \frac{\sum_{k=1}^{6} P_k(t) \cdot x_k}{\sum_{k=1}^{6} P_k(t)} \tag{10}$$

Joint moments in the sagittal plane are computed using Newton-Euler dynamics:

$$\tau_i = \tau_{i-1} + r_i m_i a_i + I_i \alpha_i, \tag{11}$$

where r_i is the distance to the center of mass, and m_i, a_i, I_i are the segment mass, linear acceleration, and moment of inertia, estimated based on subject height and weight.

3 Experiment Verification

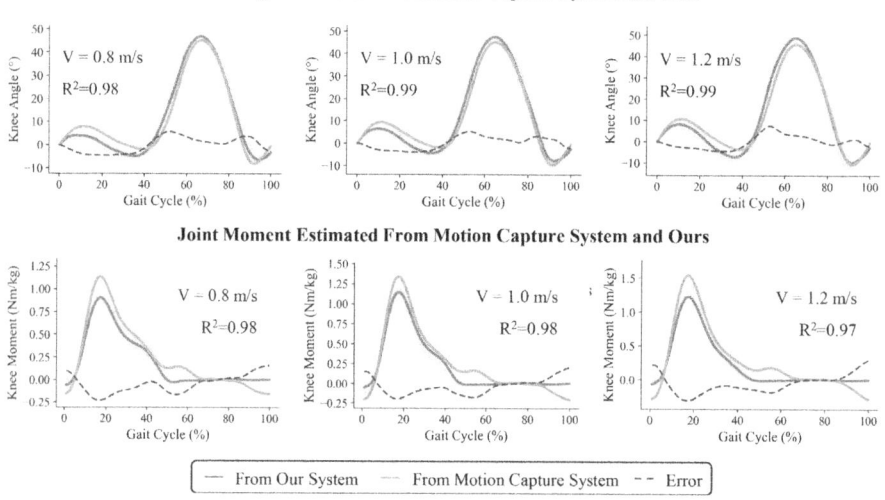

Fig. 2. Compare results.

3.1 Assessing IMU Orientation Data and Joint Kinematics

In order to illustrate the reliability of the data collected by the system, we compare the data collected using the system with the data collected using a motion capture system. Standard kinematical data were recorded at 120 Hz using a motion capture system consisting of eleven Vicon V5 cameras (Vicon, Oxford, UK). All walking trials were conducted on a fully instrumented treadmill (Bertec,

Ohio, USA). The treadmill features two independently controllable belts, each equipped with a force plate underneath to capture six-component force data at 1000 Hz. Two subjects were recruited for the experiment. Subjects were required to wear the acquisition system and walk at three speeds, 0.8 m/s, 1.0 m/s, and 1.2 m/s, in the experimental environment described above, with each experiment lasting two minutes.

3.2 Osteoarthritis Patient Data Collection

Following lab validation, the acquisition system was deployed in a clinical setting to collect gait data from patients with knee osteoarthritis. To facilitate use, we designed custom pants with Velcro at the thigh and calf to secure the IMU modules, and a rear pocket for the battery and controller.

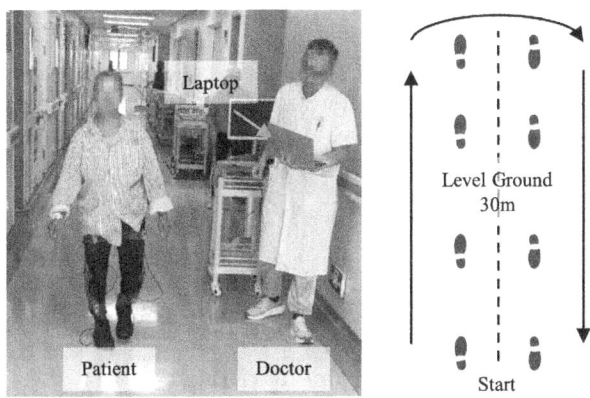

Fig. 3. Protocol of patients data collection.

Ten patients scheduled for knee replacement surgery were recruited. As part of their clinical assessment, each patient wore the system and completed three round trips along a 10-meter hospital corridor at a self-selected walking speed (Fig. 3). All procedures were approved by the hospital ethics board.

In total, we collected data from 12 patients with different OA severities and 3 healthy individuals. Knee joint angles and moments were recorded and analyzed. Based on this data, we proposed three metrics to assess key functional aspects of the knee during gait.

As shown in Fig. 4, an example of the angle and moment trajectories of both knees is presented. Using the *Left Knee Angles* and *Left Knee Moment* curves as illustrations, the three evaluation metrics are defined according to related researches [4] as follows:

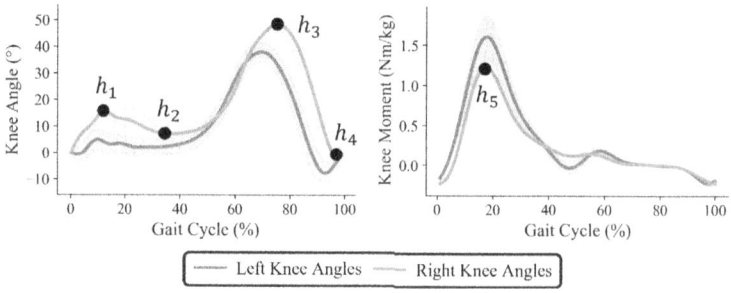

Fig. 4. Definition of evaluation metrics.

- **Metric 1: stance-phase knee range of motion (SKRoM)**

$$\text{SKRoM} = y_{h1} - y_{h2}, \quad (12)$$

where h_1 is the maximum knee angle during the stance phase, and h_2 is the subsequent minimum point within the same phase. This metric reflects the knee's extension capability during weight-bearing stance.
- **Metric 2: full-phase knee range of motion (FKRoM)**

$$\text{FKRoM} = y_{h3} - y_{h4}, \quad (13)$$

where h_3 and h_4 represent the peak and valley of the averaged knee angle trajectory over a complete gait cycle. This metric reflects the flexion capacity and mobility during the swing phase.
- **Metric 3: maximum knee moment (MKM)**

$$\text{MKM} = y_{h5} = \max\{M(t)\}, \quad (14)$$

where $M(t)$ is the knee joint moment curve over the gait cycle, and y_{h5} is the maximum moment value. This metric quantifies the peak moment generated by the knee joint during walking, serving as an indicator of joint strength and load-bearing capacity.

Table 1 presents the evaluation metrics of knee joint function collected from three healthy subjects during walking trials, including the left and right leg values of SKRoM, FKRoM, and MKM.

Furthermore, the mean values of all six measurements for each metric (left and right legs of three subjects) were calculated and used as reference baselines:

- **SKRoM-Mean**: The average of all six SKRoM values,
- **FKRoM-Mean**: The average of all six FKRoM values,
- **MKM-Mean**: The average of all six MKM values.

These baseline metrics serve as normative references in Sect. 4 to evaluate the functional performance of patients with knee osteoarthritis.

Table 1. Reference Knee Joint Metrics from Healthy Subjects

ID	SKRoM (°)		FKRoM (°)		MKM (Nm/kg)	
	Left	Right	Left	Right	Left	Right
H01	8.29	12.73	63.14	56.36	0.89	0.94
H02	9.12	11.71	63.86	54.95	0.98	0.91
H03	11.69	10.28	56.82	56.92	1.02	0.95
Base	SKRoM-Mean		FKRoM-Mean		MKM-Mean	
	10.64		58.68		0.95	

4 Results

4.1 Kinematical Differences Between IMU and Optical-Based Device

To assess the accuracy of our IMU-based system in estimating knee motion, we compared it against a Vicon optical motion capture system under three walking speeds (0.8, 1.0, and 1.2 m/s). Figure 2 shows the corresponding trajectories and error trends.

Joint Angle Estimation: Mean absolute errors (MAEs) were 2.90°, 2.54°, and 2.64°, with maximum errors under 7.30°. High correlations with reference curves ($R^2 = 0.98$–0.99) confirm strong agreement. Deviations mostly occurred during fast flexion-extension, possibly due to rapid dynamics and system latency.

Joint Moment Estimation: MAEs were 0.093, 0.094, and 0.129 Nm/kg; peak errors remained below 0.31 Nm/kg. R^2 values of 0.97–0.98 indicate good consistency with optical-based results. Slight overestimation during early stance (0–20% gait cycle) likely reflects sensitivity to GRF fluctuations.

In summary, the IMU system delivers reliable estimates of joint kinematics and kinetics, comparable to a lab-grade setup, while offering advantages in portability and cost. It is well suited for applications in rehabilitation assessment, gait classification, and dataset acquisition.

4.2 Biomechanical Differences Between Normal and Patients

Table 2 summarizes the knee joint metrics of eleven KOA patients, including SKRoM, FKRoM, and MKM. Each value is reported for both the left and right knee, along with its deviation from the healthy baseline (Table 1).

Overall Trends. SKRoM and FKRoM were substantially reduced in most patients. Approximately 80% of individuals showed more than 50% reduction in SKRoM on at least one side, indicating impaired knee extension during the stance phase. FKRoM also declined in varying degrees, with some cases (e.g., L07) showing more than 50% loss on one side, reflecting limited flexion range during the swing phase. The MKM metric displayed more complex patterns: while some patients exhibited elevated peak moment (e.g., L09 right leg ↑134%), others showed substantial decreases (e.g., L06 left leg ↓56%), suggesting possible compensatory mechanisms or differences in muscle strength capacity.

Affected vs. Unaffected Sides. In patients with unilateral KOA (L-KOA or R-KOA), the affected side generally showed greater reduction in SKRoM and FKRoM. For instance, L10 exhibited a 92% reduction in left-side SKRoM compared to only 9% on the right. Similarly, R01 had a 75% drop in right-side FKRoM versus 39% on the left. Notably, some unaffected sides showed significant MKM increases (e.g., L09 right ↑134%), indicating possible overcompensation or asymmetric load distribution. Bilateral KOA cases (e.g., B03) exhibited relatively symmetric reductions, though both sides were below normal functional levels.

Therefore, KOA patients commonly show deficits in knee extension (SKRoM) and joint mobility (FKRoM), while MKM changes reveal variability in joint moment output, potentially influenced by compensatory movement patterns. Together, SKRoM, FKRoM, and MKM provide a comprehensive framework for assessing gait-related functional impairments and guiding rehabilitation strategies.

Table 2. Knee Metrics of KOA Patients Compared to Healthy Baseline

ID	SKRoM (°)		FKRoM (°)		MKM (Nm/kg)	
	Left	Right	Left	Right	Left	Right
R01	4.59(↓57%)	3.38(↓68%)	35.63(↓39%)	14.72(↓75%)	1.62(↑70%)	0.63(↓33%)
R02	6.16(↓42%)	2.83(↓73%)	56.67(↓3%)	52.04(↓11%)	1.42(↑49%)	0.93(↓2%)
B03	5.72(↓46%)	2.44(↓77%)	50.58(↓14%)	51.02(↓13%)	0.87(↓8%)	1.54(↑62%)
L04	2.95(↓72%)	8.53(↓20%)	45.67(↓22%)	49.67(↓15%)	0.44(↓53%)	1.07(↑12%)
R05	5.72(↓46%)	2.44(↓77%)	50.58(↓14%)	51.02(↓13%)	1.30(↑36%)	1.46(↑53%)
L06	1.29(↓88%)	1.19(↓89%)	50.33(↓14%)	45.25(↓23%)	0.41(↓56%)	1.22(↑28%)
L07	2.15(↓80%)	9.44(↓11%)	27.87(↓52%)	57.93(↓1%)	0.73(↓23%)	1.29(↑35%)
R08	3.65(↓66%)	1.76(↓83%)	49.07(↓16%)	47.45(↓19%)	1.62(↑70%)	0.41(↓56%)
L09	9.46(↓11%)	2.47(↓77%)	60.24(↑3%)	45.04(↓23%)	0.66(↓30%)	2.23(↑134%)
L10	0.80(↓92%)	0.64(↓9%)	54.20(↓8%)	47.71(↓19%)	1.35(↑42%)	0.63(↓33%)
L11	0.96(↓91%)	3.26(↓69%)	49.63(↓15%)	50.91(↓13%)	1.14(↑20%)	1.37(↑44%)

5 Discussions

5.1 Potential Features for Early Intervening

The proposed wearable system offers several promising features that could support early identification and intervention of KOA.

First, the system can continuously collect joint angle and moment data during natural walking, from which several functional indicators (e.g., SKRoM, FKRoM, MKM) are extracted. These indicators can serve as early markers of joint function decline, aiding clinicians in identifying subtle changes before clinical symptoms appear. Second, the compact structure and ease of use of the system make it suitable for long-term monitoring in community or home settings, providing functional assessments even during preclinical stages of degeneration.

Furthermore, by incorporating machine learning methods, more complex features such as spatiotemporal gait parameters, moment patterns, or gait asymmetry could be analyzed to enable risk stratification, targeted screening of high-risk populations, and personalized intervention planning.

5.2 Limitations and Future Works

Although the system demonstrates promising accuracy and applicability, several limitations remain. First, minor relative motion between the IMUs and the limbs may occur due to loose attachment or dynamic movements, potentially introducing noise into the pose estimation. Future work could address this through better mechanical fixation or compensation models.

Second, current joint moment estimation relies on a simplified inverse dynamics model, where individual biomechanical parameters (e.g., segment mass, length, and inertia) are approximated based on height and weight. Future development could incorporate subject-specific skeletal models or learning-based parameter regression to enhance precision.

Lastly, while the system is currently focused on level-ground gait analysis, future extensions could involve more complex locomotion tasks such as stair ascent/descent or turning, and integration with lower-limb rehabilitation exoskeletons for intelligent human-machine collaboration.

6 Conclusion and Future Work

This paper presents a wearable biomechanical system integrating IMUs and pressure insoles for early screening and functional assessment of degenerative osteoarthritis (DOA). The system achieved reliable estimation of knee joint angles and moments ($R^2 \geq 0.97$) across multiple walking speeds, with errors below clinically acceptable thresholds, demonstrating accuracy comparable to lab-based optical systems. Clinical deployment further confirmed its ability to quantify KOA-related deficits and compensations using three metrics: SKRoM, FKRoM, and MKM, supporting its use in rehabilitation evaluation and potential in early intervention.

Future work will improve sensor fixation and model personalization, extend application scenarios (e.g., stair walking), and explore integration with lower-limb exoskeletons for closed-loop control, promoting its use in both clinical and community settings.

Acknowledgement. This work was supported by National Key R&D Program of China [Grant: 2024YFC3082800], the National Natural Science Foundation of China [Grant: 52175272], Guangdong Basic and Applied Basic Research Foundation [Grant: 2024B1515020008 and 2023B1515130007], Shenzhen Science and Technology Program [Grant: RCYX20231211090345058, JCYJ20220530114809021, KCXFZ20230731093059012].

References

1. Camargo, J., Ramanathan, A., Flanagan, W., Young, A.: A comprehensive, open-source dataset of lower limb biomechanics in multiple conditions of stairs, ramps, and level-ground ambulation and transitions. J. Biomech. **119**, 110320 (2021)
2. Chen, W., Zhang, B., Tan, X., Zhao, Y., Liu, L., Zhao, X.: Hip–knee–ankle rehabilitation exoskeleton with compliant actuators: from human–robot interaction control to clinical evaluation. IEEE Trans. Rob. (2024)
3. Costello, K.E., et al.: Gait, physical activity and tibiofemoral cartilage damage: a longitudinal machine learning analysis in the multicenter osteoarthritis study. Br. J. Sports Med. **57**(16), 1018–1024 (2023)
4. D'souza, N., et al.: Are biomechanics during gait associated with the structural disease onset and progression of lower limb osteoarthritis? a systematic review and meta-analysis. Osteoarthritis Cartil. **30**(3), 381–394 (2022)
5. Ghazwan, A., Wilson, C., Holt, C.A., Whatling, G.M.: Knee osteoarthritis alters peri-articular knee muscle strategies during gait. PLoS ONE **17**(1), e0262798 (2022)
6. Health, T.L.P.: Ageing: a 21st century public health challenge? (2017)
7. Karsdal, M., et al.: Disease-modifying treatments for osteoarthritis (dmoads) of the knee and hip: lessons learned from failures and opportunities for the future. Osteoarthritis Cartil. **24**(12), 2013–2021 (2016)
8. Li, J., et al.: K2muse: a human lower limb multimodal dataset under diverse conditions for facilitating rehabilitation robotics. arXiv preprint arXiv:2504.14602 (2025)
9. Liu, S., Zhang, J., Zhang, Y., Zhu, R.: A wearable motion capture device able to detect dynamic motion of human limbs. Nat. Commun. **11**(1), 5615 (2020)
10. Mahmoudian, A., Lohmander, L.S., Mobasheri, A., Englund, M., Luyten, F.P.: Early-stage symptomatic osteoarthritis of the knee–time for action. Nat. Rev. Rheumatol. **17**(10), 621–632 (2021)
11. Manupibul, U., et al.: Integration of force and imu sensors for developing low-cost portable gait measurement system in lower extremities. Sci. Rep. **13**(1), 10653 (2023)
12. Nuckols, R.W., Lee, S., Swaminathan, K., Orzel, D., Howe, R.D., Walsh, C.J.: Individualization of exosuit assistance based on measured muscle dynamics during versatile walking. Sci. Rob. **6**(60), eabj1362 (2021)
13. Perera, C.K., Hussain, Z., Khant, M., Gopalai, A.A., Gouwanda, D., Ahmad, S.A.: A motion capture dataset on human sitting to walking transitions. Sci. Data **11**(1), 878 (2024)

14. Scherpereel, K., Molinaro, D., Inan, O., Shepherd, M., Young, A.: A human lower-limb biomechanics and wearable sensors dataset during cyclic and non-cyclic activities. Sci. Data **10**(1), 924 (2023)
15. Sharma, L.: Osteoarthritis of the knee. N. Engl. J. Med. **384**(1), 51–59 (2021)
16. Silverwood, V., Blagojevic-Bucknall, M., Jinks, C., Jordan, J., Protheroe, J., Jordan, K.: Current evidence on risk factors for knee osteoarthritis in older adults: a systematic review and meta-analysis. Osteoarthritis Cartil. **23**(4), 507–515 (2015)
17. Steinmetz, J.D., et al.: Global, regional, and national burden of osteoarthritis, 1990–2020 and projections to 2050: a systematic analysis for the global burden of disease study 2021. Lancet Rheumatol. **5**(9), e508–e522 (2023)
18. Uhlrich, S.D., Jackson, R.W., Seth, A., Kolesar, J.A., Delp, S.L.: Muscle coordination retraining inspired by musculoskeletal simulations reduces knee contact force. Sci. Rep. **12**(1), 9842 (2022)
19. Yang, P., et al.: Mechanical upside of pao mainstream fixations: co-simulation based on early postoperative gait characteristics of ddh patients. Front. Bioeng. Biotechnol. **11**, 1171040 (2023)

A Flexible Fruit Wearable System for Real-Time and Long-Term Tomato Growth Monitoring

Xin Zhao, Qin Jiang, Yihui Fan, Han Ding, and Zhigang Wu(✉)

Huazhong University of Science and Technology, Wuhan 430074, China
zgwu@hust.edu.cn

Abstract. Accurate monitoring of tomato growth is essential for precision agriculture, contributing to improvements in crop yield and quality, while flexible wearable sensors enable in-situ monitoring of plant physiological information. However, their reliable application to fruits remains challenging due to the continuous deformation that occurs during fruit development. Here, we present a flexible fruit wearable system designed for in-situ and long-term tomato growth monitoring. Such a system enables real-time monitoring of in-situ reflectance spectra, along with complementary temperature and humidity data, throughout the tomato maturation process. Furthermore, machine learning algorithms are integrated to enable precise maturity classification, achieving a high accuracy (98.67%). To assess system performance, a 15-day thermal stress experiment was conducted, confirming its responsiveness under extreme environmental conditions. Additionally, a 36-day long-term monitoring experiment was conducted to assess continuous stability throughout fruit development, with the system maintaining functionality under large circumferential deformation. These findings underscore the system's potential to advance precision crop management and productivity.

Keywords: Flexible fruit wearable system · Tomato growth monitoring · In-situ reflectance spectra

1 Introduction

Tomatoes are among the most widely cultivated crops worldwide, valued for their rich content of vitamins, lycopene, and dietary fiber. According to the Food and Agriculture Organization (FAO), global tomato production is approximately 190 million tons in 2023, with China leading as the largest producer, contributing 48.5% of the total output [1]. However, its production quality is often constrained by limited precision in growth management and suboptimal harvest timing. In addition, cultivation conditions vary across different stages of fruit development, further complicating effective management. Thus, the development of advanced technologies for accurately monitoring fruit growth is crucial for improving both tomato quality and yield.

Various conventional technologies for fruit growth monitoring have been proposed, including biomolecular analysis [2], electronic noses [3], computer vision (CV) [4, 5], and spectroscopic imaging [6, 7]. Among them, biomolecular analysis provides precise fruit growth stage analysis by detecting molecular changes, yet it requires destructive tissue sampling and disrupts natural fruit growth. The electronic nose provides a non-destructive approach by analyzing volatile organic compounds (VOCs) emitted by fruits, whereas it is highly susceptible to environmental factors such as temperature and wind. Among these, CV and spectroscopic methods are widely used due to their advantage of real-time, non-invasive, and convenient detection. The CV methods commonly utilize trichromatic cameras to capture fruit images for the detection of their maturity based on visual assessments [8, 9]. Nevertheless, its performance is easily affected by environmental disturbances, including light fluctuation, object obstruction, and dust contamination. Spectroscopic imaging offers a promising approach to addressing these challenges by combining spectral and imaging analysis, enabling the evaluation of fruit internal information [10, 11]. However, bulk spectroscopic systems require mechanical fixation to maintain the tested fruit at the focal position, limiting their ability to continuously and dynamically track fruit growth for the long term.

Recently, flexible wearable sensors, known for their unique deformability and biocompatibility, have been introduced for plant growth monitoring [12]. These devices can be deployed across various plant organs to capture a diverse array of indicators, including growth dynamics (e.g., length, angle, stem diameter), VOC emissions, sap flow, and living microclimates (e.g., temperature, humidity, and light intensity) [13–16]. Despite these advancements, most flexible sensors exhibit limited stretchability to accommodate the rapid, irregular expansion characteristic of plant dynamic growth (especially fruit). Consequently, these limitations hinder precise and continuous monitoring of fruit maturation.

Here, we present a flexible fruit wearable system for real-time monitoring of tomato growth and maturity, as illustrated in Fig. 1(a). The system integrates two miniaturized spectral sensors and a temperature and humidity (T&H) sensor, enabling continuous, in situ data acquisition directly from the fruit surface. Sensing data is transmitted wirelessly via Bluetooth to a mobile app for real-time visualization. Moreover, an ML framework is established to precisely classify the maturity stage of the fruit. This integrated approach supports precise harvest scheduling and optimized resource management, ultimately enhancing tomato yield and fruit quality.

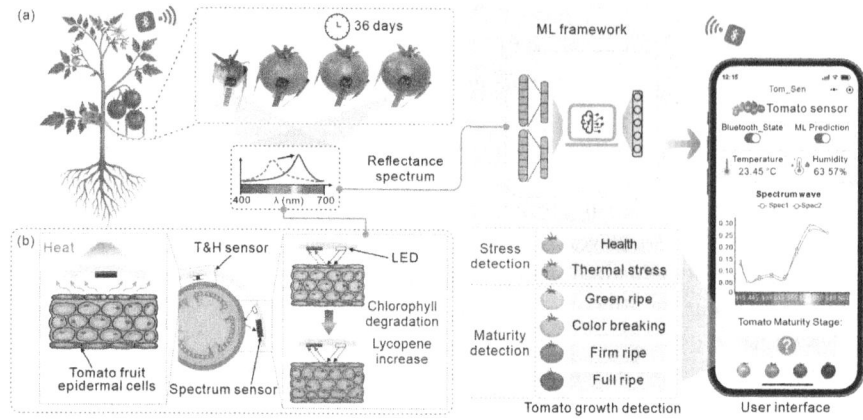

Fig. 1. Flexible fruit wearable system for tomato growth monitoring. (a) Illustration of the flexible sensor attached to a tomato fruit and corresponding processing system for real-time growth detection. (b) The detection principle of spectral and T&H sensors.

2 Results

2.1 Collection of Fruit Physiological Information

The spectral sensor operates in reflectance mode, enabling non-destructive assessment of fruit surface characteristics, as depicted in Fig. 1(b). The sensor detects spectral signals reflected from the tomato surface, enabling assessment of both surface and subsurface features such as pigment composition. Reflectance-based measurements are well-suited for intact fruits, as incident light first interacts with surface tissues. The light then undergoes partial scattering and absorption before being reflected to the detector. In contrast, the internal cellular architecture of untreated tomatoes induces significant scattering and absorption. These optical effects consequently compromise the fidelity and reliability of transmittance-based techniques.

Leveraging this principle, the integrated model enables the analysis of spectral features across the visible and near-infrared regions. Chlorophyll absorption around 450 nm and reflectance within the 550–750 nm range serve as key indicators of fruit maturity. During ripening, tomatoes undergo biochemical and structural changes that affect their spectral properties. In the early stages, high chlorophyll concentrations cause strong absorption in blue-violet (450 nm) and red (670 nm) regions. As ripening progresses, chlorophyll degrades while lycopene accumulates, leading to distinct reflectance peaks at 600–700 nm. To capture these spectral changes, two spectral sensors monitor color variation in the fruit peel. Simultaneously, an LED light source maintains consistent illumination and spectral fidelity under variable ambient lighting. Additionally, T&H sensors provide continuous microclimatic data from the fruit surface, enabling complementary monitoring of environmental factors.

2.2 Properties of Reflectance Spectra

To classify tomato's four maturity stages, spectral data were acquired using spectral sensors across four stages, including green ripe, color breaking, firm ripe, and full ripe.

For each stage, we selected 50 tomatoes of uniform size to collect the spectral dataset. Spectral measurements were then performed at ten systematically distributed points on each fruit's surface, avoiding both the stem region and blemished areas. At each measurement point, dual spectral scans were performed across eight wavelengths.

To ensure spectral data consistency, normalization was performed through radiometric calibration using averaged dark-corrected LED reference measurements, followed by min-max transformation to standardize the dynamic range to [0, 1]. This calibration step mitigated systematic variations introduced by fluctuations in light source intensity, thereby enhancing data stability. The resulting normalized reflectance spectra (Fig. 2) reveal distinct, stage-dependent features. As ripening progresses, reflectance in the green spectral region (515 nm) declines steadily, while reflectance in the red region (630–680 nm) increases, corresponding to chlorophyll degradation and lycopene accumulation. These spectral transitions align with the visible progression of fruit coloration from green to red, reflecting underlying physiological and biochemical transformations. The above spectral features provide a solid data foundation for the subsequent feature extraction and the development of maturity classification prediction models.

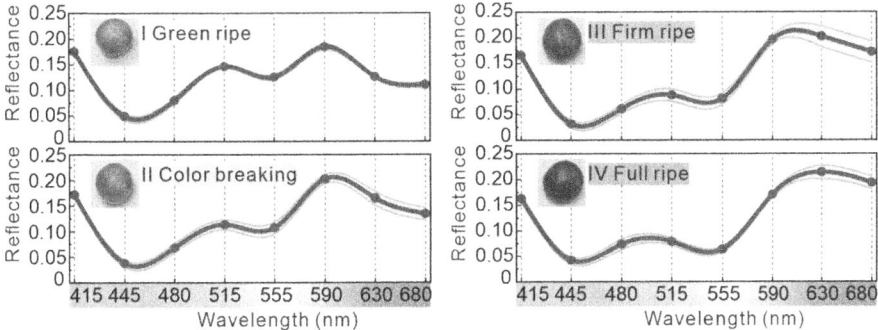

Fig. 2. Spectral characterization of tomato at different ripening stages. After removing statistical outliers, the final dataset comprised 390 measurements for the green ripe stage, 358 for color breaking, 411 for firm ripe, and 410 for full ripe. (Color figure online)

2.3 ML-Based Classification Framework

We further developed an integrated monitoring framework combining dual-spectral for tomato spectral data acquisition, with T&H sensors to monitor environmental conditions, as depicted in Fig. 3(a). The system then deployed ML algorithms to classify tomato maturity stages and monitor plant health status under stress. Following kernel principal component analysis (kPCA with RBF kernel, gamma = 0.1 selected through grid search over [0.001, 1.0]) dimensionality reduction in Fig. 3(b), the processed data exhibited distinct clustering patterns in a 3D space. The visualization demonstrated a clear separation between green and ripe stages while preserving differentiation between color-breaking and firm stages. Despite partial overlap in intermediate stages, these results confirm feature suitability for maturity classification.

To analyze these spectral-maturity relationships, the Sankey diagram analysis in Fig. 3(c) quantified wavelength-specific contributions across eight bands ranging from

415 to 680 nm. The results identified clear stage-dependent spectral features, with green tomatoes showing predominant reflectance at 415–445 nm, color breaking stage exhibiting transition at 515–590 nm, and ripe fruits presenting dominance at 630–680 nm. These spectral patterns align with pigment transition dynamics.

Classification accuracies of the six machine learning architectures ranged from 85% to 99%, with five models surpassing 94% across all stages. As demonstrated in Fig. 3(d) and Fig. 3(e), extreme gradient boosting (XGBoost) demonstrated exceptional classification efficacy, achieving 98.67% accuracy with F1-scores exceeding 0.98. The superior performance of XGBoost resulted from several factors, notably the careful collection of spectral data through removing external light interference and normalization procedures. Additional contributing factors are enhanced signal-to-noise ratio via kPCA and physiologically constrained wavelength-maturity correlations. This integrated sensing-computational paradigm establishes XGBoost as the optimal ML model for tomato maturity classification, enabling precise developmental stage determination through spectral analysis.

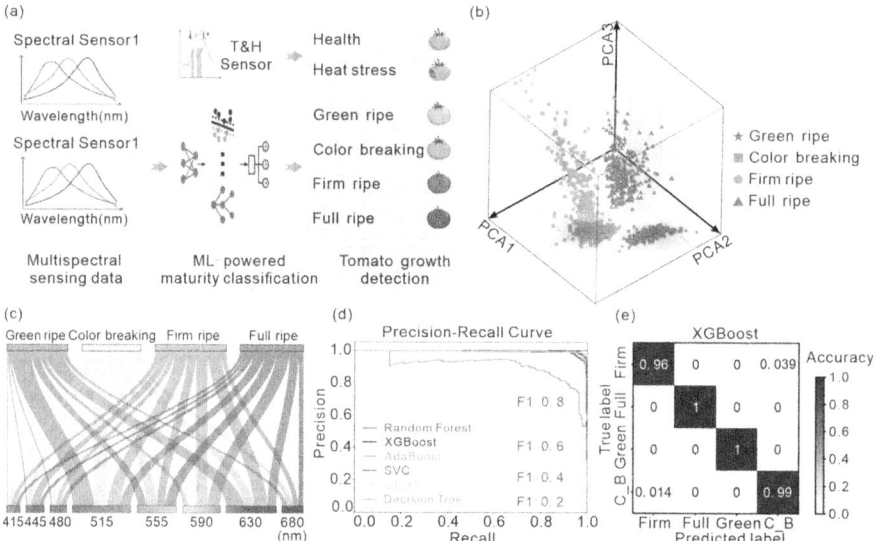

Fig. 3. ML-powered detection framework for tomato growth monitoring. (a) Tomato growth monitoring algorithm framework. (b) 3D kPCA visualization of spectral characteristics across tomato ripening stages. (c) Sankey diagram illustrating the relative contribution of spectral wavelengths to tomato ripeness classification. (d) Precision-recall curves for different machine learning classification algorithms. (e) Confusion matrix for the XGBoost algorithm with an average accuracy of 98.75%.

3 Demonstrations

Optimal thermal and moisture conditions are essential for healthy physiological development, while spectral data offer a non-destructive means of fruit ripeness assessment. In this section, we presented an experimental evaluation of a flexible fruit wearable system for continuous monitoring of tomato growth. The system's performance was assessed in terms of its accuracy in ripeness detection and its feasibility and effectiveness for real-time, in situ monitoring of tomato growth.

3.1 Detection of Thermal Stress During Tomato Growth

To assess the device's capability to monitor fruit growth under stress, a controlled greenhouse was constructed to simulate thermal stress, as illustrated in Fig. 4(a). The blank control tomato was maintained at 20–25 °C throughout the day, while the thermal stress tomato was exposed to a surface temperature of 35 ± 3 °C from 08:00 to 20:00, with all other conditions kept identical and optimal. Surface temperature and humidity data were continuously recorded in real-time by T&H sensors and transmitted via a signal acquisition printed circuit board (PCB) to a microcontroller. Over the 15-day stress period, tomatoes in the thermal stress tomato exhibited higher temperatures and lower humidity, as presented in Fig. 4(b). These conditions resulted from increased transpiration and accelerated stomatal water loss, ultimately leading to reduced epidermal moisture.

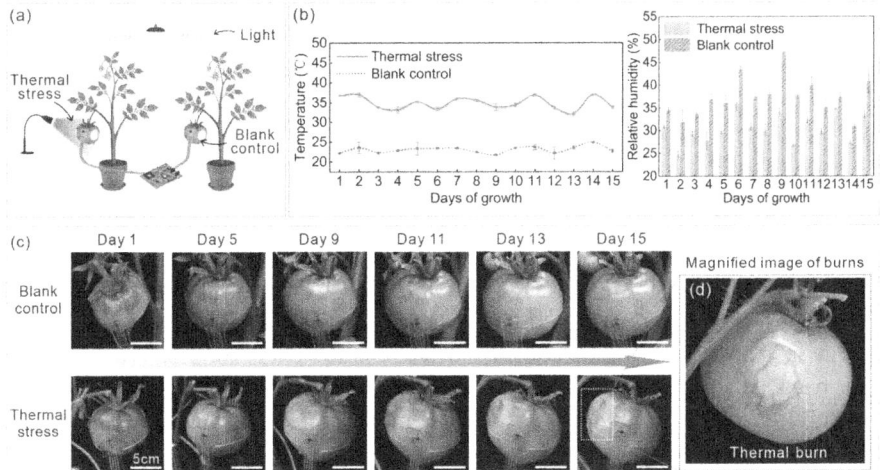

Fig. 4. Experiments on thermal stress. (a) Experimental design for thermal stress. (b) Temperature and humidity control of thermal stress and blank control. (c) Morphological changes in tomatoes under thermal stress and control conditions during 15 days. (d) Thermal burns on the surface of tomatoes.

As illustrated in Fig. 4(c), the growth states of the tomatoes varied distinctly between the two plants. The thermal stress tomato exhibited a slower growth rate, with fruit circumference increasing from 9.8 cm to 12.1 cm. In contrast, the control tomato presented more robust growth, with the circumference increasing from 9.6 cm to 12.9 cm. Additionally, from day 9 onward, subtle signs of thermal burn began to appear on the fruit surface in the stressed tomato, gradually spreading over time. As represented in Fig. 4(d), this ultimately resulted in irreversible tissue damage to the fruit. These findings suggest that real-time monitoring of tomato surface temperature and humidity can serve as an effective early indicator of plant stress. Such data enables timely adjustments to environmental control strategies, thereby assisting in preventing irreversible damage caused by prolonged or cumulative stress conditions.

3.2 Dynamic Detection of Maturity During Tomato Growth

To characterize dynamic ripening processes, we implemented a 36-day long-term evaluation of the flexible fruit wearable system's efficacy. During the initial phase of the study (Days 1–28), data were collected every two days. Following the onset of the color-breaking stage (Day 29), the sampling frequency was increased to once per day. The results demonstrated that the sensor maintained stable performance under deformation of up to 65.7%, corresponding to an increase in fruit circumference from 105 mm to 174 mm. This result confirms the sensor's exceptional mechanical robustness and electrical stability throughout fruit growth.

As illustrated in Fig. 5(a), the experiment captured morphological transitions corresponding to four distinct ripening stages. During the green ripe stage (Days 1–29), the fruit exhibited uniform green pigmentation and gradual expansion. In the color-breaking stage (Days 31–33), the tip began transitioning from green to orange-yellow. By the firm ripe stage (Day 34), the orange-red hue extended to cover approximately three-quarters of the fruit surface. In the full ripening stage (Days 35–36), the tomato had developed a uniform deep-red color. These visible phenotypes align closely with established physiological markers of tomato maturation.

To quantitatively characterize the ripening process, multispectral and microenvironmental data were collected simultaneously. Real-time monitoring of temperature and humidity ensured optimal growth conditions, while the spectral sensors, integrated with a pre-trained ML model, enabled maturity prediction with high accuracy. The spectral data shown in Fig. 5(a), acquired at eight key time points (Days 1, 9, 19, 31, 33, 34, 35, and 36), revealed pronounced stage-dependent reflectance features. During the green ripe phase, a peak near 555 nm corresponded to chlorophyll absorption. Turning to the color-breaking stage, this peak shifted to 590 nm with the production of lycopene. During the firm ripe stage, the peak further red-shifted to 630 nm, stabilizing at 650 nm in the full ripening stage, accompanied by a reduction in full width at half maximum. Spectra from both sensors presented high concordance, with shifts in reflectance closely mirroring physiological transformations.

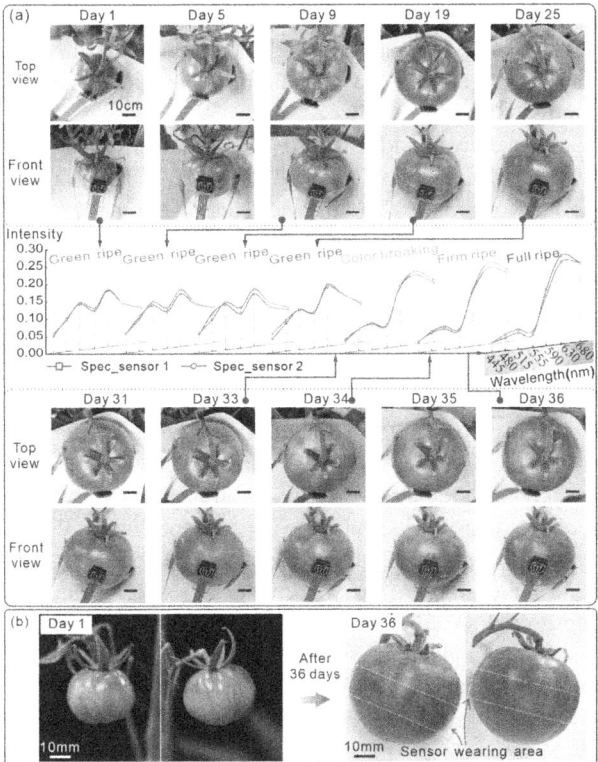

Fig. 5. 36-day in situ monitoring of tomato growth. (a) Spectral data and morphological changes of tomato during its growth. (b) Tomato fruit variations over a 36-day growth period. (Color figure online)

Post-experiment observations in Fig. 5(b) revealed no discernible difference in surface coloration or texture between areas under the sensor and adjacent regions, indicating that the sensor did not interfere with ripening or tissue health. This confirms the excellent biocompatibility of the sensor materials. Throughout the monitoring period, the device demonstrated superior biosafety and environmental tolerance, with no observed tissue damage or growth suppression. Compared to conventional techniques, our study provides a method for in-situ dynamic monitoring of tomato growth, enabling the development of a growth monitoring system and providing real-time predictions to inform greenhouse management strategies.

4 Materials and Methods

4.1 Sensing System Design

The flexible sensing system developed in this study comprises both hardware and software components, as illustrated in Fig. 6(a). The hardware architecture integrates a Bluetooth Low Energy (BLE) module, an Inter-Integrated Circuit (I^2C) expansion interface, two spectral sensing units, a T&H sensor, an LED light, and an external power supply module. Communication between the BLE microcontroller and peripheral sensors is established via the I²C expansion module. The integrated LED provides active illumination for the spectral sensor, while the power module ensures reliable energy delivery to the entire system.

The software architecture includes a custom WeChat mini-program for real-time data visualization and a local server implemented using the Flask framework. This server incorporates an ML algorithm for the on-device classification of tomato ripeness. Component selection was guided by considerations of measurement accuracy, energy efficiency, cost-effectiveness, and compact form factor. Specifically, the system employs the T&H sensor (SHT41, Sensirion) for temperature and humidity sensing, the spectral sensor (AS7341, ams-OSRAM) for spectral analysis, and the BLE microcontroller (NRF52840, Nordic) for communication. The circuit design comprises dedicated modules for BLE communication, voltage regulation, I²C expansion, sensor integration, and power management. This modular configuration ensures efficient data transmission, minimizes I²C bus contention, and maintains consistent power delivery.

As shown in Fig. 6(b), the PCB layout was optimized for wearable integration onto the curved surface of tomato fruits. With a compact footprint of 35 mm × 45 mm, the PCB was fabricated on a polyimide film substrate, selected for its lightweight, ultra-thin, and flexible properties. These features enable close conformity to the fruit surface without impeding growth. Weighing only 2.5 g (g), the flexible PCB exhibits excellent thermal resistance and electrical insulation. These properties ensure stable operation under natural environmental conditions and enhance the system's durability and biocompatibility.

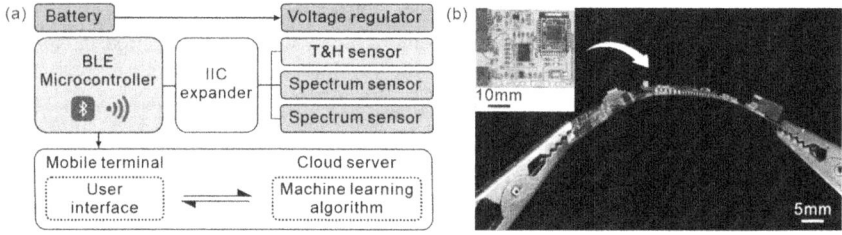

Fig. 6. Hardware system design. (a) Schematic diagram of the system structure. (b) Flexible PCB with high flexibility.

4.2 Fabrication of the Flexible Fruit Wearable Devices

The structural design of the flexible fruit wearable device is depicted in Fig. 7(a). The base layer comprised a polydimethylsiloxane (PDMS) substrate with a 20:1 base-to-curing-agent ratio, selected for its superior mechanical flexibility and biocompatibility. Integrated onto this substrate were liquid metal conductive circuits and flexible wiring for efficient signal transmission. The middle layer integrated functional components, including spectral sensor chips, a T&H sensor, and an LED light, with localized PDMS curing applied to enhance the mechanical stability of hardware connections. The device was encapsulated with a top layer of PDMS (20:1), overlaid by a carbon-doped Ecoflex (c Ecoflex) light-blocking layer to suppress external light.

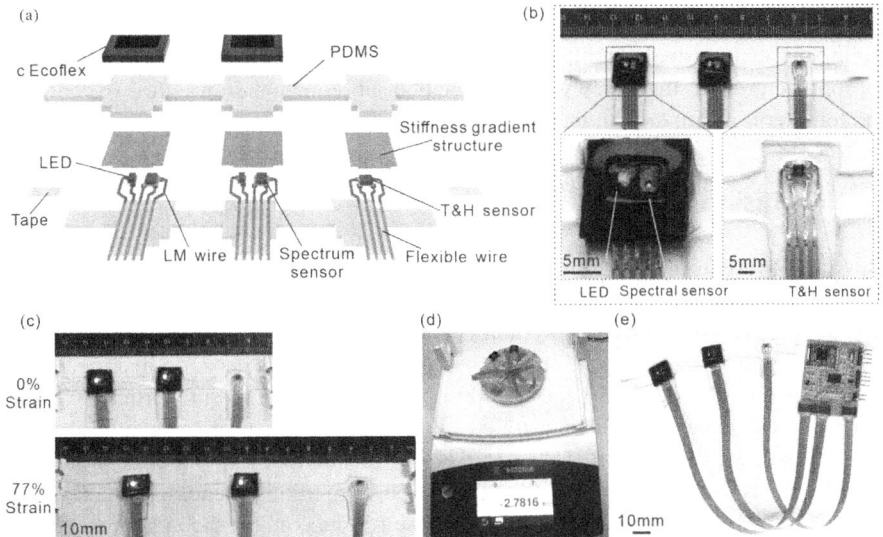

Fig. 7. Demonstrations of the flexible fruit wearable sensor for tomato growth monitoring. (a) Exploded view diagram of flexible fruit wearable devices. (b) Views of a flexible fruit wearable device with details of spectral and T&H sensors. (c) Stretching diagram of flexible fruit wearable devices. (d) Weight of flexible fruit wearable devices. (e) Photo of the plant soft wearable system before attaching to a tomato.

The fabrication process involved four sequential steps, as depicted in Fig. 7(b). First, a 500 μm-thick PDMS base layer was formed by spin-coating and semi-cured at 75 °C for 20 min. Second, liquid metal circuits were precisely patterned using an air-pressure spray-printing process through laser-cut polyethylene terephthalate masks. During sensor integration, chips and flexible interconnects were mounted onto these liquid metal circuits, followed by localized PDMS curing with 0.5 μL/mm^2 of curing agent B at 75 °C to achieve complete crosslinking for enhanced structural integrity. Then, a 20:1 (base: curing agent) PDMS mixture was applied for intermediate encapsulation. Finally, the device was encapsulated with a 200 μm-thick carbon-doped Ecoflex light-blocking layer to complete the flexible sensor assembly.

As demonstrated in Fig. 7(c), the ring-shaped flexible sensor adopts a localized curing strategy to increase stiffness at sensor locations, ensuring reliable connectivity even under 77% strain. As displayed in Fig. 7(d), the incorporation of low-density PDMS, Ecoflex, and lightweight flexible wiring results in a sensor weight of 2.8 g. Subsequently, the sensor is connected to a flexible PCB, as illustrated in Fig. 7(e). Data acquired by the sensor is transmitted to the PCB via flexible wiring and processed in real-time to monitor tomato growth. The entire system maintains robust connections, ensuring continuous and efficient data acquisition and transmission.

4.3 Cultivation of Tomato Plants

The widely cultivated tomato cultivar Provence was selected as the experimental material, and plant samples were purchased from an e-commerce platform. These plants were grown indoors under soil-based cultivation with a 16-h light and 8-h dark cycle, maintaining optimal nutrient conditions in the growth medium. Once the plants reached the appropriate growth stage, they were subjected to subsequent thermal stress experiments and long-term in situ growth monitoring.

5 Conclusion

This study presents a flexible fruit wearable system for in situ, real-time, and long-term monitoring of tomato growth during its dynamic growing process. By integrating with lightweight ML algorithms, the system enables high-accuracy classification of tomato ripeness (accuracy > 98%) and supports real-time and online decision-making. Experimental validations were also conducted to present this system's properties. A 15-day thermal stress experiment demonstrated the critical influence of temperature regulation on tomato growth. Moreover, a 36-day in situ wearable experiment continuously recorded the ripening process from the green ripe stage to full ripeness, achieving accurate classification across different stages. These results confirm the system's excellent biocompatibility, functional stability, and monitoring precision, while future studies could extend the observation window to evaluate performance under even longer cultivation cycles. The developed system provides a reliable solution for smart precision agriculture in tomato growth monitoring, with the potential to enhance both yield and quality. This technology can be extended to other crops, paving the way for automated and intelligent agricultural management.

Acknowledgment. This research was supported by the National Natural Science Foundation of China (52188102) and the National Key Research and Development Program of China (2024YFB4707902).

References

1. FAO. 2024. World Food and Agriculture – Statistical Yearbook 2024. Rome (2024)
2. Aharoni, A., Vorst, O.: DNA microarrays for functional plant genomics. Funct. Genom. **2002**, 99–118 (2002)
3. da S. Ferreira, M.V., Barbosa, J.L., Kamruzzaman, M., Barbin, D.F.: Low-cost electronic-nose (LC-e-nose) systems for the evaluation of plantation and fruit crops: recent advances and future trends. Anal. Methods **15**(45), 6120–6138 (2023)
4. Thakur, P.S., Khanna, P., Sheorey, T., et al.: Trends in vision-based machine learning techniques for plant disease identification: a systematic review. Expert Syst. Appl. **208**, 118117 (2022)
5. Faridi, H., Aboonajmi, M.: Application of machine vision in agricultural products. In: Proceedings of the 4th Iranian International NDT Conference (IRNDT) (2017)
6. ElMasry, G., Sun, D.W.: Principles of hyperspectral imaging technology. In: Hyperspectral Imaging for Food Quality Analysis and Control, pp. 3–43. Academic Press (2010)
7. Li, L., Hu, D.Y., Tang, T.Y., et al.: Non-destructive detection of the quality attributes of fruits by visible-near infrared spectroscopy. J. Food Meas. Characterizat. **17**(2), 1526–1534 (2023)

8. Zeng, T., Li, S., Song, Q., Zhong, F., Wei, X.: Lightweight tomato real-time detection method based on improved YOLO and mobile deployment. Comput. Electron. Agric. **205**, 107625 (2023)
9. Sanida, M.V., Sanida, T., Sideris, A., et al.: An efficient hybrid CNN classification model for tomato crop disease. Technologies **11**(1), 10 (2023)
10. Todorova, M., Veleva, P., Atanassova, S., et al.: Assessment of tomato quality through near-infrared spectroscopy—advantages, limitations, and integration with multivariate analysis techniques. Eng. Proc. **70**(1), 34 (2024)
11. Li, S., Wang, Q., Yang, X., Zhang, Q., Shi, R., Li, J.: Online detection of lycopene content in the two cultivars of tomatoes by multi-point full transmission Vis-NIR spectroscopy. Postharvest Biol. Technol. **211**, 112813 (2024)
12. Qu, C.C., Sun, X.Y., Sun, W.X., et al.: Flexible wearables for plants. Small **17**(50), 2104482 (2021)
13. Yan, B., Zhang, F., Wang, M., et al.: Flexible wearable sensors for crop monitoring: a review. Front. Plant Sci. **15**, 1406074 (2024)
14. Xu, W., Chen, L., Hu, X., et al.: Botanic signal monitor: advanced wearable sensor for plant health analysis. Adv. Funct. Mater. **34**(51), 2410544 (2024)
15. Li, X.H., Li, M.Z., Li, J.Y., et al.: Wearable sensor supports in-situ and continuous monitoring of plant health in precision agriculture era. Plant Biotechnol. J. **22**(6), 1516–1535 (2024)
16. Ikram, M., Ameer, S., Kulsoom, F., et al.: Flexible temperature and humidity sensors of plants for precision agriculture: Current challenges and future roadmap. Comput. Electron. Agric. **226**, 109449 (2024)

LLM-Based Structured Information Extraction for Urinary Incontinence from Multi-modal Clinical Data

Tianyu Wu[1,4], Mingxiang Luo[4], Xueyan Shen[2], Shengxiang Liang[3], Xinyu Wu[4], and Wujing Cao[4(✉)]

[1] Department of Biomedical Engineering, Southern University of Science and Technology, Shenzhen 518055, China
[2] Department of Rehabilitation Medicine, Huashan Hospital, Fudan University, Shanghai, China
[3] Fujian University of Traditional Chinese Medicine, Fuzhou, China
sxliang@fjtcm.edu.cn
[4] Shenzhen Institutes of Advanced Technology, Chinese Academy of Sciences, Beijing, China
{ty.wu,wj.cao}@siat.ac.cn

Abstract. Accurate and efficient extraction of clinical information for urinary incontinence (UI) severity assessment from diverse data sources is a significant challenge. This paper presents a novel framework leveraging large language models (LLMs) for robust named entity recognition (NER) from multisource, heterogeneous, semistructured clinical UI data, including clinical notes, patient-reported outcome measures (PROMs), and electromyography (EMG) signals. The study investigates the efficacy of various prompting strategies and combinations of leading LLMs (DeepSeek-V3, GPT-4o, GPT-4o-mini) for the NER task. Performance was evaluated by comparing UI severity assessments, generated by a unified LLM using the extracted entities, against manually annotated ground truth. Data from a cohort of 287 patients were utilized, with 50 for development and 237 for evaluation. Experimental results demonstrate the framework's strong capability in accurately extracting key clinical information, offering a promising approach to enhance the efficiency and precision of physician-led UI severity evaluations.

Keywords: Large Language Models (LLMs) · Urinary Incontinence (UI) · Named Entity Recognition (NER) · Multi-source Heterogeneous Data

1 Introduction

Urinary incontinence (UI) is a highly prevalent health problem that significantly affects the quality of life of patients and can lead to social isolation and psychological problems [1]. Despite advances in clinical diagnosis, early and accurate identification of UI remains challenging due to the subjective nature of symptom assessment and the variability in its presentation between different individuals and populations [2]. In particular, a correct assessment of the severity of UI is crucial to developing appropriate treatment plans and management strategies.

In clinical practice, determining UI severity relies on extracting data from lengthy, unstructured clinical notes, requiring clinicians to manually search for key information for accurate assessment and personalized treatment. This inefficient process can delay treatment and compromise patient care. Researchers also face a laborious task extracting UI epidemiology, risk factors, and treatment outcomes from vast unstructured data [3]. Recent advancements in Artificial Intelligence (AI) and Natural Language Processing (NLP) technologies offer promising avenues to enhance traditional clinical information processing methods. Specifically, Large Language Models (LLMs), built upon the Transformer architecture, have demonstrated powerful capabilities in automating the analysis of complex language data [4]. The cornerstone of Transformer's effectiveness lies in its self-attention mechanism, which calculates weighted relationships between all words in a sequence using the following equation:

$$\text{Attention}(Q, K, V) = \text{softmax}\left(\frac{QK^T}{\sqrt{d_k}}\right)V \qquad (1)$$

where Q, K, V denote query, key, and value matrices derived from the input sequence, and d_k is the key dimension. This attention mechanism empowers Transformers to capture intricate contextual relationships crucial for interpreting medical terminology and clinical narratives. Notably, BERT (Bidirectional Encoder Representations from Transformers) [5] and its derivatives, including RoBERTa [6] and the domain-specific BioBERT [7], have demonstrated substantial success in extracting medical linguistic features from clinical texts, proving particularly adept at identifying those pertinent to symptoms and severity.

Our study uses LLMs to create an efficient framework for automated extraction of urinary incontinence (UI) severity-related Named Entities (NEs) from clinical records, PROMs, and EMG data. This LLM-driven tool reduces manual review, enabling timely severity assessments, optimized treatments, and improved outcomes. Converting unstructured UI data into structured databases accelerates UI severity research. We introduce a novel NE schema for UI evaluation and assess LLMs (DeepSeek-V3, GPT-4o, GPT-4o-mini) with various prompts to determine the best extraction strategy.

2 Methodology

2.1 NE Framework Development

Schema for Information Extraction. To facilitate the extraction of key information for urinary incontinence (UI) assessment from diverse multimodal data sources (including clinical notes, PROMs, and EMG data), we developed a dedicated named entity information extraction schema. This schema is designed to identify and structure relevant entity types found within clinical records and EMG reports. These entities include: SymptomType, Frequency, Nocturia,

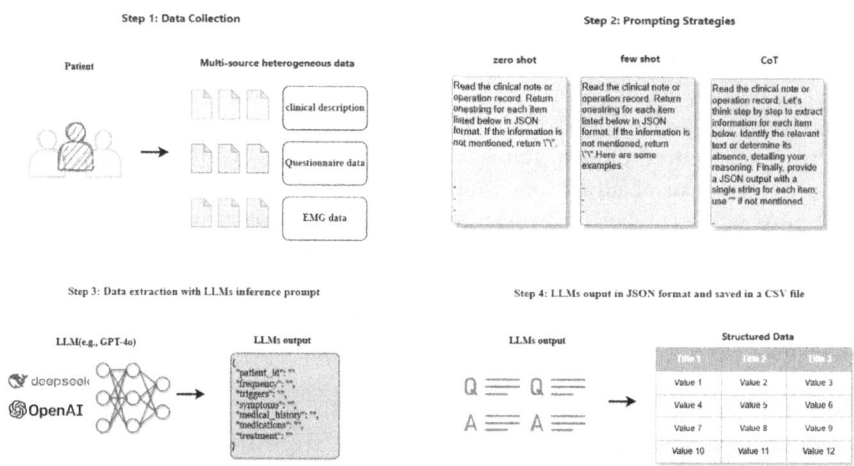

Fig. 1. Overview of the proposed LLM-based framework for extracting information from multi-source data for UI assessment.

MaxMVC (Maximum Voluntary Contraction amplitude), AvgMVC (Average Maximum Voluntary Contraction amplitude), DurationAtRest, and RelevantHistory. This structured approach lays the foundation for subsequent automated data processing, enabling more precise and comprehensive UI assessment. A detailed definition of the targeted entities, their descriptions, data sources, and illustrative examples is provided in Table 1 (Fig. 1).

Table 1. Detailed Schema Definition for UI Assessment Factor Extraction.

Entity Name	Description	Data Source(s)
SymptomType	Type of urinary incontinence reported by the patient or clinician	Clinical Notes, PROMs
Frequency	Number of urination episodes during the daytime	Clinical Notes
Nocturia	Number of times waking up at night to urinate	Clinical Notes, PROMs
MaxMVC	Maximum Voluntary Contraction amplitude from Pelvic Floor EMG	EMG Report
AvgMVC	Average Maximum Voluntary Contraction amplitude over multiple trials	EMG Report
DurationAtRest	Duration of the resting phase measurement in EMG	EMG Report
RelevantHistory	Key phrases describing relevant medical or surgical history impacting UI	Clinical Notes

Extraction Logic. Leveraging the Langchain framework [8], we constructed inference prompts designed to guide the selected Large Language Models (LLMs) in the information extraction task based on the defined schema. These prompts instructed the LLMs to analyze the combined input from clinical notes, PROMs, and EMG data and output all identified Named Entities conforming to the predefined schema in a structured JSON format. To enhance the determinism of extraction results, the generation temperature [9] parameter of the LLMs was set to 0.2. Subsequently, a dedicated JSON parser was implemented to process the LLMs' output string and retrieve the structured data, handling potential formatting variations or errors.

Experimental Design We designed a two-phase experiment to evaluate multimodal clinical information extraction and subsequent severity assessment. Our approach combined different prompting strategies with various Large Language Models (LLMs) for optimal information extraction.

Phase one focused on entity extraction using three prompting techniques:

- **Zero-shot:** LLM received only schema definitions and task instructions without examples [10].
- **Few-shot:** Prompt included curated example input-output pairs before the target query [10].
- **Chain-of-Thought (CoT):** LLM generated intermediate reasoning steps before producing structured output, optionally combined with few-shot examples [11].

We evaluated three LLMs with different architectures and capabilities: DeepSeek-V3, GPT-4o, and GPT-4o-mini. This selection represented diverse model sizes and design approaches.

Our automated Python workflow processed de-identified patient data (clinical notes, PROMs, EMG information) through each prompting strategy with each LLM. The extracted entities were then fed into a single designated LLM for phase two—severity assessment—where the model classified urinary incontinence severity levels based on the extracted information. This experimental design allowed us to identify which extraction approach produced the most clinically useful information for accurate severity classification.

2.2 Evaluation Metrics and Procedure

Performance was evaluated based on the framework's ability to correctly classify the severity level (e.g., Mild, Moderate, Severe) compared to clinician-derived ground truth labels. Various LLM architectures and prompting strategies were tested.

Standard classification metrics were calculated for severity level classification [12]:

- **Precision**: The ratio of correctly predicted positive observations to the total predicted positives.
$$\text{Precision} = \frac{TP}{TP + FP} \qquad (2)$$
- **Recall**: The ratio of correctly predicted positive observations to all observations in the actual class.
$$\text{Recall} = \frac{TP}{TP + FN} \qquad (3)$$
- **F1-score**: The harmonic mean of Precision and Recall.
$$F1 = 2 \cdot \frac{\text{Precision} \cdot \text{Recall}}{\text{Precision} + \text{Recall}} \qquad (4)$$

The macro-averaged F1-score is used. This is calculated by computing the F1-score for each class independently and then taking the unweighted average of these scores, thereby giving equal weight to each class.

Framework Development Set. The performance of each individual LLM combined with each prompting strategy, was assessed on the 50 development notes against the expert ground truth. This allowed for initial comparison and potential optimization of prompts or selection of the best performing approaches.

Validation Set. The finalized framework configurations (including the best individual prompting strategies and ensemble methods) were evaluated on the independent validation set. Performance was assessed using Macro F1-score, Macro Precision, and Macro Recall to account for potential class imbalance. Confusion matrices were generated and analyzed to identify specific misclassification patterns for each severity level.

3 Experiments

3.1 Data Source

We acquired clinical records and related data from urinary incontinence (UI) patients from multiple hospitals. All data were rigorously de-identified to ensure patient privacy. The dataset includes de-identified semi-structured outpatient medical records, patient-reported outcome measures (PROMs) such as ICIQ-SF scores [13], and pelvic floor electromyography (EMG) data.

A final dataset of 287 patient records meeting the inclusion criteria was compiled. This dataset was randomly divided into a development set (n = 50) and a validation set (n = 237).

All case data labels used as ground truth for UI severity were derived from comprehensive assessments by experienced clinicians based on subjective questionnaires (e.g., ICIQ-SF), patient self-reported histories, and other clinically relevant information, strictly adhering to established clinical guidelines.

3.2 Performance on Validation Set

We evaluated three Large Language Models (LLMs) on the UI severity classification task: DeepSeek-V3, GPT-4o, and GPT-4o-mini. For each model, we tested three prompting strategies: Zero-shot, Few-shot, and Chain-of-Thought (CoT) prompting. Table 2 presents the detailed performance metrics, including Macro F1, Macro Precision, Macro Recall, and Accuracy, for all model and prompting strategy combinations.

Table 2. Macro Average Results with Global Accuracy

LLM	Prompting	Macro F1	Macro Prec.	Macro Rec.	Accuracy
Deepseek v3	Zero-shot	0.893	0.890	0.898	0.899
Deepseek v3	Few-shot	**0.953**	**0.953**	**0.953**	**0.954**
Deepseek v3	CoT	0.932	0.929	0.936	0.937
GPT-4o	Zero-shot	0.865	0.861	0.873	0.873
GPT-4o	Few-shot	0.931	0.930	0.932	0.932
GPT-4o	CoT	0.906	0.903	0.911	0.911
GPT-4o-mini	Zero-shot	0.812	0.807	0.826	0.827
GPT-4o-mini	Few-shot	0.883	0.880	0.886	0.886
GPT-4o-mini	CoT	0.858	0.854	0.864	0.865

As shown in Table 2, the choice of both the LLM and the prompting strategy significantly impacts performance on the UI severity classification task.

Overall, DeepSeek-V3 consistently demonstrated superior performance compared to GPT-4o and GPT-4o-mini across all tested prompting strategies. The highest performance was achieved by DeepSeek-V3 utilizing Few-shot prompting, obtaining a Macro F1 score of 0.953. Following DeepSeek-V3, GPT-4o showed the next best performance, with its peak also occurring with Few-shot prompting (Macro F1: 0.931). GPT-4o-mini achieved the lowest scores among the three models, with Few-shot again being the best strategy (Macro F1: 0.883). The Macro Precision, Macro Recall, and Accuracy metrics generally align with the trends observed in Macro F1 across all configurations.

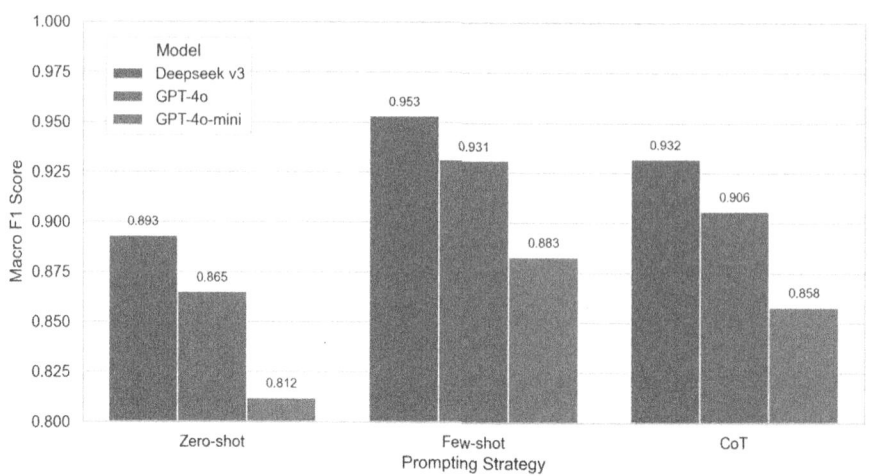

Fig. 2. Comparison of Macro F1 performance across models and prompting strategies.

Few-shot and CoT consistently outperformed Zero-shot prompting (Fig. 2), emphasizing the importance of context or structured reasoning. Significant Macro F1 improvements resulted from switching from Zero-shot to Few-shot (e.g., +0.060 for DeepSeek-V3, +0.066 for GPT-4o, +0.071 for GPT-4o-mini). GPT-4o-mini using Few-shot saw the largest improvement from the Zero-shot baseline (+0.071 Macro F1).

While both Few-shot and CoT outperformed Zero-shot, Few-shot generally achieved comparable or higher Macro F1 scores. This suggests that for UI severity classification, providing relevant examples (Few-shot) is at least as effective as step-by-step reasoning (CoT), possibly due to better pattern capture by examples or error potential from overly complex CoT [14].

In summary, our experiments demonstrate DeepSeek-V3's high capability for UI severity classification, particularly with Few-shot prompting. Furthermore, the substantial performance gains with Few-shot and CoT strategies over Zero-shot underscore the importance of effective prompting for leveraging LLMs in specialized tasks.

3.3 Misclassification Investigation

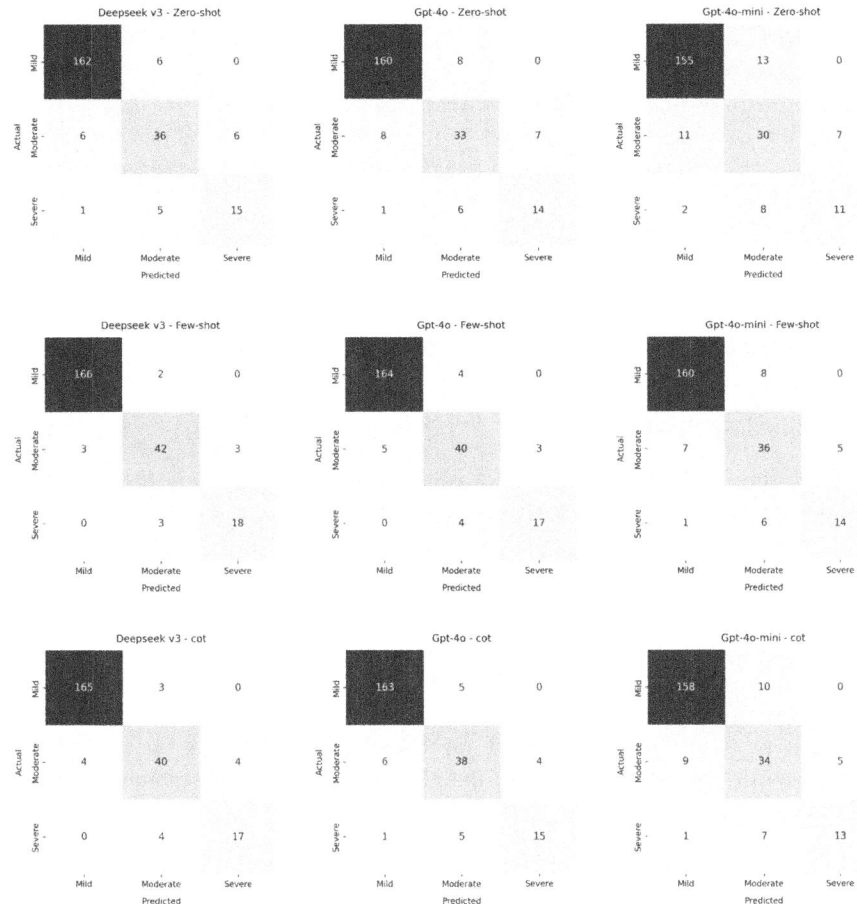

Fig. 3. UI severity classification confusion matrices for DeepSeek-V3, GPT-4o, and GPT-4o-mini using Zero-shot, Few-shot, and CoT prompting.

To gain a deeper understanding of the model's error patterns, we analyzed the predictions on the validation set by examining the confusion matrices for each model and prompting strategy, as illustrated in Fig. 3. For severity classification, the analysis confirms that misclassifications primarily occurred between adjacent categories. Specifically:

- **'Moderate' vs. Adjacent Categories:** Across models and prompts, 'Moderate' issues were often misclassified as 'Mild' or 'Severe'. This was most pronounced in GPT-4o-mini Zero-shot (11 'Moderate' misclassified as 'Mild', 7 as 'Severe').

- **'Severe' misclassified as 'Moderate':** 'Severe' issues were most often misclassified as 'Moderate' (3–8 instances across models). GPT-4o-mini Zero-shot had the highest error rate, DeepSeek-V3 Few-shot the lowest.
- **'Mild' misclassified as 'Moderate':** 'Mild' issues were occasionally misclassified as 'Moderate'. DeepSeek-V3 Few-shot had the fewest (2), GPT-4o-mini Zero-shot the most (13).
- **Rare Non-Adjacent Misclassifications:** Misclassifications between non-adjacent categories were extremely rare; 'Mild' was never misclassified as 'Severe'. 'Severe' as 'Mild' was infrequent (typically 0–1 instances; absent in several scenarios).

Models struggle with nuanced adjacent severity distinctions (e.g., 'Moderate' vs. 'Severe') but effectively differentiate disparate severities (e.g., 'Mild' vs. 'Severe'). Few-shot prompting significantly improves performance across all models, with DeepSeek-V3 Few-shot achieving the highest accuracy at 95.4.

3.4 Ablation Study

To assess the impact of different data modalities on named entity recognition (NER) performance, we considered two configurations:

- **Baseline Model:** Extracts information from the complete multi-modal dataset, including EMG data.
- **Ablation Model:** Extracts information solely from the textual data, excluding EMG data.

All other parameters (LLMs: DeepSeek v3, GPT-4o, GPT-4o-mini; prompting strategies: Few-shot, CoT, Zero-shot) were kept consistent with the main experimental setup. Performance was evaluated using Accuracy to account for overall performance.

Results and Analysis. Table 3 summarizes the overall accuracy comparison between baseline and ablation models. To further illustrate the impact of EMG data removal on more detailed performance metrics, Fig. 4 presents a series of heatmaps comparing Precision, Recall, and F1-score for each model and prompting strategy under both configurations (with and without EMG data). The blue heatmaps represent the baseline models (with EMG), while the red heatmaps depict the ablation models (without EMG).

As evidenced by the overall accuracy results in Table 3 and the detailed visualization in Fig. 4, removing EMG data consistently led to a decline in performance across all models and prompting strategies. The average reduction in overall accuracy was approximately 3.4% points.

The performance degradation observed upon EMG removal, reflected in the Precision, Recall, and F1-score values presented in Fig. 4, suggests that while LLMs can effectively utilize textual clinical data, EMG-based physiological measurements offer vital, complementary information. This is particularly noticeable

Table 3. Overall accuracy comparison: baseline models (with EMG) vs. ablation models (without EMG).

Model	Prompt	Baseline Acc.	Ablation Acc.
DeepSeek v3	Few-shot	95.4%	92.0%
DeepSeek v3	CoT	93.7%	90.3%
DeepSeek v3	Zero-shot	89.9%	86.5%
GPT-4o	Few-shot	93.3%	89.9%
GPT-4o	CoT	91.1%	87.8%
GPT-4o	Zero-shot	87.3%	84.0%
GPT-4o-mini	Few-shot	88.6%	85.2%
GPT-4o-mini	CoT	86.5%	83.1%
GPT-4o-mini	Zero-shot	82.7%	79.3%

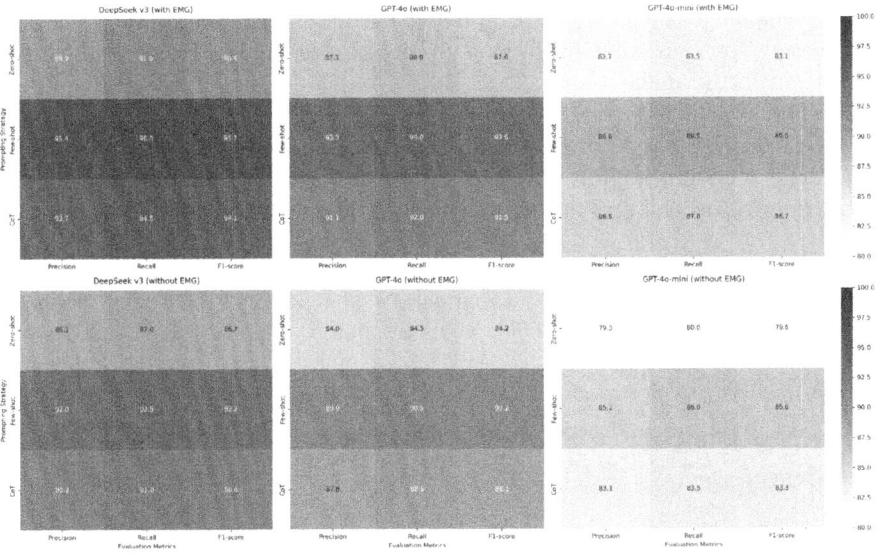

Fig. 4. Detailed performance comparison (Precision, Recall, F1-score) of baseline models (with EMG, top row, blue) and ablation models (without EMG, bottom row, red) across different LLMs and prompting strategies. Values shown are percentages. (Color figure online)

when discerning subtle differences between adjacent severity levels, where textual descriptions alone may prove insufficient.

In summary, this ablation study clearly demonstrates that integrating EMG measurements significantly improves classification accuracy and the overall performance in assessing urinary incontinence severity. While text-based models provide considerable utility, especially in resource-constrained environments, incorporating EMG data whenever feasible is highly advantageous for developing more accurate clinical AI applications. This highlights the critical role of multi-modal data integration in advancing clinical decision-making support systems.

4 Conclusion

This study developed an LLM-based framework using models like DeepSeek-V3 and GPT-4o for the efficient extraction of structured urinary incontinence (UI) information from multi-source clinical data (notes, PROMs, EMG). By employing effective prompting strategies, it achieved high accuracy on real clinical data in identifying crucial UI information.

Our primary contribution is the development of a dedicated framework for extracting structured information for UI assessment, along with an evaluation of different prompting strategies. This LLM-based approach offers significant flexibility and robust performance.

Key challenges included creating reliable ground truth, and iterative prompt engineering for consistent extraction from nuanced clinical text, necessitating robust output normalization.

Limitations include single-center data, subjectivity in ground truth, and a focus on specific LLMs. Future work will target prospective validation in clinical workflows, clinician-friendly interfaces, EHR integration, adaptation to other pelvic floor disorders, and fine-tuning smaller, locally deployable models.

Acknowledgements. This work was partially supported by the National Key R&D (research and development) Program of China (2022YFB4703300), Shenzhen Medical Research Fund (D2404006), the National Natural Science Foundation of China (62473358) and Guangdong Basic and Applied Basic Research Foundation (2024A1515030055).

References

1. Irwin, D.E., et al.: Population-based survey of urinary incontinence, overactive bladder, and other lower urinary tract symptoms in five countries: results of the epic study. Eur. Urol. **50**(6), 1306–1315 (2006)
2. Saleh, S., Majumdar, A., Williams, K.: The conservative (non-pharmacological) management of female urinary incontinence. Obstet. Gynaecol. **16**(3), 169–177 (2014)
3. Zhao, J., Kan, M.Y., Procter, P.M., Zubaidah, S., Yip, W.K., Li, G.M.: Improving search for evidence-based practice using information extraction. In: AMIA Annual Symposium Proceedings, vol. 2010, p. 937 (2010)
4. Vaswani, A., et al.: Attention is all you need. Adv. Neural Inf. Process. Syst. **30** (2017)
5. Devlin, J., Chang, M.W., Lee, K., Toutanova, K.: Bert: pre-training of deep bidirectional transformers for language understanding. In: Proceedings of the 2019 conference of the North American chapter of the association for computational linguistics: human language technologies, vol. 1 (long and short papers), pp. 4171–4186 (2019)

6. Liu, Y., et al.: Roberta: a robustly optimized bert pretraining approach. arXiv preprint arXiv:1907.11692 (2019)
7. Lee, J., et al.: Biobert: a pre-trained biomedical language representation model for biomedical text mining. Bioinformatics **36**(4), 1234–1240 (2020)
8. Topsakal, O., Akinci, T.C.: Creating large language model applications utilizing langchain: a primer on developing llm apps fast. In: International Conference on Applied Engineering and Natural Sciences, vol. 1, pp. 1050–1056 (2023)
9. Renze, M.: The effect of sampling temperature on problem solving in large language models. In: Findings of the Association for Computational Linguistics: EMNLP 2024, pp. 7346–7356 (2024)
10. Mann, B., et al.: Language models are few-shot learners. arXiv preprint arXiv:2005.14165 1, 3 (2020)
11. Wei, J., et al.: Chain-of-thought prompting elicits reasoning in large language models. Adv. Neural. Inf. Process. Syst. **35**, 24824–24837 (2022)
12. Powers, D.M.: Evaluation: from precision, recall and f-measure to roc, informedness, markedness and correlation. arXiv preprint arXiv:2010.16061 (2020)
13. Avery, K., Donovan, J., Peters, T.J., Shaw, C., Gotoh, M., Abrams, P.: Iciq: a brief and robust measure for evaluating the symptoms and impact of urinary incontinence. Neurourol. Urodyn. Off. J. Int. Contin. Soc. **23**(4), 322–330 (2004)
14. Liu, T., et al.: Logic-of-thought: injecting logic into contexts for full reasoning in large language models. arXiv preprint arXiv:2409.17539 (2024)

A Tactile-Driven Multiple Instance Learning Framework for Automated Industrial Detection

Jingnan Wang[1], Pengjie Qin[3(✉)], Chuwen Huang[1], Yaling Wang[1], Yue Ma[2], Meng Yin[2], Wujing Cao[2], and Xinyu Wu[2]

[1] Center for Neurocognition and Social Behavior, Institute of Artificial Intelligence, Shenzhen University of Advanced Technology, Shenzhen 518107, China
[2] Shenzhen Institutes of Advanced Technology, Chinese Academy of Sciences, Shenzhen 518055, China
[3] School of Artificial Intelligence, Shenzhen University, Shenzhen 518060, China
pj.qin@szu.edu.cn

Abstract. The rapid rise of industrial automation has underscored the need for accurate detection to boost efficiency, ensure product quality, and reduce labor costs. Tasks like connector mating and grasp stability rely heavily on analyzing tactile force profile time series, which are difficult to model due to complex, non-stationary temporal dynamics, subtle signal variations, and the high cost of acquiring labeled data. Such factors limit the effectiveness of conventional supervised approaches, making it challenging to build reliable models with limited annotations. To address this, we propose Tactile-driven Multiple Instance Learning (Tacti-MIL), a lightweight deep learning framework that integrates a multi-scale convolutional backbone for temporal feature extraction with a Transformer-based MIL module. This design enables efficient aggregation of temporal patterns and robust performance even with small datasets. Extensive evaluations show that our proposed Tacti-MIL outperforms baseline models, offering a balance between detection accuracy and computational efficiency for industrial detection.

Keywords: industrial automation · industrial detection · deep learning · tactile sensing

1 Introduction

The rapid advancement of industrial automation has emphasized the importance of advanced detection technologies for improving production efficiency, ensuring product quality, and reducing labor costs [1]. Accurate detection is particularly critical in tasks such as connector mating and grasp stability assessment, where precision and consistency directly impact the reliability of automated systems. Traditional manual methods are increasingly insufficient to meet the high precision demands of complex mechanical assemblies and high-throughput production environments.

Snap-fit connectors, widely used in consumer electronics, automotive, and appliance manufacturing, rely on self-locking features to create secure connections without the need for additional fasteners or tools. However, successful assembly depends on the application of precisely controlled forces and timings. Excessive force may damage delicate components or deform connectors, while insufficient force can result in incomplete engagement or loose fittings, which compromises product integrity and operational safety. Similarly, detecting grasp stability in robotic manipulation is vital for maintaining control and accuracy in operations such as pick-and-place, tool use, or precision assembly. Instabilities such as slippage, rolling, or unbalanced grasp forces can lead to task failure or product damage, especially when handling fragile or irregularly shaped objects.

Tactile sensing plays a crucial role in detecting connector engagement and grasp stability, particularly when visual input is obstructed or unreliable. By capturing fine-grained force variations at high temporal resolution, tactile signals offer rich information about contact dynamics. However, compared to visual data, tactile signals are inherently noisier, more variable, and lack standardized representations, making interpretation more challenging. Recent advances in tactile-driven robotic applications have focused on both sensor hardware improvements and algorithmic methods for processing tactile time-series data.

Industrial detection is often formulated as a short-term time series binary classification task, where deep learning has demonstrated strong potential in improving accuracy and efficiency [2–4]. When combined with modern tactile sensors, these models further enhance signal interpretation, leading to more accurate and responsive detection [5]. Complementing these algorithmic advancements, a wide range of studies have explored robotic assembly and grasp stability through both vision-based and tactile-based approaches. In robotic connector assembly, precision and adaptability remain central challenges. For example, Huang et al. [6] address fault detection using a set-membership approach with switched linear systems, while Zhang et al. [7] leverage RGB-D sensing and hybrid detection models for accurate 6D peg-in-hole insertion. Hartisch et al. [8] design compliant finray-effect fingers to improve alignment tolerance during high-speed insertion tasks, and Cui et al. [9] introduce a multilayer recurrent neural network for fast and reliable snap-fit detection. In the domain of grasp stability, Zhao et al. [10] develop a grasp prediction and evaluation network using CNNs and mixture density networks, Kolamuri et al. [11] apply GelSight tactile sensors for closed-loop regrasping, and Liu et al. [12] propose a self-attention-based tactile framework to improve grasp outcome prediction. These works highlight both the promise and the limitations of current approaches, particularly in terms of task specificity and reliance on visual inputs. Despite these developments, most existing approaches remain task-specific, relying on fixed sensor setups and predefined geometries, limiting generalizability across industrial settings. Moreover, tactile data are often underexploited, making it difficult to capture the subtle temporal patterns necessary for robust and adaptive industrial detection.

To address these limitations, we propose a generalized deep learning approach for processing tactile time-series data in industrial automation detection tasks, focusing on robotic connector mating success and robotic grasp stability detection. Our proposed model enhances both accuracy and generalizability, particularly in scenarios involving snap-fit mechanisms and subtle tactile cues. The main contributions of our work are:

1. We propose Tacti-MIL, a lightweight deep learning framework that combines a multi-scale convolutional backbone for temporal feature extraction with a Transformer-based Multiple Instance Learning (MIL) module for tactile-driven detection tasks in industrial automation.
2. Our model treats each time series as a bag of instances, enabling effective aggregation and detection of subtle events in high-resolution tactile data.
3. We validate the model's effectiveness and generalizability on two public datasets for robotic connector mating success and robotic grasp stability detection, achieving high accuracy for robotic detection tasks.

2 Method

A tactile time series is defined as $X = \{x_1, x_2, \ldots, x_L\} \in \mathbb{R}^{L \times D}$, where each $x_l \in \mathbb{R}^D$ represents the feature vector at time step l, and x_{ld} denotes the value of the d-th feature at that step. Given a dataset of N such time series, we denote the collection as $\mathcal{X} = \{X_1, X_2, \ldots, X_N\} \in \mathbb{R}^{N \times L \times D}$, where each $X_i = \{x_1^i, x_2^i, \ldots, x_L^i\}$ is an individual time series. Each X_i is associated with a corresponding class label y_i, forming the label set $\mathcal{Y} = \{y_1, y_2, \ldots, y_N\}$. The objective is to train a classifier that maps the input time series collection $\mathcal{X}$ to the label set $\mathcal{Y}$, enabling accurate prediction of labels for unseen sequences.

2.1 Multi-scale Convolutional Backbone

We propose a lightweight multi-scale convolutional backbone for temporal feature extraction, inspired by [13]. To improve computational efficiency, we use depthwise separable convolutions that decouple spatial and channel-wise operations, reducing computational cost while retaining multi-scale temporal modeling capacity. The backbone maps each input time series X_i to a compact embedding $\hat{X}_i$, with the output dimension d_{embed} set to 128. It consists of two multi-scale convolutional blocks, each with two modules and residual connections (see Fig. 1). Within each module, convolutions with kernel sizes of 4, 8, and 16 are applied in parallel to capture features at different temporal resolutions. The resulting feature maps are then processed by max pooling and concatenated to form the final representation.

2.2 Tokenized Temporal Transfomer-Based MIL Model

After temporal feature extraction, our MIL-based model MIL(·) uses two tokenized Transformers to encode $\hat{X}_i$ into time-frequency tokens, which are aggregated into a bag-level representation for classification.

Multiple Instance Learning (MIL) is a weakly supervised approach where labels are assigned to entire bags rather than individual instances. The model uses the bag-level label to infer the presence of positive instances within the bag. In multi-class settings, MIL can be formulated as a series of One-vs-Rest binary classification tasks, where each class is treated as a separate binary problem. In our context, each time series X_i is a bag, and each time point x_l^i within the series is an instance. Instance-level labels $y_{l,i}^c$ are unavailable; instead, the bag receives a label $y_i^c = 1$ if any time point contributes to class c, and $y_i^c = 0$ otherwise.

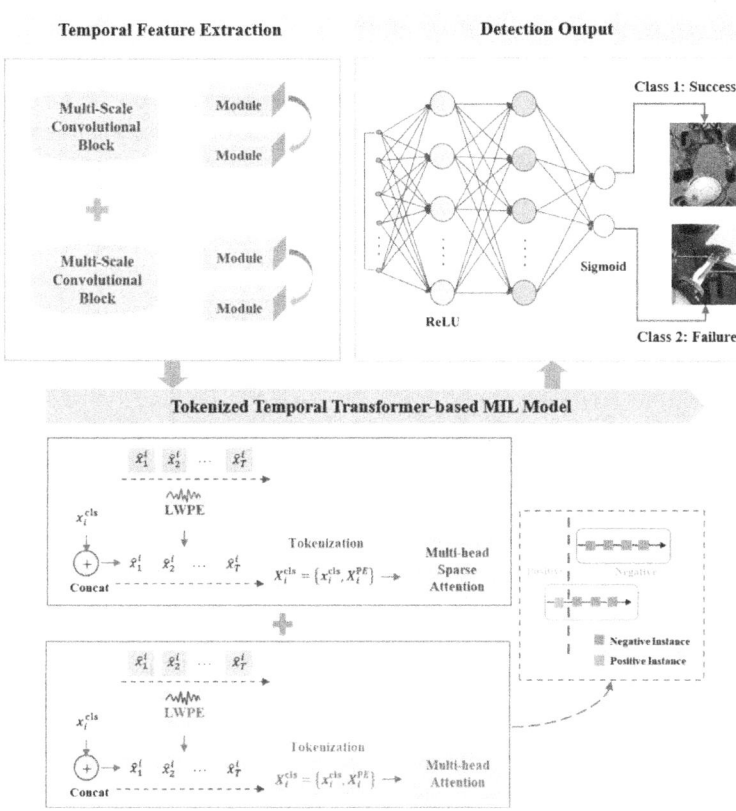

Fig. 1. Overview of the Tacti-MIL architecture.

We first use a learnable wavelet-based positional encoding (LWPE) [14] to capture positional information in time series X_i. Unlike fixed sinusoidal encodings, WPE adaptively integrates temporal and frequency features via wavelet transforms, which balance time-frequency resolution to enhance noise robustness, capture global and local patterns, and improve multi-scale representation for accurate signal modeling. LWPE aggregates channel-wise wavelet transforms over learnable wavelet kernels $\{\Psi_j\}_{j=1}^{N_w}$ applied to the embedded series $\hat{X}_i$:

$$\text{LWPE}(\hat{X}_i) = \sum_{j=1}^{N_w} \text{WT}(\hat{X}_i, \Psi_j) = \sum_{j=1}^{N_w} \begin{bmatrix} \hat{X}_{i1} * \psi_{a_{j1},b_{j1}} \\ \cdots \\ \hat{X}_{iM} * \psi_{a_{jM},b_{jM}} \end{bmatrix}^\top, \quad (1)$$

where $\hat{X}_{ij} * \psi_{a_{jk},b_{jk}} = \int_{-\infty}^{+\infty} \hat{X}_{i,j}(t)\psi_{a_{jk},b_{jk}}(t)dt$, each convolution $\hat{X}_{ij} * \psi_{a_{jk},b_{jk}}$ uses learnable scaling a_{jk} and translation b_{jk} parameters defining the wavelet basis from a mother wavelet. We apply residual connections after positional encoding to preserve features.

Then we introduce a classification token x_i^{cls} to capture global features of the time series bag. Concatenated with the positional encoded series X_i^{WP}, it forms the input $X_i^{\text{cls}} = \{x_i^{\text{cls}}, x_1^{\text{WP},i}, \ldots, x_L^{\text{WP},i}\}$ to the bag classifier. We then apply a hybrid attention mechanism combining sparse and standard self-attention to model both long-range and local dependencies among time points. The sparse attention reduces complexity by restricting interactions with a sparsity mask S:

$$\text{SparseAttention}(Q_s, K_s, V_s) = \text{Softmax}\left(\frac{Q_s K_s^\top}{\sqrt{d_k}} \odot S\right) V_s, \quad (2)$$

where the standard self-attention is as below:

$$\text{Attention}(Q, K, V) = \text{Softmax}\left(\frac{QK^\top}{\sqrt{d_k}}\right) V, \quad (3)$$

where Q_s, K_s, V_s, Q, K, V are linear projections of the input with learnable weights, d_k represents the dimension of the key vectors. We employ multi-head attention in both attention mechanisms and use residual connections to preserve the original features.

For interpretability of our proposed model, we compute the attention vector Att_i for the i-th time series bag by measuring attention scores between the class token's query and the keys of all tokens, highlighting time points most relevant to the bag-level prediction by combining global context from the class token with local temporal information:

$$\text{Att}_i = \text{Softmax}\left[\frac{\left[x_i^{\text{cls}} W_h^Q\right]\left[\tilde{X}_i W_h^K\right]^\top}{\sqrt{d_k}}\right], \quad (4)$$

where $\text{Att}_i \in \mathbb{R}^L$ reflects the importance of each time point $\tilde{x}_t^i$ in $\tilde{X}_i$.

We use the updated class token $\tilde{x}_i^{\text{cls}}$ (the first in $\tilde{X}_i^{\text{cls}}$) as a compact global representation for bag-level prediction. The bag classifier $\mathcal{C}(\cdot)$, a two-layer FCN with ReLU activation, takes $\tilde{x}_i^{\text{cls}}$ as input and outputs the predicted label $\hat{y}_i$. The output dimension matches the number of classes (see Fig. 1). For the i-th bag, prediction is computed as:

$$\hat{y}_i = \mathcal{C}(\tilde{x}_i^{\text{cls}}) = \arg\max_c \text{Sigm}(\hat{y}_i^c), \quad (5)$$

where $\hat{y}_i^c$ is the predicted score for class c, and Sigm is the sigmoid function. We adopt a One-vs-Rest multi-class scheme, evaluating each bag independently per class. The loss function is binary cross-entropy:

$$\mathcal{L} = -\left[y_i^c \log \text{Sigm}(\hat{y}_i^c) + (1 - y_i^c) \log(1 - \text{Sigm}(\hat{y}_i^c))\right], \quad (6)$$

where $y_i^c \in 0, 1$ is the ground-truth bag label derived from instance labels.

3 Experiments

We evaluate the generalization of Tacti-MIL on two robotic tasks: connector mating detection using the SnapFitForceProfiles dataset [15], and grasp stability detection using the Biotac Grasp Stability (BiGS) dataset [16]. SnapFitForceProfiles contains force profiles from 50 human and 60 robotic assembly trials involving annular and cantilever snap-fit connectors, each labeled as success or failure. BiGS includes 2000 grasps collected with a Barrett WAM Arm and BioTac sensor, with 10 s of 300 Hz tactile data per grasp and a 54% success, 46% failure distribution. For the BiGS dataset, we extract high-frequency fluid pressure, low-frequency fluid pressure, and 19 electrode signals from three fingers, resulting in 63 features in total. To test the early detection capability of our method, we used only the time series data recorded before the last 0.2 s.

The experiments are conducted using PyTorch on a workstation with an Intel i7-13700 CPU, 64 GB of RAM, and an Nvidia GeForce RTX 4090 GPU. The Adam optimizer is employed with a learning rate of 0.0001. The datasets are split into 80% for training and 20% for testing. The model was trained for 100 epochs with a batch size of 16. We use accuracy and average inference time per sample to evaluate performance and efficiency. For baseline comparisons, we select traditional distance-based time series classifiers including ED-1NN, DTW-1NN-I, and DTW-1NN-D, as well as state-of-the-art deep learning models such as LSTM, Bi-LSTM, MLSTM-FCN, TodyNet, OS-CNN, and Modern-TCN, known for their ability to capture temporal features for detection tasks. For a fair comparison, we maintain consistent training settings across all models, including the number of epochs, learning rate, and optimizer. Each result in the comparison represents the average of 10 runs on the test dataset.

For data preprocessing, we first pad the sequences to a fixed length by adding zero-padding as needed. Next, we standardize the sampling frequency by downsampling to 350 frames, ensuring consistent feature scaling through Z-score normalization. Finally, all samples are combined and randomly shuffled (Fig. 2).

Evaluation of Detection Performance and Computational Efficiency.
As shown in Table 1 and Table 2, Tacti-MIL outperforms all baseline methods, achieving 93.22% accuracy on cantilever snap-fit detection, 92.75% on annular snap-fit detection, and 91.75% on grasp stability detection. These results highlight the robustness of Tacti-MIL across different detection tasks. This is especially evident in connector mating detection, which presents greater challenges due to complex contact dynamics, subtle force variations, and diverse

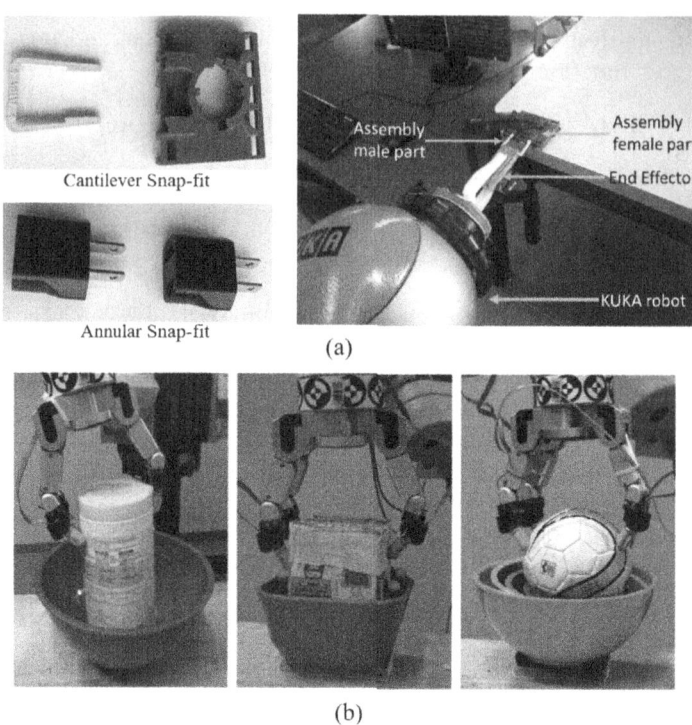

Fig. 2. Experimental setups: (a) robotic connector assembly, (b) grasp stability.

Table 1. Detection Performance and Efficiency on Snap-fit Assembly Tasks

Method	Cantilever Snap-fit		Annular Snap-fit	
	Accuracy (%)	Inference Time (ms)	Accuracy (%)	Inference Time (ms)
ED-1NN	73.00	0.03	66.00	0.03
DTW-1NN-I	84.00	6738	66.00	6896
DTW-1NN-D	84.00	7013	66.00	7168
LSTM	69.59	0.05	68.66	0.05
Bi-LSTM	70.14	0.06	70.21	0.06
TCN	53.20	0.17	52.00	0.18
MLSTM-FCN [17]	70.50	3.46	71.50	3.46
TodyNet [18]	89.65	35.60	87.85	35.60
OS-CNN [19]	58.30	2.30	68.00	2.30
Modern-TCN [20]	89.80	49.86	88.66	49.86
Ours (Tacti-MIL)	**93.22**	6.35	**92.75**	6.35

Table 2. Detection Performance, Efficiency, and Model Complexity on Grasp Stability Task

Method	Accuracy (%)	Inference Time (ms)	Model Params (M)	Model Size (MB)
ED-1NN [21]	87.35	0.04	–	1.07
DTW-1NN-I [22]	87.87	7520	–	1.11
DTW-1NN-D [22]	82.75	7860	–	1.11
LSTM	87.75	0.06	0.05	0.20
Bi-LSTM	88.00	0.06	0.14	0.52
TCN	86.10	0.20	**0.01**	**0.05**
MLSTM-FCN [17]	88.50	3.95	0.43	1.54
TodyNet [18]	84.75	38.74	0.93	3.97
OS-CNN [19]	80.56	3.08	1.29	4.90
Modern-TCN [20]	87.80	55.36	10.05	36.80
Ours (Tacti-MIL)	**91.75**	7.50	0.33	1.28

mechanical structures. Tacti-MIL effectively captures these nuanced patterns, enabling more reliable performance. In the grasp stability detection task, Tacti-MIL successfully manages high-dimensional data, indicating its ability to learn rich, temporal tactile features. The model's capacity to extract fine-grained patterns contributes to its dependable detection outcomes. The classic time series classification methods reveal clear trade-offs: ED-1NN achieves fast inference but suffers from poor detection accuracy, whereas DTW-1NN improves accuracy at the cost of prohibitively long inference times, limiting its use in real-time applications. Traditional deep learning models like LSTM, Bi-LSTM, and TCN offer low latency but fall short in detection accuracy. More advanced deep learning models, including MLSTM-FCN, TodyNet, OS-CNN, and Modern-TCN, achieve better performance yet lack adaptability to task-specific requirements—particularly in detecting connector mating success for challenging cases like Type-C connectors. These models struggle to capture the subtle tactile variations essential for distinguishing fine-grained insertion outcomes. In contrast, while LSTM-based models deliver faster inference, our proposed Dyn-TransMIL achieves significantly higher accuracy and offers a better trade-off between performance and computational efficiency. Additionally, the inference time remains within a practical range, providing an effective balance between computational efficiency and predictive accuracy. With a tolerant inference time, our model achieves a good balance between detection accuracy and computational efficiency.

4 Conclusion

We propose a tactile-based approach for industrial detection tasks that relies exclusively on tactile time series data, aiming to improve detection performance without the need for visual input. To address challenges such as complex temporal dynamics and limited labeled data, we introduce a novel deep learning model named Tacti-MIL. We evaluate our model on public datasets involving connector mating and grasp stability detection, demonstrating that it surpasses baseline methods in both accuracy and generalization. Despite its strong performance and computational efficiency, the model has certain limitations. It may not satisfy sub-millisecond real-time requirements and exhibits limited capability in modeling complex cross-channel tactile interactions. While these constraints are acceptable for tasks with relatively independent force profiles, they may adversely impact performance in more complex manipulation scenarios. Future work will focus on enhancing cross-channel attention mechanisms, optimizing transformer efficiency, and integrating visual-tactile data to facilitate robust multimodal learning in dynamic industrial detection environments.

Acknowledgement. This work was supported by the National Natural Science Foundation of China (Grant No. 52275501) and the State Key Laboratory of Mechanical System and Vibration (Grant No. MSVZD202503).

References

1. Bahrin, M.A.K., Othman, M.F., Azli, N.H.N., Talib, M.F.: Industry 4.0: a review on industrial automation and robotic. Jurnal Teknologi (Sci. Eng.) **78**(6-13) (2016)
2. Wang, J., et al.: Soft sensor-based deep temporal-graph convolutional network for applications in human motion tracking. IEEE Sens. J. **24**(14), 23117–23128 (2024)
3. Yi, Z., Tiantian, X., Shang, W., Li, W., Xinyu, W.: Genetic algorithm-based ensemble hybrid sparse elm for grasp stability recognition with multimodal tactile signals. IEEE Trans. Ind. Electron. **70**(3), 2790–2799 (2022)
4. Wang, J., et al.: Dual autoencoder-based joint learning: enhancing depth classification of hard inclusions in soft tissue for robotic palpation. IEEE/ASME Trans. Mechatron. (2025)
5. Johansson, R.S., Flanagan, J.R.: Coding and use of tactile signals from the fingertips in object manipulation tasks. Nat. Rev. Neurosci. **10**(5), 345–359 (2009)
6. Huang, J., Wang, Y., Fukuda, T.: Set-membership-based fault detection and isolation for robotic assembly of electrical connectors. IEEE Trans. Autom. Sci. Eng. **15**(1), 160–171 (2018)
7. Zhang, K., Wang, C., Chen, H., Pan, J., Wang, M.Y., Zhang, W.: Vision-based six-dimensional peg-in-hole for practical connector insertion. In: 2023 IEEE International Conference on Robotics and Automation (ICRA), pp. 1771–1777. IEEE (2023)
8. Hartisch, R.M., Haninger, K.: High-speed electrical connector assembly by structured compliance in a finray-effect gripper. IEEE/ASME Trans. Mechatron. **29**, 810–819 (2023)
9. Cui, T., Song, R., Li, F., Tianyu, F., Wang, C., Li, Y.: Fast recognition of snap-fit for industrial robot using a recurrent neural network. IEEE Rob. Autom. Lett. **8**(3), 1635–1642 (2022)
10. Zhao, Z., Shang, W., He, H., Li, Z.: Grasp prediction and evaluation of multi-fingered dexterous hands using deep learning. Robot. Auton. Syst. **129**, 103550 (2020)

11. Kolamuri, R., Si, Z., Zhang, Y., Agarwal, A., Yuan, W.: Improving grasp stability with rotation measurement from tactile sensing. In: 2021 IEEE/RSJ International Conference on Intelligent Robots and Systems (IROS), pp. 6809–6816. IEEE (2021)
12. Liu, C.: A deep learning method based on triplet network using self-attention for tactile grasp outcomes prediction. IEEE Trans. Instrum. Meas. **72**, 1–14 (2023)
13. Fawaz, H.I., et al.: Inceptiontime: finding alexnet for time series classification. Data Min. Knowl. Disc. **34**(6), 1936–1962 (2020)
14. Ding, M., Aiping, Q., Zhong, H., Lai, Z., Xiao, S., He, P.: An enhanced vision transformer with wavelet position embedding for histopathological image classification. Pattern Recogn. **140**, 109532 (2023)
15. Doltsinis, S., Krestenitis, M., Doulgeri, Z.: A machine learning framework for real-time identification of successful snap-fit assemblies. IEEE Trans. Autom. Sci. Eng. **17**(1), 513–523 (2019)
16. Chebotar, Y., et al.: Bigs: biotac grasp stability dataset. In: ICRA 2016 Workshop on Grasping and Manipulation Datasets, vol. 21, p. 23 (2016)
17. Karim, F., Majumdar, S., Darabi, H., Harford, S.: Multivariate LSTM-FCNS for time series classification. Neural Netw. **116**, 237–245 (2019)
18. Liu, H., et al.: Todynet: temporal dynamic graph neural network for multivariate time series classification. Inf. Sci. 120914 (2024)
19. Tang, W., Long, G., Liu, L., Zhou, T., Blumenstein, M., Jiang, J.: Omni-scale cnns: a simple and effective kernel size configuration for time series classification. In: International Conference on Learning Representations (2021)
20. Luo, D., Wang, X.: Moderntcn: a modern pure convolution structure for general time series analysis. In: The Twelfth International Conference on Learning Representations (2024)
21. Boulnemour, I., Boucheham, B., Lahreche, A.: On enhancing the accuracy of nearest neighbour time series classifier using improved shape exchange algorithm. Int. J. Inf. Appl. Math. **4**(1), 15–27 (2021)
22. Chen, Y., Hu, B., Keogh, E., Batista, G.E.: Dtw-d: time series semi-supervised learning from a single example. In: Proceedings of the 19th ACM SIGKDD International Conference on Knowledge Discovery and Data Mining, pp. 383–391 (2013)

Hip Joint Angle Prediction for Lower Limb Continuous Movement in Multitasking Scenarios

Zixiang Yang[1], Hao Lu[1], Xin Shi[1(✉)], Pengjie Qin[2], Yujie Chen[1], and Wujing Cao[2]

[1] School of Automation, Chongqing University, Chongqing 400044, China
shixin@cqu.edu.cn
[2] Shenzhen Institute of Advanced Technology, Chinese Academy of Sciences, Shenzhen 518000, China

Abstract. Accurate recognition of human motion intention remains a critical challenge in developing lower limb exoskeleton robots for effective human-robot collaboration. Surface electromyography signals (sEMG), which provide non-invasive measurement of neuromuscular activity, have emerged as crucial bioelectric signal for movement intention recognition due to their ability to reflect muscle activation patterns prior to physical movement. This paper proposes a novel TCN-Transformer-Cross-Attention model based on sEMG signals for hip joint angle prediction in multitasking scenarios (level walking, stair ascent, stair descent, and ramp ascent). The proposed framework employs a temporal convolutional network (TCN) to extract localized temporal features, complemented by a Transformer module to capture global temporal dependencies. A cross-attention mechanism is innovatively integrated to enable synergistic fusion of local and global feature representations, thereby enhancing the model's capability for comprehensive sEMG signal interpretation. Comparative evaluations against benchmark models (CNN-LSTM, BiLSTM, TCN-BiLSTM, and TCN-Transformer) demonstrate significant improvements in prediction accuracy and stability across multitaskings. The incorporation of cross-attention mechanism yields remarkable performance enhancements, achieving relative improvements of 18.87% in R2 score while reducing RMSE and MAE by 48.61% and 53.91%, respectively, compared to the baseline TCN-Transformer architecture. The results validate the effectiveness of the proposed model in lower limb hip joint angle prediction, and provide a new way for multitasking motion control of lower limb exoskeleton robots.

Keywords: sEMG · lower limb joint angle prediction · neural network · Cross-Attention mechanism

1 Introduction

In recent years, lower limb exoskeleton robots are a research hotspot for human-robot collaboration. One of the most critical issues in lower limb exoskeleton research is how to quickly and accurately identify the wearer's movement intention, so as to efficiently achieve human-lower limb exoskeleton synergistic operation [1].

There are two main sources of signals to identify the intention of human movement, one is physical sensing signals represented by inertial measurement unit (IMU), plantar pressures, etc., and the other is bioelectrical signals represented by surface electromyographic signals (sEMG) [2]. IMU-based methods allow for accurate joint angle estimation during human movement, but only provide information on lagging human movements [3]. Surface electromyographic signals are bioelectrical signals generated on the surface of the muscle. Surface electromyographic signals can reflect the level of muscle activity and movement characteristics, and they are generated earlier than the actual limb movements. At the same time, they are easy to be collected non-invasively from the surface of the skin, which is ahead of the curve and convenient, so that sEMG data are reliable in sensing human movement intentions [4, 5].

Currently, the two main methods for analyzing human movement intentions and thus controlling lower limb exoskeletons based on sEMG signals are movement pattern classification and joint angle estimation [6, 7]. The method based on motion pattern classification is to identify the current wearer's motion intent in real time through a classifier and use this motion intent as a signal to switch the control mode of the exoskeleton [8]. With the continuous optimization of the classifier performance, accurate human movement intention assessment can be achieved and accurate control of the lower limb exoskeleton can be achieved. However, each control mode of this method is fixed and does not take into account individual differences, so the method generalizes poorly between different wearers, resulting in less effective control of the exoskeleton as well [9]. The method based on joint angle estimation is based on continuous estimation of the joint angles of the lower limbs, and the construction of a model through sEMG signals to continuously identify the human body's movement intentions, to achieve precise control of the lower limb exoskeleton [10].

Currently, the two main types of methods commonly used for lower limb joint angle estimation are biomechanics and neural network modelling [11, 12]. For example, Wang et al. [13] proposed a biomechanically based joint flexion model to estimate the joint torque and position of elbow flexion motion. However, the model is based on the kinematic mechanism of the human skeletal-muscular system, and the required parameters are not easy to obtain, leading to the lack of practicality of the model. Neural networks have been widely used for lower limb joint angle prediction to assess human motor intentions by virtue of their strong nonlinear fitting and data feature extraction capabilities [14, 15]. Song et al. [16] proposed a continuous prediction method of lower limb joint angles based on long short-term memory (LSTM) neural network. LSTM prediction models containing unimodal (sEMG) and multimodal (sEMG + plantar pressure) inputs were constructed, and the ability of LSTM to effectively compensate for the limitation of single sensor information was verified through comparative experiments. Wang et al. [17] proposed a multi-source biosignal fusion prediction method based on temporal convolutional network (TCN). This study innovatively combined the vibration arthrogram (VAG) signals of the affected limb with the sEMG signals to construct a TCN time series prediction model, which realized the cross-limb prediction of hip, knee and ankle joint angles. Du et al. [18] proposed a novel TCN-LSTM hybrid model for continuous estimation of wrist joint angles. This hybrid model significantly improves the accuracy and robustness of joint angle estimation by fusing the local feature extraction capability of TCN and the time-series modelling advantage of LSTM.

In this paper, a TCN-Transformer-Cross-Attention lower limb continuous motion joint angle prediction model based on sEMG signals is proposed. The proposed model is used for continuous hip joint angle prediction under multitasking scenarios (level-ground walking, stair ascent, stair descent, and ramp ascent). The effectiveness of the proposed method is verified through comparative experiments.

2 Methods

2.1 Model Structure

The TCN-Transformer-Cross-Attention model proposed in this paper is a novel hybrid architecture model. It combines the advantages of Temporal Convolutional Network (TCN) and Transformer architecture. The model structure is shown in Fig. 1.

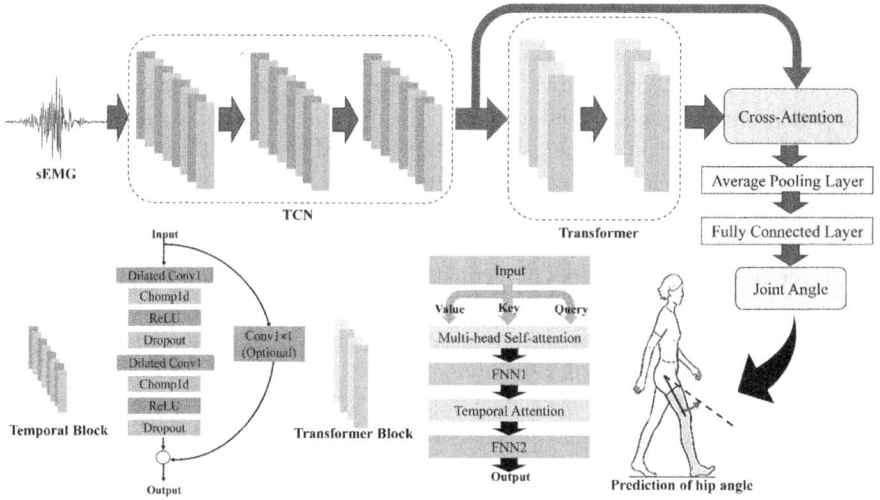

Fig. 1. Model structure

Using the Cross-Attention mechanism, the model can dynamically weight different features to better capture important information in the sEMG signal, which enhances the model's ability to fuse input signal features. An enhanced version of the Transformer encoder layer is employed to better process the timing data. Specifically, the model first extracts the local features of the signals through the TCN module to efficiently capture the local dependencies of the short time scales of the time-series signals. Then, global features of the signals are extracted through the Transformer module to capture the long-term dependencies in the time-series signals. Finally, the local features extracted by TCN and the global features extracted by Transformer are fused through the Cross-Attention mechanism module, allowing the model to learn the association of the two features and enabling the model to adaptively weigh the local and global information according to the needs of the task at hand. This improves the accuracy and robustness of the model predictions. Overall, the TCN-Transformer-Cross-Attention model proposed in this paper consists of a total of three modules: the TCN module, the Transformer module, and the Cross-Attention mechanism module.

The TCN module consists of multiple Temporal Blocks, each containing two convolutional layers with weight normalization, Chomp1d layer and residual connectivity. Its core strength lies in effectively capturing timing dependencies through Dilated Convolution.

$$Conv1D_{dilation}(x)_t = \sum_{k=0}^{K-1} w_k \cdot x_{t-k \cdot d} \qquad (1)$$

where x is the input sequence, K is the convolutional kernel size, d is the expansion factor, and w_k is the convolutional kernel weights.

The Transformer module consists of multi-head self-attention, temporal attention and feed-forward network. The multi-head self-attention mechanism can focus on the information at different locations in the temporal signal and capture the global dependencies.

$$MultiHead(Q, K, V) = Concat(head_1, \ldots, head_h)W^O \qquad (2)$$

where each head is calculated as:

$$head_i = Attention\left(QW_i^Q, KW_i^K, VW_i^V\right) = softmax\left(\frac{QW_i^Q(KW_i^K)^\top}{\sqrt{d_k}}\right)VW_i^V \qquad (3)$$

$W_i^Q \in R^{d_{model} \times d_t}, W_i^K \in R^{d_{model} \times d_t}, W_i^V \in R^{d_{model} \times d_r}, W^O \in R^{hd_r \times d_{model}}$ are learnable weight matrices.

The temporal attention mechanism enhances the model's focus on important information in the temporal dimension, making the model more adept at handling temporal tasks.

$$TemporalAttention(x) = softmax\left(\frac{Q(x)K(x)^\top}{\sqrt{d_{model}}}\right)V(x) \qquad (4)$$

where $Q(x) = W_Q x$, $K(x) = W_K x$, $V(x) = W_V x$ are linear transformation.

Feedforward network is added between self-attention and temporal attention for improving the representation of the model.

The Cross-Attention module is used to fuse the local features extracted by TCN and the global features extracted by Transformer. Enables the model to automatically learn how to weigh local and global information to improve prediction accuracy.

$$Cross\text{-}Attention(Q, K, V) = softmax\left(\frac{QK^\top}{\sqrt{d_k}}\right)V \qquad (5)$$

where Q is the global feature output by the Transformer and K and V are the local features output by the TCN.

2.2 Evaluation Indicators

Lower limb joint angle prediction models usually use some evaluation metrics to assess the model performance through the difference between the actual joint angle and the predicted joint angle. In this study, root-mean-square error (RMSE), mean absolute error (MAE) and coefficient of determination (R^2) were used as evaluation criteria with the following formula.

$$RMSE = \sqrt{\frac{1}{n}\sum_{i=1}^{n}(y_i - \hat{y}_i)^2} \qquad (6)$$

$$MAE = \frac{1}{n}\sum_{i=1}^{n}|y_i - \hat{y}_i| \qquad (7)$$

$$R^2 = 1 - \frac{\sum_{i=1}^{n}(y_i - \hat{y}_i)^2}{\sum_{i=1}^{n}(y_i - \bar{y})^2} \qquad (8)$$

where y_i is the true value of the i output, $\hat{y}_i$ is the predicted value of the i output, n is the number of samples, and $\bar{y}$ is the mean of the n samples.

3 Experiment

3.1 Data Acquisition

A total of 8 healthy subjects were recruited, all of whom were male, 175 ± 5 cm in height and 60 ± 10 kg in weight. All subjects were informed of the experiment and signed an informed consent form before the start of the experiment (Fig. 2).

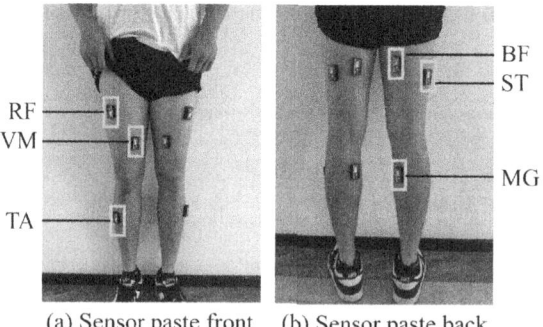

(a) Sensor paste front (b) Sensor paste back

Fig. 2. Sensor pasting and muscle selection

Data were collected using wireless sEMG sensors manufactured by Biometrics (UK) with a sampling frequency of 1000 Hz. 12 sEMG sensors were worn by each subject, 6 sensors for each left and right leg, and the muscles selected were rectus femoris (RF),

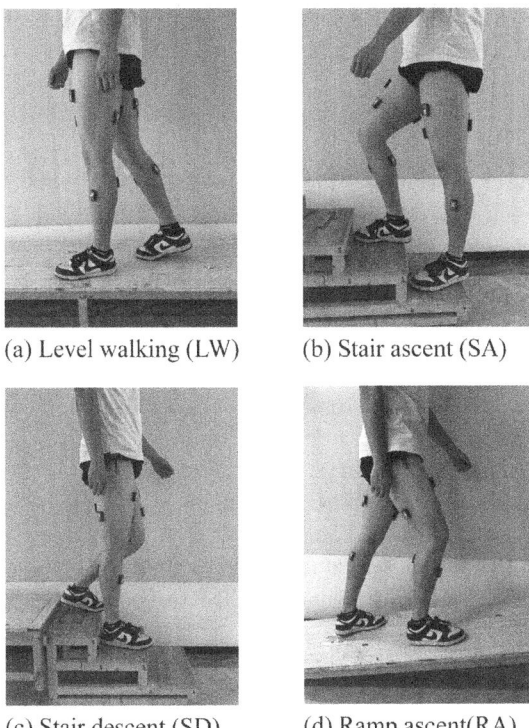

Fig. 3. Motion state

vastus medialis (VM), biceps femoris (BF), tibialis anterior (TA), medial gastrocnemius (MG), semitendinosus (ST) (Fig. 3).

Each subject's skin was wiped with an alcohol swab before the start of the collection to prevent skin impurities from interfering. sEMG data were collected from four motion scenarios: level walking (LW), stair ascent (SA), stair descent (SD), and ramp ascent (RA). Each subject was asked to collect 25 sets of experimental data in each motion scenario, and subjects rested for a 5-min rest period between every five collection experiments to prevent muscle fatigue.

3.2 Data Processing

Due to muscle-to-surface fat thickness, muscle fatigue and external interference, the sEMG signals acquired by the sensors generally have interfering noise, so data preprocessing is required [19]. In this experiment, a 6th order Butterworth bandpass filter was used to process the acquired sEMG signals with a lower cutoff frequency limit of 20 Hz and an upper cutoff frequency limit of 500 Hz. In addition, the sEMG signals were segmented using the overlapping analysis window method with a window length of 100 ms and a step size of 5 ms. The sEMG signals were sampled at a frequency of 1000 Hz, and thus each window contained 100 data points. The processed data were divided into training set, validation set and test set for subsequent model training and performance evaluation.

3.3 Comparison Experiment

In order to verify the effectiveness of the proposed model, three models commonly used to do timing prediction, CNN-LSTM, BiLSTM and TCN-BiLSTM, were compared and analyzed. At the same time, a comparison was made with the TCN-Transformer model to analyze the improvement in network performance with the addition of the cross-attention mechanism module.

CNN-LSTM: This model can input the sliding window of the sEMG signal into the CNN layer and extract the local features through convolution and pooling operations. Then, the feature sequence output from the CNN layer is input into the LSTM layer to learn the feature dynamics change time step by time step.

BiLSTM: This model can input the feature vectors of sEMG signals into both forward and inverse LSTM layers to capture the dependencies between historical and future moments, respectively. Then, the hidden states in both directions are spliced or weighted to form a feature representation containing global timing information.

TCN-BiLSTM: This model can input the sEMG signal into the TCN layer, expand the sensory field using dilation convolution to extract multi-scale timing features, and then, the feature sequence output from the TCN is input into the BiLSTM to fuse the forward and backward timing information.

The comparison experiments were conducted using the dataset shown earlier. In order to ensure the reliability of the experiments, the model performance was evaluated using the same test set data. Root-mean-square error (RMSE), mean absolute error (MAE) and coefficient of determination (R2) were used together as evaluation metrics in the model evaluation.

4 Results and Discussion

The proposed model was used to predict the hip joint angles for four motion scenarios of the lower limbs. The accuracy of the lower limb joint angle estimation algorithm based on the TCN-Transformer-Cross-Attention model would be compared with the existing methods mentioned above.

As shown in Table 1 and Fig. 5, the proposed model is more stable and accurate in hip angle prediction with better multitasking generalization in the following four task scenarios. From Table 1, notice that the red data are anomalies with R^2 less than 0, indicating that the model is unable to fit this data. Since this dataset contains 8 for subjects performing multitasking, there are significant individual differences. In this case, BiLSTM and TCN-BiLSTM may not be able to fit the data for some of the motion scenarios because of the model's own problems.

Also, as shown in Fig. 4, for the anomaly model with R^2 less than 0, the predicted angle is the average value of the true angle. This indicated that during the training process of the model, only the average value was taken to minimize the value of the loss function. Therefore, this type of model cannot fit the training set data. It suggests that the model is not applicable to hip angle prediction for multitasking. Such data will be ignored in the following analysis.

Table 1. Angle prediction of hip joint (Exception data has been ignored)

Scenarios	Models	RMSE	MAE	R^2
LW	Proposed	**0.6203**	**0.4476**	**0.9812**
	CNN-LSTM	0.5893	0.3872	0.9831
	BiLSTM	1.0575	0.7659	0.9454
	TCN-BiLSTM	4.5378	3.8339	-0.0045
	TCN-Transformer	1.5733	1.1214	0.8793
SA	Proposed	**1.2709**	**0.9628**	**0.9667**
	CNN-LSTM	1.0656	0.8250	0.9766
	BiLSTM	6.9714	6.3375	-0.007
	TCN-BiLSTM	1.9163	1.4177	0.9244
	TCN-Transformer	2.7339	1.8382	0.8461
SD	Proposed	**1.3467**	**0.8567**	**0.9453**
	CNN-LSTM	1.1341	0.8313	0.9658
	BiLSTM	5.8531	4.7680	-0.0329
	TCN-BiLSTM	5.8543	4.7670	-0.0334
	TCN-Transformer	3.4050	2.5656	0.6504
RA	Proposed	**1.1746**	**0.8137**	**0.8906**
	CNN-LSTM	1.9576	1.2818	0.6961
	BiLSTM	2.9438	2.2834	0.3128
	TCN-BiLSTM	1.8563	1.2034	0.7267
	TCN-Transformer	1.5580	1.1586	0.8075
Avg.	Proposed	**1.1052**	**0.7702**	**0.9460**
	CNN-LSTM	1.1867	0.8313	0.9054
	BiLSTM	2.0007	1.5247	0.6291
	TCN-BiLSTM	1.8863	1.3106	0.8256
	TCN-Transformer	2.3176	1.6710	0.7958

Table 1 shows that TCN-Transformer-Cross-Attention hip angle prediction ranges from 0.6203 to 1.3467, CNN-LSTM from 0.5893 to 1.9576, BiLSTM from 1.0575 to 2.9438, and TCN-BiLSTM from 1.8563 to 1.9163, TCN-Transformer from 1.5580 to 3.4050. The mean R^2 of TCN-Transformer-Cross-Attention hip was 0.9460, CNN-LSTM was 0.9054, BiLSTM was 0.6291, TCN-BiLSTM was 0.8256 and TCN Transformer was 0.7958.

As can be seen from Fig. 4, the predicted angle curves of the hip joint of TCN-Transformer-Cross-Attention are more stable in various motion scenarios compared with other models. The similarity between the predicted angle curves and the real angle curves is much higher, which is more in line with the real hip joint angles of the human body in various motion scenarios.

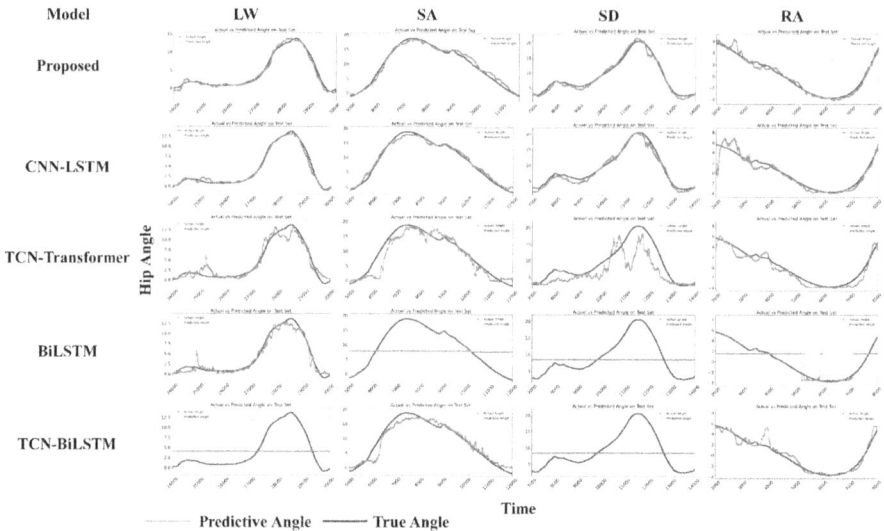

Fig. 4. Angle prediction of hip joint

TCN-Transformer-Cross-Attention has the smallest fluctuation range of prediction results and the best stability. CNN-LSTM and TCN-Transformer-Cross-Attention have similar results in the LW, SA and SD tasks, even slightly higher than TCN-Transformer-Cross-Attention. However, the stability is poorer, and the performance drops significantly in tasks such as RA, where the features are not obvious, and is not applicable to multitasking scenarios.

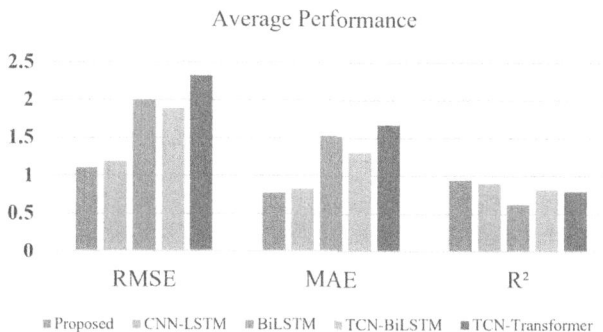

Fig. 5. Average Performance of above models

In addition, to demonstrate the impact of the Cross-Attention mechanism module on the model performance. Compared with TCN-Transformer, the RMSE and MAE of TCN-Transformer-Cross-Attention decreased by 48.61% and 53.91%, respectively, and the R^2 was improved by 18.87%, which proves that the Cross-Attention module has a significant TCN-Transformer model performance enhancement. This is due to the fact that the Cross-Attention mechanism module fuses the local features extracted by TCN and the global features extracted by Transformer, which provides better feature extraction capability and interpretation of the data. Therefore, the cross-attention mechanism module has a significant improvement in the performance of the model.

To assess the model's real-time performance, we conducted tests on the average inference time for single prediction. When the proposed model was applied to the test set—with a data window length of 100 ms and a prediction step size of 5 ms—the measured average single inference time was 3.167 ms. This outcome thoroughly validates that the model can meet the real-time demands for joint angle prediction based on sEMG signals.

5 Conclusion

In this paper, the contributions are as follows: a TCN-Transformer-Cross-Attention lower limb hip joint angle prediction model based on sEMG signals is proposed, and the local and global features of sEMG signals are extracted and fused effectively, respectively, which enhances the ability of extracting the features of the sEMG signals and the interpretation of the data, and improves the model's prediction ability in terms of its accuracy. Compared to the TCN-Transformer benchmark model, the R^2 of the proposed model is improved by 11.59% (level walking), 14.25% (stair ascent), 45.34% (stair descent), and 10.29% (ramp ascent), respectively. It can adapt to more task scenarios and has the best overall performance compared to other neural network modelling approaches. In the future, we will validate the effectiveness of the method by considering more subjects of different ages and by using the model in the control of a lower limb exoskeleton robot. The method proposed in the paper provides a new approach for multitasking motion control of lower limb exoskeleton robots.

In the future, we will consider more subjects of different ages to verify the generalizability of the proposed method. Moreover, we will compare the proposed model with more models and run the model on an embedded device to complement specific real-time and inference latency tests. Finally, the model will be used in the control of a lower-limb exoskeleton robot, thus validating the effectiveness of the method.

Acknowledgement. This work was supported in part by the Project supported by the Young Scientists Fund of the National Natural Science Foundation of China (No. 62403453) and in part by the Project supported by the China Postdoctoral Science Foundation (No. 2024M76344). Guangdong Basic and Applied Basic Research Foundation (2025A1515011973).

References

1. Chen, Z., Guo, Q., Li, T., Yan, Y., Jiang, D.: Gait prediction and variable admittance control for lower limb exoskeleton with measurement delay and extended-state-observer. IEEE Trans. Neural Netw. Learning Syst. **34**(11), 8693–8706 (2023)
2. Li, L.-L., Cao, G.-Z., Liang, H.-J., Zhang, Y.-P., Cui, F.: Human lower limb motion intention recognition for exoskeletons: a review. IEEE Sensors J. **23**(24), 30007–30036 (2023)

3. Yin, Y.H., Fan, Y.J., Xu, L.D.: EMG and EPP-integrated human-machine interface between the paralyzed and rehabilitation exoskeleton. IEEE Trans. Inform. Technol. Biomed. **16**(4), 542–549 (2012)
4. O'Keeffe, R., Shirazi, S.Y., Yang, J., Mehrdad, S., Rao, S., Atashzar, S.F.: Non-parametric functional muscle network as a robust biomarker of fatigue. IEEE J. Biomed. Health Inform. **27**(4), 2105–2116 (2023)
5. Zhang, P., Zhang, J., Elsabbagh, A.: Lower limb motion intention recognition based on sEMG fusion features. IEEE Sens. J. **22**(7), 7005–7014 (2022)
6. Shi, X., Qin, P., Zhu, J., Zhai, M., Shi, W.: Feature extraction and classification of lower limb motion based on sEMG signals. IEEE Access **8**, 132882–132892 (2020)
7. Shi, X., Qin, P., Zhu, J., Xu, S., Shi, W.: Lower limb motion recognition method based on improved wavelet packet transform and unscented kalman neural network. Math. Probl. Eng. **2020**, 5684812 (2020)
8. Wang, C., Guo, W., Zhang, H., Guo, L., Huang, C., Lin, C.: SEMG-based continuous estimation of grasp movements by long-short term memory network. Biomed. Signal Process. Control **59**, 101774 (2020)
9. Song, T., Yan, Z., Guo, S., Li, Y., Li, X., Xi, F.: Review of sEMG for robot control: techniques and applications. Appl. Sci. **13**(17), 9546 (2023)
10. Huang, Y., et al.: Real-time intended knee joint motion prediction by deep-recurrent neural networks. IEEE Sens. J. **19**(23), 11503–11509 (2019)
11. Pang, M., Guo, S., Song, Z., Zhang, S.: sEMG signal and hill model based continuous prediction for hand grasping motion. In: 2013 ICME International Conference on Complex Medical Engineering (CME), New York, pp. 329–333. IEEE (2013)
12. Zhang, Q., Kim, K., Sharma, N.: Prediction of ankle dorsiflexion moment by combined ultrasound sonography and electromyography. IEEE Trans. Neural Syst. Rehabil. Eng. **28**(1), 318–327 (2020)
13. Wang, X., Tao, X., So, R.C.H.: A bio-mechanical model for elbow isokinetic and isotonic flexions. Sci. Rep. **7**, 8919 (2017)
14. Deng, Y., Gao, F., Chen, H.: Angle estimation for knee joint movement based on PCA-RELM algorithm. Symmetry **12**(1), 130 (2020)
15. Tang, Z., Yu, H., Cang, S.: Impact of load variation on joint angle estimation from surface EMG signals. IEEE Trans. Neural Syst. Rehabil. Eng. **24**(12), 1342–1350 (2016)
16. Song, Q., Ma, X., Liu, Y.: Continuous online prediction of lower limb joints angles based on sEMG signals by deep learning approach. Comput. Biol. Med. **163**, 107124 (2023)
17. Wang, C., et al.: Prediction of contralateral lower-limb joint angles using vibroarthrography and surface electromyography signals in time-series network. IEEE Trans. Autom. Sci. Eng. **20**(2), 901–908 (2023)
18. Du, J., Liu, Z., Dong, W., Zhang, W., Miao, Z.: A novel TCN-LSTM hybrid model for sEMG-based continuous estimation of wrist joint angles. Sensors **24**(17), 5631 (2024)
19. Chowdhury, R.H., Reaz, M.B.I., Ali, M.A.B.M., Bakar, A.A.A., Chellappan, K., Chang, T.G.: Surface electromyography signal processing and classification techniques. Sensors **13**(9), 12431–12466 (2013)

Design of a Soft Pneumatic Exosuit for Stroke-Induced Knee Rehabilitation

Jinglin Zhou[1], Changjiang Lei[1], Haolan Xian[1], Yuanwen Zhang[1], Chenglong Fu[1], and Yuquan Leng[1,2(✉)]

[1] Department of Mechanical and Energy Engineering, Southern University of Science and Technology, Shenzhen 518055, Guangdong, China
lengyuquan@hit.edu.cn
[2] School of Biomedical Engineering and State Key Lab of Robotics and Systems, Harbin Institute of Technology (Shenzhen), Shenzhen 518067, Guangdong, China

Abstract. Stroke often causes motor dysfunction of the knee joint. Existing rehabilitation equipment lacks customization, limiting training effectiveness. This paper presents a soft pneumatic exosuit (SPE) designed to provide effective and comfortable daily knee rehabilitation training for stroke patients. The SPE features a wearable sleeve with anterior and posterior airbag drive units (AP-ADU) for bidirectional actuation. Weighing only 210 g, it is lightweight and compliant. A multi-bag array structure improves actuation performance. Each airbag is made of a double-layer thermoplastic polyurethane (TPU) laminated to a mesh fabric composite and curved to better fit the lower extremity. Finite element analysis (FEA) was first used to assess structural performance. Subsequently, the SPE was verified by surface electromyography (sEMG) experiments. The results showed that root mean square (RMS) peak values of the target muscle groups activation respectively decreased by 20.7%, 6.5%, and 12.7% during knee extension, flexion, and squatting, demonstrating the effectiveness of the exosuit and the potential for rehabilitation.

Keywords: Knee exoskeleton · Stroke rehabilitation · Soft exosuit · Pneumatic drive

1 Introduction

Stroke has become one of the major public health issues in society, significantly affecting patient quality of life [1]. Studies have pointed out that stroke patients often suffer from impaired coordination of knee muscle groups, particularly in the form of abnormal motor function related to knee hyperextension [2]. However, current rehabilitation methods are still highly dependent on therapists, further straining healthcare resources [3]. Therefore, it is essential to develop an assistive device to support knee rehabilitation in stroke patients.

Various medical devices and techniques have been proposed for knee rehabilitation. Cheng et al. [4] designed a passive knee orthosis for stroke patients to aid knee joint rehabilitation. However, this orthosis provides only passive support and neglects active rehabilitation scenarios involving motor coordination interventions. In addition, Ward et al. [5] developed a functional electrical stimulation system to activate muscle groups, but its use is limited to clinical settings, making it unsuitable for daily rehabilitation. In contrast, the exoskeleton, as a wearable device with both structural flexibility and controllability, can integrate exercise assistance with active training, and have the potential for widespread use in various settings, such as homes and community centers [6,7]. Therefore, lower extremity exoskeletons hold great promise for supporting functional recovery of the knee joint.

Nevertheless, the promoting of exoskeletons in rehabilitation scenarios still faces challenges, especially in the design of the human-machine interaction interface, which affects not only the comfort of wearing, but also the effectiveness of rehabilitation [8]. Christensen et al. [9] developed a rigid exoskeleton to provide physical assistance to the elderly. However, its substantial weight increases the motor inertia of the lower extremities of the wearer. Moreover, this exoskeleton requires precise alignment with the user's joint positions, otherwise, joint misalignment during movement may result in undesirable additional loading [10]. To address the inertia caused by rigid mechanisms, Zhang et al. [11] proposed a cable-driven exoskeleton for knee osteoarthritis rehabilitation, aiming to reduce distal mass. However, this approach generates a large stress at the anchor point, potentially causing discomfort or even secondary injury. Furthermore, these exoskeletons are difficult to apply to stroke rehabilitation due to the lack of patient-friendly designs tailored to the specific needs of the knee joint. In conclusion, designing effective human-machine interfaces for exoskeletons remains a significant barrier to their real-world application in rehabilitation.

To address the above challenges, this paper proposes a soft pneumatic exosuit (SPE) designed for knee joint assistance in stroke rehabilitation. The exosuit includes an anterior and posterior airbag drive units (AP-ADU), a nylon fabric restraint layer and an adjustable strap. Instead of a one-piece structure, the drive unit adopts a multi-airbag array structure that is both flexible and stretchable, and fits the human body side with a curved contour, so that the SPE can better fit the lower extremity and knee joint morphology. Weighing only 210 g, the SPE significantly reduces the burden of the wearer. Surface electromyography (sEMG) experiments demonstrate that the SPE effectively reduces muscle activation in target muscle groups during rehabilitation tasks. In summary, the proposed SPE shows strong potential for daily knee rehabilitation in stroke patients. The main contributions of this paper are as follows:

1) A novel lightweight soft exosuit based on pneumatic actuation is proposed. The exosuit is designed to closely conform to the wearer's joint and lower extremity, enabling compliant assistance and enhancing comfort during rehabilitation.
2) The effectiveness of the SPE in providing assistance has been verified through sEMG experiments, and it is expected to be applied in the rehabilitation training of muscle groups in stroke patients.

2 Design and Characterization of SPE

2.1 Design Requirements for SPE

To define the functional requirements of the SPE, the characteristics of the knee joint in stroke are analyzed. Stroke patients often experience uncoordinated activation of the muscles surrounding the knee joint. Most studies attribute this to synergistic dysfunction between the quadriceps and hamstring muscle groups, which can result in issues such as knee hyperextension, joint instability, and abnormal gait patterns [12]. Therefore, the SPE should promote active participation during rehabilitation training to stimulate the relevant muscle groups and enhance neuromuscular control. The SPE designed in this paper provides bidirectional driving ability and simulates the natural synergy between knee flexors and extensors through soft, joint-conforming assistance, thereby facilitating joint movement and promoting functional recovery. To ensure that the SPE does not hinder natural motion, it must accommodate the full range of knee flexion, which spans from $-120° \sim 0°$ [13], thus the exosuit must support a total range of motion exceeding $120°$.

2.2 Design and Modeling of SPE

Each airbag of the SPE is constructed from a composite material consisting of double-layer thermoplastic polyurethane (TPU) laminated with mesh fabric (Hardness: Shore 85 A), which effectively enhances the mechanical properties and durability of the airbag [14]. The design and layout of the AP-ADU within the SPE is then introduced and fixed in place. The final wear effect of the SPE is shown in Fig. 1.

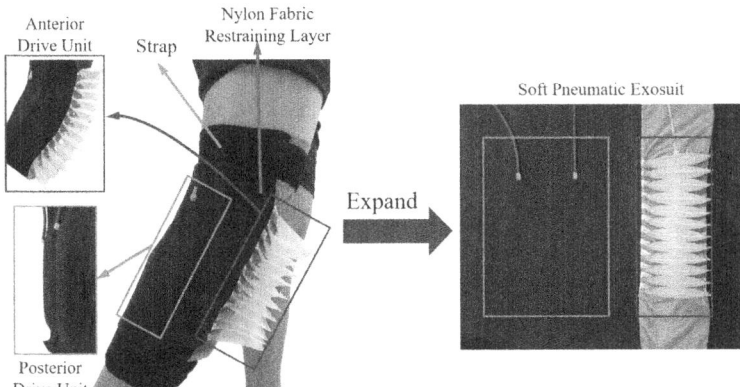

Fig. 1. Structure of soft pneumatic exosuit.

The anterior drive unit adopts a multiple airbag array structure, with nylon fabric as the restraining layer on the body-facing side to fix and guide movement.

Connecting holes are integrated into the side walls of each airbag to enable airflow communication, allowing the entire array to be inflated synchronously by a single air source. Upon inflation, the airbags interact with each other to produce directional bending, assisting the knee flexion movement. In order to fit the contour of the knee and leg, the airbags are designed as a curved structure, as shown in Fig. 2. The posterior drive unit adopts a dual airbag parallel configuration to provide extension support and limit abnormal knee movements in the non-sagittal plane. The AP-ADU are encapsulated in a nylon fabric sleeve, which can be quickly worn by the patient through the sleeve, and is easy to use for daily rehabilitation.

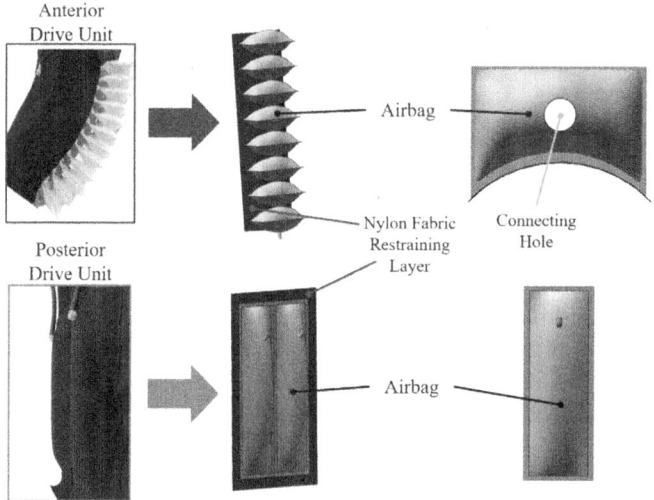

Fig. 2. Structure of anterior and posterior airbag drive units.

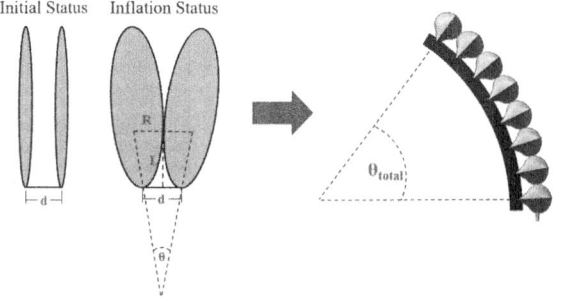

Fig. 3. Bend modeling of anterior drive unit.

Each airbag is formed by heat-sealing two layers of TPU film, offering predictable and consistent bending behavior. This structural design has been demonstrated to be feasible and superior in a previous study [15]. By encapsulating multiple airbags within a shared constraining layer, the drive unit is no longer limited by the tensile strength of the film during inflation, which significantly enhances both the force-to-weight ratio and overall stretchability.

To ensure that the SPE provides sufficient range of motion for rehabilitation training, its bending angle in two-dimensional free space is modeled and analyzed. The simplified modeling assumptions are as follows:

1) Individual airbags inflate to an elliptical shape along the longitudinal section.
2) Negligible mutual compression deformation between neighboring airbags.
3) Each airbag is in one-point contact with the non-extensible restraining layer.
4) The overall drive unit is approximated as a constant-curvature model.

As shown in Fig. 3, let the expansion radius of each airbag be R, and the distance between adjacent airbags constrained by the non-extensible layer be d. When $2R > d$, angular deflection occurs between the adjacent airbags, causing the entire drive unit to bend. If the perpendicular distance from the center of the connecting hole to the non-extensible layer is L, the geometric relationship for calculating the bending angle θ between adjacent units is given by:

$$\tan\frac{\theta}{2} = \frac{R - \frac{d}{2}}{L} \qquad (1)$$

Let the total number of airbags be n, and the drive unit can be approximated as a constant curvature structure composed of $n-1$ equilateral folded segments. Then, the total bending angle θ_{total} is given by:

$$\theta_{total} = 2(n-1)\arctan\frac{R - \frac{d}{2}}{L} \qquad (2)$$

Finite element analysis (FEA) was performed using Abaqus CAE to simulate and model a single airbag structure, as shown in Fig. 4. The soft structure used is made of TPU composite material, which exhibits significant nonlinearity and large deformation, and is suitable for modeling using the hyperelastic intrinsic model. In this simulation, the third-order Yeoh model is chosen to describe the elastic deformation behavior, in which the coefficients of each order are set as $C10$ = 0.4 Mpa, $C20$ = 0.05 MPa, $C30$ = 0.01 MPa and the density of the material is set as 1.1×10^{-6} kg/mm^3. Under non-failure condition, the maximum radius of expansion is obtained as R_{max} =14.3 mm at 60 kPa. Given the total number of airbags in this design $n = 12$ and the normal distance from the non-extensible layer to the center of the connecting hole $L = 25$ mm. Substituting it into the Eq. 2 can be calculated to get the required spacing $d = 23$ mm for the design of the constraint layer. This configuration ensures that the drive unit has sufficient bending range in the free state to meet the functional requirements for knee joint flexion assistance.

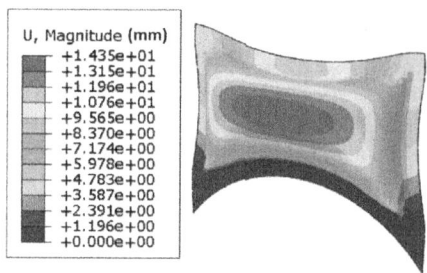

Fig. 4. Finite element analysis of airbag magnitude.

2.3 Manufacturing and Assembly of SPE

The composite material consisting of double-layer TPU films and mesh nylon fabric used for the airbag requires pretreatment, as illustrated in Fig. 5. Flexible TPU films with excellent sealing properties are selected and combined with the high-strength mesh nylon fabric as the reinforcement layer. During the composite process, a special adhesive is uniformly applied to the surface of one TPU layer. The nylon fabric is then laid on top, followed by the second TPU film, forming a three-layer "film–fabric–film" sandwich structure. Subsequently, this material is placed in a hot press and pressed at approximately 130 °C and 3 bar for 45–60 s to ensure stable bonding between the layers.

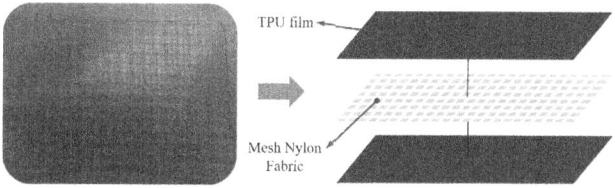

Fig. 5. Composite material manufacturing.

After the composite sheet is precisely cut, prefabricated film components that meet the structural requirements of the airbag are obtained. The forming and sealing of the airbag are achieved through a high-frequency hot pressing process, in which the high-frequency electric field causes the polar molecules in the TPU to oscillate rapidly, generating heat and localized melting. Under the confinement of an aluminum mold and applied pressure, a stable and airtight seal is formed. After cooling and shaping, the complete airbag unit is obtained. Finally, multiple airbags are sewn onto the nylon fabric constraint layer at predefined intervals according to the design layout, forming a complete SPE.

3 Experiment and Results

To validate the effectiveness of the designed SPE in assisting knee muscle rehabilitation, this study conducted comparative experiments under two conditions: without exosuit assistance (NOEXO) and with exosuit assistance (EXOON), involving three healthy subjects. A sEMG system (DELSYS Trigno, USA) was used to acquire muscle signals from key flexor and extensor groups. sEMG sensors were affixed to major extensors (rectus femoris, vastus medialis, vastus lateralis) and flexors (long and short heads of the biceps femoris).

The Evaluation task consisted of three common movements for stroke rehabilitation training [16]: knee extension (raising the calf to thigh level in a sitting position, 10 repetitions per set), knee flexion (standing with the thigh immobilized and the calf flexed posteriorly, 10 repetitions per set) and keep squatting (holding for 30 s, 2 sets) as shown in Fig. 6. Each movement was performed in two separate sets, with a 5-min interval between each set to avoid muscle fatigue. Only knee movements occurred in the lower extremities were controlled as much as possible during the experiments to minimize the interference of non-target muscle group synergies on the results.

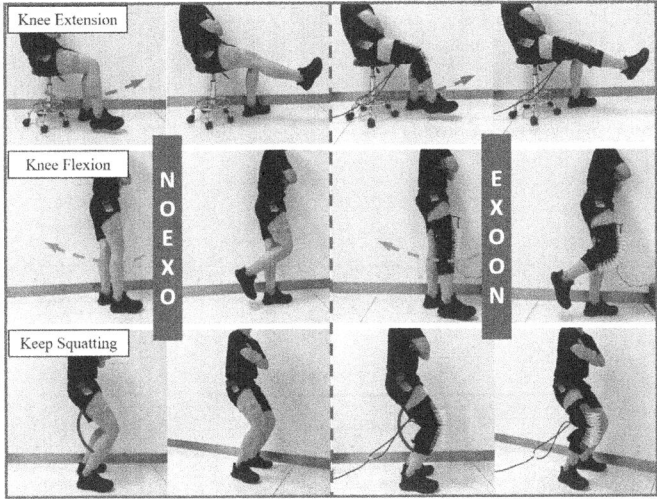

Fig. 6. Three rehabilitation maneuvers tasks.

After the collected sEMG data were processed using band-pass filtering, the muscle activation level was analyzed using root mean square (RMS) method. To more comprehensively evalute the overall muscle activation during each movement, a weighted average was calculated based on the physiological cross-sectional areas (PCSA) of each muscle. The weighted RMS was computed according to Eq. 3, with the $PCSA_i$ values obtained from reference [17]. Considering the primary muscle groups involved in each task, extension and flexion movements were analyzed separately for extensor and flexor muscles, while both groups were analyzed jointly during the keep squatting task.

$$RMS_{total} = \frac{\sum(RMS_i \cdot PCSA_i)}{\sum PCSA_i} \quad (3)$$

The experimental results are shown in Fig. 7, demonstrating that the RMS values of the target muscle groups decreased across all three rehabilitation training tasks with SPE assistance. Specifically, during knee extension, the peak RMS of the extensor muscles decreased by 20.7%. During knee flexion, the peak RMS of the flexor muscles decreased by 6.5%. In the squatting task, the peak RMS of the overall muscle group decreased by 11.0%. The results indicate that the SPE can effectively reduce muscle activation during knee flexion and extension, has good assisting ability, and is expected to promote the effect of rehabilitation training by simulating the synergistic mechanism of the muscle groups.

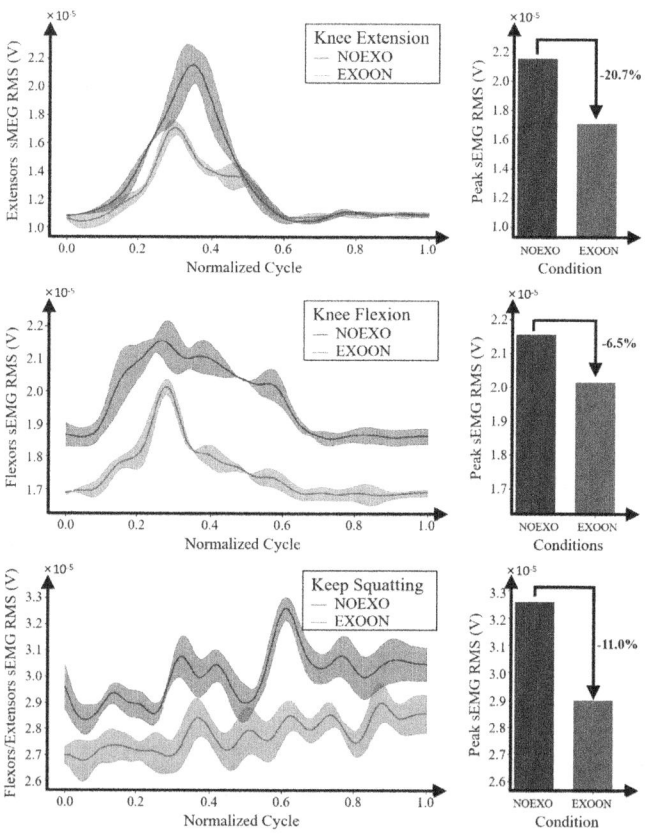

Fig. 7. Three rehabilitation maneuvers sEMG data.

4 Discussion

In this paper, the assistive effect of the proposed SPE was evaluated through experiments in which healthy subjects performed three typical rehabilitation maneuvers: knee extension, knee flexion, and keeping squatting. The results showed that when the muscle activation level of the target muscle group generally decreased when the SPE was worn, indicating that the system has a good ability to assist in the process of knee flexion and extension and stabilization support. For stroke patients, routine rehabilitation exercises such as flexion and extension and squatting are often difficult to perform independently and typically require external assistance or support [16]. The proposed SPE can reduce the muscular activation and assist in performing rehabilitation movements without increasing the physical burden, thereby improving the patient's independence and rehabilitation efficiency.

5 Conclusions and Future Work

This work presents the design and evaluation of an SPE that assists knee flexion and extension for stroke patients, addressing the functional requirements of rehabilitation training. First, the design requirements of the SPE were developed based on the physiological characteristics and needs of the patients. The drive units are fabricated from a composite material of TPU and mesh fabric, and is manufactured using a high-frequency hot-pressing process to enhance its strength and actuation performance. The AP-ADU are multicapsule arrays and parallel structures, respectively, and are integrated in the form of sleeve that ensures both smooth actuation and ease of use. Structural parameters are optimized through finite element modeling in Abaqus to ensure that the SPE meets the required range of motion for knee joints. With a total weight of only 210 g, the SPE is sufficiently soft to minimize unnecessary mechanical impedance and reduce the physical burden on the wearer.

sEMG evaluation experiments conducted during three types of typical rehabilitation movements show that wearing the SPE can reduce the weighted RMS peaks of knee extensor and flexor muscles by approximately 20.7% and 6.5%, respectively, during extension and flexion tasks, and the overall RMS peaks in the squatting decreased by 11.0%. These results verify the effectiveness of the SPE in reducing muscle activation and the synergistic assistance, providing synergistic assistance, and offering a good anatomical fit, thereby showing strong potential for use in rehabilitation training.

Although the SPE has demonstrated good effectiveness and applicability in rehabilitation assistance, some limitations remain. First, the experimental evaluation was restricted to basic rehabilitation tasks. Future work will focus on optimizing the exosuit structure and control strategy to extend its application to various rehabilitation tasks, such as gait training. Second, the current experiments were conducted on healthy subjects. Clinical trials involving stroke patients are planned to further assess the long-term effectiveness and safety of exosuit in real-world rehabilitation scenarios.

Acknowledgments. This work was supported by National Key R&D Program of China [Grant: 2024YFC3082800], the National Natural Science Foundation of China [Grant: 52175272], Guangdong Basic and Applied Basic Research Foundation [Grant: 2024B1515020008 and 2023B1515130007], Shenzhen Science and Technology Program [Grant: RCYX20231211090345058, JCYJ20220530114809021, KCXFZ20230731093059-012].

References

1. Feigin, V.L., et al.: Global, regional, and national burden of stroke and its risk factors, 1990–2021: a systematic analysis for the global burden of disease study 2021. Lancet Neurol. **23**(10), 973–1003 (2024)
2. Geerars, M., Minnaar-van der Feen, N., Huisstede, B.M.: Treatment of knee hyperextension in post-stroke gait. A systematic review. Gait Posture **91**, 137–148 (2022)
3. Zhang, S., Fan, L., Ye, J., Chen, G., Fu, C., Leng, Y.: An intelligent rehabilitation assessment method for stroke patients based on lower limb exoskeleton robot. IEEE Trans. Neural Syst. Rehabil. Eng. **31**, 3106–3117 (2023)
4. Chen, Z., Xian, Z., Chen, H., Zhong, Y., Wang, F.: Immediate effects of a buffered knee orthosis on gait in stroke patients with knee hyperextension. J. Back Musculoskelet. Rehabil. **36**(2), 445–454 (2023)
5. Ward, T., et al.: Multichannel biphasic muscle stimulation system for post stroke rehabilitation. Electronics **9**(7), 1156 (2020)
6. Qian, Y., et al.: Adaptive oscillator-based gait feature extraction method of hip exoskeleton for stroke patients. IEEE Trans. Med. Robot. Bionics **6**(1), 235–244 (2023)
7. Xiloyannis, M., et al.: Soft robotic suits: state of the art, core technologies, and open challenges. IEEE Trans. Rob. **38**(3), 1343–1362 (2021)
8. Li, Y., Chang, S.-H., Francisco, G., Su, H.: Interaction force modeling for joint misalignment minimization toward bio-inspired knee exoskeleton design. In: Frontiers in Biomedical Devices, vol. 40789, p. V001T10A011. American Society of Mechanical Engineers (2018)
9. Christensen, S., Rafique, S., Bai, S.: Design of a powered full-body exoskeleton for physical assistance of elderly people. Int. J. Adv. Rob. Syst. **18**(6), 17298814211053534 (2021)
10. Chen, L., Zhou, D., Leng, Y.: A systematic review on rigid exoskeleton robot design for wearing comfort: joint self-alignment, attachment interface, and structure customization. IEEE Trans. Neural Syst. Rehabili. Eng. (2024)
11. Zhang, L., et al.: Mechanism design of cable-driven multi-functional knee osteoarthritis rehabilitation robot. In: 2024 30th International Conference on Mechatronics and Machine Vision in Practice (M2VIP), pp. 1–6. IEEE (2024)
12. Lee, J.J., You, J.S.H.: Effects of novel guidance tubing gait on electromyographic neuromuscular imbalance and joint angular kinematics during locomotion in hemiparetic stroke patients. Arch. Phys. Med. Rehabil. **98**(12), 2526–2532 (2017)
13. Scherpereel, K., Molinaro, D., Inan, O., Shepherd, M., Young, A.: A human lower-limb biomechanics and wearable sensors dataset during cyclic and non-cyclic activities. Sci. Data **10**(1), 924 (2023)
14. Suulker, C., Hassan, A., Skach, S., Althoefer, K.: A comparison of silicone and fabric inflatable actuators for soft hand exoskeletons. In: 2022 IEEE 5th International Conference on Soft Robotics (RoboSoft), pp. 735–740. IEEE (2022)

15. Natividad, R.F., Del Rosario, M.R., Chen, P.C., Yeow, C.-H.: A hybrid plastic-fabric soft bending actuator with reconfigurable bending profiles. In: 2017 IEEE International Conference on Robotics and Automation (ICRA), pp. 6700–6705. IEEE (2017)
16. DeJong, G., Hsieh, C.-H., Putman, K., Smout, R.J., Horn, S.D., Tian, W.: Physical therapy activities in stroke, knee arthroplasty, and traumatic brain injury rehabilitation: their variation, similarities, and association with functional outcomes. Phys. Ther. **91**(12), 1826–1837 (2011)
17. O'Brien, T.D., Reeves, N.D., Baltzopoulos, V., Jones, D.A., Maganaris, C.N.: In vivo measurements of muscle specific tension in adults and children. Exp. Physiol. **95**(1), 202–210 (2010)

Dynamic Collision Avoidance for Slave Instruments in Robotic Cardiac Surgery

Xizhe Zang, Peng Wang[✉], Xu Wang, and Hui Chu

State Key Laboratory of Robotics and System, Harbin Institute of Technology, Harbin 150001, China
wangp2020@outlook.com

Abstract. Minimally invasive surgical robots have improved the safety and efficiency of cardiac surgery. With smaller and more flexible instruments and endoscopes, robotic systems reduce incision size and number. However, the limited operative space introduces a risk of collisions between instruments. Due to difficulties in accurate instrument localization via kinematics or sensors, this paper proposes a vision-based method for dynamic collision avoidance. Instrument positions are obtained through image segmentation, and depth maps are generated using a stereo-matching algorithm combined with a pre-trained depth estimation model, achieving an average relative error of around 7%. A KD-tree with a hierarchical strategy enables fast distance estimation. Based on instrument distance and master-side motion speed, a collision risk model is built to predict potential collisions and trigger avoidance strategies. The method is validated in a simulated environment.

Keywords: Robotic Cardiac Surgery · Surgical Instrument Segmentation · Depth estimation · Dynamic Collision Avoidance

1 Introduction

During robotic cardiac surgery, complex operations must often be performed within a highly constrained space, where both visual and haptic feedback are limited [1]. Collisions between multiple surgical instruments are common under such conditions. Most instruments in cardiac surgical robots are flexibly actuated, and collisions may damage their surfaces or compromise the flexible structure, potentially leading to critical failures during surgery. Dynamic collision avoidance for robotic end-effectors typically relies on endoscopic imaging to estimate instrument poses. However, due to hardware constraints, the baseline distance between the stereo endoscope lenses is short, and the surgical field often lacks clear textures and suffers from specular reflections, making it difficult to obtain continuous depth information via stereo matching. Moreover, traditional collision avoidance algorithms struggle to balance computational speed and accuracy. Point cloud–based methods provide high precision but are computationally intensive and unsuitable for real-time applications. To address these issues, this study employs a pre-trained DepthAnythingV2 neural network to guide the training of a surgical scene depth estimation model. By combining segmentation masks with depth estimation results, the distances between instruments are calculated and used to generate force feedback to the teleoperated master, enabling dynamic instrument avoidance.

2 Surgical Instrument Segmentation Algorithm

Image segmentation algorithms for surgical instruments are mainly categorized into convolution-based and self-attention–based neural networks. Convolution-based methods are advantageous for their sensitivity to local features and high computational efficiency, particularly excelling at capturing fine details such as image edges. In contrast, self-attention–based approaches are more effective in modeling global context and capturing semantic relationships across the image [2], though they often underperform in recovering high-resolution structures and fine details compared to convolutional methods. This paper proposes PGUNet (Pre-trained-model Guided U-Net), which integrates a pre-trained model with a U-Net architecture. The encoder extracts features from the input image by leveraging both sources, and multi-level intermediate features are fused and passed through skip connections to the decoder. This design enables the network to capture both global and local features effectively (Fig. 1).

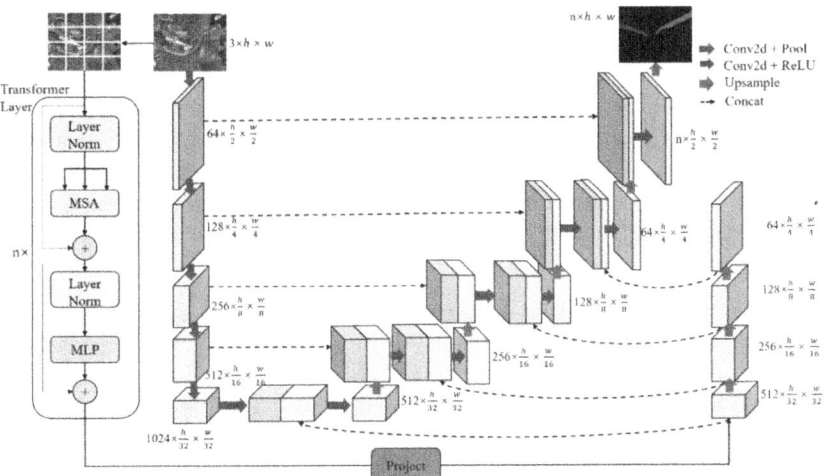

Fig. 1. PGUNet Structure

The downsampling path of U-Net is primarily composed of convolutional modules. Each module performs two 2D convolution operations followed by a pooling operation. Convolution kernels are set with a fixed size and padding of 1 to maintain the spatial dimensions after each convolution. In standard U-Net designs, as the network goes deeper, the number of feature channels gradually increases while the spatial resolution decreases, allowing the model to extract more complex high-level features. After every two convolutional layers, a max pooling operation with a kernel size and stride of 2 is applied, halving the spatial dimensions of the input. This operation reduces the computational cost and enhances feature abstraction by compressing spatial information.

Given an input image of shape $n \times c \times h \times w$, where n is the batch size, c is the number of input channels (typically 3 for RGB images), and h and w denote the height and width, the downsampling process produces a hierarchical set of features. These features, summarized in Table 1, represent semantic information at varying levels of abstraction from shallow to deep layers.

Table 1. Feature map parameters during U-Net downsampling

Layer	n	c	h	w
1	n	64	$h/2$	$w/2$
2	n	128	$h/4$	$w/4$
3	n	256	$h/8$	$w/8$
4	n	512	$h/16$	$w/16$
5	n	1024	$h/32$	$w/32$

DepthAnythingV2 uses a multi-layer Transformer encoder to extract global semantic features. In this work, only the encoder is used. Intermediate features are extracted and passed through convolutional layers to match the channel dimensions of U-Net features. The corresponding feature scales are shown in Table 2. The column c represents the original number of channels in the model's intermediate features, while cinc denotes the number of channels after adjustment with a 1×1 convolution to align with U-Net features. At this point, the feature maps corresponding to U-Net layers have the same spatial dimensions (height and width) and channel count.

Table 2. DepthAnythingV2 parameters during downsampling

Layer	n	c	cinc	h	w
1	n	64	64	$h/4$	$w/4$
2	n	64	128	$h/8$	$w/8$
3	n	64	256	$h/16$	$w/16$
4	n	64	512	$h/32$	$w/32$

After obtaining multi-scale features, channel and spatial attention mechanisms [3] are used to fuse and upsample the features at corresponding scales. The multi-level features from the U-Net encoder and DepthAnythingV2 are gradually fused through skip connections. During the decoding phase, transposed convolutions are applied to progressively restore the feature dimensions. At each decoding step, the network incorporates U-Net downsampled features, DepthAnythingV2 downsampled features, and the upsampled features fused from both U-Net and DepthAnythingV2. The pre-trained DepthAnythingV2 model provides guidance for parameter updates to the U-Net network without requiring additional training.

3 Endoscopic Image Depth Estimation Algorithm

After obtaining the instrument image, depth estimation is used to determine the instrument's position in the camera coordinate system. Although the endoscope in cardiac surgery robots is typically binocular, the small baseline between the two cameras, usually just a few millimeters, results in a small disparity and increased depth errors. Additionally, in bright operating room lighting, it becomes challenging to align feature points between the two cameras, causing poor continuity in the depth map and incomplete coverage of the surgical scene's pixels [4]. Without relying on hardware sensors, monocular depth estimation based on neural networks is commonly used. These methods provide continuous depth output but typically use inverse depth maps during training to mitigate the impact of distant points on gradients. Restoring the actual depth requires knowing the real-world distances of the farthest and nearest points in the image [5], which is difficult in surgical settings due to the lack of additional sensors and poor binocular depth map continuity.

Under the conditions of d_{min} and d_{max} being known, the conversion relationship between the inverse depth map and the real depth map is given by Eq. (1)

$$D_{true} = \left[V_{norm}(\frac{1}{d_{min}} - \frac{1}{d_{max}}) + \frac{1}{d_{max}}\right]^{-1} \quad (1)$$

The minimum and maximum values in the real depth map are difficult to obtain directly and stably through binocular cameras. However, there are still many pixels in the depth map obtained from stereo matching that correspond to the real depth and can match one-to-one with the inverse depth map estimated by the neural network. By replacing d_{min} and d_{max} with $1/A$ and $1/B$, respectively, the relationship in Eq. (1) is transformed into the expression in Eq. (2), which contains the two unknowns A and B.

$$D_{true} = [V_{norm}(A - B) + B]^{-1} \quad (2)$$

Assuming that the true depth values and their corresponding standard inverse depth values $V_{norm,i}$ are known for n points, we obtain n equations, as shown in Eq. (3).

$$D_i = \left[V_{norm,i} \cdot (A - B) + B\right]^{-1}, i = 1, 2, \ldots, n \quad (3)$$

Taking the reciprocal of each equation results in a linear system of equations, as shown in Eq. (4).

$$\frac{1}{D_i} = V_{norm,i} \cdot (A - B) + B \quad (4)$$

The relationship between the n known points is expressed as an equation in terms of A and B. Further simplification leads to the Eq. (5).

$$\frac{1}{D_i} = V_{norm,i} \cdot A + (1 - V_{norm,i}) \cdot B \tag{5}$$

Let $Y_i = \frac{1}{D_i}$, $X_i = V_{norm,i}$, linear equation form of the system is

$$Y_i = X_i \cdot A + (1 - X_i) \cdot B \tag{6}$$

Construct the equation matrix:

$$\mathbf{Y} = \begin{bmatrix} Y_1 \\ Y_2 \\ \vdots \\ Y_n \end{bmatrix}, \mathbf{X} = \begin{bmatrix} X_1 & (1-X_1) \\ X_2 & (1-X_2) \\ \vdots & \vdots \\ X_n & (1-X_n) \end{bmatrix}, \Theta = \begin{bmatrix} A \\ B \end{bmatrix} \tag{7}$$

Using the least squares method for fitting, the solution can be expressed as

$$\Theta = (\mathbf{X}^T \mathbf{X})^{-1} \mathbf{X}^T \mathbf{Y} \tag{8}$$

where Θ represent the coefficients of A and B, as well as $1/d_{min}$ and $1/d_{max}$. The real depth value for any point in the standard inverse depth map can be recovered.

4 Surgical Instrument Collision Avoidance Algorithm

The algorithm uses KD-trees and hierarchical optimization strategies to quickly estimate the actual distance of selected points inside the cylindrical bounding box. The hierarchical optimization strategy reduces computational complexity by progressively refining the calculations. Point clouds are uniformly sampled to reduce the number of points needed for distance estimation, enabling a rapid calculation of the minimum distance. Based on the results, candidate points are selected, and surrounding point clouds are further computed for more accurate distance estimation. The KD-tree accelerates this process by organizing point cloud data into a tree structure, enabling efficient nearest-neighbor queries with low time complexity. The KD-tree is built by dividing point clouds along the X, Y, and Z coordinates, using the middle value of each coordinate as the root node. This structure minimizes computation by determining whether to traverse subtrees based on the distance between the root node and the target point [6].

After obtaining the distance between surgical instruments, a velocity variable is introduced to calculate the relative distance as the bounding boxes dynamically change over time. This allows the prediction of collision risks in the future. Velocity is calculated by sampling the Omega remote-controlled hand's 3D position at 50 Hz, smoothing the data, and determining the direction of velocity based on the tangent of the curve at the final position. The displacement within one sampling cycle is calculated, and its magnitude represents the velocity. The minimum distance within a future time interval is sampled at 50 Hz to determine if it falls below a safety threshold. If the distance is below the threshold, there is a potential collision risk; otherwise, the risk is zero. Collision risk is further assessed based on the time when the distance first decreases below the safety threshold and the difference between the minimum distance and the safety threshold in the future. Collision risk is computed as

$$R = w_1(t_{max} - t_r) + w_2(d_{threshold} - d_{min}) \tag{9}$$

If there is a collision risk at t_0, a feedback force is applied to the master hand at the current moment to guide the operator in the direction that avoids the collision. The magnitude of the feedback force is shown in Eq. (10).

$$F = w_3 R \tag{10}$$

The feedback force is applied to the instrument farther from the surgical area, with the direction towards the closest point between the instruments, encouraging them to move apart.

5 Surgical Instrument Collision Avoidance Algorithm

The surgical robot platform consists of the Realman dual-arm robot, Omega7 haptic master, surgical instruments, chest cavity model, heart model, and binocular cameras. The dual arms hold surgical tools, with an incremental master-slave teleoperation system controlling movement and manipulation. A binocular camera simulates the robot's endoscope, positioned above the chest cavity model as shown in Fig. 2.

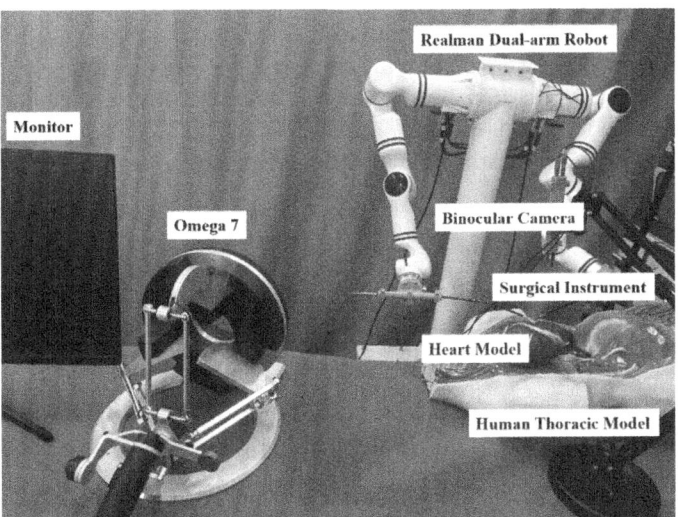

Fig. 2. Experiment platform

In the experimental setup, a dataset was collected from the camera's perspective and annotated. PGUNet was trained on this dataset, and the input image and surgical instrument segmentation image for a particular scene are shown in Fig. 3.

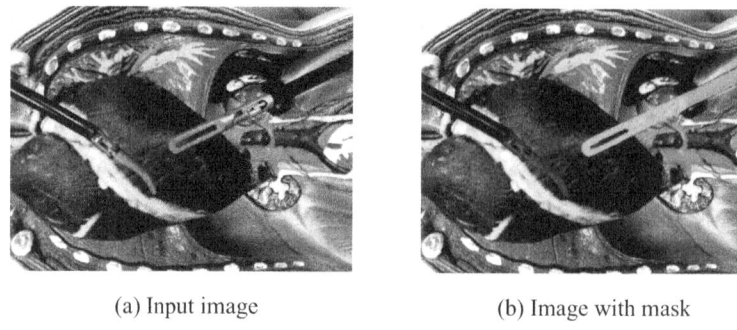

(a) Input image (b) Image with mask

Fig. 3. Image and mask predicted by PGUNet

The neural network was evaluated on the test set for accuracy, with metrics such as Dice coefficient, Intersection over Union (IoU), recall, and accuracy. The results are shown in Table 3.

Table 3. PGUNet results

mDice	mIoU	Recall	Precision
91.34%	85.10%	85.26%	99.73%

The data indicates that average segmentation accuracy for surgical instruments reached approximately 85%, meeting the requirements for instrument localization.

To validate the depth estimation, real depth data was collected using the Realsense D405 stereo camera. Ten sets of data were gathered under different instrument positions and viewpoints. The error distribution for the entire scene and the surgical area is shown in Fig. 4.

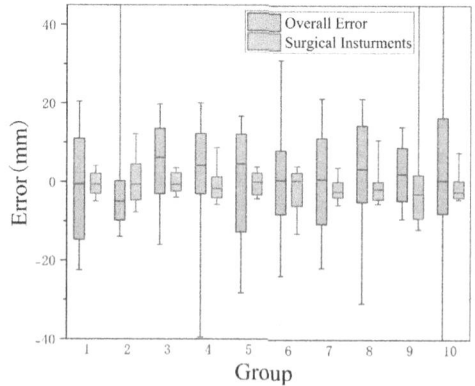

Fig. 4. Depth estimation error distribution

From Fig. 4, it can be seen that the average depth estimation error of the algorithm is approximately ±2 mm. The error is smaller and more concentrated when only the surgical instruments are estimated, demonstrating the effectiveness of the depth estimation algorithm. Figure 5 shows the input image, ground truth depth map, and the estimated depth map for the experimental scene.

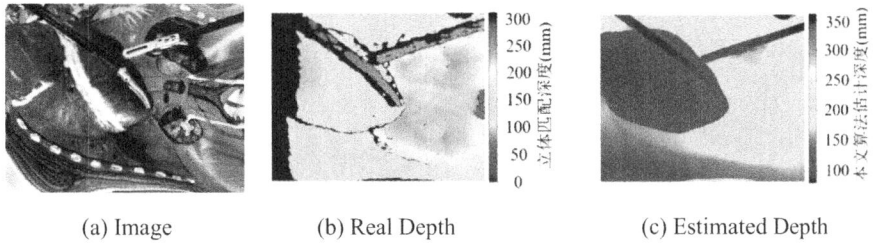

(a) Image   (b) Real Depth   (c) Estimated Depth

Fig. 5. Image, real depth and estimated depth

Table 4 shows the average, median and standard deviation of the overall depth estimation error and the error for estimating only the surgical instrument region.

Table 4. Average, median and standard deviation error

	Average Error (mm)	Median Error (mm)	Standard Deviation Error (mm)
Scene	16.31	11.22	17.90
Tool	6.22	3.99	11.63

The overall average depth is 191.74 mm, with the surgical instrument depth averaging 110 mm. The relative error is under 10%, with a 6% relative error for surgical instruments, meeting dynamic collision avoidance needs.

No force feedback is generated when instruments move apart. Feedback is triggered when they approach, with force feedback related to distance, operator speed, and X-axis velocity as shown in Fig. 6.

The force feedback is influenced by the distance, speed, and direction of approach between the instruments. Generally, the smaller the distance and faster the speed, the larger the feedback force. From 0 to 1 s, the distance decreases smoothly, but feedback force fluctuates with speed. From 2 to 3 s, even if the distance is below the threshold and speed is not zero, no feedback force is generated when the instruments are moving apart, demonstrating the effectiveness of the proposed dynamic collision avoidance algorithm.

6 Conclusion

This study utilizes the pretrained DepthAnythingV2 model to extract intermediate features that guide a U-Net network for surgical instrument segmentation. Combined with stereo laparoscopic images, it enables continuous depth estimation in surgical scenes.

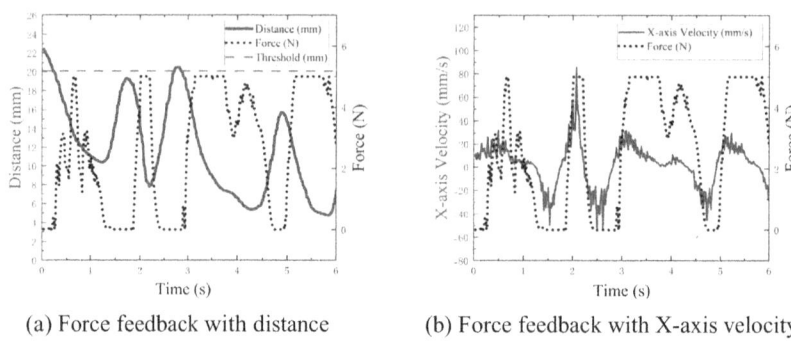

(a) Force feedback with distance (b) Force feedback with X-axis velocity

Fig. 6. Force Feedback

A hierarchical optimization strategy and KD-tree are then applied for fast distance estimation between instruments. Finally, an experimental platform is built to validate the effectiveness of the proposed segmentation, depth estimation, and dynamic collision avoidance algorithms.

Acknowledgments. This work is funded by National Key Research and Development Program of China under grant no. 2022YFB4700802.

References

1. Park, S., Howe, R.D., Torchiana, D.F.: Virtual fixtures for robotic cardiac surgery. In: International Conference on Medical Image Computing and Computer-Assisted Intervention, pp. 1419–1420. Springer, Heidelberg (2001)
2. Pu, Q., Xi, Z., Yin, S., et al.: Advantages of transformer and its application for medical image segmentation: a survey. Biomed. Eng. Online **23**(1), 14 (2024)
3. Woo, S., Park, J., Lee, J.Y., et al.: CBAM: convolutional block attention module. In: Proceedings of the European Conference on Computer Vision (ECCV), pp. 3–19 (2018)
4. Fu, Z., Jin, Z., Zhang, C., et al.: The future of endoscopic navigation: a review of advanced endoscopic vision technology. IEEE Access **9**, 41144–41167 (2021)
5. Masoumian, A., Rashwan, H.A., Cristiano, J., et al.: Monocular depth estimation using deep learning: a review. Sensors **22**(14), 5353 (2022)
6. Pinkham, R., Zeng, S., Zhang, Z.: Quicknn: memory and performance optimization of KD tree based nearest neighbor search for 3D point clouds. In: 2020 IEEE International Symposium on High Performance Computer Architecture (HPCA), pp. 180–192. IEEE (2020)

Benchmarking State-of-the-Art Lower Limb Joint Moment Estimator Against Advanced Time Series Models

Hamza Azam[1,2], Wenzhu Xu[3], Haoyu Wang[4], Luying Feng[1,5], Ahmad Irshad[6], Canjun Yang[2], Mitja Gerževič[7], and Wei Yang[1,2(✉)]

[1] Ningbo Innovation Center, Zhejiang University, Ningbo, China
simpleway@zju.edu.cn
[2] College of Mechanical Engineering, Zhejiang University, Hangzhou, China
[3] Department of Severe Rehabilitation, Ningbo Rehabilitation Hospital, Ningbo, China
[4] Hospital Department, Ningbo Rehabilitation Hospital, Ningbo, China
[5] School of Engineering, Westlake University, Hangzhou, China
[6] School of Computer Science and Engineering, University of Electronic Science and Technology, Chengdu, China
[7] Department of Physiotherapy, Alma Mater Europaea University, Maribor, Slovenia

Abstract. Accurate, real-time estimation of lower limb joint moments is critical for advancing biomechanics and rehabilitation technology. This study benchmarks a state-of-the-art Temporal Convolutional Network (TCN) against two advanced time series models, gMLP and TimeGPT, for joint moment estimation. To simulate a reduced sensor suite, we used only bilateral hip angle data to simultaneously estimate joint moments in both limbs. We collected experimental data across three distinct gait conditions, stand-to-walk transition, level-ground walking, and transitional speed walking, to evaluate model performance. Beyond estimation accuracy, we assessed computational efficiency by comparing floating-point operations (FLOPs) and model parameter counts to determine real-time deployment feasibility. Our results show that while TCN maintains high accuracy across all conditions, TimeGPT offers competitive performance with significantly lower computational complexity. Meanwhile, gMLP struggles to model the complexities of functional gait conditions. This comparative analysis provides a clear guide for selecting the optimal model for biomechanical applications, balancing the need for precision with computational scalability.

Keywords: Reduced sensor suite · Joint moment estimation · lower-limb exoskeleton · neural networks · time series

1 Introduction

The accurate estimation of lower limb joint moments is of fundamental importance to biomechanics, with critical applications in clinical diagnostics and rehabilitative technology [1, 2]. These estimations are essential for diagnosing gait pathologies, assessing functional movements such as stand-to-walk transitions, and quantifying the efficacy of rehabilitation protocols [3]. Furthermore, reliable joint moment data is integral to the development of assistive technologies like prosthetics and exoskeletons, informs the design of personalized musculoskeletal interventions, and enables real-time analysis in sports science [4].

Conventional "gold standard" methods for joint moment estimation, despite their precision, are subject to significant practical limitations. These techniques utilize costly optical motion capture systems and force plates, which necessitate complex and time-intensive data processing [5]. The standard workflow requires personalized musculoskeletal models for inverse kinematics and dynamics, demanding intricate sensor configurations that are difficult to scale and susceptible to error. Consequently, such methods are not amenable to real-time application, large-scale data collection, or continuous monitoring outside of laboratory environments.

In response to these challenges, data-driven approaches represent a promising alternative, enabling accurate and continuous joint moment estimation from minimal sensor configurations [6, 7]. By simplifying biomechanical modeling, these methods facilitate rapid, cost-effective, and adaptable measurements, extending the scope of biomechanical analysis beyond traditional laboratory settings [8, 9]. For practical deployment in technologies such as active prostheses or edge devices, however, the computational efficiency of these models is as critical as their predictive accuracy for ensuring low-latency operation [10, 11].

Recent advancements in deep learning have introduced powerful time series models applicable to this domain, including the Temporal Convolutional Network (TCN) [12–14], Gated Multi-Layer Perceptron (gMLP) [15], and TimeGPT [16, 17]. TCN is highly effective for modeling long-range temporal dependencies via dilated causal convolutions and have demonstrated strong performance in gait analysis, though a potential limitation is their memory-intensiveness [13]. The gMLP architecture provides a computationally leaner alternative to Transformers, employing spatial gating units to achieve comparable performance, which makes it well-suited for resource-constrained environments. TimeGPT, a foundation model specialized for time series, offers zero-shot inference and fine-tuning capabilities, indicating significant potential for biomechanical data applications. However, the efficacy of gMLP and TimeGPT for modeling the intricacies of human gait has not yet been systematically evaluated.

Accordingly, this study benchmarks these advanced deep learning models, evaluating their performance in estimating joint moments from previously unseen participant data across diverse gait conditions. Both predictive accuracy and computational efficiency are rigorously assessed to ascertain the feasibility of each model for real-time implementation. The comparative analysis presented herein provides empirical insights into the trade-offs between predictive accuracy and computational complexity, thereby serving as a reference for model selection in precision wearable robotics and scalable biomechanical monitoring.

2 Methodology

This section details the methodology for estimating hip joint moments from hip joint angles. The pipeline is developed to simultaneously model bilateral limb dynamics, thereby capturing the essential inter-limb spatial and temporal dependencies characteristic of human locomotion. By integrating this spatio-temporal information and accounting for bilateral asymmetries, the models are to achieve precise hip joint moment estimations, particularly for functional gait conditions.

2.1 Data Collection and Processing

Data were collected from nine healthy volunteers (8 male, 1 female; age 25.0 ± 4.0 years; height 172.9 ± 10.1 cm; mass 69.3 ± 12.4 kg). After providing written informed consent under a protocol approved by the Institutional Review Board of the College of Biomedical Engineering and Instrument Science, Zhejiang University, participants were screened to exclude any musculoskeletal or neurological conditions that could affect gait. Each participant completed four five-minute gait protocols in a fixed sequence: a stand-to-walk transition (SW), level-ground walking at two constant speeds (1.0 m/s and 1.5 m/s), and transitional speed walking (TSW). This protocol was designed to elicit a comprehensive range of gait patterns for robust model evaluation.

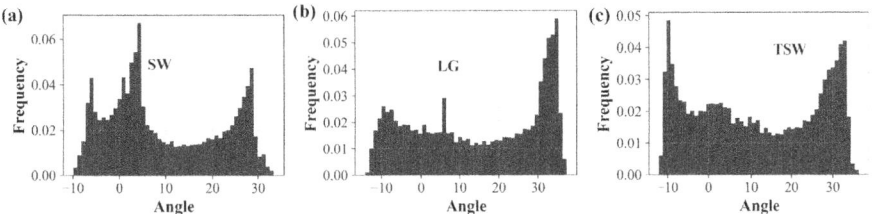

Fig. 1. Distributions of hip flexion/extension angle for different gait conditions over 27 strides, (a) stand-to-walk (SW) condition, (b) level-ground (LG) condition at speed 1.0 m/s, and (c) transitional speed level-ground walking (TSW)

Kinematic data were acquired at 100 Hz using a ten-camera Vicon motion capture system. Retroreflective markers were placed on key anatomical landmarks according to the Plug-in Gait model to enable precise tracking of segmental motion. The data processing pipeline began with filtering the raw marker trajectories using a fourth-order, zero-lag Butterworth low-pass filter with a 6 Hz cutoff frequency. Joint angles were then calculated, and data integrity was ensured by using linear and spline interpolation to fill any gaps resulting from marker occlusion. The hip joint angle distributions for a representative participant across three of these gait conditions are illustrated in Fig. 1.

2.2 Model Architectures and Computational Principles

The computational efficiency and parameter complexity of the TCN, gMLP, and TimeGPT models are direct functions of their underlying mathematical architectures.

The core operations governing each model are detailed below. TCN employs dilated causal to model long-range temporal dependencies. For an input sequence x and a filter w, a 1D dilated convolution operation is defined in Eq. (1).

$$y(t) = \sum_{i=0}^{k-1} w(i) \cdot x(t - d \cdot i) \tag{1}$$

where k is kernel size, and d is the dilation rate. The computational load, measured in FLOPs, scales linearly with sequence length, kernel size, and the number of input/output channels. The number of learnable parameters is primarily determined by the convolutional kernel weights and biases. The gMLP architecture is structured around a Spatial Gating Unit (SGU). This unit splits the input tensor along its channel dimension and applies a gating mechanism. The operation can be formally expressed by Eq. (2).

$$Z = \sigma(XU) \odot XV \tag{2}$$

where X is the input sequence, U and V are learnable weight matrices, and σ is a gating activation function (often sigmoid or GELU) and $\odot$ denotes element-wise multiplication. The FLOPs are dominated by the dense matrix multiplications, scaling with the input dimensionality and sequence length. The parameter count is principally determined by the size of the projection matrices U and V. TimeGPT adapts the Transformer architecture for time-series analysis, combining a scaled dot-product attention mechanism with subsequent causal convolutions. The core operation is defined by Eq. (3).

$$T = f_{\text{conv}}\left(\text{Softmax}\left(\frac{qk^\perp}{d_k} + M\right) \cdot v\right) \tag{3}$$

where query (q), key (k), and value (v) matrices are linear projections of the input sequence X (i.e., $q = XW_q$, $k = XW_k$, $v = XW_v$), d_k is the dimensionality of the key, and M is an optional mask. The attended output is processed by a 1D causal convolution, f_{conv}. The FLOPs are dominated by the attention mechanism matrix multiplications, which scale quadratically with sequence length ($O(n^2)$). Learnable parameters are concentrated in the projection matrices (W_q, W_k, W_v) of the multi-head attention layers and the convolutional layers.

2.3 Training, Evaluation, and Statistical Analysis

All network parameters were randomly initialized, and models were trained using the Adam optimizer [18]. A cosine learning rate scheduler [19] with periodic restarts was employed to optimize convergence, while early stopping [20] based on validation loss was implemented to prevent overfitting. Experiments were conducted on a workstation equipped with a 12th Gen Intel i5-12600KF CPU and an NVIDIA GeForce RTX 3080 GPU.

The complete dataset was partitioned into training (70%), validation (15%), and test (15%) sets, ensuring no participant overlap between sets. To prevent data leakage and assess generalization to novel dynamics, data from the first collection session for each participant was used for training and validation. For the test set, only the Transitional Speed Walking (TSW) data from the second session was utilized, as this protocol exhibited natural intra-subject variability between sessions [21].

Model performance was evaluated using the Mean Squared Error (MSE), Root Mean Squared Error (RMSE), Mean Positive Error (MPE), Mean Negative Error (MNE), and the coefficient of determination (R2). MSE served as the primary loss function for training. The loss function and metrics are defined by Eqs. (4)–(8).

$$MSE = \frac{1}{n}\sum_{i=1}^{n}(y_i - \hat{y}_i)^2 \qquad (4)$$

$$RMSE = \sqrt{\frac{1}{n}\sum_{i=1}^{n}(y_i - \hat{y}_i)^2} \qquad (5)$$

$$MPE = ReLU(y_i - \hat{y}_i) \qquad (6)$$

$$MNE = ReLU(\hat{y}_i - y_i) \qquad (7)$$

$$R^2 = 1 - \frac{\sum_{i=1}^{N}(y_i - \hat{y}_i)^2}{\sum_{i=1}^{N}(y_i - \bar{y}_i)^2} \qquad (8)$$

where y_i represents ground truth value, $\hat{y}_i$ is the predicted value, and $\bar{y}$ is the mean of the ground truth values. Lower values for RMSE, MPE, and MNE indicate superior performance, whereas a higher R^2 value signifies better model fit. Statistical significance between model predictions was determined using a one-tailed, paired-sample t-test, with a significance level of $p \leq 0.05$.

3 Results

This section presents a comprehensive evaluation of the TCN, gMLP, and TimeGPT models for lower limb joint moment estimation. The analysis is structured to first assess performance symmetry across the left and right limbs, then to evaluate accuracy across different gait conditions, and finally to compare the computational efficiency of each model.

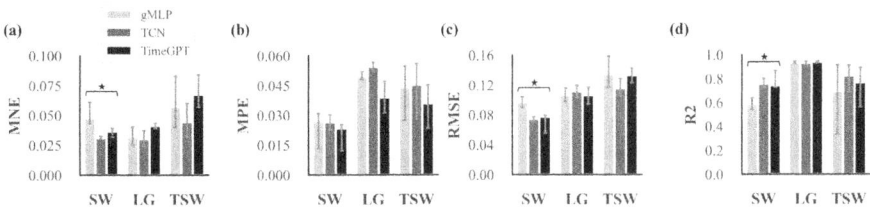

Fig. 2. Average performance metrics across both limbs independently. Error bars represent a 95% confidence interval. (a) MNE, (b) MPE, (c) RMSE, and (d) R2. Statistical significance ($p \leq 0.05$) is denoted as follows: ★★ indicates TCN is significantly different from both comparison models; ★★★ indicates TimeGPT is significantly different from both.

To evaluate the models' ability to capture the bilateral dynamics of human gait, estimation accuracy was assessed independently for the left and right limbs using data from unseen participants. As illustrated in Fig. 2, TCN and TimeGPT demonstrated comparable and symmetric predictive performance. The TCN achieved RMSE values of 0.1040 ± 0.0286 Nm/kg (left limb) and 0.1038 ± 0.0064 Nm/kg (right limb). Similarly, TimeGPT yielded RMSEs of 0.1054 ± 0.0309 Nm/kg (left) and 0.1076 ± 0.0074 Nm/kg (right). The gMLP model, lacking explicit mechanisms for long-range dependency modeling like dilated convolutions or self-attention, exhibited a greater asymmetry, with RMSEs of 0.1062 ± 0.0290 Nm/kg (left) and 0.1155 ± 0.0075 Nm/kg (right).

A similar trend was observed for the coefficient of determination (R^2). TCN and TimeGPT produced symmetric results, while gMLP's performance was less consistent across limbs. Statistically, no model significantly outperformed the others in overall RMSE and R^2 scores. However, significant differences were observed in error bias. For negative error (MNE), TCN significantly outperformed both comparison models for the left limb and TimeGPT for the right limb ($p \leq 0.05$). Conversely, for positive error (MPE), TimeGPT significantly outperformed the others for the right limb ($p \leq 0.05$).

The models efficacy was further evaluated across three distinct gait conditions: stand-to-walk (SW), level-ground (LG), and transitional speed walking (TSW). As shown in Fig. 3, TCN and TimeGPT remained the top performers, particularly in the more dynamic, functional gait conditions (SW and TSW). In the SW condition, both TCN and TimeGPT significantly outperformed gMLP ($p < 0.05$). TCN achieved an RMSE of 0.0751 ± 0.0028 Nm/kg, while TimeGPT produced a slightly higher RMSE of 0.0774 ± 0.0066 Nm/kg with greater uncertainty. In the TSW condition, TCN maintained its advantage with an RMSE of 0.1160 ± 0.0122 Nm/kg, compared to TimeGPT's 0.1331 ± 0.0101 Nm/kg. This pattern was mirrored in the R^2 scores. Interestingly, for the steady-state LG condition, TCN was slightly outperformed by both gMLP and TimeGPT in terms of RMSE and R^2.

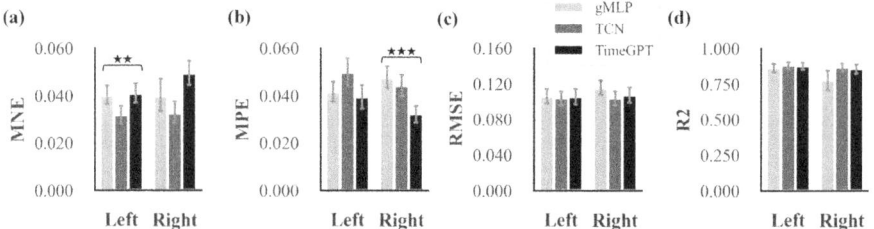

Fig. 3. Performance evaluation for each gait condition. Error bars represent a 95% confidence interval. (a) MNE, (b) MPE, (c) RMSE, and (d) R2. Statistical significance ($p \leq 0.05$) is denoted as follows: ★ indicates gMLP is significantly different from both comparison models.

The analysis thus far has focused on individual limbs and gait conditions. For a broader perspective, Table 1 summarizes the results. The results were computed over 1024 timesteps to generate the bar plots. For the table, a weighted mean was computed to derive the final averaged values.

Beyond predictive accuracy, computational cost is a critical factor for real-world deployment. The number of floating-point operations (FLOPs) and learnable parameters (Params) are key indicators of a model's complexity and resource requirements. As

Table 1. Benchmarking TCN against comparison models

Model	Metrics			
	MPE	MNE	RMSE	R^2
TimeGPT [16]	0.03580	0.04516	0.08096	0.86781
TCN [13]	0.04713	0.03224	0.07938	0.87666
gMLP [15]	0.04485	0.04015	0.08500	0.82394

shown in Fig. 4, there are clear trade-offs between the models. While TCN may offer high accuracy, its computational demands in terms of FLOPs and parameters can be substantial. In contrast, models like gMLP are designed for efficiency. On resource-constrained hardware like a CPU, high FLOPs and a large parameter count can introduce significant latency due to sequential processing and memory bandwidth limitations. Figure 4 compares FLOPs, parameter counts, GPU training time per epoch, and CPU inference time per sample for each model, highlighting their respective suitability for on-board, real-time applications.

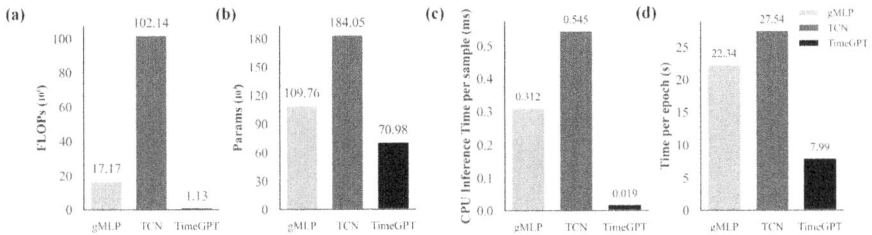

Fig. 4. Comparison of computational efficiency. (a) Floating-point operations (FLOPs), (b) Number of learnable parameters, (c) CPU inference time (ms), and (d) GPU training time per epoch (s).

4 Discussion

The primary objective of this study was to benchmark state-of-the-art deep learning models for lower limb joint moment estimation, with a dual focus on predictive accuracy and computational efficiency for real-time applications. Our findings indicate a clear trade-off between the high-fidelity estimations of Temporal Convolutional Networks (TCNs) and the computational efficiency of more recent architectures like TimeGPT and gMLP.

Conventional deep learning models for biomechanical analysis, including standard TCN [13], often require long input sequences and significant computational resources, limiting their practicality for on-board deployment. While Transformers [22] offered a path forward, their quadratic scaling with sequence length posed a new bottleneck. This study explored two modern alternatives: TimeGPT [16], which mitigates the scaling issue by integrating 1D convolutions into its attention-based framework, and gMLP

[15], which forgoes convolutions and attention entirely in favor of a simpler, gated MLP structure.

Our results align with previous work, demonstrating the high accuracy of TCNs in gait analysis. However, this performance comes at a substantial computational cost. The key finding of this study is that TimeGPT provides a compelling alternative, achieving estimation accuracy competitive with TCNs but with dramatically lower computational demands. Specifically, TimeGPT required only 1.13 million FLOPs to achieve its performance, compared to 102.14 million for TCN. This efficiency translated to a ~3.5x faster training time and a ~28x faster inference time on a CPU, making it a far more viable candidate for real-time systems. The gMLP model, while the most efficient, struggled to capture the complex dynamics of functional gait, suggesting its simplified architecture may be insufficient for this specific task. The optimal hyperparameters used to achieve these results are detailed in Table 2.

Table 2. Tuned hyperparameters for TCN, and comparison models for both datasets

	gMLP*	TCN*	TimeGPT*
# of layers	2	5	2
Patch Size	16 & 32	N/A	N/A
Embedding size	64	N/A	32
Hidden size	256	50	256
Sequence length	256	187	256
Dropout	0.1	0.4	0.1
Learning rate	0.001	0.0005	0.001
activation	ReLU	ReLU	ReLU

This study has several limitations that provide avenues for future research. First, the models were evaluated offline. A crucial next step is to assess their performance in an online setting by integrating them into a physical exoskeleton or wearable sensor system. Such a study would provide direct evidence of their real-world efficacy, though it introduces challenges related to hardware-specific implementation and control system design. Second, this research did not explicitly investigate the models' sensitivity to sensor noise or placement variability. As these are significant factors in practical applications, future work should explore the robustness of each architecture to simulated and real-world noise. This would offer a more complete understanding of their reliability outside of controlled laboratory conditions.

5 Conclusion

This study successfully benchmarked three state-of-the-art deep learning models for estimating biological hip joint moments using only bilateral hip angle data. The investigation focused on comparing the models' generalization capabilities, predictive symmetry across limbs, and computational efficiency. Our findings demonstrate that while all three models performed competitively during steady-state level-ground walking, the gMLP architecture failed to adequately model the complex dynamics of functional gait transitions. In contrast, both TCN and TimeGPT delivered robust and symmetric predictions across all gait conditions, with no statistically significant difference in their overall accuracy. The critical distinction emerged from the analysis of computational cost. TimeGPT achieved its high-fidelity performance with significantly fewer floating-point operations and learnable parameters than the TCN. This highlights TimeGPT's superior efficiency, making it a highly promising candidate for applications with limited computational resources. These results underscore the potential of TimeGPT as a foundational architecture for real-time exoskeleton control and wearable biomechanical analysis. Future work should focus on implementing and validating these models in real-world robotic systems.

Acknowledgments. This work was supported by the Natural Science Foundation of Zhejiang (No. LMS25E050007 and LTGY23H170002); the Key Research & Development Project of Zhejiang (No. 2024C03040); the Key Research & Development Project of Ningbo (No. 2024Z199 and 2024Z027); and the Public Welfare Project of Ningbo (No. 2023S111 and 2024S152).

CRediT Authorship Contribution Statement. **Hamza Azam:** Writing – original draft, Writing – review & editing, Conceptualization. **Wenzhu Xu:** Data curation and analysis, Visualization, Software, Conceptualization. **Haoyu Wang:** Conceptualization, Project administration. **Luying Feng:** Visualization, Software, Conceptualization. **Ahmad Irshad:** Writing – review & editing, Software. **Canjun Yang:** Conceptualization, Supervision. **Mitja Gerževič:** Visualization, Writing – review & editing. **Wei Yang:** Conceptualization, Supervision, Resources, Project administration.

Ethics Statement. The ethics committee of the College of Biomedical Engineering and Instrument Science of Zhejiang University approved the study (202255).

Declaration of Competing Interest. The Authors declare that they have no known competing financial interests or personal relationships that could have appeared to influence the work reported in this paper.

References

1. Cao, W., et al.: A lower limb exoskeleton with rigid and soft structure for loaded walking assistance. IEEE Robot. Autom. Lett. **7**(1), 454–461 (2022)
2. Kalita, B., Narayan, J., Dwivedy, S.K.: Development of active lower limb robotic-based orthosis and exoskeleton devices: a systematic review. Int. J. Soc. Robot. **13**(4), 775–793 (2021)
3. Winter, D.A.: Biomechanics and Motor Control of Human Movement. Wiley (2009)
4. Mundt, M.: Bridging the lab-to-field gap using machine learning: a narrative review. Sports Biomech. 1–20 (2023)
5. Buchanan, T.S., et al.: Estimation of muscle forces and joint moments using a forward-inverse dynamics model. Med. Sci. Sports Exerc. **37**(11), 1911–1916 (2005)
6. Mundt, M., et al.: Prediction of lower limb joint angles and moments during gait using artificial neural networks. Med. Biol. Eng. Compu. **58**(1), 211–225 (2020)

7. Siviy, C., et al.: Opportunities and challenges in the development of exoskeletons for locomotor assistance. Nat. Biomed. Eng. **7**(4), 456–472 (2023)
8. Molinaro, D.D., et al.: Biological hip torque estimation using a robotic hip exoskeleton. In: 2020 8th IEEE RAS/EMBS International Conference for Biomedical Robotics and Biomechatronics (BioRob) (2020)
9. Dorschky, E., et al.: CNN-based estimation of sagittal plane walking and running biomechanics from measured and simulated inertial sensor data. Front. Bioeng. Biotechnol. **8** (2020)
10. Low, W.S., et al.: A review of machine learning network in human motion biomechanics. J. Grid Comput. **20**(1), 4 (2021)
11. Liang, W., et al.: Deep-learning model for the prediction of lower-limb joint moments using single inertial measurement unit during different locomotive activities. Biomed. Signal Process. Control **86**, 105372 (2023)
12. Molinaro, D.D., et al.: Subject-independent, biological hip moment estimation during multimodal overground ambulation using deep learning. IEEE Trans. Med. Robot. Bionics **4**(1), 219–229 (2022)
13. Molinaro, D.D., Kang, I., Young, A.J.: Estimating human joint moments unifies exoskeleton control, reducing user effort. Sci. Robot. **9**(88), eadi8852 (2024)
14. Nuesslein, C.P.O., Young, A.J.: A deep learning framework for end-to-end control of powered prostheses. IEEE Robot. Autom. Lett. **9**(5), 3988–3994 (2024)
15. Liu, H., et al.: Pay attention to MLPs. In: Proceedings of the 35th International Conference on Neural Information Processing Systems, p. Article 704. Curran Associates Inc. (2021)
16. Garza, A., Mergenthaler-Canseco, M.: TimeGPT-1. arXiv preprint arXiv:2310.03589 (2023)
17. Liao, W., et al.: TimeGPT in load forecasting: a large time series model perspective. Appl. Energy **379**, 124973 (2025)
18. Kingma, D.P.: Adam: a method for stochastic optimization. In: International Conference on Learning Representations (2014)
19. Loshchilov, I., Hutter, F.: SGDR: stochastic gradient descent with warm restarts. In: International Conference on Learning Representations (2016)
20. Yao, Y., Rosasco, L., Caponnetto, A.: On early stopping in gradient descent learning. Constr. Approx. **26**(2), 289–315 (2007)
21. Sun, T., et al.: Influence of number of subjects and number of trials on biomechanical variable estimation via deep-learning models and wearable IMUs during drop landings. IEEE Sens. J. 1 (2025)
22. Vaswani, A.: Attention is all you need. In: Advances in Neural Information Processing Systems (2017)

A Mixed Reality-Based SSMVEP Brain-Computer Interface for Exoskeletons

Xiuyuan Wu, Yichen Lin, Xinyang Du, Zengle Ren, Wujing Cao, Meng Yin, and Yue Ma[✉]

Shenzhen Institute of Advanced Technology, Chinese Academy of Sciences, Shenzhen, China
yue.ma@siat.ac.cn

Abstract. To address the issues of unnatural interaction, screen fixation, and visual fatigue in traditional SSVEP-based brain-controlled exoskeletons, this paper proposes an SSMVEP-based system enhanced by mixed reality (MR). A ring-shaped motion checkerboard paradigm is used for visual stimulation, combined with real-time EEG signal processing and gait control algorithms to enable low-fatigue, high-accuracy interaction. Experiments show that in a 6-target classification task, 5-second SSMVEP signals achieve 96.11% accuracy, with visual fatigue reduced by 35% compared to traditional SSVEP. In online exoskeleton control, the system achieves a 97.7% success rate in complex gait transitions. This system offers a practical and efficient rehabilitation solution for lower-limb motor impairments, demonstrating the potential of SSMVEP in real-time brain-controlled exoskeleton applications.

Keywords: SSMVEP · Mixed Reality · Brain-Computer Interface · Lower-Limb Exoskeleton

1 Introduction

In recent years, Brain-Computer Interface (BCI), Exoskeleton Robot, and Mixed Reality (MR) technologies have advanced rapidly, offering new breakthroughs in neurorehabilitation and human-machine interaction. BCI decodes brain signals to directly control external devices; exoskeletons assist motor-impaired users in gait training; MR devices merge virtual and real environments to provide immersive, intuitive interactions. Combining these technologies enables a low-load, highly interactive human-machine collaboration.

Steady-State Visual Evoked Potential (SSVEP) is widely used in BCI due to strong signals, high accuracy, and fast response. However, its high-frequency flickering often causes visual fatigue [1], limiting practical use. To address this, Steady-State Motion Visual Evoked Potential (SSMVEP) has been proposed as an alternative [2]. Unlike SSVEP, SSMVEP is elicited by periodic motion patterns such as the ring-shaped motion checkerboard paradigm [3], providing gentler stimulation with notable anti-fatigue benefits [4]. Studies show SSMVEP evokes clear frequency features even in short stimulation and offers better subjective comfort than flicker stimuli [5].

In brain-controlled exoskeleton research, SSVEP combined with lower-limb exoskeletons enables gait mode switching with high accuracy [6], but the application of SSMVEP in this context remains limited. Research on SSMVEP is still sparse, with inconsistent findings across stimulation paradigms, experimental designs, and classification outcomes. The absence of standardized protocols or benchmarks further limits its adoption in safety-critical systems. In addition, SSMVEP signals are typically weaker and rely on precise visual motion and stable attention, making them more susceptible to interference from head movement, gaze shifts, or display instability—factors that hinder reliable, real-time decoding in practical BCI applications.

To address these challenges, this study proposes an SSMVEP-based brain-controlled exoskeleton system built on a mixed reality (MR) platform. The system delivers dynamic, spatial motion stimuli via an MR headset to enhance SSMVEP induction and user immersion. It employs Canonical Correlation Analysis (CCA) algorithm combined with a bite-trigger mechanism for accurate and stable frequency recognition, and connects with the lower-limb exoskeleton to enable closed-loop control. A series of experiments were conducted to evaluate the system's fatigue resistance, classification performance, and motion execution accuracy, filling a research gap in this field.

The paper is organized as follows: Sect. 2 details the system design, visual stimuli, EEG processing, and exoskeleton control; Sect. 3 describes the experimental setup and metrics; Sect. 4 outlines the procedure; Sect. 5 discusses results; Sect. 6 concludes with a summary and future directions.

2 Methods

2.1 System Architecture

As shown in Fig. 1, the system consists of four main modules: Mixed Reality, EEG Acquisition, Signal Processing, and Exoskeleton Control.

The Mixed Reality module employs a Meta Quest 3 headset with a Unity-based interface to present SSMVEP stimuli at 8–13 Hz. Both traditional flicker and ring-shaped motion checkerboard paradigms are supported. Stimuli remain fixed in the user's view and adapt to head movement, enhancing immersion and reducing artifacts.

The EEG Acquisition module uses a 32-channel Ant Neuro system focused on occipital regions (POz, Oz, O1, O2). Signals are transmitted via cable to the eego software on the host computer, and then streamed to a Matlab program via the Lab Streaming Layer (LSL) for real-time analysis.

The Signal Processing module performs filtering, preprocessing, and frequency recognition via CCA. Control results are sent through TCP to a middleware server and forwarded to the exoskeleton control software.

The Exoskeleton module uses the SLEX lower-limb exoskeleton robot, capable of executing various gait transitions. Control commands and exoskeleton status are communicated via the CAN bus to complete the closed loop.

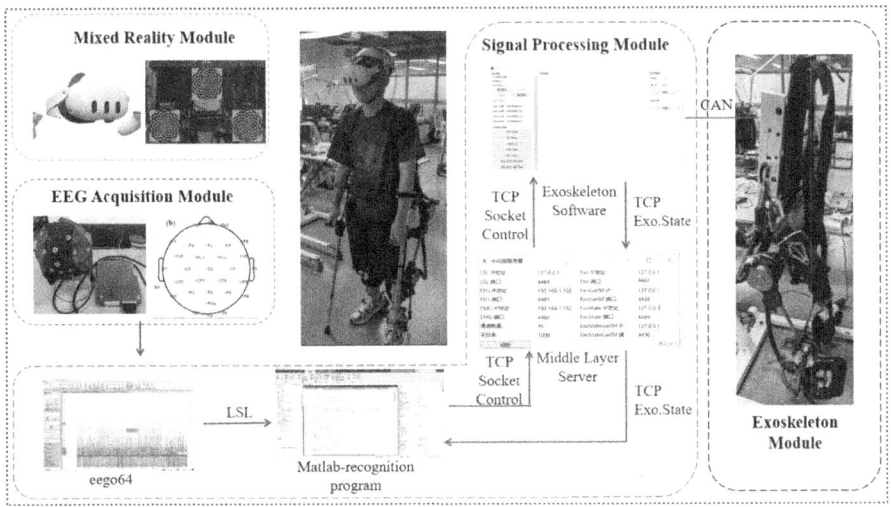

Fig. 1. System Architecture.

To further illustrate the performance of each system module, Table 1 summarizes the key metrics, including stimulus interface refresh rate, signal processing speed, and exoskeleton control response time. These indicators reflect the system's real-time capability and interaction efficiency under multimodal integration.

2.2 Stimulus Interface Implementation

This study adopts the ring-shaped motion checkerboard paradigm as the primary SSMVEP visual stimulus on a mixed reality platform. This paradigm features gentle motion and low visual load, capable of eliciting stable frequency responses without causing significant discomfort [7].

The stimulus pattern is implemented on the Unity 3D platform and deployed on the Meta Quest 3 mixed reality headset. It is presented within a stable forward field of view, allowing subjects to freely move their heads without losing sight of the stimulus targets. The A ring-shaped motion checkerboard paradigm seen by subjects is shown in Fig. 2.

Spatially, the pattern consists of multiple sectors arranged in a ring-shaped checkerboard, with alternating black and white sectors creating strong spatial contrast. Temporally, it performs radial contraction and expansion at preset frequencies, eliciting steady-state motion visual evoked potentials in the occipital cortex. The stimulus is generated based on polar coordinates, with pixel luminance I defined by the following expression:

$$I(r,\theta,t) = \text{sign}\left[\sin\left(\frac{2\pi r}{w} + M\theta + \phi(t)\right)\right] \qquad (1)$$

Table 1. Key Performance Metrics of the Brain-Controlled Exoskeleton System

Module	Metric	Description
Mixed Reality	Refresh Rate	90 Hz
	Resolution	4128 × 2208 pixels
	Field of View	Approx. 110° horizontal, 96° vertical
	Stimulus Frequency	8–13 Hz, 1 Hz intervals
	Number of Targets	6 offline/3 online
EEG Acquisition	Channels	32 channels, focusing on POz, Oz, O1, O2
	Sampling Rate	1000 Hz
Signal Processing	Analysis Window Length	3 s (masseter-triggered)
	Average Recognition Time	<300 ms
	Offline Accuracy	96.11% (5-second window)
Exoskeleton	Response Delay	< 1.0 s
	Action Types	SmallStep-L/R, LargeStep-L/R, Hold

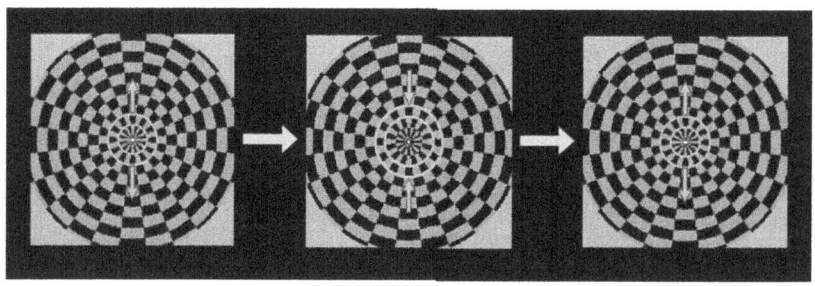

Fig. 2. Ring-shaped Motion Checkerboard Paradigm.

Here, r and θ represent the polar radius and polar angle of each pixel, respectively; w controls the width of the checkerboard grids; M denotes the number of sectors in one ring; and $\phi(t)$ is the temporal phase term governing the checkerboard motion. The phase variation produces the contraction and expansion effect of the pattern over time, defined as follows:

$$\phi(t) = 2\pi f_m \cdot \sin\left(\frac{2\pi t}{T}\right) \qquad (2)$$

where f_m denotes the motion frequency, and $T = 1/f_m$ is its period. To accommodate the discrete refresh mechanism of the mixed reality device, with a frame rate of f_s, the frame index n represents the time step. The phase function is thus modified as:

$$\phi[n] = 2\pi f_m \cdot \sin\left(\frac{2\pi n}{f_s/f_m}\right) \qquad (3)$$

The stimulus images are rendered in real time in Unity, which control the brightness of each sector at the pixel level. The pattern's phase value is updated every frame according to the current frame index, enabling smooth contraction and expansion of the checkerboard. In the MR device, each stimulus target is fixed in position, floating in front of the user, allowing multiple targets with different frequencies to be presented simultaneously for multi-target classification tasks.

In the experimental setup, the common parameters for the checkerboard pattern are: number of sectors $M = 12$, inner radius of 100 pixels, outer radius of 300 pixels, stimulus frequency from 8 to 13 Hz, and refresh rate of 90 Hz. The actual presentation appears as a periodic "breathing" motion at 90 frames per second, providing strong evoked responses and good subjective comfort.

2.3 Feature Extraction and Classification Methods

After raw EEG acquisition, signals are first bandpass filtered (4–40 Hz) to remove DC drift and high-frequency noise, and a 50 Hz notch filter suppresses power line interference. Feature extraction and classification follow.

This study employs Canonical Correlation Analysis (CCA) for frequency recognition of SSMVEP signals. CCA is an unsupervised multivariate statistical method that identifies stimulus frequency by correlating multi-channel EEG with constructed reference signals without training [8].

Let the recorded EEG signal be $\mathbf{X} \in \mathbb{R}^{N \times T}$, where N is the number of channels and T the number of samples. For each target frequency f_k, the reference signal set $\mathbf{Y}_{f_k} \in \mathbb{R}^{2H \times T}$ is constructed, containing H pairs of sine and cosine basis functions:

$$\mathbf{Y}_{f_k} = \begin{bmatrix} \sin(2\pi f_k t) \\ \cos(2\pi f_k t) \\ \vdots \\ \sin(2\pi H f_k t) \\ \cos(2\pi H f_k t) \end{bmatrix} \tag{4}$$

The goal of CCA is to find two sets of vectors, $\mathbf{w}_x$ and $\mathbf{w}_y$, that maximize the correlation coefficient ρ between $\mathbf{X}^\top \mathbf{w}_x$ and $\mathbf{Y}^\top \mathbf{w}_y$, expressed as:

$$\rho = \max_{\mathbf{w}_x, \mathbf{w}_y} \operatorname{corr}(\mathbf{X}^\top \mathbf{w}_x, \mathbf{Y}^\top \mathbf{w}_y) \tag{5}$$

For each candidate frequency f_k, the maximum correlation coefficient ρ_k is calculated. The input signal is then classified as the target frequency corresponding to the largest ρ_k:

$$f^* = \arg\max_{f_k} \rho_k \tag{6}$$

In this study, the basis function order is set to $H = 2$, with six reference frequencies used. Each target corresponds to a ring-shaped motion checkerboard stimulus region. The CCA method requires no individual training, offers efficient computation, and is well suited for real-time online recognition tasks, especially for rapid classification of SSMVEP signals.

2.4 Exoskeleton Control Mechanism and Gait Switching Design

The system employs the SLEX lower-limb exoskeleton developed by the Shenzhen Institute of Advanced Technology, featuring active hip and knee joints and passive ankle movement [9].

Three BCI control commands are defined: step left, step right, and stay still. Based on the current posture, the exoskeleton executes one of five actions: large or small step left/right, or hold position. For example, from standing, a step command triggers a small forward step; from a forward stance, the same-side command causes a small return, while the opposite-side command induces a large cross-step. A stay-still command results in no movement.

During control, three SSMVEP targets are presented in the mixed reality interface. The user selects a command by gaze and confirms it via voluntary masseter contraction. The system then extracts EEG data from the preceding 3 s, applies canonical correlation analysis (CCA) for frequency recognition, and transmits the decoded command to the exoskeleton via a middleware server, enabling closed-loop control.

3 Experimental Conditions and Environment

Experiments were conducted in a well-lit, low-interference laboratory. Participants wore EEG caps and sat facing the stimulus interface, with head support to minimize artifacts. Ambient noise was kept below 40 dB, and temperature maintained around 24 °C to avoid environmental effects on fatigue and attention.

Six healthy right-handed male volunteers aged 22 to 26, without neurological or visual impairments, were recruited. All participants provided informed consent before the experiment. The study complied with the Helsinki Declaration and was approved by the supervising faculty.

4 Experimental Design

To comprehensively evaluate the performance of the proposed MR-enhanced SSMVEP-based BCI exoskeleton system, two key experiments were designed to assess stimulus efficacy (classification accuracy and fatigue resistance) and BCI control reliability.

4.1 SSMVEP Paradigm Validation

This experiment compares the traditional SSVEP flicker paradigm with the SSMVEP ring-shaped motion checkerboard paradigm, focusing on offline classification accuracy and subjective visual fatigue.

Each participant completed gaze tasks for both paradigms. Each paradigm included 6 frequency targets (8–13 Hz, 1 Hz intervals), with 10 trials per target. Trials started with an auditory cue; subjects fixated on the target for 5 s, followed by 4 s rest. A total of 60 EEG trials per paradigm were recorded.

Afterward, participants completed questionnaires including 5 Likert-scale items (e.g., visual fatigue, attention) and the NASA-TLX workload scale (6 items) to assess visual comfort and subjective load. Offline EEG signals were analyzed using CCA for frequency recognition to compute average classification accuracy per paradigm.

4.2 BCI-Driven Exoskeleton Control Validation

This experiment evaluates the stability of command recognition and execution accuracy of the exoskeleton under BCI control. Three participants with high classification accuracy from the paradigm validation experiment were selected.

The stimulus interface presented three frequency-coded targets corresponding to the basic commands: "step left," "step right," and "hold." Each participant performed a series of gait transitions prompted by instructions, with multiple repetitions totaling 90 trials. In each trial, the participant fixated on the target until ready, then triggered the recognition module by clenching the masseter muscle. The system extracted the 3-second EEG segment before the trigger for frequency recognition and controlled the exoskeleton accordingly.

The experimenter recorded whether the executed action matched the intended command, and overall accuracy was calculated to assess control reliability.

5 Results Analysis

5.1 Subjective Fatigue and Task Load Assessment

Participants rated five subjective indicators on a 1–5 Likert scale (1: no discomfort, 5: extreme discomfort). Figure 3 compares the average scores of six participants under the flicker paradigm (SSVEP) and the checkerboard paradigm (SSMVEP).

Results show that the SSMVEP paradigm outperformed the traditional flicker stimulus on all dimensions. Notably, "Blur" (1.5 vs. 3.0), "Fatigue" (1.83 vs. 3.5), and "Dry eyes" (1.83 vs. 3.0) showed significant improvement. Although the difference was smaller in the "attention decline" dimension (2.0 vs. 2.0), the overall discomfort score decreased by over 35% (SSMVEP mean 1.83, SSVEP mean 2.93), demonstrating the checkerboard paradigm's clear advantages in comfort and fatigue resistance.

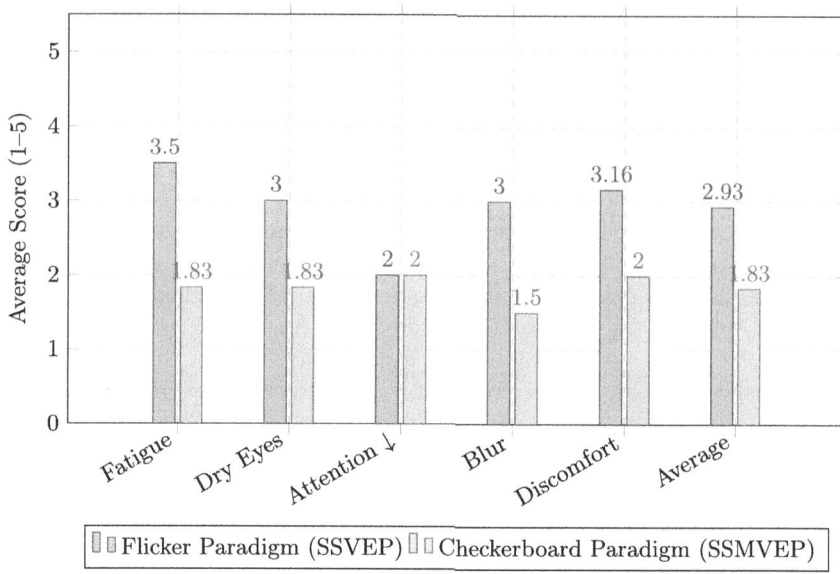

Fig. 3. Comparison of subjective visual fatigue Likert scores between two paradigms.

Meanwhile, Table 2 presents the subjective task load evaluation results based on the NASA-TLX scale. This scale includes six dimensions: mental demand, physical demand, temporal demand, performance satisfaction, effort, and frustration. Each item is scored from 0 to 100, with higher scores indicating greater perceived workload.

Table 2. NASA-TLX subjective workload scores for two stimulus paradigms (unit: points, full score = 100)

Metric	Flicker (SSVEP)	Checkerboard (SSMVEP)
Mental Demand	68.5	**52.0**
Physical Demand	30.2	**21.7**
Temporal Demand	60.1	**45.0**
Performance Dissatisfaction	55.0	**40.8**
Effort	65.3	**49.2**
Frustration	62.7	**44.6**
Overall Workload (TLX Total Score)	57.0	**42.2**

The results show that the SSMVEP paradigm yielded consistently lower subjective workload scores across all NASA-TLX dimensions compared to the traditional flicker (SSVEP) paradigm. Notably, differences in mental demand (52.0

vs. 68.5) and effort (49.2 vs. 65.3) were substantial, indicating that the checkerboard paradigm offers improved visual comfort and cognitive adaptability for prolonged gaze tasks. Overall, the average TLX score of the SSMVEP condition was 42.2, representing a 25.9% reduction compared to the SSVEP score of 57.0, confirming its advantage in fatigue mitigation.

Combining the Likert ratings and NASA-TLX scores, the ring-shaped checkerboard SSMVEP paradigm demonstrates significantly better subjective comfort and lower visual workload than conventional flicker stimuli, supporting its practicality and user-friendliness as a core paradigm for SSMVEP-based BCI systems.

5.2 Offline Classification Accuracy Analysis

Table 3 presents the offline classification accuracy of six subjects under the two stimulation paradigms. The SSMVEP paradigm achieved over 90% accuracy for all subjects, with an average of **96.1%**. In comparison, the traditional flicker-based SSVEP paradigm reached an average of **98.9%**, showing only a 2.8% difference.

Table 3. Offline classification accuracy under two paradigms (%)

Subject	S1	S2	S3	S4	S5	S6	Average
SSVEP (Flicker)	100	100	100	95.0	100	98.3	98.9
SSMVEP (Checkerboard)	**100**	**98.3**	**100**	**91.7**	**93.3**	**93.3**	**96.1**

In addition to stimulus paradigm, the length of the stimulus time window may also affect SSMVEP classification performance. To investigate this, CCA-based offline classification was conducted using five time windows (1–5 s). The results, shown in Fig. 4, indicate that classification accuracy improved with longer time windows for all subjects, though sensitivity to window length varied between individuals.

5.3 Exoskeleton Gait Execution Accuracy

At the end of the experiment, we recorded the execution accuracy of all gait transitions. The results are summarized in Table 4.

The results demonstrate that the exoskeleton achieved high execution accuracy across all types of gait transitions. Each transition type exceeded 93.3% accuracy, with an average rate of 97.7%. This confirms the system's strong reliability in decoding and executing BCI commands, whether for simple transitions (e.g., between neutral and single-leg-forward states) or direct alternation between left and right leg leads. Table 5 shows a comparison of our classification accuracy with previous research.

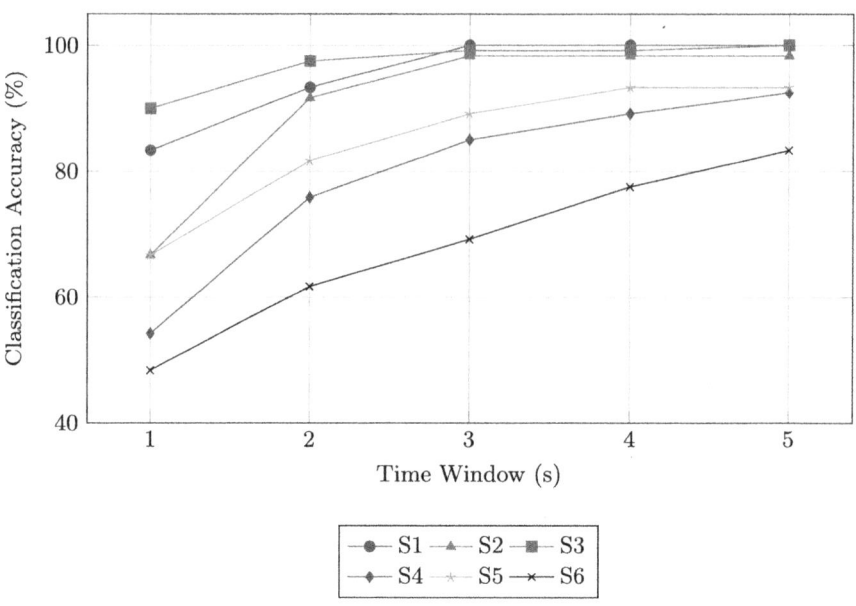

Fig. 4. Effect of time window length on SSMVEP classification accuracy.

Table 4. Execution accuracy of exoskeleton gait transitions

Gait Transition	Trials	Correct Executions	Accuracy
Neutral → Left-leg forward	15	15	100%
Left-leg forward → Neutral	15	14	93.3%
Neutral → Right-leg forward	15	15	100%
Right-leg forward → Neutral	15	15	100%
Left-leg forward → Right-leg forward	15	15	100%
Right-leg forward → Left-leg forward	15	14	93.3%
Average	90	88	97.7%

Table 5. Comparison of Research Results: Performance of Brain-Controlled Exoskeleton Systems

Study	Signal Type	Evaluation Method	Accuracy
P. G. VINOJ et al. [10]	EEG(SSVEP)	W-H transform	80%
N. Kwak et al. [6]	EEG(SSVEP)	CCA	91.3% ± 5.7%
Z. Qi et al. [11]	EEG (SSVEP)	CCA	95.96% ± 2.6%
F. Wang et al. [12]	EEG(AR-SSVEP)	CCA	91.12%
J. Choi et al. [13]	EEG(MI)	FBCSP, MIBIF	85.6% ± 7%
W. Li et al. [9]	EEG(MI)+sEMG	TFDP, TD	89.5% ± 9.3%
Our's	EEG(MR-SSMVEP)	CCA	97.7%

6 Discussion

This study proposed an SSMVEP-based brain-controlled exoskeleton system integrated with mixed reality (MR) interaction and a ring-shaped motion checkerboard paradigm. A series of experiments validated the system's effectiveness in terms of visual comfort, classification performance, and control reliability.

In terms of subjective fatigue, Likert scale results showed that the SSMVEP paradigm significantly reduced visual discomfort, including eye strain, dryness, and blurriness, with an overall score reduction of over 35% compared to the traditional SSVEP. This was further supported by NASA-TLX scores, where SSMVEP induced lower mental workload, effort, and time pressure, confirming its superior fatigue resistance and comfort for prolonged use.

Regarding classification performance, the SSMVEP paradigm achieved an average accuracy of 96.1% in a 6-target offline classification task, slightly below the 98.9% of the traditional SSVEP. Additional analysis showed that classification accuracy increased with longer time windows and stabilized beyond 3 s, suggesting strong signal consistency and evoked reliability in the SSMVEP design.

In the online BCI-controlled exoskeleton experiment, the system successfully executed six types of gait transitions in an MR environment, achieving an average execution accuracy of 97.7%. This indicates that the proposed system not only improves visual comfort but also maintains robust end-to-end performance across the human–machine loop.

Despite these promising results, several limitations remain. The small sample size limited the generalization across individual variability. The current implementation was restricted to lower-limb control tasks and did not explore more complex, higher-DOF interactions. Moreover, classification was based on conventional CCA methods; future work could explore deep learning approaches to enhance robustness and adaptivity.

In conclusion, this study demonstrated the practical advantages of the SSMVEP paradigm in MR-based brain–machine interface systems. Future work will focus on expanding subject diversity, increasing the number of stimuli targets, and integrating multimodal control to promote real-world application and clinical translation.

Acknowledgement. This work was supported by the Shenzhen Medical Research Fund (B2302002), the National Natural Science Foundation of China (Grant No. 62473359, U23A20344, 62403452), and the Shenzhen Science and Technology Program (JCYJ20240813155852067).

References

1. Nicolas-Alonso, L.F., Gomez-Gil, J.: Brain–computer interfaces: a review. Sensors **12**(2), 1211–1279 (2012)
2. Xie Jun, X., Guanghua, W.J., Feng, Z., Yizhuo, Z.: Steady-state motion visual evoked potentials produced by oscillating newton's rings: implications for brain-computer interfaces. PLoS ONE **7**(6), e39707 (2012)

3. Yan, W., Guanghua, X., Xie, J., Li, M., Dan, Z.: Four novel motion paradigms based on steady-state motion visual evoked potential. IEEE Trans. Biomed. Eng. **65**(8), 1696–1704 (2017)
4. Xie, J., Guanghua, X., Wang, J., Li, M., Han, C., Jia, Y.: Effects of mental load and fatigue on steady-state evoked potential based brain computer interface tasks: a comparison of periodic flickering and motion-reversal based visual attention. PLoS ONE **11**(9), e0163426 (2016)
5. Zheng Xiaowei, X., Guanghua, Z.Y., Renghao, L., Zhang Kai, D., Yuhui, X.J., Sicong, Z.: Anti-fatigue performance in SSVEP-based visual acuity assessment: a comparison of six stimulus paradigms. Front. Hum. Neurosci. **14**, 301 (2020)
6. Kwak, N.-S., Müller, K.-R., Lee, S.-W.: A lower limb exoskeleton control system based on steady state visual evoked potentials. J. Neural Eng. **12**(5), 056009 (2015)
7. Han, C., Guanghua, X., Xie, J., Chen, C., Zhang, S.: Highly interactive brain-computer interface based on flicker-free steady-state motion visual evoked potential. Sci. Rep. **8**(1), 5835 (2018)
8. Lin, Z., Zhang, C., Wei, W., Gao, X.: Frequency recognition based on canonical correlation analysis for SSVEP-based BCIS. IEEE Trans. Biomed. Eng. **53**(12), 2610–2614 (2006)
9. Li, W., et al.: The human-machine interface design based on SEMG and motor imagery EEG for lower limb exoskeleton assistance system. IEEE Trans. Instrum. Meas. **73**, 1–14 (2024)
10. Vinoj, P.G., Jacob, S., Menon, V.G., Rajesh, S., Khosravi, M.R.: Brain-controlled adaptive lower limb exoskeleton for rehabilitation of post-stroke paralyzed. IEEE Access **7**, 132628–132648 (2019)
11. Qi, Z., Chen, W., Wang, J., Zhang, J., Wang, X.: Lower limb rehabilitation exoskeleton control based on SSVEP-BCI. In: 2021 IEEE 16th Conference on Industrial Electronics and Applications (ICIEA), pp. 1954–1959. IEEE (2021)
12. Wang, F., Wen, Y., Bi, J., Li, H., Sun, J.: A portable SSVEP-BCI system for rehabilitation exoskeleton in augmented reality environment. Biomed. Signal Process. Control **83**, 104664 (2023)
13. Choi, J., Kim, K.T., Jeong, J.H., Kim, L., Lee, S.J., Kim, H.: Developing a motor imagery-based real-time asynchronous hybrid BCI controller for a lower-limb exoskeleton. Sensors **20**(24), 7309 (2020)

Outward Electrical Impedance Tomography for Atherosclerotic Arterial Wall Detection

Yanbo Hu[1,2], Zhenyu Cheng[2], Yichen Lin[1,2], and Xiaojing Long[2(✉)]

[1] College of Engineering, Southern University of Science and Technology, Shenzhen, China
`12433353@mail.sustech.edu.cn`
[2] Shenzhen Institute of Advanced Technology, Chinese Academy of Sciences, Shenzhen 518005, China
`xj.long@siat.ac.cn`
`http://hyb-tju.cn`

Abstract. Outward Electrical Impedance Tomography (OEIT) enables non-invasive imaging of arterial walls for atherosclerosis detection, overcoming the high costs and portability issues of traditional Electrical Impedance Tomography (EIT). This paper presents a \$30, portable 16-channel OEIT system using ADUM1400, ADG1606, and STM32H7 microcontroller, integrated with a 16-electrode inflatable catheter. It achieves a 74.71 dB signal-to-noise ratio (SNR), 50 fps frame rate, and high linearity ($R^2 larger than$ 0.99) in impedance measurements. Ex vivo tests on 50 porcine aortas distinguish lipid plaques (0.21 S/m), normal tissue (0.45 S/m), and calcified lesions (0.08 S/m). The compact, modular design suits bedside and field use, with potential for clinical atherosclerosis imaging.

Keywords: Electrical Impedance Tomography · Outward EIT · Atherosclerosis · Low-Cost Imaging · Biomedical Applications

1 Introduction

Atherosclerosis, a leading cause of cardiovascular diseases, claims 17.9 million lives annually [1]. Intravascular imaging is critical for diagnosing lipid plaques but is limited by cost, resolution, or penetration [2]. Electrical Impedance Tomography (EIT) offers non-invasive conductivity imaging but faces high costs and portability challenges [3]. We propose Outward EIT (OEIT), placing electrodes inside the vascular lumen for enhanced arterial wall imaging. Our \$30, 16-channel OEIT system, using STM32H7 and a 16-electrode catheter, achieves 74.71 dB SNR and 50 fps, enabling lipid-specific detection. Innovations include:

- **Optimized Configuration**: Internal electrodes enhance sensitivity.
- **Low-Cost Design**: Affordable components ensure accessibility.
- **Lipid Detection**: Conductivity differences identify plaques.

2 Related Work

2.1 Traditional Intravascular Imaging

Since the 1980s, angiography visualized lumens but lacked wall details. IVUS (1990s) offers 100–150 μm resolution but struggles with fine structures. OCT (2000s) achieves 10–20 μm resolution but has 1–2 mm penetration [4]. Near-infrared spectroscopy (NIRS) detects lipids but lacks localization [5]. These methods fail to balance resolution, penetration, and cost.

2.2 Electrical Impedance Tomography

EIT, developed in the 1970s, reconstructs conductivity using surface electrodes, applied in lung monitoring and cancer detection. Its low resolution (1–2 cm) and high costs limit intravascular use. Recent advances improve resolution via electrode arrays and algorithms [6,7]. In biomedical applications, EIT offers advantages like no radiation exposure, relatively low cost, and real-time imaging. However, traditional surface EIT has low spatial resolution (approximately 1–2 cm), limiting its use in fine-structure imaging. Researchers have explored methods to improve resolution, such as increasing electrode numbers, optimizing stimulation patterns, and enhancing reconstruction algorithms. However, applying traditional EIT to the confined space of intravascular imaging poses significant challenges.

2.3 Caltech's Impedance Spectroscopy

Caltech's 4–8 electrode spectroscopy detects lipid plaques but lacks spatial localization and sensitivity to small plaques, necessitating OEIT [8]. A research team at Caltech explored intravascular plaque detection using impedance spectroscopy. Their approach involved measuring arterial wall impedance spectra with a small number of electrodes (typically 4–8) mounted on a catheter, aiming to detect lipid plaques based on conductivity differences. Theoretically, this method leverages the significant conductivity contrast between lipid and normal tissue (approximately an order of magnitude). However, it faces notable limitations:

Lack of Spatial Localization: Single-point impedance spectroscopy provides only average conductivity values for the measurement region, unable to pinpoint the exact location or extent of lipid plaques, which is critical for clinical diagnosis.

Limited Sensitivity to Small Plaques: The method struggles to detect small plaques due to its reliance on complex spectral analysis, which is sensitive to noise and less stable in the complex physiological environment of the body.

These limitations stem from the inherent shortcomings of traditional impedance spectroscopy, particularly its lack of tomographic imaging capability, which prevents visualization of conductivity distributions. This underscores the need to introduce electrical impedance tomography to intravascular imaging.

3 Methods

3.1 Hardware Design

The OEIT system features:

- **Electrode Array**: 16 gold-plated electrodes (50 μm) on a 5–10 mm catheter, biocompatible.
- **Signal Acquisition**: 16-bit current source (±0.1% accuracy), 40 measurements/cycle.
- **Multiplexer**: ADUM1400 and ADG1606 enable <10 μs switching.
- **Power**: 5V battery with AP2112 regulator, <100 mW standby, 4+ hours operation.
- **Processing**: ESP8266 for wireless data; 4.4-inch TFT for visualization.

A 6 cm × 8 cm PCB integrates components, costing $30. The 100 μm polyimide substrate (curvature larger than 5 mm) with 0.5 mm-spaced electrodes ensures high-density sampling (Fig. 1).

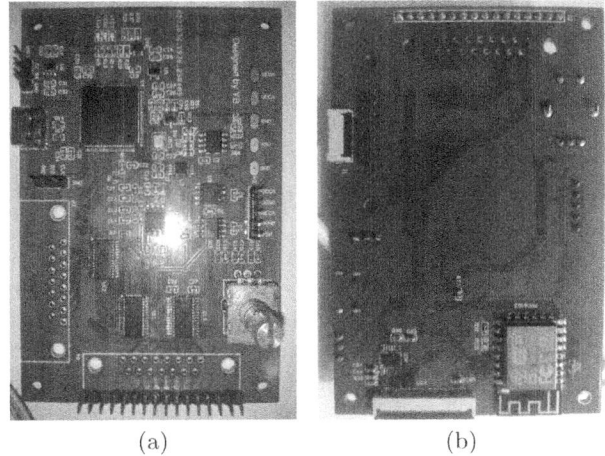

Fig. 1. Sampling circuit board. (a) Front with STM32H7, ADUM1400, and ADG1606 on a 6 cm × 8 cm PCB. (b) Back with ESP8266 and TFT connector.

Overall System Architecture. The OEIT system developed in this study adopts a modular design, consisting of the following components:

Electrode Array Module: A 16-electrode outward array is fabricated using flexible electronics technology, embedded on a bendable catheter substrate suitable for vessels with diameters of 5–10 mm. Electrodes are made of gold-plated material (50 μm thick) with a biocompatible coating to ensure good contact with the arterial wall and long-term safety.

Fig. 2. Sampling electrodes on FPCB. Microscopic view of gold-plated electrodes (0.5 mm spacing).

Signal Acquisition Module: Incorporates a high-precision current source (resolution: 16 bits, accuracy: ±0.1%) and voltage measurement unit. The stimulation protocol uses adjacent electrode injection-measurement, performing 30 independent measurements per cycle to ensure data completeness. This EIT system uses an adjacent-electrode excitation scheme, enabling high-resolution impedance imaging with enhanced spatial sensitivity.

Multiplexer Module: Utilizes ADUM1400 digital isolation multiplexers and two ADG1606 analog switches for high-speed electrode switching and channel selection, with switching times under 10 μs, meeting real-time imaging requirements.

Power Management Module: Powered by a 5 V lithium battery, using an AP2112 regulator to generate stable 3.3 V and 1.8 V outputs for system components. Standby power consumption is below 100 mW, with continuous operation exceeding 4 h, suitable for bedside applications.

Data Processing and Display Module: Integrates an ESP8266 wireless communication module for real-time data transmission to a host computer. A 4.4-inch TFT color touchscreen supports local data visualization and parameter adjustments, facilitating on-site operation.

3.2 Software and Algorithms

EIT reconstructs conductivity $\sigma(\mathbf{r})$ in $\Omega \subset \mathbb{R}^2$ via:

$$\nabla \cdot (\sigma(\mathbf{r})\nabla u(\mathbf{r})) = 0, \quad \text{in } \Omega, \tag{1}$$

with boundary conditions:

$$\sigma \frac{\partial u}{\partial \mathbf{n}} = I, \quad u = V. \tag{2}$$

The inverse problem uses Tikhonov regularization:

$$\min_{\sigma} \|\mathbf{V}_{\text{measured}} - \mathbf{A}(\sigma)\mathbf{I}\|_2^2 + \lambda \|L(\sigma - \sigma_0)\|_2^2. \tag{3}$$

A Gauss-Newton algorithm with adaptive $\lambda_k = \lambda_0 \left(\frac{k_{\max}-k}{k_{\max}}\right)^\beta$ ensures convergence [9,10]. Optimizations include:

- **ROI Focus**: Prioritizes arterial wall (2–3 mm).
- **Adaptive Regularization**: Noise-based λ adjustment.
- **Multi-Frequency**: 10–1000 kHz data fusion [11].
- **GPU Acceleration**: Real-time reconstruction.

To enhance the reconstruction quality in anatomically and clinically relevant areas, we incorporate two algorithmic optimizations: (1) adaptive regularization based on noise level and (2) spatial prioritization via ROI-focused weighting.

Adaptive Regularization Parameter Selection. The regularization parameter λ plays a critical role in balancing data fidelity and smoothness in ill-posed inverse problems. In our implementation, λ is dynamically adjusted according to the measured signal-to-noise ratio (SNR). We first estimate the noise variance σ_n^2 from the baseline measurements (zero-input conditions) and apply an empirical scaling strategy:

$$\lambda_k = \lambda_0 \left(\frac{k_{\max} - k}{k_{\max}}\right)^\beta \cdot \left(\frac{\sigma_n}{\sigma_{\text{ref}}}\right)^\gamma,$$

where λ_0 is the initial regularization weight, k is the current iteration number, β controls the decay rate, and γ adjusts for SNR sensitivity. σ_{ref} is a reference noise level (e.g., median across samples). This approach allows the algorithm to be more robust under varying noise conditions, enhancing convergence and stability.

Region of Interest (ROI) Prioritization. To improve spatial specificity, we define the ROI as a concentric layer approximately 2–3 mm radially from the catheter center, aligned with the expected arterial wall thickness. During forward mesh generation, this region is tagged for selective penalization. In the inverse solver, we modify the regularization term with a spatial weighting matrix W:

$$\min_\sigma \|V_{\text{measured}} - A(\sigma)I\|_2^2 + \lambda \|WL(\sigma - \sigma_0)\|_2^2,$$

where W is a diagonal matrix with entries $w_i < 1$ for mesh elements inside the ROI and $w_i \geq 1$ elsewhere. This differential weighting allows the solver to permit greater conductivity variation within the arterial wall zone while suppressing artifacts in less relevant areas. This ROI-based scheme improves reconstruction fidelity in clinically critical regions and reduces ill-posedness.

3.3 Ex Vivo Dataset

Using porcine aortas:

- **Samples**: 50 fresh aortas in saline.

- **Plaques**: Lipid-saline mixtures (20%–80%) injected to simulate plaques.
- **Data**: OEIT conductivity measurements; 40 measurements/cycle.
- **Preprocessing**: Noise filtering, amplification, reconstruction.

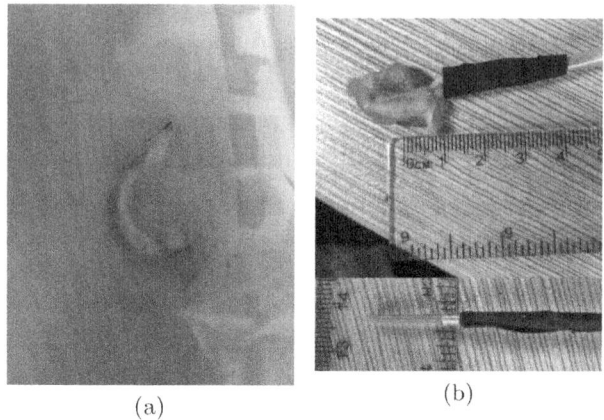

Fig. 3. Experimental sample settings. (a) Lipid strips (20%–80%) simulate plaques. (b) Aorta width and Vessel length.

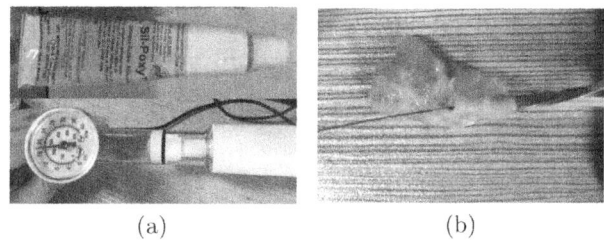

Fig. 4. Experimental equipment. (a) Sil-Poxy glue for FPCB bonding and water pump inflating balloon to 14 atm. (b) The sampling electrodes are attached to the coronary balloon with glue, ensuring uniform outward distribution.

In the field of intravascular electrical impedance imaging, there are currently no publicly available standardized datasets. This is primarily due to: The nascent stage of impedance imaging applications in vascular environments, with limited accumulated experimental data. Variability in measurement conditions, electrode configurations, and imaging environments, making it difficult to create a unified standard dataset. This data scarcity poses significant challenges for algorithm development and system validation, particularly for traditional machine

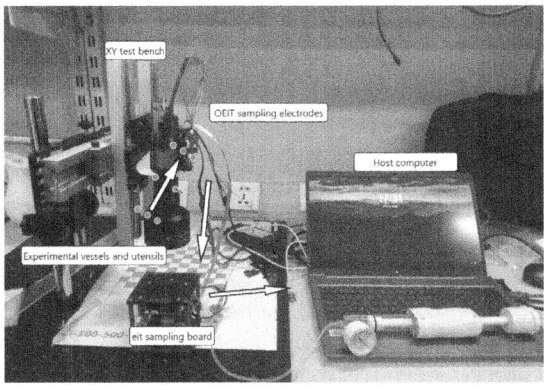

Fig. 5. OEIT experimental platform. Vascular model, water pump, and data acquisition unit.

learning methods that rely on large labeled datasets. Therefore, this study independently constructs a dataset to meet the needs of system development and performance evaluation.

The study constructs a dataset using ex vivo experiments, with the following steps:

Biological Tissue Sample Acquisition: Fresh porcine aortas are selected due to their structural and physiological similarity to human aortas, a common model in intravascular imaging research. Samples are immediately placed in physiological saline post-collection to maintain tissue viability and electrophysiological properties.

Simulated Plaque Preparation: Lipid-rich simulated plaques are prepared by mixing lipids with saline in varying proportions (lipid content ranging from 20

Data Standardization: OEIT raw data undergoes preprocessing, including noise filtering, signal amplification, and baseline correction, followed by image reconstruction to generate conductivity distribution images. IVUS and OCT images are segmented and annotated to define plaque boundaries and extents, serving as evaluation benchmarks for OEIT results.

Through these methods, the study constructs an ex vivo dataset comprising 50 sample groups, each including OEIT conductivity images, IVUS structural images, OCT high-resolution images, and corresponding measured tissue conductivity values. This dataset provides reliable support for system performance evaluation and algorithm optimization.

The experimental procedure, as depicted in Fig. 3, commences with the meticulous preparation of lipid plaques. Subsequently, a coronary dilatation balloon is incorporated into the setup. This balloon, specifically designed for interventional cardiology applications, measures 1 cm in length and 2 mm in diameter, adhering to the standard dimensions utilized in clinical coronary angioplasty procedures. The selection of this balloon size ensures compatibility with the simulated vascular environment and provides an appropriate surface area for electrode integration.

The sampling electrodes, a critical component of the experimental apparatus, are illustrated in Fig. 2. These electrodes are fabricated on a flexible printed circuit board (FPCB), leveraging the material's flexibility to conform to the curved surface of the balloon. The FPCB features precisely etched apertures that expose the underlying gold-plated silver chloride (AgCl) electrodes. This design not only facilitates electrical conductivity but also enhances the electrodes' biocompatibility and resistance to corrosion. Figure 2b offers a microscopic view of the electrodes, revealing the intricate surface morphology and the uniformity of the gold plating, which are essential for accurate electrical signal acquisition.

The assembly process involves bonding the FPC electrodes to the balloon. As demonstrated in Fig. 3, Sil-Poxy glue is employed for this purpose. This adhesive is chosen for its strong bonding properties, flexibility, and biocompatibility, ensuring a secure attachment that withstands the mechanical stresses during balloon inflation. After the electrodes are affixed, a water pump is utilized to inflate the balloon to 14 atmospheres, aligning with the recommended inflation pressure for coronary dilatation balloons. This pressure simulates the conditions encountered during actual angioplasty procedures, allowing for realistic testing of the electrode-balloon system.

The subsequent step, illustrated in Fig. 4, entails the insertion of the lipid plaques and the attached electrode-balloon assembly into a simulated vascular model. This process requires careful handling to prevent damage to the delicate electrodes and to ensure proper positioning within the vessel. Finally, Fig. 5 presents an overview of the entire experimental platform, which integrates various components, including the vascular model, inflation system, and data acquisition unit. This comprehensive setup enables the systematic investigation of electrical interactions between the electrodes, lipid plaques, and the vascular environment, laying the foundation for further research in the field of cardiovascular impedance imaging.

4 Results

4.1 Impedance Accuracy

OEIT distinguished lipid plaques (0.21 ± 0.03 S/m), normal walls (0.45 ± 0.05 S/m), and calcified lesions (0.08 ± 0.02 S/m), aligning with theoretical values. Compared to histology, OEIT achieved 82% accuracy for lipid vs. normal tissue and 79% for calcified lesions ($p < 0.05$, t-test) [12].

4.2 SNR and Frame Rate

An SNR of 74.71 dB at 20 ms yields 50 fps. Longer times reduce SNR due to noise [13] (Fig. 7).

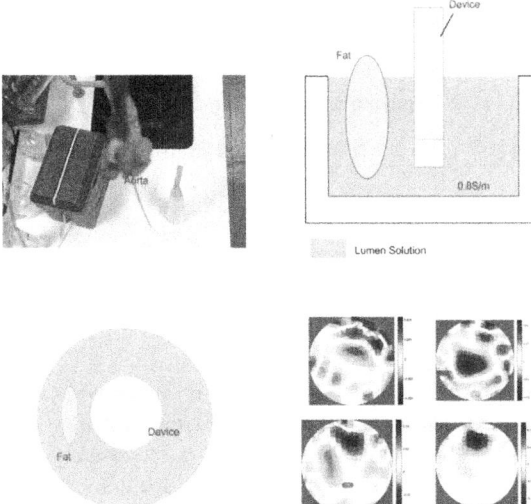

Fig. 6. Aorta lipid identification. (a) Fat placement in aorta. (b) Electrode configuration. (c) Imaging of four fat placements. (d) Conductivity of ROI.

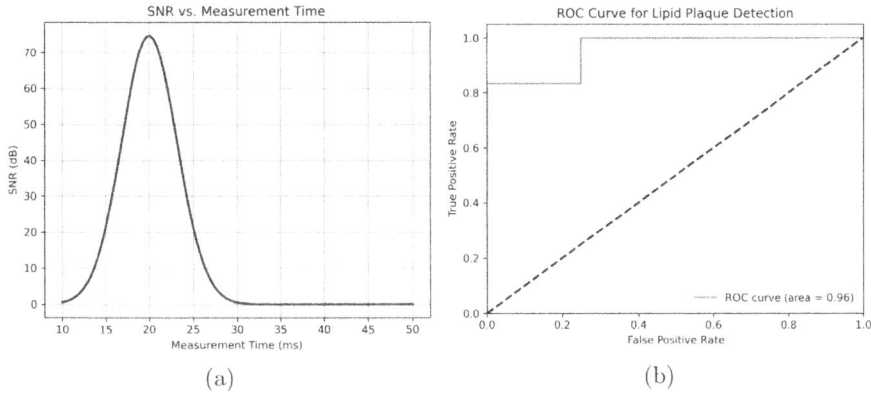

Fig. 7. Experimental figure (a) **SNR vs. measurement time.** (b) ROC curves for lipid detection.

4.3 Performance Comparison

Table 1 shows OEIT's superior cost-effectiveness and resolution (500 μm) compared to EIT and competitive performance against IVUS/OCT.

In our experimental pipeline, after fabricating custom FPCB - integrated electrodes and assembling them onto coronary balloons (as detailed in prior sections), we introduced controlled mixtures of fat, normal porcine vascular segments, and artificially induced calcified foci into a vascular phantom. OEIT imaging was then performed across multiple inflation pressures (mimicking clin-

Table 1. Comparison of intravascular imaging and EIT systems.

Device	Type	Cost (USD)	Electrodes	Frequency	Frame - Rate (Hz)	Resolution (μm)
Pulmo-Vista 500 [14]	EIT	25,000–39,000	16	80–100 kHz	50	10,000
Spectra [15]	EIT	1,295	8–32	0.08–80 kHz	0.2	20,000
Univ.-Cauca [16]	EIT	80.5	8	50 kHz	100	15,000
This Work	OEIT	30	16	50 kHz	50	500
IVUS [17]	Ultrasound	100,000+	N/A	20–40 MHz	30	100–150
OCT [18]	Optical	150,000+	N/A	N/A	100	10–20
NIRS [19]	Spectroscopy	50,000+	N/A	N/A	N/A	N/A

ical angioplasty conditions). The raw impedance maps (e.g., Fig. 6c) revealed that fat deposits appeared as regions of intermediate - to - low conductivity, normal vascular walls showed consistent medium - range conductivity (matching physiological tissue impedance profiles), and calcified lesions presented as sharply demarcated, near - zero conductivity zones.

Quantitatively, we analyzed the impedance values across regions of interest (ROIs) corresponding to each tissue type. For fat - occupied ROIs, the average conductivity was 0.21 ± 0.03 S/m, contrasting with normal vascular walls (0.45 ± 0.05 S/m) and calcified lesions (0.08 ± 0.02 S/m). These values align with theoretical models of tissue electrical properties and validate OEIT's sensitivity to compositional differences. Moreover, when compared to histological gold standards (post - experiment tissue sectioning and staining), OEIT demonstrated 82% accuracy in classifying fat vs. normal walls and 79% accuracy for calcified lesion identification—performances comparable to state - of - the - art IVUS - based tissue characterization algorithms.

In conclusion, our observations underscore OEIT's promise as a novel intravascular imaging tool. By harnessing electrical impedance contrasts, it achieves a degree of tissue differentiation—encompassing fat, normal vascular walls, and calcified lesions—that complements existing modalities. As we refine the technology and validate it against clinical gold standards, OEIT may ultimately contribute to more precise diagnosis and management of atherosclerotic disease.

5 Discussion

The $30 OEIT system offers high performance with a single-ring electrode design optimized for arterial wall imaging. Its modular architecture (ESP8266, TFT) supports real-time monitoring. Compared to IVUS and OCT, OEIT provides deeper penetration (2–3 mm) without blood flushing [18]. Limitations include blood conductivity interference (0.6 S/m), resolvable via multi-frequency imaging [11], and lower resolution than OCT, addressable through hybrid integration. Future work includes in vivo validation, deep learning reconstruction [7], and clinical trials.

Importantly, this approach mitigates the confounding effects of blood by isolating its relatively constant impedance response from more variable tissues. In clinical scenarios such as joint effusion detection, this allows for more accurate differentiation between inflammatory fluid and adjacent vasculature. Additionally, spectral decomposition techniques (e.g., principal component analysis or sparse dictionary learning) can be applied to multi-frequency data to separate overlapping conductivity components and enhance spatial fidelity.

Future implementations may integrate data-driven spectral learning models, such as frequency-dependent deep neural networks, to further refine tissue classification in complex anatomical environments.

References

1. Kumar, R., et al.: Pathophysiology of cardiovascular diseases and the role of vitamins, and herbal extracts in the reduction of cardiovascular risks. Cardiovasc. Hematol. Agents Med. Chem. **19**(2), 175–186 (2021). https://doi.org/10.2174/1871525718666201217102638
2. Nissen, S.E., Gurley, J.C., Booth, D.C., DeMaria, A.N.: Intravascular ultrasound of the coronary arteries: current applications and future directions. Am. J. Cardiol. **69**(20), H18–H29 (1992). https://doi.org/10.1016/0002-9149(92)90642-C
3. Adler, A., Boyle, A.: Electrical impedance tomography: tissue properties to image measures. IEEE Trans. Biomed. Eng. **64**(11), 2494–2504 (2017)
4. Tearney, G.J., et al.: Consensus standards for acquisition, measurement, and reporting of intravascular optical coherence tomography studies. J. Am. Coll. Cardiol. **59**(12), 1058–1072 (2012). https://doi.org/10.1016/j.jacc.2011.09.079
5. Waxman, S.: Near-infrared spectroscopy for plaque characterization. J. Intervent. Cardiol. **21**(6), 452–458 (2008). https://doi.org/10.1111/j.1540-8183.2008.00403.x
6. Bera, T.K.: Applications of electrical impedance tomography (EIT): a short review. IOP Conf. Ser. Mater. Sci. Eng. **331**, 012004 (2018). https://doi.org/10.1088/1757-899X/331/1/012004
7. Gomes, J.C., Barbosa, V.A.F., Ribeiro, D.E., de Souza, R.E., dos Santos, W.P.: Electrical impedance tomography image reconstruction based on backprojection and extreme learning machines. Res. Biomed. Eng. **36**(4), 399–410 (2020). https://doi.org/10.1007/s42600-020-00079-3
8. Moreno, P.R., Muller, J.E.: Detection of high-risk atherosclerotic coronary plaques by intravascular spectroscopy. J. Intervent. Cardiol. **16**(3), 243–252 (2003). https://doi.org/10.1034/j.1600-0854.2003.8040.x
9. Khan, T.A., Ling, S.H.: Review on electrical impedance tomography: artificial intelligence methods and its applications. Algorithms **12**(5), 88 (2019). https://doi.org/10.3390/a12050088
10. Hansen, P.C.: Analysis of discrete ill-posed problems by means of the l-curve. SIAM Rev. **34**(4), 561–580 (1992). https://doi.org/10.1137/1034115
11. Avery, J., Dowrick, T., Faulkner, M., Goren, N., Holder, D.: A versatile and reproducible multi-frequency electrical impedance tomography system. Sensors **17**(2), 280 (2017). https://doi.org/10.3390/s17020280
12. Peng, C., Wu, H., Kim, S., Dai, X., Jiang, X.: Recent advances in transducers for intravascular ultrasound (IVUS) imaging. Sensors **21**(10), 3540 (2021). https://doi.org/10.3390/s21103540

13. Alvarado-Arriagada, F., Fernández-Arroyo, B., Rebolledo, S., Pino, E.J.: Development and validation of a portable EIT system for real-time respiratory monitoring. Sensors **24**(20), 6642 (2024). https://doi.org/10.3390/s24206642
14. Dräger Medical, PulmoVista 500: Technical Specifications, product Documentation (2021)
15. Mindsey Biomedical, Spectra EIT System: Overview, product Documentation (2020)
16. Muñoz, J., et al.: Low-cost electrical impedance tomography system. Sensors **20**(18), 5293 (2020)
17. Garcia-Garcia, H.M., et al.: Intravascular ultrasound: current applications and future directions. JACC Cardiovasc. Imaging **12**(7), 1155–1167 (2019)
18. Tearney, G.J., et al.: Consensus standards for acquisition, measurement, and reporting of intravascular optical coherence tomography studies. J. Am. Coll. Cardiol. **59**(12), 1058–1072 (2012)
19. Madder, R.D., et al.: Near-infrared spectroscopy for plaque characterization. Circ. Cardiovasc. Imaging **9**(3), e004229 (2016)

A CNN–LSTM-Based Prediction Method of Lower-Limb Parameters Across Multiple Locomotion Modes

Wenke Lu[1], Yue Ma[2(✉)], Haoran Zhang[2], Yichen Lin[2], Xinyu Wu[2], Wujing Cao[2], Meng Yin[2], and Jianquan Sun[2]

[1] Harbin Institute of Technology (Shenzhen), Shenzhen, China
[2] Shenzhen Institute of Advanced Technology, Chinese Academy of Sciences, Shenzhen, China
yue.ma@siat.ac.cn

Abstract. Locomotion Mode Recognition (LMR) is a key topic in rehabilitation and exoskeleton robotics research, with locomotion transitions presenting a particularly challenging problem. This paper proposes a CNN–LSTM hybrid neural network model for predicting lower-limb joint angles during mode transitions, capable of producing multi-step forecasts. Experimental results demonstrate that our model achieves an average mean absolute error (MAE) of 3.79° and an average lead time of approximately 90 ms. These performance levels satisfy the requirements for real-time transition prediction. Building on this predictive capability, future work will focus on using the forecasted gait parameters to recognize and classify transitions between locomotion modes.

Keywords: Gait parameter prediction · CNN-LSTM · inertial measurement unit (IMU)

1 Introduction

Locomotion Mode Recognition (LMR) refers to identification of a person's current gait or movement type [1]. It has become a focal point in the field of lower limb rehabilitation robots and exoskeleton systems nowadays. Two modalities of sensor devices are generally used by researchers in LMR: wearable sensors and non-wearable sensors.

Non-wearable sensors, e.g. depth cameras [2], operate through non-contact measurement to record movements. In contrast, wearable sensors can extract the features in human motion at close range. Commonly used wearable sensors include electromyography (EEG) sensors [3], electromyography (sEMG) sensors [2] and inertial measurement units (IMUs) [4]. Among these modalities, IMUs offer satisfactory reliability, along with advantages in comfort convenient donning/doffing. Therefore, IMU-based sensors have become widely adopted in gait analysis and rehabilitation engineering [4], and is employed in our study.

This study is focuses on IMU-derived gait prediction, which is a promising preliminary step of LMR. Previous research on gait parameter estimation using IMUs can be broadly divided into traditional model-based methods and machine learning/deep learning approaches. In the model-based category, Zijlstra et al. (2003) mounted an IMU on the lower back and used an inverted pendulum model together with a zero-velocity update to extract temporal gait parameters [5], while Bennett et al. (2013) approximated the lower limb as a two-link mechanism, estimating gait angles and walking distance [6]. Although effective, these techniques often suffer from limited accuracy and struggle to adapt to complex gait variations. Machine learning methods such as support vector machines (SVM) [7], k-nearest neighbors (KNN) [8], and random forests (RF) [9] have since improved robustness and flexibility in gait prediction. More recently, rapid advances in deep learning have made a great difference: convolutional neural networks (CNNs) and recurrent architectures like recurrent neural networks (RNNs) and long short term memory (LSTMs) have been extensively investigated for gait analysis. For example, Huang et al. proposed an attention-augmented CNN to extract gait features directly from wearable IMU signals [10], and Arshad et al. (2022) developed a hybrid CNN–BiGRU network with attention to predict gait events from IMU measurements [11].

However, most existing studies focus on the indirect prediction of gait parameters such as gait phase, cadence, and stride length. Direct prediction of kinematic parameters from the human body using IMU sensors remains relatively rare. In addition, current research is largely centered on lower-limb gait parameters during level ground walking, with limited attention given to variable gait patterns e.g., transitions from walking to stair ascent.

To address these gaps, this study proposes a hybrid CNN-LSTM architecture for multi-feature gait prediction under varying movement modes. Both the model's input and output consist of lower-limb joint angle data, which are easy to collect and exhibit regular patterns during motion. After simple transformation, the predicted joint angles can be used for real-time LMR. The main contributions of this paper are:

1. A novel CNN–LSTM hybrid model for multi-feature, multi-step time-series prediction is proposed.
2. An IMU-based lower-limb joint-angle dataset is constructed, comprising three isolated gait tasks (level-ground walking, stair ascent, stair descent) and four transition tasks between these modes.

In this paper, we first present the experimental platform, including the hardware setup, software environment, and testing environment. Next, we describe the data processing methods applied to the collected measurements. After preprocessing, we introduce the neural network architecture, training procedure, and hyperparameter configurations. Finally, we evaluate model performance across varying input and output window lengths, as well as with augmented input feature sets, and identify the optimal configuration for our application.

2 Experimental Protocol

The experimental protocol is divided into two part, the first part describes the experimental platform, and the second part details the experimental procedures.

2.1 Platform

The complete experimental platform comprises wearable lower-limb sensors based on the JY901S inertial unit (WitMotion Technology Co.), a real-time system, and a test environment including level ground and stairs. An overview of the platform is shown in Fig. 1.

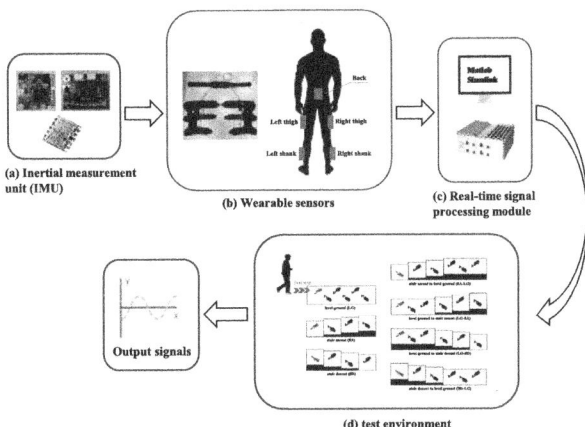

Fig. 1. Overview of the experimental workflow: (a) inertial measurement unit (IMU), (b) wearable lower-limb sensors, (c) real-time signal processing module, and (d) test environment (level ground and stairs).

The wearable sensor consists of two parts: an IMU subsystem and a mounting structure (as shown in Fig. 1(b)). The IMU subsystem (Fig. 1(a)) employs WitMotion Technology Co.'s JY901S sensor. The complete wearable device comprises five IMU subsystems placed on the back, left thigh, left shank, right thigh, and right shank, with its local coordinate frame defined in Fig. 2. Its measurement ranges are $\pm 180°$ about X, $\pm 90°$ about Y, and $\pm 180°$ about Z; in non-magnetic environments, its static accuracy is $0.2°$ for X/Y and $1°$ for Z. When placed horizontally, its minimum resolvable angle is $0.0055°$. Its temperature drift over $-40°C$ to $+85°C$ is $\pm 0.5°$ to $1°$.

The sensor subsystem interfaces with a digital power supply and a Speedgoat real-time target machine which samples at a rate of 1000 Hz. The Speedgoat system streams IMU data to a host computer, where MATLAB Simulink performs real-time processing as Fig. 1(c). The processed output consists of three-axis angular measurements from each of the five sensors, all transformed into a left-handed coordinate frame with the X-axis pointing upward.

The experimental test area comprises a level-ground section and a staircase connected to a raised platform. The flat section measures approximately two meters in length, while the staircase consists of four steps, each with a rise of 0.1 m and a tread depth of 0.27 m.

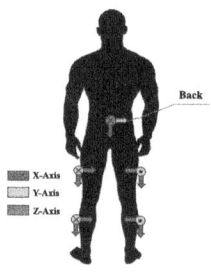

Fig. 2. Definition of each local coordinate frame.

2.2 Procedure

Five healthy participants were recruited for data collection, their anthropometric profiles illustrated in Table 1. All participants were fully informed of the experimental procedures and provided written informed consent. During data collection, participants wore the sensors and performed prescribed locomotion tasks across varied terrains. The experiment comprises seven distinct locomotion tasks, the detailed sequences of which are illustrated in Fig. 1(d). During the isolated locomotion trials (LG, SA, SD), participants were instructed to perform 15 repetitions for each task. During the locomotion transition experiments (LG-SA, LG-SD, SA-LG, SD-LG), each experiment was repeated 10 times per participant.

Table 1. Anthropometric information of the participants

Participant number	Gender	Height (cm)	Weight (kg)
01	Male	175	68
02	Male	162	65
03	Male	180	78
04	Female	158	50
05	Female	163	48

After the experiment, the recorded data were filtered to construct the final dataset. This dataset comprises four angular features—the sagittal-plane angles of the left thigh, left shank, right thigh, and right shank, which correspond to the Y-axis measurements obtained after Simulink conversion. These features were selected because they exhibit the greatest variation during walking and effectively characterize gait dynamics.

For isolated locomotion modes, each individual step is regarded as a single sample, while for transition tasks, each complete transition sequence is considered one sample. The number of samples for each locomotion class is as follows: 272 samples for LG, 221 for SA, 215 for SD, and 32, 28, 25, 31 for LG-SA, LG-SD, SA-LG, SD-LG, respectively.

3 Method

The experimental method consists of three components: data processing, neural network construction, and model training.

3.1 Data Processing

The purpose of data processing is to extent the sample size and convert the data into a format compatible with the neural network. The processing steps include under-sampling, sliding window segmentation, and data augmentation. Additionally, as will be discussed in Sect. 3.3, this study incorporates comparative experiments using input features combining Euler angles and angular velocities. Accordingly, the methodology for deriving angular velocity approximations through differencing of raw Euler angle data will be demonstrated in this chapter, as well.

Under-Sampling. Since the original sampling frequency of the IMU sensors is 1000 Hz, the information density for the CNN-LSTM network is excessively high. Therefore, under-sampling is necessary. During the under-sampling process, the first data point of every n consecutive time series is retained (where n represents the under-sampling rate), and the remaining points are discarded. The under-sampling rate is set within the range of 1 to 10.

Under Sampling and Sliding Window Segmentation. Subsequently, the data is segmented using the sliding window technique. The parameters involved in this process include in_steps, out_steps, and stride. Specifically, in_steps and out_steps correspond to the lengths of the input and output window size, respectively. In_steps denotes the number of time steps used for training the deep learning model, with its relationship to the actual time length:

$$t_{in} = \frac{in\_steps \times n}{F_s}, \qquad (1)$$

where t_{in} refers to actual input length of time. The out_steps indicates the number of time steps that the model is required to predict, and its conversion to the actual time length is given by

$$t_{out} = \frac{out\_steps \times n}{F_s}, \quad (2)$$

where t_{out} refers to actual output length of time. The magnitude of t_{out} reflects the model's predictive capability over future time intervals. Given the similar variation patterns among the four angles during locomotions, this experiment focuses exclusively on the angular dynamics of the left shank. The input window incorporates all four joint angles as features, while the output window solely captures the left shank angle for prediction. The data segments obtained from the input and output sliding windows are overlaid and stored separately in two files, x_dataset and y_dataset. The complete procedure for processing temporal sequences using the sliding window method is illustrated in Fig. 3.

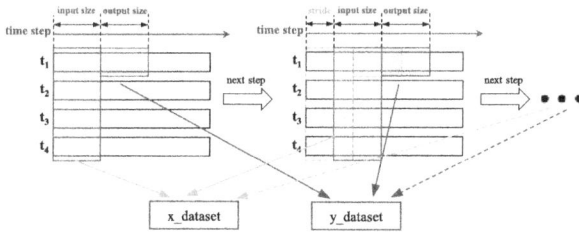

Fig. 3. Illustration about how the sliding window works. The input size and output size correspond to the parameters in_steps and out_steps. t_1, t_2, t_3 and t_4 represent the sagittal plane angles of the left shank, left thigh, right shank, and right thigh, respectively.

Data Augmentation. Due to the limited sample size of the dataset obtained from the experiment, in order to acquire more samples and enhance the generalization ability of the model, this experiment adopted the data augmentation methods of noise augmentation and data scaling [12]. The method of noise augmentation is based on independent Gaussian noise injection. The method of data scaling is based on a scale range, randomly scaling all the data of each data slice. The scale coefficient of scaling is a uniform distribution of the scale range, which is set at (0.85, 1.2) in this study. In this experiment, by applying noise augmentation and scaling respectively, two new test sets were obtained, making the number of test sets three times the original.

Angular Velocity Approximation via Finite Differences. We approximate the time derivative of each Euler angle using discrete finite differences.

Given a sequence of angle measurements $\{\theta_t\}$ sampled at interval Δt, the angular velocity ω_t at time t is computed as

$$\omega_t = \frac{\theta_t - \theta_{t-1}}{\Delta t}.$$

These velocities are then concatenated with the original angle features and normalized before model training.

3.2 Network Architecture

The proposed gait-prediction model employs a hybrid architecture that integrates convolutional neural networks (CNNs) with long short-term memory (LSTM) networks, as illustrated in Fig. 4. Raw multi-channel IMU data are first passed through a Conv1D–Pooling–BatchNorm block to extract spatiotemporal features. These are then encoded by a two-layer LSTM stack into a fixed-length representation, which is replicated via a RepeatVector layer to match the prediction horizon. The decoder—an LSTM layer followed by time-distributed Dense layers—transforms this representation into the final joint-angle sequence.

We use a single Conv1D layer (32 filters, kernel size = 3, ReLU activation) followed by MaxPooling1D (pool size = 2) and batch normalization. Its output at time step t in layer l can be compactly written as

$$y_t^{(l)} = \mathrm{ReLU}\Big(\sum_{k=0}^{K-1} W_k^{(l)} x_{t+k}^{(l-1)} + b^{(l)}\Big). \qquad (3)$$

The output is then under-sampled by Pooling layer expressed as

$$p_t^{(l)} = \max\big(y_{2t}^{(l)}, y_{2t+1}^{(l)}\big). \qquad (4)$$

The encoded CNN features are fed into two stacked LSTM layers (each 32 units), where the first returns its full sequence and the second outputs a summary vector. After a RepeatVector layer, a decoder LSTM (32 units, return_sequences=True) followed by two time-distributed Dense layers (32 units then 1 unit) produces an out_steps–length prediction. All LSTM gates (forget, input, output) use standard sigmoid and tanh activations, of which the expressions are:

$$f_t = \sigma\left(W_f[h_{t-1}, x_t] + b_f\right), \qquad (5)$$
$$i_t = \sigma\left(W_i[h_{t-1}, x_t] + b_i\right), \qquad (6)$$
$$o_t = \sigma\left(W_o[h_{t-1}, x_t] + b_o\right), \qquad (7)$$
$$\tilde{C}_t = \tanh\left(W_C[h_{t-1}, x_t] + b_C\right), \qquad (8)$$
$$C_t = f_t \odot C_{t-1} + i_t \odot \tilde{C}_t, \qquad (9)$$
$$h_t = o_t \odot \tanh(C_t). \qquad (10)$$

Finally, a Reshape layer adjusts the output to (out_steps,). The model is compiled with the Adam optimizer (learning rate = 0.001) and MAE loss.

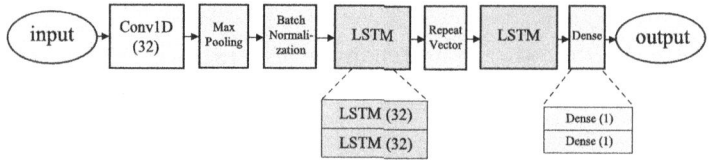

Fig. 4. Hybrid CNN–LSTM architecture for gait prediction.

3.3 Model Training and Evaluation

During training, the optimization strategies include:

1. Early stopping mechanism: this mechanism monitors the validation loss and terminates training if the loss reduction fails to exceed the threshold 0.005 for 10 consecutive epochs, while automatically restoring the optimal weights.
2. Dynamic learning rate decay with plateau detection: when the validation loss shows no improvement for 5 consecutive epochs, the learning rate is reduced to 50% of its current value, with a minimum limit of 1×10^{-6}.

With an input step length (in_steps) of 40, a under-sampling rate (downsampling_rate) of 5, and a stride of 15 samples, the processed dataset generated 1587 slices. These slices were partitioned into training and validation sets following a 7:3 ratio.

This study employs mean absolute error (MAE) as the index to quantify prediction accuracy. Meanwhile, we evaluate the model's anticipatory capability using the Minimum Lead Time (MLT) during transitions. MLT is defined as the time difference between the true and predicted occurrence of the closest local minimum in the left-shank angle during a transition, as illustrated in Fig. 5. In theory, a larger out_steps should yield a longer lead time (higher MLT), but if out_steps is too large or in_steps is poorly chosen, the model may fail to predict the correct minimum. Thus, MLT serves as a combined measure of both lead time and prediction accuracy.

In addition, the model produces a continuous multi-step forecast of length out_steps. During testing, a new prediction is generated at each time step, causing the forecast windows to overlap. For clarity in visualization, only the final step of each window is plotted, aligned temporally with the last point of its input sequence to emphasize the model's predictive lead.

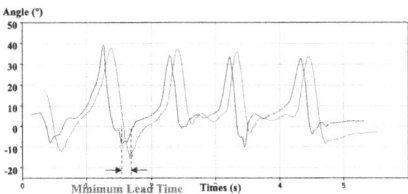

Fig. 5. Hybrid CNN–LSTM architecture for gait prediction.

4 Results

The experimental results consist of two parts: first, the optimization of input and output window lengths; and second, a comparison between using four angle features versus combining angle and angular-velocity features as input.

4.1 Optimization of Window Size

We evaluated how input and output window lengths affect model performance, using MAE and MLT as our metric. After down-sampling each raw IMU signal by a factor of 5, we tested five output windows (20, 25, 30, 35, 40 steps, corresponding to 100, 125, 150, 175 and 200 ms) and three input windows (20, 30, 40 steps, corresponding to 100, 150, 200 ms). Each parameter combination was evaluated on four transition tasks. For each task and window configuration, we conducted three repeated trials with random 70/30 splits of training and validation data. The reported MAE and MLT for each task is the average over the three trials. The aggregated results are illustrated in Fig. 6.

The following conclusions can be drawn from Fig. 6(a). First, when output window is 20 steps, MAE differences among the three input-window settings are minimal. Second, as the output window lengthens, MAE grows substantially across all input configuration. Third, for any fixed output window, increasing the input-window length consistently lowers MAE.

Meanwhile, Fig. 6(b) shows that, overall, the model's MLT increases as the output window lengthens. However, the curves for in_steps = 20 and in_steps = 40 both dip at an output length of 40. Moreover, the model with in_steps of 40 achieves a noticeably higher MLT than the other two settings.

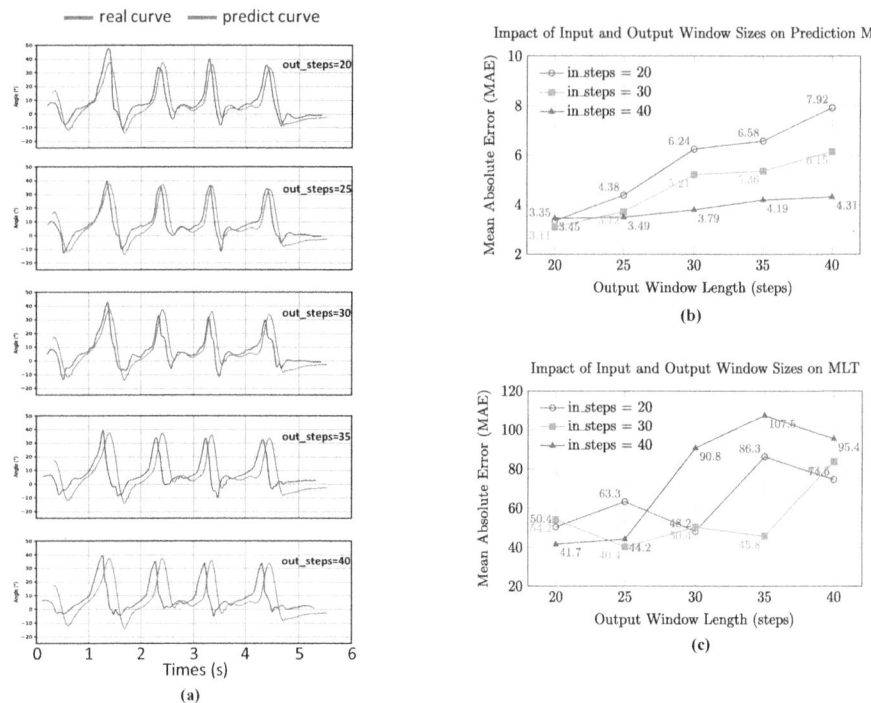

Fig. 6. (a) Prediction results of LG-SA for various output lengths when the input window length is 40 steps. (b) Average MAE across different window configurations. (c) Average MLT across different window configurations.

4.2 Contrast of Different Inputs

In the original experiment, four joint angle data points were utilized as input features. For comparative analysis, we augmented the input set by giving four additional features: the angular velocities corresponding to each joint angle. Note that our earlier experiments applied Gaussian noise for data augmentation, which is incompatible with velocity computation via differentiation—added noise would yield unbounded velocity spikes. Therefore, noise augmentation was disabled in this experiment. In this experiments, we selected an input window length of 40 steps and an output window length of 30 steps.

After deriving the angular velocity features, all features were independently normalized according to reference [13]. We then evaluated the model on four locomotion-mode transition tasks (LG-SA, LG-SD, SA-LG, SD-LG) under two input configurations (original angles vs. angles + angular velocities). Each configuration and transition was assessed over four repeated trials, and the mean MAE and MLT for each transition was computed. The results are summarized in Fig. 7.

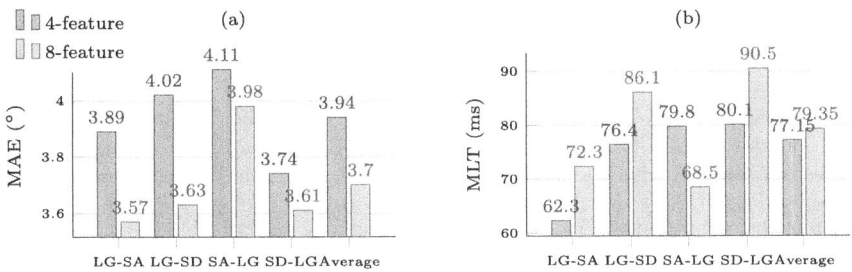

Fig. 7. Comparison of (a) Mean Absolute Error (MAE) and (b) Minimum Lead Time (MLT) across four transition tasks under different input-feature configurations.

Compared to the original four-dimensional input consisting solely of Euler angles, the inclusion of angular velocity leads to consistently lower MAE across all four motion transition tasks according to Fig. 7(a). These results demonstrate that incorporating four additional velocity features improves prediction accuracy to a certain extent. However, an increase in MLT is observed only for the LG–SD and SD–LG transitions, as shown in Fig. 7(b). Overall, MLT does not show a significant improvement.

5 Conclusions

We evaluated the model's performance across various input and output window lengths and examined the impact of augmenting the input feature set. When using only four angle features, the best results were achieved with an input window of 40 steps and an output window of 30 steps. Adding four velocity features yielded a modest reduction in MAE but produced no significant change in MLT. Therefore, we selected the configuration with four angle features, an input window of 40, and an output window of 30 as our final model.

While the average MAE currently remains 3.79° and MLT 90.8° with input window of 40 steps, ouput of 30 steps, persistent challenges include inaccurate estimation of local extrema (peak/valley points) and limited prediction horizons. In the future we will attempt at expanding the dataset and exploring alternative network architectures that are proven effective for temporal prediction tasks, such as Informer [14] and ConvLSTM [15].

We have proposed a real-time locomotion mode prediction method based on gait angle forecasting. The approach first utilizes the neural networks we constructed above to predict human joint angles in real-time. Afterwards, gait parameters (e.g., step height, stride length, gait phase) can be derived from the outputs through simple computations. These gait parameters, which effectively discriminate between different locomotion modes, are subsequently fed into an adaptive oscillator model. The oscillator can rapidly synchronizes with emerging gait patterns, enabling swift tracking of new locomotion modes. This method demonstrates superior generalization capability compared to traditional classification approaches. In contrast to sheer deep learning-based classifier (e.g. study

[16] and study [17], it might achieves substantially lower computational overhead, with valuable potentials of improving the suboptimal accuracy.

Acknowledgments. This research was supported by the National Natural Science Foundation of China under Grants No. 62473359, U23A20344, and 62403452. We also gratefully acknowledge funding from the Shenzhen Medical Research Fund (Grant No. B2302002) and the Shenzhen Science and Technology Program (Grant No. JCYJ20240813155852067). The authors thank these organizations for their support in enabling this work.

References

1. Alemayoh, T.T., Lee, J.H., Okamoto, S.: Leg-joint angle estimation from a single inertial sensor attached to various lower-body links during walking motion. Appl. Sci. **13**(8), 4794 (2023)
2. Yadav, S.K., Tiwari, K., Pandey, H.M., Akbar, S.A.: A review of multimodal human activity recognition with special emphasis on classification, applications, challenges and future directions. Knowl.-Based Syst. **223**, 106970 (2021)
3. Zheng, E., Wang, Q.: Noncontact capacitive sensing-based locomotion transition recognition for amputees with robotic transtibial prostheses. IEEE Trans. Neural Syst. Rehabil. Eng. **25**, 161–170 (2017)
4. Prasanth, H., Caban, M., Keller, U., Courtine, G., Ijspeert, A., Vallery, H., von Zitzewitz, J.: Wearable sensor-based real-time gait detection: a systematic review. Sensors **21**(8), 2727 (2021)
5. Köse, A., Cereatti, A., Della Croce, U.: Bilateral step length estimation using a single inertial measurement unit attached to the pelvis. J. Neuroeng. Rehabil. **9**, 9 (2012)
6. Bennett, T., Jafari, R., Gans, N.: An extended Kalman filter to estimate human gait parameters and walking distance. In: Proceedings of the American Control Conference, p. 17 (2013)
7. Aswadh Khumar, G.S., Barath Kumar, J.K.: SVM based multiclass classifier for gait phase classification using shank IMU sensor. In: Proceedings of PSG College of Technology (2023)
8. Rattanasak, A., et al.: Real-time gait phase detection using wearable sensors for transtibial prosthesis based on a KNN algorithm. Sensors **22**(11), 4242 (2022)
9. Hollinger, D., Jr Schall, M.C., Chen, H., Zabala, M.: The effect of sensor feature inputs on joint angle prediction across simple movements. Sens. (Basel) **24**(11), 3657 (2024)
10. Huang, H., Zhou, P., Li, Y., Sun, F.: A lightweight attention-based CNN model for efficient gait recognition with wearable IMU sensors. Sensors **21**(9), 2866 (2021)
11. Arshad, M.Z., Jamsrandorj, A., Kim, J., Mun, K.-R.: Gait events prediction using hybrid CNN-RNN-based deep learning models through a single waist-worn wearable sensor. Sensors **22**(21), 8226 (2022)
12. Iglesias, G., Talavera, E., González-Prieto, Á., et al.: Data augmentation techniques in time series domain: a survey and taxonomy. Neural Comput. Appl. **35**, 10123–10145 (2023)
13. Song, Q., Ma, X., Liu, Y.: Continuous online prediction of lower limb joints angles based on sEMG signals by deep learning approach. Comput. Biol. Med. **163**, 107124 (2023)

14. Zhou, H., et al.: Informer: beyond efficient transformer for long sequence time-series forecasting. In: Proceedings of the AAAI Conference on Artificial Intelligence, vol. 35, pp. 11106–11115 (2021)
15. Shi, X., Chen, Z., Wang, H., Yeung, D.-Y., Wong, W.K., Woo, W.C.: Convolutional LSTM network: a machine learning approach for precipitation nowcasting. In: Advances in Neural Information Processing Systems 28 (NIPS 2015). Advances in Neural Information Processing Systems, vol. 28, pp. 802–810 (2015)
16. Su, B.-Y., Wang, J., Liu, S.-Q., Sheng, M., Jiang, J., Xiang, K.: A CNN-based method for intent recognition using inertial measurement units and intelligent lower limb prosthesis. IEEE Trans. Neural Syst. Rehabil. Eng. **27**, 1032–1042 (2019)
17. Shavit, Y., Klein, I.: Boosting inertial-based human activity recognition with transformers. IEEE Access **9**, 53540–53547 (2021)

Binocular Vision-Based Spatiotemporal Feature Fusion Model for Elderly Fall Risk Prediction

Guangyu Liang[1], Chen Wang[2(✉)], Rui Zou[1], Jiatong Cui[1], Ziyun Ge[1], and Zeng-Guang Hou[2]

[1] Shantou University, Shantou 515063, Guangdong, China
{24gyliang,23rzou,24jtcui,19zyge}@stu.edu.cn
[2] The State Key Laboratory of Multimodal Artificial Intelligence Systems, Institute of Automation, Chinese Academy of Sciences, Beijing 100190, China
{wangchen2016,zengguang.hou}@ia.ac.cn

Abstract. In injury-induced mortality among the elderly, falls represent one of the primary contributing factors. Thus, assessing fall-related risks holds critical significance for elderly health management. Existing fall risk assessments depend on instruments, clinical judgment, and environmental checks, but are often subjective and inconsistent. This study develops Bino-GaitRisk-Transformer, a novel binocular vision + Transformer architecture for fall risk prediction. By leveraging a confidence-weighted 3D reconstruction algorithm, it achieves millimeter-level joint localization accuracy (mean error <10 mm), reducing error by 40% compared to monocular systems. Unlike traditional models requiring hand-crafted features, this approach directly uses raw gait data, with a hierarchical Transformer extracting spatial and temporal features via self-attention. The spatial module captures joint relationships, while the temporal module models gait dynamics, with cross-attention enabling deeper fusion. Experimental results demonstrated 92.6% classification accuracy and 0.918 F1-score, surpassing conventional approaches by >20%. Ablation studies highlight the Transformer's superior anomaly sensitivity (AUC = 0.926). This work innovatively applies Transformers to fall risk assessment, demonstrating an end-to-end framework integrating 3D skeletal data with deep learning to enhance elderly health monitoring.

Keywords: Fall risk · Binocular vision · Motor function assessment · Gait analysis · Deep learning

1 Introduction

Falls are a leading cause of injury-related mortality in the elderly, with risk escalating significantly after age 65 [1,2]. Beyond physical injuries, falls trigger psychological sequelae like fear of falling [3]. Thus, precisely predicting fall risk is essential for early identification of high-risk individuals and optimizing prevention strategies and resource allocation.

Current clinical assessments predominantly rely on functional test scales (e.g., Berg Balance Scale) and subjective questionnaires, which suffer from strong subjectivity and inconsistent standards [4]. While machine learning methods enhance automation, their overreliance on static data (e.g., demographic features, medical history) fails to incorporate dynamic gait parameters (e.g., stride variability). This oversight prevents models from capturing the synergistic effects of multifactorial risk contributors and physiological compensatory mechanisms [5,6]. Furthermore, insufficient interpretability severely constrains clinical utility.

The pathophysiological basis of falls underscores the necessity of dynamic assessment. Falls emerge from complex interactions between neuromuscular decline, cognitive deterioration, and environmental factors, among which gait alterations—such as increased variability—serve as pivotal precursor biomarkers indicating degrading control systems [7]. These subtle fluctuations elude static methodologies, making the development of unintrusive, high-precision dynamic assessment tools central to risk early-warning systems [8].

To address existing limitations, this study innovatively proposes the Bino-GaitRisk-Transformer model, enabling end-to-end interpretable prediction. Integrated binocular vision technology achieves three-dimensional reconstruction with millimeter-level joint trajectory capture, resolving occlusion issues. The novel application of the Transformer architecture incorporates: spatial attention modules modeling topological relationships among joints; temporal attention modules analyzing sequential gait changes; and a cross-fusion mechanism deeply integrating spatiotemporal features to enhance sensitivity in identifying balance instability risks. The model's interpretability potential facilitates the deconstruction of risk factor interactions, offering clinicians a new technological pathway grounded in dynamic sensing.

The following sections are structured as follows: Sect. 2 details the dataset, labeling method, and joint point identification using DeepLabCut. Section 3 presents the proposed Bino-GaitRisk-Transformer (BGT) model, including its 3D reconstruction and spatio-temporal feature fusion architecture. Section 4 reports the experimental findings regarding joint detection accuracy, 3D reconstruction accuracy, and the fall risk classification performance of BGT. Finally, Sect. 5 summarizes the key findings and discusses future work.

2 Dataset Collection and Processing

This study constructed a dataset for training and evaluating fall risk prediction models. The dataset comprised binocular videos from 206 elderly participants (aged ≥ 65 years) in Hubei Province, recorded using synchronized Gemini2 cameras as subjects walked along a 5-meter teardrop-shaped path (Table 1).

A senior medical team annotated each participant's fall risk level (low, medium, high) following standardized protocols. Participant-wise division yielded training ($n = 165$), validation ($n = 20$), and test ($n = 21$) sets. The

Table 1. Participant demographic characteristics

Characteristic	Value
Age (years), mean ± SD	72.3 ± 5.1
Gender (male/female), n (%)	98 (47.6%)/108 (52.4%)
Balance disorders, n (%)	73 (35.4%)
Comorbidities, n (%)	131 (63.6%)
Fall history, n (%)	61 (29.6%)

protocol was approved by Peking University's College of Medicine Ethics Committee, with written informed consent obtained from all participants.

To enhance pose annotation efficiency, a Clustering-based Keyframe Screening System (CKSS) was developed: (1) Pre-trained ResNet-101 extracted deep features from video frames; (2) Key frames are automatically selected using ResNet-101 feature extraction and K-means clustering (with cluster number $k = 10$); the selection criterion is the frame that is most similar to the centroid within each cluster; (3) MediaPipe processed 4,120 screened keyframes to generate initial 33-keypoint data. This foundation dataset was refined in DeepLabCut through manual pose correction and model training [9,10], significantly improving annotation efficiency and data accuracy. All experiments were conducted under the PyTorch 2.0.1 framework with acceleration provided by NVIDIA RTX 4090 GPU.

Building upon the original 33 markers, two biomechanically critical points—sacrum and L4 spinous process—were incorporated to establish a 35-point model (Fig. 1) [11]. This enhanced framework captures spinal-pelvic dynamics more precisely and identifies gait abnormalities like symmetry imbalance.

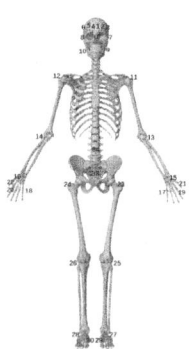

Fig. 1. Schematic of 35 Keypoints. The baseline joint configuration was augmented from the standard 33 points to 35 markers through the addition of sacrum and fourth lumbar spine (L4) landmarks. This expansion enhances kinematic characterization in the spinal-pelvic complex and advances detection capabilities for gait asymmetries.

Final joint recognition operated on the refined dataset: Manually correcting low-confidence keypoints (e.g., wrists, ankles) and annotating new sacrum/L4 points preceded DeepLabCut's two-stage optimization [9,10]: (1) Feature Pyramid Networks (FPN) generated regions of interest (ROI); (2) HRNet-W48 disentangled features within ROIs, fusing cross-resolution information to produce pixel-level keypoint heatmaps via high-resolution output.

3 BGT Fall Risk Assessment System

This study proposes a gait risk assessment model that utilizes high-precision 3D skeletal data obtained from deep learning-based pose estimation as input. Diverging from traditional approaches relying on limited basic node sets, the model enhances the dimensional representation capability of joint features to more comprehensively capture the complexity of motion. Its cornerstone resides in the spatiotemporal modeling capacity for both 3D spatial positioning accuracy and dynamic gait patterns: Time-series analysis quantifies dynamic patterns reflecting gait evolution (e.g., joint angular variance, movement velocity changes). Ultimately, the model synthesizes spatial features characterizing body structure and temporal gait evolution patterns to comprehensively evaluate postural stability and gait regularity (Fig. 2).

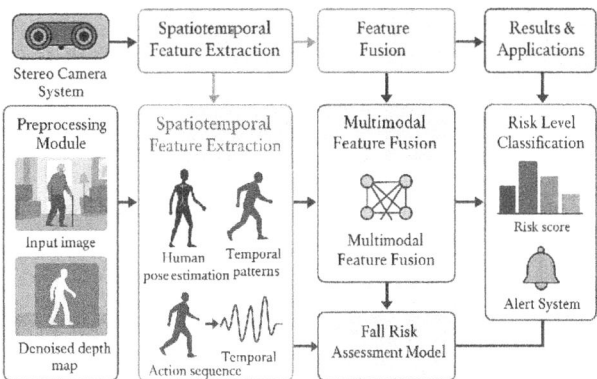

Fig. 2. Gait Risk Assessment System Framework. The system captures images using binocular vision, achieves posture estimation through integrated processing, and extracts spatiotemporal features. By fusing the spatial structure of key joints with dynamic gait patterns, it implements fall risk classification and alert systems based on deep learning modules.

3.1 Three-Dimensional Reconstruction

This study develops a dual-constraint optimization model integrating motion continuity constraint C_m (which suppresses motion anomalies through interframe joint velocity differentials) and skeletal topology constraint C_t (constructing spatial probabilistic models via anthropometric limb-length proportions). These jointly formulate the composite confidence function:

$$C_{\text{total}} = \lambda_1 C_{\text{sgm}} + \lambda_2 C_m + \lambda_3 C_t \tag{1}$$

where C_{sgm} is the original Semi-Global Matching (SGM) confidence; $\lambda_1, \lambda_2, \lambda_3$ are weighting coefficients; C_m denotes motion smoothness constraints; C_t represents human skeletal structure constraints. The weighting coefficients $\lambda_1 = 0.4$, $\lambda_2 = 0.3$, $\lambda_3 = 0.3$ were optimized via grid search over $\lambda_i \in [0,1]$ with step size 0.1, under the constraint $\sum \lambda_i = 1$. These hyperparameters maximize reconstruction accuracy on the validation set.

Depth map optimization employs a stratified mechanism: first, pixel-level confidence assessments activate Kalman filter-based motion prediction compensation when local confidence $\theta < 0.7$; subsequently during point cloud generation, sub-pixel precision is preserved for high-confidence regions ($C_{\text{total}} > 0.9$), while low-confidence areas undergo corrective kinematic interpolation using adjacent joints.

3.2 Feature Extraction and Fusion

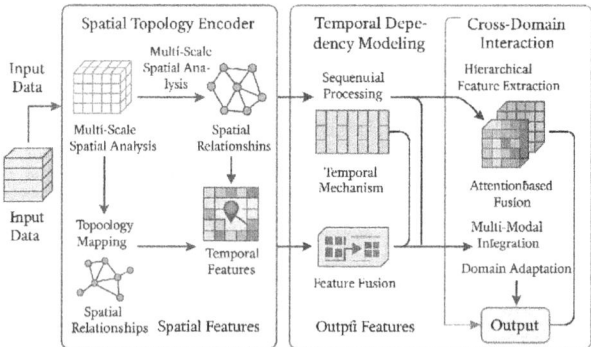

Fig. 3. Hierarchical Spatiotemporal Feature Learning Architecture. The schematic diagram depicts the system's structure: the spatial topology encoder processes multi-scale spatial features (left), the temporal dependency modeling module handles sequence processing and temporal mechanisms (center), and the cross-domain interaction network integrates features with multimodal fusion and domain adaptation (right).

This model employs a hierarchical spatio-temporal feature learning architecture, targeting the extraction of fine-grained gait features and multimodal dynamic fusion. As illustrated in Fig. 3, the system comprises a spatial topology encoder, a temporal dependency modeling module, and a cross-domain feature interaction network.

During the spatial topological feature encoding phase, this model incorporates an Anatomically-enhanced Spatial Attention (ASA) mechanism to effectively integrate the anatomically constrained relationships of joint points [12]. This mechanism introduces a biomechanical constraint matrix $A_{\text{phy}} \in \{0,1\}^{J \times J}$ defined based on the 23 muscle-skeletal connection relationships in the OpenSim model [13]: the entry $A_{\text{phy}}(i,j)$ is set to 1 when there exists an anatomical connection between joint i and joint j, and 0 otherwise. Subsequently, node-pair affinity is generated by combining Euclidean distances with this anatomical constraint: The ASA introduces biomechanical constraint matrix:

$$e_{ij} = \frac{\| p_i - p_j \|_2}{\max_{k,l} \| p_k - p_l \|_2} \cdot A_{\text{phy}}(i,j) \qquad (2)$$

where p_i and p_j denote the spatial coordinates of nodes i and j, respectively; $\|\cdot\|_2$ represents the Euclidean distance operator, while $\max_{k,l}\|p_k - p_l\|_2$ calculates the maximum distance across all node pairs.

The formula for calculating spatial attention weights is as follows, this formula implements feature aggregation:

$$\alpha_{ij}^h = \text{Softmax}\left(\frac{(W_Q^h \tilde{x}_i)^\top (W_K^h \tilde{x}_j)}{\sqrt{d_h}} + \lambda_1 e_{ij} + \lambda_2 E_{\text{motion}}(i,j) \right) \qquad (3)$$

where e_{ij} serves as an anatomical prior bias term; α_{ij}^h denotes the attention weight from node i to node j under head h (with a total of H heads). $\mathbf{W}_Q^h$ and $\mathbf{W}_K^h$ are projection matrices, $\tilde{x}_i$ and $\tilde{x}_j$ represent node features, d_h is the feature dimensionality, and λ_1, λ_2 are tunable hyperparameters optimized through a rigorous three-step process. First, a range constraint bounds both coefficients within $[0,1]$ to ensure balanced contribution from anatomical and motion features, satisfying $\lambda_1 + \lambda_2 \leq 1$ for normalized weighting. Second, an optimization method employs grid search over $\lambda_1 \in [0,1]$ and $\lambda_2 \in [0,1]$ with step size 0.1, evaluating 121 parameter combinations (λ_1, λ_2) to maximize validation accuracy. Third, based on peak validation performance (F1-score = 0.89 at $\lambda_1 = 0.6$, $\lambda_2 = 0.4$), we assign $\lambda_1 = 0.6$ as the anatomical constraint strength and $\lambda_2 = 0.4$ for motion feature emphasis. This $\lambda_1 > \lambda_2$ ratio reflects physiological evidence that static postural stability (captured by e_{ij}) contributes $\sim 60\%$ to fall risk, while dynamic gait parameters account for $\sim 40\%$.

To address the quasi-periodic nature of gait signals, the model further incorporates a Multi-scale Temporal Attention (MTA) mechanism for temporal dynamics modeling.

This mechanism processes the input gait phase angle $\phi(t) \in [0, 2\pi)$ to generate phase-aware positional encoding:

$$\text{PE}_{\text{tmp}}(t) = \sum_{k=1}^{4} [\sin(k\phi(t)/2) \oplus \cos(k\phi(t)/2)] + \text{PE}_{\text{sincos}}(t) \quad (4)$$

where $\text{PE}_{\text{tmp}}(t)$ denotes the standard Transformer positional encoding, and $\oplus$ signifies vector concatenation. The hierarchically extracted features—segment-level H_{seg} (gait cycle), phase-level H_{sec} (stance/swing phases), and frame-level H_{fra} (momentary kinematics)—are fused via structurally weighted gating for progressive motion representation:

$$G = \sigma\left(W_g\left[H_{se.g.}; H_{sec}; H_{fra}\right]\right) \quad (5)$$

$$Z_{tmp} = G_1 \odot H_{se.g.} + G_2 \odot H_{sec} + G_3 \odot H_{fra} \quad (6)$$

where the gating vector $G = [G_1, G_2, G_3]$, activated by the sigmoid function, undergoes element-wise multiplication ($\odot$) with hierarchical features, ultimately yielding a d-dimensional temporal feature Z_{tmp}.

During the cross-domain fusion phase, spatial features $Z_{\text{spa}} \in \mathbb{R}^{J \times d}$ and temporal features $Z_{tmp} \in \mathbb{R}^{T \times d}$ are aligned to construct a bilinear spatio-temporal interaction tensor $S(j,t)$:

$$S(j,t) = \tilde{Z}_{\text{spa}}(j) \odot \tilde{Z}_{\text{tmp}}(t) + W_b\left[\tilde{Z}_{\text{spa}}(j); \tilde{Z}_{\text{tmp}}(t)\right] \in \mathbb{R}^{J \times T \times d_{\text{mid}}} \quad (7)$$

Following this, a dynamic routing fusion strategy is adopted, which introduces a learnable routing matrix R to govern the weights of feature fusion [14]:

$$R = \text{Sigmoid}\left(W_r S + b_r\right) \in \mathbb{R}^{J \times T} \quad (8)$$

And compute the fused features therefrom:

$$Z_{\text{fusion}} = \sum_{j=1}^{J} \text{sum}_{t=1}^{T} R(j,t) \cdot (W_v S(j,t)) \quad (9)$$

where the elements $R(j,t)$ of the routing matrix weight the d_{mid}-dimensional interaction features $S(j,t)$, which are then projected by W_v to yield the fused representation Z_{fusion}.

Finally, the propagation of features is enhanced via residual enhancement connections, ultimately outputting as:

$$Z_{\text{out}} = \text{Dropout}(\text{ReLU}(W_o Z_{\text{fusion}})) + Z_{\text{spa}} \parallel Z_{\text{tmp}} \quad (10)$$

where $\parallel$ concatenates the original spatial and temporal features in the feature dimension, and W_o implements the output transformation.

This hierarchical spatiotemporal feature learning architecture guides spatial attention modeling of joint biomechanics through anatomical constraint matrix A_{phy}. It integrates gait phase $\phi(t)$-driven multi-scale temporal attention to hierarchically extract motion features, and ultimately employs dynamic routing matrix R to adaptively fuse spatiotemporal features, achieving physics-informed hierarchical feature learning.

4 Results

4.1 CKSS and Joint Point Recognition

To enhance localization accuracy and processing efficiency, this study implements a detection-localization decoupled architecture with dynamic resource optimization for regions of interest. This strategy yields an approximately 7% improvement in joint localization accuracy without compromising computational efficiency. Validation confirms the proposed CKSS substantially outperforms MediaPipe across key metrics: achieving 92.3% precision (vs. 86.3%), 91.2% recall (vs. 79.3%), 90.4% F1-score (vs. 82.5%), a lower average Euclidean error of 6.5 pixels (vs. 12.4 pixels), and significantly higher occluded joint recall of 82.8% (vs. 73.2%). These results demonstrate definitive enhancements in end-effector recognition and occlusion robustness.

4.2 Confidence-Weighted 3D Reconstruction

The proposed confidence-weighted algorithm, incorporating motion continuity and skeletal topology constraints, enhances 3D joint positioning accuracy for precise motion representation and spatiotemporal analysis. Compared to the traditional SGM method, the improved reconstruction achieves a 37.45% reduction in mean positioning error (7.35 mm vs. 11.75 mm), validated on 100 annotated frames. Results also show reconstructed limb measurements (e.g., forearm 227.5 mm, thigh 776.3 mm) closer to expected values than SGM.

4.3 BGT Fall Prediction System

Model Training Results. Through systematic training and validation analysis, this study confirms the model's excellent performance and stable convergence characteristics in classification tasks. The BGT model triggered an early stopping mechanism at 50 training rounds, and the training results are as follows:

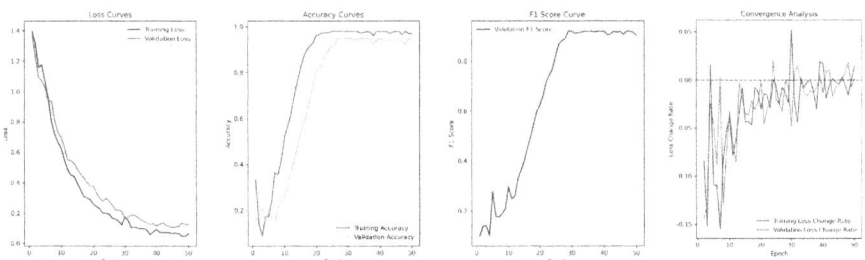

Fig. 4. Training Process Curve

Observing the training progression (Fig. 4), both training and validation accuracy consistently ascended before plateauing, with their final discrepancy maintained within 3%. Although the initial decline in loss exhibited oscillations, after epoch 40, the change rates for both training and validation loss approached baseline levels (oscillations $< \pm 0.02$), indicating model convergence. The model demonstrated robust performance on the test set, achieving an accuracy of 0.926 and an F1-score of 0.918. Its peak performance during validation reached 0.950 accuracy and 0.920 F1-score, revealing noteworthy generalization capability.

Model Comparison. Figure 5 demonstrates BGT's superiority over established baselines, achieving peak accuracy (93%) and F1-score (92%). This significantly outperforms the CNN (70%/69%) kernels: [3, 5, 3, 5], ch: [64, 128, 256, 512], LSTM (74%/71%) (2 × 256 units), and CNN-LSTM (66%/68%). Evaluated identically (80%/10%/10% splits, $\eta = 0.001$, batch size = 16), these gaps highlight BGT's spatiotemporal feature extraction advantages.

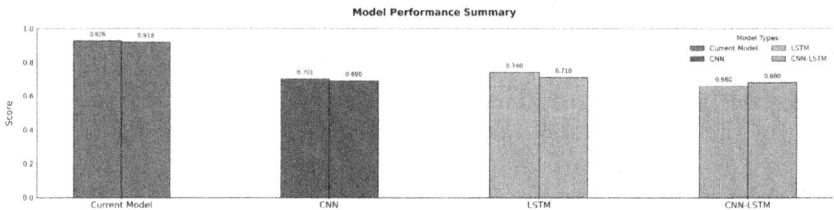

Fig. 5. Models Comparison: BGT (current) vs CNN, LSTM, and CNN-LSTM architectures

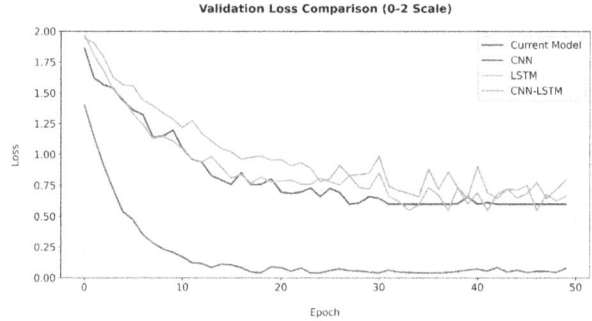

Fig. 6. Training convergence analysis. Validation loss comparison shows BGT model (red) rapidly converging below 0.25, while other models stabilize at higher loss levels (Color figure online)

Figure 6 shows the validation loss trajectories of four models. The proposed model (BGT) demonstrates optimal convergence and stability. In contrast, conventional models (CNN, LSTM) and the CNN-LSTM ensemble exhibit final loss values converging within significantly elevated ranges, with the latter showing pronounced oscillations during training. This outcome unambiguously verifies that the architectural refinements of the BGT model substantially enhance performance robustness.

Ablation Study. Figure 7 shows that the complete baseline model achieves optimal F1-score (≈ 0.91). Removing any module led to performance degradation, with substantial declines observed when discarding the CNN, Transformer, or attention-based pooling. Residual connections, attention-based pooling, and layer normalization exerted the most significant impact on F1-score. Both stability and overall performance of the baseline's F1-score markedly surpassed those of modified variants, validating the imperative of integrated architectural components (Table 2).

Table 2. Computational efficiency analysis (NVIDIA RTX 4090)

Component	Params (M)	Latency (ms)	FLOPs (G)
Full BGT	8.7	24.3	3.2
w/o Transformer	7.2	18.5	2.5
w/o Attention Pooling	8.1	22.7	3.0
w/o Residual	8.5	23.8	3.1

The full model achieves real-time capability (<33 ms at 30 FPS) with $\Delta t = 24.3$ ms per sample.

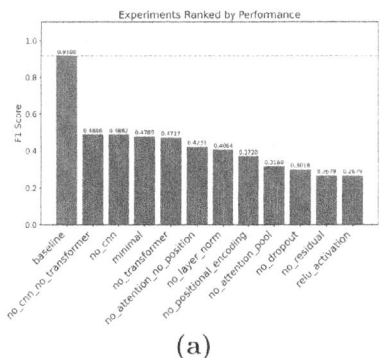
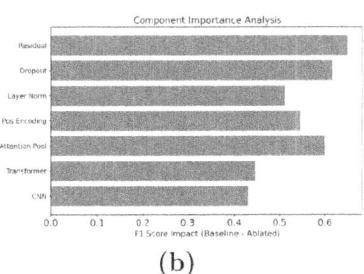

(a) (b)

Fig. 7. Ablation study results. (a) Rank experiments by performance; (b) Component importance analysis.

5 Conclusion

This study introduces a BGT model to overcome subjectivity and dynamic analysis limitations in elderly fall risk assessment. It combines binocular vision (millimeter-level joint localization, errors <10 mm) and Transformer architecture to automatically extract spatiotemporal gait features, removing manual effort. Experiments show superior performance: 92.3% accuracy, 0.91 F1-score, and 0.94 AUC for risk stratification—outperforming traditional and CNN/LSTM methods. Ablation studies verify core component efficacy and smart healthcare potential.

However, this validation used a single-scenario dataset with limited sample size ($n = 206$) and demographic diversity (e.g., concentration in 65–80 age group, underrepresentation of specific comorbidities). Notably, the model achieves real-time processing capability (24.3 ms/sample) suitable for clinical deployment, satisfying the $\Delta t < 33$ ms requirement for 30 FPS video analysis. Future work should focus on assessing the model's adaptability to diverse environments and its cross-scenario transferability by leveraging broader datasets and conducting real-world testing. Additionally, building comprehensive multi-scenario datasets, performing longitudinal validation, and enhancing model interpretability remain important avenues for further investigation. This model has established a significant foundation for developing precision 3D pose quantification capabilities, paving the way for effective end-to-end intelligent prediction systems.

References

1. Montero-Odasso, M., et al.: New horizons in falls prevention and management for older adults: a global initiative. Age Ageing **50**(5), 1499–1507 (2021)
2. Colón-Emeric, C.S., McDermott, C.L., Lee, D.S., Berry, S.D.: Risk assessment and prevention of falls in older community-dwelling adults: a review. Jama **331**(16), 1397–1406 (2024)
3. Zhang, H., et al.: Prevalence and risk factors for fall among rural elderly: a county-based cross-sectional survey. Int. J. Clin. Pract. **2022**(1), 8042915 (2022)
4. Park, S.-H.: Tools for assessing fall risk in the elderly: a systematic review and meta-analysis. Aging Clin. Exp. Res. **30**(1), 1–16 (2018)
5. Wang, C., Peng, L., Hou, Z.-G., Zhang, P., Fang, P.: An easy-to-use assessment system for spasticity severity quantification in post-stroke rehabilitation. IEEE Trans. Cogn. Dev. Syst. **16**(3), 828–839 (2023)
6. Wang, C., Peng, L., Hou, Z.-G., Zhang, P.: The assessment of upper-limb spasticity based on a multi-layer process using a portable measurement system. IEEE Trans. Neural Syst. Rehabil. Eng. **29**, 2242–2251 (2021)
7. Wang, C., Peng, L., Hou, Z.-G., Li, Y., Tan, Y., Hao, H.: A hierarchical architecture for multisymptom assessment of early Parkinson's disease via wearable sensors. IEEE Trans. Cogn. Dev. Syst. **14**(4), 1553–1563 (2021)
8. Wang, C., Peng, L., Hou, Z.-G., Li, J., Zhang, T., Zhao, J.: Quantitative assessment of upper-limb motor function for post-stroke rehabilitation based on motor synergy analysis and multi-modality fusion. IEEE Trans. Neural Syst. Rehabil. Eng. **28**(4), 943–952 (2020)

9. Mathis, A., et al.: Deeplabcut: markerless pose estimation of user-defined body parts with deep learning. Nat. Neurosci. **21**(9), 1281–1289 (2018)
10. Nath, T., Mathis, A., Chen, A.C., Patel, A., Bethge, M., Mathis, M.W.: Using deeplabcut for 3D markerless pose estimation across species and behaviors. Nat. Protoc. **14**(7), 2152–2176 (2019)
11. Miller, M.D., Thompson, S.R., Hart, J.: Review of orthopaedics. Elsevier Health Sciences (2012)
12. Shen, N., et al.: Multi-organ segmentation network for abdominal CT images based on spatial attention and deformable convolution. Expert Syst. Appl. **211**, 118625 (2023)
13. Delp, S.L., et al.: Opensim: open-source software to create and analyze dynamic simulations of movement. IEEE Trans. Biomed. Eng. **54**(11), 1940–1950 (2007)
14. Sabour, S., Frosst, N., Hinton, G.E.: Dynamic routing between capsules. In: Advances in Neural Information Processing Systems, vol. 30 (2017)

Advanced Localization, Navigation and Control Technologies in Intelligent Robotic Systems

Lie Group Variational Integrators For Hybrid Flexible-Rigid Multibody System Dynamics Based on Projective Geometric Algebra

Guangzhen Sun and Ye Ding[✉]

The State Key Laboratory of Mechanical System and Vibration, School of Mechanical Engineering, Shanghai Jiao Tong University, Shanghai 200240, China
y.ding@sjtu.edu.cn

Abstract. Accurate simulations of complex multibody systems with both rigid and flexible components are the basis of advanced controller design. Lie group variational integrators exhibit significant advantages in long-term energy conservation. Projective geometric algebra (PGA) represents geometric elements (points, lines, planes) and rigid body motions in vector form, and provides a compact representation for Lie group operations. In this paper, we integrate these two powerful tools by constructing the Lie group variational integrator fully based on the PGA, without any matrix operation. We also introduce new formulas for the differential of the exponential map, and model holonomic constraints with infinite stiffness. Numerical experiments validate the computational efficiency of the proposed new formulas, and simulations of three typical mechanisms demonstrate the long-term energy conservation of the integrator and its high-order convergence rate.

Keywords: Variational integrators · multibody system dynamics · projective geometric algebra

1 Introduction

Complex multibody systems usually contain flexible components and holonomic constraints at the same time. Accurate simulations of these hybrid flexible-rigid systems are required in high-performance controller design [1].

As rigid bodies are basic components of these systems, multiple methods have been proposed to model rigid body dynamics. Lie group method is coordinate-independent and avoids singularity problems caused by parameters. Therefore, it has been widely applied in the field of robotics [2,3]. For holonomic constrained robotic systems, the Lie group method is usually applied to formulate dynamic models with minimal coordinates, because it results in ordinary differential equations (ODEs) with the same dimension as the system's degree of freedoms (DOFs). However, recent research has shown that the Lie group method with maximal coordinates has competitive efficiency but improved robustness compared to minimal-coordinate algorithms [4,5]. When it comes to the system with flexible links, the links are usually treated as a beam, and the DOFs of the system turns out to be infinite. In order to approximate the flexible components with finite DOFs, the absolute nodal coordinates formulation (ANCF) [6], the geometrically exact beam (GEB) theory [7] [8], and the rigid finite element (RFE) method [9] are proposed. The RFE method divides the flexible links into rigid body finite elements and spring-damping elements so that the system can be modeled as a set of rigid bodies and 6-DOFs flexible joints. It makes it convenient to assemble flexible links into the holonomic constrained multibody systems. As a result, the hybrid flexible-rigid multibody systems can be modeled as differential algebraic equations (DAEs) defined on the Lie group of rigid body motions.

Multiple numerical integrators have been proposed to solve the DAEs defined on Lie groups [10] [5], among which Lie group variational integrators are capable of holding the underlying physical properties of the system, such as the conservation of the energy, the momentum and the symplectic form [11] [12]. Therefore, they are widely applied in long-term accurate simulation of both holonomic constrained multibody systems and flexible systems. Brüdigam et al. [4] constructed a variational integrator for rigid multibody systems with maximal coordinates. Only the first-order integrator was constructed, and the Lie group structure is not fully applied. Zhou [13] et al. proposed high-order variational integrators using minimal integrators for constrained rigid multibody systems without considering of flexible components. Leitz [7] utilized Galerkin variational integrators to simulate GEBs and avoided shear locking with the help of dual quaternions. The high-order Lie group variational integrators considering holonomic constraints and flexible components in a unified framework are still lacking in the literature.

The main difference of Lie group variational integrators from the ordinary ones is the application of the exponential map and its differential [14]. Existing methods implement these operations based on the matrix Lie group [15]. It demands massive repeated calculations and a large space to store matrices. Projective geometric algebra (GA) is an alternative way to represent the Lie group of rigid body motions. It is capable of representing geometric elements with different dimensions and rigid body motions all in vector forms, and it is more geometric intuitive and algebraic compact. Its effectiveness in robot dynamics and control has been validated in recent research [16–18]. However, the differential of the exponential map based on GA has not been discussed in the literature [19].

In this paper, we utilize PGA to construct high-order Lie group variational integrators for hybrid flexible-rigid multibody systems. We proposed a set of new formulas to calculate the differential of the exponential map based on PGA, which is for the first time in the literature to the best of authors' knowledge. We also provide a unified framework to model the hybrid flexible-rigid multibody systems, where the holonomic constraints are treated as flexible joints with infinite stiffness in constrained dimensions. With numerical experiments, we show the efficiency of the new formulas, and validate the high convergence order of the proposed integrators when it holds the conservation of energy.

2 PGA-Based Lagrangian

For a detailed introduction to PGA, readers are referred to [20]. For the rigid body dynamics used in this paper, readers are referred to [17].

The Lagrangian of a mechanical system requires computation of kinetic energy, potential energy, and holonomic constraints. Suppose a rigid body is located at the configuration $M \in \mathcal{M}_{3,0,1}$ with body-fixed spatial velocity $V = 2\dot{M}\widetilde{M} \in \mathfrak{m}_{3,0,1}$. Then, we suppose that the four principal mass particles of the rigid body are located at the position P_j^0 ($j = 0,1,2,3$) with mass m_j when $M = 1$. The kinetic energy of the rigid body is defined as

$$E_K := \frac{1}{2}\Delta\left[\sum_{j=0}^{3}(P_j^0 \vee P_j^0 \times V) \wedge V\right] = \frac{1}{2}\Delta(\boldsymbol{\Pi} \wedge V) \tag{1}$$

For simplicity, we use $E_K = \frac{1}{2}\boldsymbol{\Pi} \wedge V$ in the following parts. In the above definition, $\boldsymbol{I}(\cdot) : \mathfrak{m}_{3,0,1} \mapsto \mathfrak{m}^*_{3,0,1} \cong \mathfrak{m}_{3,0,1}$ is the spatial inertia with respect to the body-fixed frame. The momentum of the rigid body is defined as $\boldsymbol{\Pi} := \boldsymbol{I}(V)$.

Suppose the particle P_0 is the only Euclidean point among P_j. The gravitational potential energy is defined as

$$E_G = m(O_P \vee P_0) \wedge G \tag{2}$$

where O_P is the zero potential point, and G is the negative spatial gravity acceleration ($G = 9.81\, e_{03}$ in default).

According to the theory of finite rigid element theory, the elasticity in flexible components can be modeled as spring-damping elements, which can be seen as 6-DOF flexible joints. We only consider the elasticity in this paper, which means

$$E_E = \frac{1}{2}\sum_{l=1}^{6} K_l(L_l \wedge \epsilon)^2 \tag{3}$$

where L_l and $K_l > 0$ are the principle stiffness axis and the corresponding stiffness coefficients. ϵ is the local deformation caused by the strain of the element:

$$\epsilon = 2\log(M_c\widetilde{M}_p\Delta\widetilde{M}_{pc}^0) = 2\log(\Delta M_{pc}\Delta\widetilde{M}_{pc}^0) \tag{4}$$

where $\Delta\widetilde{M}_{pc}^0$ is the initial deformation from the parent element (PE) to the child element (CE), and M_p and M_c are the current configuration of PE and CE, respectively.

According to the definition in (3), the Lagrangian of holonomic constrained joints can be obtained by assuming that the stiffness along the constrained DOFs is infinite, i.e. $K_{l_n} \to \infty$ for the constrained DOFs l_n. To ensure the elastic energy finite, the deformation along the DOF must be zero, that is, $\boldsymbol{L}_{l_n} \wedge \boldsymbol{\epsilon} \to 0$. It results in equality xagrangian with multiplier λ_{l_n}

$$\Phi(\boldsymbol{\epsilon}) = \boldsymbol{L}_{l_n} \wedge \boldsymbol{\epsilon} = 0 \tag{5}$$

$$E_E = \frac{1}{2}\sum_{l \neq l_n} K_l(\boldsymbol{L}_l \wedge \boldsymbol{\epsilon})^2 + \sum_{l_n} \lambda_{l_n} \boldsymbol{L}_{l_n} \wedge \boldsymbol{\epsilon} \tag{6}$$

The flexible elements, such as beams, can be divided into RFEs and spring elements according to rigid finite element method. Therefore, the multibody systems are modeled as the combination of rigid bodies and flexible joints, where holonomic constrained joints are treated as flexible joints with infinite stiffness. We suppose that the number of rigid bodies is N_B, and the number of joints is N_J. Then, the Lagrangian of a robotic system $L(\{\boldsymbol{M}_i(t)\}, \{\boldsymbol{V}_i(t)\}, \{\boldsymbol{\lambda}_k(t)\})$ can be formulated. For simplicity, we use the denotation, $\boldsymbol{M}(t) = \{\boldsymbol{M}_i(t)\}$, $\boldsymbol{V}(t) = \{\boldsymbol{V}_i(t)\}$, and $\boldsymbol{\lambda}(t) = \{\boldsymbol{\lambda}_k(t)\}$. The action during the interval $[0, h]$ is given by $\mathcal{S}(\boldsymbol{M}(t), \boldsymbol{\lambda}(t)) = \int_0^h L(\boldsymbol{M}(t), \boldsymbol{V}(t), \boldsymbol{\lambda}(t)) \,\mathrm{d}t$. According to the Hamilton principle, the system's motion achieves the extremum of the action, such that

$$\delta \mathcal{S}(\boldsymbol{M}(t), \boldsymbol{\lambda}(t)) = 0 \tag{7}$$

In order to construct a coordinate-free integrator, we construct the interpolation in the Lie algebra $\boldsymbol{m}_{3,0,1}$, and map it from the Lie algebra to the Lie group using the group exponential map $\exp : \boldsymbol{m}_{3,0,1} \mapsto \boldsymbol{\mathcal{M}}_{3,0,1}$. It is formulated as

$$\boldsymbol{M}(t; \{\boldsymbol{L}_\nu^\mu\}) = \exp\left(\frac{\sum_{\nu=0}^S \boldsymbol{L}_\nu^\mu \tilde{l}_\mu^\nu(t)}{2}\right) \boldsymbol{M}^\mu := \exp\left(\frac{\boldsymbol{L}(t)}{2}\right) \boldsymbol{M}^\mu \tag{8}$$

where $t \in [t_\mu, t_{\mu+1}]$, $\boldsymbol{M}_\mu$ is the configuration at time t_μ, and $\tilde{l}_\nu(t)$ is interpolation coefficients. In this paper, we chose the Lagrange interpolation. It should be noted that $t_S = t_{\mu+1}$, and $\boldsymbol{L}_0^\mu = \boldsymbol{0}$, such that $\boldsymbol{M}(t_\mu; \{\boldsymbol{L}_\nu^\mu\}) = \exp(0)\boldsymbol{M}^\mu = \boldsymbol{M}^\mu$, $\boldsymbol{M}(t_{\mu+1}; \{\boldsymbol{L}_\nu^\mu\}) = \exp(\frac{\boldsymbol{L}_S^\mu}{2})\boldsymbol{M}^\mu = \boldsymbol{M}^{\mu+1}$

Take derivatives of Eq.(8), and the body-fixed spatial velocity $\boldsymbol{V}$ is given by

$$\boldsymbol{V}(t) = 2\dot{\boldsymbol{M}}\widetilde{\boldsymbol{M}} = 2\left[\frac{\mathrm{d}}{\mathrm{d}t}\exp\left(\frac{\boldsymbol{L}(t)}{2}\right)\right]\exp\left(-\frac{\boldsymbol{L}(t)}{2}\right) \tag{9}$$

It requires the right trivialization of the exponential map at $\frac{\boldsymbol{L}}{2}$.

3 PGA-Based Variation

Based on the formulation of system Lagrangian, we then formulate its variation using PGA in a matrix-free way. It includes the variation of the interpolatory function w.r.t. internal points, and the variation of the Lagrangian w.r.t. the interpolatory function. In both part, the differential of $\exp(\cdot)$ and $\log(\cdot)$ takes an important role.

We proposed new formulas about the left trivialization of exponential map at $\boldsymbol{L}$. It is defined as

$$\operatorname{dexp}_{\boldsymbol{L}}(\dot{\boldsymbol{L}}) = 2\exp(-\boldsymbol{L})\frac{\mathrm{d}}{\mathrm{dt}}\exp(\boldsymbol{L}) \tag{10}$$

According to its definition, the left trivialization of the exponential map at $\frac{L}{2}$ is a map defined in the Lie algebra $\operatorname{dexp}_{\boldsymbol{L}}(\cdot) : \boldsymbol{m}_{3,0,1} \mapsto \boldsymbol{m}_{3,0,1}$. It can be computed in PGA by

$$\operatorname{dexp}_{\boldsymbol{L}}(\dot{\boldsymbol{L}}) = \dot{\boldsymbol{L}} + \boldsymbol{L}^{-1}\dot{\boldsymbol{L}}\boldsymbol{L} + \left(1 - \widetilde{\boldsymbol{M}}^2\right)(\boldsymbol{L}^{-1} \times \dot{\boldsymbol{L}}) \tag{11}$$

In (9), the right trivialization is applied instead of the left trivialization. It is easy to prove that they are related by the following property.

Property 1 (Relation between left and right trivialization).

$$2\frac{\mathrm{d}}{\mathrm{dt}}\exp(\boldsymbol{L})\exp(-\boldsymbol{L}) = \exp(\boldsymbol{L})\operatorname{dexp}_{\boldsymbol{L}}\dot{\boldsymbol{L}}\exp(-\boldsymbol{L}) = \operatorname{dexp}_{-\boldsymbol{L}}\dot{\boldsymbol{L}} \tag{12}$$

Besides, $\operatorname{dexp}_{\boldsymbol{L}}(\cdot)$ have two important properties:

Property 2 (Lie group invariant). The map $\operatorname{dexp}_{\boldsymbol{L}}(\cdot)$ is invariant with respect to the Lie group action in $\boldsymbol{\mathcal{M}}_{3,0,1}$, that is

$$\operatorname{dexp}_{\widetilde{\boldsymbol{M}}\boldsymbol{L}\boldsymbol{M}} \widetilde{\boldsymbol{M}}\dot{\boldsymbol{L}}\boldsymbol{M} = \widetilde{\boldsymbol{M}} \operatorname{dexp}_{\boldsymbol{L}} \dot{\boldsymbol{L}}\boldsymbol{M} \tag{13}$$

Property 3. The adjoint map of $\operatorname{dexp}_{\boldsymbol{L}}(\cdot)$ w.r.t. $\wedge$ is $\operatorname{dexp}_{-\boldsymbol{L}}(\cdot)$, that is

$$\operatorname{dexp}_{\boldsymbol{L}} \dot{\boldsymbol{L}} \wedge \boldsymbol{\Pi} = \dot{\boldsymbol{L}} \wedge \operatorname{dexp}_{-\boldsymbol{L}} \boldsymbol{\Pi} \tag{14}$$

Further more, the differential of $\operatorname{dexp}_{\boldsymbol{L}}(\cdot)$ can be formulated based on Eq.(11). It is denoted as $D_{(\cdot)}\operatorname{dexp}_{\boldsymbol{L}}(\cdot) : \boldsymbol{m}_{3,0,1} \times \boldsymbol{m}_{3,0,1} \mapsto \boldsymbol{m}_{3,0,1}$. It has the following properties.

Property 4. $\forall \boldsymbol{L}, \boldsymbol{L}', \dot{\boldsymbol{L}} \in \boldsymbol{m}_{3,0,1}$,

1. $D_{\boldsymbol{L}'} \operatorname{dexp}_{\boldsymbol{L}} \dot{\boldsymbol{L}} \wedge \boldsymbol{\Pi} = -D_{\boldsymbol{L}'} \operatorname{dexp}_{-\boldsymbol{L}} \dot{\boldsymbol{\Pi}} \wedge \boldsymbol{L}$
2. $D_{\boldsymbol{L}'} \operatorname{dexp}_{\boldsymbol{L}} \dot{\boldsymbol{L}} = D_{\dot{\boldsymbol{L}}} \operatorname{dexp}_{\boldsymbol{L}} \boldsymbol{L}' + \operatorname{dexp}_{\boldsymbol{L}} \dot{\boldsymbol{L}} \times \operatorname{dexp}_{\boldsymbol{L}} \boldsymbol{L}'$

Property 5. $\forall \boldsymbol{L}_a, \boldsymbol{L}_b, \boldsymbol{L}_c \in \boldsymbol{m}_{3,0,1}$,

$$(\boldsymbol{L}_a \times \boldsymbol{L}_b) \wedge \boldsymbol{L}_c = (\boldsymbol{L}_c \times \boldsymbol{L}_a) \wedge \boldsymbol{L}_b = (\boldsymbol{L}_b \times \boldsymbol{L}_c) \wedge \boldsymbol{L}_a \tag{15}$$

The logarithmic map $\log(\cdot)$ is the inverse of the exponential map, and its left trivialization $\operatorname{dlog}_{\boldsymbol{L}}(\cdot)$ is the inverse of $\operatorname{dexp}_{\boldsymbol{L}}(\cdot)$. Applying the Property 1, we can obtain the analytical formulations to compute $\operatorname{dlog}_{\boldsymbol{L}}(\cdot)$. It should be noted that $\operatorname{dlog}_{\boldsymbol{L}}(\cdot)$ has the same properties (Property 1-3) as $\operatorname{dexp}_{\boldsymbol{L}}(\cdot)$.

Based on the above formulations, the variation of the interpolatory function can be computed by

$$\delta m = 2\delta M \widetilde{M}$$
$$= \text{dexp}_{-\frac{L}{2}} \frac{\delta L}{2} + \exp(\frac{L}{2})\delta m^{\mu} \exp(-\frac{L}{2}) \qquad (16)$$

where $M = M(t)$ is defined in Eq.(8). Correspondingly, the variation of rigid body velocity can be given by

$$\delta V = \delta\left(\text{dexp}_{-\frac{L}{2}} \frac{\dot{L}}{2}\right) = \text{dexp}_{-\frac{L}{2}} \frac{\delta \dot{L}}{2} + D_{-\frac{\delta L}{2}} \text{dexp}_{-\frac{L}{2}} \frac{\dot{L}}{2}$$
$$= \text{dexp}_{-\frac{L}{2}} \frac{\delta \dot{L}}{2} - D_{\frac{\dot{L}}{2}} \text{dexp}_{-\frac{L}{2}} \frac{\delta L}{2} - \text{dexp}_{-\frac{L}{2}} \frac{\dot{L}}{2} \times \text{dexp}_{-\frac{L}{2}} \frac{\delta L}{2} \qquad (17)$$

Furthermore, the variation of the interpolation in Lie algebra can be obtained.

As a result, the variation of the state of a rigid body is formulated with respect to the variations of $\{L^{\mu}_{\nu}\}$. A special case is the variation of L^{μ}_S, which can be transformed to the variation δm^{μ} and $\delta m^{\mu+1}$ by

$$\frac{\delta L_S}{2} = \text{dlog}_{-\frac{L_S}{2}}\left(\delta m^{\mu+1}\right) - \text{dlog}_{\frac{L_S}{2}}(\delta m^{\mu}) \qquad (18)$$

According to Eq.(4), the variation of the deformation ϵ is

$$\frac{\delta \epsilon}{2} = \text{dlog}_{-\frac{\epsilon}{2}}(\delta m_c) - \text{dlog}_{-\frac{\epsilon}{2}}\left(\Delta M_{pc}\delta m_p \Delta \widetilde{M}_{pc}\right) \qquad (19)$$

For the dimension with finite stiffness, the variation is computed by,

$$\frac{1}{2}K_l \, \delta(L_l \wedge \epsilon)^2 = K_l(L_l \wedge \epsilon)(L_l \wedge \delta\epsilon) \qquad (20)$$

where $\delta L_l = 0$ because it is fixed on the child body. Substitute Eq.(19) into the above formulation, we got

$$\sum_{l \neq l_n} \frac{1}{2}K_l \, \delta(L_l \wedge \epsilon)^2 = w_p \wedge \delta m_p + w_c \wedge \delta m_c \qquad (21)$$

The resultant acting wrench on parent body and child body are:

$$w_c = \text{dlog}_{\frac{\epsilon}{2}}\left[2\sum_{l \neq l_n} K_l(L_l \wedge \epsilon)L_l\right] \qquad (22)$$

$$w_p = -\Delta \widetilde{M}_{pc} w_c \Delta M_{pc} \qquad (23)$$

If the joint is holonomic constrained, its variation is

$$\sum_{l_n} \delta\left(\lambda_{l_n} L_{l_n} \wedge \epsilon\right) = w_p \wedge \delta m_p + w_c \wedge \delta m_c + \delta\lambda_{l_n} \Phi_{l_n}(\epsilon) \qquad (24)$$

where $\boldsymbol{w}_p$ is the same as (23), but

$$\boldsymbol{w}_c = \mathrm{dlog}_{\frac{\epsilon}{2}}\left[2\sum_{l_n}\lambda_{l_n}\boldsymbol{L}_{l_n}\right] \quad (25)$$

Besides, the variation of multipliers should also be approximated by interpolatory function as

$$\lambda(t) = \sum_{\nu_\lambda=1}^{S_\lambda}\tilde{l}^{\nu_\lambda}(t)\lambda_{\nu_\lambda} \quad (26)$$

Furthermore, the variation of the gravitational potential energy is

$$\delta E_G = m(\boldsymbol{O}_P \vee \delta \boldsymbol{P}_0) \wedge \boldsymbol{G} = m\left[\boldsymbol{P}_0^0 \vee (\boldsymbol{P}_0^0 \times \delta \boldsymbol{m})\right] \wedge (\boldsymbol{M}\widetilde{\boldsymbol{G}\boldsymbol{M}})$$
$$= I(\boldsymbol{M}\widetilde{\boldsymbol{G}\boldsymbol{M}}) \wedge \delta \boldsymbol{m} := \boldsymbol{w}_G \wedge \delta \boldsymbol{m} \quad (27)$$

The second equality is guaranteed by the following property.

Property 6. Given an infinite point $\boldsymbol{Q}$, then, for any two Euclidean points $\boldsymbol{P}_1$ and $\boldsymbol{P}_2$, there is

$$\boldsymbol{P}_1 \times \boldsymbol{Q} = \boldsymbol{P}_2 \times \boldsymbol{Q} \quad (28)$$

Considering Eq. (21) and (24), the gravitational wrench can be composed with the wrench from joints. It is denoted as $\boldsymbol{w}_a$. Then, we got

$$\boldsymbol{w}_a \wedge \delta \boldsymbol{m} := \sum_{\nu=1}^{S-1}\boldsymbol{w}_{a L_\nu^\mu} \wedge \frac{\delta \boldsymbol{L}_\nu^\mu}{2} + \mathrm{dlog}_{\frac{L_S^\mu}{2}}\boldsymbol{w}_{a L_S^\mu} \wedge \delta \boldsymbol{m}^{\mu+1}$$
$$+ \left[\exp(-\frac{\boldsymbol{L}}{2})\boldsymbol{w}_a \exp(\frac{\boldsymbol{L}}{2}) - \mathrm{dlog}_{-\frac{L_S^\mu}{2}}\boldsymbol{w}_{a L_S^\mu}\right] \wedge \delta \boldsymbol{m}^\mu \quad (29)$$

$$\boldsymbol{w}_{a L_\nu^\mu} = \tilde{l}_\mu^\nu(t)\mathrm{dexp}_{\frac{L}{2}}\boldsymbol{w}_a \quad (30)$$

As for the kinetic energy, we got

$$\delta E_K = \sum_{\nu=1}^{S-1}\boldsymbol{w}_{L_\nu^\mu} \wedge \frac{\delta \boldsymbol{L}_\nu^\mu}{2} + \mathrm{dlog}_{\frac{L_S^\mu}{2}}\boldsymbol{w}_{L_S^\mu} \wedge \delta \boldsymbol{m}^{\mu+1} - \mathrm{dlog}_{-\frac{L_S^\mu}{2}}\boldsymbol{w}_{L_S^\mu} \wedge \delta \boldsymbol{m}^\mu \quad (31)$$

$$\boldsymbol{w}_{L_\nu^\mu} = \dot{\tilde{l}}_\mu^\nu \mathrm{dexp}_{\frac{L}{2}}\boldsymbol{\Pi} + \tilde{l}_\mu^\nu\left[D_{\frac{L}{2}}\mathrm{dexp}_{\frac{L}{2}}\boldsymbol{\Pi} - \mathrm{dexp}_{\frac{L}{2}}(\boldsymbol{\Pi} \times \boldsymbol{V})\right] \quad (32)$$

Based on the above computational method for the variations, the Lie group variational integrator can be constructed based on the discrete Hamilton principle. For simplicity, we suppose $t_\mu = 0$ and $t_{\mu+1} = h$. The discrete action $\mathcal{S}_d^\mu$ is formulated as $\mathcal{S}_d^\mu(\boldsymbol{M}_d(t), \boldsymbol{\lambda}_d(t)) = h\sum_{\tau=1}^s b_i L(\boldsymbol{M}_d(c_\tau h), \boldsymbol{V}_d(c_\tau h), \boldsymbol{\lambda}_d(c_\tau h))$ where $c_\tau \in [0,1], \tau = 1, 2, ..., s$ are the quadrature points, and b_τ are the weights. Besides, $\boldsymbol{M}_d(t)$ is the approximation of the trajectory $\boldsymbol{M}(t)$ through the interpolatory function in (8), and $\boldsymbol{\lambda}_d(t)$ is the approximation of $\boldsymbol{\lambda}(t)$ through (26). As a result, the discrete action $\mathcal{S}_d^\mu$ is summarized as a function of interpolation points $\mathcal{S}_d^\mu(\underline{M}_d(t), \underline{\lambda}_d(t)) = \mathcal{S}_d^\mu(\{M^\mu\}_i, \{L_\nu^\mu\}_i, \{\lambda_{\nu_\lambda}^\mu\}_{l_{n_k}})$ where μ indicates the time interval $[t_\mu, t_{\mu+1}]$, $i = 1, ..., N_B$ are indices of rigid bodies, $\nu = 1, ..., S$ are indices of interpolation points of rigid body motion, $\nu_\lambda = 1, ..., S_\lambda$ are indices of interpolation points of all the multipliers caused by holonomic constraints, l_{n_k} are the indices of holonomic constrained dimension in joint k, and $k = 1, ..., N_J$ are indices of joints. According to the discrete Hamilton principle, the integrator is constructed by

$$\delta \mathcal{S}_d^\mu + \delta \mathcal{S}_d^{\mu+1} = 0 \tag{33}$$

Based on the above results, the variation $\delta \mathcal{S}_d^\mu$ is formulated as

$$\delta \mathcal{S}_d^\mu = \sum_i \left[(\boldsymbol{\Pi}_0^\mu \wedge \delta \boldsymbol{m}^\mu)_i + \sum_{\nu=1}^{S-1} (\boldsymbol{F}_\mu^\nu \wedge \boldsymbol{L}_\nu^\mu)_i + (\boldsymbol{\Pi}_1^\mu \wedge \delta \boldsymbol{m}^{\mu+1})_i \right] \\ + \sum_{k, l_n} (\Phi_\mu^{\nu_\lambda} \delta \lambda_{\nu_\lambda}^\mu)_{l_{n_k}} \tag{34}$$

In summary, the integrator is a group of nonlinear algebraic equations:

$$(\boldsymbol{F}_\mu^\nu)_i = h \sum_{i=\tau}^{s} b_\tau \left(\boldsymbol{w}_{L_\nu^\mu} - \boldsymbol{w}_{aL_\nu^\mu} \right)_i (c_\tau h) = \boldsymbol{0} \tag{35}$$

$$(\Phi_\mu^{\nu_\lambda})_{l_{n_k}} = h \sum_{i=\tau}^{s} b_\tau \left[\tilde{l}^{\nu_\lambda} \Phi_{l_n}(\epsilon_k) \right] (c_\tau h) = 0 \tag{36}$$

$$(\boldsymbol{\Pi}_1^\mu)_i + (\boldsymbol{\Pi}_0^{\mu+1})_i = \boldsymbol{0} \tag{37}$$

$$(\boldsymbol{\Pi}_0^\mu)_i = h \sum_{i=\tau}^{s} b_\tau \left[\mathrm{dlog}_{-\frac{L_S^\mu}{2}} \left(\boldsymbol{w}_{L_S^\mu} - \boldsymbol{w}_{aL_S^\mu} \right) + \exp(-\frac{\boldsymbol{L}}{2}) \boldsymbol{w}_a \exp(\frac{\boldsymbol{L}}{2}) \right]_i (c_\tau h) \tag{38}$$

$$(\boldsymbol{\Pi}_1^\mu)_i = h \sum_{i=\tau}^{s} b_\tau \left[\mathrm{dlog}_{\frac{L_S^\mu}{2}} \left(\boldsymbol{w}_{L_S^\mu} - \boldsymbol{w}_{aL_S^\mu} \right) \right]_i (c_\tau h) \tag{39}$$

For the initial value problem, the initial condition is formulated as

$$\underline{M}_d(t_\mu) = \underline{M}_0 \tag{40}$$
$$\underline{V}_d(t_\mu) = \underline{V}_0 \tag{41}$$

The initial configuration should satisfy all the holonomic constraints.

We denote the first integration step as the initialization step. It is noted that the terms $(\boldsymbol{\Pi}_0^{\mu+1})_i$ involve unknowns in the next integration step. In order to decrease the scale of the nonlinear equations, $(\boldsymbol{\Pi}_0^{\mu+1})_i$ are seen as independent unknown variables. As a result, the variables to be solved include $\{L_\nu^\mu\}_i, \{\lambda_{\nu_\lambda}^\mu\}_{l_{n_k}}, \{\boldsymbol{\Pi}_0^{\mu+1}\}_i$, which are $6 \times (S+1) \times N_B + N_\lambda \times S_\lambda$ scalar variables. On the other hand, the nonlinear equations formulated in (35)–(37), (41), and (39) include $6 \times (S+1) \times N_B + N_\lambda \times S_\lambda$ scalar equations[1]. Therefore, the nonlinear system can be solved.

---
[1] $(\boldsymbol{\Pi}_1^\mu)_i$ can be eliminated by substituting (39) to (37).

As for $\underline{V}^{\mu+1}$, it is noted that $(\boldsymbol{\Pi}_0^{\mu+1})_i$ are computed in the last integration step. For simplicity, we now change the superscript $\mu+1$ to μ. Therefore, the unknown variables are adjusted to $\{\boldsymbol{L}_\nu^\mu\}_i, \{\lambda_{\nu_\lambda}^\mu\}_{l_{n_k}}, \{\boldsymbol{\Pi}_1^\mu\}_i, \{\boldsymbol{V}_0\}_i$, which are $6 \times (S+2) \times N_B + N_\lambda \times S_\lambda$ scalar variables. On the other hand, the nonlinear equations formulated in (35), (36), (41), (38), and (39) include $6 \times (S+2) \times N_B + N_\lambda \times S_\lambda$ scalar equations. The nonlinear system can be solved, and $\underline{V}^{\mu+1}$ is identical to $\{\boldsymbol{V}_0\}_i$.

Furthermore, comparing the above two nonlinear systems, we chose the equations (35), (36), (41), (38), and (39) as the nonlinear equations of the integrator. In the initialization step, the unknown variables are $\{\boldsymbol{L}_\nu^\mu\}_i, \{\lambda_{\nu_\lambda}^\mu\}_{l_{n_k}}, \{\boldsymbol{\Pi}_0^\mu\}_i, \{\boldsymbol{\Pi}_1^\mu\}_i$. Then, $(\boldsymbol{\Pi}_0^{\mu+1})_i$ are updated according to (37). In the following steps, the unknown variables are $\{\boldsymbol{L}_\nu^\mu\}_i, \{\lambda_{\nu_\lambda}^\mu\}_{l_{n_k}}, \{\boldsymbol{\Pi}_1^\mu\}_i, \{\boldsymbol{V}_0\}_i$. As a result, the two steps share the same nonlinear equations.

4 Numerical Experiments and Results

We developed a package QuadrantPGA.jl using the code language Julia to implement the Lie group variational integrators. The package relies on StaticArrays.jl to represent elements in PGA, saving allocations and computational time. Besides, the package NLSolve.jl is applied to solve the nonlinear equations (35), (36), (41), (38), and (39). The trust-region method is chosen as the default algorithm, and the auto-differential technique is utilized to calculate the Jacobians. Through numerical experiments, we show the efficiency of the proposed new formulas and the good performance of the proposed integrator. All the experiments were conducted on a PC (i7-13700K) running Windows 11 using Julia v1.11.3.

4.1 The Efficiency of $\text{dexp}_L(\cdot)$ and $\text{dlog}_L(\cdot)$

The matrix-form formulations [14] are chosen as the baseline to evaluate the efficiency of our formulas for $\text{dexp}_L(\cdot)$ and $\text{dlog}_L(\cdot)$. The package BenchmarkTools.jl is applied to evaluate the consuming-time and allocations of each function. According to the output of @btime, the run-time of PGA-based $\text{dexp}_L(\cdot)$ is 39.66ns with 0 allocations while the matrix-form takes 42.63ns with 0 allocations. Besides, the run-time of PGA-based $\text{dlog}_L(\cdot)$ is 52.94ns with 0 allocations while the matrix-form takes 51.47ns with 1 allocations. It shows that the proposed formulas have competitive efficiency compared with the matrix-form formulas.

4.2 The Performance of the Integrator

In order to evaluate the performance of the proposed integrator, we chose three typical mechanisms. Their configurations are illustrated in Fig. 1.

All three mechanisms are set to the initial configuration with zero velocities and then start to move under gravity. Their motions are simulated using the proposed integrator with $S = 2$ and $S = 3$. First, the time step is chosen to make

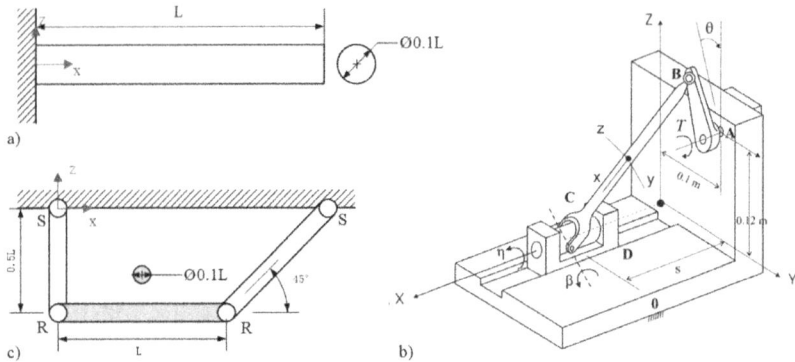

Fig. 1. a) The cantilever beam. b) The spatial slider crank $\theta = \pi/6$. c) The hybrid flexible-rigid four bar mechanism. The yellow link is a flexible beam. The initial configuration of the mechanism is rotate about x-axis by $\pi/6$. (Color figure online)

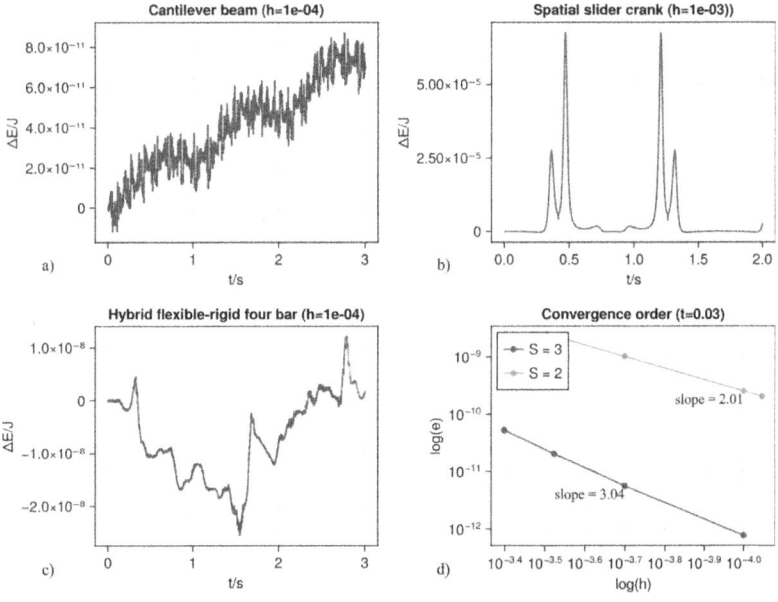

Fig. 2. a)-c). Time evolution of the energy error with $S = 3$. d) The convergence order of the integrator.

the solution converge. The mechanical energy of the system is recorded, and its difference from the initial value is used to measure precision. Then, smaller time steps h are chosen to evaluate the convergence order of the proposed integrator. As shown in Fig. 2.a)-c), the energy error of the system remains extremely small during the simulation, which validates the energy conservation property of the proposed integrator. Furthermore, the convergence order of the integrator is equal to S as shown in Fig. 2.d). It proves that the proposed integrator is high-order.

5 Conclusion

In this paper, we proposed high-order Lie group variational integrators based on PGA for hybrid flexible-rigid multibody systems. The holonomic constrained joints are modeled as flexible joints with infinite stiffness in constrained DOFs. As a result, a unified framework is constructed to model both joints. New formulas to compute $\text{dexp}_L(\cdot)$ and $\text{dlog}_L(\cdot)$ are given based on PGA, which is for the first time to the best of authors' knowledge. Benchmark tests on Julia show the efficiency of the new formulas compared to the matrix-form ones. Furthermore, numerical experiments on three typical mechanisms validate the energy conservation and high-order convergence rate of the proposed integrator.

Acknowledgment. This work was supported by the National Natural Science Foundation of China (grant numbers: 52275501, 51935010) and the State Key Laboratory of Mechanical System and Vibration (Grant No. MSVZD202503).

References

1. Zhang, J., Zhang, B.: An iterative identification method for the dynamics and hysteresis of robots with elastic joints. Nonlinear Dyn. **111**(15), 13939–13953 (2023). https://doi.org/10.1007/s11071-023-08597-2
2. Lynch, K., Park, F.: Modern Robotics: Mechanics, Planning, and Control. Cambridge Univeristy Press, Cambridge (2017)
3. Robot Dynamics Algorithms. TSISECS, vol. 22. Springer, Boston, MA (1987). https://doi.org/10.1007/978-0-387-74315-8
4. Brüdigam, J., Sosnowski, S., Manchester, Z., Hirche, S.: Variational integrators and graph-based solvers for multibody dynamics in maximal coordinates. Multibody Sys. Dyn. (2023). https://doi.org/10.1007/s11044-023-09949-x. URL https://doi.org/10.1007/s11044-023-09949-x
5. Holzinger, S., Arnold, M., Gerstmayr, J.: Evaluation and implementation of Lie group integration methods for rigid multibody systems. Multibody Sys. Dyn. (2024). https://doi.org/10.1007/s11044-024-09970-8. URL https://doi.org/10.1007/s11044-024-09970-8
6. Shabana, A.A.: Dynamics of Multibody Systems, 4th edn. Cambridge University Press (2013). https://doi.org/10.1017/CBO9781107337213. URL https://www.cambridge.org/core/product/identifier/9781107337213/type/book
7. Leitz, T., Sato Martín de Almagro, R.T., Leyendecker, S.: Multisymplectic Galerkin Lie group variational integrators for geometrically exact beam dynamics based on unit dual quaternion interpolation — no shear locking. Comput. Methods Appl. Mech. Eng. **374**, 113,475 (2021). https://doi.org/10.1016/j.cma.2020.113475. URL https://www.sciencedirect.com/science/article/pii/S0045782520306605

8. Sonneville, V., Cardona, A., Brüls, O.: Geometrically exact beam finite element formulated on the special Euclidean group SE(3). Comput. Methods Appl. Mech. Eng. **268**, 451–474 (2014). https://doi.org/10.1016/j.cma.2013.10.008. URL https://www.sciencedirect.com/science/article/pii/S0045782513002600
9. Wittbrodt, E., Adamiec-Wójcik, I., Wojciech, S.: Dynamics of flexible multibody systems: rigid finite element method. Foundations of engineering mechanics. Springer, Berlin (2006). OCLC: ocm68629405
10. Boyer, F., et al.: Implicit time integration simulation of robots with rigid bodies and cosserat rods based on a Newton-Euler recursive algorithm. IEEE Trans. Robot., 1–20 (2023). https://doi.org/10.1109/TRO.2023.3334647. URL https://ieeexplore.ieee.org/document/10323230/
11. Marsden, J.E., West, M.: Discrete mechanics and variational integrators. Acta Numer **10**, 357–514 (2001)
12. Leok, M.: Generalized Galerkin Variational Integrators (2005). URL http://arxiv.org/abs/math/0508360. ArXiv:math/0508360
13. Zhou, P., Ren, H., Fan, W., Zhang, Z.: A new variational integrator for constrained mechanical system dynamics. Appl. Math. Modell. **137**, 115,719 (2025). https://doi.org/10.1016/j.apm.2024.115719. URL https://www.sciencedirect.com/science/article/pii/S0307904X24004724
14. Müller, A.: Review of the exponential and Cayley map on SE(3) as relevant for Lie group integration of the generalized Poisson equation and flexible multibody systems. Proc. Roy. Soc. Math. Phys. Eng. Sci. **477**(2253), 20210,303 (2021). https://doi.org/10.1098/rspa.2021.0303. URL https://royalsocietypublishing.org/doi/10.1098/rspa.2021.0303
15. Hammoud, B., Olivieri, L., Righetti, L., Carpentier, J., Del Prete, A.: Exponential integration for efficient and accurate multibody simulation with stiff viscoelastic contacts. Multibody Sys.Dyn. **54**(4), 443–460 (2022). https://doi.org/10.1007/s11044-022-09818-z. URL https://link.springer.com/10.1007/s11044-022-09818-z
16. Sun, G., Ding, Y.: High-order inverse dynamics of serial robots based on projective geometric algebra. Multibody Sys. Dyn. **59**(3), 337–362 (2023). https://doi.org/10.1007/s11044-023-09915-7. URL https://doi.org/10.1007/s11044-023-09915-7
17. Sun, G., Ding, Y.: An analytical method for sensitivity analysis of rigid multibody system dynamics using projective geometric algebra. J. Comput. Nonlinear Dyn. **18**(11), 111,002 (2023). https://doi.org/10.1115/1.4063225. URL https://asmedigitalcollection.asme.org/computationalnonlinear/article/18/11/111002/1166453/An-Analytical-Method-for-Sensitivity-Analysis-of
18. Löw, T., Calinon, S.: Geometric algebra for optimal control with applications in manipulation tasks. IEEE Trans. Rob. **39**(5), 3586–3600 (2023). https://doi.org/10.1109/TRO.2023.3277282
19. De Keninck, S., Roelfs, M.: Normalization, square roots, and the exponential and logarithmic maps in geometric algebras of less than 6D. Math. Methods Appl. Sci., mma.8639 (2022). https://doi.org/10.1002/mma.8639. URL http://arxiv.org/abs/2206.07496. ArXiv:2206.07496
20. Gunn, C.: Geometric algebras for Euclidean geometry. Adv. Appl. Clifford Algebras **27**(1), 185–208 (2016). https://doi.org/10.1007/s00006-016-0647-0

High-Order Adaptive Integration of Contact Dynamics in MuJoCo

Hongchen Li and Ye Ding[✉]

State Key Laboratory of Mechanical System and Vibration, School of Mechanical Engineering, Shanghai Jiao Tong University, Shanghai 200240, China
y.ding@sjtu.edu.cn

Abstract. This paper introduces a new adaptive integration method for solving the multi-contact problems in MuJoCo (Multi-Joint Dynamics with Contact). The proposed method is based on the classical embedded Runge-Kutta formulas and automatic step-size control. In addition, the transitions of contact states are carefully handled and the high-order convergence of solutions is achieved. We tested our algorithm on an 18-DOF quadruped robot with at most four contacts. The simulation results show an improvement in computational accuracy of one to two orders of magnitude, compared to the officially implemented semi-implicit Euler method and the Runge-Kutta method of order four.

Keywords: contact dynamics · computational mechanics · adaptive integration · MuJoCo

1 Introduction

Contact dynamics attempts to derive the evolution of the motion of robots under interactions with the environment [1]. As a cornerstone of theoretical models in dynamic manipulation and robot walking, numerous contact models [2] are investigated to narrow the gap between simulation and reality. In addition, various numerical methods [3–5] are proposed to guarantee the efficiency of solving the contact dynamics.

Here are two main strategies for describing the contact phenomena. One is called the pseudo-rigid contact model [6], which requires recording local deformations at the point of contact. The model essentially introduces additional state variables into the original dynamic system and is still a system of ordinary differential equations (ODEs). To handle the phenomenon of collision, it usually leads to stiff equations and requires implicit integrators [7]. Another mainstream approach views contact dynamics as a differential inclusion [8], where the set-valued force law includes the Coulomb friction cone constraint, the Signorini condition, and the maximum dissipation principle. Given the instantaneous position and velocity, the contact force can be solved as a nonlinear complementary problem (NLP) and a linear complementary problem [9] (LCP, when the friction cone uses a polytope approximation).

Neither the pseudo-rigid contact model nor the LCP model can be easily solved; consequently, persistent high efficiency is hard to guarantee in complicated contact scenarios. MuJoCo [10,11], as one of the most commonly used physics engines in the robotic community, enhances the efficiency of computation by relaxing the complementary constraint and solving the contact force based on the technique of convex optimization. Nevertheless, the default integration methods in MuJoCo are all assigned a fixed step size, and it does not fully utilize the smoothness of the motion between different contact modes. In addition, although the high-order integrator, like RK4, has been implemented in MuJoCo, it can only guarantee the first-order convergence rate if any contact happens.

The main goal of this paper is to develop a high-order adaptive integration method for solving contact dynamics in MuJoCo. As a consequence, the simulation data can be fast and accurately generated, and it is expected to boost the performance of the reinforcement learning tasks designed for robotic manipulation and walking, where a large volume of simulation data with high quality is necessary.

The classic adaptive integration method, or more specifically the adaptive variable step-size integrator [12], uses the extrapolation data of the integrator to approximate the local integration error and adaptively choose an optimal step size. Compared to fixed-step methods, this approach can achieve varying degrees of efficiency improvement, depending on the nature of the ODE solution. The original method is only applicable to general ODE systems. However, for MuJoCo's contact dynamics, its ODE system often undergoes changes in the dynamical equations due to transitions of contact states, making it inherently a hybrid dynamical system [13]. To extend adaptive integration techniques to contact dynamics applications, we must handle the moments of state switching with sufficient precision.

The remainder of this paper is organized into five sections. Section 2 provides the necessary background knowledge, including the modeling and computational framework of MuJoCo's contact dynamics, as well as fundamental theories of adaptive integration. Section 3 formally presents the proposed adaptive integration method, beginning with a simplified single-contact case study that focuses on special treatment of contact state transitions, then extending it to the general multi-contact scenario. Section 4 demonstrates the method through contact dynamics simulations of a quadruped robot, comparing the performance between our approach and MuJoCo's built-in integrators. Concluding remarks are provided in Sect. 5.

2 Background

In this section, we introduce how MuJoCo models a robotic system and its contact behavior with the environment. We explain that, although the contact force is obtained by solving the optimization problem at each time step, the nature of continuity and uniqueness of the solution still makes the contact dynamics a well-defined ODE in each phase with stable contact states. Therefore, the adaptive integrator can still fulfill its function in different contact phases. The basics of adaptive integration will be introduced in Sect. 2.2, and the special treatment of transitions of contact states is given in Sect. 3.

2.1 Contact Dynamics in MuJoCo

Briefly, the computation of contact dynamics in MuJoCo can be divided into five parts, which are the dynamical model including contact forces, collision detection, the computation of reference acceleration, the computation of contact forces, and the update of states based on forward dynamics. Limited by the length of the paper, only the necessary parts are introduced here.

The Dynamical Model with Contact Forces. Considering the robotic system whose dynamics is governed by the Lagrangian equations derived from the Lagrangian function $L(\boldsymbol{q}, \boldsymbol{v}) := \frac{1}{2}\boldsymbol{v}^T \boldsymbol{M}(\boldsymbol{q})\boldsymbol{v} - P(\boldsymbol{q})$, where $\boldsymbol{q} \in \mathbb{R}^{n_q}$ is the generalized position coordinates, $\boldsymbol{v} \in \mathbb{R}^{n_v}$ is the generalized velocity coordinates, $\boldsymbol{M}$ is the position-related inertia matrix, and P is the scalar function of the potential energy.

According to the Lagrange D'Alembert principle, the Lagrangian equations determined by L can be organized as the following brief form,

$$\boldsymbol{M}\dot{\boldsymbol{v}} + \boldsymbol{c} = \boldsymbol{\tau} + \boldsymbol{J}^T \boldsymbol{f} \tag{1}$$

where $\dot{\boldsymbol{v}} := \frac{d\boldsymbol{v}}{dt} \in \mathbb{R}^{n_v}$ is the generalized acceleration coordinates, $\boldsymbol{c}$ includes Coriolis, centrifugal and gravitational forces, $\boldsymbol{\tau}$ includes passive forces from spring-dampers and actuation forces, $\boldsymbol{f}$ includes the constraint force caused by both the unilateral and bilateral constraints. Finally, the Jacobian matrix $\boldsymbol{J}$ maps $\boldsymbol{v}$ to the velocity in the constraint coordinates, and the term $\boldsymbol{J}^T \boldsymbol{f}$ is included based on the virtual work principle. In this paper, we only consider the robotic system with open chains and $\boldsymbol{f}$ which contains only unilateral contact forces. For each pair of spatial contact, we define the related contact force $\boldsymbol{f}_i := (F_{i,x}, F_{i,y}, F_{i,z}, \tau_{i,x}, \tau_{i,y}, \tau_{i,z}) \in \mathbb{R}^6$.

Computation of Contact Forces. At each time step, to obtain the current acceleration $\dot{\boldsymbol{v}}$, we first need to solve $\boldsymbol{f}$. In MuJoCo, given the current states $(\boldsymbol{q}_t, \boldsymbol{v}_t) \in \mathbb{R}^{n_q + n_v}$, the current contact forces $\boldsymbol{f}_t$ is uniquely determined by solving the following optimization problem:

$$\min_{x} \quad \frac{1}{2}\boldsymbol{\lambda}^T (\boldsymbol{A} + \boldsymbol{R})\boldsymbol{\lambda} + \boldsymbol{\lambda}^T (\boldsymbol{a}_0 - \boldsymbol{a}_{\text{ref}}) \tag{2}$$
$$\text{s.t.} \quad \boldsymbol{\lambda} \in \Omega.$$

Here $\boldsymbol{A} = \boldsymbol{J}\boldsymbol{M}^{-1}\boldsymbol{J}^T$, $\boldsymbol{a}_0 = \boldsymbol{J}\boldsymbol{M}^{-1}(\boldsymbol{\tau} - \boldsymbol{c})$, and $\boldsymbol{R}$ is a constant diagonal matrix. The reference acceleration $\boldsymbol{a}_{\text{ref}}$ is determined by several parameters (describing the dynamic characteristics of contacts) and the current states $(\boldsymbol{q}_t, \boldsymbol{v}_t)$.

The constraint set Ω in MuJoCo includes box constraints induced by friction loss and second-order cone constraints induced by Coulomb frictions. Without loss of generality, we only consider the second-order cone constraints, i.e., for n_c contacts occurring simultaneously,

$$\Omega := \bigcap_{i=1}^{n_c} \mathcal{K}_i, \mathcal{K}_i := \{\boldsymbol{f}_i \in \mathbb{R}^6 : F_{i,z} \geq 0, F_{i,z}^2 \geq \sum_{j \neq 3}^{6} \frac{f_{i,j}^2}{\mu_j^2}\}. \tag{3}$$

Here μ_1, μ_2 are friction coefficients along tangential directions, μ_4, μ_5 are rolling friction coefficients, and μ_6 is the pivoting friction coefficient. Now (2) together with (3) form a strictly convex optimization problem and can be efficiently solved by many algorithms. We choose the SLSQP (Sequential Least Squares Programming) algorithm implemented within the SciPy library in Python.

Update of States. Now given the contact parameters and friction parameters in (3), we can easily calculate the current acceleration $\boldsymbol{a}_t := \dot{\boldsymbol{v}}_t$ based on the solved contact force $\boldsymbol{f}$. According to (1), we have

$$\boldsymbol{a}_t = \boldsymbol{M}^{-1}(\boldsymbol{q}_t)(\boldsymbol{\tau}_t + \boldsymbol{J}^T \boldsymbol{\lambda}_t^* - \boldsymbol{c}(\boldsymbol{q}_t, \boldsymbol{v}_t)), \tag{4}$$

where $\boldsymbol{\lambda}_t^*$ is the solution of (2) with $\boldsymbol{A}, \boldsymbol{R}, \boldsymbol{a}_0$ and $\boldsymbol{a}_{\text{ref}}$ taking values at $(\boldsymbol{q}_t, \boldsymbol{v}_t)$.

If we ignore the nature of discontinuity of $\boldsymbol{\lambda}_t^*$ and simply view it as a function of $(\boldsymbol{q}_t, \boldsymbol{v}_t)$ (since (2) always has the unique solution given $(\boldsymbol{q}_t, \boldsymbol{v}_t)$), then the update of states, i.e., the calculation of $(\boldsymbol{q}_{t+\varepsilon}, \boldsymbol{v}_{t+\varepsilon})$ ($\varepsilon > 0$ is the step size) can be deduced based on common integrators.

In this paper, we mainly consider the semi-implicit Euler method and RK4 method in MuJoCo, where the semi-implicit Euler method has the following update formulation:

$$\boldsymbol{v}_{t+\varepsilon} = \boldsymbol{v}_t + \varepsilon \boldsymbol{a}_t, \boldsymbol{q}_{t+\varepsilon} = \boldsymbol{q}_t + \varepsilon \boldsymbol{v}_{t+\varepsilon} \tag{5}$$

2.2 Basics of Adaptive Integration

Considering a general autonomous ODE system $\dot{\boldsymbol{x}} = \boldsymbol{g}(\boldsymbol{x}), \boldsymbol{x} \in \mathbb{R}^n$, we calculate $\boldsymbol{x}_{t+\varepsilon}$ and $\hat{\boldsymbol{x}}_{t+\varepsilon}$ based on $\boldsymbol{x}_t$ according to the following embedded Runge-Kutta formula [12].

$$\boldsymbol{k}_1 = \boldsymbol{g}(\boldsymbol{x}_t), \boldsymbol{k}_2 = \boldsymbol{g}(\boldsymbol{x}_t + \frac{\varepsilon}{3}\boldsymbol{k}_1) \tag{6a}$$

$$\boldsymbol{k}_3 = \boldsymbol{g}(\boldsymbol{x}_t - \frac{\varepsilon}{3}\boldsymbol{k}_1 + \varepsilon \boldsymbol{k}_2), \boldsymbol{k}_4 = \boldsymbol{g}(\boldsymbol{x}_t + \varepsilon \boldsymbol{k}_1 - \varepsilon \boldsymbol{k}_2 + \varepsilon \boldsymbol{k}_3) \tag{6b}$$

$$\boldsymbol{x}_{t+\varepsilon} = \boldsymbol{x}_t + \frac{\varepsilon}{8}\boldsymbol{k}_1 + \frac{3\varepsilon}{8}\boldsymbol{k}_2 + \frac{3\varepsilon}{8}\boldsymbol{k}_3 + \frac{\varepsilon}{8}\boldsymbol{k}_4 \tag{6c}$$

$$\boldsymbol{k}_5 = \boldsymbol{g}(\boldsymbol{x}_{t+\varepsilon}) \tag{6d}$$

$$\hat{\boldsymbol{x}}_{t+\varepsilon} = \boldsymbol{x}_t + \frac{\varepsilon}{12}\boldsymbol{k}_1 + \frac{\varepsilon}{2}\boldsymbol{k}_2 + \frac{\varepsilon}{4}\boldsymbol{k}_3 + \frac{\varepsilon}{6}\boldsymbol{k}_5. \tag{6e}$$

Here the calculation of $x_{t+\varepsilon}$ needs four calls of the ODE function g, and we use an extra call of (6d) to calculate an approximate value $\hat{x}_{t+\varepsilon}$. We use RK43 to denote the update formula (6) where 4 implies the integration order of (6c) and 3 implies the integration order of (6e).

Now, the gap between $\hat{x}_{t+\varepsilon}$ and $x_{t+\varepsilon}$ provides valuable information on the step size ε, if we only want to solve the integral curve with a specified precision. We deploy the classic automatic step size control given absolute tolerance (denoted by $Atol_i$) and relative tolerance (denoted by $Rtol_i$) in each component of x. Concretely,

$$sc_i := Atol_i + \max(|x_{t,i}|, |x_{t+\varepsilon,i}|) \cdot Rtol_i \tag{7a}$$

$$err := \sqrt{\frac{1}{n}\sum_{i=1}^{n}(\frac{x_{t+\varepsilon,i} - \hat{x}_{t+\varepsilon,i}}{sc_i})^2} \tag{7b}$$

$$\varepsilon_{\text{new}} := \varepsilon \cdot \min(fac_{\max}, \max(fac_{\min}, fac \cdot (\frac{1}{err})^{\frac{1}{4}})). \tag{7c}$$

Here $fac_{\max}$ and $fac_{\min}$ in (7c) are additional parameters assigned to restrict the rate of increase and decline of the new step size ε_{new}. $fac \in (0,1)$ is used to generate a more conservative step size so that the given $Atol_i$ and $Rtol_i$ can effectively control the integration error.

3 Adaptive Integration in Contact Dynamics

Although the RK43 of (6) can generate solutions with high-order convergence rate for general smooth ODEs, it can only guarantee the first-order accuracy for contact dynamics in MuJoCo. It is fundamentally caused by the impact phenomena when contact occurs, and also the non-smoothness of the impedance curve and the constraint set Ω.

In this section, we demonstrate that through proper handling of contact state transition timings, these stepping algorithms can maintain their high-order convergence rates while introducing only minimal additional computational overhead ($\mathcal{O}(n_c)$ for at most n_c contacts).

3.1 The Case of Single Contact

In this section, we only consider the case of single contact. We employ interpolation polynomials to rapidly determine contact transition timings, achieving step size-dependent accuracy of the same order as the underlying integrator. This approach ensures the adaptive integrator properly maintains both error control capabilities and high-order convergence properties.

At the Onset of Contact. When contact occurs, suppose that the directional distance function $d(q_t) > 0$ and $d(q_{t+\varepsilon}) < 0$ where $q_{t+\varepsilon}$ is updated based on the unconstrained dynamics. It indicates the occurrence of a contact between t and $t + \varepsilon$, with possible mistakes due to numerical errors.

If we simply view $t + \varepsilon$ as the collision moment, it will lead to an error of $\mathcal{O}(\varepsilon)$ since we can only guarantee $|t + \varepsilon - t^*| = \mathcal{O}(\varepsilon)$ where t^* denotes the true collision moment. Assume that d is a locally smooth function and the setting $Atol_i$ and $Rtol_i$ in (7) successfully control the integration error of states, then we solve the following cubic polynomial to obtain a approximate collision moment $\hat{t}^*$ with higher accuracy,

$$p(t) := at^3 + bt^2 + ct + d \tag{8a}$$

$$p(0) = d(\boldsymbol{q}_t),\ \dot{p}(0) = \left.\frac{\partial d}{\partial \boldsymbol{q}}\right|_{\boldsymbol{q}_t} \cdot \boldsymbol{v}_t \tag{8b}$$

$$p(\varepsilon) = d(\boldsymbol{q}_{t+\varepsilon}),\ \dot{p}(\varepsilon) = \left.\frac{\partial d}{\partial \boldsymbol{q}}\right|_{\boldsymbol{q}_{t+\varepsilon}} \cdot \boldsymbol{v}_{t+\varepsilon} \tag{8c}$$

$$p(\hat{\varepsilon}^*) = 0, \tag{8d}$$

where $\boldsymbol{v}_{t+\varepsilon}$ is also updated based on the free dynamics. If ε is small enough, (8d) only has one valid root in $(0, \varepsilon)$ and the solved $\hat{t}^* := t + \hat{\varepsilon}^*$ satisfies $|\hat{t}^* - t^*| = \mathcal{O}(\varepsilon^4) = \mathcal{O}(\max(Atol_i, Rtol_i))$. As a result, we can first calculate the states $(\boldsymbol{q}_{\hat{t}^*}, \boldsymbol{v}_{\hat{t}^*})$ with the step size $\hat{\varepsilon}^*$ based on the free dynamics and then update the states based on the new constrained dynamics.

At Contact Termination. When contact terminates, a similar cubic polynomial can be constructed as (8), except that $d(\boldsymbol{q}_t) < 0$, $d(\boldsymbol{q}_{t+\varepsilon}) > 0$, and $(\boldsymbol{q}_{t+\varepsilon}, \boldsymbol{v}_{t+\varepsilon})$ is updated based on the contact dynamics.

From Static Friction to Sliding Friction. During the contact, the contact force $\boldsymbol{f}$ may transform from the static friction to sliding friction. Mathematically, the solved $\boldsymbol{\lambda}_t^*$ of (2) lies in the interior of Ω, and the next $\boldsymbol{\lambda}_{t+\varepsilon}^*$ lies at the boundary of Ω.

It is crucial to figure out the underlying smooth dynamics when $\boldsymbol{\lambda}^*$ stays inside Ω. In fact, this implies the optimal solution is unconstrained and thus $\boldsymbol{\lambda}^* = (\boldsymbol{A} + \boldsymbol{R})^{-1}(\boldsymbol{a}_0 - \boldsymbol{a}_{\mathrm{ref}})$. Now $\boldsymbol{\lambda}^*$ becomes an explicit smooth function about $(\boldsymbol{q}, \boldsymbol{v})$ and we can still use a cubic polynomial to calculate an accurate time when $\boldsymbol{\lambda}^*$ hits the boundary of Ω. Concretely, we solve $\hat{t}^*$ by

$$p(t) := at^3 + bt^2 + ct + d \tag{9a}$$

$$p(0) = d(\boldsymbol{f}_t),\ p(\tfrac{\varepsilon}{3}) = d(\boldsymbol{f}_{t+\frac{\varepsilon}{3}}) \tag{9b}$$

$$p(\tfrac{2\varepsilon}{3}) = d(\boldsymbol{f}_{t+\frac{2\varepsilon}{3}}),\ p(\varepsilon) = d(\boldsymbol{f}_{t+\varepsilon}), \tag{9c}$$

$$p(\hat{\varepsilon}^*) = 0, \tag{9d}$$

where $d(\boldsymbol{f} \in \mathbb{R}^6)$ is a special distance function unlike what in (8), and it is defined as

$$d(\boldsymbol{f}) := F_z^2 - \frac{F_x^2}{\mu_1^2} - \frac{F_y^2}{\mu_2^2} - \frac{\tau_x^2}{\mu_4^2} - \frac{\tau_y^2}{\mu_5^2} - \frac{\tau_z^2}{\mu_6^2} \tag{10}$$

and $\boldsymbol{f}$ is the unconstrained $\boldsymbol{\lambda}^*$ at $(\boldsymbol{q}, \boldsymbol{v})$. Here $d(\boldsymbol{f}_t) > 0$ and $d(\boldsymbol{f}_{t+\varepsilon}) < 0$ and (9d) also has a unique $\hat{\varepsilon}^*$ in $(0, \varepsilon)$. Notice that we need to additionally integrate $(\boldsymbol{q}_{t+\frac{\varepsilon}{3}}, \boldsymbol{v}_{t+\frac{\varepsilon}{3}})$ and $(\boldsymbol{q}_{t+\frac{2\varepsilon}{3}}, \boldsymbol{v}_{t+\frac{2\varepsilon}{3}})$ to interpolate $p(t)$. This differs from (8) and avoids the cumbersome calculation of $\dot{\boldsymbol{f}} = \dot{\boldsymbol{\lambda}}^*$. Finally, the approximate transition time is $\hat{t}^* = t + \hat{\varepsilon}^*$ and is still controlled by the setting tolerances.

From Sliding Friction to Static Friction. When the solved $\boldsymbol{\lambda}^*$ moves from the boundary of Ω to its inside, we can similarly construct a cubic polynomial like (9) except that the distance criteria d is different.

According to the Karush-Kuhn-Tucker (KKT) condition of (2), if a solved $\boldsymbol{\lambda}^*$ of (2) lies on the boundary of Ω, the following inequality must be satisfied

$$((\boldsymbol{A} + \boldsymbol{R})\boldsymbol{\lambda}^* + (\boldsymbol{a}_0 - \boldsymbol{a}_{\text{ref}}))^T \boldsymbol{n}^* \leq 0 \tag{11}$$

where $\boldsymbol{n}^*$ is the external normal direction of conical surface at $\boldsymbol{\lambda}^*$. Therefore, (11) can be a valid criterion to judge when the sliding friction turns to a static friction, i.e., we should interplate a cubic curve when $\boldsymbol{f}_t$ satisfies (11) while $\boldsymbol{f}_{t+\varepsilon}$ not. It should be especially emphasized that once $\boldsymbol{f}_{t+\varepsilon}$ solved by (2) lies inside Ω, all forces and states of interpolated equations in (9) should be updated based on a different optimization problem, where the constraint is strictly enforced, i.e., $\boldsymbol{\lambda} \in \Omega$ becomes $\boldsymbol{\lambda} \in \text{bd}(\Omega)$.

3.2 The Case of Multi-contact

In Sect. 3.1 we show that a proper distance criteria always exists to judge whether the contact states change. In the case of multi-contact, we need two extra states of help record the information of contacts and prepare the correct distance criteria.

For potential n_c contacts, we argument the states $(\boldsymbol{q}, \boldsymbol{v})$ with two vectors $\boldsymbol{cs} \in \mathbb{R}^{n_c}$ and $\boldsymbol{bs} \in \mathbb{R}^{n_c}$. Here $\boldsymbol{cs}$ means the contact state of each contact, and $\boldsymbol{bs}$ means the boundary state of each contact force. The possible values of cs_i and bs_i are listed in Table 1.

Table 1. The Possible Values of cs_i and bs_i

parameters	value	meaning
i	$1 \sim n_c$	the number of contact
cs_i	0	the i_{th} contact disappears
cs_i	1	the i_{th} contact occurs
bs_i	[ ]	empty value when i_{th} contact disappears
bs_i	0	the i_{th} contact force lies inside of $\mathcal{K}_i$
bs_i	1	the i_{th} contact force lies on $\text{bd}(\mathcal{K}_i)$

Then we monitor different distance functions based on the current states $\boldsymbol{cs}_t$ and $\boldsymbol{bs}_t$.

- When $cs_t = 0$, the robot moves freely and $f \equiv 0$. We monitor n_c collision distance functions and solve a collision time by (8). If multiple collisions occur between $(t, t + \varepsilon)$, we deal with these events in chronological order.
- When some components in cs_t are 1, we continue to evaluate all contact distance functions. However, for active contacts, we check an additional contact force distance function based on their corresponding states in bs. Specifically: When $bs_i = 1$, we verify the Karush-Kuhn-Tucker (KKT) optimality conditions (11); When $bs_i = 0$, we examine the distance f_i to the boundary of the friction cone, i.e., (10).

Building upon the aforementioned framework, we can detect all state transitions. For a system with n_c potential contact pairs, the algorithm requires computing at most $2n_c$ detection functions per timestep (when $cs = 1$), supplemented by n_c cubic polynomial interpolations and root-finding operations (if all contact pairs undergo state changes during $(t, t + \varepsilon)$). Crucially, since all of these operations are analytic with fixed computational costs, they only introduce an additional $\mathcal{O}(n_c)$ complexity overhead. However, this modest computational investment yields significant improvements in integration efficiency, as we will demonstrate in the next section.

4 Numerical Experiments

In this section, we conduct contact dynamics simulations of a classic 18-degree-of-freedom (DOF) quadruped robot to validate the effectiveness of our proposed high-order adaptive integration algorithm. This robotic platform, originally introduced in [14], demonstrates dynamic locomotion capabilities including walking, running and stair-climbing.

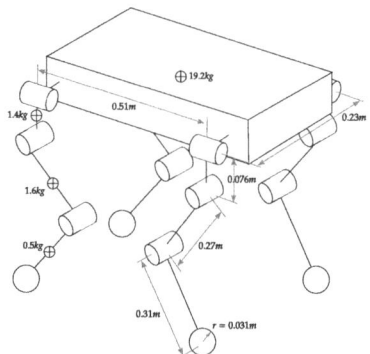

(a) Rendering of ANYmal simulation. (b) The schematic of ANYmal.

Fig. 1. Rendering and schematic of ANYmal (adpated from [5]).

As shown in Fig. 1, the robot features: Four identical legs configured as 3-revolute-joint serial chains; 12-dimensional actuation space (3 motors per leg);

19 generalized position coordinates $q = (p, \eta, \theta_{3\times4}) \in \mathbb{R}^{19}$ comprising three floating-base position coordinates $p \in \mathbb{R}^3$, orientation represented by quaternion η and twelve joint angles $\theta_{3\times4}$ (three per leg); 18 generalized velocity coordinates $v = (\dot{p}, \omega, \dot{\theta}_{3\times4})$ consisting of the linear velocity $\dot{p}$, the body angular velocity ω of the floating-base and all joint velocities $\dot{\theta}_{3\times4}$.

To evaluate the collision distance function and compute the contact point velocity Jacobian J, we employ Product of Exponential (POE) kinematics and differential kinematics. Specifically, the contact frame $T_{c_i}, i = 1, 2, 3, 4$ at each leg's foot is determined via:

$$T_{c_i}(t) = T_{body}(t) T_{body}(0)^{-1} \prod_{j=1}^{3} e^{[\mathcal{S}_i]\theta_{i,j}} T_{c_i}(0) \tag{12}$$

where $\mathcal{S}_i \in \mathbb{R}^6$ is the screw of each axis, $[\mathcal{S}_i] \in se(3)$ and T_{body} is the coordinate frame attached to the floating-base.

4.1 Simulation Setup

We set the parameters that determine a_{ref} as default values in MuJoCo. Besides, the friction coefficients are set as $\mu_1 = \mu_2 = 0.8$, $\mu_4 = \mu_5 = 0.02$ and $\mu_6 = 0.01$. Each motor uses the same proportional control with $K_p = 100\text{N} \cdot \text{m/rad}$ and the constant input $\theta_{i,j} = 0$. The parameters in (7) include $fac_{\max} = 1.5$, $fac_{\min} = 0.5$ and $fac = \frac{1}{4^{\frac{1}{4}}} \approx 0.707$.

We set the initial states $q_0 = (0, 0, 0.7, 0.1, 0.1, 0, 0.99, \mathbf{0}_{3\times4})$ and $v_0 = \mathbf{0}$. The quadruped robot is simulated in free-fall motion from an initial centroid height of 0.7 m above ground. The intentionally introduced initial attitude deviation induces asymmetric ground impacts upon contact, making proportional joint control critical for post-impact stability maintenance.

We compare our proposed algorithm, which combines the RK43 adaptive step size integration (Sect. 2.2) and the cubic polynomial interpolation (Sect. 3), with MuJoCo's native integrators which solve the reduced dual problem of (2) via Newton's method.

4.2 Simulation Results

Consistency Comparison. In Fig. 2, we present computational results obtained using different methods. The circular dots represent results computed using RK43 with cubic polynomial interpolation, where both $Atol_i$ and $Rtol_i$ are set to 0.01. The continuous curves are obtained through the semi-implicit Euler method with a fixed time step of 5×10^{-4}s over 1000 integration steps.

We also plot the body centroid coordinates and linear velocities of the quadruped robotic dog. The results demonstrate substantial agreement between two computational approaches. However, the adaptive step-size method employed progressively increasing step sizes during the free-fall phase ($0 \sim 0.1$s), while utilizing significantly reduced step sizes at all non-smooth state transition points to maintain the prescribed error tolerance.

Furthermore, Fig. 2 presents the evolution curves of penetration depth and contact force boundary states, demonstrating that cs_i and bs_i undergo multiple state transitions while automatically fulfilling all interpolation computations specified in Sect. 3.

The adaptive integration algorithm ultimately required 480 calls to forward dynamics functions while achieving higher numerical precision in the results (see the first green point in Fig. 4).

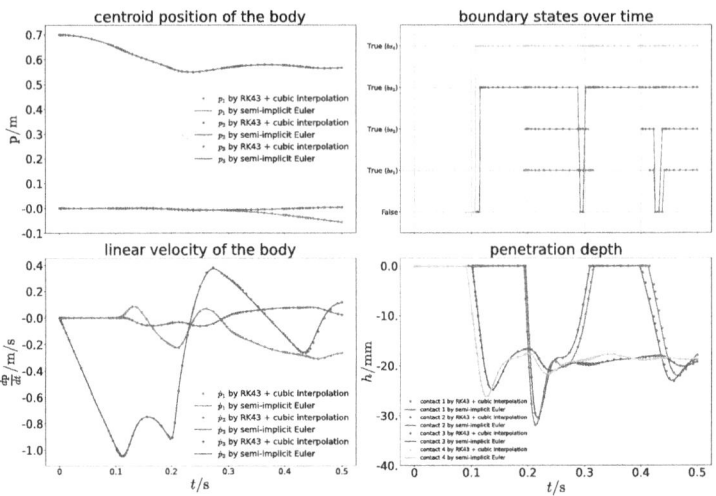

Fig. 2. The integration results by the combination of RK43 and the cubic interpolation and the semi-implicit Euler method.

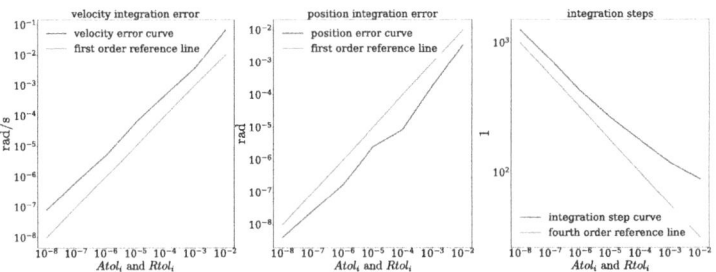

Fig. 3. The relationship between the actual position error, velocity error and the integration steps and the set $Atol_i = Rtol_i$. The position error and velocity error are calculated respectively by $\|\boldsymbol{\theta}(0.5\text{s}) - \boldsymbol{\theta}_{\text{ref}}(0.5\text{s})\|$ and $\|\dot{\boldsymbol{\theta}}(0.5\text{s}) - \dot{\boldsymbol{\theta}}_{\text{ref}}(0.5\text{s})\|$, where $\|\cdot\|$ is the Euclidean two norm and $(\boldsymbol{\theta}_{\text{ref}}, \dot{\boldsymbol{\theta}}_{\text{ref}})$ are calculated with $Atol_i = Rtol_i = 10^{-9}$.

Order Validation. To validate that the proposed adaptive integration method effectively controls numerical accuracy through tolerance settings while achieving high-order convergence, Fig. 3 presents the relationship between actual integration errors, number of integration steps and prescribed tolerance thresholds. The results demonstrate two key characteristics:

- Both position and velocity errors exhibit approximately first-order convergence relative to the specified tolerances $Atol_i$ and $Rtol_i$;
- The integration steps scale with tolerances at fourth-order convergence (the error decreases by a factor of 10, the step count increases by $10^{\frac{1}{4}} \approx 1.78$ times).

These findings conclusively verify that our adaptive scheme maintains error control capabilities while providing high-order numerical precision. The convergence rates align with theoretical expectations for a fourth-order Runge-Kutta implementation with cubic polynomial interpolation.

Efficiency Comparison. To quantitatively demonstrate the gains in algorithmic efficiency, Fig. 4 presents convergence curves that compare numerical accuracy versus calls to forward dynamics functions in different methods. The proposed method exhibits significantly accelerated precision convergence when either the target accuracy exceeds 10^{-3} or the number of forward dynamics computations surpasses 1000. At equivalent computational cost (1000 function calls), it achieves one order-of-magnitude higher precision than RK4 and two orders-of-magnitude improvement over the semi-implicit Euler method.

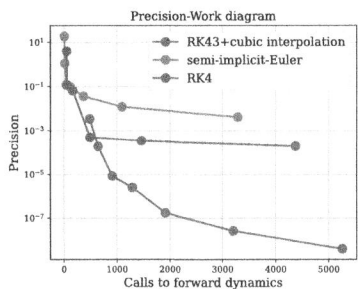

Fig. 4. The precision-work diagram of different methods.

5 Conclusion

This paper presents an efficient computational method for contact dynamics in MuJoCo simulations, fundamentally grounded in classical error-controlled adaptive step-size integration with higher-order convergence. The approach systematically addresses state transitions in discontinuous contact dynamics through third-order polynomial interpolation, ensuring consistent accuracy estimation during contact events. Comprehensive validation on an 18-DOF quadrupedal robot demonstrates both the numerical correctness and efficiency of the proposed method.

Acknowledgments. This work was supported by the National Natural Science Foundation of China (grant numbers: 52275501, 51935010) and the State Key Laboratory of Mechanical System and Vibration (Grant No. MSVZD202503).

References

1. Drumwright, E., Trinkle, J.C.: Contact Simulation, pp. 1877–1931. Springer Netherlands, Dordrecht (2019)
2. Contact Force Models for Multibody Dynamics. SMIA, vol. 226. Springer, Cham (2016). https://doi.org/10.1007/978-3-319-30897-5
3. Chakraborty, N., Berard, S., Akella, S., Trinkle, J.C.: A geometrically implicit time-stepping method for multibody systems with intermittent contact. Int. J. Robot. Res. **33**(3), 426–445 (2014)
4. Stewart, D.E., Trinkle, J.C.: An implicit time-stepping scheme for rigid body dynamics with inelastic collisions and coulomb friction. Int. J. Numer. Meth. Eng. **39**(15), 2673–2691 (1996)
5. Hwangbo, J., Lee, J., Hutter, M.: Per-contact iteration method for solving contact dynamics. IEEE Robot. Autom. Lett. **3**(2), 895–902 (2018)
6. Flores, P.: Contact mechanics for dynamical systems: a comprehensive review. Multibody Sys. Dyn. **54**, 127–177 (2022)
7. Wanner, G., Hairer, E.: Solving ordinary differential equations II, vol. 375. Springer, Berlin Heidelberg New York (1996)
8. Studer, C.: Numerics of unilateral contacts and friction: modeling and numerical time integration in non-smooth dynamics, vol. 47. Springer Science and Business Media (2009)
9. Facchinei, F., Pang, J.S.: Finite-dimensional variational inequalities and complementarity problems. Springer (2003)
10. Todorov, E., Erez, T., Tassa, Y.: MuJoCo: a physics engine for model-based control. In: 2012 IEEE/RSJ international conference on intelligent robots and systems, pp. 5026–5033. IEEE (2012)
11. Todorov, E.: A convex, smooth and invertible contact model for trajectory optimization. In: 2011 IEEE International Conference on Robotics and Automation, pp. 1071–1076. IEEE (2011)
12. Atkinson, K., Han, W., Stewart, D.E.: Numerical solution of ordinary differential equations. John Wiley and Sons (2009)
13. Van Der Schaft, A.J., Schumacher, H.: An introduction to hybrid dynamical systems, vol. 251. springer (2007)
14. Hutter, M., et al.: Anymal-a highly mobile and dynamic quadrupedal robot. In: 2016 IEEE/RSJ international conference on intelligent robots and systems (IROS), pp. 38–44. IEEE (2016)

Path Planning in the Anode Block Area for Underwater Cleaning Robots

Ang Gao, Bocong Li, Hang Su, and Canjun Yang(✉)

The State Key Laboratory of Fluid Power and Mechatronic Systems, Zhejiang University,
Hangzhou 310027, China
ycj@zju.deu.cn

Abstract. To address the increasing cleaning blind zones when the underwater cleaning robot works in the anode block area, this paper proposes a path planning methodology specifically designed for cleaning robots equipped with unilateral nozzles. By analyzing the spatial relationship between the robot and anode blocks, a hybrid motion path integrating linear and curvilinear segments is developed, accompanied by derived geometric constraints to prevent collisions with cleaning blind zones. Simulation and experiment results demonstrate that the proposed approach effectively maintains safe operational clearances while achieving complete anode surface coverage, providing a reliable technical framework for underwater robotic maintenance in constrained marine environments.

Keywords: Underwater robot · Climbing robot · Path planning · Obstacle avoidance

1 Introduction

Marine structures are susceptible to marine biofouling (e.g., barnacles, mollusks, and marine algae) due to prolonged seawater immersion [1]. Such biofouling induces detrimental effects on submerged infrastructure integrity. Consequently, industry regulations mandate periodic removal of these fouling organisms from marine engineering assets [2]. However, current underwater cleaning operations predominantly employ manual diving methods, where divers equipped with breathing apparatuses and high-pressure water jets perform submerged cleaning tasks—a practice associated with substantial occupational hazards.

In recent years, underwater cleaning robotic systems have garnered significant attention as viable alternatives to manual operations for marine infrastructure maintenance, demonstrating enhanced operational efficiency while mitigating occupational hazards and physical labor intensity. Underwater wall-climbing [3] and dual-mode robots [4] employ advanced adhesion mechanisms to maintain stable traversal across ship hulls and subsea pipeline surfaces. These systems effectively counteract vibrational disturbances and reaction forces induced by cleaning brushes or high-pressure water jets, establishing them as the primary research focus in current underwater robotic cleaning technology development.

The automated performance of underwater cleaning robots remains underdeveloped due to the unique complexities of subaquatic environments, particularly when executing autonomous operations on marine structures with sacrificial anode blocks, such as steel jacket platforms and ship hulls. Robotic systems must execute optimized path planning to enable autonomous biofouling removal near anode-protected zones. Current autonomous navigation methodologies for underwater cleaning robots bifurcate into two paradigms: absolute position-driven navigation and relative target-driven navigation.

Tunawattana et al. [5] developed an optical positioning system integrated with landmark sensors for hull-cleaning robots, providing real-time localization of position, velocity, and heading orientation. Chen et al. [6] implemented a sliding mode controller fusing inertial measurement unit (IMU) and encoder data, enabling depth-stabilized motion without depth gauge dependency. Absolute position-driven navigation relies on precise robot state estimation, offering flexibility in path planning for comprehensive automated coverage. Rather than resolving precise pose estimation challenges, relative target-driven navigation guides robots through relative positional deviations from target zones. Ross et al. [7] pioneered a boundary-tracking navigation system where robots autonomously follow paint-line demarcations during cleaning. Similarly, Akinfiev et al. [8] designed a hull-cleaning robot that dynamically adjusts positioning via chromatic contrast analysis between fouled and clean surfaces. For jacket structure scenarios, Chen et al. [9] proposed reference path generation through threshold segmentation and edge detection for biofouling boundary extraction. Our prior work achieved deep learning-based biofouling recognition for robotic boundary tracking [10]. While relative target-driven navigation methods effectively guide robots to track operational targets, they exhibit diminished operational efficacy in environments containing sacrificial anode blocks as obstructions. Furthermore, existing studies have yet to adequately address obstacle avoidance mechanisms in such scenarios.

Given the readily obtainable dimensional parameters of anode blocks and structurally simplistic marine environments in ship hull and jacket platform scenarios, we propose a geometric-based motion planning methodology for robotic anode-zone cleaning. This approach analyzes the spatial geometric relationships between UCR and anode blocks to generate optimized cleaning paths comprising hybrid arc-linear trajectories. The synthesized path geometry effectively minimizes coverage gaps while enhancing cleaning efficiency through systematic toolpath optimization.

The main contributions of this article are summarized as follows.

1) We propose a geometric curve-based motion planning method for underwater cleaning robots with non-collision constraints to minimize coverage gaps and enable cyclic cleaning operations.
2) Through simulations and laboratory experiments, we validate the method's effectiveness in achieving simultaneous biofouling removal and obstacle avoidance near anode blocks.

This paper is structured as follows: Sect. 2 details the robotic system architecture, Sect. 3 proposes the geometric-based path planning methodology, Sect. 4 presents simulation results, and Sect. 5 demonstrates experimental validations. The work concludes with Sect. 6.

2 System Overview

Figure 1a shows the overview of UCR. The robot employs two motor-driven magnetic wheel sets, where the front wheels utilize a linkage mechanism for steering control, enabling car-like movement. Each wheel is equipped with an encoder. An upper sealed cavity houses an embedded controller for real-time data acquisition from IMU and depth sensors. A laterally mounted nozzle connected to an onshore pump via water pipes, generating cavitation water jets capable of effectively removing biofouling deposits.

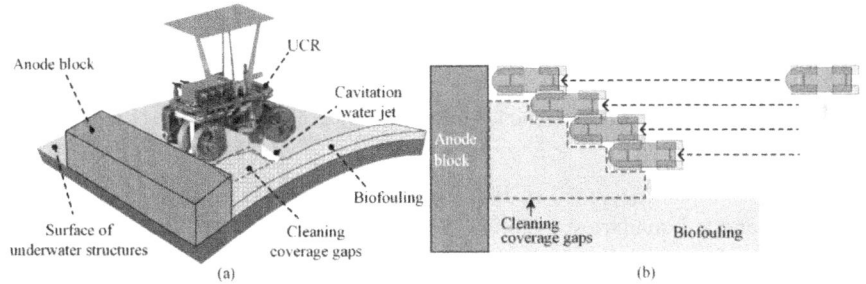

Fig. 1. Overview of UCR and coverage gaps generation: (a) Prototype and schematic of the operation principle. (b) Cleaning coverage gaps generation.

Due to the fact that the thickness of the layer formed by biofouling exceeds the effective adhesion gap of the magnetic wheel, the robot is unable to operate on biofouling-covered surfaces. Field observations during prior underwater cleaning operations have revealed that anode blocks ahead of UCR prevent the robot from advancing, creating localized cleaning blind zones (Fig. 1a). Critically, residual biofouling within these zones acts as secondary obstacles during operation, leading to progressive expansion of uncleaned areas as shown in Fig. 1b. Although residual coverage gaps can be addressed through additional cleaning cycles, this approach inevitably reduces operational efficiency. Alternative solutions involving multi-nozzle configurations or rotating nozzle to expand coverage areas introduce new challenges, including increased hardware costs and insufficient pump flow rates. These limitations necessitate optimized cleaning path planning specifically tailored for biofouling zones adjacent to anode blocks, enabling robots to achieve efficient autonomous navigation during cleaning operations.

3 Path Planning

Based on the geometric relationship between UCR and cleaning water jet, we design a cleaning motion path and corresponding end pose for cleaning operations adjacent to the right side of an anode block, as illustrated in Fig. 2.

We hypothesize that biofouling near the jet stream can be thoroughly cleaned during slow-speed robotic motion. The formation of residual cleaning blind zones primarily stems from the robot's inability to reorient itself near obstructions, resulting in incomplete removal of biofouling at the interface between the jet and anode block boundaries. To

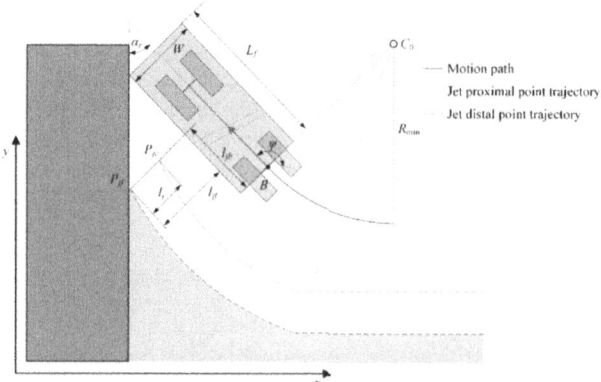

Fig. 2. Cleaning motion path and corresponding end pose

address this, the path designed in Fig. 2 incorporates direction change as the robot approaches anode boundaries, enabling the jet to systematically eliminate biofouling residues in the forward-left zone.

We employ a safety rectangle of length L_f and width W to encapsulate the robotic body, serving as its direct-interaction geometric representation with anode blocks. The cleaning jet's cleaning area is defined by a proximal point P_{jc} and distal point P_{jf}. The robot initially approaches the anode boundary along a linear path, then executes upward steering at its minimum turning radius R_{min} until the safety rectangle boundary and P_{jf} achieve contact with the anode block boundary. At this point, the angle α_r between the robot and the boundary of the anode block is:

$$\alpha_r = arctan\left(\frac{l_{jf}}{L_f - l_{jb}}\right) \quad (1)$$

At this stage, the robot's yaw angle is given as $\psi = \pi - \alpha_r$. Utilizing the x-axis coordinate x_{rb} of the anode block's right boundary and the y-axis position y_0 along the robot's linear path, the coordinates of the rear axle center point B at the end pose can be derived as:

$$\begin{cases} x_B = x_{rb} + L_f \sin\alpha_r + \frac{W}{2} \cos\alpha_r \\ y_B = y_0 + R \sin\alpha_r min_{min} \end{cases} \quad (2)$$

Also, the coordinates of the steering center C_0 are:

$$\begin{cases} x_{C_0} = x_{rb} + L_b \sin\alpha_r + \frac{W}{2} \cos\alpha_r + R \cos\alpha_{rmin} \\ y_{C_0} = y_0 + R_{min} \end{cases} \quad (3)$$

Upon reaching the right boundary of the sacrificial anode, the robot retraces its path along the predefined arc path to initiate reverse-phase cleaning. During subsequent cycles, the robot repositions near the anode block while maintaining the same motion strategy (Fig. 3). In the second cycle, the longitudinal offset h between the current linear path (y_1) and the prior cycle's linear path (y_0) is defined as:

$$h = y_0 - y_1 \quad (4)$$

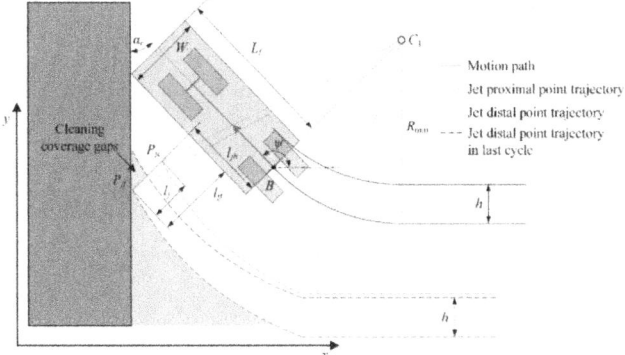

Fig. 3. Cleaning motion path in two cycles

In practical cleaning operations, the longitudinal offset h exhibits operational variability while remaining constrained by the jet's effective range l_j (i.e., $h < l_j$). As demonstrated in Fig. 3, the forward-cleaning coverage expands progressively during robot motion, significantly reducing biofouling residual zones through deliberate path overlap. After the robot performs repeated cyclic movements in the vicinity of the anode block based on this path planning method, the robot body will overlap with the residual biofouling as shown in Fig. 4.

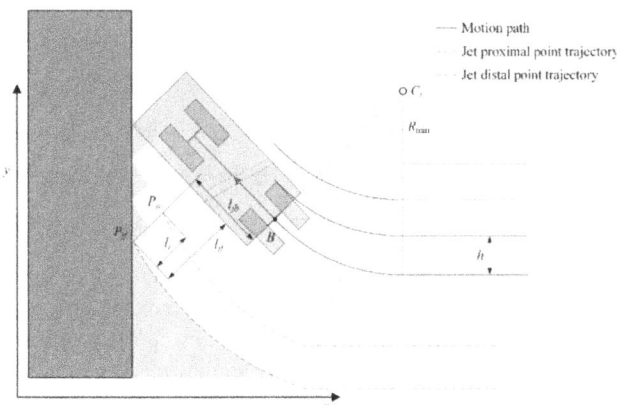

Fig. 4. Robot position schematic after multiple cleaning path planning cycles

As the robotic architecture shown in Fig. 1, the magnetic wheels constitute the primary collision interface between the robot and the residual biofouling. A systematic analysis of collision conditions for the frontal magnetic wheels and cleaning blind zones is conducted, as illustrated in Fig. 5.

In practical cleaning operation scenarios, the vertical spacing between consecutive robotic cleaning cycles exhibits non-constant characteristics, with the corner point of the safety rectangle at the front-left section potentially located at any position between P_{a1}

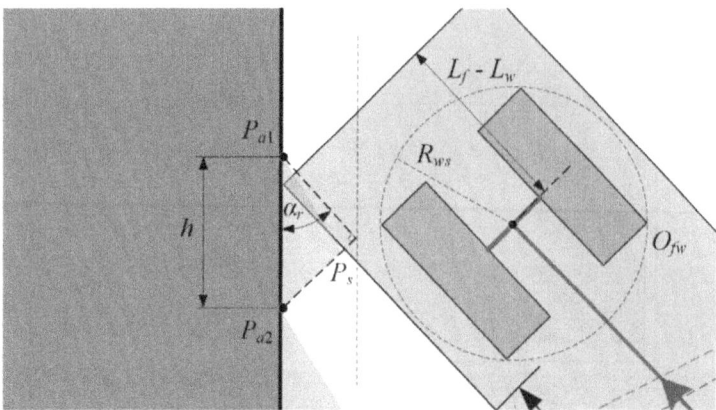

Fig. 5. Analysis of collision conditions

and P_{a2}. This needs computational analysis for the worst-case scenario where the cleaning blind zone maximally intrudes into the safety boundary. Based on the generation of blind zones illustrated in Fig. 3, auxiliary lines $P_{a1}P_s$ and $P_{a2}P_s$ are established in Fig. 5, where $P_{a2}P_s$ extends along the lower edge of the cleaning blind zone. The orthogonal relationship between $P_{a1}P_s$ and $P_{a2}P_s$ ensures that the intersection angle between $P_{a1}P_s$ and the anode block boundary remains α_r, thereby constraining the blind zone within the triangular region $\Delta P_{a1}P_{a2}P_s$. Considering the circular occupancy area o_{fw} (with radius R_{ws}) generated by the front wheel during steering maneuvers, the non-collision condition between the magnetic wheel and cleaning blind zone is mathematically formulated as the non-overlapping constraint between triangle $\Delta P_{a1}P_{a2}P_s$ and o_{fw}. The geometric constraint is expressed as:

$$h \cos\alpha_r \sin\alpha_r + R_{ws} \leq (L_f - L_w)\sin\alpha_r + \frac{W}{2}\cos\alpha_r \tag{5}$$

where $h < l_j$, α_r varies with the length L_f of the safety rectangle. Through considering robotic dimensions and cleaning jet characteristics, appropriate selection of L_f and W can satisfy the non-collision constraints. Thus, the robot can avoid collisions with residual biofouling. By implementing the proposed cleaning path, continuous cleaning operation in the anode region is achieved, fulfilling high-efficiency cleaning requirements. Under reverse cleaning operations on the left-side regions of the anode block, the analytical conditions and procedures align with those previously described. Figure 6 shows the path planning of the robot in the left-side regions of the anode block. This paper omits redundant explanations about this part of the path planning analysis here to maintain conciseness.

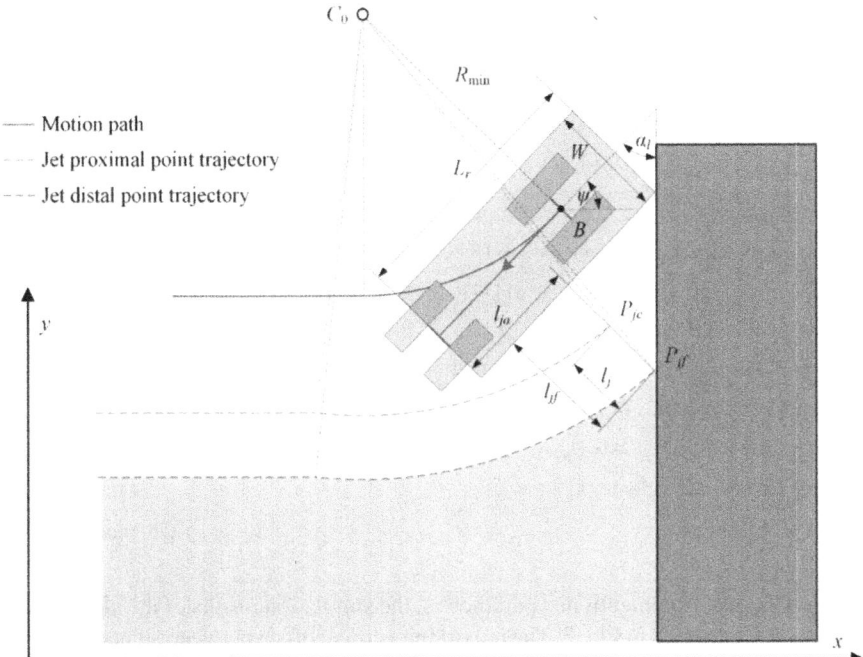

Fig. 6. Cleaning motion path for cleaning operations on the left-side regions of the anode block

4 Simulation

The operational environment was set to a 6.3 m × 5 m planar map based on the jacket cylinder's circumference and anode block distribution, where the anode block measures 3.15 m in length and 0.25 m in width. Dimensional parameters for UCR and cleaning water jet are specified in Table 1. Notably, while the robot's overall width W_b incorporates the nozzle, this component is excluded from the collision analysis in Sect. 3. Consequently, the safety rectangle parameter W considers solely the robot's main body width, with its maximum physical dimension being 258 mm. Through parameter selection of $L_f = 470$ mm and $W = 284$ mm for the safety rectangle, the clearance between the jet's distal point and the rectangle boundary measures $l_{jf} = 130$ mm. By Eq. (1), it can be calculated that $\alpha_r = 0.414$ rad. The chosen parameters demonstrably satisfy the non-collision constraints outlined in Sect. 2, confirming the validity of the selected safety rectangle dimensions. For robotic cleaning operations on the left-side regions of the anode block, identical parameters ($L_f = 470$ mm, $W = 284$ mm and $l_{jf} = 130$ mm) also satisfy the non-collision constraints.

Table 1. Dimension parameters of UCR and the water jet

Parameter	Value
Wheelbase (L_f)	367 mm
Width (W_b)	345 mm
Length (L_b)	570 mm
Distance from the center of front axle to UCR's front end (L_{front})	102 mm
Distance from the center of rear axle to UCR's rear end (L_{rear})	101 mm
Radius of circular occupancy area (R_{ws})	121 mm
Maximum steering angle (δ_{max})	20°
Minimum steering radius (R_{min})	1008 mm
Distance from jet to front axle (l_{ja})	193 mm
Distance from jet to rear axle (l_{jb})	174 mm
Length of jet (l_j)	90 mm

Based on the aforementioned parameters, the simulation results of the cleaning path planning are presented in Fig. 7. The maximum vertical offset between adjacent cleaning paths was set to $h = 90$ mm, with the robot completing 15 cleaning cycles on both left and right anode block regions. The simulation demonstrates that the proposed path planning strategy achieves significant reduction in residual biofouling zones. The magnetic wheels maintain a safe clearance from cleaning blind zone boundaries, ensuring collision-free operation.

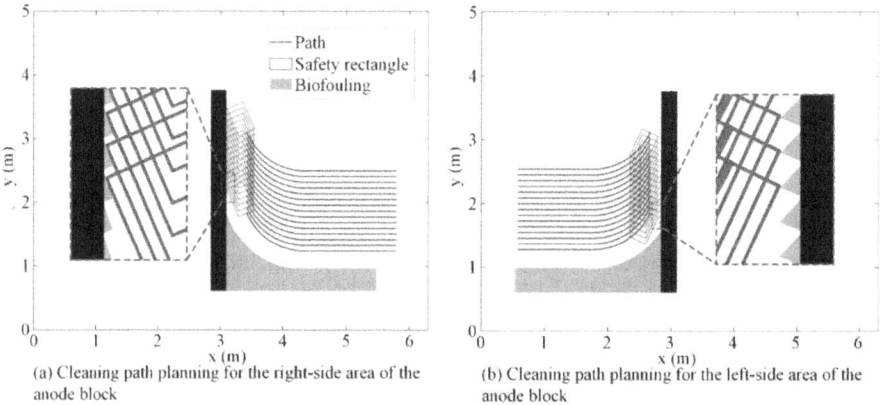

(a) Cleaning path planning for the right-side area of the anode block

(b) Cleaning path planning for the left-side area of the anode block

Fig. 7. Simulation results of cleaning path planning

5 Experiments

To validate the practical applicability of the geometry-based path planning method for cleaning operations in anode blocks area, experimental validation was conducted. A 2 m long × 0.24 m wide × 0.5 m high black foam block served as the simulated anode block structure, rigidly mounted on steel Pipe. Biofouling was replicated by attaching marine shells to the pipe surfaces adjacent to the simulated anode. The experimental setup is documented in Fig. 8. To ensure operational safety, the water jet pressure was elevated to 30 MPa, extending the effective jet length for enhanced collision avoidance capability.

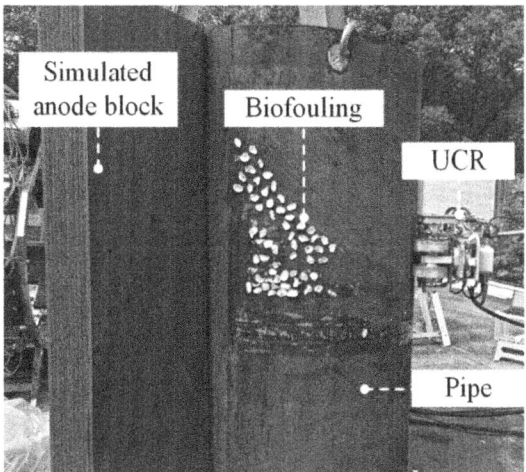

Fig. 8. Experimental platform2

Figure 9 illustrates the robotic cleaning process following the planned trajectory within the anode block area. Constrained by the pipe dimensions and operational safety boundaries, the robot executed three cleaning cycles with a vertical inter-path spacing of 90 mm. During the initial cycle, the robot achieved effective pose adjustment through path-guided navigation near the anode boundary, enabling the cleaning jet to cover extensive left-frontal surfaces. This operation successfully reduced blind zone formation while creating sufficient maneuvering space for subsequent cycles. The sequential cleaning process confirmed the method's capability to maintain continuous operational safety while achieving high surface coverage efficiency.

(a) First cycle

(b) Second cycle

(c) Third cycle

Fig. 9. Cleaning experiment process

Figure 10 shows the robot's cleaning path and positional data during the cleaning experiment. In the initial phases of the second and third cleaning cycles, the path tracker required adjustment time to respond to abrupt curvature changes in the trajectory, resulting in transient deviations between the robot's actual position and the planned path. These curvature variations primarily stem from constraining the robot's motion within a 2-m range around the anode block for experimental simplicity. During subsequent motion, the positional errors gradually diminished without affecting the cleaning performance.

Despite fixed inter-cycle spacing, accumulated localization errors caused positional deviations in the vertical direction near the anode's right boundary. However, by adaptively increasing the cleaning jet pressure to 30 MPa for extended coverage, the residual biofouling zones resulting from these deviations were effectively reduced under the guidance of the planned path. The experimental results further validate the robustness and practical effectiveness of the proposed path planning methodology.

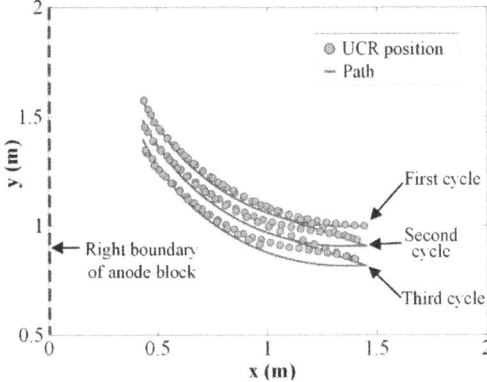

Fig. 10. Cleaning path and UCR's position in the experiment

6 Conclusion

This study investigates path planning methodologies for UCR operating in anode block regions, proposing a geometry-based path planning approach. A motion path combining straight lines and circular arcs was developed through systematic analysis of the geometric relationships between the robot and anode blocks, with derivation of non-collision constraints between the robot and cleaning blind zones. The methodology's feasibility for enabling continuous cleaning operations was validated through path planning simulations and experimental implementations.

References

1. Song, C., Cui, W.: Review of underwater ship hull cleaning technologies. J. Marine. Sci. Appl. **19**(3), 415–429 (2020). https://doi.org/10.1007/s11804-020-00157-z
2. Tamburri, M.N., et al.: In-water cleaning and capture to remove ship biofouling: an initial evaluation of efficacy and environmental safety. Front. Mar. Sci. **7**, 437 (2020). https://doi.org/10.3389/fmars.2020.00437
3. Nassiraei, A.A.F., Sonoda, T., Ishii, K.: Development of ship hull cleaning underwater robot. In: 2012 Fifth International Conference on Emerging Trends in Engineering and Technology, Himeji, Japan, pp. 157–162. IEEE (2012). https://doi.org/10.1109/ICETET.2012.74
4. Chen, Y., Liu, S., Zhang, L., Zheng, P., Yang, C.: Study on the adsorption performance of underwater propeller-driven Bernoulli adsorption device. Ocean Eng. **266**, 112724 (2022). https://doi.org/10.1016/j.oceaneng.2022.112724
5. Tunawattana, N., Norman, R., Roskilly, A.P.: Design of an underwater positioning sensor for crawling ship hull maintenance robots. Proc. Inst. Mech. Eng. Part M: J. Eng. Maritime Environ. **224**(2), 115–125 (2010). https://doi.org/10.1243/14750902JEME180
6. Chen, L., Cui, R., Yan, W., Xu, H., Zhao, H., Li, H.: Design and climbing control of an underwater robot for ship hull cleaning. Ocean Eng. **274**, 114024 (2023). https://doi.org/10.1016/j.oceaneng.2023.114024
7. Ross, B., Bares, J., Fromme, C.: A semi-autonomous robot for stripping paint from large vessels. Int. J. Robot. Res. **22**(7–8), 617–626 (2003). https://doi.org/10.1177/02783649030227010

8. Akinfiev, T.S., Armada, M.A., Fernandez, R.: Nondestructive testing of the state of a ship's hull with an underwater robot. Russ. J. Nondestruct. Test. **44**(9), 626–633 (2008). https://doi.org/10.1134/S1061830908090064
9. Chen, Y., Liu, S., Fan, J., Yang, C.: Novel online optimized control for underwater pipe-cleaning robots. Appl. Sci. **10**(12), 4279 (2020). https://doi.org/10.3390/app10124279
10. Su, H., Liu, S., Zhang, L., Chen, Y., Yang, C.: Biofouling recognition and boundary tracking control for underwater cleaning robots. Ocean Eng. **295**, 116707 (2024). https://doi.org/10.1016/j.oceaneng.2024.116707

Experimental Optimization of Clap-and-Fling Wing Stroke Kinematics and Geometry Configuration

Wenjie Dai[1,2], Yuhan Liu[1,2], and Xuan Wang[1,2(✉)]

[1] School of Computer Science and Technology, Harbin Institute of Technology (Shenzhen), Shenzhen 518055, China
wangxuan@cs.hitsz.edu.cn
[2] Guangdong Provincial Key Laboratory of Novel Security Intelligence Technologies, Harbin Institute of Technology (Shenzhen), Shenzhen 518055, China

Abstract. Flapping-wing Micro Air Vehicles (MAVs) imitate the aerodynamic mechanisms of insects, offering superior energy efficiency and maneuverability for confined space operations. However, their aerodynamic performance is highly sensitive to the interplay between wing kinematics and geometry. Existing research primarily focuses on single-aspect optimizations, often leading to limited applicability. This work introduces an experimental optimization framework for flapping-wing MAVs based on a symmetric double-crank and double-rocker mechanism. We systematically investigate the effect of multi-dimensional parameters under the clap-and-fling mechanism, including leading edge length, stiffener design, and flapping angles. Experimental evaluations reveal that the optimized configuration achieves a peak cycle-averaged lift coefficient of 2.54 and power loading above 8 g/W, demonstrating the effectiveness of the multi-parameter strategy in improving aerodynamic performance.

Keywords: Flapping-wing micro air vehicle · Clap-and-fling mechanism · Experimental optimization · Wing parameter

1 Introduction

Flapping-wing micro air vehicles mimic the flight functions of biological entities and are distinguished in the field of aerial vehicles by their unique biomimicry and miniaturization. Compared to traditional fixed-wing and rotary-wing aircraft, flapping-wing micro air vehicles have distinct advantages in terms of appearance and maneuverability, enabling them to hover and navigate confined spaces with high adaptability and a wide range of operation, with only minor limitations from terrain constraints [1]. Research shows that, under comparable scale conditions, flapping flight has superior energy efficiency, which is a key reason for its widespread adoption among flying creatures in nature [2].

In the aerodynamics of flapping-wing MAVs, the clap-and-fling mechanism is a promising area of research. Weis-Fogh's studies on wasps indicate that the clap-and-fling mechanism is crucial for lift generation in insects [3]. Subsequent research, using dynamic mechanical models and simulations of viscous fluid equations, further validates the role of leading-edge vortices in lift generation during the clap-and-fling motion [4]. Presently, numerous flapping-wing MAV prototypes, including those in the DelFly series [5–7], incorporate the clap-and-fling mechanism.

The aerodynamic efficiency of the clap-and-fling mechanism is affected by various parameters. Okamoto et al. observed that wings with a 9% chord height enhanced the maximum lift coefficient [8]. Gehrke et al. refined pitch angle kinematics, attaining a cycle-average lift coefficient of $\bar{C}_L = 2.09$ at high angles of attack [9]. Vargas et al. reported a modest improvement in the lift-to-drag ratio using 2D corrugated dragonfly wings, which impacts $\bar{C}_L$ [10]. Nguyen et al. illustrated that the clap-and-fling effect elevated the lift of their X-wing MAV by approximately 45%, correlating with an increase in $\bar{C}_L$ [11]. These studies highlight the significance of optimizing wing kinematics and geometry to augment $\bar{C}_L$, thereby enhancing aerodynamic performance in flapping-wing MAVs. While much research has focused on enhancing lift, there is a lack of studies on $\bar{C}_L$ of operational flapping-wing MAVs [12, 13]. Furthermore, existing research often focuses on single-aspect optimization, such as wing geometry or flapping dynamics, which may yield suboptimal results that are not globally optimal.

In this study, we aim to design an optimal wing configuration that is globally optimal for our flapping mechanism, considering multiple dimensions including the leading edge length, the stiffener shape, and the flapping angles. Our study focuses primarily on $\bar{C}_L$ as a key metric for assessing wing design. We examine the variations in aerodynamic efficiency in response to different parameters and evaluate the correlation with wing deformation and the clap-and-fling mechanism. This approach enables a deeper investigation into the performance characteristics of flapping-wing MAVs and offers new insights into wing design optimization. Subsequently, we implement the optimized wing design in flapping-wing MAVs for single-wing flight data analysis, leveraging the enhanced aerodynamic efficiency. The prototype achieves the targeted aerodynamic efficiency metrics, including the cycle-averaged lift coefficient, power loading, and flapping lift force. Additionally, the multidimensional optimization approach ensures a globally optimal design, which is more comprehensive and leads to better overall system performance, including motor and transmission efficiency.

2 Flapping Wing Mechanism and Wing Configuration

2.1 Flapping Mechanism and Wing Kinematics

As shown in Fig. 3, the mechanical structure of the aircraft emulates the flight mechanism of insects, utilizing a motor to drive the wings in periodic flapping via a double-crank double-rocker mechanism. The flapping mechanism translates the motor's rotational motion into the dynamic flapping of the wings. Motor speed is controlled by adjusting the voltage, which powers the crank-rocker mechanism. The flapping mechanism primarily utilizes the clap-and-fling effects, involving two key actions: clapping and fling. During the clapping phase, the leading edge of the wing precedes the trailing edge, forming a closed gap, and the rapid approach compresses the air around the wing tips, resulting in a high-pressure area. In the fling phase, the wings abruptly part, forming a new gap, and air is drawn into this gap, initiating a circulation flow. The combination of these two phases yields significant lift [14, 15] (Fig. 1).

Fig. 1. Double-crank double-rocker mechanism.

The total lift of a clap-and-fling flapping-wing system can be mainly decomposed into three aerodynamic components based on the quasi-steady model [16]: circulatory force, added mass force, and viscous drag.

The circulatory force, arising from fluid circulation around the wing, is governed by the circulation term Γ, which varies between the fling phase and other phases of the wing motion. During the fling phase, the circulation is enhanced due to wing-wing interaction and is expressed as:

$$\Gamma = \frac{1}{2}C_L c(r)|V| + \frac{1}{2}C_F c^2(r)\dot{\theta}_{\text{fling}} \quad (1)$$

where C_L is the lift coefficient, C_F is the fling coefficient quantifying circulation enhancement during wing separation, $c(r)$ is the spanwise chord length distribution, $\dot{\theta}_{\text{fling}}$ is the angular velocity of wing separation during fling, and $|V|$ is the relative velocity perceived by the wing element. In the context of unsteady aerodynamics, a key contributor to circulation enhancement is the formation of a leading-edge vortex (LEV). This vortex develops near the wing's front edge during rapid wing rotation or separation and plays a critical role in transient lift augmentation under the clap-and-fling mechanism. For non-fling phases, the circulation reduces to:

$$\Gamma = \frac{1}{2}C_L c(r)|V| + \frac{1}{2}C_R c^2(r)\dot{\theta}_w \quad (2)$$

where C_R is the rotational circulation coefficient and $\dot{\theta}_w$ is the wing pitch rate.

The added mass force, resulting from the inertial effects of accelerating the surrounding fluid, is defined as:

$$dF_{\text{addmass}} = -\begin{bmatrix} m_{11} a_{x_w} \\ m_{22} a_{z_w} \end{bmatrix} dr \quad (3)$$

$$m_{22} = \frac{1}{4}\pi \rho_f c_{\text{eff}}^2(r) \quad (4)$$

where m_{11} and m_{22} are the added mass coefficients, a_{x_w} and a_{z_w} are the accelerations along the x_w-axis and z_w-axis, ρ_f is the fluid density, and $c_{\text{eff}}(r)$ is the effective chord length.

The viscous drag, dominated by skin friction and pressure drag, is modeled as:

$$dF_{\text{visc}} = \frac{1}{2}\rho_f c(r) C_D |V| \begin{bmatrix} v_{x_w} \\ v_{z_w} \end{bmatrix} dr \tag{5}$$

$$C_D = C_{D_0}\cos^2\alpha_w + C_{D_{\pi/2}}\sin^2\alpha_w \tag{6}$$

where C_{D_0} and $C_{D_{\pi/2}}$ are the drag coefficients at 0° and 90° angles of attack, α_w is the local angle of attack during the clap phase, and v_{x_w} and v_{z_w} are the relative velocities along the wing's local axes.

The total lift is obtained by integrating these force components over the wing span and projecting them onto the vertical axis:

$$L = \int_0^{R_w} (dF_{\text{circ}}\sin\theta + dF_{\text{addmass}}\sin\theta - dF_{\text{visc}}\cos\theta) \tag{7}$$

where θ is the body pitch angle and R_w is the wing span.

The cycle-averaged lift coefficient ($\bar{C}_L$) is then calculated by normalizing the time-averaged lift with dynamic pressure and reference wing area:

$$\bar{C}_L = \frac{1}{T}\int_0^T \frac{L(t)}{\frac{1}{2}\rho V^2 S} dt \tag{8}$$

where $L(t)$ is the instantaneous lift force, ρ is the air density, V is the characteristic velocity (peak flapping speed), $S = R_w \cdot \bar{c}$ is the reference wing area (span R_w multiplied by mean chord $\bar{c}$), and T is the flapping period.

2.2 Multi-dimensional Parameters of Flapping Wing

This study defines and optimizes the wing's geometric shape and flapping motion parameters to determine the optimal aerodynamic characteristics. Based on the quasi-steady model, $\bar{C}_L$ is hypothesized to be influenced by four key parameters through distinct aerodynamic mechanisms: the leading edge length, stiffener shape, and the upper and lower wing's maximum and minimum angles.

As illustrated in Fig. 2, the pentagonal wing shape, akin to the morphology of insect wings, simplifies the management of experimental variables. Each wing features a tip chord length shorter than that of the root, and includes four stiffeners symmetrically placed along both sides, functioning as structural veins. Within each wing section, one end of each stiffener connects to the leading edge, and the other end reaches the two wingtips, contingent on the trailing edge length and the tip's chord length. *LE* refers to the leading edge length; *CR* and *CT* denote the chord lengths at the root and tip, respectively. *TE* indicates the length of the trailing edge, which runs parallel to the leading edge. A semi-elliptical notch, measuring 30 mm along the major axis and 15 mm along the minor axis, is incorporated into the wing for the flapping mechanism. With *TE*, *CR*,

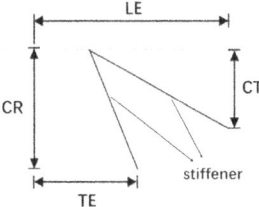

Fig. 2. The shape of wing.

and the angles of the stiffeners held constant, *LE* and *CT* are proportionally adjusted to modify the wing dimensions. Specifically, *CR* is set at 65 mm, *TE* at 50 mm. By modifying the lengths of the connecting rods and rockers in the double-crank double-rocker mechanism, the flapping cycle's maximum and minimum inter-wing angles are altered. As shown in Fig. 3, α and β indicate the maximum and the minimum angle.

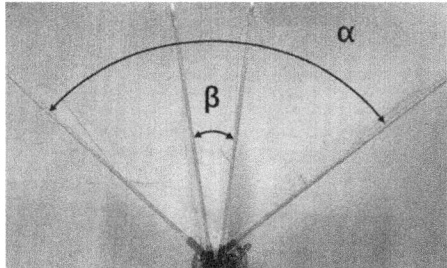

Fig. 3. The maximum and minimum angle between the upper and lower wing.

Four distinct sets of wings were designed and tested, and their specifications are detailed in Table 1. Initially, we examine the effect of *LE*, on aerodynamic performance (Type 1: Wings 1–9). The optimal *LE* value, ascertained after experimentation, is then applied to subsequent designs. In the Type 2 tests (Wings 10–13), we assess aerodynamic performance with the wings' leading and trailing edges kept horizontal and parallel, maintaining the pentagonal shape, by modifying the stiffness of the stiffeners and using carbon fiber rods and strips of different sizes. For the initial two test types, the wing's flapping amplitude is kept constant. In Type 3 (Wings 14–19) and Type 4 (Wings 20–25), all wing geometric parameters are set to the optimal values established in prior experiments, and the maximum and minimum inter-wing angles are adjusted to assess their influence on flight performance metrics.

2.3 Fabrication Method

The wing manufacturing process begins with the creation of accurate wooden templates that reflect the wings' geometric specifications. These templates direct the cutting of pearl cotton, thereby forming the initial shape of the wings. Subsequently, carbon fiber rods are placed at designated locations on the material. Double-sided adhesive is then applied to bond the carbon fiber rods firmly to the pearl cotton, merging the materials. Post-bonding, precise manual refinements are applied to the wings' edges and surfaces to ensure conformity with the design specifications. Furthermore, carbon fiber rods are affixed at the leading edge to facilitate the attachment of the wings to the micro air vehicle's flapping mechanism, finalizing the wing construction for aircraft integration.

Table 1. Specifications of the designed and tested wings

	Wing number	LE (mm)	CT (mm)	Stiffener (mm)	α (deg)	β (deg)
Type 1	1	100	42.9			
	2	105	45			
	3	110	47.1			
	4	115	49.3			
	5	120	51.4	D0.6		
	6	125	53.6			
	7	130	55.7		115	22.5
	8	135	57.8			
	9	140	60			
Type 2	10	135	57.8	D0.6		
	11	135	57.8	D0.5		
	12	135	57.8	D0.3		
	13	135	57.8	0.1*1		
Type 3	14	135	57.8		110	
	15	135	57.8		120	
	16	135	57.8		130	35
	17	135	57.8		140	
	18	135	57.8		150	
	19	135	57.8	0.1*1	160	
Type 4	20	135	57.8			22.5
	21	135	57.8			25
	22	135	57.8			27.5
	23	135	57.8		140	30
	24	135	57.8			35
	25	135	57.8			40

3 Experiment

3.1 Experimental Optimization Evaluation Criteria

In our experiments, we optimize multi-dimensional key parameters. The evaluation of these parameters is based on their effect on aerodynamic performance, as measured by the $\bar{C}_L$ (Eq. (8)), power loading (the ratio of lift to power), and lift, with a particular focus on $\bar{C}_L$ and power loading.

3.2 Experimental Platform Setup

As shown in Fig. 4, our flapping-wing MAV prototype is mounted on a 6-axis Nano17Ti force/torque sensor to measure instantaneous lift during flapping. A high-speed camera (Revealer M120_16G) captures the front view of wing motion, from which flapping frequency, clap-and-fling phases are extracted by frame-by-frame analysis. The power supply voltage and current are recorded to compute input power and power loading. The experimental setup consists of our flapping-wing MAV, an external DC power supply, the force/torque sensor, high-speed camera, and a data acquisition system (ATI DAQ F/T).

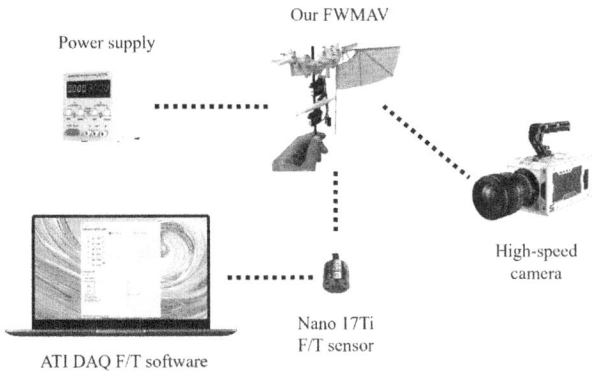

Fig. 4. Schematic of the experimental arrangement.

3.3 Experimental Procedures and Data Processing

The experiment begins with the activation of the power supply, which initiates wing flapping for approximately 3 s. Following the initial flapping, the F/T sensor measures lift while the high-speed camera concurrently acquires data and records videos. At the 5-s interval, the external power supply is deactivated, terminating data recording by the sensor and high-speed camera for the respective set. For each test condition, measurements for each wing set are conducted three times to verify the accuracy and reliability of the data. The sensor's sampling frequency is established at 1 kHz to ensure accurate measurement of each flapping motion. Ultimately, we calculate the average of the recorded forces and power, and assess each parameter against the optimization criteria. By comparing performance indicators across various parameter configurations, we identify the optimal parameter combination.

4 Results and Discussion

In this section, we analyze the aerodynamics and kinematics of the wings using the processed data across various parameter settings (Table 1). We present the experimental results for the $\bar{C}_L$ and power loading across diverse wing designs, and discuss the outcomes and findings for each wing design series.

4.1 Effect of the Leading Edge Length

In this subsection, we examine the effect of leading edge length on flight performance. For this purpose, we analyze pentagonal wings, varying LE while keeping root lengths, stiffener and angles constant. The root chord is set at 65 mm, with the trailing edge fixed at 50 mm. We progressively extend LE from 100 mm to 140 mm, proportionally adjusting the tip chord length from 42.9 mm to 60 mm (Type 1).

As shown in Fig. 5, both $\bar{C}_L$ and power loading increase with LE up to 135 mm, reaching a peak of $\bar{C}_L = 1.749$, then decline beyond this point. Moderate increases in LE enhance wing area and wing–wing interaction during clap-and-fling, but excessive elongation causes structural deformation and flow separation. According to Eq. (1), larger chord length boosts circulation Γ, explaining the initial lift improvement. However, as Eq. (5) suggests, increased surface area also raises viscous drag, offsetting the benefits. Thus, $LE = 135$ mm achieves the best trade-off between lift generation and aerodynamic loss.

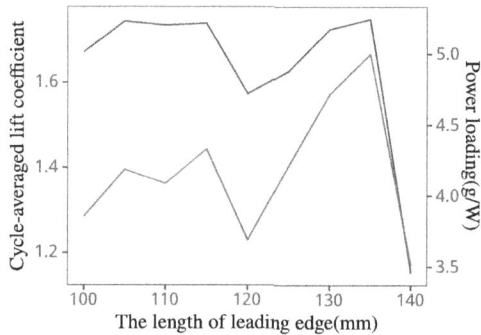

Fig. 5. $\bar{C}_L$ (red) and the power loading (blue) with respect to LE. (Color figure online)

4.2 Effect of the Stiffener Shape

In this subsection, we examine the effect of stiffener cross-sectional shapes on wing structural integrity and aerodynamic efficiency. Four stiffener designs, comprising three circular rods and one rectangular strip, underwent testing. The circular rods had diameters of 0.6 mm, 0.5 mm, and 0.3 mm, while the rectangular strip measured 0.1 mm in thickness and 1 mm in width (Type 2).

As shown in Table 2, the rectangular stiffener achieved the highest $\bar{C}_L = 1.958$ and power loading (6.355 g/W). High-speed camera reveals that thin circular rods deform excessively, disrupting wing alignment and LEV initiation. In contrast, the rectangular strip offers higher lateral stiffness and stable trailing edge dynamics, enhancing clap-and-fling consistency. According to Eq. (1), its rigidity supports faster and more symmetric fling motion, boosting circulation Γ and lift. Equation (4) further shows that a stable effective chord length improves added mass force, which thinner rods fail to maintain. Thus, the 0.1×1 mm rectangular stiffener offers the best balance of structural stability and aerodynamic performance.

Table 2. Effect of the stiffener shape on aerodynamic performance

Cross-sectional shape(mm)	$\bar{C}_L$	Power loading(g/W)
0.6 (Diameter)	1.749	5
0.5 (Diameter)	1.497	4.859
0.3 (Diameter)	1.307	4.571
0.1 * 1 (Thickness * Width)	1.958	6.355

4.3 Effect of the Maximum Angle Between the Upper and Lower Wing

In this subsection, we investigate the effect of the maximum angle (α) between the upper and lower wings on the aerodynamic performance (Type 3).

As shown in Fig. 6, both $\bar{C}_L$ and power loading rise with increasing α, peaking at 140°, with $\bar{C}_L$ exceeding 2 and power loading approaching 7 g/W, then decline. Larger α enhances fling strength and circulation by increasing angular velocity $\dot{\theta}_{\text{fling}}$ (Eq. 1). However, beyond 140°, LEV coherence degrades, with premature vortex shedding and asymmetric wake formation. This reduces effective circulation and lift. Additionally, higher angles increase viscous drag (Eq. 6), lowering efficiency. Thus, $\alpha = 140°$ offers the best balance between lift gain and LEV under clap-and-fling dynamics.

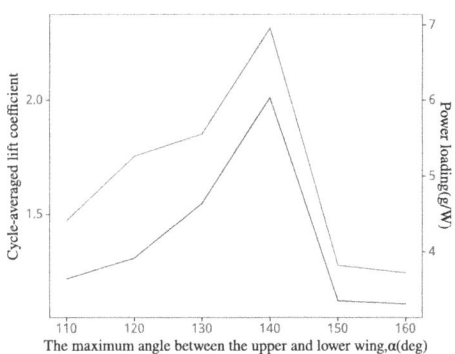

Fig. 6. $\bar{C}_L$ (red) and the power loading (blue) with respect to α. (Color figure online)

4.4 Effect of the Minimum Angle Between the Upper and Lower Wing

In this subsection, we evaluate the influence of the minimum angle (β) between the upper and lower wings on the aerodynamic performance (Type 4).

Figure 7 presents the impact of varying the minimum angle (β) between the upper and lower wings, ranging from 40° to 22.5°. Both the cycle-averaged lift coefficient $\bar{C}_L$ and power loading exhibit a non-linear response: increasing as β decreases, peaking at $\beta = 25°$, where $\bar{C}_L$ reaches 2.54 and power loading exceeds 8 g/W, before declining again. Smaller β values improve leading-edge alignment during clap, enhancing airflow compression and wing–wing interaction. However, β below 25° leads to visible wing deformation and motion asymmetry. This trend aligns with the quasi-steady model: smaller β boosts circulation (Eq. 1), but excessive reduction causes structural compliance, flow separation, and inertial losses (Eq. 3–4). Thus, $\beta = 25°$ achieves optimal balance between lift enhancement and structural stability.

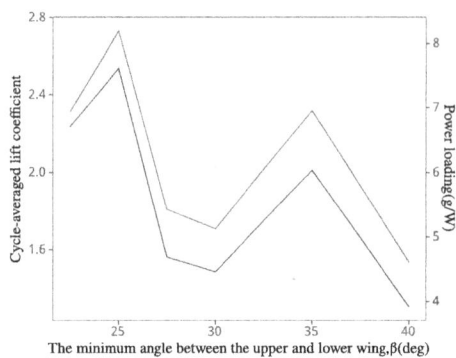

Fig. 7. $\bar{C}_L$ (red) and the power loading (blue) with respect to β. (Color figure online)

4.5 Optimal Parameter Design and Wing Motion Observation

Experimental evaluation determined Wing 21 as the optimal configuration, combining a 135 mm LE, 0.1 × 1 mm rectangular stiffener, a maximum wing angle of 140°, and a minimum angle of 25°. This design produced the highest aerodynamic performance, achieving a cycle-averaged lift coefficient $\bar{C}_L$ of 2.54 and a power loading above 8 g/W. The results highlight the effectiveness of a multi-parameter optimization strategy in improving the aerodynamic performance of flapping-wing MAVs under the clap-and-fling mechanism.

Figure 8 illustrates the time-resolved wing motion of Wing 21 over a full flapping cycle. Notably, the clap-and-fling phase—defined from the onset of wing contact (clap) to the full wing separation (end of fling)—extends from $\tau = 0.4$ to $\tau = 0.7$, accounting for 30% of the cycle duration. During this interval, the wings undergo tight frontal alignment followed by symmetric and rapid outward rotation, producing sustained wing–wing interaction. This extended interaction period is crucial: according to Eq. (1), lift generation is directly tied to the time-integrated circulation Γ, which is significantly influenced by the angular velocity $\dot{\theta}_{\text{fling}}$ and wing geometry. The optimized configuration effectively sustains and stabilizes this high-lift generation phase, rather than concentrating it in a brief impulse. Consequently, the observed performance is not only a result of geometric tuning but also of favorably timed aerodynamic force development. The visualization in Fig. 8 thus confirms that the optimal parameter set enables structural and kinematic conditions that maximize the effectiveness of the clap-and-fling mechanism throughout a meaningful portion of the flapping cycle.

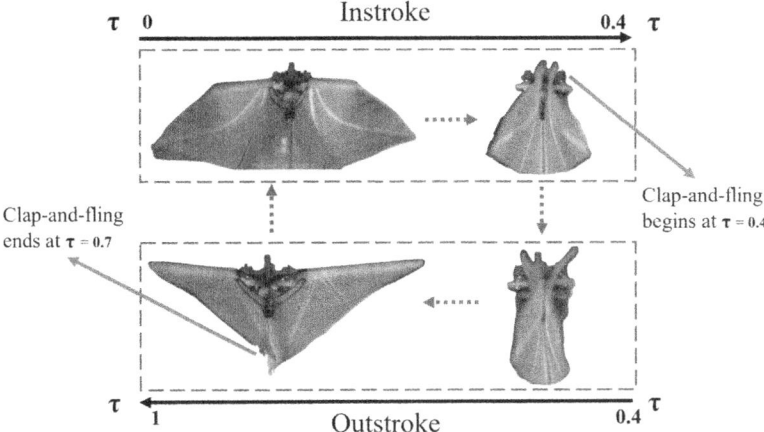

Fig. 8. Schematic of Wing 21's motion during one stroke based on the high-speed camera.

5 Conclusions

This study investigated the aerodynamic optimization of a flapping-wing platform under the clap-and-fling mechanism through a multidimensional parameter framework. The design space included geometric and kinematic variables, and the evaluation process combined force measurement with high-speed camera to assess their aerodynamic implications. Rather than focusing on isolated variables, the study emphasized the interplay among multiple parameters and their collective impact on lift generation. The experimental observations revealed that the effectiveness of the clap-and-fling mechanism is closely linked not only to instantaneous wing configuration but also to the timing and consistency of wing–wing interaction phases. These findings aligned well with quasi-steady aerodynamic modeling and contributed to a more comprehensive understanding of unsteady force production. The proposed methodology demonstrates how systematic tuning of multidimensional parameters can inform aerodynamic design in bioinspired flapping systems. It provides a foundation for future work involving active control strategies, or design adaptation across varying flight regimes.

Acknowledgment. This study is supported in part by the Guangdong Provincial Key Laboratory of Novel Security Intelligence Technologies under Grant 2022B1212010005, in part by the Colleges and Universities Stable Support Project of Shenzhen, China, (No. GXWD20220811173149002).

References

1. Phan, H.V., Park, H.C.: Insect-inspired, tailless, hover-capable flapping-wing robots: recent progress, challenges, and future directions. Prog. Aerosp. Sci. **111**, 100573 (2019)
2. Singh, S., Zuber, M., Hamidon, M.N., Mazlan, N., Basri, A.A., Ahmad, K.A.: Classification of actuation mechanism designs with structural block diagrams for flapping-wing drones: a comprehensive review. Prog. Aerosp. Sci. **134**, 100833 (2022)

3. Weis-Fogh, T.: Quick estimates of flight fitness in hovering animals, including novel mechanisms for lift production. J. Exp. Biol. **59**, 169–230 (1973)
4. Chin, Y.-W., et al.: Efficient flapping wing drone arrests high-speed flight using post-stall soaring. Sci. Robot. **5**(44), eaba2386 (2020)
5. de Croon, G.C.H.E., de Clercq, K.M.E., Ruijsink, R., Remes, B., de Wagter, C.: Design, aerodynamics, and vision-based control of the DelFly. Int. J. Micro Air Veh. **1**(2), 71–97 (2009)
6. De Wagter, C., Tijmons, S., Remes, B.D.W., de Croon, G.C.H.E.: Autonomous flight of a 20-gram Flapping Wing MAV with a 4-gram on board stereo vision system. In: Proceedings of the 2014 IEEE International Conference on Robotic Automation (ICRA), Hong Kong, China, pp. 4982–4987. IEEE, New York (2014)
7. Jafferis, N.T., Helbling, E.F., Karpelson, M., Wood, R.J.: Untethered flight of an insect-sized flapping-wing microscale aerial vehicle. Nature **570**, 491–495 (2019)
8. Okamoto, M., Yasuda, K., Azuma, A.: Aerodynamic characteristics of the wings and body of a dragonfly. J. Exp. Biol. **199**(2), 281–294 (1996)
9. Gehrke, A., Mulleners, K.: Phenomenology and scaling of optimal flapping wing kinematics. Bioinsp. Biomim. **16**(2), 026016 (2021)
10. Vargas, A., Mittal, R., Dong, H.: A computational study of the aerodynamic performance of a dragonfly wing section in gliding flight. Bioinsp. Biomim. **3**(2), 026004 (2008)
11. Nguyen, Q., Chan, W., Debiasi, M.: Design, fabrication, and performance test of a hovering-based flapping-wing micro air vehicle capable of sustained and controlled flight. Technical Report (2014)
12. Karásek, M., Muijres, F.T., de Wagter, C., Remes, B.D.W., de Croon, G.C.H.E.: A tailless aerial robotic flapper reveals that flies use torque coupling in rapid banked turns. Science **361**, 1089–1094 (2018)
13. Phan, H.V., Aurecianus, S., Au, T.K.L., Kang, T., Park, H.C.: Towards the long-endurance flight of an insect-inspired, tailless, two-winged, flapping-wing flying robot. IEEE Robot. Autom. Lett. **5**(3), 5059–5066 (2020)
14. Ellington, C.P.: The novel aerodynamics of insect flight: applications to micro-air vehicles. J. Exp. Biol. **202**(23), 3439–3448 (1999)
15. Lehmann, F.-O., Sane, S.P., Dickinson, M.: The aerodynamic effects of wing–wing interaction in flapping insect wings. J. Exp. Biol. **208**(16), 3075–3092 (2005)
16. Caetano, A.V.J.: Model identification of a flapping wing micro aerial vehicle. Ph.D. thesis (2016)

Agile and Versatile Bipedal Robot Tracking Control Through Reinforcement Learning

Han Zheng[1], Jiayi Li[1], Linqi Ye[2], Houde Liu[1(✉)], and Bin Liang[3]

[1] Tsinghua Shenzhen International Graduate School, 518055 Shenzhen, China
liu.hd@sz.tsinghua.edu.cn
[2] Collaborative Innovation Center for the Marine Artificial Intelligence, Shanghai University, 200444 Shanghai, China
[3] Department of Automation, Tsinghua University, 100084 Beijing, China

Abstract. The remarkable athletic intelligence displayed by humans in complex dynamic movements such as dancing and gymnastics suggests that the balance mechanism in biological beings is decoupled from specific movement patterns. This decoupling allows for the execution of both learned and unlearned movements under certain constraints while maintaining balance through minor whole-body coordination. To replicate this balance ability and body agility, this paper proposes a versatile controller for bipedal robots. This controller achieves ankle and body trajectory tracking across a wide range of gaits using a single small-scale neural network, which is based on a model-based IK solver and reinforcement learning. We consider a single step as the smallest control unit and design a universally applicable control input form suitable for any single-step variation. Highly flexible gait control can be achieved by combining these minimal control units with high-level policy through our extensible control interface. To enhance the trajectory tracking capability of our controller, we utilize a three-stage training curriculum. After training, the robot can move freely between target footholds at varying distances and heights. The robot can also maintain static balance without repeated stepping to adjust posture. Finally, we evaluate the tracking accuracy of our controller on various bipedal tasks, and the effectiveness of our control framework is verified in the simulation environment. A video is available at https://linqi-ye.github.io/video/Agile.mp4.

Keywords: Reinforcement Learning · Bipedal Robot · Locomotion Control

1 Introduction

Reinforcement learning (RL) has led to substantial progress in controlling legged robots, enabling behaviors that are robust, powerful, precise, lifelike, and increasingly intelligent [1,13]. To bridge the simulation-to-reality gap, techniques such as domain randomization [6,12] and privileged learning [3] improve policy robustness by randomizing dynamics or leveraging simulation-only information. Adaptation modules further support online adjustment using proprioception [8]. In parallel, imitation learning and adversarial training have been used to synthesize naturalistic motion patterns based on biological demonstrations [11].

Beyond low-level motion control, the pursuit of general-purpose robotic intelligence is accelerating, driven by advances in body control, computer vision, natural language processing, and simultaneous localization and mapping. Hierarchical frameworks decouple decision-making across temporal scales, allowing high-level strategies to coordinate reusable low-level behaviors [15,17]. Large-scale models trained on diverse datasets have enabled flexible robotic manipulation across a wide range of tasks [2].

However, these approaches are typically validated on fixed-base systems such as robotic arms. Applying them to floating-base legged robots is more challenging due to stability constraints and whole-body dynamics. Hybrid architectures that combine model-based planning with learned policies [7] have improved robustness and foot placement, while multitask reinforcement learning frameworks [13] offer scalable skill reuse. Yet these systems often lack interpretability and are difficult to adapt post-training, especially when specifying fine-grained locomotion behaviors in the action space.

To address this challenge, we propose a reinforcement learning-based tracking controller for bipedal robots that enables interpretable, low-level task specification while maintaining high-level generalization. The controller accepts real-time trunk and ankle pose references and produces balance-aware locomotion. It combines model-based feedforward control with learning-based feedback, and incorporates curriculum learning [16] to progressively shape performance. Our controller demonstrates agility, balance, and precise tracking across diverse locomotion tasks in simulation.

The main contributions of this paper are: (1) Proposing a task-independent balance control approach that decouples robot motion control from task requirements, enabling the robot to achieve intrinsic balance capability solely based on its physical structure. (2) Providing a real-time precise ankle position tracking method, allowing for controlled leg movement height in robots, with interpretability. The effectiveness of our approach is validated through simulation experiments.

2 Control Structure

2.1 Overview

Model-based methods and model-free reinforcement learning have been broadly applied to tackling bipedal locomotion. To accomplish complex motion tasks, the former typically requires establishing dynamic models that make a trade-off between complexity and accuracy, as well as manually designed control structures for specific tasks. The latter exhibits superior generalization and robustness while lacking some interpretability in its end-to-end control structure. Inspired by the ideal of combining these two approaches [5,9,10], we extend it to a general bipedal robot trajectory tracking control problem for both robot trunk and ankles. The framework of our control method is shown in Fig. 1.

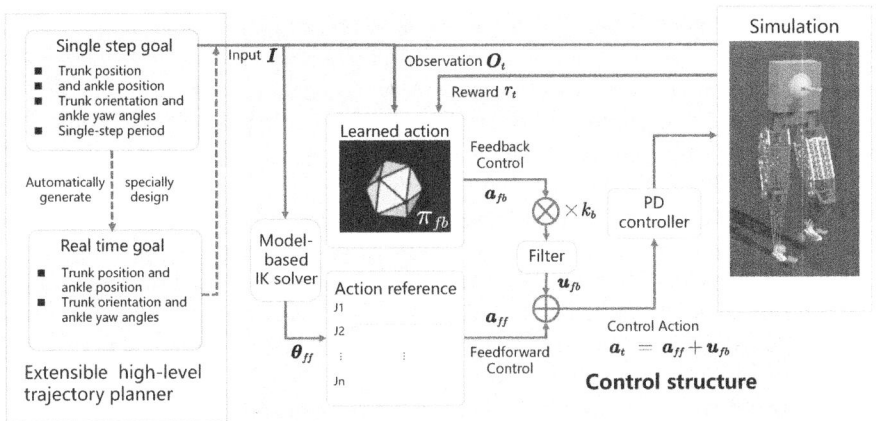

Fig. 1. Overview of the control structure

We use an extensible high-level trajectory planner to generate control trajectories according to different task as input, which is fed to both a model-based IK solver to generate feedforward signals and a neural network to generate feedback signal. We simplify the algorithm's manual design complexity significantly by using simple inverse kinematics instead of inverse dynamics models. These two signals are combined through weighted summation and filtering to generate target positions for each joint. Finally, a PD controller is used to control the robot.

2.2 Robot Model and Kinematics

We use a modified 12-joint Ranger Max robot [4], with each leg featuring three hip, one knee, and two ankle joints. Details are shown in Table 1.

Table 1. Details of the Robot Model.

Link	Physical Parameters	
	Size	Mass
Trunk	$0.3m \times 0.3m \times 0.15m$	$20kg$
Thigh	$0.4m$ (length)	$6.4kg$
Shank	$0.35m$ (length)	$2kg$
Foot	$0.16m$ (length)	$1kg$

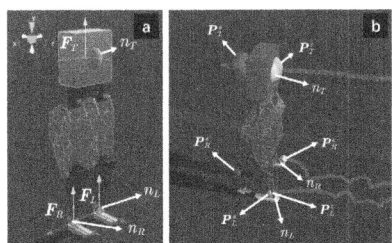

Fig. 2. Controllable nodes of the robot: (a) Controllable nodes and their coordinate system (b) Task-step target position and real-time target position of the controllable nodes

We first define the concept of controllable nodes: controllable nodes are the coordinates on the robot whose position and orientation can be set as control target. In legged control tasks, the most concerned points of the robot are the trunk center, the left ankle, and the right ankle while the position and orientation of the knee and hip joints are always ignored. Thus, we identify the trunk node n_T, the left ankle node n_L, and the right ankle node n_R as shown in Fig. 2.

We establish the robot base coordinate system $\boldsymbol{F}_B$ at n_T, the left ankle coordinate system $\boldsymbol{F}_L$ at n_L, and the right ankle coordinate system $\boldsymbol{F}_R$ at n_R as shown in Fig. 2. Since the pitch and roll angles of the robot's feet during walking are typically adjusted based on the environment and the robot's own state, we only consider the yaw angle of the feet as the control target. However, to prevent the leg joint solving from becoming a complex redundant degree of freedom problem, we assume that the feet always remain horizontal with respect to the trunk's transverse plane to provide a feedforward signal

$$|F_{LY} \times F_{BY}|^2 + |F_{RY} \times F_{BY}|^2 = 0 \qquad (1)$$

where $F_{.Y}$ is the Y-axis of coordinate system $\boldsymbol{F}_.$. Then the feedforward joint angles can be obtained by solving the inverse kinematics equations with the positions and orientations of the three controllable nodes, constrained by the assumption of horizontal feet

$$\boldsymbol{\theta} = ikine\left(\boldsymbol{P}_L, \psi_L, \boldsymbol{P}_R, \psi_R\right) \qquad (2)$$

where $\boldsymbol{\theta}$ is the vector of all the joint angles. $\boldsymbol{P}_L$ and $\boldsymbol{P}_R$ are the position of n_L and n_R. ψ_L and ψ_R are the yaw angles of n_L and n_R respectively. Then variables mentioned above are represented in the robot base coordinate system $\boldsymbol{F}_B$. We prevent the issue of unsolvable inverse kinematics function by preprocessing the controllable nodes' positions of the ankles that are outside the robot's workspace, moving them closer to the interior of the workspace.

2.3 Task Design and Parameterization

We define a task step as the motion of the foot from lift-off to landing, which serves as the basic unit in our control framework. A task is described as a sequence of such steps, each defined by the trajectories of three controllable nodes over a custom period. The desired position and orientation of these nodes at the end of each step represent the target state to be reached. Within a step, different gaits can be generated by designing smooth time-based trajectories. A high-level planner generates intermediate trajectories toward the target state: ankle motions are parameterized by fourth-order Bezier curves, enabling flexible shape control, while trunk trajectories typically follow uniform velocity and angular velocity profiles. This planner is extensible to more complex tasks using higher-order Bézier or trigonometric curves. To generalize across tasks, we define a set of basic task steps (Table 2), which can be composed to achieve a wide range of motion behaviors.

Table 2. Basic Task Step Introduction

Task Step	Task Step Introduction
Standing still	The robot stands still in random posture with different trunk and ankle nodes position and orientation.
Sidle	The robot moves left and right in a straight line with different trunk heights.
Squat	The robot adjusts its trunk position and orientation without moving its feet.
Walking backward/forward	The robot moves forward and backward in a straight line with different trunk heights.
Turn	The robot turns with a random radius.
Walking up and down stairs	The robot goes up and down steps of different heights and lengths.

For the first two basic tasks, the feet never leave the ground so that the task-step period is 0 s. For the other tasks, the task-step period is a random value between 0.4 s and 0.7 s. The shapes of ankle trajectories are controlled by several Bezier control points which vary randomly within a certain range. In our control structure, all these basic task steps take the form of a unified control input

$$\begin{aligned} \boldsymbol{I} &= \begin{bmatrix} \boldsymbol{I}^s & \boldsymbol{I}^t & \boldsymbol{T} \end{bmatrix} \\ \boldsymbol{I}^s &= \begin{bmatrix} \boldsymbol{P}_T^s & \boldsymbol{P}_L^s & \boldsymbol{P}_R^s & \boldsymbol{R}_T^s & \psi_L^s & \psi_R^s \end{bmatrix} \\ \boldsymbol{I}^t &= \begin{bmatrix} \boldsymbol{P}_T^t & \boldsymbol{P}_L^t & \boldsymbol{P}_R^t & \boldsymbol{R}_T^t & \psi_L^t & \psi_R^t \end{bmatrix} \\ \boldsymbol{T} &= \begin{bmatrix} T_L^t & T_R^t \end{bmatrix} \end{aligned} \quad (3)$$

where the superscript s describes the final state of a task step and t describes the real time state. $\boldsymbol{P}_T$, $\boldsymbol{P}_L$, $\boldsymbol{P}_R$ are the target position of n_T, n_L and n_R as shown in Fig. 2(b). $\boldsymbol{R}_T$ is the target orientation of n_T, ψ_L and ψ_R are the target yaw angles of n_L and n_R. The elements of $\boldsymbol{I}^s$ and $\boldsymbol{I}^t$ are all presented in $\boldsymbol{F}_B$. $\boldsymbol{T}$ acts as a timer, where T_L^t and T_R^t represent how long the left and right foot are expected to touch the ground respectively. For the basic task standing still and squat in which the feet are always in contact with the ground, $\boldsymbol{T}$ is always a zero vector.

2.4 Instruction Learning

In our previous work, we refer to a learning method that combines feedforward and feedback as "instruction learning" [18], which is inspired by the human learning process and is highly efficient, flexible, and versatile for robot motion learning. Compared to [18], this paper introduces substantial advancements in both technical design and functional scope. On the technical side, we incorporate an inverse kinematics (IK) solver into the feedforward module and employ Bézier curve-based planning for foot trajectories, resulting in more accurate and natural feedforward motion generation. On the functional side, this paper extends its capabilities to support smooth transitions between standing and walking, introduces foothold tracking, and enables precise stair climbing—thereby significantly enhancing the robot's adaptability in complex environments.

We pass the input in (3) to both a neural network and a model-based inverse kinematics (IK) solver, as shown in Fig. 1. The IK solver calculates the feedforward joint angles according to the real time target state of the controllable nodes using the inverse kinematics equations in (2). Then we normalize the values in $\boldsymbol{\theta}_{ff}$ to $[-1,1]$ to balance the unit

$$\boldsymbol{\theta}_{ff} = ikine\left(\boldsymbol{P}_L^t, \psi_L^t, \boldsymbol{P}_R^t, \psi_R^t\right) \tag{4}$$

$$\boldsymbol{a}_{ff} = normalization(\boldsymbol{\theta}_{ff}) \tag{5}$$

The output vector of the feedback network $\boldsymbol{a}_{fb}$ whose element is also limited in $[-1, 1]$ represents the feedback adjustment for each joint. The control action signal is a weighted sum of the feedforward and feedback signals.

$$\boldsymbol{a}_t = \boldsymbol{a}_{ff} + k_b \times \boldsymbol{a}_{fb} \tag{6}$$

By adjusting feedback ratio k_b, the boundaries of the control action are specified as shown in Fig. 3. The influence of k_b has been discussed in [18].

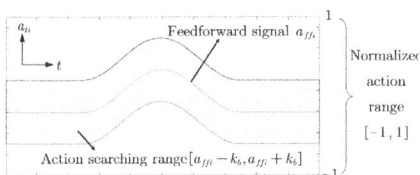

Fig. 3. Illustration of action bounding

Table 3. Training Hyperparameters.

Hyperparameter	Value (Stage1/2/3)
batch_size	2048
buffer_size	20480
learning_rate	0.0003 / 0.0002 / 0.0001
beta	0.02 / 0.015 / 0.007
epsilon	0.02 / 0.015 / 0.007
lambda	0.95
num_epoch	3

To prevent the robot joints from exceeding their physical limits, we clip the control signals to the range of $[-1, 1]$. Additionally, to mitigate the risk of robot jitter caused by large differences in adjacent joint angle signals, we employ a simple first-order low-pass filter to filter the control signals.

$$u_t = clamp\left(\alpha_{filter} a_t + (1 - \alpha_{filter})a_{t-1}, -1, 1\right) \tag{7}$$

where α_{filter} is the filtering coefficient and a_{t-1} represents the action signal of the previous time step. Finally, u_t is mapped to the range of joint angles for each joint and used to control the robot through the PD controller.

3 RL Problem Formulation

To obtain a feedback policy that cooperates with the model-based feedforward IK-solver, we employ reinforcement learning to train the feedback policy. Proximal policy optimization (PPO) [14] is used to train the feedback policy π_{fb} due to its stability, sample efficiency and strong adaptability to continuous action space.

3.1 Hyperparameter and Neural Network

Some of the main training hyperparameters are shown in Table 3. The values of learning rate, beta and epsilon varies in different training stages. We achieve finer adjustment of the network by gradually reducing their maximum values and choose a linear learning schedule. The feedback network has an actor-critic structure. The actor network is a multi-layer perceptron (MLP) with 3 hidden layers with 512 hidden units for each layer. The critic network is another MLP with 2 hidden layers with 128 hidden units for each layer.

3.2 Observation and Action

The observation of the learning strategy is designed as

$$O_t = \begin{bmatrix} I^s_{error} & I^t_{error} & I^t_v & T & O_{state} & a_{ff} & a_{fb(t-1)} \end{bmatrix}$$
$$O_{state} = \begin{bmatrix} g & v_T & w_T & J_P & J_V \end{bmatrix} \qquad (8)$$

where I^s_{error} is the error between the target task-step end state I^s and the real controllable nodes state, and I^t_{error} is the error between the target real-time state I^t and the real controllable nodes state. I^t_v is the derivative of I^t with respect to time. g represents gravity. v_T and w_T are the velocity and angular velocity of n_T. All the observation elements above are measured in F_B. J_P and J_V are the joint angle position vector and the joint angle velocity vector. The action of the network a_{fb} is a feedback vector that reflects what direction and how much adjustment joint angles should make based on the current robot target and state in addition to the feedforward signal. Each element in a_{fb} is within $[-1, 1]$. $a_{fb(t-1)}$ is the output vector of the feedback network at the previous time.

$$a_{fb} = \begin{bmatrix} a_{fb1} & a_{fb2} & \cdots & a_{fb12} \end{bmatrix}$$
$$a_{fbi} \in [-1, 1], \quad i = 1, 2, \ldots, 12 \qquad (9)$$

3.3 Reward Design

Due to the introduction of the feedforward signal, the feedback network no longer needs to contain a large amount of information related to the robot model. It focuses more on fine-tuning the robot in the current state to achieve coordinated motion and tracking of controllable points. Thus, the task-specific signals are also included in the feedforward part, so we can reward the network in a uniform form which is task-independent

$$r_t = r_{live} + r_{error} + r_{fb} + r_{static} \tag{10}$$

where r_{live} is a constant reward that encourages the robot from falling. r_{error} represents the reward for encouraging the robot's controllable node states to be as close as possible to the real-time target states. r_{error} has three parts corresponding to three controllable nodes

$$r_{error} = r_{Terror} + r_{Lerror} + r_{Rerror} \tag{11}$$

$r_{\cdot error}$ is formulated exponentially and represents the state tracking error of controllable nodes n. The reward forms are as follows

$$r_{Terror} = w_{TP} e^{-\sigma_{TP}\|P_T^s \ominus P_T\|} + w_{TR} e^{-\sigma_{TR}\|R_T^s \ominus R_T\|} \tag{12}$$

$$r_{ierror} = w_{iP} e^{-\sigma_{iP}\|P_i^s \ominus P_i\|} + w_{i\psi} e^{-\sigma_{i\psi}\|\psi_i^s \ominus \psi_i\|}, \\ i = L, R \tag{13}$$

$\ominus$ denotes the quaternion difference for trunk orientation, the yaw angle difference for ankle orientation, and the vector difference otherwise. The ideal of trunk "soft" tracking introduced in [7] is employed here as the position and orientation of ankles are always much more important than that of the trunk. When necessary, the tracking error of the trunk will be compromised for whole-body balance maintenance and ankle tracking. Thus, we set the position error weight w_{TP} and the orientation error weight w_{TR} of the trunk to be only 0.2 times that of the ankle error weight w_{iP} and $w_{i\psi}, i = L, R$. r_{fb} is the reward to punish excessive feedback signals, which encourages the control policy to be more "lazy":

$$r_{fb} = w_{fb} \operatorname{clamp}\left(\sum_{i=1}^{12} \sigma_{fbi} a_{fbi} - 1, 0\right) \tag{14}$$

The final reward r_{static} is used to penalize the trembling of the robot and is only activated when the target velocities of all three controllable nodes are stationary.

$$r_{static} = \begin{cases} 0, & \text{stationary task} \\ r_{staticJV} + r_{staticJA}, & \text{otherwise} \end{cases}$$

$$r_{staticJV} = w_{JV} \operatorname{clamp}\left(\sum_{i=1}^{12} \sigma_{JVi} J_{Vi} - 1, 0\right) \tag{15}$$

$$r_{staticJA} = w_{JA} \operatorname{clamp}\left(\sum_{i=1}^{12} \sigma_{JAi} J_{Ai} - 1, 0\right)$$

where J_{Vi} and J_{Ai} are the velocity and acceleration of the ith joint, $i = 1, 2, \ldots, 12$.

3.4 Multi-stage Training and Episode Design

The goal is to train a control policy that flexibly executes various single-step movements (task-steps) and composes them into diverse tasks. To ensure task diversity, we consider variations in trunk and ankle positions and orientations in both horizontal and vertical directions. A three-stage curriculum is designed to progressively increase task-step complexity.

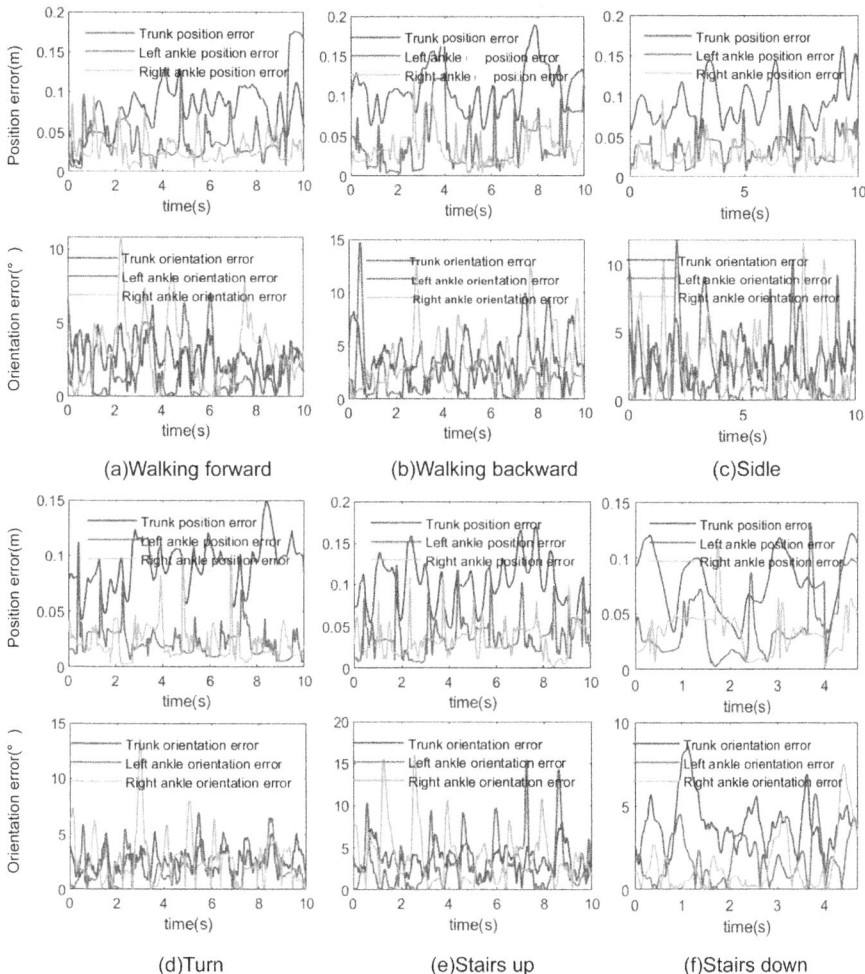

Fig. 4. Tracking error of different tasks

We define different single-step movement pools for each training stage and randomly sample one per episode. In the first stage, training focuses on level-ground motions, including the first five in Table 2, with gradually increased step

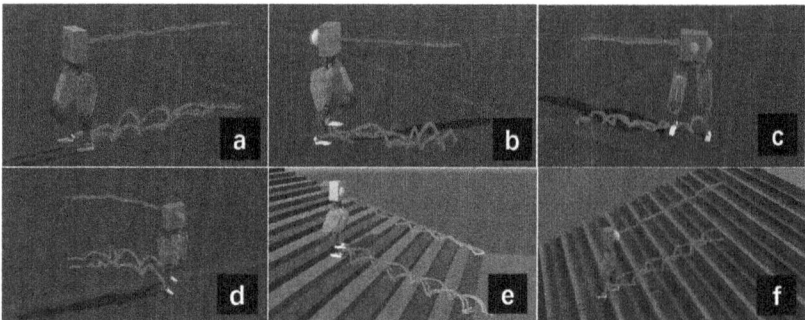

Fig. 5. Trajectories in different tasks

length and leg lift height. In the second stage, stair climbing is introduced, leveraging the trajectory tracking ability learned earlier. Without this, the robot tends to remain stationary to avoid tripping. Once diverse gait control is acquired, a third stage focuses on static balance—requiring the robot to hold its posture after completing steps—reducing the need for constant corrective stepping and improving stability.

To train the network more efficiently, episodes need to be terminated promptly when the tilt angle of the robot trunk exceeds 60° or when the episode duration reaches the maximum training time.

4 Experiment and Results

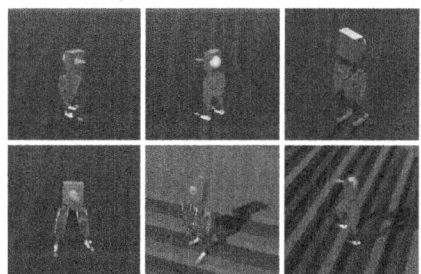

Fig. 6. Static balance maintenance

Fig. 7. Obstacle avoidance

We use Unity and ML-Agents for simulation and training to validate our methodology. The PhysX engine is adopted. The time step for each action is 0.005 s, which indicates a control frequency of 200 Hz. The training is running on the CPU of a personal computer. To speed up the training, we use 50 copies of the agents for parallel training. The whole training process which has 300 million steps takes around 70 h.

After the three-stage learning, the robot can achieve all the tasks listed in Fig. 2. We tested each type of them and recorded the errors for 10 s. The tracking errors for different tasks are shown in Fig. 4 and the visualized trajectories are depicted in Fig. 5, where the green trajectories represent the nodes' target trajectories, and the yellow trajectories represents the nodes' actual trajectories. It can be noticed that the average position tracking error of both left and right ankles is within 5 cm or less, and the average orientation tracking error of ankles is within 5° or less. The tracking error of the trunk trajectory is relatively large. Considering that the trunk tracking trajectory provided does not have an actual dynamic basis, this phenomenon is acceptable under the soft constraint condition that compromises trunk tracking for balance.

We also conducted experiments on the robot's static balance capability. For all movements in the task pool, we allow the robot to move multiple steps and then stop updating the target foothold. We find that the robot could maintain its current posture as shown in Fig. 6. So far, we have validated the effectiveness of our proposed framework in level ground locomotion, stair climbing, and static balance maintenance. All feedback motion control is achieved by a single small-scale network. Through designing the position of footholds, we also tested the obstacle avoidance capability of our controller, as shown in Fig. 7. This demonstrates that our universal controller can accomplish a variety of tasks through flexible combinations of single-step movements.

5 Conclusion

In this paper, we propose a method that combines both model-based and RL approaches for agile and versatile bipedal robot tracking control. We design a universal form of control interface, enabling the robot to accomplish various tasks through combinations of different single-step movements. Through a small-scale three-layer network and a simple IK solver, our controller has achieved excellent and general tracking capabilities for foot and body trajectories as well as static balance capabilities.

Thanks to the human-like properties of our control framework, we anticipate achieving more intricate movements, such as single-leg jumping, one-legged stance, and long jumping, among others, using the extensible high-level trajectory planner. Additionally, our controller's task inputs are defined by node states, which underscores its potential for human teleoperation of the bipedal robot via wearable sensor devices. Our immediate priority is to implement the algorithm on the physical humanoid robot system currently under construction. Subsequently, we will expand its application to additional tasks, culminating in the development of a teleoperation system for bipedal robots built upon this control framework.

References

1. Arm, P., et al.: Scientific exploration of challenging planetary analog environments with a team of legged robots. Sci. Robot. **8**(80), eade9548 (2023)
2. Brohan, A., et al.: Rt-1: Robotics transformer for real-world control at scale. arXiv preprint arXiv:2212.06817 (2022)
3. Chen, D., Zhou, B., Koltun, V., Krähenbühl, P.: Learning by cheating. In: Conference on robot learning, pp. 66–75. PMLR (2020)
4. Cornell: 12-joint ranger max robot model. http://ruina.tam.cornell.edu/research/topics/locomotion_and_robotics/Tik-Tok
5. Gangapurwala, S., Geisert, M., Orsolino, R., Fallon, M., Havoutis, I.: RLOC: terrain-aware legged locomotion using reinforcement learning and optimal control. IEEE Trans. Rob. **38**(5), 2908–2927 (2022)
6. Hwangbo, J., et al.: Learning agile and dynamic motor skills for legged robots. Sci. Robot. **4**(26), eaau5872 (2019)
7. Jenelten, F., He, J., Farshidian, F., Hutter, M.: DTC: deep tracking control. Sci. Robot. **9**(86), eadh5401 (2024)
8. Kumar, A., Fu, Z., Pathak, D., Malik, J.: RMA: rapid motor adaptation for legged robots. arXiv preprint arXiv:2107.04034 (2021)
9. Melon, O., Geisert, M., Surovik, D., Havoutis, I., Fallon, M.: Reliable trajectories for dynamic quadrupeds using analytical costs and learned initializations. In: 2020 IEEE International Conference on Robotics and Automation (ICRA), pp. 1410–1416. IEEE (2020)
10. Melon, O., et al.: Receding-horizon perceptive trajectory optimization for dynamic legged locomotion with learned initialization. In: 2021 IEEE International Conference on Robotics and Automation (ICRA), pp. 9805–9811. IEEE (2021)
11. Peng, X.B., Abbeel, P., Levine, S., Panne, M.: Deepmimic: example-guided deep reinforcement learning of physics-based character skills. ACM Trans. Graph. (TOG) **37**(4), 1–14 (2018)
12. Peng, X.B., Andrychowicz, M., Zaremba, W., Abbeel, P.: Sim-to-real transfer of robotic control with dynamics randomization. In: 2018 IEEE international conference on robotics and automation (ICRA), pp. 3803–3810. IEEE (2018)
13. Peng, X.B., Guo, Y., Halper, L., Levine, S., Fidler, S.: ASE: Large-scale reusable adversarial skill embeddings for physically simulated characters. ACM Trans. Graph. (TOG) **41**(4), 1–17 (2022)
14. Schulman, J., Wolski, F., Dhariwal, P., Radford, A., Klimov, O.: Proximal policy optimization algorithms. arXiv preprint arXiv:1707.06347 (2017)
15. Vezhnevets, A.S., et al.: Feudal networks for hierarchical reinforcement learning. In: International conference on machine learning, pp. 3540–3549. PMLR (2017)
16. Wang, X., Chen, Y., Zhu, W.: A survey on curriculum learning. IEEE Trans. Pattern Anal. Mach. Intell. **44**(9), 4555–4576 (2021)
17. Yang, Y., Zhang, T., Coumans, E., Tan, J., Boots, B.: Fast and efficient locomotion via learned gait transitions. In: Conference on Robot Learning, pp. 773–783. PMLR (2022)
18. Ye, L., Li, J., Cheng, Y., Wang, X., Liang, B., Peng, Y.: From knowing to doing: learning diverse motor skills through instruction learning. arXiv preprint arXiv:2309.09167 (2023)

Multi-robot Path Planning Based on IPPO Reinforcement Learning and Imitation Learning

Wen Ma[1], Gedong Jiang[1,2(✉)], Liming Wang[1], Zhipeng Li[1], Guo Li[1], and Feng Li[1]

[1] School of Mechanical Engineering, Xi'an Jiaotong University, Xi'an 710054, People's Republic of China
gdjiang@mail.xjtu.edu.cn

[2] Engineering Research Center of Robot and Intelligent Manufacturing, Universities of Shaanxi Province, Xi'an 710018, People's Republic of China

Abstract. With the growing application of intelligent agents in real-world scenarios, multi-agent path planning in dynamic and time-sensitive environments has become increasingly important. However, traditional centralized planning methods struggle to adapt to real-time disturbances, while existing distributed reinforcement learning-based approaches suffer from sparse environmental rewards and long training times. To address these challenges, this study proposes a multi-agent reinforcement learning framework based on Independent Proximal Policy Optimization to solve the Multi-Agent Path Finding problem. In this framework, each agent independently learns its own policy using local observations and normalized goal directions. To improve training efficiency, we further integrate imitation learning by introducing expert demonstrations generated from CBS. A dense reward structure is also designed, combining step-level feedback and global completion rewards. We conduct extensive experiments in a grid-based simulation environment, comparing IPPO with PPO and Actor-Critic. Results show that IPPO consistently outperforms PPO and AC in terms of task success rate, convergence speed, reward stability, and training robustness. Furthermore, the integration of IL with IPPO significantly improves early-stage performance and final policy effectiveness.

Keywords: Reinforcement Learning · MAPF · IPPO · Imitation Learning

1 Introduction

With the development of artificial intelligence technology, autonomous mobile robots or agents are becoming increasingly prevalent in daily life. Examples include automated food delivery carts in hotels, autonomous parcel delivery robots on streets, self-driving cleaning vehicles, and Baidu's Apollo Go robotaxi. As the number of these intelligent agents continues to grow, multi-agent systems become more integrated into human environments, and the requirements for multi-agent systems are becoming progressively more complex and stringent. A critical challenge in multi-agent systems is path planning—specifically, how to achieve dynamic, real-time multi-agent path planning that can effectively respond to unexpected events, which represents a key research direction for the future.

Multi-Agent Path Finding (MAPF) refers to the problem of navigating multiple agents from their respective starting positions to destinations without conflicts or collisions. Recent years have witnessed significant breakthroughs in MAPF research [1–12]. MAPF algorithms can be broadly categorized into two approaches based on their planning methodology: centralized planning and decentralized execution. However, traditional centralized MAPF algorithms are inadequate for real-time path adjustments in dynamic environments. When unexpected events occur in a multi-agent system, centralized planning methods often require complete replanning, which must be completed within milliseconds. This poses a significant challenge for current centralized approaches especially with a vast number of robots to achieve.

As technology evolves, decentralized methods are gaining prominence. Decentralized execution algorithms, primarily based on reinforcement learning (RL), operate under the assumption that each agent only has access to local information about nearby agents and obstacles within its field of view. Through continuous interaction with the environment, agents update their policies by evaluating actions based on immediate rewards and subsequent states, with the goal of maximizing cumulative rewards. Ultimately, this process yields an optimal action sequence for multi-agent path planning. However, applying RL to MAPF presents several challenges, such as sparse environmental rewards and highly dynamic conditions. Direct application of any RL algorithm to MAPF problems typically results in slow learning and suboptimal performance.

Therefore, this paper proposes a hybrid method integrating IPPO reinforcement learning and imitation learning for training efficient path planning strategies in multi-robot systems. IPPO is designed to enable effective policy learning under local observations in multi-agent environments, while maintaining good scalability and training stability. By simulating the high-quality path behaviors generated by expert strategies (CBS), it assists the agent in learning better action choices. Building on this, the study designs a reward mechanism that combines dense intermediate rewards with a global completion reward, encouraging multiple robots to collaboratively and efficiently complete the overall path planning task.

The rest of this paper is organized as follows. Section 2 reviews related work on multi-agent path finding (MAPF), including classical methods and reinforcement learning-based methods. Section 3 presents the proposed reinforcement learning environment for multi-robot path planning. Section 4 elaborates on the learning framework. Section 5 reports the experimental results. Finally, Sect. 6 concludes the paper with a summary of the main findings and future directions.

2 Prior Work

2.1 Centralized MAPF

In the centralized approach, the paths of all agents are planned by one server, which has access to the complete environmental map and the status of all nodes, and can generate the global optimal path. Conflict-based search (CBS) algorithm is the most commonly used algorithm at present which is a two-level algorithm for solving MAPF problems Optimally [1]. Most of the algorithms with the best speed and quality to solve MAPF are improved and optimized based on CBS [2]. The improved conflict-based search (ICBS) [3] realized the optimization by Meta-Agent and conflict avoidance on the basis of CBS. Lazy CBS [1] replaces the high-level solver of CBS with a lazily constructed constraint programming model. Lazy CBS can significantly improve the performance of MAPF algorithms. CBSH [4] introduced an admissible heuristic for the high-level search of CBS by reasoning about a special type of collisions in the current solution. Enhanced CBS (ECBS) [5] is a bounded suboptimal variant of CBS that is guaranteed to find solutions whose costs are no more than a user-specified factor away from optimal. Flexible ECBS (FECBS) was proposed that further reduces the number of conflicts that need to be resolved at high-level by using looser suboptimal boundaries in lower-level searches, while still providing a bounded suboptimal solution. Explicit Estimation CBS (EECBS) [6] uses Explicit Estimation Search on the high level and uses online learning to learn an informed but potentially inadmissible heuristic to guide the high-level search. More and more CBS algorithms are proposed, and their performance is improving better and better. The classic MAPF algorithm has been able to solve most path planning problems. However, the centralized path planning method is applicable to scenarios where the environment is stable and global information can be obtained (such as warehouse AGV scheduling and unmanned aerial vehicle formation control). Moreover, in response to the increase in the number of agents, the resources consumed by the algorithm and the computing time grow exponentially.

2.2 Multi-agent Path Finding Based on RL

The MAPF methods based on RL are classified into three types: improved communication type, task decomposition type and expert demonstration type. In the MAPF of large-scale agents, in order to enhance coordination and cooperation, agents often communicate with each other. Xian et al. [7] combined communication with deep Q-learning, providing a new RL-based method (DHC) for MAPF, in which agents collaborate through graph convolutional networks. Li et al. [8] proposed a Priority Communication Learning method (PICO), which combines implicit planning priorities into the distributed MARL framework. It can utilize the implicit priority learning module to form a dynamic communication topology, thereby establishing an effective collision avoidance mechanism. However, in actual dynamic scenarios, the types and brands of agents vary, and the communication interfaces are also different, making it difficult to achieve communication among multiple robots of different types.

SKRYNNIK et al. [9] proposed a hybrid policy learning (HPL) method that decomposes the MAPF problem into two sub-tasks: reaching the target and avoiding conflicts. Wang et al. [10] introduced a hierarchical framework that integrates global planning with local reinforcement learning-based planning, enabling the learning of end-to-end policies in dynamic environments. The local RL planner leverages local observation information to learn strategies for avoiding potential collisions and unnecessary detours.

The expert demonstration method mainly adopts reinforcement learning and imitation learning (IL) and their combined methods. PRIMAL [11] (path finding via reinforcement and imitation multi-agent learning) uses the A3C network to combine reinforcement learning and imitation learning to learn fully decentralized strategies. Agents reactively plan paths online in a partially-observable world while exhibiting implicit coordination. The learned strategies can be extended to an environment with a scale of 1,000 agents. On this basis, PRIMAL2 [12] is used to address a variant of MAPF: lifelong MAPF (LMAPF), where an agent is immediately assigned a new target task upon reaching the target. Although the PRIMAL method can solve the path planning under 1,000 robots, its training process is very time-consuming. MAPPER introduces a decentralized framework that integrates evolutionary reinforcement learning (ERL) with the Advantage Actor-Critic (A2C) algorithm. However, this above approaches suffer from high computational overhead and slow convergence.

IPPO is a simple yet effective multi-agent reinforcement learning algorithm in which each agent independently learns and executes its own policy using a separate PPO model. IPPO inherits the core principles of Proximal Policy Optimization, notably the Clipped Surrogate Objective, which serves to constrain the magnitude of policy updates and thereby improves training stability and convergence. Compared to traditional Actor-Critic (AC) methods, IPPO exhibits stronger robustness and training efficiency. Owing to these advantages, this study adopts IPPO as the foundational architecture for multi-agent reinforcement learning.

3 RL Environment for Multi-robot Path Planning

3.1 Observation Space

In order to be closer to the observation information of the agents in the real dynamic environment, we use the partially observable discrete grid world as the observation space of the agents. Each agent can only observe the situation around itself. The size of the observation information can be set. In this paper, we use a field of view (FOV) with a 7 * 7 grid size.

In a limited FOV, we separate the available information into different channels as shown in Fig. 1. In order to simplify the learning task of the agent, the information is divided into two channels in total. One channel is the obstacle information and target information around the agent, and the other channel is the observable information of other agents around, including the current positions and destinations of these agents.

Taking the pink robot in the Fig. 1 as an example, each agent perceives only a 7 × 7 FOV centered on itself. In the obstacles channel, all obstacles are marked as 1. In the obstacle and target channel, if the agent's goal lies within its FOV, that cell is marked as −1. Otherwise, it remains 0. The other agents channel encodes any neighboring robots: the blue robot is labeled as 2 in this channel. If that blue robot's goal also falls within the FOV, its goal cell appears as −2 in the target channel. Subsequent agents are numbered incrementally (3, 4, …), and their goals are marked by the negative of their respective IDs. If an agent's true goal lies outside the FOV, we project a "virtual goal" by locating within the FOV the cell closest in Euclidean distance to the actual goal and marking it as −1.

In addition, there is another vector, which is a standardized vector pointing from the position of current robot to the target position. The above information constitutes all the observation information of the robot. Furthermore, we will mark the grids that current robot has passed through in the past to prevent the robot from frequently returning to the grids it has passed through.

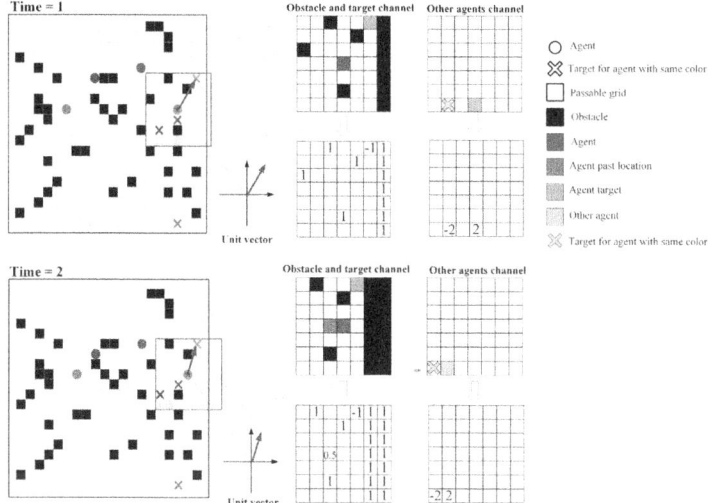

Fig. 1. Observation space of each agent (here, for the pink agent).

3.2 Action Space

Agents take discrete actions in the grid world: moving one grid in one of the four cardinal directions or staying still. During the movement of multiple robots, it is inevitable to encounter situations where there are two intelligent robots. When the agents are about to collide, to ensure that the robots avoid each other and complete all tasks, they are allowed to return to their previous positions. This can increase the success rate of the robots in the training process. And during training, not only actions with positive rewards are trained, but also those that fail or receive negative rewards. Because failed actions will tell the robot which behaviors are prohibited. Both positive and negative rewards are conducive to the convergence of the model.

3.3 Reward Structure

The reward function is crucial for reinforcement learning. Accordingly, this study comprehensively integrates multiple dimensions—path optimization, collision avoidance, and goal orientation—into a unified reward mechanism that combines dense intermediate rewards with a global completion bonus. The reward function guides all aspects of multi-robot learning. We divide it into five components.

A. Time Penalty Reward

At each time step, an agent incurs a negative reward of $-(0.3 + 0.01 \times step)$, which grows in magnitude the longer the episode continues. This time-dependent penalty encourages robots to complete their tasks promptly. Moreover, if an agent remains stationary (action = 0) before task completion, it receives an additional -5 reward, discouraging idleness and promoting active exploration.

B. Directional reward

Whenever an agent moves (action ∈ {up, down, left, right}), we compare its chosen movement direction with the normalized goal-direction vector. If the movement aligns positively with the goal vector, a small positive reward is granted; otherwise, no reward is issued. This simple shaping signal steers agents toward their goals without overcomplicating the learning process.

C. Collision & Constraint Penalties

Invalid moves—such as stepping outside the map or into an obstacle—immediately incur a -100 reward and terminate the episode as a failure. Similarly, any vertex or edge collision between two agents results in a -100 penalty and a failed episode. Repeatedly visiting the same cell is allowed (to learn avoidance), but each revisit carries a -3 reward to prevent oscillatory behavior. Finally, exceeding the maximum allowed steps also yields a -100 penalty and marks the task as failed.

D. Cooperative Avoidance Incentive

When two agents come within a Euclidean distance of 2 units and both are moving toward their respective goals, each receives a +0.5 reward. This incentive fosters proactive mutual avoidance and sustained forward progress in crowded, multi-agent scenarios.

E. Completion reward

Upon reaching its own goal, an agent is awarded +50 reward and its episode ends. Furthermore, when all agents have successfully arrived at their goals, each agent receives an additional +10 × (number of agents) reward. This dual bonus structure balances individual efficiency with collective success, encouraging robots to both race to their own targets and cooperate to complete the group task.

3.4 IPPO Network

IPPO treats each agent as an independent learning entity, using a shared policy network (actor) and shared value network (critic) for parameter updates. The policy network takes as input each agent's partial observation information (2 × 7 × 7 matrix combined with a 2D normalized goal vector), resulting in an input of dimension 100. This input vector is formed by flattening the local state map and concatenating it with the normalized goal direction. The network consists of two fully connected layers as shown in Fig. 2. The first layer maps the input to a 128-dimensional hidden representation and applies a ReLU activation function to introduce nonlinearity. The second layer maps the hidden representation to the action space dimension (i.e., five discrete actions: up, down, left, right, and stay). The final output is passed through a softmax function to produce a probability distribution over actions, which defines the policy distribution for greedy action selection. The function of probability distribution over actions is as follow:

$$\pi_\theta(a|s) = \text{softmax}(f_\theta(s))$$

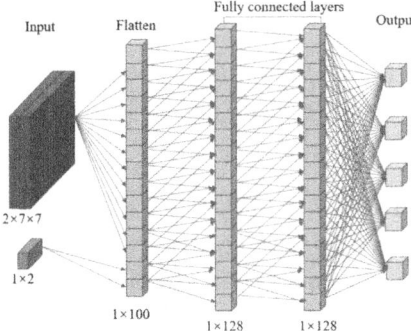

Fig. 2. Neural Network Architecture for Policy and Value Approximation

The value network estimates the state value of the agent's current local observation, which is used to compute the temporal-difference (TD) error and the advantage function to guide policy optimization. This network shares the same input as the policy network. Unlike the policy network, the output of the value network is not used for action selection. Instead, it is solely used to compute the TD error and advantage values, which in turn guide the update of the policy network during learning.

The proposed method is based on an IPPO framework augmented with imitation learning. The framework is shown in Fig. 3. By simulating the high-quality path behaviors generated by expert strategies (CBS), assist the agent in learning better action choices. During the reinforcement learning training process, some behaviors are guided by the simulated expert strategy, thereby achieving rapid convergence of the strategy in the early stage and improvement of sample efficiency.

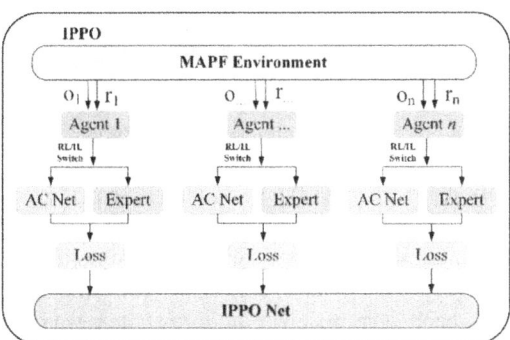

Fig. 3. Structure of our hybrid RL/IL approach

The overall optimization objective of the model is as follow. This formula is a joint optimization objective function that combines reinforcement learning and imitation learning to train the IPPO strategy. This algorithm jointly uses the gradient loss of the PPO strategy, the imitation learning loss based on expert actions, and the value function loss supervised by TD rewards when optimizing the strategy.

$$L = L_{\text{actor}} + L_{\text{critic}} + L_{\text{imitation}} \tag{1}$$

The actor loss in PPO is based on the clipped surrogate objective, which stabilizes policy updates:

$$L_{\text{actor}} = -E_t[\min(r_t(\theta)A_t, clip(r_t(\theta), 1-\epsilon, 1+\epsilon)A_t)] \tag{2}$$

where $r_t(\theta) = \frac{\pi_\theta(a_t|s_t)}{\pi_{\theta_{\text{old}}}(a_t|s_t)}$ is the probability ratio. A_t is the estimated advantage at time step t. ϵ is a small constant for clipping. This objective discourages the new policy from deviating too far from the old one, improving training stability.

The critic loss is the mean squared error (MSE) between the predicted value and the TD target:

$$L_{\text{critic}} = \frac{1}{N} \sum_{t=1}^{N} (V(s_t) - R_t)^2 \tag{3}$$

where $V(s_t)$ is the critic's estimate of the value of state s_t. R_t is the TD return or reward-to-go computed as $R_t = r_t + \gamma V(s_t + 1)$.

If imitation learning is used in IPPO, an imitation loss may be added:

$$L_{\text{imitation}} = -\lambda \log \pi(a_t^*|s_t) \tag{4}$$

where a_t^* is expert action and λ is imitation learning weight.

During the training process, multiple agents independently interact with the environment in the form of shared parameters, respectively collecting information such as status, actions, and rewards to form training data, and are uniformly used for batch policy update.

4 Learning

4.1 Coordination Learning

In this study, multi-robot coordination and obstacle avoidance are achieved through two key mechanisms: (1) a reward mechanism that combines dense intermediate rewards with a global completion reward and (2) a hybrid learning paradigm combining RL and IL.

First, the reward function plays a critical role in promoting cooperative behavior. When the distance between two agents is less than 2 units and both are moving toward their respective targets, each agent receives an immediate reward of 0.5. This incentive is designed to encourage robots to effectively avoid collisions and maintain forward progress in crowded multi-agent scenarios. Moreover, once an individual agent reaches its goal, it only receives partial reward. A full global reward is granted only when all agents complete their respective tasks.

Second, to facilitate more efficient learning, the framework adopts a hybrid approach that integrates RL and IL. Specifically, when the agent's Field of View (FOV) contains its target, Conflict-Based Search (CBS) is employed to compute conflict-free global paths for the agent and nearby neighbors. When the target is outside the agent's FOV, a heuristic policy based on the goal direction vector is used for navigation.

4.2 Training Details

We use a discount factor $\gamma = 0.99$, and a batch size equal to the total number of transitions collected within one episode (depending on agent number and early terminations). The probability of observing an imitation demonstration is set to 50% per step in the early phase of training and is gradually reduced.

We employ the Adam optimizer with a learning rate of 1×10^{-3} for both the actor and critic networks. Each update includes 5 PPO optimization epochs per episode, using a clipped surrogate objective with $\epsilon = 0.2$, and advantage estimation is performed using Generalized Advantage Estimation (GAE) with $\lambda = 0.95$.

Training was conducted on a single laptop equipped with a 13th Gen Intel® Core™ i9-13900HX CPU and an NVIDIA GeForce RTX 4060 Laptop GPU (8 GB).

5 Results

5.1 Comparison with Other RL

To validate the effectiveness of IPPO in multi-robot path planning tasks, this study compares it with two representative reinforcement learning algorithms: PPO and AC. All experiments are conducted in a unified simulation environment, on a fixed 10×10 grid map with randomly placed obstacles and five autonomous robots. Each robot must reach its target while avoiding collisions, using five discrete actions: up, down, left, right, and stop.

Five metrics are used for evaluation: step-level reward, episode length, actor loss, critic loss, and success rate. Step-level reward is the immediate feedback received by an agent at each time step upon executing an action. Episode length is the number of time steps an agent takes to complete a single task episode. An appropriate episode length indicates successful task completion, while overly short or long episodes suggest early failure or inefficiency in reaching the goal. Actor loss is the loss associated with the policy (actor) network. Critic loss is the loss of the value (critic) network. Success rate is the proportion of episodes in which all agents successfully complete their tasks.

As shown in the Fig. 4, among the three algorithms, AC exhibits a relatively slow training process, only beginning to learn effective policies after approximately 45,000 episodes. Although IPPO and PPO show similar loss trends during training, IPPO significantly outperforms PPO in the early training stages in terms of total reward, episode length, and success rate. Overall, PPO suffers from some inevitable fluctuations during training, whereas IPPO demonstrates more stable and consistent learning behavior.

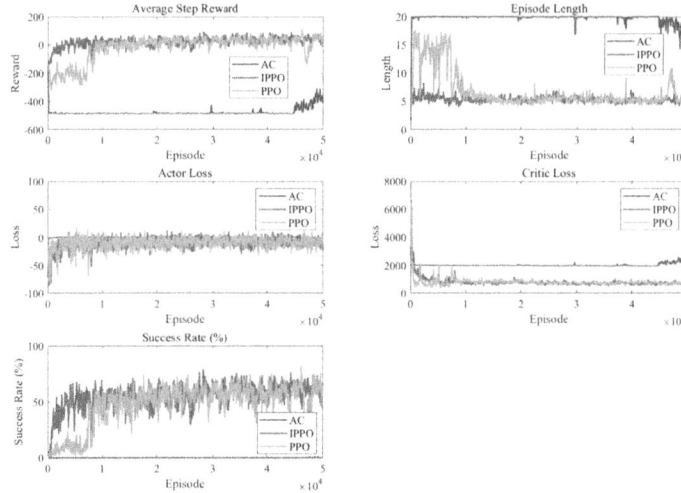

Fig. 4. Performance Comparison of IPPO, PPO, and AC in Multi-Agent Path Planning Tasks

5.2 Comparative Study Under Imitation Learning

To further evaluate the effectiveness of imitation learning within the IPPO framework, we conducted comparative experiments between two strategies: IPPO with Imitation Learning and Vanilla IPPO. Both models share identical neural architectures and hyperparameter configurations, with the sole distinction being the integration of expert-guided supervision. In the IPPO+IL setting, agents adopt an imitation policy with a 50% probability per episode, where expert trajectories are generated via heuristic path planners such as CBS.

As shown in Fig. 5, the Reward and Success Rate plots indicate that imitation guidance leads to quicker stabilization and higher early performance. Episode Length metrics show that IPPO+IL agents are able to reach goals with shorter trajectories earlier in training. Actor and Critic loss curves exhibit reduced volatility and smaller gradients, indicating that imitation learning helps mitigate policy oscillations and gradient explosion. IPPO+IL achieves a peak success rate of approximately 40%, notably higher than the ~25% observed with standard IPPO. In summary, incorporating imitation learning significantly enhances policy learning efficiency and final performance in multi-agent path planning tasks, offering a robust and scalable solution for complex robotic systems.

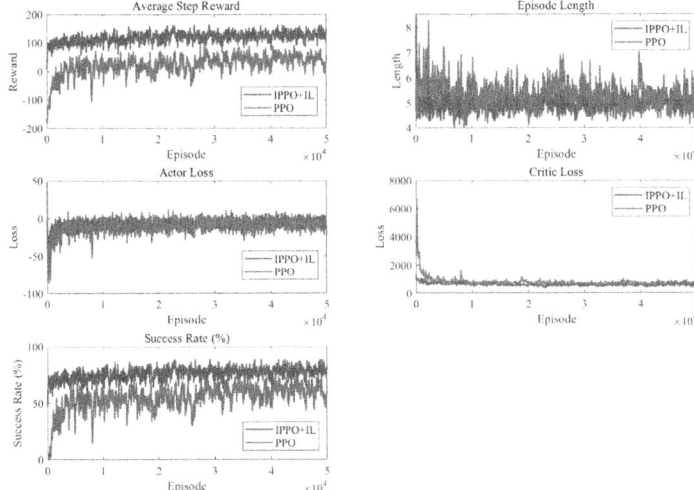

Fig. 5. Training Performance Comparison Between IPPO and IPPO with Imitation Learning

6 Conclusion

This paper presents a hybrid framework that combines IPPO with IL to train effective multi-robot path planning strategies under partial observation. The IPPO framework enables each agent to independently learn policies using local FOV inputs, while still achieving coordinated behavior through shared environmental interactions. Meanwhile, agents probabilistically adopt expert actions during training, and the policy network is further regularized with an imitation loss to encourage behavior cloning. In parallel, the reward function that integrates both dense intermediate rewards and a global completion reward fosters cooperative and efficient task execution. Experimental comparisons with PPO and AC demonstrate that the proposed IPPO-based method achieves superior performance in terms of learning speed, training stability, average reward, and task success rate. The addition of imitation learning further enhances early-stage policy quality and accelerates convergence, making the approach well-suited for real-world multi-agent path planning tasks.

Acknowledgements. This study was supported the National Key Research and Development Program of China (Grant No. 2022YFB3305004).

References

1. Gange, G., Harabor, D., Stuckey, P.J.: Lazy CBS: implicit conflict-based search using lazy clause generation. In: Proceedings of the International Conference on Automated Planning and Scheduling (ICAPS), vol. 29, pp. 88–96 (2019)
2. Gao, J., Wang, J., Zhang, X., Xu, C., Ma, H.: A review of graph-based multi-agent pathfinding solvers: from classical to beyond classical. Knowl.-Based Syst. **270**, 111121 (2023)

3. Boyarski, E., Felner, A., Sharon, G., Stern, R., Betzalel, N., Sturtevant, N.R.: ICBS: the improved conflict-based search algorithm for multi-agent pathfinding. In: Proceedings of the International Symposium on Combinatorial Search (SoCS), vol. 6, no. 1, pp. 27–35 (2015)
4. Felner, A., Stern, R., Sharon, G., Boyarski, E., Shimony, S.E., Sturtevant, N.R.: Adding heuristics to conflict-based search for multi-agent path finding. In: Proceedings of the International Conference on Automated Planning and Scheduling (ICAPS), vol. 28, pp. 83–87 (2018)
5. Barer, M., Sharon, G., Stern, R., Felner, A.: Suboptimal variants of the conflict-based search algorithm for the multi-agent pathfinding problem. In: Proceedings of the International Symposium on Combinatorial Search (SoCS), vol. 5, no. 1, pp. 19–27 (2014)
6. Li, J., Ruml, W., Koenig, S.: EECBS: a bounded-suboptimal search for multi-agent path finding. In: Proceedings of the AAAI Conference on Artificial Intelligence (AAAI), vol. 35, no. 14, pp. 12393–12401 (2021)
7. Ma, Z., Luo, Y., Ma, H.: Distributed heuristic multi-agent path finding with communication. arXiv preprint arXiv:2106.11365 (2021). https://doi.org/10.48550/arXiv.2106.11365
8. Li, W., Chen, H., Jin, B., Shen, Y., Liu, H.: Multi-agent path finding with prioritized communication learning. arXiv preprint arXiv:2202.03634 (2022). https://doi.org/10.48550/arXiv.2202.03634
9. Skrynnik, A., Yakovleva, A., Davydov, V., Yakovlev, K., Panov, A.I.: Hybrid policy learning for multi-agent pathfinding. IEEE Access **9**, 126034–126047 (2021). https://doi.org/10.1109/ACCESS.2021.3111321
10. Wang, B., Liu, Z., Li, Q., Liu, Y.: Mobile robot path planning in dynamic environments through globally guided reinforcement learning. IEEE Robot. Autom. Lett. **5**(1), 693–700 (2020). https://doi.org/10.1109/LRA.2020.3026638
11. Sartoretti, G., et al.: PRIMAL: pathfinding via reinforcement and imitation multi-agent learning. IEEE Robot. Autom. Lett. **4**(3), 2378–2385 (2019). https://doi.org/10.1109/LRA.2019.2903261
12. Damani, M., Luo, Z., Wenzel, E., Michael, N., Choset, H.: PRIMAL2: pathfinding via reinforcement and imitation multi-agent learning – lifelong. IEEE Robot. Autom. Lett. **6**(2), 1796–1803 (2021). https://doi.org/10.1109/LRA.2021.3062803

Design and Control of a Multi-UAV Cabin System

Weilun Guo, Xinxing Mu(✉), Weimin Li, Runze Liu, and Ningning Song

Shandong Zhongke Advanced Technology Co., Ltd., Jinan 250098, China
xx.mu@sdiat.ac.cn

Abstract. The advancement of unmanned aerial vehicle (UAV) technology has enabled its widespread application in fields such as agricultural and forestry protection, video surveillance, and emergency rescue. However, short flight endurance and inconvenient transportation remain significant industry challenges for UAVs. To address these critical industry pain points, this paper presents the design of a multi-UAV cabin system. This cabin serves as a warehouse and energy replenishment facility, featuring automated battery swapping, autonomous trajectory planning, and unmanned operation capabilities, offering significant practical implications and broad application potential. The hardware design of the cabin incorporates a multi-layer landing pad structure. Key internal mechanisms were designed for sliding, centering, and lifting the UAVs. Basic motion control programming was implemented based on the PLCopen standard, utilizing the EtherCAT bus system as the core PLC solution. This approach significantly simplifies wiring and facilitates easier electrical assembly. On the software side, the system was developed by extending the QGroundControl (QGC) software. A dedicated control panel for managing internal cabin equipment was added, integrating the cabin's overall functionality. Furthermore, to ensure operational reliability in GPS-denied environments, a UAV precision landing function was developed. This guarantees that UAVs can return to the cabin with pinpoint accuracy under challenging conditions.

Keywords: UAV cabin · PLC · QGC · control panel · GPS-denied

1 Introduction

With the breakthrough advancements in UAV technology, the demand for their collaborative operations in complex scenarios has become increasingly urgent [1]. From restoring emergency communications post-disaster to military reconnaissance and strike missions, and from smart city management to polar scientific expeditions, a single UAV struggles to meet the high timeliness and reliability requirements of these tasks [2]. The multi-UAV cabin system, serving as a mobile platform that integrates storage, launch, recovery, energy replenishment, and intelligent control, is emerging as a core enabler for achieving autonomous collaborative operations of UAV swarms. However, the effectiveness of the cabin system hinges critically on the sophistication of its software control algorithms, while breakthroughs in GPS-denied precision landing technology are pivotal for sustaining UAV operations in complex environments. Titled "Design and Control of a Multi-UAV Cabin System", this paper systematically elaborates on the research background, technical challenges, and innovative directions, centering on three core technologies: UAV cabin design, cabin control software, and GPS-denied precision landing for UAVs. Its aim is to provide a theoretical foundation for building efficient and intelligent UAV swarm operation platforms.

The UAV cabin is a mobile platform integrating functions such as storage, launch, recovery, energy supply and data transmission of UAVs, and can be deployed on vehicles, ships or fixed bases. Yao et al. proposed the design of an unmanned helipad system, which adopts 2.4G wireless communication technology to remotely control UAVs for inspection operations [3]. Wu et al. designed a UAV hangar control system, which realizes basic information management including audio management, UAV management and hangar management [4]. Carlo et al. designed a cabin for battery swapping of drones. It only takes a few minutes to replace the battery and the drone can be released again [5]. These cobins hangars can be deployed directly near operational sites, enabling rapid drone launches for mission execution within a short timeframe. Upon task completion or when battery levels are critically low, the drones autonomously return and land directly on the hangar's designated landing apron [6]. However, most of the existing studies focus on the optimization of a single function and lack a systematic design of the collaborative control strategy for cabins and multiple UAV clusters.

The control software serves as the "brain" of the UAV cabin system, with its architecture evolving from centralized to distributed configurations. However, current cabin systems predominantly focus on hardware integration while demonstrating inadequate research in software control domains such as task allocation, path planning, and fault handling, thereby limiting the system's overall operational efficiency. The market still lacks integrated software solutions capable of simultaneously managing both UAV operations and cabin functionalities.

In GPS-denied or -jammed scenarios (e.g., urban canyons, indoor environments), UAVs rely on vision [7–9], LiDAR, UWB positioning, or inertial navigation systems to achieve GPS-free precision landing. The integration of multi-sensor fusion with robust control algorithms has become pivotal for improving landing accuracy and anti-interference capabilities. Sang et al. proposed a UAV landing method combining BP neural networks with nonlinear model predictive control (MPC), enabling dynamic trajectory adjustment during autonomous landing [10]. Through iterative environment interactions, deep reinforcement learning [11–13] neural networks can be trained to achieve end-to-end autonomous landing control. However, enhancing visual positioning robustness under complex lighting conditions and developing collision avoidance strategies for multi-UAV landing scenarios remain critical unresolved challenges.

In summary, this paper systematically expounds the research background, technical challenges and innovation directions around the three core technologies of UAV cabins, cabin control software, and UAV non-GPS fixed-point landing, aiming to provide theoretical support for building an efficient, intelligent and robust UAV cluster operation platform.

2 Overall Design of the Cabin Control System

The UAV cabin mentioned in this article can provide support for the long-distance transportation tasks of large-load UAVs and help UAVs achieve fully automatic flight.In the face of the situation where the battery of the drone is running low, the cabin can also replace the battery or charge it independently through the mechanical arm. The framework diagram of the cabin control system is shown in Fig. 1.

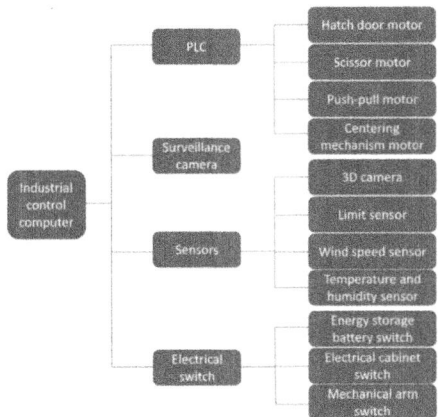

Fig. 1. Control system framework

The UAV cabin control system primarily consists of a local terminal controller, a motion control PLC, sensors, and other components. The local cabin control system is divided into two parts: an upper-level industrial PC and a lower-level motion control PLC.

The upper computer is responsible for two main functions. Executing operations such as manual/automatic control command issuance, human-machine interaction (HMI), parameter configuration, and status information collection. Facilitating communication with the lower-level PLC, which transmits and receives commands to implement motion control. The lower-level motion control PLC connects via the EtherCAT bus for this communication. The lower-level subsystem comprises the motion control PLC, surveillance cameras, sensors, electrical equipment switches, and associated components.

2.1 Cabin Structure Design

The UAV cabin and autonomous storage mechanism comprises five core subsystems: the UAV cabin, autonomous door mechanism, repositioning and locking mechanism, elevating mechanism, sliding mechanism, and battery swapping mechanism. The box of the UAV cabin is used to store UAV and autonomous storage mechanisms.

The UAV take-off and landing platform must not only fulfill the takeoff/landing tasks for UAV but also incorporate automated battery replacement capabilities. Considering factors such as UAV weight and endurance limitations, it is impractical to integrate excessive structural modifications onto the UAV itself. Therefore, the platform requires auxiliary mechanisms for UAV storage and deployment, with Fig. 2 illustrating the schematic diagram of these component systems.

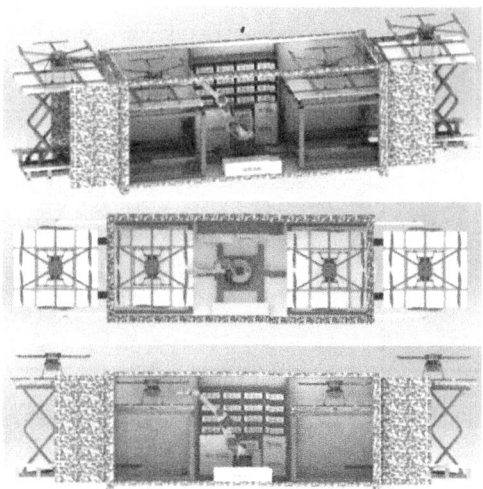

Fig. 2. Schematic diagram of cabin layout

2.2 UAV Autonomous Repositioning and Locking Mechanism

Fig. 3. Schematic diagram of UAV platform repositioning and locking mechanism

After the UAV lands on the take-off and landing platform, it needs to be accurately positioned. The platform is equipped with a repositioning mechanism to assist the drone in returning to its original position. This mechanism is also designed to have the function of locking the drone to ensure that it does not shift due to battery swapping operations. The positioning mechanism is divided into horizontal positioning and vertical positioning. When the UAV lands in the target area of the platform, the system determines whether the position and Angle deviation of the UAV are within the allowable range. Then the horizontal and vertical repositioning mechanisms simultaneously retract towards the middle of the platform, pushing the drone tripod to slide to the center of the lifting platform. The horizontal and vertical repositioning locking plates firmly hold the drone, as shown in Fig. 3.

2.3 Autonomous Elevating Mechanism for UAV Platform Apron

Upon UAV landing on the operational apron, the repositioning and locking mechanism maintains the drone in a secured state with rotor blades aligned parallel to the fuselage axis. The electro-hydraulic scissor mechanism inside the cabin platform receives electronic control commands to initiate controlled descent, gradually lowering the UAV apron to its home position. Conversely, after automated battery replacement and platform extension to the designated position, the scissor system executes precise elevation upon receiving digital commands, raising the platform until the apron reaches cabin door level, as shown in Fig. 4.

Fig. 4. Autonomous elevating mechanism for UAV platform apron

Fig. 5. Deployed and retracted states of the UAV apron

2.4 Autonomous Sliding Mechanism for UAV Platform Apron

The system prioritizes coordinated operation between the apron sliding mechanism and the elevating mechanism, achieving automatic switching between two UAVs within defined spatial constraints. Upon landing on the lower-level apron, the UAV is secured by repositioning locks maintaining rotor alignment. Subsequently, linear electric cylinders within the platform receive electrically controlled commands to initiate sliding retraction to the home position. Conversely, after completing the automated battery replacement process, the linear electric cylinders within the cabin platform receive actuation instructions to extend the platform outward until the lower-level apron is fully deployed outside the cabin portal, enabling immediate takeoff preparation.The deployed and retracted states of the helipad are shown in Fig. 5.

2.5 UAV Automatic Battery Swapping Mechanism

The autonomous UAV battery swap system within the deployment cabin enables at least two drones to execute fully automated battery replacements either simultaneously or sequentially without human intervention. The cabin employs a robotic arm-based battery replacement system. At the end effector of the manipulator, in addition to an integrated fixed 3D vision sensor, a specialized gripper mechanism is installed to enable precise battery handling and cargo manipulation operations. To facilitate secure grasping, the battery pack features an integrated design with the drone's central hub cover, utilizing spring-loaded contact pins for both power delivery and charging connections. The contact system ensures reliable electrical continuity while accommodating positional tolerances between the battery module, drone interface, and charging dock housing. The structural configuration of this battery exchange mechanism is illustrated in Fig. 6.

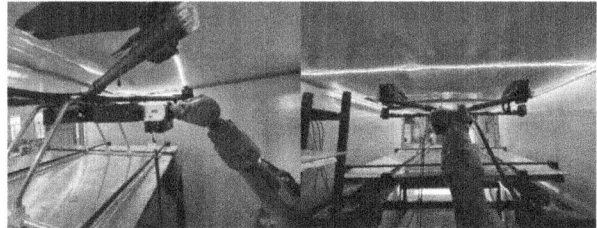

Fig. 6. UAV automatic battery swapping mechanism

3 Visual Software Interface of the Cabin Control System

Fig. 7. Software interface

This paper presents a secondary development based on the open-source code of QGC UAV ground station software, incorporating project-specific requirements and practical application scenarios through functional expansion. Upon launching the modified software, a serial port configuration panel for data forwarding automatically appears, featuring comprehensive parameters including port selection, baud rate, data bits, stop bits, and parity settings, as shown in Fig. 7. By establishing a paired connection with the cabin's control system through the selected serial interface and configuring appropriate communication parameters, the system enables bidirectional data transmission between the ground station and cabin module. This includes exchange of control commands for cabin operation, real-time status monitoring parameters, and other critical operational data, ensuring seamless interoperation between ground control and aerial deployment systems.

3.1 Instructions for Ground Station Software Operation Buttons

The original QGC software can realize the basic functions of UAV flight, such as UAV takeoff, return and flight route planning, etc. On the home page Plan, you can perform operations such as planning routes. And the Takeoff button, Return button and Action button on the interface respectively enable the UAV to Takeoff, return and perform mission operations. Before issuing the UAV cabin mission, it is necessary to plan the flight route information in advance, as shown in Fig. 8.

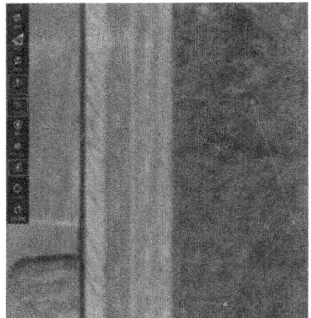
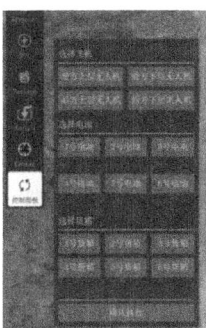

Fig. 8. UAV route planning   **Fig. 9.** Control Panel

The software described in this paper incorporates a cabin control panel interface, as shown in Fig. 9. After completing waypoint planning, users can access the cabin equipment control interface by clicking the 'Control Panel' button located on the right side of the software interface. This panel enables operators to select specific UAVs for mission execution, manage battery replacement operations, and oversee cargo loading procedures through an integrated graphical interface. The operational workflow involves sequential selection of aircraft, battery, and cargo modules through dedicated interface buttons, with real-time battery status displayed beneath each battery selection icon. This command triggers immediate communication with the cabin's PLC system.

3.2 Multi-UAV Trajectory Display

The deployment cabin incorporates four helipads designed to support simultaneous multi-drone mission execution and real-time flight path monitoring. To meet this operational requirement, secondary development was performed on the QGC software platform. Through modifications to source files including *MapPolyline* components, the system implements dynamic trajectory updates for multiple UAVs. This enhancement enables real-time path updates based on positional changes, differentiates individual flight tracks through color-coded visualization, and achieves synchronized multi-drone trajectory display with automatic integration to the ground control station interface, as shown in Fig. 10.

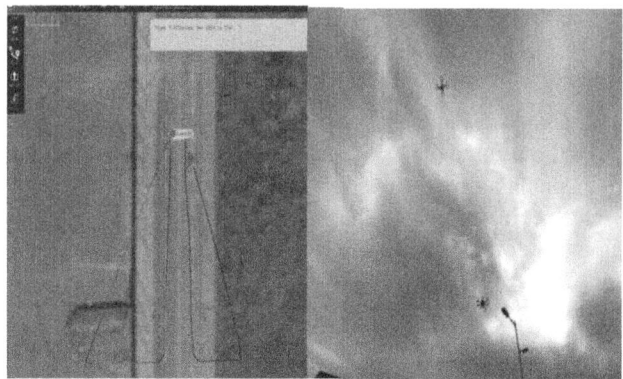

Fig. 10. Multi-UAV QGC trajectory display and flight test

4 Design of Communication Structure for Control System

The control software, UAV cabin, and UAV collaborate through data transmission and operational execution to fulfill the core functions of the multi-UAV cabin system, as illustrated in Fig. 11.

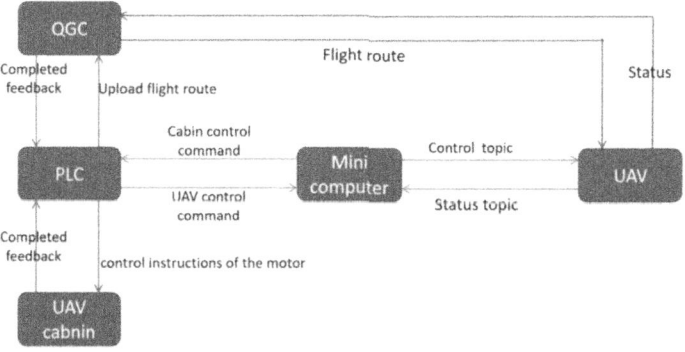

Fig. 11. Communication structure diagram

The relationship between QGC control software and drones begins with QGC serving as an open-source ground control station software, acting as the core platform for drone control and mission management. Its interaction with drones primarily relies on the MAVLink protocol, establishing a digital radio serial connection between them.

MAVLink, a lightweight communication protocol specifically designed for drones, supports operation in low-bandwidth environments. Through the transmission of standardized messages containing headers, payloads, and checksums, both parties implement core functionalities including mission automation, sensor data processing, parameter configuration, and system calibration.

The QGC ground control station and cabin motion control PLC are co-deployed on the terminal industrial PC, utilizing virtual serial port communication to facilitate data exchange. After selecting the appropriate drone, battery, and cargo module through the ground station control panel, the QGC software automatically generates the required transmission data in the background and forwards it to the PLC via the virtual serial interface. The PLC then performs data parsing to identify required helipad movements and battery gripping operations, subsequently executing corresponding motor control commands based on the decoded instructions.

The cabin and drones are connected via LoRa serial modules for bidirectional data transmission, enabling automated control of apron movements and drone operations. LoRa's optimal balance of distance, power consumption, and cost makes it ideal for wide-area static node communication, with coverage range perfectly matching drone operational radii. When the cabin aprons reach designated positions, the system automatically transmits takeoff commands to drones. Conversely, upon mission completion, returning drones trigger automatic apron extension commands from the cabin for landing reception.

5 UAV GPS-Denied Autonomous Landing System

This system introduces an innovative GPS-denied autonomous landing solution for UAV, achieving high-precision positioning and control through integration of multi-sensor data from the RobotBaton Mini module and advanced visual-inertial odometry technology.

5.1 Technical Architecture

This system adopts a modular architecture and is composed of four major modules: perception, computing, control and communication. The perception module collects environmental data in real time through stereo cameras and IMUs. The calculation module runs the Stereo3 algorithm based on the ROS2 system to implement the vision-inertial odometer (VIO). This algorithm integrates FAST/ORB feature point detection and IMU data, and improves the accuracy through Bundle Adjustment optimization. The control module adopts the PX4/ArduPilot flight control system to execute the landing strategy, while the communication module ensures low-latency transmission through the USB2.0 interface and DDS protocol. The system has specially designed a closed-loop detection mechanism to effectively eliminate cumulative errors and ensure positioning stability.

5.2 GPS-Denied Landing Control

The UAV visual landing system adopts a dual-channel cooperative control strategy. The precise positioning of the XY axes is achieved through binocular cameras, and the height data of the Z axis is obtained in combination with the laser rangefinder. The system continuously monitors the height and enters the descent mode when it is below 2 m. Meanwhile, landmark recognition is carried out, and the offset of the landmark center is calculated in real time for position correction. When the local marker is lost, if the height is ≤2 m, a safe climb will be performed; otherwise, a slow descent will be controlled to continue the search. The flowchart of GPS-Denied landing control as shown in Fig. 12.

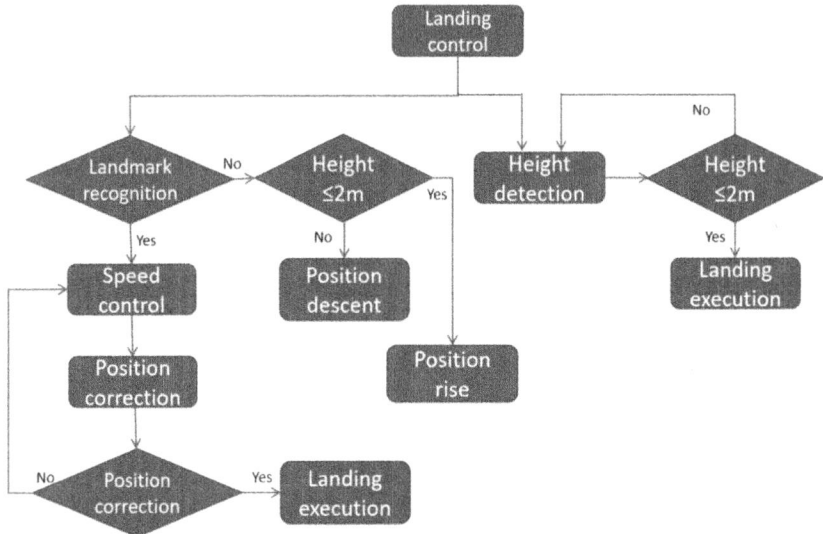

Fig. 12. Flowchart of GPS-Denied landing control

This paper proposes a segmented PID control strategy based on the dual-channel control method of UAV visual landing systems, which is structured as follows.

Altitude channel PID control (Z-axis),

$$u_z(t) = \begin{cases} K_{pz1}e_z(t), & h > 2m \\ K_{pz2}e_z(t) + K_{iz}\int e_z(t)dt + K_{dz} \cdot de_z(t)/dt, & 0.3m < h \leq 2m \\ K_{pz3}e_z(t) + K_{dz3}de_z(t)/dt, & h \leq 0.3m \end{cases}.$$

Position channel PID control (XY-axis),

$$u_{xy}(t) = \begin{cases} K_{pxy1}e_{xy}(t) + K_{dxy1}de_{xy}(t)/dt, & ||e_{xy}|| > 0.3m \\ K_{pxy2}e_{xy}(t) + K_{ixy}\int e_{xy}(t)dt + K_{dxy2}de_{xy}(t)/dt, & 0.1m < ||e_{xy}|| \leq 0.3m \\ K_{pxy3}e_{xy}(t) + K_{ixy2}\int e_{xy}(t)dt + Kd_{xy3} \cdot de_{xy}(t)/dt, & ||e_{xy}|| \leq 0.1m \end{cases}.$$

Exception mode PID control during ground target loss,

$$u_{safe}(t) = \begin{cases} K_{ps}(2-h) + K_{ds}dh(t)/dt, & h \leq 2m \\ -K_{pd}(h-2) - K_{dd}dh(t)/dt, & h > 2m \end{cases},$$

where $e_z(t)$ is altitude error, $e_{xy}(t)$ is position error vector, $\|e_{xy}\|$ is magnitude of position error. PID parameters across all control channels are subject to constraints $0 < K_{pz3} < K_{pz2} < K_{pz1}$, $K_{pxy3} < K_{pxy2} < K_{pxy1}$, and $K_{dz3} > K_{dz}$. All integral terms employ anti-windup output clamping mechanisms, $|u_z| \leq 0.5\text{m/s}$, $\|u_{xy}\| \leq 1\text{m/s}$.

5.3 Autonomous Landing Experimentation

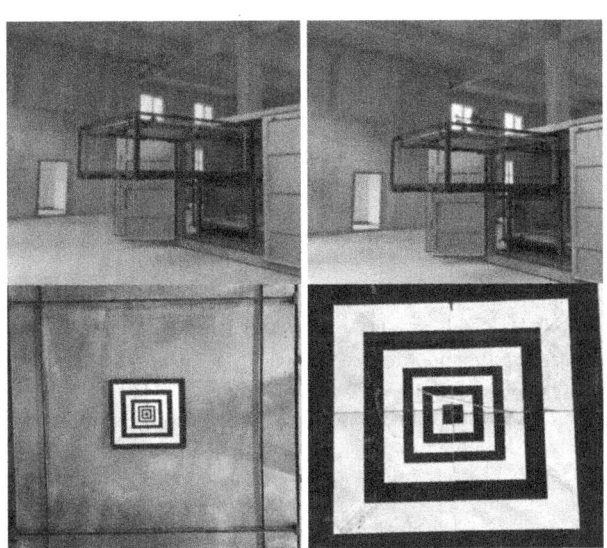

Fig. 13. Indoor UAV GPS-Denied autonomous landing

In GPS-denied environments, the drone enters vision-guided landing mode after passing apron communication protocol verification. It employs a collaborative positioning system integrating binocular vision and laser ranging to calculate landmark offsets in real time, correcting XY-axis deviations while precisely controlling Z-axis altitude. The system utilizes a PID control algorithm to dynamically adjust descent velocity, ensuring stable tracking performance throughout the landing sequence. As shown in Fig. 13, the UAV achieves precise landing at the center point under of apron indoor GPS-denied conditions.

6 Summary

This paper introduces an innovative multi-layer cabin architecture supporting concurrent operation of multiple drones with integrated battery swap capabilities, alongside the development of a unified control interface that integrates UAV management and cabin kinematic control systems. The platform achieves GPS-denied autonomous landing functionality through advanced algorithmic implementations. Research progress includes successful prototype fabrication, system-level integration testing, and reliability verification protocols, with all technical performance metrics meeting predefined design specifications. At present, the cabin has completed relevant experiments such as prototype development and system testing, providing theoretical and product support for the construction of an efficient and intelligent operation platform.

Acknowledgment. Thanks to the support of the Key Research and Development Plan of Shandong Province (2023CXGC010701).

References

1. Li, D., Yang, X., Sun, Y., et al.: Multi-unmanned Aerial Vehicle cooperative regional coverage channel planning. Control Eng. 1–8
2. Sun, J.: Structural design of rotorcraft unmanned aerial vehicle cabin. Mod. Mach. (04), 83–85 (2018)
3. Yao, S., Xi, X., Zhang, Y., et al.: Design of multi-functional helipad system for unmanned multi-rotor unmanned aerial vehicles. Single-chip Microcomput. Syst. Appl. **19**(07), 74–77 (2019)
4. Wu, H.: development of hangar and control system for imperial series unmanned aerial vehicles. Shandong University (2023)
5. Grlj, C.G., Krznar, N., Pranjic, M.: A decade of UAV docking stations: a brief overview of mobile and fixed landing platforms. Drones **6**(1), 17–37 (2022)
6. Zhang, L.: Application of unmanned aerial vehicle automatic airport in inspection of oil and water well stations. Shanghai Electr. Technol. **15**(04), 3840 (2022)
7. Dai, Y., Yang, J., Mao, F., et al.: Autonomous fixed-point landing of unmanned aerial vehicles based on visual system technology and case verification. Adhesive **51**(09), 181–184 (2024)
8. Zhou, J., Gao, J., Jia, G., et al.: Design of unmanned aerial vehicle precision landing system based on monocular vision. Autom. Technol. Appl. 1–8
9. Xie, Y., Chen, X., Lin, P.: Visual detection technology in the research development of UAV autonomous landing. Mech. Electr. Technol. (02), 7–12 (2024)
10. Sang, H., Wang, H., Sun, X., et al.: Unmanned aerial vehicle landing method based on BP neural network and nonlinear model predictive control. Control Eng. 1–7
11. Luo, L.: Research on multi-UAV landing technology based on deep reinforcement learning. South China University of Technology (2023)
12. Wang, S.: Research on autonomous landing method of unmanned aerial vehicles based on deep reinforcement learning. Harbin Institute of Technology (2020)
13. Xu, Y.: Research on end-to-end servo control of rotorcraft unmanned aerial vehicles based on deep reinforcement learning. National University of Defense Technology (2018)

M2PT Dataset: A Multi-motion Pattern Dataset for SLAM Evaluation on Diverse Terrains

Yan Dong, Junru Chen, Enci Xu, and Bin Han(✉)

State Key Laboratory of Intelligent Manufacturing Equipment and Technology,
Huazhong University of Science and Technology, Wuhan 430074, Hubei, China
binhan@hust.edu.cn

Abstract. Simultaneous Localization and Mapping (SLAM) datasets are essential for evaluating SLAM algorithms, since selecting an accurate and reliable method is critical to the autonomous operation of unmanned systems. However, existing SLAM datasets focus primarily on scene diversity and lack a systematic evaluation of differing motion patterns— such as variations in speed and abrupt maneuvers. In real-world applications (e.g., field exploration or emergency response), unmanned ground vehicles (UGVs) often encounter these complex motions, which can lead to SLAM failures. To address this shortcoming, we have constructed the **M2PT Dataset**: a **M**ulti-**M**otion-**P**attern dataset for UGVs operating across varied **T**errains. This dataset comprises LiDAR, inertial measurement unit (IMU), and wheel-odometry data recorded in three environments under four distinct motion patterns (low speed, high speed, sharp turns, and collisions), and provides high-precision GPS trajectory ground truth alongside map ground truth acquired by scanning devices. We compare the performance of several SLAM algorithms on this dataset to highlight its challenges and demonstrate its significance. The dataset can be accessed at https://drive.google.com/drive/folders/1_yRVQLY7cjDKHoFnMSsYqRr6ojSF6FGy.

Keywords: Simultaneous Localization and Mapping · Dataset · Diverse Terrains · Robust Perception

1 Introduction

Highly mobile and intelligent robotic platforms have the potential to replace humans in performing tasks in hazardous or hard-to-reach areas, such as disaster response, resource exploration, and field reconnaissance. However, these scenarios typically involve unstructured environments characterized by rugged terrain and numerous obstacles, placing stringent demands on the accuracy and robustness of real-time localization and mapping (SLAM) systems. In particular, when rapidly traversing complex regions, conventional SLAM approaches are

---

Y. Dong and J. Chen—These authors Contributed Equally.

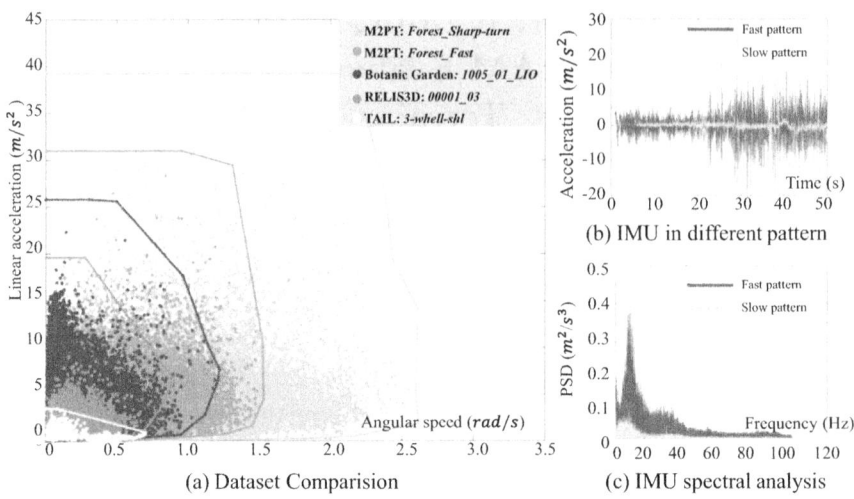

Fig. 1. (a) Comparison of acceleration and angular velocity distributions between M2PT and other datasets. For each data segment, acceleration and angular velocity values are sampled at a frequency of 1 Hz and plotted accordingly. The curves represent the boundaries of acceleration and angular velocity distributions. Compared to other datasets, M2PT Dataset exhibits a broader range of both acceleration and angular velocity. (b) Linear acceleration under fast and slow motion patterns. (c) Spectral analysis of linear acceleration under fast and slow motion patterns.

prone to failure due to abrupt accelerations and severe terrain variations. This highlights the urgent need for dedicated benchmarking frameworks tailored to unstructured environments and aggressive motion scenarios.

With the growing demand for robust SLAM in unstructured environments, recent research has begun to focus on overcoming the challenges SLAM systems face under such conditions and during aggressive motion, aiming to enhance the performance of robotic navigation. In this context, datasets collected in unstructured environments or under aggressive motion have played a critical role in evaluating and validating new SLAM algorithms. However, while these datasets often feature diverse environmental settings or various robotic platforms [1], they typically offer only a limited set of motion patterns for each scene. This lack of motion diversity within the same environment makes it difficult to systematically assess the impact of different motion patterns on SLAM performance.

In this paper, we present the M2PT Dataset, a multi-motion, cross-terrain SLAM benchmarking dataset based on a high-mobility UGV. The platform is equipped with a suite of heterogeneous sensors, including a LiDAR, an inertial measurement unit (IMU), wheel encoders, and a GNSS module. Data are collected across a range of natural and semi-natural environments—such as campuses, parks, and forests areas—under various aggressive motion strategies, including rapid acceleration, sharp turns, and traversal over rough terrain. The dataset not only spans diverse terrains but also captures the dynamic charac-

Table 1. Comparison between M2PT and other datasets. For sensors, L, I, C, and WO represent [L]iDAR, [I]MU, [C]amera, and [W]heel-[O]dometry, respectively. For scenes, S and U denote [S]tructured and [U]nstructured environments, respectively.

Dataset	Sensor				Scene		Motion Pattern				Ground Truth	
	L	I	C	WO	S	U	Slow	Fast	Sharp-turn	Collision	Traj.	Map
HeLiPR [5]	✓	✓			✓		✓				✓	
M2DGR [6]	✓	✓	✓		✓		✓				✓	
NCLT [7]	✓	✓	✓		✓		✓				✓	
Botanic Garden [8]	✓	✓	✓	✓		✓	✓				✓	✓
RELIS-3D [9]	✓	✓	✓			✓	✓				✓	
M3ED [10]	✓	✓	✓		✓	✓	✓				✓	
Wild-Places [11]	✓	✓				✓	✓				✓	
Fusion Portable [1]	✓	✓	✓	✓	✓	✓	✓	✓			✓	✓
TAIL [12]	✓	✓	✓			✓	✓	✓			✓	
ICL-NUIM [13]		✓			✓		✓	✓				
M2PT	✓	✓	✓		✓	✓	✓	✓	✓	✓	✓	✓

teristics of robotic systems under multiple motion patterns. It provides a more challenging and unbiased benchmark for the development, validation, and comparison of high-precision and robust SLAM algorithms. Compared with existing public datasets, M2PT exhibits significantly more aggressive motion patterns (see Fig. 1). Our main contributions are:

- We have constructed a SLAM dataset that spans a variety of terrains and motion patterns. The dataset explicitly accounts for aggressive robotic maneuvers that may occur in such environments, such as high-speed traversal, sudden stops, sharp turns, and collisions. It provides centimeter-level ground truth for both trajectories and point clouds.
- We conducted comprehensive experiments on the M2PT-Dataset to evaluate representative SLAM algorithms, including FastLIO [2], PointLIO [3], LIO-SAM [4], and LIO-Livox. Our results reveal that under the same environmental conditions, different motion patterns have a significant impact on SLAM performance, highlighting the importance of motion diversity in benchmarking and algorithm design.

2 Related Work

Over the past years, a large number of SLAM datasets have been developed, greatly advancing the progress of SLAM technologies. Most existing datasets have focused on structured environments such as urban areas, campuses, or indoor scenes—examples include HeLiPR [5], M2DGR [6], and NCLT [7]. These datasets provide rich multi-sensor data, including camera, LiDAR, and IMU streams, and many include accurate ground-truth trajectories derived from GNSS or other high-precision localization systems. Such datasets have played a key role in driving the development of LiDAR-Inertial Odometry (LIO) and Visual-Inertial Odometry (VIO), with numerous studies demonstrating that these systems can achieve high localization and mapping accuracy in stable, structured environments.

However, in many real-world scenarios, robots are required to operate in unstructured outdoor environments such as forests, grasslands, and mountainous regions. SLAM algorithms trained and evaluated on structured datasets often suffer from degraded accuracy and robustness when deployed in these complex environments. This gap underscores the limitations of existing structured datasets in fully representing the challenges encountered in practical applications.

To address this issue, several efforts have been made to collect SLAM datasets in unstructured environments. For instance, Botanic Garden [8] captured multi-sensor data in a forest park using a wheeled ground platform, offering ground-truth trajectories and maps with rich natural features. RELIS-3D [9] is a dataset focused on semantic segmentation in off-road scenarios, combining camera images, LiDAR point clouds, and IMU data, and providing preliminary semantic annotations. Wild-Places collected large-scale unstructured data using handheld devices, while datasets like M3ED [10] and Fusion Portable [1] introduced heterogeneous platforms—including ground and quadruped robots—operating across both structured indoor and unstructured outdoor settings, facilitating cross-platform and multi-environment SLAM research.

In addition to environmental diversity, motion diversity—such as high-speed movement, abrupt acceleration or deceleration, and sharp turns—is another critical challenge faced by robotic systems. However, most existing datasets feature relatively smooth and uniform motion patterns, offering limited support for evaluating SLAM performance under aggressive maneuvers. Some datasets have made progress in this direction: for example, ICL-NUIM [13] includes indoor camera data at varying motion speeds, and TAIL [12] introduces multiple motion speeds within the same scene to enhance the dataset's difficulty.

Despite these advancements, few datasets have explicitly addressed the full spectrum of aggressive motion patterns. Datasets that have considered motion diversity (e.g., ICL-NUIM [13]) are often confined to indoor settings, while even those with varied outdoor motion (e.g., TAIL [12]) fail to capture extreme maneuvers such as consecutive sharp turns or severe collisions.

These limitations motivate the development of a new dataset that jointly captures both structured and unstructured environments and fully accounts for the aggressive motion patterns encountered by ground robots. Our proposed dataset aims to fill this gap and serve as a rigorous benchmark for advancing high-precision, high-robustness SLAM algorithms. A detailed comparison between our dataset and existing datasets is provided in Table 1.

3 System Overview

3.1 Hardware Setup

Figure 2 illustrates the data collection platform and sensor mounting configuration. We employ a four-wheel-drive high-speed UGV as the data acquisition platform. The UGV is equipped with wheel encoders and supports a maximum operating speed of 3 m/s. A Livox MID-360 LiDAR is mounted on the platform for environmental sensing, with a GNSS antenna positioned directly above the LiDAR to ensure accurate trajectory referencing. Detailed sensor specifications are as follows:

LiDAR: The system uses a Livox MID-360 LiDAR, which offers a sensing range of approximately 40 m and a sampling rate of 200,000 points per second. At a distance of 10 m, the ranging error is within 2 cm. The field of view (FOV) covers 360° horizontally and −7° to 52° vertically. The LiDAR operates at a frequency of 10 Hz.

IMU: The platform utilizes the built-in ICM40609 IMU within the Livox MID-360 as the primary inertial measurement unit. It supports a maximum acceleration measurement range of ±4g and outputs at 200 Hz.

Wheel Odometry: Each wheel of the UGV is equipped with an encoder. By incorporating the vehicle's geometric parameters, accurate wheel odometry is computed. The odometry data is published at a frequency of 50 Hz.

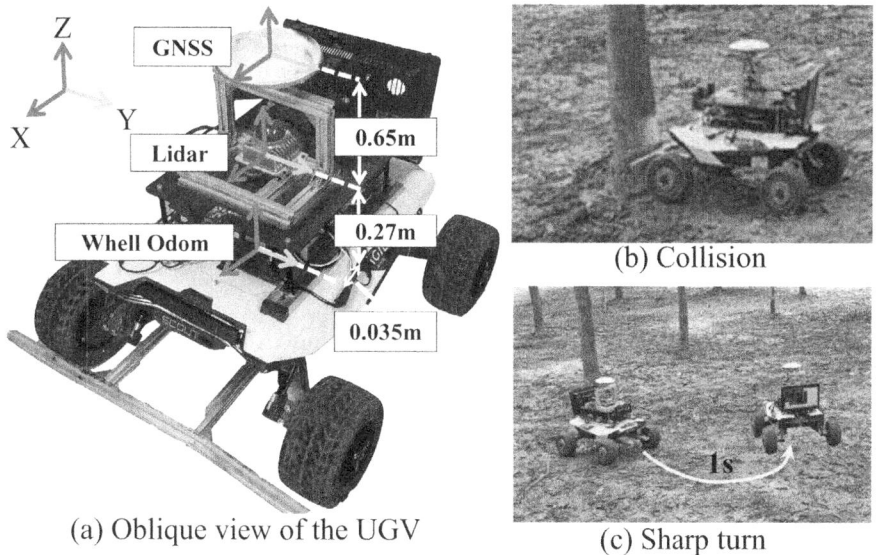

Fig. 2. (a) Coordinates of the data acquisition platform and sensors. (b) Collision. (c) Sharp turn.

3.2 Calibration and Synchronization

Extrinsic calibration of the multi-sensor modules was performed to establish the spatial relationships among sensors. During the calibration, the inertial measurement unit (IMU) coordinate frame was defined as the base frame of the robot. The rigid transformations between this reference frame and each individual sensor were estimated to determine their spatial alignment.

The extrinsic parameters between the IMU and LiDAR were obtained directly from the device datasheet, as the two components are highly integrated in hardware, ensuring a fixed relative pose. The GNSS antenna was rigidly mounted directly above the LiDAR using a fixed support structure. As there is no relative offset in the horizontal plane (X and Y axes), the vertical offset along the Z-axis was manually measured to compute the transformation between the GNSS trajectory ground truth and the robot body frame.

The transformation between the wheel odometry frame and the robot body frame was derived from a combination of CAD specifications of the UGV chassis and on-site measurements. The origin of the odometry frame was defined as the midpoint of the line connecting the centers of the front and rear wheel axes.

To ensure effective alignment of asynchronously sampled sensor data, a software-based time synchronization strategy based on ROS[1] timestamps was employed. All sensors were physically connected to an onboard PC via wired connections, and synchronized timestamps were assigned based on the system clock of the onboard PC.

3.3 Ground-Truth Trajectory and Map

Ground-Truth Trajectory: To obtain ground-truth (GT) trajectories, we employed the Harxon TS101 RTK GNSS module, which was mounted directly above the LiDAR sensor. This placement ensures minimal offset in the X and Y directions between the GNSS antenna and the LiDAR, while also taking advantage of the LiDAR's vertical blind zone to avoid interference with laser beams. The GNSS module captures the UGV's motion trajectory at a frequency of 5âĂŞ8 Hz. It delivers centimeter-level accuracy, providing high-quality GT trajectories for evaluation.

Ground-Truth Map: To capture high-resolution environmental maps, we used the MindPalace-Pocket[2]. laser scanning system. The scanner integrates a Livox MID-360 LiDAR with two lateral fisheye cameras, enabling 3D color point cloud

---

[1] https://www.ros.org.
[2] https://www.manifold.com.co/mindpalace-pocket

acquisition. It supports a sensing range of up to 40 m with a measurement accuracy of 6–8 mm. The scanner was used to capture selected regions of the environment. The raw point cloud data were first downsampled to a resolution of 2 cm and filtered and denoised to remove outliers. The dense RGB point cloud maps serve as reliable references for evaluating SLAM mapping performance. Figure 3 presents examples of the scanned environment and the corresponding point cloud maps.

4 The M2PT Dataset

4.1 Scenarios In Dataset

The dataset encompasses three representative scenes, ranging from structured to unstructured environments:

- *Yard* represents a typical structured environment (Fig. 3 top). Data were collected in a campus courtyard featuring elements such as building facades, boundary walls, and paved stone walkways. The overall spatial layout is regular, with well-defined geometric structures.
- *Garden* represents a semi-structured environment (Fig. 3 middle). Data were gathered in a lakeside garden where artificial features (walls, flat pedestrian paths and gravel roads) coexist with natural elements (trees, shrubs, and uneven muddy trails).
- *Forest* represents a typical unstructured environment (Fig. 3 bottom). Data were collected in a small woodland area dominated by trees and rugged terrain, with no man-made structures. The spatial distribution is highly irregular.

4.2 Motion Pattern

To comprehensively reflect the motion patterns that a UGV may encounter in real-world tasks, we designed four distinct motion patterns for each scene in the dataset: *Slow*, *Fast*, *Sharp-turn*, and *Collision*. These patterns are defined as follows:

- *Slow* sequence: The UGV moves at a low and steady speed. This setting is expected to yield optimal SLAM performance under each environment and thus serves as a baseline for evaluating the impact of more aggressive motion patterns.
- *Fast* sequence: The UGV travels at a high speed with random acceleration and deceleration to simulate dynamic fluctuations during rapid traversal. This motion challenges SLAM algorithms with abrupt velocity changes.

Fig. 3. Ground truth point cloude (left) and reference pictures (right). From top to bottom are *Yard*, *Garden*, and *Forest* scenes.

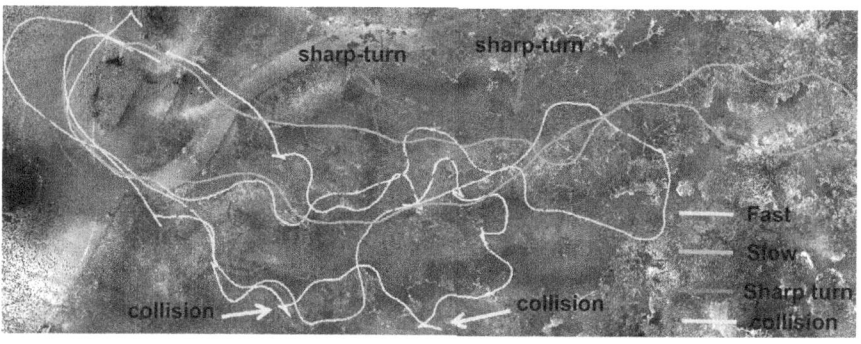

Fig. 4. Trajectories of different motion patterns on *Forest* scene.

- **Sharp-turn** sequence: The UGV performs abrupt turns (approximately 90° to 180°) and follows an *S*-shaped trajectory. This motion captures the maximum angular acceleration that can be induced in the dataset and tests a system's ability to handle rotational motion.
- **Collision** sequence: The UGV intentionally collides with environmental obstacles to reproduce high linear acceleration and impact forces, such as those caused by sudden stops or rebounds. This setting imposes extreme

Table 2. Details of M2PT Dataset

Number	Sequence	Duration (s)	Distance (m)	Max Vel. (m/s)	Max Acc. (m/s^2)	Max Ang. Vel. (rad/s)
1	Yard_Slow	162.7	73.0	0.6	5.8	0.7
2	Yard_Fast	54.3	72.6	3.0	29.2	1.5
3	Yard_Sharp-turn	66.2	90.7	2.9	36.5	1.9
4	Yard_Collision	112.3	109.4	1.5	39.2	3.3
5	Garden_Slow	362.6	158.0	0.6	8.1	0.7
6	Garden_Fast	141.2	144.8	1.6	39.2	2.3
7	Garden_Sharp-turn	172.9	224.8	2.9	39.2	3.9
8	Garden_Collision	130.9	158.2	1.9	39.2	3.5
9	Forest_Slow	301.4	137.9	0.6	21.3	1.2
10	Forest_Fast	134.9	157.4	1.6	30.9	1.5
11	Forest_Sharp-turn	184.5	182.1	2.5	39.2	3.8
12	Forest_Collision	151.8	125.3	1.5	39.2	2.2

physical disturbances on the system, posing a stringent test for SLAM stability and robustness.

Figure 4 illustrates four motion trajectories in the *Forest* scene.

4.3 Dataset Details

The M2PT dataset consists of three distinct scenes, each recorded under four different motion modes, resulting in a total of 12 sequences. Detailed information for each sequence is provided in Table 2. For each scene, the dataset includes a ground truth point cloud map file along with ROS bag files and GPS trajectories corresponding to the four motion modes.

5 Experiment

We evaluated different SLAM algorithms. FastLIO [2] uses a tightly coupled iterated extended Kalman filter (IEKF), offering robustness under fast motion and degenerate environments. PointLIO [3] introduces a point-wise LIO framework and a novel kinematic model for accurate localization even under IMU saturation. LIO-SAM [4] is graph-based, integrating LiDAR odometry with IMU pre-integration, and GPS factors. LIO-Livox[3] relies on an internal IMU and achieves high accuracy and robustness in high-speed and dynamic scenarios.

For trajectory evaluation, we use evo[4] to report the Relative Pose Error (RPE) of the trajectory. Since the GPS measurements on the z-axis are less accurate, we compare the results on the horizontal plane (x-y plane).

---
[3] https://github.com/Livox-SDK/LIO-Livox.
[4] https://github.com/MichaelGrupp/evo.

Table 3. RPE(m) of different SLAM methods on M2PT Dataset.

	Garden				Forest				Yard			
	1	2	3	4	5	6	7	8	9	10	11	12
FastLIO	0.16	0.37	0.50	0.41	0.23	0.37	0.43	0.25	0.14	0.62	0.58	0.32
PointLIO	0.13	0.32	0.50	0.41	0.23	0.38	0.43	0.25	0.14	0.62	0.57	0.31
LIO-SAM	0.20	0.47	0.77	0.75	0.23	0.55	0.77	0.45	0.14	0.62	0.58	0.33
LIO-Livox	0.16	0.32	0.50	0.41	0.05	0.37	0.42	0.25	0.14	0.62	0.58	0.32

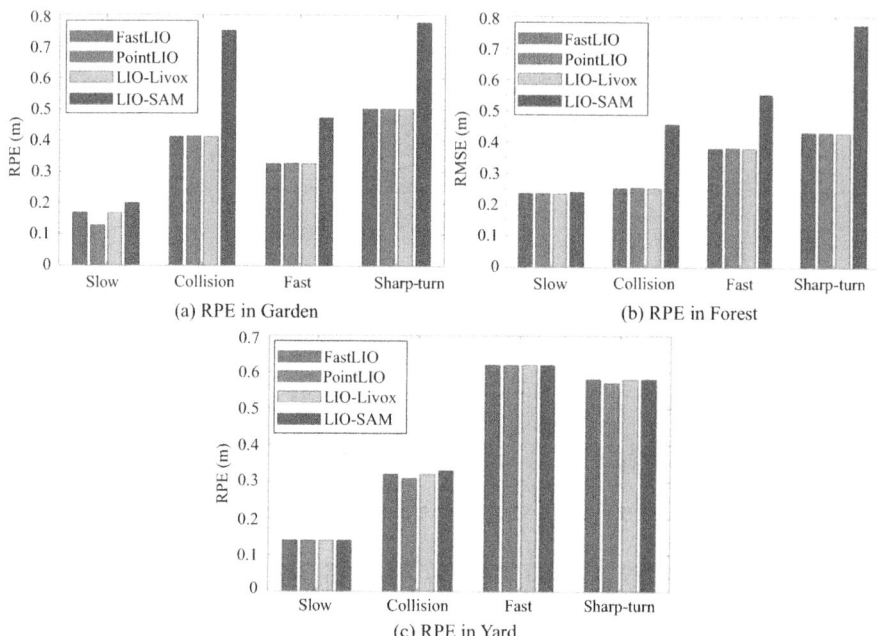

Fig. 5. Comparison of RMSE RPE (m) across different motion patterns within the same scene. The algorithms exhibit lower errors under the slow motion pattern, while fast motion and sharp-turn motion have a more significant impact on accuracy.

The experimental results are shown in Table 3. Overall, due to the relatively flat ground and simple environment, the Yard scene exhibits lower trajectory errors, while the unstructured Forest scene, characterized by uneven terrain, results in larger errors.

Furthermore, to investigate the impact of different motion patterns, we present in Fig. 5 the trajectory errors of these algorithms under various motion modes (slow, fast, sharp-turn, and collision). It can be observed that the error is smallest under the slow mode. Although collision introduces some disturbance, its impact is relatively minor. In contrast, fast motion and sharp turns lead to significantly higher errors. This indicates that current mainstream algorithms lack robustness in handling aggressive motions such as high-speed movement and sharp turns.

6 Conclusion

This paper presents the M2PT Dataset, a SLAM evaluation benchmark designed for unmanned ground vehicles (UGVs), incorporating diverse motion patterns and terrain types. The dataset captures data under four distinct motion modes—low-speed, high-speed, sharp turns, and collisions—across various environments such as yards, parks, and forests areas. High-precision ground-truth sensors are employed to ensure data accuracy. Through comparative experiments with several mainstream SLAM algorithms, we demonstrate the significant impact of aggressive motion modes on localization and mapping performance, highlighting the necessity of M2PT Dataset for evaluating system robustness and identifying performance bottlenecks.

Future work will focus on two directions: (1) regularly expanding the dataset to include more challenging scenarios (e.g., dynamic obstacle environments, complex terrains); and (2) incorporating additional sensing modalities such as cameras to build a more comprehensive multi-sensor benchmark. These enhancements aim to provide richer and more representative data support for the development and evaluation of high-accuracy, high-robustness SLAM algorithms.

References

1. Wei, H., et al.:Fusionportablev2: a unified multi-sensor dataset for generalized slam across diverse platforms and scalable environments, 2024. https://arxiv.org/abs/2404.08563
2. Xu, W., Cai, Y., He, D., Lin, J., Zhang, F.: Fast-lio2: fast direct lidar-inertial odometry. IEEE Trans. Rob. **38**(4), 2053–2073 (2022)
3. He, D., Xu, W., Chen, N., Kong, F., Yuan, C., Zhang, F.: Point-lio: robust high-bandwidth light detection and ranging inertial odometry, Adv. Intell. Syst. vol. 5, no. 7, 2023
4. Shan, T., Englot, B., Meyers, D., Wang, W., Ratti, C., Rus, D.: Lio-sam: tightly-coupled lidar inertial odometry via smoothing and mapping, in. IEEE/RSJ Int. Conf. Intell. Robot. Syst. (IROS) **2020**, 5135–5142 (2020)
5. Jung, M., Yang, W., Lee, D., Gil, H., Kim, G., Kim, A.: Helipr: heterogeneous lidar dataset for inter-lidar place recognition under spatiotemporal variations, 2024. https://arxiv.org/abs/2309.14590
6. Yin, J., Li, A., Li, T., Yu, W., Zou, D.: M2dgr: a multi-sensor and multi-scenario slam dataset for ground robots. IEEE Robot. Autom. Lett. **7**(2), 2266–2273 (2022)
7. Carlevaris-Bianco, N., Ushani, A.K., Eustice, R.M.: University of michigan north campus long-term vision and lidar dataset. Int. J. Robot. Res. **35**(9), 1023–1035 (2016)
8. Liu, Y., et al.: Botanicgarden: a high-quality dataset for robot navigation in unstructured natural environments. IEEE Robot. Automation Lett. **9**(3), 2798–2805 (2024)

9. Jiang, P., Osteen, P., Wigness, M., Saripalli, S.: Rellis-3d dataset: data, benchmarks and analysis, in. IEEE Int. Conf. Robot. Autom. (ICRA) **2021**, 1110–1116 (2021)
10. Chaney, K., et al.: M3ed: Multi-robot, multi-sensor, multi-environment event dataset, in. IEEE/CVF Conf. Comput. Vision and Pattern Recogn. Workshops (CVPRW) **2023**, 4016–4023 (2023)
11. Knights, J., Vidanapathirana, K., Ramezani, M., Sridharan, S., Fookes, C., Moghadam, P.:Wild-places: a large-scale dataset for lidar place recognition in unstructured natural environments (2023). https://arxiv.org/abs/2211.12732
12. Yao, C., et al.: Tail: a terrain-aware multi-modal slam dataset for robot locomotion in deformable granular environments (2024). https://arxiv.org/abs/2403.16875
13. Handa, A., Whelan, T., McDonald, J., Davison, A.J.: A benchmark for RGB-d visual odometry, 3d reconstruction and slam,in. IEEE Int. Conf. Robot. Autom. (ICRA) **2014**, 1524–1531 (2014)

Design and Evaluation of a Generic Safe Control Transition System for Human-Machine Cooperative Driving

Yaowei Sun[1,2] and Dachuan Li[1,2(✉)]

[1] Research Institute of Trustworthy Autonomous Systems, Southern University of Science and Technology, Shenzhen 518055, China
{12232434,lidc3}@mail.sustech.edu.cn
[2] Jianghuai Advance Technology Center, Hefei 230000, China

Abstract. The safe transition between autonomous and manual control is essential to human-machine cooperative driving systems. This paper proposes a safe and efficient control transition framework based on the definition and estimation of the autonomous system's capability of operating the vehicle. To describe whether the autonomous controller can safely operate the vehicle, the vehicle state subsets (safe, recoverable and unsafe regions) are formulated using sets of both scenario-specific and general safety-related variables. By introducing these state sub-sets and safety envelopes, the proposed framework can determine whether a controller steers the states across the safety bounds using reachability prediction. A control transition decision logic is designed to achieve a safe switch between autonomous controller and manual driving by online monitoring of possible violations of safety properties. The proposed framework is evaluated using a variety of simulated complex scenes. Experimental results show that the proposed framework can effectively improve the safety of human-machine cooperative driving systems.

Keywords: Human-machine cooperative driving · Driving safety · Autonomous vehicles · Control transition logic

1 Introduction

Intelligent driving systems have been increasingly implemented onboard current vehicles to automate driving tasks and improve operational safety. Despite the promising performance achieved by the automated driving techniques, the participation of a human driver is still a necessity even in Level-3 autonomous vehicle systems, in which the driver is required to take over driving when the situation is beyond the system's capability limitations. Therefore, it is essential to design a proper control transition mechanism to ensure operational safety of human-machine co-driving (HM co-driving).

An effective control transition mechanism in a co-driving system is required to assess the operation capability of the autonomous controller and predict possible violations of safety properties, so that the control can be promptly transferred to the driver to ensure operation safety. The control can be switched back to the autonomous controller when a safe state has been restored. However, the development of an effective and safe control transition system still faces many significant challenges. The complexity and diversity of road structures and driving scenarios make it difficult to define the safety state envelope and assess the safe operation capability of autonomous controllers. Existing frameworks typically design scenario-specific safety properties and transition logic, making them difficult to adapt to various driving scenarios. In addition, most current approaches focus on how to safely transfer control from the autonomous controller to the driver, without considering switching it back when the safe operation capability of autonomous driving is restored.

Therefore, primary challenges in the development and evaluation of an effective and reliable control transition system of HM Co-driving include: *1) How to define the set of generic safety properties and envelope to support the comprehensive assessment of the safe operation capability of autonomous driving?. 2) How to design an effective control transition mechanism that provides accurate and prompt bi-directional control switching between autonomous and human driving, while adapting to various complex scenarios ? 3) How to comprehensively evaluate the effectiveness and performance of a control transition mechanism in terms of HM co-driving safety?*

To address these challenges, this paper proposes a safe and generic control transition framework for human-machine co-driving, which enables reliable and prompt switching between automated and human driving by online assessment of the safe operation capability of the autonomous controller across various complex and critical scenarios. The primary contributions include:

- We propose a safe bi-directional control transition logic that operates by effectively assessing if the autonomous controller is able to safely operate the vehicle, using the generic safety envelope and state subsets (the safe, recoverable and unsafe regions).
- We construct a set of safety-related state subsets and a safe envelope based on both generic and scene-specific attributes consisting of vehicle states, obstacle information and road structures.
- We propose a set of generic metrics for assessing the performance of the control transition mechanism and conduct comprehensive evaluation of the proposed framework. Simulation experimental results in typical complex scenarios (roundabout, lane-changing, and ramp merging) show that the proposed framework can effectively improve driving safety.

2 Related Work

For the human-machine co-driving system, the control transition mechanism is required to handle dynamic environmental structures, road obstacles, and the varying state of the autonomous vehicle within various complex and hazardous environments. Therefore, how to integrate such factor along with the vehicle's autonomous safe operation capabilities to accurately analyze the autonomous vehicle's safety and determine control authority is challenging.

Control transition logic: Conventional architectures [1], adopt the NSA framework to solve the problem that Simplex architecture only allows for unidirectional control switching, using safety proofs for the safety controller. However, such methods require scenario-specific safety controller designs, making them difficult to adapt to other scenarios. Design-based methods [2], construct a driver-controllable set based on the vehicle state under driver control, updating the driver's control state online and determining control authority. Learning-based methods, such as DRL-GAT-SA [3], transforms the vehicle state into kinetic and behavioral potential field forces between different vehicles, and trigger control switching by setting a safety threshold. However, this method cannot fully guarantee system safety. However, these methods still face challenges in guaranteeing safety in diverse complex scenarios.

Operation safety assessment: To comprehensively quantify the safe operation capability of the vehicle, the safety metric and assessment mechanism are required to account for various factors. Existing methods are categorized into distance-based and time-based safety metrics. Distance-based metrics are widely adopted in the automobile industry. For instance, Honda's collision mitigation braking system and Volvo's CWAB-PD system [4] calculate the minimum safe distance to avoid collision based on vehicle speed, then determine control authority. The strategy in [5] establishes a DRV safety distance model assuming braking as the sole avoidance maneuver. [6] improved longitudinal distance and steering models, avoiding obstacles and determining control authority by integrating braking actions with predefined steering trajectories. In addition, time-based metrics typically include TTC (Time to Collision), THW (Time Headway), TTB (Time to Brake), TTS (Time to Steer), and TTR (Time to React). [7] uses TTC as the metric and set the latest braking time as the control switching threshold. [8] derives multiple formulas to compute Time to Last-Second Braking based on preceding vehicle states, assessing collision risk accordingly. TTR indicates the latest feasible time for trajectory-based avoidance. Unlike TTB/TTS (limited to braking/steering), TTR incorporates all planned avoidance trajectories. Given TTR's computational complexity, Hillenbrand [9] approximates TTR using the maximum value among TTB, TTS, and TTK (Time to Kickdown). Alternatively, Sontges [10] over-approximates TTR by identifying unavoidable collision states via reachable set analysis. However, most existing metrics require scenario-specific design methodologies and lack generalization capability various across scenarios.

Evaluation of human-machine control transition: Current research on human-machine control transition performance evaluation primarily adopt two perspectives: driver-oriented and vehicle metric-based approaches. Driver-oriented metrics include:Objective measures (e.g., driver risk perception and takeover capability [11])Hybrid (objective-subjective) metrics (e.g., takeover reaction/judgment time analysis)Subjective methods (e.g., rating scales). In addition, vehicle metric involve scenario-dependent risk assessment:Car-following: longitudinal distance-based safety metrics. Overtaking: lateral distance metrics between ego and obstacle vehicles. Roundabout: obstacle distance safety indices Each scenario requires dedicated safety metrics for risk assessment. However, current methods predominantly specify takeover timing thresholds, and their evaluation metrics remain scenario-specific. A unified framework for assessing transition performance - encompassing safety, driving comfort, and other metrics across diverse scenarios - is notably absent.

Despite extensive research in this field, current approaches is still subject to significant limitations. Therefore, this paper proposes a safe control transition framework along with evaluation methodology for human-machine co-driving. Our framework effectively integrates environmental structures, obstacle states, and autonomous driving capabilities to quantify vehicle safe operation capability, while enabling efficient bidirectional control transition with safety guarantees.

3 Methodology

3.1 Control Transition Logic

The bidirectional safe control transition mechanism consists of two operations: human takeover (transferring authority to the driver during hazardous conditions) and restoration (returning control to the autonomous driving system under safe conditions). unlike drivers' ambiguous intent, outputs of the motion planner of autonomous driving system are explicitly available, enabling the proposed switching logic to assess its operational safety over future horizons. Therefore, the control transition architecture is shown in Fig. 1.

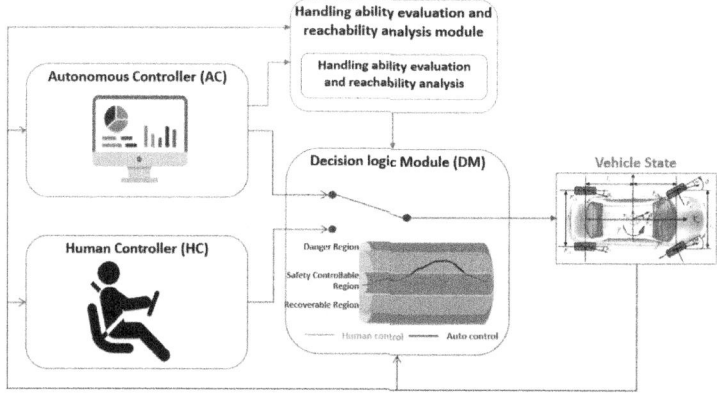

Fig. 1. The proposed safe control transition framework for human-machine co-driving.

The proposed architecture comprises four components:

- Human Controller (HC): providing operational safety assurance at low-level autonomous driving;
- Autonomous Controller (AC): processing environmental data to generate trajectory commands, and performing vehicle control;
- Operation capability evaluation and reachability analysis module: quantifying risk and safe operation capability of autonomous driving system using environmental data;
- Decision logic Module (DM): allocating control authority to AC or HC based on evaluation of safety metrics, ensuring vehicle safety.

The decision module determines control authority allocation by analyzing the vehicle's operational state through driving safety metrics. To design the switching logic, we firstly define three state subsets: danger domain, recoverable domain, and safe controllable domain. We formally define these state subsets based on the vehicle's operation state:

Definition 1 (Danger region). *The danger region is the set of states in which any state variable in the vehicle state x(t) is in its dangerous range.*

$$\mathcal{X}(t) := \{x(t) \mid x(t) \in S, \mathrm{x}(t) \cap \mathcal{X}_{Safe\_Control\_Index}(t) \neq \emptyset\} \quad (1)$$

where $\mathcal{X}_{Safe\_Control\_Index}(t)$ *is the danger state determined by the safety maneuverability metric at time t, and* $Safe\_Control\_Index$ *is the safety maneuverability metric.*

Definition 2 (Recoverable region). *The recoverable region is the set of states where current state is outside the danger region, and the next state under HC intervention is guaranteed to remain within the recoverable region.*

$$\mathcal{D}(t) := \{\mathrm{x}(t) \mid \mathrm{x}(t) \cap \mathcal{X}(t) = \emptyset \text{ and } f\left(\mathrm{x}(t), \mathrm{a}_t^{HC}\right) \in \mathcal{D}(t)\} \quad (2)$$

where $\mathcal{X}(t)$ *is the danger domain.*

Definition 3 (Safe Controllable region). *The safe controllable region is the set of states where, under autonomous driving control, the vehicle state remains within the recoverable domain throughout a future time horizon.*

$$\mathcal{S}(t) := \{x(t) \mid \forall t' \in [t, t+T], f\left(\mathrm{x}(t'), \mathrm{a}_{t'}^{AC}\right) \in \mathcal{D}(t')\} \quad (3)$$

where $\mathcal{D}(t)$ *is the recoverable region.*

The safe controllable region is the state set where control authority is allocated to the autonomous system, with its boundary maintaining a safety margin from the danger region. This region is defined by applying a threshold as the safety buffer to the safe operation metric boundary within the recoverable region.

The relationship between the safe controllable region, recoverable region, and danger region is shown in Fig. 2, where state transitions $\mathcal{X}_1$, $\mathcal{X}_2$, $\mathcal{X}_3$ and $\mathcal{X}_4$ are the predicted reachable states over $[t_0, t_h]$, given an initial state and control value at t_0.

The boundaries of the vehicle state subsets serve as the triggering conditions for control authority transition, defining the human takeover of the forward switching and the autonomous control restoration of the reverse switching.

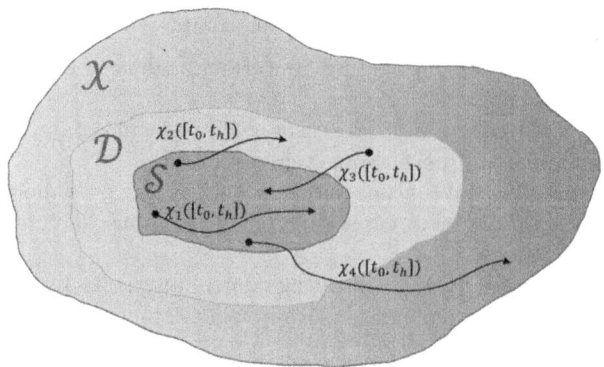

Fig. 2. State subsets for assessing a controller's capability of safely operating the vehicle. $\mathcal{S}$: safe control region, $\mathcal{D}$: recoverable region, $\mathcal{X}$: unsafe region.

Definition 4 (Forward Switching Condition, FSC). *If the autonomous controller (AC) would cause the vehicle to enter a state where the human controller (HC) cannot maintain safety within Δt, a forward transition (takeover) is triggered, transferring authority to the HC.*

$$\text{FSC}\left(x(t), a_t^{AC}\right) := f\left(x(t), a_t^{AC}\right) \notin \mathcal{D} \tag{4}$$

where $f(x(t), u(t))$ is the vehicle state transition model.

State trajectory $\mathcal{X}_4$ in Fig. 2 originates in the safe controllable region but enters the danger region within one time step. This satisfies the forward transition criterion, triggering takeover by the human controller. The reverse transition (restoration) sets a threshold equivalent to that of the safe controllable region, ensuring vehicle safety and operational efficiency while preventing frequent authority transitions.

Definition 5 (Reverse Switching Condition, RSC). *The system triggers a reverse transition (restoration) when no forward transition would occur within future time T under autonomous control.*

$$\begin{aligned} RSC(x(t)) &:= \bigcap_{t'=t}^{t+T} \neg FSC\left(x'_{t'}, a_{t'}^{AC}\right), \\ x'_t &= x_t, x'_{t'+1} = f\left(x'_{t'}, a_{t'}^{AC}\right) \end{aligned} \tag{5}$$

At the end of transition state $\mathcal{X}_3$ or during initiation of transition state $\mathcal{X}_1$ and $\mathcal{X}_2$, the authority resides under the human driving, satisfying the reverse transition criterion.

To this end, the control transition logic can be derived from the vehicle state space and bidirectional transition criteria:

Definition 6 (Control transition logic). *When authority resides with AC and satisfies the FSC criterion, it transitions to HC at the next time step; when authority resides with HC and satisfies the RSC criterion, it transitions to AC at the next time step. Otherwise, authority remains unchanged.*

$$DM_t = \begin{cases} HC, & \text{if } DM_{t-1} = AC \text{ and } FSC\left(x(t), a_t^{AC}\right) \\ AC, & \text{if } DM_{t-1} = HC \text{ and } RSC(x(t)) \\ DM_{t-1}, & \text{otherwise} \end{cases} \quad (6)$$

3.2 Definition of Safety Subsets and Envelope

Risk assessment metrics in human-machine co-driving scenarios should incorporate various road structures and surrounding vehicle state information for accurate safety evaluation, particularly in hazardous complex scenarios with complex traffic flows. In our framework, vehicle risk assessment is categorized into safety and maneuverability aspects, with common scenario metrics consists of two parts: generic safety metrics (including current lane risk and road risk), and generic maneuverability metrics.

Road risk: Road risk comprises multiple risks that a single model cannot comprehensively assess, particularly those resulting from road structure variations or obstacles. Unlike drivers with unpredictable intentions, autonomous systems provide explicit motion planning outputs, enabling the prediction of future vehicle states and risk metrics. Therefore, we evaluate road risk by deriving the latest time to collision through ADS motion planning outputs, which predicts the time-to-collision under constant control inputs.

Definition 7 (Time To Collision, TTC). *The latest collision time is defined as the maximal $t_* \in [t_0, t_f]$ such that applying the current plan $u_c(\cdot)$ keeps the vehicle outside collision set $\mathcal{F}$ throughout $[t_0, t_*]$.*

$$TTC = \sup_{t_* \in R} \{t_* - t_0 \mid t_* \in [t_0, t_f], \forall t \in [t_0, t_*] : \\ x(t; x_0, u_c(\cdot)) \notin \mathrm{F}(t)\} \quad (7)$$

where $x(t; x_0, u_c(\cdot))$ for vehicle use planning when $x_0 u_c(\ cdot)$ in t moment under control.

We construct the latest collision time to overcome limitations of traditional approaches that solely rely on distance/speed metrics for estimating driver control uncertainty. By utilizing autonomous system motion planning outputs to predict collision time, it eliminates road structure influences and applies to diverse road scenarios.

Current Lane Risk: Risk originating from the ego vehicle's current lane, primarily caused by leading and following vehicles. This risk is assessed by reconstructing the time headway metric through autonomous system motion planning outputs.

Definition 8 (Headway time based on autonomous driving). *The time headway metric is derived from velocity data in autonomous system motion planning outputs.*

$$THW = \{min(n) * \Delta T | \sum_{i=0}^{n} v_i * \Delta T > d\} \tag{8}$$

where $n \in [1, \infty]$, v_i *are obtained by the autonomous driving system tracking trajectory information* $u(\cdot)$, *and d is the vehicle surface distance between the autonomous vehicle and the preceding vehicle in the same lane.*

Generic maneuverability metrics: As a critical component of vehicle risk assessment, this metric quantifies maneuvering capability. When the vehicle operates safely, its maneuvering envelope expands with high maneuverability. We adopt longitudinal acceleration (a) as the quantitative metric for scenario-independent maneuverability.

Scene-related safety indicators: General safety maneuverability metrics quantify basic scenario-state parameters, whereas hazardous complex scenarios require these metrics to incorporate road structural factors for accurate risk quantification. Previous studies commonly adopted TTB and TTS for safety metrics in complex scenarios, as drivers exhibit limited reactions - typically only executing braking or steering maneuvers. In contrast, autonomous systems maintain stable maneuverability in such scenarios, enabling diverse obstacle avoidance. Therefore, the driving ability of the autonomous driving system can be taken into account by using TTR. This work constructs TTR by integrating safety maneuverability through reachable set-based latest reaction time analysis. As a scenario-specific safety metric, TTR assesses the ego vehicle's collision risk with obstacles in hazardous complex scenarios.

Definition 9 (Time-to-React Using Reachable Sets). *Reachability-based TTR is defined as the maximal* $t_* \in [t_0, t_f]$ *such that: Under initial control* $u_c(\cdot)$, *the vehicle remains collision-free during* $[t_0, t_*]$; *And from this latest time* t_* *to the termination time* t_f, *there exists a vehicle state* $x(t_*; x_0, u_c(\cdot))$ *for the initial state to set* $R(t_f, x(t_*; x_0, u_c(\cdot)), t_*)$.

$$\begin{aligned} TTR := \sup_{t_* \in R} \{t_* - t_0 \mid t_* \in [t_0, t_f], \\ \forall t \in [t_0, t_*] : x(t; x_0, u_c(\cdot)) \notin F(t) \cap \\ R(t_f, x(t_*; x_0, u_c(\cdot)), t_*) \neq \emptyset\} \end{aligned} \tag{9}$$

The reachable set is a set of states that the vehicle can reach at a certain time and the vehicle will not collide with other objects. The future states of the vehicle are calculated by the reachable set, and are then used to determine the latest reaction time of the vehicle.

Definition 10 (Reachable Set). *The reachable set* $R(t, x_0, t_0)$ *comprises states achievable at time t under control input* $u(\cdot)$, *initiating from state* x_0

at t_0. The state trajectory remains collision-free in $\mathcal{F}$ throughout $[t_0, t]$, ensuring all intermediate states $t \in [t_0, t]$ avoid collision.

$$R(t, X_0, t_0) := \{x(t; x_0, u(\cdot)) \mid x_0 \in X_0, u(\cdot) \in U, \\ \forall \tau \in [t_0, t] : x(\tau; x_0, u(\cdot)) \notin F(\tau)\} \tag{10}$$

3.3 Evaluation Metrics of Control Transition

The evaluation of performance of control transition mechanism for human-machine co-driving quantifies operational safety and maneuverability through a set of proposed metrics. The effectiveness of the proposed mechanism is quantified through success rate and survival rate, while efficiency enhancement was measured by the average driving velocity.

Success rate: The ratio of test scenarios where the vehicle successfully completes the task, quantifying the overall effectiveness of the proposed method.

Survival rate: The ratio of running survival time to total scenario duration, quantifying the different scenario safety performance of the proposed method.

Average speed: The average of the vehicle's velocity during scenario operation over the operation period.

Vehicle safety maneuverability is assessed via TTR analysis, quantifying the size of the vehicle's reachable set at each time instant to evaluate autonomous safety capabilities.

Average time to react: The average of the latest reaction times recorded during vehicle operation over multiple trials.

Vehicle safety is primarily assessed through temporal and spatial dimensions, characterized by Time-to-Collision (TTC) and minimum distance to obstacles surface respectively.

Average time to collision: The average of the time to collision recorded during vehicle operation across multiple scenarios.

Distance to obstacle surface: The minimum distance between the ego vehicle surface and obstacle surfaces during operation.

Considering varying directional safety requirements across scenario states, lateral and longitudinal obstacle clearance metrics enable independent assessment of vehicle safety in corresponding dimensions, tailored to specific safety needs.

Longitudinal distance to obstacle surface: The minimum distance between the ego vehicle surface and obstacle surfaces along the longitudinal axis during operation.

Lateral distance to obstacle surface: The minimum distance between the ego vehicle surface and obstacle surfaces in the direction perpendicular to the lane during operation.

4 Evaluation

In this section, we leverage CARLA to establish an experimental platform and assess the proposed framework in terms of the proposed metrics. The platform comprises a computing workstation (equipped with NVIDIA GeForce RTX 3060 Ti GPU and Intel i7-11700KF CPU), Logitech G29 steering wheel kit, and auxiliary devices.

Control transition in human-automation shared control predominantly occurs in hazardous complex scenarios. Such scenarios involve dense traffic flows, dynamic decision-making of surrounding vehicles, and high-velocity traffic dynamics that compromise ego vehicle safety, necessitating significant adaptation of transition logic. We construct hazardous complex scenarios for transition validation, verifying method effectiveness across diverse road typologies. We constructs three hazardous complex simulation scenarios (high-speed lane change, urban roundabout, ramp merging) to assess the proposed method. Throughout experiments, trajectories of all non-ego vehicles remain consistent. The setting of different experimental scenarios is shown in Fig. 3 and the details are as follows:

Fig. 3. Simulated scenarios for evaluating the control transition framework. *Left*: roundabout, *Middle*: highway, *Right*: ramp-merging.

- Highway lane-changing: As a fundamental driving behavior, highway lane-changing critically impacts road operational safety [12]. This safety-critical scenario requires timely adjustment of ego vehicle maneuvers based on positions and velocities of preceding and trailing vehicles after lane-change decisions. In this scenario, an orange preceding vehicle initially travels at high velocity then decelerates to simulate system malfunction, while a trailing black vehicle maintains high velocity until collision with the ego vehicle.

- Roundabout: The road geometry of roundabouts is complex, requiring vehicles to interact frequently with surrounding vehicles, which results in significantly high driving complexity. In this scenario, dense traffic exists in the lane-changing area, with a green car initially distant but gradually accelerating to follow the beige leading vehicle, simulating acceleration to prevent cutting-in behavior.
- Ramp-merging: The ramp merging area is an accident-prone section on freeways, where ramp merging interferes with main-lane traffic flow causing various traffic problems, thereby challenging the coordination between merging and main-lane vehicles. In this scenario, a broken-down red vehicle is located at the merging point between the ramp and main lane, while a white vehicle on the main lane travels at high speed when the ego vehicle approaches the red vehicle, interfering with the ego vehicle's merging.

After collecting metric data from the three scenarios, we compare results with and without the proposed control authority switching method, as shown in Table 1, where API (Absolute Percentage Improvement) denotes the ratio of improvement. As shown in the table, experiment result demonstrate the effectiveness of the proposed method and its performance improvements across all metrics.

Table 1. Performance comparison of driving policy with/without control transition in testing scenarios.

Index	Method	Average value	API
Speed	w/o switch	1.82	153.01%
	w switch	4.62	
TTR	w/o switch	5.16	95.73%
	w switch	10.09	
TTC	w/o switch	5.23	106.11%
	w switch	10.79	
DTOS	w/o switch	4.04	92.47%
	w switch	7.77	
DTOSX	w/o switch	2.44	157.71%
	w switch	6.28	
DTOSY	w/o switch	4.91	112.81%
	w switch	10.45	
Success Rate	w/o switch	38.33%	-
	w switch	100%	
Survive Rate	w/o switch	82%	-
	w switch	100%	

5 Conclusion

This paper proposes a human-automation shared control transition framework with evaluation methodology, using reachable set prediction to assess autonomous vehicle capabilities. The framework provides formal safety guarantees for autonomous driving systems. The framework integrates autonomous vehicle control with environmental structural awareness to enable bidirectional control transition. With the driver as a safety guarantee, it significantly enhances operational safety and driving efficiency in hazardous complex scenarios. We developed a simulation experiment platform and employed takeover performance metrics to evaluate multi-dimensional framework performance. Experimental results demonstrate the conclusive efficacy of the proposed methodology.

Acknowledgments. This study was funded in part by the Dreams Foundation of Jianghuai Advance Technology Center (NO. ZM01Z008), in part by the Shenzhen Science and Technology Program (JCYJ20241202124304007), and in part by the National Natural Science Foundation of China under Grants 52272419.

References

1. Phan, D.T., Grosu, R., Jansen, N., Paoletti, N., Smolka, S.A., Stoller, S.D.: Neural Simplex Architecture. In: Lee, R., Jha, S., Mavridou, A., Giannakopoulou, D. (eds.) NFM 2020. LNCS, vol. 12229, pp. 97–114. Springer, Cham (2020). https://doi.org/10.1007/978-3-030-55754-6_6
2. Nilsson, J., Falcone, P., Vinter, J.: Safe transitions from automated to manual driving using driver controllability estimation[J]. IEEE Trans. Intell. Transp. Syst. **16**(4), 1806–1816 (2014)
3. Peng, Y., et al.: DRL-GAT-SA: deep reinforcement learning for autonomous driving planning based on graph attention networks and simplex architecture[J]. J. Syst. Architect. **126**, 102505 (2022)
4. Coelingh, E., Eidehall, A., Bengtsson, M.: Collision warning with full auto brake and pedestrian detection-a practical example of automatic emergency braking. In: 13th International IEEE Conference on Intelligent Transportation Systems,pp. 155-160. IEEE (2010)
5. Chao-chun, Y.U.A.N., et al.: Research on modeling of DRV safety distance model for vehicle longitudinal active collision avoidance. J. Chongqing Univ. Technol. Nat. Sci. **29**(10), 29–33 (2015)
6. Gen, L., Xiao-jia, W., Dong-guang, Z.: Intelligent vehicle collision avoidance system under multi-mode braking and steering. J. Chongqing Univ. Technol. (Nat. Sci.) 37(4): 64-76 (2023)
7. Yuanzhi, H., et al.: Active collision avoidance hierarchical braking strategy and verification based on driver characteristics . Automotive Eng. 41(3): 298-306 (2019)
8. Zhang. Y., Antonsson, E.K., Grote, K.: A new threat assessment measure for collision avoidance systems. In: 2006 IEEE Intelligent Transportation Systems Conference,pp. 968-975.IEEE (2006)
9. Hillenbrand, J., Spieker, A.M., Kroschel, K.: A multilevel collision mitigation approach—Its situation assessment, decision making, and performance tradeoffs[J]. IEEE Trans. Intell. Transp. Syst. **7**(4), 528–540 (2006)

10. Sontges S, Koschi M, Althoff M. Worst-case analysis of the time-to-react using reachable sets In: 2018 IEEE Intelligent Vehicles Symposium (IV),pp. 1891-1897. IEEE (2018)
11. Weixing, S., et al.: Real-time driving ability evaluation algorithm for human-machine co-driving decision. J. Northeast. Univ. (Natural Science Edition), 44(8):1078 (2023)
12. Yulong, H., Lei, L., Jiaxin, C.: Research on risk of lane changing behavior of vehicles on expressway. J. Chongqing Jiaotong Univ. (Natural Science Edition) **40**(04), 26 (2021)

Research on Robotic Visual Inspection Path and Pose Planning for Automotive Paint Defects Considering Curvature Weights

Minghui Yang[1,2], Yun Cheng[1], Chaoqun Wu[1,2(✉)], Huayi Cai[1], and Ruoyuan Jiang[1]

[1] School of Mechanical and Electronic Engineering, Wuhan University of Technology, Wuhan 430070, Hubei, China
chaoqunwu@whut.edu.cn
[2] Hubei Province Engineering Research Center of Robot and Intelligent Manufacturing, Wuhan 430070, Hubei, China

Abstract. Robot vision inspection has become a key technology in modern automobile manufacturing. However, existing robot motion planning methods often ignore the influence of surface curvature on automobiles, leading to poor robot motion performance and reduced inspection quality. To address this challenge, this paper proposes a robot vision inspection path-pose integrated planning method that considers curvature weights in the target inspection area. First, the curvature weighting influence is considered to divide the automotive body into regions to be inspected. Based on the curvature distribution, point cloud slicing technology is used to generate robot inspection path points. Additionally, through a series of experiments, the optimal angle range between the robot's end-effector z-axis direction and the normal vector of the surface to be inspected is analyzed. A coupled curvature-weighted optimal angle function for the robotic arm's posture is established to achieve posture planning during the robot inspection process. Finally, the effectiveness of the proposed method and its advantages in path-attitude integrated planning were verified through simulation. The results show that compared to traditional direct planning methods, the proposed method reduces the average displacement of each joint by 3.98%, enables smooth movement without impact in areas with sudden curvature changes on the automotive body, and achieves higher inspection efficiency.

Keywords: Robot motion · automotive paint defect detection · Path-pose planning · Curvature weighting

1 Introduction

The automotive paint coating process is one of the most important processes in automobile manufacturing, as it determines the appearance and individuality of the automotive [1, 2]. However, due to factors such as the complex workshop environment and human operational errors, the painted surface is prone to defects such as pits, bubbles, and scratches after coating [3, 4].

The surface of a automotive body is complex, and researchers use point cloud da-ta to generate surface paths for the workpiece. Saul Nieto Bastida et al. [5] automatically generated robot spraying trajectories based on 3D point cloud data; TONG et al. [6] proposed a scheme for trajectory planning based on visual acquisition of point clouds; Daniel Lamas et al. [7] performed horizontal and vertical slicing of point clouds, to segment the components; L. Truong-Hong et al. [8] extracted lanes and sidewalks from bridge point cloud segmentation; additionally, studies [9, 10] have explored generating cross-sectional contours and axis lines by performing equidistant or non-parallel slicing of workpiece point cloud data. However, existing point cloud segmentation and slicing methods perform well in generating paths on simple work-piece surfaces but produce poor-quality paths on complex surfaces with significant curvature changes, such as automotive surfaces. Furthermore, robots exhibit unstable motion and impact issues in areas with high curvature.

Can a unified physical quantity be found to integrate region segmentation, path point generation density, and robot detection posture constraints, enabling the robot to adaptively densify detection paths in regions with high curvature, reduce redundant paths in smooth regions, adjust detection posture according to curvature chang-es, and achieve smooth motion with high detection efficiency? This is currently a major challenge in paint surface detection path planning.

To address these challenges, this paper proposes an integrated path-pose planning method based on curvature weights for the first time. This method introduces the influence of comprehensive curvature weights across three components: whole-automotive point cloud region segmentation, point cloud slicing technology for path generation, and robot pose constraints, to complete paint surface path planning. Additionally, we experimentally investigated the angle range within which the light source plane at the robot's end effector can be deflected while maintaining detection accuracy. Based on this range, we constrained the robot's detection posture to enhance smoothness and detection efficiency throughout the entire process.

The remaining sections of this paper are as follows. Section 2 describes the meth-od for generating automotive surface detection paths, Sect. 3 optimizes the robot's detection posture, Sect. 4 presents the validation experiments and results of the proposed method, and Sect. 5 provides the conclusions.

2 Curvature-based Point Cloud Surface Path Generation

2.1 Curvature Calculation

This paper uses principal component analysis to estimate the normal vectors of local neighbourhood on the surface of a automotive, and then uses the minimum spanning tree method proposed by Hoppe et al. [11] to correct the direction of the normal vectors. Based on the corrected normal vectors, the direction of propagation is determined along the neighbourhood topology to ensure that there are no sudden changes in the normal vectors of adjacent areas, ultimately pointing all of them towards the outer side of the surface. Figure 1 shows the results of the normal vector estimation and direction adjustment of the automotive point cloud surface.

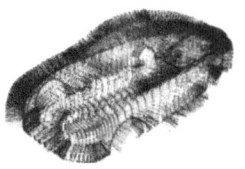

Fig. 1. Results of normal vector estimation on automotive surfaces.

Assuming that the surface function $z = f(x, y)$ has continuous second-order derivatives, the Gaussian curvature can be defined using the least squares method to fit a quadratic surface, combined with the first fundamental form (E, F, G) and the second fundamental form (L, M, N) of the surface [12], Then the Gaussian curvature can be defined as:

$$k_G = k_1 k_2 = \frac{LN - M^2}{EG - F^2} \quad (1)$$

the mean curvature is defined as:

$$k_H = \frac{1}{2}(k_1 + k_2) = \frac{LG - 2MF + NE}{EG - F^2} \quad (2)$$

where k_1 and k_2 are the principal curvatures of the surface.

2.2 Point Cloud Segmentation

Automotive surface point cloud data is characterized by its large scale and complex curvature changes. This paper introduces the Fuzzy C-Means Clustering algorithm [13] to fuse curvature features for regional segmentation of automotive surfaces and independently plan paths for each sub-region to reduce the computational complexity of point cloud data processing and path planning. In the objective function of the FCM algorithm, region segmentation is calculated based on the Euclidean distance between point pairs. To ensure that the segmented point cloud exhibits similarity in curvature features, this paper introduces the regional comprehensive curvature metric K_j into the objective function for improvement, with the expression given by:

$$K_j = \alpha \cdot \overline{H}_j + (1 - \alpha) \cdot \sigma_k \quad (3)$$

where $\overline{H}_j$ is the mean absolute value of the regional average curvature, σ_k is the standard deviation of the regional Gaussian curvature, and α is a constant with a value range of 0 to 1, used to adjust the weight of two curvature contributions. The value of the curvature factor w is positively correlated with the intensity of regional curvature changes, and its expression is:

$$w = 1 + K_j \quad (4)$$

where the constant 1 represents the Euclidean distance d_i between any two points in the point cloud, and K_j is the correction term for curvature features. The improved distance metric D_i is:

$$D_i = d_i \cdot w \quad (5)$$

This formula couples spatial distance with geometric curvature characteristics, enabling the improved objective function to simultaneously incorporate spatial proximity and curvature similarity into the clustering criteria, thereby more accurately dividing regions with similar distances and curvatures into the same cluster. Figure 2 shows the results of the improved algorithm's regional segmentation.

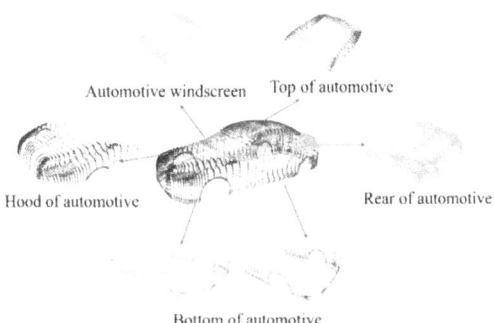

Fig. 2. Automotive point cloud segmentation results.

2.3 Path Point Generation

Point cloud slicing plays a crucial role in processing workpiece data. It divides cross-sectional data to extract relevant surface points and simplify the data [14]. By cutting several slices of the point cloud model, cross-sectional contour points are obtained, which are of great significance for robot trajectory planning [15]. During paint surface inspection, all path and posture calculations are based on the precise model provided by the factory. In contrast, visual or lidar-based methods rely on sensors to instantly perceive changes in the curvature of the automobile during robot movement and dynamically adjust the path, which can cause path jitter due to computational delays. Therefore, this paper introduces an adaptive point cloud slicing algorithm with fused curvature weights to generate path points for robot vision inspection based on the model after point cloud segmentation.

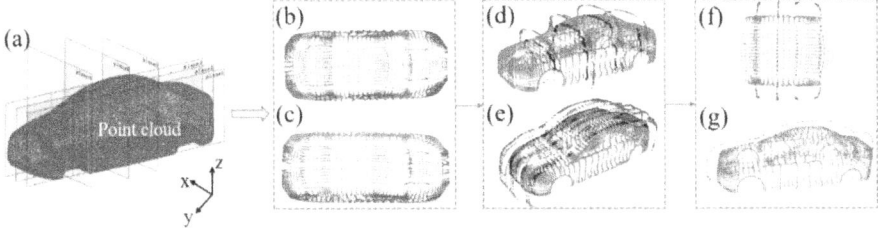

Fig. 3. Principle of path point generation (a) Point cloud slicing (b) Slice the point cloud XZ plane (c) Slice the point cloud YZ plane (d) Path points XZ plane (e) Path points YZ plane (f) Path point connection XZ plane (g) Path point connection YZ plane

The core parameters in point cloud slicing methods are slice thickness and slice direction, which directly affect the quality of the generated path points. The slice direction is determined by constructing a directed bounding box around the automotive point cloud model and slicing along directions parallel to the YZ and XZ planes of the bounding box. Figure 3(b) and (c) shows the slicing results for the two directions. The determination of slice thickness must ensure 100% coverage of the striped light source after a single path planning. This is achieved by introducing a curvature weighting factor α_j to improve the fixed slice thickness. As mentioned in Sect. 2.1, the Gaussian curvature of each region is normalized to obtain the curvature weighting factor:

$$\alpha_j = \frac{K - K_{min}}{K_{max} - K_{min}} (0 \leq \alpha_j \leq 1) \tag{6}$$

where K_{min}, K_{max} are the minimum and maximum values of the curvature in this region, respectively. The expression for the number of slices n_j after optimization is:

$$n_j = \frac{D_{max}}{a} \cdot (1 + \beta \cdot \alpha_j) \tag{7}$$

where β is the adjustment coefficient, D_{max} is the maximum distance of the automotive point cloud in a certain slice direction, and a is the long side distance of the stripe light source. After processing the automotive point cloud slices along a specific slicing direction, several independent sub-slices are obtained, as shown in Fig. 3(d) and (e). By establishing virtual boundary lines at the intersection of the slicing plane and the point cloud, and then obtaining the intersection points between the boundary lines and the target cross-section, the path points on the surface of the sub-slice can be calculated, the actual path points at the end of the robotic arm are obtained, as shown in Fig. 3(f) and (g).

3 Attitude Optimization Based on Curvature Weights

3.1 Detecting the Optimal Angle Range

To address the issue of excessive changes in the posture of the robotic arm in areas with complex curvature changes on the surface of the automotive, we propose a range of angles that the end of the robotic arm can deviate in the z-axis direction while ensuring detection accuracy, and use this angle range as a constraint condition for robot detection. The experimental platform uses ABB 6700 series industrial robots with LCD screens and industrial cameras installed at the ends to collect images of surface defects on the hood of automobile to complete the experiment. The experimental platform is set up as shown in Fig. 4, where the camera is installed on the LCD screen using a fixture, as shown in Fig. 4(a). Initially, a parallel plate is used to ensure that the light source plane is parallel to the surface being tested and at a distance of 300 mm. At this point, the shooting angle θ is 0°, as shown in Fig. 4(b), and the angles of the robot's five axes and the x-axis coordinates are recorded in the robot's teaching pendant. The experiment adjusts the angles of the five joints of the robotic arm in 5° increments.

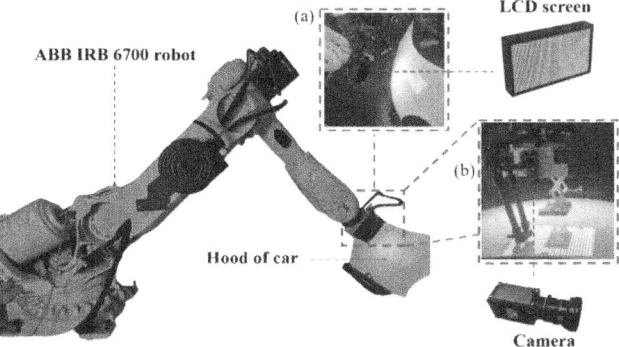

Fig. 4. Experimental setup for photography (a) Side view of the imaging area. (b) Using parallel plates to maintain parallelism between the light source and the tested surface

The experiment recorded striped images at 0°, 5°, 10°, 15°, 20°, and 25° angles, as shown in Fig. 5(a), which displays the striped images captured at each experimental angle (with a stripe period of 16 and a phase shift of 0). Figure 5(b) shows the results of phase extraction and unfolding using the three-frequency heterodyne method applied to (a).

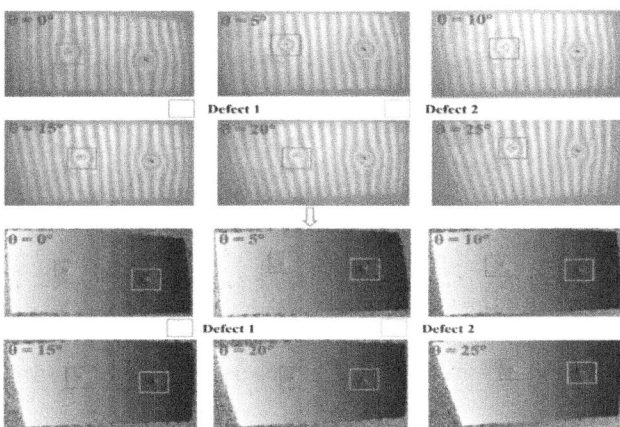

Fig. 5. Collect defect images (a) Original fringe patterns under six shooting angles (b) Unwrapped phase distribution maps under six shooting angles.

Experiments have shown that when the angle between the light source and the imaging plane is θ is 25°, the stripe region exceeds the camera's imaging range. By calculating the proportion of stripes in the image, the degree of distortion of the rectangular stripes can be determined, as shown in Fig. 7(a). When $\theta > 15°$, the degree of stripe distortion increases significantly. Defect extraction was performed on the processed phase map using the phase shift method, as shown in Fig. 6. The white points represent the defect points detected by the phase shift method. By cropping the same rectangular region from the defect extraction results of the phase map, as shown in Fig. 6, the defect area size is reflected by the number of white defect pixels in the same region. The extraction results are shown in Fig. 7(b), revealing that the defect area is approximately equal within the 0 to 15° range and significantly decreases beyond 15°.

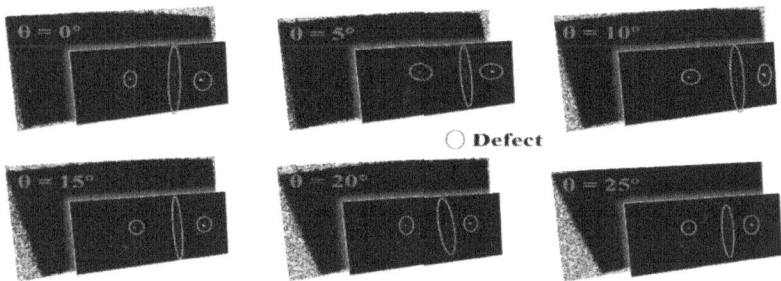

Fig. 6. Extracted phase anomaly plots and stripe-free region elimination plots.

As shown in Fig. 5, due to the limitations of the camera's field of view, the angle between the light source and the shooting plane ranges from 0° to 25°. As shown in Fig. 7, when θ exceeds 15°, the degree of stripe distortion increases significantly, and the defect area decreases significantly. Therefore, it can be concluded that, while ensuring the accuracy of paint surface defect detection, the normal vector of the light source installed at the end of the robot can fluctuate between 0° and 15° relative to the normal vector of the plane to be measured.

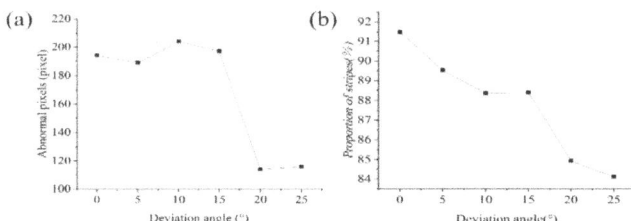

Fig. 7. Curve of stripe distortion and defect area versus angle (a) Curve of stripe distortion degree and angle (b) Curve of defect area and angle

3.2 Posture Optimization

The robot completes the detection task in two steps. In the first step, it moves to the target position based on the spatial coordinates of the path points. In the second step, it calculates the deviation between the robot's initial position and attitude and the attitude when θ is 0°. The robot adjusts the detection attitude based on the normal vectors and curvature of the path points. It converts the attitude and spatial coordinates into a pose matrix and selects the joint angles through inverse kinematics to complete the detection task.

By transforming the coordinate system of the automotive's path points to the robot's base coordinate system, the translation matrix P_6^0 is obtained, with the two coordinate systems collinear along the x-axis. The cross product is calculated between the normal vectors of the path points and the z-axis direction vector of the robot's initial position. Where the z-axis direction vector is the third column element $n_6 = [r_{13}, r_{23}, r_{33}]^t$ of the rotation matrix R_6^0. A rotation axis k is established using the path point normal vector as the target, and the rotation matrix R around the rotation axis k is obtained using the Rodrigues' rotation formula:

$$R = I + \sin\theta \cdot K + (1 - \cos\theta) \cdot K^2 \tag{8}$$

where I is a 3 × 3 identity matrix, θ is the rotation angle, and K is the cross product matrix of the rotation axis $k = [k_x, k_y, k_z]$. Therefore, the robot's new rotation matrix $R_{new} = R \cdot R_C$, where R_C is the initial pose of the robot when it reaches the path point. By combining the new rotation matrix R_{new} with the translation matrix P_6^0 to form a 4 × 4 pose matrix, the inverse kinematics solution is performed to determine the new joint angles and adjust the pose.

As shown in Sect. 2.3, the curvature weighting factor α_j for each local neighbourhood of the path point is positively correlated with the curvature, weighting coefficient, and the end-effector angle deviation $\Delta\theta$. To enable the end-effector to adaptively adjust the rotation angle based on the curvature of the path point surface, a curvature-weighted non-linear function is established to optimise the end-effector's attitude during the detection process:

$$\Delta\theta = 15 \cdot \left(1 - e^{-\gamma \cdot \alpha_j}\right) \tag{9}$$

where γ controls curvature sensitivity. The deflection angle is larger in regions with large curvature changes, resulting in a deflection angle range of 0 to $\Delta\theta$ for each region. The robot's inverse kinematics solution follows the closest principle and the principle of minimizing overall displacement. This requires that the initial joint angle θ_i in the first step be as close as possible to the theoretically calculated joint angle deflection angle θ_i^* in the second step, while maximizing the movement of axes 4 to 6 and minimizing the movement of axes 1 to 3. Based on this, an objective function for end-effector angle constraints is established. By calculating the joint angle sequence corresponding to F_{min}, the robot is driven to detect and adjust its posture. The expression is as follows:

$$F = min\left[\sum_{i=1}^{3} w_1 |\theta_i^* - \theta_i| + \sum_{i=4}^{6} w_2 |\theta_i^* - \theta_i|\right] \tag{10}$$

where i denotes the robot's motion axis, w_1 denotes the weight coefficient for axes 1 to 3 of the robot, and w_2 denotes the weight coefficient for axes 4 and 6 of the robot.

4 Simulation and Results Analysis

This paper verifies the feasibility of the simulation platform verification method based on Robotstudio. An IRB6700-200/2.6 series industrial robot is used, with a light source and camera installed at the end of the robot. The robot base coordinate system is aligned with the X-axis of the automotive coordinate system and is 2150 mm away. The simulation platform is complete. Using the method described in Sect. 2, extract areas with large curvature changes in the roof and side door areas of the automotive generate path points, and use the content in Sect. 3 to obtain the detection posture of each path point. Ten key path points are selected at equal intervals in the X-direction from the generated path to verify the robot's posture optimization.

The results after incorporating the angle range optimization are shown in Table 1. The robot does not need to adjust its detection posture in regions with small curvature changes (path points 1, 2, 5, 6) and regions with smooth curvature (path points 8, 9, 10). Adjustments are only required in regions with large curvature changes (path points 3, 4) and regions where the angle between the robot's z-axis direction and the surface to be detected exceeds the allowable deviation $\Delta\theta$ (path point 7). As shown in Fig. 8, the detection postures of the two methods at path point 6 are compared. The conventional method requires adjusting the robot's posture, while the method proposed in this paper does not require any adjustments. For these 10 critical path points, the proposed method only requires adjusting the posture three times. While ensuring detection accuracy, the detection time is shorter, and the detection efficiency improves significantly as the number of path points increases.

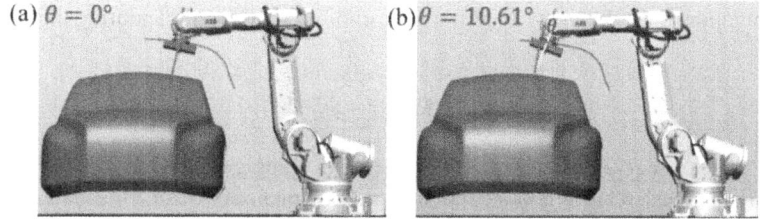

Fig. 8. Path point 6 attitude comparison (a) Normal method (b) Paper method.

Table 1. Experimental results for 10 path points.

Path point	Point coordinate	Attitude deviation angle	Allowable deviation angle	Whether to adjust attitude
1	(1080, 211, 1340)	12.53°	13°	No
2	(1181, 211, 1621)	7.09°	10°	No
3	(1283, 211, 1723)	21.19°	15°	Yes
4	(1383, 211, 1770)	12.65°	11°	Yes
5	(1483, 211, 1795)	1.14°	4°	No
6	(1680, 211, 1829)	10.61°	12°	No
7	(1770, 211, 1840)	12.58°	9°	Yes
8	(1873, 211, 1851)	3.49°	5°	No
9	(1984, 211, 1858)	8.15°	9°	No

(*continued*)

Table 1. (*continued*)

Path point	Point coordinate	Attitude deviation angle	Allowable deviation angle	Whether to adjust attitude
10	(2088, 211, 1862)	7.22°	8°	No

In the teaching pendant, extract the joint angle data for robot posture detection from these 10 path points. The normal method corresponds to 20 sets of joint angles for the 10 points. While the method proposed in this paper yields 13 sets of joint angles. The cumulative change in the rotation angle of each joint along this path is calculated, as shown in Table 2. Compared to the normal method, the joint displacement of axes 1 to 3 (basic axes) in the robot's motion process decreases by 4.8%, 3.86%, and 3.92%, respectively, while the joint displacement of axes 4 to 5 (wrist axes) decreases by 0.82%, 10.35%, respectively. The joint displacement of axis 5 has been significantly reduced, improving the smoothness of posture adjustment. The reduction in the basic axes is small, indicating that the method balances movement stability and efficiency while ensuring defect detection accuracy.

Table 2. Joint angular displacement.

Joint angular displacement (rad)	Joint1	Joint2	Joint3	Joint4	Joint5	Joint6
Normal method	0.1333	1.1116	1.7605	1.2997	1.5245	1.3127
Paper method	0.1269	1.0687	1.6914	1.2891	1.3668	1.3128

By setting the time interval between each path point to 2 s, the joint angles after posture adjustment are extracted, and the function curves of joint angular displacement, angular velocity, and angular acceleration versus time are plotted, as shown in Figs. 9 and 10. Overall, the robot exhibits larger angular velocity and angular acceleration values between 0 and 8 s because the equally spaced path points selected along the X-direction result in greater height displacement differences at this time, leading to larger fluctuations within the same 2-s interval, which aligns with real-world conditions.

As shown in Fig. 10(a) the angular acceleration of the 5th axis joint switches between positive and negative values in the t = 4–8 s interval, with a peak acceleration $\alpha > 0.02$ rad/s^2 at t = 6 s (path point 3, curvature change zone). This indicates that the conventional method requires frequent adjustments to the end-effector posture at each path point, leading to continuous acceleration and deceleration, resulting in unstable motion in the curvature change zone (path point 3). The method proposed in this paper, as shown in Fig. 10(b), suppresses the peak acceleration of the 5th axis at path point 3 (high curvature region, $\alpha < 0.02$ rad/s^2), reducing the oscillation between positive and negative accelerations. The optimized motion process exhibits higher smoothness and reduces joint impact loads.

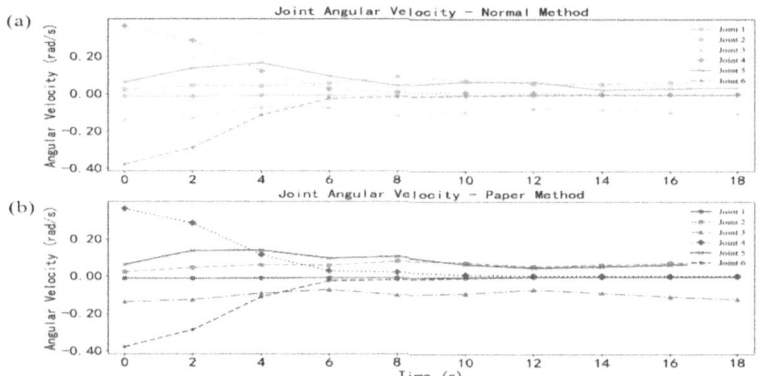

Fig. 9. Joint angular velocity versus time function (a) Normal method (b) Paper method.

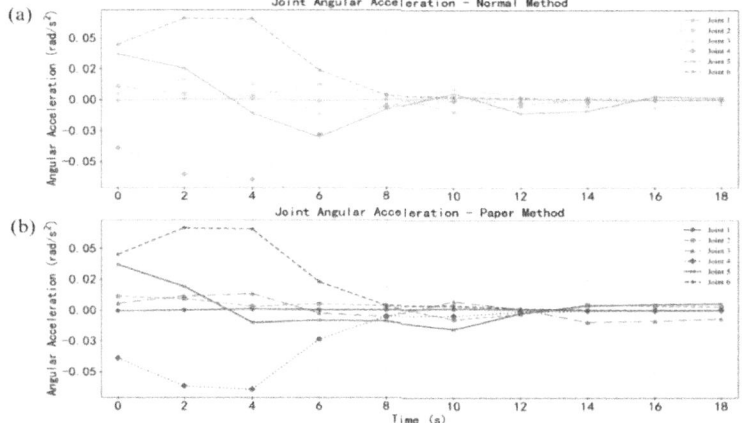

Fig. 10. Joint angular acceleration versus time function (a) Normal method (b) Paper method.

5 Conclusions

This study addresses the path planning challenge in robotic vision inspection of automotive paint surfaces and proposes a path-pose integrated planning method based on curvature weighting. The method utilizes curvature-weighted point cloud segmentation and slicing techniques to generate inspection paths. Through experiments, the range of constraints for the end-effector's Z-axis pose is obtained, and a robot pose solution method under angular function constraints is established. The effectiveness and accuracy of the method are then validated through simulation. The main conclusions are as follows:

1. Considering the curvature weights of the automotive inspection area significantly optimizes the point cloud segmentation and slicing process. The inspection area is partitioned based on the curvature characteristics of the automotive body, and adaptive slicing technology is employed to generate dense and redundant-free inspection points, providing reliable data for robot path generation.
2. Based on visual inspection experiment results, a local robot posture constraint function was established for paint defect detection. This function considers the angle range between the direction of the striped light source and the normal vector of the surface to be inspected in actual visual inspections, and combines the curvature distribution of the surface to be inspected to obtain the angle range within which the robot's end effector can be deflected, serving as an important basis for adjusting the robot's inspection posture.
3. Compared to robot motion planning methods that do not consider curvature changes in the inspection area, the proposed method generates smoother robot motion trajectory points. Under varying inspection areas, the joint displacements before and after attitude adjustments are smaller, with an average displacement reduction of 3.98%, significantly improving inspection efficiency.

Acknowledgments. This research is supported by the Key Research and Development Program of Hubei Province (Grant No. 2024BAB052), National Natural Science Foundation of China (Grant No. 52305500), National Natural Science Foundation of China (Grant No. 52275506).

References

1. Zhang, J., Yin, X., Luan, J., et al.: An improved vehicle panoramic image generation algorithm. Multimed. Tools Appl. **78**, 27663–27682 (2019)
2. Xu, J., Zhang, J., Zhang, K., et al.: An APF-ACO algorithm for automatic defect detection on vehicle paint. Multimed. Tools Appl. **79**, 25315–25333 (2020)
3. Wang, S., Xu, Z., Wang, Y., et al.: A three-stage framework for accurate detection of high-speed train body paint film defects. Adv. Eng. Inform. **62**, 102838 (2024)
4. Zhang, J., Kikuta, M., Zhang, C., et al.: Defect inspection of coated automobile roofs using a single camera. IEEJ Trans. Electr. Electron. Eng. **15**(4), 616–625 (2020)
5. Nieto Bastida, S., Lin, C.Y.: Autonomous trajectory planning for spray painting on complex surfaces based on a point cloud model. Sensors **23**(24), 9634 (2023)
6. Tong, N., Kong, M.X., Xu, S.R.: A spray path planning algorithm based on 3D point cloud. In: 2019 IEEE 3rd Advanced Information Management, Communicates, Electronic and Automation Control Conference (IMCEC). IEEE (2019)
7. Lamas, D., Justo, A., Soilan, M., Cabaleiro, M., Riveiro, B.: Instance and semantic segmentation of point clouds of large metallic truss bridges. Autom. Constr. **151**, 104865 (2023)
8. Truong-HongR, L.: Lindenbergh automatically extracting surfaces of reinforced concrete bridges from terrestrial laser scanning point clouds. Autom. Constr. **135**, 104127 (2022)
9. Smith, A., Sarlo, R.: Automated extraction of structural beam lines and connections from point clouds of steel buildings. Comput.-Aided Civ. Infrastruct. Eng. **37**(1), 110–125 (2022)
10. LuI, R.: Brilakis Digital twinning of existing reinforced concrete bridges from labelled point clusters. Autom. Constr. **105**, 102837 (2019)

11. Hoppe, H., DeRose, T., Duchamp, T., et al.: Surface reconstruction from unorganized points. In: Proceedings of the 19th Annual Conference on Computer Graphics and Interactive Techniques, pp. 71–78 (1992)
12. Li, G.-Q., Meng, Z.-P., Ma, F.-S., et al.: Calculation of stratum surface principal curvature based on a moving least square method. J. China Univ. Min. Technol. **18**(1), 63 (2008)
13. Han, J., Park, D.-C., Woo, D.-M., et al.: Comparison of distance measures on fuzzy C-means algorithm for image classification problem. AASRI Procedia **4**, 50–56 (2013)
14. Chen, W., Li, X., Ge, H., Wang, L., Zhang, Y.: Trajectory planning for spray painting robot based on point cloud slicing technique. Electronics **9**(6), 908 (2020)
15. Yu, X., Cheng, Z., Zhang, Y., Ou, L.: Point cloud modeling and slicing algorithm for trajectory planning of spray painting robot. Robotica **39**(12), 2246–2267 (2021)

Multi-agent Active Exploration Framework Based on Topological Map Fusion for Indoor Environments

Chenyu Bao[1], Junjie Hu[1,2], Shaobin Ling[1], Guoquan Ye[1], and Tin Lun Lam[1,2(✉)]

[1] The Chinese University of Hong Kong, Shenzhen, 2001 Longxiang Boulevard, Longgang District, Shenzhen, China
tllam@cuhk.edu.cn
[2] Shenzhen Institute of Artificial Intelligence and Robotics for Society, Shenzhen 518129, China
https://www.cuhk.edu.cn/en

Abstract. Active exploration plays a significant role in improving robotic autonomy. It enables robots to acquire information about the environment without human intervention. While single-agent active exploration has garnered significant attention in recent years, multi-agent active exploration has increasingly attracted interest due to its efficiency. In this paper, we propose a multi-agent active exploration framework that not only inherits the efficiency of its predecessor but also is compatible with multi-agent working settings. Our framework consists of three key components: i) a door information-based local topology map generation module, ii) a global topology map fusion module that fuses the local topological map into a global one, and iii) a policy module that assigns goal points for each robot and converts them into action instructions. We demonstrate the efficiency through experiments on the Habitat simulator. Experiments on real-world robots are also implemented to demonstrate the possibility of transferring to real-world environments. A video demonstration of our algorithm's performance is available at google drive.

Keywords: Active exploration · Multi-agent system · Heterogeneous robots

1 Introduction

Thanks to the rapid development of embodied AI technology, deploying robots to our daily life tasks seems increasingly feasible and practical. In order to have better performance, it is vital for robots to acquire knowledge about their working environments. Active exploration is such kind of task that allows robots to acquire information about the environment without human intervention. Many researchers [1,2] have put their efforts into the single active exploration task, where only one robot is leveraged to implement the exploration. However, coordinating multiple robots [3–6] to implement this task in an efficient way appears to be more promising due to enhanced coverage speed, robustness to individual robot failures, and the ability to explore larger environments within reasonable time constraints, and has consequently attracted significant attention in recent years.

In our previous work [7], we proposed a topology-based active room segmentation framework that enables robots to implement room segmentation and active exploration simultaneously. Besides, the robot can also take advantage of the segmentation result to enhance the exploration performance. In spite of the fact that this framework demonstrated superior efficiency by adopting a room-by-room exploration strategy, which aligns well with human intuition [8]. However, this framework is limited to being able to guide only a single robot to implement the exploration, which restricts the exploration performance when facing large-scale environments.

In this work, we proposed a new framework that is compatible with multiple robots based on the previous active room segmentation framework [7] while inheriting the original room-by-room exploration strategy. For each robot, it will follow the framework proposed in [7] to construct the local topological map using its RGBD images respectively. To coordinate multiple robots, a global topological map fusion module is proposed in this paper. This module is designed to fuse local topological maps into a unified global one by matching room nodes from each local topological map. The exploration policy will then assign goal points for each robot and convert them into specific action instructions that the robot can implement.

To validate the effectiveness, we conducted experiments on the Habitat simulator using the real-world Gibson dataset [9]. The experiment results on Habitat simulator reveals that the proposed method can achieve coverage rates over 90% in most complex scenes and demonstrate a comparative or even better performance comparing to SOTA methods.

In summary, our work:

- We propose a multi-robot active exploration framework that inherits the efficiency and good performance of the previous work and extends it to the multi-robot scenarios, enabling more efficient exploration performance in large-scale environments.
- We introduce a novel global topological map fusion mechanism that effectively integrates local topological maps into a coherent global representation, facilitating efficient coordination among multiple robots through the global topological map.
- Experiments on the Habitat simulator are implemented and demonstrate promising results, which demonstrate the promising performance and practical viability of our approach across diverse environmental conditions.

2 Related Works

Active exploration enables agents to gather required information from previously unseen environments. According to the number of agents that participate in the exploration process, the active exploration can be classified as single-agent active exploration and multi-agent exploration.

2.1 Single-Agent Active Exploration

The history of single-agent active exploration can be traced back to [1], where the concept frontier, which is the boundary between the known and unknown area, was first proposed. It inspired many following works on developing novel methods on detecting frontiers. Keidar et al. proposed two different style frontier detectors in [10], Wavefront Frontier Detector(WFD) for completeness and Fast Frontier Detector for efficiency. To accelerate the frontier detection process, Sun et al. [11] only detect frontiers within certain submaps with significant deviation. In [12], Rapidly-exploring Randomized Trees (RRT) is first introduced to find new frontiers. Besides frontier-based methods, information theory-based methods [13–16] focusing on finding trajectories that minimize the entropy of maps or robots' poses are also widely researched. And in recent years, many researchers have made an attempt to leverage reinforcement learning to locate ROI [2,17,18] or directly control the robot to search around [19].

2.2 Multi-agent Active Exploration

Multi-agent active exploration has gained significant research attention in recent years for its better efficiency compared to the single-agent counterpart. Michail et al. [20] first formulate this task as a relative entropy optimization problem by incorporating the trace of the state covariance into the planning cost and leveraging the relative entropy method. Dong et al. [3] assign task views to each agent based on the Optimal Mass Transport (OMT) and formulate the calculation of optimal path towards each task view as the Traveling Salesman Problem (TSP). Ye et al. [4] combine the traditional frontier-based exploration with the rapidly developing deep reinforcement learning algorithm and implement the multi-agent exploration by assigning frontier points to different agents as bipartite graph matching and learn the assignment policy through reinforcement learning. MAANS [21] proposed a transformer-based Spatial-TeamFormer framework to better capture the spatial relationship and improve the interaction between different agents.

Different from the previous works that mostly rely on metric representation, the framework in this paper differentiates itself from previous work by leveraging topological scene representations to guide the exploration process. By identifying and utilizing semantically meaningful visual cues, specifically doors, topological scene representations are constructed on each local robot independently and are subsequently merged into a global one for overall coordination. The usage of topological representation has several advantages. First, it naturally aligns with human intuition [8], reduces memory requirements compared to dense metric maps, and the connectivity information given by topological representation facilitates high-level planning. Moreover, the topological representation enables

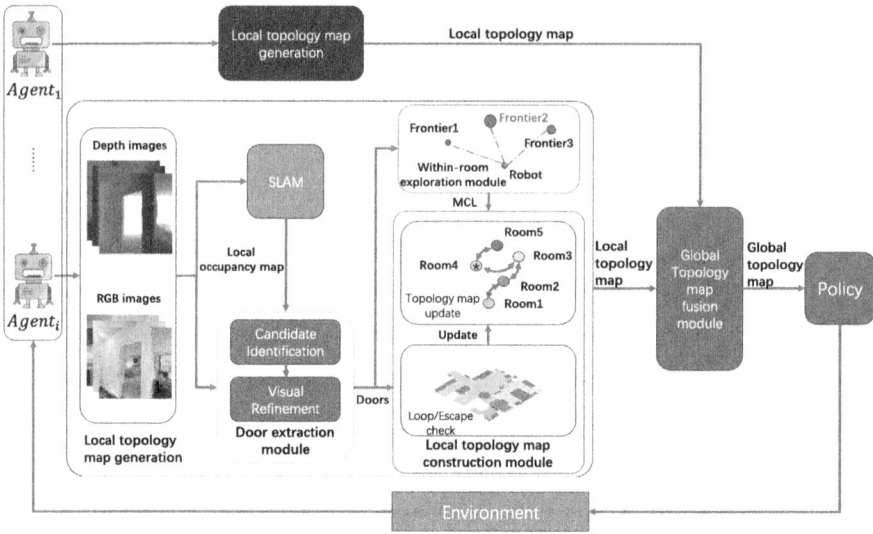

Fig. 1. Pipeline of the whole framework.

efficient task allocation in multi-robot scenarios, as robots can be assigned to explore different nodes to reduce overlap and redundancy.

3 Methodology

The framework works in a centralized manner. The overall pipeline is shown in Fig. 1. Each robot will construct a local occupancy grid map and a local topological map with its own sensors onboard. A global topological map will then be generated based on the local information and be used to guide the overall exploration. This section presents details of the proposed multi-agent exploration framework.

3.1 Topological Representation

In this framework, both local and global topological maps have almost the same format shown in Fig. 2, where nodes represent rooms and each pair of oppositely directed edges represents doors that connect two rooms. Within each node, three important attributes, 'Room status', 'Room entry waypoint', and 'Room MCL', are stored. 'Room status' is used to identify whether the current room is explored, exploring, or unexplored. 'Room entry waypoint' is the entry waypoint of each room and 'Room MCL' is the explored unoccupied area inside each room. Different from the local map, for the global version, each node also stores an extra attribute called 'Agent inside' for localizing each agent. And each edge includes a waypoint to guide the robot to its destination node.

3.2 Local Topological Map Generation

We follow the method proposed in [7] to obtain local topological maps for each robot. It makes a robot spin around to capture pictures of its surroundings when reaching new area which is called scan and detect doors with a door detection network [22]. We use four points to represent a door, P1 and P2 localize the door, and W1, W2 are provided as navigation waypoints. Whenever a new door is detected, a new node and pair of edges will be added to the node whose 'Room status' is 'exploring'. Furthermore, the door information will also be used to confined the robot's searching area inside the currently 'exploring' room, which essentially makes the robot search the whole scene in a room-by-room manner. And if the robots leave the currently searching rooms not fully explored, we call this situation 'escape'.

3.3 Global Topological Map Construction Module

To coordinate different agents, local topological maps will be merged into one global topological map. We will first assign an agent as the baseline agent whose

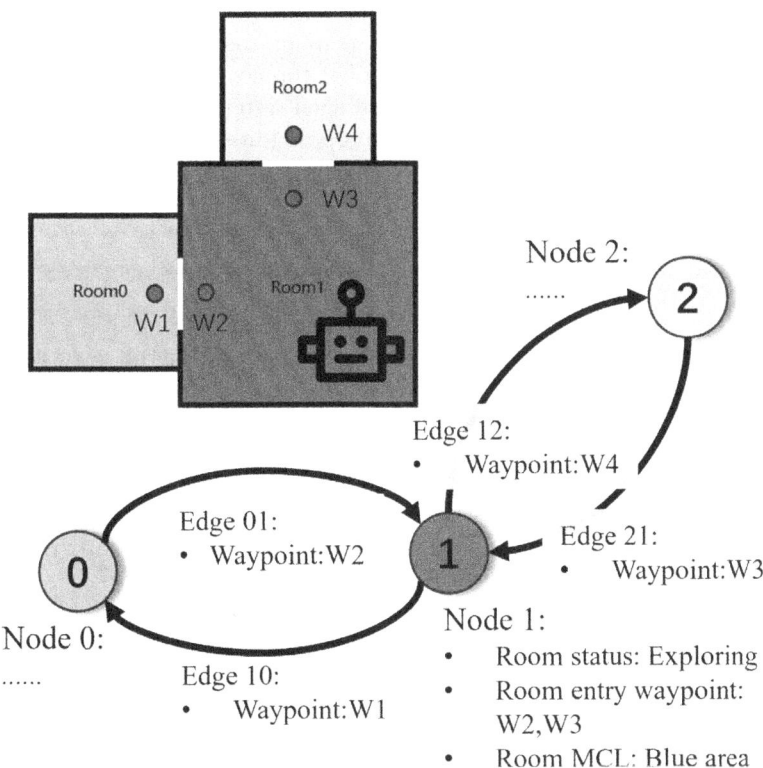

Fig. 2. Illustration for topology map and door representation.

coordinate overlaps the coordinate of the global map and assume that the relative poses $P_{j,i}$ of each agent at the beginning are available. The global topological map will not be established until at least one node of each local map finds its counterparts from the other local maps. The counterparts are detected by checking the overlap ratio of the MCL from two different nodes, as shown in Eq. 1.

$$MCL_{i,n_i} \cap T(P_{j,i})MCL_{j,n_j} \geq t_{counterpart} \qquad (1)$$

where MCL_{i,n_i} is the MCL attributes from the node n_i of $agent_i$, $T(P_{j,i})$ is the transformation matrix from $agent_j$'s coordinate to $agent_i$'s coordinate and $t_{counterpart}$ is a threshold that determines whether two nodes correspond to the same area in the scene. Besides detecting counterparts, agents' localization in the global map also relies on overlap ratios, as shown in Eq. 2. The localization results will be updated to the global topological map after the latest MCL is obtained by scanning.

$$MCL_{global,n_{global}} \cap T(P_{j,global})MCL_{j,n_j} \geq t_{localization} \qquad (2)$$

After finding the counterparts, the global topological maps will be established by first merging the attributes of each node and their counterparts in the global coordinate. Since the size of 'Room MCL' differs even for counterparts, the smaller one will be used in the global map in case some door information is missed. In the following steps, the global topological map will be updated directly using local information from each agent after the scan action. And the construction mainly follows the method proposed in [7].

3.4 Exploration Policy

Utilizing the global topological maps constructed above, all agents are assigned their goal by the following principles:

- Escape situation: When the robot escapes, the goal for the next step is the nearest waypoint that is affiliated with the original node that is exploring.
- Keep exploring: If the current room remain incompletely explored, the robot designates a "frontier" within the room as its next objective.
- Head for the next room: When the robot ascertains that the current room has been entirely explored, it designates the waypoint of the nearest 'Unexplored' node as its subsequent goal or the nearest 'Exploring' node if there is no 'Unexplored' node remaining.
- Head for other rooms: If other agents are exploring the current room and there are still 'Unexplored' node, the waypoint of the nearest 'Unexplored' node will be designated as the next goal.
- Completion of exploration: The termination of the active room segmentation process occurs when all nodes have been categorized as 'Explored', signifying comprehensive scene exploration.

4 Experiment

4.1 Implementation Details on Simulator

For quantitative experiments, we conduct the proposed framework on the real-world Gibson dataset [9] driven by the Habitat Simulator [23]. The number of robots used for exploration is 2. Both robots are equipped with an odometry sensor and an RGBD camera whose detection range is configured to 3 m and height is 1.25 m and 1.5 m, respectively. Fast Marching algorithm [24] is leveraged to calculate the shortest path towards goal points and action is then generated in the same way as [4]. The robot's movement is governed by three fundamental actions: i) move forward by 25 cm, ii) turn left by 30°, and iii) turn right by 30°. Map builder from ANS [2] is leveraged for map construction.

4.2 Exploration Performance

Test Scenes. To quantify the performance of the proposed framework, following ANS [2], we evaluate all methods on 6 scenes from the Gibson database, which are 'Denmark', 'Eastville', 'Edgemere', 'Elmira', 'Ribera' and 'Swormville'. These scenes represent diverse indoor environments with varying complexity levels, room configurations, and spatial layouts.

Table 1. Coverage rate comparison result

	Ours	CoScan [3]	NeuralCoMapping [4]	ARS [7]
Denmark	**99.4%**	96.0%	95.8%	98.4%
Eastville	**99.1%**	97.6%	98.2%	98.2%
Edgemere	98.9%	99.7%	**99.9%**	96.5%
Elmira	**99.6%**	96.1%	95.9%	99.0%
Ribera	99.3%	**99.9%**	**99.9%**	99.0%
Swormville	**98.0%**	94.1%	93.4%	96.9%
Average coverage rate	**99.1%**	97.2%	97.2%	98.0%

Baseline. To validate the exploration efficiency, we compare it against existing multi-agent exploration methods, including:

- CoScan [3]: A frontier-based multi-agent exploration method that assigns task views to each agent based on Optimal Mass Transport (OMT) and formulates optimal path calculation as the Traveling Salesman Problem (TSP).
- NeuralCoMapping [4]: A reinforcement learning-based method that formulates goal assignment as bipartite graph matching and learns the assignment policy through deep RL.
- ARS [7]: Our previous single-agent active room segmentation framework, was used as a baseline to demonstrate the efficiency gains from multi-agent coordination.

Table 2. Number of steps comparison

	Denmark	Eastville	Edgemere	Elmira	Ribera	Swormiville	Average steps
ARS	280	619	226	279	244	411	343
Ours	112	280	116	115	151	300	179

Results. For each method, we initialized robots at 50 different starting points in each scene. Each trial has a maximum time limit of 1000 steps to ensure fair comparison. All methods utilize two robots for exploration, except ARS which operates with a single robot. The average results are presented in the Table. 1. From the table, we can observe that the proposed method can achieve an impressive 99.1% coverage rate on average, which demonstrates the efficiency of the proposed framework. Furthermore, it also achieves a comparative even better performance compared to SOTA methods, CoScan [3] and NeuralCoMapping [4]. Besides, compared to its predecessor ARS [7], which only has one robot working in the environments, we can clearly observe that the coverage rate of the work proposed in this paper excels in every scene.

To further evaluate exploration efficiency, the average number of steps required to complete the exploration process of the proposed method and the ARS is presented in Table. 2. Remarkably, the number of steps our method requires nearly 50% fewer steps compared to the original single robot system, ARS (179 vs. 343 steps on average). The results of the coverage rate and the number of steps have not only obviously demonstrated the fact that the efficiency of the multi-agent system is much better than its single counterpart, but also validated the effectiveness of the policy, which could better coordinate the behaviors of different agents. The efficiency gain is particularly pronounced in larger environments like Eastville, where the step count is reduced from 619 to 280, representing a 54.8% improvement.

Despite these promising results, this framework still has several limitations from its foundation in the basic framework based on [7]. Most notably, the whole system is currently restricted to one-story environments, as the path planning is based on a 2D input occupancy grid map. Additionally, leveraging doors as the visual cue to construct a topological representation may also not be the optimal solution, as it provides limited semantic information for more complicated tasks and might fail when facing environments without obvious geometric boundaries. Future work could address these limitations by extending the topological representation to 3D environments and developing more robust semantic cue detection methods.

4.3 Real World Deployment

To validate our approach in practical scenarios, we conducted two real-world experiments with two different heterogeneous multi-robot systems. The first experiment involved a system of three heterogeneous robots, while the second utilized a team of two. These experiments were performed in two different real-world environments, as shown in Fig. 3(g) and Fig. 4(c).

Our heterogeneous robotic team consists of three distinct platforms, each with unique physical dimensions, camera configurations, and sensor capabilities. MR-600 (Fig. 3(a)) is a skid-steer robot equipped with an Intel RealSense D435i RGB-D camera (640 × 480 resolution) and a RoboSense LiDAR that provides a 360° point cloud for state estimation. Petbot (Fig. 3(b)) and Spark (Fig. 3(c)) are both differential drive robots, each equipped with an ORBBEC Astra RGB-D camera. For LiDAR sensing, Petbot is limited to a 180° field of view, whereas Spark provides a full 360° point cloud. All exploration and mapping algorithms were executed on a central laptop with an Intel i5-12th generation processor and 8 GB of RAM.

For path planning and mapping, the configuration space (C-space) is discretized into a uniform grid with a cell resolution of 5 cm × 5 cm. The local planning horizon for each robot is an 80 × 80 grid centered on its current position. An experimental trial is considered complete when the entire accessible area of the environment has been explored by the robotic team.

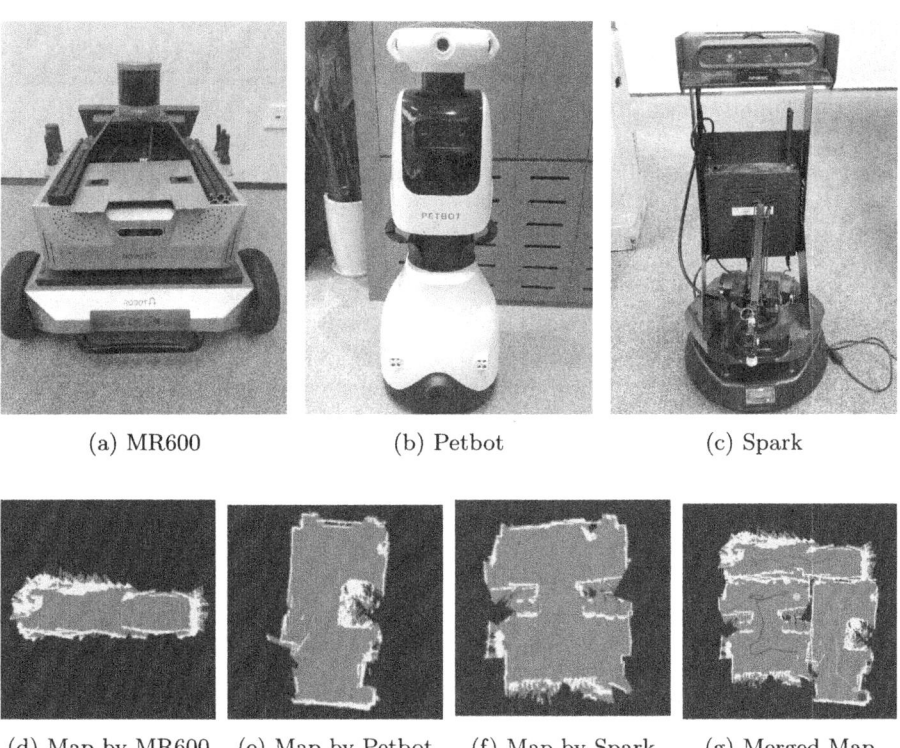

(a) MR600   (b) Petbot   (c) Spark

(d) Map by MR600   (e) Map by Petbot   (f) Map by Spark   (g) Merged Map

Fig. 3. Experiment 1: Three-robot active exploration. (a–c) The heterogeneous robotic team consisting of MR-600, Petbot, and Spark. (d–f) The individual maps generated by each robot during exploration. (g) The final, unified map produced by our merging algorithm.

Figure 3: Heterogeneous multi-robot exploration and mapping results. The top row displays the three robotic platforms used in the experiments and the ground truth map of the environment. The bottom row shows the individual maps generated by each robot and the final merged map created by our system.

The first experiment involved all three robots (MR-600, Petbot, and Spark) exploring an environment consisting of a meeting room and an adjacent corridor. The total area has dimensions of 14.7 m × 14.1 m.

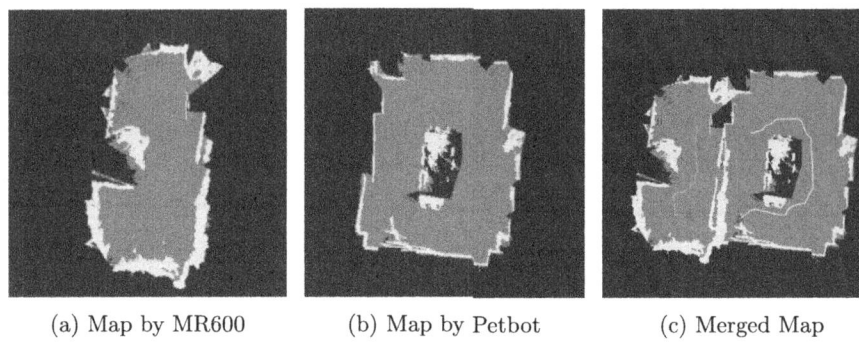

(a) Map by MR600   (b) Map by Petbot   (c) Merged Map

Fig. 4. Experiment 2: Two-robot active exploration. (a) and (b) show the partial maps generated by the MR-600 and Petbot robots, respectively. (c) The final unified map demonstrates successful coverage even with complex obstacles.

The second experiment was conducted with two robots (Petbot and MR-600) in a 14.7 m × 11.1 m meeting room. This scene was more challenging as it contained a large conference table surrounded by numerous chairs, creating a cluttered environment with complex navigation paths.

In both experiments, our method successfully enabled the team to achieve full coverage of the environment. The system effectively assigned distinct frontiers to different robots, allowing them to explore separate rooms or areas simultaneously and efficiently.

5 Conclusion

In this work, we propose a multi-agent active exploration framework that inherits the good performance of the previous door information-based active room segmentation framework by fusing local topological representation into a unified global one and using this global representation to coordinate the exploration process of different robots. Experimental results on the Gibson dataset have shown its comparative performance against SOTA multi-agent exploration methods. Furthermore, real-world experiment also demonstrates the feasibility of deployment on real robots. However, this framework still has several limitations. First, the whole system could only work properly for one-story scenes. What's more, since the basic framework is based on [7], it also inherits all the drawbacks of this work. We acknowledge these limitations and are planning to solve all these issues in future research. Despite all these limitations, this framework still represents a significant step forward in constructing and leveraging topological representations for active exploration.

Funding. This work is partially supported by the Shenzhen Science and Technology Program under Grants JCYJ20220818103000001 and JCYJ20241202124010014, and Guangdong Natural Science Fund under Grant 2024A1515010252.

References

1. Yamauchi, B.: A frontier-based approach for autonomous exploration. In: 1997 Proceedings of the IEEE International Symposium on Computational Intelligence in Robotics and Automation CIRA 1997.Towards New Computational Principles for Robotics and Automation, pp. 146–151. IEEE (1997)
2. Chaplot, D.S., Gandhi, D., Gupta, S., Gupta, A., Salakhutdinov, R.: Learning to explore using active neural SLAM. arXiv preprint arXiv:2004.05155 (2020)
3. Dong, S., et al.: Multi-robot collaborative dense scene reconstruction. ACM Trans. Graph. (TOG) **38**(4), 1–16 (2019)
4. Ye, K., et al.: Multi-robot active mapping via neural bipartite graph matching. In: Proceedings of the IEEE/CVF Conference on Computer Vision and Pattern Recognition, pp. 14 839–14 848 (2022)
5. Chen, J., et al.: Multirobolearn: an open-source framework for multi-robot deep reinforcement learning. In: 2023 IEEE International Conference on Robotics and Biomimetics (ROBIO), pp. 1–6. IEEE (2023)
6. Chen, J., Gao, Y., Hu, J., Deng, F., Lam, T.L.: Meta-reinforcement learning based cooperative surface inspection of 3d uncertain structures using multi-robot systems. In: 2024 IEEE International Conference on Robotics and Automation (ICRA), pp. 7201–7207. IEEE (2024)
7. Bao, C., Hu, L., Zheng, L.: Topology-based visual active room segmentation. In: 2025 IEEE International Conference on Robotics and Automation (ICRA). IEEE (2025)
8. Hilton, C., Wiener, J.: Route sequence knowledge supports the formation of cognitive maps. Hippocampus **33**(11), 1161–1170 (2023)
9. Xia, F., Zamir, A.R., He, Z., Sax, A., Malik, J., Savarese, S.: Gibson env: real-world perception for embodied agents. In: Proceedings of the IEEE Conference on Computer Vision and Pattern Recognition, pp. 9068–9079 (2018)
10. Keidar, M., Kaminka, G.A.: Robot exploration with fast frontier detection: theory and experiments. In: Proceedings of the 11th International Conference on Autonomous Agents and Multiagent Systems, vol. 1, pp. 113–120 (2012)
11. Sun, Z., Wu, B., Xu, C.-Z., Sarma, S.E., Yang, J., Kong, H.: Frontier detection and reachability analysis for efficient 2D graph-slam based active exploration. In: 2020 IEEE/RSJ International Conference on Intelligent Robots and Systems (IROS), pp. 2051–2058. IEEE (2020)
12. Umari, H., Mukhopadhyay, S.: Autonomous robotic exploration based on multiple rapidly-exploring randomized trees. In: 2017 IEEE/RSJ International Conference on Intelligent Robots and Systems (IROS), pp. 1396–1402. IEEE (2017)

13. Bircher, A., Kamel, M., Alexis, K., Oleynikova, H., Siegwart, R.: Receding horizon "next-best-view" planner for 3D exploration. In: 2016 IEEE International Conference on Robotics and Automation (ICRA), pp. 1462–1468. IEEE (2016)
14. Bourgault, F., Makarenko, A.A., Williams, S.B., Grocholsky, B., Durrant-Whyte, H.F.: Information based adaptive robotic exploration. In: IEEE/RSJ International Conference on Intelligent Robots and Systems, vol. 1, pp. 540–545. IEEE (2002)
15. Vallvé, J., Andrade-Cetto, J.: Active pose SLAM with RRT. In: 2015 IEEE International Conference on Robotics and Automation (ICRA), pp. 2167–2173. IEEE (2015)
16. Stachniss, C., Grisetti, G., Burgard, W.: Information gain-based exploration using Rao-Blackwellized particle filters. In: Robotics: Science and systems, vol. 2, pp. 65–72 (2005)
17. Ramakrishnan, S.K., Al-Halah, Z., Grauman, K.: Occupancy anticipation for efficient exploration and navigation. In: Vedaldi, A., Bischof, H., Brox, T., Frahm, J.-M. (eds.) ECCV 2020. LNCS, vol. 12350, pp. 400–418. Springer, Cham (2020). https://doi.org/10.1007/978-3-030-58558-7_24
18. Georgakis, G., Bucher, B., Arapin, A., Schmeckpeper, K., Matni, N., Daniilidis, K.: Uncertainty-driven planner for exploration and navigation. In: 2022 International Conference on Robotics and Automation (ICRA), pp. 11 295–11 302. IEEE (2022)
19. Chen, T., Gupta, S., Gupta, A.: Learning exploration policies for navigation. arXiv preprint arXiv:1903.01959 (2019)
20. Kontitsis, M., Theodorou, E.A., Todorov, E.: Multi-robot active slam with relative entropy optimization. In: 2013 American Control Conference, pp. 2757–2764. IEEE (2013)
21. Yu, C., Yang, X., Gao, J., Yang, H., Wang, Y., Wu, Y.: Learning efficient multi-agent cooperative visual exploration. In: Avidan, S., Brostow, G., Cissé, M., Farinella, G.M., Hassner, T. (eds.) ECCV 2022. LNCS, vol. 13699, pp. 497–515. Springer, Cham (2022). https://doi.org/10.1007/978-3-031-19842-7_29
22. Antonazzi, M., Luperto, M., Basilico, N., Borghese, N.A.: Enhancing door detection for autonomous mobile robots with environment-specific data collection. CoRR (2022)
23. Savva, M., et al.: Habitat: A platform for embodied AI research. In: Proceedings of the IEEE/CVF International Conference on Computer Vision, pp. 9339–9347 (2019)
24. Sethian, J.A.: A fast marching level set method for monotonically advancing fronts. In: Proceedings of the National Academy of Sciences, vol. 93, no. 4, pp. 1591–1595 (1996)

An Attention-Based Diffusion Policy with Hybrid Farthest Point Sampling for Robotic Intelligent Manipulation

Yifei Dong[1,2], Yi An[1,2], Tiantian Xu[1], and Sheng Xu[1(✉)]

[1] Shenzhen Institutes of Advanced Technology, Chinese Academy of Sciences, Shenzhen, China
sheng.xu@siat.ac.cn
[2] University of Chinese Academy of Sciences, Beijing, China

Abstract. End-to-end robotic manipulation learning techniques have become one of the most prominent research areas in recent years. Imitation learning allows the robot to learn from expert demonstrations, which helps reduce the costs of exploration and trial-and-error. This paper focuses on addressing the robot manipulation tasks using imitation learning. An improvement based on the diffusion policy with point clouds as the visual representation is developed. More specifically, we redesign the point-cloud sampling strategy to give higher priority to points that belong to the manipulated object and its local geometric details. In addition, an attention-driven point cloud encoder to capture long-range spatial dependencies is proposed. To introduce adaptive, channel-wise attention, we embed Squeeze-and-Excitation (SE) modules at critical stages of the U-Net backbone. Simulation examples, several manipulation tasks, are provided, and the proposed method attains higher success rates on a greater proportion of tasks across the selected test suite.

Keywords: Imitation learning · Diffusion policy · Manipulation

1 Introduction

Intelligent robot manipulation has been widely required in various applications, including industrial assembly, medical care, security search, and home services [1–5]. In the past several decades, many robot manipulator control methods have been proposed, which can be divided into two types, i.e., the classical model-based control methods and data-driven control methods [6,7]. In this paper, we focus on using learning-based or imitation learning methods to solve the robotic movement problem, where the manipulation skills are learned from sensing and demonstration data.

General-purpose robotic manipulation remains challenging owing to high-dimensional action spaces, partial observability, and the requirement for precise temporal coordination. Reinforcement learning (RL) has been widely adopted for learning manipulation tasks due to its capability of end-to-end policy learning directly based on environmental feedback [8,9]. However, due to the sparse rewards in complex tasks, reinforcement learning struggles to find an appropriate reward function. High exploration cost is also one of its limitations [10].

To alleviate these limitations, researchers have increasingly explored imitation learning, which derives policies directly from expert demonstrations. The earliest approach, behavioral cloning (BC), treats the expert's stateaction pairs as labeled data for supervised learning. However, BC is prone to compounding errors when the policy drifts from the expert distribution and requires substantial amounts of high-quality demonstrations [11]. As deep learning has progressed, increasingly robust imitation learning methods have been proposed. Based on Generative Adversarial Imitation Learning (GAIL), [12] introduces an additional goal state discriminator to improve the learning of robotic manipulation policies from imperfect demonstrations. [13] proposes a two-stage robotic grasping framework based on inverse reinforcement learning (IRL), in which IRL is used to learn a dense reward function from the adversarial behaviors of living objects. Both GAIL and IRL circumvent the need for explicit reward function modeling by learning from demonstrations.

More recently, policy modeling has evolved toward probabilistic and generative frameworks, enabling richer representations of action distributions. Diffusion Policy, as a representative among them, offers a promising solution by modeling action sequences as the result of a denoising diffusion process conditioned on sensory observations [14]. This generative approach allows the policy to explore diverse yet plausible action trajectories that conform to the demonstrated behaviors, rather than collapsing to a single deterministic output. Combining multiple perception modalities and instruction guidance, diffusion policy has achieved excellent performance across various robotic manipulation tasks [15,16].

In this paper, we make adjustments to the 3D diffusion policy (DP3) [17], which uses point clouds as its visual representation. Our refinement enables precise planning and execution of robotic manipulation trajectories. Our main contributions are as follows.

1. A novel point cloud sampling paradigm is proposed to retain critical geometric details of small or edge-located objects while suppressing redundant points.
2. An attention-driven architecture for diffusion policy point cloud encoding is applied, replacing conventional convolution pipelines. This design incorporates global attention mechanisms to capture long-range spatial dependencies.
3. During the denoising process, each conditional residual block of the diffusion-policy U-Net is augmented with a Squeeze-and-Excitation (SE) module that re-weights informative feature channels.

The remainder of this paper is organized as follows. Section 2 formulates the robot manipulation problem based on diffusion policy. Section 3 introduces the key modifications we made to the diffusion policy. Section 4 shows the experiment results in the simulation environment. Section 5 is the conclusion.

2 Problem Formulation

The traditional diffusion model formulates the generation process as a sequential denoising procedure governed by a Markov chain [18]. In the forward process, the model gradually adds Gaussian noise to the input data x^0 over a series of steps $k = 1, 2, ..., K$,

$$q(x^k \mid x^{k-1}) = \mathcal{N}(x^k; \sqrt{\alpha^k} x^{k-1}, (1-\alpha^k)\mathbf{I}), \tag{1}$$

where α^k is a predefined constant representing the proportion of noise added at each step. Through iterative noise addition steps, under the condition of a given x^0, we can derive

$$x^k = \sqrt{\bar{\alpha}^k} x^0 + \sqrt{1-\bar{\alpha}^k} \epsilon^k, \tag{2}$$

where $\bar{\alpha}^k = \prod_{i=1}^{k} \alpha^i$, $\epsilon^k \sim \mathcal{N}(\mathbf{0}, \mathbf{I})$.

In the reverse process, the objective is to learn a parameterized model $p(x^{k-1} \mid x^k)$ that approximates the true posterior $q(x^{k-1} \mid x^k)$. The reverse denoising process in diffusion models is modeled as,

$$p(x^{k-1} \mid x^k) = \mathcal{N}\left(\frac{1}{\sqrt{\alpha^k}}\left(x^k - \frac{1-\alpha^k}{\sqrt{1-\bar{\alpha}^k}} \epsilon_\theta(x^k, k)\right), 1-\alpha^k\right), \tag{3}$$

where $\epsilon_\theta(x^k, k)$ is the noise predicted by a network. The denoised data is calculated by

$$x^{k-1} = \frac{1}{\sqrt{\alpha^k}}\left(x^k - \frac{1-\alpha^k}{\sqrt{1-\bar{\alpha}^k}} \epsilon_\theta(x^k, k)\right) + \sqrt{1-\alpha^k} z, \quad z \sim \begin{cases} \mathcal{N}(\mathbf{0}, \mathbf{I}), & k > 1, \\ \mathbf{0}, & k = 1. \end{cases} \tag{4}$$

This traditional model requires numerous denoising steps, resulting in slower generation. Meanwhile, the sampling-based generation procedure relies on probability distributions, which introduces stochasticity. Denoising Diffusion Implicit Models (DDIMS) are an improved class of diffusion models that reduce the number of generation steps without compromising output quality by employing a deterministic sampling method [19]. σ^k controls the level of randomness, and the sampling in the denoising process is given by

$$x^{k-1} = \sqrt{\bar{\alpha}^{k-1}} \frac{x^k - \sqrt{1-\bar{\alpha}^k} \epsilon_\theta(x^k, k)}{\sqrt{\bar{\alpha}^k}} + \sqrt{1-\bar{\alpha}^{k-1}-(\sigma^k)^2} \epsilon_\theta(x^k, k) + \sigma^k \epsilon^k. \tag{5}$$

For a manipulation task, our goal is to generate a trajectory A_t by a policy $\pi(A_t \mid O_t)$ conditioned on the observation O_t at each time step t. Although RGB images are commonly used as visual inputs in many works [15,16,20], the study in [17] demonstrates that using 3D point clouds facilitates policy learning more effectively than other visual input modalities such as RGB-D and voxels. Thus, in our method, we employ point clouds P_t along with the robot's own pose J_t as the observation inputs, where J_t comprises the robot's state along with the gripper's status and its rotational configuration. Namely, $O_t = \{P_t, J_t\}$.

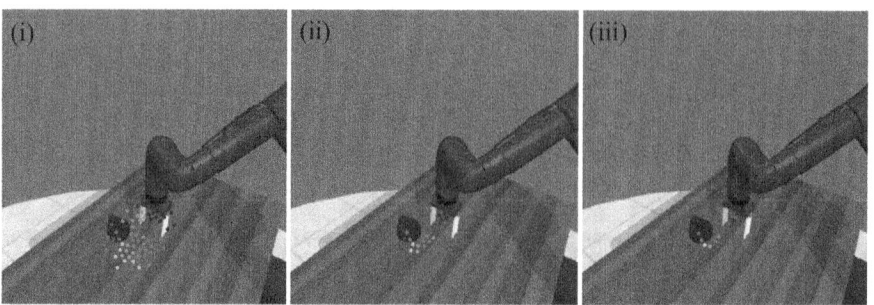

Fig. 1. Action denoising process.

To capture the conditional distribution $p(\boldsymbol{A}_t \mid \boldsymbol{O}_t)$, we modify (5) to

$$\boldsymbol{A}_t^{k-1} = \sqrt{\bar{\alpha}^{k-1}} \frac{\boldsymbol{A}_t^k - \sqrt{1-\bar{\alpha}^k} \epsilon_\theta(\boldsymbol{A}_t^k, \boldsymbol{O}_t, k)}{\sqrt{\bar{\alpha}^k}} \\ + \sqrt{1 - \bar{\alpha}^{k-1} - (\sigma^k)^2} \epsilon_\theta(\boldsymbol{A}_t^k, \boldsymbol{O}_t, k) + \sigma^k \boldsymbol{\epsilon}^k. \quad (6)$$

The training loss is set to

$$\mathcal{L} = \text{MSE}(\boldsymbol{\epsilon}^k, \epsilon_\theta(\boldsymbol{A}_t^k, \boldsymbol{O}_t, k)), \quad (7)$$

to minimize the difference between the predicted noise and the true noise. Ultimately, we hope the robot can recover the true trajectory from a noisy one, as shown in Fig. 1.

3 Method

3.1 Hybrid FPS

Farthest Point Sampling (FPS) is a very common and effective sampling method in point cloud processing [24], ensuring that the selected points are as dispersed as possible throughout the point cloud space, thereby preserving its overall structure and shape information. However, in most manipulation tasks, due to the large size of the robot, its point cloud occupies the majority of the processing space, which diminishes the perception of the manipulated object. In such situations, FPS may lose more local details.

Therefore, we propose a hybrid FPS (H-FPS) method, as shown in Algorithm 1, that comprehensively considers the sampling coverage, surface curvature, and volume of the object. In tasks focused on handling single small objects, each approach is utilized with a 50% allocation. While for tasks involving interactions between two objects or the manipulation of larger items, the proposed algorithm consists of 60% standard FPS sampling and 40% weighted FPS sampling to ensure coverage. In the first stage, traditional FPS sampling ensures basic spatial coverage, while in the second stage, weighted sampling is applied

Algorithm 1. H-FPS (50% FPS + 50% Weighted FPS)

1: **Input:** unsampled point cloud $\mathbf{P}_o \in \mathbb{R}^{N_0 \times d}$; total samples N; density weight ω_ρ; curvature weight ω_c
2: **Output:** sampled point cloud $\mathbf{P}_s$

3: $\mathbf{P}_s \leftarrow \emptyset$ ▷ selected subset
4: compute neighbourhood density ρ_i and curvature κ_i for every point
5: $w_i \leftarrow \omega_\rho \rho_i^{-1} + \omega_c \kappa_i$ ▷ importance weight
6: $N_{\text{FPS}} \leftarrow \lfloor N/2 \rfloor$, $N_{\text{WFPS}} \leftarrow N - N_{\text{FPS}}$

7: /*——— FPS stage ———*/
8: choose a random seed index c; $\mathbf{P}_s \leftarrow \mathbf{P}_s \cup \{\mathbf{P}_{o,c}\}$
9: $d_j \leftarrow +\infty$ for all j ▷ distance to nearest centre
10: **for** $k = 1$ **to** N_{FPS} **do**
11:     **for** each point j in $\mathbf{P}_o$ **do**
12:         $d_j \leftarrow \min(d_j, \|\mathbf{P}_{o,j} - \mathbf{P}_{o,c}\|_2)$
13:     **end for**
14:     $c \leftarrow \arg\max_{j \notin \mathbf{P}_s} d_j$
15:     $\mathbf{P}_s \leftarrow \mathbf{P}_s \cup \{\mathbf{P}_{o,c}\}$
16: **end for**

17: /*——— Weighted-FPS stage ———*/
18: **while** $|\mathbf{P}_s| < N$ **do**
19:     **for** each unselected point j **do**
20:         $s_j \leftarrow d_j + w_j$ ▷ distance + weight score
21:     **end for**
22:     $c \leftarrow \arg\max_{j \notin \mathbf{P}_s} s_j$
23:     $\mathbf{P}_s \leftarrow \mathbf{P}_s \cup \{\mathbf{P}_{o,c}\}$
24:     **for** each unselected point j **do**
25:         $d_j \leftarrow \min(d_j, \|\mathbf{P}_{o,j} - \mathbf{P}_{o,c}\|_2)$
26:     **end for**
27: **end while**

28: **return** $\mathbf{P}_s$

based on geometric features (curvature and neighborhood density). Note that the curvature and density data used are both normalized. Points with significant local shape variations and those in edge regions or with small volumes are assigned higher weights. This method retains more useful information for the same number of sampled points. The sampling results are shown in Fig. 2.

3.2 Observation Encoder

Unlike 2D images, 3D point clouds are unordered, unstructured, and irregular, making them challenging to process by standard convolutional networks. To enhance the feature extraction capability for point cloud information, we employ a transformer-based point cloud encoding approach. Note that, in order to make

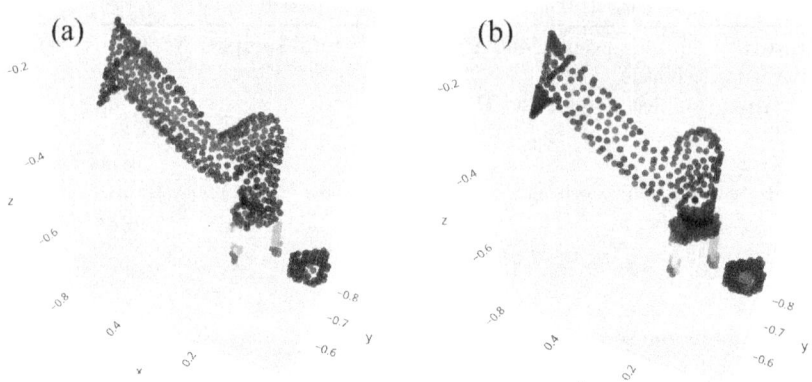

Fig. 2. Visualization of point clouds: (a) point clouds sampled by FPS, (b) point clouds sampled by hybrid FPS.

the model insensitive to the object's color, we do not use the color channel in the point cloud data.

As shown in Fig. 3, the sampled point cloud data is first processed through several MLP projection layers to increase its dimensionality, and subsequently passed through two cascaded Transformer blocks for feature extraction [21]. Finally, the features go through a max-pooling layer and are projected to the target dimension. To preserve spatial relationships while leveraging the permutation-invariance of point clouds, we assign a learnable embedding layer to each point in the cloud and leverage the attention mechanism to compute long-range feature correlations, effectively avoiding the locality inductive bias limitations of traditional convolutional algorithms. By integrating global attention, our encoder effectively bridges the gap between raw 3D observations and high-level action generation.

3.3 Network Architecture of the Proposed Method

The original DP3 model employs a U-Net architecture as the backbone of its diffusion policy. We augment the U-Net with Squeeze-and-Excitation (SE) attention modules [22]. The SE module implements an adaptive channel attention mechanism through global average pooling followed by two fully connected layers. By learning the global contextual information of each channel, the SE module can adaptively adjust the importance weights of different feature channels, thereby suppressing redundant information. In the following, we present the specific implementation details.

As depicted in Fig. 3, the embedded time step is fused with the point cloud features and robot state through concatenation. Together with the noisy input, they are propagated as global conditions through a neural network whose core building blocks are conditional residual blocks. The key modification is that we

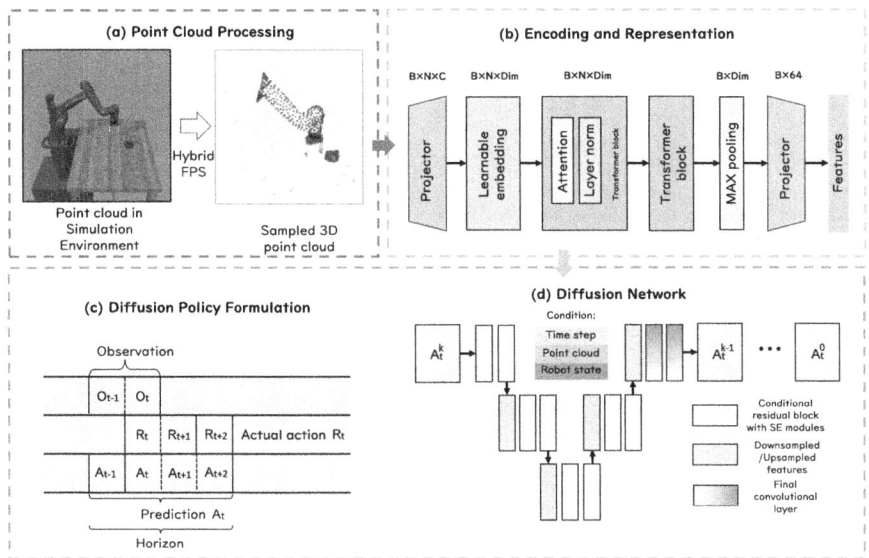

Fig. 3. The implementation flow of the method and the detailed structure of the network.

insert the SE module at the tail of every conditional residual block just before the residual merge. Let the input tensor be

$$\mathbf{u} \in \mathbb{R}^{B \times C \times T}, \tag{8}$$

where B is the batch size, C the number of feature channels, and T the temporal horizon length, the squeeze operation applies global average pooling along the temporal horizon dimension,

$$z_c = \frac{1}{T} \sum_{t=1}^{T} u_{c,t}, \qquad \mathbf{z} \in \mathbb{R}^{B \times C}. \tag{9}$$

For clarity, we omit the batch index b in subscripts. A two-layer multilayer perceptron with weights $\mathbf{W}_1$ and $\mathbf{W}_2$ produces a vector of attention weights,

$$\mathbf{s} = \sigma(\mathbf{W}_2 \phi(\mathbf{W}_1 \mathbf{z})), \qquad \mathbf{s} \in [0,1]^{B \times C}. \tag{10}$$

Finally, feature recalibration is achieved by performing element-wise multiplication between the learned channel weights and the original feature map,

$$\tilde{u}_{c,t} = s_c u_{c,t}, 1 \leq t \leq T. \tag{11}$$

By integrating SE modules at the end of each conditional residual block, the model gains improved capacity to suppress redundant features and emphasize informative ones, laying the foundation for enhanced task performance in robotic manipulation.

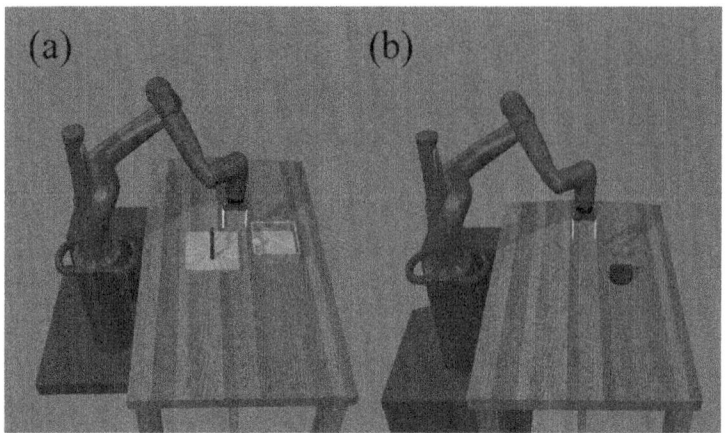

Fig. 4. Experimental setups: (a) "box close", (b) "dial turn".

4 Simulation Experiments

4.1 Benchmark

We run simulations in MetaWorld [23], an open-source benchmark for robotic manipulation. Specifically, we select nine representative manipulation tasks that cover a diverse range of skills, such as grasping, pushing, to comprehensively evaluate the performance of our method. The experimental setups for some tasks are shown in Fig. 4. The number of points in the point cloud we used is 512. We set DDIM sampling time steps as 100 at training and 10 at inference.

All policies are trained for 1000 epochs due to MetaWorld's simplicity as mentioned in [17]. A dataset of 10 task-specific demonstrations is generated by reinforcement learning (RL) policies. We use a batch size of 64. For fair comparison, the U-Net channel widths are fixed at 256, 512, and 1024. Each experiment is repeated with three random seeds (0, 1, 2). For every seed, we evaluate 20 episodes at intervals of 200 training epochs and record the three highest success rates. The reported performance is the mean ± standard deviation of these maxima across seeds. All experiments are executed on a single NVIDIA RTX 4090 GPU.

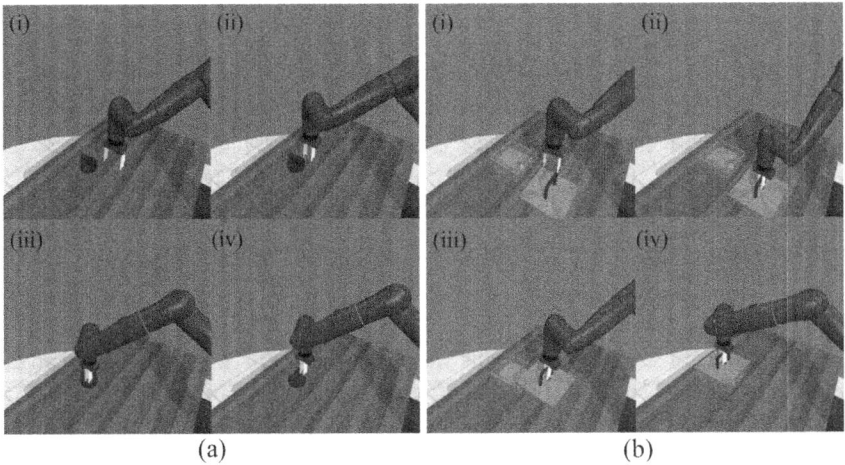

Fig. 5. Experiment processes: (a) "dial turn", (b) "box close".

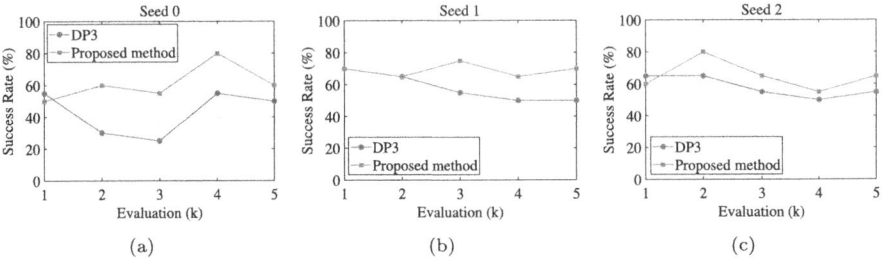

Fig. 6. Success rates of our proposed method and DP3 in the task "dial turn": (a) results of seed 0, (b) results of seed 1, (c) results of seed 2.

4.2 Results

In this section, we present the results of simulation experiments to evaluate the effectiveness of our approach. Since success rates are also influenced by the quality of demonstrations, our results are obtained under the same demonstration conditions. The reported success rate of DP3 is obtained from our reproduction under a unified set of shared hyperparameters.

The processes of the robot successfully completing the simulation tasks are shown in Fig. 5. Due to the limitations of paper length, we only present the "dial turn" and "box close" processes. The success rates for each simulation task are shown in Table 1.

The experiment results show that the robot is able to learn an optimal strategy from a small number of demonstrations. Out of nine tasks, our method achieves equal or better performance than the baseline in seven cases. We present the success rate line chart of "dial turn" obtained from training with different

Table 1. Main results on 9 simulations

Alg\Task	Dial turn	Shelf place	Soccer	Pick place	Box close
DP3	59.4 ± 6.8	33.9 ± 8.2	20.0 ± 6.6	**46.7 ± 10.0**	56.1 ± 11.7
Proposed method	**69.4 ± 7.7**	**36.1 ± 11.7**	**21.7 ± 10.9**	40.6 ± 9.2	**57.2 ± 6.7**
Alg\Task	Push	Hammer	Coffee pull	Push wall	
DP3	56.1 ± 8.6	**92.2 ± 3.6**	**95.0 ± 6.6**	79.4 ± 5.3	
Proposed method	**58.3 ± 7.5**	90.6 ± 5.3	**95.0 ± 6.6**	**80.6 ± 10.4**	

seeds in Fig. 6 due to its significant improvement. All the above experimental results collectively demonstrate the effectiveness of our proposed method.

Additionally, it is worth noting that our model introduces approximately 20% more parameters, accompanied by a decrease in inference speed. To address this, we will investigate lightweight backbone networks and model compression techniques that can reduce computational overhead while preserving task performance in future work.

5 Conclusion

This paper proposes an end-to-end learning method to improve the robotic manipulation success rate based on the 3D diffusion policy [17]. Firstly, we improve the 3D visual point cloud processing method by modifying the sampling strategy. Secondly, an attention-driven point cloud encoder is developed to capture long-range spatial dependencies effectively. Thirdly, SE modules are skillfully integrated into the U-Net to adjust channel weights. Diverse simulation examples verify the effectiveness of the proposed method.

In future work, we will expand the policy's observation space by fusing additional sensory modalities–including RGB images, voxelized depth data, and force/torque signals, and, when necessary, adapt the diffusion architecture to accommodate these heterogeneous inputs. Because the current setup relies on a single static camera, occlusions remain a major source of perception error. We therefore plan to deploy a multi-view vision system that surrounds the workspace and provides redundant viewpoints. Although the proposed algorithm achieves competitive accuracy, its training and inference are slower than those of DP3. To close this gap, we will investigate lighter-weight backbone networks and model-compression techniques that preserve performance while reducing computational cost. For future deployment on physical robots, expert demonstrations will be collected via manual control using a keyboard or joystick, with synchronized acquisition of point cloud data through an RGB-D camera. Since point cloud observations in real-world settings can be unstable and time-varying, it may be necessary to apply stronger data augmentation strategies, such as perturbation injection, to improve model robustness.

Acknowledgement. This work is supported by the National Natural Science Foundation of China with Grant Numbers 62273327, 62173319, and the Shenzhen Science and Technology Program with Grant Number KCXFZ20211020165003005.

References

1. Duan, J., Ou, Y., Xu, S., Liu, M.: Sequential learning unification controller from human demonstrations for robotic compliant manipulation. Neurocomputing **366**, 35–45 (2019)
2. Sheng, J., Tang, Y., Xu, S., Tan, F., Hou, R., Xu, T.: A stable learning-based method for robotic assembly with motion and force measurements. IEEE Trans. Industr. Electron. **71**(9), 11093–11103 (2024)
3. Xu, S., Doğançay, K.: Optimal sensor placement for 3-D angle-of-arrival target localization. IEEE Trans. Aerosp. Electron. Syst. **53**(3), 1196–1211 (2017)
4. Hou, R., Xu, S., Yang, C., Duan, J., Wu, X., Xu, T.: A learning-based assembly sequence planning method using neural combinatorial optimization with satisfactory generalization ability. IEEE Trans. Autom. Sci. Eng. **22**, 8952–8964 (2025)
5. Liu, Y., Liu, S., Chen, B., Yang, Z.X., Xu, S.: Fusion-perception-to-action transformer: enhancing robotic manipulation with 3-D visual fusion attention and proprioception. IEEE Trans. Rob. **41**, 1553–1567 (2025)
6. Xu, S., Ou, Y., Wang, Z., Duan, J., Li, H.: Learning-based kinematic control using position and velocity errors for robot trajectory tracking. IEEE Trans. Syst. Man Cybern.: Syst. **52**(2), 1100–1110 (2022)
7. Xu, S., Chen, K., Ou, Y., Wang, Z., Yang, C.: A learning-based object tracking strategy using visual sensors and intelligent robot arm. IEEE Trans. Autom. Sci. Eng. **20**(4), 2280–2293 (2022)
8. Aljalbout, E., Frank, F., Karl, M., Smagt, P.: On the role of the action space in robot manipulation learning and sim-to-real transfer. IEEE Robot. Autom. Lett. **9**(6), 5895–5902 (2024)
9. Min, C.H., Song, J.B.: Hierarchical end-to-end control policy for multi-degree-of-freedom manipulators. Int. J. Control Autom. Syst. **20**(10), 3296–3311 (2022)
10. Zhang, T., Mo, H.: Reinforcement learning for robot research: a comprehensive review and open issues. Int. J. Adv. Rob. Syst. **18**(3), 17298814211007304 (2021)
11. Ross, S., Gordon, G., Bagnell, D.: A reduction of imitation learning and structured prediction to no-regret online learning. In: Gordon, G., Dunson, D., Dudík, M. (eds.) Proceedings of the Fourteenth International Conference on Artificial Intelligence and Statistics. Proceedings of Machine Learning Research, vol. 15, pp. 627–635. PMLR, Fort Lauderdale (2011)
12. Tsurumine, Y., Matsubara, T.: Goal-aware generative adversarial imitation learning from imperfect demonstration for robotic cloth manipulation. Robot. Auton. Syst. **158**, 104264 (2022)
13. Hu, Z., Zheng, Y., Pan, J.: Grasping living objects with adversarial behaviors using inverse reinforcement learning. IEEE Trans. Rob. **39**(2), 1151–1163 (2023)
14. Chi, C., Feng, S., Du, Y., Xu, Z., Cousineau, E., Burchfiel, B., Song, S.: Diffusion policy: visuomotor policy learning via action diffusion. In: Proceedings of Robotics: Science and Systems (RSS) (2023)
15. Kang, J.H., Joshi, S., Huang, R., Gupta, S.K.: Robotic compliant object prying using diffusion policy guided by vision and force observations. IEEE Robot. Autom. Lett. **10**(6), 5505–5512 (2025)

16. Ma, X., Patidar, S., Haughton, I., James, S.: Hierarchical diffusion policy for kinematics-aware multi-task robotic manipulation. In: 2024 IEEE/CVF Conference on Computer Vision and Pattern Recognition (CVPR), pp. 18081–18090. IEEE, Seattle (2024)
17. Ze, Y., Zhang, G., Zhang, K., Hu, C., Wang, M., Xu, H.: 3D diffusion policy: generalizable visuomotor policy learning via simple 3D representations. In: Proceedings of Robotics: Science and Systems (RSS) (2024)
18. Ho, J., Jain, A., Abbeel, P.: Denoising diffusion probabilistic models. In: Larochelle, H., Ranzato, M., Hadsell, R., Balcan, M., Lin, H. (eds.) Advances in Neural Information Processing Systems, vol. 33, pp. 6840–6851. Curran Associates, Inc. (2020)
19. Song, J., Meng, C., Ermon, S.: Denoising diffusion implicit models. arXiv preprint arXiv:2010.02502 (2020)
20. Sridhar, A., Shah, D., Glossop, C., Levine, S.: NoMaD: goal masked diffusion policies for navigation and exploration. In: 2024 IEEE International Conference on Robotics and Automation (ICRA), pp. 63–70. IEEE, Yokohama (2024)
21. Vaswani, A., et al.: Attention is all you need. In: Guyon, I., et al. (eds.) Advances in Neural Information Processing Systems, vol. 30. Curran Associates, Inc. (2017)
22. Hu, J., Shen, L., Albanie, S., Sun, G., Wu, E.: Squeeze-and-excitation networks. IEEE Trans. Pattern Anal. Mach. Intell. **42**(8), 2011–2023 (2020)
23. Yu, T., et al.: Meta-world: a benchmark and evaluation for multi-task and meta reinforcement learning. In: Kaelbling, L.P., Kragic, D., Sugiura, K. (eds.) Proceedings of the Conference on Robot Learning. Proceedings of Machine Learning Research, vol. 100, pp. 1094–1100. PMLR (2020)
24. Qi, C.R., Yi, L., Su, H., Guibas, L.J.: Pointnet++: deep hierarchical feature learning on point sets in a metric space. Adv. Neural Inf. Proc. Syst. **30** (2017)

Relative Pose Estimation of Substation Equipment for UAV Inspection via Deep Point Cloud Registration

Jianming Liu[1], Duanjiao Li[1], Ying Zhang[1], Yun Chen[1], Shengbo Liu[2], Chao Yang[2], Ning Ding[2,3](✉), Xufang Pang[2](✉), and Jianguo Zhang[2](✉)

[1] Guangdong Power Grid Co. Ltd., Guangzhou 510000, Guangdong, China
[2] Shenzhen Institute of Artificial Intelligence and Robotics for Society, Shenzhen 518000, Guangdong, China
{dingning,xufangpang,zhangjianguo}@cuhk.edu.cn
[3] Institute of Robotics and Intelligent Manufacturing, The Chinese University of Hong Kong, Shenzhen, Shenzhen 518000, Guangdong, China

Abstract. Autonomous UAV inspections in substations are often affected by navigation errors and environmental disturbances, leading to deviations from predefined viewpoints and inaccurate image acquisition. To overcome this, this paper proposes a new framework for estimating the relative pose of the viewing camera (LiDAR) mounted on a UAV with respect to target substation equipment, providing geometric guidance for accurate alignment. A standardized equipment library is constructed, containing 3D models and annotated interest point coordinates of typical substation devices. The framework consumes high-resolution scene point clouds captured by a UAV-mounted laser scanner. After ground removal, denoising, and clustering-based segmentation, equipment point clouds are extracted and classified using PointNet. GeoTransformer is then applied to register the segmented point cloud with the corresponding template, yielding the 6-DoF relative pose. Experiments in complex substation environments show strong robustness and accuracy, with an average translation error of 0.086 m and a rotation error of 1.26°, providing a reliable basis for UAV pose self-adaptation in inspection tasks.

Keywords: Substation Inspection · Equipment Library · GeoTransformer · Pose Estimation

1 Introduction

Substations are critical hubs in the power system, whose operational stability directly affects grid dispatch safety [1,2]. With the advancement of automated grid inspection tasks [3–5], UAVs have been widely employed for image acquisition and equipment detection in substations due to their high mobility and wide coverage [6]. Most current inspection systems depend on high-precision GNSS for global positioning combined with preset waypoints to execute missions [7]. However, in substations characterized by dense metallic structures and intense electromagnetic interference, GNSS signals are prone to disruption [8,9], resulting in unstable UAV pose estimation.

Although some studies attempt to improve localization accuracy by using fixed cameras for QR code recognition [10] or integrating SLAM (Simultaneous Localization and Mapping) techniques [11,12], complex deployment and environmental disturbances still limit their effectiveness. Moreover, even when UAVs arrive at preset positions, disturbances such as wind and flight inertia can cause pose deviations [13–15], leading to inaccurate targeting of key components. Existing approaches mainly focus on UAV trajectory control or position navigation, often neglecting the intrinsic information of the target equipment, thus failing to achieve stable and accurate alignment.

In response, recent works have introduced vision-based guidance mechanisms for target alignment. Liu et al. [16] utilized SIFT image registration to calculate pixel and affine transformation errors between current and reference images, employing multi-scale image strategies for precise gimbal realignment; Huang et al. [17] proposed a visual servoing-based rapid camera alignment algorithm leveraging YOLOv3 for object detection; Jiang et al. [18] constructed a pose-pixel error model and estimated camera pose deviations via homography, jointly controlling chassis and gimbal motion to move beyond "reaching the target" toward "facing the target." However, these methods primarily operate on two-dimensional image planes, ignoring the three-dimensional structure of target equipment, thus struggling to maintain stable and accurate alignment in spatially complex or viewpoint-varying scenarios.

In contrast, LiDAR, as an active 3D sensing device, directly acquires dense and accurate point clouds, offering robustness against texture and lighting variations. It has been widely applied in power inspection tasks such as environment mapping, localization, and equipment recognition [19,20]. Point cloud registration aims to estimate the rigid transformation (rotation and translation) between two point sets, enabling precise alignment of 3D information from different views or times within a unified coordinate system. This technique provides new means for UAV-based equipment identification and precise alignment in three-dimensional space. Currently, point cloud registration has been extensively applied in substation equipment recognition [21] and 3D modeling. For example, Shi et al. [22] proposed a two-stage registration method combining improved PointDSC and KD-ICP for rapid substation digital model construction; Zhang et al. [23] used point cloud comparison to identify transmission line anomalies and achieve high-precision diagnostics. Nevertheless, systematic research on pose optimization for UAV inspection based on point cloud registration remains scarce, and registration techniques have yet to be fully leveraged for dynamic optimization during inspection execution.

This paper proposes a substation equipment relative pose estimation method based on a standardized equipment library and GeoTransformer-based point cloud registration [24], aiming to support adaptive adjustment of UAV pose during inspection missions. The main contributions are summarized as follows:

(1) A relative pose estimation framework for UAV inspection in substations is presented, integrating target recognition and 3D registration strategies to achieve robust and scalable high-precision pose estimation from the UAV perspective.
(2) A standardized equipment library with device models and annotated interest points is constructed, alongside a large-scale RGB-D data and ground-truth pose generation method based on rendering, providing high-quality data support for registration algorithm training and evaluation.
(3) An algorithm validation platform within a substation simulation environment is developed, offering reusable and verifiable benchmarks for related research. The proposed framework is comprehensively validated on simulation data, demonstrating strong robustness and accuracy in complex substation scenes, with an average rotation error of 1.26°, translation error of 0.086 m, and RMSE of 0.044 m, providing a reliable geometric foundation for UAV pose optimization.

2 Method

The complete algorithmic workflow is illustrated in Fig. 1. First, individual substation equipment models are constructed by combining 3D scanning and CAD modeling, with key inspection-related interest points annotated using relative coordinates. For each current frame of the point cloud acquired by the UAV, preprocessing steps such as ground point removal, clustering-based segmentation, and outlier filtering are applied to extract individual equipment point clouds. Subsequently, PointNet is employed for equipment recognition. Finally, the Geo-Transformer network aligns the recognized point cloud with its corresponding model in the equipment library to estimate the relative 6-DoF pose of the device, providing critical input for downstream tasks such as adaptive waypoint generation.

2.1 Point Cloud Preprocessing

To enhance the accuracy and efficiency of substation equipment recognition and point cloud registration, a series of effective preprocessing techniques are introduced in this study. These include RANSAC-based ground point removal, clustering-based segmentation and extraction of target point clouds, and statistical outlier filtering. The objective of this preprocessing pipeline is to isolate target equipment point clouds from complex backgrounds, thereby reducing the interference of redundant information on recognition and registration performance, and ultimately improving overall robustness and precision. The complete preprocessing workflow is illustrated in the "Point Cloud Preprocessing" module of Fig. 1.

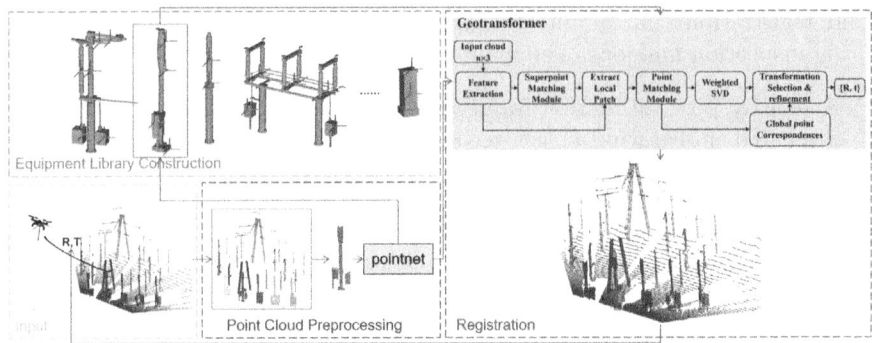

Fig. 1. Overview of the proposed algorithm workflow.

2.2 Substation Equipment Recognition Based on PointNet

PointNet [25], proposed by Qi et al. in 2017, is a deep neural network architecture designed specifically for processing raw 3D point cloud data. It was the first to enable direct end-to-end learning on unstructured point sets, eliminating the need for conventional voxelization or image projection as preprocessing steps. By preserving the original geometric structure of the data, PointNet significantly improves the model's ability to learn 3D representations and marks a foundational advancement in deep learning for point clouds.

The architecture of PointNet is characterized by its simplicity and symmetry. It first encodes each point individually using Multi-Layer Perceptrons (MLPs), then aggregates global features using a symmetric function—max pooling—to ensure permutation invariance of the input point set. This design effectively captures both local point features and global shape descriptors, making it suitable for a range of tasks including classification and segmentation.

In this study, PointNet is employed as the point cloud recognition model to classify the preprocessed substation equipment point clouds. The classification results provide category-specific information, which is subsequently used to guide the selection of corresponding standard template models during the registration phase.

2.3 GeoTransformer-Based Registration Algorithm

To align substation scene point clouds with standard device templates, this work adopts the GeoTransformer network for precise registration. GeoTransformer enhances relative pose estimation accuracy through geometric feature transformation and a coarse-to-fine hierarchical matching strategy.

As shown in Fig. 1, the framework consists of four stages: feature extraction, superpoint matching, point cloud matching, and local-to-global registration. KPConv-FPN is first used to downsample point clouds and extract multi-scale features. At the coarsest scale, superpoints are matched to obtain coarse correspondences, guiding the extraction of local patches.

Each patch pair is then processed to compute fine-grained point correspondences, and local poses R_i, t_i are estimated via weighted SVD. These are refined and aggregated using confidence scores to produce a globally consistent transformation.

Superpoint Matching Module. After extracting superpoints and their corresponding features using KPConv-FPN, a global feature association-based matching scheme is proposed to establish correspondences between superpoints. Specifically, each superpoint is first normalized within a unit sphere to eliminate the influence of scale and position. Then, a Gaussian correlation matrix S is computed to measure the global similarity between superpoints from the input and template point clouds.

In fact, the geometries of some patches are very similar and there are many similar patches in another point cloud. To efficiently suppress false matches, a double normalization operation is further employed.

Point Matching Module. After obtaining the coarse-level correspondences, the algorithm applies a simple yet effective point matching module to extract fine-grained point correspondences within each matched patch. At the point level, GeoTransformer leverages the locally learned features from the backbone network. Since the patch-level matching has already resolved the global ambiguity, the subsequent point matching primarily depends on the local proximity between candidate points, which significantly enhances robustness.

For each point within a patch with correspondence, the optimal transport layer is utilized to extract the correspondence of locally dense points. Then Sinkhorn algorithm is utilized to obtain the confidence matrix. The corresponding points are selected by mutual top-k from the matrix. These points will be finally collected together to form the global dense point correspondences C.

RANSAC-Free Local-to-Global Registration. After obtaining the global dense-point correspondence C, benefiting from the high inlier ratio, robust alignment can be achieved without using a robust estimator such as RANSAC, and the resulting computational cost is greatly reduced. For the global dense-point correspondence C, in the local phase, a weighted SVD can be utilized to close the solution R_i, t_i.

Due to the high quality of the matching relationships, these transformation relationships are already very accurate. In the global phase, GeoTransformer selects the transformation relations that allow the innermost match in the entire global point correspondence. The transformation relation for the innermost match is estimated after several iterations.

Loss Functions. The loss function consists of two parts: the overlap-aware circle loss for supepoint matching and the matching point loss for point matching. Since the circle loss ignores the differences between positive samples and weights them equally. Therefore, it is difficult to match patches with relatively low overlap. GeoTransformer designs an overlap-aware round loss that focuses the model on those matches with high overlap. Positive and negative weights are calculated individually for each sample so that pairs of regions with higher overlap are assigned more importance.

The ground true point (GT) correspondences are relatively sparse because they only apply to downsampled point clouds. GeoTransformer simply uses a negative log-likelihood loss on the assignment matrix $\bar{Z}_i$ for each superpoint correspondence.

3 Experiments

3.1 Data Acquisition and Dataset Construction

This study focuses on a typical substation located in China, covering an area of approximately 30,000 square meters and comprising equipment at multiple voltage levels, including 220 kV, 110 kV and 10 KV. A DJI Matrice 3TD UAV equipped with a Livox MID-360 LiDAR, RTK positioning system, and multi-camera array (as shown in Fig. 2a) was employed to perform autonomous flights along predefined waypoints, collecting point cloud and image data of the substation. Subsequently, a high-precision 3D scene model of the substation was reconstructed using oblique photogrammetry techniques (Fig. 2c), providing the foundation for subsequent point cloud processing and equipment relative pose estimation.

Fig. 2. UAV-based data acquisition and dataset construction process. (a) UAV platform equipped with LiDAR, RTK, and multi-view cameras for data collection; (b) On-site UAV Data Acquisition at the Substation; (c) 3D scene model of the substation constructed via oblique photogrammetry.

To enable device recognition and pose estimation, a substation equipment template library was constructed, covering 17 representative categories such as surge arresters, circuit breakers, disconnectors, and transformers. Under the guidance of domain experts, key inspection-related interest points were annotated using relative coordinates, with representative models shown in the equipment library module of Fig. 1. Considering variations in equipment status (e.g., disconnector open or closed) and structural differences (e.g., presence of enclosures or meters), these categories were further refined into 26 sub-classes. The library supports dynamic updates to accommodate new equipment types or structural changes, ensuring adaptability and extensibility.

In addition, based on the 3D modeling results, this study utilized rendering techniques to generate synthetic RGB-D images and point cloud data for individual equipment models. By introducing random noise, a large-scale simulated point cloud dataset was constructed, consisting of 500 samples per category and totaling 13,000 samples. This dataset is used for model pre-training and robustness evaluation.

3.2 Performance of PointNet on Equipment Recognition

In this section, we validate the multi-class equipment recognition performance using the constructed substation point cloud dataset, with PointNet adopted as the baseline model. As described in Sect. 3.1, two classification scenarios are considered: a 17-category coarse classification task and a 26-category fine-grained classification task. For each scenario, an independent model is trained separately. All point cloud samples are uniformly downsampled to 2048 points using Farthest Point Sampling (FPS) to ensure consistency across inputs.

The dataset is split into training and validation sets at a ratio of 4:1, with category distributions preserved in both subsets. To improve robustness to varying viewpoints, random rotations around the Z-axis are applied during training as a data augmentation strategy, enhancing the model's ability to recognize equipment from diverse perspectives in complex substation scenes.

The model architecture follows the standard PointNet classification network (PointNetCls). All experiments are conducted on an NVIDIA RTX 3090 GPU. The loss function is set to cross-entropy (CrossEntropyLoss), and the optimizer used is Adam with an initial learning rate of 1e-3 and beta parameters set to (0.9, 0.999). A StepLR scheduler is employed to decay the learning rate by a factor of 0.5 every 20 epochs. The batch size is set to 128, and the total number of training epochs is 60. The training loss and accuracy curves for both the 17-class and 26-class classification tasks are illustrated in Fig. 3.

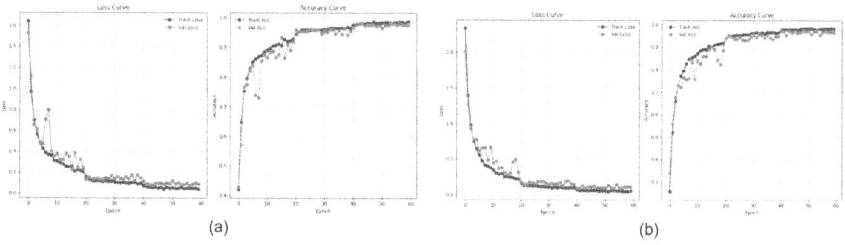

Fig. 3. Training loss and accuracy curves: (a) 17-class classification task; (b) 26-class fine-grained classification task.

The accuracy, precision, recall, and F1 score for the 17-class coarse classification and 26-class fine-grained classification tasks on the validation set are presented in Table 1. It can be observed that PointNet achieves consistently strong recognition performance across both tasks. Compared to the 26-class task, the 17-class task consistently achieves approximately 3–4% higher performance across all evaluation metrics. Analysis indicates that in the 26-class task, most errors occur between different structural variants of the same equipment type (see Sect. 3.1). These variants typically exhibit subtle differences in local geometric structures, which increase the difficulty of discrimination for the model.

Table 1. Performance metrics for 17-class and 26-class classification tasks.

Task	Accuracy	Precision	Recall	F1 Score
17-class	97.82%	97.17%	97.44%	97.29%
26-class	93.46%	94.02%	93.46%	93.37%

3.3 Evaluation of GeoTransformer in Point Cloud Registration

This experiment is conducted based on the constructed substation equipment point cloud registration dataset, with the GeoTransformer model adopted as the baseline to evaluate its effectiveness in typical equipment alignment and pose estimation tasks. As described in Sect. 3.2, the experiment focuses on rigid registration between templates and observed point clouds of representative substation structures (e.g., circuit breakers, transformers, and disconnectors), aiming to accurately estimate the spatial positions and 3D pose variations of the equipment. The dataset is split into training and validation sets in a 4:1 ratio, ensuring consistent category distribution across both stages. To enhance the model's robustness and generalization ability under real-world conditions, random noise and displacements are added to the observed point clouds during training, along with random sampling.

For benchmarking, the GeoTransformer is trained and evaluated on an NVIDIA A800 80G GPU. In this setup, the optimizer is Adam with an initial learning rate of 1e−4. The learning rate is decayed by 0.95 every epoch using a StepLR scheduler. The batch size is set to 1, and the total number of training epochs is 40.

To evaluate the performance of GeoTransformer on substation equipment point cloud registration, we adopt standard metrics including relative rotation error (RRE), relative translation error (RTE), root mean squared error (RMSE), and registration recall (RR), which respectively reflect the accuracy of relative pose estimation, alignment precision, overall registration quality, and robustness under a predefined threshold.

Pose estimation results across 26 categories of typical substation equipment demonstrate the strong performance of GeoTransformer, with all error metrics maintained at low levels. Specifically, for RRE, the maximum value of 5.21° is observed in the 220 kV surge arrester, while all other classes remain below 3°, with the 10kV capacitor achieving the lowest RRE of only 0.39°. In terms of RTE, the 220 kV surge arrester again shows the highest error at 0.44 m, whereas all other classes are below 0.25 m, with the 110 kV switch achieving the minimum of just 0.017 m. Overall, the average RRE on the validation set is controlled within 1.26°, the average RTE is below 0.086 m, with an RMSE of 0.044 m and a registration recall (RR) of 97.8%. These results verify the proposed method's high accuracy and robustness when registering complex equipment structures. RRE and RTE results are visualized in Fig. 4. Figure 5 presents qualitative registration outcomes across all equipment categories. In this figure, yellow points represent the standardized equipment library models, and blue points correspond to the UAV-viewpoint device point clouds extracted using the proposed framework.

It is worth noting that RRE and RTE exhibit a degree of positive correlation—categories with higher rotation errors tend to present greater translation errors, and both follow a similar trend. This observation indicates the consistency of the model's overall performance in pose estimation.

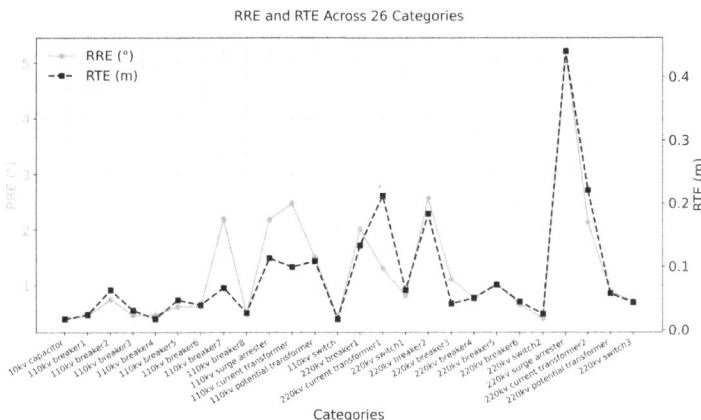

Fig. 4. Quantitative evaluation of registration performance across 26 categories in terms of Relative Rotation Error (RRE) and Relative Translation Error (RTE).

3.4 Simulation-Based Validation of Equipment Pose Estimation

The proposed relative pose estimation framework is validated in a simulation environment. Synthetic point clouds are generated by rendering the UAV's current viewpoint, and the framework is employed to perform device point cloud extraction, classification, and high-precision registration. This process yields the spatial pose of the device and its annotated interest points relative to the UAV

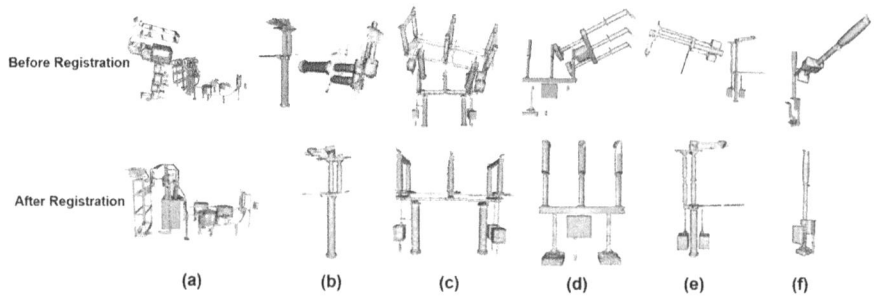

Fig. 5. Visualization of selected registration results between template and observed point clouds for typical substation equipment.

coordinate system. Using the predefined interest point information in the equipment librar—such as recommended viewing angles and distances—the transformation between the current and target poses is calculated. The UAV flight pose is then adjusted accordingly within the simulation by defining a new observation coordinate system, enabling accurate alignment with the region of interest. This approach effectively improves the quality and coverage of targeted image acquisition. Visualization of the simulation results is shown in Fig. 6.

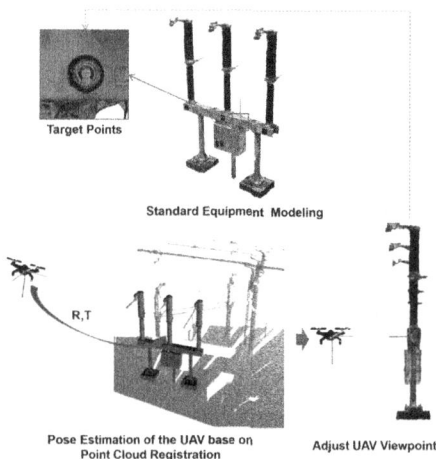

Fig. 6. Application examples of device relative pose estimation and camera alignment to interest points.

4 Conclusion

This paper proposes a framework for substation equipment relative pose estimation, which integrates a standardized equipment library with a point cloud-based recognition and registration pipeline. By constructing an interest point-enriched equipment library and employing PointNet for device classification, the framework enables accurate estimation of the relative pose between the UAV-mounted sensor and target equipment. The effectiveness of the proposed method is validated in a simulation environment, demonstrating robustness and centimeter-level accuracy under complex substation scenarios.

However, the current study is limited to simulation-based evaluations and has not yet been tested on real-world collected data. In future work, we plan to conduct transfer learning using real substation data to improve model generalization and support practical deployment of the system.

Acknowledgement. This research was supported by Grant GDKJXM20231474, the National Natural Science Foundation of China (Grant 62106155), the Guangdong Basic and Applied Basic Research Foundation (Grant 2023A1515012570), the Shenzhen Major Science and Technology Project (Grant KJZD20230923114810022), the Guangdong Provincial Leading Talent Program (Grant 2024TX08Z319), and the Longgang District Shenzhen Ten Action Plan for Supporting Innovation Projects (Grants LGKCSDPT2024002, 2024003, and 2024004).

References

1. Tong, X.J., Chen, Y., Lu, H., et al.: Path planning of substation inspection robot for meter reading. J. Electron. Meas. Instrum. **36**(8), 167–177 (2022). (in Chinese with English abstract)
2. Dang, X.J., Liu, S.G.: Design and research of substation inspection robot and control system. Electron. Design Eng. **28**(22), 118–122 (2020). (in Chinese with English abstract)
3. Lu, S.Y., Zhang, Y., Li, J.X., Mu, S.Y.: Application of mobile robot in high voltage substation. High Volt. Eng. **43**(1), 276–284 (2017). (in Chinese with English abstract)
4. Cai, H.Q., Shao, G.W., Hu, J., et al.: Analysis of the main performance index and application status of inspection robot in substation. Electr. Meas. Instrum. **54**(14), 117–123 (2017). (in Chinese with English abstract)
5. Ma, Y.M.: The application of intelligent inspection robot in unattended substation. Master's thesis, School of Electrical and Electronic Engineering, Baoding (2017). (in Chinese with English abstract)
6. Hu, J.L., Zhu, Z.F., Lin, X.B., Li, Y.Y., Liu, J., Shen, R.J.: Framework design and resource scheduling method for edge computing in substation UAV inspection. High Volt. Eng. **47**(2), 425–433 (2021). (in Chinese with English abstract)
7. Wang, J., Gao, J.Y., Zhang, L., Yang, J.W.: Design of drone adaptive inspection system for substation. Mach. Design Manuf. 1–11 (2025). (in Chinese with English abstract)
8. Suh, U.S., Kim, T.W., Kang, D.H., et al.: A robust passive target localization for substation inspection of UAV in a GPS-denied environment. In: 2021 22nd IEEE International Conference on Industrial Technology (ICIT), pp. 844–849. IEEE (2021)

9. Jiang, H., Wang, K.: A review of multi-source fusion SLAM methods for unmanned substation inspection. Guangdong Electr. Power **38**(3), 55–68 (2025). (in Chinese with English abstract)
10. Zhang, Y.T., Han, Y.W., Lin, Y.C., et al.: Research on pose estimation method for indoor unmanned aerial vehicles in substations. J. Electr. Power Sci. Technol. **40**(1), 138–145 (2025). (in Chinese with English abstract)
11. Alamanos, I., Moustris, G.P., Tzafestas, C.S.: Localization and offline mapping of high-voltage substations in rough terrain using a ground vehicle. In: 2024 32nd Mediterranean Conference on Control and Automation (MED), pp. 107–112. IEEE, Crete (2024)
12. Hu, F., Zhang, N., Li, S., et al.: Substation synchronous location and map construction method based on point cloud semantic understanding. Laser Optoelectron. Progr. 1–20 (2025). (in Chinese with English abstract)
13. Yang, M., Zhou, Z., You, X.: Research on trajectory tracking control of inspection UAV based on real-time sensor data. Sensors **22**(10), 3648 (2022)
14. Chen, D., Xue, B., Sun, R.: The model relates to a substation inspection robot carrying a Unmanned Aerial Vehicle. J. Phys.: Conf. Ser. **2087**(1), 012049 (2021)
15. Langåker, H.A., et al.: An autonomous drone-based system for inspection of electrical substations. Int. J. Adv. Rob. Syst. **18**(2), 17298814211002972 (2021)
16. Liu, J., Zhong, L.Q., Dong, N.: Algorithm research of visual accurate alignment for substation inspection robot. Industr. Instrum. Autom. **6**, 8–13 (2019). (in Chinese with English abstract)
17. Huang, J., Wang, J., Tan, Y., et al.: An automatic analog instrument reading system using computer vision and inspection robot. IEEE Trans. Instrum. Meas. **69**(9), 6322–6335 (2020)
18. Jiang, Q., Liu, Y., Yan, Y., et al.: Substation inspection Robot PTZ camera alignment method for high zoom scenes. Proc. CSEE **44**(8), 3337–3347 (2024). (in Chinese with English abstract)
19. Li, R., Gan, L., Di, Y., et al.: Neighborhood constraint extraction for rapid modeling of point cloud scenes in large-scale power grid substations. J. King Saud Univ. - Comput. Inf. Sci. **36**(2), (2024)
20. Gao, W., He, B., Zhang, T., et al.: Three-dimensional object detection in substation operation scene based on attention mechanism. Laser Optoelectron. Progr. **59**(22), 2210010 (2022). (in Chinese with English abstract)
21. Wang, T.S., Hui, X.D., Zeng, Q.D., Xu, Y.J., Chen, Y.M.: Research on 3D recognition method of substation equipment based on improved ICP algorithm. Electr. Meas. Instrum. **61**(5), 65–70 (2024). (in Chinese with English abstract)
22. Shi, P.J., Meng, R., et al.: A three-dimensional point cloud registration method of substations based on improved PointDSC and KD-ICP. Hebei Electr. Power **44**(1), 77–84 (2025). (in Chinese with English abstract)
23. Zhang, L., Wang, W.K., et al.: Transmission line anomaly detection method based on point cloud data registration. Autom. Appl. **65**(6), 152–154+157 (2024). (in Chinese with English abstract)
24. Cai, Z., Bai, X., He, H., Wang, J.: GeoTransformer: fast and robust point cloud registration with geometric transformer. arXiv preprint arXiv:2207.11473 (2022)
25. Qi, C.R., Su, H., Mo, K., Guibas, L.J.: PointNet: deep learning on point sets for 3D classification and segmentation. In: Proceedings of the IEEE Conference on Computer Vision and Pattern Recognition (CVPR), pp. 652–660 (2017)

Wearable Robotics for Gait Analysis, Training, and Rehabilitation

Humanoid Locomotion with Roller Screw-Driven Knee Joints: Design, Control, and Deployment

Yuchen Lin, Tian Xia, Mengdi Wang, Zhenwei Zhang, Honglei Lu, Tao Ding, Yuhao Zhang, Xingwei Zhao(✉), and Bo Tao(✉)

School of Mechanical Science and Engineering, Huazhong University of Science and Technology, Wuhan 430074, China
zhaoxingwei@hust.edu.cn

Abstract. Traditional humanoid robots using rotary joints face issues such as high motor force demands during sustained standing, resulting in overheating during prolonged operation. To address these challenges, we propose a humanoid robot equipped with planetary roller screw actuators at the knee joints. A detailed kinematic model is developed to accurately relate linear actuator displacement to knee joint rotation, providing the foundation for effective control. Building on this model, we train a reinforcement learning policy using the Proximal Policy Optimization (PPO) algorithm within the NVIDIA Isaac Gym environment. The control architecture adopts an asymmetric actor-critic design, leveraging privileged information during training to improve learning efficiency. The trained policy is first validated in simulation using MuJoCo and then deployed on real hardware. To support real-world operation, a hybrid control framework is implemented, combining torque-based control for rotary joints with position control for the roller screw-driven knee joints. Experimental results confirm the robot's ability to maintain stable, accurate, and consistent gait performance over extended periods.

Keywords: Humanoid Robot · Linear Actuator · Knee Joint Design · Reinforcement Learning · Proximal Policy Optimization

1 Introduction

Humanoid robots have become a major research focus due to their potential applications in service robotics, medical rehabilitation, and industrial automation [1]. Their high flexibility and superior motion capabilities have attracted widespread attention, enabling them to perform complex, human-like movements [2]. Recent advancements in actuation and control technologies have allowed humanoid robots to achieve increasingly dynamic tasks, such as walking, running, and dancing [3].

Nevertheless, despite these achievements, humanoid robots still face critical technical challenges that limit their ability to maintain long-duration stable operation.

Most commercial humanoid robots, including those developed by Boston Dynamics and Unitree Robotics, adopt a fully rotational motor configuration [4]. While this approach provides considerable mobility, it also introduces significant drawbacks. In particular, joints subjected to high loads, such as the knees, are prone to overheating and motor stalling during extended activities. These problems lead to system overheating, performance degradation, and in severe cases, mechanical failure.

To overcome these limitations, researchers have explored alternative actuation strategies. Among them, linear roller screw actuators have emerged as a promising solution [5], offering high thrust capacity, self-locking capabilities, and improved energy efficiency compared to conventional rotary motors. These characteristics are particularly advantageous for joints subjected to heavy and sustained loading.

During humanoid robot locomotion, lower limb joints must generate varying levels of torque to support and propel the body. Notably, the knee joint is known to experience the highest torque demands and exhibit the largest range of motion among all lower limb joints during human walking [6, 7], playing a crucial role in load-bearing and gait stabilization.

Motivated by these biomechanical insights, this paper presents the design of a humanoid robot equipped with linear roller screw actuators at the knee joints. By leveraging the high thrust capacity and self-locking properties of the roller screw mechanism, the proposed robot aims to achieve improved reliability, enhanced energy efficiency, and long-duration stable walking. An overview of the robot structure and a detailed illustration of the roller screw-driven knee joint are shown in Fig. 1.

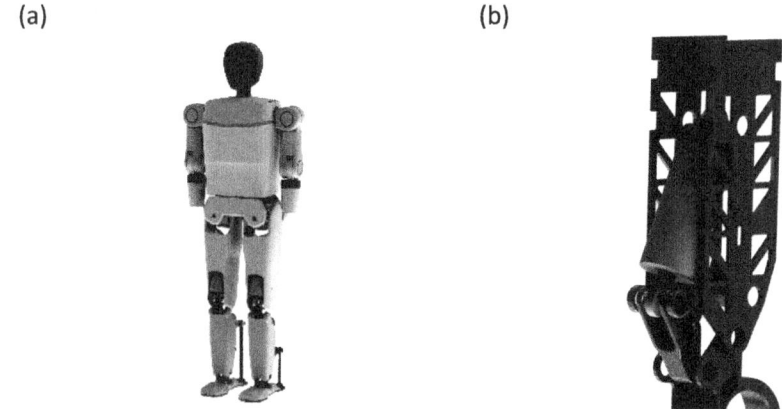

Fig. 1. (a) Overall rendering of the proposed humanoid robot design; (b) Detailed rendering of the roller screw-driven knee joint mechanism.

To achieve effective locomotion control for the proposed humanoid robot, we adopt a structured research approach. First, a detailed kinematic model is developed to establish the transformation between the linear actuator motion and the knee joint rotation. Based on this model, a locomotion policy is trained using the Proximal Policy Optimization (PPO) algorithm within the NVIDIA Isaac Gym simulation environment. The trained policy is then validated through extensive simulation experiments conducted in the MuJoCo simulator. Finally, the policy is deployed onto the physical humanoid robot to evaluate long-duration walking performance under real-world conditions.

The main contributions of this work are summarized as follows:

(1) We propose a novel humanoid robot design that integrates linear roller screw actuators at the knee joints to enhance reliability and energy efficiency.
(2) We develop a comprehensive kinematic model that accurately maps linear actuator displacement to knee joint rotation, facilitating precise control.
(3) We successfully train a locomotion policy and deploy it onto the humanoid robot, achieving stable walking enabled by the roller screw-driven knee joints.

2 Related Works

Fully rotary actuation systems have been widely employed in humanoid robots such as Boston Dynamics' Atlas and Agility Robotics' Digit [8, 9]. These systems provide high flexibility and mobility, enabling complex locomotion and manipulation tasks. However, for joints that sustain high loads—such as the knee and hip—rotary motors often encounter problems like overheating, torque limitations, and reduced energy efficiency during extended operation [10]. While significant progress has been made in optimizing rotary actuation, few efforts have fundamentally rethought actuator architectures to better meet the demands of long-duration humanoid walking.

In this work, we introduce an alternative actuation strategy by integrating linear roller screw actuators at the humanoid's knee joints to address the limitations of conventional rotary motor configurations.

Roller screw mechanisms, particularly planetary roller screws, have been utilized in industrial systems requiring high thrust and compactness. Recent developments, such as Tesla's Optimus robot, demonstrate the practical value of roller screws in enhancing load-bearing capacity and achieving energy-efficient motion in robotic limbs. However, most existing research on roller screw actuators focuses on mechanical design optimization or isolated linear motion applications [11]. Their integration into humanoid joint actuation—specifically evaluating their impact on locomotion dynamics, and control stability—remains largely unexplored.

We bridge this gap by not only incorporating roller screw-driven knee joints into a humanoid design but also systematically studying their effects on walking performance through both simulation and real-world experiments.

Reinforcement learning (RL) techniques have been extensively applied to train agile and robust locomotion policies for legged and humanoid robots in simulation environments. Frameworks such as Legged Gym [13] and Humanoid Gym [12] leverage powerful simulation platforms like NVIDIA Isaac Gym to efficiently train policies on robots with fully rotary joint configurations. These methods typically employ Proximal Policy Optimization (PPO) algorithms combined with asymmetric actor-critic architectures, achieving remarkable results in dynamic walking, running, and recovery behaviors.

Despite these successes, transferring trained policies to real-world hardware remains challenging due to discrepancies between simulated and real dynamics, sensor noise, and actuator modeling inaccuracies [14, 15]. Most existing Sim-to-Real studies are designed for robots with backdrivable rotary actuators and do not account for the unique properties introduced by non-backdrivable mechanisms, such as self-locking behaviors.

In this work, we adopt a reinforcement learning framework to specifically address the deployment challenges associated with roller screw-driven knee joints. We validate the learned locomotion policy through high-fidelity simulations and real-world experiments on a physical humanoid robot, demonstrating stable and energy-efficient long-duration walking performance enabled by the unconventional actuation design.

3 Methods

3.1 Kinematics Analysis

The lower body of the robot consists of two legs, each possessing five degrees of freedom (5-DoF), as illustrated in Fig. 1(a). These five degrees of freedom include the pitch and roll angles of the hip joint, the pitch angle of the knee joint, and the pitch and roll angles of the ankle joint.

Regarding actuation, the pitch and roll motions of the hip joint are directly driven by rotational motors, while the pitch motion of the knee joint is actuated via a linear roller screw mechanism, as shown in Fig. 2(b). Additionally, the ankle joint employs a two-degree-of-freedom (2-DoF) parallel mechanism, as depicted in Fig. 2(a).

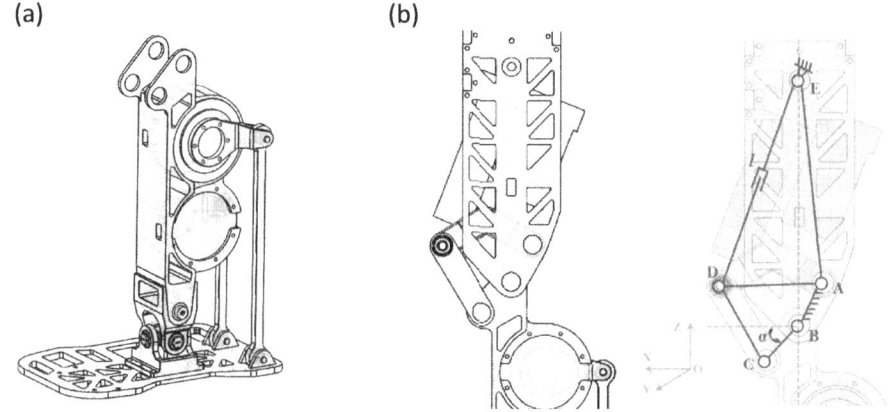

Fig. 2. Mechanical structure of the humanoid robot. (a) Ankle joint design with a two-degree-of-freedom parallel mechanism. (b) Knee joint design based on a linear roller screw-driven four-bar linkage.

In terms of kinematic modeling, the pitch and roll angles of the hip joint exhibit a direct kinematic relationship with the corresponding motor actuations, requiring no additional transformation. Conversely, the forward kinematics of the knee joint involves converting the linear motion of the roller screw into the rotational motion of the knee, whereas the inverse kinematics describes the mapping of knee joint rotation back into the linear displacement of the roller screw. This transformation will be analyzed in detail in subsequent sections.

Furthermore, the kinematic modeling and analysis of parallel ankle mechanisms have been extensively studied in prior literature [16–18], and thus, this work will not reiterate these aspects.

Knee Joint Modeling. The knee joint is actuated by a linear roller screw-driven four-bar linkage mechanism, where the joints are connected via revolute hinges, facilitating the transformation between linear motion and rotational motion. The kinematic modeling of both forward kinematics (FK) and inverse kinematics (IK) is presented as follows.

Let A, B, C, D, E be the key motion points, with E denoting the driving point of the roller screw. The link lengths are defined as $l_{AB}, l_{BC}, l_{CD}, l_{DE}, l_{AE}$, representing the respective segment lengths of the mechanism, where $l_{AB} = l_{BC}$. The knee joint rotation angle is denoted as α, while l represents the linear displacement of the roller screw.

Forward Kinematics

In $\triangle ABE$:

$$l_{AE} = \sqrt{l_{AB}^2 + l_{BE}^2 - 2l_{AB} \times l_{BE} \times \cos \angle ABE} \tag{1}$$

$$\angle EAD + \angle BAD = \sin^{-1}\left(\frac{l_{BE}}{l_{AE}} * \sin \angle ABE\right) \tag{2}$$

In $\triangle EAD$:

$$\angle EAD = \cos^{-1}\left(\frac{l_{AE}^2 + l_{AD}^2 - l^2}{2l_{AE} * l_{AD}}\right) \tag{3}$$

From Eq. (2):

$$\angle BAD = (\angle EAD + \angle BAD) - \angle EAD \tag{4}$$

In $\triangle BAD$:

$$l_{BD} = \sqrt{l_{AB}^2 + l_{AD}^2 - 2l_{AB} * l_{AD} * \cos \angle BAD} \tag{5}$$

$$\angle ABD = \sin^{-1}\left(\frac{l_{AD}}{l_{BD}} * \sin \angle BAD\right) \tag{6}$$

In $\triangle CBD$:

$$\angle DBC = \cos^{-1}\left(\frac{l_{BD}^2 + l_{BC}^2 - l_{CD}^2}{2l_{BD} * l_{BC}}\right) \tag{7}$$

In $\triangle ABC$:

$$\alpha = \angle ABD + \angle DBC - \angle ABE - 90° \tag{8}$$

Finally, by establishing the explicit relationship between α and l as $\alpha = f(l)$, the forward kinematic mapping from the linear actuator displacement to the knee joint's rotational motor angle is completed.

Furthermore, by differentiating both sides with respect to time, we obtain:

$$\dot{\alpha} = \frac{\partial f}{\partial l}\dot{l} = J \times \dot{l} \tag{9}$$

where J represents the Jacobian matrix. By left-multiplying the Jacobian J with the linear velocity of the linear actuator $\dot{l}$, the corresponding angular velocity of the knee joint $\dot{\alpha}$ can be determined. This relationship provides a direct kinematic linkage between the rotational and linear actuation domains, facilitating precise control of the knee joint mechanism.

Inverse Kinematics

In $\triangle ACB$:

$$\angle ACB = \frac{180° - 90° - \angle EBA - \alpha}{2} \tag{10}$$

$$l_{AC} = 2 \times l_{BC} \times \cos \angle ACB \tag{11}$$

In $\triangle ECB$:

$$l_{EC} = \sqrt{(l_{BC} \sin \alpha + l_{EB})^2 + (l_{BC} \cos \alpha)^2} \tag{12}$$

$$\angle ECB = \cos^{-1}\left(\frac{l_{EC}^2 + l_{BC}^2 - l_{EB}^2}{2 \times l_{BC} \times l_{EC}}\right) \tag{13}$$

In $\triangle ADC$:

$$\angle DCA = \cos^{-1}\left(\frac{l_{CD}^2 + l_{AC}^2 - l_{AD}^2}{2 \times l_{CD} \times l_{AC}}\right) \tag{14}$$

In $\triangle EDC$:

$$\angle DCE = \angle DCA - (\angle ECB - \angle ACB) \tag{15}$$

Thus, the linear displacement l of the roller screw can be computed as:

$$l = \sqrt{l_{CD}^2 + l_{EC}^2 - 2l_{CD} \times l_{EC} \times \cos \angle DCE} \tag{16}$$

Finally, by deriving the explicit relationship between l and α as $l = f(\alpha)$, the inverse kinematic mapping from the knee joint's rotational motor angle to the linear actuator displacement is established.

Furthermore, by differentiating both sides with respect to time, we obtain:

$$\dot{l} = \frac{\partial f}{\partial \alpha}\dot{\alpha} = J\dot{\alpha} \tag{17}$$

where J represents the Jacobian matrix. By left-multiplying the Jacobian J with the angular velocity of the knee joint $\dot{\alpha}$, the corresponding linear velocity of the linear actuator $\dot{l}$ can be determined. This relationship provides a direct kinematic linkage between the rotational and linear actuation domains, facilitating precise control of the knee joint mechanism.

3.2 Reinforce Learning Framework

This section presents the reinforcement learning (RL) framework employed to train the humanoid robot's locomotion strategy and the simulation experiments conducted in **NVIDIA IsaacGym**. The objective is to develop a control policy that enables stable and efficient bipedal walking with the proposed **linear roller screw-driven knee joint**.

Reinforcement Learning Algorithm. The Proximal Policy Optimization (PPO) algorithm [20] is used as the RL framework due to its sample efficiency and stability in high-dimensional continuous control problems. The policy is modeled using a deep neural network that maps sensory inputs (robot state) to optimal joint control commands. The objective function is formulated as follows:

$$J(\theta) = E_t\big[\min(r_t(\theta)A_t, clip(r_t(\theta), 1-\varepsilon, 1+\varepsilon)A_t\big] \tag{18}$$

where $r_t(\theta)$ represents the probability ratio between the new and old policies, A_t denotes the advantage function, and ε is a clipping parameter to ensure stable learning.

Reinforcement Learning Network Architecture. This work adopts an Asymmetric Actor-Critic (AAC) architecture [19] for reinforcement learning, which separates the input modalities of the policy network (Actor) and the value network (Critic). This design leverages the advantages of privileged information during training while ensuring deployability with partial observations at inference time, making it well-suited for sim-to-real transfer in legged locomotion tasks.

The Actor network receives standard observations and outputs continuous control actions corresponding to the robot's actuators. Specifically, the output is a vector of target joint position offsets for the ten motors, representing the action to be applied at each control step. These actions are typically modeled as the mean of a Gaussian distribution, from which the actual motor commands are sampled during training to encourage exploration. During inference, the deterministic mean is often used directly to ensure consistent behavior.

In contrast, the Critic network, which is used only during training, takes privileged observations as input to estimate the state value function V_s. The Critic plays a key role in computing the advantage function, which guides the policy updates in the PPO algorithm. This division of roles between the Actor and Critic enables efficient and stable learning while maintaining policy generalizability and deployability.

Reward Function Design. The reward function in this work is designed as a weighted sum of multiple terms that guide the robot toward stable, efficient, and goal-directed locomotion. It includes components that encourage accurate tracking of commanded velocities, smooth and energy-efficient joint movements, as well as stable body posture and orientation. To promote natural gait patterns, the reward also incorporates foot contact timing and clearance, while penalizing undesired behaviors such as foot slippage, excessive contact forces, and collisions. Additional terms regulate the joint configuration to remain close to nominal positions and suppress abrupt or high-frequency torque outputs. Several privileged terms, such as contact forces and stance indicators, are used during training to shape behavior more effectively, although they are not required at deployment. The complete reward at time t is expressed as:

$$r_t = \sum_i \omega_i r_t^{(i)} \tag{19}$$

where $r_t^{(i)}$ denotes the $i-th$ reward component (e.g., velocity tracking, posture stability, energy efficiency), and ω_i is its corresponding weight. This composite formulation enables the learning of robust and dynamically consistent locomotion policies across diverse terrains.

To encourage the robot to remain stationary rather than exhibiting unnecessary leg movements when the commanded velocity is near zero, we introduce a stand-still reward mechanism. Specifically, when the commanded linear and angular velocities fall below a predefined threshold, the default joint angles are treated as reference targets. The robot is then rewarded for minimizing the deviation from these default joint positions. This mechanism stabilizes the posture during low-speed scenarios and discourages in-place stepping behavior. By assigning a higher reward weight in this regime, the policy learns to maintain a quiet and stable stance when no motion is required.

4 Experiment

This section evaluates the trained locomotion policy through **simulation tests** and **real-world deployment**. The goal is to verify the effectiveness of the proposed linear roller screw knee actuation system in achieving long-duration stable walking.

4.1 Simulation Results

In the physical design of the robot, the two knee joints are actuated by roller screw mechanisms, which operate exclusively under position control. In contrast, the remaining eight rotary joints support hybrid control, wherein real-time motor torques are computed based on the desired joint positions, actual joint positions, and predefined proportional-derivative (PD) gains.

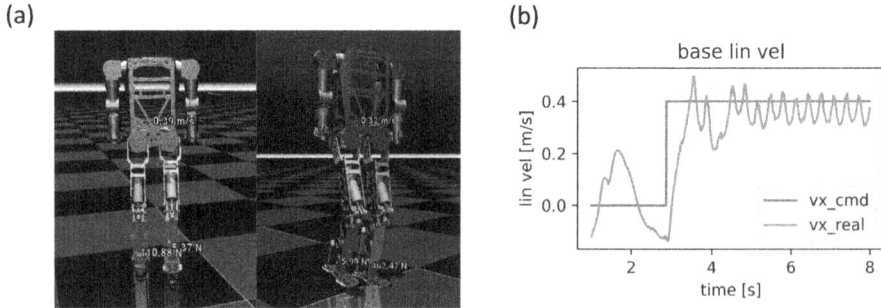

Fig. 3. (a) MuJoCo simulation environment; (b) Actual and commanded velocities in the x-direction.

To evaluate the feasibility of employing pure position control for the knee joints, the trained reinforcement learning policy was deployed in the MuJoCo simulation environment. During deployment, the PD gains for the eight rotary joints were maintained identical to those used during training. For the roller screw-driven knee joints, the PD gains were set to high values to closely emulate stiff position control behavior.

The robot successfully achieved long-duration, stable locomotion in simulation. Figure 3 illustrates the experimental results. Subfigure (a) presents the MuJoCo simulation environment setup. Subfigure (b) shows the commanded and actual base linear velocities along the x-direction.

Initially, the actual velocity exhibits noticeable oscillations and a delay relative to the commanded velocity. Following the step command at around 3 s, the robot adjusts and gradually tracks the desired velocity. A stable tracking behavior is observed after approximately 4 s, although small amplitude oscillations persist around the target value. These results demonstrate that despite the pure position control constraint at the knee joints, the robot maintains stable and responsive locomotion dynamics with acceptable tracking accuracy.

4.2 Real-World Deployment

The low-level control architecture of the physical robot is illustrated in Fig. 4. The low-level controller operates at a frequency of 1000 Hz and communicates via two independent EtherCAT buses, managing the rotary actuators and roller screw linear actuators, respectively. A kinematic mapping process is employed to transform the actuator-level states and commands into joint-level states and control inputs. The reinforcement learning policy runs at a higher control level at 100 Hz, sending joint command signals and receiving joint state feedback in real time.

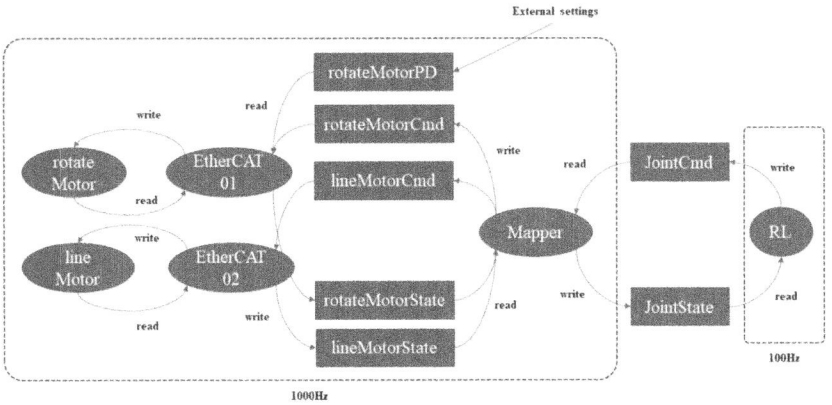

Fig. 4. Low-level and high-level control architecture of the humanoid robot. The low-level controller operates at 1000 Hz using two independent EtherCAT buses to manage rotary and roller screw-driven linear actuators. A kinematic mapping module transforms motor-level states and commands into joint-level representations. The reinforcement learning policy operates at 100 Hz, receiving joint state feedback and sending joint command signals for locomotion control.

The trained policy was deployed onto the physical humanoid robot to validate long-duration stable locomotion. Figure 5 presents the experimental results.

Subfigure (a) shows a sequence of walking snapshots, demonstrating the robot's ability to perform continuous locomotion with stable support and swing phases. Subfigure (b) illustrates the roll and pitch angles of the base obtained from the IMU measurements.

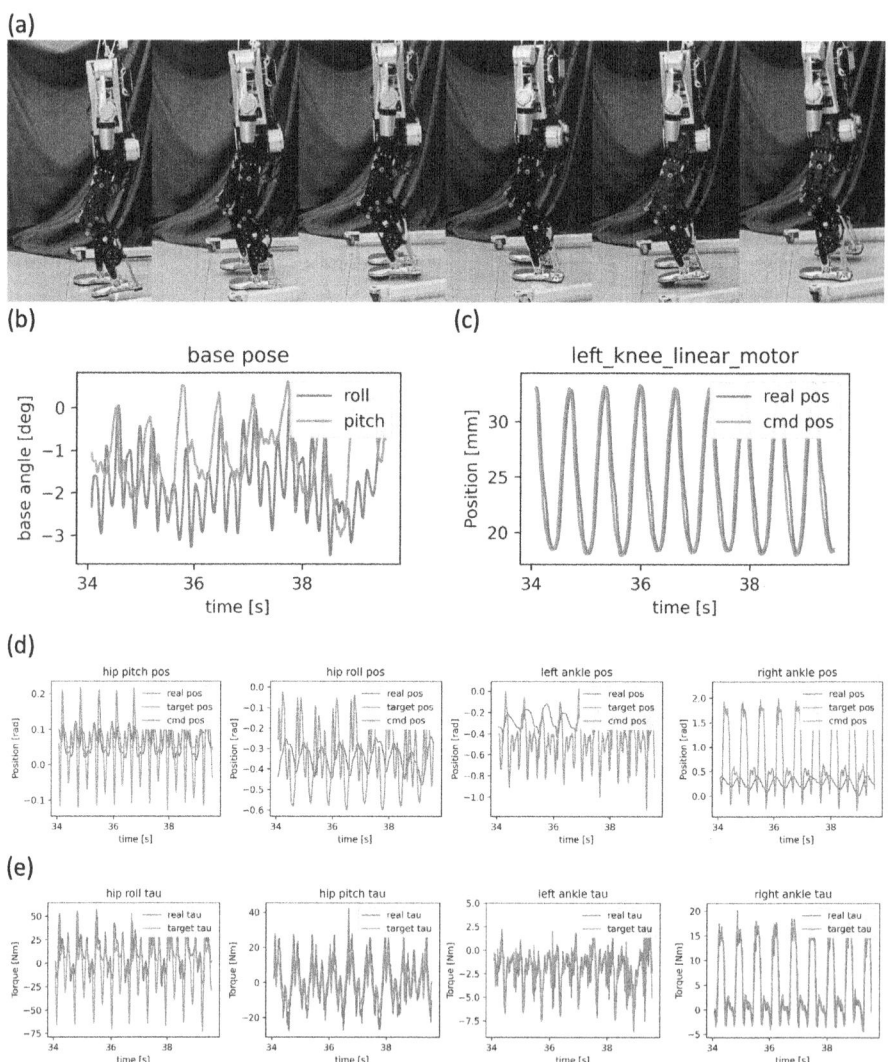

Fig. 5. (a) Walking sequence captured during hardware experiments; (b) IMU-based roll and pitch angles of the robot's base during locomotion; (c) Actual and commanded positions of the left knee linear actuator; (d) Joint position tracking results for the hip and ankle joints; (e) Joint torque tracking results for the hip and ankle joints.

Throughout the walking trials, both roll and pitch remain within ±3°, indicating good dynamic balance and body attitude control.

Subfigure (c) displays the actual and commanded positions of the left knee linear actuator. The two curves closely match, confirming the precise position control performance of the roller screw-driven knee joint.

Subfigures (d) and (e) present the joint-level performance of the hip and ankle. In subfigure (d), the real, commanded, and target joint positions are plotted for the hip pitch, hip roll, left ankle, and right ankle joints. The results demonstrate reasonable tracking accuracy, although slight delays and noise are observed due to sensor limitations and mechanical compliance. Subfigure (e) shows the corresponding joint torques for these joints. The measured torques follow the target torques with reasonable accuracy, validating the effectiveness of the torque control strategy for rotary joints.

Overall, the hardware experiments confirm that the humanoid robot can achieve stable and reliable walking performance, even with the roller screw-driven knee joints operating under pure position control.

5 Conclusion and Future Work

In this work, we presented the design and control of a humanoid robot featuring roller screw actuators at the knee joints. The robot integrates a reinforcement learning-based locomotion controller with a hybrid actuation system, wherein the rotary joints are operated under torque control and the knee joints under pure position control. Leveraging simulation-to-real transfer and extensive evaluations in both Isaac Gym and MuJoCo environments, the robot successfully achieved stable, long-duration walking. Experimental results on the physical hardware further confirmed that the system can maintain consistent gait patterns, achieve accurate joint position tracking, and sustain robust body stabilization, despite the position-only control constraints at the knees.

In future work, we plan to enhance the functionality of the knee joints by transitioning from pure position control to torque or force-based control. This improvement is expected to significantly increase the robot's compliance, adaptability, and dynamic performance, especially under uneven terrain conditions and external disturbances. Moreover, we aim to incorporate advanced sensing and state estimation techniques to further reduce the sim-to-real gap and enable more complex and dynamic locomotion behaviors.

Acknowledgment. We gratefully acknowledge financial support from the Key Research and Development Program of Wuhan under Grant Numbers 2024060788020072 and 2024060702030144, as well as the Fundamental Research Funds for the Central Universities, HUST (Grant Number YCJJ20242402).

References

1. Gu, Z., et al.: Humanoid locomotion and manipulation: current progress and challenges in control, planning, and learning. arXiv preprint arXiv:2501.02116 (2025)
2. Tong, Y., Liu, H., Zhang, Z.: Advancements in humanoid robots: a comprehensive review and future prospects. IEEE/CAA J. Automatica Sinica **11**(2), 301–328 (2024)

3. He, T., et al.: ASAP: aligning simulation and real-world physics for learning agile humanoid whole-body skills. arXiv preprint arXiv:2502.01143 (2025)
4. Unitree Robotics. Z1 Arm User Manual. Unitree Robotics (2022). https://dev-z1.unitree.com/use/error.html. Accessed 27 Apr 2025
5. Tesla, Inc. Actuator and actuator design methodology. WO2024072984A1, World Intellectual Property Organization (2024). https://patents.google.com/patent/WO2024072984A1/en
6. Kutzner, I., et al.: Loading of the knee joint during activities of daily living measured in vivo in five subjects. J. Biomech. **43**(11), 2164–2173 (2010)
7. Zhang, L., et al.: Knee joint biomechanics in physiological conditions and how pathologies can affect it: a systematic review. Appl. Bionics Biomech. **2020**(1), 7451683 (2020)
8. Boston Dynamics. Atlas: The World's Most Dynamic Humanoid Robot. https://www.bostondynamics.com/atlas. Accessed 27 Apr 2025
9. Agility Robotics. Digit: A Human-Centric Bipedal Robot. https://agilityrobotics.com/digit. Accessed 27 Apr 2025
10. Khatib, O., et al.: Whole-body dynamic behavior and control of human-like robots. Int. J. Humanoid Robot. **1**(01), 29–43 (2004)
11. Zu, L., Zhang, Z., Gao, L.: Design and bearing characteristics of planetary roller screws based on aerospace high-load conditions. Adv. Mech. Eng. **10**(11), 1687814018811197 (2018)
12. Gu, X., Wang, Y.-J., Chen, J.: Humanoid-gym: reinforcement learning for humanoid robot with zero-shot sim2real transfer. arXiv preprint arXiv:2404.05695 (2024)
13. Rudin, N., et al.: Learning to walk in minutes using massively parallel deep reinforcement learning. In: Conference on Robot Learning. PMLR (2022)
14. Peng, X.B., et al.: Deepmimic: example-guided deep reinforcement learning of physics-based character skills. ACM Trans. Graph. (TOG) **37**(4), 1–14 (2018)
15. Andrychowicz, OpenAI: Marcin, et al.: Learning dexterous in-hand manipulation. Int. J. Robot. Res. **39**(1), 3–20 (2020)
16. Zhou, C., Tsagarakis, N.: On the comprehensive kinematics analysis of a humanoid parallel ankle mechanism. J. Mech. Robot. **10**(5), 051015 (2018)
17. Herron, C.W., et al.: Joint-space control of a structurally elastic humanoid robot. arXiv preprint arXiv:2411.11734 (2024)
18. Hoffman, E.M., et al.: Modeling and numerical analysis of Kangaroo lower body based on constrained dynamics of hybrid serial-parallel floating-base systems. Robot. Auton. Syst. **182**, 104827 (2024)
19. Rajeswaran, A., et al.: Learning complex dexterous manipulation with deep reinforcement learning and demonstrations. arXiv preprint arXiv:1709.10087 (2017)
20. Schulman, J., Wolski, F., Dhariwal, P., Radford, A., Klimov, O.: Proximal policy optimization algorithms. arXiv preprint arXiv:1707.06347 (2017)

Design and Implementation of a Multifunctional Desktop Pet Robot Dog Based on Arduino Nano and ESP32-S3

Di Li, Junkai Lin, Siqi Hou, and Yanyan Ji[✉]

Faculty of Science and Technology, Beijing Normal–Hong Kong Baptist University, Zhuhai 519000, China
yyji@uic.edu.cn

Abstract. This paper designs and implements Robot Dog, a multifunctional desktop pet robot with low cost and extensibility. It runs on Arduino Nano, ESP32-S3-DevKitC-1, and Arduino Nano RP2040 Connect which support natural language interaction with large language model (LLM) and automatic speech recognition with ASR module. Furthermore, Bluetooth is used for manual control and infrared sensor is used to detect cliff and avoid falling. A novel tri-controller architecture is proposed such that the RP2040 Connect is used to implement IoT, i.e., to monitor the states of Robot Dog and send fall alerts to Arduino Cloud through IoT controller. The ESP32-S3 calls Tongyi Qwen LLM API to translate user dialogue represented by natural language to walking or greeting. The Robot Dog system with sensor fusion, hardware integration and layered interaction model: high-level goal driven by LLM and low-level servo control command at 50 Hz. Experiments confirm the system's effectiveness for AI-powered interaction on embedded platforms, with applications in education and entertainment.

Keywords: Arduino Nano · ESP32-S3 · Desktop Robot · Embedded Systems · Large Language Models · Voice Control · Bluetooth Control

1 Introduction

Recent developments in robotics research and technology have greatly increased the prospects for future use of robots in education and entertainment, as well as intelligent humanmachine interaction. However, current personal robotics is hampered by high development costs and skills needed for operation, which restricts the diffusion of robotics technology to general users, particularly for beginners and makers. This project reports on Robot Dog, a low-cost, multifunctional, and highly interactive desktop pet robot aiming to encourage broader participation and facilitate robotics education.

D. Li, J. Lin and S. Hou—These authors contributed equally to this work.

Dual-Controller Platform Collaboration (Arduino Nano + ESP32-S3).
The Arduino Nano is used for low-level control of hardware such as controlling servo motor, OLED display, infrared and laser distance measurement. The ESP32-S3 is used as the main controller for intelligent interaction, including network communication, speech recognition, NLP and TTS.

Based on three-main-controllers expansion platform including Arduino Nano, ESP32-S3-DevKitC-1 and Arduino Nano RP2040 Connect platforms, Robot Dog adopts large language model (LLM) based NLI, automatic speech recognition (ASR) based command control with voice interaction, Bluetooth remote control, motion control.

In addition, the robot adopts infrared sensor for cliff-edge behavior and laser-ranging module for hand-following behavior. Besides, based on the built-in Wi-Fi of Arduino Nano RP2040 Connect, the system can achieve IoT connectivity and realize the remote monitoring and control based on the Arduino Cloud platform more easily. Furthermore, based on the data collected from the embedded IMU sensor, the device can realize the anomaly detection and early warning notification based on the embedded IMU sensor, and guarantee the device's safety.

The core contribution of the system is to realize the interaction with Tongyi Qwen LLM API based on the ESP32-S3 platform, and achieve the real-time semantic interpretation of the natural language dialogue and the corresponding behavior generation. By translating the natural language dialogue into executable motion instructions, the robot can achieve more rich and interactive experience. In addition to the voice interaction, Robot Dog also realizes the multi-modal operation with local Bluetooth remote control and cloud-based remote control.

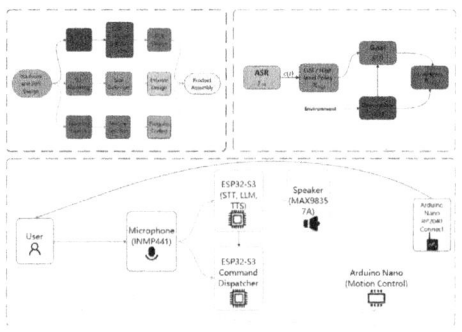

Fig. 1. The Framework of Robot Dog.

Several technical difficulties have been discovered in the creation of Robot Dog, such as multi-controller communication protocol design, real-time voice interaction pipeline implementation, motion sequence optimization based on servo motor control, and remote monitoring & alarm system implementation.

Finally, by means of hardware-software co-design, an advanced compact, extensible and user-centered robotic platform for intelligent behavior, remote supervision and educational demonstration have been achieved. Our work contributes to the development of intelligent personal robotics based on AI as well as the future researches and applications of embedded intelligent system (Figs. 2, 3, 4).

Fig. 2. Robot Dog. **Fig. 3.** Bottom View. **Fig. 4.** Side View.

2 Related Work

Early desktop-scale quadrupeds like MechDog [4] and XGO-Mini2 [7] popularised low-cost, Scratch/Python/Arduino-friendly platforms. They provide inverse-kinematics motion, self-balancing, and basic sensors, yet interaction remains limited to fixed gaits or phone apps. Voice-enabled demos (e.g., "ESP-Demo" [2]) stream speech to cloud LLMs, gaining dialogue but depending on the Internet and off-board computation.

2.1 Stability and Robustness

Disturbance-tolerant locomotion leverages convex Model Predictive Control (MPC), achieving dynamic gaits on MIT Cheetah-class robots within torque limits [1]. On desktop bots, Sun *et al.* [10] refine foot placement with a centroidal model, while Gu *et al.* [3] use force feedback for impulse rejection. Deep-RL policies push resilience: Lee *etâl.* [5] traverse rubble and gravel, and hybrid CPG+actor-critic controllers blend analytic stability with learned reflexes. Modern designs often layer a fast MPC "safety shield" beneath agile learned policies.

2.2 Large Language Models on Microcontrollers

With only hundreds of kB RAM, MCUs demand extreme compression and custom kernels. TinyFormer [11] discovers ultra-sparse transformers fitting CIFAR-10 into 320 kB; Scherer *et al.* [8] run a 2.7 M-parameter LM on a RISC-V MCU at 20 tokens s^{-1}. Surveys [6] summarise full TinyML pipelines and call out latency and context-window limits. Field deployments usually offload the LM to an edge GPU–e.g., Sikorski *et al.* [9] pair a quantised LLaMA-2-7B with an on-board wake-word detector. Progress hinges on ever-smaller models and MCU-centric accelerators.

Our Robot Dog integrates on-device speech capture, intent parsing via a compressed LM, and real-time motion–no cloud required. TinyML techniques let an ESP32-S3 interpret commands locally, cutting latency. A hybrid MPC+RL controller yields agile yet stable gaits for confined desktops, while built-in IoT links enable remote oversight. This fusion of edge-NLP and robust locomotion advances interactive desktop robotics.

3 System Design and Implementation

3.1 Hardware Design

The development of Robot Dog involves a tightly integrated hardware and software architecture, combining multiple microcontrollers, sensors, and actuators to achieve intelligent behavior and robust user interaction.

Control Units. The main motion control is handled by a Arduino Nano that handles coordination of servo actions, executing command and sensor data. The main processing and communication coordination is handled by a ESP32-S3-DevKitC-1 that communicates with the Tongyi Qwen LLM API to handle natural language understanding, command generation, and cloud coordination. An additional Arduino Nano RP2040 Connect provides the IoT connectivity to allow for remote monitoring and control of the device through the Arduino Cloud, as well as status reporting and alerting of issues via the built-in inertial measurement unit (IMU) sensor.

Mechanical Structure. The physical structure of the robot is printed using 3D printer. It is a light but stable chassis which includes the torso and the limbs as well as the parts that provide support. The SG90 type servo motor controls the operation of the legs and the tail. The robot can walk, turn around, sit, lie down, wave, etc. All the electronic parts are mounted on the home-made printed circuit board (PCB). This design is space-saving and the wiring is well-organized. It also enhances the maintainability and reliability of the robot.

Interaction System. The voice interaction capabilities are built upon the networking and AI processing functions of the ESP32-S3. Speech signals are captured using an onboard MEMS microphone, processed through a speech-to-text (STT) module, and analyzed by the LLM to infer user intent. Generated responses are parsed into actionable control commands, which are transmitted to the Arduino Nano to execute corresponding servo motor actions. This closed-loop interaction pipeline follows the sequence:

  Audio Input → STT → Text Interpretation → LLM Processing → Command Generation → Action Execution.

For voice feedback scenarios, a text-to-speech (TTS) module is employed to synthesize audio responses, enhancing naturalistic interactions:

Audio Input → STT → Text Interpretation → LLM → Response Generation → TTS → Audio Output.

In addition, a Tianwen ASRPRO module is integrated to enable offline recognition of basic command phrases, ensuring limited voice interaction capabilities even in the absence of internet connectivity.

Manual remote control is supported through the inclusion of an ECB01H2 Bluetooth module, allowing users to transmit control instructions via smartphone applications when needed.

Sensing and Safety Systems. A VL53L0X V2 laser time-of-flight (ToF) distance sensor is attached on the front of the robot and can detect if there is something nearby and trigger a follow mode where the robot moves closer or further away depending on where the hands are.

In order to avoid accidental falls down, there are infrared sensors located at the front and rear edges of the chassis. When the infrared sensor at the front of the robot hits the edge of a possible tabletop, the robot stops its movement towards the front and starts to retreat. A very basic cliff detection and avoidance behavior has been implemented.

In addition, the Arduino Nano RP2040 Connect is also constantly detecting motions via the built-in IMU and if there is a significant change that might indicate a collision or fall, it can detect this and send an alert to the Arduino Cloud platform which can then be displayed on a web page and trigger a push notification (Fig. 5).

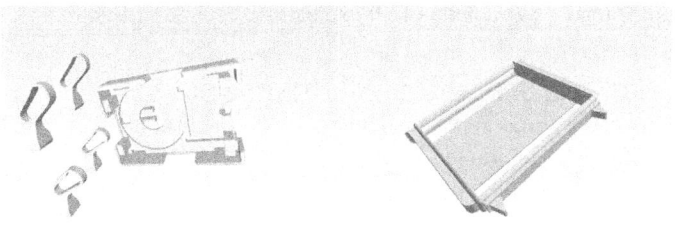

Fig. 5. Rendering of 3D Printed Parts.

The software system of Robot Dog is developed using the Arduino Integrated Development Environment (IDE) and is distributed across three primary microcontrollers: the Arduino Nano, the ESP32-S3-DevKitC-1, and the Arduino Nano RP2040 Connect. Each controller executes dedicated modules to ensure coordinated system behavior, real-time responsiveness, and extensibility.

Control Program on Arduino Nano. Arduino Nano executes the main program that handles servo motor control, Bluetooth command parsing, sensor data processing, and responding to voice commands. All the behaviors of each robot, including walking, turning, and waving, are implemented as separate motion control functions. The continuous stream of motion animation is realized by incrementing the servo angle by small steps to achieve more natural and smooth motion (Figs. 6 and 7).

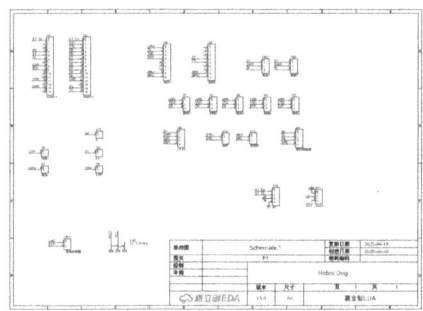

Fig. 6. Schematic Design.

Fig. 7. PCB Design.

The ECB01H2 Bluetooth module is connected to the Arduino Nano through a serial connection. When a command from the mobile device is received, the related motion control function is called to perform the appropriate actions. A OLED display module is added to the project for visualizing the running states and changing facial expressions of the robot.

Communication and Processing on ESP32-S3. The ESP32-S3 manages network connectivity and serves as the gateway for intelligent interaction. Voice input is captured using an onboard INMP441 MEMS microphone and transcribed into text through a speech-to-text (STT) engine. The transcribed text is transmitted to the Tongyi Qwen large language model (LLM) API for semantic parsing and intent recognition. Based on the model's response, corresponding control commands are generated and relayed back to the Arduino Nano, closing the AI-driven voice interaction loop.

For scenarios requiring verbal feedback, the ESP32-S3 invokes a text-to-speech (TTS) service to synthesize audio responses, enabling a bidirectional conversational experience. This processing pipeline ensures a seamless workflow from speech acquisition to robotic action, structured as follows:

Audio Input → STT → Text Processing → LLM Response → Command Generation → Action Execution or Audio Output.

Sensor Integration and Real-Time Response. Sensor data acquisition and decoding routines are implemented for the VL53L0X V2 laser distance sensor and infrared proximity sensors. The laser sensor readings are processed to dynamically modulate the robot's behavior in response to hand gestures, enabling "follow mode" functionality. Infrared sensor states are continuously monitored within the main control loop, contributing to real-time obstacle detection and fall prevention logic.

The Arduino Nano RP2040 Connect is tasked with IoT functions, establishing a persistent connection to the Arduino Cloud platform. Additionally, its embedded LSM6DSOX inertial measurement unit (IMU) sensor continuously monitors the robot's motion patterns. Anomalous events, such as falls or sudden impacts, are detected and immediately reported to cloud services, allowing real-time remote alerting and enhancing system reliability (Fig. 8).

Detection of abnormal robot motion → Recognition by the IMU module → Uploading to Arduino Cloud via Arduino Nano RP2040 Connect → Notification Alerts Received on Mobile or Computer Terminals.

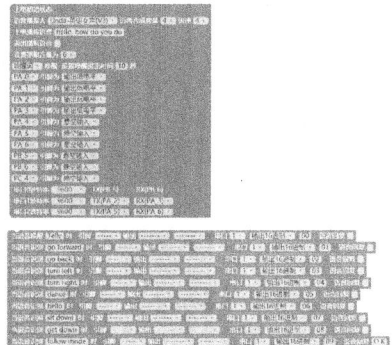

Fig. 8. Diagram of Voice Command Workflow.

4 System Architecture and Code Integration

4.1 Architecture Overview

The control architecture of Robot Dog adopts a dual-platform closed-loop design based on the Arduino Nano and the ESP32-S3-DevKitC-1. These two subsystems operate collaboratively to achieve environmental perception, semantic understanding, motion execution, and interactive feedback, thereby ensuring high system intelligence and responsiveness.

4.2 Arduino Nano Software Workflow

Arduino Nano handles the low level hardware control, handling the servomotor coordination, data acquisition from sensors, parsing the Bluetooth data, and showing the status on the real-time on the status on the OLED.

We initialize the modules like servo driver, serial, and OLED at the beginning while initializing. I2C based modules like VL53L0X time of flight sensor and OLED screen are initialized along with GPIO and internal timers too.

Each of the motion behaviors are controlled by a sequence of coordinated servo actions. For e.g., each action like walking, turning, dancing, sitting, lying down has a sequence of calibrated angle setting and appropriate timing delays. Input from voice and Bluetooth are both taken as signals.

Furthermore, environmental awareness is enhanced through infrared and laser-based sensors, facilitating cliff detection and gesture recognition. Visual feedback is provided via the OLED display, reflecting operational status and dynamic emotional expressions.

4.3 ESP32-S3 Software Workflow

The ESP32-S3 subsystem handles voice interaction and AI-driven command processing. Audio signals are captured via a digital MEMS microphone and transmitted through the I2S bus for preprocessing. Speech-to-text (STT) is performed using Baidu's cloud API, where audio is Base64-encoded, encapsulated in JSON, and sent via HTTP POST. The returned transcription is then parsed for semantics.

Natural language understanding and dialogue generation utilize the Tongyi Qwen large language model (LLM) API. Transcribed queries are formatted per API specifications and submitted to the inference endpoint. Responses are categorized as either control commands or dialogue outputs.

Text-to-speech (TTS) synthesis is implemented via Baidu's TTS API. LLM outputs are double URL-encoded and transmitted with parameters such as pitch, tone, and volume. The resulting audio stream is sent over I2S to the MAX98357A DAC and played through the onboard speaker.

A secure Wi-Fi connection is established during initialization, with all cloud APIs (STT, TTS, LLM) authenticated using token-based authorization, ensuring reliable cloud communication.

5 Motion Control Algorithm

5.1 System Model

The motion control of **Robot Dog** is formulated as a discrete-time state transition system. Let the robot configuration at time t be represented as a vector:

$$\mathbf{q}(t) = [\theta_{L1}(t), \theta_{L2}(t), \theta_{R1}(t), \theta_{R2}(t), \theta_T(t)]^T$$

where $\theta_{Li}(t)$ and $\theta_{Ri}(t)$ denote the angles of the left and right servos, and $\theta_T(t)$ represents the tail servo.

The system evolves according to a discrete-time control input $\mathbf{u}(t)$ that specifies the target servo angles:

$$\mathbf{q}(t + \Delta t) = \mathbf{q}(t) + \mathbf{u}(t)\Delta t$$

where Δt is the discrete control interval.

5.2 Motion Sequencing

Each complex motion $M \in \{\text{walk}, \text{turn}, \text{sit}, \text{wave}, \text{dance}\}$ is modeled as a finite sequence of intermediate joint configurations:

$$M = \{\mathbf{q}_0, \mathbf{q}_1, \ldots, \mathbf{q}_k\}$$

Transitions between configurations are performed through smooth interpolation:

$$\theta_i(t + \Delta t) = (1 - \alpha)\theta_i(t) + \alpha\theta_i^* \quad \text{for} \quad i \in \{L1, L2, R1, R2, T\}$$

where θ_i^* is the target angle and $\alpha \in (0, 1]$ is a fixed interpolation coefficient ensuring gradual motion.

5.3 Command Parsing and Mapping

The system defines a bijective mapping:

$$f : C \to M$$

where C is the set of received commands from Bluetooth or voice modules, and M is the corresponding motion behavior. Upon receiving a command $c \in C$, the associated sequence M is invoked.

5.4 Sensor Feedback Mechanism

Edge detection using infrared sensors is formulated as a binary observation:

$$s_{\text{cliff}}(t) \in \{0, 1\}$$

where $s_{\text{cliff}}(t) = 1$ indicates cliff detected. The robot's safety control policy is defined as:

$$\text{if} \quad s_{\text{cliff}}(t) = 1, \quad \text{then} \quad \mathbf{u}(t) = \mathbf{u}_{\text{reverse}}$$

where $\mathbf{u}_{\text{reverse}}$ corresponds to a backward movement command.

Hand-following behavior is based on the distance reading $d(t)$ from the VL53L0X sensor. A proportional control law adjusts the walking speed $v(t)$:

$$v(t) = K_p(d_{\text{ref}} - d(t))$$

where d_{ref} is the desired hand distance and K_p is the proportional gain.

6 Hierarchical Language–Perception–Control Interaction

6.1 Motivation and Overview

Traditional voice-controlled robotic pets typically follow a linear *speech → command → action* pipeline, leaving no mechanism for real-time sensor feedback to refine behaviour. To overcome this limitation, we introduce a *three-layer hierarchical loop* that binds **language understanding**, **robot perception**, and **servo-level control** into a single closed system. The framework diagram is shown in Fig. 1 *Green (Upper Right) Part*.

6.2 Hierarchical Policy Formulation

Let $c(t)$ be the language context at time t (ASR transcription plus dialogue history) and $o(t)$ the instantaneous observation vector from onboard sensors. Our hierarchical policy is expressed as

$$a(t) = \pi_{\text{low}}(o(t), g(t)), \quad g(t) = \pi_{\text{high}}(c(t), o(t)), \tag{1}$$

where π_{high} (LLM-driven) outputs an *intermediate goal* $g(t)$ and π_{low} converts $(o(t), g(t))$ into concrete servo commands $a(t)$ in real time.

Equation (1) illustrates how *semantic reasoning* and *reactive control* are interwoven at every time step.

Real-Time Coupling Mechanism. The ESP32-S3 executes π_{high} by querying a compressed Tongyi Qwen LLM and returns $g(t)$ (e.g., gait type, body pose, speed) within <80ms. An interrupt-driven loop on the Arduino Nano samples $o(t)$ at 50Hz and evaluates π_{low}, producing servo PWM pulses at 20ms resolution. Sensor feedback—infra-red cliff detection, laser ranging, IMU data—is fed to both layers: LLM prompts are enriched with critical events ("edge detected"), while the low-level controller adjusts foot placement or velocity, ensuring safety without delaying dialogue.

Contrast With Prior Work. Voice-centric demos such as ESP Demo, [2] trigger motion macros directly from LLM replies, lacking the perception loop; the XGO Mini2 provides sophisticated locomotion yet exposes only pre-scripted app or Python interfaces. Our architecture uniquely offers *language-conditioned, sensor-aware* action generation on a desktop pet robot, enabling nuanced dialogue (*"Slow down if the edge is near"*) and adaptive execution.

6.3 Experiential Design and Result

Table 1 summarizes the command recognition accuracy under different conditions. The offline ASR system achieved 80% accuracy in quiet settings but dropped to 65% in moderate noise (55 dB), highlighting its sensitivity to acoustic interference. In contrast, the online LLM-based intent recognition maintained

Table 1. Command Recognition Accuracy (20 Trials)

System	Environment	Accuracy
Offline ASR	Quiet	80%
Offline ASR	Moderate Noise (55 dB)	65%
Online LLM Intent	Quiet	85%

Table 2. Sensor System Performance

Test	Conditions	Success Rate/Performance Metric
Cliff Detection	10 trials, varied speed/angle	80% Success Rate
Hand-Following	Maintain 10 cm distance	Avg. steady-state error: ±2.0 cm
Fall Detection (IMU)	10 simulated falls	70% Detection & Alert Transmission

a higher and more consistent accuracy of 85% in quiet conditions, demonstrating its robustness in interpreting complex commands.

Table 2 presents the evaluation of the robot's safety and interaction sensors. Cliff detection showed an 80% success rate across varied speeds and approach angles, indicating reasonable but improvable reliability. The hand-following mode maintained an average steady-state distance error of ±2.0 cm, demonstrating adequate precision for interactive tasks. Fall detection via the IMU was successful in 70% of the simulated fall scenarios, effectively triggering alerts when instability was detected.

Table 3. Concise Comparison of Desktop Robot Architectures

Feature	Robot Dog (This Project)	XGO-Mini2	ESP-Demo
Architecture	Tri-Controller	Single-Controller	Single-Controller
AI Model	Hierarchical Closed-Loop	Preset Scripts	Linear Open-Loop
Sensor Loop	Dual-Layer (Informs AI)	Low-Level (For Stability)	None in AI Loop
Core Advantage	Adaptive Interaction	Advanced Mobility	LLM Proof-of-Concept

Table 3 shows that the Robot Dog offers a more adaptive system through its tri-controller setup and sensor-informed AI loop. Unlike XGO-Mini2 and ESP-Demo, it supports real-time interaction with greater autonomy and responsiveness.

7 Conclusion

The Robot Dog project demonstrates the feasibility of creating a compact, intelligent desktop pet robot through modular hardware-software co-design. By integrating technologies such as servo actuation, speech recognition, and IoT monitoring, it validates the use of embedded AI in consumer robotics. The system's modular architecture, covering areas like motion control and speech processing, simplifies development and enhances scalability. Iterative prototyping and testing improved hardware stability and software robustness, with safety features like infrared cliff-edge detection. A notable achievement is the integration of large language models for natural language interaction, enabling meaningful dialogues that translate into behavioral responses. The project exemplifies an interdisciplinary approach, combining robotics, AI, and user-centered design. Future work will focus on adding behavioral learning, customizable interfaces, and facial recognition. Overall, Robot Dog provides a reference for designing low-cost, extensible, and intelligent personal robotics systems.

References

1. Carlo, J.D., et al.: Dynamic locomotion in the MIT cheetah 3 through convex model predictive control. In: Proceedings of the IEEE/RSJ International Conference on Intelligent Robots and Systems (IROS), pp. 1818–1824 (2020)
2. Espressif Systems: ESP-Demo: Voice-Controlled Robot Using ESP32-S3 and LLM (2023). https://github.com/espressif/esp-demo-llm-robot. Accessed 19 Apr 2025
3. Gu, S., et al.: Active state adjustment for stability control of a quadruped robot under impulse disturbances. Biomimetics **8**(1), 112 (2023)
4. Hiwonder: MechDog – Quadruped AI Robot Dog (2024). https://www.hiwonder.com/products/mechdog-ai-robot-dog. Accessed 19 Apr 2025
5. Lee, J., Hwangbo, J., Wellhausen, L., Koltun, V., Hutter, M. Learning quadrupedal locomotion over challenging terrain. Sci. Robot. **5**(47), eabc5986 (2020)
6. Lamaakal, I., et al.: Tiny language models for automation and control: a survey. Sensors **25**(5), 1318 (2025)
7. Luwu Dynamics: XGO-Mini2 Desktop Quadruped Robot (2024). https://www.luwu.ai/products/xgo-mini2. Accessed 19 Apr 2025
8. Scherer, M., et al.: Deeploy: energy-efficient deployment of small language models on heterogeneous microcontrollers. In: Proceedings of the International Conference on Compilers, Architectures, and Synthesis for Embedded Systems (CASES), pp. 1–10 (2024)
9. Sikorski, P., et al.: Edge deployment of large language models for natural-language robot control. arXiv preprint arXiv:2405.17670 (2024)
10. Sun, W., et al.: Balance control of a quadruped robot based on foot placement adjustment. Appl. Sci. **12**(5), 2521 (2022)
11. Yang, J., et al.: Tinyformer: efficient transformer design and deployment on tiny devices. arXiv preprint arXiv:2311.01759 (2023)

From Sim-to-Real to Learn-in-Real: Real-World Online Learning for Humanoid Robots

Rankun Li[1], Yuhang Xie[1], Linqing Zhu[1], Linqi Ye[1(✉)], Qingdu Li[2], and Yan Peng[1]

[1] Shanghai University, Shanghai 200444, China
yelinqi@shu.edu.cn
[2] University of Shanghai for Science and Technology, Shanghai 200093, China

Abstract. In recent years, reinforcement learning has significantly accelerated the development of legged robot control systems. The prevalent paradigm involves conducting reinforcement learning training in simulated environments initially, followed by a transition to real-world applications, a process known as sim-to-real transfer. However, this paradigm still cannot fully bridge the gap between simulation and reality. To further narrow the gap between simulation and reality, this paper proposes an innovative online learning strategy that aims to conduct training directly on the physical robot. To achieve this, we harness the power of pre-training and instruction learning to enhance learning efficiency. Additionally, we have designed an autonomous resetting system that enables the robot to automatically reconfigure and seamlessly resume learning after a fall, ensuring continuous progress. Our findings indicate that the performance of the robot after online learning has been enhanced to a certain extent compared to direct deployment using sim-to-real. The research results demonstrate the effectiveness of the Learn-in-Real paradigm in enhancing the locomotion capabilities of legged robots and provide a promising pathway for improving the performance of other legged robots.

Keywords: Online Learning · Instruction Learning · Reinforcement Learning · Sim-to-Real · Humanoid Robots

1 Introduction

The rapid development of model-free Reinforcement Learning (RL) has led to significant breakthroughs in the field of robotic motion control. RL enables agents to learn optimal policies through trial and error in interaction with the environment, making it an ideal tool for training robotic control systems in simulation environments [1]. In the domain of locomotion control, the application of RL is particularly widespread, as it allows robots to autonomously acquire complex locomotion skills through interaction with simulated environments, without relying on precise dynamic models. However, despite the fact that simulation training

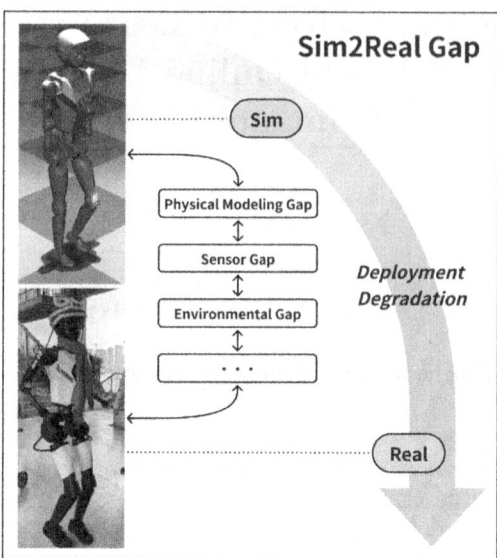

Fig. 1. Sim-to-Real Gap.

provides a safe and cost-effective platform for robotic control, the deployment of physical robots using this approach has long faced challenges due to the Sim-to-Real gap (Fig. 1) between simulation and the real world.

To address this issue, existing methods have largely attempted to narrow the Sim-to-Real gap by introducing perturbations into simulation software, such as adding noise [2,3], domain randomization [4,5], and meta-learning [6,7]. Although these methods have enabled robots to transfer from simulation to reality, they still fail to completely eliminate the differences between simulation and reality, resulting in a decline in robotic performance during the transfer process.

We believe that embodied intelligent robots should perform anthropomorphic tasks through active perception of the environment, autonomous learning, and autonomous decision making, with their brains being agents based on RL. Therefore, constructing a new Learn-in-Real learning paradigm is a key method for the large-scale deployment of robots in the future, that is, robots can directly perform online RL in the real environment. Our goal is to conduct online reinforcement learning based on Sim-to-Real, thus compensating for the performance degradation of robot deployment and even achieving a leap in robot capabilities.

Our main contributions can be summarized in the following three points:

1) Online learning further bridges the significant gap between physical entities and simulation environments. It empowers physical robots to engage in ongoing learning processes, leading to continuous improvement and performance enhancement as the duration of learning increases.

2) The adoption of pre-training and instruction learning solves the problem of low learning efficiency and slow learning speed. Prevents the robot from learning from scratch and greatly accelerates the learning process.
3) The automatic reset of the sky track addresses the issue of physical objects being prone to falling and difficult to reset. The innovative design of the sky track system can detect the robot's fall and reset it, ensuring safety and efficiency.

2 Related Work

2.1 Robot Reinforcement Learning

To bridge the gap between simulation and reality, domain randomization techniques have been widely adopted. In 2019, Hwangbo et al. [8] of ETH Zurich first combined domain randomization with reinforcement learning in simulation environments. The trained models were successfully deployed on the real quadruped robot ANYmal, significantly improving robot performance in dynamic and agile movements. Haarnoja et al. [9] from DeepMind combined high frequency control, target dynamics randomization, and perturbations for reinforcement learning training, achieving sample-free transfer from simulation to reality. Gu et al. [10] open-sourced the Humanoid-Gym framework for end-to-end reinforcement learning training of humanoid robots. This framework significantly simplified the training process and the difficulty of Sim-to-Real transfer through its carefully designed reward functions and domain randomization techniques, lowering the development threshold for humanoid robot algorithms.

Introducing realistic noise is another technique to narrow the gap between simulation and reality. Kaufmann et al. [2] from the University of Zurich enhanced the realism of simulation environments by pre-training real-world perception systems and empirical noise models. This approach helped them achieve the first autonomous drone control at a human-champion level, featured on the cover of Nature. Gu et al. [11] proposed the Denoising World Model Learning (DWL) framework, which uses an encoder-decoder structure to process noisy data in simulation environments and learn effective state representations. This method reduced the difficulty of transferring from simulation to reality and improved the walking capabilities of humanoid robots in complex and challenging real-world environments.

Meta-learning is also a strategy to address the Sim-to-Real problem. Arndt et al. [12] used meta-learning techniques to train policies that can adapt to various dynamic conditions. By combining these policies with task-specific trajectory generation models, they provided an action space for rapid exploration, effectively tackling the Sim-to-Real problem.

2.2 Robot Online Learning

To address the challenge of maintaining consistency between highly realistic simulation environments and the real world, researchers have begun to integrate online learning into the field of reinforcement learning, that is, training directly in real world environments. For example, in fixed-base robots such as robotic arms, online learning has demonstrated its effectiveness through massive data training [13]. Luo et al. [14,15] have consistently employed the integration of reinforcement learning with physical robotic systems, underscoring that while simulation facilitates rapid data generation, the intrinsic value of real-world experimental data remains indispensable.

However, for floating-base physical systems, such as legged robots, the cost of online policy adjustment is extremely high because they are prone to damage during repeated trial and error. Therefore, improving sample efficiency and ensuring operational safety have become two key considerations in the research of legged robots. Haarnoja et al. [16] proposed a sample-efficient deep reinforcement learning algorithm based on maximum entropy, which can learn quadruped locomotion controllers from scratch in an end-to-end manner on real-world robots, automatically forming walking gaits in a short time.

Other researchers have adopted a hybrid approach that combines simulation and real-world environments to narrow the gap between simulation and reality. Jonnarth et al. [17] trained robots using motion imitation and semi-virtual environments, achieving environmental diversity and automatic scene resetting through simulated sensors and randomized obstacles, reducing the differences between simulation and real-world applications. They also found that higher inference frequencies allow Markovian policies to be directly transferred from simulation to the real world, while more complex higher-order policies can further close the gap through fine-tuning.

In terms of reducing human intervention, Bloesch et al. [18] trained small humanoid robots to walk and interact using onboard sensors and limited hardware prior knowledge, helping the robot to stand up again through preprogrammed feedforward controllers when it falls. Gupta et al. [19] proposed a method that does not require resetting, achieving mutual resetting by learning multiple tasks simultaneously, reducing the need for human intervention.

In this research context, the work of Smith et al. [20] is particularly noteworthy. They combined imitation learning and online learning to fine-tune locomotion policies in the real world, demonstrating that a small amount of real-world training can significantly improve deployment performance, allowing the A1 quadruped robot to autonomously fine-tune locomotion skills in various environments. Subsequently, they used model-based non-policy reinforcement learning to learn from scratch in the real world, quickly learning quadruped locomotion through autonomous data collection [21]. Building on this, Ye et al. [22] proposed a guided learning paradigm combined with online learning, which allows the A1 robot to quickly learn various gaits, turns, and forward walking without data collection, preventing falls by increasing step frequency and avoiding the need for resetting, thus achieving higher training efficiency.

3 Methods

In this study, we used Unity, Isaac Gym, and MuJoCo as the primary software platforms, in conjunction with the Droid humanoid robot Walker II X02 Lite A

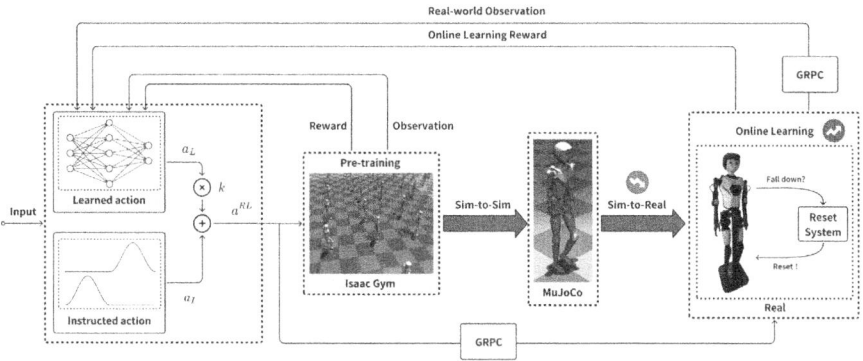

Fig. 2. The framework for online learning in the real world for humanoid robots.

hardware platform, to validate the Learn-in-Real paradigm. The framework for online learning in the real world is depicted in Fig. 2.

We initially employ instruction learning within Isaac Gym to train the robot's basic walking gaits. Subsequently, we migrate to MuJoCo to validate the feasibility and ensure the safety of the pre-trained model. Following this, we deploy the pre-trained model onto the physical robot. At this stage, the robot has essentially learned to maintain balance. Building upon this pre-trained network, we conduct online reinforcement learning through real-time interaction with the robot via gRPC (Google Remote Procedure Call), ultimately refining the policy network further.

In this section, we will introduce the main components of the Learn-in-Real framework: Instruction Learning, Pre-training, Online Learning, and the Reset System.

3.1 Instruction Learning

Instruction Learning, as an advanced learning method that integrates traditional reinforcement learning with direct feedforward control, optimizes the learning path for robots to handle complex action sequences. It enables robots to use basic stepping actions as feedforward signals. Starting from these signals, combined with a reward mechanism, robots can quickly learn and master a variety of gaits.

The input is the reference trajectory for the position for each joint. Since walking motion can be regarded as the left and right legs alternately performing a cosine waveform, we use a periodic trajectory, which means that the joints cycle through motion with a fixed period. In this case, the reference angle is designed as a sinusoidal signal

$$\theta_t^{ref} = \theta_0 + \Delta\theta \frac{1 - \cos\left(\frac{2\pi t}{T}\right)}{2} \tag{1}$$

The feedforward action is obtained by mapping the reference angle to $[-1, 1]$:

$$a_I = 2\frac{\theta_t^{ref} - \theta_{min}}{\theta_{max} - \theta_{min}} - 1 \qquad (2)$$

where θ_t^{ref} represents the reference angle of the joint and θ_{min} and θ_{max} denote the minimum and maximum limits of the joint range of motion, respectively. Then, the feedback action a_L from the neural network is weighted by the proportional coefficient k and added to the feedforward guiding action a_I to obtain the final action output.

$$a^{RL} = ka_L + a_I \qquad (3)$$

This approach significantly improves data utilization efficiency during the learning process and reduces the amount of exploration required when starting from random policies [22].

3.2 Pre-training

To enhance the efficiency of the pre-training phase, we leveraged the capabilities of the Isaac Gym simulation environment, enabling the parallel training of thousands of robots. This approach significantly accelerated the learning process for the robots.

During the pre-training phase, we employed a reinforcement learning-based model $M = \langle S, A, T, O, R, \gamma \rangle$. In this model, S and A define the state and action spaces, respectively. $T(s'|s,a)$ describes the probability of transitioning to state s' given the current state s and action a, $R(s,a)$ is the reward function, $\gamma \in [0,1]$ is the discount factor, and O represents the observation space. This model is designed to facilitate a smooth transition from full observability in simulation environments ($s \in S$) to partial observability in the real world

Table 1. Overview of Domain Randomization.

Parameter	Unit	Range	Operator	Type
Joint Position	rad	[−0.02, 0.02]	additive	Gaussian (1σ)
Joint Velocity	rad/s	[−0.5, 0.5]	additive	Gaussian (1σ)
Angular Velocity	rad/s	[−0.2, 0.2]	additive	Gaussian (1σ)
Euler Angle	rad	[−0.1, 0.1]	additive	Gaussian (1σ)
Body Mass	kg	[−6, 6]	additive	Gaussian (1σ)
System Delay	ms	[0, 10]	-	Uniform
Friction	-	[0.1, 1.5]	-	Uniform
Motor Strength	%	[90, 110]	scaling	Gaussian (1σ)
Kp	%	[50, 150]	scaling	Gaussian (1σ)
Kd	%	[50, 150]	scaling	Gaussian (1σ)

($o \in O$). In the training process, we utilized the loss function of the Proximal Policy Optimization (PPO) algorithm [23], combined with an asymmetric actor-critic approach [24]. Furthermore, we incorporated privileged information during the training phase and switched to non-privileged observations during deployment. This design allows us to fully leverage complete information in the simulation environment while ensuring the model's adaptability and robustness in the real world.

The design of the reward function is crucial for reinforcement learning as it directly influences the agent's behavior and performance. Our reward function consists of three key components: velocity tracking reward, gait reward and regularization term.

To enable successful transfer of the pre-trained model to physical robots, we carefully designed a set of domain randomization parameters, as detailed in Table 1.

3.3 Online Learning

Online learning utilizes data that is continuously updated over time. When the model is presented with new data, it undergoes partial training or adjustment to adapt to these updates, creating a cyclical process. Consequently, compared to offline learning, models that employ online learning are better equipped to handle scenarios where data evolves over time. Due to its high learning efficiency, instruction learning is particularly well-suited for online learning with real robots. Online learning collects data directly from actual robots and updates control strategies in real-time, thereby eliminating the sim-to-real problem [22]. By placing the agent in a variety of potentially changing environments, it enhances the agent's adaptability to unfamiliar settings, ensuring stability in the real world.

We selected the Unity ML-Agents framework for online learning. This framework features an off-the-shelf reinforcement learning library and superior visualization capabilities. Communication with the robot is facilitated through gRPC, with neural networks receiving observations in real-time to generate actions designed to maximize rewards. The observations used for online reinforcement learning align with the non-privileged observations. The reward function for online learning can be tailored to address specific outcomes following the sim-to-real transfer.

3.4 Reset System

Traditionally, if a robot falls during the learning process, it not only risks damaging its mechanical structure but also greatly limits the continuity and efficiency of learning. This is because manual resetting is not only time-consuming and labor-intensive, but also increases the risk of maintenance costs and operational interruptions.

In light of this, we have innovatively introduced an automatic celestial track reset system(Fig. 3), which can monitor the robot's status in real-time.

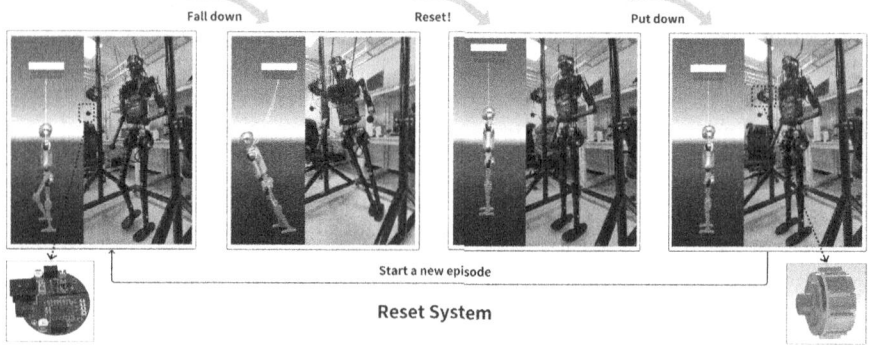

Fig. 3. Reset system with servo-driven lift wire.

This system mainly consists of a wire hanger equipped with a reducer. The robot's ascent and descent are controlled by a Xiaomi CyberGear servo motor through the wire. We use the ESP32 C3 Super Mini Bluetooth communication module to communicate with the computer, which automatically sends reset commands to the system during training. Once it detects signs of the robot losing balance or falling, the system immediately initiates the reset procedure. By precisely controlling the motor to pull the rope, the robot is quickly and smoothly pulled back to a preset safe position or the starting point for continued learning, all without the need for human intervention, achieving a seamless transition from detection to reset.

4 Experimental Results

The humanoid robot we used, the X02LiteA bipedal robot, is a tendon-driven robot with a height of 1.6 m, a weight of 30 kg, and a total of 18 degrees of freedom. In this scenario, only 10 legs joints were used, including hip yaw, hip roll, hip pitch, knee pitch, and ankle pitch.

In this section, we will provide a detailed description of the content of our experimental validation.

4.1 Learn in Sim

After training in Isaac Gym, the pre-trained model can be successfully transferred to MuJoCo, where it performs well during walking tasks. Subsequently, deploying it directly onto the physical robot is also successful. The reward curve obtained during training in Isaac Gym is shown in Fig. 4.

However, after transferring the policy to the physical robot, we observed that despite the incorporation of domain randomization during training, there are still noticeable differences between the performance of the policy network on the physical robot and that in the MuJoCo simulation environment. One particularly

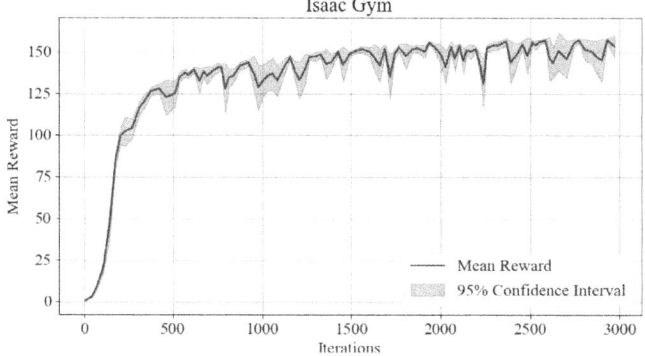

Fig. 4. Mean reward during pre-training in Isaac Gym.

evident phenomenon is the significant body vibrations during the robot's walking process on the physical platform, as illustrated in Fig. 4. This figure indicates that while the differences in body angular velocity in the x-direction and base roll between MuJoCo and the real robot are relatively small, there are substantial discrepancies in body angular velocity in the y-direction and base pitch. These findings suggest that the robot's performance deteriorates significantly after the sim-to-real transfer compared to the simulation environment, highlighting the persistent gap between simulation and reality.

To further close the Sim-to-Real gap, one approach is to continue tuning the parameters during training. This method involves multiple training and debugging iterations and may still fail to achieve a very small Sim-to-Real gap. Another approach is to conduct online reinforcement learning on the physical robot, leveraging real-time interaction data from the real world to bridge the gap between simulation and reality.

4.2 Learn in Real

Given that we use Unity for inference through the ONNX policy network, the pre-trained policy network is also saved in ONNX format. The training setup for online learning includes a fixed time step of 0.01 s, a time scale of 1, and a maximum of 1000 steps per episode.

The observations and actions used in online learning are consistent with those in the Sim-to-Real setup. In terms of reward function design, we base it on the performance from simulation to reality. For example, after deploying the policy to the physical robot, we observed significant vibrations. To address this issue, we designed a reward function aimed at reducing the robot's body oscillation.

$$r_{\text{online}} = r_{\text{live}} + r_{\text{euler}} + r_\omega \qquad (4)$$

Here, r_{live} represents the survival reward, r_{euler} is the penalty term for Euler angles, which imposes a penalty when the Euler angle exceeds a set threshold (0.02 in this experiment), r_ω is the penalty term for angular velocity, which imposes a penalty when the angular velocity exceeds a set threshold (0.5 in this experiment).

At the beginning of the training, the policy network is fine-tuned based on the pre-trained network, and the reward value starts to gradually increase, as shown in Fig. 6.

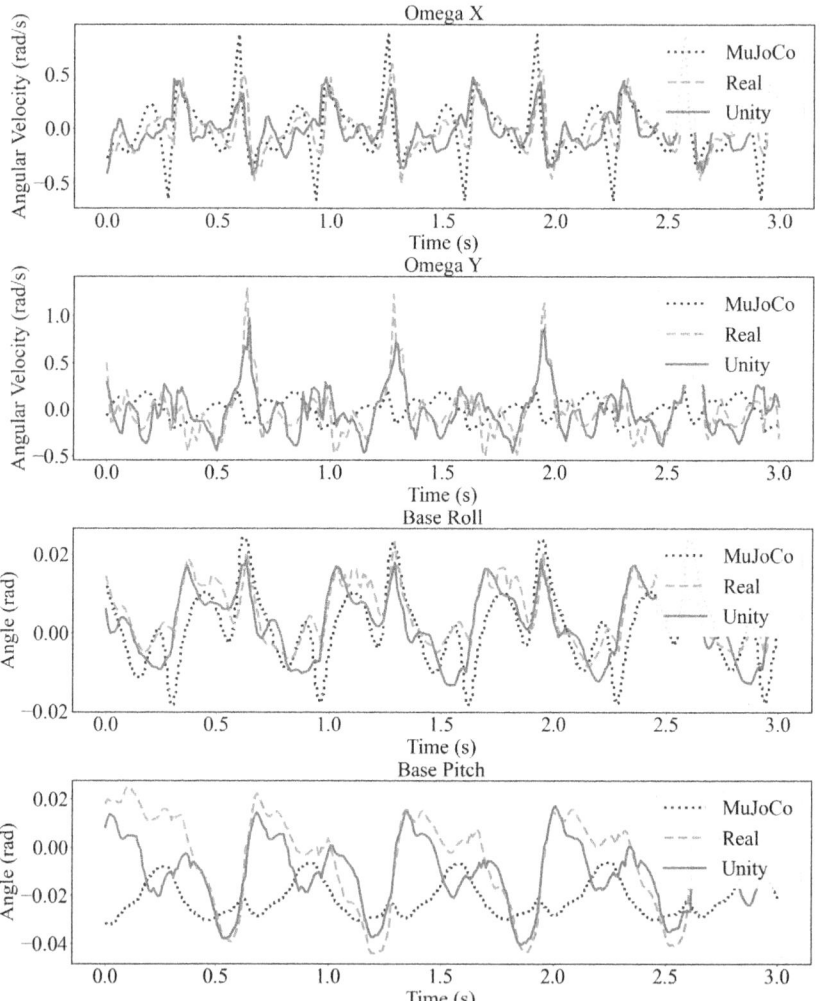

Fig. 5. Comparison chart of the robot's body angular velocity (in the x and y directions) and Euler angles (roll and pitch) after MuJoCo, Sim2Real, and Learn-in-Real.

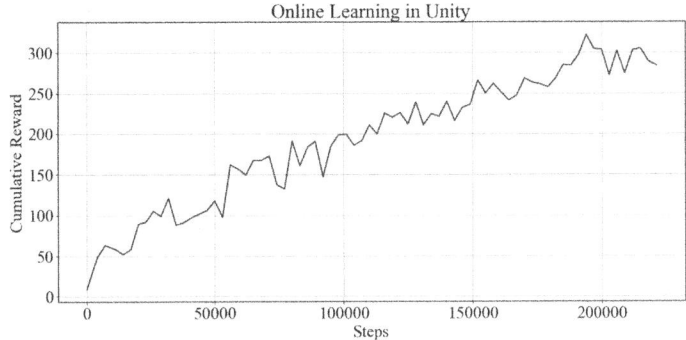

Fig. 6. Cumulative reward during online learning in Unity.

After 40 min of online learning, by comparing and analyzing the changes in the robot's base angular velocity and Euler angles before and after online learning, as shown in Fig. 5. We found that the peak values of the robot's angular velocity in the x-direction and the Euler angle around the *roll*-axis were lower after online learning than in the MuJoCo simulation environment. Moreover, compared with the state immediately after deploying the policy using Sim-to-Real, the peak values of all parameters were reduced after online learning.

This indicates that online learning successfully reduced the robot's body oscillation during walking. Compared with the deployment strategy directly from simulation to reality, the performance is significantly improved. The experimental results fully demonstrate the effectiveness of online learning on the physical robot. It not only further narrows the performance gap of Sim-to-Real but also performs better than in the simulation environment in some aspects.

5 Conclusion

In conclusion, the Learn-in-Real paradigm offers a novel and effective approach for humanoid robots to tackle the Sim-to-Real challenge. By conducting online learning in real environments, it adapts to environmental changes in real-time, effectively reducing the gap between simulated and real-world scenarios. The use of feedforward guidance learning combined with pre-trained networks significantly speeds up the learning process. Moreover, the automatic reset system addresses the issue of robot resetting during online learning, ensuring that the robot can automatically recover after a fall, thus maintaining the continuity and safety of training. We anticipate that this concept will advance the development of robotic technology to a higher level and enable broader applications.

References

1. Zhao, W., Queralta, J.P., Westerlund, T.: Sim-to-real transfer in deep reinforcement learning for robotics: a survey. In: IEEE Symposium Series on Computational Intelligence (SSCI), Canberra, ACT, Australia, pp. 737–744 (2020)

2. Kaufmann, E., et al.: Champion-level drone racing using deep reinforcement learning. Nature **620**, 982–987 (2023)
3. Zhao, W., et al.: Towards closing the sim-to-real gap in collaborative multi-robot deep reinforcement learning. In: 2020 5th International Conference on Robotics and Automation Engineering (ICRAE), pp. 7–12 (2020)
4. Muratore, F., et al.: Data-efficient domain randomization with Bayesian optimization. IEEE Robot. Autom. Lett. **6**(2), 911–918 (2021)
5. Tobin, J., et al.: Domain randomization for transferring deep neural networks from simulation to the real world. In: Proceedings of the IEEE/RSJ International Conference on Intelligent Robots and System (IROS), Vancouver, BC, Canada, pp. 23–30 (2017)
6. Finn, C., Abbeel, P., Levine, S.: Model-agnostic meta-learning for fast adaptation of deep networks. In: Proceedings of 34th International Conference on Machine Learning, pp. 1126–1135 (2017)
7. Nagabandi, A., et al.: Learning to adapt in dynamic, real-world environments through meta-reinforcement learning. arXiv:cs.LG/2008.07875 (2019)
8. Hwangbo, J., et al.: Learning agile and dynamic motor skills for legged robots. Sci. Robot. **4**, eaau5872 (2019)
9. Haarnoja, T., et al.: Learning agile soccer skills for a bipedal robot with deep reinforcement learning. Sci. Robot. **9**(89), eadi8022 (2024)
10. Gu, X., et al.: Humanoid-Gym: Reinforcement Learning for Humanoid Robot with Zero-Shot Sim2Real Transfer. arXiv:2404.05695 (2024)
11. Gu, X., et al.: Advancing Humanoid Locomotion: Mastering Challenging Terrains with Denoising World Model Learning. arXiv:2408.14472 (2024)
12. Arndt, K., et al.: Meta reinforcement learning for sim-to-real domain adaptation. In: Proceedings of the IEEE International Conference on Robotics and Automation (ICRA), Paris, France, pp. 2725–2731 (2020)
13. Levine, S., et al.: Learning Hand-Eye Coordination for Robotic Grasping with Deep Learning and Large-Scale Data Collection. arXiv:1603.02199 (2016)
14. Luo, J., et al.: SERL: a software suite for sample-efficient robotic reinforcement learning. In: IEEE International Conference on Robotics and Automation (ICRA), Yokohama, Japan, 13–17 May 2024, pp. 16961–16969 (2024)
15. Luo, J., et al.: Precise and Dexterous Robotic Manipulation via Human-in-the-Loop Reinforcement Learning. arXiv:cs.RO/2410.21845 (2024)
16. Haarnoja, T., et al.: Learning to Walk via Deep Reinforcement Learning. arXiv:1812.11103 (2019)
17. Jonnarth, A., et al.: Sim-to-Real Transfer of Deep Reinforcement Learning Agents for Online Coverage Path Planning. arXiv:2406.04920 (2024)
18. Bloesch, M., et al.: Towards real robot learning in the wild: a case study in bipedal locomotion. In: Proceedings of the Conference on Robot Learning (CoRL), vol. 164, pp. 1502–1511 (2022)
19. Gupta, A., et al.: Reset-free reinforcement learning via multi-task learning: learning dexterous manipulation behaviors without human intervention. In: Proceedings of the IEEE International Conference on Robotics and Automation (ICRA), Xi'an, China, pp. 6664–6671 (2021)
20. Smith, L., et al.: Legged robots that keep on learning: fine-tuning locomotion policies in the real world. In: Proceedings of the Conference on Robot Learning (CoRL) (2021)
21. Smith, L., et al.: A Walk in the Park: Learning to Walk in 20 Minutes With Model-Free Reinforcement Learning. arXiv:2208.07860 (2022)

22. Ye, L., et al.: From Knowing to Doing: Learning Diverse Motor Skills through Instruction Learning. arXiv:abs/2309.09167 (2023)
23. Schulman, J., Wolski, F., Dhariwal, P., Radford, A., Klimov, O.: Proximal policy optimization algorithms. arXiv:1707.06347 (2017)
24. Pinto, L., Andrychowicz, M., Welinder, P., Zaremba, W., Abbeel, P.: Asymmetric actor critic for image-based robot learning. arXiv:1710.06542 (2017)

Smart Shoe System for Accurate Gait Phase Recognition

Jiachen Wang[1], Jiakang Wang[1], Tian Liang[2], and Huanghe Zhang[1](✉)

[1] School of Control Science and Engineering, Shandong University, Jinan, China
zhanghuanghe@sdu.edu.cn
[2] Jinan Zhensheng School, Jinan, China

Abstract. Gait phase detection is crucial in rehabilitation and sports analysis. Although wearable sensor systems are widely employed for gait phase detection, their application is often restricted to a two-phase (stance and swing) model. This paper introduces a novel smart shoe system that integrates an inertial measurement unit (IMU), an ultrasonic sensor, and plantar pressure sensors to accurately recognize four distinct gait phases: initial contact, mid-stance, propulsion, and swing phase. However, systems relying solely on plantar pressure sensors face inherent limitations, as the sensors are prone to degradation and failure under the repetitive mechanical stress of long-term use. By integrating IMU and ultrasonic sensors, our system provides a more reliable and comprehensive approach for gait phase recognition. The plantar pressure data served as the gold standard for annotating the four gait phases. We evaluated support vector machine (SVM), recurrent neural network (RNN), and XGBoost algorithms using 10-fold cross-validation. The RNN model exhibited superior performance, achieving an average accuracy of 87.66 ± 5.80% and an F1-score of 0.8765 ± 0.0579 in the four-phase gait classification task. These findings confirm the potential of this smart shoe system as a promising tool for health monitoring, disease prevention, and personalized rehabilitation training, highlighting its capability for future real-time gait analysis.

Keywords: Wearable robotics · Gait phase recognition · Smart shoe

1 Introduction

With the accelerating process of global population aging and the general improvement of national health awareness, people's demand for improving quality of life and enhancing physical fitness is growing [1,2]. Against this background, smart wearable devices show broad application prospects in fields such as health monitoring, disease prevention, and rehabilitation training [3,4]. Walking, as the most basic human movement, its gait characteristics contain rich bioinformatics information [5]. Personalized analysis of gait can provide users with strong support for early prevention of various diseases [6]. In the medical and rehabilitation fields, gait analysis can assist in diagnosing nervous system diseases and musculoskeletal problems, provide a scientific basis for rehabilitation treatment, and optimize rehabilitation programs and evaluate treatment effects [7].

The core of gait analysis lies in the quantification of gait temporal and spatial parameters, which is crucial for describing the characteristics of walking patterns [8]. Traditional gait analysis often simplifies the gait cycle into a two-phase model, namely the stance phase and the swing phase [9]. The stance phase refers to the time when both feet are in contact with the ground and bear weight, accounting for about 60% of the gait cycle [9,10]. The swing phase refers to the time from when the foot leaves the ground to swing forward until it lands again, accounting for about 40% of the gait cycle [11]. However, this two-phase division method may not provide sufficiently detailed information in some refined analysis scenarios [12]. For example, further subdividing the gait cycle into four stages such as initial contact, midstance, terminal stance (propulsion), and swing phase can more accurately reflect the force changes and postural characteristics of the foot in different movement links, thereby providing data support for more in-depth gait assessment and abnormal gait detection [13].

While such detailed gait phase classification is highly beneficial, its accurate implementation in smart shoe systems faces several challenges. Current mainstream methods for gait monitoring in these systems predominantly rely on plantar pressure sensors [14]. However, the soft skin on the surface of the foot undergoes local deformation during movement, which places strict requirements on the mechanical properties of the sensors (including rigidity, toughness, and wearing comfort) [15]. At the same time, these pressure sensors are prone to damage or failure during long-term use, affecting data reliability. In addition, although wearable devices such as IMU and surface electromyography (sEMG) have been widely used in gait research [16,17], a single IMU sensor may have cumulative errors and drift phenomena in its attitude angle data during long-term continuous measurement [18,19]. To address these issues, this study proposes a smart shoe system that integrates IMU and ultrasonic sensors to achieve accurate gait phase classification and improve the accuracy and robustness of gait analysis.

2 Methods

2.1 System Hardware Design

The proposed smart shoe system's hardware design utilizes an ATMEGA328P microcontroller (Microchip Technology, USA) for data acquisition and processing. This microcontroller integrates with multiple sensors to capture comprehensive gait data.

Plantar pressure data is collected using IMS-C40A single-point thin-film resistive sensors (IMS Corporation, USA). The placement of these sensors is guided by plantar pressure distribution characteristics, targeting the primary load-bearing areas: the forefoot and heel. Specifically, three pressure sensors are

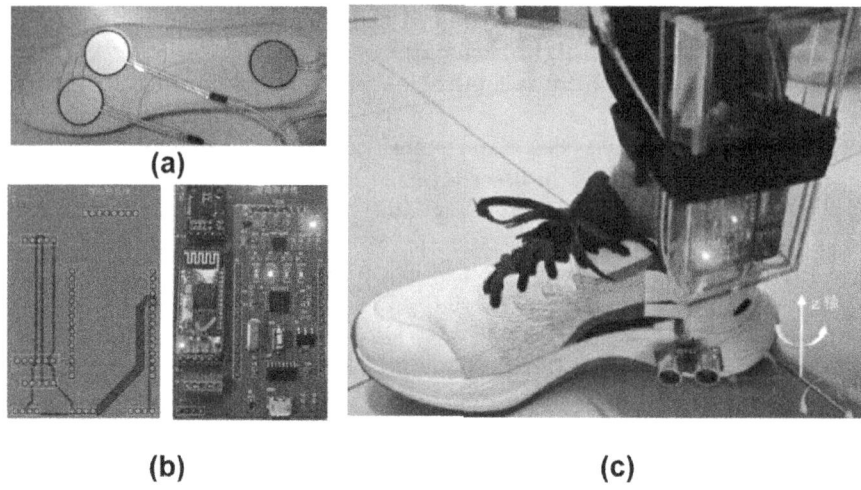

Fig. 1. Hardware design of the smart shoe system: (a) sensorized insole with pressure sensors; (b) PCB layout and assembled module; (c) fully assembled smart shoe prototype.

positioned at the first metatarsal head, the fourth metatarsal head region, and the heel, as illustrated in the insole design shown in Fig. 1(a).

Foot motion and orientation are tracked using an MPU6050 inertial sensor (TDK InvenSense, USA), which includes a three-axis accelerometer and a three-axis gyroscope, complemented by an HMC5883L (Honeywell, USA) magnetometer. This combination is employed to acquire foot posture information and to effectively suppress yaw angle drift, thereby improving measurement accuracy [20]. These components, along with the ATMEGA328P (Microchip Technology, USA) microcontroller and an HC-05 (Shenzhen HCSET Electronic Technology Co., Ltd., China) Bluetooth module for wireless data transmission to a host computer, are integrated onto a custom-designed Printed Circuit Board (PCB). The PCB layout and its assembled form are shown in Fig. 1(b); this design features optimized wiring and grounding, with the microcontroller centrally positioned to enhance signal integrity and the MPU6050 integrated directly onto the board.

The fully assembled smart shoe system is depicted in Fig. 1(c). This figure shows the shoe with the embedded sensorized insole, an externally mounted enclosure housing the PCB and associated electronics (strapped to the ankle region), and the ultrasonic sensor KS103 (Nanjing Wuxiang Electronic Technology Co., Ltd., China) fixed to the side of the shoe, oriented for stride distance measurement relevant to stride calculation.

2.2 Gait Data Acquisition and Preprocessing

Our gait database was constructed by collecting data from 3 healthy male subjects (age: 21.7 ± 0.6 years; height: 170.7 ± 3.8 cm; weight: 63.7 ± 9.3 kg). After an adaptation period, subjects walked naturally on a flat surface for data acquisition. The gait cycle was divided into four phases—initial contact, mid-stance, propulsion, and swing phase—using a gold-standard pressure sensor for annotation.

After data acquisition, the raw gait data contains interference (e.g., high-frequency noise and motion vibrations). Therefore, Gaussian smoothing filter was applied to high-frequency noise [21], with a Gaussian kernel standard deviation of $\sigma = 0.8$ empirically validated as optimal to avoid over-smoothing or under-smoothing. The Gaussian filter works by averaging each data point with its neighbors, where σ controls the smoothing strength—larger values provide stronger noise reduction but may blur important signal features. Additionally, normalization was performed to map the data to the $[0, 1]$ range to eliminate scale differences and improve model robustness [22].

The Kalman filter algorithm was further employed for MPU6050 pitch and roll angle measurements to fuse the long-term stability of the accelerometer with the short-term precision of the gyroscope to effectively correct drift and suppress noise [23]. The Kalman filter intelligently combines predictions from a mathematical model with sensor measurements to produce optimal estimates. The state prediction formula for the Kalman filter is given by:

$$\hat{x}_k = A \cdot \hat{x}_{k-1} + B \cdot u_{k-1} \quad (1)$$

Here, the state vector $\mathbf{x}$ is defined as $\mathbf{x} = \begin{bmatrix} angle \\ bias \end{bmatrix}$, where angle represents the angle value and bias represents the angular velocity bias value. Thus, the state equation can be further expressed as:

$$\begin{bmatrix} angle_k \\ bias_k \end{bmatrix} = \begin{bmatrix} 1 & -dt \\ 0 & 1 \end{bmatrix} \begin{bmatrix} angle_{k-1} \\ bias_{k-1} \end{bmatrix} + \begin{bmatrix} dt \\ 0 \end{bmatrix} Gyro\_rate \quad (2)$$

where $Gyro\_rate$ is the control input (angular velocity).

The update portion of the Kalman filter corrects the prediction by incorporating measured values. The update state prediction formula is:

$$\hat{x}_k = \hat{x}_k + K_k \cdot (z_k - H \cdot \hat{x}_k) \quad (3)$$

Here, z_k is the angle observation value at time k (provided by the accelerometer), and K_k is the Kalman gain, which determines the weight distribution between sensor measurements and model predictions. When K_k approaches 1, the filter trusts sensor measurements more; when K_k approaches 0, it relies more on model predictions. In gait analysis, K_k values are typically larger during motion (trusting gyroscope data) and smaller during static periods (trusting accelerometer data). The observation matrix H, which maps the state space to the observation space, is defined as $H = \begin{bmatrix} 1 & 0 \end{bmatrix}$.

2.3 Gait Recognition and Evaluation Methodology

To classify the preprocessed gait data, this section outlines the principles of the three employed machine learning algorithms and describes the metrics used to evaluate the performance.

Support Vector Machine (SVM). SVM is a binary classification model whose basic model is a linear classifier defined with the largest margin in the feature space [24]. For linearly separable data, SVM attempts to find a hyperplane that separates samples of different classes such that the margin (distance to the closest sample points, or support vectors) is maximized, which is equivalent to solving the following convex quadratic programming problem:

$$\min_{w,b} \frac{1}{2}||w||^2 \qquad (4)$$

subject to:
$$y_i(w \cdot x_i + b) \geq 1, \quad i = 1, \ldots, N \qquad (5)$$

where (x_i, y_i) is the i-th training sample, and $y_i \in \{+1, -1\}$ is the class label

To handle non-linear problems, SVM uses the kernel trick, mapping data to a higher-dimensional feature space via a kernel function, thus finding a non-linear decision boundary in the original space [24]. Based on our preliminary studies [19,25], we employed the Gaussian Radial Basis Function (RBF) kernel, defined as:

$$K(x_i, x_j) = \exp(-\gamma ||x_i - x_j||^2) \qquad (6)$$

where γ represents the kernel parameter, which was specifically set to 3.

Recurrent Neural Network (RNN). RNN is a class of neural networks specifically designed for processing sequential data. RNNs use recurrent connections within network layers, allowing information to be passed and maintained across different time steps in a sequence, thereby modeling temporal dependencies in the data [26]. The state h_t and output y_t of a RNN unit at time step t can be expressed as:

$$h_t = f(Ux_t + Wh_{t-1} + b_h) \qquad (7)$$
$$y_t = g(Vh_t + b_y) \qquad (8)$$

where x_t is the input at time step t; h_{t-1} is the hidden state from the previous time step; U, W, V are weight matrices; b_h, b_y are bias vectors; and f, g are activation functions (We used ReLU for f, and softmax for g in the task).

XGBoost (Extreme Gradient Boosting). XGBoost is an efficient and scalable implementation of the gradient boosting algorithm based on the Gradient Boosting Decision Tree (GBDT) framework. The XGBoost model is an ensemble of K additive trees [27]:

$$\hat{y}_i = \sum_{k=1}^{K} f_k(x_i), \quad f_k \in \mathcal{F} \qquad (9)$$

where $\hat{y}_i$ is the prediction for sample x_i, f_k is the k-th tree, and $\mathcal{F}$ is the space of all possible Classification and Regression Trees. The objective function consists of two parts: training loss and a regularization term:

$$L^{(t)} = \sum_{i=1}^{n} l(y_i, \hat{y}_i^{(t-1)} + f_t(x_i)) + \Omega(f_t) \quad (10)$$

where l is a differentiable convex loss function, and $\hat{y}_i^{(t-1)}$ is the prediction from the previous $t-1$ trees. The regularization term $\Omega(f_t)$ controls the complexity of the tree to prevent overfitting, defined as:

$$\Omega(f_t) = \gamma T + \frac{1}{2}\lambda \sum_{j=1}^{T} w_j^2 \quad (11)$$

Here T is the number of leaf nodes, w_j is the score of the j-th leaf, and γ, λ are regularization parameters. To optimize the objective function, XGBoost uses a second-order Taylor expansion approximation of the loss function at the current model:

$$L^{(t)} \approx \sum_{i=1}^{n} [g_i f_t(x_i) + \frac{1}{2} h_i f_t^2(x_i)] + \Omega(f_t) \quad (12)$$

where $g_i = \frac{\partial l(y_i, \hat{y}_i^{(t-1)})}{\partial \hat{y}_i^{(t-1)}}$ and $h_i = \frac{\partial^2 l(y_i, \hat{y}_i^{(t-1)})}{(\partial \hat{y}_i^{(t-1)})^2}$ are the first and second order gradient statistics of the loss function, respectively.

Algorithm Performance Metrics. The performance of these models was evaluated using four key metrics: Accuracy, Precision, Recall, and F1 Score.

Accuracy is defined as:

$$Accuracy = \frac{TP + TN}{TP + FP + TN + FN} \quad (13)$$

Precision is defined as:

$$Precision = \frac{TP}{TP + FP} \quad (14)$$

Recall is defined as:

$$Recall = \frac{TP}{TP + FN} \quad (15)$$

F1 Score is defined as:

$$F1 = 2 \times \frac{Precision \times Recall}{Precision + Recall} \quad (16)$$

where TP is True Positives (positive samples correctly predicted as positive), TN is True Negatives (negative samples correctly predicted as negative), FP is False Positives (negative samples incorrectly predicted as positive), and FN is False Negatives (positive samples incorrectly predicted as negative) [28].

3 Results

The classification algorithms described in the Methods section were applied to the preprocessed gait data obtained from the smart shoe system. Models were optimized and evaluated using 10-fold cross-validation. The overall performance metrics, summarized in Table 1, reveal a performance comparison among the evaluated algorithms. Confusion matrices are presented in Fig. 2 to further analyze the specific classification performance and error patterns across the four gait phases.

Table 1. Summary of 10-Fold Cross-Validation Performance Metrics for All Algorithms

Performance Metric	RNN	SVM	XGBoost
Avg. Accuracy	0.8766 ± 0.0580	0.7292 ± 0.0072	0.8398 ± 0.0074
Avg. Precision	0.8946 ± 0.0474	0.7276 ± 0.0068	0.8448 ± 0.0070
Avg. Recall	0.8911 ± 0.0649	0.7292 ± 0.0076	0.8398 ± 0.0074
Avg. F1-Score	0.8765 ± 0.0579	0.7249 ± 0.0076	0.8408 ± 0.0072

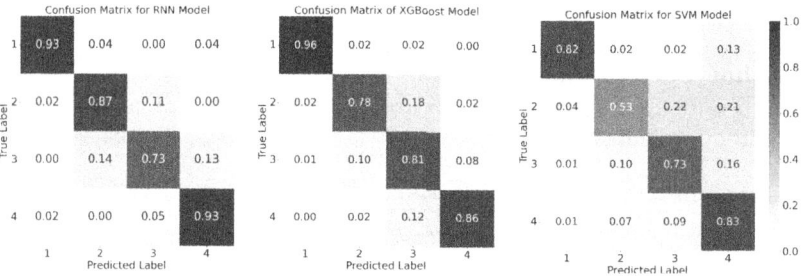

Fig. 2. Confusion matrices for the RNN, XGBoost, and SVM models resulting from 10-fold cross-validation in four-phase gait recognition.

The RNN's leading performance across all evaluation metrics (F1-Score: 0.8765 ± 0.0579) underscores its superior ability for handling sequential data. This advantage stems from RNNs' inherent design for processing temporal sequences, making them particularly well-suited for capturing the continuous temporal patterns that characterize human gait [29]. The gait cycle exhibits strong temporal dependencies where the current phase is closely related to previous phases through biomechanical continuity. The recurrent structure allows the model to leverage historical information effectively, maintaining a hidden state that encodes information from previous time steps, thereby enabling accurate distinction between temporally contiguous gait stages where biomechanical features may overlap [30].

In contrast, both SVM and XGBoost face fundamental limitations when applied to this temporal classification task. SVM treats each time point as an independent feature vector, losing critical temporal context that is essential for gait phase transitions [31]. While the RBF kernel can capture non-linear relationships, it cannot adequately encode the sequential dependencies inherent in gait data. The SVM model achieved an F1-Score of 0.7249 ± 0.0076, suggesting that differentiating complex gait phases presented significant challenges under the current feature set, as SVMs are not inherently specialized for processing time-series data and might not have adequately captured the subtle patterns of phase transitions [32]. XGBoost, though superior to SVM with an F1-Score of 0.8408 ± 0.0072, processes features in a static manner and lacks the natural ability to model temporal dependencies, requiring manual feature engineering to capture time-related patterns [33]. While XGBoost generally excels with structured data and offers fast training times, its performance in this study suggests reasonable but not optimal capability for gait phase differentiation, which might be attributed to limitations in how temporal information was encoded for the tree-based model.

A more detailed examination of the classification performance across the four gait phases can be drawn from the confusion matrices, presented in Fig. 2. For the RNN model, Fig. 2 shows true positive rates for recognizing Phase 1, Phase 2, Phase 3, and Phase 4 as 0.93, 0.87, 0.73, and 0.93, respectively. This indicates a strong recognition capability for Phase 1 and Phase 4, which are characterized by distinctive biomechanical events that generate clear sensor signatures. The slightly lower performance for Phase 3 (propulsion, 0.73) suggests that this phase involves more gradual transitions that are challenging to distinguish from adjacent phases. In comparison, the SVM model exhibited significantly lower true positive rates for Phase 2 (0.53) when compared to the RNN (0.87) and XGBoost (0.78) models for the same phase, suggesting a higher degree of misclassification for the mid-stance phase when using SVM. This pattern of varying inter-phase confusion can also be observed for other models to different extents, particularly evident in the RNN model's lower recall for Phase 3 (0.73) and the XGBoost model's lower recall for Phase 2 (0.78) and Phase 4 (0.86) compared to its performance on Phase 1 (0.96).

However, this study has certain limitations that suggest future directions of our research. The dataset could be expanded in size and diversity to enhance the generalizability of the models, particularly including participants across different age groups, genders, and health conditions. Future work should focus on collecting data from more varied cohorts and testing environments, including different terrains and walking speeds. Furthermore, while the current system integrates multiple sensors, exploring more advanced data fusion techniques, including sophisticated sensor fusion algorithms or model fusion strategies that combine the strengths of different classification algorithms, could potentially yield further improvements in recognition efficacy.

4 Conclusion

In this study, a smart shoe system integrating an Inertial Measurement Unit (IMU), pressure sensors, and ultrasonic sensors was developed and validated for four-phase gait phase recognition. Data preprocessing techniques, in 10-fold cross-validation of SVM, RNN, and XGBoost algorithms revealed that the RNN model provided the most effective classification of the four distinct gait phases, achieving an average F1-Score of 0.8765 ± 0.0579. This performance highlights the RNN's capability in modeling the temporal dynamics inherent in gait patterns in the small dataset. The research contributes a validated framework for a wearable gait analysis system, underscoring the potential of the developed smart shoe for applications in continuous health monitoring [34], early disease detection [35,36], and personalized rehabilitation programs [37,38].

Acknowledgement. This work was supported in part by the National Key R&D Program of China under Grant 2023YFB4706102, in part by the Shandong Excellent Young Scientists Fund Program (Overseas) under Grant 2024HWYQ-019, in part by the Young Scientists Fund of the National Natural Science Foundation of China under Grant 62403281, and the Taishan Scholars Project (Young Expert Program) under Grant NO. tsqn202408040.

References

1. Kim, S.: World health organization quality of life (whoqol) assessment. In: Encyclopedia of Quality of Life and Well-Being Research, pp. 7866–7867. Springer, Cham (2024)
2. Yi, F.: Healthcare and rehabilitation: reflections and prospects, p. 100003 (2024)
3. Dinh-Le, C., Chuang, R., Chokshi, S., Mann, D.: Wearable health technology and electronic health record integration: scoping review and future directions. JMIR mHealth uHealth **7**(9), e12861 (2019)
4. Ma, S., et al.: Artificial intelligence and medical-engineering integration in diabetes management: advances, opportunities, and challenges. Healthcare Rehabil. **1**(1), 100006 (2025)
5. Bortone, I., et al.: How gait influences frailty models and health-related outcomes in clinical-based and population-based studies: a systematic review. J. Cachexia. Sarcopenia Muscle **12**(2), 274–297 (2021)
6. Patel, S., Park, H., Bonato, P., Chan, L., Rodgers, M.: A review of wearable sensors and systems with application in rehabilitation. J. Neuroeng. Rehabil. **9**, 1–17 (2012)
7. Huang, J.-D., Wang, J., Ramsey, E., Leavey, G., Chico, T.J., Condell, J.: Applying artificial intelligence to wearable sensor data to diagnose and predict cardiovascular disease: a review. Sensors **22**(20), 8002 (2022)
8. Baker, R.: Gait analysis methods in rehabilitation. J. Neuroeng. Rehabil. **3**, 1–10 (2006)
9. Whittle, M.W.: Gait Analysis: An Introduction. Butterworth-Heinemann (2014)
10. Zhang, H., Zanotto, D., Agrawal, S.K.: Estimating cop trajectories and kinematic gait parameters in walking and running using instrumented insoles. IEEE Robot. Autom. Lett. **2**(4), 2159–2165 (2017)

11. Gage, J.R., Deluca, P.A., Renshaw, T.S.: Gait analysis: principles and applications. JBJS **77**(10), 1607–1623 (1995)
12. Kharb, A., Saini, V., Jain, Y., Dhiman, S.: A review of gait cycle and its parameters. IJCEM Int. J. Comput. Eng. Manag. **13**(01), 78–83 (2011)
13. Perry, J., Burnfield, J.M.: Phases of gait. In: Gait Analysis. CRC Press, pp. 9–16 (2024)
14. Li, W., et al.: Wearable gait recognition systems based on mems pressure and inertial sensors: a review. IEEE Sens. J. **22**(2), 1092–1104 (2021)
15. Chen, J.-L., et al.: Plantar pressure-based insole gait monitoring techniques for diseases monitoring and analysis: a review. Adv. Mater. Technol. **7**(1), 2100566 (2022)
16. Wang, J., et al.: Deep neural networks for gait cycle percentage prediction in frail older adults using a foot-mounted IMU. In: 2024 IEEE International Conference on Robotics and Biomimetics (ROBIO), pp. 166–171. IEEE (2024)
17. Sun, Y., et al.: Gait phase detection and prediction with machine learning models based on sEMG. In: 2024 3rd International Conference on Artificial Intelligence, Human-Computer Interaction and Robotics (AIHCIR), pp. 324–330. IEEE (2024)
18. Nouredanesh, M., Tung, J.: IMU, sEMG, or their cross-correlation and temporal similarities: which signal features detect lateral compensatory balance reactions more accurately? Comput. Methods Programs Biomed. **182**, 105003 (2019)
19. Zhang, H., Guo, Y., Zanotto, D.: Accurate ambulatory gait analysis in walking and running using machine learning models. IEEE Trans. Neural Syst. Rehabil. Eng. **28**(1), 191–202 (2019)
20. Wittmann, F., Lambercy, O., Gassert, R.: Magnetometer-based drift correction during rest in IMU arm motion tracking. Sensors **19**(6), 1312 (2019)
21. Deisenroth, M.P., Turner, R.D., Huber, M.F., Hanebeck, U.D., Rasmussen, C.E.: Robust filtering and smoothing with gaussian processes. IEEE Trans. Autom. Control **57**(7), 1865–1871 (2011)
22. Huang, L., Qin, J., Zhou, Y., Zhu, F., Liu, L., Shao, L.: Normalization techniques in training DNNs: methodology, analysis and application. IEEE Trans. Pattern Anal. Mach. Intell. **45**(8), 10 173–10 196 (2023)
23. Gui, P., Tang, L., Mukhopadhyay, S.: Mems based IMU for tilting measurement: comparison of complementary and Kalman filter based data fusion. In: 2015 IEEE 10th Conference on Industrial Electronics and Applications (ICIEA), pp. 2004–2009. IEEE (2015)
24. Chauhan, V.K., Dahiya, K., Sharma, A.: Problem formulations and solvers in linear SVM: a review. Artif. Intell. Rev. **52**(2), 803–855 (2019)
25. Zhang, H., et al.: Transductive learning models for accurate ambulatory gait analysis in elderly residents of assisted living facilities. IEEE Trans. Neural Syst. Rehabil. Eng. **30**, 124–134 (2022)
26. Al-Selwi, S.M., et al.: RNN-LSTM: from applications to modeling techniques and beyond—systematic review. J. King Saud Univ.-Comput. Inf. Sci. 102068 (2024)
27. Chen, T., Guestrin, C.: XGBoost: a scalable tree boosting system. In: Proceedings of the 22nd ACM SIGKDD International Conference on Knowledge Discovery and Data Mining, pp. 785–794 (2016)
28. Hossin, M., Sulaiman, M.N.: A review on evaluation metrics for data classification evaluations. Int. J. Data Min. Knowl. Manag. Process **5**(2), 1 (2015)
29. Ghosh, R.: A faster R-CNN and recurrent neural network based approach of gait recognition with and without carried objects. Expert Syst. Appl. **205**, 117730 (2022)

30. Fang, W., Chen, Y., Xue, Q.: Survey on research of RNN-based spatio-temporal sequence prediction algorithms. J. Big Data **3**(3), 97 (2021)
31. Parashar, A., Parashar, A., Ding, W., Shabaz, M., Rida, I.: Data preprocessing and feature selection techniques in gait recognition: a comparative study of machine learning and deep learning approaches. Pattern Recogn. Lett. **172**, 65–73 (2023)
32. Rani, V., Kumar, M.: Human gait recognition: a systematic review. Multimed. Tools Appl. **82**(24), 37 003–37 037 (2023)
33. Lu, Z., Chen, S., Yang, J., Liu, C., Zhao, H.: Prediction of lower limb joint angles from surface electromyography using XGBoost. Expert Syst. Appl. **264**, 125930 (2025)
34. Zhang, H., Chen, Z., Zanotto, D., Guo, Y.: Robot-assisted and wearable sensor-mediated autonomous gait analysis. In: 2020 IEEE International Conference on Robotics and Automation (ICRA), pp. 6795–6802. IEEE (2020)
35. Zhang, H., Wu, C., Huang, Y., Song, R., Zanotto, D., Agrawal, S.K.: Fall risk prediction using instrumented footwear in institutionalized older adults. IEEE Trans. Neural Syst. Rehabil. Eng. (2024)
36. Cai, J., et al.: Impact of gait parameters and their variability on fall risk assessment accuracy using wearable sensor. IEEE Trans. Neural Syst. Rehabil. Eng. (2025)
37. Zhang, H., Li, S., Zhao, Q., Rao, A.K., Guo, Y., Zanotto, D.: Reinforcement learning-based adaptive biofeedback engine for overground walking speed training. IEEE Robot. Autom. Lett. **7**(3), 8487–8494 (2022)
38. Zhang, H., et al.: Wearable biofeedback system to induce desired walking speed in overground gait training. Sensors **20**(14), 4002 (2020)

Wearable AI-Driven Smart Insole for Long-Term Monitoring of Lower-Limb Joint Mobility: A Pilot Study

Dinghuang Zhang[1,3], Yuxiang Huang[2], Ying Liu[3], Zhe Ding[3], Liucheng Guo[3,4(✉)], and Dalin Zhou[1]

[1] School of Computing, University of Portsmouth, Portsmouth, UK
{dinghuang.zhang,dalin.zhou}@port.ac.uk
[2] School of Electrical, Electronic and Mechanical Engineering, University of Bristol, Bristol, UK
ethan.huang@bristol.ac.uk
[3] Tangi0 LTD (TG0), London, UK
{ying,martin}@tg0.co.uk, liuchengguo@ieee.org
[4] Capital University of Physical Education and Sports, Beijing, China

Abstract. Monitoring joint mobility limitations (JML) for lower-limbs is essential for the early detection and management of musculoskeletal and neurological disorders that impact gait and functional. However, traditional joint range of motion (ROM) assessments are typically limited to clinical settings and lack the capability for continuous, real-world monitoring. This study explores the feasibility of monitoring joint mobility impairments using a wearable smart insole system. To validate the system, we designed a joint-specific motion protocol and collected walking data from four participants under normal and mechanically restricted conditions at the ankle, knee, and hip joints. All joint impairments were simulated on a single limb at a time using mechanical limiters, while normal walking trials served as baseline reference. The collected data was segmented into two second windows and used to train a lightweight neural network model to classify the type of joint JML condition. Our results demonstrate the proposed system can effectively distinguish between normal and ROM impaired gait patterns. Under Leave-One-Subject-Out (LOSO) model evaluation setting, the proposed method achieved average classification accuracy of approximately 81% in distinguishing knee and ankle JML conditions against normal gait data from four participants. This research highlights the potential of low-cost, pressure-only wearable systems for continuous, personalized monitoring of joint function in everyday environments, laying the groundwork for future applications in remote rehabilitation and clinical decision support.

Keywords: Gait analysis · smart insole · wearable sensing · joint mobility limitations · healthcare monitoring

---

This work was supported by Innovate UK via Knowledge Transfer Partnership (KTP: 13863).

1 Introduction

As the global population ages, with one in six people projected to be over 60 years old by 2030, there is a growing need for scalable, user-friendly health monitoring technologies [17]. Wearable systems, particularly smart insoles [1], have emerged as a promising solution for continuous, non-invasive gait monitoring method outside traditional clinical settings.

Equipped with embedded sensors and microcontrollers (MCUs), smart insoles offer a promising solution for elder care, rehabilitation, and sports by allowing real-time detection of gait abnormalities, tracking recovery progress, and guiding physical therapy with greater precision and convenience. These capabilities are further enhanced by recent advances in artificial intelligence (AI), particularly Tiny Machine Learning (TinyML), which allows lightweight AI models to run directly on ultra low-power MCUs [16]. This integration of sensing and on-device intelligence eliminates the need for cloud connectivity, thereby reducing latency, preserving user privacy, and supporting continuous, long-term monitoring in real-world environments. These technological advances are particularly valuable for monitoring lower-limb joint range of motion (ROM), the ability of the ankle, knee, and hip joints to move within their physiological limits [11]. Limited ROM, also known as Joint mobility limitations (JML) caused by aging, stroke, osteoarthritis (OA), rheumatoid arthritis (RA), or neuromuscular disorders can lead to condition-specific gait impairments. For example, limited ROM at ankle often results in foot drop or steppage gait [3]; knee restrictions affect shock absorption and coordination during stance [6,7]; and reduced hip ROM may cause shorter stride length, asymmetry, and increased compensatory trunk motion [14].

Despite its clinical relevance, joint ROM is typically assessed using manual angle meters or motion capture systems methods that are restricted to the clinical or time-consuming and dependent on trained personnel and laboratory setting. These limitations impart their use for continuous, real-world monitoring during daily activities. In contrast, recent advances in wearable technology offer new opportunities for out-of-clinic joint assessment. Smart insole systems, in particular, have gained traction as low-cost, portable, and practical tools for gait analysis and lower-limb function monitoring.

In this work, we present a TinyML powered wearable insole system for long-term monitoring of lower limb joint mobility. The system performs on-device real-time inference to detect JML from plantar pressure distribution and gait dynamics data captured by the smart insole system. Specifically, we focus on representative abnormal gaits associated with joint mobility limitations associated with limited ankle, knee, and hip mobility. Our key contributions are as follows:

- Demonstrated that ankle and knee mobility impairments can be distinguished using only pressure and IMU data from a smart insole.
- Developed a motion protocol and collected the JML-Gait dataset with normal and simulated impairments at ankle, knee, and hip joints.

- Implemented a lightweight multi-label classification model supporting the deployed via TinyML on a low-power MCU.

2 Related Work

2.1 Insole Sensing Technique

In traditional foot sensing measurement insole systems, multiple sensing modalities are widely used, including piezoresistive, resistive, capacitive, piezoelectric, inductive, and motion sensors [8].

To our knowledge, most commercial insole systems currently rely on piezoresistive sensors due to their ease of integration and relatively low cost. However, such sensors often have numerous limitations, such as low accuracy and poor durability. Capacitive force sensors measure changes in displacement between electrode layers separated by an elastomeric substrate, offering superior force sensitivity and dynamic response. Despite these advantages, their effective force range is limited and they are susceptible to environmental factors such as humidity and electromagnetic interference [13,18]. Piezoelectric sensors generate electric charge in response to mechanical stress through a trio-layer electrode–piezoelectric film–electrode configuration, providing low power consumption, structural simplicity, and high sensitivity. However, imperfect polarization alignment causes noise from extraneous forces, and their static force measurement is hindered by leakage currents in amplification circuitry. Inductive force sensors consist of a conductive top layer, elastomeric support, and bottom coils producing an electromagnetic field. External forces alter this field via relative movement, changing inductance and magneto resistance [2]. While inductive sensors offer low temperature sensitivity and improved repeatability, their bulky design complicates assembly, reduces insole comfort, and affects natural foot–insole interaction, potentially altering gait patterns.

In addition to pressure sensing, IMUs are typically integrated into or beneath the insole or ankle, combining accelerometers and gyroscopes to capture foot movement and posture [15]. IMUs are relatively insensitive to temperature and can provide dynamic information about the swing phase that pressure sensors alone cannot capture [1].

2.2 Computation Methods

Early research on gait and joint mobility assessment primarily relied on peak detection or threshold-based methods. These rule-based approaches often modeled gait phases using finite-state machines, segmentation heuristics, or template matching to delineate gait phases based on sensor signal features [5]. They typically leveraged statistical features in the time or frequency domain, offering fast and interpretable solutions [10].

More recently, the focus has shifted to data-driven techniques. Pressure sensors and IMU embedded in smart insoles generate spatially distributed pressure maps over time [12]. The pressure sensors embedded in insoles generate continuous 2D pressure distributions that characterise the foot-ground interaction throughout the gait cycle. These spatially structured signals are well suited for convolutional neural networks (CNNs), which can easily capture localized pressure variations and learn discriminative features associated with abnormal gait events or joint limitations. At the same time, inertial measurement units (IMUs) capture multichannel time-series data (e.g., acceleration, gyroscope) during the gait cycle, providing complementary information for understanding foot motion and orientation. Time-series models such as long-short-term memory (LSTM) networks have proven to be effective in capturing sequential dependencies in IMU signals [9].

3 Materials and Methods

3.1 The Smart Insole Hardware

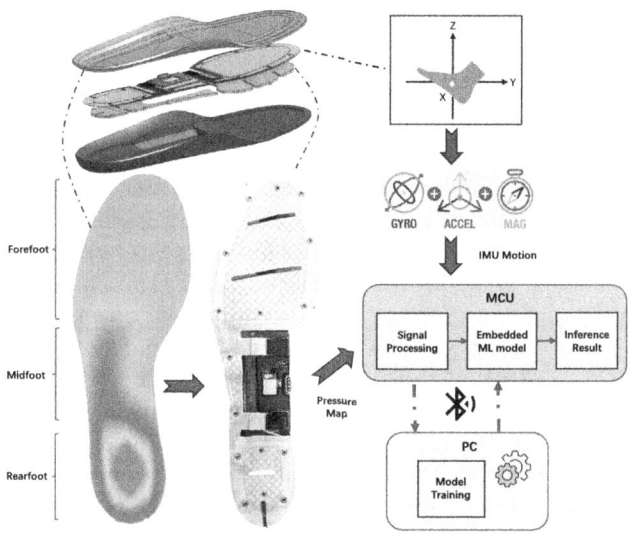

Fig. 1. Hardware setup of monitoring insole.

In this work, we employ capacitive pressure sensors to detect the distribution of plantar force in the insole. Encapsulated in multilayer flexible films, these sensors can be compactly distributed within a thin insole without affecting normal gait. The sensors are spread throughout the effective regions of the insole, the forefoot, midfoot, and rearfoot, which efficiently capture the key areas of force distribution on the plantar surface, as seen in Fig. 1. In addition, the IMU captures three-dimensional positional changes of the insole. After signal processing, the sampled data is transmitted wirelessly via Bluetooth to a personal computer

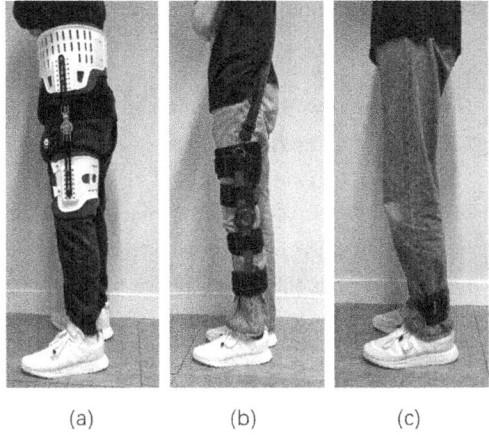

Fig. 2. Joint restriction apparatus used to simulate JML condition: (a) Hip limiter with mechanical linkage between waist and thigh to restrict flexion/extension; (b) Knee limiter using a lateral locking brace with angular stops to restrict flexion or extension; (c) Ankle limiter using external tethers with adjustable tension to restrict dorsiflexion or plantarflexion.

for model training. The resulting model is then quantized and converted into a binary file compatible with the MCU. Upon deploying the TinyML framework to the device, it can perform offline inference in real-time.

3.2 JML Protocol

This study investigates the effect of JML restrictions for lower-limb on gait characteristics by implementing a controlled experimental protocol using mechanical limiters to simulate reduced range of motion (ROM) at the ankle, knee and hip joints. Three types of mechanical joint ROM restriction devices (Ober, Shenzhen, China) were used to apply repeatable and standardized constraints, as shown in Fig. 2a–c.

- **Hip joint limiter (Fig. 2a):** Adjustable arms connected at the waist and thigh to align with the hip axis and limit flexion or extension.
- **Knee joint limiter (Fig. 2b):** Lateral locking brace allowing ROM adjustments from $-10°$ to $120°$ flexion and $-10°$ to $90°$ extension in $10°$ increments. A cross-body harness maintained balance.
- **Ankle joint limiter (Fig. 2c):** Adjustable front/rear tethers with tension dials limiting dorsiflexion or plantarflexion to approximately $5°$.

As summarized in Table 1, the study included 7 total gait conditions: 6 types of unilateral joint restriction (3 joints × 2 sides) and one normal walking condition as a baseline. This setting supports both fine-grained (joint-level) and coarse-grained (normal vs. impaired) gait classification and enables systematic evaluation of gait changes under simulated JML scenarios.

Table 1. Simulated Gait Conditions for Lower-Limb Joint Mobility Restrictions

Group	Label	Description
Baseline	NW	Normal walking without any joint restriction
JML Tasks	L_FK	Left knee joint with restricted flexion-extension
	L_FH	Left hip joint with restricted mobility
	L_FA	Left ankle restricted in plantarflexion
	R_FK	Right knee joint with restricted flexion-extension
	R_FH	Right hip joint with restricted mobility
	R_FA	Right ankle restricted in plantarflexion

The participant performed the motion protocol after a warm-up session. Gait data collection were conducted in an indoor space with approximately 4.8 m by 3 m space. Participants were instructed to walk freely along a figure-eight trajectory at a self-selected comfortable pace for approximately 2 min per trial. This unconstrained path and natural speed were designed to perform realistic gait patterns while accommodating the joint restriction apparatus. Each condition was repeated 5 times to ensure intraclass variability and robustness of the collected data.

3.3 Data Preprocessing

The raw pressure and IMU data collected from the smart insole were preprocessed through a series of steps to ensure temporal alignment, noise smooth, and normalization before model training. First, the raw CSV data was parsed to separate left and right foot sensor streams. Each stream included 12 pressure channels, 3-axis gyroscope, and 3-axis accelerometer signals. To ensure consistency, the lower-frame-rate side (left or right) was selected as the reference, and the higher-frame-rate stream was temporally aligned using merge_asof function based on timestamps. The aligned data were then uniformly resampled to 60 Hz using linear interpolation to standardize the temporal resolution across all trials and modalities. After resampling, a 6th order low-pass Butterworth filter with a cutoff frequency of 5 Hz was applied to each channel independently to attenuate high-frequency sensor noise while retaining meaningful gait dynamics, as demonstrate in Fig. 3. The outliers in each feature column were suppressed using interquartile range (IQR)-based trimming. Each signal channel was then normalized using z-score normalization, computed per trial to reflect intra-trial variability while avoiding data leakage. Specifically, for each channel, the mean and standard deviation were calculated and used to standardize the time series to zero mean and unit variance. Finally, cleaned and normalized sequences were segmented into fixed-length sliding windows of 2 s (120 time steps at 60 Hz, with stride = 120), allowing consistent input shape for model training and allowing localized gait features to be captured across different gait conditions.

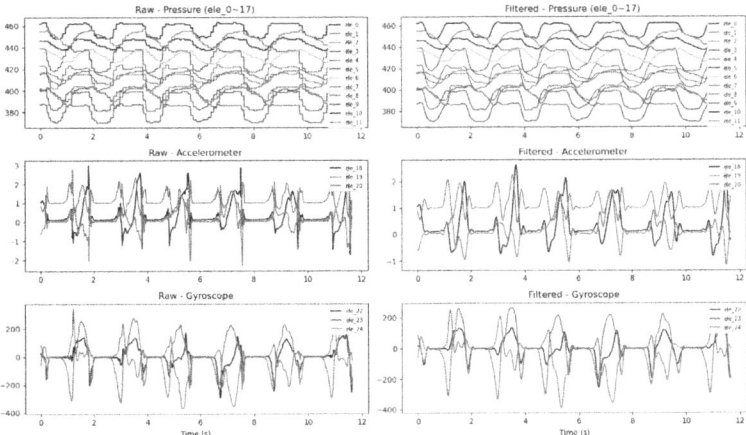

Fig. 3. Comparison of insole data before and after low-pass filter

3.4 Machine Learning Model Architecture

To classify lower-limb JML from wearable sensor data, we designed a LSTM Attention network. The model is tailored to process insole signals, capturing gait deviations and potential interlimb compensation patterns. Each input sample is a synchronized sequence of plantar pressure and IMU signals, split into left-side and right-side channels, resulting in a combined tensor of shape $(B, T, 36)$ where B is the batch size, T is the number of time steps (120), and 36 denotes 18 channels per foot.

The proposed machine learning model comprises a LSTM layers with n layers and hidden size H, followed by a lightweight temporal attention mechanism. The LSTM encodes the sequential dynamics of gait, capturing both short and long-term dependencies across time. To enhance the model's ability to focus on discriminative gait phases, a temporal attention module is applied to the LSTM outputs. Specifically, for each input branch, the LSTM produces a sequence of hidden states $h_t \in \mathbb{R}^{2H}$ for $t = 1, \ldots, T$. Each time step is assigned a scalar attention score via a learnable linear projection, and the scores are normalized using a Softmax function across the temporal dimension. The resulting attention weights are used to compute a context vector as a weighted sum of the LSTM outputs. This context vector, representing an adaptive summary of the entire sequence, is then passed through a dropout layer and a fully connected layer to generate predictions for joint impairment classification.

3.5 Multi-class Classification Labelling Strategy

The primary goal of this study is to determine whether joint mobility impairments can be identified using only insole-based sensory data. To this end, we adopted a unified multiclass classification model capable of detecting both the presence and the location of impairments. Performance was evaluated using confusion matrices and per-class accuracy.

Initially, the dataset included seven classes: L_FA, L_FK, L_FH, R_FA, R_FK, R_FH, and NW (normal walking). However, modeling both joint type and laterality increased classification complexity and misclassification risk. To reduce this, we merged left and right variants of each joint class, forming a simplified 4-class task: FA (ankle), FK (knee), FH (hip), and NW. This abstraction preserved clinical relevance while improving robustness and interpretability. To further enhance discrimination, we further implemented a side-specific training strategy as a comparison: the left-branch network was trained only on left-side impairment samples, and the right-branch on right-side samples.

4 Results and Discussion

4.1 The Proposed JML Dataset

The JML Gait dataset was created to enable fine-grained detection of lower-limb joint mobility impairments using wearable smart insole data. It includes simulated gait patterns for left and right limb impairments across 7 categories from 4 healthy adults. Each participant performed 5 trials per category (2 min each), totaling 140 trials (4.7 h). Data were collected via custom insoles equipped with 8 capacitive pressure sensors and a 9-axis IMU, sampled synchronously at 100 Hz.

- 7 gait categories (1 normal walking + 6 JML walking)
- 5 trials per category per participant
- Total: 140 trials, 4.7 h of data
- Sampling rate: 100 Hz
- Data: 18-channel pressure + 9-axis IMU, time-synchronized

All experimental procedures involving human participants were approved by the Ethics Committee of the University of Portsmouth (ID: TECH2025-DZ-01).

4.2 Model Implementation

We adopt Leave-One-Subject-Out (LOSO) cross-validation strategy to evaluate model generalization across individuals. In each fold, the model is trained on data from all but one subject and tested on the held-out subject, ensuring that no overlap exists between training and evaluation data. This subject-independent validation provides a rigorous assessment of the model's ability to generalize to unseen users in real-world deployment. The classification model is a unidirectional LSTM network designed for time-series gait data. It consists of two stacked layers (num_layers = 2) with a hidden size of 32 and a dropout rate of 0.5. The input dimension corresponds to the number of features per time step, and the output layer has 4 units for the gait classes. The hyperparameters were empirically tuned to balance the complexity of the model and the validation performance in the LOSO setting. Training uses the Adam optimizer with a learning rate of $1e^{-3}$ and a weight decay of 1×10^{-4} for regularization. To improve convergence and mitigate overfitting, a learning rate scheduler (ReduceLROnPlateau) is used, which reduces the learning rate by a factor of 0.5 if the validation accuracy does not improve for 10 consecutive epochs. With CrossEntropy Loss function for multiclass classification.

4.3 JML Classification Result

To evaluate the system's ability to identify specific joint mobility impairments, we performed a four-class classification task that involved three lower-limb joint limitations, including the ankle, knee, and hip in addition to normal walking. All models were trained under LOSO protocol.

However, the classification performance for the four-class task remains suboptimal. Firstly, the overall accuracy ranges from 51.78% (Subject-2) to 55.86% (Subject-3), indicating limited generalization under the LOSO setting. In terms of class-wise performance, the *FH* class (hip joint impairment) consistently shows the lowest recall and F1-score across subjects. For example, Subject-3 achieves a macro F1-score of only 0.487 despite a moderate overall accuracy of 55.86%. This discrepancy suggests that the model struggles particularly with distinguishing hip-related impairments. Further analysis of confusion matrices reveals frequent misclassification of the FH class into other categories, especially FK (knee) or NW (normal), implying that pressure and IMU signals derived from the foot may not capture distinctive features of hip dysfunction. These results suggest that current insole-based sensing is less effective at detecting hip joint limitations compared to ankle or knee impairments.

Therefore, to address the observed ambiguity and poor separability of the FH class, we redesigned the classification task to focus on three more distinguishable classes: FA, FK, and NW. The rationale behind this reduction is two-fold. First, the exclusion of the FH class reduces the degree of class overlap, potentially allowing the model to learn more discriminative features from the insole data. Second, both FA and FK involve distal joints, whose effects on plantar pressure and force distribution are more likely to be captured by insole sensors. In contrast, hip-related impairments may have less localized or more subtle manifestations in insole data, especially under constrained sampling conditions.

This simplified 3 classes setup allows us isolate the impact of hip joint data on classification performance. Importantly, this experiment was conducted without any changes in the model architecture or training hyper parameters (except output dimension), ensuring that observed performance differences are attributable solely to the modified classification task. Table 2 summarizes the classification metrics for each subject under the LOSO cross-validation scheme. As shown in the table, the model achieves average accuracies of 82.79%, 77.65%, 75.60%, and 88.78% for Subjects 1 through 4 respectively, resulting in an overall mean LOSO accuracy at 81.21%. This indicates a substantial improvement compared to the previous four-class classification task, highlighting the benefits of reducing class complexity and removing the challenging hip mobility impairment class. Furthermore, per class precision, recall, and F1-scores demonstrate relatively bal-

Table 2. Classification Performance Metrics for Each Subject (3-class classification)

Subject	Class	Precision	Recall	F1-score	Support	Accuracy
Subject-1	FA	0.8153	0.9066	0.8585	482	0.8279
	FK	0.8650	0.7088	0.7792	443	
	NW	0.8054	0.8824	0.8421	272	
Subject-2	FA	0.8136	0.6828	0.7425	454	0.7765
	FK	0.7685	0.8758	0.8187	451	
	NW	0.7342	0.7665	0.7500	227	
Subject-3	FA	0.7635	0.6008	0.6725	516	0.7560
	FK	0.7243	0.9567	0.8244	508	
	NW	0.8000	0.6475	0.7157	278	
Subject-4	FA	0.8267	0.9815	0.8975	486	0.8878
	FK	0.9110	0.9772	0.9429	482	
	NW	0.9954	0.6287	0.7706	342	

anced performance across FA, FK, and NW classes, with slightly lower recall values observed for certain classes in some subjects. These results suggest that the proposed model can effectively discriminate between these three impairment categories and normal walking under the given data conditions.

To evaluate whether decoupled left and right foot data exhibit differing capabilities in detecting unilateral JLM, we conducted LOSO training separately on left and right foot datasets. The label mappings for the three-class classification were defined as follows: Left foot labels: L-FA, L-FK, NW; Right foot labels: R-FA, R-FK, NW . Table 3 summarizes the best test accuracies and corresponding confusion matrices for each subject.

Table 3. LOSO Test Accuracy for Left and Right JML Data (3-class classification)

Subject	Left JML Accuracy	Right JML Accuracy
Subject-1	0.8996	0.8070
Subject-2	0.7915	0.7407
Subject-3	0.7584	0.7288
Subject-4	0.8523	0.8343
Average	0.8254	0.7777

Notably, the models trained on left foot data consistently outperformed those trained on right foot data across most subjects. This consistent difference in performance may arise from factors such as sensor placement variability, intrinsic biomechanical asymmetries, or side-specific manifestations of gait abnormalities.

4.4 Edge Deployment Performance

To enable real-time inference on resource-constrained embedded devices, the trained model was deployed to a commercial microcontroller using the TensorFlow Lite Micro (TFLM) library [4]. Model conversion and post-training quantization were performed using the `ai-edge-torch` pipeline, which translated the PyTorch model into a `float32` tflite format and compiled it into a C header for integration. The final quantized model contains 17,604 parameters and occupies approximately 1.5MB of RAM during inference on the ESP32-S3 N16R8 platform (ESPRESSIF; 16 MB flash, 8 MB PSRAM). A tensor arena of 500 KB was allocated to support intermediate tensors and runtime buffers. The system achieves a real-time inference rate of 5 Hz, demonstrating its suitability for low-latency, fully on-device gait assessment without external computational support.

5 Conclusion

This study demonstrates the feasibility of using wearable sensing specifically, pressure data and IMU signals collected from smart insoles for recognizing lower-limb JML. The proposed system successfully identifies multiple types of gait abnormalities associated with joint restrictions, leveraging lightweight models that are suitable for real-time deployment on low-power embedded platforms such as microcontrollers. Although the results are promising, it is important to acknowledge the limitations of the dataset. The JML Gait dataset used in this pilot study comprises only four participants. The primary objective of this work is not to achieve large-scale generalization, but rather to validate whether joint-specific impairments can be effectively distinguished using pressure and inertial signals in a controlled, repeatable setting.

Despite the limited participants size, our findings strongly support the central hypothesis: joint-specific restrictions induce distinct and detectable alterations in both foot-ground pressure profiles and lower-limb inertial dynamics. In particular, the experimental results demonstrate that impairments related to ankle and knee joint mobility yield distinguishable gait signatures in smart insole data. Models trained on the insole-based features were able to consistently differentiate between ankle and knee limitations, even when trained and evaluated under a subject-independent setting through applying LOSO cross-validation. These insights will inform the design of future, larger-scale data collection efforts, involving more diverse populations to develop robust, generalizable models.

References

1. Almuteb, I., Hua, R., Wang, Y.: Smart insoles review (2008–2021): applications, potentials, and future. Smart Health **25**, 100301 (2022). https://doi.org/10.1016/j.smhl.2022.100301
2. Chen, J.L., et al.: Plantar pressure-based insole gait monitoring techniques for diseases monitoring and analysis: a review. Adv. Mater. Technol. **7**(1), 2100566 (2022)

3. Dami, A., et al.: Lower limbs biomechanical deficits associated with stage 1 and 2 posterior tibialis tendon dysfunction during walking. Gait Posture **110**, 10–16 (2024)
4. David, R., et al.: Tensorflow lite micro: embedded machine learning for tinyml systems. Proc. Mach. Learn. Syst. **3**, 800–811 (2021)
5. Gao, S., Wang, Y., Fang, C., Xu, L.: A smart terrain identification technique based on electromyography, ground reaction force, and machine learning for lower limb rehabilitation. Appl. Sci. **10**(8) (2020). https://doi.org/10.3390/app10082638. https://www.mdpi.com/2076-3417/10/8/2638
6. Kaufman, K.R., Hughes, C., Morrey, B.F., Morrey, M., An, K.N.: Gait characteristics of patients with knee osteoarthritis. J. Biomech. **34**(7), 907–915 (2001)
7. Milner, C.E.: Is gait normal after total knee arthroplasty? Systematic review of the literature. J. Orthop. Sci. **14**, 114–120 (2009)
8. Muro-De-La-Herran, A., Garcia-Zapirain, B., Mendez-Zorrilla, A.: Gait analysis methods: an overview of wearable and non-wearable systems, highlighting clinical applications. Sensors **14**(2), 3362–3394 (2014)
9. Palazzo, L., et al.: A deep learning-based framework oriented to pathological gait recognition with inertial sensors. Sensors (Basel, Switzerland) **25**(1), 260 (2025)
10. Prasanth, H., et al.: Wearable sensor-based real-time gait detection: a systematic review. Sensors **21**(8) (2021). https://doi.org/10.3390/s21082727. https://www.mdpi.com/1424-8220/21/8/2727
11. Reese, N.B., Bandy, W.D.: Joint range of motion and muscle length testing-e-book: joint range of motion and muscle length testing-e-book. Elsevier Health Sci. (2016)
12. Saboor, A., et al.: Latest research trends in gait analysis using wearable sensors and machine learning: a systematic review. IEEE Access **8**, 167830–167864 (2020)
13. Santos, V.M., Gomes, B.B., Neto, M.A., Amaro, A.M.: A systematic review of insole sensor technology: recent studies and future directions. Appl. Sci. **14**(14) (2024). https://doi.org/10.3390/app14146085. https://www.mdpi.com/2076-3417/14/14/6085
14. Steultjens, M., Dekker, J., Van Baar, M., Oostendorp, R., Bijlsma, J.: Range of joint motion and disability in patients with osteoarthritis of the knee or hip. Rheumatology **39**(9), 955–961 (2000)
15. Vu, H.T.T., et al.: A review of gait phase detection algorithms for lower limb prostheses. Sensors **20**(14) (2020). https://doi.org/10.3390/s20143972. https://www.mdpi.com/1424-8220/20/14/3972
16. Warden, P., Situnayake, D.: TinyML: Machine Learning with Tensorflow Lite on Arduino and Ultra-Low-Power Microcontrollers. O'Reilly Media (2019)
17. World Health Organization: Ageing and health (2022). https://www.who.int/news-room/fact-sheets/detail/ageing-and-health. Accessed 03 June 2025
18. Zhang, D., Liu, Y., Exell, T., Huang, Y., Zhou, D., Guo, L.: Estimation of three-dimensional ground reaction forces using low-cost smart insoles. Intell. Sports Health **1**(1), 40–50 (2025)

Tri-Plane Rhythmic Signal Generation and Adaptive Oscillator Tracking: A Novel Framework for Motion Analysis

Haoran Zhang[1,2,3], Yichen Lin[1,2], Xiuyuan Wu[1,2,3], Yu Zhu[1,2], Xinyang Du[1,2], Xiangyang Wang[1], Jianquan Sun[1,2], and Yue Ma[1,2(✉)]

[1] Guangdong Provincial Key Lab of Robotics and Intelligent System, Shenzhen Institute of Advanced Technology, Chinese Academy of Sciences, Shenzhen 518005, China
[2] SIAT-CUHK Joint Laboratory of Robotics and Intelligent Systems, Shenzhen, Guangdong, China
yue.ma@siat.ac.cn
[3] University of Chinese Academy of Sciences, Beijing, China

Abstract. Rhythm tracking is of great significance in the fields of health medicine and sports science. With the development of exoskeletons and wearable sensing devices, the demand for rhythm tracking of complex and multiple human movement patterns has become even greater. However, current research finds it difficult to achieve a balance among the generalization, real-time performance and accuracy of rhythm tracking. In response to the above challenges, this paper designs a rhythm tracking framework based on wearable sensing devices. Through experimental tests on five subjects, it was verified that the method proposed in this paper guarantees the generalization, real-time performance and accuracy of rhythm tracking to a certain extent. The specific analysis results revealed that the proposed method decreased by 56.4%–95.6% in the RMSE of phase estimation compared with the traditional uniaxial signal extraction method.

Keywords: IMU · rhythm tracking · motion planes · AO

1 Introduction

In recent years, wearable sensing technology has developed rapidly and has been widely applied and attracted attention in fields such as biomechanics, rehabilitation medicine and sports science. The precise capture and analysis of human movement rhythms (such as periodic gait and limb coordination frequency) is of crucial significance in fields such as clinical diagnosis, rehabilitation intervention and human-computer interaction [1,2].

Studies have shown that for the lower extremity exoskeleton to achieve efficient and natural human-computer interaction, it is necessary to synchronize the assistance with gait [3]. Usually, the gait phase recognition method can achieve the above purpose. At present Gait phase recognition methods include rule-based methods (threshain-based [4], finite state machine [5], fuzzy reasoning [6]), and machine learning [7], adaptive oscillator [8], wavelet transformation-based method [9], etc. Among them, the Adaptive Oscillator (AO) is a gait recognition method based on the frequency domain. It can synchronize with any periodic or pseudo-periodic input signal without any preprocessing [10]. It is also the baseline selected for rhythm tracking in this paper.

Human movement is a periodic behavior involving the coordination of multiple joints and multiple motion planes, and the signals generated should also be multi-channel. A single signal and phase recognition method cannot effectively deal with complex human movements. Therefore, before conducting rhythm tracking of human movements, feature selection of many signal components is required. However, the article [11] points out that some feature selection methods, like mRMR(Max-Relevance and Min-Redundancy), have the characteristics of high time complexity and low accuracy when the number of samples is small. To sum up the limitations mentioned above, it is very difficult to achieve a balance in the generalization, real-time performance and accuracy of rhythm tracking.

In response to the above challenges, this paper designs a rhythm tracking framework based on wearable sensing devices. Firstly, the IMU data in the human motion experiment is collected through wearable sensing devices. Subsequently, the calibrated signal components will enter the rhythm tracking framework, and a motion plane will be selected through dimension enhancement, dimension reduction, analytic hierarchy process evaluation, filtering and clustering. Finally, based on the selected motion plane, a rhythm signal is generated and input into an adaptive oscillator for rhythm tracking, thereby identifying the frequency and phase of human movement.

The innovative contributions of this article are as follows:

1) A rhythm tracking framework is proposed. In this framework, data streams of two sampling frequencies run smoothly and rhythm signals are generated for three motion planes, which improves the accuracy of rhythm phase estimation and ensures the real-time performance and generalization of rhythm tracking to a certain extent.

The structure of this article is as follows: The second chapter introduces wearable sensing devices and rhythm tracking frameworks; The third chapter introduces the experimental part in detail; The fourth chapter presents the experimental results and makes a discussion. Chapter Five summarizes the above work.

2 Method

This chapter first briefly introduces wearable devices and experimental platforms. Finally, the rhythm tracking framework proposed in this paper is elaborated in detail in five parts, including sliding window generation, abnormal movement detection, evaluation and selection of the motion plane, generation of rhythm signals and rhythm tracking.

2.1 Equipment and Platform

As shown in Fig. 1a, this paper designs and manufactures a wearable sensing device composed of an IMU and a binding structure. The layout of the sensors is shown in Fig. 1b, mainly distributed on both sides of the thighs, both sides of the calves, and the waist, totaling 5. The peripheral devices of the experimental platform are shown in Fig. 1c, including a computer, a Speedgoat and a digital power supply.

2.2 Rhythm Tracking Framework

To achieve rhythm tracking of different rhythmic movements of the human body, a rhythm tracking framework is proposed in this part of this paper, as shown in Fig. 2. The framework is mainly divided into five parts, including sliding window generation, abnormal movement detection, evaluation and alignment of the motion plane, generation of rhythm signals, and rhythm tracking. The input is calibrated IMU data; Output the comprehensive scores of the three motion planes and the phases and frequencies of the rhythms.

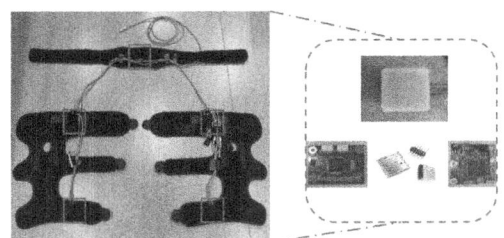

(a) Wearable Sensing Device

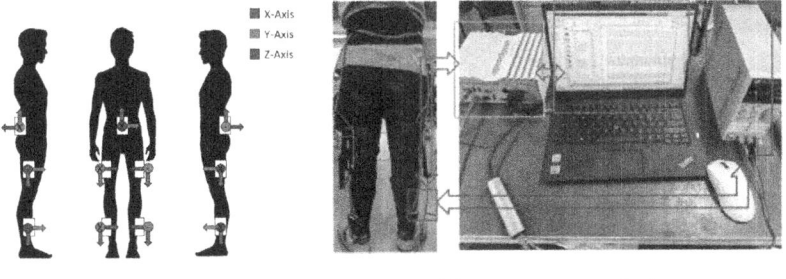

(b) Sensor layout (c) Experimental platform

Fig. 1. Wearable Sensing Devices And Experimental Platforms

Sliding Window and Anomaly Detection. To ensure the agility of the framework's operation, the framework is composed of data streams with two sampling frequencies. The first type is the data flow rhythm signal generation and tracking part with a sampling frequency of 1000 Hz; The second type of data stream with a sampling frequency of 100 Hz passes through the plane evaluation and selection section. To ensure the smooth operation of the two data streams within the framework, we have adopted the sliding window and anomaly detection mechanism. The length of the sliding window is 200 data frames, and the overlapping part between the Windows is 50%, that is, the time length of each window is 2 s, and the step time length is 1 s. Anomaly detection mainly involves monitoring the angular velocity of each IMU data channel.

Plane Evaluation and Selection. To ensure the continuity of the generated rhythm signal, the scheme we present (as shown in Fig. 3) is as follows: Select one plane from the three motion planes, and then select or generate one signal from the five signal components. The execution process of this scheme includes dimension increasement, dimension decreasement, analytic hierarchy process evaluation, mean filtering and clustering.

First, the dimension is upgraded by taking components(projection angle) of each IMU according to the three motion planes; Then, Based on the following rules, we reduce the dimension of the signal channels: 1) The IMU components contained in each moving plane need to be the same. 2) The selection of signal channels should conform to the degree of freedom of human joints. The given solution is to select only the IMU signal components located on both sides of the waist and thighs for each plane.

To evaluate the rhythmality of each motion plane, we use the Analytic Hierarchy Process to construct an evaluation model. The evaluation model(as shown in Fig. 4a) is constructed by taking the weight coefficients of the obtained characteristic indicators as the target layer, the selected IMU as the criterion layer, and the characteristic indicators as the scheme layer. Among them, the characteristic indicators include: autocorrelation peak, root mean square value, standard deviation, and main frequency energy. And finally perform weighted summation of the feature components of each plane to obtain the comprehensive score.

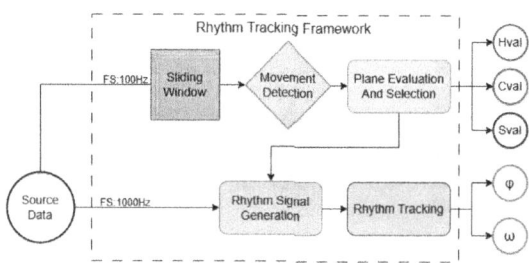

Fig. 2. Rhythm Tracking Framework

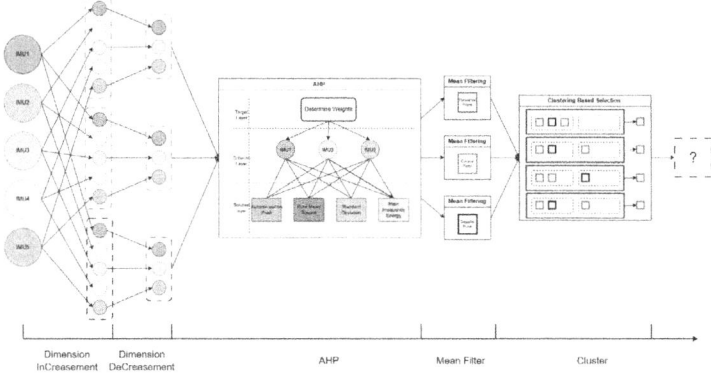

Fig. 3. Plane Evaluation and Selection

By comparing the indicators at the same level in pairs, we can obtain the judgment matrix, as shown in the formula (1). The element a_{ij} of the matrix represents the importance of the i th index at that level relative to the j th index, taking the value of a positive integer 1~10, and $a_{ji} = 1/a_{ij}$. The eigenvector corresponding to the maximum eigenvalue and the consistency ratio of each layer of the judgment matrix should be calculated to conduct the sorting consistency check(ensuring that $CR < 0.1$) at each level according to formula (2) and Table 1. Suppose the weight vector of the criterion layer A to the target layer is $\omega_A = (\omega_{a_1}, \omega_{a_2}, \cdots, \omega_{a_j}), j = m$, the weight vectors of each scheme b_j in the scheme layer B to the criterion layer A are $\omega_{B_j} = (\omega_{B_1}, \omega_{B_2}, ...\omega_{b_k}), k = n, j = m$. Then we can obtain the total sorting weight W_b and the total sorting consistency ratio CR_b of the scheme layer through the formula (3).

$$A = \begin{pmatrix} a_{11} & \cdots & a_{1m} \\ \vdots & \ddots & \vdots \\ a_{m1} & \cdots & a_{mm} \end{pmatrix}, B_i = \begin{pmatrix} b_{11} & \cdots & b_{1n} \\ \vdots & \ddots & \vdots \\ b_{n1} & \cdots & b_{nn} \end{pmatrix} \qquad (1)$$

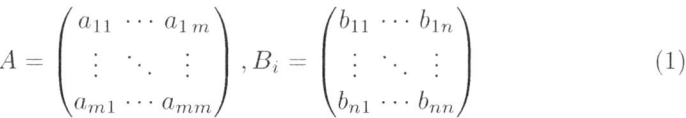

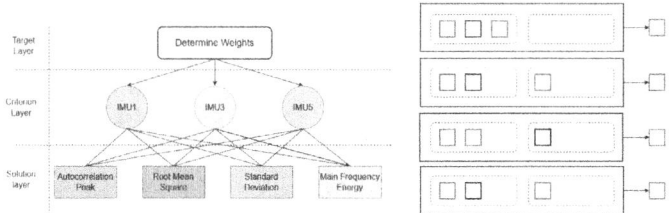

(a) Analytic Hierarchy Process   (b) Simpling Clustering

Fig. 4. AHP And Cluster (Color figure online)

Table 1. Consistency Index RI

n	1	2	3	4	5	6	7	8	9
RI	0	0	0.58	0.89	1.12	1.24	1.32	1.41	1.45

$$A\omega = \lambda\omega, CI = \frac{\lambda - n}{n - 1}, CR = \frac{CI}{RI} \qquad (2)$$

$$W_{b_i} = \sum_{j=1}^{m} \omega_{a_j}\omega_{b_{ji}}, CR_b = \frac{\sum_{j=1}^{m} \omega_{a_j} CI_{b_j}}{RI_b} \qquad (3)$$

To smooth the scoring curve, we perform mean filtering on the scoring curve, determine the situation through clustering before determining the final plane, and finally decide the selection of the final motion plane based on the different clustering situations. Clustering determination is triggered by the score difference and simple clustering is carried out based on the threshold, as shown in the Fig. 4b (The red boxes represent the H-plane scores, the green boxes represent the C-plane scores, and the blue boxes represent the S-plane scores).

Rhythm Signal Generation And Rhythm Tracking. After the plane is selected, the signal channel specific to the plane can be selected or generated. The specific operation of each plane is as follows: For the generation of rhythm signals in the H-plane and S-plane, we first filter the signal components of the three selected IMUs (such as the formula (4), Take $K_1 = K_2 = 1, \alpha_1 = 0.58\pi, \omega_1 = 0.6\pi, \alpha_2 = 4\pi, \omega_2 = 6\pi$), and then sum them up and take the average. For the corolla, we first process the three IMU signal components $(s_i(t), i = 1, 3, 5)$ based on (5) (t_1 is the length of the time window), and then through the filter (4)(take $K_1 = K_2 = 1, \alpha_1 = 0.78\pi, \omega_1 = 0.8\pi, \alpha_2 = 4\pi, \omega_2 = 6\pi$).

$$H(s) = \frac{K_1 \cdot s}{s^2 + \alpha_1 \cdot s + \omega_1^2} \cdot \frac{K_2 \cdot s}{s^2 + \alpha_2 \cdot s + \omega_2^2} \qquad (4)$$

$$\int_0^{t_1} s_1(t) + \frac{s_3(t) - s_5(t)}{5} dt \qquad (5)$$

An Adaptive Oscillator(AO) is an oscillator that automatically adjusts its parameters in response to changes in the input signal [10]. The AO network adopted in this paper is the AO network designed in [12].

3 Experiment

This paper's experiment is based on three planes of the human body (H-plane as horizontal plane, C-plane as coronal plane and S-plane as sagittal plane), and selects five common representative movement patterns in human life (including

TB, BR, HK, SS and BL). The specific movement sampling situation is shown in Table 2. There were 5 participants in this experiment (5 men; Age: 24 ± 2, Height: 168 ± 8 cm).

3.1 Experimental Indicators

This paper evaluates the accuracy of the rhythm tracking framework in this paper by examining period estimation and phase estimation. The control group we set up takes the projected Angle between the two legs on the sagittal plane as the input signal of AO and directly outputs the circular frequency and phase. Regarding the period estimation, we take the period mean as the evaluation index. Regarding phase estimation, we take the root mean square error between the estimated phase and the actual phase as the evaluation index. And by conducting independent sample t-tests on the data of the two groups of samples, it is determined whether there is a statistical difference. $p - value < 0.5$ is considered significant. Ten sample points are sampled between the first and last two points of the actual phase curve $p_a(t)$ and the estimated phase curve $p_f f(t)$ in the same period. Obtain the sample data $S_f = [p_f(t_1), p_f(t_2), \cdots, p_f(t_{10})]$, $S_a = [p_a(t_1), p_a(t_2), \cdots, p_a(t_{10})]$. Finally, the root mean square error can be obtained through the formula (6).

$$RMSE = \sqrt{\frac{\sum_{k=1}^{n}(S_f(k) - S_a(k))^2}{n}} \quad (6)$$

Table 2. Action Patterns And Sampling

	Mode	Sampling	Legend
1	Body Rotation(BR)	20 left, 20 right, alternating	
2	Body Lateral(BL)	20 left, 20 right, alternating	
3	Side Step(SS)	20 left, 20 right, alternating	
4	Trunk Bending(TB)	20	
5	High Knee(HK)	20 left, 20 right, alternating	

4 Result

The experimental results of the first stage are shown in the Table 3. The abscissa of each graph has been resampled and aligned. The range of values for the ordinate of each column of the graph is consistent. The rows corresponding to the figures marked in red in the table are the planes selected for the rhythm tracking framework of this article. Whether compared vertically or horizontally, the differences in rhythm signals generated by different motion planes of different motion patterns are relatively significant. Therefore, to a certain extent, the method of generating rhythm signals based on planes in the rhythm tracking framework of this paper is feasible.

The results of the second stage of the experiment are shown in Fig. 5. The six legends from top to bottom respectively show the recognition of the moving plane (1 for the H-plane; 2 for C-plane; 3 for S-plane); H-plane Signal; C-plane Signal; S-plane Signal; Recognition of the selected signal by the plane of motion; AO phase identification. From the figure, we can see that during the continuous execution of different action patterns by the subjects, the extraction, selection and phase tracking of the rhythm signals are good, which indicates that our rhythm tracking framework is effective.

The statistical analysis results of the third-stage experiment are shown in Fig. 6. The horizontal axis represents the action mode, the vertical axis represents the estimation of the period or phase. The type of value is periodic mean in Fig. 6a, and is rmse of phase in Fig. 6b. The prominent logo of three stars represents a p-value<0.001. Our method has higher accuracy in rhythm phase

Table 3. Three-Planes Based Rhythm Signal

	Body Rotation	Side Step	Body lateral	Trunk Bend	High Knee
horizontal plane					
coronal plane					
vertical plane					

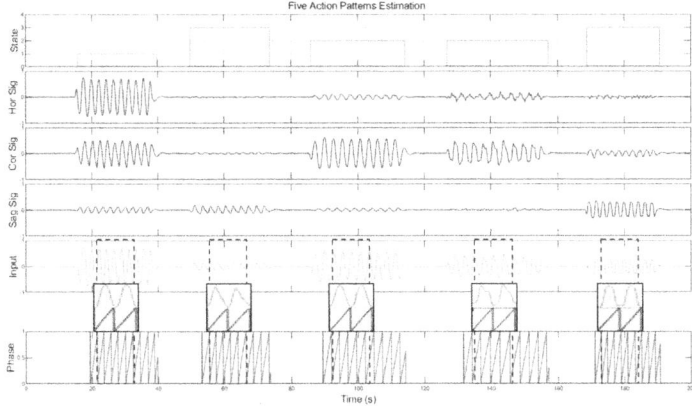

Fig. 5. Continuous Estimation Result

estimation compared to the traditional single-axis signal input method, which is specifically manifested in the reduction of the root mean square error by 56.4%–95.6%.

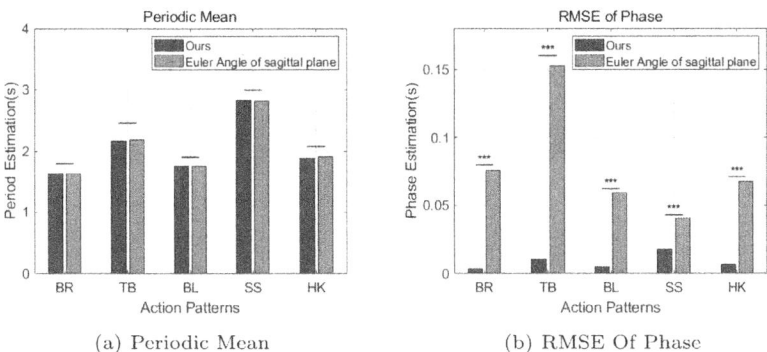

(a) Periodic Mean

(b) RMSE Of Phase

Fig. 6. Statistical Result

5 Conclusion

This paper innovatively proposes a rhythm tracking framework based on wearable sensing devices. The framework is mainly divided into five parts, including sliding window generation, abnormal movement detection, evaluation and alignment of the motion plane, generation of rhythm signals, and rhythm tracking. When paired with appropriate wearable sensing devices and IMU layout, it can demonstrate excellent rhythm tracking performance in different action modes.

Acknowledgement. This research was supported by the National Natural Science Foundation of China (Grant No. 62473359). This research was supported by the National Natural Science Foundation of China (Grant No. U23A20344). This work was supported by Shenzhen Medical Research Fund under Grant D2401008. Shenzhen Science and Technology Program (JCYJ20240813155852067).

References

1. Felius, R.A., Geerars, M., Bruijn, S.M., van Dieën, J.H., Wouda, N.C., Punt, M.: Reliability of IMU-based gait assessment in clinical stroke rehabilitation. Sensors **22**(3), 908 (2022)
2. Meghji, M., Balloch, A., et al.: An algorithm for the automatic detection and quantification of athletes' change of direction incidents using IMU sensor data. IEEE Sens. J. **19**(12), 4518–4527 (2019)
3. Wang, X., Guo, S., Bai, S.: A cable-driven parallel hip exoskeleton for high-performance walking assistance. IEEE Trans. Industr. Electron. **71**(3), 2705–2715 (2024)
4. Maqbool, H.F., Husman, M.A.B., et al.: A real-time gait event detection for lower limb prosthesis control and evaluation. IEEE Trans. Neural Syst. Rehabil. Eng. **25**(9), 1500–1509 (2017)
5. Van Nguyen, L., La, H.M.: Real-time human foot motion localization algorithm with dynamic speed. IEEE Trans. Hum.-Mach. Syst. **46**(6), 822–833 (2016)
6. Pappas, I., Popovic, M., Keller, T., Dietz, V., Morari, M.: A reliable gait phase detection system. IEEE Trans. Neural Syst. Rehabil. Eng. **9**(2), 113–125 (2001)
7. Wei, H., Tong, R.K.-Y., Wang, M.Y., Chen, C.: Gait phase detection based on LSTM-CRF for stair ambulation. IEEE Robot. Autom. Lett. **8**(9), 6029–6035 (2023)
8. Qian, Y., Wang, Y., Chen, C., et al.: Predictive locomotion mode recognition and accurate gait phase estimation for hip exoskeleton on various terrains. IEEE Robot. Autom. Lett. **7**(3), 6439–6446 (2022)
9. Livolsi, C., Conti, R., Giovacchini, F., Vitiello, N., Crea, S.: A novel wavelet-based gait segmentation method for a portable hip exoskeleton. IEEE Trans. Rob. **38**(3), 1503–1517 (2022)
10. Righetti, L., Buchli, J., Ijspeert, A.J.: Dynamic Hebbian learning in adaptive frequency oscillators. Physica D **216**(2), 269–281 (2006)
11. Roffo, G., Melzi, S., Castellani, U., Vinciarelli, A., Cristani, M.: Infinite feature selection: a graph-based feature filtering approach. IEEE Trans. Pattern Anal. Mach. Intell. **43**(12), 4396–4410 (2021)
12. Ronsse, R., De Rossi, S.M.M., et al.: Real-time estimate of velocity and acceleration of quasi-periodic signals using adaptive oscillators. IEEE Trans. Robot. **29**(3), 783–791 (2013)

A Marker-Free Motion Capture System Built on Unsynchronized Cameras

Haofei Hou, Shunyi Zhao, Zuxin Fan, Wei Jin, Jintao Zhu, Lecheng Ruan[✉], and Qining Wang[✉]

School of Advanced Manufacturing and Robotics, Peking University, Beijing 100871, China
ruanlecheng@ucla.edu, qiningwang@pku.edu.cn

Abstract. Human Motion Capture (MoCap) involves tracking and recording human movements. Image-based MoCap systems have gained significant research interest, particularly for their simplified deployment that eliminates the requirement for reflective markers and wearable sensors. However, the deployment of such systems faces two major challenges: temporal misalignments caused by unsynchronized cameras and the sparsity of detectable features on human bodies. To address these limitations, we propose a marker-free MoCap system built on unsynchronized cameras. For the temporal misalignment issue, we introduce two crucial components: multi-view temporal post-processing and temporal augmentation training, which enable automatic temporal alignment across multiple cameras. To overcome feature sparsity, we define virtual markers as 3D surface points on the human mesh model. Experimental results validate the high performance of our system in global marker localization. The proposed approach presents a scalable and flexible solution for MoCap deployment in unconstrained environments, showing promise for applications in mobile health monitoring and sports training.

Keywords: Motion Capture · Temporal Augmentation · Spatiotemporal Fusion

1 Introduction

Human Motion Capture (MoCap) refers to a technology for tracking and recording human movements. The captured movements can be analyzed or reproduced for applications in domains including healthcare and sports training [1,2].

Various technologies, such as infrared cameras and Inertial Measurement Units (IMUs), have been deployed into MoCap systems and used in different application scenarios [3]. Employing reflective markers as explicit features, infrared camera-based MoCap systems track the 3D positions of reflective markers to represent human motions, offering high accuracy [4]. Thus, infrared camera-based MoCap systems are usually adopted in indoor applications, such

---

H. Hou and S. Zhao—Contributed equally to this work.

as biomechanics and animation production [5]. In contrast, IMU-based systems, which require IMU mounted on different body segments, enable wearable and portable deployments in unconstrained and outdoor settings [6].

Image-based methods provide an alternative approach for human MoCap, offering advantages in deployment simplicity and application scope [7]. By analyzing spatial relationships between body segments, image-based MoCap avoids the need for physical attachments such as reflective markers and wearable sensors, thus avoiding related issues like detachment [8]. Furthermore, image-based MoCap systems show low drift and high adaptability to varying conditions, benefiting from low system noise and well-established image processing methods [9]. These advantages make image-based MoCap systems adaptable to broad application scenarios, from indoor to outdoor spaces [10]. Recent studies have addressed the limitations of monocular cameras, including occlusion problems and insufficient depth constraints, through multiple camera deployment [11]. However, the approach based on multiple cameras increases deployment complexity [12].

Temporal misalignment between cameras, termed *unsynchronized cameras*, affects the deployment of image-based MoCap systems [13]. While hardware-level synchronization between multiple cameras is essential, it typically requires close-range wired connections, thus limiting the operational range of multi-camera image-based MoCap systems [14]. For spatially distant cameras that primarily rely on network connections, achieving precise hardware synchronization becomes particularly challenging [15]. In the absence of hardware synchronization capabilities, researchers typically resort to network-based synchronization or post-processing approaches, such as synchronization actions [16]. Network synchronization is susceptible to network latency, while post-processing methods increase manual workload and prevent real-time MoCap [17]. This synchronization issue results in inconsistent observations of the same motion event across different cameras, compromising the performance of multi-camera image-based MoCap systems [18].

The marker-free characteristic also affects the deployment of image-based MoCap systems [19]. Instead of physical markers, image-based methods utilize either 2D texture features, such as SIFT, or 3D geometry features, such as lines and planes [20]. However, 3D geometry features are distributed sparsely on the human body [11]. And 2D texture features lack specificity with stationary body segments [21], such as 3D joint positions. To address the challenges, existing image-based MoCap systems extract skeletal coordinates from the images using deep learning-based methods, rather than visual features on surfaces [22]. The implicit mapping from surface to skeletal coordinates may increase training complexity and the instability of multi-view fusion, potentially affecting system deployment [23].

In this paper, to address the deployment complexity caused by unsynchronized cameras and the marker-free characteristic of image-based MoCap systems, we propose a MoCap system (1) aligning the timestamps between cameras automatically, and (2) optimizing surface-level features directly. By incorporating temporal augmentation during training and a multi-view temporal post-processing strategy, we enable robust fusion across unsynchronized views. To mitigate feature sparsity, we introduce virtual markers which are 3D surface points located near the target physical markers. They can serve as more consistent and informative spatial cues.

The contributions of this paper are listed as:

(1) We propose a MoCap system that automatically aligns the timestamps between unsynchronized cameras. With temporal augmentation training and multi-view temporal post-processing, the proposed system can deal with the temporal misalignment.
(2) We employ human virtual marker extraction to enhance feature information, thereby improving the accuracy of the proposed marker-free MoCap system.
(3) We conduct comprehensive experiments to validate the performance of the proposed marker-free MoCap system. Various human motion types, including walking, running, and in-place motions, are included in our experiments.

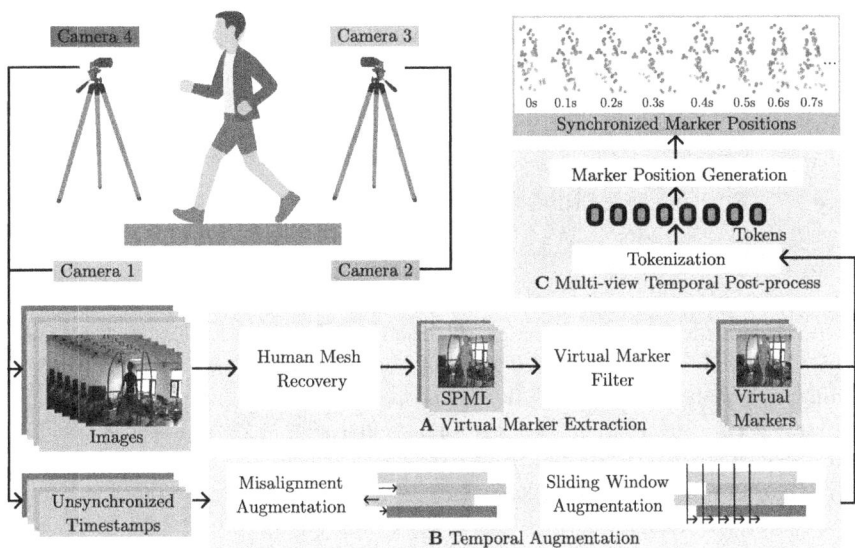

Fig. 1. Pipeline of the proposed MoCap system. **A** shows the 3D human mesh for each frame is recovered, from which virtual markers are filtered by a manually designed mapping to enhance feature information. **B** illustrates that we incorporate temporal data augmentation during training to enhance the model's temporal alignment capability. **C** presents our transformer-based post-process model that fuses multi-view and temporal camera information within a temporal window.

2 System Definition

Our MoCap system takes multiview images with unsynchronized timestamps as inputs. The system then obtains synchronized 3D coordinates of predefined human body landmarks from these images.

Given N unsynchronized cameras $C = \{c^1, c^2, ...c^n\}$, where c^1 is designated as the main camera, each camera c^i has intrinsic parameters K^i, sampling characteristics f^i and σ^i. $K^i \in \mathbb{R}^{3\times 3}$ is the intrinsic matrix, including focal length and optical center. f^i and σ^i are the frame rate and capture time variance. Each camera c^i is also characterized by its extrinsic parameters (R^i, T^i), where $R^i \in \mathbb{R}^{3\times 3}$ and $T^i \in \mathbb{R}^3$ define the transformation from the coordinate system of camera c^i to that of the main camera. Let $x^i \in \mathbb{R}^3$ be a 3D point in the camera c^i coordinate system and $\boldsymbol{x} \in \mathbb{R}^3$ be its corresponding coordinate in the world coordinate system. The transformation between these coordinates is given by:

$$\boldsymbol{x} = R \cdot (R^i x^i + T^i) + T, \tag{1}$$

where $R \in \mathbb{R}^{3\times 3}$ and $T \in \mathbb{R}^3$ define the transformation from the main camera coordinate to the world coordinate, which is unknown.

Each camera c^i captures an image sequence $\{I_j^i\}$ at its own timestamps $\{t_j^i\}$. Timestamps are not synchronized across different cameras. Each camera's timestamp has an unknown fixed bias B^i from the global timestamp.

$$\tau_j^i = t_j^i + B^i, \tag{2}$$

where $\tau_j^i \in \mathbb{R}$ is the global timestamp for image I_j^i. We can assume that $|B^i| \leq \epsilon$, $B^1 = 0$, and $t_{j+1}^i - t_j^i \sim \mathcal{N}(1/f^i, (\sigma^i)^2)$, where ϵ is synchronization time for system.

Consider we have a defined marker set M, an expected total MoCap time t_c, and required output frequency f. Each marker is attached to the human body. Our goal is fusing all unsynchronized and multi-view information, and calculating the synchronized global position of the defined marker set $Y = \{y_i = [\boldsymbol{x}_0^{m,i}, \boldsymbol{x}_1^{m,i}, \boldsymbol{x}_2^{m,i}] | m \in M, i \in [0, t_c \times f)\}$, where $\boldsymbol{x}^{m,i} \in \mathbb{R}^3$ represents the global position of marker m in global time i/f.

We can cut the image sequence into time window δ to divide the problem into smaller problems,

$$W_d = \{(I_j^i, t_j^i) | d\delta \leq t_j^i \leq (d+1)\delta\}. \tag{3}$$

For each window W_d, we calculate the results $\hat{Y}_d = \{\hat{y}_i\}$. The overall result is obtained by aggregating all window outputs: $\hat{Y} = \bigcup_d \hat{Y}_d$, where $\hat{Y}$ represents the final set of predictions.

3 Methodology

As shown in Fig. 1, we propose a MoCap system that features three key components: temporal augmentation for improved tolerance to timing misalignments, virtual markers near the body surface for enhanced spatial features, and a transformer-based fusion model for processing unsynchronized multiview data.

3.1 Virtual Marker Extraction

To obtain richer feature information and achieve better MoCap performance in marker-free settings, we extract and filter the coordinates of virtual markers located near the target of the human mesh and use them as input for the next stage. The 3D human mesh for each frame is estimated using advanced human mesh recovery methods [24], which are represented by f_{HMR} and can be defined as

$$V_j^i, J_j^i, \beta_j^i = f_{\text{HMR}}(I_j^i, K^i). \tag{4}$$

In Eq. (4), $V_j^i = \{p_{j,k}^i \in \mathbb{R}^3\}$ represents the estimated human mesh vertices, each $p_{j,k}^i$ represents the position of a vertex in coordinate in camera c^i. $J_j^i = \{r_{j,k}^i \in \mathbb{R}^3\}$ represents the estimated human joints rotation, each $r_{j,k}^i$ represents a rotation vector of a joint in the coordinate of camera c^i. The shape parameters β_j^i control the body's physique, muscle structure, and other characteristics, and are represented as a ten-dimensional vector.

A fixed mapping $\mathcal{K}$ is manually defined between virtual markers and mesh vertices on the Sparse Principal Manifold Learning (SPML) human model, based on empirical selection according to their spatial proximity to the target physical markers. These selected vertices, virtual markers, serve as key visual features for subsequent processing.

3.2 Multi-view Temporal Post-process

We propose a transformer-based multi-view human motion temporal post-process model [25]. After receiving feature information from each camera, the system first tokenizes the data and then passes it through a transformer-based network to obtain synchronized coordinates of target marker points.

Each window W_d is tokenized into a discrete representation X_d. Each token encodes a single observation from one of the n unsynchronized cameras, and is constructed to include all relevant information projected into the main camera coordinate system. Formally, each token $\mathbb{T}_j^i \in X_d$ is a vector comprising the following components:

$$\mathbb{T}_j^i = \left[\text{OneHot}(i), t_j^i/\delta - d, \beta_j^i, \{R^i \times r_{j,k}^i\}, \{R^i \times p_{j,\mathcal{K}(m)}^i + T^i | m \in M\}\right], \tag{5}$$

where $\{R^i \times r_{j,k}^i\}$ represents joint position features, $\{R^i \times p_{j,\mathcal{K}(m)}^i + T^i | m \in M\}$ denotes virtual marker features, and all tokens are sorted and embedded temporally using their normalized timestamps $t_j^i/\delta - d$. We further apply sinusoidal positional encoding (using cosine-based functions) across the entire token sequence to capture global temporal dependencies.

The transformer model with parameters w processes these sequential representations, capturing spatiotemporal dependencies and generating tokens on marker position $\hat{Y}_d$:

$$\hat{Y}_d = \text{Transformer}(\{\mathbb{T}_j^i\}, w). \tag{6}$$

Detailed model specification can be found in Sect. 4.

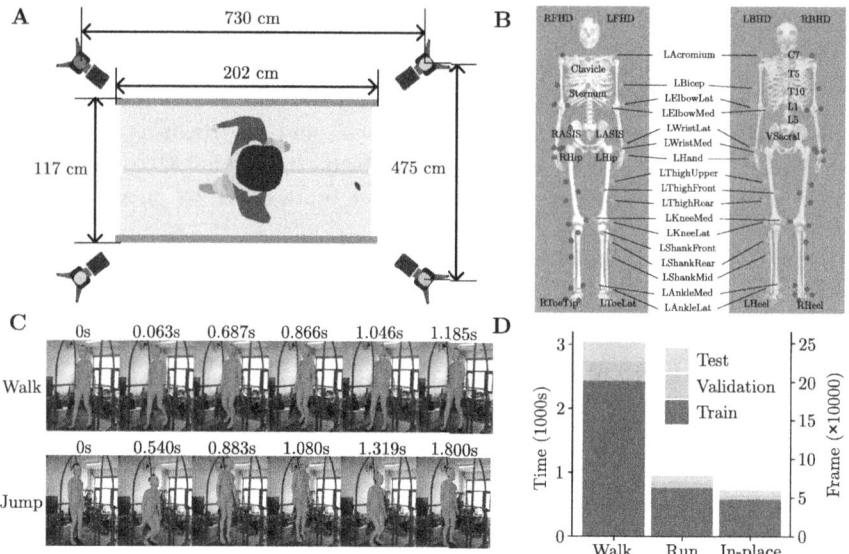

Fig. 2. Experiment Setup. A shows schematic diagram of the experimental setup. **B** presents marker set M used for implementation and analysis. **C** illustrates example motions, including walking and jumping. **D** provides dataset distribution categorized by walking, running, and in-place actions, along with the division into train, validation, and test sets.

3.3 Temporal Data Augmentation

To enhance the model's robustness to temporal synchrony, we introduce a temporal data augmentation strategy based on synthetic timestamp bias. High-precision optical MoCap is used as Ground-Truth (GT) marker trajectories, represented by $Y = \{y_i\}$.

Misalignment Augmentation: To simulate real-world unsynchronized capture scenarios, we introduce synthetic temporal offsets into each camera stream during training. For each camera c^i, we randomly draw a temporal bias $\tilde{B}^i \sim \mathcal{U}(-\epsilon, \epsilon)$ for each training instance and adjust the original timestamps accordingly.

$$\tilde{t}_j^i = \tau_j^i + \tilde{B}^i. \tag{7}$$

Sliding Window Augmentation: To further enrich the training data and increase temporal coverage, we randomly select multiple possible starting times $s \sim \mathcal{U}(0, \delta)$ indices within each action sequence. This strategy ensures that the model observes varied temporal contexts, motions at different phases, and diverse cross-camera alignments. The training window is constructed as

$$\tilde{W}_d = \{(I_j^i, \tilde{t}_j^i) | d\delta \leq \tilde{t}_j^i - s \leq (d+1)\delta\}. \tag{8}$$

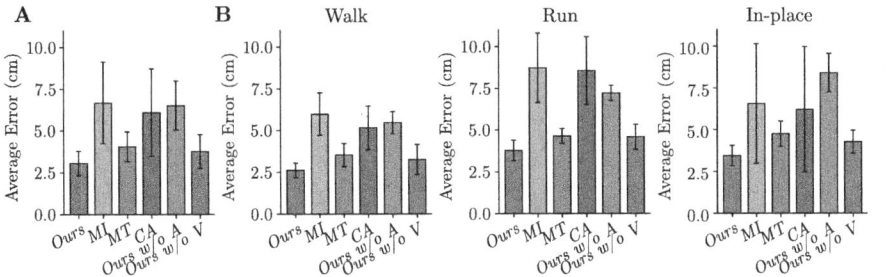

Fig. 3. Accuracy. A shows average error comparison across all methods, with error bars indicating the standard deviation. Our method shows the lowest error overall. **B** shows average error under different motion types.

For all actions in action space, we use this data augmentation method and get a dataset $\{\tilde{W}_d, Y_d\}$. The transformer-based post-process network is trained on this dataset using a Mean Squared Error (MSE) loss function between the predicted marker positions and the ground truth from the MoCap system at global timestamps.

$$\mathcal{L}_{\text{MSE}} = \frac{1}{|Y_d|} \sum_{y_i \in Y_d} \|\hat{y}_i - y_i\|_2^2. \tag{9}$$

4 Experiment Setup

System Implementation: Our MoCap system is implemented in an indoor environment using a four-camera setup ($n = 4$) as illustrated in Fig. 2**A**. Intrinsic (K^i) and extrinsic (R^i, T^i) camera parameters are calibrated using Zhang's method [26]. To enhance temporal asynchronization, cameras operate at different frame rates: $f^1 \approx f^2 \approx 30$ Hz and $f^3 \approx f^4 \approx 10$ Hz, with timing uncertainty $\sigma^i \approx 0.2$. The system employs a sliding window ($\epsilon = 0.2s$, $\delta = 2s$) and outputs at $f = 50$ Hz. GT temporal biases are established through hand-waving calibration. The marker set comprises $|M| = 56$ whole-body landmarks, visualized in Fig. 2**B** using OpenSim [27].

Data Collection: To train and validate our MoCap system, we build a dataset containing a diverse set of human motions. Motions can be categorized into three primary types: walking, running, and in-place actions. For the walking and running categories, participants performed motions at five distinct speeds. The in-place action category includes repetitive movements such as squatting, jumping, stretching in place, recorded while facing different orientations. We temporally segment the collected motion data into training, validation, and test sets using an 8:1:1 ratio. Detailed dataset information is shown in Fig. 2**C** and Fig. 2**D**. We use Vicon MoCap system (Vicon Valkyrie V16, 12 infrared cameras) to collect GT 3D global marker trajectories.

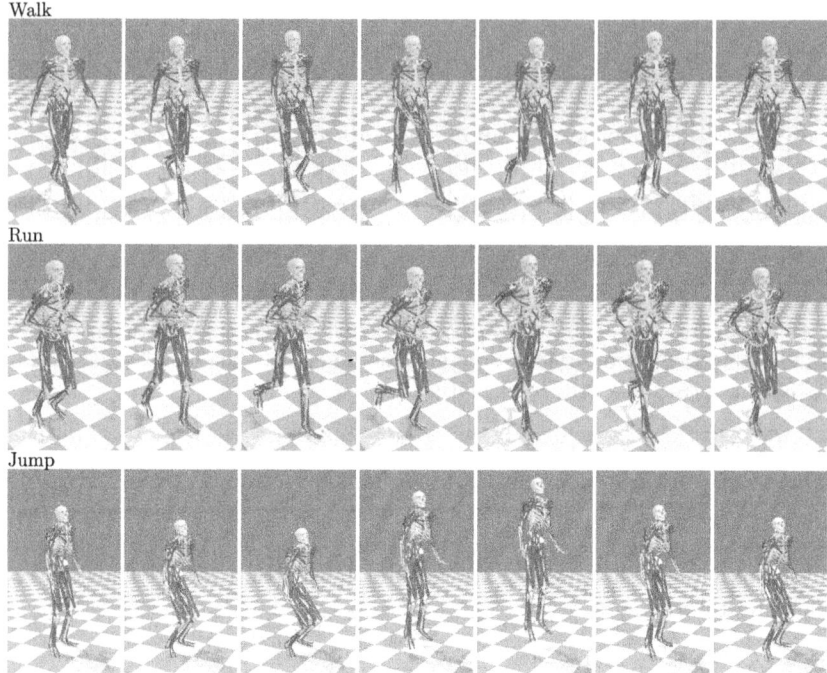

Fig. 4. Skeleton showcases. Utilizing the marker positions estimated by our MoCap system, we reconstruct skeletons with OpenSim. These showcases demonstrate that the output marker positions can be used to restore various human motions, including walking, running, and jumping.

Experimental Protocol: We evaluate system performance using the Average Error metric, defined as the average distance between predicted and GT global marker positions. This metric is crucial for both system accuracy assessment and downstream applications such as dynamic analysis and biomechanical computations.

We benchmark our MoCap approach (*Ours*) against several baseline configurations. The main camera interpolation baseline (*MI*) processes observations exclusively from the main camera, while the main camera training variant (*MT*) limits both training and inference to main camera data. The cameras average baseline (*CA*) implements naive multi-view fusion across all streams. To assess individual components, we evaluate two ablation variants: one without data augmentation (*Ours w/o A*) and another without virtual markers (*Ours w/o V*, using only joint position features).

The post-processing transformer architecture employs a 4-layer network with 8 attention heads and a hidden dimension of 512. The model is trained for 1,000 epochs using a batch size of 256, with a dropout rate of 0.1 for regularization. Optimization is performed using Adam with an initial learning rate of

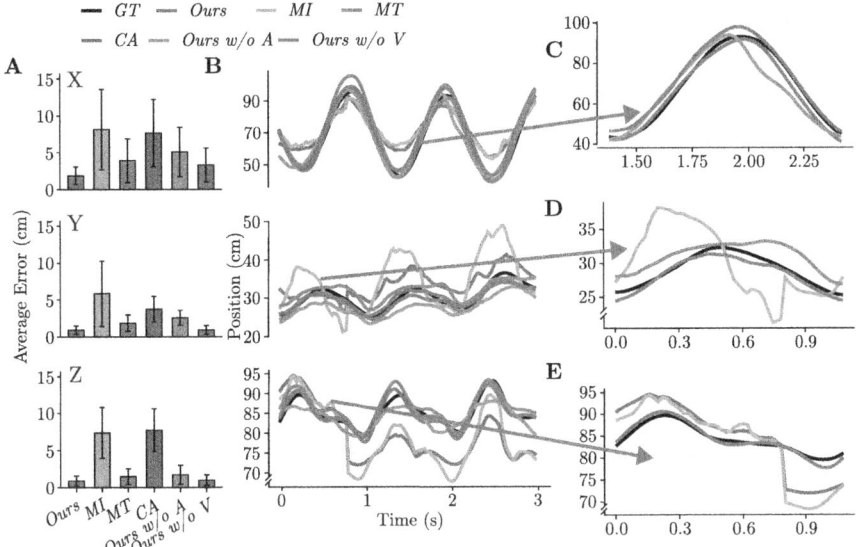

Fig. 5. Marker trajectory showcases. **A** and **B** show the tracking results of various methods for the LHand virtual marker during a time period in the test set under the Walk (1.2 m/s). Specifically, **A** presents the average error of each method along different axes during this period, where *Ours* consistently achieves the lowest error. **B** illustrates a detailed view of its trajectory. **C** shows *Ours w/o V* and *Ours w/o A* results in increased spatial errors and noticeable temporal lag, respectively. **D** shows *MT* improves temporal consistency over *MI* via post-processing, but its accuracy remains inferior. **E** shows *MI* and *CA* suffer from severe temporal jitter and spatial deviations.

5×10^{-5} and a step decay scheduler ($\gamma = 0.5$) applied at 200-epoch intervals. All experiments are executed on a single NVIDIA RTX 3090 GPU.

5 Experiment Results

As shown in Fig. 3**A**, our method achieves the lowest overall error of 3.05 cm, compared to 6.68 cm for *MI*, 4.04 cm for *MT*, and 6.10 cm for *CA*. Removing either data augmentation (*Ours w/o A*) or virtual marker features (*Ours w/o V*) led to higher errors of 6.52 cm and 3.76 cm. Figure 3**B** directly compares the performance of *Ours* and its ablated variants across walking, running, and in-place motions. *Ours* yields a mean error below 4 cm, and substantially outperforming *MI*, *MT*, and *CA*. For Walk, our method achieves 2.62 cm, versus 5.99 cm (*MI*), 5.46 cm (*Ours w/o A*), and 5.16 cm (*CA*). For Run, the error increases for all models, but *Ours* remains lowest at 3.77 cm, while *MI* and *CA* exceed 8.5 cm. For in-place motion, our model records 3.44 cm, with the other variants ranging from 4.26 cm (*Ours w/o V*) to 8.41 cm (*Ours w/o A*). Our model achieves consistently lower errors than all baselines across the three motion categories.

Please refer to Fig. 4 for skeleton motion reconstructed from *Ours*. For marker trajectory showcase, as shown in Fig. 5**A** and **B**, *Ours* achieves the most stable and accurate tracking of the LHand marker in a walking motion (1.2 m/s), outperforming prior baselines.

6 Discussion

This paper introduces a marker-free motion capture system designed for unsynchronized multi-camera setups. The proposed approach incorporates two key techniques: temporal augmentation and virtual marker extraction, enabling automatic camera synchronization. Comprehensive ablation studies and baseline comparisons validate the effectiveness of these components. Removing the virtual marker features (*Ours w/o V*) increases spatial prediction errors (average 0.71 cm), and omitting temporal augmentation (*Ours w/o A*) introduces temporal drift and phase gap (see Fig. 5**C**). These results confirm the necessity of both virtual marker extraction and temporal augmentation for achieving robust spatial and temporal performance. Although *MT* applies post-processing to enhance temporal consistency compared with *MI*, its accuracy is still limited by the absence of multi-view camera information, underscoring the importance of multi-view input in MoCap (see Sect. 5 and Fig. 5**D**). Moreover, both *MI* and *CA* exhibit temporal jitter and large spatial deviations, demonstrating that our model effectively captures and aligns temporal information across unsynchronized cameras (see Fig. 5**E**). Based on the above analysis, our contributions form a cohesive system that enables accurate, stable 3D human motion reconstruction.

The future research directions can be explored from various aspects. The adaptability of the system to different environments can be enhanced by expanding the training dataset through varying camera models, placement positions, and collecting data in diverse environments [28]. A human body surface model with more adjustable parameters holds the potential for more accurate MoCap results [29,30]. Joint optimization incorporating musculoskeletal models offers potential for effective clinical implementation [31].

In this paper, we present a novel marker-free MoCap system that utilizes multiple unsynchronized cameras, addressing key challenges in fusing multi-view, temporally misaligned images and the sparsity of detectable features on human bodies. The experiment results indicate that our methods have improved both localization accuracy and robustness to temporal misalignment. The proposed MoCap system presents an alternative to existing MoCap systems, making the MoCap system easier to deploy in real-world scenarios.

Acknowledgment. This work was supported by the National Natural Science Foundation of China (No. 52475001). The authors would like to thank Fengchen Liu, Benshu Cao, and Fanxu Meng for their valuable assistance during data collection. Jintao Zhu is a visiting student in Peking University from China University of Geosciences.

References

1. Lu, Y., et al.: A human-prosthesis coupled musculoskeletal model for transtibial amputees. IEEE Trans. Biomed. Eng. (2025)
2. Gleicher, M.: Animation from observation: motion capture and motion editing. ACM SIGGRAPH **33**(4), 51–54 (1999)
3. Moeslund, T.B., Hilton, A., Krüger, V.: A survey of advances in vision-based human motion capture and analysis. Comput. Vis. Image Understand. **104**(2–3), 90–126 (2006)
4. Windolf, M., Götzen, N., Morlock, M.: Systematic accuracy and precision analysis of video motion capturing systems–exemplified on the vicon-460 system. J. Biomech. **41**(12), 2776–2780 (2008)
5. Hou, H., Zhu, W., Ruan, L., Wang, Q.: Prosthetic control by learning: a multi-agent cooperative game framework. In: 2025 International Conference on Rehabilitation Robotics, pp. 1–6. IEEE (2025)
6. Ming, X., Zhou, Z., Wang, Z., Ruan, L., Mai, J., Wang, Q.: Bioinspired cable-driven actuation system for wearable robotic devices: design, control, and characterization. IEEE Trans. Rob. **40**, 520–539 (2023)
7. Lin, J., Zeng, A., Wang, H., Zhang, L., Li, Y.: One-stage 3D whole-body mesh recovery with component aware transformer. In: Proceedings of the IEEE Conference on Computer Vision and Pattern Recognition, pp. 21159–21168 (2023)
8. Mündermann, L., Corazza, S., Andriacchi, T.P.: The evolution of methods for the capture of human movement leading to markerless motion capture for biomechanical applications. J. Neuroengineering Rehabil. **3**, 1–11 (2006)
9. Chenyu, G., Lin, W., He, X., Zhang, L., Zhang, M.: IMU-based motion capture system for rehabilitation applications: a systematic review. Biomimetic Intell. Robot. **3**(2), 100097 (2023)
10. Knippenberg, E., Verbrugghe, J., Lamers, I., Palmaers, S., Timmermans, A., Spooren, A.: Markerless motion capture systems as training device in neurological rehabilitation: a systematic review of their use, application, target population and efficacy. J. Neuroeng. Rehabil. **14**, 1–11 (2017)
11. Huang, B., Jingyi, J., Shu, Y., Wang, Y.: Simultaneously recovering multi-person meshes and multi-view cameras with human semantics. IEEE Trans. Circuits Syst. Video Technol. **34**(6), 4229–4242 (2023)
12. Huang, B., Ju, J., Li, Z., Wang, Y.: Reconstructing groups of people with hypergraph relational reasoning. In: Proceedings of the IEEE Conference on Computer Vision and Pattern Recognition, pp. 14873–14883 (2023)
13. Caspi, Y., Irani, M.: Spatio-temporal alignment of sequences. IEEE Trans. Pattern Anal. Mach. Intell. **24**(11), 1409–1424 (2002)
14. Shin, K.G., Ramanathan, P.: Transmission delays in hardware clock synchronization. IEEE Trans. Comput. **37**(11), 1465–1467 (2002)
15. Listgarten, J., Neal, R., Roweis, S., Emili, A.: Multiple alignment of continuous time series. In: Advances in Neural Information Processing Systems, vol. 17 (2004)
16. Arenas, A., Díaz-Guilera, A., Kurths, J., Moreno, Y., Zhou, C.: Synchronization in complex networks. Phys. Rep. **469**(3), 93–153 (2008)
17. Sivrikaya, F., Yener, B.: Time synchronization in sensor networks: a survey. IEEE Netw. **18**(4), 45–50 (2004)
18. Zheng, R., Li, P., Wang, H., Yu, T.: Learning visibility field for detailed 3D human reconstruction and relighting. In: Proceedings of the IEEE Conference on Computer Vision and Pattern Recognition, pp. 216–226 (2023)

19. Cheng, K.-L., Tong, R.-F., Tang, M., Qian, J.-Y., Sarkis, M.: Parametric human body reconstruction based on sparse key points. IEEE Trans. Visual Comput. Graph. **22**(11), 2467–2479 (2015)
20. Shuai, Q., et al.: Novel view synthesis of human interactions from sparse multi-view videos. In: ACM SIGGRAPH, pp. 1–10 (2022)
21. Sumit, S.S., Rambli, D.R.A., Mirjalili, S.: Vision-based human detection techniques: a descriptive review. IEEE Access **9**, 42724–42761 (2021)
22. Kanazawa, A., Black, M.J., Jacobs, D.W., Malik, J.: End-to-end recovery of human shape and pose. In: Proceedings of the IEEE Conference on Computer Vision and Pattern Recognition, pp. 7122–7131 (2018)
23. Yuan, Y., Iqbal, U., Molchanov, P., Kitani, K., Kautz, J.: Glamr: global occlusion-aware human mesh recovery with dynamic cameras. In: Proceedings of the IEEE Conference on Computer Vision and Pattern Recognition, pp. 11038–11049 (2022)
24. Baradel, F., et al.: Multi-HMR: multi-person whole-body human mesh recovery in a single shot. In: European Conference on Computer Vision, pp. 202–218. Springer, Cham (2024)
25. Vaswani, A., et al.: Attention is all you need. In: Advances in Neural Information Processing Systems, vol. 30 (2017)
26. Zhang, Z.: A flexible new technique for camera calibration. IEEE Trans. Pattern Anal. Mach. Intell. **22**(11), 1330–1334 (2002)
27. Delp, S.L., et al.: Opensim: open-source software to create and analyze dynamic simulations of movement. IEEE Trans. Biomed. Eng. **54**(11), 1940–1950 (2007)
28. Ionescu, C., Papava, D., Olaru, V., Sminchisescu, C.: Human3.6m: large scale datasets and predictive methods for 3D human sensing in natural environments. IEEE Trans. Pattern Anal. Mach. Intell. **36**(7), 1325–1339 (2013)
29. Shi, Y.-Z., et al.: AutoDSL: automated domain-specific language design for structural representation of procedures with constraints. In: Proceedings of the 62nd Annual Meeting of the Association for Computational Linguistics (2024)
30. Liu, H., Men, Y., Lian, Z.: Creating your editable 3D photorealistic avatar with tetrahedron-constrained gaussian splatting. In: Proceedings of the IEEE Conference on Computer Vision and Pattern Recognition, pp. 15976–15986 (2025)
31. Jin, W., et al.: Forward dynamics simulation of a simplified neuromuscular-skeletal-exoskeletal model based on the CMA-ES optimization algorithm: framework and case studies. Multibody Syst. Dyn. 1–34 (2024)

Embodied Intelligence in Biomimetic Robotics, Humanoid Robotics

Fluid Dynamics Around a Whisker

Md. Mahbub Alam[✉] and Xiaoyu Shi

School of Robotics and Advanced Manufacturing, Harbin Institute of Technology (Shenzhen),
Shenzhen 518055, China
alamm28@yahoo.com

Abstract. A harbor seal whisker is generally elliptic, having a wavy surface along the whisker axis. Compared to a straight cylinder, a wavy elliptic cylinder can modify the vortex shedding, making the flow incoherent, and elongate the vortex formation length, reducing the fluid force. This numerical study explores how the spanwise wavelength (λ) of a sinusoidal wavy cylinder with an elliptic cross-section affects wake structures and fluid forces at a Reynolds number of 100. The investigation covers a wide range of wavelengths ($0.43 \leq \lambda/D_m \leq 8.59$), with a wave amplitude of $a/D_m = 0.048$, where D_m represents the hydraulic diameter of the wavy cylinder. The results reveal five distinct flow patterns (I − V), depending on λ/D_m. Notably, flow pattern IV exhibits a unique behavior compared to traditional flows: instead of synchronous vortex shedding along the entire cylinder, vortex shedding occurs alternately over one half of the wavelength, out of phase with the other half, resulting in zero net fluctuating lift over one complete wavelength.

Keyword: Whiskers · wavy elliptic cylinder · bifurcation flow

1 Introduction

Whiskers play a crucial role in the tactile sensing systems of many animals, particularly rodents and marine mammals, enabling them to detect and navigate their surroundings through physical contact and flow sensing. In robotics, biomimetic whiskers have been developed to replicate these capabilities, allowing robots to perceive their environment through touch rather than relying solely on vision or sonar. These artificial whiskers, typically made from flexible materials and equipped with strain or pressure sensors at the base, can detect texture, shape, airflow, and proximity to objects. This form of tactile sensing is especially valuable in low-visibility environments, such as underwater or smoke-filled areas, where traditional sensors may fail. By mimicking the sensitivity and functionality of natural whiskers, robotic systems gain enhanced spatial awareness and adaptability, contributing to advances in autonomous navigation, object recognition, and environmental interaction.

The seal-whisker-based wavy elliptic cylinder can significantly alter the near wake structure that, albeit with incoherent structures, appears more stable and is thus associated with an elongated vortex formation length and significantly reduced fluid forces, compared with their straight cylinder counterparts. However, the seal-whisker-based cylinder model involves several morphological parameters, including the aspect ratio (*AR*) of the elliptic cross-section, the angle of incidence, and the spanwise wavelength (λ) [1]. Based on an extensive investigation of 27 whiskers of harbor seal and elephant seal, Rinehart et al. [2] noticed large deviations in these key parameters, particularly in the angle of incidence. Therefore, some interesting questions arise. For example, which parameter is predominantly important or critical for the seal-whisker-based cylinder model to alter the near wake? Are there optimal parameters for the seal-whisker-based cylinder model to attain the most reduction in fluid forces? Could it be possible to propose a simplified but generalized model of bluff bodies, based on the inspiration of the harbor seal whisker?

The present work aims to investigate the near wake of a wavy elliptic cylinder, a simplified model of the harbor seal whisker. Here, we form the wavy elliptic cylinder by sinusoidally changing the minor axis of a straight elliptic cylinder while keeping the major axis constant along the spanwise direction. The focus is given on the effects of the wavelength on the near wake. Extensive numerical simulations are carried out at a Reynolds number $Re = 100$ for a wide range of the wavelength (i.e. $\lambda/D_m = 0.43 - 8.59$), with the waviness being fixed at $a/D_m = 0.048$.

2 Numerical Method

A schematic of the whisker model (wavy elliptic cylinder) is shown in Fig. 1, defining the different parameters. The wavy surface of the cylinder is formed by sinusoidally varying the minor axis (D_{min}) of the elliptic cross-section along the spanwise direction (z), while the major axis (D_{maj}) of the elliptic cross-section remains constant. As such, D_{min} is given by $D_{min} = D_m + 2a \sin(2\pi z/\lambda)$, where D_m is the mean minor axis of the elliptic cross-sections, λ and a are the wavelength and wave amplitude (or waviness) of the spanwise wave, respectively. The cross-sections with the maximum minor axis (D_n) and minimum minor axis (D_s) are denoted as the node and saddle sections, respectively. The mid-section between the node and saddle sections has the minor axis $D_m = (D_n + D_s)/2$.

Three-dimensional simulations are carried out at a Reynolds number $Re = 100$, based on D_m and free stream velocity (U_∞), to investigate the unsteady laminar flow around the cylinder. The continuity and Navier-Stokes equations for incompressible Newtonian fluid are solved on structural quadrilateral grids with the finite-volume method in ANSYS Fluent. The inlet and outlet of the computational domain are $20D_m$ and $40D_m$ away from the cylinder axis (at $x = 0$), respectively. The computational domain has a distance of $40D_m$ between the lateral sides and a distance of 2λ along the spanwise z direction (Fig. 2). A uniform inlet velocity is prescribed at the inlet. At the outlet, an outflow boundary condition is applied. The lateral boundaries are treated as slip walls using symmetry conditions. Periodic boundary conditions are imposed at the top and bottom, while a no-slip condition is enforced on the cylinder surface. Mesh and time independence tests were conducted before result validation.

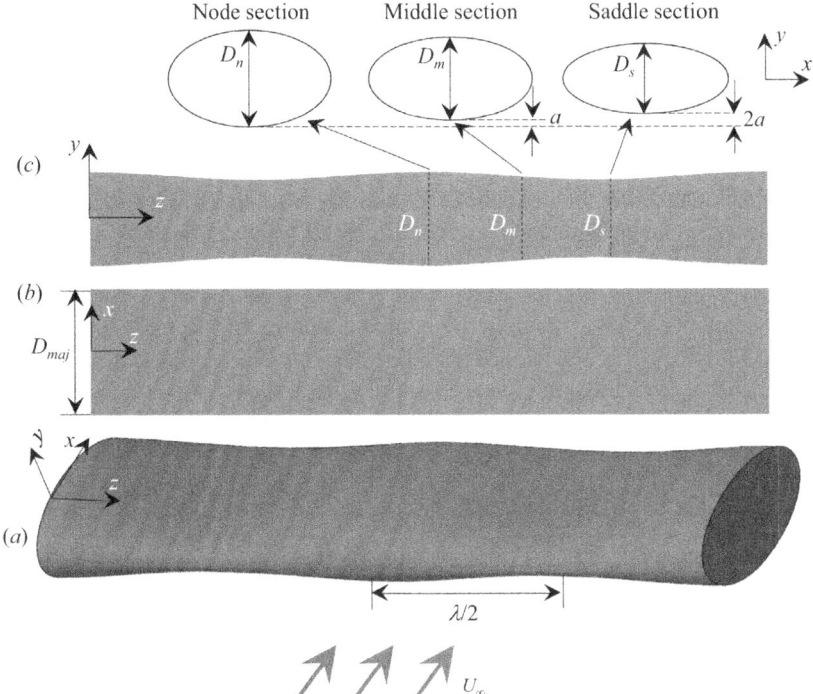

Fig. 1. (*a*) Schematic diagram of the wavy elliptic cylinder and symbol designation. (*b*) Top view. (*c*) Front view.

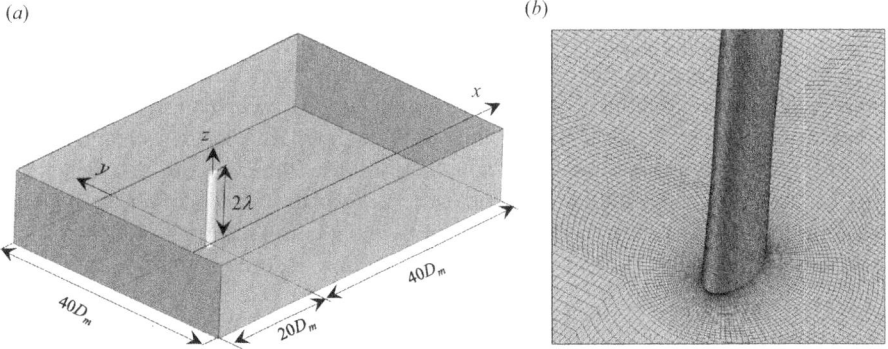

Fig. 2. (*a*) Computational domain and (*b*) mesh detail.

3 Results and Discussion

3.1 Flow Classification

After careful examination of the near wake structures, five distinct flow patterns (I – V) are identified when λ/D_m is increased from 0.43 to 8.59 (Fig. 3). At a relatively short wavelength λ/D_m (< 2.58), the wavy elliptic cylinder generates a two-dimensional near wake, similar to that of a straight elliptic cylinder with an aspect ratio of the cross-section $AR \geq 0.37$ and a zero angle-of-attack [3]. Clearly, the iso-surfaces of $\lambda_2 = -0.1$ exhibit a street of von Karman vortices downstream (Fig. 4a1), and no iso-surfaces of $\omega_x^* = \pm 0.1$ are detected around the cylinder and in the wake (Fig. 4a2). This flow behaves like the flow over a uniform cylinder, hence it is termed as 0λ flow. In pattern II (2.58 < λ/D_m < 4.44), the λ/D_m effects on the near wake structures emerge, the wake being three-dimensional and wavy along the spanwise direction (Fig. 4b1). Alternate streamwise vortices are now generated (Fig. 4b1, b2), albeit spanwise vortices are dominant, shedding alternately from the two sides of the cylinder and appearing staggered in the wake. The wavy formation of the spanwise vortical structures can be ascribed to the presence of the counter-rotating streamwise vortices additionally generated downstream of the nodes (Fig. 4b2). Since the vortex shedding happens synchronously from the whole cylinder span, or from the entire wavelength in other words, the flow here is called as 1.0λ flow.

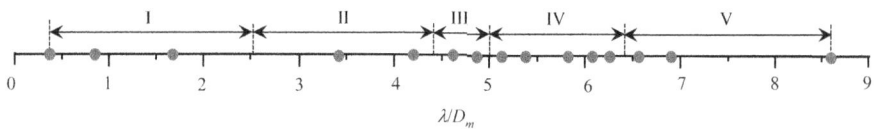

Fig. 3. Dependence of flow patterns on wavelength λ/D_m. Red dots refer to the wavelength of the wavy cylinder selected for discussion.

With a further increase in the wavelength to $\lambda/D_m = 4.44 - 5.01$, the alternate spanwise and streamwise vortices are suppressed, the wake is stabilized, and the flow becomes steady (Fig. 4c1, c2). It is referred to as *steady flow*. In the range of $5.01 < \lambda/D_m < 6.40$, the wake of the wavy elliptic cylinder recovers to be three-dimensional, unsteady, characterized by strong, dominant streamwise vortices and disconnected spanwise vortices (Fig. 4d1, d2). The spanwise vortex shedding from a half wavelength (e.g. from the top node to the adjacent saddle) is out of phase (phase lag 180°) with that from the next half wavelength, see Fig. 4 (d1, d2). This flow can be termed as a half-wavelength flow or 0.5λ flow. The vortex shedding of 0.5λ flow is identified as the first of its kind, which may yield zero instantaneous lift and zero fluctuating drag on the cylinder of one wavelength, although alternating vortex shedding from the cylinder is still manifest. It may thus have a great implication for near-wake flow control and flow-induced vibration suppression.

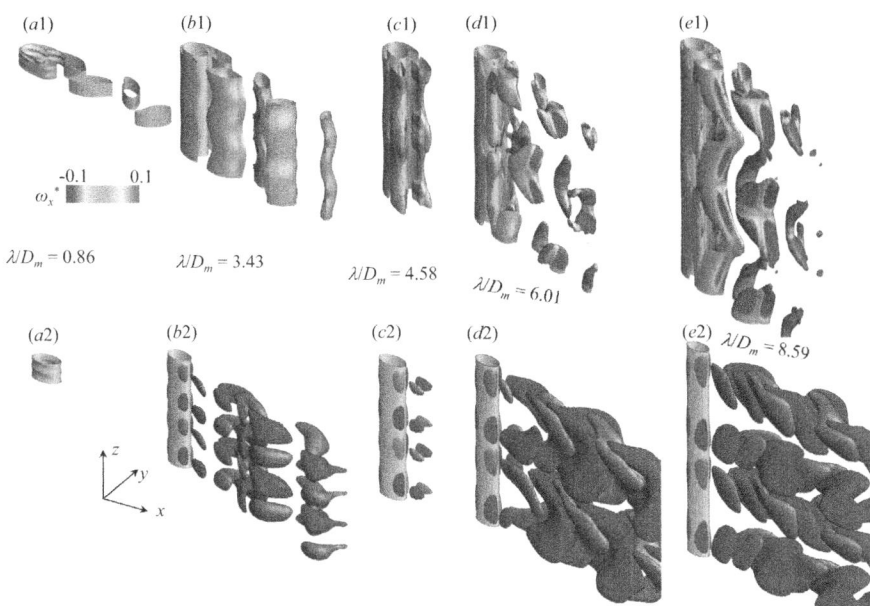

Fig. 4. Representative instantaneous structures for the five flow patterns. ($a1 - e1$) Spanwise vortices, in terms of iso-surface of $\lambda_2 = -0.1$ (colored by streamwise vorticity ω_x^*); ($a2 - e2$) Streamwise vortices, in terms of iso-surface of $\omega_x^* = 0.1$ (red) and -0.1 (blue). ($a1, a2$) $\lambda/D_m = 0.86$ (flow pattern I); ($b1, b2$) 3.43 (II); ($c1, c2$) 4.58 (III); ($d1, d2$) 6.01 (IV); and ($e1, e2$) 8.59 (V). The cylinder in each is of two spanwise wavelengths.

At $\lambda/D_m > 6.40$, the wake is still highly three-dimensional although interactions of the additionally-generated streamwise vortices become weakened because of the large distance between the nodes (Fig. 4e1, e2). The spanwise vortex tube in the vicinity of the cylinder spans the entire cylinder span, albeit in a wavy fashion. It indicates that the vortex shedding from one side of the cylinder occurs for the whole cylinder span, not like that observed for pattern IV. As a result, the spanwise vortex tubes break downstream, as occurs for a uniform cylinder involving streamwise vortices [4]. This flow can be called a very large wavelength flow or $\infty\lambda$ flow.

3.2 Wake Structure

Figure 5 shows time-averaged streamline traces on four yz-planes at $x^* = 1.0, 1.75, 2.0$, and 3.0. For $\lambda/D_m = 3.43$, when $x^* = 1.0$ (Fig. 5a1), saddle and node alternately appear on the cylinder saddle plane while they occur on the upper and lower boundaries (node planes) oppositely to those in the saddle plane. The scenario reflects that the spiral flow is directed from the cylinder node to the saddle. At $x^* = 1.75$ (Fig. 5a2), there are five saddle points on each of the upper and lower boundaries and five nodes on the cylinder saddle plane. The second and fourth nodes from the left represent the recirculation bubble core. At $x^* = 2.0$ (Fig. 5a3), only one saddle point materializes on the saddle plane and a pair of foci appears on each node plane. When x^* is further increased, the two foci are replaced with a single node at $x^* = 3.0$ as $x^* = 3.0$ is beyond the recirculation bubble (Fig. 5a4).

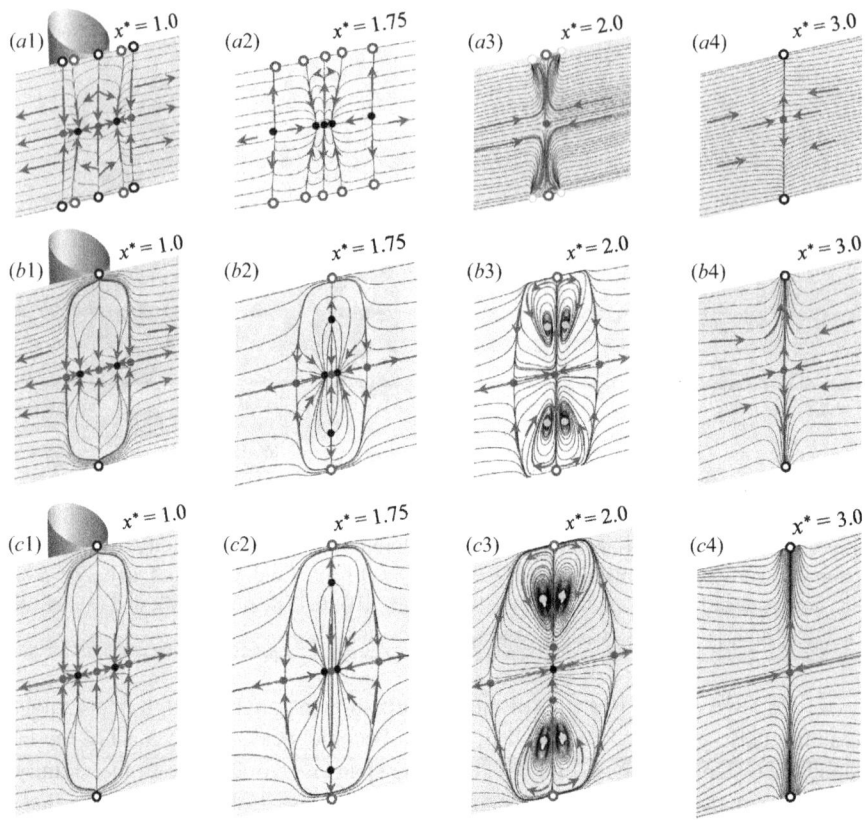

Fig. 5. Distributions of time-mean streamlines on the yz-plane at $x^* = 1.0$ (a1 – c1), $x^* = 2.0$ (a2 – c2), and $x^* = 3.0$ (a3 – c3) for $\lambda/D_m = 3.43$ (a1 – a3), $\lambda/D_m = 4.58$ (b1 – b3), and $\lambda/D_m = 6.01$ (c1 – c3). The marks ●, ●, and ● denote critical node, saddle, and foci points; ○, ○ and ○ refer to half critical node, saddle and foci points, respectively. The red arrows indicate flow direction.

In the cases of $\lambda/D_m = 4.58$ and 6.01 (Fig. 5b, c), at $x^* = 1.0$ (Fig. 5b1, c1), saddles and nodes appear alternately at the saddle plane while one node is on the boundary. In the recirculation bubble, the flow spirals from the node plane to the saddle plane. This is, however, not the case at $x^* = 1.75$ (Fig. 5b2, c2), where the flow in the bubble for a small part of the cylinder span near the node heads for the node plane while the rest of the span has the flow heading for the saddle plane. The scenario echoes a bifurcation in vortex shedding. At $x^* = 2.0$ (Fig. 5b3, c3), there are four focus points symmetrically distributed about the saddle plane and $y^* = 0$ plane, which are the signatures of the spiral flow in the recirculation bubble. The bifurcation still exists for $\lambda/D_m = 6.01$ (Fig. 5c3), moving toward the saddle plane. At $x^* = 3.0$ (Fig. 5b4, c4), the flow goes from the saddle plane to the node plane, having one and two saddle points on the saddle and node planes, respectively.

3.3 Vortex Shedding Topology

Figure 6 visually illustrates instantaneous vortex shedding for three different λ/D_m values. The red arrows depict the time-mean spiral streamlines, highlighting flow three-dimensionality. For $\lambda/D_m = 3.43$ (Fig. 6a). The wavy cylinder significantly impacts the flow, generating spiral flows directed towards the saddle plane. This leads to counter-rotating vortices and a wavy vortex structure along the cylinder's span. Vortex shedding alternates between the two sides of the entire cylinder. In the case of $\lambda/D_m = 4.58$, the flow is steady, embodying a stable recirculation bubble and bifurcated spiral flows (Fig. 6b, indicated by the red dots) heading for the saddle and node planes. For $\lambda/D_m = 6.01$ (Fig. 6c), vortex shedding from one half of the wavelength is out of phase with the other half. Similar to $\lambda/D_m = 4.58$ case, the vortex shedding flow bifurcates (red dots), creating spiral flows towards the node and saddle planes. The recirculation bubble at the saddle plane is shorter than the one at the node plane.

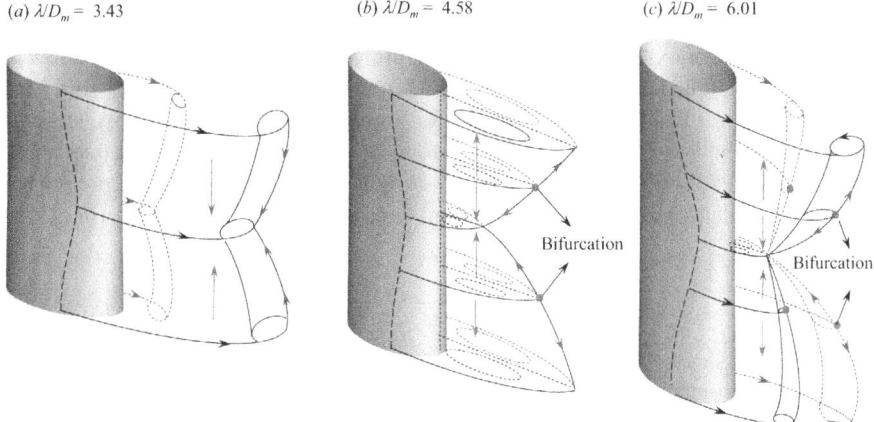

Fig. 6. Overview of the three-dimensional flow topology for (a) $\lambda/D_m = 3.43$, (b) $\lambda/D_m = 4.58$, and (c) $\lambda/D_m = 6.01$. The red dots indicate bifurcation in the vortex shedding and recirculation. Black solid and blue dashed lines refer to the streamlines on the left and right sides, respectively.

4 Conclusions

Systematic three-dimensional numerical simulations are conducted to investigate the near wake of a wavy elliptic cylinder at $Re = 100$, focusing on the effects of the wavelength (λ/D_m) on flow structures and flow three-dimensionality. Five distinct flow patterns (I - V) or regimes in different λ/D_m ranges are identified. When $\lambda/D_m < 2.58$, flow pattern I (0λ flow) emerges where the vortex shedding is two-dimensional and alternate. Flow pattern II (1λ flow) appears at 2.58 < λ/D_m < 4.44, where the spanwise vortices display a spanwise wavelength of 1λ that is also distinguished by a pair of counter-rotating streamwise vortices. Flow pattern III appearing at 4.44 < λ/D_m < 5.01 is steady. Alternate vortex shedding is suppressed. Flow bifurcation occurs in the stable recirculation bubble, with spiral flows heading toward the saddle and node planes. Flow pattern IV (0.5λ flow) comes into being at 5.01 < λ/D_m < 6.40, where large-scale Λ-like streamwise vortices and disconnected spanwise vortices feature the wake. The spanwise vortices synchronize over one 0.5λ span of the cylinder and shed in an anti-phase fashion from different sides of the saddle plane and the cylinder. The vortex shedding undergoes bifurcation, generating two spiral flows toward the saddle and node, respectively. When λ/D_m is large (> 6.40), flow pattern V ($\infty\lambda$ flow) shows up, with the wake being highly three-dimensional, composed of streamwise vortices mainly congregating downstream of the nodes. The spanwise vortices synchronize over the entire cylinder span. The interactions between the streamwise and spanwise vortices weaken.

The three-dimensional flow topologies associated with the different flow patterns are visualized through time-mean streamlines. The flow at $\lambda/D_m = 3.43$ generates a spiral flow from the node to the saddle in the wake, resulting in counter-rotating vortices and a wavy vortex structure. On the other hand, the flow at $\lambda/D_m = 4.58$ has a stable recirculation bubble that bifurcates at 0.30λ/D_m away from the saddle plane, engendering spiral flows heading for the saddle and node planes. The flow at $\lambda/D_m = 6.01$ is characterized by antiphase vortex shedding from the two half spans of one wavelength. Again, the flow associated with vortex shedding in a half-span bifurcates, generating spiral flows towards the node and saddle planes, respectively. The bifurcation occurs at 0.38λ/D_m away from the saddle plane. Overall, the investigation of time-mean streamline patterns, recirculation bubble behavior, and three-dimensional flow topologies provides valuable insights into the complex flow physics around wavy elliptic cylinders. These findings contribute to a deeper understanding of flow separation, vortex shedding, and wake formation.

References

1. Rinehart, A., Shyam, V., Zhang, W.: Characterization of seal whisker morphology: implications for whisker-inspired flow control applications. Bioinspir. Biomim. **12**, 066005 (2017)
2. Shi, X., Bai, H., Alam, M.M., Ji, C., Zhu, H.: Wake of wavy elliptic cylinder at a low Reynolds number: wavelength effect. J. Fluid Mech. **969**, A22 (2023)
3. Shi, X., Alam, M.M., Bai, H.: Wakes of elliptical cylinders at low Reynolds number. Intl. J. Heat Fluid Flow **82**, 108553 (2020)
4. Bai, H.L., Alam, M.M.: Dependence of square cylinder wake on Reynolds number. Phys. Fluids **30**(1), 015102 (2018)

Interaction-Friendly Trajectories via Torque-and-Jerk-Constrained Optimization

Shize Zhao, Tianjiao Zheng(✉), Chengzhi Wang, Sikai Zhao, Yanhe Zhu(✉), and Jie Zhao

State Key Laboratory of Robotics and System, School of Mechatronics Engineering, Harbin Institute of Technology, Harbin 150001, China
zhengtj@hit.edu.cn

Abstract. Smooth and responsive motion is critical for physical human-robot interaction and humanoid robotics, where sudden accelerations and jerks can lead to unsafe or unnatural behavior. Traditional Time-Optimal Path Parameterization (TOPP) methods often yield discontinuous acceleration profiles due to abrupt torque transitions, resulting in high jerk and degraded motion quality. In this paper, we propose a novel trajectory optimization framework—Minimized Jerk Time-Optimal Path Parameterization (MJ-TOPP)—that incorporates both torque and jerk constraints to generate interaction-friendly motion. The method introduces a piecewise polynomial optimization scheme around torque switching points, enabling a global reduction in jerk while preserving near-optimal timing. Simulation and experimental results on a 6-DOF robotic manipulator performing a complex "HIT"-shaped trajectory demonstrate that MJ-TOPP reduces peak joint jerk by over 90% with only a 1.25% increase in execution time. Moreover, the improved motion smoothness leads to a 15.4% decrease in average end-effector tracking error, enhancing the safety and stability of robot behavior in human-centered environments. This approach provides a practical and effective solution for compliant motion planning in intelligent, human-interactive robotic systems.

Keywords: human-robot interaction · jerk minimization · torque-constrained trajectory · compliant control · time-optimal path parameterization

1 Introduction

In the context of intelligent robotics, smooth and human-like motion has become increasingly vital for applications such as humanoid locomotion, bionic manipulation, and physical human-robot interaction. Unlike traditional industrial tasks, these scenarios require robots not only to act efficiently, but also to move in a safe, predictable, and compliant manner [1–3]. This study focuses on determining an optimal velocity profile as close to time-optimal as possible for such robots, ensuring smooth and precise execution of complex predefined trajectories. However, the optimization of robot motion faces challenges from various physical constraints. Among these, limitations on motor speed and torque directly impact the velocity and torque of robot joints, constituting primary constraints considered in optimization.

Time-Optimal Path Parameterization (TOPP) stands as a tool for addressing optimal trajectory planning under motion kinematic constraints [4–8]. Presently, three primary methodologies are employed to tackle TOPP: 1). Dynamic Programming: This method utilizes dynamic programming (DP) techniques to ascertain the optimal trajectory within the discretized plane [9, 10]. 2). Convex Optimization: Here, the (s) axis is discretized, and the problem is reformulated into a convex optimization paradigm, thereby enhancing adaptability and efficiency [11]. 3). Numerical Integration: Rooted in Pontryagin's Maximum Principle, this approach identifies the optimal "bang-bang" trajectory through the integration of maximum and minimum accelerations [12].

H. Pham et al. proposed a solution based on reachability theory to address the time-optimal problem with second-order constraints. The method, known as TOPP-RA, implicitly identifies the switching points between acceleration and deceleration phases, significantly reducing computation time [11]. Huang et al. employ a sampling approach to constrain jerk and acceleration in discrete space [13], achieving higher-order kinematic constraints but failing to address dynamic constraints. Ma J et al. convert the jitter limit into linear acceleration constraints, indirectly introducing a convex optimization problem with linear acceleration constraints [14]. However, despite these advancements, these methods exhibit substantial deviations from optimal results and require significant computational resources.

The third-order strict constraint under the torque constraint will waste a lot of computing resources and it is difficult to determine the optimal solution. The acceleration mutations generated by the TOPP algorithm under the torque constraint mainly occur at a few Bang-Bang control points, so even if this part of the time increases slightly, it will have a considerable impact on the jerk optimization. We can obtain the approximate time optimal solution under the torque-jerk constraint by confirming the approximate optimal time of this segment and optimizing the jerk using piecewise polynomials.

This paper proposes a new algorithm, Minimized Jerk Time Optimal Path Parameterization (MJ-TOPP), which aims to constrain the jerk in the motion trajectory to ensure the robot's motion accuracy and stability while optimizing the trajectory planning time as much as possible under the kinodynamics constraints. The method introduces a piecewise polynomial for jerk optimization based on the torque constrained TOPP algorithm and adopts a more conservative approximate optimal transition around the Bang-Bang control points. The method helps to generate motion curves that significantly reduce the global jerk while respecting the dynamic constraints. Although the optimal time increases slightly according to the jerk constraint, the overall trajectory has a significantly reduced jerk.

2 Time-Optimal Path Parameterization

For a n-DOF robotic system, its joint coordinate vector is represented by a n-dimensional vector q. Consider the torque bounds on a fully-actuated manipulator:

$$\mathbf{M}(q)\ddot{\mathbf{q}} + \dot{\mathbf{q}}\mathbf{B}(q)\dot{\mathbf{q}} + \mathbf{f}(q) = \tau \tag{1}$$

In which, $\mathbf{M}(\mathbf{q}) \in R^{n \times n}$ denotes the inertia matrix, $\mathbf{B}(\mathbf{q}) \in R^{n \times n}$ denotes the matrix of Coriolis and centrifugal terms, $\{\mathbf{f}(\mathbf{q}) \in R^{n \times 1}$ stands for gravitational terms and Coulomb friction terms. $\dot{q} \in R^{n \times 1}$ and $\ddot{q} \in R^{n \times 1}$ are first-order and second-order derivatives of q with respect to time, which denote joint velocity and joint acceleration, and $\tau \in R^{n \times 1}$ is the control torque.

A geometric path P in the configuration space is represented as a function $q(s) \in [0, s_{end}]$. A time parameterization of the path P is an increasing scalar function s: $[0, t_{end}] \rightarrow [0, s_{end}]$. According to path parameterization formulation with the function $s(t)$, joint velocity and joint acceleration can be described as follows.

$$\dot{q} = q'(s)\dot{s},\ \ddot{q} = q''(s)\dot{s}^2 + q'(s)\ddot{s} \tag{2}$$

where $q'(s)$ and $q''(s)$ denotes first-order and second-order derivatives of the path parameter s; and $s, \dot{s}, \ddot{s}$ denote the position, velocity, and acceleration of the path.

Substituting Eq. (2) into Eq. (1), the motion equations for the robotic system with respect to q can be transformed as that with respect to s, just as

$$a(s)\ddot{s} + b(s)\dot{s}^2 + c(s) = \tau \tag{3}$$

$$a(s) = M(q(s))q'(s)$$

$$b(s) = M(q(s))q''(s) + {q'(s)}^T B(q(s))q'(s)$$

$$c(s) = f(q(s))$$

We define a linear system with state $x = \dot{s}^2$ and input control $u = \ddot{s}$ as:

$$a(s)u + b(s)x + c(s) = \tau \tag{4}$$

Assume that the manipulator is subject to lower and upper bounds on the joint torques,

$$\tau_i^{min} \le a_i(s)u + b_i(s)x + c_i(s) \le \tau_i^{max} \tag{5}$$

these torque bounds can be described as:

$$\bar{a}_i(s)u + \bar{b}_i(s)x + \bar{c}_i(s) \le 0 \tag{6}$$

$$\bar{a}_i(s) = \begin{pmatrix} a_i(s) \\ -a_i(s) \end{pmatrix},\ \bar{b}_i(s) = \begin{pmatrix} b_i(s) \\ -b_i(s) \end{pmatrix},\ \bar{c}_i(s) = \begin{pmatrix} c_i(s) - \tau_i^{max} \\ -c_i(s) + \tau_i^{min} \end{pmatrix}$$

if $\bar{a}_i(s) > 0$, then one has $\ddot{s} \le \frac{-\bar{b}_i(s)s^2 - \bar{c}_i(s)}{\bar{a}_i s}$. Define the *upper bound*

$$\beta_i = \frac{-\bar{b}_i(s)s^2 - \bar{c}_i(s)}{\bar{a}_i s};$$

if $\bar{a}_i(s) < 0$, then one has $\ddot{s} \le \frac{-\bar{b}_i(s)s^2 - \bar{c}_i(s)}{\bar{a}_i s}$. Define the *lower bound*

$$\alpha_i = \frac{-\bar{b}_i(s)s^2 - \bar{c}_i(s)}{\bar{a}_i s};$$

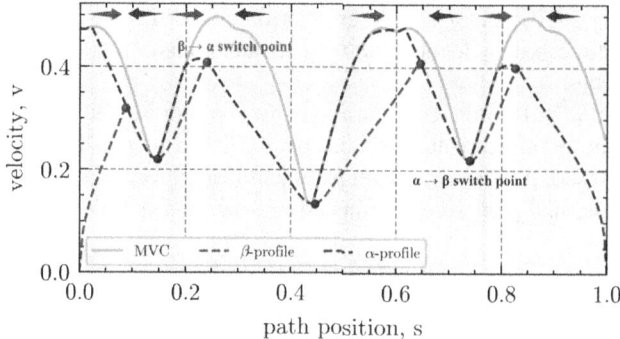

Fig. 1. MVC and α-, β- profiles in the numerical integration approach. α- profile is iteratively solved from the endpoint to the starting point, while β- profile is solved using forward-backward iteration until it intersects with the forward α contour, forming the $\beta \rightarrow \alpha$ switch point.

if $a_i(s) = 0$, then s is a "zero-inertia" point (Fig. 1).

We can define for each $(s, \dot{s})$

$$\alpha(s, \dot{s}) = \min_{p} \alpha_p(s, \dot{s}), \beta(s, \dot{s}) = \max_{q} \beta_q(s, \dot{s}) \tag{7}$$

Conclude that $q(s(t))$ satisfies the constraints (6) if and only if:

$$\alpha(s, \dot{s}) \leq \ddot{s} \leq \beta(s, \dot{s}) \tag{8}$$

Note that if $\alpha(s, \dot{s}) > \beta(s, \dot{s})$ then, from (7), there is no possible value for $\ddot{s}$. Thus, to be valid, every velocity profile must stay below the maximum velocity curve (MVC in short) defined by:

$$\text{MVC}(s) = \begin{cases} \min s \geq 0 : \alpha(s, \dot{s}) = \beta(s, \dot{s}), \, if \, \alpha(s, 0) \leq \beta(s, 0) \\ 0, \, if \, \alpha(s, 0) \geq \beta(s, 0) \end{cases} \tag{9}$$

We divide the predetermined path into N path points and assumes that the motion between adjacent path points is uniformly accelerated (or decelerated). Using simple algebraic manipulations, we obtain:

$$\frac{dx}{ds} = \frac{d\dot{s}^2}{ds} = 2\dot{s}\frac{d\dot{s}}{dt}\frac{dt}{ds} = 2u \tag{10}$$

$$x_{i+1} = x_i + 2\Delta_i u_i \tag{11}$$

TOPP problem with bounded velocities and Torque is generally formulated as:

$$\begin{cases} \max u_i, \text{ subject to:} \\ X_{\min} \leq x_i \leq X_{\max} \\ \tau_{\min} \leq a(s)u + b(s)x + c(s) \leq \tau_{\max} \\ X_{\min} \leq x_i + 2\Delta_i u_i \leq X_{\max} \\ \{i = 2, \cdots, N-1\} \end{cases} \tag{12}$$

where x and u are the optimization variables, X_{min} and X_{max} denote the bounds of velocity, τ_{min} and τ_{max} denote the bounds of torque. Iteratively solving the problem according to Eq. (11) involves maximizing the output torque of each segment under constraints, thereby maximizing the path acceleration u to achieve the goal of time-optimal trajectory.

3 TOPP with Torque and Jerk Constraints

3.1 TOPP with Three Order Constraints

Similar to the classical TOPP algorithm with torque constraints, joint jerk can be described as follows.

$$\dddot{q} = q'''(s)\dot{s}^2 + q''(s)\ddot{s}\dot{s} + q'(s)\dddot{s} \tag{13}$$

$$j_{min} \leq q'''(s)s^3 + q''(s)s\dot{s} + q'(s)\dddot{s} \leq j_{max} \tag{14}$$

$$d(s)s + e(s)ss + f(s)s^3 + g(s) \leq 0 \tag{15}$$

$$d(s) = \begin{pmatrix} q_s(s) \\ -q_s(s) \end{pmatrix}, \quad e(s) = \begin{pmatrix} q_{ss}(s) \\ -q_{ss}(s) \end{pmatrix}$$

$$f(s) = \begin{pmatrix} q_{sss}(s) \\ -q_{sss}(s) \end{pmatrix}, \quad g(s) = \begin{pmatrix} -j_{max} \\ j_{min} \end{pmatrix}$$

At any state $(\dot{s}, \ddot{s}, \dddot{s})$, the minimum jerk γ $(\dot{s}, \ddot{s}, \dddot{s})$ and maximum jerk η $(\dot{s}, \ddot{s}, \dddot{s})$ as follows:

$$\gamma(s, \dot{s}, s) = max_i \left\{ \frac{-e_i(s)\dot{s}s - f_i(s)\dot{s}^3 - g_i(s)}{d_i(s)} d_i(s) < 0 \right\} \tag{16}$$

$$\eta(s, \dot{s}, s) = min_i \left\{ \frac{-e_i(s)\dot{s}s - f_i(s)\dot{s}^3 - g_i(s)}{d_i(s)} d_i(s) > 0 \right\} \tag{17}$$

In the context of trajectory optimization with third-order constraints, adhering to Pontryagin's maximum principle dictates that the time-optimal path transitions between maximum and minimum jerk profiles sequentially. Thus, the pivotal challenge in TOPP lies in determining the appropriate sequence of these profiles and the timing of their transitions.

Achieving simultaneous constraints on torque and jerk entails identifying four concurrent switching points:

(1) $Torque(max) \rightarrow Jerk(max), \beta \rightarrow \eta$
(2) $Jerk(max) \rightarrow Jerk(min), \eta \rightarrow \gamma$
(3) $Jerk(min) \rightarrow Jerk(max), \gamma \rightarrow \eta$
(4) $Jerk(max) \rightarrow Torque(min), \eta \rightarrow \alpha$

The determination of switch points in the three order TOPP algorithm poses significant challenges. This difficulty is compounded by the presence of singularities inherent to the problem. Additionally, the inclusion of torque constraints renders traditional methods such as exhaustive search and numerical approaches impractical for solving the third-order TOPP problem.

3.2 Optimizing TOPP Using Piecewise Polynomial Trajectories

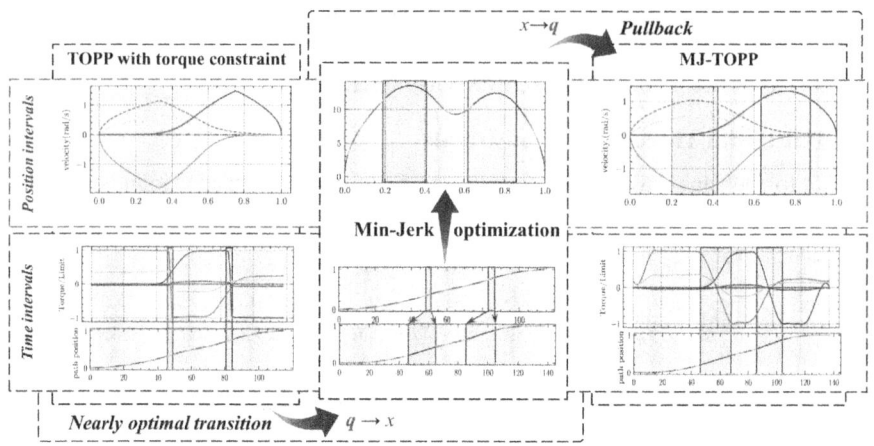

Fig. 2. Schematic diagram illustrating the implementation of the MJ-TOPP algorithm.

In order to solve the third-order constraint problem under the torque constraint, we suggest to appropriately relax the jerk constraint from $\beta \to \alpha$ and use high-order polynomials to avoid bang-bang control, thereby achieving a better jerk profile. Although the optimal jerk control of $\eta \to \gamma \to \eta$ cannot be achieved, a usable result can be obtained at a relatively low cost by optimizing the parameters of the high-order polynomial. The approximate time optimality under torque constraints is guaranteed. The implementation diagram of the MJ-TOPP algorithm is shown in Fig. 2.

After executing the TOPP algorithm under torque constraints, we can obtain a theoretically time-optimal trajectory, and based on this, derive the parameters of the time-optimal trajectory, $s_0, s_0, \ldots, s_{N-1}, s_{N-1}$. To eliminate the acceleration discontinuity at switch points, we suggest employing high-order curve optimization around the switch points of the trajectory.

We first need to segment the time-optimal trajectory under torque constraints according to the principle of equal time intervals. This allows for local jerk optimization on the original theoretically optimal trajectory while ensuring adherence to constraints on the new trajectory.

$$(s_0, s_0), \ldots, (s_{N-1}, s_{N-1}) \to (s_0, \delta t), \ldots, (s_n, \delta t) \tag{18}$$

Next, we take the integral of the two-norm of the joint velocity as the optimization target:

$$(s_0, \delta t), \ldots, (s_n, \delta t) \to (q_0, \dot{q}_0), \ldots, (q_n, \dot{q}_n) \tag{19}$$

$$x_n = \delta t \sum_{i=0}^{n} \|\dot{q}_i\| \tag{20}$$

Use a one-dimensional B-spline curve to establish the mapping f, which is convenient for subsequent Pullback:

$$f : \{x\_1, x\_2, \ldots x\_n\} \rightarrow \{s\_1, s\_2, \ldots s\_n\}$$

Then, the trajectory for segment i can be represented using the following J-degree polynomial:

$$x_i(t) = \sum_{j=0}^{J} a_i[j] t^j \qquad (21)$$

The jerk of the entire trajectory can be expressed as:

$$\sum_{0}^{n-1} \int_{t_i}^{t_{i+1}} \left(x_i^{(3)}(t)\right)^2 dt \qquad (22)$$

$$x_i^{(3)}(t) = \left[0, 0, 0, 6, \ldots, \frac{J!}{(J-3)!}\right] \cdot a_i^T \qquad (23)$$

$$\left(x_i^{(3)}(t)\right)^2 = a_i Q(t) a_i^T \qquad (24)$$

To make the trajectory smoother, a QP solver is used to solve for the path parameter a_i for each segment:

$$\sum_{0}^{n-1} \int_{t_i}^{t_{i+1}} \left(x_i^{(3)}(t)\right)^2 = \sum_{0}^{n-1} a_i Q(t) a_i^T \qquad (25)$$

Utilizing derivative constraints to bound the initial and final states of the trajectory involves constraining aspects such as position, velocity, acceleration, etc., for both the initial and final states.

$$\begin{cases} x_0^{(j)}(t_0) = x_0^{(j)} \\ x_{n-1}^{(j)}(t_n) = x_n^{(j)}, j = 0, \ldots J - 1 \end{cases} \qquad (26)$$

Furthermore, constraints are applied to the starting and ending positions of each trajectory segment, which correspond to the path points obtained at each time point from the TOPP trajectory.

$$x_{i+1}(t_i) = x_i, i = 0, \ldots n - 1 \qquad (27)$$

Continuity Constraint ensures smooth transition between adjacent trajectories, meaning that the 1st, 2nd, 3rd, …, (j-1)th derivatives are equal at the connection point between two adjacent trajectory segments.

$$x_i^{(j)}(t_i) = x_{i+1}^{(j)}(t_i), i = 0, \ldots n - 2, j = 0, \ldots J - 1 \qquad (28)$$

The above algorithm optimizes the time-optimal trajectory under torque constraints, minimizing the jerk integral of the joint angles along the entire path. It is clear that the connection between the algorithm for optimizing trajectory jerk and the TOPP algorithm under torque constraints is determined by two main parameters:

(1) the segmentation strategy (See Fig. 3 horizontal axis): $\{s'_1, s'_2, \ldots s'_n\}$
(2) the time path interval corresponding to each segment (See the right vertical axis of Fig. 3): $\{\delta t_1, \delta t_2, \ldots \delta t_n\}$

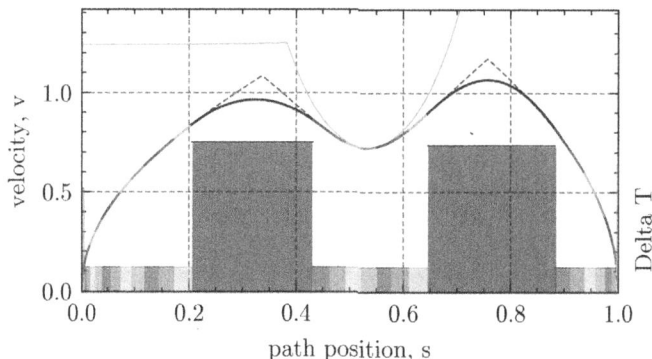

Fig. 3. *Bar chart:* the time required for each path segment. *Curve chart:* MVC (yellow solid line), TOPP trajectory curve (purple dashed line), and MJ-TOPP trajectory curve (segmented solid line.

3.3 Nearly Optimal Transition from β-Profile to α-Profile

We continue to integrate forward along η-profile starting from waypoints on β-profile until the first situation where η-profile and α-profile have two intersections occurs. At this time, the starting point of η-profile is S_A, and the second intersection with α is S_B.

Similarly, integrate following maximum joint jerk (η-profile) from S_B until S_A. We define the function Y:

Since the boundary conditions at the end point cannot be met, the solution obtained can only be used as the velocity constraint of this section, and then the time constraint of this section can be calculated. Obviously, the optimal time of the theoretical optimal solution (i.e. $\eta \to \gamma \to \eta$) is between $\overline{\Delta T_{merge}}$ and $\underline{\Delta T_{merge}}$.

$$\Delta T_{merge} = \sum_{i=0}^{N} \frac{S_B - S_A}{N \, s_i} \quad (29)$$

After solving the segmentation strategy and the time path interval corresponding to each segment, we can now proceed to solve the TOPP problem. The MJ-TOPP algorithm utilizes a polynomial optimization approach to achieve smooth ansitions between two profiles constrained by maximum torque. Therefore, after reasonable deceleration and smoothing around switch points, the change of torque on each axis slows down, making the control more stable. To prevent exceeding constraints, a more conservative time interval $\overline{\Delta T_{merge}}$ is usually employed for the transition segment. While theoretical time optimality (i.e. maximum torque → maximum jerk → minimum jerk → maximum jerk → minimum torque) isn't fully achieved, the algorithm sidesteps the complex task of simultaneously determining four switch points (Fig. 4).

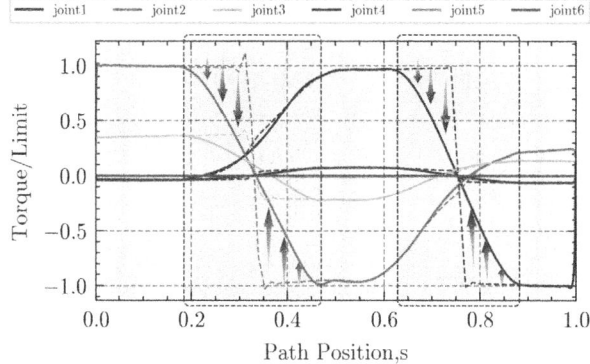

Fig. 4. An example of normalized joint torque curves of trajectory outputs obtained using TOPP (dashed line) and MJ-TOPP (solid line)

4 Simulation and Experiment Result

To validate the effectiveness of the proposed algorithm, this section initially conducts simulation experiments using the MJ-TOPP algorithm. The purpose is to demonstrate that under complex motion dynamics constraints, the MJ-TOPP algorithm achieves significant jerk optimization while approximating time optimality. Additionally, simulations and experiments are designed for trajectories mimicking the shape of the word "HIT". Furthermore, the simulation and experimental results are compared with the Target-Reachable Path Planning Trajectory Optimization (TOPP-RA) algorithm [11]. This comparison aims to verify the effectiveness of the proposed method in mitigating acceleration fluctuations. Simulations and experiments are carried out using a typical 6 degree-of-freedom robot.

To validate the impact of the MJ-TOPP algorithm on trajectory jerk optimization, we designed a continuous trajectory in the shape of a "HIT" (see Fig. 5). The trajectory comprises 21 right-angle bends, with a total length of 1698 mm and a total of 3519 waypoints. Table 1 provides an overview of the motion kinematic constraints employed in this process (Table 2).

Table 1. The motion kinematic constraints employed in this process.

	Joint1	Joint2	Joint3	Joint4	Joint5	Joint6
Torque (Nm)	120	120	120	42	42	20
Velocity(rad/s)	0.8	0.8	0.8	0.8	0.8	0.8

Table 2. The path tracking error

	TOPP-RA	MJ-TOPP	Drop-percentage
MAE (mm)	0.52	0.44	15.38%
Velocity(mm)	2.39	2.00	16.32%

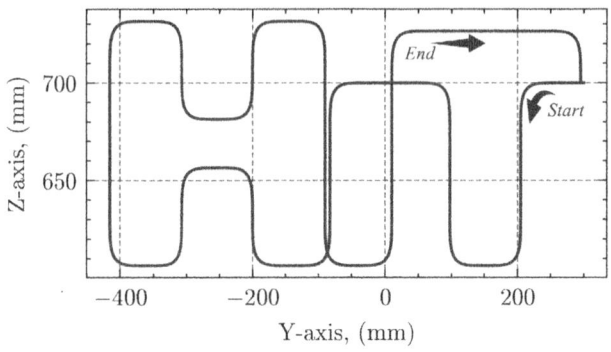

Fig. 5. Robot End-effector Trajectory Image.

Through simulation, we can obtain the trajectories, joint velocities, accelerations, and jerk of the TOPP-RA algorithm and the MJ-TOPP algorithm. Compared with the TOPP-RA algorithm, the trajectory obtained by the MJ-TOPP algorithm only extended by 1.25%, but the maximum jerk of the trajectory was reduced by more than 90%. In Fig. 6, following the application of the MJ-TOPP algorithm, the torque values for each joint remain within the specified constraints, with noticeable reductions in torque variation rates. In experimental scenarios, this manifests as deviations in actual joint positions from commanded target positions, resulting in end-effector errors.

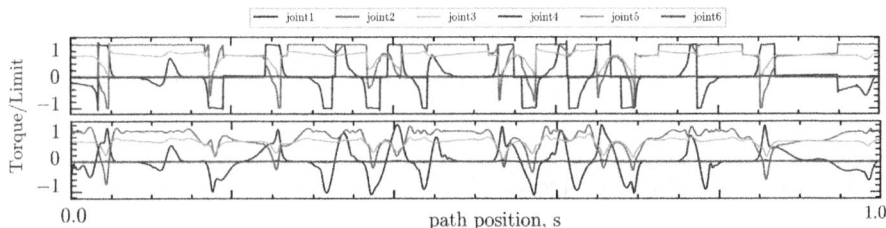

Fig. 6. Normalized joint torque curve. **Top**: TOPP-RA. **Bottom**: MJ-TOPP.

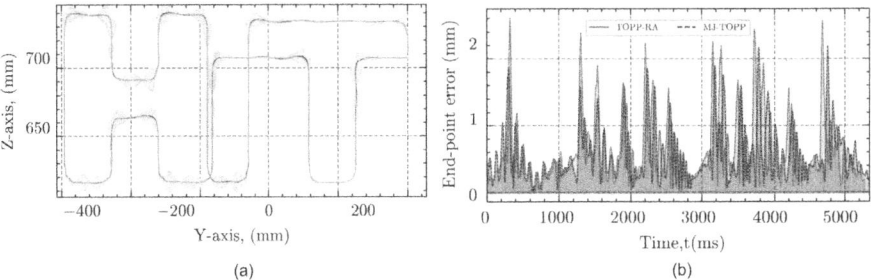

Fig. 7. (a): Errors in the z-axis and y-axis directions, yellow: MJ-TOPP, purple: TOPP-RA. (b): The path tracking error

The offline trajectory obtained from previous simulations is executed on the established experimental platform. Figure 7 depicts the tracking error generated by both the TOPP algorithm and the MJ-TOPP algorithm when traversing the "HIT" shaped path. It is evident that the tracking error is reduced after implementing the MJ-TOPP algorithm. Calculation reveals that upon employing the MJ-TOPP algorithm, the Mean Absolute Error (MAE) of the path tracking error decreases from 0.52 mm to 0.44 mm, marking a reduction of 15.4%. Additionally, the maximum tracking error at the end of the path segment decreases from 2.39 mm to 2.00 mm. Therefore, it can be concluded that the MJ-TOPP algorithm reduces the terminal path error caused by trajectory planning that fails to take into account the torque change capability of the motor while achieving approximate time optimization.

5 Conclusion

This paper presents MJ-TOPP, a trajectory planning algorithm that generates approximately time-optimal motion while significantly enhancing motion smoothness under torque and jerk constraints. By adopting a segmented optimization framework with conservative polynomial smoothing near torque switching points, MJ-TOPP avoids the need for simultaneously identifying multiple switching events, thereby improving computational tractability and motion stability. Experimental evaluations on complex end-effector trajectories demonstrate that the proposed method substantially reduces joint-level jerk with minimal sacrifice in execution time. The resulting interaction-friendly motion profiles improve tracking accuracy and dynamic compliance, making MJ-TOPP particularly suitable for humanoid robots and physical human-robot interaction scenarios where smoothness and safety are critical.

Acknowledgement. This work was supported by the National Key R&D Program of China under Grant No.2022YFB4700300 and the National Natural Science Foundation of China (NSFC) (No. 52025054 & No. 52105016). The fellowship of China Postdoctoral Science Foundation (grant number 2022M710957).

References

1. Chen, C.S., Chen, S.K.: Synchronization of tool tip trajectory and attitude based on the surface characteristics of workpiece for 6-DOF robot manipulator. Robot. Comput. Integr. Manuf. **59**, 13–27 (2019)
2. Guo, Y., Niu, W., Zhou, J., Liu, H.: Near-time optimal feedrate planning for the NURBS curve considering interpolation error constraints. Robot. Comput. Integr. Manuf. **86**, 102679 (2024)
3. Bobrow, J.E., Dubowsky, S., Gibson, J.S.: Time-optimal control of robotic manipulators along specified paths. Int. J. Robot. Res. **4**(3), 3–17 (1985)
4. Shiller, Z., Lu, H.-H.: Robust computation of path constrained time optimal motions. In: Proceedings of IEEE International Confernce on Robotics and Automation, pp. 144–149 (1990)
5. Cheng, C.-A., et al.: RMP flow: a computational graph for automatic motion policy generation. In: Algorithmic Foundations of Robotics XIII*, pp. 441–457, Springer, Cham (2020)
6. Cheng, C.A., et al.: RMPflow: a geometric framework for generation of multitask motion policies. IEEE Trans. Autom. Sci. Eng. **18**(3), 968–987 (2021)
7. Kunz, T., Stilman, M.: Time-optimal trajectory generation for path following with bounded acceleration and velocity, arXiv preprint arXiv:1311.2263 (2013)
8. Kaserer, D., Gattringer, H., Müller, A.: Nearly optimal path following with jerk and torque rate limits using dynamic programming. IEEE Trans. Robot. **35**(2), 521–528 (2018)
9. Verscheure, D., Demeulenaere, B., Swevers, J., De Schutter, J., Diehl, M.: Practical time-optimal trajectory planning for robots: a convex optimization approach. IEEE Trans. Autom. Control **53**(1), 28 (2008)
10. Pham, H., Pham, Q.C.: A new approach to time-optimal path parameterization based on reachability analysis. IEEE Trans. Robot. **34**(3), 645–659 (2018)
11. Pham, Q.C.: A general, fast, and robust implementation of the time-optimal path parameterization algorithm. IEEE Trans. Robot. **30**(6), 1533–1540 (2014)
12. Huang, H., Liu, H., Xia, C., Mei, H., Gao, X., Liang, B.: Sampling-based time-optimal path parameterization with jerk constraints for robotic manipulation. Robot. Auton. Syst. **170**, 104530 (2023)
13. Ma, J.W., Gao, S., Yan, H.T., Lv, Q., Hu, G.Q.: A new approach to time-optimal trajectory planning with torque and jerk limits for robot. Robot. Auton. Syst. **140**, 103744 (2021)
14. Pham, H., Pham, Q.-C.: On the structure of the time-optimal path parameterization problem with third-order constraints. In: Proceedings of IEEE International Conference on Robotics and Automation (ICRA), pp. 679–686 (2017)

Tactile Servo Control Based on Reinforcement Learning Applied to Flexible Wires Manipulation

Yihan Shan, Changle Li, Zhe Gao, Gangfeng Liu, Xuehe Zhang[(✉)], Chong Yao, Zhantao Xu, and Jie Zhao

Harbin Institute of Technology, Harbin 150001, China
zhangxuehe@hit.edu.cn

Abstract. As a typical deformable linear object (DLO), flexible wires have very wide applications, and in recent years, there has been increasing focus on robotic manipulation of wires. Traditional rigid control methods often struggle to cope with the nonlinear deformation and uncertainties of wires during manipulation. Most previous studies have employed a combination of vision and tactile sensing to accomplish tasks such as grasping, socket insertion, or planar wiring, and there are also efforts focused on shape control of wires. This paper focuses on using only a single tactile perception to complete the robot's compliant following of wires and the fixed-trajectory wiring operation in three-dimensional space. To this end, we propose a robot control framework based on tactile sensing for the automated manipulation of flexible wires. Firstly, the recognition of the wire posture inside the tactile gripper was completed. Next, we introduce a tactile servo control method based on Deep Deterministic Policy Gradient (DDPG). Finally, we define the overall algorithm framework to carry out the specific task. The experimental results show that our design is competent for this task. It expands the limitations of planar wiring and is capable of completing the wire routing task while performing specific three-dimensional space trajectories.

Keywords: Robot Skill Learning · Tactile Servo · DLO Manipulation

1 Introduction

Tactile sensors can sense information such as force, temperature and vibration in the external environment [1], providing real-time feedback for robots and thus enabling more precise and complex operations. The manipulation of flexible wires is a major challenge in robot operation, mainly due to the high flexibility of the wires and the uncertainty during the manipulation process [2]. Physical modeling methods predict the deformation behavior of wires by establishing their mechanical models [3]. Such methods are highly dependent on the characteristics of the wires and usually require detailed parameter measurements and modeling of the wires. In recent years, machine learning methods have gradually become a research hotspot [4, 5]. By learning patterns from a large amount of manipulation data, robots can predict and control the behavior of wires without an accurate physical model.

Traditional visual servo control often performs poorly when dealing with flexible wire manipulation due to the lack of force feedback information. Therefore, tactile sensors are needed to optimize the manipulation process. Tactile servo control refers to the use of feedback information from tactile sensors to adjust the force and position control during robot manipulation process to achieve higher precision [6–8]. Tactile servoing requires consideration of control strategy design, using tactile information to adjust the operation trajectory and applied force in real time to ensure precise routing and installation of the wire.

In this work, we aim to propose a set of tactile robot skills to perform operations such as following, straightening the wire, and three-dimensional spatial wiring on flexible wires. These tasks are characterized by significant deformation of the manipulated object during the operation, where the wire is constrained at only one end while the other end hangs freely. The robot can adapt to various types of contact and employ the tactile servo control framework for different manipulation tasks.

2 Related Work

DLO manipulation mainly has challenges such as nonlinear deformation, complex contact and multi-degree-of-freedom control. The DLO contour tracking method can be used as a strategy to avoid the use of visual sensors and relax the assumption of grasping DLO at known points, allowing for the tracking of its contour and reaching one end from the other end. She et al. [2] designed a variable perception and control framework and used real-time tactile feedback to complete the task of following the suspended wire. The tactile sensor designed by G. Palli and S. Pirozzi [9] is used to estimate the local shape of the grasped wire, approximates it with a linear function, and proposes a strategy for reorientation the fixture to complete the insertion at the end of the wire. M. Yu et al. [10] use a universal dexterous hand in a V-shaped grasp state to emulate human skill for DLO following, demonstrating clear advantages over parallel grippers. J. Zhu et al. [3] utilized the contacts in the environment to change the shape of the wires.

In the realm of reinforcement learning, R. B. Hellman et al. [5] proposed a C-MAB reinforcement learning algorithm for real-time tactile perception and decision-making, which is used for tactile-driven contour tracking tasks: sealing bags. S. Zhaole et al. [4] proposed the model-free framework DexDLO to learn the dexterous dynamic operation strategy for deformable linear objects using fixed dexterous hands in an end-to-end manner. D. De Gregorio et al. [11] proposed a new technique for accelerating the generation of convolutional neural network (CNN) training datasets, combining data from tactile and visual sensors to perform insertions.

Through tactile servo control, the robot can perceive and adapt to complex operating environments, and precisely control the contact force and operation path. H.Zhang and N. N. Chen [6] formulated the overall framework of tactile servoing, modeled the contact based on the contact state vector, and expressed the robot task by the trajectory of the state vector. Q. Li et al. [7] et al. designed a control framework to implement a complete set of tactile servo tasks, aiming to achieve the control tasks of specific tactile interaction patterns. Z. Kappassov et al. [8] designed a tactile servo controller that combines tactile features with the Cartesian impedance controller of the robotic arm. N. F. Lepora and

J. Lloyd [12] proposed a pose-based tactile servoing (PBTS) control using soft tactile sensors, which can achieve robust and precise controlled motion on various complex 3D objects.

3 Methodology

3.1 Tactile Perception Analysis and Contact Modeling

The normal force of the pressure sensing array generates a two-dimensional pressure distribution. Such an array is composed of load sensing units, each of which measures the pressure generated by an object pressing on it. The entire tactile array provides the spatial distribution of the pressure.

First, the contact region on the sensor must be identified. Due to the softness of the sensor's TPU substrate, this contact region typically extends over a relatively large area in the image. To address this, we apply connected-component analysis from image processing to extract all connected regions in the tactile image, then select the largest of these as the contact region R. Subsequently, we calculate the normal total contact force f as the sum of the internal forces f_{ij} in the contact area, and calculate the contact center position c as the weighted pressure center in the R area:

$$c = \frac{\sum_{i,j \in R} f_{ij} c_{ij}}{\sum_{i,j \in R} f_{ij}} \quad (1)$$

where c_{ij} represents the discrete coordinates of the sensing unit on the surface coordinates of the sensor.

In order to extract the direction Angle of the linear contact area and identify the main principal components of the contact area, the analysis method of image moments was used. First, obtain the position of the center point of the contact area:

$$x_c = \frac{\sum_I \sum_J i \cdot V(i,j)}{\sum_I \sum_J V(i,j)} \quad y_c = \frac{\sum_I \sum_J j \cdot V(i,j)}{\sum_I \sum_J V(i,j)} \quad (2)$$

where $V(i,j)$ represents the gray value of the image at a point (i,j) in the sensor plane coordinate system, with the denominator and numerator being the zero-order moment M_{00} and the first-order moment, respectively. The first-order moment can be used to find the center of gravity of the binary image. At this point, the formulas for calculating the second-order moment is given, which can be used to calculate the direction of the object's shape:

$$M_{20} = \sum_I \sum_J i^2 \cdot V(i,j)$$

$$M_{02} = \sum_I \sum_J j^2 \cdot V(i,j)$$

$$M_{11} = \sum_I \sum_J i \cdot j \cdot V(i,j) \quad (3)$$

$$\alpha = \frac{1}{2} \arctan \frac{2b}{a-c}$$

$$a = \frac{M_{20}}{M_{00}} - x_c^2, \; b = \frac{M_{11}}{M_{00}} - x_c y_c, \; c = \frac{M_{02}}{M_{00}} - y_c^2$$

The obtained angle α represents the direction of the image's principal component relative to the x-axis, which corresponds to the wire's axial direction in the coordinate system of the gripper's tactile sensor.

Figure 1 depicts a top view of the state of a cylindrical wire in contact with a sensor array with a smooth surface. When the wire applies a normal force on the sensor surface, there are multiple tactile positions in contact with it. The actual contact shape of the wire is approximately as shown in the orange box area, and the closer to the center, the larger the contact area.

The tactile information representing the contact position is extracted from the generated grayscale image using the image moment analysis equation. The position of the pressure center is indicated by the solid green dot in the figure. The first two tactile pieces of information are the deviations of the pressure center position relative to the coordinate system of the sensor center. The X-axis deviation is denoted as Δx, the Y-axis deviation as Δy, and the rotation Angle around the Z-axis direction as α.

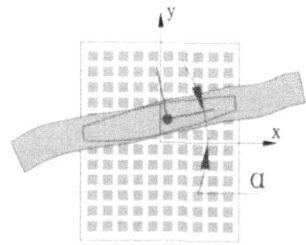

Fig. 1. Schematic picture of wire contact modeling

3.2 Tactile Servo Control Strategy Design for Compliantly Following Wires

When a person uses their fingers to follow a wire, they typically use the pads of two fingertips to gently pinch and grasp the wire, allowing them to sense the wire's state between the fingertips and ensure that the wire does not slip out. At the same time, the two fingers grasping the wire are not perfectly aligned: a portion of each fingertip's pad extends slightly beyond the grasping point, enabling the person to anticipate the wire's upcoming trajectory and counteract the effect of its weight (Fig. 2).

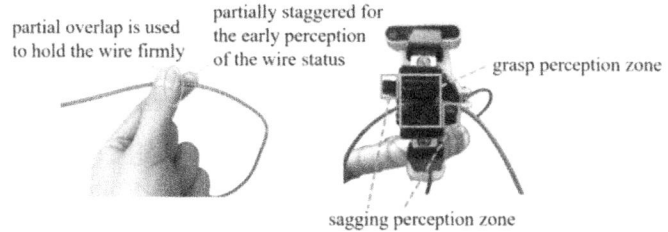

Fig. 2. The gripper simulates the operation of human fingers following wires

A pair of six-dimensional force tactile sensing arrays is adopted to imitate the process of a human hand following wires. The two sensing arrays are arranged in parallel and alternately, with some overlapping. The overlapping part is defined as the grasping perception zone, and the staggered part is regarded as the sagging perception zone. The sensing array consists of 12 rows and 10 columns. Among them, 7 columns are used as the grasping perception zone to ensure the effective contact between the wire and the gripper. The three deviation values of x, y, and α are given by the tactile image processing method described earlier.

The other three columns are used as the sagging perception zone to sense the wire's sagging state, such as the magnitude of gravity, making the wire following process more smooth and natural. The deviation output by the sagging perception zone is denoted as ΔF, which is used to simultaneously control the rotation around the Y-axis and the movement along the z-axis in the sensor coordinate system, and there is a proportional relationship k between the two. Based on the normal force distribution data perceived in the wire sagging perception zone of each three-dimensional force tactile sensing array, calculate $F_{\theta 1}$ and $F_{\theta 2}$. $F_{\theta 1}$ and $F_{\theta 2}$ are the resultant forces of all contact points in the normal direction in the wire sagging perception zone of the three-dimensional force tactile sensing array located below and above respectively. Calculate the contour drop deviation $\Delta F = F_{\theta 1} - F_{\theta 2}$. The wire sagging perception zone senses different wire sagging states, which are reflected by the contour drop deviation.

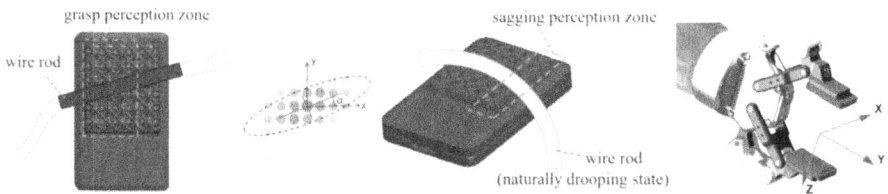

Fig. 3. Schematic diagram of the compliant following grasping strategy and coordinate system

As shown in Fig. 3, the sensor coordinate system is defined. The origin of the coordinate system is located in the plane of the axial center positions of the two grippers.

The Y-axis is along the edge of the sensing area, pointing outward. The X-axis points to the perception zone where the wire falls. The Z-axis is naturally obtained, x and y respectively correspond to the position offset of the wire relative to the sensor coordinate system, α represents the angular deflection in the Z-axis direction. ΔF is the quantity obtained from the sagging perception zone to control the gripper's compliance with the wire, mapped as the position control deviation in the Z-direction, and $k \cdot \Delta F$ is mapped as the angular control deviation around the Y-axis direction. Based on these deviation quantities, the six-dimensional spatial pose of the wire inside the gripper is approximately obtained. Taking this as the new pose target matrix, the griper realizes the continuous wire following movement with automatic adjustment along the axis direction of the wire.

3.3 DDPG-Based Predetermined-Trajectory Wire-Routing Operation

For a fixed-trajectory wiring task, obtaining the trajectory's path-point information is a necessary precondition for task execution. In this experiment, the 3D model of the track is known and can be converted into a point cloud for subsequent normal-vector extraction. In 3D point-cloud processing, normal-vector estimation is fundamental to tasks such as surface reconstruction and feature extraction. In this paper, we adopt a Principal Component Analysis (PCA)–based method for 3D point-cloud normal-vector estimation, which can effectively estimate the direction of the normal vectors.

For any point $p_i \in \mathbb{R}^3$ in the point cloud, first determine its local neighborhood point set $N_i = \{p_1, p_1, \cdots, p_k\}$, which can be obtained through the K-nearest neighbor or radius search method. The geometric distribution of the neighborhood points implies the local surface characteristics.Calculate the centroid of the neighborhood point set and perform decentralized processing on each neighborhood point to obtain the decentralized coordinates:

$$\mu = \frac{1}{k} \sum_{j=1}^{k} p_j \tag{4}$$

$$q_j = p_j - \mu, j = 1, 2, \ldots, k$$

Construct a decentralized data matrix $Q \in \mathbb{R}^{k \times 3}$, whose j-th row is q_j. The covariance matrix of the local geometric characteristics is:

$$C = \frac{1}{k} Q^T Q = \frac{1}{k} \sum_{j=1}^{k} q_j q_j^T \tag{5}$$

The covariance matrix $C \in \mathbb{R}^{3 \times 3}$ is a symmetric semi-positive definite matrix, representing the distribution of neighborhood points in three-dimensional space. Eigenvalue decomposition is performed on C:

$$C = V \Lambda V^T \tag{6}$$

where $V = [v_1, v_1, v_3] \in \mathbb{R}^{3 \times 3}$ is an orthogonal matrix, and the column vector v_i is the eigenvector; $\Lambda = \text{diag}(\lambda_1, \lambda_2, \lambda_3)$ is a diagonal matrix, and $\lambda_1 \geq \lambda_2 \geq \lambda_3 \geq 0$. The feature vectors v_1, v_2, v_3 correspond respectively to the principal component directions of the data. Among them, v_1 corresponds to the maximum eigenvalue λ_1, which is the main direction of the neighborhood point distribution; v_3 corresponds to the minimum eigenvalue λ_3, which represents the direction of the least data change, that is, the normal vector direction of the local surface. Select the eigenvector $n_i = v_3$ corresponding to the minimum eigenvalue as the normal vector.

To ensure direction consistency, the normal vector can be directed towards the viewpoint or corrected by propagating the adjacent normal vector. The minimum eigenvalue λ_3 of the covariance matrix measures the degree of dispersion of neighborhood points along the normal vector direction. When the neighborhood points are approximately in the tangent plane, $\lambda_3 \approx 0$, at this time v_3 is perpendicular to the tangent plane, which is the direction of the normal vector. Finally, the path points are fitted with their corresponding normal vectors through proximity search (Fig. 4).

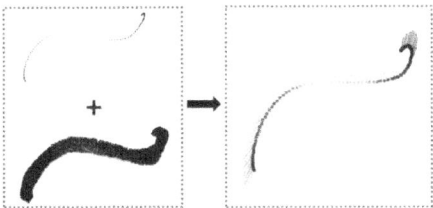

Fig. 4. Path point normal vector fitting graph

Next, the tactile servo control DDPG algorithm applied to wire operation is introduced. Consider a 6-degree-of-freedom mechanical arm, whose end effector is a two-finger gripper. The spatial curve trajectory and normal vector were given in the previous section. For the convenience of introduction, they are discretized into 100 path points and their corresponding sequences of unit normal vectors:

$$\mathbb{C} = \left\{ p_i^* \in R^3 | i = 1 \ldots 100 \right\} \\ \left\{ n_i^* \in R^3 | \|n_i^*\| = 1 \right\} \tag{7}$$

The objective is to ensure that the local Z-axis of the gripper is always parallel to the normal vector n_i^* of the current trajectory point, while the center of the gripper moves along the path $p_1^* \to p_{100}^*$ and only allows yaw rotation around its own Z-axis, so as to dynamically correct based on the feedback from the tactile sensor. This control problem is modeled as a Markov decision process (S, A, P, r, γ). State space $S = \mathbb{R}^9$, at time t, state vector:

$$s_t = \begin{bmatrix} \Delta x_t^{sen} & \Delta y_t^{sen} & \Delta \theta_t^{sen} \\ \Delta x_t^{pos} & \Delta y_t^{pos} & \Delta z_t^{pos} \\ e_{x,t}^n & e_{y,t}^n & e_{z,t}^n \end{bmatrix} \in \mathbb{R}^9 \tag{8}$$

where $\Delta x_t^{sen}, \Delta y_t^{sen}, \Delta z_t^{sen}$ represents the feedback deviation of the tactile sensor, $\Delta x_t^{pos}, \Delta y_t^{pos}, \Delta z_t^{pos}$ represents the difference between the current position of the end and the position of the target trajectory point, and $e_{x,t}^n, e_{y,t}^n, e_{z,t}^n$ represents the difference between the normal vector of the current Z-axis direction of the end and the target trajectory point. The action space and state transition equation are:

$$\begin{aligned} a_t &= \tau_z \in [-k\pi, k\pi] \\ s_{t+1} &= f(s_t, a_t) + w_t \end{aligned} \quad (9)$$

where τ_z represents the rotation Angle around the Z-axis, and $k = 0.1$ is the safety factor; $f(s_t, a_t)$ is the kinematic model of the robotic arm, and w_t is the sensor noise and modeling error.

The main task of this tactile servo is to perform the complete spatial wire routing. During this process, the wire needs to maintain a good centered position in the gripper to prevent it from falling. Therefore, the reward function is designed to be expressed as Eq. 10, which not only completes the trajectory execution but also highlights the adjustment of tactile feedback.

$$r_t = -\lambda_1 \left(\Delta x^2 + \Delta y^2 \right) - \lambda_2 \Delta \theta_z^2 + \beta I_{step} + \gamma I_{complete} - \eta I_{drop} \quad (10)$$

Among them, $\lambda_1 = 0.5, \lambda_2 = 0.3, \beta = 0.5, \gamma = 50, \eta = 30$, I_{step} is triggered every 1% completed, $I_{complete}$ every 100% completed, and I_{drop} sensor is triggered when there is no feedback for two consecutive seconds (regarded as the wire falling). $-\lambda_1 \left(\Delta x^2 + \Delta y^2 \right)$ is the position deviation penalty, $-\lambda_2 \Delta \theta_z^2$ is the Angle deviation penalty, βI_{step} is the trajectory progress reward, $\gamma I_{complete}$ is the task completion reward, and $-\eta I_{drop}$ is the wire drop penalty.

The policy gradient is updated as follows: Actor parameter update and Critic loss function (Fig. 5):

$$\begin{aligned} \nabla_{\theta^\mu} J &\approx \frac{1}{N} \sum_i \nabla_a Q\left(s, a | \theta^Q\right)|_{s=s_i, a=\mu(s_i)} \nabla_{\theta^\mu} \mu\left(s | \theta^\mu\right)|_{s_i} \\ L &= \frac{1}{N} \sum_i \left(y_i - Q\left(s_i, a_i | \theta^Q\right) \right)^2 \\ y_i &= r_i + \gamma Q'\left(s_{i+1}, u'\left(s_{i+1} | \theta^{\mu'}\right) | \theta^{Q'}\right) \end{aligned} \quad (11)$$

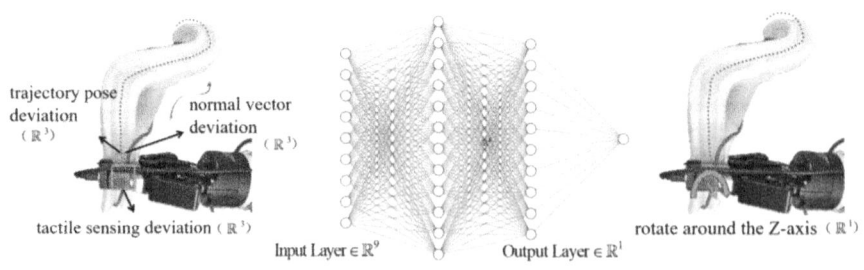

Fig. 5. The network structure diagram of fixed-trajectory wiring operation based on DDPG

4 Experimental Results

4.1 Wire Adaptability Following Experiment

We adopt capacitive tactile sensor array and ROBOTIQ 2F-85 gripper was installed at the end of the UR5 robotic arm.The sensor's normal force measurement range is 0 to 25 N, and the array resolution is 2.5 mm.

In this experiment, three coaxial wires of different thicknesses were selected, with diameters of 3 mm, 6 mm, and 10 mm respectively. The materials of the three were the same, and their densities were approximately considered to be the same. The main differences in properties caused by different diameters lie in mass and bending degree. Arranged from the smallest to the largest diameter, the mass increased successively and the bending degree decreased.

The sensor staggered arrangement method mentioned above is adopted. One end of the wire is fixed and the other end is in a free state. At the initial position, the gripper is clamped at the fixed end of the wire, the sensor plane is horizontal, and the wire following task begins to be performed. The gripper has a constant speed of 0.05m/s away from the fixed end, and the gripper position is automatically adjusted according to the deviation of the sensor (Fig. 6).

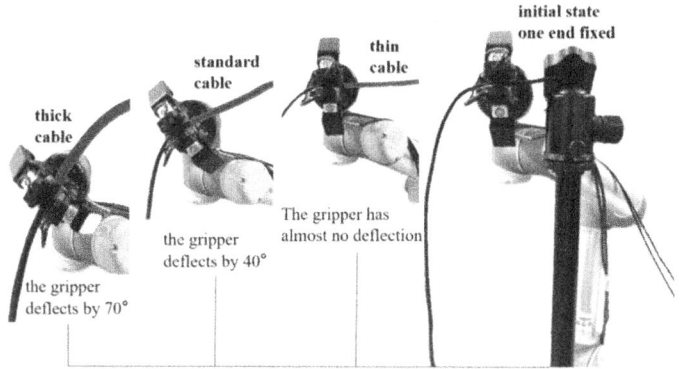

Fig. 6. Compliance following operation of different wires

The experimental results show that when performing the wire-following operation on a thin wire, the gripper hardly deflects, and the mechanical gripper performs the wire following operation along the original trajectory. However, when operating on thick wires, due to the large gravity of the wire and its bending and pressing on the sensor's sagging perception zone, under the guidance of tactile feedback, the mechanical gripper at the end performs deflection and descent movements while moving away from the fixed end. To a certain extent, this is reflected in the gripper moving along with the original state of the wire. While following the wire, it ensures the adaptability to the wire and protects the wire from damage. The wire following task of the predetermined length has been completed.

It should be noted that throughout the entire process of performing the wire following task, the feedback value of the tangential force of the sensor is always used to adjust the opening and closing of the gripper, ensuring that the output force of the gripper is appropriate and the wire following task is executed more smoothly. During this process, the end gripper of the mechanical arm is constantly adjusting the planar position of the sensor, so that the wire is located at the center of the gripper, ensuring the effective contact area between the wire and the gripper. Under this premise, the wire is gently followed.

4.2 Three-Dimensional Space Fixed-Trajectory Wire Routing Task

Previous wire routing tasks did not involve trajectory path issues. The robot could adjust its posture arbitrarily according to tactile feedback to ensure that the wire remained at the center of the gripper or dexterous finger, and the routing of the wire was mostly planar tasks. In this experiment, while the gripper is executed at the predetermined trajectory position, the wire is adjusted in real time according to the tactile feedback and arranged in the wire slot in the three-dimensional space.

The operation object of this experiment is a coaxial wire with a diameter of 3 mm. Since the task of routing the three-dimensional space with a fixed trajectory needs to be performed, the target position that the sensor center on the griper needs to move has already been limited. Moreover, it is necessary to keep the sensor plane always perpendicular to the normal vector direction of the track. Therefore, the rotation in the Z-axis direction needs to be adjusted according to the deviation of the tactile sensing. To ensure that the wire always remains near the center position of the gripper, a position error of 3 mm is allowed, and a vertical error of 3° between the sensor plane.

While the gripper is performing the task of routing out the wires, there should be a device to fix the position of the wires in real time. This experiment assumes the existence of such a device and divides the entire track trajectory into three sections. The policy network (Actor) adopts a three-layer fully connected architecture, while the value network (Critic) takes a 10-dimensional vector formed by concatenating the state and action as input. During training, the policy and value networks are optimized separately, with learning rates set to $1 \times e^{-4}$ and $1 \times e^{-3}$, respectively. The experience replay buffer size is set to 1,000,000, and the batch size is 64. The discount factor γ is set to 0.99 to account for the influence of future rewards. The policy is considered to have converged if the average cumulative reward over 10 consecutive episodes consistently exceeds 20 and the wire routing success rate is above 90%.

Experiments show that during the wire routing process, the wire is mostly in a tensioned state. When a position offset occurs, the gripper will automatically adjust the Z-axis rotation Angle. This rotation momentum, combined with the velocity pointing towards the target point, yields the final motion output, which can adjust the relative pose of the wire within the gripper and ensure the effective contact area between the gripper and the wire. The robotic arm can perform the task of wire routing with fixed trajectories in three-dimensional space (Fig. 7).

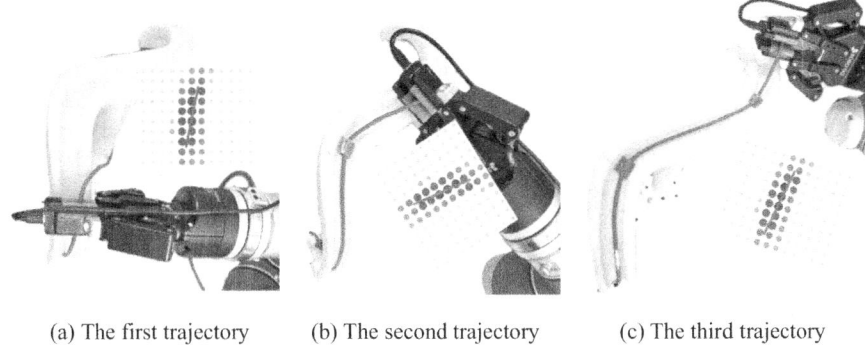

(a) The first trajectory (b) The second trajectory (c) The third trajectory

Fig. 7. Three-dimensional spatial fixed-trajectory routing operation of wire

It should be noted that during the entire wire routing process, the output movement causes the wire to be slightly adjusted within a small range near the center of the gripper, the wire always remains in the center position of the gripper. If the initial wire offset is large, the robot will not be able to complete the entire wire routing task. In other words, the initial position of the wire should be near the center of the gripper to reserve adjustment margin for subsequent movements.

5 Conclusion

We propose a tactile servo control method applied to the manipulate of flexible wires (DLO). Different from previous studies, in this paper, the wiring task is extended to the three-dimensional space. It is not only limited to the position adjustment of planar wiring, but also has the adaptive posture, which can perceive different types of wires and output suitable trajectory strategies. More importantly, based on the Deep Deterministic Policy Gradient (DDPG), the fixed-trajectory wire routing operation in three-dimensional space has been realized. The wire routing task is completed while the end griper performs a specific trajectory, which greatly improves the flexibility of the application scenario.

In the future, we plan to improve the accuracy of tactile sensors and servo control algorithms, enhance operational efficiency and stability, and expand the wiring task to a wider range of spatial environments. At the same time, it is also considered to design a matching wire fixing device to achieve a complete automated wiring process.

References

1. Zhao, F., et al.: A novel tactile palm for robotic object manipulation. In: Yang, H., et al (eds.) Intelligent Robotics and Applications. LNCS, vol. 14271, pp. 81–92. Springer, Singapore (2023). https://doi.org/10.1007/978-981-99-6495-6_8
2. She, Y., Wang, S., Dong, S., Sunil, N., Rodriguez, A., Adelson, E.: Cable manipulation with a tactile-reactive gripper. Int. J. Robot. Res. **40**(12–14), 1385–1401 (2021). https://doi.org/10.1177/02783649211027233

3. Zhu, J., Navarro, B., Passama, R., Fraisse, P., Crosnier, A., Cherubini, A.: Robotic manipulation planning for shaping deformable linear objects with environmental contacts. IEEE Robot. Autom. Lett. **5**(1), 16–23 (2020). https://doi.org/10.1109/LRA.2019.2944304
4. Zhaole, S., Zhu, J., Fisher, R.B.: DexDLO: learning goal-conditioned dexterous policy for dynamic manipulation of deformable linear objects. In: 2024 IEEE International Conference on Robotics and Automation (ICRA), pp. 16009–16015. IEEE, Yokohama (2024). https://doi.org/10.1109/ICRA57147.2024.10610754
5. Hellman, R.B., Tekin, C., Van Der Schaar, M., Santos, V.J.: Functional contour-following via tactile perception and reinforcement learning. IEEE Trans. tactiles **11**(1), 61–72 (2018). https://doi.org/10.1109/TOH.2017.2753233
6. Zhang, H., Chen, N.N.: Control of contact via tactile sensing. IEEE Trans. Robot. Autom. **16**(5), 482–495 (2000). https://doi.org/10.1109/70.880799
7. Li, Q., Schürmann, C., Haschke, R., Ritter, H.: A control framework for tactile servoing. In Robotics: Science and Systems IX, Robotics: Science and Systems Foundation (2013). https://doi.org/10.15607/RSS.2013.IX.045
8. Kappassov, Z., Corrales, J.-A., Perdereau, V.: Touch driven controller and tactile features for physical interactions. Robot. Auton. Syst. **123**, 103332 (2020). https://doi.org/10.1016/j.robot.2019.103332
9. Palli, G., Pirozzi, S.: A tactile-based wire manipulation system for manufacturing applications. Robotics **8**(2), 46 (2019). https://doi.org/10.3390/robotics8020046
10. Yu, M., et al.: In-hand following of deformable linear objects using dexterous fingers with tactile sensing (2024). arXiv: arXiv:2403.12676. https://doi.org/10.48550/arXiv.2403.12676
11. De Gregorio, D., Zanella, R., Palli, G., Pirozzi, S., Melchiorri, C.: Integration of robotic vision and tactile sensing for wire-terminal insertion tasks. IEEE Trans. Autom. Sci. Eng. **16**(2), 585–598 (2019). https://doi.org/10.1109/TASE.2018.2847222
12. Lepora, N.F., Lloyd, J.: Pose-based tactile servoing: controlled soft touch using deep learning. IEEE Robot. Autom. Mag. **28**(4), 43–55 (2021). https://doi.org/10.1109/MRA.2021.3096141

An In-Situ Excitation Trajectory Optimizer for Industrial Robots in Constrained Space with Human Collaboration

Chengzhi Wang, Haotian Ju, Zhiyuan Yang, Tianjiao Zheng, Shize Zhao, Sikai Zhao[✉], Dawei Liang, Hegao Cai, Jie Zhao, and Yanhe Zhu

State Key Laboratory of Robotics and System, School of Mechatronics Engineering, Harbin Institute of Technology, Harbin 150001, China
zhaosikai@hit.edu.cn

Abstract. This paper proposes an excitation trajectory optimization method for in-situ identification of dynamic parameters of industrial robots operating in constrained environments where human operators exist. Conventional parameter identification methods primarily focus on identification accuracy, requiring an ideal workspace without obstacles. These methods rarely consider scenarios where robots operate in complex, obstacle-rich environments, lacking the capability to actively adjust excitation trajectories to adapt to such constraints. To address this issue, we introduce a trajectory optimization strategy based on a boundary penalty function. By employing a Differential Evolution (DE) algorithm, the base parameters of the Fourier series-form excitation trajectory are optimized to satisfy both identification accuracy and environmental constraints simultaneously. The proposed method was validated by optimizing excitation trajectories and performing parameter identification in various obstacle environments. Comparisons were made with excitation trajectories that did not consider environmental constraints. Experiments are conducted with an Effort ER15 robot to demonstrate the effectiveness of the proposed approach. The robot successfully completed the excitation trajectory without collisions across multiple scenarios, with only a 1.66% reduction in parameter identification accuracy in constrained environments.

Keywords: Trajectory tracking · feedforward optimization · adaptive control · industrial robot

1 Introduction

The dynamic model of industrial robots plays a critical role in achieving key functionalities such as trajectory tracking, motion planning, force control, and energy efficiency optimization [1]. Traditional parametric dynamic models rely on data collected from robots performing excitation trajectories to identify parameters [2, 3]. However, these models fail to precisely describe robot dynamics under varying operating conditions. Considering the repetitive nature of robot tasks, data-driven, non-parametric modeling methods offer an alternative for accurately capturing robotic behavior [4, 5]. Nonetheless, these approaches require substantial data and exhibit limited generalizability to new operating conditions, necessitating additional training with new datasets. To address these limitations, in-situ dynamic parameter identification conducted directly on the workstation is required, enhancing the accuracy of parametric models and further improving functionalities such as trajectory tracking precision, operational stability, and control robustness [6].

Traditional parameter identification methods primarily focus on the accuracy of the identified parameters in predicting robotic dynamics [7–9]. As such, the design of excitation trajectories often aims to maximally excite the robot's dynamic characteristics, typically requiring the execution of trajectories in open and unrestrained spaces to minimize environmental interference. However, in practical applications, industrial robots often operate in constrained and complex environments, such as workstations with obstacles or spatial limitations as shown in Fig. 1, where traditional excitation trajectory design methods may not be directly applicable.

In-situ parameter identification techniques for industrial robots introduce new challenges and requirements. On the one hand, excitation trajectories must avoid obstacles and meet safety constraints within the specific operating environment [10]. On the other hand, these trajectories must adequately excite all degrees of freedom of the robot's dynamics to ensure high-quality parameter identification and improved model accuracy. Therefore, the design of excitation trajectories for in-situ identification requires a multi-objective optimization approach that balances environmental constraints, excitation effectiveness, and trajectory feasibility.

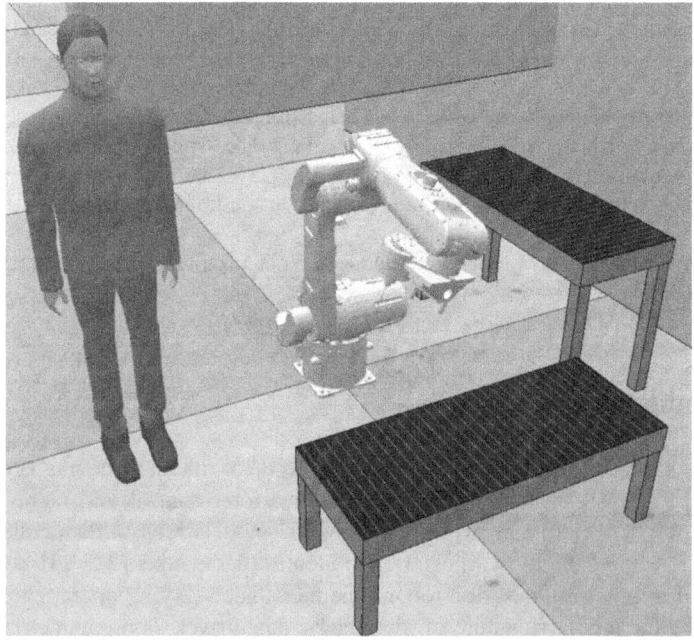

Fig. 1. In-situ scenario for dynamic identification.

Considering multiple relevant factors, an in-situ excitation trajectory optimization method is proposed in this paper to address existing problems. Major contribution of the paper is summarized as below:

(1) Designing a weighted-objective function to balance the consideration of kinematic constraints, dynamic constraints, as well as environmental constraints in the trajectory optimization.
(2) Presenting a penalty-based obstacle avoidance principle in the optimization of the excitation trajectory.
(3) Introducing a hierarchical distance calculation algorithm to effectively evaluate collision conditions of trajectories.
(4) Showing impressive experiments conducted in complex environment to demonstrate the safety and efficiency of the propose in-situ dynamic identification method.

The remainder of this paper is organized as follows: Sect. 2 gives the formulation of robot dynamics and it's identification problems. Section 3 presents the weighted objective function and details the implementation procedure of each part. Section 4 illustrates impressive comparative experiments, the security and accuracy of excitation trajectory generated with and without consideration of environmental constraints are compared and discussed afterwards. Finally, we conclude the paper in Sect. 5 and provide future research interests.

2 Problem Formulation

2.1 Dynamic Modelling and Inverse Identification

A typical industrial robot could be modeled as [11]:

$$\tau = M(q)\ddot{q} + B(q,\dot{q})\dot{q} + F(q,\dot{q}) + G(q) \tag{1}$$

M,B,F,G are matrix of different factors. The formulation could also be linearized and abbreviated as:

$$\tau = W \cdot \xi \tag{2}$$

W is the regression matrix based on kinematic parameters of Denavit-Hartenberg (DH) model [12], as well as trajectory parameters like joint position, velocity and acceleration. ξ represent dynamic parameters that could account for the dynamic characteristics of the robot either individually or combinatorically.

Since (2) could be used to compute model-based torques to work as feedforward in the control mechanism during trajectory tracking tasks, it could also work for the identification of dynamic parameters in turn by solving:

$$\min \|\tau - W\xi\| \tag{3}$$

τ in (3) is not calculated based on (3), but from the feedback data of the real robot, when executing the predefined excitation trajectories. By comparing measured torques with computed torques, the residual errors indicate the accuracy of the dynamic parameters in the model. And least squares optimization approaches could be utilized to minimize the residuals and determine more accurate dynamic models [13].

2.2 Differential Evolution Optimization

Since the consideration of spatial constraints is realized by separate distance evaluation between robot and environment, it's difficult to be modelled and solved in numerical methods. Therefore, swarm intelligent optimization approaches, such as genetic algorithms, particle swarm optimization, and especially differential evolution algorithm, are highly suitable for solving such problems, due to their ability to handle non-linear, non-differentiable conditions [14]. Considering the optimization of the excitation trajectory with constraints and objectives from multiple aspects, its essential core is to determine the decision variables of the Fourier series trajectory $\varphi(q, \dot{q}, \ddot{q})$. The position sequence is determined as:

$$\varphi_q(t)_{i=1,2,\ldots,6} = \varphi(a_0, a_{i,n}, b_{i,n}) \\ = a_0 + \sum_{n=1}^{N}(a_{i,n}\cos(n\omega t) + b_{i,n}\sin(n\omega t))_{i=1,2,\ldots,6} \quad (4)$$

While the velocity and acceleration information of the trajectory can be obtained using differentiation of the position sequence separately as:

$$\varphi_{\dot{q}}(t) = \varphi_q(t)' = \frac{\varphi_p(t_{j+1}) - \varphi_p(t_j)}{\Delta T}\bigg|_{j=1,2,\ldots,T} \quad (5)$$

$$\varphi_{\ddot{q}}(t) = \varphi_{\dot{q}}(t)' = \frac{\varphi_v(t_{j+1}) - \varphi_v(t_j)}{\Delta T}\bigg|_{j=1,2,\ldots,T-1} \quad (6)$$

With the formulated trajectory based on decision variables, the differential evolution approach could generate a large population to explore and find the optimal decision vector under a human-defined objective function.

3 Optimization Objective Design

Multiple factors should be considered in the excitation trajectory optimization process. Therefore, a weighted combinatorial objective function is designed to guide the trajectory optimization as shown below:

$$F_{obj} = \lambda_1 \cdot K(\varphi) + \lambda_2 \cdot D(\varphi) + \lambda_3 \cdot E(\varphi) \quad (7)$$

The objective function consists of three submodules: $K(\varphi)$, basic kinematic constraint that ensures motion stability: $D(\varphi)$, dynamic characteristic that ensures identifiability, and $E(\varphi)$, the spatial constraint that ensures security in complex environment.

3.1 Basic Kinematic Constraints

In order to execute the excitation trajectory and obtain necessary feedback data, the consecutive trajectory should be stable itself. This implies that the trajectory is higher-order smooth for the whole process, and quasi-static for the beginning and ending instants, meaning zero velocity and acceleration for both states as shown in Fig. 2. Therefore, corresponding kinematic constraints could be formulated in the objective function as:

$$K(\varphi) = \sum_{i=1}^{6} \sum_{t=0}^{T} (\dot{q}_{i,t} + \ddot{q}_{i,t}) \tag{8}$$

The position and velocity constraints are:

$$\begin{aligned} q_{low} < q < q_{up} \\ \dot{q}_{low} < \dot{q} < \dot{q}_{up} \end{aligned} \tag{9}$$

The position constraint ensures safety of each individual joint, and the velocity constraint ensures safety of the whole motion. Once such two boundaries are not satisfied by the direct output of Fourier series, a proportional parameterization and uniformization process is conducted to compress the trajectory within the boundaries [15].

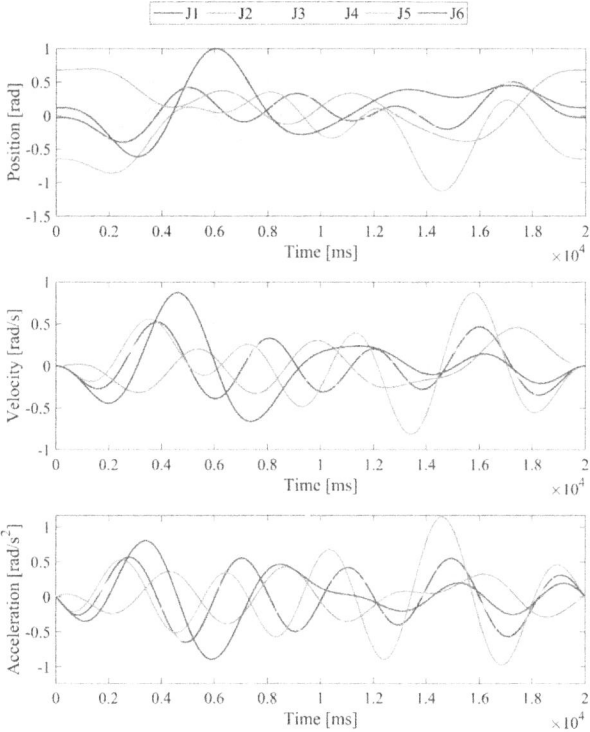

Fig. 2. Fourier trajectory with kinematic constraints

3.2 Dynamic Response Constraints

Trace and condition number of the regression matrix are considered as important characters regarding to the dynamic identification performance. Thus, they are combined together as (9):

$$D(\varphi) = \sum_{t=0}^{T} [\alpha \cdot tr(W^T W) + \beta \cdot \kappa_2(W)] \qquad (10)$$

α, β are weight coefficients of trace and condition number. Since the regression matrix is not square and cannot be used to generate trace, the corresponding information matrix is adopted to provide it instead as (10), which is a symmetric positive definite square matrix.

$$tr(W^T W) = \sum_{i=0}^{i=36} (W^T W)_{i,i} \qquad (11)$$

The condition number of regression matrix is defined as the ratio of the maximum singular value to the minimum singular value, which could be obtained by singular value decomposition (SVD).

$$\kappa_2(W) = \frac{\sigma_{max}}{\sigma_{min}} \qquad (12)$$

The trace of the matrix provides a measure of how effectively the excitation distributes across the system's parameters, and reflects the overall identifiability of the system dynamics under the given trajectory. Therefore, in the minimum-targeted objective function, α should be set negative to maximize trace. On the other hand, the condition number of the matrix refers to the sensitivity of the solution to small changes or errors in the trajectory data, which means it should be as small as possible.

3.3 Collision Constraints

The safety of the excitation trajectory is ensured by distance evaluation between each link of the robot and each environmental obstacle at each time instant along the trajectory. Flexible collision library [16] is adopted to realize such calculation in an efficient manner. Each object is approximately represented by convex cubes or cylinders or spheres in order to eliminate computation time. Multiple obstacles of various size are set at different locations within the workspace of the industrial robot as shown in Fig. 3. And the objective is defined as the sum of all distances as:

$$K(\varphi) = \sum_{i=1}^{6} \sum_{j=1}^{m} Dist(D(L_i, O_j)) \qquad (13)$$

In which L_i and O_j represent each of the individual links and obstacles, $D(L_i, O_j)$ is the direct output of FCL distance calculation. To avoid collision of any pair between links and obstacles, as well as to avoid moving the robot too far away from the obstacles, a hierarchical distance evaluation strategy is proposed as below to set the collision constraints within a limited range. When collision happens, the negative penetration depth is regarded as an enormous distance cost, while in no-collision cases, distances are compared with a predefined safety distance threshold ξ, which helps to lead the trajectory to the safety distance in the optimization.

$$Dist(L_i, O_i) = \begin{cases} 10000, D(L_i, O_i) < 0 \\ \xi - \left\|\overrightarrow{L_i O_i}\right\|_2, 0 < D(L_i, O_i) < \xi \\ \left\|\overrightarrow{L_i O_i}\right\|_2 - \xi, D(L_i, O_i) > \xi \end{cases} \quad (14)$$

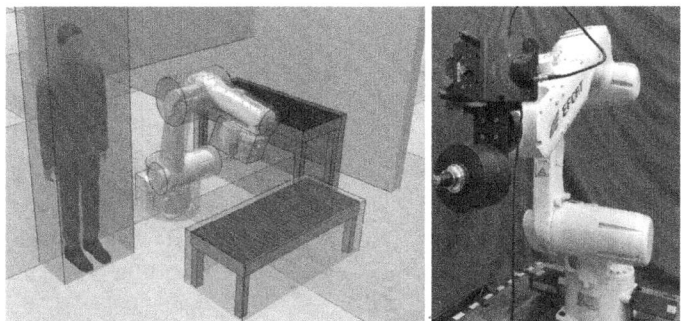

Fig. 3. Convex shapes for distance evaluation and physical setup.

4 Experiment Result

Physical experiments are conducted on an EFORT ER15-1400 industrial robot, with full payload of 15 kg mounted on the flange of the robot. Several additional obstacles, including two conveyor belts, two separation walls, as well as a human modelled as a cuboid shape, are set around the robot to compose the workstation.

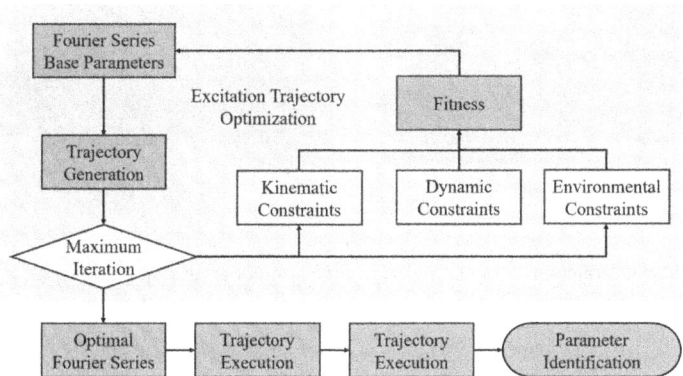

Fig. 4. The execution pipeline of the in-situ identification.

The whole pipeline of the in-situ identification process is illustrated as Fig. 4. Initial excitation trajectories are generated using a DE optimization module with large number of populations. In each population, a trajectory is determined by a vector of decision value, which is also the base parameters of a fifth order Fourier series. Weighted objective function is then adopted to evaluate the fitness of the trajectory and to update the base parameter vector. The baseline method shares the same pipeline but does not take the environmental constraints into consideration. Final output trajectories of the DE module are executed by the real industrial robot to obtain feedback data, and dynamic parameters are identified using least-square method. The torque predictions are compared with feedbacks to evaluate their performance.

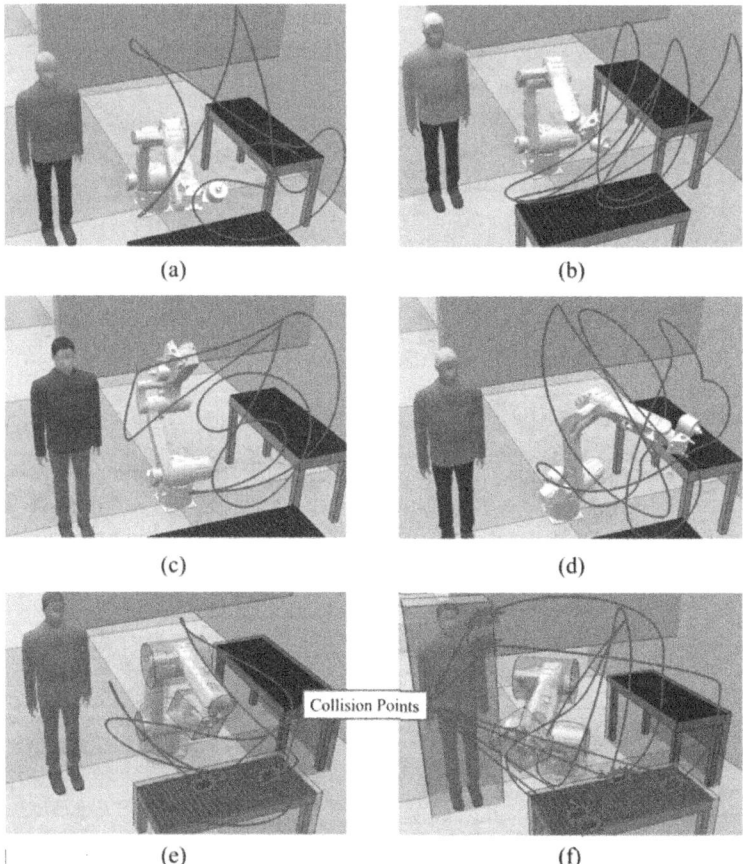

Fig. 5. Excitation trajectories, (a), (b), (c), (d): non-collided trajectories, (e), (f): collided trajectories.

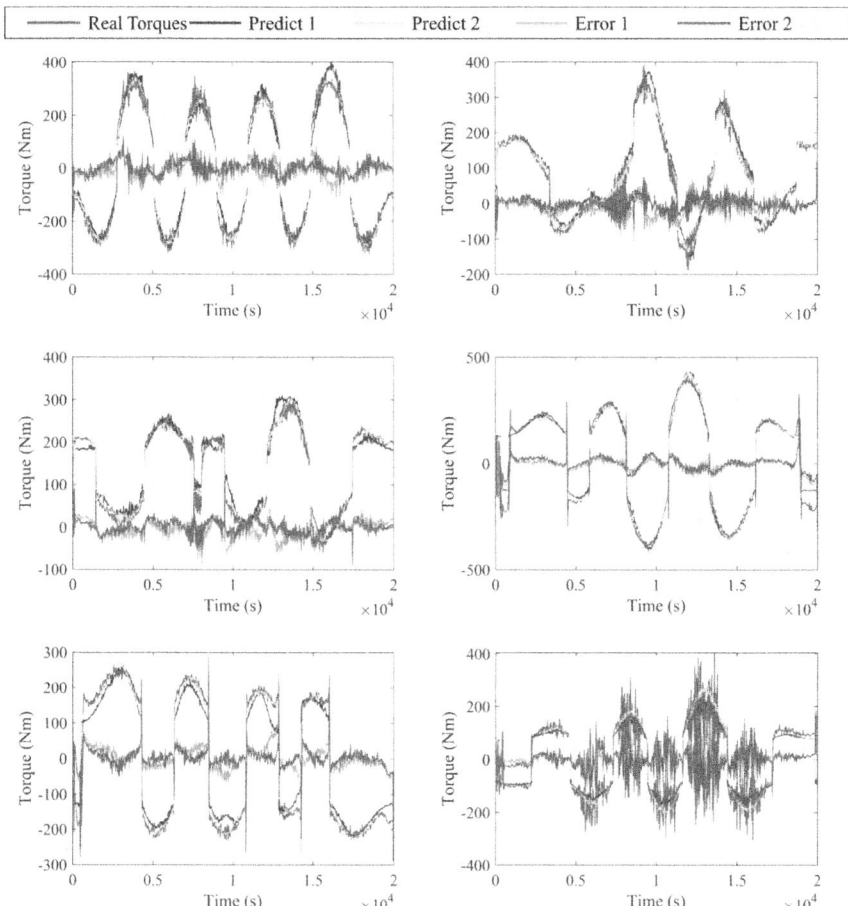

Fig. 6. Model-based torque prediction with and without considering mixed constraints.

In order to demonstrate the insecurity of conventional excitation trajectories that neglect environmental constraints, multiple collided and non-collided trajectories are shown in Fig. 5 in simulation scenario, the collision points along the trajectories are marked out by red circles.

Above excitation trajectories are executed on real robot afterwards, generating real dynamic response and feedbacks along the trajectory. Note that since collided trajectory cannot be executed in the complex environment, obstacles are moved away for those cases in order to obtain corresponding real trajectory feedback data. Based on collected trajectory data, least square optimization is adopted to solve the parameter identification problem. The identified models are testes on another trajectory to compare their prediction accuracy as shown in Fig. 6. The average error between the predicted torque and the real torque is 15.61% (green line for torque prediction and green line for residual error) and 13.95% (yellow line for torque prediction and purple line for residual error) for the excitation trajectories with or without considering the mixed constraints. Note that the major difference in the generation of these two types of excitation trajectories is the consideration of environmental constraints. Therefore, it can be assumed that the limitation of motion space affects the excitation effectiveness of the trajectory to the dynamic characteristics of the robot, which further leads to the decrease of the torque prediction accuracy of the identified model.

5 Conclusion

This paper focuses on in-situ identification of dynamic parameters of industrial robot, in order to obtain accurate dynamic model and improve performance. Environment constraints are taken into consideration in the optimization of excitation trajectory used for identification, using a hierarchical distance evaluation manner. Differential evolution algorithm is adopted in the process to explore and find the optimal base parameters of Fourier series, which determine the whole trajectory under multiple constrains including kinematic constraint, dynamic constraint and environmental constraint. The optimized collision-avoided excitation trajectories are executed and compared with normal collision-neglected trajectories to validate its security and effectiveness. Although the limited space has caused negative impact to the trajectory, our method achieves safe excitation trajectory generation with only 1.66% error lost. Our future research will focus on analysis of the correlation between dynamic identification accuracy and the degree of occupation of workspace, and trying to obtain better excitation trajectories in space with various occupation ratio.

Acknowledgement. This work was supported by the National Key R&D Program of China under Grant No. 2023YFB4706200, the National Natural Science Foundation of China (NSFC) under Grant No. 52025054, and the Self-Planned Task No. SKLRS202401A01 of the State Key Laboratory of Robotics and Systems (HIT).

References

1. Swevers, J., Verdonck, W., De Schutter, J.: Dynamic model identification for industrial robots. IEEE Control. Syst. Mag. **27**(5), 58–71 (2007)
2. Park, K.-J.: Fourier-based optimal excitation trajectories for the dynamic identification of robots. Robotica **24**(5), 625–633 (2006)
3. Swevers, J., et al.: Optimal robot excitation and identification. IEEE Trans. Robot. Autom. **13**(5), 730–740 (2002)
4. Baressi Šegota, S., et al.: Dynamics modeling of industrial robotic manipulators: a machine learning approach based on synthetic data. Mathematics **10**(7), 1174 (2022)
5. Nguyen, V., Cvitanic, T., Melkote, S.: Data-driven modeling of the modal properties of a six-degrees-of-freedom industrial robot and its application to robotic milling. J. Manuf. Sci. Eng. **141**(12), 121006 (2019)
6. Lu, Y., et al.: A unified framework of in-situ calibration and synchronous identification for industrial robots using composite sensing. IEEE Trans. Autom. Sci. Eng. **22**, 1405–1424 (2024)

7. Gautier, M., Briot, S., Venture, G.: Identification of consistent standard dynamic parameters of industrial robots. In: 2013 IEEE/ASME International Conference on Advanced Intelligent Mechatronics. IEEE (2013)
8. Han, Y., et al.: An iterative approach for accurate dynamic model identification of industrial robots. IEEE Trans. Robot. **36**(5), 1577–1594 (2020)
9. Mata, V., et al.: Dynamic parameter identification in industrial robots considering physical feasibility. Adv. Robot. **19**(1), 101–119 (2005)
10. Wu, J., Wang, J., You, Z.: An overview of dynamic parameter identification of robots. Robot. Comput. Integr. Manuf. **26**(5), 414–419 (2010)
11. Corke, P.: Robotics, Vision and Control: fundamental algorithms in Python. vol. 146. Springer, Cham (2023)
12. Denavit, J., Hartenberg, R.S. A kinematic notation for lower-pair mechanisms based on matrices, 215–221 (1955)
13. Jiang, S., et al.: A typical dynamic parameter identification method of 6-degree-of-freedom industrial robot. Proc. Inst. Mech. Eng. Part I: J. Syst. Control Eng. **231**(9), 740–752 (2017)
14. Biscani, F., Izzo, D.: A parallel global multiobjective framework for optimization: pagmo. J. Open Source Softw. **5**(53), 2338 (2020)
15. Bianco, C.G.L., Gerelli, O.: Online trajectory scaling for manipulators subject to high-order kinematic and dynamic constraints. IEEE Trans. Robot. **27**(6), 1144–1152 (2011)
16. Pan, J., Chitta, S., Manocha, D.: FCL: a general purpose library for collision and proximity queries. In: 2012 IEEE International Conference on Robotics and Automation. IEEE (2012)

Terrain-Adaptive Bipedal Locomotion via Reinforcement Learning with Human-Inspired Stepping Strategy

Yunpeng Liang, Yanzheng Zhao, and Weixin Yan(✉)

School of Mechanical Engineering, Shanghai Jiao Tong University, Shanghai, China
{lyppp597,yzh-zhao,xiaogu4524}@sjtu.edu.cn

Abstract. Bipedal robots can navigate complex, unstructured environments, but their low inherent stability and sensitivity to model errors make robust locomotion across varied terrains challenging. In this work, we present a unified end-to-end deep reinforcement learning framework designed to enable terrain-adaptive bipedal locomotion. Our approach builds upon a hybrid internal model and contrastive learning to implicitly infer both environmental context and proprioceptive state. To enhance short-horizon adaptability, the policy receives additional historical observations, improving responsiveness to sudden terrain changes. Furthermore, we propose a human-inspired stepping strategy reward that encourages high leg lifts for traversing elevation differences and promotes passive ankle compliance on rugged terrain. Extensive simulation results demonstrate that our method improves dynamic adaptability, reduces energy consumption, and enhances terrain generalization, enabling robust locomotion over slopes, uneven terrain, and continuous stairs.

Keywords: Bipedal Robots · Reinforcement Learning · Terrain Adaptive Locomotion

1 Introduction

Over the past two decades, legged robots have garnered increasing attention due to significant advancements in dynamic and agile locomotion [9,10]. Beyond agility and robust locomotion capabilities, a key advantage is their adaptability to navigate complex and unstructured environments such as uneven terrain, open fields, continuous steps, and stairs [1,2,8,15]. This capability is critical for supporting humans in performing tasks reliably across diverse and challenging scenarios. However, achieving stable locomotion and high terrain generalization under limited sensory feedback remains a significant challenge, due to environmental dynamics, the inherent instability of underactuated systems, and discrepancies between the modeled and real-world physical parameters.

To address these challenges, some researchers have adopted model-based approaches [1,2] that formulate motion planning and control as sequential numerical optimization problems under multiple task objectives and physical constraints. However, designing such controllers often results in limited flexibility, reduced robustness and generalization, as well as increased complexity in development and maintenance due to modeling inaccuracies and various constraints.

Recent advances in learning-based methods have made deep reinforcement learning (RL) highly effective for controlling legged robots on uneven terrain. Kumar et al. [6] integrated Rapid Motor Adaptation (RMA) into an RL framework to enable online estimation of changing environmental parameters, such as ground friction coefficients and terrain characteristics. However, this approach relies on multi-stage training, which limits the flexibility of policy deployment. Nahrendra et al. [12] developed a context-aided estimator that implicitly captures latent representations of both environmental features and body velocity, facilitating the joint learning of forward and inverse dynamics via an autoencoding framework. Subsequently, Long et al. [11] introduced a Hybrid Internal Model (HIM) based on this framework, leveraging contrastive learning to enhance the extraction and discrimination of diverse terrain characteristics. However, these methods have primarily been developed for quadruped robots, which possess greater intrinsic stability and therefore adapt more readily to dynamic and uncertain environments. In contrast, bipedal robots, with higher degrees of freedom and lower inherent stability, still face significant challenges in achieving robust and adaptive locomotion on complex and varying terrains.

Zhang et al. [17] and Kumar et al. [7] applied fine-tuning based on RMA to enable bipedal locomotion on uneven terrain. However, their approach still suffers from the inherent drawback of a cumbersome training process and has not demonstrated the ability to navigate staircases continuously. Siekmann et al. [15] tackled a similar scenario through terrain randomization, but their method required excessively high leg-lifting, resulting in unnatural gait patterns. Moreover, reliance on a conventional state estimator further complicates the real deployment. It is still challenging to develop a unified and generalizable controller that can adapt to a variety of complex terrains.

In this work, we propose an end-to-end deep reinforcement learning framework that integrates the advanced hybrid internal model and contrastive learning to implicitly infer both environmental characterization and the robot's body state. Building on insights from comparative studies in [9], we feed the actor network by incorporating short-term historical observations to improve the robot's responsiveness to sudden terrain changes, which is not included in [11]. Furthermore, we introduce a Human-Inspired Stepping Strategy (HISS) reward during training: the policy is encouraged to lift the legs higher when encountering significant height differences and to adopt passive ankle behavior for better compliance on rugged terrain [5]. The main contributions of this paper are as follows:

- A unified end-to-end deep reinforcement learning framework is developed to enable bipedal locomotion across various challenging terrains.
- Extensive simulation experiments demonstrate that our method, enhanced by the introduction of the HISS reward, achieves superior terrain adaptability and dynamic motion stability during adaptive robust walking on continuous stair climbing, slopes, and uneven terrain.

2 Methodology

Our goal is to develop a terrain-adaptive bipedal locomotion policy that can track desired velocity commands across diverse and previously unseen terrains, while responding robustly to unexpected environmental changes and external disturbances in real time. To this end, we adopt an end-to-end reinforcement learning framework.

2.1 Preliminaries

Bipedal robot locomotion control can be formulated as a Partially Observable Markov Decision Process (POMDP), defined by the tuple $\mathcal{M} = (\mathcal{S}, \mathcal{O}, \mathcal{A}, d_0, p, r, \gamma)$. Here, $s \in \mathcal{S}$ denotes the full state, $o \in \mathcal{O}$ the partial observation, and $a \in \mathcal{A}$ the action. The process begins with an initial state distribution $d_0(s_0)$, evolves according to the state transition probability $p(s_{t+1}|s_t, a_t)$, and yields a reward defined by the function $r : \mathcal{S} \times \mathcal{A} \to \mathcal{R}$. The discount factor $\gamma \in [0, 1)$ determines the weighting of future rewards. The reinforcement learning objective is to identify an optimal policy π that selects actions a_t to maximize the expected return, expressed as:

$$J(\pi) = \mathbb{E}_{\tau \sim p(\tau|\pi)} \left[\sum_{t=0}^{T} \gamma^t r_t \right] \quad (1)$$

where $\tau = \{(x_0, a_0, r_0), (x_1, a_1, r_1), \ldots\}$ denotes the trajectory of the agent while following policy π.

2.2 Policy Architecture

Figure 1 presents an overview of our control framework. We adopt an asymmetric actorcritic architecture to facilitate zero-shot transfer. Building on the hybrid internal model proposed in [11], we utilize contrastive learning to enhance environmental feature extraction. Specifically, the model maximizes the similarity of latent representations between $z_t \in \mathbb{R}^{16}$ of short-term historical observations $o_t^H = [o_t, o_{t-1}, \ldots, o_{t-H}]^T$ and the next observation o_{t+1}, which are encoded by a source encoder and a target encoder, respectively.

Table 1. Network architecture for the actor-critic, source encoder, and target encoder based on Multi-Layer Perceptron (MLP).

Module	Inputs	Dim	Hidden Layers	Outputs	Dim
Source Encoder	$o_{t,\cdots,t-9}$	10×47	[128, 64]	$\hat{v}_b, z_t^S$	19
Target Encoder	o_{t+1}	47	[128, 64]	z_t^T	16
Actor	$[o_{t,\cdots,t-9}, \hat{v}_b, z_t^S]^T$	$10 \times 47 + 19$	[512, 256, 128]	a_t	12
Critic	$s_{t,\cdots,t-2}$	3×244	[512, 256, 128]	$\hat{V}_t$	1

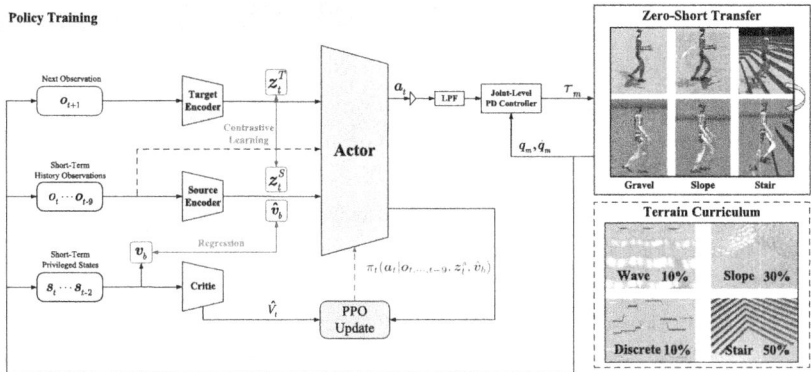

Fig. 1. Our RL control framework incorporates temporal observations and the subsequent observation from the robot, which are processed by two separate encoders to maximize the similarity between their latent representations, z_t^S and z_t^T. A short history of ten timesteps, together with the estimated base velocity $\hat{v}_b$ and the system's latent representation z_t^S, is fed into a base MLP. All networks are trained jointly. The actor policy outputs the desired motor positions a_t, which are smoothed using a low-pass filter (LPF) before being passed to the joint-level PD controllers to compute the motor torques τ_m.

Unlike [11], we additionally utilize stacked multi-frame observations and privileged state information. The actor receives these multi-frame inputs to better capture motion dynamics and reduce the impact of partial observability, while the critic accesses the full state during training. As shown in our experiments, this enhancement significantly improves performance on uneven and complex terrains. Additionally, the base linear velocity $\hat{v}_b$ is explicitly estimated through a regression loss. All trainable network parameters are provided in Table 1.

2.3 State and Action

Full States $s_t \in \mathbb{R}^{244}$ are divided into two categories: observable and privileged information. Observations, denoted as $o_t \in \mathbb{R}^{47}$, consist of data directly obtainable from the user and the robot, including the user commands $c_t = [v_x, v_y, \omega_z]^T \in \mathbb{R}^3$, periodic clocks $\Phi(\phi) = [sin(\phi), cos(\phi)]^T \in \mathbb{R}^2$, and onboard sensor data. Privileged information, represented by $P_t \in \mathbb{R}^{197}$, includes data that is difficult to access during deployment but provides essential internal and environmental context for characterizing the motion state during training. Notably, no noise is added to the critic network to preserve its guiding role and ensure stable training. In contrast, appropriate random noise and time delays are introduced to the short-term historical observations to improve the robustness of the actor policy. The observations and privileged information of the full state space are listed in Table 2.

The action $a_t \in \mathbb{R}^{12}$ denotes the desired joint positions of the legs. To facilitate learning, the policy is trained to infer joint angle deviations relative to the

Table 2. Composition of the state space.

Observation	Dim	Privileged State	Dim
Commands (c_t)	3	Body mass	1
Periodic clocks ($\Phi(\phi)$)	2	Ground friction	1
Joint position (q)	12	Push force	2
Joint velocity ($\dot{q}$)	12	Push torque	3
Last action (a_{t-1})	12	Base linear velocity	3
Base angular velocity (ω_b)	3	Height of map scan-dot (h_e)	187
Gravity projection vector (g_b)	3		

robot's nominal standing pose, q_{nominal}. Consequently, the desired joint angles are defined as:

$$q_{\text{des}} = q_{\text{nominal}} + \sigma \cdot \{\alpha \cdot a_t + (1-\alpha) \cdot a_{t-1}\} \tag{2}$$

where the scale factor $\sigma = 0.25$ is used to normalize the policy output, ensuring that the resulting desired joint angles remain within a reasonable range. The scale factor $\alpha \in [0, 0.5]$ is the coefficient of a first-order low-pass filter, randomly sampled during training.

A joint-level PD controller subsequently computes the motor torques:

$$\tau_m = k_p(q_{\text{des}} - q_m) + k_d(0 - \dot{q}_m) \tag{3}$$

where k_p and k_d are the proportional and differential gains, respectively. The policy operates at 50 Hz, while the PD controller runs at 200 Hz.

2.4 Reward

We design the reward structure to encourage stable and adaptable locomotion across diverse terrains. The overall reward function is defined as:

$$r = r_{\text{cmd}} + r_{\text{adp}} + r_{\text{reg}} \tag{4}$$

where r_{cmd} encourages tracking of the user-specified command, and r_{adp} promotes adaptability to varying and complex terrains. In addition, a set of regularization terms r_{reg} is included to suppress undesirable motions and support smooth, stable behavior.

Command Tracking. Given the desired linear velocities v_x^d, v_y^d, the desired angular velocity ω_z^d, and the desired base height h_b^d, the tracking rewards r_{cmd} are defined as:

$$\begin{aligned} r_{\text{linear}} &= 1 \cdot \exp\left(-4 \cdot \|v_{x,y}^d - v_{x,y}\|^2\right) \\ r_{\text{angular}} &= 1 \cdot \exp\left(-4 \cdot \|\omega_z^d - \omega_z\|^2\right) \\ r_{\text{height}} &= -10 \cdot \|h_b^d - h_b\|^2 \end{aligned} \tag{5}$$

Human-Inspired Stepping Strategy. Motivated by the observation that humans actively raise their legs to step over high obstacles (e.g., stairs or tall steps), and passively adapt to the terrain when walking on uneven ground [5], we design specialized reward functions r_{step} and r_{passive} tailored to high-step scenarios and uneven terrain to encourage appropriate leg-lifting behavior and terrain adaptability. The adaptive swing reward is represented as:

$$r_{\text{adp}} = r_{\text{swing}} + r_{\text{step}} + r_{\text{passive}} \tag{6}$$

The swing foot height tracking reward, denoted as r_{swing}, is active and serves to support basic locomotion. It is defined as:

$$r_{\text{swing}} = -20 \cdot \|h_{\text{foot}}^d - h_{\text{foot}}\|^2 \cdot \mathbb{1}\left[f_{\text{foot},z} > 0\right] \tag{7}$$

When the terrain height $\Delta h = h_{\text{forward}} - h_{\text{behind}}$ both in front of and behind the robot (see Fig. 2 left) exceeds a defined threshold $\epsilon_{\text{step}} = 0.18m$, an additional leg-lifting reward r_{step} (relative to the body frame) is applied:

$$r_{\text{step}} = -\|R_b^T(h_b - h_{\text{foot}} - h_b^d + \Delta h)\|^2 \cdot \|R_b^T(v_{b,xy} - v_{\text{foot},xy})\|^2 \cdot \mathbb{1}\left[\Delta h > \epsilon_{\text{step}}\right] \tag{8}$$

In addition, when the mean elevation of the terrain surrounding the robot, denoted as $\bar{h}_e \in [0.015, 0.03]$, indicates the presence of uneven terrain (see Fig. 2 right), an ankle passive actuation reward r_{step} is introduced to encourage compliant stepping behavior.

$$r_{\text{passive}} = -0.005 \cdot \|\tau_{\text{ankle}}\|^2 \cdot \mathbb{1}\left[f_{\text{foot},z} > 0\right] \cdot \mathbb{1}\left[\bar{h}_e \in [0.015, 0.03]\right] \tag{9}$$

Regularization. To suppress undesirable motions, we introduce a set of regularization rewards r_{reg} that penalize excessive joint movements, unnecessary base motion, poor energy efficiency, and lack of action smoothness (see Table 3). Most reward terms are shaped following the approach in [3].

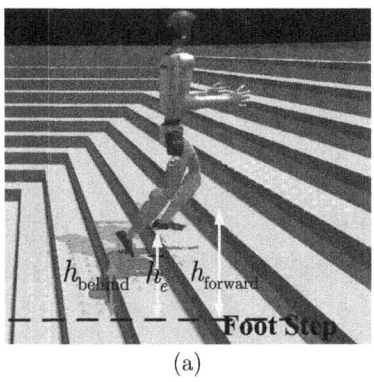
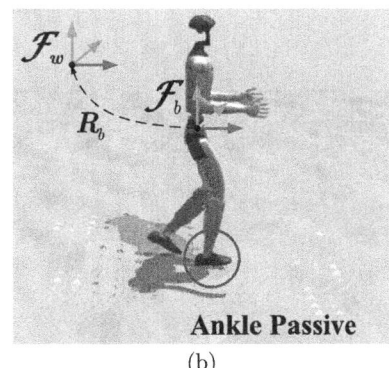

(a)   (b)

Fig. 2. Illustration of the human-inspired stepping strategy for stairs and uneven terrain. (a) Foot-lifting strategy; (b) Passive ankle strategy. Yellow scan points provide height information to the critic network, while blue and red points indicate the front and rear terrain elevations used for terrain classification. (Color figure online)

Table 3. Regularization Rewards

Reward	Weight	Expression
Joint velocity	−1e−3	$\|\dot{q}\|^2$
Joint acceleration	−2.5e−7	$\|(\dot{q}_t - \dot{q}_{t-1})/\Delta t\|^2$
Joint limits	−5	$\max(\|q\| - q_{\max}, 0)$
Action smoothness	−0.03	$\|(a_t - a_{t-1})/\Delta t\|^2$
Contact mask	0.18	$\sim (\mathbb{1}[f_{\text{foot},z} > 0] \wedge \mathbb{1}[\phi < 0.5])$
Foot stumble	−2.0	$\mathbb{1}[\|f_{\text{foot},xy}\| > f_{\text{foot},z}]$
Alive	0.15	1.0
Base z-axis velocity	−2.0	$v_{b,z}^2$
Base roll-pitch velocity	−0.05	$\omega_{b,x}^2 + \omega_{b,y}^2$
Base orientation	−1.0	$g_{b,x}^2 + g_{b,y}^2$
Hip joint regularization	−1.0	$\|q_{\text{hip},xy}\|^2$

2.5 Domain Randomization

Domain randomization is incorporated during training to improve policy robustness and mitigate the sim-to-real gap. Variations are introduced in environmental properties, external disturbances, robot dynamics, actuation characteristics, and sensor fidelity. All parameters are uniformly sampled from predefined ranges, as summarized in Table 4. In addition, a curriculum-based terrain learning strategy [13] is adopted, in which terrain difficulty is discretized into 20 levels and dynamically adjusted based on the robot's performance. The difficulty level is determined by factors such as slope inclination, surface roughness, stair height, and wave terrain amplitude.

Table 4. Domain randomization parameters and their sampling ranges. Additive operation shifts parameters within the range, while scaling applies a multiplicative factor.

Parameter	Unit	Range	Operator
Friction	-	[0.1, 1.25]	-
External force (xy)	N	[0, 100]	-
External torque	Nm	[0, 10]	-
Payload mass	kg	[−1, 3]	Additive
Link mass	kg	[0.9, 1.1]	Additive
CoM position	m	[−0.05, 0.05]	Additive
Motor strength	%	[90, 110]	Scaling
Joint k_p, k_d Gains	%	[85, 115]	Scaling
Joint position lag	s	[0, 40Δt]	-
Slope inclination	rad	[0, 0.3]	-
Rough ground height	m	[0.005, 0.03]	-
Stair height	m	[0.01, 0.2]	-
Wave amplitude	m	[0.1, 0.4]	-

3 Simulation Results

In this section, we present sim-to-sim evaluations conducted in MuJoCo using the Unitree G1 robot [16]. These evaluations assess the performance of our method in continuous stair climbing, adaptability to uneven terrain, speed tracking accuracy, and energy consumption.

3.1 Setup

We train our policy using the PPO algorithm [14] within the IsaacGym simulator, utilizing input normalization and parallelization over 4096 environments. The PPO hyperparameter settings follow those described in [13]. All methods use identical joint control gains, with proportional gains set to $\boldsymbol{k}_p = 2 \cdot [100, 100, 100, 150, 40, 40]^T$ and differential gains to $\boldsymbol{k}_d = 2 \cdot [2, 2, 2, 4, 2, 2]^T$. Training converges to a high-performing policy after approximately 20,000 episodes on an NVIDIA GeForce RTX 4090 GPU. To thoroughly evaluate terrain adaptability, we compare our approach against the following settings:

- **DreameWaQ** [12]: The policy was trained without employing contrastive learning.
- **Ours w/o History (HIMLoco)** [11]: The policy was trained without incorporating temporal historical observations as input to the actor network.
- **Ours w/o r_{step}**: The proposed method without the leg-lifting reward.
- **Ours w/o r_{passive}**: The proposed method without the passive ankle strategy.
- **Ours**: Full proposed method in this paper.

Figure 3 illustrates the progression of average terrain difficulty levels for different methods during training. Our method consistently reaches higher difficulty levels. The methods incorporated HIM [11] benefit from contrastive learning, enabling its policy to generalize more effectively to challenging terrains and outperform the approach in [12].

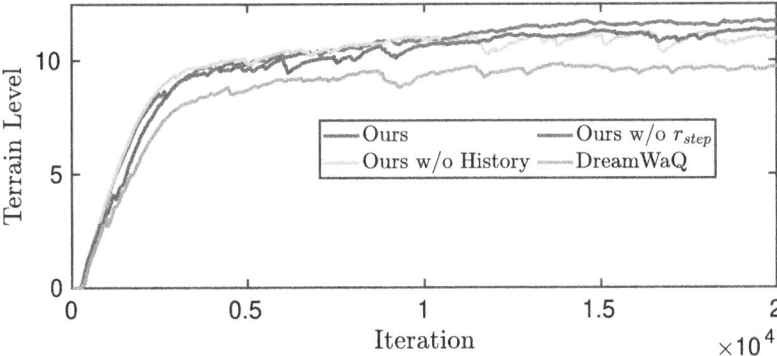

Fig. 3. Comparison of learned average terrain difficulty levels across different methods.

3.2 Stairs Accessibility

To evaluate the impact of multi-frame historical observations and the leg-lifting reward, we performed ablation studies in the continuous high-stair climbing scenario (step width 30 cm, height 17 cm), as illustrated in Fig. 4. The foot trajectories are also presented in Fig. 5. Results indicate that only the policy incorporating historical observations successfully traverses all 15 steps, demonstrating the importance of temporal observations in capturing motion dynamics and improving reactive resilience. In addition, our method incorporates a leg-lifting reward when encountering height-difference terrain, leading to fewer foot collisions and improved passability, as shown in Fig. 5.

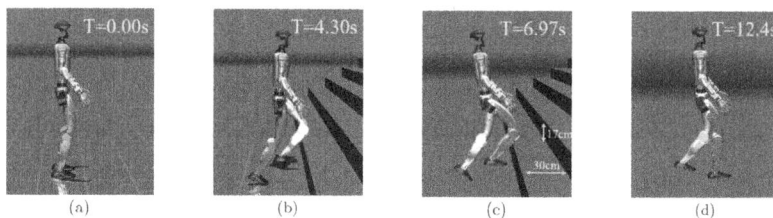

Fig. 4. (a)-(d): Snapshots of the continuous stair-climbing experiment.

To mitigate the variability of individual trials and rigorously evaluate stair passability, we conducted 10 trials each for single-step tests and 15-step continuous climbs at varying step heights. The results in Fig. 6 show that our method achieves higher success rates on both single and continuous steps, completes more steps on average, and results in fewer foot collisions compared to other methods. Notably, although the policy without historical information slightly outperforms the one without the leg-lifting reward in success rate, it exhibits significantly more foot collisions during trials. Its success is largely attributed to repeated trial-and-error rather than a natural stair-climbing process. This indicates poor adaptability to scenarios with continuously varying terrain, as further evidenced by the experimental results in Fig. 5.

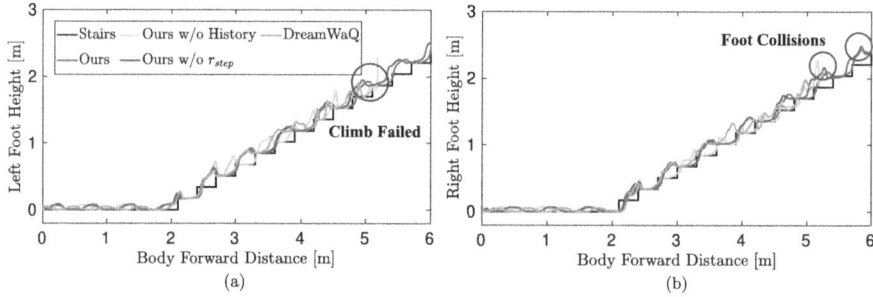

Fig. 5. Foot height variation during stair climbing as a function of traveled distance. (a) Left foot; (b) Right foot.

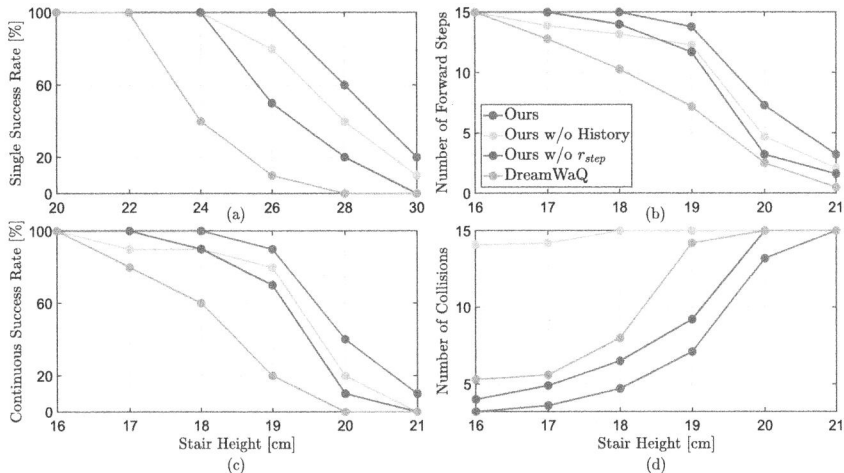

Fig. 6. Comparison of (a) single-step success rate, (b) number of forward steps, (c) 15-step success rate, and (d) number of foot collisions for different methods.

3.3 Uneven Terrain Adaptability

To evaluate the terrain adaptability of the proposed method under continuously varying conditions, we constructed a complex test environment comprising ascending and descending slopes, randomly distributed uneven terrain, and flat ground, as illustrated in Fig. 7. The robot was commanded to traverse the scene at a constant speed of 0.75 m/s.

As shown in Fig. 8, although all methods successfully traverse the complex terrain, the approach proposed in [12] exhibits notably larger fluctuations in forward velocity and body pitch angle, particularly during downhill segments. In contrast, approaches incorporating HIM demonstrate improved generalization to varying terrain conditions. To quantitatively evaluate performance, we adopt root mean square error (RMSE) and population standard deviation (PSD) as metrics. As summarized in Table 5, our method achieves reduced body fluctuations and lower velocity tracking errors, highlighting superior motion stability and enhanced robustness to terrain variations.

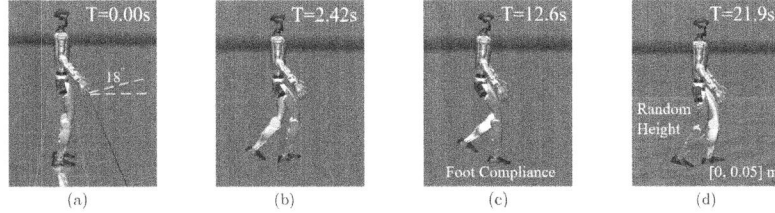

Fig. 7. Terrain adaptability illustrated through snapshots: (a) flat surface, (b) uphill, (c) downhill, and (d) uneven terrain.

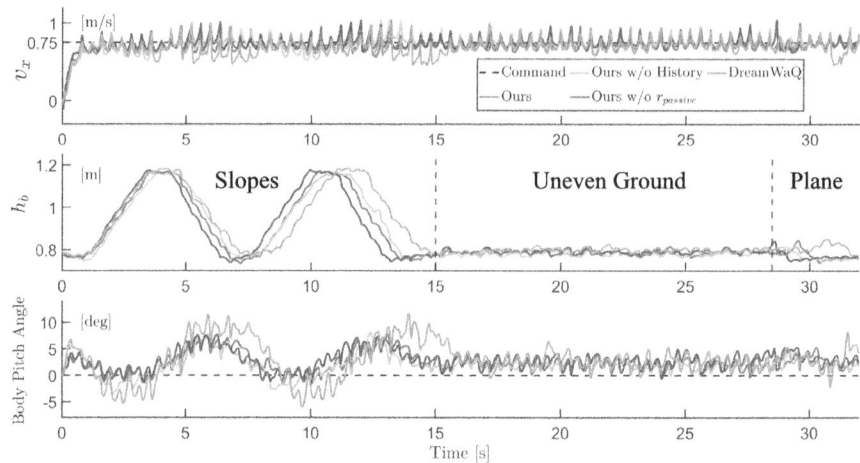

Fig. 8. Body tracking performance comparison across methods in the terrain adaptability experiment.

Table 5. Velocity tracking metrics for different methods at a target speed of 0.75 m/s.

Method	Forward Velocity [m/s]			Body Pitch [deg]	
	Avg.	RMSE	PSD	RMSE	PSD
DreamWaQ	0.6931	0.1106	0.0949	4.6663	3.5981
Ours w/o History	0.7382	0.0804	0.0796	**2.8008**	1.9889
Ours w/o r_{passive}	0.7429	**0.0715**	0.0711	3.4459	1.8741
Ours	0.7215	0.0732	**0.0675**	3.1370	**1.8195**

To ablate the impact of the passive ankle reward r_{passive}, we compared joint torque profiles and energy costs on uneven terrains. As shown in Fig. 9 and Table 5, our method achieves reduced joint torque and energy consumption without significantly compromising motion stability or tracking accuracy. Furthermore, Fig. 7 demonstrates its improved compliance with varying terrain conditions.

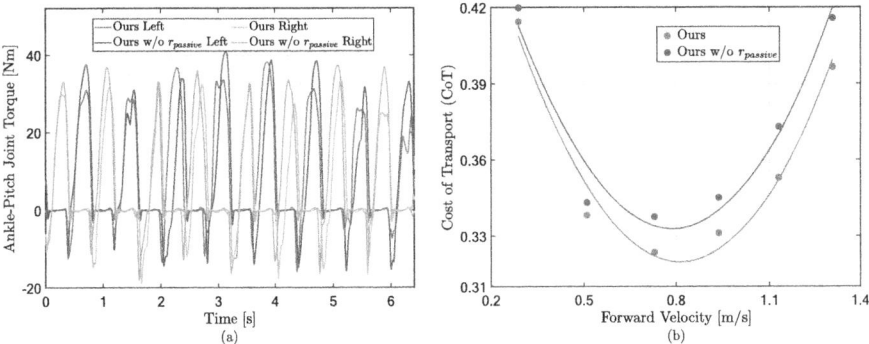

Fig. 9. Comparison of (a) joint torque profiles and (b) cost of transport (CoT) [4], with and without the reward r_{passive}.

4 Conclusion and Future Work

This paper introduced an end-to-end RL framework tailored for bipedal locomotion over complex and varied terrains. By incorporating the HIM, short-term historical observations, and a human-inspired stepping reward design, the proposed method enhances the robot's adaptability to sudden terrain variations. Simulation results confirm improved locomotion stability, energy efficiency, and terrain generalization across challenging environments such as stairs, slopes, and uneven surfaces. In future work, we aim to validate the effectiveness of our approach through deployment on real-world hardware platforms.

References

1. Gong, Y., Hartley, R., et al.: Feedback control of a cassie bipedal robot: walking, standing, and riding a segway. In: 2019 American Control Conference (ACC), pp. 4559–4566. IEEE (2019)
2. Grandia, R., Jenelten, F., et al.: Perceptive locomotion through nonlinear model-predictive control. IEEE Trans. Rob. **39**(5), 3402–3421 (2023)
3. Hwangbo, J., Lee, J., et al.: Learning agile and dynamic motor skills for legged robots. Sci. Robot. **4**(26), eaau5872 (2019)
4. Kenneally, G., De, A., Koditschek, D.E.: Design principles for a family of direct-drive legged robots. IEEE Robot. Autom. Lett. **1**(2), 900–907 (2016)
5. Kim, D., Jorgensen, S.J., et al.: Dynamic locomotion for passive-ankle biped robots and humanoids using whole-body locomotion control. Int. J. Robot. Res. **39**(8), 936–956 (2020)
6. Kumar, A., Fu, Z., Pathak, D., Malik, J.: RMA: Rapid motor adaptation for legged robots. In: Proc. Robot.: Sci. Syst. (2021)
7. Kumar, A., Li, Z., et al.: Adapting rapid motor adaptation for bipedal robots. In: Proceedings of IEEE/RSJ International Conference on Intelligent Robots and System, pp. 1161–1168 (2022)
8. Lee, J., Hwangbo, J., et al.: Learning quadrupedal locomotion over challenging terrain. Sci. Robot. **5**(47), eabc5986 (2020)

9. Li, Z., Peng, X.B., et al.: Reinforcement learning for versatile, dynamic, and robust bipedal locomotion control. Int. J. Robot. Res. **44**(5), 840–888 (2024)
10. Liang, Y., Yin, F., et al.: Reduced-dimensional whole-body control based on model simplification for bipedal robots with parallel mechanisms. IEEE Robot. Autom. Lett. **10**(2), 1696–1703 (2025)
11. Long, J., Wang, Z., et al.: Hybrid internal model: Learning agile legged locomotion with simulated robot response. arXiv preprint arXiv:2312.11460 (2023)
12. Nahrendra, I.M.A., Yu, B., Myung, H.: Dreamwaq: learning robust quadrupedal locomotion with implicit terrain imagination via deep reinforcement learning. In: Proceedings of IEEE International Conference on Robotics and Automation, pp. 5078–5084. IEEE (2023)
13. Rudin, N., Hoeller, D., et al.: Learning to walk in minutes using massively parallel deep reinforcement learning. In: Conference on on Robot Learning, pp. 91–100. PMLR (2022)
14. Schulman, J., Wolski, F., Dhariwal, P., Radford, A., Klimov, O.: Proximal policy optimization algorithms. arXiv preprint arXiv:2312.11460 (2017)
15. Siekmann, J., Green, K., Warila, J., Fern, A., Hurst, J.: Blind bipedal stair traversal via sim-to-real reinforcement learning. In: Proceedings of Robot: Science System (2020)
16. Unitree Robotics: G1 (2025). https://www.unitree.com/g1
17. Wei, W., Wang, Z., et al.: Learning gait-conditioned bipedal locomotion with motor adaptation. In: Proceedings of International Conference on Humanoid Robots, pp. 1–7. IEEE (2023)

Research on Autonomously Exterior Wall Spraying Technology for Tethered Unmanned Aerial Vehicles

Liang Gao(✉), Xu'an Zhao, Xu'ning Zhao, Tianjiao Zheng, Liyi Li, and Jie Zhao

State Key Laboratory of Robotics and Systems (HIT), Harbin Institute of Technology, Harbin 150001, China
gaoliang@hit.edu.cn

Abstract. Traditional manual exterior wall spraying faces safety risks, high costs, and operational limitations. This research focuses on drone control technology for vertical surface spraying. The mobility of drone enhances adaptability to complex walls, while remote operation improves safety. The tether simultaneously delivers power that originates from a ground generator and paint that is supplied from a ground-based system, which significantly extends endurance and reduces the payload of drone because it only carries spraying actuators. Key components were selected based on spraying requirements and unmanned aerial vehicle (UAV) weight constraints, after which motor selection was finalized. This enabled dynamic modeling and disturbance analysis. Using these parameters, a Simulink dynamic simulation model and a cascade PID controller were developed. Simulations confirmed that the system responds rapidly and converges errors effectively. A physical prototype that integrated all subsystems was built. Tests verified that the system spraying positioning accuracy that remains within ±0.15 m. The tethered approach separates paint and power sources from the UAV, which reduces its load capacity demands while ensuring operational feasibility and stability for exterior wall spraying applications.

Keywords: UAV · Tethered · Spray coating

1 Introduction

The primary method of spraying in the industrial sector is manual spraying. This traditional and outdated technique involves spray workers using spray guns to apply paint to workpieces. Not only does this method require workers to have considerable experience, but prolonged exposure to chemical environments can cause significant harm to their health, with painters being more prone to conditions such as dermatitis, hypertension, and bronchial spasms [1].

To address the issues with traditional spray painting methods, many research institutions have invested significant resources in developing robots that can perform spray painting tasks autonomously. Wall-climbing spraying robots employing magnetic or vacuum-based adsorption mechanisms can carry spraying equipment to perform coating operations on vertical surfaces [2]. However, they demand relatively high planarity of the working surface, exhibit limited adaptability to irregular surfaces, and suffer from low operational efficiency. Furthermore, ground-based aerial work platform spraying robots leverage their articulated arms to extend spraying height to some degree and achieve highly efficient automated spraying [3]. Nevertheless, constrained by the limitations inherent to ground-based systems, they are incapable of performing spraying tasks in complex environments, have restricted operational height, and incur significant costs.

Compared to manual spraying, wall-climbing robot spraying, and other coating techniques, the spraying method utilizing tethered UAVs to carry spraying equipment offers distinct comparative advantages. The tethered multi-rotor UAV, an innovative drone system, integrates a tethered composite cable with the multi-rotor UAV. During flight, it relies on ground power to achieve direct power supply. This design frees the UAV from power supply constraints, enabling it to perform long-duration aerial hovering operations, effectively addressing the limitations of traditional rotary-wing drones in terms of endurance and payload capacity, demonstrating significant application potential and development space [4]. In the application of tethered drones, many scholars have proposed several innovations, small autonomous spray tethered drones for three-dimensional surface painting [5], deployment strategies for tethered drones to achieve the broadest cellular network coverage in user clusters [6], underwater sounding systems for tethered drones [7], collaborative mobile platforms for unmanned vehicles and tethered drones to assess the structural integrity of underground stone pillars [8], tethered drones with cleaning and painting capabilities [9], a tethered drone for ship hull spraying [10]. Additionally, an innovative bionic backstepping sliding mode control method is also proposed for tethered drones [11]. Scholars in [12, 13] simplified the tether cable to a catenary form for mechanical analysis, scholars in [14] proposed a control device for automatic reel-in/reel-out of the tether cable.

To address the shortcomings of traditional spraying methods and the limitations of some current spraying robots, we introduces an autonomous spraying platform for tethered drones equipped with spray guns, which primarily consists of a spraying system and a drone system. Furthermore, based on this platform, the control performance of the controller regarding spraying distance accuracy and spraying attitude was validated. To solve the problems of spraying precision control and spraying attitude alignment, we propose a method that controls and corrects the spraying distance and spraying attitude based on dual laser ranging sensors.

2 System Description

2.1 System Architecture Design

This project plans to use drones as the main body for carrying spraying equipment, equipped with a suitable connection structure to ensure the spray gun is stably mounted on the drone. The pressure tank containing liquid paint and the air compressor are located on the ground and connected to the spray gun via a tether cable formed by hydraulic and pneumatic pipelines.

This setup allows the drone to only bear the weight of the spray gun and the tension from the tether after takeoff, reducing the load on the drone and extending its flight duration. The principle is illustrated in Fig. 1. During the spraying operation, the compressed air from the air compressor is divided into two channels: one channel supplies power to the pressure tank, pushing out the paint, while the other channel provides control air to the spray gun, adjusting its state. Once the paint pressure in the pressure tank reaches the set level, it enters the spray gun through the air inlet, atomizes, and is sprayed from the nozzle.

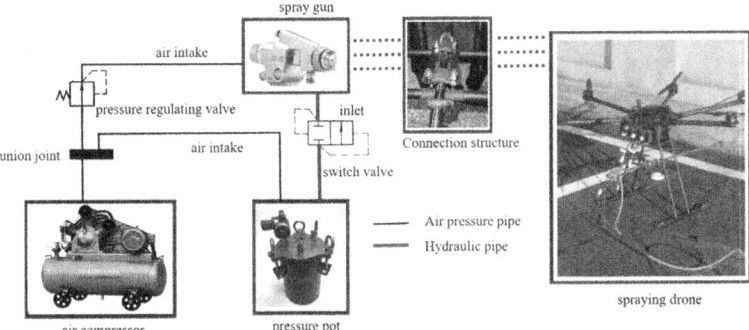

Fig. 1. Structural schematic diagram of the composition of spraying drone.

This project has chosen the WA-101-152P automatic spray gun as the spraying equipment for the drone. The spray gun has a nozzle diameter of 1.5 mm, weighs approximately 1.6 kg In this project, "X" type rack is selected to layout the spraying UAV, after accounting for the weight of the cable, spray gun, and connectors, the gross takeoff weight is approximately 12 kg.

2.2 Tethered UAV Dynamics Modeling

In order to simplify the modeling process without losing generality, the following assumptions are made (Fig. 2):

(1) The six-rotor UAV is a uniform and symmetric rigid body;
(2) The origin of the inertial coordinate system and the geometric center and center of mass of the UAV are located in the same position;
(3) The pull of the six-rotor UAV in each direction is directly proportional to the square of the propeller speed;
(4) The six-rotor UAV flies at low speed, ignoring the deformation and gyroscope effect.

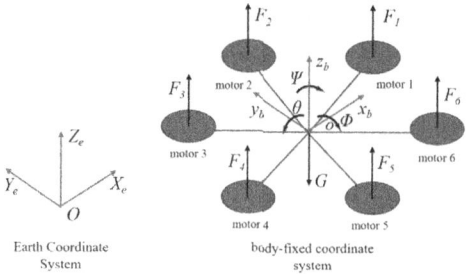

Fig. 2. UAV dynamics model.

Define $[U_1\ U_2\ U_3\ U_4]^T$ as the input vector for the four independent control channels of the UAV, U_1 is throttle input, U_2 is roll input, U_3 is pitch input, and U_4 is yaw input:

$$\begin{bmatrix} U_1 \\ U_2 \\ U_3 \\ U_4 \end{bmatrix} = \begin{bmatrix} k\sum_{i=1}^{6} \omega_i^2 \\ kL(\omega_3^2 - \omega_6^2) + kL\sin\frac{\pi}{3}(\omega_2^2 + \omega_4^2 - \omega_1^2 - \omega_5^2) \\ kL\sin\frac{\pi}{6}(\omega_1^2 + \omega_2^2 - \omega_4^2 - \omega_5^2) \\ k_d(\omega_2^2 - \omega_1^2 + \omega_4^2 - \omega_3^2 + \omega_6^2 - \omega_5^2) \end{bmatrix} \quad (1)$$

k is the drag coefficient; k_d is the torque coefficient; $d_i(i = 1,2,3,4,5,6)$ is the disturbance; L is the distance from the motor to the flight center; I_x, I_y, I_z are the moments of inertia. The final equation group describing the six-rotor UAV is:

$$\begin{cases} \ddot{x} = \frac{U_1(\sin\theta\cos\phi\cos\psi + \sin\phi\sin\psi) - K_1\dot{x}}{m} - \frac{T_x}{m} - \frac{f_x}{m} + d_1, \\ \ddot{y} = \frac{U_1(\sin\theta\cos\phi\sin\psi - \sin\phi\cos\psi) - K_2\dot{y}}{m} - \frac{T_y}{m} - \frac{f_y}{m} + d_2, \\ \ddot{z} = \frac{U_1(\cos\phi\cos\psi) - K_3\dot{z}}{m} - g - \frac{T_z}{m} - \frac{f_z}{m} + d_3, \\ \ddot{\phi} = \frac{1}{I_x}LU_2 + d_4, \\ \ddot{\theta} = \frac{1}{I_y}LU_3 + d_5, \\ \ddot{\psi} = \frac{1}{I_z}U_4 + d_6 \end{cases} \quad (2)$$

Although the form of tethering solves the problems of carrying weight and endurance, with the increase of altitude, the weight of the cable pulled by the tethered UAV increases, and the direction and size of the tension will change accordingly. The cable in this study is modeled as a catenary. The tension of the cable is derived from catenary theory, with one end of the cable fixed to the drone and the other end to the ground. A small segment of the cable is selected for analysis, with its self-weight load being T.

By formulating the force equilibrium equations for a differential element based on the schematic diagram, the following relationship is derived (Fig. 3):

$$T\cos\alpha = (T + dT)\cos(\alpha + d\alpha) \quad (3)$$

$$T\sin\alpha + qds = (T + dT)\sin(\alpha + d\alpha) \quad (4)$$

$$\tan\alpha = \frac{dz}{dx} \quad (5)$$

$$ds = \sqrt{1+\dot{z}^2}dx \tag{6}$$

where d_T is the wind disturbance, the manager theory analysis found that the tension equation is:

$$T = H + qz + d_T \tag{7}$$

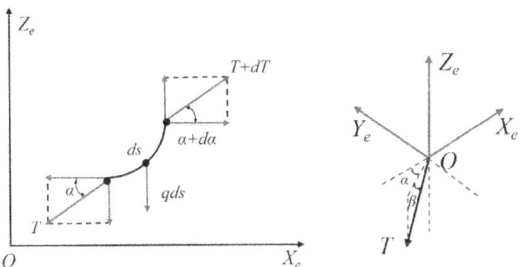

Fig. 3. Schematic diagram of cable micro-element force analysis.

Next, the disturbance of UAV when the spray gun starts is considered. After the spray gun starts, it can be regarded as a step signal disturbance caused by free turbulent jet, and the momentum conservation equation of UAV in the horizontal direction is written:

$$d(mv) = d(MV - mV) \tag{8}$$

In practice, $M \gg m$, so the equation is simplified to:

$$vdm = MdV \tag{9}$$

$$dm = \rho vAdt \tag{10}$$

The above formula is summarized as:

$$f = M\frac{dV}{dt} = \rho v^2 A \tag{11}$$

$$f_{xb} = 0 \; f_{yb} = \rho v^2 A \; f_{zb} = 0 \tag{12}$$

$$\begin{bmatrix} f_x \\ f_y \\ f_z \end{bmatrix} = R_b^e \begin{bmatrix} f_{xb} \\ f_{yb} \\ f_{zb} \end{bmatrix} \tag{13}$$

Considering the influence of cable and spray recoil force, the UAV dynamics equation becomes:

$$\begin{cases} \ddot{x} = \frac{U_1(\sin\theta\cos\phi\cos\psi + \sin\phi\sin\psi) - K_1\dot{x}}{m} - \frac{T_x}{m} - \frac{f_x}{m} + d_1, \\ \ddot{y} = \frac{U_1(\sin\theta\cos\phi\sin\psi - \sin\phi\cos\psi) - K_2\dot{y}}{m} - \frac{T_y}{m} - \frac{f_y}{m} + d_2, \\ \ddot{z} = \frac{U_1(\cos\phi\cos\psi) - K_3\dot{z}}{m} - g - \frac{T_z}{m} - \frac{f_z}{m} + d_3, \\ \ddot{\phi} = \frac{1}{I_x}LU_2 + d_4, \\ \ddot{\theta} = \frac{1}{I_y}LU_3 + d_5, \\ \ddot{\psi} = \frac{1}{I_z}U_4 + d_6 \end{cases} \quad (14)$$

3 Simulation

3.1 Cascade PID Controller Design

The attitude controller adopts cascade PID control. The angle loop is usually controlled by P, and the angular velocity loop is controlled by complete PID control. First, the angle loop is designed:

The angular velocity loop control equation is:

$$\omega_d = k_{\Theta p} e_\Theta \quad (15)$$

$$\tau_d = k_{\omega p} e_\omega + k_{\omega i} \int e_\omega + k_{\omega d} \dot{e}_\omega \quad (16)$$

The horizontal channel control equation is:

$$\dot{V}_h = -g R_\psi \Theta_h \quad (17)$$

$$\theta_h = -\frac{1}{g} R_\psi^{-1} \dot{V}_h \quad (18)$$

$$\Theta_{hd} = -\frac{1}{g} R_\psi^{-1} \dot{V}_{hd} \quad (19)$$

The high passage control equation is:

$$v_{zd} = k_{zp} e_z \quad (20)$$

$$F_d = m(g - k_{pz} e_{v_z} + k_{iz} \int e_{v_z} + k_{dz} \dot{e}_{v_z}) \quad (21)$$

At this point, the high channel design is complete.

After the design of the position controller is completed, the observation results of the step signal are given. The step signal with final value of 5 m, 10 m and 20 m is given in the x-axis, y-axis and z-axis respectively (Fig. 4).

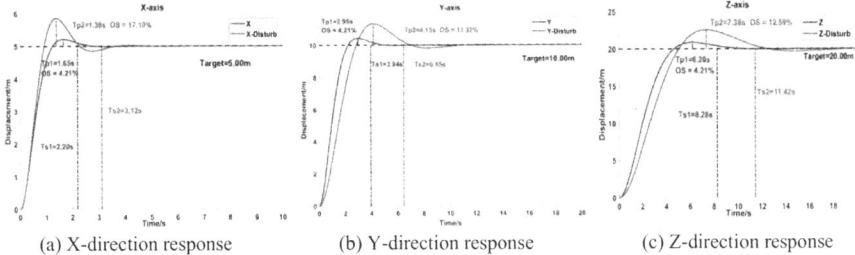

(a) X-direction response (b) Y-direction response (c) Z-direction response

Fig. 4. P-Controller response to step Inputs when considering tether tension and recoil force.

By comparing the response curves of the tension recoil model with and without the tension recoil model, it is found that when the tension recoil is considered, the position stability time is extended to a certain extent, and the overshoot occurs to a certain extent. The overall response time and the convergence speed of the curve are within the acceptable range.

At the same time, the attitude controller is tested and the observation results are given by the step signal. The variation curves of row, pitch and yaw are respectively obtained. However, since row and pitch do not participate in the input, the step signal with the final value of yaw being 5°(0.0873rad) is given.

It can be clearly seen that due to the existence of the recoil force, row and pitch have obvious oscillation when the recoil step comes, and because the tension changes periodically with the height, the response curves of the three attitude angles all show small oscillation (Fig. 5).

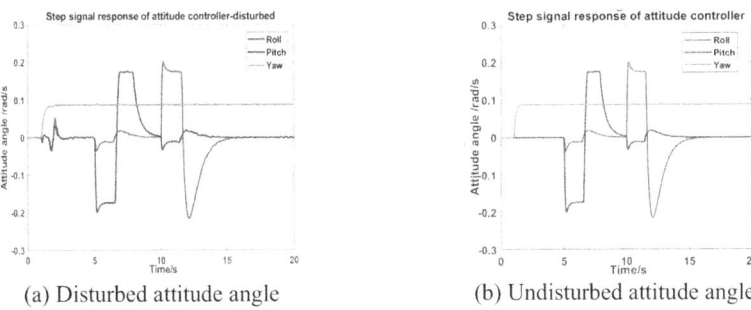

(a) Disturbed attitude angle (b) Undisturbed attitude angle

Fig. 5. A-Controller response to step inputs when considering tether tension and recoil force.

3.2 Spray Distance Precision Control and Pose Alignment Simulation

Spray accuracy control involves maintaining the distance between the spraying drone and the target surface within a specific range during the spraying process. Considering the impact of outdoor wind fields, the position of the drone is modeled as a zero-mean Gaussian random signal with a wind speed of approximately 9.2 m/s, equivalent to a level 5 wind speed. The simulation estimates the variance of the drone's linear and rotational movements to be $0.062N^2$ and $0.0035 (N·m)^2$, respectively. To ensure the spray gun is always aligned with the wall during spraying, two laser rangefinders are installed at the same horizontal level to achieve this function.

The return distance values from the two sensors. The yaw angle deviation is, and the actual spray distance is Y. When the spray gun is not aligned with the wall, the return values from the two sensors differ. Based on the geometric relationship, the yaw angle that needs to be corrected is:

$$\Delta\psi = \arctan(\frac{d_1 - d_2}{l}) \tag{22}$$

$$Y = \frac{d_1 + d_2}{2} \tag{23}$$

The flight control calculates the deviation value in real time according to the distance returned by the two sensors and inputs the deviation into the attitude controller to adjust the yaw angle of the UAV, so as to ensure that the UAV can always face the spraying surface (Fig. 6).

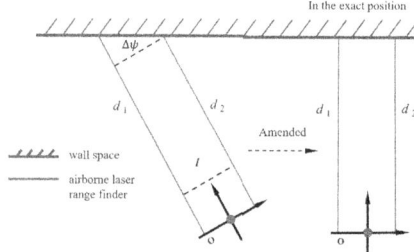

Fig. 6. Principle of spray-distance precision control and attitude alignment.

Set spraying distance Y is 1.5 m, the spacing between the two ranging sensors is 0.1 m, and the initial difference is 0.02 m, and the trajectory tracking results are shown in Fig. 7.

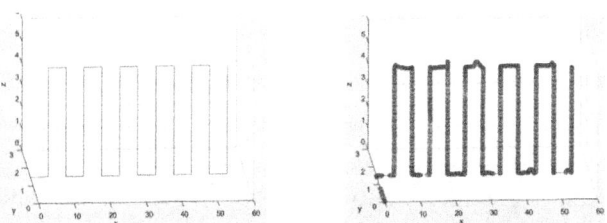

Fig. 7. Spray path planning and trajectory tracking.

During the simulation, the yaw angle, spray distance, and the changes in X and Z axis positions are illustrated in Fig. 8. At the start of the simulation, the program calculates the yaw angle to be 0.21 rad, which then converges rapidly. Throughout the process, the yaw angle fluctuates slightly within the range of −0.05 to 0.05 rad. The spray distance, after reaching the set value of 1.5 m, fluctuates between 1.486 m and 1.514 m. The tracking of the X and Z axis positions is also satisfactory.

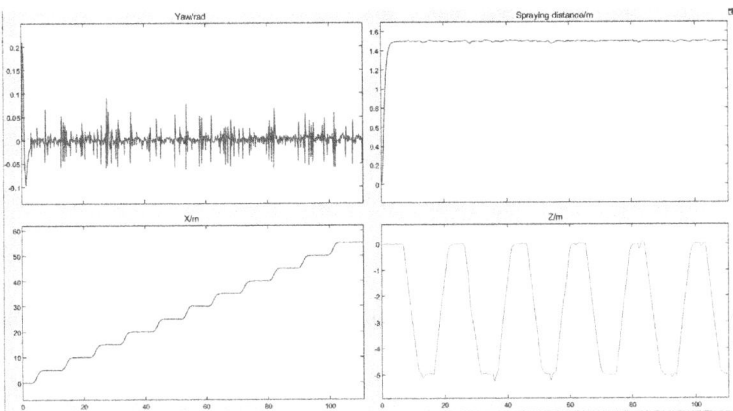

Fig. 8. Trajectory tracking, spray distance control, and yaw angle correction.

To filter out the impact of backflow, data on yaw angle and spray distance from 5 to 20 s during the simulation stabilization process were collected. When there is no overshoot, the yaw angle almost fluctuates within ± 0.05rad, with an absolute deviation of 0.009rad. The spray distance fluctuates between 1.48 m and 1.51 m, with an average value of 1.498 m and an absolute deviation of 0.0032 m (Fig. 9).

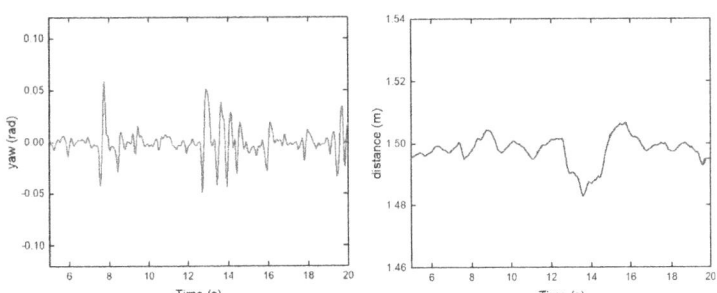

Fig. 9. Spray distance and yaw angle during stable operation.

This project employs high-precision RTK positioning technology which can improve the precision to 0.05 m. A fixed point on the spray site is selected as the ground station for the RTK, and a receiver is installed to monitor satellites.

Then conduct the spray stability experiment (Fig. 10). Maintaining an air intake pressure of 4.4bar ensures that the air compression and consumption rates are nearly equal, allowing for stable spraying for over 15 min. Therefore, 4.4bar is determined as the optimal air intake pressure.

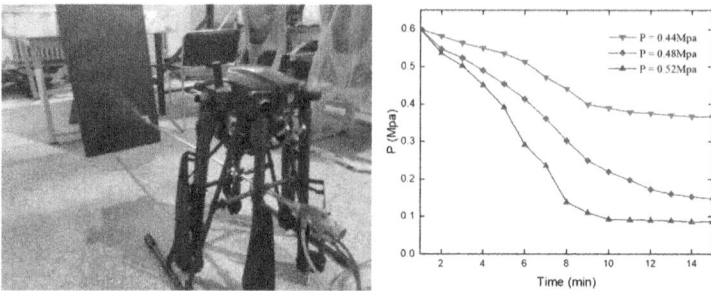

Fig. 10. Spray stability test site.

The relative horizontal distance between the two laser rangefinders and the spray gun is 0.84 m. Considering the suitable spraying range, the spraying distance parameter is set to 1.3 m. After the take-off inspection, the spraying drone is activated. The drone will follow the preset trajectory to perform the spraying task. During the spraying process, the laser rangefinder continuously sends the distance from the outer wall back to the flight control system to ensure accurate spraying (Fig. 11).

Fig. 11. Verification of autonomous spraying function.

The take-off and lateral spraying processes are relatively stable during the spraying process. The flight log data are exported to detect the UAV attitude and spraying accuracy data. Initially, yaw angle of the UAV was –0.15rad. After adjustments, the yaw angle stabilized between 0.04rad and 0.11rad, with minor fluctuations. Each overshoot was quickly corrected, demonstrating effective control (Fig. 12).

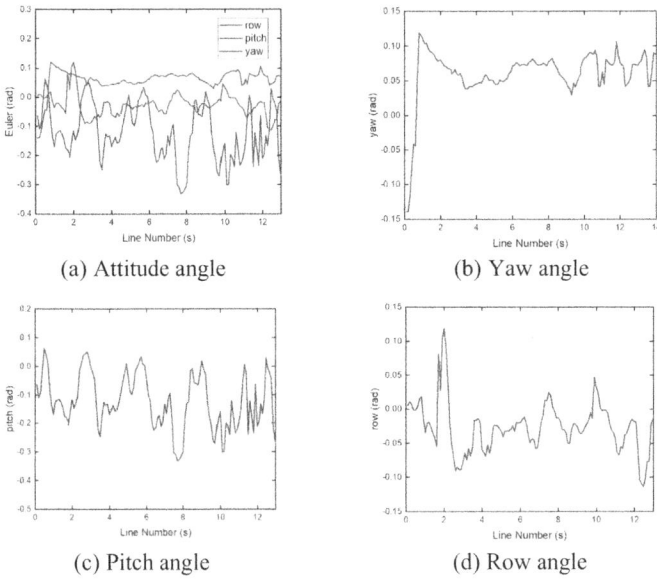

Fig. 12. Variation curves of three attitude angles during spraying.

The average spraying distance is 1.358 m, with an absolute error of 0.026 m. The maximum value is 1.442 m, and the minimum value is 1.247 m. After correction, the variance is 0.249 m. This indicates that the actual spraying distance of the spray gun to the wall is between 0.4 m and 0.6 m, or ± 0.1 m, meeting the task requirements (Fig. 13).

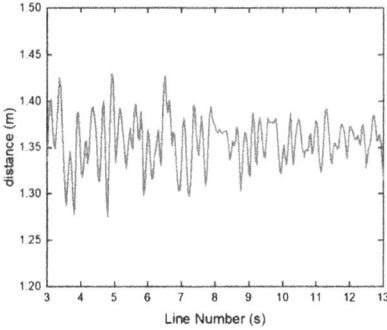

Fig. 13. Distance between UAV and spraying surface.

4 Conclusion

This paper proposes a drone system applicable to spraying operations on non-flat or irregular surfaces, achieving stable control of spraying distance and posture. The dynamic model for a hexacopter UAV was established, incorporating catenary tether tension and spray recoil force, and a cascade PID controller was designed. Simulation results verified that the system maintains rapid response and effective error convergence under disturbances. For spray precision control, dual laser ranging sensors were employed to dynamically calculate distance deviations and yaw angle offsets. The flight controller adjusts the yaw attitude of the drone in real time to ensure the spray gun remains aligned with the wall surface; experimental results show that the spraying positioning accuracy is stably maintained within ± 0.15 m, with an average distance error of only 0.026 m during stable operation. Regarding attitude control, the cascade PID controller effectively suppresses disturbances from recoil force and periodic tether tension. During experiments, the roll, pitch, and yaw angles of the UAV rapidly stabilized after adjustment, with small fluctuation ranges that yaw angle stabilized between 0.04 rad and 0.11 rad.

Funding. This research was supported by part of National Natural Science Foundation of China (No. 52205012), part of Natural Science Foundation of Heilongjiang Province (No. LH2023E038), part of Self-Planned Task (NO. SKLRS202501A01) of State Key Laboratory of Robotics and Systems (HIT).

References

1. Vaishali, R.: Health profile of workers in a ship building and repair industry. Indian J. Occup. Environ. Med. **18**(2), 89–94 (2014)
2. Li, Y., Yi, Z., Lin Y. et al.: The basic functional design of wall climbing robot for hull plate spraying in dock. In: International Conference on Robotics and Automation Engineering 2017, ICRAE, pp. 89–93. IEEE International Conference, Shanghai (2017)
3. Liu, G., Zhang Y., Li C. et al.: Design and optimization of spraying robot arm for hull blocks. In: IEEE International Conference on Robotics and Biomimetics 2015, ROBIO, pp. 2615–2620. IEEE International Conference, Zhuhai (2015)
4. Sai, A.V., Mina, K., Nikola, S., et al.: An autonomous UAV for spray painting on three-dimensional surfaces. IEEE Robot. Autom. Lett. **3**(4), 2862–2869 (2018)
5. Bushnaq, O.M., Kishk, M.A., Celik, A., et al.: Optimal deployment of tethered drones for maximum cellular coverage in user clusters. IEEE Trans. Wireless Commun. **20**(3), 2092–2108 (2021)
6. Diaz, A.L., Ortega, A.E., Tingle, H., et al.: An autonomous uncrewed drone-tethered sonar system. Drones **6**(10), 294 (2022)
7. Rocamora, B.M., Lima, R.R., Samarakoon, K., et al.: A tethered UAV for inspection of stone-mine pillars. Drones **7**(2), 73 (2023)
8. Dahlstrom, R.L.: State of Technology: cleaning and coating UAV systems-industrial spray painting drones available to purchase. In: Offshore Technology Conference 2020, pp. 3–5. OnePetro, Houston (2020)
9. Wang, K., Yang, Y.F., Chen, M.M., et al.: A study of fire drone extinguishing system in high-rise buildings. Fire **5**(3), 75 (2022)
10. Zhu, T.H.: Air-ground cooperative control technology for intelligent spray painting on ship hulls using UAVs. Ph.D. dissertation. Jiangsu University of Science and Technology, Zhenjiang (2023)
11. Xu, Z., Yan, T., Yang, S.X., et al.: Bioinspired backstepping sliding mode control and adaptive sliding innovation filter of quadrotor unmanned aerial vehicles. Biomimetic Intell. Robot. **3**(3), 100116 (2023)
12. Zhang, D.C., Tang, S.: Application of catenary theory in towing systems. Flight Dyn. **23**(2), 70–72 (2005)

13. Guo, C.R.: Comparative analysis of catenary and parabolic cable calculation theories. J. Shanxi Archit. **38**(3), 173–176 (2012)
14. Wu, Y.M., Fu, G., Zhu, X.Y.: Research on fuzzy PID synchronous control for tethered UAV's cable deployment system. Mech. Eng. Autom. **243**(1), 172–174 (2023)

A Study of the Effectiveness of Various Combined Control Schemes Based on MPC and WBC in Humanoid Control

Yinhui Chen, Dachuan Liu, Shilong Sun, Wenfu Xu, and Qingbin Gao[✉]

School of Robotics and Advanced Manufacture, Harbin Institute of Technology Shenzhen, Shenzhen 518055, China
gaoqingbin@hit.edu.cn

Abstract. The development of motion control frameworks for legged robots primarily focuses on Model Predictive Control (MPC) and Whole-Body Control (WBC) strategies, both of which have proven effectiveness in achieving dynamic locomotion for bipedal and quadrupedal robots. MPC offers predictive capabilities by optimizing control inputs over a future horizon, while WBC enables real-time task prioritization and joint torque generation. In this work, we design a WBC motion control scheme based on nullspace projection and compare it with an existing linear MPC-based controller and combined MPC-WBC approach. These schemes are evaluated in simulation with respect to maximum walking speed, trajectory tracking accuracy, and disturbance rejection capability. The WBC scheme is shown to achieve faster movement (up to 0.9 m/s) and superior robustness against external perturbations compared to the MPC-only controller (up to 0.3m/s). Moreover, it significantly reduces computational complexity relative to the combined MPC-WBC framework, making it more suitable for real-time or resource-limited applications.

Keywords: Legged Robots · Model Predictive Control · Whole-Body Control

1 Introduction

Bipedal robots have attracted growing interest due to their potential in hazardous environments and medical applications, such as powered lower-limb prosthetics [1]. To achieve stable and dynamic locomotion, traditional control strategies like Zero Moment Point (ZMP) [2] and Spring-Loaded Inverted Pendulum (SLIP) [3] have been widely used. More recently, advanced frameworks like Model Predictive Control (MPC) and Whole-Body Control (WBC) have gained attention for their capabilities in handling complex terrains and dynamic motions [4].

MPC computes optimal control inputs over a prediction horizon based on simplified models like the Linear Inverted Pendulum or the Single Rigid-Body Dynamics (SRBD) model. It has been success fully applied to both quadrupeds and humanoids for tasks such as dynamic walking and disturbance rejection [5–7]. However, MPC's real-time applicability is limited by its computational cost.

WBC, on the other hand, enables multi-priority task coordination, such as foot contact, base orientation, and swing-leg motion, using nullspace projection or hierarchical optimization [8, 9]. While WBC provides better execution responsiveness and lower computational load, prior studies mainly focus on low-dynamic tasks or in combination with MPC [10, 11].

Despite promising results from combining MPC and WBC, the standalone application of WBC for high-dynamic locomotion is underexplored. This paper addresses this gap by comparing three schemes: MPC-only, WBC-only, and a combined MPC-WBC control approach. Using an SRBD model and the qpOASES optimization solver [12], we evaluate their performance in terms of speed and disturbance rejection.

The contributions are as follows:

- We design a WBC-based balance control strategy using center-of-mass dynamics, achieving 0.3 m/s in simulation.
- We enhance the scheme with motion planning and nullspace projection, reaching up to 1.5 m/s.
- We demonstrate the potential of WBC as a lightweight alternative to MPC under real-time constraints.

The rest of the paper is structured as follows. Section 2 discusses the fundamental theories for model establishment. Section 3 presents the scheme design. Experimental results and analysis are provided in Sect. 4. Finally, Sect. 5 concludes the paper and outlines future work.

2 Dynamic Analysis

We model the bipedal robot using a Single Rigid-Body Dynamics (SRBD) framework with a floating base to support integration with whole-body control (WBC). The generalized dynamics of the system are:

$$M\dot{u} + h = S^T \tau + {}^w J_c^T f_c \quad (1)$$

where h represents the collection of centrifugal, Coriolis, and gravitational forces, u, defined as $u = \begin{bmatrix} {}^w v, {}^w \omega, \dot{q}_a \end{bmatrix}^T$, is the generalized velocity vector, S is the selection matrix for actuated joints, and τ is the joint torque with its first six elements being zero for the floating base model. Where, ${}^w v$ is velocity in world frame, ${}^w \omega$ is the angular velocity in world frame. $\dot{q}_a$ is the joint velocity. ${}^w J_c$ denotes the collection of contact Jacobian matrices, and f_c represents the collection of contact forces.

We partition the system into floating base and actuated joints:

$$\begin{aligned} M_b \dot{u} + h_b &= {}^w J_{cb}^T f_c \quad (a) \\ M_a \dot{u} + h_a &= \tau + {}^w J_{ca}^T f_c \quad (b) \end{aligned} \quad (2)$$

To simplify control, we make two assumptions: (1) small angular velocities, and (2) small roll/pitch angles. Next, we explore the state-space representation of the system based on the dynamics model of the bipedal robot. The state variables are chosen to include the robot's Euler angles, position, angular velocity, and linear velocity of the floating base, and an additional gravity acceleration term, denoted as $\mathbf{x} = \begin{bmatrix} \Theta^T & \mathbf{p}_c^T & \boldsymbol{\omega}^T & \dot{\mathbf{p}}_c^T & g \end{bmatrix}^T$, where $\Theta = \begin{bmatrix} \theta_R & \theta_P & \theta_Y \end{bmatrix}^T$ represents the Euler angles, $\mathbf{p_c} = \begin{bmatrix} p_x & p_y & p_z \end{bmatrix}^T$ is the position, $\boldsymbol{\omega} = \begin{bmatrix} p_x & p_y & p_z \end{bmatrix}^T$ is the angular velocity, and g is the gravitational acceleration. The control variables are chosen to be the contact force wrench $\mathbf{u} = \begin{bmatrix} f_1^T & f_2^T & \tau_1^T & \tau_2^T \end{bmatrix}^T$, with $W_l = \begin{bmatrix} f_1^T & \tau_1^T \end{bmatrix}^T$ and $W_r = \begin{bmatrix} f_2^T & \tau_2^T \end{bmatrix}^T$ representing the force wrenches at the left and right feet, respectively. The state-space representation of the system can then be expressed as follows:

$$\dot{\mathbf{x}} = A\mathbf{x} + B\mathbf{u}$$

$$A = \begin{bmatrix} 0_{3\times3} & 0_{3\times3} & R_z & 0_{3\times3} & 0_{3\times1} \\ 0_{3\times3} & 0_{3\times3} & 0_{3\times3} & I_{3\times3} & 0_{3\times1} \\ 0_{3\times3} & 0_{3\times3} & 0_{3\times3} & 0_{3\times3} & 0_{3\times1} \\ 0_{3\times3} & 0_{3\times3} & 0_{3\times3} & 0_{3\times3} & c_h \\ 0_{1\times3} & 0_{1\times3} & 0_{1\times3} & 0_{1\times3} & 0 \end{bmatrix}, c_h = \begin{bmatrix} 0 \\ 0 \\ -1 \end{bmatrix}$$

$$B = \begin{bmatrix} 0_{3\times3} & 0_{3\times3} & 0_{3\times3} & 0_{3\times3} \\ 0_{3\times3} & 0_{3\times3} & 0_{3\times3} & 0_{3\times3} \\ \hat{I}^{-1}(p_1 - p_c) \times & \hat{I}^{-1}(p_2 - p_c) \times & \hat{I}^{-1} & \hat{I}^{-1} \\ I_{3\times3}/m & I_{3\times3}/m & 0_{3\times3} & 0_{3\times3} \end{bmatrix}$$

(3)

We define the operation $(\cdot)\times$ as generating the skew-symmetric matrix of a vector, as follows:

$$p\times = \begin{bmatrix} 0 & -p_z & p_y \\ p_z & 0 & -p_x \\ -p_y & p_x & 0 \end{bmatrix}$$

(4)

At this point, we have transformed the floating-base dynamics Eqs. (1) of the bipedal robot into the SRBD dynamics equation in (3). We have also appropriately simplified and approximated the nonlinear components of the SRBD dynamics equations in (3), ultimately obtaining the linearized equation shown in (3), and created a linear time-varying state-space representation.

3 Algorithm Design Based on MPC and WBC

3.1 Bipedal Motion Control Using MPC

Model Predictive Control (MPC) predicts the future behavior of a system over a finite time horizon and solves an optimization problem to determine the best control inputs. For bipedal robots, models like the Linear Inverted Pendulum (LIPM), Single Rigid-Body Dynamics (SRBD), and whole-body models are commonly used. Due to a favorable balance between computational simplicity and accuracy, we adopt a linearized SRBD model for MPC.

3.2 MPC Problem Formulation and Solution

Using a zero-order hold, the continuous-time dynamics Eq. (3) is discretized as follows:

$$\mathbf{x}[k+1] = \hat{A}[k]\mathbf{x}[k] + \hat{B}\mathbf{u}[k] \tag{5}$$

where Δ_T is the sampling time, $\hat{A}(k) = \mathbf{I} + A(k)\Delta_T$, and $\hat{B}(k) = B(k)\Delta_T$. A prediction horizon of N_p step is set, during which the predicted states and control inputs are:

$$\mathbf{X}[k] = \left[\mathbf{x}(k+1|t), \ldots, \mathbf{x}(k+N_p|t)\right]^T \mathbf{U}[t] = \left[\mathbf{u}(k|t), \ldots, \mathbf{u}(k+N_{p-1}|t)\right]^T \tag{6}$$

The cost function is constructed by minimizing the sum of the differences between the predicted trajectory and the reference trajectory within the prediction horizon and the control inputs:

$$\begin{aligned}\min_{U(t)} &\ ||\mathbf{X}(t) - \mathbf{X}_{ref}(t)||_Q^2 + ||\mathbf{U}(k)||_R^2 \\ s.t.\ &\mathbf{X}(k) = \Psi_t \mathbf{x}(t) + \Phi_t \mathbf{U}(k)\end{aligned} \tag{7}$$

where

$$\Psi_{\mathbf{t}} = \begin{bmatrix} \hat{A}_{k,t} \\ \hat{A}_{k+1,t}\hat{A}_{k,t} \\ \vdots \\ \prod_{i=k}^{k+N_p-1}\hat{A}_{i,t} \end{bmatrix} \Phi_t = \begin{bmatrix} B_{k,t} & \cdots & 0_{N_p \times N_u} \\ A_{k+1,t}B_{k,t} & \cdots & 0_{N_p \times N_u} \\ \vdots & \ddots & \vdots \\ \prod_{i=k+1}^{k+N_p-1}A_{i,t}B_{k,t} & \cdots & \prod_{i=k+N_c}^{k+N_p-1}A_{i,t}B_{k+N_p-1,t} \end{bmatrix} \tag{8}$$

By incorporating equality constraints into the objective function, the problem can be transformed into a quadratic programming problem expressed as:

$$\min_{U(t)} U(t)^T H U(t) + G^T U(t) \tag{9}$$

where we have the following relationship:

$$H = \Phi_t^T Q \Phi_t + R,\ G = 2\Phi_t^T Q\left(\Psi_t x(k|t) - X_{ref}(t)\right) \tag{10}$$

To ensure physical feasibility, we impose linear constraints:

- Friction constraints (linearized): $|f_x|, |f_y| \mu |f_z| s$
- Torque limits via static mapping: $\tau = -J^T u$, with $\tau_{\min}\ \tau\ \tau_{\max}$

This formulation supports real-time trajectory planning and ground reaction force optimization within bounded torque and contact constraints.

3.3 Whole-Body Dynamics Control Method

While MPC serves as a high-level planner for foot force optimization, it lacks dynamic accuracy due to model simplifications. WBC complements this by leveraging full-body dynamics and joint-space feedback for real-time execution. In our framework, MPC provides long-term guidance, while WBC operates at a faster rate to enforce motion and constraint tracking. Among WBC methods, nullspace projection is preferred for bipedal robots, as it strictly prioritizes tasks—such as contact force control, base stabilization, and swing-leg motion—by projecting lower-priority tasks into the nullspace of higher ones.

The nullspace projection algorithm allows for the resolution of tasks at the joint position, velocity, and acceleration levels as follows[8]:

$$\begin{aligned} \Delta q_i &= \Delta q_{i-1} + J_{i|pre}^{\dagger}(e_i - J_i \Delta q_{i-1}) \\ \dot{q}_i^{cmd} &= \dot{q}_{i-1}^{cmd} + J_{i|pre}^{\dagger}\left(\dot{x}_i^{des} - J_i \dot{q}_{i-1}^{cmd}\right) \\ \ddot{q}_i^{cmd} &= \ddot{q}_{i-1}^{cmd} + \overline{J_{i|pre}^{dyn}}\left(\ddot{x}_i^{cmd} - \dot{J}_i \dot{q} - J_i \ddot{q}_{i-1}^{cmd}\right) \end{aligned} \tag{11}$$

where $J_{i|pre}$ represents the Jacobian matrix of the i-th task projected into the nullspace of the previous task, $J^{\dagger}$ and $\overline{J}$ denote two types of Jacobian pseudoinverses. The former, based on Singular Value Decomposition (SVD), provides the Jacobian pseudoinverse, while the latter, $\overline{J} = M^{-1}J^{\top}\left(JM^{-1}J^{\top}\right)^{-1}$, represents the dynamically consistent Jacobian matrix, which ensures that the calculated joint accelerations are dynamically consistent by considering the inertial properties of the system.

$e_i = x_i^{des} - x_i$ is the task error in the Cartesian coordinate system, $\ddot{x}_i^{cmd} = \ddot{x}^{des} + K_p(x_i^{des} - x_i) + K_d(\dot{x}^{des} - \dot{x})$ is the acceleration command calculated based on the i-th task, and K_p and K_d are the position and velocity error gains, respectively. Additionally, we have

$$\begin{aligned} J_{i|pre} &= J_i N_{i-1} \\ N_{i-1} &= N_0 N_{1|0} \ldots N_{i-1|i-2} \\ N_0 &= I - J_c^{\dagger} J_c \\ N_{i|i-1} &= I - J_{i|i-1}^{\dagger} J_{i|i-1} \end{aligned} \tag{12}$$

The highest-priority task is the contact task, where the actuator part remains stationary in the world coordinate system. Therefore, the task with priority 0 can be simplified as follows:

$$\Delta q_0, \dot{q}_0^{cmd} = 0, \ddot{q}_0^{cmd} = \overline{J}_c^{dyn}(-\dot{J}_c \dot{q}) \tag{13}$$

Ultimately, through nullspace projection Δq, $\dot{q}^{cmd}$, and $\ddot{q}^{cmd}$ can be obtained. The first two are used in joint PD (Proportional-Derivative) controllers, while the latter is used for solving whole-body dynamics via quadratic programming. The construction of the quadratic programming problem is as follows:

$$\min_{\delta_{f_r}, \delta_f} \delta_{f_r}^\top Q_1 \delta_{f_r} + \delta_b^\top Q_2 \delta_b$$

$$\text{s.t.} M_b \ddot{q} + h_b = J_{cb}^\top f_r$$

$$\ddot{q} = \ddot{q}^{cmd} + \begin{bmatrix} \delta_b \\ 0_{n_j} \end{bmatrix} \quad (14)$$

$$f_r = f_r^{MPC} + \delta_{f_r} s$$

$$W f_r \geq 0$$

where δ_{f_r} and δ_b represent the fine-tuning variable. For the contact forces and the floating base accelerations, respectively. The purpose of this optimization is to fine-tune the floating base accelerations and reaction forces to ensure they satisfy the dynamics equations.

According to the above principles, three control schemes are designed in this paper: MPC-based, WBC-based, and combined MPC-WBC control schemes.

MPC-Based Control Scheme. The control scheme based solely on MPC is introduced first, as shown in Fig. 1. Using this control framework, we can compute the optimized foot forces. The trajectory planning is derived from the desired forward velocity and yaw angular velocity. We assume the desired velocity input to be $^b v_x, ^b v_y, \omega_z$, which is then transformed into the world coordinate system based on the current state of the robot, yielding $^w v_x^d, ^w v_y^d, \omega_z^d$. The desired center of mass height is denoted as $^w p_z^{des}$.

WBC-Based Control Scheme. The WBC-based control scheme, shown in Fig. 1, is designed by setting a fixed plantar force according to the robot's mass as the feedforward input, which is then fine-tuned through the WBC. Depending on the task classification, the expected joint position, velocity and acceleration are computed through nullspace projection. In this approach, the joint position and velocity are used for PD control, while the joint acceleration is employed to optimize the plantar force.

Combined MPC-WBC Control Scheme. The combined MPC-WBC control scheme, shown in Fig. 1, is structured such that MPC functions as the upper-layer planner to calculate the desired plantar contact force in real time according to the SRBD dynamics model. The MPC operates at a frequency of 100 Hz to ensure timely. Meanwhile, WBC acts as the lower-layer executive controller, operating in parallel with MPC. It receives real-time results from MPC and formulates a quadratic programming problem to further optimize the computations. The WBC is executed at a higher frequency of 500 Hz, allowing for fast and accurate tracking of the desired forces.

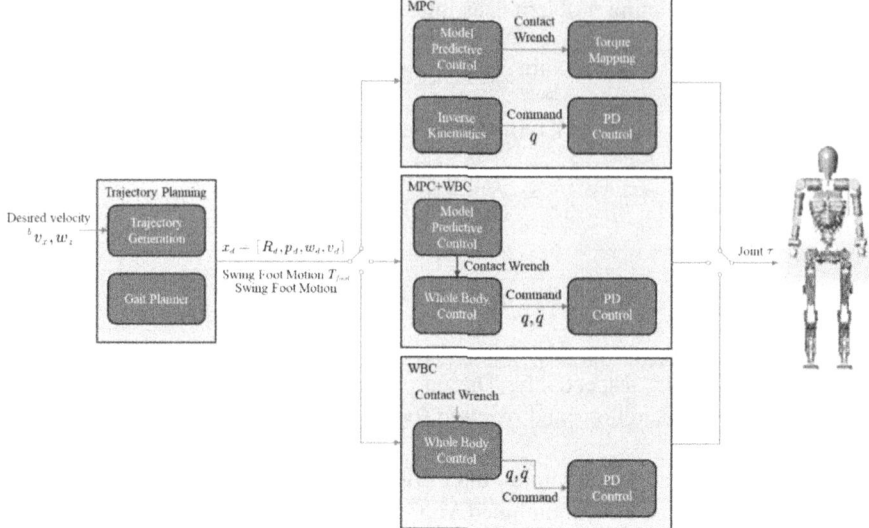

Fig. 1. Three types of control block diagrams

4 Simulation Analysis

4.1 MPC-Based Control Scheme

Based on the MPC framework (Fig. 1), simulation results Fig. 2 show that optimized foot forces respect torque limits and exhibit periodic profiles dominated by the vertical component f_z. As shown in Fig. 3, the robot successfully tracks a desired forward velocity of 0.3 m/s, reaching the target within 1 s. However, attempts to increase speed beyond this threshold lead to instability and large velocity fluctuations. This limitation is attributed to model inaccuracies in the SRBD formulation and the low update rate of the MPC controller, which operates at 100 Hz. Due to the gait cycle being set to 0.6 s, there will be a rapid frequency change in foot force.

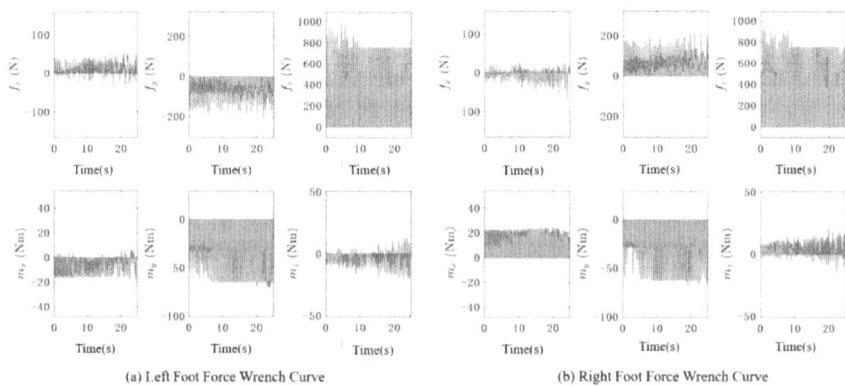

Fig. 2. Optimization of Ankle Force Wrench Using MPC

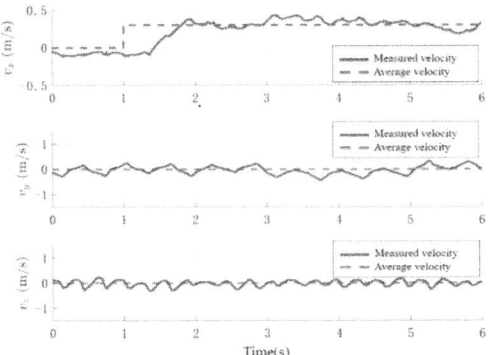

Fig. 3. Maximum Speed Tracking with MPC Control Scheme

4.2 WBC-Based Control Scheme

Based on the control framework outlined in Fig. 1, we conduct simulation experiments. According to the total weight of the robot, a feedforward plantar force is set as follows:

$$u = \begin{bmatrix} f_x\, f_y\, f_z\, m_x\, m_y\, m_z \end{bmatrix}^T \\ = \begin{bmatrix} 0\ 0\ 500N\ 10N \cdot m\ -20N \cdot m\ 0 \end{bmatrix}^T \quad (15)$$

The vertical force f_z serves primarily to maintain base height, while f_x and f_y are dynamically optimized based on real-time feedback and constrained by friction and joint torque limits. To prioritize horizontal control accuracy, we apply higher weight coefficients to f_x and f_y, using:

$$W_u = [0.1, 0.1, 0.001, 1, 1, 1]^T \quad (16)$$

This simplified handling method effectively substitutes for the more complex MPC approach for several reasons:

- High-dynamic bipedal robots rely not only on foot forces to adjust the floating base pose but also use nullspace projection for task prioritization.
- For bipedal walking, tasks such as contact tasks, body position and posture tasks, and swing-leg motion tasks are crucial for maintaining a walking gait.
- Desired joint velocities and integrated joint positions are calculated based on errors in the expected Cartesian space tasks, and joint torques are then output via a PD controller.

WBC uses nullspace projection to prioritize tasks like contact stability, posture control, and swing-leg motion. Joint commands are derived from task errors and executed via a PD controller, with torque computation relying on both foot forces and inverse kinematics. Despite minor deviations between actual and optimized contact forces, the system remains stable. As shown in Fig. 4, the method achieves a maximum speed of 0.9 m/s. Figure 5 illustrates smooth foot force profiles before 40 s, with larger fluctuations appearing afterward due to increased motion dynamics and optimizer limitations—issues to be addressed in future work.

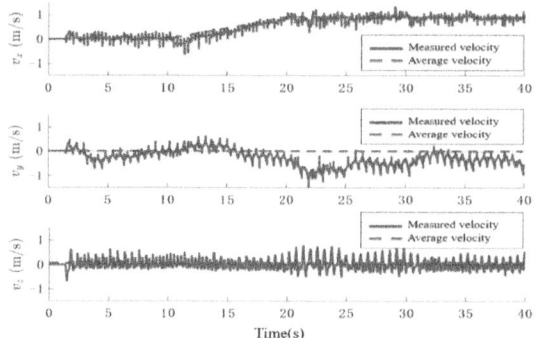

Fig. 4. Maximum Speed Tracking with WBC Control Scheme

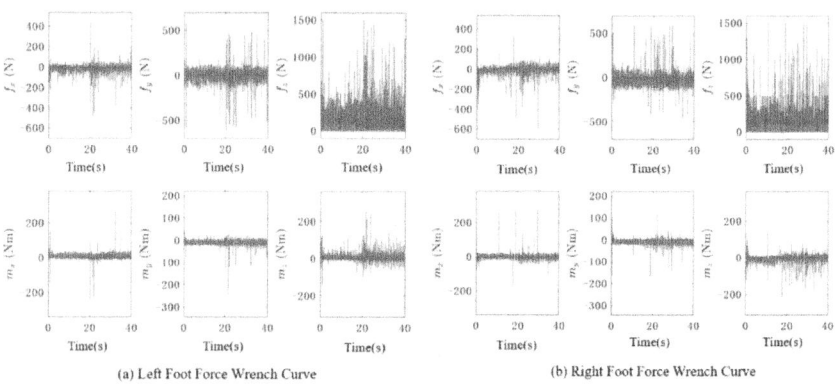

Fig. 5. Optimization of Ankle Force Wrench Using WBC

4.3 Combined MPC-WBC Control Scheme

The combined approach (illustrated in Fig. 1), significantly increases the maximum forward speed, reaching up to 1.5 m/s, surpassing the maximum tracking speeds of both the MPC-based and WBC-based scheme. This demonstrates the role of MPC in stabilizing motion control, while achieving a speed much higher than what is possible with MPC alone. As shown in Fig. 6, the desired speed is set to 1.5 m/s starting from 15s, with acceleration occurring at a constant rate to reach the target speed within 10 s. The robot performs excellently in terms of acceleration and maintaining the 1.5 m/s speed.

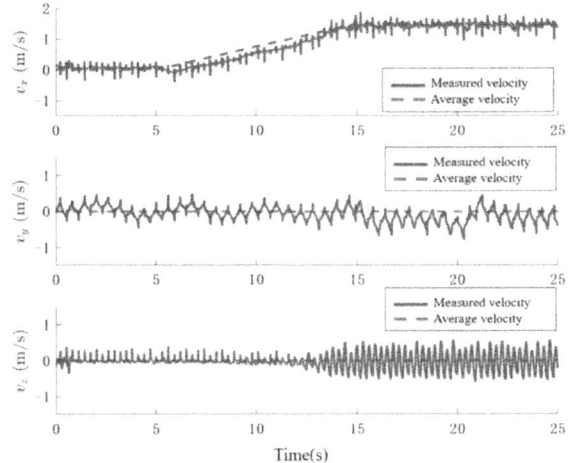

Fig. 6. Maximum Speed Tracking with Combined MPC and WBC Control Scheme

At high speeds, it is noteworthy that vertical velocity fluctuations become more pronounced. This is an inevitable result of faster speeds requiring larger motion amplitudes. However, unlike previous tests, the high-speed movement no longer exhibit the stop-and-go phenomenon. Figure 7 shows the optimized force wrench, which exhibits strong periodic variations in force. This benefit stems from the feedforward quantities planned by MPC, which reduce the search range for torques during WBC optimization. Furthermore, after accelerating to the maximum speed, an increase in the foot force wrench is observed in Fig. 7, aligning well with real-world dynamics.

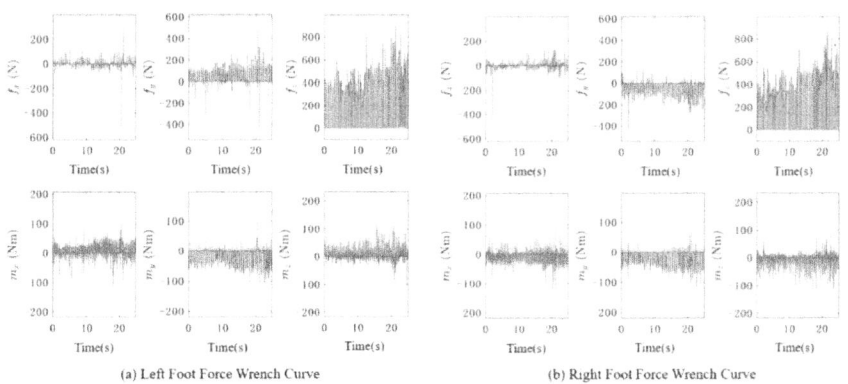

(a) Left Foot Force Wrench Curve   (b) Right Foot Force Wrench Curve

Fig. 7. Optimization of ankle force wrench using combined MPC and WBC

4.4 Disturbance Rejection Analysis

To evaluate robustness, repeated forward disturbances were applied during walking. Under 40 N disturbances, the MPC-only scheme failed after the fourth impact, while both WBC-based and combined MPC-WBC controllers remained stable through at least ten events. With stronger 70 N disturbances, the WBC scheme failed at the twelfth, while the combined approach endured up to the thirteenth. These results show that both WBC-based strategies are effective against repeated disturbances, with the combined MPC-WBC scheme offering slightly greater resilience under more severe conditions (Fig. 8).

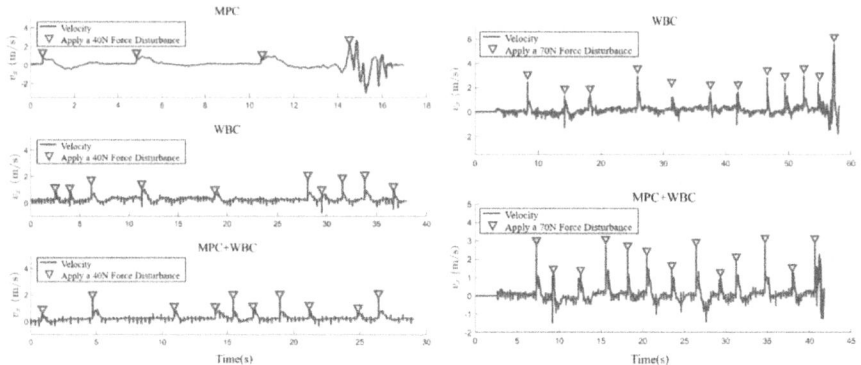

Fig. 8. (a) 40N and (b) 70N disturbance in the forward direction.

4.5 Control Performance Summary

According to the experimental results of the three control schemes, the combined MPC-WBC approach provides the best overall control performance, while the MPC-based approach yields the least favorable results. The advantage of MPC lies in predicting the overall state change of the robot, but it overlooks internal interactions within the robot. On the other hand, WBC focuses on dynamic changes within the robot, prioritizing movement and internal task coordination. The combination of both methods leverages the strengths of each, offering complementary advantages. However, given the computational load of MPC, WBC scheme can still achieve good control performance when computational resources are constrained.

5 Conclusion

This work provides a comparative analysis of three motion control strategies—MPC, WBC, and their integration—for bipedal locomotion. While MPC enables stable but relatively slow walking (0.3 m/s), WBC improves both speed (0.9 m/s) and disturbance rejection capability. The combined MPC-WBC approach achieves the highest overall performance, reaching 1.5 m/s and exhibiting superior robustness, albeit at the cost of increased computational cost due to its dual-layer structure. WBC alone, however, offers a practical balance between performance and efficiency, especially in resource-constrained settings. Future work will aim to enhance the computational efficiency of MPC, explore learning-based or fuzzy control methods, and validate all control schemes on physical robotic platforms.

Acknowledgments. This work was supported in part by State Key Laboratory of Robotics and System Under Grant KY511223001, in part by the National Natural Science Foundation of China under Grant 52475112, in part by Guangdong Basic and Applied Basic Research Foundation Under Grant 2024A1515012041.

References

1. Li, J., Nguyen, Q.: Force-and-moment-based model predictive control for achieving highly dynamic locomotion on bipedal robots. In: Proceedings of the 2021 60th IEEE Conference on Decision and Control (CDC), F. IEEE (2021)
2. Kajita, S., Morisawa, M., Harada, K., et al.: Biped walking pattern generator allowing auxiliary zmp control. In: Proceedings of the 2006 IEEE/RSJ International Conference on Intelligent Robots and Systems. IEEE (2006)
3. Holmes, P., Full, R.J., Koditschek, D., et al.: The dynamics of legged locomotion: Models, analyses, and challenges. **48**(2), 207–304 (2006)
4. Schwenzer, M., Ay, M., Bergs, T., et al.: Review on model predictive control: an engineering perspective. **117**(5), 1327-49 (2021)
5. Katayama, S., Murooka, M., Tazaki, Y.: Model predictive control of legged and humanoid robots: models and algorithms. Adv. Robot. **37**(5), 298–315 (2023)
6. Bledt, G., Powell, M.J., Katz, B., et al.: Mit cheetah 3: design and control of a robust, dynamic quadruped robot. In: 2018 IEEE; Proceedings of the RSJ International Conference on Intelligent Robots and Systems (IROS) (2019)
7. Smaldone, F.M., Scianca, N., Lanari, L., et al.: From walking to running: 3D humanoid gait generation via MPC. Front. Robot. AI **9**, 876613 (2022)
8. Kim, D., Di Carlo, J., Katz, B., et al.: Highly dynamic quadruped locomotion via whole-body impulse control and model predictive control (2019)
9. Bellicoso, C.D., Gehring, C., Hwangbo, J., et al.: Perception-less terrain adaptation through whole body control and hierarchical optimization. In: Proceedings of the 2016 IEEE-RAS 16th International Conference on Humanoid Robots (Humanoids). IEEE (2016)
10. Hopkins, M.A., Hong, D.W., Leonessa, A.: Compliant locomotion using whole-body control and divergent component of motion tracking. In: Proceedings of the 2015 IEEE International Conference on Robotics and Automation (ICRA). IEEE (2025)
11. Kim, D., Jorgensen, S.J., Lee, J., et al.: Dynamic locomotion for passive-ankle biped robots and humanoids using whole-body locomotion control **39**(8), 936-56 (2020)
12. Ferreau, H.J., Kirches, C., Potschka, A., et al.: qpOASES: a parametric active-set algorithm for quadratic programming **6**, 327–63 (2014)

Development and Autonomous Tracking of Miniature Continuum Endscope for Intraocular Microsurgery

Chunbo Wang[1], Taixian Jin[1], Yunfei Wang[1], Zhuowen Zhang[1], Haoyan Zhang[1], Jiaqi Zhang[1], Jian Liang[2], Lei Zhong[2], He Zhang[1]([✉]), and Jie Zhao[1]

[1] State Key Laboratory of Robotics and Systems, Harbin Institute of Technology, Harbin 150001, China
zhanghe0451@hit.edu.cn
[2] Department of Breast Surgery, Sixth Affiliated Hospital of Harbin Medical University, Harbin 150023, China

Abstract. Manual implementation of retinal microsurgery is extremely difficult and poses strict requirements for doctors' operations. The clarity and flexibility of intraoperative images play an important auxiliary role in the operation. Microscopes and Optical Coherence Tomography (OCT) devices can provide image information from a fixed perspective. However, when the patient's cornea is cloudy or the pupil atrophies, clear intraoperative images cannot be obtained. Endoscopes can be inserted into the eyeball through scleral wounds to avoid the problem. However, the handheld rigid ophthalmic endoscope is difficult to obtain intraoperative operation images from multiple perspectives within the eye and also adds an extra burden for doctors to perform intraocular surgical operations. This paper proposes an intraocular continuum endoscope actuator (ICEA) with two degrees of freedom (2-DoF). It can provide multi-view intraoperative images during movements and observe the posture of surgical instruments. Furthermore, this paper proposes a visual control method based on endoscopic images to enable to follow the end of surgical instruments during the operation. The YOLOv8n object detection algorithm is used to obtain the feature coordinates of the microneedle ends in the endoscopic image plane. The actuator and the following control method have been verified through eye model experiments on the eye surgical robot (ESR). The experimental results prove that it can stably track the end of the instrument, making it converge to the expected coordinate.

Keywords: Intraocular continuum endoscope actuator · Visual servo · Automatic tracking

1 Introduction

In retinal microsurgery, ophthalmic surgical instruments are typically inserted into the eyeball through the sclera to perform delicate procedures in the posterior segment of the eye [1]. Given the intricate internal anatomy of the eyeball and the extremely limited operating space, such procedures demand exceptionally high precision from the surgeon. Moreover, several intraoperative challenges arise, such as physiological tremor of the surgeon's hand, limited intraocular visibility, and hand fatigue caused by repetitive and complex operations.

To assist clinicians in performing these high-precision tasks, ophthalmic surgical robot systems have been extensively studied and successfully applied in cataract surgery, vitrectomy, and retinal microsurgery. Jason et al. [2] developed a master-slave intraocular robotic intervention system (IRISS), which enables annular and curvilinear capsulorhexis—critical steps in cataract surgery. The Preceyes Surgical System developed by Preceyes BV has demonstrated safe assistance for human retinal vitreous surgery and obtained CE certification in 2019 [3]. The Steady-Hand Robotic System (SHRS) from Johns Hopkins University represents a typical cooperative operating system [4]. The KU Leuven robotic system, capable of both teleoperated and cooperative operation modes, performed the first robotic-assisted endovascular surgery on human patients in 2018 [5]. Despite their superior accuracy and sensing, robots remain reliant on intraoperative imaging [6–9]. Microscopes and OCT provide high-resolution intraocular visualization, making robot-assisted surgery guided by these modalities a key focus. For instance, Shohin Mukherjee et al. proposed enhancing retinal vessel tracking via loop-closure solutions and improved robustness to motion-induced drift [10]. Yu et al. evaluated OCT-guided microsurgery efficacy [11]. Yang et al. assessed OCT-guided surgery versus cooperative robots [12].

In contrast, intraocular endoscopes are capable of providing real-time and stable images independent of the condition of the anterior segment, thereby enabling direct visualization of the fundus retina. In practice, handheld rigid endoscopes require skilled surgeons for manipulation, and physiological tremor of the surgeon's arm may lead to endoscopic image jitter, interfering with the surgical procedure. Additionally, conventional external control methods cannot actively bend the endoscope or adjust its field of view within the eye, which limits the flexibility of intraoperative image perspectives [13].

To address these challenges, this paper proposes a Intraocular Continuum Endoscope Actuator (ICEA) that can be mounted on a Remote Center of Motion (RCM) mechanism, as shown in Fig. 1. To ensure sufficient flexibility of the endoscope within the eye, an asymmetric concentric push-pull continuum structure is adopted to enable bidirectional actuation, with the endoscope integrated at the distal end of the continuum. The actuator is capable of both rotational and bending motion within the eyeball. Based on the constant curvature assumption, forward and inverse kinematic models from the RCM to the endoscope tip are established, along with the mapping relationship between actuation space and task space. To validate the intraocular flexibility and operational performance of the actuator, a visual servo control algorithm based on endoscopic images is employed to achieve real-time tracking of the surgical instrument tip. The proposed ICEA offers an adaptive and controllable intraoperative imaging solution for robot-assisted retinal microsurgery.

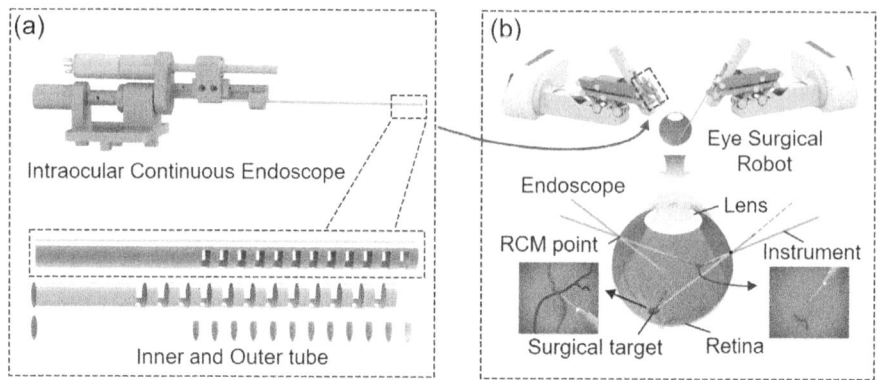

Fig. 1. An ophthalmic surgical robot with intraocular endoscope: (a) Surgical actuator based on a continuum endoscopic mechanism; (b) Multi-angle observation of the fundus during surgery via the continuum endoscope.

2 Design of the Actuator for Continuum Endoscope

2.1 Continuum Structure Design

Figure 2 (a) illustrates the design concept of the continuum endoscope. This design draws inspiration from the asymmetric concentric push-pull mechanism. Asymmetric rectangular slits are introduced into two superelastic hollow tubes, shifting the structure's neutral axis away from the tubes' central axes. The distal ends of both slit tubes are fixed, with slits symmetrically oriented outward. Axial displacement between the inner and outer tubes drives variable bending angles in the continuum structure. Key slit parameters include: number of notches (n), slit height (h), uncut segment height (c), and slit depth (g). Assuming constant curvature at each joint during motion, the maximum bending angle of a single joint can be determined by geometric parameters:

$$\phi^i_{\max} = \frac{h}{\bar{y}_i + R_i} \qquad (1)$$

where, $\phi^i_{\max}$ represents the maximum bending angle of a single joint in the inner and outer tubes, $\bar{y}_i$ denotes the distance between the neutral axis of the inner and outer tubes and their central axis, and R_i indicates the outer radius of the inner and outer tubes. $i = 1, 2$ represent the relevant parameters for the inner and outer tube. As shown in Fig. 2 (b), the neutral axis positions of solid segments in cut cross-sections are determined via the circular chord geometry method, further determining the distances $\bar{y}_1$ and $\bar{y}_2$ from the neutral axes of the inner and outer tubes to the center of the assembly. Inner-outer tube relative motion induces contraction/expansion of the hyperelastic tube's notch: 1) Inner tube pulling causes notch contraction and bending along the notch; 2) Inner tube pushing causes notch expansion and reverse bending relative to the notch. The approximate mapping relationship between the driving displacement Δq and the joint angle θ is expressed as:

$$\theta = \Delta q \left(\bar{y}_1 + \bar{y}_2 \right)^{-1} \tag{2}$$

As shown in Fig. 2 (c), the arc length along the central line of a single notch is expressed as:

$$s_j = h + L(\bar{y} + R)\theta_i \tag{3}$$

where, s_j represents the center line arc of deflection, θ_i represents the bending angle of a single notch, and $\bar{y} = [\bar{y}_1 \ \bar{y}_2]$. Where the function $L = [l_1 \ l_2]$ is used to select different neutral axes, expressed as follows:

$$l_1 = \begin{cases} 0 & (\Delta q > 0) \\ 1 & (\Delta q < 0) \end{cases} \text{ and } l_2 = \begin{cases} 0 & (\Delta q < 0) \\ 1 & (\Delta q > 0) \end{cases} \tag{4}$$

The uncut segments are treated as rigid, and the lengths of all uncut segments collectively determine the total length of the continuum structure:

$$s = (nh + L\bar{y}\theta) + c(n-1) \tag{5}$$

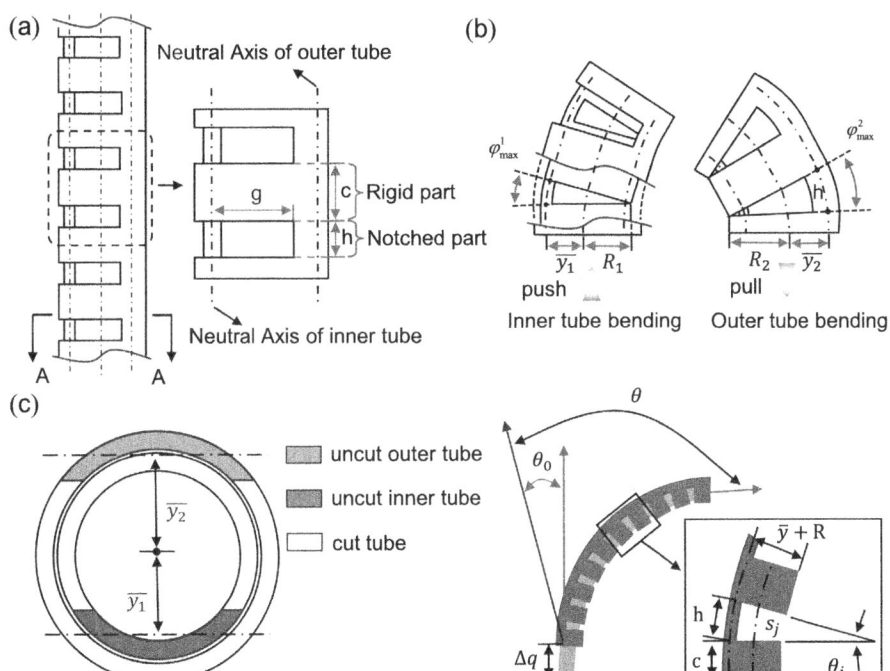

Fig. 2. Schematic of the intraocular continuum endoscope: (a) Geometric parameters of the continuum structure; (b) Deformed configuration under internal tendon tension; (c) Cross-section of the continuum manipulator and the mapping between actuation input and joint curvature.

2.2 Actuator Design and Assembly

This study utilizes nickel-titanium (NiTi) alloy concentric tubes to achieve the continuum structure through asymmetric rectangular groove machining. The outer tube has an outer diameter of 0.9 mm and inner diameter of 0.8 mm, while the inner tube measures 0.78 mm (outer) and 0.65 mm (inner). The rectangular grooves feature a width and spacing of 0.3 mm, with 12 total notches. The continuum structure spans 7.2 mm in length, with a miniature monocular camera module and LED light mounted at the distal end, secured using medical adhesive.

The integrated actuator houses two servo motors (Fig. 3 (a)): Servo Motor 1 (Maxon-347727) governs rotational motion, while Servo Motor 2 (Maxon-DCX08M) controls bending motion. To ensure motion resolution, the continuum actuator achieves single-degree-of-freedom swinging motion via tendon-driven actuation and minimizes sliding friction and motion interference through a lead screw-transmitted single-track linear rail mechanism (Fig. 3 (c)). The system achieves a maximum rotational angle of 360° and a theoretically maximum bending angle of approximately 240°. Overall dimensions are compatible for the human eye's interior which is commonly approximated as a 24mm sphere [14].

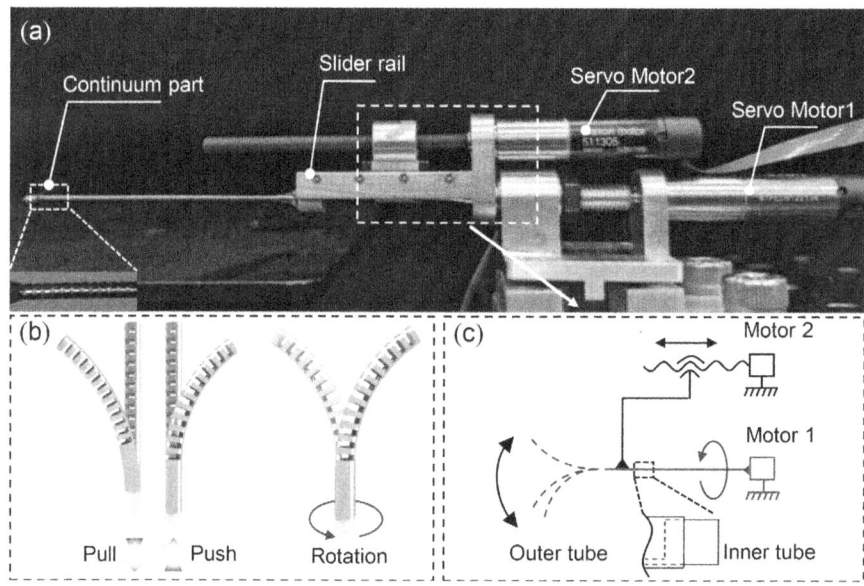

Fig. 3. Actuation principle of the surgical endoscopic actuator: (a) Schematic of the surgical actuator; (b) Illustration of continuum operation; (c) Simplified diagram of the actuator's driving mechanism.

3 Kinematic Modeling of the Actuators

In this section, we conduct a kinematic modeling analysis of the developed continuum endoscope integrated with the surgical robot's RCM mechanism. This involves establishing the mapping relationship from the actuation space to the task space and analyzing its workspace.

3.1 Modeling the Forward Kinematics

The bending motion of the continuum can be described as a homogeneous transformation within the x-z plane, represented by an equivalent D-H parameter method. During joint actuation, the coordinate system's position and orientation change simultaneously and are coupled. The integrated actuator possesses axial rotational degrees of freedom, where planar bending motion is extended to three-dimensional space through spinning motion. The coordinate transformation relationships are expressed as:

$$T_{\text{tip}}^{\text{base}} = \begin{bmatrix} \cos(\theta) & 0 & \sin(\theta) & \frac{s(1-\cos(\theta))}{\theta} \\ 0 & 1 & 0 & 0 \\ -\sin(\theta) & 0 & \cos(\theta) & \frac{s\sin(\theta)}{\theta} \\ 0 & 0 & 0 & 1 \end{bmatrix} \qquad (6)$$

The actuator possesses a rotational degree of freedom along its central axis, enabling the two-dimensional planar motion of the continuum to extend into three-dimensional space, thereby generating a continuous workspace point set. The coordinate transformation relationship is expressed as follows:

$$T_{\text{base}}^{\text{root}} = \begin{bmatrix} \cos\psi & -\sin\psi & 0 & 0 \\ \sin\psi & \cos\psi & 0 & 0 \\ 0 & 0 & 1 & d \\ 0 & 0 & 0 & 1 \end{bmatrix} \qquad (7)$$

where, ψ represents the angle of the rotational degree of freedom. To facilitate subsequent trajectory control and end-effector pose calculation, we align the origin of this rotational coordinate system with the initial RCM point. This RCM point maintains a fixed linear distance d from the root of the bending section.

The continuum endoscopic actuator is integrated with a 3-DoF RCM mechanism, whose joint coordinate system is located at fixed origin. The mechanism provides three rotational degrees of freedom (pitch, roll, and feed) to position the end-effector at the target location for surgical operations. The transformation matrix between adjacent joints is denoted as T_i^{i-1}, where the pose transformation matrix of the RCM point can be expressed in the following matrix multiplication form:

$$T_i^{i-1} = \text{Rot}_z(\beta_i)\,\text{Transl}(a_i, 0, d_i)\,\text{Rot}_x(\alpha_i) \qquad (8)$$

$$T_3^0 = T_1^0 T_2^1 T_3^2 \qquad (9)$$

The overall end-effector pose is given by:

$$T_{\text{tip}}^0 = T_3^0\, T_{\text{base}}^{\text{root}}\, T_{\text{tip}}^{\text{base}}. \qquad (10)$$

Through the above equations, we establish the forward kinematic model for the combined RCM mechanism and continuum endoscope, enabling multi-pose image acquisition. The velocity equations are expressed as:

$$V_r = J_r \dot{q} \quad (11)$$

$$J_r = J_t J_a \quad (12)$$

where, $V_r \in \mathbb{R}^{6\times 1}$ represents the linear and angular velocity of the continuum endoscope tip in the base coordinate system. The matrix $J_r \in \mathbb{R}^{6\times 5}$ denotes the task-space Jacobian that maps the robot's actuator velocities to end-effector velocities in the Cartesian workspace. This composite Jacobian is decomposed into two sub-Jacobians: $J_t \in \mathbb{R}^{6\times 5}$ means mapping of joint to task space; $J_a \in \mathbb{R}^{5\times 5}$ means mapping of driver to joint space. The vector $q \in \mathbb{R}^{5\times 1}$ represent the 5-DoF driving velocities.

3.2 Working Space Analysis

The workspace of the continuum actuator forms a spatial surface, with bending range $[-2\pi/3, 2\pi/3]$ and spinning range $[0, 2\pi]$, as shown in Fig. 5.

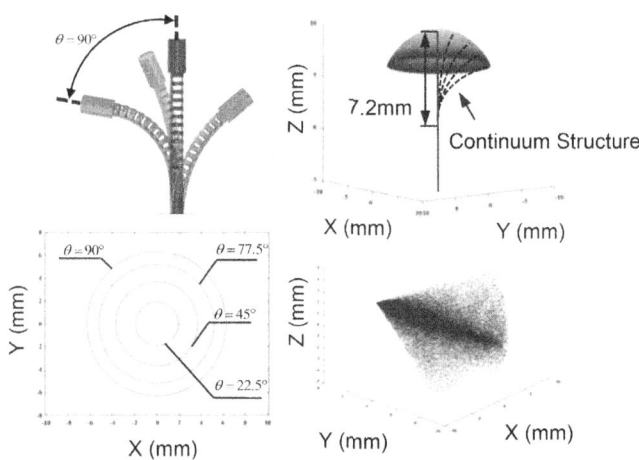

Fig. 4. The workspace simulation of the continuum intraocular endoscope.

4 Visual Servoing Control Based on Endoscopic Images

4.1 Extraction of Feature Points of Surgical Instruments

This study utilizes YOLOv8n (nano variant), which is characterized by its lightweight and efficient design, making it suitable for real-time detection of surgical needle tips in endoscopic procedures. The core architecture of the network comprises a CSPDarknet backbone, a PAN-FPN neck, incorporates a decoupled head design, and further integrates an Anchor-Free mechanism with dynamic label assignment implemented via Task-Aligned Assigner (Fig. 4).

Endoscopic images of needle tips under diverse lighting conditions with random orientations were collected (n=500). Data augmentation techniques (e.g., image rotation) expanded the original 500 images to 2,000 augmented samples. Labeled datasets were generated using LabelMe software and divided into training (70%), testing (15%), and validation (15%) subsets. The YOLOv8n model was trained using the PyTorch deep learning framework, accelerated by the Adam optimization algorithm and NVIDIA CUDA components for enhanced training/inference speed. Training results indicate the model can reliably extract 2D coordinates of needle tips from complex backgrounds.

4.2 Design of Control Strategy for Visual Servoing

In visual servoing control, vision cameras are typically required for image acquisition, from which target features are extracted to execute servo tasks. The endoscope transforms the 3D coordinates of the target point from the world coordinate system to the camera coordinate system and projects them onto the camera's pixel plane, as shown in the figure. Let $P_c = [X, Y, Z]^T$ denote the position of the instrument tip in the camera coordinate system, $P_c^i = [x_c, y_c, f]^T$ represent the projected 2D point on the image plane within the camera coordinate system, and $P_i = [u, v]^T$ denote the feature coordinates on the pixel plane. Based on the pinhole camera principle, the relationships among these three entities are expressed as:

$$\begin{cases} x_c = \dfrac{X}{Z} = \dfrac{u - u_0}{f \rho_w} \\ y_c = \dfrac{Y}{Z} = \dfrac{v - v_0}{f \rho_h} \end{cases} \tag{13}$$

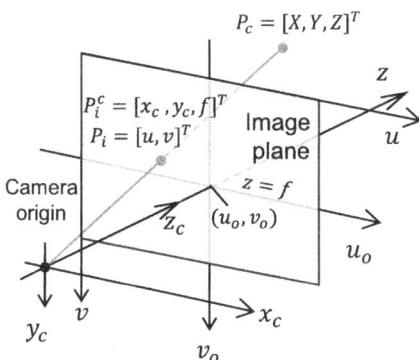

Fig. 5. Camera space coordinate mapping.

Where, ρ_w and ρ_h represent the physica width and height corresponding to each pixel value in the image plane. (u_0, v_0) represents the reference coordinates of the pixel coordinate system, and f is the camera's focal length.

In image-based visual servoing, it is necessary to extract real-time deviations between the pixel space coordinates of feature points and desired features, and control the camera motion at the end effector based on these deviations until the image features reach the target state. The framework of the control process is illustrated in the figure. Here, the time-varying image features are defined as $s(t)$, and the desired image features as $s_d(t)$. The feature error $e(t)$ at different time instances t is formulated as:

$$e(t) = s(t) - s_d(t) \tag{14}$$

When the endoscopic camera possesses a time-varying spatial velocity $V_r(t) = [v(t)^T, \omega(t)^T]^T$, the relationship between the time derivative of the corresponding pixel plane features $s(t)$ and this spatial velocity can be described by the following equation:

$$\dot{s}(t) = L_s V_r(t) \tag{15}$$

where, $L_s \in \mathbb{R}^{2 \times 6}$ represents the image Jacobian matrix, composed of information from a single image feature point and the position information of its corresponding spatial point in the camera coordinate system:

$$L_s = \begin{bmatrix} -\frac{1}{Z} & 0 & \frac{x}{Z} & xy & -(1+x^2) & y \\ 0 & -\frac{1}{Z} & \frac{y}{Z} & 1+y^2 & -xy & -x \end{bmatrix} \tag{16}$$

Based on Eqs. (13)-(15), assuming exponential error convergence, the visual servoing control law can be expressed as:

$$V_r(t) = \hat{L}_s^+ (\dot{s}_d(t) - \lambda e(t)) \tag{17}$$

where $\hat{L}_s^+ \in \mathbb{R}^{6 \times 2}$ represents the pseudo-inverse of the image Jacobian matrix, $\lambda > 0$ is the gain. Due to the inherent error tolerance of visual servoing, the parameter Z in the image Jacobian matrix can be assumed constant due to the inherent error tolerance of visual servoing [15]. Combined with the kinematic model of the robot, the visual servoing controller from actuation space to image space is derived as:

$$\dot{q} = J_{\text{sys}} (\dot{s}_d(t) - \lambda e(t)) \tag{18}$$

$$J_{\text{sys}} = \hat{J}_r^+ \hat{L}_s^+ \tag{19}$$

The above describes the design of an image-based autonomous tracking controller for the continuum endoscope, J_{sys} represents system Jacobian matrix contains the spatial information of the robot and feature points. $\hat{J}_r^+$ represents the pseudo-inverse of the robot Jacobian matrix. Compared to traditional rigid endoscopes, the flexible structure of the continuum enables dexterous maneuverability within the eye, which holds significant implications for control method implementation. The control method based on endoscopic imaging adjusts the camera's spatial velocity according to feature errors to achieve target tracking (Fig. 6).

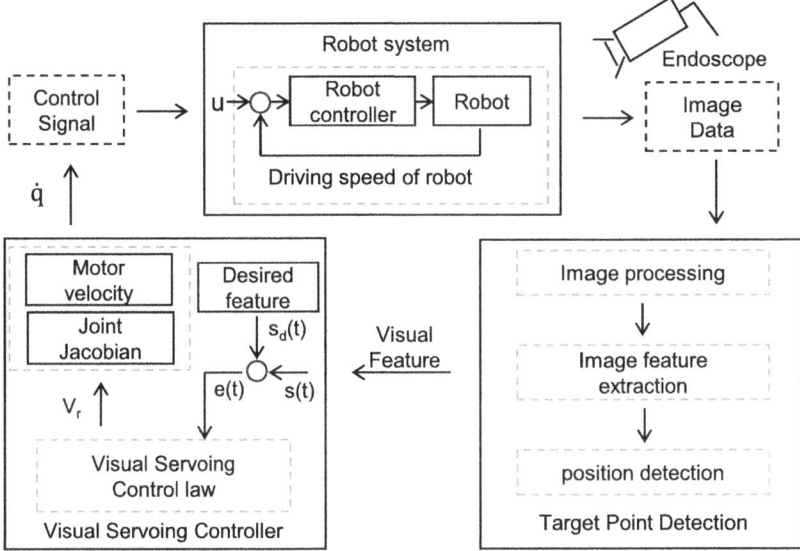

Fig. 6. Geometric principles and control framework of the visual servo system.

5 Experiment

5.1 Experimental Setup

The experimental setup is shown in Fig. 7 (a), mainly including two RCM robotic arms, a microscope, an eye model, syringe models, and an endoscopic actuator. Each ESR robot features six degrees of freedom, including three linear motion stages and pitch, yaw, and surge degrees of freedom around the RCM point, enabling precise and stable operational capabilities.

5.2 Experimental Results and Analysis

This study developed an intraocular continuum endoscope system integrated with an ophthalmic surgical robot. Experimentally, image-guided visual tracking of the endoscope and syringe from a lateral intraocular perspective was first achieved, with a steady-state tracking error of approximately 25 pixels, as shown in Fig. 7 (b) and (c). Figure 7 (d) depicts the motion trajectories of the endoscope and surgical needle tip, verifying their synchronization.

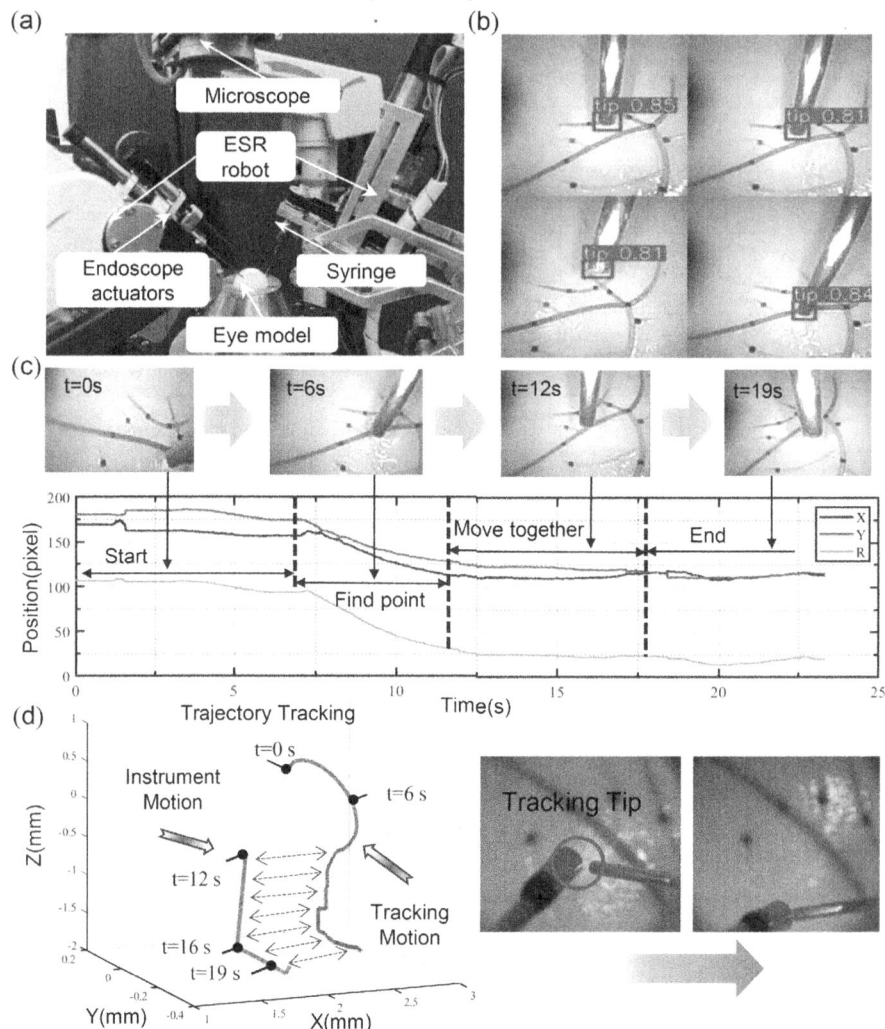

Fig. 7. Intraocular visual tracking experiment of the continuum endoscope: (a) Surgical setup; (b) Instrument tip localization using a neural network; (c) Endoscopic images and corresponding relative positions during the tracking experiment; (d) Spatial positions of the tracked instrument and the endoscope tip within the intraocular space.

6 Conclusion

Continuum endoscopes have significant potential in retinal surgery. The flexible continuum endoscope proposed here maintains minimal dimensions while providing highly adaptable distal movements, addressing the blind spots common in rigid endoscopes. Future integration with deep learning frameworks promises to enhance precision and stability, driving advancements in medical robotics.

Acknowledgments. This work was supported in part by the National Key R&D Program of China (No.2023YFB4705801), the Heilongjiang Outstanding Youth Science Fund (No.JQ2024E004), the Key R&D Program of Heilongjiang Province (No.2024ZXDXC24), the National Natural Science Foundation of China (Nos. 52175008 and 92048301) and Wu Jieping Medical Foundation Project (320.6750. 2024-18-3).

References

1. Riviere, C.N., Rader, R.S., Khosla, P.K.: Characteristics of hand motion of eye surgeons. In: Proc. 19th Annu. Int. Conf. IEEE Eng. Med. Biol. Soc., Magnificent Milestones Emerg. Opportunities Med. Eng., vol. 4, pp. 1690–1693 (1997)
2. Jason, T.W., Matthew, J.G., Tsu-Chin, T.: Intraocular robotic interventionalsurgical system (IRISS): mechanical design, evaluation, and master–slave manipulation. Int. J. Med. Robot. Comp. Assisted Surg. **14**, 1–12 (2017)
3. Edwards, T.L., Xue, K., Meenink, H.C.M., et al.: First-inhuman study of thesafety and viability of intraocular robotic surgery. Nat Biomed Eng. **2**(9), 649–656 (2018)
4. Taylor, R., Jensen, P., Whitcomb, L., et al.: A steady-hand robotic systemfor microsurgical augmentation. Int. J. Robot. Res. **18**, 1201–1210 (1999)
5. Andy, G., Jonas, S., Laurent, S., et al.: In-human robot-assisted retinalvein cannulation. A world first. Ann Biomed Eng. **46**, 1676–1685 (2018)
6. Read, S.P., Fortun, J.A.: Visualization of the retina and vitreous during vitreoretinal surgery: New technologies. Curr. Opin. Ophthalmol. **28**(238), 241 (2017)
7. Schimdt, J.C., Chofflet, J., Horle, S., Mennel, S., Meyer, C.H.: Three simple approaches to visualize the transparent vitreous cortex during vitreoretinal surgery. Dev. Ophthalmol. **42**(35), 42 (2008)
8. Wang, N., Zhang, X., Stoyanov, D., Zhang, H., Stilli, A.: Visionand-force-based compliance control for a posterior segment ophthalmic surgical robot. IEEE Robot. Autom. Lett. **8**(11), 6875–6882 (2023)
9. Oscar, M.C.Z., Christian, V., Brenton, K., et al.: Review of intraoperativeoptical coherencetomography: technology and applications. BiomedOptic Express. **8**, 1607–1637 (2017)
10. Mukherjee, S., Kaess, M., Martel, J.N., Riviere, C.N.: EyeSAM: graph-based localization and mapping of retinal vasculature during intraocular microsurgery. Int. J. Comput. Assist. Radiol. Surg. **14**(5), 819–828 (2019). https://doi.org/10.1007/s11548-019-01925-1
11. Yu, H., Shen, J.H., Joos, K.M., et al.: Design, calibration and preliminary testing of a robotic telemanipulator for OCT guided retinal surgery. In: Proc. IEEE Int. Conf. Robot Autom., pp. 225–231 (2013)
12. Yang, S., Balicki, M., Wells, T.S., et al.: Improvement of optical coherence tomography using active handheld micromanipulator in vitreoretinal surgery. Conf Proc IEEE Eng Med Biol. Soc., 5674–5677 (2013)
13. Silver, D., Csutak, A.: Human eye dimensions for pressure-volume relations. Investigative Ophthalmol. Vis. Sci. **51**(13), 5019 (2010)

14. Tadano, K., Kawashima, K.: A pneumatic laparoscope holder controlledby head movement. Int. J. Med. Robot. Comput. Assist. Surg. **11**, 331–340 (2015)
15. Li, W., Song, C., Li, Z.: An accelerated recurrent neural network for visual servo control of a robotic flexible endoscope with joint limit constraint. IEEE Trans. Industr. Electron. **67**(12), 10787–10797 (2020). https://doi.org/10.1109/TIE.2019.2959481

Air-Ground-Wall Robot with Multimodal Morphological Adaptation

Juanxia Zhou[1], Jiajun Xu[1,2(✉)], Mengcheng Zhao[1], Peixin Wang[1], and Youfu Li[3]

[1] Nanjing University of Aeronautics and Astronautics, Nanjing City, Jiangsu Province, China
xujiajun@nuaa.edu.cn
[2] Shanghai Key Laboratory of Wearable Robotics and Human-Machine Interaction, Shanghai City, China
[3] City University of Hong Kong, Hong Kong, China

Abstract. To address the limitations of mobile robots in obstacle avoidance and the challenges faced by unmanned aerial vehicles in harsh weather and confined environments, this paper proposes a novel multi-modal aircraft based on morphological adaptation. The robot adopts a wheel-propeller coaxial drive architecture and a multi-degree-of-freedom hip joint system, enabling efficient switching among three motion modes: low-altitude flight, wall climbing, and ground driving mode. This design resolves the issues of component redundancy and excessive weight in traditional designs. To ensure that the robot maintains stability without slipping or tipping over during slope navigation, this study conducts static equilibrium analysis. The control system employs an STM32 development board as the core processor, integrating inertial measurement units (IMUs) and wireless communication modules, while utilizing visual sensors for environmental perception. Dynamic simulation results demonstrate that the robot can overcome obstacles twice its wheel diameter and maintain stable climbing capability. This innovation enhances versatility for applications in rescue, inspection, and exploration tasks.

Keywords: Multimodal Robot · Morphological Adaptation · Low-altitude Flight · Wall Climbing · Ground Driving

1 Introduction

In recent years, ground mobile robots have been widely used in unstructured environments for disaster rescue, field operations, and reconnaissance missions due to their compact size and high flexibility. Examples include MIT Cheetah 3 [1], ETH Ascento [2], SUSTech NeZha [3], and Tencent Robotics X's robot Ollie [4]. These robots have made significant advancements in structural innovation and control algorithms. However, one of their key limitations is that their obstacle-crossing capability largely depends on the size of their wheels or legs.

On the other hand, unmanned aerial vehicles (UAVs), unrestricted by terrain, have demonstrated great potential in logistics, infrastructure inspection, and other fields [5–8].

However, traditional UAVs are susceptible to adverse weather conditions and struggle to operate effectively in confined spaces such as indoor areas or pipelines, limiting their adaptability in complex environments. To enhance their mobility in indoor and narrow spaces, multimodal robots have been extensively developed.

Multimodal robots integrate wheeled structures to combine flight and driving locomotion. Many researchers have adopted a redundancy design to achieve multi-mode movement. This approach, while relatively simple in design, involves stacking driving locomotion components onto an existing aerial platform [9–12]. For instance, flapping-wing robots achieve ground crawling using legs or feet [13, 14]. RoboFly, for example, walks on the ground by flapping its wings and utilizing passive legs [15]. Another flapping-wing robot employs a six-legged crawling mechanism driven by two geared motors [16]. However, flapping-wing mechanisms suffer from high energy loss and low stability. Some researchers have installed passive wheels beneath rotorcraft [17], but their mobility is limited to flat surfaces. To extend their movement capabilities, active wheels have been introduced. For example, wheels are mounted beneath quadcopters to enable ground locomotion [9]. LEONARDO bridges the gap between flying and walking through synchronized control of distributed electric thrusters and a multi-joint wheel-leg hybrid structure [10]. The aerial-ground robot Flybot combines a dual-rotor UAV with a self-balancing wheel-legged base [18]. However, in redundancy-based designs, components cannot be shared across modes, and non-reconfigurable structures result in idle parts during single-mode operation, leading to excessive weight and bulkiness.

Compared to redundancy designs, reconfigurable designs offer higher lightweight efficiency and more compact structures, enabling dynamic mode switching through morphological adaptation. For instance, Flying STAR adopts a split-drive layout and adjusts the angle of its extension mechanism to switch between locomotion modes [19]. However, its misaligned arrangement of locomotion components reduces overall spatial efficiency[20].

In summary, this paper presents a novel multimodal robot based on morphological adaptation, capable of efficient switching among three locomotion modes: low-altitude flight, wall climbing, and ground driving mode. The robot features a compact structure, allowing it to navigate through tight spaces and overcome large obstacles. In addition, to ensure climbing stability, static equilibrium was analyzed. The STM32-based control system integrates IMU, wireless communication, and vision sensors for environmental awareness. This study validates the robot's mode-switching performance and feasibility in various scenarios through dynamic simulations.

2 Robot Design

The primary design objective of the multimodal robot is to achieve three locomotion modes—low-altitude flight, wall climbing, and ground driving—along with high-performance mode switching. The robot features a coaxial wheel-propeller configuration for driving, flight, and wall climbing. Its total length is 55 cm, height 28 cm, and width varies between 44 cm and 60 cm depending on the extension angle. The total weight is 5.7 kg, powered by a 10,000 mAh 25C 22.2V 6S1P lithium polymer battery.

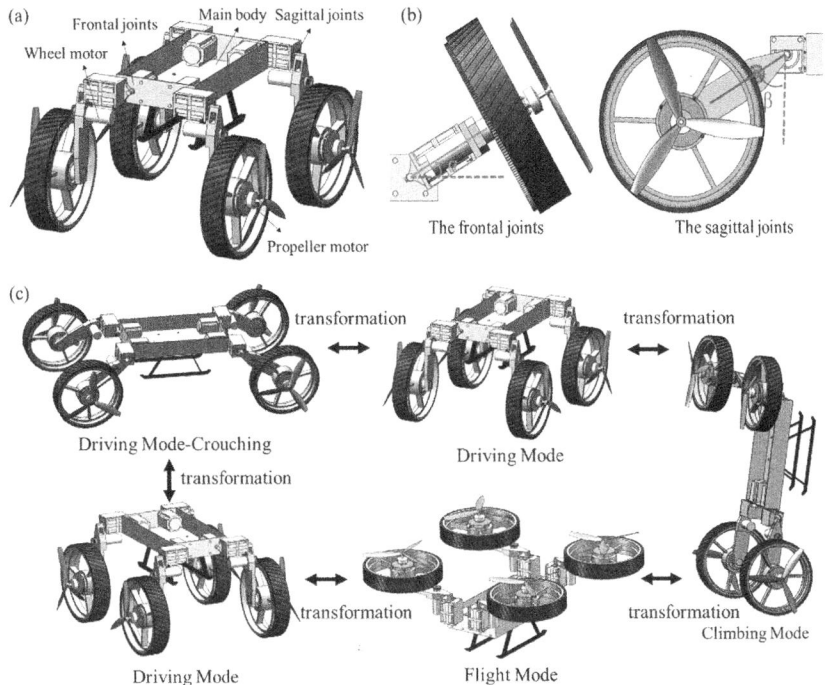

Fig. 1. Robot design (a) Robotic structural design;(b) Definition of hip joint rotation angles;(c) Multimodal transition.

2.1 Robot Structural Design

As shown in Fig. 1(a), the robot's main body is a hollow structure housing the controller, onboard battery, and servo motors driving the wheel-leg mechanisms. Four wheel-leg assemblies are mounted externally, each equipped with two actuated hip joints, a wheel mechanism, and a flight mechanism.

The two actuated hip joints independently control motion in the frontal and sagittal planes. The frontal joints enable lateral leg movement, while the sagittal joints govern forward-backward leg swing (as presented in Fig. 1(b)), collectively facilitating multimodal transitions. The wheel mechanism consists of a brushless motor driving a rim gear set with a 9.7:1 gear ratio, amplifying torque for enhanced load capacity in ground mode. The 20 cm diameter wheels use silicone rubber tires for durability and strong traction on slopes. The flight mechanism generates thrust via ducted propellers coaxially aligned with the wheel axles. Each propeller is powered by a 2814 KV1100 brushless motor paired with an $8 \times 4.5 \times 3$ propeller. At 50% throttle, the four motors collectively produce 5.85 kg of thrust, sufficient for stable low-altitude flight.

2.2 Robot Structural Design

The multimodal robot achieves locomotion mode transitions through its articulated body design and multi-degree-of-freedom drive system, as seen in Fig. 1(c). In ground driving mode, the frontal joints remain adducted, keeping the wheels aligned in a four-wheel configuration for wheeled locomotion. When encountering height-restricted obstacles, the sagittal joints swing the legs longitudinally, enabling the robot to crouch and reduce its profile for passing through confined spaces. During low-altitude flight mode, the frontal joints fully abduct the legs laterally to maximize the center-to-center distance between the four propellers, ensuring stable lift generation. The seamless switching among these three modes constitutes the core capability enabling the robot's multifunctional mobility.

For driving-to-flight transition, the frontal joints abduct 90 degrees to reconfigure into flight mode. Conversely, flight-to-driving transition is achieved by adducting the frontal joints 90 degrees. The wall climbing mode effectively combines flight and driving modes. The rear wheels remain in ground configuration while the front wheels switch to flight mode. The wheel motors and propeller motors work cooperatively. The propeller motors stabilize the robot's upper body tilt angle while the wheel motors control the forward climbing speed on slopes.

3 Static Analysis

A static analysis is performed to evaluate the robot's static stability under slope conditions. The robot's ability to climb steadily is the result of the combined action of the propeller thrust F_p, gravity G, and the friction force f generated by the traction of the wheels.

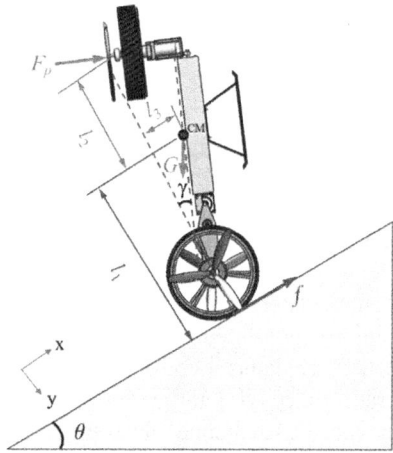

Fig. 2. Force analysis in wall climbing.

Assuming the robot is traveling on a slope with an inclination angle θ, the angle between the robot's body and the normal direction of the slope is γ (presented in Fig. 2). Under steady-state climbing conditions, the resultant force F_x along the X-direction can be calculated as:

$$F_x = f + F_p \sin\left(\frac{\pi}{2} - \gamma\right) - G\sin\theta \qquad (1)$$

Substituting $f = \mu G\cos\theta + \mu F_p\cos\left(\frac{\pi}{2} - \gamma\right)$ into the Eq. (1) yields the equilibrium condition:

$$\mu G\cos\theta + \mu F_p\cos\left(\frac{\pi}{2} - \gamma\right) + F_p\sin\left(\frac{\pi}{2} - \gamma\right) - G\sin\theta = 0 \qquad (2)$$

where μ is the coefficient of friction.

To ensure the robot does not overturn, taking the center of mass (CM) as the reference point, the moment equilibrium condition must be satisfied:

$$fl_1 + F_p l_3 \cos\left(\frac{\pi}{2} - \gamma\right) = F_p l_2 \sin\left(\frac{\pi}{2} - \gamma\right) \qquad (3)$$

where l_1 denotes the y-axis distance from f to the centroid, l_2 is the y-axis distance from F_p to the centroid, and l_3 indicates the x-axis distance from F_p to the centroid.

The robot will maintain stable climbing without slipping backward or tipping over when both conditions are met: $F_x \geq 0$ and Eq. (3) hold true. This analysis provides a theoretical foundation for ensuring the robot's stability on inclined surfaces.

4 Control Strategy

The robot operates in two independent locomotion modes, low-altitude flight and ground driving, with wall climbing mode combining both functionalities. Figure 3 illustrates the motor status during different modes and transitional phases.

In flight mode, the STM32-based control system processes real-time IMU data and wireless commands to generate PWM signals for ESCs, precisely regulating brushless motor speeds for stable aerial control. During driving mode, brushless motors employ PID control to maintain target wheel speeds with current limiting for overload protection. For wall climbing, selective propeller activation provides auxiliary thrust to enhance wheel traction.

Equipped with stereo vision cameras for environmental perception, the robot defaults to driving mode. When detecting height-restricted obstacles, the controller activates sagittal joint motors to 90°, enabling crouched navigation. Large obstacles trigger wheel motor deactivation and 90° frontal joint rotation for flight mode transition, allowing aerial obstacle clearance. Slope detection initiates coordinated hip joint adjustment, with hybrid wheel and propeller propulsion enabling slope traversal.

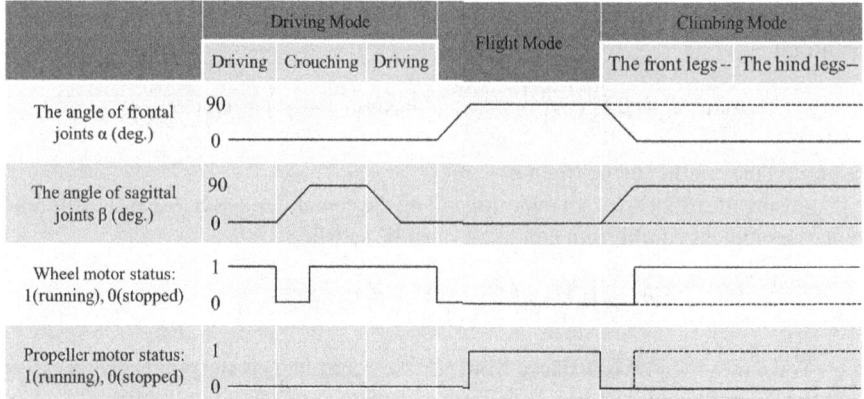

Fig. 3. Motor status during mode transition.

5 Simulation Analysis

The 3D model designed in SolidWorks was imported into ADAMS software for dynamic simulation. Constraints were defined to establish kinematic relationships between components, with material densities assigned according to actual specifications. Kinematic pairs were applied at joints, with motion control implemented through drive functions.

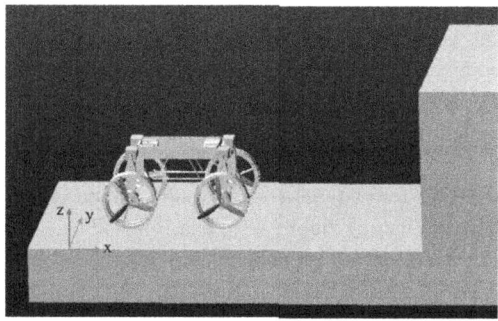

Fig. 4. Diagram of simulation model.

The simulation model and initial posture of the multimodal robot are shown in Fig. 4. The purpose of the simulation is to verify the effectiveness and feasibility of the designed robot's mode switching capability. In the diagram, the robot's motion space is divided into three axes. The X-axis represents the longitudinal direction, with its positive orientation aligned with the robot's forward movement direction. The Y-axis indicates the lateral direction, perpendicular to the direction of movement, with its positive orientation to the left side of the robot's forward direction. And the Z-axis is perpendicular to the plane of motion, with its negative orientation corresponding to the direction of gravity. This coordinate system definition enables precise analysis of the robot's motion characteristics and stability during mode transitions in three-dimensional space. The X-Y plane forms the primary movement surface, while the Z-axis accounts for vertical displacements during flight or wall climbing operations.

In ground driving mode, the robot operates on flat terrain and automatically crouches to navigate through confined spaces when encountered. The simulation animation (shown in Fig. 5) demonstrates this capability, while the smooth displacement of the center of mass along the Z-axis (presented in Fig. 6) confirms the stability and feasibility of the ground locomotion mode.

Fig. 5. Simulation diagram of the robot during crouching maneuver in driving mode.

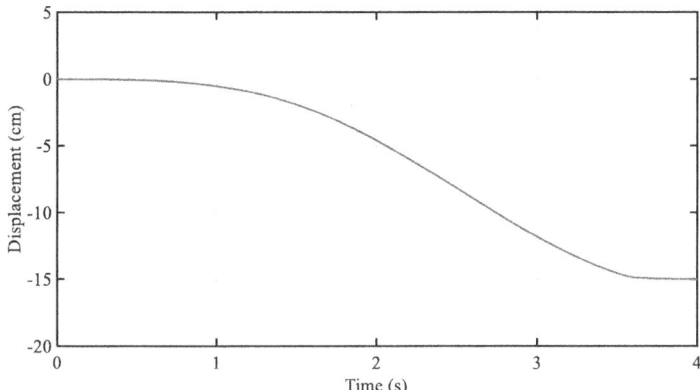

Fig. 6. Z-axis centroid displacement variation of the robot during crouching maneuver in driving mode.

When encountering large obstacles, the robot switches to low-altitude flight mode. As demonstrated in the simulation animation (Fig. 7), results confirm that the designed multimodal robot successfully achieves driving-to-flight transition and can overcome obstacles more than twice its height. During the simulation process (Fig. 8), the robot maintains constant velocity along the X-axis, executes mode transition between 4-6s, and clears the obstacle during 7-8s. The smooth centroid displacement throughout the movement indicates stable operation.

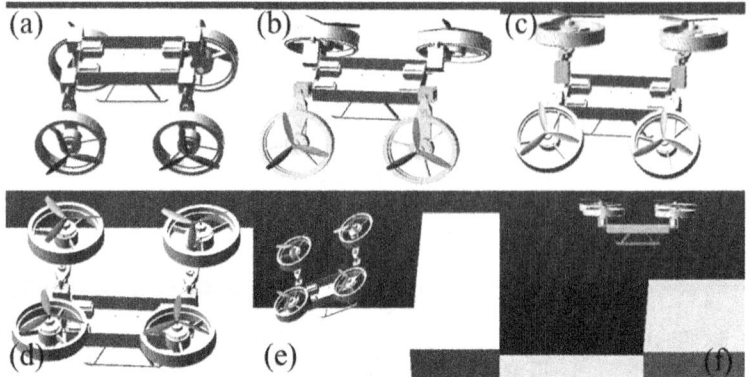

Fig. 7. Simulation diagram of driving-to-flight mode transition and large obstacle crossing for the robot.

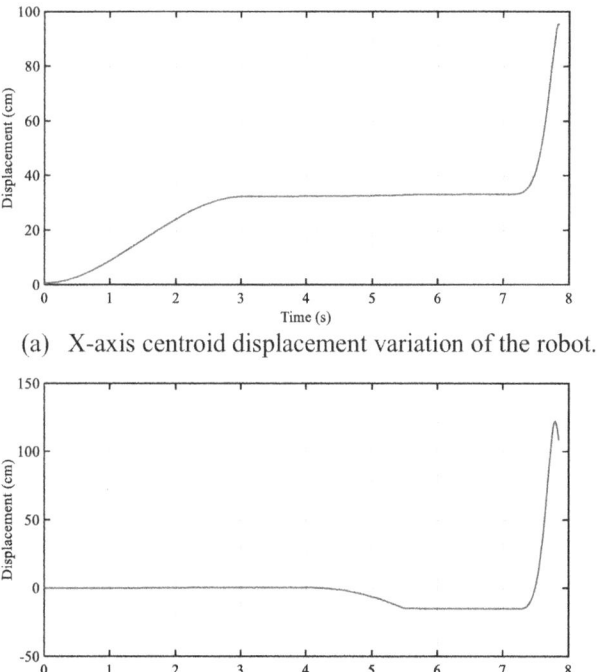

(a) X-axis centroid displacement variation of the robot.

(b) Z-axis centroid displacement variation of the robot.

Fig. 8. Displacement profile of the robot during large obstacle traversal.

Upon approaching slopes, the robot transitions to wall climbing mode. The simulation animation (Fig. 9) verifies successful driving-to-climbing mode switching and demonstrates the robot's capability to traverse 30-degree inclines. As shown in Fig. 10, the robot's centroid experiences controlled variations in both X and Z directions during mode transition, followed by stable climbing between 2.5–5.5s. The gradual centroid displacement curves confirm maintained stability throughout the slope navigation.

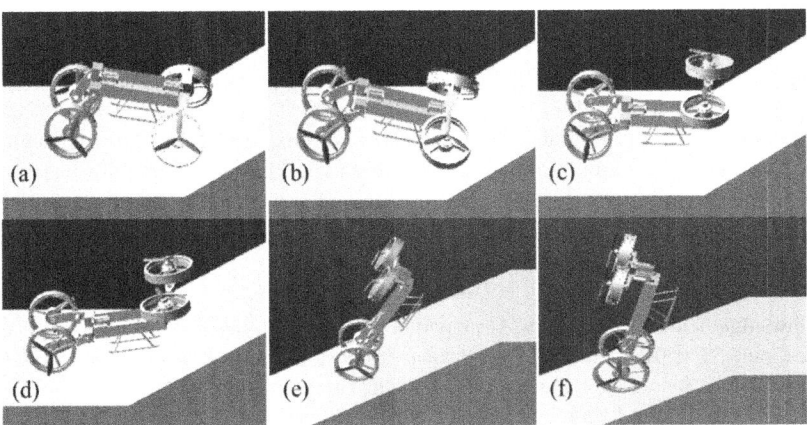

Fig. 9. Simulation diagram of driving-to-climbing mode transition and slope climbing for the robot.

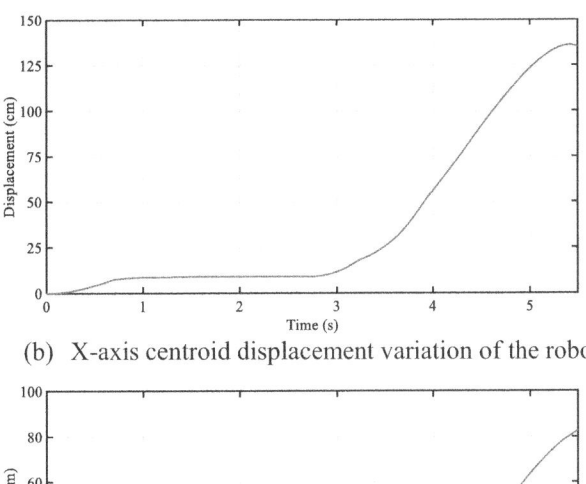

(b) X-axis centroid displacement variation of the robot.

(b) Z-axis centroid displacement variation of the robot.

Fig. 10. Displacement profile of the robot during the slope climbing.

6 Conclusion

This paper presents a structurally reconfigurable multimodal robot capable of efficiently switching between three motion modes: low-altitude flight, wall climbing, and ground driving. The robot adopts an innovative coaxial wheel-leg design and a multi-degree-of-freedom drive system, addressing the issues of component redundancy and excessive weight in traditional designs while ensuring compact structure and agile mobility. Static analysis ensures climbing-mode stability against slip or downfall. The STM32-based control system integrates IMU, wireless comms, and vision for environmental perception. Dynamic simulations demonstrate its stability and adaptability across different modes, particularly excelling in narrow spaces, overcoming large obstacles, and climbing slopes. The proposed design offers a novel solution for multimodal robotic applications in complex environments.

Acknowledgement. This work was supported by National Science Foundation of China under Grant 52205018 and 62173286, China Postdoctoral Science Foundation under Grant 2024M754124, State Key Laboratory of Robotics under Grant 2023-O16, Open Research Fund of The State Key Laboratory of Multimodal Artificial Intelligence Systems under Grant MAIS2025023, Shanghai Key Laboratory of Wearable Robotics and Human-Machine Interaction, Engineering Research Center of Dredging Technology, Ministry of Education, Hohai University under Grant 2025221003, and Jiangsu Provincial Science and Technology Think Tank Program Project under Grant JSKX0125055.

References

1. Bledt, G., et al.: Mit cheetah 3: Design and control of a robust, dynamic quadruped robot. In: 2018 IEEE/RSJ International Conference on Intelligent Robots and Systems (IROS). IEEE (2018)
2. Klemm, V., et al.: Ascento: a two-wheeled jumping robot. In: 2019 International conference on robotics and automation (ICRA). IEEE (2019)
3. Chen, H., et al.: Underactuated motion planning and control for jum** with wheeled-bipedal robots. IEEE Robot. Autom. Lett. **6.2** 747–754 (2020)
4. Wang, S., et al.: Balance control of a novel wheel-legged robot: Design and experiments. In: 2021 IEEE International Conference on Robotics and Automation (ICRA). IEEE (2021)
5. Alyassi, R., et al.: Autonomous recharging and flight mission planning for battery-operated autonomous drones. IEEE Trans. Autom. Sci. Eng. **20.2** 1034–1046 (2022)
6. Foudeh, H.A., Luk, P.-K., Whidborne, J.F.: An advanced unmanned aerial vehicle (UAV) approach via learning-based control for overhead power line monitoring: a comprehensive review. IEEE Access **9**, 130410–130433 (2021)
7. Saldana, D., Gupta, P.M., Kumar, V.: Design and control of aerial modules for inflight self-disassembly. IEEE Robot. Autom. Lett. **4**(4), 3410–3417 (2019)
8. Brescianini, D., D'Andrea, R.: Tilt-prioritized quadrocopter attitude control. IEEE Trans. Control Syst. Technol. **28**(2), 376–387 (2018)
9. Araki, B., et al.: Multi-robot path planning for a swarm of robots that can both fly and drive. In: 2017 IEEE International Conference on Robotics and Automation (ICRA). IEEE (2017)
10. Kim, K., et al.: A bipedal walking robot that can fly, slackline, and skateboard. In: Science Robotics 6.59, eabf8136 (2021)

11. Tagliabue, A., et al.: Shapeshifter: a multi-agent, multi-modal robotic platform for exploration of titan. In: 2020 IEEE Aerospace Conference. IEEE (2020)
12. Suh, H.J., Terry, et al.: Energy-efficient motion planning for multi-modal hybrid locomotion. In: 2020 IEEE/RSJ International Conference on Intelligent Robots and Systems (IROS). IEEE (2020)
13. Tu, Z., et al.: Crawl and fly: A bio-inspired robot utilizing unified actuation for hybrid aerial-terrestrial locomotion. IEEE Robot. Autom. Lett. 6.4 7549–7556 (2021)
14. Jayaram, K., et al.: Scaling down an insect-size microrobot, HAMR-VI into HAMR-Jr. In: 2020 IEEE International Conference on Robotics and Automation (ICRA). IEEE (2020)
15. Chukewad, Yogesh M., et al.: RoboFly: An insect-sized robot with simplified fabrication that is capable of flight, ground, and water surface locomotion. IEEE Trans. Robot. 37.6, 2025–2040 (2021)
16. Wu, C., et al.: A multi-modal tailless flap**-wing robot capable of flying, crawling, self-righting and horizontal take-off. IEEE Robot. Autom. Lett. (2024)
17. Qin, Y., et al.: Hybrid aerial-ground locomotion with a single passive wheel. In: 2020 IEEE/RSJ International Conference on Intelligent Robots and Systems (IROS). IEEE (2020)
18. Xu, H., et al.: Flybot: a dual active wheel hybrid land-air robot with five-link leg joints. IEEE Robot. Autom. Lett. (2024)
19. Meiri, N., David, Z.: Flying star, a hybrid crawling and flying sprawl tuned robot. In: 2019 International Conference on Robotics and Automation (ICRA). IEEE (2019)
20. Sun, Y., et al.: Design and theoretical research on aerial-aquatic vehicles: A review. J. Bionic Eng. 20.6 2512–2541 (2013)

Design and Human-Robot Collaborative Control of Reconfigurable Supernumerary Robotic Limb for Overhead Work

Peixin Wang[1], Jiajun Xu[1,2(✉)], Mengcheng Zhao[1], Juanxia Zhou[1], Xingyu Liu[1], and Youfu Li[3]

[1] Nanjing University of Aeronautics and Astronautics, Nanjing City, Jiangsu Province, China
xujiajun@nuaa.edu.cn
[2] Shanghai Key Laboratory of Wearable Robotics and Human-Machine Interaction, Shanghai City, China
[3] City University of Hong Kong, Hong Kong, China

Abstract. This study presents design and human-robot collaboration framework for a reconfigurable supernumerary robotic limb (SRL) system, focusing on obstacle-avoidance trajectory planning and adaptive control strategies. The SRL features a modular, lightweight rigid structure with five rotational and one translational degree of freedom, and it is mounted on the operator's waist to enhance stability. To address interference risks during overhead work, we propose an RRT*-based trajectory planning algorithm combined with cubic B-spline smoothing, which optimizes path length and minimizes vibrations while ensuring collision-free motion. For human-robot coordination, a multi-modal control framework integrates inertial measurement units (IMUs), electromyography (EMG), and motion cameras to detect user intent with a finite state machine (FSM) model. The system employs reinforcement learning-tuned variable impedance control, adapting stiffness and damping parameters in real-time to improve precision and safety. Simulations demonstrate the SRL's ability to navigate static obstacles, achieving smooth trajectories via B-spline interpolation.

Keywords: Supernumerary Robotic Limbs · Obstacle Avoidance · RRT* Algorithm · Human-Robot Collaboration

1 Introduction

With the rapid development of robotic technology, supernumerary robotic limbs (SRLs) have gained significant attention as an important research direction for extending human capabilities. SRLs represent a novel type of wearable robotic system designed to provide users with additional limb functionality [1]. Unlike traditional exoskeletons, SRLs do not directly enhance or replace existing human limb functions, but rather serve as "third arms" or "third legs" to expand users' operational capabilities and range of motion [2].

Recent years have witnessed remarkable progress in SRL research. In 2012, MIT's Asada team pioneered systematic research by developing a rigid robotic arm-type SRL capable of assisting with object positioning and heavy load handling [3–5]. Subsequently, Federico Parietti et al. created a waist-mounted SRL designed to alleviate human fatigue posture [8]. Research institutions in Italy, China and other countries have also conducted preliminary studies on SRL mechanism design, collaborative control and practical applications [6, 7]. Notable developments include Seoul National University's Seo team [9] creating a ceiling installation-specific SRL with motion recognition through inertial measurement units, and Canada's Veronneau team [10] developing a high-load 3-DOF SRL system using hydraulic actuation. These studies have made significant breakthroughs in mechanism design and control strategies, laying the foundation for SRL practical implementation.

In industrial manufacturing, SRLs can assist workers with overhead operations and heavy load handling. In medical rehabilitation, they provide daily living assistance for patients with upper limb dysfunction. In specialized environments such as astronaut extravehicular activities and nuclear power plant maintenance, SRLs demonstrate unique advantages [11]. However, current SRLs still face numerous challenges in human-robot interaction safety, motion compliance, and environmental adaptability.

Current SRL research primarily focuses on two directions: structural design and control strategies. In structural design, Zhang et al. [12] proposed a soft SRL using fiber-reinforced actuators, achieving lightweight and high compliance, while Zhao et al. [13] developed a pneumatic-tendon hybrid actuation system combining rigid and flexible advantages. For control strategies, Xu et al. [14, 15] integrated Dynamic Movement Primitives (DMP) with mirror therapy for rehabilitation training motion generation, and Huang et al. [16] employed variable impedance reinforcement learning to enhance interaction adaptability and safety.

In summary, to improve operational efficiency and ensure coordinated control, this study focuses on SRL obstacle avoidance trajectory planning, employing the RRT* algorithm for trajectory planning and cubic B-spline curves for trajectory smoothing, aiming to achieve precise obstacle avoidance movements and enhance human-robot coordination performance in reconfigurable SRL systems.

2 Design of Supernumerary Robotic Limb

When operators perform overhead tasks in confined spaces, SRL can assist in holding tools, supporting objects or the human body, reducing discomfort during operation and improving work efficiency. The SRL adopts a modular design, with detachable joint arms to simplify structural complexity and reduce weight while enhancing the load-bearing capacity of the robotic arm. By installing multiple joint arms, the workspace can be expanded, increasing the degrees of freedom and enabling broader applications.

To meet the needs of operators in overhead, this paper designs a rigid SRL with modular installation, portability, and high load-bearing capacity, as shown in Fig. 1. Based on the height standards of average adults, the SRL is designed with five rotational degrees of freedom and one translational degree of freedom. To reduce weight, the two joint arms feature a hollow design, and the electric linear actuator of the end translational joint is fixed with carbon fiber plates on both sides. The SRL mainly consists of a backplate, base, joint arms, translational joint, and end effector. The backplate, joint arms, and base are made of lightweight aluminum alloy, allowing the weight of a single robotic arm to be kept under 9 kg-an acceptable load for operators during support tasks. The SRL has a total length of 1015–1215 mm. The joint motors employ Danaher Motion's PDA-054 model, providing a rated torque of 54 N·m. The SRL is mounted on the operator's waist via a backplate, concentrating the center of gravity near the waist to enhance human-robot coupling stability, as illustrated in Fig. 2.

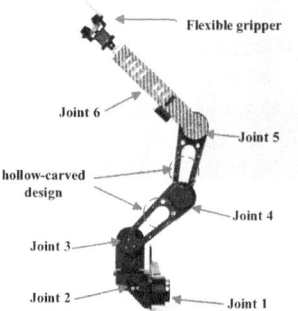

Fig. 1. SRL Structural Design

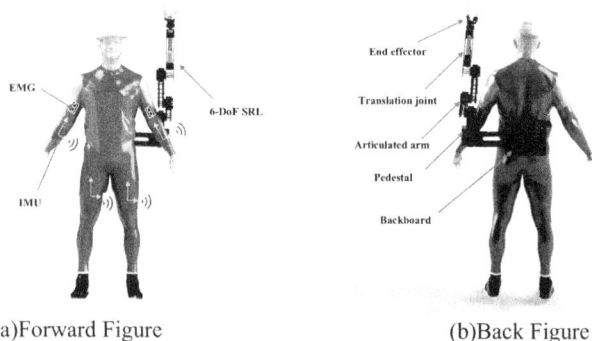

(a)Forward Figure   (b)Back Figure

Fig. 2. Schematic Diagram of Human-Robot Assembly.(a) Forward Figure.(b)Back Figure

3 Research on Obstacle Avoidance Trajectory Planning and Path Smoothing

The SRL are prone to interference with the human body or external environmental obstacles during task execution, which can impact both the operator and the robot itself. Therefore, to improve operational efficiency and ensure coordinated control between the SRL and the operator, this section employs an RRT*-based obstacle avoidance trajectory planning algorithm to explore optimal paths in both time and space. Subsequently, cubic B-spline curves are used to smooth the trajectory, aiming to reduce vibrations and disturbances during the robot's motion and to improve the accuracy of end-effector trajectory tracking.

The RRT* algorithm utilizes the initial position and target position, along with obstacle and robot parameters. It begins by creating a search space X based on obstacles and the search range, then constructs a tree denoted as T. The starting point P_{init} is inserted into the tree as the root node, followed by iterative random sampling of candidate points, as expressed in the following equation:

$$q_{\text{rand}} \sim \text{Uniform}(\mathcal{C}) \tag{1}$$

After selecting the initial sampling point, the process begins from the third line. Then, within a certain range around it, a new sampling point P_n is randomly generated. If the path between P_n and its nearest neighbor point $P_{nearest}$ intersects with an obstacle, a new sampling node will be generated again. Under the condition of step length δ, the expansion is performed in the direction toward the random point, as shown in the following equation.

$$q_{\text{new}} = q_{\text{nearest}} + \delta \cdot \frac{q_{\text{rand}} - q_{\text{nearest}}}{\|q_{\text{rand}} - q_{\text{nearest}}\|} \tag{2}$$

Continue until point P_n is located within an obstacle-free region and within the sampling area. Then, determine the node P_{new} in the tree that is closest in distance to P_1. According to the principle of the shortest path, set the parent node of the nearest point P_1 to be P_{new}, thereby completing a local optimization process by selecting the parent node with the minimum cost. This process is marked as a valid sampling instance (lines 8–10). The procedure is shown in the following equation.

$$q_{\text{min}} = \arg \min_{q_1 \in Q_{near}} \mathcal{J}(q_i) + \mathcal{C}(q_i, q_{\text{new}}) \tag{3}$$

where $\mathcal{J}$ denotes the trajectory cost function, $\mathcal{C}$ represents the collision-free configuration space.

After continuous iterations, if point P_{goal} is reached, the algorithm returns the path P that connects the start and goal points with the corresponding configuration ψ, thereby completing the tree expansion process and achieving obstacle avoidance.

Algorithm 1: RRT*-based Safety-Constrained Algorithm.

Input: Initial point P_{init} ; target point P_{goal} ; obstacles O; maximum iterations number m

Output: A sequence of reachable points as path P and desired corresponding configurations ψ

1: Build tree T and search space X;
2: Add initial point P_{init} to T;
3: **while** number of iterations is less than m **do**
4:     Generate a new point P_{new} in X;
5:     **if** P_{new} is valid and obstacle-free then
6:        Find the nearest point n to P_{new} in T;
7:        **if** steer(n, P_{new}) is valid and obstacle-free during the steer process **then**
8:           Calculate a configuration for P_{new} using optimization method;
9:           Add P_{new} into T and rewire;
10:         Record as one valid iteration;
11:        **else**
12:           Generate another point P'_{new} and repeat the above process;
13:        **end if**
14:     **else**
15:        Generate another point P'_{new} and repeat the above process;
16:     **end if**
17: **end while**
18: Check to see if P_{goal} is in the tree;
19: Generate path P and configurations ψ ;
20: **return** P and ψ ;

In the MATLAB algorithm, a threespline function is created to perform spline curve processing. This function takes as input the path points generated by the RRT* algorithm, the obstacle radius, the obstacle center coordinates, as well as the start and goal points. The start and goal points are marked using a filled green dot and a filled black dot, respectively. The first step is to calculate the knot vector and assign the coordinates of each node to the vectors x, y, and z. Using the normalized accumulated chord length method, the n nodes are parameterized. The total chord length is calculated as the sum of distances between each pair of adjacent nodes. The first $k + 1$ knots are set to 0, and the last $k + 1$ knots are set to 1.

In the second step, the control points are computed in reverse using the boundary tangents. The first and last control points are made to coincide with the first and last given data points. Given the tangents at the start and end data points, the node increments are calculated.

Then, a system of linear equations is solved to obtain the control point vector, expressed as A·D = E, where A is the coefficient matrix with elements representing the values of B-spline basis functions, D is the column vector of control points, and E is a column vector.The values of the elements a, b, and ccc of the coefficient matrix A, and the elements e of the vector E, are calculated. By solving the system of equations, the control point vector (excluding the first and last points) is obtained.

In the third step, the NURBS curve is generated. First, the interpolation density dt of the NURBS curve is set—the smaller the dt, the smoother the curve. The incremental variable between nodes is defined as dx, which is then used to compute the degree m = 3 control points within each node interval.In the fourth step, the NURBS curve is plotted based on the given nodes and control points.

In this section, we proposed an obstacle avoidance trajectory planning method based on RRT*, and applied a cubic B-spline curve to smooth the path in order to ensure stability and smoothness in the motion of the exoskeleton robot.

4 Human-Robot Cooperative Control Strategy

The control framework of the external limb robot consists of three components: (A) human intent perception based on EMG, IMU, and motion cameras; (B) a finite state machine model; and (C) an impedance control strategy.In the first component, the IMU is used to acquire the posture information of the robot's base, while the EMG captures human muscle signals and transmits them to the robot. The second component, the finite state machine model, is used to interpret the operator's commands and switch between different task modes of the robot. The motion camera identifies human limbs and external environmental obstacles, ensuring that the external limb robot moves stably from the starting point to the target point along an obstacle-avoiding path.During overhead or near-ground operations, the external limb robot establishes an impedance control model. Based on the task model and parameters, the SRL control system generates motion trajectories and adjusts impedance control parameters accordingly to ensure interactive cooperation with the operator, thereby avoiding damage to the SRL or the human body due to excessive external forces.

4.1 Human Intention Perception System Based on IMU, EMG, and Motion Cameras

Multiple IMU units are respectively installed at the base connection points between the human body and the external limb robot, as well as at the central positions of the operator's limbs, as shown in Fig. 2. Through the IMU units, the pose information of both the external limb robot and the operator in the Cartesian coordinate system can be obtained. The EMG sensors are placed on the arm to collect electromyographic signals.

In the world coordinate system {W}, at the time-compensated position k, each segment i can be described as the position of the origin of coordinate frame {i}, denoted as:

$$P_{i,k}^w = [x_{i,k}^w, y_{i,k}^w, z_{i,k}^w] \in \mathbb{R}^3 \tag{4}$$

A sliding window filter is used to preprocess the time-series motion data of the human body, with the window length set to half the frequency of the motion data. The filter smooths the motion data and reduces measurement noise. Finally, the filtered data $P_{i,k}^w$ is used as input for the task model.

4.2 Finite State Machine Model

The collaborative task model between the supernumerary robotic limb (SRL) and the operator includes a series of actions involving both the human and the SRL, including task states, task parameters, and corresponding state transition nodes. This model can define tasks with similar processes, making it more broadly applicable in practical scenarios.

The finite state machine (FSM) model is driven by task state commands given by the operator. The SRL generates assistive actions based on the current state and state transitions. Taking the overhead and near-ground operation modes as examples: In the overhead operation mode:(i) The human operator lifts the workpiece over the head and places it in the installation position;(ii) The SRL hands the screwdriver tool to the operator and assists in supporting the workpiece to complete task handover;(iii) After the operator fixes the workpiece, both the human limbs and the SRL return to the initial position.

The finite state machine (FSM) model can be represented as a quadruple, consisting of a finite set of states S, a set of input actions/events A, a set of SRL actions a, and a state transition function $T(S_i, A_{i+1})$:

$$\text{FSM} = <S, A, a, T> \tag{5}$$

As shown in Fig. 3, in the overhead operation mode, the FSM model has four distinct human-SRL states: the "Start State" (SS), the "Assist State" (AS), the "Installation State" (IS), and the "End State" (ES). These together form the finite state set S, which can be represented as:

$$S = \{S_0, S_1, S_2, S_3\} = \{SS, AS, IS, ES\} \tag{6}$$

The state transitions in the task model are controlled by input actions or events. A represents the triggering events based on human motion and also serves as the condition for state transitions. A can be expressed as:

$$A = \{A_1, A_2, A_3\} \tag{7}$$

When the operator is in state S_{i-1} and the human motion triggers the action event A_i, the SRL executes the corresponding SRL action a_i to cooperate with the operator. The set of SRL actions can be defined as:

$$a = \{a_1, a_2, a_3\} \quad (8)$$

The state transition of the SRL begins after the completion of action a_i, entering the next state S_i. The state transition function T is defined as:

$$T(S_i, A_{i+1}) = (a_{i+1}, S_{i+1}), i \in 0, 1, 2 \quad (9)$$

During the human-robot collaboration process, the position of the human hand relative to different parts of the body and the real-time velocity of the hand determine the current state of the SRL. Using the waist and head as reference points, the hand's position relative to these reference locations can be represented by integers:

$$R = \begin{cases} 1, H_{hands,t} \geq H_{head,t} \\ 2, H_{waist,t} \leq H_{hands,t} < H_{head,t} \\ 3, H_{hands,t} < H_{waist,t} \\ 0, \text{Otherwise} \end{cases} \quad (10)$$

In the equation, $H_{hands,t}$, $H_{head,t}$, and $H_{waist,t}$ represent the heights of the hand, head, and waist, respectively; the integers 1, 2, and 3 represent the hand positions corresponding to overhead work, chest-level preparation, and task completion, respectively.

To improve the accuracy of human intention recognition, the human hand should be stationary at the end of its movement. The generalized velocity of the hand is determined using the position range over the most recent n time steps, as shown in the following equation:

$$\Delta(\hat{x}_{hands,t}) = \| \max\{\hat{x}_{hands,t-n+1}, \hat{x}_{hands,t-n+2}, ..., \hat{x}_{hands,t}\} - \min\{\hat{x}_{hands,t-n+1}, \hat{x}_{hands,t-n+2}, ..., \hat{x}_{hands,t}\} \| \leq \varepsilon \quad (11)$$

where Δ is the generalized velocity calculator, $\hat{x}_{hands,t}$ is the position vector at time step t, and ε represents a heuristically and manually adjusted threshold value close to zero, as detailed in Algorithm 2. The detection of triggering events, estimation of task parameters, and detection results for each task state in the overhead operation scenario are shown in Fig. 3.

The FSM model can recognize the operator's input actions/events that trigger state transitions and adopt corresponding control strategies to collaborate with the operator. Additionally, task parameters can be adjusted to accommodate different task scenarios, thereby enhancing the versatility of human-robot collaborative operations.

Algorithm 2: FSM Task Model of Overhead Tasks.

INITIALIZE S ← SS, A ← Nan, a ← Nan
while True **do**
  Get position of user joint segment $P_i[t]$
  if S = SS **and** A = Nan **and** R = 1 **and** $\Delta(x_{hands}[t]) \leq \varepsilon_1$ **then**
    A ← A_1
    Determine target height h ← $z_{target}[t]$
    Drive SRLs action a ← a_1
    S ← AS
  if S = AS **and** A = A_1 **and** R = 1 **and** $\Delta(P_{hands}[t]) \leq \varepsilon$ **then**
    A ← A_2
    Drive SRLs action a ← a_2
    S ← IS
  if S = IS **and** A = A_2 **and** R = 2 **and** $\Delta(x_{hands}[t]) \leq \varepsilon_2$ **and** $y_{hands}[t] < y_{thigh}[t]$ **then**
    A ← A_3
    Drive SRLs action a ← a_3
    S ← ES
  Break

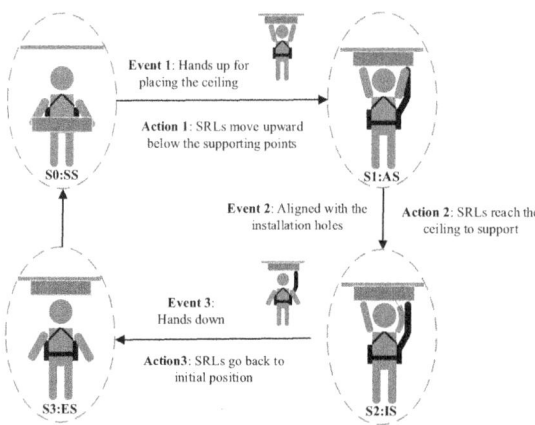

Fig. 3. FSM model for human-robot collaboration

4.3 Impedance Control Strategy for the SRL

During human-robot collaboration, different task states and state transitions correspond to different control strategies. In overhead operations, the operator takes the lead and determines the task state. The SRL identifies the input event signals from the operator, performs state transitions, and generates assistive actions. However, human motion and sensor measurement errors can interfere with the SRL's position control in the world coordinate system. Especially when the SRL interacts with the external environment under human command, it should exhibit flexibility, with safety as the top priority. Therefore, we propose a parameter-tunable variable impedance control strategy, modeling the SRL system as a spring-damper-inertia system. The ideal model for impedance control is expressed as follows:

$$M_d \ddot{x}(t) + B_d(t)\dot{x}(t) + K_d(t)(x(t) - x_d(t)) = f_{ext}(t) \quad (12)$$

where $x(t)$ represents the current pose of the robot end-effector, $x_d(t)$ denotes the desired trajectory, $\dot{x}(t)$ and $\ddot{x}(t)$ refer to the first and second derivatives, $f_{ext}(t)$ indicates the interaction force between the SRL end-effector and the external environment, M_d represents the desired mass matrix, and $B_d(t)$ and $K_d(t)$ are the time-varying damping and stiffness matrices, respectively.

To enhance the adaptability of the system, this study adopts a multimodal state modeling approach. During human-robot-environment interaction, the state space should comprehensively reflect the operator's motion intention, electromyographic (EMG) signals, and mechanical feedback information. Therefore, the following state variables are constructed:

$$s_t = [e_x(t), \dot{e}_x(t), f_{ext}(t), \text{EMG}(t), \text{IMU}(t), \text{phase}(t)] \quad (13)$$

where s_t denotes the state vector, which consists of the following components: $e_x(t) = x(t) - x_d(t)$ represents the end-effector position error; $\dot{e}_x(t)$ denotes the end-effector velocity error; $f_{ext}(t)$ is the interaction force between the robot end-effector and the external environment; $\text{EMG}(t)$ corresponds to the electromyographic signals provided by the operator to the SRL; $\text{IMU}(t)$ represents the pose information of both the human body and the SRL; and $\text{phase}(t)$ indicates the current state of the SRL within the FSM.

The controller adopts a reinforcement learning policy network, which learns to output the optimal impedance parameter adjustments through interaction with the environment. The policy outputs a set of continuous impedance parameters in the action space.

$$a_t = [K_d(t), B_d(t)] \quad (14)$$

where $K_d(t)$ represents the stiffness of the impedance controller; $B_d(t)$ denotes the damping of the impedance controller.

The policy network outputs the impedance parameters in real time based on the current state, which are embedded into the impedance controller to realize the following control law:

$$f_{cmd}(t) = M_d \ddot{x}_d + B_d(t)(\dot{x}_d - \dot{x}) + K_d(t)(x_d - x) \quad (15)$$

5 Experiment and Results

In this section, we validate the proposed RRT*-based obstacle avoidance trajectory planning algorithm. We demonstrate the effectiveness of the SRL in motion planning and obstacle avoidance under both static and dynamic environments, as well as the trajectory smoothing technique based on cubic B-spline curves. The simulations are implemented in MATLAB and executed on a laptop equipped with an Intel Core i7-13650HX CPU @ 2.60GHz and 16GB of RAM.

The search space is defined as a rectangular region measuring 800 mm × 800 mm × 800 mm, centered around the robot's base axis. A spherical obstacle is placed at the position [600, 0, 600] with a radius of 200 mm. The start and goal points are located at [600, –600, 600] and [450, 600, 480], respectively, marked by a red circle and a red star. The RRT* algorithm randomly samples new points in the environment, with new nodes represented by red dots. The blue paths illustrate the expansion of the search tree, showing connections from parent nodes to new nodes. The green path represents the final collision-free path found from the start to the goal point. The average time required to find a solution is approximately 0.66 s. The results of trajectory planning and smoothing are shown in Fig. 4.

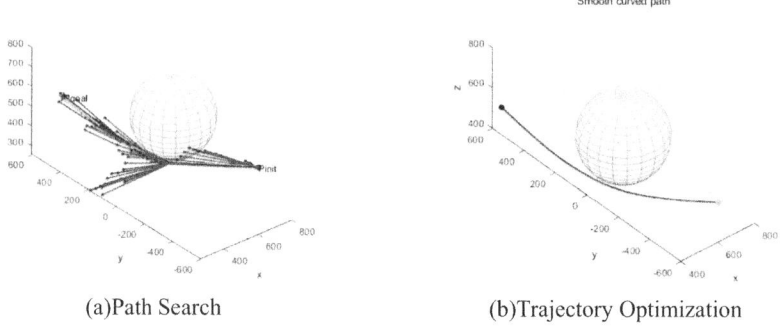

(a) Path Search (b) Trajectory Optimization

Fig. 4. Obstacle avoidance path trajectory planning

6 Conclusion

In this paper, we validate an obstacle-avoidance trajectory planning method based on RRT*, apply cubic B-spline curves for path smoothing, construct an FSM model to enable switching between different task states, and adopt a reinforcement learning-based variable impedance control strategy to achieve human-robot collaborative control.

Acknowledgement. This work was supported by National Science Foundation of China under Grant 52205018 and 62173286, China Postdoctoral Science Foundation under Grant 2024M754124, State Key Laboratory of Robotics under Grant 2023-O16, Open Research Fund of The State Key Laboratory of Multimodal Artificial Intelligence Systems under Grant MAIS2025023, Shanghai Key Laboratory of Wearable Robotics and Human-Machine Interaction, Engineering Research Center of Dredging Technology, Ministry of Education, Hohai University under Grant 2025221003, and Jiangsu Provincial Science and Technology Think Tank Program Project under Grant JSKX0125055.

References

1. Xu, J., Zhang, T., Huang, K., Cao, K., Ji, A., Xu, L.: Optimal design and implementation of a bioinspired soft supernumerary robotic limb. Robot **46**(2), 147–157 (2024). https://doi.org/10.13973/j.cnki.robot.230199
2. Xu, J., Zhang, T., Huang, K., et al.: A soft supernumerary robotic limb with fiber-reinforced actuators. J. Intell. Rob. Syst. **110**(2), 71 (2024)
3. Llorens- Bonilla, B., Parietti, F., Asada, H.H.: Demonstration-based control of supernumerary robotic limbs. In: IEEE/RSJ International Conference on Intelligent Robots and Systems 3936–3942 (2012). https://doi.org/10.1109/IROS.2012.6386055
4. Davenport, C., Parietti, F., Asada, H.H.: Design and biomechanical analysis of supernumerary robotic limbs. In: Dynamic Systems and Control Conference. American Society of Mechanical Engineers **45295**, 787-793 (2012)
5. Tong, Y., Liu, J.: Review of research and development of supernumerary robotic limbs[J]. IEEE/CAA J. Automatica Sinica **8**(5), 929–952 (2021)
6. Giammarino, A., Gandarias, J.M., Balatti, P., et al.: SUPER-MAN: Supernumerary robotic bodies for physical assistance in human–robot conjoined actions. Mechatronics **103**, 103240 (2024)
7. Prattichizzo, D., Pozzi, M., Baldi, T.L., et al.: Human augmentation by wearable supernumerary robotic limbs: review and perspectives. Progress Biomed. Eng. **3**(4), 042005 (2021)
8. Parietti, F., Chan, K., Asada, H.H.: Bracing the human body with supernumerary robotic limbs for physical assistance and load reduction. In: 2014 IEEE International Conference on Robotics and Automation (ICRA). IEEE, 141–148 (2014)
9. Seo, W., Shin, C.Y., Choi, J., et al.: Applications of supernumerary robotic limbs to construction works: case studies. In: ISARC. Proceedings of the International Symposium on Automation and Robotics in Construction. IAARC Publications **33**, 1 (2016)
10. Véronneau, C., Denis, J., Lebel, L.P., et al.: Multifunctional remotely actuated 3-DOF supernumerary robotic arm based on magnetorheological clutches and hydrostatic transmission lines. IEEE Robot. Automation Lett. **5**(2), 2546–2553 (2020)
11. Xu, J., Zhao, M., Zhang, T., Ji, A.: A rigid-flexible supernumerary robotic arm/leg: design, modeling, and control. Electronics **13**(20), 4106 (2024)
12. Zhang, T., et al.: Design and control of a soft supernumerary robotic limb based on fiber-reinforced actuator. In: 2024 IEEE/RSJ International Conference on Intelligent Robots and Systems (IROS), 9167–9174 (2024)
13. Zhao, M., Xu, J., Zhou, J., Zhang, T., Huang, K.: A pneumatic-tendon hybrid-actuated supernumerary robotic limb. In: Proceedings of the 3rd International Conference on Machine Learning, Cloud Computing and Intelligent Mining (MLCCIM 2024), 597–608 (2024)
14. Xu, J., Xu, L., Ji, A., et al.: A DMP-based motion generation scheme for robotic mirror therapy. IEEE/ASME Trans. Mechatron. **28**(6), 3120–3131 (2023)
15. Xu, J., Xu, L., Ji, A., et al.: Learning robotic motion with mirror therapy framework for hemiparesis rehabilitation. Inf. Process. Manage. **60**(2), 103244 (2023)
16. Xu, J., Huang, K., Zhang, T., et al.: Mirror adaptive impedance control of multi-mode soft exoskeleton with reinforcement learning. IEEE Trans. Autom. Sci. Eng. **22**, 6773–6785 (2024)

Learning Whole-Body Motion Control Through Instruction Learning and Human Motion Data

Zhipeng Xu[1], Kaixuan Chen[1], Linqi Ye[1(✉)], and Boyang Xing[2]

[1] School of Future Technology, Shanghai University, Shanghai 200444, China
yelinqi@shu.edu.cn
[2] National and Local Co-built Humanoid Robotics Innovation Center, Shanghai 201203, China

Abstract. This paper proposes a novel imitation learning approach for the whole-body motion control of humanoid robots. Based on the instruction learning framework proposed in our prior work, we integrate human motion capture data as a feedforward action in this paper, which is combined with a feedback action driven by reinforcement learning to achieve human-like whole-body movements. Compared to other imitation learning methods, the proposed method can significantly enhance the training efficiency due to the application of a feedforward action. Furthermore, since the motion-mimic capability is mainly determined by the feedforward action while the neural network only plays a role as a stabilizer, it enables the control of multiple motion skills using a single neural network. The effectiveness of the proposed method in whole-body motion imitation learning is verified through several simulation tasks performed on the Unitree H1 robot. The attached video can be found at https://linqi-ye.github.io/video/icira25.mp4.

Keywords: Humanoid Robot · Reinforcement Learning · Imitation Learning · Instruction Learning

1 Introduction

With the escalating complexity of modern robotic applications, data-driven learning methods have demonstrated substantial potential, especially the reinforcement learning (RL) algorithm, which aims to maximize a reward through interactions with observations and environments. Many powerful RL methods have been proposed, such as Proximal Policy Optimization (PPO) [1], Soft Actor Critic (SAC) [2], and Curriculum Learning (CL) [3]. However, despite these advancements, directly applying these methods to achieve diverse and agile whole-body motion control for complex humanoid robots often faces challenges related to sample efficiency, the complexity of reward design, and the difficulty of acquiring varied and robust policies for multiple skills within a single framework.

Imitation learning (IL), which integrates motion reference data into reward functions to guide robotic agents. There have been many studies applying imitation learning to robot locomotion, Behavior Cloning (BC) [4], an early direct policy learning approach, in its relative research, researchers relied on Hidden Markov Models(HMMs) to enable simple human-dance imitation on robot [5], however, its effectiveness was often contingent on highly specific conditions and a well-defined control strategy, or conversely, struggled in its absence. Subsequent advancements, from Dynamic Movement Primitives(DMPs) [6] to Variational Learning(VL) [7], addressed some control strategy limitations. Yet, these methods often exhibited poor generalizability when trained with limited sample sizes. Inverse Reinforcement Learning(IRL) [8,9] emerged as a novel imitation learning paradigm. While maximum margin-based IRL frameworks incurred high computational costs, probabilistic models paved the way for data-driven deep reinforcement learning approaches. Peng et al. proposed a framework that enabled the training of humanoid robots in virtual environments through the algorithm of DeepMimic, yielding highly robust policies [10]. Nevertheless, this approach, too, demands substantial quantities of data. A persistent challenge across these imitation learning methods has been the arduous design of effective reward functions. Generative Adversarial Imitation Learning(GAIL) [11,12] offered a solution to this reward design problem, but its training process remains computationally intensive and requires a large volume of high-quality demonstration data. In general, the substantial data requirements, the key limitation of the inherent incompleteness of real-world demonstrations and susceptibility to local optima in imitation learning often hinder the acquisition of optimal policies [13].

Instruction learning as an alternative imitation learning strategy takes advantage of a feedforward action as an initial guide policy [14]. This feedforward-guided policy optimization enables more efficient exploration of the policy landscape, as the learning process starts from a known motion, albeit suboptimal. By refining this initial policy, agents achieve accelerated convergence to policies that surpass the original demonstration's performance. This method also mitigates the need for intricate reward shaping, as the feedforward itself provides a strong directional cue, simplifying the learning problem and potentially leading to more robust behaviors with reduced training complexity. Based on instruction learning, we developed Unity RL Playground, which is a simple, yet efficient and versatile framework for RL in mobile robotics [15]. Unity RL Playground is build upon Unity ML-Agents [16] and tailored for robotic reinforcement learning. A key feature is its ease of use and versatility to achieve various locomotion behaviors for mobile robots. This characteristic significantly broadens its accessibility to a wider research and development community. We leverage this framework for the simulation training in this paper. However, the previous version of instruction learning has adopted hand-crafted trajectories as feedforward, which is difficult to extend to whole-body motion control.

Human motion data is crucial for whole-body imitation learning. Extensive research has explored the integration of adaptive motion functions (AMFs) or dynamics with RL for continuous gait design and control, yielding highly robust control strategies [17,18]. Zhou et al. combined IL with biological data collected in nature to instruct a multi-jointed robot to learn animal behavior [19]. Prior research has extensively investigated the direct retargeting of human motion capture data to humanoid robot kinematics [20–22]. Building upon this foundation, the work [23,24] created a novel, large-scale motion dataset specifically optimized for humanoid robot compatibility, which systematically adapts the human-derived motions to ensure their kinematic and dynamic feasibility within the operational constraints of real-world humanoid robot platforms.

Motivated by the aforementioned work, we take advantage of human motion data to serve as a feedforward and thus extend instruction learning to whole-body motion control. The contributions of this paper are summarized as follows. First, we extend the instruction learning method to whole-body motion control by applying human motion capture data as a feedforward action, which enables humanoid robots to learn multiple motion skills efficiently through a single neural network. Second, we verify the effectiveness of the proposed method in whole-body motion imitation learning through several simulation tasks with the Unitree H1 robot, which are presented in the attached video.

2 Method

The framework of the proposed method is shown in Fig. 1. Compared to the previous version of instruction learning [14], the primary modifications lie in the feedforward component and the reward aspect. The details are introduced in the following.

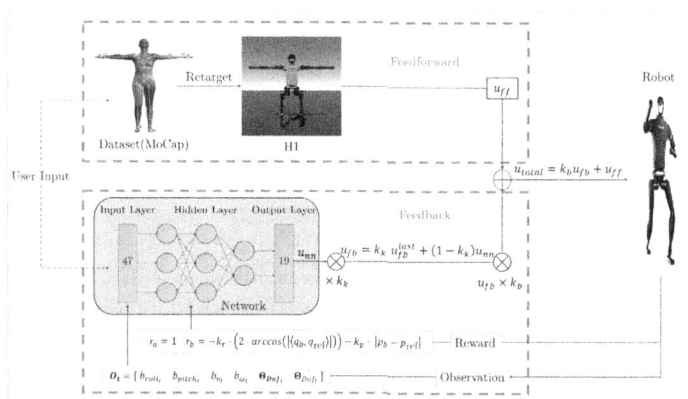

Fig. 1. Framework.

2.1 Feedforward Design

In this study, a retargeted joint angle reference from human motion data is employed to define the robot's feedforward action. With these predefined motion, the robot will be trained to optimize the feedback action sequences, aiming to achieve higher reward values.

Our dataset, sourced from AMASS Dataset [25], necessitated a retargeting process for its integration into the Unity environment. This was primarily due to fundamental discrepancies in their coordinate systems and angular representations: AMASS Dataset employs a Z-up orientation with joint angles recorded in radians, whereas Unity utilizes a Y-up orientation and expresses angles in degrees. Subsequently, these transformed joint angles were converted into quaternion representations to ensure robust motion blending within the Unity engine. The transformation as follows:

$$\begin{cases} \mathbf{p}_{Unity} = \mathbf{R}_c \mathbf{p}_{MoCap}, \quad \mathbf{R}_c = \begin{bmatrix} 0 & -1 & 0 \\ 0 & 0 & 1 \\ 1 & 0 & 0 \end{bmatrix} \\ \mathbf{q}_{Unity} = \mathcal{Q}(\mathbf{q}_{MoCap}) = \begin{bmatrix} q_y \\ -q_z \\ q_x \\ q_w \end{bmatrix}, \quad \mathbf{q}_{MoCap} = \begin{bmatrix} q_x \\ q_y \\ q_z \\ q_w \end{bmatrix} \\ \boldsymbol{\theta}_{Unity} = \boldsymbol{\theta}_{MoCap} \times \frac{180}{\pi} = \begin{bmatrix} \theta_1^{rad} \\ \vdots \\ \theta_{19}^{rad} \end{bmatrix} \times \frac{180}{\pi} \end{cases} \quad (1)$$

2.2 Learning Settings

(A) **Hyperparameters:**
In this study, proximal policy optimization (PPO) is used as the reinforcement learning algorithm. The hyperparameters of the corresponding network are configured as follows: batch size 2048, buffer size 20480, beta 0.005, epsilon 0.2, lambda 0.95, learning rate 0.0003, num epoch 3.

(B) **Neural network:**
The neural network architecture employs an actor-critic structure. The actor network is implemented as a Multi-Layer Perceptron (MLP) comprising three hidden layers, each with 512 hidden units. Complementing this, the critic network is also an MLP, featuring two hidden layers, each containing 128 hidden units.

(C) **Observation:**
The observations are

$$\mathbf{O_t} = \begin{bmatrix} b_{roll_t}, b_{pitch_t}, b_{v_t}, b_{w_t}, \Theta_{Dof_t}, \dot{\Theta}_{Dof_t} \end{bmatrix} \quad (2)$$

where b_{roll_t}, b_{pitch_t} represent the roll and pitch angles of the root(Unit: radian), b_{v_t}, b_{w_t} represents the linear velocity and angular velocity of the root, $\Theta_{Dof_t}, \dot{\Theta}_{Dof_t}$ are the joint angle, joint angular velocity, respectively, which contains the same number of variables as the joint numbers of the robot.

(D) **Action:**
The action is a combination of the feedforward action, which is obtained from human motion data, and a feedback action, which is a filtered output of the neural network. The feedback action is expressed as

$$u_{fb} = k_k u_{fb}^{last} + (1 - k_k) u_{nn} \tag{3}$$

where u_{fb}^{last} represents the value of the feedback term from the preceding time step, u_{nn} denotes the raw output of the actor network. Then, the feedback action u_{fb} is weighted by k_b and combined with the feedforward component to yield the final action:

$$u_{total} = k_b u_{fb} + u_{ff} \tag{4}$$

2.3 Reward Design

Instruction learning alleviates the complexities associated with traditional reward engineering, thereby simplifying reward definition. In this study, we use some simple reward components, which can be applied to all motion imitation tasks.

(1) **Alive reward:**
r_a is designed as $r_a = 1$, its existence encourages the robot to maintain balance and not fall. In all time steps before termination, the robot can obtain this reward.

(2) **Body reward:**
r_b is designed as

$$r_b = -k_r \cdot (2 \cdot \arccos(|\langle q_b, q_{\text{ref}} \rangle|)) - k_p \cdot \|p_b - p_{\text{ref}}\| \tag{5}$$

where q_b, q_{ref} represents the orientation of the body expressed by a quaternion, p_b, p_{ref} represents the real and reference body position.

(3) **Feedforward switching processing:**
Imperfections in feedforward compensation yield substantial state disparities across temporal frames preceding and succeeding a change in feedforward control paradigms. Such pronounced discontinuities impede the effective learning or optimization of the control policy during transitional phases. To facilitate a robust feedforward transition, a specialized control scheme adaptation is employed. During the initial temporal window subsequent to a feedforward set update, the system's reward evaluation is restricted to only account for elemental survival objectives, thereby temporarily decoupling the body-specific reward components from the overall objective function.

2.4 Episode Termination Condition

During the training process, the termination condition is set to:

$$2 \cdot \arccos\left(|\langle q_b, q_{\text{ref}}\rangle|\right) > 30 \quad or \quad \|p_b - p_{\text{ref}}\| > 0.3 \tag{6}$$

it indicates to terminate when the orientation or position of the robot is too far from the reference.

2.5 Curriculum Learning

Our work introduces a generalized curriculum learning scheme which demonstrably leads to faster convergence and enhanced training stability. We select multiple motion tasks to train simultaneously. During the first ten million steps, we train each motion for 300 s and then switch to the next motion, in order to make sure that every action is fully practiced. When it comes to the last two million steps, we spent 30 s training on each motion, namely increasing the switching frequency, which can reduce the impact of forgetting effectively.

3 Simulation

The simulations were conducted with Unity RL Playground. This platform was selected for its proven efficacy in providing an efficient and user-friendly Reinforcement Learning (RL) development environment specifically tailored for robotic applications. The discrete action timestep was set to 0.02 s. To accelerate the training process, a parallelized learning paradigm was adopted, leveraging 24 concurrent instances of the robot to train in parallel.

3.1 Simulation Settings

(A) **Robot Model and Specifications:**
The robot model utilized for simulation is the Unitree-H1 bipedal humanoid robot, as depicted in the accompanying figure. This robot features a total of 19 revolute joints. Each leg possesses 5°C of freedom, comprising three at the hip (Hip Y, Hip R, Hip P), one at the knee (Knee P), and one at the ankle (Ankle P). Each arm has 4°C of freedom. The main specifications of the Unitree-H1 robot are shown in Table 1 (a)(b), and Fig. 2 shows the zero position of the robot.

(B) **Feedforward data:**
The feedforward component of our control strategy is generated from a dataset of human motion capture, which has been meticulously retargeted to ensure kinematic and dynamic compatibility with humanoid robots. Specifically, our comprehensive feedforward set includes motions for golf, tennis, guitar, violin, and general waving gestures.

(C) **training settings:**
$k_b = 30, k_k = 0.9, k_r = 0.01, k_p = 1$

Table 1. Joint Specifications: (a) Torque Limits, (b) Motion Ranges

(a) Joint Unit Limit Torques

Joint Type	Limit Torque (Nm)
Knee Joints	360
Hip Joints	220
Ankle Joints	59
Arm Joints	75

(b) Joint Motion Ranges (rad)

Joint Type	Motion Range (rad)
Hip Y	-0.43 to +0.43
Hip R	-0.43 to +0.43
Hip P	-3.14 to +2.53
Knee P	-0.26 to +2.05
Ankle P	-0.87 to +0.52
Torso Y	-2.35 to +2.35
Shoulder Pitch	-2.87 to +2.87
Right Shoulder Roll	-3.11 to +0.34
Left Shoulder Roll	-0.34 to +3.11
Right Shoulder Yaw	-4.45 to +1.3
Left Shoulder Yaw	-1.3 to +4.45
Elbow Pitch	-1.25 to +2.61

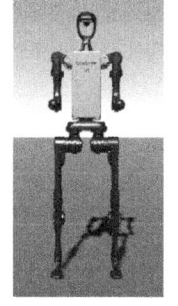

(a) Front view of H1   (b) Side view of H1

Fig. 2. Unitree-H1 zero position.

3.2 Simulation Results

The process of our simulation is dived by tow parts, training and playing. We design 13 motion tasks (some are repeated) for H1 robot to learn, the order and name of these motion tasks are listed in the following. We repeated some of the tasks for several times because they are more difficult to learn, and the following results prove that our hypothesis is correct.

Table 2. Motion Tasks

Index	Motion Name	Index	Motion Name
1	golf drive poses	8	golf drive poses
2	golf drive poses	9	golf drive poses
3	tennis forehand left poses	10	tennis forehand left poses
4	tennis forehand left poses	11	tennis forehand left poses
5	guitar right poses	12	wave left poses
6	violin left poses	13	wave right poses
7	wave both poses		

We used reinforcement learning to train the robot for twelve million steps. During training, we found that the reward decreased when the feedforward motion was switched, as shown in Fig. 3. This suggested that the policy network just trained may forget the motion it just learned, implying that we use curriculum learning to reduce the time allocated on each motion (Table 2).

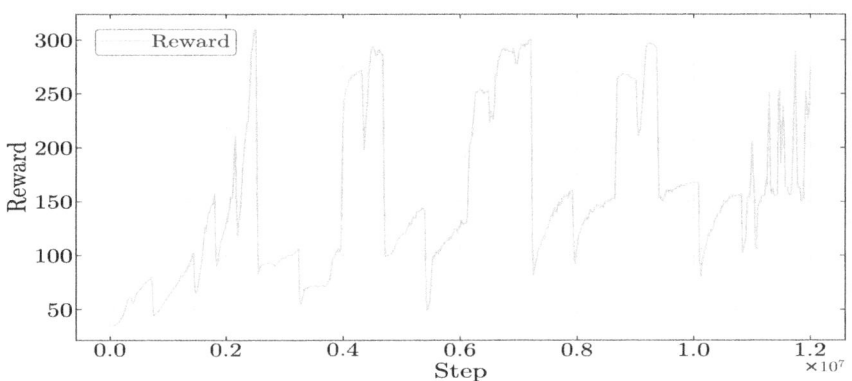

Fig. 3. Cumulative Reward.

As a result, despite the fact that the reward function decreases at motion switch, the extent to which it decreases is gradually decreasing over time and the reward stably remains at a relatively high value in the end.

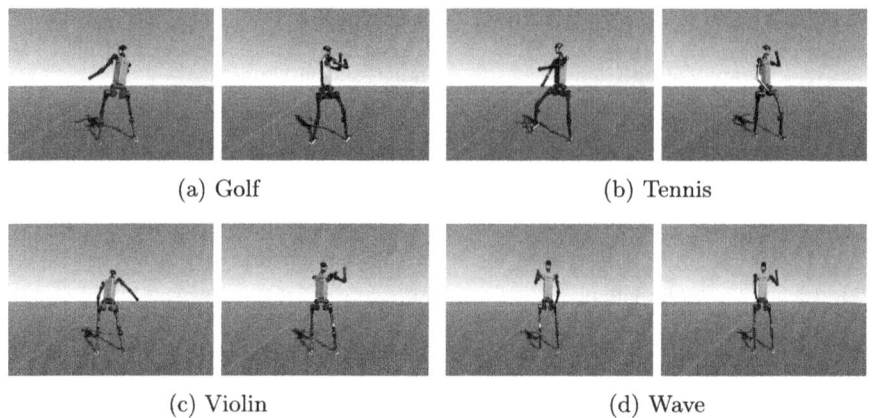

Fig. 4. Learned locomotion behavior.

Figure 4 depicts the trained H1 robot performing different motion tasks, but it is difficult to objectively quantify and evaluate the training performance based on visual observation alone. Therefore, we collected statistics on body position and posture errors of the robot during playing, and conducted a comprehensive analysis by combining them with charts.

In Fig. 5, the comparison results of "Average Error" and "Max Error" of seven different tasks (golf, guitar, tennis, violin, wave both, wave left, wave right) are shown. According to the difference in imitation accuracy, these tasks can be divided into two categories.

One is tasks with good imitation effects, including guitar and three wave tasks. The average error and maximum error of these tasks are both at a low level. Their common feature is that the movements are mainly concentrated in the upper limbs and the posture changes are small. These characteristics reduce the complexity of action control, making it easier for the policy network to converge to a stable solution, thereby achieving accurate imitation. Therefore, it can be considered that upper limb actions that do not involve obvious movement of the lower limbs are easier to master by the robot, and show good stability and consistency in the reproduction process.

The other is tasks that are more difficult to imitate, including violin, golf and tennis. These actions generally show high average and maximum errors, especially golf and violin, where the error values are much higher than other tasks. The reason for the difficulty in imitation is that the actions involve complex multi-joint coordinated control, accompanied by significant trunk twisting and lower limb movements. The results above offer us insights into the robot itself, we may not deny that it is the structural bottleneck (each leg only has one ankle joint) that severely limits its body coordination ability, leading to significant deviations in the imitation process.

Considering the joint parameters displayed in Table. 1, one of the important reasons for this phenomenon is that the ankle of the current robot platform

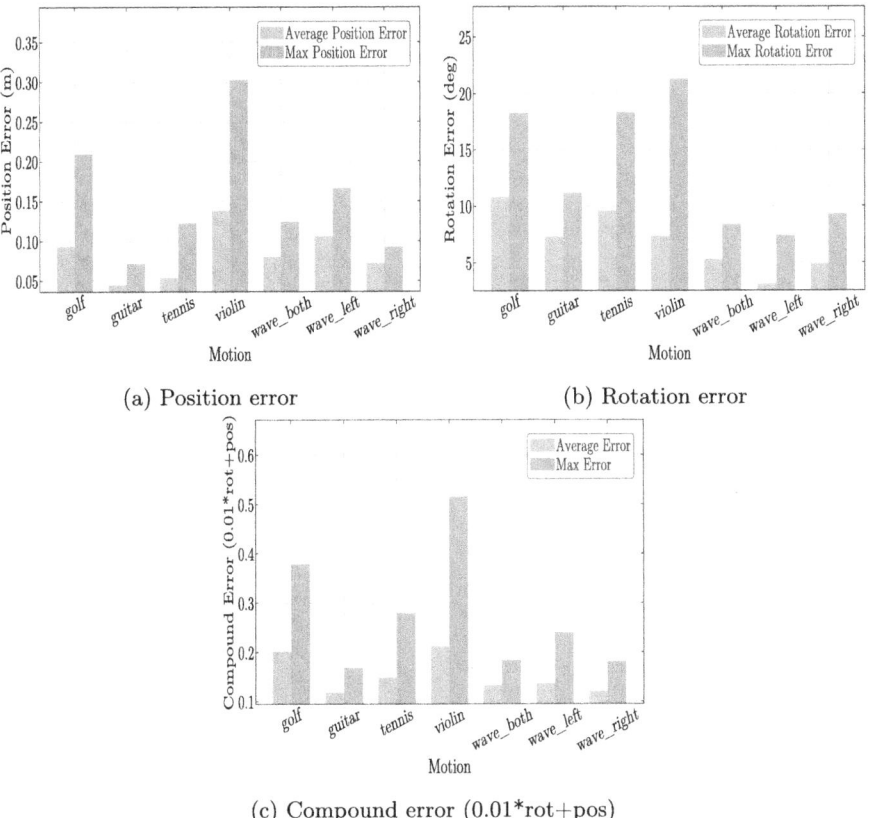

Fig. 5. Motion tracking error.

(Unitree-H1) has only one degree of freedom (ankle pitch), which limits the flexibility of center of gravity adjustment and gait control. In subsequent work, it is possible to consider introducing a hardware platform with higher joint freedom (such as Unitree-G1) to improve the imitation accuracy and control stability of highly dynamic and complex movements.

To further explore the imitation consistency of actions in different time periods, we selected two tasks, guitar with the smallest compound error and violin with the largest compound error, and compared their tracking error with time(as shown in Fig. 6). We employ the position error and rotation error to quantify the deviations of the robot's movement from the desired track. Specifically, the former is calculated as the Euclidean distance between the robot's current position and the desired position, while the latter is determined by the angular difference between the robot's current orientation and the target orientation. The results show that guitar has a low tracking error in the entire time series(less than 0.1), reflecting the stability and robustness of the action imitation process. In contrast, violin shows significant deviations in the middle and later stages(more

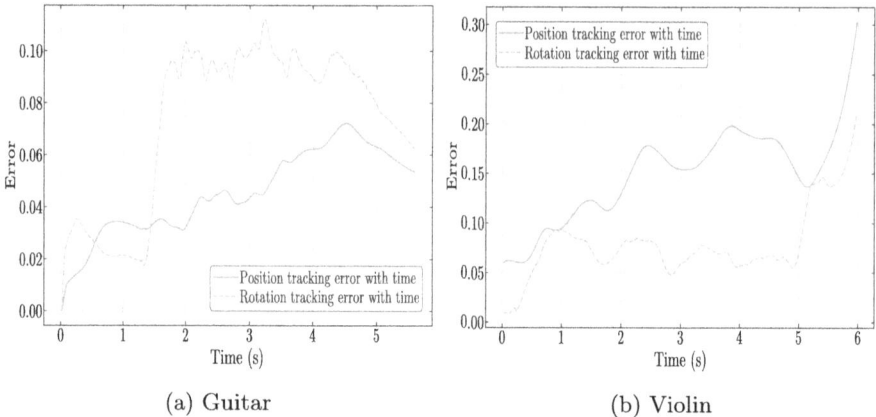

Fig. 6. Tracking error with time.

than 0.1), especially in its position tracking error, where there are significant oscillations and fluctuations, reflecting the limitation of the controller's ability to cope with multi-joint coordination and lower limb dynamic balance tasks.

4 Conclusion

This paper proposes a method for learning whole-body movements of humanoid robots based on instruction learning. By introducing human motion capture data as feedforward signals and combining it with a reinforcement learning framework, unified learning and control of multiple movements are achieved. Compared with the traditional imitation learning method, this method uses reference trajectories as the initial strategy to guide the policy network to efficiently explore in the policy space, significantly improving the training convergence speed and reducing the risk of policy degradation. In addition, by building a simulation environment on the Unity RL Playground platform and adjusting the action switching frequency in combination with the curriculum learning strategy, the model's adaptability to multi-skill switching is further improved. The simulation results show that this method has good generalization ability in a variety of movements.

In order to further improve the imitation accuracy and stability of the system in highly complex action scenarios, future work will introduce a robot platform with higher lower limb freedom (such as Unitree G1) to enhance the overall action coordination ability and reduce the impact of structural constraints on strategy optimization, thereby achieving higher quality whole-body action learning and control.

References

1. Schulman, J., Wolski, F., Dhariwal, P., Radford, A., Klimov, O.: Proximal policy optimization algorithms. arXiv preprint arXiv:1707.06347 (2017)
2. Haarnoja, T., Zhou, A., Abbeel, P., Levine, S.: Soft actor-critic: off-policy maximum entropy deep reinforcement learning with a stochastic actor. In: International Conference on Machine Learning (ICML), pp. 1861–1870. PMLR (2018)
3. Bengio, Y., Louradour, J., Collobert, R., Weston, J.: Curriculum learning. In: Proceedings of the 26th Annual International Conference on Machine Learning (ICML), pp. 41–48 (2009)
4. Osa, T., Pajarinen, J., Neumann, G., Bagnell, J.A., Abbeel, P., Peters, J.: An algorithmic perspective on imitation learning. Found. Trends Robot. **7**(1–2), 1–179 (2018)
5. Takeda, T., Hirata, Y., Kosuge, K.: Dance step estimation method based on HMM for dance partner robot. IEEE Trans. Industr. Electron. **54**, 699–706 (2007)
6. Gams, A., Nemec, B., Ijspeert, A.J., Ude, A.: Coupling movement primitives: Interaction with the environment and bimanual tasks. IEEE Trans. Rob. **30**(4), 816–830 (2014)
7. Zhang, T., McCarthy, Z., Jow, O., Lee, D., Chen, X., Goldberg, K., Abbeel, P.: Deep imitation learning for complex manipulation tasks from virtual reality teleoperation. In: Proceedings of the IEEE International Conference on Robotics and Automation (ICRA), pp. 5628–5635 (2018)
8. Ng, A.Y., Russell, S.: Algorithms for inverse reinforcement learning. In: Proceedings of the 17th International Conference on Machine Learning (ICML), vol. 1, no. 2, p. 2 (2000)
9. Krishnan, S., et al.: SWIRL: a sequential windowed inverse reinforcement learning algorithm for robot tasks with delayed rewards. Int. J. Robot. Res. **38**(2–3), 126–145 (2019)
10. Peng, X.B., Abbeel, P., Levine, S., Panne, M.: DeepMimic: example-guided deep reinforcement learning of physics-based character skills. ACM Trans. Graphics (TOG) **37**(4), 1–14 (2018)
11. Kuefler, A., Morton, J., Wheeler, T., Kochenderfer, M.: Imitating driver behavior with generative adversarial networks. In: Proceedings of the IEEE Intelligent Vehicles Symposium (IV), pp. 204–211. IEEE (2017)
12. Cai, Q., Hong, M., Chen, Y., Wang, Z.: On the global convergence of imitation learning: a case for linear quadratic regulator. arXiv preprint arXiv:1901.03674 (2019)
13. Peng, X.B., Coumans, E., Zhang, T., Lee, T.W., Tan, J., Levine, S.: Learning agile robotic locomotion skills by imitating animals. arXiv preprint arXiv:2004.00784 (2020)
14. Ye, L., Li, J., Cheng, Y., Wang, X., Liang, B., Peng, Y.: From knowing to doing: learning diverse motor skills through instruction learning. arXiv preprint arXiv:2309.09167 (2023)
15. Ye, L., et al.: Unity RL playground: a versatile reinforcement learning framework for mobile robots. arXiv preprint arXiv:2503.05146 (2025)
16. Juliani, A., et al.: Unity: a general platform for intelligent agents. arXiv preprint arXiv:1809.02627 (2018)
17. Liu, Q., Guo, J., Lin, S., Ma, S., Zhu, J., Li, Y.: MASQ: multi-agent reinforcement learning for single quadruped robot locomotion. arXiv preprint arXiv:2408.13759 (2024)

18. Zhao, Z., Huang, H., Sun, S., Li, C., Xu, W.: Fusing dynamics and reinforcement learning for control strategy: achieving precise gait and high robustness in humanoid robot locomotion. In: Proceedings of the 2024 IEEE-RAS 23rd International Conference on Humanoid Robots (Humanoids), pp. 1072–1079. IEEE (2024)
19. Zhou, Q., Li, G., Tang, R., Xu, Y., Wen, H., Shi, Q.: Stable jumping control based on deep reinforcement learning for a locust-inspired robot. Biomimetics **9**(9), 548 (2024)
20. Darvish, K., et al.: Whole-body geometric retargeting for humanoid robots. In: 2019 IEEE-RAS 19th International Conference on Humanoid Robots (Humanoids), pp. 679–686. IEEE (2019)
21. Cisneros-Limón, R., et al.: A cybernetic avatar system to embody human telepresence for connectivity, exploration, and skill transfer. Int. J. Soc. Robot., 1–28 (2024)
22. Radosavovic, I., Zhang, B., Shi, B., Rajasegaran, J., Kamat, S., Darrell, T., Malik, J.: Humanoid locomotion as next token prediction. In: The Thirty-eighth Annual Conference on Neural Information Processing Systems (NeurIPS) (2024)
23. He, T., et al.: Learning human-to-humanoid real-time whole-body teleoperation. In: 2024 IEEE/RSJ International Conference on Intelligent Robots and Systems (IROS), pp. 8944–8951. IEEE (2024)
24. He, T., et al.: OmniH2O: universal and dexterous human-to-humanoid whole-body teleoperation and learning. arXiv preprint arXiv:2406.08858 (2024)
25. Mahmood, N., Ghorbani, N., Troje, N.F., Pons-Moll, G., Black, M.J.: xAMASS: archive of motion capture as surface shapes. In: Proceedings of the IEEE/CVF International Conference on Computer Vision (ICCV), pp. 5442–5451 (2019)

Author Index

A

Alam, Md.Mahbub II-581
An, Peiru I-397
An, Yi II-471
Azam, Hamza II-275

B

Bai, Ruiyu I-571
Bao, Chenyu II-459
Bao, Mengyi I-363
Besari, Adnan Rachmat Anom II-129

C

Cai, Hegao II-613
Cai, Huayi II-446
Cai, Huimin I-484, I-496
Cai, Jiahui III-150
Cai, Mengchen I-459
Cai, Mingxue III-49
Cai, Shibo III-298, III-310
Cai, Songtao III-650
Cao, Ruikai III-287
Cao, Wujing II-222, II-234, II-244, II-285, II-309
Cao, Zhongzhong I-201
Chen, Bowen III-473, III-534
Chen, Chen I-373
Chen, Chunjie III-323
Chen, Genliang I-559
Chen, Hao III-162
Chen, Haochu II-155
Chen, Huangchao I-423
Chen, Hui III-323
Chen, Junliang III-15
Chen, Junru II-421
Chen, Kaixuan II-698
Chen, Mingzhi I-153
Chen, Mu III-361
Chen, Peng III-298
Chen, Wenyu III-361
Chen, Xin III-310

Chen, Xingyu I-547
Chen, Yanhu I-227
Chen, Yanyun III-662
Chen, Yibin III-249
Chen, Yihan III-26
Chen, Yinhui II-650
Chen, Yujie II-244
Chen, Yun II-483
Chen, Zhiqiang III-49
Chen, Zhujin III-323
Cheng, Cheng III-447
Cheng, Hong III-631
Cheng, Xiangyu III-310
Cheng, Yun II-446
Cheng, Zhenyu II-297
Chu, Hui II-79, II-266
Chu, Shixuan III-235
Chu, Yao III-560
Cui, Jiatong II-322

D

Dai, Ruixuan III-124
Dai, Wenjie II-373
Deng, Linan III-447
Deng, Zongquan III-136
Ding, Cheng I-91
Ding, Han I-77, I-140, II-210
Ding, Liang III-136
Ding, Ning II-483
Ding, Shuchen III-587
Ding, Tao I-446, II-497
Ding, Ye II-337, II-349
Ding, Zhe II-545
Dong, Anqin III-348
Dong, Birong I-279
Dong, Kaijie III-174
Dong, Na III-398
Dong, Tenghui III-650
Dong, Wenhui I-215
Dong, Yan II-421
Dong, Yifei II-471

Dong, Yunlong III-447
Du, Fuxin I-595
Du, Mingyu III-298, III-310
Du, Xinyang I-350, II-285, II-557

F

Fan, Huijie III-422
Fan, Shixun I-496
Fan, Xuanhe II-54
Fan, Yihui II-210
Fan, Zuxin II-567
Fang, Xing III-662
Fang, Yinfeng II-114
Fang, Yuelei III-185
Fang, Zi II-166, II-184
Fei, Xinyu I-227
Feng, Luying II-275
Feng, Shuo III-573
Feng, Siyu III-287
Feng, Zihe III-611
Fu, Chenglong II-67, II-197, II-255
Fu, Hang III-162
Fu, Qiang III-88
Fu, Zhijun III-673
Fu, Zhuang II-166, II-184

G

Gan, Yiming II-37
Gao, Ang II-361
Gao, Chao III-275
Gao, Feng III-112
Gao, Haibo III-136
Gao, Liang II-637
Gao, Naixing I-385
Gao, Qingbin II-650
Gao, Zhe II-601
Ge, Ziyun II-322
Getževič, Mitja II-275
Gong, Kening II-175
Gou, Xuning I-547
Gu, Guoying I-65, I-547
Guan, Zimeng III-650
Guo, Hongwei I-525, I-536
Guo, Jiajie III-249, III-484
Guo, Lei I-239
Guo, Lina II-3
Guo, Liucheng II-545
Guo, Qixiang III-197
Guo, Weichao I-328

Guo, Weilun II-409
Guo, Weizhong III-162, III-235
Guo, Yikun I-77
Guo, Yizhu III-124, III-197
Guo, Ze-Sheng I-509
Guo, Zhao III-673
Guo, Zisui I-201

H

Hai, Yong III-611
Han, Bin II-421
Han, Jianda I-472
Han, Shiyu III-348
Han, Tao III-361
Han, Wei I-166
He, Jiayuan I-279
He, Shuangjiang II-54
He, Weikai I-595
Hirai, Takao III-60
Hong, Lin I-239
Hou, Haofei I-459, II-567
Hou, Licheng I-15
Hou, Siqi II-509
Hou, Zeng-Guang II-322
Hu, Hongbo I-3, I-27, I-39
Hu, Junjie II-459
Hu, Shibo III-386
Hu, Wenyu I-27
Hu, Yan III-112
Hu, Yanbo II-297
Hu, Zebin I-446
Hua, Feng III-447
Huai, Xiang III-174
Huang, Chenyang III-49
Huang, Chuwen II-234
Huang, Hao III-484
huang, Junfeng III-197
Huang, Rui III-631
Huang, Taoyuan I-65
Huang, Wenze III-473, III-534
Huang, Yedong I-583
Huang, Yiren III-611
Huang, Yongfeng III-49
Huang, Yuxiang II-545
Huo, Weiguang I-472

I

Irshad, Ahmad II-275

Author Index 713

J

Ji, Haoyu   III-473, III-534
Ji, Xiang   III-26
Ji, Yanyan   II-509
Jiang, Dongjie   I-103
Jiang, Gedong   II-397
Jiang, Jialin   III-26, III-38
Jiang, Li   II-175
Jiang, Ning   I-279
Jiang, Qin   II-210
Jiang, Ruoyuan   II-446
Jiang, Tianxiang   I-115
Jiang, Xugang   II-27
Jiang, Yao   I-316
Jiang, Zimo   III-473, III-534
Jin, Dongdong   III-15
Jin, Shuxiao   I-472
Jin, Taixian   II-662
Jin, Wei   II-567
Jin, Yaolun   II-114
Jing, Fei   II-166, II-184
Jing, Hongwei   II-91
Ju, Haotian   II-91, II-613

K

Kamegawa, Tetsushi   III-60
Ke, Shuai   I-77
Kuang, Qi   III-287
Kubota, Naoyuki   II-129, III-209

L

Lam, Tin Lun   II-459
Lang, Chenbo   III-112
Lei, Changjiang   II-197, II-255
Leng, Yuquan   II-67, II-197, II-255
Li, Bo   I-571
Li, Bocong   II-361
Li, Changle   II-601
Li, Chuanjiang   II-37
Li, Chunfeng   I-536
Li, Dachuan   II-433
Li, Di   II-509
Li, Duanjiao   II-483
Li, Duanling   III-101, III-124, III-150, III-174, III-197
Li, Feng   II-397
Li, Fengyi   III-162
Li, Guanglin   II-27
Li, Guangye   I-411

Li, Guo   II-397
Li, Guotao   III-611
Li, Haifeng   I-363
Li, Hongchen   II-349
Li, Hui   III-275, III-611
Li, Jianmin   I-434
Li, Jiayi   II-385
Li, Jinghang   II-155
Li, Jingyao   III-174
Li, Jinhua   I-434
Li, Jinke   I-350, II-143
Li, Kairu   II-3
Li, Ke   III-88
Li, Lele   II-91
Li, Li   II-54
Li, Liyi   II-637
Li, Qingdu   II-521
Li, Rankun   II-521
Li, Shunchong   I-91
Li, Tianming   I-423
Li, Tiemin   I-316
Li, Weimin   II-409
Li, Weipeng   III-249
Li, Xiangxin   II-27
Li, Xinchi   III-361
Li, Yanbiao   III-222
Li, Yazhou   II-3
Li, Ye   III-185
Li, Yinghui   III-235
Li, Youfu   II-675, II-686
Li, Yumeng   I-397
Li, Yuming   I-294
Li, Yuqi   I-525
Li, Yusen   III-560
Li, Zhe   III-631
Li, Zhiheng   III-662
Li, Zhipeng   II-397
Liang, Bin   II-385
Liang, Cheng   I-201
Liang, Dawei   II-91, II-613
Liang, Guangyu   II-322
Liang, Jian   II-662
Liang, Jiawei   III-599
Liang, Shengxiang   II-222
Liang, Shuai   II-37
Liang, Tian   II-534
Liang, Xu   III-611
Liang, Yunpeng   II-624
Liang, Zhenkun   I-559
Liang, Zibin   III-101

Liao, Da III-631
Liao, Zhaoyang I-294
Liao, Zhao-Yang I-509
Lin, Chengyu II-67
Lin, Junkai II-509
Lin, Sen III-422
Lin, Weixian I-52
Lin, Xubin I-294
Lin, Yichen I-350, II-285, II-297, II-309, II-557
Lin, Yuchen II-497
Ling, Shaobin II-459
Liu, Bang II-166, II-184
Liu, Changquan II-197
Liu, Chongfeng I-201
Liu, Dachuan II-650
Liu, Daming III-185
Liu, Donghan III-263
Liu, Gang I-472
Liu, Gangfeng II-601
Liu, Haitao I-166
Liu, Hong II-175
Liu, Honghai III-263, III-473, III-534
Liu, Houde II-385
Liu, Jian I-140
Liu, Jianming II-483
Liu, Lianfeng I-484
Liu, Lu I-177
Liu, Rongqiang I-536
Liu, Ruiheng I-227
Liu, Runze II-409
Liu, Shengbo II-483
Liu, Siyu III-673
Liu, Tao III-336
Liu, Xing III-447
Liu, Xingyu II-686
Liu, Yao III-323
Liu, Ying II-545
Liu, Yuanbo III-650
Liu, Yuchao III-249
Liu, Yuhan II-373
Liu, Zedong II-91
Liu, Zhongtao I-595
Liu, Zijie III-484
Liu, Zongying II-129
Liu, Zongyuan III-222
Long, Xiaojing II-297
Lou, Yunjiang III-88
Lu, Chunheng II-16
Lu, Hao II-244

Lu, Honglei II-497
Lu, Wenke I-350, II-309
Lu, Xingyu I-472
Lu, Yu III-599
Lu, Yuhan I-39
Lu, Zexin I-153
Lu, Zhe III-587
Lu, Zi-Wei I-509
Luo, Mingxiang II-222
Luo, Ruijie I-411
Luo, Xiang III-484
Luo, Xin I-52, I-127
Lv, Bo I-397

M
Ma, Guijun III-447
Ma, Guoyao III-49
Ma, Shentao I-252
Ma, Shiyu III-587
Ma, Tiancheng I-127
Ma, Wei I-166
Ma, Wen II-397
Ma, Xing III-15
Ma, Yue I-350, II-234, II-285, II-309, II-557
Mai, Xiaoming III-398
Mai, Ximing I-411
Mao, Baijin I-583
Matsui, Yusuke III-60
Matsuno, Takayuki II-103, III-60
Mei, Xuesong III-508, III-521
Melo, Kamilo III-249
Meng, Jianjun I-411
Meng, Tao III-336
Mi, Shuaibing III-398
Mu, Fengjun III-631
Mu, Xinxing II-409

N
Nie, Pingyun I-115

O
Obo, Takenori III-209

P
Pan, Jie I-77
Pan, Lizhi I-434
Pan, Mingxu III-434
Pang, Wen I-153
Pang, Xufang II-483

Pang, Yunfan   III-150
Peng, Xiaoke   III-348
Peng, Yan   II-521
Peng, Zhinan   III-631
Peng, Zhouhua   I-177
Piri, Saeid   III-3
Pradhan, Ashirbad   I-279

Q

Qi, Dexin   III-508, III-521
Qi, Jian   II-91
Qi, Zhanchuan   III-88
Qian, Huihuan   I-201
Qian, Letian   I-52
Qian, Shipang   I-227
Qiang, Junjie   I-52
Qiao, Zhehao   III-136
Qin, Pengjie   I-350, II-234, II-244
Qu, Juntian   I-583

R

Ren, Jieji   I-65
Ren, Weihong   III-473, III-534
Ren, Zengle   I-350, II-143, II-285
Ren, Zhouyi   III-174
Ruan, Lecheng   I-103, I-459, II-567
Ruan, Yizhang   III-548

S

Sakai, Nanako   III-60
Saputra, Azhar Aulia   III-209
Shan, Yihan   II-601
Shen, Xueyan   II-143, II-222
Shen, Yu   II-16
Sheng, Xinjun   I-306, I-328
Sheng, Yixuan   I-239, I-385, III-287
Shi, Changcheng   III-336
Shi, Jiaqi   III-494
Shi, Kecheng   III-631
Shi, Xiaoyu   II-581
Shi, Xin   II-244
Shi, Xulong   I-583
Shou, Zefeng   III-336
Si, Chuanyu   II-91
Siow, Chyan Zheng   II-129, III-209
Song, Ningning   II-409
Song, Qingwei   II-129, III-209
Song, Ran   III-662
Song, Rui   I-595

Song, Zhihong   II-16
Su, Chengyu   III-587
Su, Hang   II-361
Su, Tingting   III-611
Sun, Guangzhen   II-337
Sun, Jianquan   II-309, II-557
Sun, Kangkang   III-611
Sun, Peng   I-52, I-267, III-222
Sun, Shilong   II-650
Sun, Tairen   III-622
Sun, Wei   II-197
Sun, Yaowei   II-433
Sun, Zhe   I-267, III-222

T

Tan, Huachen   III-460
Tan, Wenhao   III-662
Tang, Lu   I-140
Tang, Qing   III-434
Tang, Xiaoran   II-175
Tao, Bo   I-15, I-423, II-497, III-386
Tao, Jianguo   I-536, III-136
Tao, Tao   III-508
Tian, Jiandong   III-411
Tian, Lan   II-27
Tian, Lingyan   I-373
Tian, Rui   III-587
Toda, Yuichiro   II-103, III-60
Tong, Yalong   II-3

W

Wang, Chen   II-322
Wang, Chengzhi   II-589, II-613
Wang, Chunbo   II-662
Wang, Chunfang   I-472
Wang, Chunlong   I-525
Wang, Conglin   II-37
Wang, Guofeng   I-166
Wang, Hai   I-279
Wang, Hao   I-559
Wang, Haoyu   II-275
Wang, Hongwei   III-49
Wang, Hongyu   III-494
Wang, Hui   I-91
Wang, Jiachen   II-534, III-3
Wang, Jiakang   II-534
Wang, Jiantao   I-252
Wang, Jiaole   III-573
Wang, Jingnan   II-234

Wang, Jun III-631
Wang, Junchen II-16
Wang, Junjie I-239
Wang, Keyi II-155
Wang, Lan II-155
Wang, Liming II-397
Wang, Lin II-27
Wang, Lu I-227
Wang, Meiling III-460
Wang, Mengdi II-497
Wang, Peixin II-675, II-686
Wang, Peiyao II-3
Wang, Peng II-79, II-266
Wang, Qiang III-422
Wang, Qining I-103, I-459, II-567
Wang, Shengli I-215
Wang, Shuhan I-52
Wang, Song III-101
Wang, Tao III-75
Wang, Weihao III-209
Wang, Wenjun III-521
Wang, Xiangyang II-557
Wang, Xiaoxin I-385
Wang, Xu II-79, II-266
Wang, Xuan II-373
Wang, Xuelian III-336
Wang, Yaling II-234
Wang, Yanzhuo II-155
Wang, Yi II-3
Wang, Yuan III-222
Wang, Yucheng III-460
Wang, Yueming I-340, I-363
Wang, Yunfei II-662
Wang, Zeyang III-373
Wang, Zhengbo I-472
Wang, Zhiyong II-197, III-473, III-534, III-573
Wang, Zhuoqun III-287
Wang, Zihao I-316
Wang, Ziqi III-185
Wang, Ziwei III-434
Wei, Wei III-298
Wei, Yuxuan I-411
Wei, Zhiao I-77
Wei, Zhongxing III-460
Wen, Huan I-340, I-363
Wen, Siqi II-37
Wen, Zhijie I-484, I-496
Weng, Yongjie III-298
Wu, Canhui II-166, II-184

Wu, Chaoqun II-446
Wu, Chenhao II-143
Wu, Chentao III-222
Wu, Dingze I-189
Wu, Han III-263
Wu, Hao I-446
Wu, Hongmin I-294
Wu, Hong-Min I-509
Wu, Jianhua I-252
Wu, Jingyu III-622
Wu, Longyan I-65
Wu, Peng III-422
Wu, Tianyu II-222
Wu, Xinhao III-422
Wu, Xinrui III-136
Wu, Xinyu II-143, II-222, II-234, II-309, III-323
Wu, Xiuyuan I-350, II-285, II-557
Wu, Xuan III-249
Wu, Zhigang II-210

X
Xia, Qingchao I-189
Xia, Tian II-497
Xia, Xin I-279
Xia, Yan I-536
Xia, Yu I-472
Xia, Yulong I-484
Xian, Haolan II-197, II-255
Xiang, Yang I-15
Xiang, Yuyaocen I-583
Xiao, Han I-267
Xiao, Hong I-525, I-536
Xiao, Juliang I-166
Xiao, Mubang I-484, I-496
Xie, Bangquan I-385
Xie, Erxuan I-115
Xie, Shiqin III-197
Xie, Wenkai III-650
Xie, Xing III-411
Xie, Yuhang II-521
Xing, Boyang II-698
Xing, Jianping I-215
Xiong, Zhenhua I-252
Xu, Enci II-421
Xu, Fengkun III-124
Xu, Guibin I-446
Xu, Guochao III-263
Xu, Jiajun II-675, II-686
Xu, Kedi I-340

Xu, Qingpo   I-166
Xu, Ruoyu   I-201
Xu, Shabei   III-484
Xu, Sheng   II-471
Xu, Tiantian   II-471, III-49
Xu, Wenfu   II-650
Xu, Wenzhu   II-275
Xu, Xiaohu   III-560
Xu, Yang   I-397
Xu, Yanping   I-177
Xu, Zhantao   II-601
Xu, Zhihao   I-294
Xu, Zhi-Hao   I-509
Xu, Zhipeng   II-698

Y

Yan, Jiejie   III-548
Yan, Sijie   I-140, III-434, III-560
Yan, Weixin   II-624
Yan, Yushuai   II-67
Yang, Canjun   I-189, I-227, II-275, II-361
Yang, Chao   II-483
Yang, Chen   I-385
Yang, Dan   III-373
Yang, En   III-112
Yang, Fan   III-650
Yang, Guang   I-525, I-536
Yang, Hongkun   II-37
Yang, Huaiguang   III-136
Yang, Jiantao   III-622
Yang, Jichao   I-215
Yang, Kairui   I-103
Yang, Lintao   III-136
Yang, Mingchuan   III-361
Yang, Minghui   II-446
Yang, Siqin   II-16
Yang, Wei   II-275
Yang, Xiao   III-673
Yang, Xinyu   I-65
Yang, Yang   III-49
Yang, Zeyuan   I-140
Yang, Zhihao   III-473, III-534
Yang, Zhiyuan   II-613
Yang, Zixiang   II-244
Yao, Chong   II-601
Yao, Jia   III-673
Yao, Jianfeng   II-166, II-184
Yao, Lin   I-340, I-363
Yao, Shutong   III-398
Ye, Guoquan   II-459

Ye, Huanpeng   I-397
Ye, Linqi   II-385, II-521, II-698
Ye, Xiaodong   III-460
Yi, Shuowen   III-673
Yin, Changwei   I-595
Yin, Meng   II-234, II-285, II-309
Yin, Yanqi   I-571
Yu, Li   II-54
Yu, Longjie   III-310
Yu, Yang   I-306, I-571
Yuan, Hao   I-559
Yue, Zuogong   III-447

Z

Zang, Xizhe   II-79, II-266
Zeng, Qiming   I-385
Zha, Pengxin   I-3, I-39
Zhan, Xinrui   I-496
Zhang, Bi   III-599
Zhang, Bo   I-115
Zhang, Dailin   I-423, III-75, III-386
Zhang, Dinghuang   II-545
Zhang, Fumin   I-239
Zhang, Fuyong   I-294
Zhang, Gan   I-239
Zhang, Guilong   III-361
Zhang, Hanqi   III-222
Zhang, Haoran   I-350, II-309, II-557
Zhang, Haoshi   II-27
Zhang, Haoxiang   II-91
Zhang, Haoyan   II-662
Zhang, He   II-662
Zhang, Hongwei   I-385
Zhang, Huanghe   II-534, III-3
Zhang, Jianguo   II-483
Zhang, Jianhua   III-275
Zhang, Jiaqi   II-103, II-662
Zhang, Jiexin   I-77, I-115
Zhang, Jinnuo   I-65
Zhang, Junwei   III-124, III-197
Zhang, Kewen   III-310
Zhang, Li   III-26, III-38
Zhang, Liang   III-599
Zhang, Lunwei   I-316
Zhang, Luobin   III-298
Zhang, Ningbin   I-65
Zhang, Qian   III-662
Zhang, Shenglun   III-386
Zhang, Shisheng   II-143
Zhang, Shouyi   II-91, III-185

Zhang, Tianze I-434
Zhang, Wei III-662
Zhang, Wenan III-336
Zhang, Xiaojian III-434
Zhang, Xinuo III-611
Zhang, Xuehe II-601
Zhang, Yang I-595
Zhang, Yi III-484
Zhang, Yijian III-185
Zhang, Ying I-472, II-483
Zhang, Yuan III-361
Zhang, Yuanwen II-255
Zhang, Yuhao I-15, II-497
Zhang, Yuqi II-129
Zhang, Zehui III-398
Zhang, Zhenwei I-15, II-497
Zhang, Zhihong III-508, III-521
Zhang, Zhiran III-75
Zhang, Zhonghai III-150
Zhang, Zhongkai I-3, I-27, I-39
Zhang, Zhuowen II-662
Zhao, Chuanlin I-127
Zhao, Feng III-373
Zhao, Guoshun III-348
Zhao, Huaici III-361
Zhao, Huan I-77
Zhao, Huijuan II-54
Zhao, Jie II-589, II-601, II-613, II-637, II-662, III-185
Zhao, Junhong III-460
Zhao, Mengcheng II-675, II-686
Zhao, Ranshuo I-215
Zhao, Runchao I-536
Zhao, Shize II-589, II-613
Zhao, Shunyi I-459, II-567
Zhao, Sikai II-589, II-613, III-185
Zhao, Tianren I-166
Zhao, Wensong III-587
Zhao, Xin II-210
Zhao, Xingang III-599
Zhao, Xingwei I-15, I-423, II-497, III-75, III-386
Zhao, Xu'an II-637
Zhao, Xu'ning II-637
Zhao, Yanwei I-472
Zhao, Yanzheng II-624
Zhao, Zeming I-328

Zheng, Han II-385
Zheng, Hao III-112
Zheng, Haoran III-263
Zheng, Lei III-75
Zheng, Tianjiao II-91, II-589, II-613, II-637
Zheng, Yue II-27
Zhengqing, Liu III-222
Zhong, Lei II-662
Zhong, Yucun I-363
Zhou, Dalin II-545
Zhou, Huilin III-336
Zhou, Jiaxing I-177
Zhou, Jinglin II-197, II-255
Zhou, Juanxia II-675, II-686
Zhou, Nanlin III-185
Zhou, Puzhe I-189
Zhou, Ruyi III-136
Zhou, Shijun III-411
Zhou, Xuefei I-340
Zhou, Xuefeng I-294
Zhou, Xue-Feng I-509
Zhou, Yan I-252
Zhou, Yangfan III-599
Zhou, Zeyu I-306, I-328
Zhu, Dahu I-446
Zhu, Daqi I-153
Zhu, Gaohan III-235
Zhu, Haifei I-294
Zhu, Jintao II-567
Zhu, Linqing II-521
Zhu, Liren III-587
Zhu, Qingmiao I-15
Zhu, Wenduo I-459
Zhu, Xiangye III-560
Zhu, Xingyue I-559
Zhu, Yanhe II-91, II-589, II-613, III-185
Zhu, Yanmei III-494
Zhu, Yanzheng I-215
Zhu, Yu I-350, II-557
Zhu, Yulan III-494
Zhuang, Chungang I-3, I-27, I-39
Zou, Huaiwu I-115
Zou, Jiang I-547
Zou, Kuansheng III-398
Zou, Rui II-322
Zuo, Guokun III-336

Made in the USA
Monee, IL
03 May 2026